OWAIN GLYNDŴR

A Casebook

'Owain Glyndŵr was and is a great many things to a great many people: a prince and a savage, a rebel and a patriot, a gentleman and an outlaw, a scholar and a magician. If he was for the Welsh a symbol of their hopes and dreams, then he was for the English a figuration of their fears and nightmares. Owain is, simply put, one of those extraordinary figures of history who were, even in their own time, legend.'

— from the Introduction

This casebook is the most extensive collection of documents, poems, letters, and laws ever assembled to illustrate the life of Owain Glyndŵr and the rebellion against the English crown that began under his banner on 16 September 1400. An international team of experts has gathered, edited, and translated 101 sources concerning this fascinating leader and his prominent role in the turmoil of fifteenth-century Britain. Eleven essays provide historical context and literary background to help interpret Owain's career and his vision for Wales. Here we see Owain Glyndŵr as never before, through the eyes of the poets who loved him, the enemies who fought him, the people of Wales and England who were caught up in his wake, and the chroniclers and poets, even Shakespeare himself, who told and retold his tale.

Michael Livingston is an Associate Professor at The Citadel, The Military College of South Carolina. He is the editor of *The Battle of Brunanburh: A Casebook* (2011), along with scholarly editions of *Siege of Jerusalem* (2004), *In Praise of Peace* (2005), and *The Middle English Metrical Paraphrase of the Old Testament* (2011).

John K. Bollard is a Medieval Welsh scholar, editor, and lexicographer. He has published extensively on *The Mabinogi* and other early Welsh works, including popular translations of *The Mabinogi* (2006), *Companion Tales to The Mabinogi* (2007), and *Tales of Arthur* (2010).

EXETER MEDIEVAL TEXTS AND STUDIES
Series Editors: Vincent Gillespie and Richard Dance

Founded by M.J. Swanton
and later co-edited by Marion Glasscoe

Owain Glyndŵr

A Casebook

edited by
Michael Livingston
and
John K. Bollard

LIVERPOOL UNIVERSITY PRESS

Cover image courtesy the National Museum of Wales.

First published in 2013 by
Liverpool University Press
4 Cambridge Street
Liverpool L69 7ZU
UK

www.liverpooluniversitypress.co.uk

British Library Cataloguing in Publication Data
A catalogue record for this book is available
from the British Library.

Hardback ISBN 978-0-85989-884-3
Paperback ISBN 978-0-85989-883-6

Typeset in 10/13 New Baskerville with Golden Cockerel Ornaments display
by Michael Livingston, after layout design by Linda K. Judy.

Printed in Great Britain by Short Run Press Ltd, Exeter.

CONTENTS

🐉 ILLUSTRATIONS

Cover Art. Gilt-bronze armorial, probably a martingale harness mount for a horse. This artifact, unearthed at Harlech Castle in 1923, shows the arms of Owain Glyndŵr: the four lions rampant of the Gwynedd dynasty. Courtesy of the National Museum of Wales.

 ABBREVIATIONS

Certain terms and works appear often enough that we have opted to abbreviate them.

GPC	*Geiriadur Prifysgol Cymru*
ME	Middle English
MED	*Middle English Dictionary*
ModW	Modern Welsh
MW	Middle Welsh
NLW	National Library of Wales
OED	*Oxford English Dictionary*
OF	Old French
PPC	*Proceedings and Ordinance of the Privy Council*, ed. Nicolas
PROME	*Parliamentary Rolls of Medieval England*, ed. Given-Wilson
RCAHMW	Royal Commission on the Ancient and Historical Monuments of Wales
W	Welsh

CONTRIBUTORS

John K. Bollard is a Medieval Welsh scholar, editor, and lexicographer. He has published extensively on *The Mabinogi* and other early Welsh works, including popular translations of *The Mabinogi* (2006), *Companion Tales to The Mabinogi* (2007), and *Tales of Arthur* (2010).

Kelly DeVries is a Professor of History at Loyola University. He has authored many books on military history, including a biography of *Joan of Arc* (1999; reissued 2011) and the widely used textbook *Medieval Military Technology*, now entering its second edition (2012).

Helen Fulton is a Professor of Medieval Literature at the University of York. She has published widely on medieval English and Welsh literatures, with a particular interest in relations between medieval Wales and England as represented in political and prophetic poetry.

Rhidian Griffiths was formerly Keeper of Printed Books and Director of Public Services at the National Library of Wales, Aberystwyth. He has published articles on Prince Henry's campaigns against Owain.

Elissa R. Henken, a Professor at the University of Georgia, teaches Folklore and Celtic studies. She holds degrees in Folklore, Mythology, and Welsh Language and Literature. Her published works include *Traditions of the Welsh Saints* and *National Redeemer*, a study of Owain.

Michael Livingston holds degrees in History, Medieval Studies, and English. He is an Associate Professor at The Citadel, The Military College of South Carolina. He is the editor of *The Battle of Brunanburh: A Casebook* (2011), along with several other scholarly editions.

Scott Lucas is a Professor of English at The Citadel, the Military College of South Carolina. He is the author of *"A Mirror for Magistrates" and the Politics of the English Reformation* (2009) and of a number of articles on early modern English literature, historiography, and culture.

Alicia Marchant is currently a Research Associate at the ARC Centre of Excellence for the History of Emotions at the University of Western Australia. She is author of a forthcoming monograph from York Medieval Press on Owain in medieval English chronicle narratives.

William A. Oram is the Helen Means Professor of English at Smith College. He is the coordinating editor of the Yale Edition of the *Shorter Poems of Edmund Spenser* (1989) and the author of *Edmund Spenser* (1997) and of essays about many Renaissance writers.

Gruffydd Aled Williams is Emeritus Professor of Welsh and former Head of the Department of Welsh at Aberystwyth University. He has published extensively in the fields of medieval Welsh poetry, and he was raised in Owain's own fields of Glyndyfrdwy.

MICHAEL LIVINGSTON
PREFACE: OWAIN GLYNDŴR'S CASEBOOK

These signs have mark'd me extraordinary,
And all the courses of my life do show
I am not in the roll of common men.
                    — Owain Glyndŵr, in William Shakespeare's *1 Henry IV* (Item 101.43–45)

Owain Glyndŵr was and is a great many things to a great many people: a prince and a savage, a rebel and a patriot, a gentleman and an outlaw, a scholar and a magician. If he was for the Welsh a symbol of their hopes and dreams, then he was for the English a figuration of their fears and nightmares. Owain is, simply put, one of those extraordinary figures of history who were, even in their own time, legend.

This book is to some degree built upon this indisputable fact about the man: who he was depends on who is telling his story, and so we have gathered here one hundred and one of our earliest and most essential sources related to the life and legend of Owain Glyndŵr — regardless of their language of origin — from works of his own hand to Shakespeare's fascinating presentation of him in *1 Henry IV*, the most comprehensive collection of these sources ever assembled. An international team of scholars has selected and gathered these texts, annotated them, and translated or glossed them into English in order to make them available to a wide range of both academics and common readers alike. These sources, some of them printed here for the first time, are the heart of the book. Built upon this core, however, we have included nine essays that put these many sources into historical context while addressing many of our questions about this extraordinary character: from his very real military life to his equally real (if legendary) after-life over the centuries. Throughout, it has been our aim to make this material and this man available not just to researchers but to a wider public audience, too.

THE NAMES

Following the model established by *The Battle of Brunanburh: A Casebook*, which I edited for Exeter Medieval Texts and Studies in 2011, our intent in constructing this volume has been to gather in one place the essential material for understanding Owain Glyndŵr. I have been very fortunate, given the necessity to work with so much Welsh material as a result, to have John K. Bollard as my co-editor. At all stages of the project John and I have worked with one common vision for this final product.

Our task as editors, all too often, has been to instill a well-intended sense of regularization across works that might rightly lack it. A multi-faceted volume such as this, however, by its nature introduces still more problems in a search for consistency, perhaps most noticeably in regards to the spelling of names.

An obvious example, of course, is the name of the man himself, which can appear in a striking number of forms: *Owain Glyndŵr*, *Owain Glyn Dŵr*, *Owein Glyndour*, *Owenus de Glyndor*, or, as Shakespeare has it, *Owen Glendower* — just to name a few. While we have generally left

these various spellings of Owain's name in their original textual contexts, we have endeavored
to be consistent in otherwise referring to this man in commentary and translations using the
single representation *Owain Glyndŵr*, a common modern spelling. More troubling than this,
perhaps, is the question of how to navigate the charged waters of representing place-names
in the text: especially those names for locations (or people) whose Welsh names, while arguably more accurate, are far less likely to be known outside Wales than are the Anglicized or
English versions. In many such cases we have opted for the highest clarity to the most readers,
thus favoring English spellings. At the same time, however, we have tried to incorporate Welsh
names where the subject is less likely to be widely known by an English spelling. Thus, on the
map for this volume, readers will find both English *Kidwelly* (rather than Welsh *Cydweli*) and
Welsh *Bryn Glas* (rather than English *Pilleth*). The result may seem an unsettling mix to two
cultures, but to some degree this discomfort is inevitable given the history of this book's subject. It is likewise inevitable due to the fact that it has been our intent throughout this project
to present a balanced (i.e., neither pro-Welsh or anti-Welsh) perspective on Owain Glyndŵr's
character and actions. The same rationale applies to the presentation of the names or titles
of the sources we have included: we have regularized the majority of references to the form
that will, we hope, be the most recognizable to the most readers. None of this volume's orthographical presentations should be viewed, therefore, as statements of either Anglo-centrism
or Welsh nationalism.

THE SOURCES
    Given the complexities inherent in presenting texts compiled over two centuries and
written in many different languages from a variety of cultures, it seems most helpful to present the sources collected here in something close to chronological order. Such an arrangement has the advantage of allowing the reader to trace Owain Glyndŵr's career as it shifts
from reported events to legends. Yet, as anyone familiar with medieval literature can confirm, determining a firm date for medieval texts is a frustrating and largely fruitless task:
often the best we can manage is a range counted in decades, if not centuries. The issue is
even more problematic when it comes to medieval chronicles, passages from many of which
appear in this volume. We have endeavored — with the help of our contributors, though in
the final count they should remain blameless for our faults — to determine a suitable origin
date for the preserved texts, though in some cases we have simply opted to date the text to
its point of preservation. Thus the fascinating work of Thomas Walsingham, which may very
well contain some material that is contemporaneous with the events it records, survives in
a chronicle account probably written down almost twenty years later. It appears, therefore,
as Item 68 in our accounts with the date c.1423 rather than somewhere earlier. Despite our
efforts to rationalize these decisions, however, the order of texts that results is inevitably
speculative, and readers are encouraged to make their own determinations on the matter.
    While the final selection of texts to include in the volume was also editorial, we have
once again leaned heavily on the findings and opinions of the contributors. As already
stated, the volume is intended to preserve the essential sources for study of the historical
figure, thus omitting many later legendary accounts. For reasons of space and sanity, we also
could not include every reference to the war in Wales, which was the subject of a great deal
of official correspondence to and from the English crown, for instance. In sifting through
this material we have tried to identify the works that would be most useful for understanding
Owain, rather than the totality of the conflict itself. Our cut-off date is William Shakespeare.

Acknowledgments

Michael Livingston

This volume began even before its forebear (*The Battle of Brunanburh: A Casebook*) was in print. John Bollard had been an indispensable contributor in the formation of that book, and we began to discuss how it might provide a model for other subjects. I suggested Owain Glyndŵr, and John not only heartily agreed to take on oversight of the Welsh materials that would be necessary for such a volume, he also agreed (to my great relief) to take on the task of co-editing the whole of the book. I could not have asked for a better partner in the execution of such a complex project.

I owe no small debt to Debbe Causey and Terri Johnson, Interlibrary Loan specialists of the Daniel Library at The Citadel. My departmental secretary, Alisa Whittle, was also indispensable: from photocopies to transcriptions, from sound advice to simple good humor, she has fulfilled many a favor that helped move this project along. I am also pleased to acknowledge The Citadel Foundation for providing funds to send me on a highly productive trip to Wales to do research — during which I took those photos appearing herein.

Above all I happily acknowledge my debt to the ever-present good humor and love of my family for keeping me sane and smiling despite the long nights.

John K. Bollard

I must first say what a pleasure it is to work with Michael Livingston, a lucid writer, subtle thinker, scrupulous editor, and a careful — and amazingly quick — researcher, not to mention his good humor and fine wit. While we both owe a great debt to all of the contributors to this book, I must particularly thank Bill Oram, Aled Williams, and Elissa Henken for their willingness to listen to my own ideas, read my drafts and translations, and generally keep me on track. Dafydd Johnston, Rhiannon Ifans, Aled Williams, and Iestyn Daniel graciously agreed to let us reprint their edited texts of various poems; they were unfailingly kind in their responses to my queries and gentle in offering improvements to my translations of their work. Thanks are also due to J. Beverley Smith, Brynley F. Roberts, Marged Haycock, and Ceridwen Lloyd-Morgan for their encouragement at the earliest stages of this project; their enthusiastic response to the idea of this book provided a foundation of confidence for us to build on. My debt to my wife, Margaret Lloyd, for both her tolerance and her sound and detailed criticism is, as always, greater than I can express, and Brynley and Catrin Lloyd-Bollard listened patiently and offered helpful advice on matters both general and specific.

Collective Thanks
- Denbighshire Historical Society for permission to reprint from *Transactions* 37 (1988) the Welsh text of Madog ap Gronw Gethin's poem praising the river Dee (Item 53).
- Hereford Museum and Art Gallery for permission to reproduce images of Owain Glyndŵr's Privy Seal and the Canon Pyon Hoard.
- The National Museum of Wales for permission to reproduce images of the armorial mount and Owain Glyndŵr's Great Seal.
- Oxford University Press, for permission to reprint material from *The Chronicle of Adam Usk 1377–1421*, ed. and trans. Chris Given-Wilson (1997), and *The St Albans Chronicle: The Chronica Maiora of Thomas Walsingham*, ed. and trans. John Taylor, Wendy R. Childs, and Leslie Watkiss (2003–11). These items have been regularized orthographically.
- York Medieval Press and Boydell and Brewer, for permission to reprint six translations from Alicia Marchant's forthcoming monograph on Owain Glyndŵr (2014).

Map of Wales at the time of Owain Glyndŵr's revolt, showing major geological features and important locations mentioned in the text.

# Owain Glyndŵr: A Chronology

The following chronology provides a summary not only of Owain's life but also of the course of the Welsh rebellion with which he is associated.

A Brief Note on the Pronunciation of Welsh Names
Pronounce *a* as in f*a*ther; *ae, ai, au, ei* as in *ai*sle; *aw* as in n*ow*; *c* as in *c*at; *ch* as in Scottish lo*ch*; *dd* as in *th*en; *e* as in b*e*d; *f* as in o*f*; *ff* as in e*ff*ect; *g* as in *g*o; *i* as in b*i*d; *th* as in *th*ink; *u* as in b*u*sy or b*ea*d; *w* as in *w*ith or as the vowel in r*oo*f; *y* as in m*y*th or lad*y* in a single or final syllable and as *a*live or gl*o*ve in other syllables. Pronounce the *h* in *rh*, as in *Rh*ys. Pronounce *ll* with the tip of the tongue in the same position as for the *l* in *l*ike but gently blowing air, without voice, past the side of the tongue (the *l* in English c*l*ean is very similar). An *r* should be rolled or trilled, as in Scottish. The stressed syllable in Welsh is usually the penultimate.

1357–59?	Born, probably at Sycharth.
1380?	Studies at Inns of Court.
1383?	Marries Margaret Hanmer
1384	March. With his brother Tudur, the poet/prophet Crach Ffinnant, and others in retinue of Sir Gregory Sais garrisoned at Berwick.
1385	August. With Richard II's campaign in Scotland.
1386	3 September. In Chester, gives evidence for the Scrope-Grosvenor trial.
1387	In retinue of Richard Fitzalan, earl of Arundel.
1399	*30 September. Richard II deposed by Henry, duke of Lancaster.*
1400	*January. Epiphany Rising defeated by Henry IV.*
	September. Henry IV invades Scotland.
	September. Quarrels with Lord Grey of Ruthin.
	16 September. Declared prince of Wales.
	18 September. Burns Ruthin, along with Denbigh, Flint, Rhuddlan, Hawarden, Holt, Oswestry, and Welshpool.
	19 September. Henry IV summons levies against Wales.
	24 September. Battle of Welshpool. Defeated by Hugh Burnell of Shropshire.
	Rhys and Gwilym ap Tudur, Owain's cousins, seize Anglesey.

October. Henry IV invades North Wales.

Rhys and Gwilym ap Tudur attack king at Beaumaris.

8 November. Henry IV grants Owain's lands to the earl of Somerset.

11 November. Trials for rebels.

30 November. Henry IV offers protection to submitting Welsh rebels.

1401   21 February. Parliament, with many anti-Welsh measures.

10 March. Henry IV pardons Welsh rebels, except for Owain, Rhys and Gwilym ap Tudur.

1 April. Rhys and Gwilym ap Tudur seize Conwy Castle.

Henry IV orders Hotspur to take command of Wales.

25/26 May. Henry IV issues commission to prepare to defend against Welsh.

31 May. Battle of Cader Idris. Hotspur defeats a Welsh force.

1 June. Battle of Mawddwy. John Charlton, lord of Powys, defeats Owain in Wales.

14 June. Henry IV dismisses his army from Worcester.

24 June. Rhys and Gwilym ap Tudur surrender Conwy Castle to Hotspur.

Summer. Battle of Hyddgen. Defeats the English.

? Rumored to have executed 60 Englishmen at New Radnor Castle.

18 September. Henry IV issues proclamation against Owain and the rebels.

October. Henry IV invades South Wales, executes many Welshmen.

? Attends funeral for two of them.

? Sends letters to Scotland and Ireland, seeking support against England.

2 November. Battle of Tuthill. Displays standard of the golden dragon of Uther Pendragon at Caernarfon.

November. Owain and Percy parley.

1402   Before 18 April. Captures Lord Grey of Ruthin.

22 June. Battle of Bryn Glas. Captures Edmund Mortimer.

31 July. English execute three-pronged attack on Wales.

14 September. Battle of Homildon Hill. Hotspur defeats Scots.

30 September. Parliament enacts statutes against Wales.

October. Henry IV begins to seize Mortimer's estates.

November. Mortimer marries Owain's daughter.

13 December. Mortimer announces defection to Owain.

1403   8 March. Prince Henry made royal lieutenant in Wales.

21 April. Terror in Shropshire.

May. Prince Henry razes Owain's homes.

3 July. Siege of Llandovery.

10 July. Hotspur declares rebellion against Henry IV.

11 or 12 July. Defeated by Thomas, lord Carew, near St. Clears.

21 July. Battle of Shrewsbury. Hotspur killed.

3 September. Henry IV invades Wales, crossing to Carmarthen.

3 October. French and Breton ships seen off Kidwelly.

1404   May. Opens dialogue with France through John Hanmer and Gruffudd Young.

Holds a parliament in Machynlleth.

14 July. Treaty between Wales and France executed in Paris.

? Guillaume sieur de Chastel raids Dartmouth, defeated by English.

August. Jacques de Bourbon, count de La Marche, readies a fleet to attack the English in support of Owain.

November. After months of delay and channel harassment, the French fleet lands in England, burns Plymouth, then retreats.

1405   12 January. Treaty between Wales and France signed by Owain.

28 February. *Tripartite Indenture* signed by Owain, Mortimer, and Henry Percy.

11 March. Battle of Grosmont. English victory.

Battle of Craig-y-dorth near Monmouth. Welsh victory.

5 May. Battle of Pwll Melyn. English victory. Owain's son Gruffudd taken prisoner, his brother Tudur killed along with John ap Hywel.

8 June. Richard le Scrope, archbishop of York, beheaded for rebelling against Henry IV.

July. Summons a parliament to Harlech.

22 July. A larger French invasion of Wales begins in support of Owain, led by Jean de Rieux, marshal of France; Jean VI de Hengest, lord of Hugueville and master of crossbows; and Robert de la Heuse, lord of Ventes.

7 August. Henry IV orders forces to Hereford against invasion.

By September. Welsh-French force retreats from confrontation with Henry IV.

1406   31 March. Writes Pennal Letter to king of France.

1408   *19 February. Battle of Bramham Moor. Henry Percy is defeated.*

1409   February. Harlech Castle recaptured by English; Edmund Mortimer dies.

Owain's men raid Shropshire, are captured and executed.

1411   23 June. Welsh outlaw in protection of Owain's son, Maredudd.

22 December. Pardons to Welsh excluding Owain.

1412   Spring. Captures Dafydd Gam.

1413   19 February. Exchequer pays for information about Owain.[1]

20 March. Death of Henry IV; crowning of Henry V.

27 June. Owain's wife and daughter in prison.[2]

1 December. Owain's daughter dies in prison.[3]

1414   May. Parliament declares the Welsh rebellion over.

1415   5 July. Offered pardon.

11 August. Henry V sails for France.

?20/21 September. Owain dies.

25 October. Battle of Agincourt in France; Henry relies on Welsh archers.

1416   24 February. Owain's son, Maredudd, offered pardon.

---

[1] "To a certain Welshman, coming to London, and there continuing for a certain time to give information respecting the conduct and designs of 'Ewain Glendourdy.' In money paid to his own hands for his expenses, and as an especial reward for the cause aforesaid. By direction of the Treasurer and Chamberlains of the Exchequer, £1." In *Issues of the Exchequer*, ed. Devon, p. 332.

[2] "To John Weele, esquire. In money paid to his own hands, for the expenses of the wife of Owen Glendourdi, the wife of Edmund Mortimer, and others, their sons and daughters, in his custody in the city of London at the King's charge, by his command. By writ of privy seal, £30." In *Issues of the Exchequer*, ed. Devon, p. 321.

[3] "To William del Chaumbre, valet of the said Earl [Arundel]. In money paid to his own hands, for expenses and other charges incurred for the burial and exequies of the wife of Edward [sic] Mortimer and her daughters, buried within Saint Swithin's Church, London. By write of privy seal amongst the mandates of this term, £1." In *Issues of the Exchequer*, ed. Devon, p. 327.

SOURCES ON OWAIN GLYNDŴR

Privy Seal of Owain Glyndŵr, showing a dragon and a lion framing the crowned arms of the Gwynedd dynasty: four lions rampant. The inscription is unknown. Courtesy of the Hereford Museum and Art Gallery.

1. *PROPHECY OF SIX KINGS*

**English
c. 1370 CE**

Quod Merlyn:

In þe yere of Incarnacioun of oure Lorde Jhesu Crist MCCXV þere shal come a Lambe oute of Wynchestre þat shal have a white tong and trew lippis, and he shal have wryten in his hert Holynesse.

5   Þis Lambe shal make meny Goddes house, and he shal have pees þe most parte of his lif. And he shal make one of þe faireste places of þe worlde þat in his tyme shal nouht fully ben made an ende. And in þe ende of his lif a Wolf of a straunge lande shal do him grete harme; but at þe ende þe Lambe shal be maistre, þrouh helpe of a rede Fox þat shal come out of þe Northwest, and him shal overcome.
10 And þe Wolfe shal dye in water, and after þat tyme þe Lambe shal leve no while þat he ne shal dye.

His sede þan shal bene in strange lande, and þe lande shal bene wiþout a governoure a litil tyme.

And after him shal come a Dragoun, mellede wiþ mercy and ek wodenesse, þat
15 shal have a berde as a goot. Þat shal geve in Engeland shadewe, and shal kepe the lande from colde and hete: and his o foote shal be sette in Wik, and þat oþere in London. And he shal unbrace iij habitacions, and he shal oppen his mouþ toward Walys, and þe tremblyng of þe hidure of his mouþe, his heres shal strecche towarde meny habitaciouns and contres. And his breþ shal bene ful suete in straunge landes.
20 And in his tyme shal ryvers renne wiþ bloode and wiþ brayne, and he shal make in places of his lande, walles, þat shal done miche harme to his seede after his tyme.

Þan shal þere come a peple out of þe Northwest duryng his regne þat shal bene lade þrouh an wickede Hare, þat þe Dragoun shal done crone kyng, þat afterwarde shal flee over þe see wiþout comyng ageyne, for drede of þe Dragoun.

25 In þat tyme þe sonne shal bene also rede as blode, as meny men shul see þrouh al þe worlde. Þat shal bitoken grete pestilence, and deþ of folc þrouh dent of swerde. And þis peple shal bene faderles til þe tyme þat þe Dragon shal dye þrouh an Hare þat shal meve ageynes him werr in þe ende of his lif, þat shal nouht bene fulliche endede in his tyme.

30 Þis Dragoun shal bene holden in his tyme þe best body of al þe worlde; and he shal dye bisides þe marche of a straunge lande. And þe lande shalle duelle faderlesse, wiþouten a gode governoure; and me shal wepe for his deþ fram þe Ile of Shepe unto þe haven of Marcill. Wherfore, "Allas!" shal bene þe commune songe of faderles folc, þat shal overleven in his land destroiede.

Sources Regarding Owain Glyndŵr (Translations)

1. PROPHECY OF SIX KINGS

Notes: pp. 247–61

Said Merlin:

In the year 1215 of the Incarnation of our Lord Jesus Christ there shall come a Lamb out of Winchester who will have a pure tongue and true lips, and he will have Holiness written on his heart.

This Lamb shall remember God's house, and he shall have peace through most of his life. He will build one of the fairest places of the world, but it will not be completed in his time. At the end of his life, a Wolf from a strange land will do him great harm; but in the end the Lamb will be the victor through the help of a red Fox who will come out of the Northwest and will overcome the Wolf. The Wolf will die in water, and after that time the Lamb, too, shall die.

His seed shall then be in a strange land, and the land will be without a governor for a short time.

And after him shall come a Dragon with a goat's beard, speaking with both mercy and mania. He shall cast upon England a shadow, and he will keep the land from cold and heat: his one foot will be set upon Berwick and the other upon London. He shall engulf three habitations, and he will open his mouth toward Wales, and the trembling of the terror of his mouth and his hairs will stretch toward many habitations and countries. His breath will be full sweet in strange lands. And in his time the rivers shall run with blood and with brains, and he will make in places of his land walls that will do much harm to his seed after his time.

There shall come during his reign a people out of the Northwest who will be led by a wicked Hare. The Dragon shall crown the Hare as king, and afterward it will flee over the sea never to return for fear of the Dragon.

In that time the sun shall be as red as blood, as men shall see throughout all the world. That will betoken great pestilence, and the death of the people through the clash of swords. This people shall be fatherless until the time that the Dragon will die through a Hare who will wage a war against him in the end of his life, a war that will not end in his time.

This Dragon shall be held in his time the best body of all the world; and he will die beside the border of a strange land. The land will go on fatherless, without a good governor, and men shall weep for his death from the Isle of Sheppey to the haven of Marseille. As a result, "Alas!" shall be the common song of the fatherless folk who will remain in his destroyed land.

35   And after þis Dragone shal come a Gote oute of a kar, þat shal have hornes and
berde of silver. And þere shal come out of his noseþelles a drop þat shal bitoken
hunger and sorw and grete deþ of þe peple; and miche of his lande in þe bigyn-
nyng of his regne shal be wastede.

Þis Goot shal go over into Fraunce, and shal oppon þe Floure of Lif and of Deþ.
40   In his tyme þere shal arise an Egle in Cornewaile þat shal have feþeres of golde, þat
of pride shal bene wiþouten pere of alle þe lande. And he shal despise lordes of
blode. And after he shal flee shamefully by a Bere at Gaversiche; and after shal bene
made brigges of men oppon þe costes of þe see. And stones shal falle fram castelles,
and meny oþere tounes shal ben made pleyne. And a bataile shalle bene done
45   uppon an arme of þe see in a felde ordeynede as a shelde, and at þat bataile shal
dye meny white hedes. Wherfore þat bataile shal bene callede "þe white bataile."
And þe forsaide Beere shal done þis Goote michel harme, and it shal bene oute of
þe Southwest. And of his bloode þan shal þe Goote lese miche of his lande, til at þe
tyme þat shendeship shal him overcomen. And þan shal he cloþen him in a lyonez
50   skyn, and þan shal he wynne þat he hade loste — and more þerto — ffor a peple
shal come out of þe northwest þat shal make þe Goot sore to bene adrade. And he
shal avenge him oppon his enemys, þrouh conseil of ij Oweles, þat ferst shal bene
in peril forto bene undone. But þe olde owel shal wende over þe se into a straunge
lande, and þere he shal duelle unto a certeyne tyme. And after, he shal come a-
55   geyne into þis lande.

þise ij Oweles shullen do grete harme to meny on, and so þai shullen counseil
þe Gote þat he shal arere werre ageynes þe forsaid Bere. And at þe last þe Goot and
þe Oweles shullen come atte Bur-up-Trent and shullen wende over. And for drede
þe Bere shal flee, and a Swan wiþ him, for his company, to Bur towarde þe north,
60   and þere þai shal bene wiþ an harde shoure. And þan þe Swan shal bene slayne wiþ
sorwe, and þe Bere taken and biheuedede, alþer nexte his neste, þat shal stand
uppon a broken brigge, up wham þe sone shal caste his beemes. And meny shal him
seche, for vertu þat fro hym shal come.

In þat same tyme shal dye, for sorwe and care, a peple of his lande, so þat meny
65   shal bene oppon him þe more bolder afterward. And þo ij Oweles shullen do miche
harme to þe forsaide Floure of Lif, and here shul lede in distresse, so þat she shal
passe over into Fraunce, forto make pees bituene þe Gote and þe Flour Delice. And
þere she shal duelle to a tyme þat her sede shal come to seche here; and þere þai
shul bene stille til a tyme þat þai shul ham cloþe with grace: and þai shul seche the
70   Owelyn, and put ham unto despitous deþ. And after shal þis Goot bene brouht to
disese, and in grete anguisshe and sorwe he shal leve al his lif.

Aftre þis Goote shal come out of Wyndesore a Boor þat shal have an heuede of
witte, a lyons hert, a pitouse lokyng. His vesage shal be reste to sike men. His breþ
shal bene stanchyn of þerst to ham þat bene aþreste þerof shal. His worde shal bene
75   gospelle. His beryng shal bene meke as a Lambe. In þe ferste yere of his regne he
shal have grete payne to justifien ham þat bene untrew; and in his tyme shal his
lande bene multipliede wiþ aliens.

After this Dragon shall come a Goat out of a bog who will have horns and a beard of silver. And there shall come out of his nostrils a drop that will betoken hunger and sorrow and great death among the people; and much of his land in the beginning of his reign shall be wasted.

This Goat will go over into France, and he will reveal the Flower of Life and of Death. In his time there will arise an Eagle in Cornwall who will have feathers of gold and who in pride will be without peer in all the land. He will despise lords of blood. Afterwards he shall flee shamefully from a Bear at Blacklow Hill; and then shall be made bridges of men upon the coasts of the sea. Stones shall fall from castles, and many other towns will be made level. A battle will be fought upon an arm of the sea in a field ordained as a shield, and at that battle shall die many white heads. Therefore that battle shall henceforth be called "the white battle." The aforesaid Bear shall do this Goat great harm, and it shall be out of the Southwest. From his blood then shall the Goat lose much of his land, until the time that ignominy shall overcome him. Then will he clothe himself in a lion's skin, and he will win back what he had lost — and even more — for a people will come out of the Northwest who will make the Goat loathe to be fearful. So he shall avenge himself upon his enemies, through the counsel of two Owls, who at first shall be in peril to be destroyed. But the old Owl will cross over the sea into a strange land, and there he will dwell until a certain time. Afterward he will come again into this land.

These two Owls will do great harm to many people, and so they shall counsel the Goat that he should raise war against the aforesaid Bear. In the end the Goat and the Owls will come to Burton-upon-Trent and will cross over. And for dread the Bear will flee, with a Swan for his company, to Boroughbridge in the north, and there they will be in a hard battle. And then the Swan shall be sorrowfully slain, and the Bear taken and beheaded, close beside her nest, and his head will stand upon a broken bridge, upon which the sun shall cast its beams. Many will seek him out, because of the blessings that from him shall come.

In that same time shall die, for sorrow and care, a people of his land, so that many shall be against him the more bolder afterward. Those two Owls shall do much harm to the aforesaid Flower of Life, and will lead her to distress, so that she shall pass over into France, to make peace between the Goat and the Fleur-de-lis. There she will dwell until a time when her seed will come to seek here; and there they will remain until that time when they will be clothed with grace: and they will seek out the Owls and put them unto dispiteous death. Afterwards this Goat will be brought to disease, and in great anguish and sorrow he will leave all his life.

After this Goat shall come out of Windsor a Boar who will have a head of white, a lion's heart, a piteous appearance. His face will be a balm for sick men. His breath will quench the thirst of those who thirst for it. His word will be gospel. His bearing will be meek as a lamb. In the first year of his reign he will have great pain to justify those who have been untrue, and in his time his land will be multiplied with foreigners.

And þis Boor, þrouh fersenesse of hert þat he shal have, shal make wolfes bicome lambes. And he shal bene callede þrouh-oute þe worlde "Boor of holynesse
80   and of fersenesse, of nobeleye and of mekenesse." And he shal do mesurabli al þat he shal have to done unto þe Burgh of Jerusalem; and he shal whet his teiþ uppon þe gates of Parys, and uppon iiij landes. Spayne shal tremble for drede of him. Gascoyne shal swete. In Fraunce he shal put his wynge. His grete taile shal reste in Engeland softely. Almayn shal quake for drede of him.

85   Þis Boor shal geve mantels to ij tounes of Engeland, and he shal make þe ryver rynne wiþ blode and wiþ brayn, and he shal make meny medowes reede. And he shal gete as miche as his auncestres deden; and er þat he bene dede he shal bere iij crones. And he shal put on lande into gret subjeccioun. And after hit shal bene relevede, but nouht in his tyme.

90   Þis Boor, after þat he is dede, for his douhtynesse shal bene enterede at Coloigne, and his lande shal bene þan fulfillede wiþ al goode.

After þis Boor shal come a Lambe, þat shal have feete of leede, an heuede of bras, an hert of a loppe, and a swynes skyn, and herde. And in his tyme his land shal bene in pees. Þe ferst yere of his regne he shal do make a citee, þat al þe
95   worlde shal speke þerof. Þis lambe shal lese in his tyme a grete parte of his lande þrouh an hidouse Wolf, but he shal recover it, an gif an Lordeship to an Egle of his landes. And þis Egle shal wel governe hit, til þe tyme þat pride shal him overgone. Allas þe sorwe, for he shal dye þrouh his broþeres suorde. And after shal þe lande falle to þe forsaide Lambe, þat shal governe in pees al his lifes tyme. And after he
100   shal dye, and þe lande bene fulfillede wiþ al maner gode.

After þis Lambe shal come a Moldewerpe acursede of Godes mouþ, a caitif, a cowarde as an here. He shal have an elderliche skyn as a goot; and vengeance shal fal uppon him for synne. In þe ferst yere of his regne he shal have of al gode grete plente in his lande, and toward him also. And in his lande he shal have grete
105   praising til þe tyme þat he shal soffre his peple lyven in to miche pride wiþouten chastisyng, wherfore God wil ben wroþ.

Þan shal arisen up a Dragoun in þe North þat shal bene ful fers, and shal meve werre ageynes þe forsaide Moldewerpe, and shal geve him bataile uppon a ston. Þis Dragoun shal gadre ageyne into his company a Wolf þat shal come oute of the West,
110   þat shal bygynne werre ageynes þe forsaide Moldewerp in his side. And so shal þe Dragoun and he bynde here tailes togeder.

Þan shal come a Lyon oute of Irlande, þat shal fal in company wiþ ham. And þan shal tremble þe lande, þat þan shal bene callede Engeland, as an aspe lef. And in þat tyme shal castelles bene fellede adoune uppon Tamise, and it shal semen þat
115   Severne shal bene drye, for þe bodyes þat shal fallen dede þerin.

Þe iiij chief flodes of Engeland shal rynne in blode. And grete drede shal bene, and anguisshe, þat shul arisen after þe Moldewerpe shal fle for drede. And þe Dragoun, þe Lyoun and þe Wolf, him shal dryven away, and the lande shal bene wiþout ham, and þe Moldewerpe shal have no maner power, saf onely a shipp
120   wherto he may wende. And after þat, he shal come to lande when þe see is wiþdraw.

This Boar, through the fierceness of heart that he will have, shall make wolves become lambs. He shall be called throughout the world the "Boar of holiness and of fierceness, of nobility and of meekness." He will do measurably all that he will have to do unto the city of Jerusalem; and he will whet his teeth upon the gates of Paris, and upon four lands. Spain shall tremble for fear of him. Gascony shall sweat. In France he shall put his wing. His great tail shall softly rest in England. Germany shall quake for dread of him.

This Boar will give mantels to two towns of England, and he will make the river run with blood and with brain, and he will make many meadows red. He will get as much as his ancestors held, and before he dies he will bear three crowns. He will put one land into great subjection. Afterward it will be relieved, but not in his time.

After he is dead this Boar for his stoutheartedness will be buried at Cologne, and his land will then be filled with all goodness.

After this Boar will come a Lamb who will have feet of lead, a head of brass, the heart of a rabbit, and a swine's hard skin. In his time his land shall be in peace. The first year of his reign he will cause a city to be made, so that all the world will speak of it. This Lamb will lose in his time a great part of his land to a hideous Wolf, but he will recover it and give lordship to an Eagle of his lands. This Eagle will well-govern it, until the time that pride will overtake him. Alas the sorrow, for the Eagle will die through his brother's sword! Afterward will the land return to the aforesaid Lamb, who will govern in peace all his lifetime. Then he will die, and the land will be filled with all manner of goodness.

After this Lamb shall come a Mole accursed by God's mouth, a caitiff, cowardly as a rabbit. He will have leathered skin like a goat, and vengeance will fall upon him for his sinfulness. In the first year of his reign he will have of all goodness great plenty in his land, and toward him also. In his land he will have great praising until the time when he shall suffer his people to live in too much pride without chastising, wherefore God will be angry.

Then shall rise up a Dragon in the north who will be very fierce, and who will bring war against the aforesaid Mole, and who will give him battle upon a stone. This Dragon will gather again into his company a Wolf that will come out of the west, who will begin war against the aforesaid Mole in his side. So shall the Dragon and he bind their tails together.

Then shall come a Lion out of Ireland, who will fall in company with them. Then the land called England will quake like an aspen leaf. In that time castles will fall down upon the Thames, and it will seem that the Severn will be dry, because of the bodies that will fall dead in its depths.

The four chief rivers of England shall run in blood. And great dread there will be, and anguish that will arise after the Mole will flee for fear. The Dragon, the Lion, and the Wolf will drive him away, and the land will be without them, and the Mole will have no power remaining, save only a ship to which he may go. After that he will come to land when the sea is withdrawn.

And after þat he shal geve þe þride part of his lande forto have þe ferþe part in pees and reste. And after he shal leve in sorw al his lif-tyme; and in his tyme þe hote baþes shullen bicome colde. And after þat shal þe Moldewerp dye aventurly and sodeynely: allas þe sorwe, for he shal bene drenchede in a flode of þe see. His seede shal bicome pure faderles in straunge lande forevermore, and þan shal the lande bene departede in iij parties. Þat is to seyn, to the Wolf, to þe Dragoune, and to þe Lioun. And so shal it bene forevermore. And þan shal þis land bene callede "þe lande of conquest," and so shal þe riht heires of Engeland ende.

2. IOLO GOCH, *YMDDIDDAN YR ENAID Â'R CORFF*

Welsh
1375x82

[Corff:] "Od ei byth o'r Deau barth,
os iach, pa waeth i Sycharth?
105 Pan elych, edrych adref,
trig, od gwn, tro gydag ef.
Duw fydd porth i ŵr difeth,
a help it i hel pob peth.
Yta ac wyna a gawn,
110 rhad drwy'r Berfeddwlad fuddlawn.
Oni mynny ddal tŷ teg
nid rhaid i ti ond rhedeg,
dwg ruthr deg ar Ithel
i Goedymynydd dan gêl.
115 Rhwyddaf dyn, rhydd yr eiddaw,
neu ry gâi dlawd ged o'i law."

3. GRUFFUDD LLWYD, *I OWAIN GLYNDŴR*

Welsh
1385x86?

Hen gowydd da i Owain Glyndyfrdwy a wnaed iddo kyn codi o hono yn erbyn Arglwydd Grae, pan fysei ef yn capten yn Ffrainc dros Richard yr Ail, rhwn a garai Owein, ac am i deposio i codes ef.

Eryr digrif afrifed,
Owain helm gain, hael am ged,
eurfab, agwrdd ei arfod,
Gruffudd Fychan, glân ei glod;
5 mur Glyn, menestr rhoddlyn rhydd,
Dyfrdwy fawr dwfr diferydd:
llafar, ymannos noswaith,
oeddwn wrth gyfedd medd maith,
fy nghrair, i'th aml gellweiriaw
10 i'th lys, lle cawn win o'th law;
medd fynfyr, mwy oedd f'anfoes
a gwaeth dros fy maeth fy moes,

And afterward he shall give three parts of his land to have the fourth part in peace and rest. He will live in sorrow all his lifetime; in his days the hot baths will become cold. After that the Mole will die accidentally and suddenly: alas the sorrow, for he will be drowned in a flood of the sea! Forevermore his seed will be completely fatherless in strange lands, and then shall the land be broken into three parts. That is to say, one to the Wolf, one to the Dragon, and one to the Lion. So shall it be forevermore. Then shall this land be called "the land of conquest," and so shall the right heirs of England end.

2. IOLO GOCH, *CONVERSATION BETWEEN THE SOUL AND BODY*   Notes: pp. 261–63

[Body:] "If you ever leave the Southland,
if you are well, why not go to Sycharth?
105   When you go, looking homeward,
stay, indeed, a while with him.
God will be a support to an unfailing man,
and a help for you to gather everything.
We shall gather corn and lambs
110   freely throughout the profitable Perfeddwlad.
If you do not wish to remain in that fair house,
you need but to run,
make a fair rush to Ithel
in Coedymynydd secretly.
115   Most generous man, he gives away what is his.
A poor man will certainly get a gift from his hand."

3. GRUFFUDD LLWYD, *OWAIN'S EXPLOITS IN SCOTLAND*   Notes: pp. 263–69

A fine old cywydd to Owain Glyndŵr that was made for him before he rose up against Lord Grey, when he had been a captain in France for Richard II, who loved Owain, and because he was deposed, he rose up.

Eagle delightful beyond measure,
fine-helmed Owain, generous with a gift,
golden son — mighty his stroke —
of Gruffudd Fychan — fair his fame,
5   protector of great Glyn — cupbearer of abundant drink —
Dyfrdwy of lively waters,
I was voluble, last evening,
at the feast of abundant mead,
my treasure, frequently jesting with you
10   in your court, where I had wine from your hand.
Lord of the mead, greater was my discourtesy
and my behavior towards you worse,

nêr mawlair nawrym milwr,
nag ar fy nhad, arnad, ŵr.

15   Yr awr yr aethost ar ŵyth
dir Prydyn, darpar adwyth,
agos i hiraeth, gaeth gad,
a'm dwyn i farw amdanad.
Nid aeth dy gof drosof draw,

20   aur baladr, awr heb wylaw;
dagrau dros y grudd dugrych,
dyfriw glaw fal dwfr a'i gwlych.
Pan oedd drymaf fy nhrafael
amdanad, mab y tad hael,

25   cefais o ben rhyw gennad,
cei ras Duw, cywir ystad,
cael yn yr aer, calon rwydd,
ohonod fawrglod, f'arglwydd.
Daroganawdd, drymlawdd dro,

30   duw a dyn, o doud yno,
f'enaid uwch Dyfrdwy faenawr,
fy nêr, fwrw llawer i'r llawr.
Dewin, os mi a'i dywawd,
fûm yma gwarwyfa gwawd.

35   Cefaist ramant yn d'antur
Uthr Bendragon, gofion gur,
pan ddialawdd, gawdd goddef,
ei frawd, â'i rwysg, ei frwydr ef.
Hwyliaist, siwrneiaist helynt

40   Owain ab Urien gain gynt,
pan oedd fuan ymwanwr
y marchog duog o'r dŵr;
gŵr fu ef wrth ymguraw,
a phen draig y ffynnon draw;

45   gwŷr a fuant, llwyddiant llu,
gwrdd ddewrnerth, gwewyr ddarnu.
Tithau Owain, taith ewybr,
taer y gwnaut, drafn, â llafn, llwybr.
Brawd unweithred y'th edir,

50   barwn hoff, mab Urien hir
pan gyhyrddawdd, ryglawdd rôn,
â phen marchog y ffynnon.
Pan oedd drymaf dy lafur
draw yn ymwriaw â'r mur,

55   torres dy onnen gennyd,
tirion grair taer yn y gryd,
dewredd Ffwg, dur oedd ei phen,
dors garw, yn dair ysgyren;
gwelodd pawb draw i'th law lân,

lord of great praise with nine times the strength of a warrior,
in return for my support, man, than towards my father.

15 The hour you went in anger
to the land of Scotland, intending destruction,
nearly did longing, fierce struggle,
bring me to death because of you.
Your memory did not leave me there,

20 golden spear, an hour without weeping;
tears across the dark furrowed cheek,
droplets of rain wetting it like water.
When my worry over you was heaviest,
son of a generous father,

25 I received from the mouth of some messenger
— you have God's grace, true status —
that you won in battle, generous heart,
great fame, my lord.
God and man prophesied, occasion of profound praise,

30 if you went there,
my friend who rules over the lordship of Dyfrdwy,
my lord, the overthrow of many to the ground.
A sage — if I may say so —
was I here on the playground of praise poetry.

35 You had in your adventure the likes of the tale
of Uthr Bendragon, pangs of memory,
when he avenged, sadness of suffering,
his brother with his sudden attack, his battle.
You sailed, you journeyed in the chase

40 of fine Owain ab Urien of old,
when he was a swift jouster
with the Black Knight from the water;
he was a man for fighting,
and chief warrior at that spring.

45 They were men, the success of an army,
brave, strong and fierce, shattering spears.
You, too, Owain — an easy voyage —
fiercely made, lord, with a sword, a path.
You are considered a brother, having performed the same deed,

50 praiseworthy baron, of the tall son of Urien
when he met, piercing lance,
with the chief Knight of the Spring.
When your labor was heaviest
there, fighting with the wall of men,

55 your spear of ash broke
— gentle treasure, terrible in the fight,
with the bravery of Ffwg — its head was of steel,
a cruel torch — into three pieces.
Everyone saw there in your fair hand,

60   gwiw fawldaith, gwayw ufeldan;
        drylliaist, duliaist ar dalwrn,
        dy ddart hyd ymron dy ddwrn.
        O nerth ac arial calon,
        a braich ac ysgwydd a bron
65   peraist, fy naf, o'th lafur
        pyst mellt rhwng y dellt a'r dur;
        gyrraist yno, gwrs doniog,
        y llu, gyriad ychen llog,
        bob ddau, bob dri, rhi rhoddfawr,
70   ar darf oll o'r dyrfa fawr.
        Hyd Ddydd Brawd, medd dy wawdydd,
        hanwyd o feilch, hynod fydd,
        dyfyn glwys, daufiniog lain,
        dêl brwydr, dy hwyl i Brydain,
75   wrth dorri brisg i'th wisg wen
        a'th ruthr i'r maes â'th rethren,
        a'th hyrddwayw rhudd, cythrudd cant,
        a'th ddeg enw a'th ddigoniant.
        Clywsam, ddinam ddaioni,
80   hort teg gan herod i ti,
        iach wyd, ddiarswyd ddursiamp,
        a chrio i Gymro'r gamp;
        a gawr drist gwedy'r garw dro
        brydnawn am Brydyn yno,
85   a'r gair i Gymry, hy hwyl,
        ŵyth archoll brwydr, o'th orchwyl,
        a'r gwiw rwysg, a'r goresgyn,
        a'r glod i'r marchog o'r Glyn.

Teityl Owain i'r dywysogaeth oedd i fod ef yn dyfod o ferch Llywelyn ap Gruff[udd] a las o dwyll ym Muellt.

4. IOLO GOCH, *MOLIANT OWAIN GLYNDŴR*   Welsh
                                                           after 1385

        Mawr o symud a hud hydr
        a welwn ni ar welydr.
        Archwn i Fair, arch iawn fu,
        noddi'r bual gwineuddu,
5   arglwydd terwyn o'r Glyn glwys
        yw'r Pywer Lew, iôr Powys.
        Pwy adwaenai bai'n y byd,
        pwy ond Owain, paun diwyd?
        Rhwysg y iarll balch gwyarllwybr,
10   rhysgyr mab Llŷr ym mhob llwybr.
        Anoberi un barwn

60   fitting praiseworthy attack, a fiery spear.
       You shattered — you struck in the field —
       your dart almost to your fist.
       From strength and fierceness of heart
       and arm and shoulder and breast
65   you caused, my lord, by your labor
       lightning bolts between the splintered bits and the steel.
       There you drove, fortunate course,
       the host, a driving of hired oxen,
       by twos, by threes, lord of great gifts,
70   scattering all the great crowd.
       Until Judgment Day, says your poet,
       — you come from a proud line — remarkable will be
       — fair summons — with a two-edged blade,
       should battle come, your attack, to the people of Britain,
75   cutting a path in your white garments
       and your rush to the field with your lance,
       and your red thrusting-spear, affliction of a hundred,
       and your fair name and your accomplishment.
       We heard, faultless bravery,
80   a fair declaration by a herald about you,
       that you are hale, fearless coat of mail,
       and crying that the contest goes to a Welshman;
       and a sad shout after the harsh turn of events
       in the afternoon for Scotland there,
85   and the decision going to the Welsh, bold attack,
       — wrath of the wound of battle — because of your undertaking,
       and the fitting authority, and the conquest,
       and the fame of the knight of the Glyn.

Owain's title to the Principality was that he was descended from a daughter of Llywelyn ap Gruffudd, who was slain by treachery at Builth.

4. Iolo Goch, *Owain's Exploits in Scotland*   Notes: pp. 269–73

       Great movement and mighty magic
       do we see among lords.
       Let us ask Mary — it was a proper request —
       to protect the bay-black bison,
5   — a fiery lord from the fair Glyn
       is the Pywer Lew — the lord of Powys.
       Who would recognize a fault in the world,
       who but Owain, faithful peacock?
       The authority of the proud earl, bloody his path,
10   the force of Llŷr's son in every path.
       Any baron is a man of no account

ond y rhyw yr henyw hwn;
hynod yw henw ei daid,
brenin ar y barwniaid;
15   ei dad, pawb a wyddiad pwy,
iôr Glyn, daeardor, Dyfrdwy;
Hiriell, Cymru ddihaereb,
oedd ei dad yn anad neb;
pwy bynnag fo'r Cymro call,
20   bythorud? — gwn beth arall;
gorau mab rhwng gŵr a mam
o Bowys, foddlwys fuddlam;
os mab, mab yn adnabod
caru clêr, felly ceir clod.
25   Ni fyn i un ofyn ach
i feibion, ni bu fwbach;
ni ddug degan o'i anfodd
gan fab ond a gâi o'i fodd;
ni pheris drwy gis neu gur
30   iddo â'i ddwylo ddolur;
ni chamodd fys na chymwyll
cymain' â bw, cymen bwyll.

Pan aeth mewn gwroliaeth gwrdd,
gorugwr fu garw agwrdd,
35   ni wnaeth ond marchogaeth meirch,
gorau amser, mewn gwrmseirch,
dwyn paladr, gwaladr gwiwlew,
soced dur a siaced tew,
arwain rhest a phenffestin
40   a helm wen, gŵr hael am win,
ac yn ei phen, nen iawnraifft,
adain rudd o edn yr Aifft.
Gorau sawdwr gwrs ydoedd
gyda Syr Grigor, iôr oedd,
45   ym Merwig, hirdrig herwdref,
maer i gadw'r gaer gydag ef.
Gair mawr am fwrw y gŵr march
a gafas pan fu gyfarch,
a'i gwympio yno'n gampus
50   i lawr, a'i aesawr yn us.
A'r ail grwydr a fu brwydr brid,
a dryll ei wayw o drallid;
cof a chyfliw heddiw hyn,
cannwyll brwydr, can holl Brydyn;
55   rhai'n llefain, rhai'n druain draw,
pob drygddyn, pawb dioer rhagddaw
yn gweiddi megis gwyddeifr,

but one of the lineage that this one is descended from.
Notable is the name of his grandfather,
king of the barons;
15 his father — everyone knew who —
the Lord of Glyn — narrow valley — Dyfrdwy;
a Hiriell, the exemplar of Wales,
was his father, more than anyone.
Whoever the wise Welshman might be,
20 what does it matter to you? I know something else:
The best boy between a man and a mother
of Powys, fine its custom, fortunate its faith.
If a boy, a boy who knew
to love poets. (Thus is fame achieved!)
25 He does not wish that anyone ask their lineage
of boys. He was never a bully.
He never took a toy against his will
from a boy, only what he would get willingly.
He never caused by stroke or blow
30 grief to him with his hands.
He never beckoned nor said
so much as "boo"; wise discretion.

When he reached stout manhood,
he was a rough, mighty slasher.
35 He did nothing but ride horses —
best of times — in dark armor,
carrying a lance, a brave proper lord,
an iron socket and a thick jacket,
a spear rest and a mail coif
40 and a fair helmet — a man generous with wine —
and on its top — finely-plumed lord —
a red plume of the bird of Egypt.
He was the best soldier of the time
with Sir Gregory — he was a lord —
45 in Berwick, a town long subject to raids,
a steward to keep the town with him.
Great praise for overthrowing a horseman
did he get when there was an encounter,
and he threw him there skilfully
50 to the ground, with his shield in bits.
And a second rout was a costly battle,
and he broke his spear with (his) ferocity.
Today this is a memory and a reproach
— he is the candle of battle — to all of Scotland,
55 some crying out, some wretched there,
each bad man, everyone indeed before him
bleating like wild goats.

gyrrodd ofn, garw fu i Ddeifr.
Mawr fu y llwybr drwy'r crwybr crau,
60   blwyddyn yn porthi bleiddiau;
ni thyfodd gwellt na thafol
hefyd na'r ŷd ar ei ôl,
o Ferwig Seisnig ei sail
hyd Faesbwrch, hydr fu ysbail.

5. Gruffudd Llwyd, *Mael Ni Wn I Mwy*   **Welsh 1386x87**

Byd dudrist, bywyd hydraul,
ydyw hwn hyd y daw haul.
Llawn yw, ac nid llawen neb,
a llonaid y naill wyneb
5   o dda i rai nid oedd raid;
aml iawn gan y mileiniaid
ariant ac aur, ni roent ged,
a golud, byd gogaled;
Cymry, rhag maint eu camrwysg,
10   cenedl druain fal brain brwysg:
gallwn, nid erfynnwn fudd,
eu galw yn gallor goludd.
A fu isaf ei foesau
uchaf yw, mawr yw'r och fau,
15   a'r uchaf cyn awr echwydd
isaf ac ufyddaf fydd.
A fu dincwd, hwd hudawl,
y sy bencwd, tancwd diawl!
Myned yn weilch bob eilchwyl
20   mae'r berïon cylion cul;
hyn a wna, hen a newydd,
y drygfyd. Pa fyd a fydd?
Methu y mae y ddaear
hyd nad oes nac ŷd nac âr.
25   Cadarnaf, blaenaf un blaid
o fryd dyn fu Frytaniaid;
atgnithion wedi cnithiaw
ŷnt weithion, cyfoedion Caw.
Tri amherodr tra moroedd
30   a fu onaddun'; un oedd,
brenin brwydr, Brân briodawr,
brawd Beli camwri mawr;
Custennin a wnaeth drin draw,
Arthur, chwith fu neb wrthaw.
35   Diau o beth ydyw bod
brenhinoedd, bro iawn hynod,

He caused fear. He was rough to the Scots.
Great was the path through the bloody hoar-frost,
60   a year feeding wolves.
Neither grass nor dock grew,
nor corn, in his track
from Berwick, English its foundation,
to Maesbury, mighty was the spoil.

5. GRUFFUDD LLWYD, *I KNOW NO GREATER LORD*   Notes: pp. 273–81

A gloomy world, a transitory life,
is this as far as the sun shines.
It is full — and no one is happy —
with a surfeit, on the one side,
5   of goods for those who had no need.
Very often the villains have
silver and gold — they give no gift —
and wealth. A harsh world.
The Welsh, because their oppression is so great,
10   are a kindred of wretches like drunken crows;
I could — I would not beg for gain —
call them a kettle of tripe.
Whoever was lowest in his mores
is highest — great is this moan of mine —
15   and the highest before midday
will be lowest and most humble.
Who was a codpiece — deceiving hood —
is a headpiece, devil's scrotum.
The slender feathered kites are
20   behaving like hawks at every turn.
It is this that causes, old and new,
the troubled world. What sort of world is to come?
The earth is failing
because there is neither corn nor ploughed land.
25   The strongest, foremost single group
in man's mind were the Britons —
feeble strokes after striking
are they now — the contemporaries of Caw.
Three emperors (whose rule extended) beyond the seas
30   were among them; one was
a king of battle, Brân the rightful ruler,
brother of Beli of great deeds;
Custennin, who made battle yonder;
Arthur, awkward was anyone compared to him.
35   It is a certain thing that there were
kings, quite remarkable region,

bum hugain ar Lundain lys,
coronog, ceirw yr ynys.
Oes farchog urddawl, hawl hy,
40   trais ac amraint, tros Gymry
ond Dafydd, uswydd aesawr,
jestus a meddiannus mawr,
o Hanmer, llwydner llednais,
a Grigor, ail Sain Siôr, Sais,
45   er pan estynnwyd, rhwyd trin,
gwayw ufelfellt gafaelfin
a phensel Syr Hywel hoyw,
air Otiel, aur ei otoyw?
Bu amser caid blinder blwng
50   anystwyth yny ostwng,
lle profed gerllaw Profyns
llew praff yn gwarchadw llu pryns;
diwedd farchog, deddf orchest,
dewredd grym, dur oedd ei grest.
55   O hil Ednywain hoywlyw
hyd yr aeth ei had a'i ryw
ni bu genedl ddiledlyth
heb adu neb yn y nyth
a gwarthol loyw, os hoyw swydd,
60   oreuraid ar ei orwydd.
Pa un weithion, pan ethyw,
piau'r swydd? Parhäus yw
Owain, mael ni wn i mwy,
iôr Glyn, daeardor, Dyfrdwy;
65   arglwyddfab o ryw gwleddfawr
Sycharth, cadfuarth, ced fawr.
Henyw, hen ei ryw erioed
er cyn cof a'r can cyfoed,
o Gymro, fam dinam dad;
70   gwisgo wrls ac ysgarlad,
a harnais aur goreuryw
a gra mân, barwn grym yw.
Os iach a rhydd fydd efô,
ef a ennill, pan fynno,
75   esgidiau, gwindasau gwaisg,
cordwalfrith, carw diwylfraisg,
yn ymwan ar dwrneimant,
yn briwio cyrff, yn bwrw cant;
eistedd a gaiff ar osteg
80   ar y bwrdd tâl, byrddaid teg;
anneddf a cham ni oddef,
ymysg ieirll ydd ymwaisg ef.

five score, at the London court,
crowned, stags of the island.
Is there an ordained knight, bold claim,
40 tyranny and disgrace, in all of Wales,
except for Dafydd — splintered shields,
a justice and very powerful —
of Hanmer, a gentle venerable lord,
and Grigor — a second Saint George — Sais,
45 since the lightning-sparked, biting-edged spear
was extended, snare of battle,
and the pennon of lively Sir Hywel,
with the reputation of Otiel, gold his spur?
There was a time when there was dreary weariness of battle,
50 unyielding, until he prevailed,
as when put to the test near Provence,
a stout lion guarding the host of a prince,
the last knight, custom of excellence,
stout bravery, his crest was steel.
55 From Ednywain's line, lively leader,
as far as his seed and his kind extend
there was never a mighty generation
that did not leave someone in the nest
and a shining stirrup, if it is a fine office,
60 brightly gilded on his steed.
Who now, since he has gone,
will hold the office? It is continuous:
Owain, I know no greater lord,
the Lord of Glyn, narrow valley, Dyfrdwy,
65 lord's son of the lineage of the lavish feasts
of Sycharth, fortress of great bounty.
He is descended — his lineage ever ancient
since before memory and a hundred equal ages —
from a Welshman, and from a mother with a faultless father.
70 Wearing borders and scarlet,
and gold harness of the best sort,
and small fur; he is a powerful baron.
If he is well and free,
he will win, whenever he wishes,
75 boots, fine buskins,
of speckled cordovan — bold powerful stag —
jousting in a tournament,
bruising bodies, overthrowing a hundred.
A seat he shall get at the call to silence
80 at the head table, fair tableful.
He will not tolerate lawlessness and wrong.
He will include himself amongst earls.

6. IOLO GOCH, *ACHAU OWAIN GLYNDŴR*

Welsh
1385x1400

Myfyrio bûm i farwn
moliant dyhuddiant i hwn;
arwyrain Owain a wnaf,
ar eiriau mydr yr euraf
5   peunydd, nid naddiad gwŷdd gwern,
pensaerwawd paun y Sirwern.
Pwy yng nghlawr holl Faelawr hir,
paun, rhwy Glyndyfrdwy dyfrdir,
pwy a ddylai, ped fai fyd,
10   — pwy ond Owain, paun diwyd —
y ddwy Faelawr mawr eu mâl,
eithr efo, a Mathrafal?
Pwy a ostwng Powystir,
pe bai gyfraith a gwaith gwir?
15   Pwy eithr y mab penaethryw,
Owain Gruffudd, Nudd in yw,
fab Gruffudd, llafnrudd yw'r llall,
gryfgorff gymen ddigrifgall,
orwyr Madog, iôr medeingl,
20   Fychan yn ymseingian Eingl,
goresgynnydd Ruffudd rwydd
Maelawr, gywirglawr arglwydd,
hil Fadog hiroediog hen,
Gymro ger hoywfro Hafren,
25   hwyliwr yr holl Ddeheuwlad,
hil Arglwydd Rhys, gwŷs i gad,
hil Fleddyn, hil Gynfyn gynt,
hil Aedd, o ryw hael oeddynt,
hil Faredudd rudd ei rôn,
30   tëyrn Carneddau Teon,
hil y Gwinau Dau Freuddwyd,
hil Bywer Lew, fy llew llwyd,
hil Ednyfed, lifed lafn,
hil Uchdryd lwyd, hael wychdrafn,
35   hil Dewdwr mawr, gwawr gwerin,
heliwr â gweilch, heiliwr gwin,
hil Faig Mygrfras, gwas gwaywsyth,
heirdd fydd ei feirdd o'i fodd fyth.
Hawddamor pôr eurddor pert,
40   hwyl racw ym mrwydr, hil Ricert,
barwn mi a wn ei ach,
ni bu barwn bybyrach;
anoberi un barwn
eithr y rhyw yr henyw hwn.
45   Gorwyr, dioer, o gaer Dwyrain,

6. Iolo Goch, *Owain Glyndŵr's Lineage*   **Notes: pp. 282–92**

I have been contemplating for a baron
the solace of praise for him.
I shall exalt Owain;
in metered words I will gild
5   daily — this is not the hewing of alder trees —
the master craftsman's praise of the peacock of Sirwern.
Who in the whole land of extensive Maelor,
peacock, lord of Glyndyfrdwy's watery land,
who would have the right, if the world were fair,
10 — who but Owain, faithful peacock? —
to the two Maelors, great their rent,
and Mathrafal, except for him.
Who would subdue the land of Powys,
if there were law and just deeds?
15 Who but the son of noble descent,
Owain Gruffudd — he is Nudd to us —
son of Gruffudd — the other is bloody-bladed —
strong-bodied, wise, delightful and discerning,
great-grandson of Madog — Angle-reaping lord —
20 Fychan, trampling Angles,
descendant of generous Gruffudd
Maelor, lord of a true land,
of the line of long-lived ancient Madog,
a Welshman by the splendid vale of the Severn,
25 leader of the entire Southland,
of the line of the Lord Rhys, a summons to battle,
of the line of Bleddyn, of the line of Cynfyn of old,
of the line of Aedd, they were from a generous stock,
of the line of Maredudd, red his spear,
30 monarch of Carneddau Teon,
of the line of Gwinau Dau Freuddwyd,
of the line of Pywer Lew, my tawny lion,
of the line of Ednyfed, whetted blade,
of the line of Uchdryd the grey, generous splendid lord,
35 of the line of Tewdwr the Great, people's hero,
hunter with hawks, dispenser of wine,
of the line of Maig Mygrfras, straight-speared lad —
handsome will his poets be always, at his will.
Hail, sovereign, fine golden protector,
40 a rush yonder in battle, of the line of Rhicert.
A baron whose lineage I know,
there was no baron more zealous.
Any baron is a man of no account
except one of the stock that this one is descended from.
45 Great-grandson, God knows, from a fortress of the East,

Gwenllian o Gynan gain.
Medd y ddwy Wynedd einym,
Da yw, a gatwo Duw ym,
wrth bawb ei ortho a'i bwyll,
50   Arth o Ddeheubarth hoywbwyll,
cynyddwr pobl cyneiddwng,
cnyw blaidd ydyw'r cenau blwng,
balch a dewr, bylchai darian,
Beli y Glyn, bual glân,
55   llew Prydain, llaw Peredur,
llew siaced tew soced dur,
pestel cad, arglwydd-dad glew,
post ardal Lloegr, pais durdew,
edling o hen genhedlaeth
60   yw ef o ben Tref y Traeth;
ei gyfoeth, ef a'i gofyn,
Tref y Garn, a'i farn a fyn;
Gwrthrych fydd, gorthrech ei farn,
gwrthrychiad gorthir Acharn.
65   Mab da arab dihaereb
hyd hyn fu, ni wybu neb;
gŵr bellach a grybwyllir,
ni wneir dwyn un erw o'i dir;
marchog ffyrf rhieddog rhwydd,
70   mawrchwyrn lle bu'r ymorchwydd;
neur aeth, asgwrn nerth esgud,
ei floedd, o'i droed mae'n flaidd drud.
Garw wrth arw, gŵr wrth eraill,
ufudd a llonydd i'r llaill,
75   llonydd wrth wan, rhan ei raid,
aflonydd i fileiniaid.
Llew Is Coed, lluosog ged,
llaw a wna llu eniwed,
llithio'r brain, llethu Brynaich
80   â llath bren mwy na llwyth braich.
Be magwn, byw ymogor,
genau i neb, egin iôr,
hael eurddrem, hwyl awyrddraig,
i hwn y magwn, ail Maig.
85   Tawwn, gorau yw tewi,
am hwn ni ynganwn ni;
da daint rhag tafod, daw dydd,
yng nghilfach safn anghelfydd,
cael o hwn, coel a honnir,
90   calon Is Aeron a'i sir,
ac iechyd a phlant gwycheirdd
yn Sycharth, buarth y beirdd.

of Gwenllian descended from fair Cynan.
Our two Gwynedds say,
"He is good — may God keep him for us —
to everyone in his patience and his understanding."
50   A bear from Deheubarth of lively understanding,
a conqueror of a stubborn people,
a young wolf is the angry cub,
proud and brave, he would hew a shield.
Beli of the Glyn, a beautiful bison,
55   lion of Britain, the hand of Peredur,
thick-jacketed lion with a socket of steel,
pestle of battle, a brave lordly father,
pillar of the region of Lloegr, a thick iron surcoat,
heir of an ancient clan
60   is he, from the head of Tref y Traeth.
His realm — he claims it —
is Tref-y-Garn, and he desires his judgment.
He will be heir, his judgment will prevail,
heir to the highlands of Acharn.
65   A good, gracious, exemplary lad
was he up to now, no one knew;
as a man is he praised henceforth.
Not one acre of his land will be taken.
A firm, noble, generous knight,
70   fierce where the battle-surge was.
There came — bone of quick strength —
his war-cry, from his foot up he is a fierce wolf.
Harsh to the harsh, a man to others,
humble and gentle to the rest,
75   gentle to the weak — he shares his necessities,
ungentle to villains.
Lion of Is Coed, numerous gifts,
a hand that does harm to a host,
feeding the ravens, overpowering Scots
80   with a wooden spear heavier than an armload.
If I were to nurture, a living abode,
a cub for anyone, offspring of a lord,
a generous beautiful visage, the temper of a flying dragon,
for him I would do it, a second Maig.
85   Let us be silent — being silent is best;
let us not mention this man.
Teeth are good in front of the tongue — a day will come —
in the depths of an unskilled mouth —
when he shall get — the belief is declared —
90   the heart of Is Aeron and its cheer,
and health and splendid, beautiful children
in Sycharth, the poets' rendezvous.

Corwen, Dyfrdwy, Conwy, Cain,
Cai fath hoyw, cyfoeth Owain;
95   un gad, un llygad, un llaw,
aur burffrwyth iôr Aberffraw;
un pen ar Gymru, wen wedd,
ac un enaid gan Wynedd,
un llygad, cymyniad caith,
100   ac unllaw yw i Gynllaith.

7. SCROPE-GROSVENOR TRIAL REPORT

Anglo-Norman
3 Sept. 1386

Oweyn, sire de Glendore, del age xxvij anz et pluys — jurre admys et diligente-
ment examine de et sur le droit de Monsieur Robert le Grosvenour de porter les
armes cestassavoir d'azure ov un bender d'ore — dit que les ditz armes de droit
appertinent a Monsieur Robert le Grovenour. Requys coment il ce sciet dit q'il ad
5   oie des anxiens gentz as queux il croia que les auncestres du dit Monsieur Robert
al temps de Conquest d'Engleterre ont portez les ditz armes sanz ascun reclamacion
et unques n'ad oie de la contraire tanque a ceste presente debate moeve. Requys
auxi s'il unques vist le dit Monsieur Robert arme en les ditz armez dit que oille
cestassavoir en le derein viage nostre seignur le Roy qore est en Escoce. Requyst
10   outre s'il vist aucuns charteres ou autres munimentz, auncientz ensealez ov sealx
eantz les ditz armes engravez dit que oil. Et dit q'ils estoient molt aunciens come il
sembloit per vieu de perchemyn et del cere. Lettre dit le dit jurre qen le conte de
Cestre et Flynt et autres lieux et contees percheinz publik vois et fame est que les
ditz armes ont apperteine et appertinent come desuz. au dit monsieur Robert et a
15   cez auncestres.

8. IOLO GOCH, LLYS OWAIN GLYNDŴR

Welsh
1387–95

Addewais hyd hyn ddwywaith,
addewid teg, addo taith;
taled bawb, tâl hyd y bo,
ei addewid a addawo.
5   Pererindawd, ffawd ffyddlawn,
perwyl mor annwyl, mawr iawn,
myned, eidduned oddáin,
lles yw, tua llys Owain;
yn oddáin yno ydd af,
10   nid drwg, yno y trigaf
i gymryd i'm bywyd barch
gydag ef o gydgyfarch;
fo all fy naf, uchaf ach,
eurben claer, erbyn cleiriach;

Corwen, Dyfrdwy, Conwy, Cain
— the like of sprightly Cai — Owain's realm;
95   the same battle, the same eye, the same hand,
golden pure fruit of the lord of Aberffraw;
the one head of Wales, fair in appearance,
and Gwynedd's one darling,
one eye, slayer of slaves,
100   and one hand is he to Cynllaith.

7. *SCROPE-GROSVENOR TRIAL REPORT*   Notes: p. 292

Owain, knight of Glyndyfrdwy, aged twenty-seven years and more — whom the jury accepted and diligently examined on the right of Sir Robert Grosvenor to carry the arms here known as the *azure a bend or* — said that these said arms were rightly associated with Sir Robert Grosvenor. He reported how he knew he said that he had heard that of the ancient people by means of which he believed that the ancestors of the said Sir Robert at the time of the Conquest of England had carried the said arms without any complaint and he had never heard of the contrary until the stirring of this present debate. He reported also that he had always seen the said Sir Robert carrying the said arms, that he had seen this with his own eyes in the most recent expedition of our lord the present king into Scotland. He reported further that he had seen with his eye some charters or other muniments, ancient markings, or inherited seals on which the said arms were engraved. And he said that they were very ancient as it seemed on account of the parchment and the value of it. By letter he said to the same jury that in the counties of Chester and Flint and other places and counties the public voice and fame is that the said arms had belonged and do belong to the said Sir Robert and to his ancestors.

8. IOLO GOCH, *OWAIN GLYNDŴR'S COURT*   Notes: pp. 292–97

I have promised twice so far
— fair promise — to promise a journey.
Let each one fulfil, as much as he might,
the promise that he promises.
5   A very great pilgrimage — faithful fortune,
a purpose so dear —
is going — swift oath,
it is good — toward Owain's court.
Swiftly shall I go there;
10   — it is not bad — there I shall stay
to gain in my life honor
with him at our mutual greeting.
My lord is able — highest lineage,
bright golden leader — to welcome a decrepit old man.

15   clod bod, cyd boed alusen,
        ddiwarth hwyl, yn dda wrth hen.
        I'w lys ar ddyfrys ydd af,
        o'r deucant odidocaf.
        Llys barwn, lle syberwyd,
20   lle daw beirdd aml, lle da byd;
        gwawr Bowys fawr, beues Faig,
        gofuned gwiw ofynaig.

        Llyna'r modd a'r llun y mae
        mewn eurgylch dwfr mewn argae:
25   (pand da'r llys?) pont ar y llyn,
        ac unporth lle'r ai ganpyn;
        cyplau sydd, gwaith cwplws ŷnt,
        cwpledig pob cwpl ydynt;
        clochdy Padrig, Ffrengig ffrwyth,
30   clostr Wesmustr, clostir esmwyth;
        cynglynrhwym pob congl unrhyw,
        cangell aur, cyngan oll yw;
        cynglynion yn fronfron fry,
        dordor megis daeardy,
35   a phob un fal llun llyngwlm
        sydd yn ei gilydd yn gwlm;
        tai nawplad fold deunawplas,
        tai pren glân mewn top bryn glas;
        ar bedwar piler eres
40   mae'i lys ef i nef yn nes;
        ar ben pob piler pren praff
        llofft ar dalgrofft adeilgraff,
        a'r pedair llofft o hoffter
        yn gydgwplws lle cwsg clêr;
45   aeth y pedair disgleirlofft,
        nyth lwyth teg iawn, yn wyth lofft;
        to teils ar bob tŷ talwg,
        a simnai lle magai'r mwg;
        naw neuadd gyfladd gyflun,
50   a naw gwardrob ar bob un,
        siopau glân glwys cynnwys cain,
        siop lawndeg fel Siêp Lundain;
        croes eglwys gylchlwys galchliw,
        capelau â gwydrau gwiw;
55   popty llawn poptu i'r llys,
        perllan, gwinllan ger gwenllys;
        melin deg ar ddifreg ddŵr,
        a'i glomendy gloyw maendwr;
        pysgodlyn, cudduglyn cau,
60   a fo rhaid i fwrw rhwydau;

15   It brings fame, though it be alms,
        — a course without shame — to be good to the old.
      To his court I will go in haste;
        out of two hundred it is the most remarkable.
      A baron's court, a place of nobility,
20   a place where many poets come, a place of the good life,
      a lady of great Powys, Maig's land,
      a fitting promise of hope.

      Here is the manner and the image that it has
      in a bright ring of water within an embankment:
25   Isn't the court fine? — a bridge over the lake,
      and a single gate where a hundred packloads could go;
      there are couples — they are couples-work —
      each couple is coupled;
      Patrick's bell-house, French fruit,
30   Westminster cloisters, a comfortable enclosure;
      each corner bound in the same way,
      golden chancel, it is fully harmonious;
      the binding joists breast to breast above,
      belly to belly like an earthen house,
35   and each one like the image of a tight knot
      which is knotted with its fellow;
      nine-plate houses in the mold of eighteen mansions,
      beautiful wooden houses atop a green hill;
      on four wonderful pillars,
40   his house is nearer to heaven;
      on top of each stout wooden pillar,
      a strongly built loft on top of a croft,
      and the four lofts of loveliness
      coupled together, where poets sleep;
45   the four bright lofts became —
      a very fair nest load — eight lofts;
      A roof of tiles on every frowning gabled house,
      and a chimney where the smoke would rise;
      nine symmetrical halls all alike,
50   and nine wardrobes in each one,
      clean, comely shops with fine contents,
      a fair full shop like London's Cheapside;
      the cross of a church whitewashed all around,
      chapels with wonderful glass windows,
55   a full bakery on every side of the court,
      an orchard, a vineyard near the bright court,
      a fair mill on the smooth water,
      and his dovecote, a bright stone tower;
      a fishpond, a little hollow enclosure,
60   where nets may be thrown at need,

amlaf lle, nid er ymliw,
penhwyaid a gwyniaid gwiw,
a'i dir bwrdd a'i adar byw,
peunod, crehyrod hoywryw;
65   dolydd glân gwyran a gwair,
ydau mewn caeau cywair,
parc cwning ein pôr cenedl,
erydr a meirch hydr, mawr chwedl;
gerllaw'r llys, gorlliwio'r llall,
70   y pawr ceirw mewn parc arall;
ei gaith a wna pob gwaith gwiw,
cyfreidiau cyfar ydiw,
dwyn blaendrwyth cwrw Amwythig,
gwirodau bragodau brig,
75   pob llyn, bara gwyn a gwin,
a'i gig, a'i dân i'w gegin;
pebyll y beirdd, pawb lle bo,
pe beunydd, caiff pawb yno;
tecaf llys bren, pen heb bai,
80   o'r deyrnas, nawdd Duw arnai;
a gwraig orau o'r gwragedd,
gwyn fy myd o'i gwin a'i medd!
Merch eglur llin marchoglyw,
urddol hael anianol yw;
85   a'i blant a ddeuant bob ddau,
nythaid teg o benaethau.
Anfynych iawn fu yno
weled na chliced na chlo,
na phorthoriaeth ni wnaeth neb;
90   ni bydd eisiau, budd oseb,
na gwall na newyn na gwarth,
na syched fyth yn Sycharth.
Gorau Cymro, tro trylew,
piau'r wlad, lin Pywer Lew,
95   gŵr meingryf, gorau mangre,
a phiau'r llys, hoff yw'r lle.

9. OWAIN GLYNDŴR, *GRANT OF LANDS*

Latin
17 June 1392

Sciant, presentes et futuri, quod nos, Oweyn ap Gruffuth, dominus de Glyndyvyrdoy, dedimus, concessimus, et hac presenti carta nostra confirmauimus Gruffuth
ap Ieuan Lloyt totum jus et clameum necessariis et tenementis que condam Davidi
Goch ap Madoc tenuit in villa de Mystwyr, cum omnibus suis libertatibus, commodi-
5   tatibus, et pertinentiis universis, habendum et tenendum totum praedictum jus et
clameum necessariis et tenementis ibidem cum omnibus suis libertatibus, commodi-

a place of great abundance, no doubt about it,
for pike and wonderful whiting;
and his bord-land and his live birds,
peacocks, elegant herons;
65   excellent meadows of pasture and hay,
corn in orderly fields,
a rabbit park for our people's lord,
ploughs and strong horses — a great tale;
beside the court, outshining the other,
70   deer graze in another park;
his bondmen who do each fitting task,
these are the necessities for cooperation,
bringing the best brewing of Shrewsbury beer,
strong liquors, foamy braggets,
75   every drink, white bread and wine,
and his meat and his fire for his kitchen.
A shelter for poets, everyone wherever he may be;
even if it were every day, he will receive everyone there.
The fairest wooden court — chief without fault —
80   of the kingdom, God's protection be upon it!
And the best woman among women —
I am blessed by her wine and her mead!
A bright girl from the line of a knightly ruler,
she is noble and generous by nature.
85   And his children come by twos,
a fair brood of chieftains.
It was very infrequent there
to see either latch or lock;
nor did anyone fulfil the function of porter.
90   There will be no need — beneficial gift —
nor want, nor hunger, nor shame,
nor thirst ever in Sycharth.
The best Welshman — brave deed —
owns the land, of the line of Pywer Lew,
95   a strong, slender man — the best dwelling —
and owns the court. The place is renowned.

9. OWAIN GLYNDŴR, *GRANT OF LANDS*   Notes: pp. 297–98

Know, those people here and those to come, that we, Owain ap Gruffudd, lord of Glyndyfrdwy, have given, granted, and by this our present charter confirmed to Gruffudd ab Ieuan Llwyd all the rights and necessary claims and tenements that were formerly held by Dafydd Goch ap Madog in the town of Mwstwr, with all its liberties, commodities, and appurtenances entire, to have and to hold all the aforesaid rights and necessary claims and these tenements with all its liberties, commod-

tatibus, et pertinnentiis universis de nobis et heredibus nostris praedicto Gruffuth ap Ieuan Lloyt heredes et assignatibus suis libere, quiete, bene, et in pace jure hereditis imperpetuum, reddendo inde nobis et heredes nostris annuatum duo-
10   decim denarius argentus in festus Sancti Michealis Archangeli pro omnibus serviciis secularibus et demandis. Et nos vero praedictus Oweyn ap Gruffuth et heredes nostram totam praedem jus et clameum in praedicto terris et tenementis cum omni-bus suis libertatibus, commoditatibus, et pertinentiis universa ibidem praedicto Gruffuth ap Ieuan Lloit, heredes, et assignatis suis imperpetuum contra omnes
15   gentes warantizabimus et imperpetuum defendemus. In cuius rei testimonium hinc praesenti carte sigilla nostra apponi fecimus. Hiis testibus Ednyfyd ap Gruffuth tunc temporis senescallo de Glyndyvyrdoy, Llewelyn ap Mereduth, rynghill ibidem, Gruffuth Lloit ap Ieuan Duy, Ednyfyd ap Ieuan ap Iorwerth, et Richard Keri et multis aliis. Datum apud Sycharth in manere ibidem die dominica proxima post
20   festum Sancti Barnabe Apostoli, anno regni regis Ricardi secundi post conquestum quintodecimo.

10. HENRY IV, *CONFISCATION OF OWAIN'S LANDS*   Latin
                                                                          8 November 1400

Rex omnibus ad quos etc., salutem.

Sciatis quod, de gratia nostra speciali, dedimus et concessimus carissimo fratri nostro Johanni, comiti Somersetiae, omnia maneria, terras, et tenementa quae fu-erunt Owini de Glyndordy, tam in Suthwallia quam in Northwallia, quae ratione
5   altae proditionis contra regiam magestatem nostram per praefatum Owinum factae et perpetratae, nobis forisfacta existent, et quae ad praesens valorem trescentarum marcarum per annum, per aestimationem (ut dicitur) non excedunt. Habenda et tenenda: omnia maneria, terras, et tenementa praedicta, una cum regaliis, regalita-tibus, feodis militum, advocationibus, et patronatibus omnimodorum beneficiorum
10   ecclesiasticorum, franchesiis, libertatibus, custumis, wardis, maritagiis, releviis, es-caetis, forisfacturis, chaceis, parcis, warennis, wrecco maris, et omnibus aliis profic-uis et commoditatibus quibuscumque, ad praedicta maneria, terras, et tenementa, spectantibus, sive pertinentibus, praefato comiti, et haeredibus suis, de nobis et hae-redibus nostris, per servitia inde debita et consueta, adeo libere, plene, et integre,
15   sicut praedictus Owinus ea habuit et tenuit aliquo tempore praeterito, absque ali-quo, nobis vel haeredibus nostris, inde reddendo, donatione et concessione per nos, nuper eidem comiti de castris, maneriis, terris, et tenementis quae fuerunt Radul-phi de Lumley chivaler, ratione forisfacturae ejusdem Radulphi, quae valent per annum eidem comiti trescentas et sexaginta libras, aut quadam annuitate viginti
20   librarum, per Richardum nuper regem Angliae secundum post Conquestum, eidem comiti pro nomine comitis Somersetiae, de exitibus comitatus Somersetiae, per manus vicecomitis ibidem percipiendarum, seu quadam alia annuitate sexaginta et sex librarum, tresdecim solidorum, et quatuor denariorum, per praefatum nuper regem, eidem comiti de exitibus honoris de Walynford percipiendarum, aut officio
25   camerarii Angliae, cujus valor non est certus, eo quod casualis existit, vactis, non obstantibus.

ities, and appurtenances entire of us and our heirs to the aforesaid Gruffudd ab Ieuan Llwyd, his heirs, and his assigns free from servitudes, without disturbance, with good will, and in peace, by lawful right of inheritance forever, rendering annually to us and our heirs twelve gold denarii at the feast of St. Michael the Archangel for all secular services and demands. And we truly the aforesaid Owain ap Gruffudd and the heirs of all our estates will warrant and forever defend to the aforesaid Gruffudd ab Ieuan Llwyd, his heirs, and his assigns forever against all men the same rights and claims in the aforesaid lands and tenements with all its liberties, commodities, and appurtenances entire. As testimony of which thing we have here affixed our current seal to this present charter. In witness whereof, Ednyfed ap Gruffudd, steward of Glyndyfrdwy, Llywelyn ap Maredudd, officer there, Gruffudd Llwyd ab Ieuan Ddu, Ednyfed ab Ieuan ab Iorwerth, Richard Keri, and many others. Dated at the manor of Sycharth, the next Sunday after the feast of St. Barnabas the Apostle, the fifteenth regnal year of King Richard the Second.

10. HENRY IV, *CONFISCATION OF OWAIN'S LANDS*   Notes: pp. 298–99

The king of all to whom etc., greetings.

Be it known that we, by our special grace, have given and granted to our beloved brother John, earl of Somerset, all the manors, lands, and tenements that previously belonged to Owain Glyndŵr, both in South Wales and in North Wales, which on account of the high treason against our royal majesty caused and committed by the aforesaid Owain are forfeited to us, and of which the values at present do not exceed an estimated three hundred marks per year (as it is said). These to be had and held: all the manors, lands, and tenements aforesaid, together with the royalties, the knights' fees, pleas, and patronages of all kinds of ecclesiastical benefices, franchises, liberties, customs, wards, marriages, reliefs, escheats, forfeitures, chases, parks, warrens, shipwrecks, and all other profits and commodities whatsoever associated with the aforesaid manors, lands, and tenements belonging or pertaining to the aforesaid earl, and to his heirs, given by us and our heirs, through the services both owed and customary, such freely, completely, and wholly, which the aforesaid Owain had and held at any time in the past. Except those of us and our heirs at the time rendered by gift and grant through us, recently to the same earl of the castles, manors, lands, and tenements which belonged to Ralph de Lumley, knight, by reason of the forfeitures of the same Ralph, to the same earl, which are valued at three hundred and sixty pounds per year, or a certain annuity of twenty pounds, given by Richard II, recent king of England, to the same earl in the name of the earl of Somerset, from the borders of the county of Somerset, these through the hands of the sheriffs receiving them there, or another annuity sixty-six pounds, thirteen shillings, and four pence, given by the aforesaid late king, to the same earl receiving them from the borders of the honor of Wallingford, or from the office of the chamberlain of England, the value of which is uncertain because the chance exists that they are empty not withstanding.

In cujus etc.
Teste rege apud Westmonasterium, octavo die Novembris.
Per ipsum regem.

11. *DE OWEINO GLENDWOREDY*   **Latin**
                                                          after 11 November 1400

Villa de Oswestry.
   Curia generalis et prima ibidem tenta vj^ti die Octobris Anno regni [Regis] Henrici iiij^ti secundo.
   Essonie: Johannes Lloitt, Ricardus Kyviley, Gruffith le Bakere, Rogerus Thom-
5   sonne, Ricardus Donn, qui sectam debent ad hanc curiam essoniati sunt de apparentia huius curie generalis.
   Inquisitio capta apud Ossestrey coram Johannes Whethales senescallo ibidem die et anno supradictis, per sacramentum Rogeri de Westbury, Ricardi Salter, Johannis Sherard, Ricardi Englys, Thomas Robinsonne, Johanne Burghall, Rogeri Glover,
10   Rogeri Yrelond, Thomas Richardsonne, Ricardi Hastonn et Johanne Gouch, qui dicunt super sacramentum summ quod Owen de Glyndowerdey, Griffinus filius eius, Tudur frater eius Oweini, Griffith Hanemer, [Phillippus Hanemer,] Robertus Pulesdon, Howell Kiffin decanus Assauensis, Ieuan Vachan ap Ieuan Gethin, Gruffith frater eius, Ieuan ap Iorwerth ap Egnion, Madoc ap Ieuan ap Madoc,
15   Ieuan ap Howell Pichull, Gruffith ap Ierwerth Gouche, Johannes Estewike, Craghe Ffynnant eorum propheta, et multi alij Wallicorum prodiciose machinantes, conspirantes et proponentes mortem et exhereditacionem domini regis predicti ac perpetuam adnullacionem corone et regalitatis sue ac omnium successorum suorum regum Anglie; mortem Henrici Principis Wallie filii regis nostri predicti primo-
20   geniti omnium magnatum et procerum Anglie; necnon mortem destruccionem et adnullacionem perpetuam tocius lingue Anglicane; erexerunt dictum Owinum ut principem eorum Wallie apud Glyndouerdey die Jovis proximo ante festum Sancti Mathei Apostoli anno regni [Regis] Henrici predicti primo insimul prodiciose insurgendo ad implendam et constentandam falsam et prodiciosam intencionem
25   suam supradictam prodiciose leuando de die in diem [de] nocte in noctem maximam multitudinem Wallicorum de pluribus partibus Wallie. Et deinde hostiliter modo guerrino transierunt directe ad villam de Ruthin et eam die Sabbati extunc proximo sequenti felonice omnibus et homines in eadem villa habitantes spoliauerunt et villam predictam immediate prodiciose combusserunt. Et deinde modo
30   guerrino hostiliter pergendo villas de Dynbighe, Rutheland, Flynt, Hawarden et Holt Anglicanas infra Walliam diebus Dominica, Lune at Martis proximis sequentibus felonice depredauerunt, ac villas de Ossestrey et Fellton Thome Comitis Arundell et Surrey in Marchia Wallie die Mercurij extunc proximo sequenti ac homines in eisdem habitantes felonice spoliauerunt ac easdem prodiciose combusserunt et
35   deinde hostiliter porrexerunt modo guerrino ad villam de la Pole et villam predictam ac homines in eadem habitantes die Jovis extunc proximo sequenti totaliter felonice spoliauerunt insimul cum exercitu modo hostilando et equitando usque in diem Veneris extunc proximum sequentem, quo die per dominum Hugonem Bur-

In whose, etc.

Witnessed by the king at Westminster, on the eighth day of November.
By the king.

11. *DE OWEINO GLENDWOREDY*   **Notes: pp. 299–303**

The Town of Oswestry.

   The General and First Court held there the sixth of October in the second year
of the reign of King Henry IV.

   Essoins: John Lloyd, Richard Kyviley, Gruffudd the Baker, Roger Thomson,
Richard Donn, who owe suit to this court, have been excused from appearing at this
General Court.

   An inquisition taken at Oswestry before John Westhales, steward of the same,
by the oath of Roger of Westbury, Richard Salter, John Sherard, Richard Englys,
Thomas Robinson, John Burghall, Roger Glover, Roger Ireland, Thomas Richard-
son, Richard Hastonn, and John Goch, who say upon their oath that Owain of Glyndyfrdwy, Gruffudd his son, Tudur brother of the same Owain, Gruffudd Hanmer,
[Philip Hanmer,] Robert Puleston, Hywel Cyffin, Dean of St. Asaph, Ieuan Fychan
ab Ieuan Gethin, Gruffudd his brother, Ieuan ab Iorwerth ab Einion, Madog ab
Ieuan ap Madog, Ieuan ap Hywel Pickhill, Gruffudd ab Iorwerth Goch, John East-
wick, Crach Ffinnant their "prophet," and many other Welshmen were treasonably
plotting, conspiring and intending the death and disinheriting of the said lord king
and the everlasting extinction of the crown and regality of himself and of all his successors, the kings of England; the death of Henry, Prince of Wales, the first-born
son of our said king, of all the magnates and nobles of England; and also the death,
destruction and the everlasting extinction of the whole English language. They
elevated the said Owain as their Prince of Wales at Glyndyfrdwy on Thursday before
the Feast of St. Matthew the Apostle in the first year of the reign of the aforesaid
[King] Henry, rising up treacherously together to carry out and affirm their above-
mentioned false and treasonable intention, treacherously levying, day after day,
night after night, a very great multitude of Welshmen from many parts of Wales.
And from thence they traveled in a warlike manner like enemies directly to the
town of Ruthin and on Saturday immediately following they feloniously despoiled
it in regards to all goods and the people living within the town, and instantly they
treacherously burnt the said town. And then proceeding hostilely in a warlike manner, they feloniously pillaged the English towns of Denbigh, Rhuddlan, Flint, Hawarden and Holt in Wales on the Sunday, Monday and Tuesday immediately following, and they despoiled the towns of Oswestry and Felton, belonging to Thomas,
Earl of Arundel and Surrey, in the Marches of Wales on the Wednesday immediately following, and they feloniously despoiled the people living in them and
treacherously burnt the same towns and then, like enemies, they made their way in
a warlike manner to the town of the Pool, and, on the Thursday immediately following, they feloniously and totally despoiled the said town and the people living
in it, attacking and riding together in a warlike manner with an army until Friday
immediately following, on which day they were defeated and scattered by Master

40   nell cum pluribus aliis ligeis eius Regis predicti de comitatibus Salope, Stafford et
      Warwicke insimul aggregatis iuxta predictam villam de la Poole super aquam Sabrine
      victi et dissipati fuerunt et deinde montanas et buscos querentes fugerunt et quam
      prius in forresti non fuissent. Dicunt eciam quod predicti Howell Kiffin, Ieuan Vach-
      unn ap Ieuan Gethen et Griffith frater eius, [Griffith filius] predicti Owini, Ieuan ap
      Ierwerth, Gruffith Hanmer ac plures alij proditores ac rebellos dominio regis in mon-
45   tanis et boscis Wallencibus commorantes et vagantes extra domanium de Chirkesland
      die Lune proximo ante festum Sancti Martini anno supradicto ac continuo prodicose
      auxiliauerunt.

      Et dicunt quod Gruffith Chaloner de villa de Ossestry, Ieuan ap Ieuan ap David
      Vachunn de Ossestry, Ieuan Laas, Phillipe ap David ap Maddoc, Madoc ap Enion,
50   Deio frater eius, Ieuan Werth, Ieuan ap Madoc ap Ieuan, Ieuan ap Ednevit, Diekes
      ap Egnion ap Ithel, Madoc ap Ieuan Graghe, Ieuan ap Ieuan Laas, Ieuan ap Madoc
      ap Gruffith, William Lloyd ap Maredudd, David ap Ieuan Lloyd, Ieuan ap Ieuan
      Vachan, Gruffith Goz de Blodewall, Ieuan ap Ierwerth de Hideslond, Johannes Sy-
      mond, William Twiford de duabus partibus de Ossestry, Atha ap Madoc ap Ierwerth,
55   Llewelyn frater eius, Llewelyn ap Ierwerth ap David, Madoc ap Ieuan ap Madoc,
      David ap Ieuan ap Madoc, Jacke Cadarne, Madoc ap Ieuan Gruffith, Deio ap Ieuan
      Lloyd, Enion ap Iorwerth, Gruffith ap Jeukes, Gruffith ap Ieuan ap Rees de Malveley
      tenens domanij dicti de Ossestry, Sir John Tuder, Grono ap David ap Maddoc et
      Maredudd ap Ierwerth ap Ieuan de Kynardisley fuerunt in comitiua predicti Oweni
60   ad dictam equitaturam suam proditoriam in exercitu victualia et auxiliis. Ideo procla-
      matum est ex parte eadem et promulgatum quod omnes et singuli tam tenentes quam
      alij quicumque Oweini proditoris ad dictam equitaturam suam extiterunt coram
      domino et eiues magno consilio compereantur ad proximam curiam ville ibidem ad
      respondendum hiis que sibi ex parte domini obicientur sub pena fortisfacture vite et
65   membrorum ac omnium aliorum que penes dictam forisfacturam pollent.

      Ad quam curiam ibidem rentam xxvijmo die Octobris anno regni Regis Henrici
      predicti secundo Madock Lloit ap Gruffith, Roger ap Gruffith, Madwin ap David
      Gethen, Gruffitjh ap Ithell de villa de Osswestry, Gruffith ap Ierwerth Vachunn,
      Ieuan ap Ieuan, Ieuan ap Einion Howell, Ieuan Vychan ap Ieuan, Deio ap Egnion
70   Tallior, Deio ap Ieuan ap Grono, Ieuan ap Maredudd ap Tudur, Ieuan Gethen,
      Ieuan Tegenn, Deio Lloit, Howell ap David ap Egneon, Deio Bille, Ieuan ap Madoc,
      Iollin ap Madoc, Owen ap Einion Vachen, Iollyn ap Davi ap Ynyr, Edwart frater
      eius, Madoc Morton, Deicos frater eius, Ieuan ap Ierwerth Duy, Llewelyn ap Mad-
      doc Lloett, Ieuan ap Iorwerth Whieth, Ieuan ap Ierwerth ap Maddoc Lloit, Ieuan
75   ap Ieuan ap David ap Meillir, Ieuan Griffith, David ap Ierwerth ap Ierwerth, Deio
      ap David ap Egnion, Ieuan ap David, Meller ap David, Yollin ap Madoc ap Atha de
      Weston, Deio ap Einion, Athe ap Mellier, Iorwerth Lloeidyn, Ithell ap David, Deio
      ap Egnion Gouch, Ieuan ap David ap Ierwerth ap Tuder, Deio ap Ierwerth ap

Hugh Burnell with many other liegemen of the aforementioned king from the counties of Salop, Stafford, and Warwick, having assembled together at the same time near the aforementioned town of the Pool on the river Severn, and then they fled, seeking the mountains and woods, and very many of the said rebels returned to their own manors, behaving just as if they had not been previously in the forests. They also say that the aforementioned Hywel Cyffin, Ieuan Fychan ab Ieuan Gethin and Gruffudd his brother, [Gruffudd son of] the aforementioned Owain, Ieuan ab Iorwerth, Gruffudd Hanmer and many others gave relief, sustenance and treacherously helped the traitors and rebels of the lord king in the mountains and woods of Wales, lingering and wandering outside the lordship of Chirkland on the Monday next before the feast of St. Martin in the aforesaid year and immediately afterwards with food, gold, silver and arms.

And they say that Gruffudd Chaloner of the town of Oswestry, Ieuan ab Ieuan ap Dafydd Fychan of Oswestry, Ieuan Las, Philip ap Dafydd ap Madog, Madog ab Einion, Deio his brother, Ieuan Werth, Ieuan ap Madog ab Ieuan, Ieuan ab Ednyfed, Deicws ab Einion ab Ithel, Madog ab Ieuan Grach, Ieuan ab Ieuan Las, Ieuan ap Madog ap Gruffudd, William Llwyd ap Maredudd, Dafydd ab Ieuan Llwyd, Ieuan ab Ieuan Fychan, Gruffudd Goch of Blodwell, Ieuan ab Iorwerth of Hideslond, John Symond, William Twyford of the Duparts of Oswestry, Adda ap Madog ab Iorwerth, Llywelyn his brother, Llywelyn ab Iorwerth ap Dafydd, Madog ab Ieuan ap Madog, Dafydd ab Ieuan ap Madog, Jack Cadarn, Madog ab Ieuan Gruffudd, Deio ab Ieuan Llwyd, Einion ab Iorwerth, Gruffudd ap Jeukes, Gruffudd ab Ieuan ap Rhys of Melverley, a tenant of the said lordship of Oswestry, Sir John Tudor, Gronw ap Dafydd ap Madog and Maredudd ab Iorwerth ab Ieuan of Kynardley were in the retinue of the aforementioned Owain with regard to his said treacherous cavalry campaign with arms, food and aid. Therefore it was proclaimed and announced by the same party that each and everyone, both tenants and all the residents, within the aforementioned lordships of Oswestry and Kynardley, who were in the retinue of the aforesaid traitor Owain in respect of his aforementioned cavalry campaign, should appear before the lord and his great council at the next court of the town in the said place in order to answer these charges which will be made against them on behalf of the lord under penalty of forfeiture of life and limb and all other things which are in force with regards to the said forfeiture.

To which court held in the same place 27 October, the second year of the reign of the said King Henry, Madog Llwyd ap Gruffudd, Roger ap Gruffudd, Madwyn ap Dafydd Gethin, Gruffudd ab Ithel of the town of Oswestry, Gruffudd ab Iorwerth Fychan, Ieuan ab Ieuan, Ieuan ab Einion ap Hywel, Ieuan Fychan ab Ieuan, Deio ab Einion Tallior, Deio ab Ieuan ap Gronw, Ieuan ap Maredudd ap Tudur, Ieuan Gethin, Ieuan Tegenn, Deio Llwyd, Hywel ap Dafydd ab Einion, Deio Bille, Ieuan ap Madog, Iolyn ap Madog, Owain ab Einion Fychan, Iolyn ap Dafydd ab Ynyr, Edwart his brother, Madog Morton, Deicws his brother, Ieuan ab Iorwerth Ddu, Llywelyn ap Madog Llwyd, Ieuan ab Iorwerth Chwith, Ieuan ab Iorwerth ap Madog Llwyd, Ieuan ab Ieuan ap Dafydd ap Meilyr, Ieuan ap Gruffudd, Dafydd ab Iorwerth ab Iorwerth, Deio ap Dafydd ab Einion, Ieuan ap Dafydd, Meilyr ap Dafydd, Iolyn ap Madog ab Adda of Weston, Deio ab Einion, Adda ap Meilyr, Iorwerth Llwydyn, Ithel ap Dafydd, Deio ab Einion Goch, Ieuan ap Dafydd ab Iorwerth

Ithell, Deio ap Ieuan ap David Vychan, Deio ap Llewelyn, Ednevett Duy, Ednevet
80   ap Ierwerth ap Grono, Llewelyn ap David ap Egnion, Egnion ap Ednevet, Madock
ap David, Jenkin ap David, Egnion ap Tudur, Deio frater eius, Ieuan ap Howell,
Howell ap David Lloyt, Howell ap Ieuan Duy, Ieaan Lloyd ap Ierwerth, Deikos ap
Egnion, Ierwor ap Kendrick, Ieuan ap Iorwerth, Ieuan ap David, Ierwerth frater
eius, Conaghe ap David ap Kendrick, Owen ap Ierwerth, Gruffeth ap Ierwerth, Ior-
85   werth ap Ierwerth, Madoc ap Atha, Owen ap Owen, Madock Lloedyn, Howell ap
David, David ap Ieuan, Ierwerth ap David ap Ieuan, Howell frater eius, Deio Person, Deio o'r Wawn, David ap Madock, Ieuan Lloyd ap Ierwerth Gouche, Madoc
Wyn, Madock Whieth, Egnion ap Iorwerth, Deio ap Ieuan de tribus partibus hundredi de Ossestry, Ieuan ap Eignion Vachan, Howell ap Gruffith, Howell ap Ieuan
90   ap Eignion, William ap Ieuan ap David, David ap Ieuan ap Rerid, Madock ap Ieuan
Lloyd, Jenkes ap Ieuan Wyne, Ririd de Llan, Deikes filius eius, Llewelyn ap Ieuan
ap Gurgene, Gruffith ap David ap Howell, Ieuan ap Grono ap Egnion, Jeukes ap
Ieuan Gouche, David ap Ierwerth Goz, Ieuan ap Howell, David ap Llewelyn, Llewelyn ap Iorwerth, Ieuan ap Iorwerth, Morgan ap Ieuan ap P'llus, Egnion ap David
100   ap Ieuan, Ieuan ap David ap Llewelyn, Ieuan ap Howell ap Ienna, Deio ap Ieuan
Cobill, Egnion ap Ieuan ap Madoc, Deio ap Ieuan ap Madoc, Evan ap David Rees,
Ieuan ap Howell, David ap Ieuan ap Phillip, Maddoc ap Ierwerth ap David, Ieuan
ap Ieuan Gam, Gruffith frater eius, Ieuan Vychan ap Ierwerth Llogawirth, Grono
ap David Gethen, Llewelyn ap Ierwerth Vaughan, Phillip ap Ieuan ap David, David
105   ap Ierwerth Vaughan, Gruffith ap David Vaughan, David ap Howell, Yollein frater
eius, Kendrick ap Iorwerth, plus Gruffith ap Ieuan Gethen, Deio ap Morgant, Ieuan
ap David Hier, Ieuan ap Maddoc ap David, Ierwerth ap Ieuan Lloit, Ieuan ap Ieuan
ap Kendrik, John ap Richard, Richard Cairck, Ieuan ap Llewelyn ap Ierwerth, Atha
ap Ieuan Padir, Thomas ap Madoc, Ybole ap Howell, Jeukes Gouche, Jeukes frater
110   eius, David ap Grono, Griffith Taillour de duabus partibus hundredi de Ossestry,
Maddoc ap David ap Athe, Yollin ap Gruffith ap Eignion, Eignion frater eius, Ieuan
ap Grono ap Cad', Ierwerth ap Ieuan ap Tudur, Ieuan ap Egnion ap Gruffith,
Owen ap Maddoc ap Richard ap Eignion, Madoc ap Gruffith ap Egnion de Melver-
deley, Madoc ap Ieuan Lloyt, Morgant ap Ieuan Lloyt, Ieuan ap Gruffith ap Ieuan
115   et Llewelyn ap Sir Madoc de Kynardeley vocati comparuerunt in propiis personis
suis coram dicto consilio et diuisim examinati cognouerunt se in comitiua predicti
Oweni ad dictam equitacionem suam proditoriam metu mortis et arsure compulsos
exitisse. Super qua recognicione sua consideratum est per eundem et eius consilium
quod hi omnes et singuli reveniant in gratiam domini tam de vita et membris quam
120   de omnibus bonis catallis terris tenamentis suis et ipsorum nemine obuersante
quousque, etc., et preceptum est Howell ap Eignion Gouche appretiatori domini
ibidem omnia bona et cattalla sua in tenementa et tenamenta sua in manus domini
saisire et extendere citra proximam [curiam], etc.

ap Tudur, Deio ab Iorwerth ab Ithel, Deio ab Ieuan ap Dafydd Fychan, Deio ap Llywelyn, Ednyfed Ddu, Ednyfed ab Iorwerth ap Gronw, Llywelyn ap Dafydd ab Einion, Einion ab Ednyfed, Madog ap Dafydd, Jenkin ap Dafydd, Einion ap Tudur, Deio his brother, Ieuan ap Hywel, Hywel ap Dafydd Llwyd, Hywel ab Ieuan Ddu, Ieuan Llwyd ab Iorwerth, Deicws ab Einion, Iorwerth ap Cynwrig, Ieuan ab Iorwerth, Ieuan ap Dafydd, Iorwerth his brother, Connak ap Dafydd ap Cynwrig, Owain ab Iorwerth, Gruffudd ab Iorwerth, Iorwerth ab Iorwerth, Madog ab Adda, Owain ab Owain, Madog Llwydyn, Hywel ap Dafydd, Dafydd ab Ieuan, Iorwerth ap Dafydd ab Ieuan, Hywel his brother, Deio Parson, Deio of Chirk, Dafydd ap Madog, Ieuan Llwyd ab Iorwerth Goch, Madog Wyn, Madog Chwith, Einion ab Iorwerth, Deio ab Ieuan of the Traean of the Hundred of Oswestry, Ieuan ab Einion Fychan, Hywel ap Gruffudd, Hywel ab Ieuan ab Einion, William ab Ieuan ap Dafydd, Dafydd ab Ieuan ap Rhirid, Madog ab Ieuan Llwyd, Jenkes ab Ieuan Wyn, Rhirid of Llan, Deicws his son, Llywelyn ab Ieuan ap Gwrgenau, Gruffudd ap Dafydd ap Hywel, Ieuan ap Gronw ab Einion, Jeukes ab Ieuan Goch, Dafydd ab Iorwerth Goch, Ieuan ap Hywel, Dafydd ap Llywelyn, Llywelyn ab Iorwerth, Ieuan ab Iorwerth, Morgan ab Ieuan ap P'llus, Einion ap Dafydd ab Ieuan, Ieuan ap Dafydd ap Llywelyn, Ieuan ap Hywel ab Ieuan, Deio ab Ieuan Cobill, Einion ab Ieuan ap Madog, Deio ab Ieuan ap Madog, Ifan ap Dafydd Rhys, Ieuan ap Hywel, Dafydd ab Ieuan ap Philip, Madog ab Iorwerth ap Dafydd, Ieuan ab Ieuan Gam, Gruffudd his brother, Ieuan Fychan ab Iorwerth Llogawirth, Gronw ap Dafydd Gethin, Llywelyn ab Iorwerth Fychan, Philip ab Ieuan ap Dafydd, Dafydd ab Iorwerth Fychan, Gruffudd ap Dafydd Fychan, Dafydd ap Hywel, Iolyn his brother, Cynwrig ab Iorwerth, together with Gruffudd ab Ieuan Gethin, Deio ap Morgant, Ieuan ap Dafydd Hir, Ieuan ap Madog ap Dafydd, Iorwerth ab Ieuan Llwyd, Ieuan ab Ieuan ap Cynwrig, John ap Richard, Richard Cairck, Ieuan ap Llywelyn ab Iorwerth, Adda ab Ieuan Padir, Thomas ap Madog, Ybole ap Hywel, Jeukes Goch, Jeukes his brother, Dafydd ap Gronw, Gruffudd Taillour of the Duparts of the Hundred of Oswestry, Madog ap Dafydd ab Adda, Iolyn ap Gruffudd ab Einion, Einion his brother, Ieuan ap Gronw ap Cad', Iorwerth ab Ieuan ap Tudur, Ieuan ab Einion ap Gruffudd, Owain ap Madog ap Richard ab Einion, Madog ap Gruffudd ab Einion of Melverley, Madog ab Ieuan Llwyd, Morgant ab Ieuan Llwyd, Ieuan ap Gruffudd ab Ieuan and Llewelyn ap Sir Madog of Kynardley having been summoned, appeared in their proper persons before the said council and having been examined individually they acknowledged that they had been in the retinue of the aforementioned Owain with regard to his said treacherous cavalry campaign compelled through fear of death and arson. Upon this their acknowledgment, it was resolved by the same lord and his council that each and every one of these people should be restored to the grace of the lord both in respect of life and limb and also in respect of all their goods, chattels, lands, tenements with no one dissenting as far as, etc., and Hywel ab Einion Goch, appraiser of the lord in the same place was commanded to set a value on all their goods and chattels having been seized into the hands of the lord and to place these things in safe custody and to seize their lands and tenements into the hands of the lord and to extend this until the next [court], etc.

Et quia supradictus Ieuan Vachan ap Ieuan Gethen, Gruffith Chalenor de Os-
125   sestry, Ieuan ap Ieuan ap David Vachan de tribus partibus hundredi de Ossestry,
Ieuan Laas, Phillipe ap David ap Maddoc, Maddoc ap Eynus, Deio frater eius, Ieuan
Wethe, Ieuan ap Madoc, Ieuan ap Ednevit, Deikos ap Egnion ap Ithell, Maddoc ap
Ithell Graghe, Ieuan ap Ieuan Laas, Ieuan ap Maddoc ap Gruffith, William Lloit ap
Maredudd, David ap Ieuan Lloit, Ieuan ap Ieuan Vychan, Gruffith Goz de Blode-
130   well, Ieuan ap Ierwerth, de Hideslond, Johannes Symons, William Twiford de duabus partibus hundredi de Ossestry, Atha ap Madoc ap Ierwerth, Llewelyn frater
eius, Llewelyn ap Ierwerth ap David, Madoc ap Ieuan ap Madoc, David ap [Ieuan
ap Madoc], Jacke Cadarne, Madoc ap Ieuan ap Grono, Deio ap Ieuan Lloyd, Egnion ap Ierwerth, Gruffith ap Jeukes, Gruffith ap Ieuan ap Richard de Malverdeley,
135   Sir John Tudor, Gruffith ap David ap Madoc, Meredudd ap Ierwerth ap Ieuan de
Kynardeley qui indictati sunt per inquisitionem predictam adeo quod ipsius in
comitiua predicti Oweni ad equitationen suam extiterunt ut eam ad curiam predictam vocati solempniter per singula nomina sua non comparuerunt sed se fugitiuos
retraxerunt ipsi omnes et singuli adiudicantur per dominum et dictum consilium
140   suum pro proditoribus et rebellis eidem domino suo qui tam vitas et membra quam
omnia bona et catalla terras et tenementa sua exinde domino suo prodito foris-
fecerunt, et preceptum est ex parte domini ballivis ville predicte tam ipsos proditores et rebellos sic adiudicatos quam alios quoscumque superius indictos qui se
in gratia domini posuerunt pro eodem corpora capere si, etc., et eciam proclam-
145   atum est appretiatori predicta omnia bona et catalla sua que infra dominia predicta
potest invenire in manus domini seista appreciare et extenderre citra proximam
[curiam]. Ad quam curiam tentam . . .

12. HENRY IV, *PROTECTION FOR SUBMITTING REBELS*   **Latin**
                                                        30 November 1400

Rex universis et singulis vicecomitibus, etc., salutem.
Sciatis quod nos, pietate misericorditer moti ac caritatis fervore accensi, de
gratia nostra speciali et ex mero motu nostro, suscepimus, et per praesentes poni-
mus et suscepimus, in protectionem, tuitionem, et defensionem nostras speciales,
universos et singulos Wallenses, eujus cumque status, gradus, seu conditionis fuer-
5   int, nuper contra nos et eorum ligeantiam in partibus illis insurgentes, qui penes
praesentiam carissimi filii nostri principis Walliae, usque civitatem nostram Ces-
triae, citra proximum parliamentum nostrum, accedere et declinare, et eos ibidem
gratiae et misericordiae nostrae humiliter submittere voluerint, usque dictam civitatem nostram veniendo, ibidem morando, et exinde, quandocumque sibi placuerit,
10   ad partes suas proprias, salvo et secure redeundo, necnon homines, servientes, et
tenentes, ac terras, res, redditus, possessiones, et bona sua quaecumque, et ideo
vobis, et cuilibet vestrum mandamus quod ipsos Wallenses, usque civitatem praedictam ex hac causa veniendo, ibidem morando, et exinde ad partes suas proprias, ut
praedictum est, redeundo, necnon homines, servientes, et tenentes, ac terras, res,
15   redditus, possessiones, et bona sua praedicta manuteneatis, protegatis, et defen-
datis, non inferentes eis, seu quantum in vobis est ab aliis inferri permittentes, in-
juriam, molestiam, dampnum, violentiam, impedimentum aliquod seu gravamen,

And since the aforementioned Ieuan Fychan ab Ieuan Gethin, Gruffudd Chalenor of Oswestry, Ieuan ab Ieuan ap Dafydd Fychan of the Traean of the Hundred of Oswestry, Ieuan Las, Philip ap Dafydd ap Madog, Madog ab Einion, Deio his brother, Ieuan Chwith, Ieuan ap Madog, Ieuan ab Ednyfed, Deicws ab Einion ab Ithel, Madog ab Ithel Grach, Ieuan ab Ieuan Las, Ieuan ap Madog ap Gruffudd, William Llwyd ap Maredudd, Dafydd ab Ieuan Llwyd, Ieuan ab Ieuan Fychan, Gruffudd Goch of Blodwell, Ieuan ab Iorwerth of Hideslond, John Symons, William Twyford of the Duparts of the Hundred of Oswestry, Adda ap Madog ab Iorwerth, Llywelyn his brother, Llywelyn ab Iorwerth ap Dafydd, Madog ab Ieuan ap Madog, Dafydd ab [Ieuan ap Madog], Jack Cadarn, Madog ab Ieuan ap Gronw, Deio ab Ieuan Llwyd, Einion ab Iorwerth, Gruffudd ap Jeukes, Gruffudd ab Ieuan ap Richard of Melverley, Sir John Tudor, Gruffudd ap Dafydd ap Madog, Maredudd ab Iorwerth ab Ieuan of Kynardley who were indicted by the aforementioned inquiry, because they were in the retinue of the aforementioned Owain himself with regard to his aforementioned cavalry campaign, when they were solemnly summoned to that aforementioned court each by his name did not appear but they themselves fled each and every one of them, they were adjudged by the lord and his said council to be traitors and rebels to their self-same lord in case of those traitors and rebels who have been adjudged in this manner and also any others indicted above who threw themselves at the mercy of the lord, if, etc., and it was also proclaimed to the aforementioned appraiser to value all their goods and chattels which he is able to find within the aforementioned lordships and, having seized them into the hands of the lord, to place them in safe custody and also to keep their lands and tenements in the hand of the lord and to extend this until the next court. To which court held . . .

12. HENRY IV, *PROTECTION FOR SUBMITTING REBELS*   Notes: pp. 303–04

The king to each and every sheriff and others, greetings.

Be it known that, moved mercifully by piety and inflamed with the fervor of charity, by our special grace and by our own volition, we take up, and we place and take up those present, into our special protection, support, and defense, each and every one in Wales, whatsoever their rank, status, or condition, who recently rebelled against us and their lieges in those lands presently of our most beloved son, the prince of Wales, all the way to our city of Chester, to accept or decline this before our next parliament. And likewise to those who wish to submit themselves humbly to our grace and mercy, to come all the way to our said city, to stay likewise, and afterwards, whenever it might please them, return safely and securely to their own regions, not only men, servants and tenants, but also lands, things, rents, possessions and whatsoever of their goods. And likewise to you and to any of yours we command those Welsh to come for this reason to the aforementioned city, likewise to stay and finally afterwards to return to their own regions, as was said above, not only men, servants, tenants, and lands, things, rents, possessions and whatsoever of their aforementioned goods, that you hold, protect and defend on your own, not harming them, or, so far as you are able, allowing others to bring injury, molestation, damage, violence, or any hindrance or grievance, and if any of those make for-

20   et si quid eis in personis aut rebus suis forisfactum vel injuriatum fuerit, id eis sine dilatione faciatis corrigi et debite reformari, proviso semper quod iidem Wallenses, penes nos et dictum regnum nostrum de caetero, bene et fideliter se gerant, ac sub ligeantia et obedientia nostris fideliter permaneant, sub poena amissionis beneficii praesentis nostrae protectionis.

In cujus etc. usque ad dictum parliamentum nostrum duraturas.

25   Teste rege apud Westmonasterium, tricesimo die Novembris.

Per ipsum regem.

13. *ROLLS OF PARLIAMENT, 1401*   **Anglo-Norman**
21 February 1401

15. Lundy le xxi jour de Feverer, les communes viendrent devaunt le roy et les seignurs en parlement et monstrerent coment les Galoises ore tarde se leverent en grande rebellioun encontre nostre dit seignur le roy, et coment mesmes nostre seignur le roy a ses grandes coustages, et a tresgrande aventure et peril de sa per-

5   sone roiale, les fist graciousement resister de leur dit rebellioun et malveis purpos; et coment ore les escolers de Gales qi feurent demurantz en les universitees d'Oxen-ford et de Cantebrigg sont departiz d'illoeqes en leur paiis; et coment auxi les labores Galoises q'estoient demurantz es diverses parties deinz le roialme d'Engle-terre se ont sodeynement retreez hors du dit roialme vers mesme leur paiis de Gales

10   et se ont purveuz fortement des armures, arks, setes et espeies, et autres defenses de guerre, autrement q'ils ne soleient unqes puis le conquest de Gales; paront il est verraisemblable q'ils se purposent de faire autre rebellioun de novel, s'ils ne soient vigerousement et fortement resistez. . . .

De faire ordinance pur la rebellion sur les marches de Gales.

15   16. Item, mesme le lundy, les ditz communes monstrerent a mesme nostre seignur le roy coment y avoient autres rebellions deins le roialme d'Engleterre et par especial sur les marches de Gales et par les ditz Galoises, encontre les meirs, custumers, et autres officers et ministres du roy, et par especial de Bristuyt et Frome; paront tresgrands riotes et debatz sont bien semblables d'advenir, si reme-

20   die ne soit mys. Empriantz a mesme nostre seignur le roy qe de celle remede ensi afaire mesmes les communes purroient avoir conisance. Sur quoi nostre dit seignur le roy ad comandez a ses justices de veier si la ley soit sufficiente en le cas pur pun-issement des tielx rebelx. Et si la ley ne soit sufficiente, qe les ditz justices mettent leur diligence, et luy facent report de leur advys, au fyn qe mesme nostre seignur

25   le roy, par conseil et advys des seignurs et communes suisditz, ent purra ordeigner ceo qe meulx leur semblera celle partie.

. . .

Hommes Galois.

77. Item, priount les communes qe nulle homme Galois entier desore enavant purchace terres ou tenementz deinz la ville de Salop', Briggenorth, Lodelowe, Leo-

30   mynstre, Hereford', Gloucestre, Wircestre, n'autres villes marchandz qeconqes

feiture or injury to persons or things, that you make these right without delay and repay the debt, always with the provision that these Welsh, are governed by us and our realm in the future, well and faithfully, and remain faithfully under allegiance and obedience to us, under penalty of losing the benefits of our current protection.

In whose etc. lasting until our said parliament.

Witnessed by the king at Westminster, November 30.

By the king himself.

13. *ROLLS OF PARLIAMENT, 1401*   **Notes: pp. 304–06**

15. An ordinance to be made concerning the Welsh rebellion. On Monday 21 February, the commons came before the king and lords in parliament and spoke of how the Welsh had recently risen up in a great rebellion against our said lord the king, and how our same lord the king, to his great cost, and incurring very great risk and danger to his royal person, had nobly forced them to desist from their said rebellion and malevolent purpose; and that now Welsh scholars who had been residing in the universities of Oxford and Cambridge had left for their country; and that also Welsh labourers who had been living in various parts of the English realm had suddenly fled the said realm for their same country of Wales, and had strongly equipped themselves with arms, bows, arrows and swords and other weapons of war, such as they had not done at any time since the conquest of Wales; on account of which it seems probable that they intend to start another, new rebellion, if they are not vigorously and forcefully resisted. . . .

An ordinance to be made concerning the rebellion on the Welsh marches.

16. An ordinance to be made concerning the rebellion on the Welsh marches. Also, on the same Monday, the said commons informed our same lord the king that there had been other rebellions in the English kingdom, and especially on the Welsh marches and by the said Welsh, against the mayors, customs officers and other royal officers and ministers, especially in Bristol and Frome, as a result of which very great riots and fights were extremely likely to arise if a remedy was not provided. And they prayed of our same lord the king that the commons be notified of this remedy to be thus provided. Whereupon our said lord the king commanded his justices to see whether the law is sufficient with regard to the punishment of such rebels; and if the law is not sufficient, that the said justices apply themselves with diligence to making for him a report of their advice, in order that our same lord the king, with the counsel and advice of the lords and aforesaid commons, might be thus able to ordain whatever seems best to them in this matter.

. . .

Restrictions on the Welsh.

Welshmen. Also, the commons request that no full-blooded Welshman shall henceforth purchase lands or tenements within the towns of Shrewsbury, Bridgnorth, Ludlow, Leominster, Hereford, Gloucester, Worcester, or any other marcher

ajoignantz as marches de Gales, ne en les suburbes d'icellez, sur la forfaiture d'icellez terres et tenementz as seignurs desqueux tielx terres et tenementz sont tenuz en
chief. Et auxi, qe nul homme Galois desore enavant soit esluz ou recieu d'estre
citezein ou burgeys en nul tiel citee, burghe, ou ville marchant. Et qe ceux Galois

35   queux ore sont en ascun tiel citee, burghe, ou ville enfraunchese, esteantz citezein
ou burgeis, troveront suffisant seurte et caucioun de lour bone porte, sibien envers
nostre tresredote seignur le roy, ses heirs et soun roialme d'Engleterre, come pur
lour loialte a les governours des tielx citees, burghes, ou villes pur le temps esteantz
en salvacioun de mesmes les citees, burghes, ou villes, s'ils vuyllent en ycelles de-

40   murrer. Issint qe nul de eux a nul office de maire, baillif, chamberleyn, conestable
ou gardein des portes ou de gaiole, ne al commune conseil des tielx citees, burghes,
ou villes, desore enavaunt soit recieu, accepte, ou occupiour en nul manere. Ne qe
nul de eux desore enavant soit si hardy de porter nul manere armure deinz ascun
tielx citees, burghes, ou villes marchandes, sur la forfaiture de l'armure suisdite; et

45   ceux qe le porteront d'estre emprisonez tanqe ils eient fait fyn en ceste partie. Et
qe suffisant ordeignance soit fait, qe en nul citee, burghe, ou ville suisdit, soit suffre
rien estre fait en contrarie.

Responsio. Le roy le voet; cestassavoir, des entiers Galois, neez en Gales, et aiantz
pier et meer neez en Galees. Adjouste a la dite peticione, qe la ville de Cestre soit

50   comprise ove les villes de Salop, Bruggenorth, Lodelowe, Leomynstre, Hereford,
Gloucestre, Wircestre, et les autres villes marchandz deinzescriptes.

. . .

Seignurs marches.
     101. Item, suppliont les ditz communes qe les seignurs marchez, chescun deinz
soun seignurie, soient chargez et comandez du par nostre seignur le roy, denaler

55   a fynalle execucion de toutz les Galees foundours, ymaginours, contrevours et
principalx faisours de les hautes tresons et insurreccions ore tarde par eux faitz,
encontre sa roialle majeste, soun roialme et ses loialx lieges d'icelle, saunz fyn,
redempcioun ou autre favour a eux faire, en garnisement et exemple d'eschuer
tieux hautz tresons et rebellions en temps advenir.

60   *Responsio*. Le roy voet sauver soun droit, et faire droit as autres.

Rebelles Galois.
     102. Item, suppliont les communes qe nulle des aultres Galoys rebelles, queux
ne fueront foundours des ditz hautes tresons et insurreccions ne soient acceptez a
pardone, fyn, ne redemptioun, pur lours ditz tresons ne rebeltez, qe fueront al

65   arsure ou roborie d'ascuns des burghes villes Engleis, soit il dedeinz Engleterre ou
Galees, tanqe il eit trove suffisant seurte d'amender et satisfier, solonc soun degree
et estat, a toutz les loialx lieges nostre seignur le roy les damages q'ils suffreront et
emporteront par lour arsure et roborie suisditz: et qe de eux soit leve, saunz delaie,

towns adjoining the Welsh marches, nor in the suburbs of the same, on pain of forfeiting these same lands and tenements to the lords of whom such lands and tenements are held in chief. And also, that no Welshman shall henceforth be elected or accepted as a citizen or burgess of any such marcher city, borough or town. And those Welshmen who are currently enfranchised in any such city, borough or town by being a citizen or burgess there shall find sufficient guarantees and pledges for their good bearing towards our most feared lord the king, his heirs and the kingdom of England, as well as for their loyalty to the governors of such cities, boroughs or towns who are then in office, for the salvation of the same cities, boroughs, or towns, if they wish to stay in them. Also that none of them shall henceforth be received or accepted to, or occupy in any way, the offices of mayor, bailiff, chamberlain, constable or warden of the ports or of the prisons, nor be accepted on to the common council of these cities, boroughs or towns. Nor that any one of them should henceforth be so bold as to carry arms in any way within any of these marcher cities, boroughs or towns, on pain of forfeiting the aforesaid arms; and that those who carry them are to be imprisoned until they have made fine in this matter. And that adequate ruling be made that in none of the aforesaid cities, boroughs or towns shall it be suffered for anything to be done to the contrary.

Answer. The king wills it; namely, with respect to full-blooded Welshmen, born in Wales, and having a father and mother born in Wales. Adding to the said petition that the town of Chester shall be included with the towns of Shrewsbury, Bridgnorth, Ludlow, Leominster, Hereford, Gloucester, Worcester and the other marcher towns mentioned within.

. . .

Marcher lords.
101. Marcher lords. Also, the said commons request that each of the marcher lords should be charged and commanded on behalf of our lord the king to go to his own lordship in order to accomplish the total destruction of all the Welsh instigators, plotters, contrivers and principal agents of the high treasons and insurrections recently committed by them against his royal majesty, his kingdom and his loyal lieges of the same, without allowing them any fine, redemption or other favour, as a warning and example to others to desist from high treasons and rebellions in time to come.

Answer. The king wishes to reserve his right, and to do right to others.

Welsh rebels not to be pardoned except on conditions.
102. Welsh rebels. Also, the commons pray that none of the other Welsh rebels who, whilst not an originator of the said high treasons and insurrections, has participated in the burning or robbery of any of the English borough towns, be it within England or Wales, should be granted a pardon, fine, or redemption for their treasons and rebellions until he shall have found sufficient surety to make amends to and satisfy, in accordance with his degree and estate, all the loyal lieges of our lord the king for all the losses they have suffered and borne as a result of the aforesaid arson and robbery: and that this should be levied from them without delay by their

70 par lours seignurs realx, et liverez a ceux queux fueront lealx lieges a nostre dit
seignur le roy par eux arsez et derobbez en manere avauntdit, par tesmoignauntz
des lettres patentes nostre dit seignur le roy, ou par les lettres des seignurs realx as
queux ils fueront tenauntz. Siqe ove les ditz sommes et autrement, les burghes
Engleis villes purront estre reedifiez et restabliez, en manere qe le noble et sage roy
Edward le primer, progenitour nostre dit seignur le roy, avaunt ces heures ordeigna
75 et devisa.

Responsio. Le roy voet estre en ses liberte et prerogative, et fair sa grace la ou luy
semblera raisonable affaire, mes il le voet faire par bon advis.

Galoys.
103. Item, suppliont les communes qe en cas qe ascun Galoys en temps avenir
80 entre les countees a ceo ajoingnauntz en la roialme d'Engleterre, et arde, tue, rape
ou ascun autre felonie ou trespas face en ycelles, de quele il soit atteint deinz Engleterre par les leys de la roialme, par utlagarie ou abjuracioun, et repeire en Galees,
tapessant illeoqes; qe fynalle execucioun soit fait sur le dit feloun par les seignurs
et lours ministres ou il soit trove en Galees, saunz fyn ou redempcioun ove luy faire.
85 Et ceo sur le certificacioun et recordes par les justices nostre seignur le roy devaunt
queux il soit issy convict desouthe lours sealx a eux faire. Et ceo sur grevous peyne
a mettre en le dit estatut, en cas qe les seignurs ou lours ministres font a contrarie.
Et ceo d'estre triez et terminez parentre nostre dit seignur le roy et les pursuantz
queux eux sentent par le manere grevez, envers les ditz seignurs marches et lours
90 ministres en les countees ou les ditz utlagaries et abjuracions soient faitz et pronunciez sur les ditz felons et trespassours.

Responsio. Le roy le voet.

Seignurs marchez.
104. Item, suppliont les communes qe les seignurs marchez soient commaundez
95 du par nostre seignur le roy, d'ordeigner et mettre tieux estouffours et gardez en
lour chastelx et seignuries Galees, qe en temps advenir nulle pierde, riot, ne
damage aveigne a nostre dit seignur le roy et soun roialme, ne a nulle de ses lieges,
par lour tenauntz, reseantz ne nullez autres Galoys, en lour default come ad avenuz
et este faitz pur default de bone governance en temps passe.

100 *Responsio*. Le roy le voet.

Galoys.
105. Item, qe chescun qe accepte ascun Galoys tenant en Engleterre, q'il
preigne seurte suffisant de soun dit tenant, q'il, et toutz ceux q'il recettera del
natioun de Galees, serront loialx lieges a nostre seignur le roy, et eux bien et loial-
105 ment emparteront a ses lieges durant le temps de lour demurre sur soun tenement,
saunz damage ou disaise faire a ascuns de ses lieges en lour default; siqe le partie,

true lords, and delivered to those who were the loyal lieges of our said lord the king who suffered arson and robbery at their hands in the aforesaid manner, by testimony of letters patent of our said lord the king, or by letters of the true lords of whom they were tenants. So that with the said sums and other things, the English borough towns might be rebuilt and re-established in the manner which the noble and wise king Edward I, progenitor of our said lord the king, ordained and directed before this time.

Answer. The king wishes to reserve his liberties and prerogatives, and to do grace when it seems reasonable to him to do it, but he wishes to do it with good advice.

Punishment of Welshmen.
    103. Welshmen. Also, the commons entreat that if any Welshman in time to come enters counties in the English kingdom adjoining Wales, and burns, kills, rapes or commits any other felony or trespass in the same, of which he shall be attainted in England by the law of the realm, by outlawry or abjuration, and returns to Wales, hiding there; that final execution of the sentence should be carried out against the said felon by the lords and ministers in that part of Wales in which he shall be found, without giving him a fine or redemption. And this upon the certification and records to be made by the justices of our lord the king before whom he shall be thus convicted under their seals; and on pain of a grievous penalty to be specified in the said statute, should the lords or their ministers act to the contrary. And this to be tried and determined between our said lord the king and the suitors who feel themselves aggrieved in this way against the said marcher lords and their ministers in the counties in which the said outlawry and abjurations should have been declared and pronounced on the said felons and trespassers.

Answer. The king wills it.

Marcher lords.
    104. Marcher lords. Also, the commons request that the marcher lords should be ordered on behalf of our lord the king to arrange and install sufficient equipment and keepers in their Welsh castles and lordships so that in time to come no loss, riot, nor harm will come to our said lord the king and his realm, nor to any of his lieges, through the actions of their tenants, residents or any other Welshman, because of their negligence, as has happened and been done through lack of good governance in times past.

Answer. The king wills it.

Welsh tenants in England.
    105. Welshmen. Also, that anyone who accepts any Welshman as a tenant in England should take a sufficient pledge from his said tenant that he, and all those whom he will receive from the nation of Wales, will be loyal lieges to our lord the king, and coexist well and loyally with his lieges during the time of their stay on his tenement, without deliberately doing damage or harm to any of his lieges; so that the party,

ou sa dit seurte, purront amender pur lour malfaitz, en cas q'ascuns yfont: autrement, qe lour seignurs desouthe queux ils sont reseantz respoignent de lour malfaitz a ceux q'ils font les trespasses et offenses.

110   *Responsio.* Trove le tenant deinzescript sufficiente seuretee, selonc le purport de cest
peticione.

Pur Engleis.
       106. Item, qe nulle entiere englies soit convict al seute de nully Galoys deinz
Galees, sy ne soit par juggement des justices englies, ou par juggement des entiers
115   englies, burges, ou enquestes des burghes villes et englies des seignuries en queux
il sont arrestuz.

Responsio. Le roy le voet pur terme de trois ans proscheins advenirs.

Galois.
       107. Item, qe nulle Galoys en temps advenir soit resceu de purchaser terre ou
120   tenement deinz Engleterre, ne deinz les burghes villes englies de Galees, sur peyne
de forffaire lours ditz purchacez as seignurs des queux les ditz terres ou tenementz
sont tenuz, come de tiel estat qe le purchasour avoit en ycelles. Ne qe nulle Galoys
soit accepte burges, ne a nulle autre libertee deinz la roialme, ne deinz les villes
avantditz.

125   *Responsio.* Le roy le voet.

14. HENRY IV, *PARDON FOR WELSH REBELS*   **Latin**
                                                                10 March 1401

Rex omnibus ballivis et fidelibus suis, ad quos etc., salutem.
       Sciatis quod, de Gratia nostra speciali, et ad supplicationem carissimi primo-
geniti nostri Henrici principis Walliae, pardonavimus, quantum in nobis est, omnibus et singulis ligeis et subditis nostris comitatuum Caernervan, Angleseye, Meryn-
5   neth, et de Dynbegh in Northwallia, sectam pacis nostrae, qae ad nos versus ipsos
et eorum quemlibet pertinet, pro omnimodis proditionibus, insurrectionibus, rebel-
lionibus, feloniis, conspirationibus, conventiculis, et confoederationibus, per ipsos
aut eorum aliquem, a Festo Sancti Hillarii, anno regni nostri primo, usque ad
Festum Epiphaniae Domini proximo praeteritum, contra nostram regiam mages-
10   tatem, et ligeantiam suam, qualitercumque factis et perpetratis, unde indictati, rec-
tati, vel appellati existunt, ac etiam utlagariae, si quae in ipsos aut eorum aliquem
hiis occasionibus fuerint promulgatae, et firmam pacem nostram eis et cuilibet
eorum inde concedimus, dum tamen erga nos et ligeantiam suam bene et fideliter
se gerant et habeant in futurum: Ita tamen quod stent recto in curia nostra, si qui,
15   versus eos vel eorum aliquem, loqui voluerint de praemissis vel aliquo praemissorum: Sub hac autem pardonationis nostrae gratia, nec Owynum de Glendourdy,
Reez ap Tudour, Willielmum ap Tudour, nec illos volumus comprehendi, qui, prae-

or his said surety, shall make amends for their misdeeds, should they commit any: otherwise, that their lords under whom they are resident shall answer for their misdeeds to those against whom they have committed the trespasses and offences.

Answer. Let the tenants mentioned here find sufficient surety, in accordance with the tenor of this petition.

On behalf of the English in Wales.

106. On behalf of the English. Also, that no full-blooded Englishman shall be convicted at the suit of any Welshman within Wales, except by judgment of English justices, or by judgment of wholly English burgesses, or by inquests of borough towns and Englishmen of the lordships in which they were arrested.

Answer. The king wills it, for the next three years to come.

Welshmen in England.

107. Welshmen. Also, that no Welshman in time to come should be allowed to purchase lands or tenements within England, nor within the English borough towns of Wales, on pain of forfeiting the said purchases to the lords of whom the said lands or tenements are held, who will then hold such estate as the purchaser had in the same. Nor should any Welshman be accepted as a burgess, nor to any other liberty within the kingdom, nor within the aforesaid towns.

Answer. The king wills it.

14. HENRY IV, *PARDON FOR WELSH REBELS* Notes: p. 306

The king to all bailiffs and to his followers, to whom etc., greetings.

Be it known from our special grace, and through the petition of our beloved firstborn Henry, prince of Wales, we pardon (insofar as we are able) each and every one of our lieges and subjects from the counties of Caernarfon, Anglesey, Merioneth and Denbigh in North Wales who broke our peace, for those things that against us they and theirs are individually responsible, for all manner of betrayals, insurrections, rebellions, felonies, conspiracies, assemblies, and confederations, for each and every one of them, from the Feast of St. Hilary, in the first year of our reign, to the Feast of the Epiphany of the Lord just past, against our royal majesty, and his lieges, no matter how committed or perpetrated, whether they have been indicted, charged, or named, even if outlawed. From this time we grant our firm peace to them and anyone of theirs, so long as they give us their own allegiance well and faithfully and will hold to that in the future: So also to each and every one from those areas who are being judged in our court, if any, who might wish to speak against them or any of them. Under this same grace of our pardon Owain Glyndŵr, Rhys ap Tudur, Gwilym ap Tudur are not included, nor are those or anyone of

missorum occasione, seu alicujus eorum, capti fuerint et modo in custodia deti-
nentur, aut illos qui hactenus in rebellione hujusmodi persistebant. In cuius, etc.

Teste rege apud Westmonasterium, decimo die Martii.

Per ipsum regem et concilium.

15. ADAM OF USK, *CHRONICLE, PART 1*   Latin
                                                    March 1401

Rex in festo decollacionis sancti Iohannis baptiste in Angliam rediit, et audito
aput Leicestriam qualiter "Oenus dominus de Glyndorédee," cum Northwalen eundem Oenum principem erigentibus, rebellando hostiliter insurrexerat, ac castra
quamplura occupauerat, burgas ubique per Anglicos inter eos inhabitatas, ipsas
5 depredando et Anglicos profugando, cremauerat, sui armata iuuentute collecta,
suas bellicosas acies in Northwaliam direxit. Quibus edomantis et deportatis, dictus
eorum princeps cum septem aliis tantum rupibus et cauernis per annum quasi deli-
tuit. Rex cum aliis se paci reddentibus, paucissimos interimendo, misericorditer
egit, ipsorum tamen principaliores secum Salopiam ducens captiuos. Et postmodo,
10 sub condicione alios adhuc in Snowdona et aliunde rebellantes prosequendi et
capiendi, dimisit eosdem.

. . .

Finitur istud parliamentum decimo die mensis Marcii, quo tamen die, modicum
ante presens, audiui plurima aspera contra Wallen' ordinanda agitari, scilicet de
non contrahendo matrimonium cum Anglicis, nec de adquirendo aut inhabitando
in Anglia, et alia plura grauia. Et, sicut nouit me Deus, nocte preuia me excitauit a
15 sompno uox ita auribus meis insonans, "Supra dorsum meum fabri," etc., "Dominus
iustus," etc., ut in psalmo, "Sepe expugnauerunt." Vnde expergefactus timens michi
eo die aliquid infortunii contingere, me Spiritus Sancti gubernacioni specialiter
timidus commisi.

16. HENRY IV, *COMMISSION: THREAT OF OWAIN*   Anglo-Norman
                                                    26 May 1401

Trescheir et foial etc.

Nous vous salvons en vous signifiant que yce Jeudy le xxvj. jour de May a nous
estoit apportee certeine nouvelle a nostre chastel de Walyngforde que Oweyn Glendourdy et autres noz rebelx de nostre pays de Gales se sont levez et de nouvelle as-
5 semblez en les marches de Kermerdyn aiant en purpos dentrer en nostre roiaume
ove fort main pour destruir nostre lange Angloys et tous noz foialx lieges et soub-
giez, qui Dieux defende! Et pour resister a la malice de noz ditz rebelx nous suymes
ordennez a departir demain de nostre dit chastel et de tener nostre chemyn vers les
parties de Wircestre. Par quoi vous mandons que ovec les chivalers, escuiers, gentz
10 d'armes, et le pluis suffisantz archiers de nostre countee dont vous estes nostre vis-

theirs whom we would understand, at that time had been arrested and detained in custody, nor those who persist in rebellion of any kind. In whose, etc.

Witnessed by the king at Westminster, the tenth day of March.

By the king and council.

15. ADAM OF USK, *CHRONICLE, PART 1*   Notes: pp. 306–07

On the feast of the Decollation of St. John the Baptist the king returned to England; while at Leicester he heard that Owain lord of Glyndyfrdwy, being put forward by the men of North Wales to be their prince, had risen up with them in armed rebellion and had seized numerous castles, and was everywhere plundering and burning the towns inhabited by the English who lived amongst them, and forcing the English to flee; so, assembling his young warriors, the king led his troops into North Wales, where he overcame them and put them to flight, leaving their prince to spend almost a year hiding away on cliffs and in caverns with no more than seven followers. Those who submitted peacefully to him, however, the king treated mercifully executing only a very few, and taking their chieftains away with him as captives to Shrewsbury, where he later released them on condition that they would pursue and capture the others who were still holding out in Snowdonia and elsewhere.

. . .

This parliament ended on 10 March, on which day — a little before the present time — I heard it being urged that all sorts of rigorous measures ought to be decreed against the Welsh, namely that they should not be allowed to intermarry with the English, or make purchases or reside in England, and many other such harsh suggestions. And, as God is my witness, the previous night I was roused from my sleep by a voice ringing in my ears saying, "The plowers plowed, upon my back" etc., "The righteous lord" etc., as in the psalm, "Oft did they vex me." As a result of which I awoke with a sense of foreboding that some disaster might occur that day, and in my fear I committed myself to the special protection of the Holy Spirit.

16. HENRY IV, *COMMISSION: THREAT OF OWAIN*   Notes: pp. 307–08

Most dear and loyal etc.

We greet you in informing you that this Thursday the 26th day of May we received certain news at our castle of Wallingford that Owain Glyndŵr and other of our rebels from our country of Wales are raising themselves and of a new assembly on the marches of Carmarthen with an intention to enter into our realm with a strong force in order to destroy our English tongue and all our loyal lieges and subjects, which God defend! And to resist the malice of our said rebels we have ordained to depart tomorrow from our said castle and to take up our way toward the area of Worcester. For this reason we mandate that with knights, squires, men at arms, and sufficient archers of your county of which you are our lord you come

counte vous soiez devers nous [par la ou nous soions] en tout hast possible sauns defaute sur la foye et ligeance que vous nous devez et come vous desirez la salvacioun de nous et de nostre roialme.

17. John Charlton, *Battle with Owain*   Anglo-Norman
                                                             1 June 1401

Mon treshonuré, tresnoble, et puissant seignur, je me recommande a vostre noblesse si avant come je scay ou plus puisse des honneurs ove touz maniers dez reverences. Et plese a vostre dit noblesse entendre coment yce lundy darrein en chivauchant ove mes gentz sur les montaignes de mon paijs de Powys, et je me departi mes gentz as diverses parties de M. bien a cccc. archiers, et sur ce en alantz vers celles parties, ils avoient veue de Oweyn et ses gentz en les montaignes, ou les espiez des miens certifierent devant mains de lour estre illoeques. Et maigntenant mes ditez [gentz] et archiers a poy lui approcherent, supposantz d'avoir la bataille de lui, et quant le dit Oweyn et ses ditz adherantz véérent mes ditez gentz hastivement approchantz a lui es ditz montaignes, il fuast et touz ses gentz ovec lui, et mes gentz eux chacirent forciblement tanque a nuyt si q'ils estoient disparpoillés es diverses parties, vers queux je [ne] say en certain a present, més a ce que on dit vers K., en quelle chace estoient prises certeine del armure du dit O[weyn], certeins chivalx et lances, et un drape de teille, peinte dez pucelles ov rouges mains, et son henxman, lequele je intende envoier a nostre seignur le Roy, vostre pere. Et celle nuyt j'estoie loggéz mesmes ovec mes autres gentz a M., gaitant celles parties et les mettant en governance pur doubte des rebelx avantditz si q'ils n'entrent illoeques. De quel drape issint painte je vous envoie un quantitee par le portour d'icestes et le remenant ay envoié a nostre seignur le Roy vostre pere susdit. Et si rien vous please devers moy que faire puisse al honneur et plesir de vous, voz tresnobles comandementz please a vostre noblesse le moy tout temps commander come a le vostre. Treshonuré etc.

De par J[ehan] Charletone a le Prince.

18. Hotspur, *Battle at Cader Idris*   Anglo-Norman
                                                             4 June 1401

Tresreverentz piers en Dieu, et treshonurez et mez treschers sieurs, jeo me recomank a vous. Et dez novellz pardeca, s'il vous pleist assavoire, jeo vous ay nadgars escript et certefiez par moun bien ame Jamez Strangways lez novellez et l'estate de ceste pais, mez puis son partier jeo voie pluis de perille et meschief en la pais que jeo ne fys adonques ensi que si bone et hastie remedy ne soit purvieu sibien par terre come par mere, tout la pais est en graund perille pur estre destruittz sanz doute par lez rebellez, si jeo parte hors de ceste pais devaunt que ordeignance soit purvieuz pur ycelle; le quelle moy faut affaire de necessitee, qar jeo ne puisse porter lez costagez que jeo face ycy sanz autre ordenaunce par vous. Et touchant ceo que ad este fait par moun treshonure uncle et lez autres sieurs en sa compaignee, j'esp[oire] q'il vous ont ad certefiez, et de moun fait en ceste chivachee, par terre et par mere, par mez souldeours, paiez a mez proprez dispencez;

to us (to the same place we are) in all possible haste without fail through the loyalty and allegiance that you owe us and as you desire the salvation of us and of our realm.

17. John Charlton, *Battle with Owain*   Notes: p. 308

My most honored, most noble, and powerful lord, I commend myself to your nobility as humbly as I know how or can do honorably with all manner of reverences. And may it please your nobility to know how this past Monday during a chevauchée with my men over the mountains of my country of Powys, I divided my good men into many parts of M. with 400 archers, and shortly after moving into these parts, they caught sight of Owain and his men on the mountains, where without question they were spotted before our hands there. Thus my said men and archers approached these few, supposing to have a battle with them. And as for the said Owain and his said adherents, they saw my men hastily approaching them in the said mountains, he and all his men with him, and my men chased them forcibly until the night so that they were scattered into diverse parts, towards where I do not know for certain at present, but it is said that it was towards K. In this chase were taken certain prizes of the armor of the said Owain, certain horses and lances, and a drape of cloth painted with maidens with red hands, as well as his henchman. These things I intend to send to our lord the king, your father. And that night I lodged myself with my other men at M., in order to guard those parts and appoint them in governance to prevent the aforesaid rebels from returning there. Of this painted cloth I send you a portion through the bearer of this letter. The remainder has been sent to our lord the king your said father. And if this thing pleases you coming from me, that it should honor and please you, then I would be pleased to have of your nobility your most noble orders, as you forever command me in all matters. Most honored etc.

By John Charlton to the Prince.

18. Hotspur, *Battle at Cader Idris*   Notes: pp. 308–09

Most reverent peers under God, and most honored and most dear lords, I recommend myself to you. Of the following news about the condition of this country, if it please you to know it, I have already written you and certified by my good friend James Strangeways; but since he departed I have seen much pillaging and mischief in the country, so good and hasty measures ought to be immediately adopted by sea as well as by land. All the country is without doubt in great peril of being destroyed by the rebels if I should leave before the arrival of my successor, which will be an affair of necessity, for I cannot bear the cost that I am put to without ordering from you. And touching this that has been done by my very honored uncle and other forces in his company, I hope that it has been certified unto you and of this work being done, by land and sea, by my soldiers, paid of my own expenses. And for the

et de le journey que j'avoie le xxx. jour de Maii darrein a Catherederys, Dieux mercye; le portour dy cestez, Johan Irby, fuist present ovesque moy illoques vous soit
15   declarer ceo q'il vist, sibien come de moun fait que jeo jay fait, et unqore face outre
poiar considerant le meschief q'est ycy. Et touchant aide promys dez sieurs marchers,
moun sieur Hughe Browe fuist ovesque moy ove xij. lancez et c. archers de moun
treshonure cosyn le Counte d'Arundelle, sanz ascun autre aide de nully, forsque a
mez dispencez proprez. Et pur ceo tiel ordeignance come vous semblera voillez
20   ordener pur c'est pais, qar jeo n'attende pas ycy mez vostre response et voluntee par
le dit Jamez Strangways dez materes suisditz. Et d'autre partie, voillez savoir que
moy sount venuz novellez, mesme c'est jour de le sieur de Pawys, coment il ad com-
batez ovesque Owane de Glendorde, et luy descomfitz, et plusours de sez gentz bles-
sez en soun chemyn vers moun treshonure uncle et moy, come il mad certefiez, dont
25   jeo mercye Dieux. Et auxi j'ay novellez c'est jour de mez gentz que j'ay ordenez sour
le meare, coment ils ont pris . . . a Bardesay, que furont pris dez Engleys par les
Escotz, et d'illeoques ils pursueront une nief d'Escoce jes qes al coste de Milforthe,
et la pristerent le dit nief, ovesque xxxv. hommez bien hornaysez, dont je mercie
Dieux. Tresreverent piers en Dieux, et treshonurez et mez treschers sieurs, autres
30   ne say a present, mez jeo prie a Dieux q'il vous eit en sa tresseinte garde.
     Escrit a Dynbiegh le .iiij. jour de Juyn.

19. HENRY IV, *PROCLAMATION AGAINST OWAIN*   **Latin**
                                                                      18 September 1401

     Rex vicecomiti Devoniae, salutem.
     Quia, certificatione plurimarum literarum, ac relatione nunciorum, quibus
fidem credulam adhibemus, certitudinaliter informamur quod Owynus Glendourdy
et alii rebelles nostri de partibus Walliae nuper contra nos et magestatem nostram
5   regiam in non modico numero insurrexerunt, ac quamplura gravamina et destruc-
tiones fidelibus subditis nostris ibidem (qui nequaquam eorum malitiosis propositis
consentire curarunt) intulerunt, et adhuc in tantum de die in diem inferre non de-
sistunt, quod magna pars hominum partium praedictarum eisdem rebellibus se reddiderunt et submiserunt, sicque residuum hominum dictarum partium et marchi-
10   arum earumdem praefatis rebellibus nostris, infra breve (quod absit) verisimiliter
se reddet et submittet, nisi eorum malitiae, divina favente clementia, virilius resista-
mus, tibi praecipimus, districtius quo possumus injungentes, quod statim, visis praesentibus, in singulis civitatibus, burgis, et villis mercatoriis, ac aliis locis comitatus
tui, ubi expediens fuerit et necesse, publice ex parte nostra proclamari facias quod
15   universi et singuli milites et armigeri, in personis ad laborandum potentes, ac Sagittarii, qui annua feoda vel vadia de nobis percipiunt, super fide et ligeantia suis quibus nobis tenentur, se trahant, properent, et festinent penes nos usque civitatem
nostram Wygorniae, ita quod sint ibidem primo die Octobris proximo futuro, vel
in crastino ejusdem diei ad ultimum, et quod venire facias coram nobis, ad diem et
20   locum praedictos, centum Sagittarios magis sufficientes comitatus tui, quilibet eorum juxta status sui exigentiam bene et sufficienter munitus et arraiatus, ad pro-
ficiscendum nobiscum in easdem partes, ad hujusmodi fideles subditos nostros pro-
tegendum et succurendum, ac dictos rebelles nostros, cum adminiculo militum,

journey I had on the 30th day of May to Cader Idris, God be praised. The bearer of this letter, John Irby, was with me and can acquaint you with the particulars. Sir Hugh Browe was with me with twelve lances and one hundred archers of my right honorable cousin the earl of Arundel, without any other aid, at my proper charges; and by such governance as you may see meet to order for this answer; for I do not here await your answer by the aforesaid James Strangeways of the under-mentioned and other matters; and please to know that news have reached me this day from the lord of Powys, as to his combat with Owain Glyndŵr, whom he hath discomfited, and wounded many of his men on his way to my much honored uncle and myself as he certified, for which I thank God. And also I have news this day from my men that I have placed on the sea, about what they have done at Bardsey Island, which was taken from the English by the Scots. To that place they pursued one Scottish ship from the coast of Milford Haven, and there they seized the said ship, with 35 men well armed, for which I thank God. Most reverent peers under God, and most honored and most dear lords, I cannot say more at present, but I pray to God that he bring you joy in his most holy custody.

Written at Denbigh on the fourth day of June.

19. Henry IV, *Proclamation against Owain*   Notes: pp. 309–10

The king to the sheriff of Devonshire, greetings.

Because, by the certification of many letters and the export of our messengers, which we consulted in faithful confidence, we have been informed with certainty that Owain Glyndŵr and other rebels of our parts of Wales recently have risen in no small number against us and our royal majesty, and because they have brought many injuries and destruction to our faithful subjects there (who by no means undertook to consent to their malicious intentions), and because they still have not stopped doing this from day to day, a large number of the men of these regions surrendered and submitted themselves to the rebels, and that the rest of the men of said regions and their marches slightly below (that is to say outside) where they had rebelled against us likewise will surrender and submit themselves unless, with divine mercy favoring us, we resist strongly their evil deeds. We command you, strictly to whomever we can, immediately after seeing this letter to proclaim publically in each city, town and markets and in other places in your county where it is expedient and necessary, on our behalf that each and every knight and esquire personally obligated to service, and archers, who take an annual fief or wages from us, or any others who hold fief from and are liege to us, take themselves, prepare quickly and rush with us to our city of Worcester, so that they are there on the first day of October next or the following day at the latest, and come to our court, on the aforementioned date and place, supplying 100 archers more from your county, each of them armed and arrayed well and sufficiently as befitting their status in your estimate, to depart with us into those parts to protect and secure all of our faithful subjects and (God willing) to resist and reprimand those rebelling against us, in support of

25   armigerorum, sagittariorum, et aliorum praedictorum (Deo dante) resistendum et reprimendum; et hoc, sub periculo quod incumbit, nullatenus omittas.

Teste rege apud Westmonasterium, decimo octavo die Septembris.

Per ipsum Regem.

20. *OWAIN AT A FUNERAL*   **Anglo-Norman**
Late 1401

Mon tresnoble, tresreverent, et trespuissant seignur, je me recommande a vostre puissant seignurie en tant come je say ou puisse. Et plese a vostre seignurie a entendre que moy est certifié de certeinetee que O[weyn] de G[lendour] et R. de B., ovec grande nombre et multitude de gentz rebelx, ont estéz ycest jour al sepulture
5   de deux escuiers de la seignurie de C., qui feurent occis a vostre darrein viage ore en Gales, et ils gisont ove lour houstez yceste nuyt un leege de ceste part de le B., et lour purposent de venir et destruir ma pais ove la seignurie de B. et ove la seignurie de C., je ne scay de certein lequel. Pur quoy, trespuissant seignur, vous plese d'estre avisé de ceste matir par vostre sage Conseil et par ycel faire ordinance par
10   lour bone avys et discrecioun, entendant, mon tresnoble seignur, que je n'ay ovec moy que poy de gentz Englois de faire aucune chivachié sur eux. Nientmains par aide de gentz de ma pais je ferra ma diligence et peine en resistence de les rebelx susditz tanque meillour eide viegne de par vous, trespuissant seignur. Et, treshonuré seignur, si les ditz rebelx lour veullent treier plus avant en Southg[ales] ou
15   en autre pais, vostre Conseil a conisance asséz de certeins lieux ou ils purront estre encontréz. Mon tresnoble, etc. des autres nouvelles que je avera de jour en autre je ferray certifier a vostre trespuissant seignurie. Et je prie a la benoite Trinité q'il vous eit etc.

21. HENRY PERCY, *OWAIN'S PARLEY*   **Anglo-Norman**
November 1401

Mon treshonuré, redoubté, et puissant seignur, je me reommans a vostre hautesse si avant come plus puisse, a laquele please assavoir que aucuns queux venoient de Oweyn de G[lendour] me disorient que le dit O[weyn] avoit desir pur parler ovec aucunes de mes gentz, sur quoy envoia par devers lui pur scavoir son entent, en
5   disant que, si il se vouldroit mettre en hault et baas en le grace nostre seignur le Roy, que je vouldroie mettre ma peine pur priere pur sa vie, sanz lui promettre riens, as queux gentz il respondist q'il ne se oseroit pur riens venir en Engleterre, car il avoit bien oïe que les communes d'Engleterre avoient tuéz des grandes seignurs encontre la voluntee du Roy nostre seignur et sanz venir a justice, et pluseurs
10   autres paroles et demandes queux ne feurent de nul effect, dont plus avant n'ad esté fait de ceste matire. Et, mon tresredoubté seignur, vous please assavoir que nostre seignur le Roy m'ad escript pur avoir esté ovec a ceste feste de Noel, et si m'en ay excuse, sibien a cause de voz sessions, come de pluseurs autres governances queux faudront estre mys sur la paijs. Et, moun redoubté seignur, si tiel ordeig-

knights, esquires, archers and others mentioned above, and that you neglect nothing under danger that it is incumbent on.

Witnessed by the king at Westminster, September 18.

By the king himself.

20. *OWAIN AT A FUNERAL* Notes: pp. 310–11

My most noble, most reverent, and most powerful lord. I commend myself to your powerful lordship in everything I think or do. And may it please your lordship to understand that it is certified for certainty that Owain Glyndŵr and R. of B., with a large number and multitude of rebel men, have been this day at the funeral of two squires of the lordship of C., who were slain at your most recent expedition in Wales, and they lie with their hosts this night a league from this part of the B., and they intend to come and destroy my lands with the lordship of B. and with the lordship of C. — I know not which for certain. Therefore, most powerful lord, may it please you to be advised about this matter through your sage Council and with their fair instruction and their good advice and discretion, hearing, my most noble lord, that I do not have enough Englishmen with me to manage a chevauchée against them. Nevertheless through the help of men from my lands I will do my diligence and sentence in resisting these aforesaid rebels until better reinforcements come from you, most powerful lord. And, most honored lord, if these said rebels desire to push further into South Wales or into other lands, your Council has knowledge enough of the certain places where they may be encountered. My most noble, etc., of other news that I have this day or another I do certify it to your most powerful lordship. And I pray to the blessed Trinity that it will aid you, etc.

21. HENRY PERCY, *OWAIN'S PARLEY* Notes: p. 311

My most honored, redoubted, and powerful lord, I commend myself to your highness in such manner as I am able, to whom it may be pleasing to know that some of these men were coming from Owain Glyndwr to mislead me that the said Owain had a desire to parley with some of my men, through which envoys I sent word back to him to know his intent, saying that if he desired to submit himself without conditions into the good graces of our lord the king, that I would make every effort to plea for his life, without promising him anything. According to those men he responded that he would not come into England for anything, because he has well heard that the commons of England have killed great lords against the wishes of the king our lord and without coming to justice, and he said many other words and demands which were not without effect, as a result of which nothing more can be done in this matter. And, my most redoubted lord, may it please you to know that our lord the king has written to invite me to be with him at the Christmas feast, and if I am excused from this, it is because of the sessions, as pleasures other than governance must be missed to be generous to the country. And, my redoubted lord, if such

15   nance purroit estre fait que a la chastel de Pole fuist un bon garnisoun que entre
      eux et Sire Edmond Mortimer et les marchiers environ celle paijs purroient venir
      ove un bon route en Northgales, et que mesme celle temps voz garnisons de C. et
      H. fuissent un autre bon route et pur entrer par autre part, et que moy ovec les
      gentz de ceste paijs venoient vers les parties de Northgales, c'est assavoir par M.,
20   et aussi pur encontrer les uns ovec les autres a lieu qui purroit estre entrepris, me
      semble que ce serroit semblable chose pur grever a voz enemys, et si di pur moy que
      je serray prest a quell jour ou temps que vous me mandréz redoubté et puissant
      seignur, autres choses a present ne vous scay escrire, méz riens vous plese moy com-
      mander, toutdis vous me troveréz prest d'accomplir en tout mon pouoir. Em priant
25   etc.
          De par un cont a le prince etc.

22. Adam of Usk, *Chronicle, Part 2*   Latin
                                                              14 February 1402

Castrum de Conwey. Wyllylmus ap Tedur et Reys ap Tedur, fratres naturales de
insula de Anglesey alias Mona, quia graciam regiam de dicti Oweny insurrexione
optenere non ualentes, eodem die parasceues castrum de Conwey, armis, uictu-
alibus tutissime instructum, duobus eius ianitoribus subtilitate cuiusdam carpentarii
5   ad opus suum solitum se uenire asserentis interfectis, cum aliis quadraginta ingressi,
      occuparunt pro tutamine. Sed statim per principem et patriam obsessi, uicesimo
      octauo die mensis Maii tunc sequenti idem castrum, uecorditer quoad se et prodi-
      torie quoad socios, quia nouem eorundem, magis dicto principi exosos, post uigilias
      nocturnas dormitantes per ipsos dolose a tergo ligatos, sub condicione sui et ali-
10   orum uitas seruandi, reddiderunt. Quos nouem, sic ligatos et principi redditos, pri-
      mo trahi, postea euiscerari, suspendi, decollari et quatriperciri, adstatim uiderunt.

                                  . . .

Oweyn. Tota illa estate Oweyn Klyndor cum pluribus Wallie proceribus, regni
exules et regis proditores habiti, in montanis et siluestribus delitentes, aliquando
depredando, aliquando insidias et insultus eis inferentes interficiendo, partes West
15   Walie et North Walie non modice infestarunt. Ac dominum de Grey captiuarunt;
      dominus de Grey per O captiuatur et pro sedecim millibus libris redimitur.

                                  . . .

Monasterium de Stratfleyr stabulum equorum. Item, isto autumpno Oweynus de
Glendor, cum tota Northewalia, Cardikan et Poysia sibi adherentibus, Anglicos in
illis partibus habitantes, cum eorum uillis et presertim uilla de Pola, ferro et flamma
20   multum infestabat. Vnde Anglici in multitudine glomerosa illas partes inuadendo,
      totaliter depopulatas et depredatas ferro, fame et flamma, eciam pueris et ecclesiis
      non parcendo, et monasterium de Stratflur, in quo rexmet hospitabatur, et eius

ordinance for it can be provided then the castle of Welshpool should have a good garrison that is established there and Sir Edmund Mortimer and the marchers around that country could come with a good route into North Wales, and then at the same time your garrisons of C. and H. would have another good route and entry into another part, and then myself, with the men of this country, could come against the parts of North Wales, that is to say M., and also in order to engage this one with the others that can take place at this undertaking, it seems to me that such a thing would be grievous to your enemies, and if it be said for my part that I pressed near at whatever day or time that you mandate, redoubted and powerful lord, other choices at present I know not to write to you, but anything you command will please me. Always you will find me ready to accomplish all in my power. In praying etc.

From an earl to the prince etc.

22. Adam of Usk, *Chronicle, Part 2*   Notes: pp. 312

Conway castle. On this same day, Good Friday, the brothers Gwilym ap Tudur and Rhys ap Tudur, who came from the island of Anglesey or Môn, since they had failed to obtain the king's pardon for their part in the rising led by the aforesaid Owain, along with another forty men entered Conway castle, which was most securely fortified with arms and provisions, and seized it as their stronghold, two of the watch having been killed after being tricked by one of the carpenters claiming that he was simply coming to do his usual work. Being immediately besieged by the prince and the people of the surrounding area, however, on 28 May following, having deceitfully bound from behind nine of their fellows, whom the prince particularly loathed, while they were sleeping following the night watch, they surrendered the castle on condition that their lives and the lives of the others would be spared — a most shameful thing for them to have done, and an act of treachery against their fellows. They then promptly stood and watched while these nine, still bound, were handed over to the prince, and firstly drawn, and then disemboweled, hanged, beheaded, and quartered.

. . .

Owain. All this summer Owain Glyndŵr and several of the Welsh chieftains, whom the king regarded as traitors and outlaws from his kingdom, severely devastated West and North Wales, taking refuge in the mountains and woodlands before emerging either to pillage or to slaughter those who tried to attack or ambush them. And they captured Lord Grey; having been captured by Owain, Lord Grey was ransomed for sixteen thousand pounds.

. . .

The monastery of Strata Florida a stable for horses. During the autumn Owain Glyndŵr, supported by the whole of North Wales, Cardigan and Powys, continually assailed with fire and sword the English living in those regions and the towns they lived in, especially the town of Welshpool. A great host of English therefore invaded the area, ravaging and utterly destroying it with fire, sword and famine, sparing neither children nor churches; even the monastery of Strata Florida, in which the

25

ecclesia et choro eciam usque ad summum altare pro stabulo utendo, ipsasque pateras penitus spoliando, et ultra mille utriusque sexus pueros secum in Angliam uehendo ipsorum seruiciis mancipandos, desolatas reliquerunt easdem. Dictus tamen Oenus non modicum Anglicis nocuit, plures eorum interimendo, arma, equos et tentoria primogeniti regis et principis Walie ac aliorum dominorum hostiliter auferendo, et eadem pro usu suo ad montana sua et tutamina de Snowdon secum transferendo. Hiis diebus ausralis Wallia, et presertim tota Landauen'

30

diocesis, ab omnimoda inuasionis siue defensionis molestia satis stetit pacifica.

Ll. ap Gr. Vayan. Rex in Wallia. Inter trucidatos per Anglicorum ingressum predictum, Ll. ap Greffit Vayan de Cayo in comitatu de Cardikan, uir multum nobilis et dapsilis, sexdecem dolia uini in familia sua omni anno expendens, quia dicto Oeno confauens, in festo sancti Dionysii apud Lanamthyury, in presencia regis, et

35

de eius mandato, cum filio suo primogenito trahitur, suspenditur, decollatur et quatripercitur. Hoc tempore, circa testum sancti Michaelis, quarterium frumenti a nobili ad duo nobilia, et in quibusdam partibus Anglie ad tria, ad annonam subito mutatur cariorem. Vbique in Walia per muros et fossata renouantur tutamina.

. . .

40

Decretum destruccionis lingue Wallice. Plebei de Cardikan, ad uite perdonacionem recepti, Oeno dimisso, licet cum magna miseria, redierunt ad propria, lingua Walicana uti permissi, licet eius destruccio per Anglicos decreta fuisset, omnipotente Deo, rege regum, infallibuli omnium iudice, huiusmodi decretum ad grauatorum appellacionem et querelam misericorditer reuocante.

45

In crastino Omnium Sanctorum, Oenus, uolens obsidionem ponere circa Caernaruon, in multitudine glomerosa uixillum suum album cum dracone aureo ibidem displicuit, tamen per intraneos aggressus, trecentis de suis interemptis, in fugam propulsus est.

Isto tempore pro maritagio filiarum suarum dominus rex totum regnum colectauit. Domini de Percy, pater et filius, Scotorum rebellionem strenue domarunt,

50

ipsos in magno numero interimendo et captiuando.

Oenus cum suis dominium de Rethyn in North Wallia et eius pagum, penultimo die Ianuarii, ferro et flamma crudeliter infestauit, predas patrie et presertim pecudum ad montana de Snowdon secum deferendo, tamen dominiis comitis Marchie de Dynby et aliis multum parcebat, duos comitatus, scilicet de Kaernaruen et Muri-

55

onnit, sibi inclinatos quoad iurisdiccionem et guerram ad uotum habendo. Quidam miles uocatus Dauit ap Ieuan Goz de comitatu de Cardigan, qui per uiginti annos continue cum rege Cypry et aliis Cristianis Sarazenos debellauerat, per regem Francie ad regem Scocie pro Oeno directus, per nautas Anglie tentus, carceribus Turris London mancipatur.

60

Nuncii Oeni cum literis infrascripti tenoris, regi Scocie et dominis Hibern directis, in Hibernia capti, decapitantur.

king himself stayed, along with its church and choir, right up to the high altar, was converted into a stable, and was completely stripped of its plate; they carried off with them to England more than a thousand children, both girls and boys, whom they forced into service for them; and they left the country desolate. Yet Owain inflicted considerable losses on the English, killing several of them, and seizing by force from the king's eldest son, the prince of Wales, and from a number of other lords, their arms, horses and tents, which he then carried off to his mountain strongholds of Snowdonia for his own use. South Wales, however, and especially the whole diocese of Llandaff, remained undisturbed by any kind of trouble, either hostile or defensive, at this time.

Llywelyn ap Gruffudd Fychan. The king in Wales. Among those killed during this invasion by the English was Llywelyn ap Gruffudd Fychan of Caeo in the county of Cardigan, an extremely well-born and generous man who used to get through sixteen tuns of wine in his household each year; on the feast of St. Denis, however, at Llandovery, in the king's presence, and at his command, he was, along with his eldest son, drawn, hanged, beheaded and quartered, because he had supported Owain. At this time, around the feast of Michaelmas, a quarter of wheat suddenly jumped in price from one to two nobles, an in some parts of England to three nobles. Throughout Wales, defences were strengthened with walls and ditches.

. . .

Decree for the destruction of the Welsh tongue. Having been pardoned their lives, the people of Cardigan deserted Owain and returned, though not without great suffering, to their homes; they were, nevertheless — even though the English had decreed that it should be suppressed — allowed to use the Welsh tongue, for God the omnipotent, the king of kings infallible judge of all things, had revoked this decree in response to the prayers and complaints of the afflicted.

Intending to lay siege to Caernarfon, Owain raised his standard, a golden dragon on a white field, in the midst of a great host there on the morrow of All Saints; following an assault by the defenders, however, in which three hundred of his men were killed, he was driven off.

At this time the king imposed a tax on the whole kingdom in order to marry his daughters. The Lords Percy, father and son, strove manfully to quell the rebellious Scots, killing and capturing a large number of them.

On 30 January [1402] Owain and his men brutally ravaged with fire and sword the lordship of Ruthin in North Wales and the surrounding area, carrying the riches of the land, including the animals, away with him to the mountains of Snowdonia; for the most part, however, he spared the earl of March's lordships of Denbigh and others; he had at his disposal the two counties of Caernarfon and Merioneth, which supported him in both the war and the administration of justice. A certain knight called Dafydd ab Ieuan Goch of the county of Cardigan, who had spent twenty years continually fighting alongside the king of Cyprus and other Christians against the Saracens, was sent by the king of France to the king of Scotland on Owain's behalf, but was captured by English ships and imprisoned in the Tower of London.

Messengers of Owain's carrying the following letters addressed to the king of Scotland and the lords of Ireland were captured in Ireland and beheaded:

Litere ad regem Scocie. "Treshaut et trespuisant et tresredoute seigneur et cosin,
je me recomande a vostre treshautisme roial mageste si humblement come suy
dygne, en toutz maneres des honors et reverencez. Et, tresredoute seigneur et tres-
65   sovereygn cosin, pleser seyt a vous et a vostre dit treshautisme mageste dasavoyr que
Brutus, vostre tresnoble auncestre et le meyn, estoyt le primer roy corone qui pri-
merment enhabita deinz cest realme dengleterre, qui jadis fuist nomme Brataygne
graunt; le quel Brutus engendera trois fitz, cest assavoir Albanactus, Loctrinus et
Kamber; de quel dit Albanactus vous estez descenduz par droit lyne, de quel dit
70   Kamber les issuez ount reygnes roialment tanque a Kadualadir, qui estoit le darrein
roy coronne de ma dit nacioun, dount je, vostre simple cosin, suy descenduz par
droit lyne. Apres que decesse mes auncestres et tout ma dit nacion avons este, et ore
sumes, en oppression et bondage desouz mes et vostres morteles enimys Sacsouns,
come vous, tresredoute seigneur et tressovereygn cosin, ent avez bone conisance.
75   Des quex oppressions et bondages le prophecie dit que je serray delivere par eid
et socour de vostre dit roial mageste. Mais, tresredoute seigneur et sovereigne cosin,
je me grauntement complaigne a vostres ditz roall mageste et tressovereigne cosi-
nage, que moi defaut graundment genz dez armez; pur quoy, tresredoute seigneur
et tressovereygne cosin, je vous supplie humblement en mez genoils engenuler, si
80   pleiser soit a dit vostre roial mageste de moy maundre certeyn nombre de gentz
darmez de moy eidir et resistre, en laide de Dieux, mes et vostres ennmys susditz;
eiant consideracion, tresredoute seigneur et tressovereigne cosin, a le eschatisme
de meschyf et meschifs que je et mes ditz auncestres de Gales susditz avons suffres
et meyntes autres passez par mez et vostres mortuels enimys susditz. Entendant,
85   tresredoute seigneur et tressovereigne cosin, que ensi soit que je serray jour de ma
vie oblige de fayr service et plesance a vostre dit roial magestre et a mendre a vous.
Et pour ceo que je ne puis vous envoir touz mex bussoignes en escript, vous envoir
les portours de cestez de toutz mez bussoygnes pleinement enformez, as quex vous
pleaise doner foy et credens de ceo quils vous durront par bouche de par moy.
90   Tresredoute seigneur et tressovereygn cosin, le trespuisant seigneur vous (garde)."

Litere ad dominos Hibern. "Salutem et amoris plenitudinem, domine reuerendis-
sime et consanguinee confidentissime. Sciatis quod maxima dissencio siue guerra
orta est inter nos et nostros uestrosque mortales inimicos Saxones, quam guerram
uiriliter sustentamus hucusque fere per duos annos elapsos, ac eciam de cetero in-
95   tendimus et speramus sustentare et ad bonum et effectualem finem perducere,
mediantibus gracia Dei saluatoris nostri uestrisque auxilio atwue fauore. Sed, quia
uulgariter dicitur per propheciam quod, antequam nos altiorem manum in hac
parte haberemus, quod uos (et) uestri carissimi consanguinei in Hibernea ad hoc
manus porrigetis adiutrices, quocirca, reuerende domine et consanguinee confi-
100   dentissime, uos corditer et effectuose requirimus quatinus de equestribus et pedi-
tatibus uestris armatis, ad succurrendum nobis et nacioni nostre, a diu per inimicos
nostros ac uestros predictos oppressis, necnon ad resistendum uoluntati fraudabili
et deceptabili eorundem inimicorum nostrorum, talem numerum qualem commode
et honeste poteritis, saluo in omnibus uestro honorabili statu, nobis tam cito quam
105   bene uidebitis expedire, necessitatem nostram considerando, transmittatis. Istud
amore nostro et sicut in uobis maxime confidamus, licet incogniti uestre reuerende

The letter to the king of Scotland. "Most excellent, powerful and esteemed lord and cousin, I commend myself to your most excellent royal majesty with fitting humility, and with honour and respect in all matters. Most esteemed lord and royal cousin, may it please you and your royal excellence to know that Brutus, your most noble ancestor and mine, was originally the first crowned king to live in this kingdom of England, which used to be known as Great Britain. Brutus fathered three sons, namely Albanactus and Locrinus and Kamber; you are descended from the direct line of this Albanactus, while the descendants of this Kamber ruled as kings until the time of Cadwaladr, who was the last crowned king of my people, and from whose direct line I, your humble cousin, am descended. Since his death, however, my forbears and all my people have been, as we still are, subjected and held in bondage by my and your mortal enemies the Saxons — a fact which you, most esteemed lord and royal cousin, know full well. The prophecy states that, with the help and support of your royal majesty, I shall be delivered from this subjection and bondage. And yet, most esteemed lord and royal cousin, it pains me greatly to inform your royal majesty that I am very short of men-at-arms; it is for this reason, most esteemed lord and royal cousin, that I beg you, humbly and with bended knee, your royal majesty, please to send me a number of men-at-arms who, with the help of God, can help me to resist my and your enemies, most esteemed lord and royal cousin, and to punish them for the evils and injuries which I and my aforesaid forbears of Wales have suffered, and for the many other things inflicted upon us by these mortal enemies of mine and your. Do not doubt, most esteemed lord and royal cousin, that I shall in consequence consider myself bound to serve and obey your royal majesty at pleasure for the rest of my days. I cannot send you all my news in writing, but these messengers whom I have sent to you are fully informed of all my affairs, and I beg you therefore to place your trust and confidence in what they tell you by word of mouth on my behalf. Most esteemed lord and royal cousin, may the Lord almighty keep you safe."

The letter to the lords of Ireland. "Greetings and much love, most esteemed lord and trusted kinsman. As you will know, a great struggle, not to say a war, has broken out between us and our, and your, mortal enemies, the Saxons, a war which we have maintained vigorously for nearly two years now, and which, by the grace of God our saviour, and with your help and support, we hope and plan to go on maintaining until it can be brought to an effective and favourable conclusion. It is commonly said in the prophecy, however, that, before we can gain the upper hand in this contest, you and your noble kinsmen in Ireland shall come to our aid in this matter; considering our plight, therefore, we warmly and earnestly request you, esteemed lord and trusted kinsman, to send over to us, as soon as you possibly can — saving your honourable estate in all things — as many mounted and unmounted men-at-arms as you can properly and honestly afford, in order to help us and our people, who have for so long been oppressed by these aforesaid enemies of ours and yours, to defeat the perfidious and deceitful purpose of these same enemies of ours. We beg you, moreover, for the love that we bear you and the great trust that we place in you, and despite the fact that we are unknown to your esteemed person, not to

persone fuerimus, facere non tardatis, intelligentes, domine et consanguinee reuer-
endissime, quod quamdiu nos ualebimus istam guerram fortiter sustentare in partibus nostris, quod uobis satis constat sine dubio, quod uos et omnes alii magnates
110   de partibus uestris Hibernie pacem desiderabilem et tranquilitatem placabilem
medio tempore impetrabitis. Et quia, domine (et) consanguinee, latores presencium
uos plenius uiua uoce informabunt, si placet, credenciam adhibeatis in omnibus que
uobis ex parte nostra dicent, et qua uolueritis, domine et consanguinee reuerende,
que per nos uestrum humilem consanguineum fieri poterunt, uos mandetis cum
115   fiducia. Domine et consanguinee reuerende, uestram reuerenciam et domina-
cionem in prosperis altissimus conseruet longeuam. Scriptum apud Northwall,
penultimo die Nouembris."

23. Henry IV, *Battle of Bryn Glas*   Anglo-Norman
                                                                    25 June 1402

Reverentes pieres en Dieu et noz treschieres et foiaulx,
      Nous vous salvons souvent. Et pour ce que certains nouvelles nous sont venuz
de present de notre pais de Gales coment noz rebelles illoesques ont pris jatarde
nostre treschier et tresame cousyn Esmon Mortymer et pluseurs autres chivalers et
5   escuiers en sa compaigniee, dont nous avons pris graunde poisauntee, volons par
tant et entendons au plaisir de Dieu de nous transporter vers les dites parties en
nostre propre personne pour resister a la malice de noz rebelles susditz. Si vous
mandons que veues cestes par votre bonne avis facez faire sibien lettres desoubz
notre prive seal as seigneurs, chivalers, et escuiers de notre retenue et a ceux qui
10   ount annuitees ou pensions de nous pour estre ovec nous, prestement armez,
montez, et arraiez solom lour degrees et estates a notre citee de Lichefelde ove le
hast que bonnement pourront, parensi que au darrein ils soient illoeques ou en
paiis pres de mesme notre citee, ou nous serroms le septisme jour de Juyllet
proschein, venant prestez daler ovesque nous as dites parties pour resister et obvier
15   a la malice de noz rebelles avantdites; come noz briefes desoubz notre graunde seal
as viscontes de noz countees de Notyngham, Warrwyk, Leycestre, Northamptoun,
Oxon, Berks, Cantebrigg, Huntyngtoun, Buks, Bedford, et Hertford, pour faire
proclamacioun en mesmes les countees et chescun de eux que sur certeines peines
grevouses, par voz sages discreciones a limiter, tous les chivalers et escuiers des
20   dites contees soy arment et arraient et quils prestement mounteez, armez, et arraiez
soient avec nous a les jour et lieu dessusditz. Et ausi noz semblables lettres et briefes
tielles come appartient a noz viscontes des contees de Nicole, Everwik, Westmorl,
Cumbr, et Northumbr, que chescun de eulx facez proclamacion que tous noz lieges
dicelles countees sur sembable peine, sibien chivalers et escuiers, come archiers et
25   gens defensables, soient prestement monteez et arraiez chescun solom soun estat
et degree, pur aler a noz marche de Scoce a quel temps qils en soient garniz par les
gardeins de noz ditz marche. Et auxi noz autres briefes a noz viscontes de noz
contees de Cornub, Devoun, Somers, Dorse, Southamt, Suure, Ken, Essex, Norff,
et Suffpour, semblable proclamacioun faire illoeques sur semblable peine que touz
30   noz lieges dicelles contees soient prestement arraiez chescun en lour degree pour
faire defense et resistence a noz enemys en salvacioun de notre roialme sibien par

delay in doing this; understand, too — as you doubtless do, most esteemed lord and kinsman — that for as long as we are able to go on maintaining this warlike struggle in our land, you and all the other lords in your land of Ireland will in the meantime be able to enjoy the sort of peace and quiet which you desire. Moreover, lord and kinsman, since the bearers of these letters shall keep you fully informed by word of mouth, may it please you to put your trust in whatever they say on our behalf, and if there is anything which you would like to see done by us, your humble kinsman, you may with confidence commit it to them. May the Almighty preserve your reverence and lordship in prosperity for many days to come, esteemed lord and kinsman. Written in North Wales, 29 November."

23. HENRY IV, *BATTLE OF BRYN GLAS*   Notes: p. 313

Reverend fathers in God and our most dear and loyal,

We greet you warmly. And because certain news has come to us at present from our country of Wales how our rebels there have lately taken our very dear and well beloved cousin Edmund Mortimer and several other knights and esquires in his company, from which we have taken great grief, we much wish and await God's pleasure to betake ourselves to the said region in our own person to combat the wickedness of our aforesaid rebels. Therefore we command you that, having seen these letters, by your good advice you will also cause to be made letters under our privy seal to the lords, knights, and esquires of our retinue and to those who receive annuities or pensions from us, to be ready with us, armed, mounted and arrayed according to their rank and standing at our city of Lichfield with all due speed, so that in the end they may be there or in the country close to our said city, where we will be on the seventh day of July next, ready to go with us to the said region to resist and combat the wickedness of our aforesaid rebels; also our writs under our great seal to the sheriffs of our counties of Nottingham, Warwick, Leicester, Northampton, Oxford, Berkshire, Cambridge, Huntingdon, Buckingham, Bedford, and Hertford, to make proclamation in each one of those same counties that on certain serious penalties, defined according to your wise discretion, all the knights and esquires of the said counties be armed and arrayed and be ready mounted, armed, and arrayed with us on the day and at the place aforesaid. And also our similar letters and writs such as relate to our sheriffs of the counties of Lincoln, York, Westmorland, Cumberland and Northumberland, that each of them should make proclamation that all our lieges of the said counties should on similar penalty, also knights and esquires, likewise archers and fighting men, be ready mounted and arrayed each one according to his standing and rank, to go to our March of Scotland at such time as they may be instructed by the guardians of our said March. And also our other writs to our sheriffs of our counties of Cornwall, Devon, Somerset, Dorset, Southampton, Sussex, Surrey, Kent, Essex, Norfolk, and Suffolk, to make similar proclamation there on similar penalty that all our lieges of these counties should be ready arrayed each according to his rank to make defence and resistance to our enemies for the saving of our kingdom also by land and by sea on their coasts,

terre come par meer en lour costiers, si ascuns y vorront faire invasioun a notre dit roiaume et noz lieges dicelle. Et notre signeur vous eit toutdys en sa seinte garde.

Donne soubz notre signet a notre chastel de Berkhamstede le xxv. Jour de Juyn.

24. HENRY PERCY, *OWAIN DENIES GENOCIDE*

**Anglo-Norman
after July 1402**

S'ensuyt le report fait au conte de Northumberland par le message par lui envoiee du congie du roy a Esmon Mortymer sur la matere expousee depar le dit conte par le dit message a Oweyn de Glyndourdy.

5

Primerement le dit message reporta au dit conte en presence du counsail qui le dit Oweyn disoit qui pour la grant affeccion et affiance qu'il porte au susdit conte il desire de parler ovesque mesme le conte devant aucun autre seignure du roiaume.

Item quant a les destruccions et gastes du paiis et les prises et occisions de gentz faitz par le dit Owein, il dit qu'il n'est pas de ce en cause, mais tresvolenters

10

voudroit il avoir pees.

Item quant a leritage qui le dit Owein cleyme davoir mesme celui Owein dit qui partie de son heritage il ad, mais nonpas atant come de droit a lui appertient. Et tresvolenters voudroit il approcher as marches d'Engleterre pur treter et parler ovec aucuns seignures sinoun qui le comun voys et claymour y est qui le dit Owein

15

voudroit et entende a destruire la lange Engloys.

25. *ROLLS OF PARLIAMENT, 1402*

**Anglo-Norman
16 October 1402**

Pur le seignur de Grey de Ruthyn.

13. Item, mesme le Lundy les ditz communes prierent a nostre dit seignur le roi: qe come le seignur de Grey de Ruthyn soit en forte et dure prisoune en Gales tresdolorousement, et ait fait soun finance et ranceon pur x. mille marcs appaiers,

5

c'estassavoir vi. mille marcs le jour de Seint Martyn proscheyn, et iiij. mille marcs deins brief temps ensuant, ou autrement d'estre mys a mort: qe pleise a mesme nostre seignur le roi grantir et conge dounir a seignur de Roos et le seignur de Wilughby, et as autres ses parentz et amys, d'ordeigner et faire chevissance pur la dite finance et ranceon, come mieultz leur semblera, sanz ent estre empeschez,

10

molestez, ou grevez par nostre dit seignur le roi ou ses heires ascunement en temps advenir.

Quel prier mesme nostre seignur le roi molt graciousement ottroia: et dist outre q'a ce faire il voet aider mesmes de sa partie; qar il sciet bien qe le dit seignur de Grey est vaillant et loial chivaler, et pur tiel il s'ad bien approvez a ceste foitz.

. . .

if any should wish to make invasion of our said kingdom and our lieges thereof. And may our Lord have you daily in his holy keeping.

Given under our signet at our castle of Berkhamsted on the 25th day of June.

24. HENRY PERCY, *OWAIN DENIES GENOCIDE*   Notes: p. 313

Here follows the report made to the earl of Northumberland by the messenger he sent by leave of the king to Edmund Mortimer regarding the matter shown by this same earl through the said message of Owain Glyndŵr.

First, this messenger reported to the said earl in the presence of the council that the said Owain, on account of the great affection and affinity that he bears toward the aforesaid earl, wishes to speak openly with the same earl before any other lord of the realm.

As to the destructions and devastations of the lands and the seizures and takings of the armies that belong to the said Owain, he says that he is not the cause of these things, but greatly he would desire to have peace.

As to the inheritance that the said Owain claims, the same Owain said that he must have that part of the inheritance that was always his, but only that which justly belongs to him. And greatly he would desire to approach the marches of England himself to entreat or talk with other lords under treaty or parley except those who through common voice and clamor have claimed that the said Owain desires and intends to destroy the English language.

25. *ROLLS OF PARLIAMENT, 1402*   Notes: p. 314

The ransom of Lord Grey of Ruthin.

13. On behalf of Lord Grey of Ruthin. Also, on the same Monday, the said commons requested our said lord the king that whereas Lord Grey of Ruthin was in a most wretched state, in a harsh and oppressive prison in Wales, and had agreed to pay 10,000 marks for his fine and ransom, namely 6,000 marks at Martinmas following and 4,000 marks shortly afterwards, or else he would be put to death: may it please our same lord the king to grant and to give leave to Lord Roos and Lord Willoughby, and to his other kinsmen and friends, to ordain and make such arrangements for the said finance and ransom as should seem best to them, without them being hindered, molested or obstructed by our said lord the king or his heirs in any way in the future.

Which request our same lord the kind most graciously granted: and he said moreover that he wished for his own part to help with this matter, because he well knows that the said Lord Grey is a brave and loyal knight, and so he had shown himself to be on this occasion.

. . .

15   102. Item, qe nulle homme Englois marie a ascune Galois de l'amiste et alliance
de Owen ap Glendourdy, traitour a nostre seignur le roy, ou autre femme Galois
puis la rebellioun du dit Owen, ou en temps advenir soi ferra marier a ascune
femme Galoys, soit mys en ascun office en Gales, ou la marche de Gales.

Responsio. Le roy le voet.

26. EDMUND MORTIMER, *DEFECTION TO OWAIN*   Anglo-Norman
                                                              13 December 1402

          Treschiers et bien amez, vouz salue mielx souvent, et vous face a entendre que
Oweyn Glyndor ad moeue une querelle la quelle est tielle, qe si le Roy Richard soit
en vie de luy restorer a sa coronne, et sinoun qe mon honore Neuewe q'est droit
heir al dit coronne serroit Roy d'Engleterre, et qe le dit Oweyn avoreit son droit en
5   Gales. Et je veiant et considerant qe la dite querelle est bone et reisonable ay
assentee de outrement estaier en la dite querele, et l'aidere et mayntener, et par la
grace de Dieu a bon fyn, Amen: Vous empriant chierement de cuer qe vous voillez
moy aider qe mon dit querele soit bonement achivee, et d'altre part voillez savoir
qe les Seignories de Mellenyth, Werthrenon, Raydre, Comot de Vdor, Arwystly,
10   Keveilloc, et Kereynon sont ore tarde venuz en nos mayns. Pourquoy vous unqore
emprie qe vous ne facez ascun journay a mes dites terres, ne nullez damages a mes
ditz tenantz, et vous eux deliverez vitailles sur certeyn resonable price come vous
voillez qieo ferray a vous le mesme, et de cestes moy voillez mander response.
          Treschiers et biens ames, Dieux vous doyve grace de bien fair al comencement
15   et vous amesne a bon fin.
          Escrite a Mellenyth le xiij. jour de Decembre.

A mes tresch. et biens ames,
          Monsr. Johan Greyndor, Howell Vougam, et touts les gentielx et comunes de
Raydenor et Preshemde.

27. IOLO GOCH, *PAN OEDD FWYAF EI RWYSG*   Welsh
                                                                   1401–03?

       Llyma fyd rhag sythfryd Sais!
       Mynych iawn y dymunais
       cael arglwydd, llawn awydd llain,
       ohonom ni ein hunain:
5   pybyr chwaen — pawb adwaen pwy —
       arf glân dewrdarf Glyndyfrdwy,
       Owain, loyw waedlain lidlorf,
       i ymwan naw tarian torf.
       Eurgledd pobl, arglwydd pybyr,
10   ergryd â'i wryd ar wŷr.
       Aed y byd, braw geinbryd gân,

102. Also, that no Englishman married to any Welshwoman of the fellowship and alliance of Owain Glyndŵr, traitor to our lord the king, or to any other Welshwoman since the rebellion of the said Owain, or who in future marries any Welshwoman, should be appointed to any office in Wales, or in the march of Wales.

Answer. The king wills it.

26. EDMUND MORTIMER, *DEFECTION TO OWAIN*   Notes: pp. 314–15

Dearest and well-beloved,

I greet you most fervently, and wish you to understand that Owain Glyndŵr has moved a grievance which is such that, if King Richard is alive, his crown will be restored to him, and if that is not so, my honored nephew, who is by right heir to the said crown, will be king of England, and the said Owain will have his right in Wales. And seeing and considering that the said grievance is good and reasonable, I have agreed to remain outside the said dispute, and to aid and uphold it, by the grace of God, to a just end, Amen: Entreating you dearly from my heart that you will assist me so that my said grievance will come to a good end, and that you will also know that the lordships of Maelienydd, Gwerthrynion, Rhayader, Cwmwd Deuddwr, Arwystli, Cyfeiliog, and Caereinion have recently come into our hands. Therefore I again entreat you that you will not make any foray into my said lands, nor do any harm to my said tenants, and that you will supply them with provisions at a reasonable price as you would wish me to do to you, and that you will send me a reply.

Dearest and well beloved, may God give you grace to do well at the beginning and lead you to a good end.

Written at Maelienydd the 13th day of December.

To my very dear and well beloved,

Sir John Greyndour, Hywel Fychan, and all the gentry and commons of Radnor and Presteigne.

27. IOLO GOCH, *WHEN HIS AUTHORITY WAS GREATEST*   Notes: pp. 315–20

Behold a world caused by English arrogance!
Very often have I wished
to have a lord — full of eagerness for a blade —
from amongst us ourselves.
5   A mighty feat — everyone knows who:
the fair, brave and fear-inspiring weapon of Glyndyfrdwy,
Owain, bright bloody blade, ferocious defender —
to contend with many shields in a host.
The golden sword of the people, mighty lord,
10   terrifies men with his bravery.
Let the world give him a gift of prophecy,

iddo reg o ddarogan.
Glân yw'r arglwydd mawrlwydd mau
yn dial cam y Deau.
15   Deall a wnair gywair gân
ohono ef ei hunan.
Trin gyrcher, goleuder glain,
tra ewybr, o'r tri Owain:
Owain, glain dwyrain, Glyndŵr,
20   baun trasyw, yn ben treisiwr;
Owain arglwyddlain, aur gledd,
derfysgwr Deifr dorf osgedd;
Owain hefyd, aerfryd ŵr,
rwysg anian, oresgynnwr.
25   Llyw llawen yw, llew a Nudd,
llyrf ffyrf ddigrif-ffyrf Gruffudd.
Llidiog wrth wŷr â llediaith,
llym gledd bryd ar wedd brwydr waith.
Llwydd brenin yn lladd Brynaich,
30   llew o brudd nerth llaw a braich.
Llew aergryd hydr llaw aergroch,
llygra gyrff holl wŷr Lloegr goch.
Llurig Dduw, ddiwall arwydd,
am Owain, iôr Rhufain rhwydd,
35   pybyr wanar bleiddgar blwng
perffaith, tair talaith teilwng.
Pur yw ei glod, pôr y Glyn,
pwyll rwysgwr, pell oresgyn.
Paun glân haul, cywaethgael coeth,
40   prifbur wayw awchddur wychddoeth.
Pôr a ladd mewn ymladdgors
pedwar can mil o hil Hors.
Pablaidd gorff, pobloedd a gur,
post addwyn hael, pais dewddur.
45   Pen nen pur, mur, mawr waladr,
pôr glew, llew llym cyflym cadr.
Prudd Nudd nêr yw'r muner mau,
pôr dôr dâr, gwanar gwinau.
Pleidiwr brwydr, paladr briwdwn,
50   poed gwir, bywyd hir i hwn!
Pedr i'w borth pa dir y bo,
pe mau swydd pumoes iddo!

a finely wrought song causing alarm.
Fair is my highly successful lord,
avenging the wrong of the South.
15   A well-made song about him
will be meaningful.
Battle may be engaged, a jewel's splendor,
very swiftly, by the three Owains:
Owain, ascendant jewel, Glyndŵr,
20   most excellent peacock, will be the chief ravager;
Owain, lordly jewel, golden sword,
agitator of the Deirans arrayed in a host;
Owain also, battle-minded man,
with an attacking nature, a conqueror.
25   He is a delightful lord, a lion and a Nudd,
with the mighty spears of pleasant, mighty Gruffudd.
Fierce towards men with a foreign accent,
the look of a sharp sword in the form of battle-work.
The success of a king in killing Bernicians,
30   a lion with skilful strength of hand and arm.
A mighty lion causing terror in battle, a hand causing battle's uproar,
he maims the bodies of all the men of bloody Lloegr.
God's breastplate, faultless sign,
for Owain, generous lord of Rome,
35   mighty leader with the fierce nature of a wolf,
perfect, worthy of three diadems.
Pure is his fame, lord of the Glyn,
wise ruler, far conquering.
Fair peacock of the sun, fine at gaining a realm,
40   Most excellent spear with a steel point, excellent and wise.
Lord who kills in the battle-bog
four hundred thousand of Horsa's line.
Vigorous body, he strikes nations,
a fine generous pillar, in a thick iron surcoat.
45   A pure chief lord, a rampart, a great spear,
brave lord, a keen, swift, brave lion.
A lord with the wisdom of Nudd is this lord of mine,
an oak door of a lord, an auburn-haired chief.
A supporter of battle with a shattered spear,
50   may it be true — long life to him!
St. Peter as his support wherever he may be.
If mine were the office — five ages to him!

28. *HISTORIA VITAE*   **Latin**
                                                                           early 1403

De execrabili scilicet insurreccione Walens, qui quendam armigerum, nomine Owyn Glendor, in suum principem, et capitaneum eorum contra pacem erexerunt. Cuius insurreccionis causa subsequitur, ut eam relatu habemus.

Cum rex in Scociam properare disponeret, inter alios misit litteras, anulo suo signatas, ad predictum Owyn, pro eo quod ipse illis diebus armiger formosus habe-
5   batur, ut illuc secum nullo modo uenire recusaret. Quarum litterarum baiulus domi-nus de Grey de Rythynn tunc constitutus erat, qui acceptas litteras usque ad pro-feccionem regis ad eum ferre differebat. Pridie igitur tercione die ante mocionem predicte regis littere sibi liberabantur. Qui de hiis ualde attonitus, respondit, quod
10   nimis tarde, subito et inopinate pro tanto uiagio premunitus erat, breuiter se ex-cusans, quod nollet, sicut nec potuisset, ea uice in Scociam ire. Dominus uero le Grey, relicto eo in Wallia, ad regem in Scociam quamtociens excessum, narrans ei modo peiori, quod predictus Owen spretis litteris suis, eum uilipendisset, eius pre-cepta ualde contempnendo.
15   Ipse uero rex tacitus pro tempore considerabat. Postea cum suo exercitu de Leycestr' egressus, Walliam intrauit cum omni festinacione, ad debellandum uel penitus eosdem destruendum, si fortuna sibi faueret. Illac istacque circuiens, et quem occideret ardenter querens, neminem uidit uel occidit. Ipse autem Owynus G[lyndor] in speluncis et montibus Wallie a facie regis se abscondebat. Videns igitur
20   rex, quod nichil proficeret, sed magis deterioracio exercitus sui fieret, cum ibidem uictualia sufficiencia minime haberent, datis prius terris, tenementis ac redditibus predicti Owyni G[lyndor] ipsi domino de Grey, reuersus est per Salopiam uersus Wigorn', ubi morabatur per dies aliquot tractaturus cum suo consilio, quid super hiis agendum esset. Et hec quidem donacio terrarum, reddituum ac tenementorum
25   nobis maioris tribulacionis et angustie fomitem ministrabat, prout lucidius inferius patebit.

Hoc eodem anno [1400], cito post recessum regis, surrexit Owynus Glyndor cum suis, et quandam uillam in Wallia, nomine Rithyn, que erat de dominio pre-dicti domini de Grey, primitus spoliatam igne penitus consumpsit.

· · ·

30   Eodem anno [1401] rex iterum propositum sumens in Walliam descendere con-tra predictum Owynum Glyndor et Wallen, adhuc sibi et regno rebellantes, in uigil-ia Corporis Christi secundo Euesham uenit, stipatus cum comitum, baronum, mili-tum, et aliorum magna multitudine. Qui illuc usque in tercium diem post prandium commoratus est. Post hec inde recedens, Wigorniam adiit, deinde in Walliam, ubi
35   per 4 septimanas cum suo excercitu moram traxit, parum proficiens ad propositum, excepto quod decapitari fecit unum Wallicum, qui asserebat, se regem ad Owynum Glyndor ducturum, nec perfecit. Iste interrogatus, cur sic regem decipere auderet,

28. *HISTORIA VITAE*   **Notes: pp. 320–21**

Regarding the hateful insurrection of the Welsh, who raised up into their ruler a certain esquire by the name of Owain Glyndŵr and their captain against the peace. The cause of this insurrection follows, as we have it related.

When the king made arrangements to hasten into Scotland he sent a letter sealed with his signet ring to the aforesaid Owain, amongst other people, because in those days he [Owain] was held to be a handsome esquire, so that in no manner could he refuse to come with him. Lord Grey of Ruthin had been appointed as the carrier of this letter, who postponed delivering the accepted letter to him up until the time of the setting out of the king. Therefore at Terce on the day before setting out the aforesaid letter of the king was freed by him. He [Owain] was deeply astonished by these happenings, and replied that he had been alerted too late, suddenly and unexpectedly for such a voyage, briefly excusing himself because he was not willing, just as he had not been able, to go into Scotland at that time. In fact Lord Grey, having left that man [Owain] in Wales, told the king, who had advanced thus far into Scotland, in an incriminating fashion, that the aforesaid Owain scorned the king's letters and considered the king of no value, vehemently condemning his commands.

Truly the king himself considered these things in silence for a time afterwards. Setting out with his army from Leicester he entered Wales with all haste to vanquish or to destroy utterly those same men if fortune should be favourable to him. Going about here and there, and seeking ardently to kill him, he neither saw nor killed anyone. However Owain Glyndŵr himself hid from the sight of the king in the caves and mountains of Wales. Therefore the king, seeing that he was achieving nothing, but rather that he was harming his army, since he barely had sufficient food there, lands having been given earlier, and the holdings and returns of the aforesaid Owain Glyndŵr to Lord Grey himself, the king turned back through Shrewsbury to Worcester, where he delayed for some days in order to discuss with his council what was to be done about these things. And indeed this giving of lands, returns and holdings prepared for us the kindling of a greater trial and poverty, as will appear more clearly below.

In this same year [1400], shortly after the return of the king, Owain Glyndŵr rose up with his people, and attacked and plundered then entirely burned a certain town in Wales, by the name of Ruthin, which was under the dominion of the said Lord Grey.

. . .

In that same year [1401] the king again formed a plan to descend into Wales against the aforementioned Owain Glyndŵr and the Welsh, until now rebelling against himself and the kingdom, and he arrived at Evesham on the evening of Corpus Christi, attended by a great multitude of earls, barons, soldiers and others. There he was delayed until after breakfast on the third day. After this, withdrawing from there, he went to Worcester, and from there into Wales, where he spent a period of four weeks with his army, achieving very little to do with his intention, except that he had one Welshman decapitated, who had claimed that he would lead the king to Owain Glyndŵr, and had not achieved it. When that man was interrogated, and they asked him why he dared to deceive the king in this way, he held

gratanter caput percussori extendens, respondit, se malle repende decollari, quam ipsius O[wyni] Glyndor consilium, eo quod duo filii sui essent cum eo, aliquo modo
40   propalare. Possumus et nos Anglici hic exemplum habere, ut discamus inter nos fideliter usque ad mortem consilia et secreta nostra tenere.

Depauperauit etiam tunc abbathiam rex de Stretflur ita ut nullum monachum in ea relinqueret. De quibus unus, qui contra regem et pacem arma portabat, iam tunc decollatus est. Ipsum uero O[wynum] Glyndor nec uidit, nec ubi esset aliquid
45   audiuit. Exercitus autem eius labore, fame, siti et frigore fatigatus, est demum occulte repedauit. Rex etiam, positis prius custodibus, licet insufficiencibus, in castellis Wallie, ubi necesse putabat, reuersus est cum suis usque London. Quod audiens O[wynus] Glyndor parum post hec surrexit de abditis, et succendebat suburbias cuiusdam uille, uocate "le Pole" et alia damna non minima ibidem perpetrauit.

. . .

50   In fine huius anni [1401] rex, tercio in Walliam properare disponens, propter sepedictum et maledictum Owynum Glyndor, qui inmania mala ibidem fecerat de die in diem.

. . .

Hoc anno [1401], dum esset rex apud Wigorn, pertractabat cum suo consilio, quid contra predictum Owynum [Glyndor] sibique adherentes agendum sit, et an
55   ipse rex in propria persona ea uice in Walliam proficissi deberet. Tandem ad id uentum est, ut rex, ordinatis prius custodibus sufficientibus in castellis et aliis fortitudinibus Wallie, London rediret.

. . .

Eodem anno [1402] in Quadragesima dominus de Grey dum esset in suo castro de Rythin in Wallia, uenerunt ad eum de sua familia, qui dicerent, O[wynum] G[lyn
60   dor] cum paucis prope assistere, et quod sibi honorem maximum nomenque sempiternum adquireret, predamque diu desiderabilem se capturum, de qua deficere non deberet, si contra eos et ad eos exire uellet. Quo audito, statim arma petit, paratisque equis, arcubus et lanceis, extra castrum ad illos animo uolente quamtocius accessit. Quem cum uidisset O[wynus] Glyndor, fugam fingendo se parum
65   retrahit, quousque dominus cum suis a castro plene et perfecte exisset. Absconderat autem O[wynus Glyndor] Wallenses per turmas, in diuersis locis latitantes, quos precepit, ut, cum tempus oportunum aduenisset, omnes in dominum predictum insurgerent.

Que plura? Mox ab hostibus circumceptus, capitur et captiuatur dominus loris
70   que fortissimis ligatur, atque cum illo in montes de Snowdonn et speluncas Wallie deducitur. Sicque factum est, ut, qui predam se capturum indubitanter dispondebat, fortuna sinistrante ipse pocius, quod condolendo referimus, uersa uice preda aduersarii effectus est.

out his head freely to the executioner, and replied that he preferred to be decapitated at once, than to divulge in any way the council of Owain Glyndŵr, especially because his own two sons were with him. We English too can hold this is an example, so that we may learn to hold our councils and secrets among ourselves faithfully to the point of death.

Then the king even rendered destitute the abbey of Strata Florida to such an extent that he left no monk in it. One of these monks, who was bearing arms against the king and the peace, was decapitated. Truly he did not see Owain Glyndŵr himself, nor did he hear at all where he was. However worn out by that labor, exhausted by hunger, thirst and cold, the army secretly turned back from there at last. The king also first posted guards, evidently insufficient, in the castles of Wales, where he supposed them necessary, and returned with his people to London. Hearing this, Owain Glyndŵr rose up a little after this from his places of concealment, and set fire with his people to the outlying areas of the town called Welshpool and carried out other terrible deeds in the same place, not at all small ones.

. . .

At the end of this year [1401] the king prepared for a third time to hasten into Wales, on account of Owain Glyndŵr, who has been spoken of often and badly, and who had committed terrible evils there day in day out.

. . .

In this year [1401], when the king was at Worcester, he was discussing with his council what should be done against the aforementioned Owain Glyndŵr and those who attached themselves to him, and whether the king himself in his own person ought to set out into Wales for that reason. At length it was decided that the king should first appoint sufficient guards in the castles and other fortified places of Wales, and return to London.

. . .

In that same year [1402] in Lent when the Lord Grey was in his castle of Ruthin in Wales, some members of his household came to him to say that Owain Glyndŵr had stopped nearby with a few men, and that he would acquire great honor and an eternal name, and plunder desirable for a long time if he should capture him, plunder which would never run out, if he wished to go to them and attack them. When he had heard this, he sought his arms at once, and when his horses had been prepared, bows and lances, he went out of the castle against them with a willing spirit and as quickly as possible. When Owain Glyndŵr had seen him, pretending to flee he withdrew himself a little, until the lord had openly and completely come out from the castle with his men. However, Owain Glyndŵr hid away the Welshmen in squadrons, lurking in various places, and ordered them, when a suitable time had come, all to rise against the aforesaid lord.

What more should I say? Soon the lord was surrounded by the enemy, was taken and made captive and was bound with the strongest bonds, and was led away with that man into the mountains of Snowdon and the caves of Wales. So it happened that he who thought that he was certainly going to take booty, rather himself, by an unlucky fortune, rather became the booty of his adversary, a thing which we relate with sympathy.

Hoc anno [1402], in festo Sancti Albani, dominus Edmundus Mortumer' miles
75   per predictum Owynum Glyndor hoc modo captus est. Existente autem illo in
propria uille de Ludlow, peruenit ad eum, quod predictus O[weynus] G[lyndor] de
montibus Wallie cum paucis descendisset, essetque super unum moncium iuxta
Pilale, ubi quedam ymago beate Marie uirginis ualde honorabatur, non longe a
dicta uilla Ludlow. Misit ergo festinater Edmundus pro hominibus et de se tenenti-
80   bus de Melenyth in Wallia, ut in adiutorium suum in hac ardua necessitate uenire
non omitterent.

Qui cum ad eum peruenissent, cum eis et aliis pluribus ualentibus dictum
montem intrepidus ascendit. Congresso igitur cum impetu magno inter eos facto,
predicti Wallenses de Melenyth non de tribu Iuda, ymmo Iude prodictoris pro-
85   creati, contra dominum proprium faciem et aciem proditorie uertebant. Cecidit
ergo fors super nostrates, captus est dominus Edmundus incontinenti, et plures alii
cum illo. Venerat quidem tunc ex parte dicti Owyni G[lyndor] quidam Wallicus,
nomine Rees a Gythe, qui et ipse inter alios mentis acerbioris erat. Hic sibi omnes
resistentes aut occidit aut mutulauit aut capiuauit. Vnde in illo conflictu occisi sunt
90   numero quasi 400 homines Anglicani, inter quos 4 milites, uidelicet dominus
Kinare de Laber.

Iacebant ergo corpora inter equorum pedes, sanguine proprio rubricata, longo
tempore post sepeliri prohibita. Hic putatur, secundum opinionen quorundam,
prodigium illud, dudum in natiuitate dicti Edmundi factum, in hoc conflictu com-
95   pletum esse. Cum enim in hanc lucem uisceribus a maternis editus esset, equi sui
in stabulo in sanguine stantes fere ad genua inuenti sunt. Sed utinam hic impletum
sit, ne nobis de cetero per ipsum, et propter ipsum, deterius contingat. Capto ergo
Edmundo, ibat de conflictu cum illo Owyn G[lyndor] in montes et speluncas de
Snowdonn in Wallia. Quam tamen humaniter simul et reuerenter pro suo modulo
100   tractauit, sperans et asserens, illum regem Anglie in proximo futurum. Ab isto
quidem die cepit pars predicti Owyni [Glyndor] nimis accrescere, nostra uero
infirmari.

. . .

Eodem anno [1402], circa festum Decollacionis beati Iohannis Baptiste,
descendit iterum rex cum manu forti in Walliam contra predictum Owynum
105   G[lyndor] et Wallenses adhuc sibi rebellantes. Qui per 20 dies ibidem extitit, non
solum nichil proficiens, sed et multa infortunia et dampna per aerearum malig-
nitatum tempestates pertulit. Vnde idem inglorious reuersus est.

. . .

Eodem anno [1402], circa festum Sancti Martini episcopi, dominus de Grey, de quo
supra fit mencio, solutis prius 5000 marcarum, liberatus est de manibus predicti
110   Owyni G[lyndor] relictis tamen duobus filiis suis obsidibus in eius custodia pro aliis
5000 marcis, adhuc remanentibus, et sibi fideliter soluendis. Eodem anno dominus

In this year [1402], on the feast of Saint Alban, Lord Edmund Mortimer, a knight, was captured in this manner by the aforesaid Owain Glyndŵr. When that man appeared in the vicinity of the town of Ludlow, news came to him, that the aforesaid Owain Glyndŵr had descended from the mountains of Wales with a few men, and he was on one of the mountains beside Pilleth, where a certain image of the blessed virgin Mary was greatly honored, not far from the said town of Ludlow. Therefore Edmund sent a message there quickly to the men and those who were attached to him in Maelienydd in Wales, asking that they not neglect to come to his aid in this dire necessity.

When these men had come to him, with these and many other strong men, he fearlessly ascended the said mountain. And so when the two forces came together with a great charge, the aforesaid Welshmen of Maelienydd, being not of the tribe of Judah, but rather descended from the line of the traitor Judas, turned against their own lord the figure and battle-line of treachery. Therefore fortune turned against our men, and Edmund was captured publicly, and many others with him. Then a certain Welshman came, of the faction of the said Owain Glyndŵr, by name Rhys ap Gruffudd, who was himself of a fiercer mind even than the others. This one either killed or mutilated or captured all those resisting him. Thus in that conflict around four hundred Englishmen were slain, among whom were four knights, including the Lord Kynard de la Bere.

Therefore the bodies were lying amongst the feet of the horses, red with their own blood, being forbidden to be buried for a long time afterwards. Here it is supposed, according to the opinion of certain people, that that prodigy, which had occurred at the birth of the said Edmund, was fulfilled in this conflict. For when he had been given forth into this light from his mother's insides, his own horses were found standing in the stables in blood almost up to their knees. But may it be so that it was fulfilled in this way, lest something worse happen to us in some other matter, through that very man and on account of that very man. So when Edmund was captured, he went from the conflict with Owain Glyndŵr into the mountains and caves of Snowdonia in Wales. Nevertheless, he treated him at the same time very humanely and respectfully as befitted his standing, anticipating and assuring, that he [Edmund] would be king of England in the near future. Indeed from this day the cause of the aforesaid Owain Glyndŵr very much increased and our cause indeed ailed.

. . .

In that same year [1402], around the feast of the Beheading of the Blessed John the Baptist, the king came down with a strong force once again into Wales against the aforesaid Owain Glyndŵr and the Welsh who were still rebelling against him. He remained in that same place for twenty days, not only achieving nothing, but bearing many misfortunes and injuries through the storms of airy malignities. So the same man returned from there ignominiously.

. . .

In that same year [1402], around the feast of Saint Martin the Bishop, Lord Grey, regarding whom mention was made above, when 5000 marks had been paid, was freed from the hands of the aforesaid Owain Glyndŵr, although two sons of his still remained in his custody upon a ransom of another 5000 marks, to be paid faithfully to him. In that same year the Lord Edmund Mortimer, about whom I have

Edmundus Mortumer, de quo etiam supra mencionem feci, circa festum Sancti
Andree Apostoli, filiam prefati Owyni Glyndor desponsauit maxima cum solemnitate, et, sicut uulgariter dicitur, conuersus est totaliter ad Wallicos.

29. *TERROR IN SHROPSHIRE*   Anglo-Norman
                                                              21 April 1403

    Tresexcellent, trespuissant, et tressoverain seignure, Nous nous recomandoms
a vostre hautesse si humblement come nous savoms et pluys poems . . . a vostre
soveraynte entendre qui voz loialx lieges de vostre countee de Salopesberia sount en
grant doute et despoir de jour en jour de malice et . . . voz rebelles Galoys et lour
5   adherdantz purposent a feare et de jour en autre fount ove tresgrant poair deinz
vostre dit countee come par . . . tuicioun de voz ditz lieges destruccioun de lour biens
et chateux — encontre queux voz ditz lieges ne sont en nulle manere de poair . . .
force affeare resistaunce sanz vostre tresgraciouse socour et eide et poair d'autres
gentz d'armes et archers estraungers tutditz vous . . . Tresexcellent seignure qui
10   plese a vostre soveraynte et tresgraciouse bounte mettre voz graciouses mayns a voz
lieges suisditz et aux enforcer . . . sonable poair des gentz d'armes et archers
estraungers tanquer al venu nostre tresdoute seignure le prince en ycestes parties.
Considerant . . . voz rebelles avanditz et lez Fraunces ore de novel a eux venuz ount
plein notice qui nullez estraunges souldiours attend . . . countee a present come ils
15   fount en autres voz countees ajoynantz a voz marches de Gales et outrement sont en
. . . sumez pleinement enfourmez de surchivacher et outrement degaster vostre dit
countee devant la venu de nostre dit seignure . . . le mischief. Trespuissant seignure
voz ditz lieges vous suppliont de eux ordeigner ent remedie par avise de vostre
tressage . . . pleise a vostre hautesse de rescrier vostre tresgraciouse volunte a voz ditz
20   lieges par voz tresgraciouses lettres et le portour d'ycestes . . . cioun et supportacioun
de vostre people avantdid. Entendant trespuissant seignure qui la tierce partie de
vostre dit countee a present . . . destruyez et degastez par voz rebelles avaunditz et
voz lieges devant illoequis enhabites fuez et retreitz hors de vostre dit . . . a gaigner
lour viandre et sustinaunce ailliours deinz vostre roialme. Tresexcellent et tres-
25   puissant et tressoverain seignure le hautisme . . . te vous yet en sa tresdigne garde.
Escript a vostre ville de Salopesberia le xxj. jour d'Apprille.
    Voz loialx lieges si vous plese, les . . . et gentils et com . . . dit . . . .

30. PRINCE HENRY, *RAZING OF OWAIN'S HOMES*   Anglo-Norman
                                                              15 May 1403

    Treschiers et tresentierment bien amez,
    Nous vous salvons tressouvent de notre entier cuer, en vous merciant treschiere-
ment de la bone consideracioun quele vous avez a les bosoignes que nous touchent
en notre absence; et vous prions treseffectuousement de votre bone et amyable con-
5   tinuance come notre fiance est en vous. Et endroit des nouvelx pardecea, si vous
vuillez savoir, entre autres, nous estions nadegaires enfourmez que Oweyn de Glyndourdy fist assembler son povair dautres rebelx de ses adherentz a grand nombre,

also made mention above, around the feast of Saint Andrew the Apostle, married the daughter of the aforesaid Owain Glyndŵr with very great solemnity, and so it is commonly said, turned entirely to the side of the Welshmen.

29. *TERROR IN SHROPSHIRE* Notes: pp. 321–22

Most excellent, most powerful, and most sovereign lord, we commend ourselves to your highness as humbly as we know and more . . . to your sovereignty that you may know how your loyal lieges of your county of Shropshire are in great doubt and despair every day because of the malice and [mischief that] your Welsh rebels and their adherents are intending to commit and which sooner or later will commit with their very great power in your said county, [threatening] your said lieges with the destruction of their goods and houses — against which your said lieges have no manner of power [or] strength to resist in this case without your most gracious succor and the help and power of other men at arms and non-local archers you quickly [could send]. Most excellent lord may it please your sovereignty and most gracious bountifulness to put your gracious hands to your aforesaid lieges and thereby to send [them some] power of the men at arms and non-local archers who came into these parts with our most redoubted lord the prince. Considering . . . your said rebels and the French now that the news of them has arrived, that they plainly see that no non-local soldiers await . . . knowing that this county is less well guarded than your other counties adjoining your marches of Wales, were intent on a chevauchée into your said county before the coming of our lord the prince . . . the mischief. Most powerful lord, your said lieges beg that you ordain a remedy for these things through the wisdom of your great sagaciousness . . . please to your highness cry out and your most gracious will to your said lieges by your gracious letters and the bearer of these . . . and support of your aforesaid people. It follows, most mighty lord, that a third part of your said county at present [has been] destroyed and devastated by your said rebels, and your lieges formerly living there have left to gain their meat and sustenance elsewhere in your realm. Most excellent and most powerful and most sovereign lord the king, . . . [we beg] of you under your most worthy watch. Written at your city of Shrewsbury on the 21st day of April.

Your loyal lieges, if it pleases you . . . men . . . said . . . .

30. PRINCE HENRY, *RAZING OF OWAIN'S HOMES* Notes: pp. 322–24

Dearest and entirely well beloved,

We greet you fully from our whole heart, thanking you very dearly for the good attention which you have for the needs which affect us in our absence; and we entreat you most earnestly for your good and courteous continuance in this, as our trust is in you. And concerning the news from here, if you wish to know, among other things, we have been informed lately that Owain of Glyndyfrdwy assembled his forces of other rebels among his adherents to a great number, with the aim of

10

15

20

25

30
purposant pur chivachier et aussi combatre si gens Englois lui voudroient resister
de son purpos, et ainsi il se avantoit a ses gens; par quoy nous prismes noz gens et
alasmes a une place du dit Oweyn bien edifie que feu son principale mansion
appelle Sagherne, la ou nous supposasmes de lui avoir trove sil vousist avoir com-
batu en manere come il disoit; et a notre venue illoeques nous ne trovasmes nul
homme, einz nous fismes ardre toute la place et pluseurs autres maisons la entour
de ses tenantz, et puis nous enalasmes droit a son autre place de Glyndourdy, pur
lui querer illoeques, et la nous fismes ardre un beau logge en son parc et toute la
paiis la entour, et nous nous loggeasmes la delies toute ce noet, et certainz de noz
gens isserent illoeques en la paiis et pristerent un grand gentil de la paiis qi feu un
des chiefteyns du dit Oweyn: li quel offrist cynk centz livres pur son ransom pur
avoir eu sa vie et davoir paie la dite some dedeinz deux semaignes. Nepurquant ce
ne feu accepte mes il avoit la mort, et diverses autres de ses compaignouns que
feurent prisez en le dit journe avoient le mesme. Et puis ce nous enalasmes en le
commote d'Edirnyoun en . . . de Merionyethe et illoeques nous fismes ardre une
beau paiis et bien enhabite. Et dilloeques nous enalasmes en Powys, et . . . setee de
vitail pur chivaux en Gales, nous fismes noz gens carier aveignes ovec eulx, et nous
hostasmes par . . . urs. Et pour vous enfourmer plus au plein de ceste journee et
[de] touz autres nouvelx pardecea de present, nous envoions pardevers vous notre
treschier escuier Johan de Watertoun, a qi vuillez adjouster ferme foy et credence
en ce qil vous reportera de notre part touchant les nouvelx desuisdites. Et notre
seigneur vous ait toudys en sa sainte garde.
        Donne soubz notre signet a Shrouesbury le xv. jour de May.

31. OWAIN GLYNDŴR, *LETTER TO HENRY DWN*   Latin
                                                               before July 1403

A noster trescher et tressentierement bon aime Henry Don.
        Salutem et amorem. Vobis narramus quod speramus auxilio Dei et vestro posse
liberare progeniem Wallicanam de captivitate inimicorum nostrorum Anglicorum,
qui oppresserunt nos et antecessores nostros a multo tempore jam elapso. Et sciatis
5   ex sensu vestro proprio quod tempus illorum desinit, et triumphus vertit versus nos,
secundum ordinacionem Dei a principio quod non refert alicui dubitare quin finis
eveniet bona, nisi amittatur per desidiam et discordiam; et quod omnes progenies
Wallicane est in dubio et periculo secundum subjectionem quam audivimus esse
penes inimicos vestros predictos versus ipsos, secundum hoc vobis mandamus, et
10   requirimus, et supplicamus quatenus satis parati venire in maxima fortitudine quam
possitis ad nos, ad locum ubi audieritis quod sumus, comburentes opprimendo inimicos nostros itinerando; et hoc erit infra breve per auxilium divinum. Et hoc non
omittatis sicut velitis habere libertatem vestram et honorem de cetero; et non admiramini quod non habuistis premonicionem primae surrectionis, nam ex nimio ti-
15   more et periculo oportuit nos surgere non premonentes. Valete et Deus vos defen-
dat a malo.
        Per Yweyn ap Gruffuth, Dominum de Glyn Dwfrdwy.

raiding and also of fighting if English men wished to resist him in his purpose, and thus he boasted to his people; because of which we took our men and went to a place of the said Owain, well built, which was his principal house named Sycharth, where we supposed to find him if he wished to fight in the manner he said; and at our coming there we found no man, and so we set fire to the whole place, and several other houses of his tenants around. And then we went straight away to his other place of Glyndyfrdwy, to seek him there, and there we fired a fine lodge in its park, and all the country around it. And we camped there all that night, and some of our men went out into the country and took an important gentleman of that land who was one of the chiefs of the said Owain. He offered five hundred pounds as ransom if his life were spared, and promised to pay the said sum within two weeks. Nevertheless this was not accepted, but he was put to death; and various others of his companions who were taken on that raid suffered the same fate. And after that we went into the commote of Edeirnion in […] of Merioneth and there we set fire to a fine and well populated country. And from there we went into Powys, and [because of shortage] of food for horses in Wales, we made our men carry oats with them, and we stayed for […] days. And to inform you more fully about this expedition, and of all other news from here at present, we are sending this with our beloved esquire John Waterton, to whom please give full faith and credence in what he will report to you on our behalf concerning the above news. And may our Lord have you always in his holy keeping.

Given under our signet at Shrewsbury on the 15th day of May.

31. Owain Glyndŵr, *Letter to Henry Dwn*   Notes: pp. 324–25

To our very dear and entirely well beloved Henry Dwn.

Greeting and love. We inform you that we hope to be able, by God's help and yours, to deliver the Welsh race from the captivity of our English enemies, who, for a long time now elapsed, have oppressed us and our ancestors. And you may know from your own perception that, now, their time draws to a close and [as] according to the ordinance of God from the beginning, success turns towards us, no one need doubt a good issue will result, unless it be lost through sloth or strife. And because all the Welsh race is in doubt and dread as to the subjection, which we have heard is within the intention of your enemies aforesaid against them, we command, require and entreat, that you will be sufficiently prepared to come to us with the greatest force possible, to the place, where you hear that we are, burning our enemies, by destroying them during the march, and this, by divine aid, shall take place shortly. And do not forget this, as you would wish to have your freedom and honor in the future. And be not surprised that you have not had warning of the first rising, because from great apprehension and danger, it behoved us to rise without fore-warnings. Farewell and God defend you from evil.

By Owain ap Gruffudd, Lord of Glyn Dyfrdwy.

32. JOHN SCUDAMORE, *PLEA FOR AID*   Middle English
                                                              5 July 1403

Worschipful sir, y recomand me to you; and for as meche as y may nouht spare
no man from this place awey fro me, to certefie neyther the kyng ne my lord the
prynce of the myschefs of this countrees abouute, ne no man may pas by no wey
hennes, y pray you and require yow that ye certefie hem how al Kermerdyn schire,
5   Kedewely, Carnwaltham, and Yskenyn ben sworyn to Oweyn yesterday, and he lay
to nyht was yn the castel of Drosselan, with Rees ap Gruffuth; and there y was and
spake with hym upon truys, and prayed of a saufconduyt under his seal to send
home my wif and hir moder and thair mayne, but he wolde none graunte me; and
on this day he is aboute the towne of Kermerdyn, and ther thenkith to abide til he
10   may have the towne and the castel; and his purpos ys from thennes into Penbroke-
schire, for he halt hym siker of al the castell and townes in Kedewelly, Gowerslonde,
and Glamorgan, for the same cuntrees have undertake the seges of hem til thei ben
wonnen. Wherfore wryteth to Sir Hugh Waterton, and to al thilke that ye suppose
wol take this mater to hert, that thei exite the kyng hederwardes in al hast to
15   vengen hym on summe of his false traytours the wheche he hath overmeche cher-
eyschid, and do rescowe the townes and casteles in these countres for y drede
fulsore there be to fewe trewe men in hem. Y can no more as nowe; but pray God
help yow and us that thenken to be trewe.
       Wreten at the castel of Carreckennen the v. day of Juil.

33. JANKYN HAVARD, *PLEA FOR AID*   Middle English
                                                              7 July 1403

Oure frende I do yow to wetyn that Oweyn Glyndour, Henri Don, Res Duy, Res
ap Gr. ap Ll., Res Gethin, han y-won the town of Kermerdyn, and Wygmor constable of the castell hadd y-yeld op the castell of Kermerdin to Oweyn; and had
ybrend the town, and y-slay of men of town mor than l. men; and thei budd yn
5   purpos to Kedweli; and a Seche ys y-ordeynyd at the castell that I kepe, and that ys
gret peril for me, and al that buth wydd ine; for thai han y-mad har avow that thei
woll al gat haue ows dede theryn. Wherfor I prei yow that ye nul not bugil ous, that
ye send to ous warning wyth yn schort time whether schull we have eny help or no;
and bot ther be help coming that we have an answer, that we may come bi niht and
10   stell away to Brechnoc; cause that we faylyth vitels and men, and namlich men. Also
Jenkyn ap Ll. hath y-yeld op the Castell of Emlyn wyth fru wyll; and also William
Gwyn, Thomas ap David ap Gruff and moni gentils bun yn person wyth Oweyn.
Warning erof I prei that ye send me bi the berer of thus lettre. Farydd well yn the
nam of the Trinite.
15   Y wryt at Dynevour, yn hast and yn dred, yn the fest of Seint Thomas the Martyr.

32. John Scudamore, *Plea for Aid* Notes: pp. 325–26

Worshipful sir, I submit myself to you. Because I may not spare a single man from this place to be away from me to certify to either the king or my lord the prince the reality of the mischiefs around us in this country, and also because no man may pass through it, I beg and require of you that you yourself certify to them how all of Carmarthenshire — Kidwelly, Carnwyllion, and Iscennen — were sworn to Owain yesterday, and he lay two nights within the castle of Dryslwyn, with Rees ap Gruffydd. I was there and spoke with him under a truce, and I asked for a safe-conduct under his seal to send home my wife and her mother and their company, but he would not grant me one. On this day he is around the town of Carmarthen, and there he plans to abide until he may have the town and the castle; and his plan is to go from there into Pembrokeshire, for he considers himself secure in all the castles and towns in Kidwelly, Gowerland, and Glamorgan, for the same countries have undertaken the sieges of them until they have been won. Therefore write to Sir Hugh Waterton, and to all those that you suppose will take this matter to heart, that they excite the king to come here in all haste to avenge himself on some of his false traitors whom he has overmuch cherished, and rescue the towns and castles in these countries, for I dread greatly that there are too few loyal men in them. I can say no more right now; but I pray to God that you will help us who hope to be true.

Written at the castle of Carreg Cennen on the fifth day of July.

33. Jankyn Havard, *Plea for Aid* Notes: pp. 326–27

Our friend, I want you to know that Owain Glyndŵr, Henry Dwn, Rhys Ddu, Rhys ap Gruffudd ap Llywelyn, and Rhys Gethin have taken the town of Carmarthen, and the constable of Wigmore Castle has yielded up the Castle of Carmarthen to Owain, and they have burned the town and slain among the men of the town more than fifty men; and they are intent on Kidwelly. A siege has begun at the castle that I keep, and that is a great peril for me and all that are within, for they have made their vow that they will have us all dead therein. Therefore I pray that you will not be false to us, that you will send to us word within a short time whether we shall have any help or not. If there is no help coming, I pray that you tell us, so that we may come by night and steal away to Brecknock because we are running out of food and men — especially men. Also, Siancyn ap Llywelyn has surrendered Newcastle Emlyn with free will; and also William Gwyn, Tomas ap Dafydd ap Gruffudd, and many landowners have joined in person with Owain. I pray that you send a response to me by the bearer of this letter. Fare you well in the name of the Trinity.

I write at Dinefwr, in haste and dread, on the feast of Saint Thomas the Martyr.

34. RICHARD KINGSTON, *PLEA FOR AID*   **Anglo-Norman and Middle English**
8 July 1403

Notre tresredoute et soverein Seigneur le Roy, je me recomande humblement
a votre hautesse come votre petite creature et continuel oratour. Et notre tresredoute et soverein Seigneur le Roy, vous plese a savoir que de jour en autre y vienent
lettres de Gales contenantz lettre illeoques par queles vous p'rez entendre que toute
5   la pais est perdu sy vous ne venez le plus hastifment. Sur quoy vous plese vous
taillor devers noz parties ave toute le poer que vous poez enchivachant si bien de
noet come de jour pur salvacioun des parties. Et vous plese a savoir que il est graunt
vergoigne, si bien come per de que vous perderez ou suffrez estre perduz le pais,
en votre comencement, que voz nobles auncestres ount gaignez, et per sy longe
10   temps peisiblement tenuz; car les gentz parlont tresmalvaisement. Et j'envoie a
votre noblesse la copie d'une lettre qu'est venuz de John Skydmore ycest matin.
Notre tresredoute et soverein Seigneur le Roy, je pry a luy toutpuissant qil vous
ottroie tresbonne vie et sainte, oue victoire de voz enemys.
Escr. en haste — grant haste — a Herford le viij. Jour de Juyll.

15   And for Godes love, my lyge lord, thinkith on your self and youre astat, or be
my trowthe all is lost elles; but and ye come youre self with haste alle othere wolle
folwin aftir. And ot on Fryday last Kermerdyn town is taken and brent, and the
castell yolden be Ro. Wygmor, and the castell Emelyn is y-yoldin; and slayn of the
toune of Kermerdyn mo thanne l. persones. Writen in ryght gret haste on Sunday;
20   and y crye yow mercy and putte me in youre hye grace that y write so schortly; for,
be my trowthe that y owe to yow, it is needful.

35. JANKYN HAVARD, *PLEA FOR AID*   **Middle English**
11 July 1403

Dure frynd, y do you to wytyng that Oweyn was in porpos to Kedewelly, and the
baron of Carewe was that day comyng wyth a gret retenu toward Seint Clere, and
so Oweyn changed is purpos and rode to yens the baron; and that nyht a logged
hym at Seint Clere and destruid al the contre about. And a Tysday they weryn at
5   tretys al day; and that nyht he logged hym at the town of Lacharn, sex miles out of
the town of Kermerdyn; thys purpos ys gef so that the baron and he acordyth in
tretys, than atornyth agein to Kermerdin for hys part of the godes, and Res Duy is
part; and mony of thes gret maistres stont yet in the castell of Kermerdyn, for they
have not y-made her ordinance whether the castell and the town schall be brend or
10   no, and therfor, yef ther is eny help comyng, hast hem with al hast toward ous for
they mowe have godes and fytelles plente, for everych hous is full aboute ous of her
pultre, and yet syn and hony ynow in the contre, and whet and ben, and al maner
vitelles. And we of the castell of Dunevor had tretys of ham Monday, Tywsday, and
Wendysday, and now a woll ordeyn for ous to have that castell for ther a castyth to
15   ben y-serkled thince, for that was the chef plas in old tyme. And Oweyn ys moster
a Monday was, as they seyyn hemselvyn, viij. mill. and xij. xx. spers, such as they
wer. Other tidyng y not now, bot God of Hevene sene yow and ous from al enemyes.
Y-wrytyn at Dynevour this Wednesday in hast.

34. RICHARD KINGSTON, *PLEA FOR AID*   Notes: p. 327

Our most redoubted and sovereign lord the king, I recommend myself humbly to your highness as your lowly creature and continual orator. And our most redoubted and sovereign lord, please you to know that from day to day letters are arriving from Wales, containing intelligence by which you may learn that the whole country is lost, if you do not go there as quick as possible. For which reason may it please you to prepare to set out with all the power you can muster, and march day and night for the salvation of those parts. And may it please you to reflect that it will be a great disgrace as well as loss, to lose or suffer to be lost, in the beginning of your reign, a country which your noble ancestors have won, and for so long a time peaceably possessed. For people talk very unfavorably. And I send to your highness the copy of a letter which came from John Scudamore this morning. Our most redoubted and sovereign lord the king, I pray to the Almighty that He may grant you a happy and holy life, with victory over your enemies.

Written in haste — great haste — at Hereford, the eighth day of July.

And for the love of God, my liege lord, think on yourself and your estate, for by my word all is lost; unless you come yourself with haste, all losses will follow after. On last Friday the town of Carmarthen was taken and burned, and the castle was handed over by Robert Wigmore, and the castle of Emlyn has been yielded; and in the town of Carmarthen more than fifty people have been slain. Written in truly great haste on Sunday; and I beg mercy of you and put myself in your high grace that I write so hastily; for, by my word that I owe to you, it is necessary.

35. JANKYN HAVARD, *PLEA FOR AID*   Notes: pp. 327–28

Dear friend, I want you to know that Owain was intent on Kidwelly, but the baron of Carew was that day coming with a great retinue toward Saint Clears, and so Owain changed his purpose and rode against the baron and that night lodged himself at Saint Clears and destroyed all of the country there. And on Tuesday they were in parley all day; and that night he lodged himself at the town of Laugharne, six miles out of the town of Carmarthen. His intention is that if he and the baron are accorded in treaty then he will return again to Carmarthen for his part of the goods, and for Rhys Ddu's parts. And many of the great masters remain yet in the castle of Carmarthen, for they have not yet made their order whether the castle and the town shall be burned or not. Therefore, if there is any help coming, speed them with all haste toward us, for they might have goods and victuals in plenty, for every house about us is full of poultry, with wine and honey enough in the country, and wheat and beans, and all manner of victuals. And we of the castle of Dinefwr had parley with them on Monday, Tuesday, and Wednesday, and now they will order us to surrender the castle that has been surrounded, for that was the chief place in old times. And Owain's muster on Monday was, as they say themselves, 8,240 spears, such as they were. Other news I do not know, but God of Heaven send you and us away from all enemies.

Written at Dinefwr this Wednesday in haste.

36. BURGESSES OF CAERLEON, *OWAIN AND THE PROPHET*   **Middle English**
                                                                  after 12 July 1403

Gretyng to yow our gode frendes and worschipful burgeis of Monemouthe. We
do yow to understonde of tydynges the weche we have y-herd of Owein Glyndour,
that is to wete of lettres under the seel the wheche were y-sende to us by the cap-
teyne of the towne of Kadewelly. And in the lettres wer y-wrete wordes that ther was
a day of batell y-take bytwyxt the worthy baroun of Carewe and Owein Glyndour;
and we do yow to understonde that thys day of bataill schuld have be do the xij. day
of Jule. And the nyht before that thys bataill schulde be do, Oweyne wes y-purpos
to have yvoidede ym to the hull ageinward. And for he wold y-wete whar his wey wer
clere ynowe to passe, gyf he hade nede, to the hull, he sende vij. c. of his meine to
serche the weyes, and thes vij. c. menne went to serche thys weyes, and ther thys vij.
c. menne were y-mette with the barones menne of Carew, and i-slay up everychone
that ther was noht on that sc . . . alyve; and thes wordes buth y-do us to understonde
that hit is sothe withowte lesyng. And fforthermor we do yow to undirstonde that
Oweine the . . . es in the ton of Kairmarthen he sende after Hopkyn ap Thomas of
Gower to come and speke with hym uppon trewes. And when Hopkyn come to
Owein, he priede hym, in as meche as he huld hym maister of Brut, that he schuld
do hym to understonde how and what maner hit schold befalle of hym; and he told
hym witterliche that he schold be take withinne a bref tyme, and the takyng schold
be twene Kayrmerthen and Gower, and the takyng schold be under a blak baner —
knowelichyd that thys blake baner scholde dessese hym, and noht that he schold be
take undir hym. No more con we say to yow at thys tyme, bote buth glad and mery,
and drede yow noht for we hope the to God that ye have no nede. And we do yow
to understonde that al thys tydynges buth sothe withoute doute.

37. RICHARD KINGSTON, *PLEA FOR AID*   **Anglo-Norman and Middle English**
                                              3 September 1403

Mon tressouverain, trespuissant, et mon tresredoute Seignour,
Jeo moi recomande [a] vostre treshaute seigneurie come vostre treshumble
oratour, et . . . . Mon tressouveraigne et tresredoute seignour, please a vostre
tresgraciouse seignourie entendre que a jourduy, apres noo[ne] . . . q'ils furent
venuz deinz nostre countie pluis de cccc. des les rebelz de Owyne Glyn Talgard, et
pluseours autres rebelz des voz Marches de Galys, et ount prisez et robbez deinz
vostre countie de Hereford pluseours gentz, et bestaille a graunte nombre, nient
contre esteant la nostre trewe, si come mon [ami] et compaignon, et vostre esquier,
Miles Walter, portur du cestez, vous dira plus pleinement par bouche que jeo ne
puisse escripte a vous a present. A qi vous please, de vostre graciouse seignourie,
donner ferme foi et credence de ceo, q'il vous enformera de part moi pur salvatioun
de vostre dit counte et dez toutz les paiis environ.
A quelle esquier vous please faire bone chire a luy, en mercier de son grant
labour et bone et loial service, q'il vous ad fait et montre deinz vostre counte, et a
Brechon — qar, mon tresredoute seignour, par la foi que jeo doy a Dieux, et a vous,
jeo luy tigne un dez lez pluis vaillantz hommez dez armez que vous avez deinz
vostre countee ou Marche, si come vous trouverez certeinment a vostre tresgra-

36. BURGESSES OF CAERLEON, *OWAIN AND THE PROPHET*   Notes: pp. 328–30

Greetings to you our good friends and honorable burgesses of Monmouth. We want you to know of the news which we have heard regarding Owain Glyndŵr, which comes from sealed letters that were sent to us by the captain of the town of Kidwelly. In these letters was written the news that there was supposed to be a day of battle between the worthy baron of Carew and Owain Glyndŵr, and this engagement was supposed to have happened on 12 July. The night before this battle was to take place, Owain was determined to flee back to the hill; and because he would know whether his way was clear enough to retreat to the hill if had the need, he sent 700 of his company to search the paths there, and these 700 men went to do so, and there these 700 men met the men of the baron of Carew, who killed every one that there was not on that . . . and these letters cause us to understand that it is truth without falsity. And furthermore we want you to know that Owain the . . . in the town of Carmarthen he sent after Hopcyn ap Tomas of Gower to come and speak with him under a truce. And when Hopcyn came to Owain, he asked him, because he considered him a master of Brut, if he would help him to understand what the future would hold for him; Hopcyn cleverly told him that he should be taken prisoner within a brief time, and the taking would happen between Carmarthen and Gower, and it would happen under a black banner — knowing that this black banner would distress him, and so nothing would be undertaken by him. No more can we say to you at this time, but be glad and merry, and dread you nought: for we hope to God that you have no need. And we urge you to understand that all this news is true without doubt.

37. RICHARD KINGSTON, *PLEA FOR AID*   Notes: pp. 330–31

My most sovereign, most mighty, and my most dread lord,
I commend me to your most high lordship as your most humble petitioner and . . . . My most sovereign and most dread lord, may it please your most gracious lordship to understand that to day, after noon [I was informed that] there had come into our county more than four hundred of the rebels of Owain Glyndŵr [from] Talgarth, and many other rebels from your Marches of Wales, and in your county of Hereford they have captured and robbed many men, and a large number of cattle, in spite of our truce, as my friend and companion, and your esquire, Miles Walter, the bearer of these letters, will tell you verbally more fully than I can write to you at present. Please grant him, of your gracious lordship, firm faith and credence in what he will relate to you on my behalf, for the protection of your said county and of all the country around.
May it please you to welcome this esquire, thanking him for his great efforts and the good and faithful service he has done and shown you in your county and at Brecon; for, my most dread lord, by the faith which I give to God and to you, I count him one of the most courageous men at arms that you have within your county or March, as you will most certainly find at your most gracious coming to us.

graciouse venue a nous — et que vous please de a luy prometter bone et graciouse
seignourie et luy comforter, qar il ad perduz tout ce q'il ad, et ceo a graunte summe.

20   Outre ceo, mon tressoveraigne et tresredoute seignour, vous please, de vostre
graciouse seignourie, et pur le salvatioun de vostre dicte countee et tout la March,
moi envoire en yceste noet, ou demeyn bien matyn a pluis tarde, mon treshonoure
Mestre Beauford, ou ascune autre vaillaunt personne, que veot et peot laborer, ove
c. launcez, et dc. archiers, tanque a vostre tresgraciouse venue en salvatioun dez
25   nous trestoutz; qar autrement, mon tresredoute seignour, en bone foy jeo tigne tout
nostre paiis destruez, qar les coers des toutz vous foialx lieges de nostre pays ove les
comyns outrement sount perduz, et pur ceo que ils oiont que vous ne vndrez illeoqes en vostre propre persone (que Dieux deffende). Qar, mon tresredoute seigneur,
vous trouverez pour certein que si vous ne venez en vostre propre persone pour
30   attendre [apres] voz rebelx en Galys, vous ne trouverez un gentil que veot attendre
deinz vostre dit countee.

War fore, for Goddesake, thinketh on your beste frende, God, and thanke Hym
as He hath deserved to yowe; and leveth nought that ye ne come for no man that
may counsaille yowe the contrarie; for, by the trouthe that I schal be to yowe yet,
35   this day the Walshment supposen and trusten that ye shculle nought come there,
and there fore, for Goddes love, make them fals men. And that hit plese yowe of
your hegh lordeship for to have me excused of my comynge to yowe, for, yn god
fey, I have nought ylafte with me over two men, that they beon sende oute with
sherref and other gentils of oure schire, for to with stande the malice of the rebelles
40   this day.

Tresexcellent, trespuissant, et tresredoute seignour, autrement say a present
nieez.

Jeo pris a la Benoit Trinite que vous ottroie bone vie ove tresentier sauntee a
treslonge durre, et sende yowe sone to ows in help and prosperitee; for, in god
45   fey, I hope to Al Mighty God that, yef ye come youre owne persone, ye schulle have
the victorie of alle youre enemyes.

And for the salvation of youre schire and Marches al aboute, treste ye nought
to no leutenaunt.

Escript a Hereford, en tresgraunte haste, a trois de la clocke apres noone, le
50   tierce jour de Septembre.

38. WILLIAM VENABLES, *OWAIN THREATENS HARLECH*   Anglo-Norman
                                                            15 January 1404

Tresexcellent et tresredoute seigneur liege, nous nous recomandons a votre
excellencie oue toutz maneres services et subjections. Et pleise a votre roial magestee
entendre que ycy Lundy darrein passee a haut nuyt Roger de Bolton receivor de
Denbiegh nous envoia parole par un vallet que le conestable de Hardelagh en
5   Northgales et deux valletz ovesque lui sont pris par les Gales et amesuez a Oweyn de
Glyndour, et que le chastell est en grand peril que Dieu pour sa mercie la sauve, qar
a ce qil nous ad certifie y ne sont paas deinz mesme le chastell forsque cynk hommes
Engleys et bien entour xvj. hommes Gales. Paront pleise a votre treshaute excellencie, par avis de votre tressage conseil, eut ordeigner remedie tiel que pleiser

And may it please you to promise him good and gracious lordship and to console him, for he has lost all that he had, to a large sum.

Besides, my most sovereign and most dread lord, may it please you of your gracious lordship and for the protection of your said county and all the March, to send me tonight or early tomorrow morning at the latest, my most honored Master Beaufort, or some other courageous man, who is willing and able to labor with one hundred lances and six hundred archers, until your most gracious arrival for the protection of us all. For otherwise, my most dread lord, I in good faith consider all our country destroyed, for the hearts of all your loyal lieges of our country, along with the commons, are utterly lost, as they hear that you are not coming here yourself, which God forbid. For, my most dread lord, you will certainly find that if you do not come yourself to await your rebels in Wales, you will not find a single gentleman remaining in your said county.

Therefore, for God's sake, think on your best friend, God, and thank Him, as He has deserved of you; and stop at nothing to come, whoever may advise you to the contrary; for, by the truth that I shall be to you yet, the Welshmen today suppose and trust that you will not come here, and therefore, for God's love, make them false men. And may it please you of your high lordship to have me excused from coming to you, for in good faith I have nothing left here with me other than two men, who have been sent out with the sheriff and other gentlemen of our shire, to withstand the wickedness of the rebels today.

Most excellent, most mighty and most dread lord, I know nothing more at present.

I pray the Blessed Trinity to give you good life and full good health, very long to last, and send you soon to us in help and prosperity; for, in good faith, I hope to Almighty God, that, if you come yourself, you shall have victory over all your enemies.

And for the protection of your shire and Marches do not trust to any lieutenant.

Written at Hereford in very great haste at three of the clock in the afternoon on the third day of September.

38. William Venables, *Owain Threatens Harlech*   Notes: pp. 331–32

Most excellent and most redoubt sovereign lord, we recommend ourselves to your excellency in all manner of services and subjections. And may it please your royal majesty to know that on this last Monday, in the middle of the night, Roger de Bolton, the receiver of Denbigh, sent word to us by a servant that the constable of Harlech in North Wales, and two servants with him, have been taken by the Welsh and carried to Owain Glyndŵr, and that the castle is in great peril, which God in his mercy prevent, for according to what he affirms, there are in that same castle no more than five Englishmen and perhaps sixteen Welshmen. Therefore may it please your most high excellency, by the advice of your wise council, to ordain a remedy as

10   soit a votre trespuissant seignorie. Et la hautisme Trinitee, notre tressovereigne et
      tresredoute seigneur liege, vous ottrois prosperitee et la victorie de touz voz enemys
      oue bone vie a long durer.
            Escrit a Cestr. le xv. jour de Janver.

39. WILLIAM VENABLES, *OWAIN ATTACKS CAERNARFON*   Anglo-Norman
                                                                    16 January 1404

      Trespuissant et tresredoute seigneur liege, nous nous recommandons a votre
      tressouvereigne seigneur oue toutz maneres honeres et reverences. Et pleise a votre
      roial magestee entendre que Robert Parys le puisne conestable du chastell de Caer-
      varvan nous ad certifee per une femme, a cause qil navoit homme ascun qi osa
5   venir, ne homme ne femme null ose ascun lettre porter pour les rebelles Gales qe
      Oweyn de Glyndour ouesque les Fraunceys et tout son autre poair se taillent d'as-
      sailler les ville et chastell de Caernarvan, et a commencer le jour de la fesance
      dicestes ovec esgynes, sowes, et laddres de tresgrand longure, et ne sont mie deinz
      mesmes les ville et chastell en tout outre xxiij. hommes defensibles, q'est trop petit
10   force, qar y sont xj. de les meillors hommes qestoient la dedeinz al darrein assege
      illeoques fait ore mortz, ascuns des plaies qils avoient a temps d'assaut a eux fait,
      et ascuns de pestilence, sique les ditz chastell et ville sont en grand peril sicome le
      portor dicestes vous savera enformer par bouche, a qi pleise a votre hautesse doner
      ferme foi et credence, qar il sciet vous enformer de tout la veritee. Et luy
15   toutpuissant Dieux vous ottrois, notre tresredoute seigneur liege, prosperitee et bon
      exploit entres touz voz affairs. Et pleise a votre hautesse regarder un lettre enclos
      dedeinz cestes quele Reignald de Baildon un des gardeins de la ville de Conewey
      nous envoia huy ce jour, touchant l'estat de votre seignorie de Northgales.
            Escrit a Cestre la xvj. jour de Januer.

40. *ROLLS OF PARLIAMENT, 1404*   Anglo-Norman
                                                                    14, 25 January 1404

      3. Primerement, a considerer coment ses rebelx de Gales luy ont fait et facent
      de jour en autre grand rebellioun encontre lour ligeance; et auxi coment le duc
      d'Orliens, et le count Seintpoule lour aient purposez de faire au roy nostre seignur
      et a soun roialme d'Engleterre les grevances et damages q'ils purront a tout lour
5   poair: et coment le dit cont Seintpoule, en accomplicement de soun malvoise enten-
      cioun, s'arriva ore tard ove grant poair en l'Isle de Wyght' — mais qe Dieu de sa
      grace ensi disposa, q'il n'osa illoeqes attendre ne demurer; et auxi considerez les
      perils iminentz, si bien de la ville de Caleys et les marches illoeqes, come de la paiis
      de Guyene, par les enemys Franceois et leur adherentz; et outre ceo, considerez les
10   guerres d'Irland et d'Escoce, et des toutz autres parties environ; et considerez auxi
      la levee de guerre nadgairs fait deins le roialme par monsire Henry Percy et mon-
      sire Thomas Percy, et plusours autres ovesqe eux, encontre nostre seignur le roy et
      lour ligeance, a le bataille de Shrouesbury: qe les ditz seignurs et comunes de lour
      comune assent et advis ent ferroient et dirroient ceo qe meulx lour sembleroit pur

shall be most pleasing to your most puissant lordship. And the high Trinity, our most sovereign and most redoubted liege Lord, grant you prosperity and victory over all your enemies and the continuation of a long, happy life.

Written at Chester on the 16th day of January.

39. WILLIAM VENABLES, *OWAIN ATTACKS CAERNARFON*   Notes: pp. 332–33

Most puissant and most redoubted liege lord, we recommend ourselves to your most sovereign lordship in all manner of honor and reverence. And may it please your royal majesty to know that Robert Paris the deputy constable of Caernarfon Castle has certified to us through a woman, because there was no man who dared to come, for neither man nor woman dare carry letters on account of the Welsh rebels that Owain Glyndŵr, with the French and all his other power, is preparing to assault the town and castle of Caernarfon, and to begin this engagement with engines, sows, and ladders of great length. And in the town and castle there are no more than 28 fighting men, which is too small a force, for 11 of the more able men who were there at the last siege of the place are dead: some from the wounds they received at the time of the assault, and others of the plague, so that the said castle and town are in great peril, as the bearer of this letter will tell you, to whom your highness will be pleased to give full faith and credence, as he can inform you of it all in truth. And may the most puissant God grant you, most redoubted lord, prosperity and success in all your affairs. And may it please you highness to look at a letter, here enclosed, which Reginald de Baildon, one of the keepers of the town of Conwy, has sent us this day, concerning the state of your lordship of North Wales.

Written at Chester on the 16th day of January.

40. *ROLLS OF PARLIAMENT, 1404*   Notes: p. 333

3. Firstly, to consider how the Welsh rebels have staged, and are constantly still staging, another great rebellion, contrary to their allegiance. And also how the duke of Orleans and the count of St. Pol have decided to do to the king our lord and to his realm of England all the harm and damage that lies within their power: and how the said count of St. Pol, in pursuit of his evil aim, landed recently in the Isle of Wight with a great force; but God in his grace so disposed it that he did not dare to remain or linger there; and also considering the imminent dangers, both to the town of Calais and its marches, and to the land of Guyenne, from the French enemy and their adherents; and besides this, considering the wars in Ireland and Scotland, and in all other regions nearby; and also considering the armed uprising recently made in the realm by Sir Henry Percy and Sir Thomas Percy, and several others with them, against our lord the king and their allegiance at the battle of Shrewsbury: so that on these matters the said lords and commons by their common assent and advice might do and say what seems advisable to them in order best to preserve peace and

15   mieulx garder paix et tranquillite deins le roialme. Et outre ceo, qe mesmes les
      seignurs et comunes par lour sages advises et discrecions ferroient lour peine et
      diligence, coment, sibien les ditz rebelx de Gales de lour rebellioun et d'estre mys
      en subjeccion a le roialme d'Engleterre, come les ditz enemys Franceois, Escotz, et
      Irroises de lour malice purroient mieultz estre guerroiez et resistez, sibien par terre
20   come par meer, et de sur ceo faire ordinance sufficiente en cest parlement.

                                         . . .

      9. Item, venderdy le xxv. jour de Janver, les comunes viendrent devant le roy
      en parlement, et luy monstrerent, coment devant le fest de Nowel darrein passe il
      avoit pleu a mesme nostre seignur le roy d'envoier pur certeines seignurs espirituelx
      et temporelx, et pur pluseurs gentilx et autres persones sufficientz de soun roialme,
25   pur estre conseillez par eux sur certeines matires alors monstrez, pur le bien et
      profit du roy et du roialme; et par especiale pur la saufe garde du meer, et pur re-
      sister la malice de ses rebelx en Gales. A quel temps, pur pleuseurs causes reson-
      ables, et pur la briefte du temps, les dites matires feurent adjournez tanq'a cest par-
      lement. Et ore en mesme cest parlement diverses articles et prieres ont este faites
30   par mesmes les comunes, sibien pur la saufe garde du meer, come pur les revenuz
      des custumes, et autres profitz du roialme, qe sont si sodeynement amesnusez, et
      de les plusours grantes des annuitees faitz devant ces heures, et diverses autres ma-
      tires: des queux ils avoient priez a nostre dit seignur le roy q'ils ent purroient avoir
      bones et graciouses responses. Et sur ceo il pleust au roy d'envoier as ditz comunes
35   en lour maisoun d'assemble, c'estassavoir en la refectorie deinz l'abbeie de Westm',
      ses honurables officers les chanceller et tresorer d'Engleterre ove mesmes les res-
      ponses, et de lour monstrer et exposer les costages et expenses necessaries affaires
      pur la saufe garde du meer, et aillours pur la defense du roialme, et les autres char-
      ges supporter pur l'ostelle du roy, et autrement. Les queux responses feurent molt
40   discretement donez par bouche de dit chanceller sur certeines des ditz articles et
      priers, et aucuns remaindroient nient responduz, et par especiale pur l'ordinance
      affaire pur Gales, sibien en le southe come en le northe, ou luy malveys rebel
      Oweyne est pluis conversant et tapissant.

                                         . . .

      Le roy de sa grace especiale ad pardonez a toutz ses lieges et subgitz de soun
45   roialme d'Engleterre, et du paiis de Gales, et de les marches d'Escoce, la seute de
      sa pees, qe a luy envers eux, et chescun de eux, appartient, pur toutz maners de
      tresons, insurreccions, rebellions, mesprisions, felonies, et trespasses, faitz ou per-
      petrez devant le xiiijme jour de Janver qe feust le primere jour de cest present
      parlement, forspris ceux qe sont en prisone ou en garde par cause de tresoun, et
50   forspris murdres, et rapes des femmes, controvours de seal du roy, fesours de fauxe
      monoie, et felons qi sont corporelement detenuz en prisone, ou lessez a mainprise
      ou en baille; et auxint les utlagaries, si nulles y soient en eux ou ascun de eux pro-
      nunciez par celles enchaisons. Et auxi nostre dit seignur le roy ad pardonez a toutz
      ses lieges et subgitz du roialme, paiis, et marches suisditz, et a chescune de eux, qi

tranquillity within the realm. And furthermore, so that the same lords and commons by their wise advice and discretion might bring their attention and consideration to bear on the question of how both the said Welsh rebels in their rebellion might be placed under subjection to the realm of England, and the said French, Scottish and Irish enemies in their malice might best be fought and resisted, both on land and on sea, and to make sufficient provision for this matter in this parliament.

. . .

9. Various requests made by the commons. Also, on Friday 25 January, the commons came before the king in parliament and explained to him how, before the feast of Christmas last, it had pleased our same lord the king to send for certain lords spiritual and temporal and for several noblemen and other capable persons of his realm, to be advised by them on certain matters which he explained at that time, for the good and advantage of the king and of the realm; and especially for the safe-keeping of the seas and to resist the malice of the rebels in Wales. At which time, for several legitimate reasons, and on account of the lack of time, the said matters were adjourned until this parliament. And now, in this same parliament, various articles and requests have been presented by the same commons, both for the safe-keeping of the seas, and concerning the revenue from the customs and other sources of income of the realm which have so suddenly been diminished, and concerning the many grants of annuities made previously, and various other matters: and they requested our said lord the king that they might have good and gracious replies to these. Whereupon it pleased the king to send to the said commons in their house of assembly, that is, in the refectory of the abbey of Westminster, his honorable officers the chancellor and treasurer of England, with these replies, and to explain and reveal to them the costs and expenses necessary for the safe-keeping of the sea and elsewhere for the defense of the realm, and the other costs to be borne for the king's household, and for other things. These replies to certain of the said articles and requests had been very wisely given by the said chancellor in person, but others remained without a reply, and especially the matter of the ordinance to be made for Wales, both in the south and in the north, where the evil rebel Owain is mostly living and hiding.

. . .

The king of his special grace has pardoned all his lieges and subjects of his realm of England, and of the country of Wales, and of the marches of Scotland, the suit of his peace which belongs to him in relation to them, and to each of them, for treasons, insurrections, rebellions, misprisions, felonies, and trespasses of all kinds, committed or perpetrated before 14 January, which was the first day of this present parliament, except for those who are in prison or in custody for treason, and except for murders, rapes of women, counterfeiters of the king's seal, forgers of false coin, and felons who are bodily kept in prison, or released on mainprise or on bail; and also outlawries, if any have been pronounced on them, or on any of them, for those reasons. And our said lord the king has also pardoned all his lieges and subjects of the aforesaid realm, country and marches, and each of them, who are at present

55   sont de present adherentz a ses enemys ou rebelx, qe veullent revenir et obeier a
       lour ligeance deinz quarant jours apres la proclamacioun de cestes grace et par-
       doun fait, la seute de sa pees pur toutz maners de tresons, insurreccions, rebellions,
       felonies, trespasses, et mesprisions, faitz ou perpetrez par eux, ou ascun de eux,
       avant lour rendre ou venue einz a lour ligeance, et auxint les utlagaries, si nulles en
60   eux ou aucun de de eux soient pronunciez par celles [enchaisons. Parainsi qe] ceux
       du paiis de Gales se rendent a nostre dit seignur le roy, ou a le prince de Gales, ou
       a duc d'Everwyk, [ou a lour lieutenantz ou] deputez, et qe ceux de les marches
       d'Escoce se rendent a nostre dit seignur le roy, ou a Johan fitz du dit roy gardein
       [de l'Estmarche, ou a le cont de Westmerland] gardein del Westmarche vers Escoce,
65   ou a lour lieutenantz ou [deputez. Purveuz toutesfoitz qe] William Serle, Thomas
       Warde de Trumpyngton' qi se pretende et [feigne] d'estre Roy Richard, et [Amye
       Donet, n'aient n'enjoient nul] avantage par cause de cestes grace et pardoun, mes
       q'ils soient expressement exceptz hors de pardoun et grace avantditz. Et quant al
       remenant du dit supplicacioun, le roy s'advisera.

41. HENRY SCARISBREC, *HARLECH NEAR SURRENDER*   Middle English
                                                                    26 February 1404

       Worschepful siris if hit like yow to wete ther is a lytil mon with Hawel Vaghan
       that was takyn when the constabull of Hardlagh wos takyn, and is sworne to Awyn
       agaynis his will, and he has send us word privyly how his maystyr has word for soche
       that Awyn has byen at Hardlagh and is accedit with all the men that arne therinne
5   save vij., for to have dilyverance of the castell at a certayn day for a certayn some of
       gold, and the day is in ryght hasty tyme bot he wot not when, and bot if hit be ryght
       sone ordaynt fore hit is lost and so is all the countre ther aboute. Worschipful sir,
       wil ye vouchesafe when ye han oversen this, to send hit to my maystir Sir John of
       Bolde, and makis ordinance as yo thenke be to do. Worschipful sirs the holy Trinite
10   kepe yow.
       Wrytyn in grete hast at Conway the xxvi. day of Feuyrzer.

42. *CHRONICLE OF DIEULACRES ABBEY*   Latin
                                                                     ca. 1404

       Anno domini millesimo cccc.^mo quidam maleficus et rebellis cum suis compli-
       cibus Wallencium de genere Britonum cuius siquidem nomen Owinus de Glyndour
       erat, figens se iure progenitorum suorum principem Wallie fore villas angligenas
       in Wallia, scilicet, Conway, Ruthyn, Oswaldistr et alias tam muratas quam nudas,
5   spoliavit et incendit. Quequidem terra Wallie tempore regis Edwardi primi
       conquesta fore dinoscitur.
       Circa idem tempus stella comata apparuit in borialibus partibus Anglie. Que
       comata sintillas vertebat versus Walliam; et quidam estimant dictam cometam
       pronosticare bellum Salopie.

adherents of his enemies or rebels, and who wish to return to and obey their allegiance within forty days of the proclamation of this grace and pardon, the suit of his peace for all kinds of treasons, insurrections, rebellions, felonies, trespasses and misprisions committed or perpetrated by them, or by any of them, before their surrender, or rather return to their allegiance, and also the outlawries, if any have been pronounced on them, or on any of them, for those reasons. Provided that those from the country of Wales should give themselves up to our said lord the king, or to the prince of Wales, or to the duke of York, or to their lieutenants or deputies, and those from the marches of Scotland should give themselves up to our said lord the king, or to John, son of the said king, warden of the East March, or to the earl of Westmorland, warden of the West March, on the border with Scotland, or to their lieutenants or deputies. Provided always, however, that William Serle, Thomas Ward of Trumpington who affects and pretends to be King Richard, and Amy Donet, do not have or enjoy any benefit from this grace and pardon, but that they should be expressly exempted from the aforesaid pardon and grace. And as to the rest of the said petition, the king will consider it further.

41. HENRY SCARISBREC, *HARLECH NEAR SURRENDER*   Notes: pp. 333–34

Honored sirs, may it please you to know that there is a little man with Hywel Fychan who was taken when the constable of Harlech was taken, who is sworn to Owain against his will, and he has secretly sent us word how his master has certain news that Owain has been at Harlech and is in agreement with all the men that are therein (except seven) that he will take delivery of the castle on a certain day for a certain sum of gold, and the day is coming soon but he does not know when, and unless action is taken immediately to prevent this it will be lost and so will be all the country thereabout. Honored sir, please promise when you have seen this, to send it to my master Sir John of Bolde, and make whatever arrangements you think best. Honored sirs, the holy Trinity protect you.

Written in great haste at Conwy the 26th day of February.

42. *CHRONICLE OF DIEULACRES ABBEY*   Notes: pp. 334–35

In the year 1400 a certain evil-doer and rebel with his Welsh companions of the race of the Britons whose name in fact was Owain Glyndŵr, setting himself up as the Prince of Wales by the law of his ancestors, plundered and burned English townships in Wales, more specifically, Conwy, Ruthin and Oswestry and others both walled and bare. The land of Wales, having been conquered in the time of Edward I, was recognised as distinct.

Around that same time a comet star appeared in the northern parts of England. This comet turned its sparks towards Wales; and certain people consider the said comet to have predicted the Battle of Shrewsbury.

10   Eodem anno Reginaldus Grey dominus de Ruthyn non longe a castro dolo et fraude Wallencium et precipue domus sue captus est et fere per biennium in arta custodia positus, ultro pro x. milibus librarum redemptus est.

      Eodem anno quidam Wallencium, Willelmus ap Tuder in die Parasceves hora tenebrarum dolo et fraude, custode absente, Iohanne Massey de Podyngton milite
15   capitaneo castellum de Conway cepit.

      Fertur siquidem in dicto castello hora supradicta tres Wallicos familiares et duos Anglicos custodes, aliis in servicio divinio in ecclesia parochiali occupatis remansisse; sicque Anglicis ab eis subdole occisis, castellum vendicarunt; parvo quoque tempore obsidio fessi, ad festum sancti Iohannis Baptiste treugis factis et pace
20   concessa omnibus octo exceptis in manum principis reddiderunt.

      Anno domini millesimo cccci. Owinus iuxta le Pole primo spoliatus contra Anglicos super undam Sabrine dimicavit suisque letaliter lesis et multis interfectis atque galea de capite proiecta sero profugit ab eis. Sed discreti reputant demenciam quando quis una manu percutit alteram. Sicque rex Henricus et princeps Henricus
25   diversis temporibus cum manu forti Walliam pergirantes omnia devestabant, quia in primeva fundacione circa ea modicum laborabant. Illi vero rebelles semper fugiendo latuerunt in montibus, boscis et cavernis terre, semper machinantes caudam anglicorum perimere.

      Hiis temporibus Anglici multa bona et precipue bestiarum omnium generum
30   quasi infinitam multitudinem abduxerunt, ut putaretur quasi impossibile tanta bona in tam modica plaga principaliter bestiarum arceri. Sed mira res, licet tempus esset clarum et tranquillum nunquam habuerunt, cum ibi essent amenum tempus ante reversionem sed inundacionem tonitruum, grandinem et precipue tempore estivali. Sed hoc non videtur difficile ex sortilegio contingere quod putatur fieri per magos
35   Owini et non est impossible per potestatem immundorum spirituum aerem commoveri; sed quampluribus discretis videbatur quod causa dictarum tempestatum principaliter fuit quia predicti iustum titulum contra eos non habuerunt: ideo proposito pene semper caruerunt et in vanum sepius laboraverunt etc.

      Eodem anno in die sancti Albani in loco qui dicitur Pilale Wallici fraude
40   circumvenerunt Anglicos interficientes ex eis mille quingentos captoque Edmundo le Mortimere a sua familia, ut dictitur, decepto et cum Owyno converso eius filiam desponsavit et in operacione istius cronice in eodem errore perseveravit.

In that same year Reginald Grey Lord of Ruthin was captured by the trickery and deceit of the Welshmen, not far from his castle and near his own home, and was placed under close guard for almost two years, until he was freed for a ransom of ten thousand libra.

In this same year on the day of Good Friday, at the hour of Tenebrae a certain Welshman, Gwilym ap Tudur, captured the castle of Conwy by fraud and treachery while the guardian John Massey of Podyngton, military captain, was absent.

It is said that in the castle at the hour mentioned above three Welsh servants and two English guards remained while the others were occupied in divine service (mass) in the church of the parish; and so when the English had treacherously been killed by them they claimed the castle; in a short time worn out by a siege, when a truce was made on the feast of St. John the Baptist, and peace conceded to all except eight of them, they returned it into the hands of their ruler.

In the year of our lord 1401, Owain, when he had first plundered near Welshpool, fought against the English over the river Severn, and, when many of his men had been mortally wounded and many killed, he threw the helm from his head and at last fled from them. But the discerning consider it madness when someone strikes one hand with the other. And in this way the King Henry and Prince Henry, at different times, were traveling through Wales with a strong hand, laying waste to everything, because they had not worked sufficiently at these things in the first place. Indeed the rebels always fled and lurked in mountains, forests and caverns of the earth, always plotting to cut off the rearguard of the English.

At this time the English took away many goods, and especially many of all kinds of beasts, an almost unlimited multitude, so that one would suppose it almost impossible that so many goods especially animals, could be gathered in such a region. But it was a miraculous thing, although the season was clear and tranquil they [the English] never had pleasant weather when they were there before going back, but there was an inundation of thunders, hail and especially in the summer season. But this does not seem difficult to give a supernatural explanation, that it is supposed to have happened through the magicians of Owain, and it is not impossible that the air be moved through the power of unclean spirits; but to many more discerning people it seemed that the cause of the said tempest was principally because the aforesaid people had no just title against them: thus they almost always failed in their plans and too often labored in vain etc.

In that same year on the day of the feast of St. Alban in the place which is called Pilleth, the Welsh deceptively surrounded the English, killing one thousand five hundred of them, and when Edmund Mortimer had been captured, deceived, so it is said, by his own family, and having been converted to Owain's cause, he married his [i.e. Owain's] daughter and continued for a long time in the same error in working with that man.

43. OWAIN GLYNDŴR, *AUTHORIZING AMBASSADORS TO FRANCE*   **Latin**
10 May 1404

Owynus, Dei gratia princeps Wallie, vniversis has litteras nostras inspecturis salutem. Noueritis quod propter affectionem et sinceram dilectionem quas erga nos et subdictos nostros illustrissimus princeps dominus Karolus eadem gratia Francorum rex hactenus gessit et sui gratia in dies gerit, sibi et suis, prout merito ad hoc
5   tenemur, adherere desideramus, Quapropter magistrum Griffinum Yonge, decretorum doctorem, cancellarium nostrum et Johannem de Hangmer consanguineos nostros predilectos, nostros veros et legitimos procuratores, actores, factores, negociorum gestores ac nuncios speciales facimus, ordinamus et constituimus per presentes; dantes et concedentes eisdem procuratoribus nostris et eorum vtrique per
10 se et in solidum potestatem generalem et mandatum speciale ita quod non sit melior condicio occupantis, sed quid vnus eorum inceperit alter eorundem prosequi valeat mediare et finire pro nobis ac nomine nostro de et super liga perpetua vel temporali cum prefato illustrissimo principe tractandi ipsamque ligam ex parte nostra iniendi, faciendi et firmandi ac quodcumque licitum iuramentum in ea parte
15 necessarium in animam nostram prestandi, litterasque obligatorias huiusmodi ligam concernentes faciendi et quamcumque aliam securitatem in ea parte forte necessariam pro nobis inueniendi et prestandi, necnon consimilem securitatem in materia premissa necessariam a prefato illustrissimo principe domino Karolo Dei gratia Francorum rege ex parte sua nobis faciendam petendi et recipiendi,
20 ceteraque omnia et singula faciendi excercendi et expediendi que in premissis et circa ea necessaria fuerint seu quomodolibet oportuna eciamsi mandatum exigant speciale et que nos facere possemus si personaliter huiusmodi tractatui interessmus. Pro dictis vero procuratoribus nostris et eorum vtraque rem ratam haberi, iudicio sisti et iudicatum solui sub ypotheca et obligacione omnium bonorum nostrorum
25 promittimus et caucionem exponimus per presentes.

In cuius rei testimonium has litteras nostras fieri fecimus patentes.

Data apud Doleguelly, x. die mensis Maii, anno Domini millesimo quadringentesimo quarto et principatus nostri quarto.

44. PRINCE HENRY, *DEFENDING THE MARCH*   **Anglo-Norman**
26 June 1404

Moun tresredoubte et tressoverain seigneur et pere,

Le plus humblement et obeissantement que je sce ou puisse me recoumande a vostre treshaulte seigneurie, humblement requerant toudys vostre gracieuses benison et tresentierement remerciant a vostre tresnoble haultesse de voz treshonur-
5   ables lettres quelles il vous plust moy darrainement envoier escritz a vostre chastel de Pontfreyt le xxi. jour de ceste present moys de Juyn. Par lesquelles lettres jay entendu la bonne prosperitee de vostre hault et roial estat, que mest le plus grand joye que me purroit avenir en ceste monde. Et jay pris tressoverain liesse et entiere joye de les nouvelles queux il vous a pleu de moy certifier, primerement de la hastive
10 venue pardevers vostre haultesse de moun treschier cousin le Conte de North-

43. OWAIN GLYNDŴR, *AUTHORIZING AMBASSADORS TO FRANCE* Notes: pp. 335–36

Owain, by the grace of God, prince of Wales, to all who will inspect these our letters, a greeting. You should understand that on account of the affection and sincere esteem which the most illustrious prince, the lord Charles, by the same grace king of the French, has displayed up to this point towards us and our subjects, and by his grace displays each day, we desire to adhere to him and his own, just as we are held to this by merit. For that reason, by those present we make, ordain and constitute our chosen kinsmen Master Gruffudd Yonge, doctor of laws, our chancellor, and John de Hanmer our true and legitimate ambassadors, managers, agents, negotiators, and special envoys; giving and conceding to our same ambassadors, and to each of them alone, complete general power and special mandate, such that there may be no better condition of negotiation, since whatever one of them may initiate, the other of them is authorised to pursue, mediate, and finish on our behalf and in our name, concerning and over a permanent or temporary allegiance with the aforementioned most illustrious prince; and negotiating that allegiance from our side, initiating, making and confirming it, and indeed being responsible for whatever necessary oath is required on that side in our place; and producing the required letters of any kind concerning the allegiance, and devising and executing on our behalf whatever other security may happen to be necessary on their side; and also seeking and receiving, in agreed format, from his side to us, any similar necessary security from the aforementioned most illustrious prince, Lord Charles, by the grace of God king of the French; and making, developing, and expediting any other things, all and singular, which might be required in or concerning the contracts, or in whatever suitable manner, even if they demand a special mandate that we would be able to make if we had been personally involved in the proceedings in any way. For the said our true ambassadors and both of them, we promise and set forth a legal bond by those here present that you shall have a ratified benefit, established by law and judicially discharged under the pledge and obligation of all our goods.

In witness of this we cause these our letters to be made patent.

Given at Dolgellau, tenth day of the month of May, in the year of our Lord 1404 and in the fourth year of our rule.

44. PRINCE HENRY, *DEFENDING THE MARCH* Notes: pp. 336–38

My most dread and most sovereign lord and father,

I recommend myself to your most high lordship in the most humble and obedient way that I know or can, humbly requesting always your gracious blessing and fully thanking your most noble highness for your most honorable letters written at your castle of Pontefract on the 21st day of this present month of June, which it pleased you to send me recently. By these letters I have heard of the great prosperity of your high and royal estate, which is the greatest joy which could befall me in this world. And I have taken enormous delight and unbroken joy in the news which it has pleased you to tell me, firstly of the speedy coming to your highness of my most dear cousin the earl of Northumberland and of William Clifford, and sec-

umbr' et de William Clifford, et secondement e la venue des messages de vostre adversaire d'Escoce et d'autres grandz de son royaume par vertue de vostre saufconduyt. Pour le bien dambedeux les royaumes que Dieux grante pour sa mercy et que vous puissez tous voz honurables desirs accomplir au plesir de lui honnour de vous et prouffit de vostre roiaume, comme jay ferme affiance en cellui qest toutpuissant que vous ferrez.

Moun tresredoubte et tressoverain seigneur et pere, a vostre hault commandement par autres voz gracieuses lettres je suy remue ovec moun petit hostiel a la ville de Wircestre, et a moun envoie y est venuz ovec moy le tresbon cuer mon treschier et tresame cousin le Conte de Warrewyk ovec une beel compaignie de ses gens a ses tresgrandes custages, peront il est bien digne pour estre bien merciez de vous pour son bon vouloir a tous temps. Et quant as nouvelles de les Galoys, sils soient vraies et quel purpos jay pris sur moun aler dont vous desirez estre acerteniez. Plese a vostre haultesse assavoir que devant mon aler et depuis par la voie je feu certiffiez que les Galoys feurent descenduz en le countee de Hereford, ardantz et destruantz mesme le countee en tresgrandz povoirs et feurent vitaillez pur xv. jours. Et voirs est qils ont arz et fait grand destruccioun en les bordures du dit countee, mes puis ma venue a paiis je noye de nul damage qils font, Dieux merciez. Mes je suy certeinement enfourmez quils sont assemblez ove tout le povair quils purront fere et eulx teignent ensemble a un grand purpos et a ce que len dit pour ardre le dit countee.

Et pour ce jay envoie a mes treschiers et tresamez cousins, Messires Richard d'Everwyk et le Conte Mareshcal, et autres des plus sufficeantz gens des countees de celle marche qils soient ovec moy a Wircestre Joedy prouchain apres la date de cestes pour moy enfourmer pleinement de la gouvernance de leures paiis et comebien des gantz ils purront fere si mestier soit et moy monstrer leure avys touchant ce que lour semble mieux affaire pour la sauve garde des parties suisdictes. Et par leur avys je vuille fere tout ce que me serra possible en resistence de les rebelx et sauvacioun de la paiis Engloys a trestout moun petit povair siavant, comme Dieux moy dorra la grace, tousdys confiant en vostre treshaulte seigneurie que vous vuillez souveigner de moun povre estat et que je ne suy pas de povoir pour continuir icy sans ce qil soit autrement ordennez pour ma demoere et que ces custages sont a moy emportables. Et fere vuillez ainsi ordener pur moy en haste que je puisse vous fere service icy a vostre honnour et sauver moun petit estat?

Moun tresredoubte et tressoverain seigneur et pere, le toutpuissant Seigneur de ciel et de terre vous doint tresgracieuse vie et longe en tresbone prosperitee a vostre plesir.

Escrit a Wircestre le xxvi. jour de Juyn.

ondly of the coming of the messages from your enemy of Scotland and of other great men of his kingdom by way of your safe conduct. For the good of both kingdoms may God grant by his mercy that you may accomplish all your honorable desires to his pleasure and your honor and the profit of your kingdom. I have firm faith in Him who is all-powerful that you will do this.

My most dread and most sovereign lord and father, at your high command by other gracious letters of yours I have removed with my small household to the town of Worcester, and at my bidding my very dear and well beloved cousin the earl of Warwick has come here with me of very good heart with a goodly company of his men at great cost to himself, for which he well deserves to be greatly thanked by you for his good will at all times. And as to the news of the Welsh, you wish to know whether it is true and what purpose I had in my going there. May it please your highness to know that before my going and since then on the road I was informed that the Welsh had descended on the county of Hereford, burning and destroying that same county in great power and that they had provisions for 15 days. And in truth they burned and wreaked great destruction in the borders of the said county, but since my coming to the area I hear of no damage which they do, God be thanked. But I am reliably informed that they are assembled with all the power which they can muster and hold themselves in readiness for a great purpose, which is to burn the countryside, so it is said.

And because of that I have sent to my very dear and well beloved cousins, Lord Richard of York and the earl marshal, and others of the most substantial men of the counties of this March that they should be with me at Worcester the next Thursday after the date of these letters to inform me more fully of the governance of their lands and how many men they could muster if needed and give me their views on what seems to them to be the best means of safeguarding the above named lands. And according to their advice I will do everything possible to resist the rebels and for the salvation of the English land as far as is within my mean power as above and, as God will give me grace, always trusting in your most high lordship that you will remember my poor estate and consider that I have not the power to continue here without other ordinance being made for my stay and that I bear my own costs. And so will you make ordinance for me with speed so that I can do service to you here to your honor and saving my small estate?

My most dread and most sovereign lord and father, may the all-powerful Lord of heaven and earth grant you a most gracious and long life and great prosperity at your pleasure.

Written at Worcester the 26th day of June.

45. LOUIS OF BOURBON, *LETTER TO HENRY III OF CASTILE*   **French**
                                                                          7 July 1404

Tres hault et très excellent prince et très cher sires et cousins, plaise à vous
savoir que j'ay receu vos lettres que envoyées m'avez par vos ambaxeurs qui
nagueres sont arrivez par deça, par lesquelles j'ay sceu le bon estat et santé de votre
personne, de très hault et puissant princesse ma très chière dame et cousine la
5   royne de Castelle et de Léon votre compaigne, et de ma très chière et très amée
cousine la infanta votre fille, de mon très chier et très honoré cousin le duc de
Penafil votre frére; dont j'ai esté très parfaitement joyeux, suis et seray toutes et
quinte foiz que óir en pourray pareilles nouvelles, etc. Et l'estat de par deça si savoir
vous plaist, Monseigneur le Roy, Madame la Royne, Monseigneur le Dolphin et les
10   autres enfans de mon dit seigneur le Roy estoient sans et en bon point ou partir de
ces lettres, et aussi estoit je, grâces à Dieu, etc. Plaise vous savoir que mon dit seigneur le Roy et les autres Messeigneurs de son sang ont oy vos diz ambaxeurs sur ce
qu'ilz leur ont exposé de par vous, comme vous voulez envoyer à mon dit seigneur
xl. nefs armées toutes prestes. De laquelle chose et du secours que vous lui presentés
15   à présent il est moult content de vous et les a très agréables, car elles viennent en
très bonne saison, mesmement pour ce qui mon dit seigneur le Roy a ordonné mon
très cher et très amé cousin le comte de la Marche d'aller briefvement ès parties de
Galles atout mil. lances et vc. arbalestriers; lequel se partira prouchainement pour
monter en mer ès parties de Bretaigne et d'illec en Galles. Pourquoy je vous prie
20   tant et si acertes comme je puis qui, en parsevérant en votre bon propos et contin-
uant les bonnes alliances tous diz continuées sans enfranidre par vous et vos bons
prédécesseurs avec mon dit seigneur le Roy et les siens, et pour le bien et avance-
ment de ceste besoigne, il vous plaise envoyer et faire avancier les dictes xl. nefs le
plus brief et hastivement que bonnement faire se pourra, en maniere que elles puis-
25   sent estre en Bretaigne dedens le xve. jour d'aoust prouchain venant afin qui mon
dit cousin de la Marche, qui en icellui temps sera ou dit païs de Bretaigne accom-
paignié comme dit est, s'en puist aider et les menner avecques lui es dites parties
de Galles, ou il trouvera bonne entrée aide et secours pour envaïr, grever et dom-
maîgéer les Anglois noz ennemis. Et à ce ne vous plaise faillir.
30   Très hault et très excellent prince et très chier sires et cousins, se chose quel-
conque vous plaist par deça que pour vous faire puisse, mandez le moij féablement,
et je le accomplirai à mon povoir de très bon cuer au plaisir de Dieu qui vous ait en
sa sainte guarde et vous doint bonne vie et longue.
Escript à Paris le viie. jour de Juillet.

46. *CONFEDERATION BETWEEN WALES AND FRANCE*   **Latin**
                                                                          12 January 1405

Owynus Dei gratia princeps Wallie, universis has litteras nostras inspecturis
salutem. Noverit universitas vestra nos litteras patentes infrascriptas ligam et con-
federacionem inter illustrissimum principem dominum Karolum Dei gratia Francorum regem et nos per procuratores suos et nostros in hac parte initas et con-
5   tractas continentes recepisse in hac verba:

45. Louis of Bourbon, *Letter to Henry III of Castile* Notes: pp. 338–39

Most high and most excellent prince and dear sires and cousins, may it please you to know that I have received your letters which you sent me by your ambassadors, who have lately arrived here, from whom I have learnt of the good estate and health of your self, of the most high and puissant princess, my very dear lady and cousin, the queen of Castile and León, your consort, and of my very dear and well-beloved cousin the Infanta, your daughter, of my very dear and very honored cousin the duke of Penafil, your brother; of which I am exceedingly glad, I am and shall be for all and the fifth time when I shall be able to hear the like news, &c. And of the state here, if it please you to know, Monseigneur the king, Madam the queen, Monseigneur the dauphin, and the other children of my said lord the king are in good health, at the moment of forwarding these letters, and I also, thanks be to God. May it please you to know that my said lord the king and the other lords of his race have heard your said ambassadors upon that question which they were to explain to them from you, that you will be pleased to send to my said lord forty ships all armed and swift. Concerning which purpose and assistance which you give him at present, he is very well content with you, and they are very acceptable, because they come at an opportune occasion, just now, for my said lord the king has ordered my very dear and well-beloved cousin, the count of March, to proceed shortly to Wales with one thousand lances and five hundred crossbowmen; who will set out shortly to embark in Brittany, and from thence to Wales. I therefore pray you as earnestly as I can, that you persevere in your good purpose, and continue in the good alliances, all the said being continued, without breach by you and your predecessors with my said lord the king and his, and for the good and advancement of his needs, may it please you to send and despatch the said forty ships as quickly and as expeditiously as can be properly done, in such a way that they can arrive in Brittany about the fifteenth day of August next, in order that my said cousin de la Marche, who shall, at that time, be in the said country of Brittany, accompanied as explained, if it is possible to aid him and conduct them with him to the said part of Wales, where he will find a good entry aided and assisted, in order to attack, harass, and injure the English, our enemies. And in this may you not fail us.

Most high and most excellent prince and very dear sires and cousins, whatever may please you here, that can be done for you, acquaint me with it faithfully, and I shall accomplish it according to my power and the good will and pleasure of God, and may He keep you in his holy care and grant you a good and a long life.

Written at Paris the seventh day of July.

46. *Confederation between Wales and France* Notes: pp. 339–41

Owain, by the grace of God, prince of Wales, to all who are about to view these our letters greeting. Be it known to all that we have received the letters patent following containing the league and covenant between the most illustrious Lord Charles, by the grace of God, king of France, and us, commenced and completed by his ambassadors and ours on this part, in these words:

"Nos Jacobus de Borbonio, comes Marchie, procurator et nuncius specialis ser-
enissimi principis domini mei metuendissimi domini Karoli, Dei gratia Francorum
regis, et nos Griffinus Yonge decretorum doctor, cancellarius et Johannes de Hanmer, scutifer, consanguinei, ambaxiatores, procuratores, et nuncii speciales illustris
et metuendissimi domini nostri Owyni principis Walliarum prout de potestatibus
et procuratoriis utrique nostrum datis per dominos nostros supradictos plene
constat per litteras patentes ipsorum dominorum quarum tenores inferius sunt in-
serte ad infrascripta a dictis dominis specialiter depputati et commissi, notum facimus universis quod nos virtute mandatorum dictorum dominorum nostrorum regis
et principis et potestatem per eos nobis atributarum et datarum de et super ligis,
confederacionibus et amiciciis inter ipsos dominos regem et principem iniendis et
firmadis invicem convenimus in certis capittulis seu articulis continentibus formam
que sequitur et tenorem:

"Primo quod ipsi domini rex et princeps erunt amodo ad invicem conjuncti,
confederati, uniti et ligati vinculo veri federis et vere amicicie certeque et bone
unionis potissime contra Henricum de Lencastria utriusque ipsorum adversarium
et hostem suosque adherentes et fautores. Item quod alter ipsorum dominorum
honorem et commodum alterius volet, prosequetur ac eciam procurabit, dampnaque et gravamina que ad unius noticiam devenerint per dictum Henricum ejusque
complices, adherentes et fautores aut alios quoscumque alteri inferenda impedient
bona fide, alter quoque ipsorum apud alteram aget et faciet ea omnia et singula que
per bonum verum et fidum amicum bono, vero et fido amico agi et fieri debent et
pertinent fraude et dolo cessantibus quibuscumque. Item si et quociens alter eorum
sciverit vel cognoverit prefatum Henricum de Lencastria seu adherentes aut fautores suos aliquid gravaminis sive dampni procurare vel machinari contra alium,
ipse sibi quamcicius commode fieri poterit ea significabit et ipsum de et super hoc
advisabit ut adversus malicias suas prout ei visum fuerit sibi valeat providere; soliciti
quoque erunt quilibet ipsorum dominorum impedire gravamina et dampna predicta bona fide. Item quod quilibet dominorum predictorum nullatenus pacietur
quod aliquis subditorum suorum det, faciat aut procuret dicto Henrico de Lencastria fautoribusve aut adherentibus suis auxilium vel consilium aliquod seu favorem
nec quod ipsum juvent cum ipsius stipendiis neque eciam sine stipendiis contra aliquem eorundem dominorum. Quod si contra facere presumerent taliter punientur
quod ceteris cedet in exemplum. Item quod aliquis dominorum regis et principis
predictorum non faciet seu capiet treugas nec faciet pacem cum dicto Henrico Lencastrie quin alter si voluerit comprehendatur in ipsis treugis sive pace nisi in eisdem
treugis vel pace renuerit sive noluerint comprehendi, et de qua noluntate seu recu-
sacione constabit illi qui dictas treugas sive pacem tractare voluerit infra mensem
postquam alteri treugas seu pacem predictas significaverit per suas patentes litteras
suo sigillo sigillatas. Item quod omnes subditi regni Francie cum eorum navigiis,
mercimoniis sive mercanciis, rebus et bonis quibuscumque recipientur et recolli-
gentur ac pacientur moram facere in omnibus terris et portubus regni Francie sine
fraude dum tamen subditi hujusmodi hinc inde habeant litteras testimoniales sub
sigillis dominorum predictorum seu justiciorum aut officiariorum suorum de et

"We, James de Bourbon, count of March, procurator and special ambassador of most serene lord prince and our most dreaded master, the lord Charles, by the grace of God, king of France, and we, Gruffudd Yonge, doctor of the Canon Law, chancellor, and John Hanmer, esquire, kinsman, ambassadors, procurators, and special nuncios to the illustrious and most dreaded Lord Owain, prince of the Welsh, as is fully given by powers and commissions given us both parties by our lords aforesaid, by letters patent of the same lords, copies of which are inserted below, being specially deputed and commissioned by the said lords, we make known to all that we, by virtue of the commands and powers of our said lords the king and the prince, attributed and given to us by them, concerning and over leagues, covenants, and friendships between the said lords the king and the prince, we have mutually agreed upon the commencing and completing in certain chapters or successive articles, which follows in form and tenor:

"In the first place, that the said lords the king and the prince shall be mutually joined, confederated, united, and leagued by the bond of a true covenant and real friendship, and of a sure, good, and most powerful union against Henry of Lancaster, and adversary and enemy of both parties, and his adherents and supporters. Again that one of the said lords shall desire, follow, and even will procure the honor and advantage of the other, and should any damage or injury intended against the one by the said Henry, his accomplices, adherents, supporters, or other whomsoever, come to the notice of one, he shall prevent that in good faith. The one, also, of these shall urge and make with the other each and every thing, which, by a good, true and faithful friend, ought and pertains to be urged and done to a good, true, and faithful friend, yielding to no one by fraud or guile. Again, if and as often as the one of them shall know or shall understand that any injury or damage is procured or plotted against the other by the aforesaid Henry of Lancaster, or by his adherents or supporters, he shall, as many times as it shall become necessary signify that fact, and shall advise him concerning and over that, so that the other shall be able to prepare against his malice as far as he shall have foreseen; also, both of the same lords, without distinction, shall be anxious to hinder the aforesaid injury or damage in good faith. Again, if anyone of the said lords be pacified in any manner, if anyone of his subjects gives, makes, or procures aid, advice of any kind, or favor to the said Henry of Lancaster, his followers or adherents, or promise that for rewards, or even without rewards, against any one of their lords. That if they shall presume to withstand, they shall be punished in such a manner that shall give an example to the others. Again, that one of the lords, the king and the prince aforesaid, shall not make or take truce nor make peace with the aforesaid Henry of Lancaster, but that the other might be included if he had wished in the same truce or peace, unless he is united or did not wish to be included in the same truce or peace, and he shall determine, concerning such refusal or rejection, who wished to treat for the said truce or peace, within a month after the one shall have signified the said truce or peace, by his letters patent, sealed by his seal. Again, that all the subjects of the kingdom of France, with their ships, merchant or mercenary, chattels, and goods whatsoever shall be taken, collected, and surrendered without fraud, to cause delay in all the lands and ports of the kingdom of France, provided that subjects of every degree have, from this time forth, letters of testimony under the seal of the aforesaid lords, or their justiciars, or their

50   super subjectione et fidelitate eorumdem confectas. Item quod si discordia, violen-
        cia, pugna, riota, spoliacio, vel alia quevis injuria in mari sive in terra inter subditos
        dictorum dominorum, quod absit, committatur seu oriri contigerit, causeque super
        hoc emergerit amicabiliter secundum merita eorumdem et locorum existenciam ubi
        premissa committentur per dominos utriusque partis vel justiciarios et officiarios
55   suos ad quos pertinebit tractentur et per eos commissa hujusmodi legitime refor-
        mentur, discordieque predicte pacificentur. Item quod quocienscumque alter pre-
        fatorum dominorum pro parte alterius fuerit requisitus confederaciones predictas
        sic per eorum procuratores factas et initas tenebitur per suas litteras cum promis-
        sionibus debitis ratificare, confirmare ac eciam validare. Item quod quelibet pars
60   procuratorum predictorum promictet et jurabit in animam domini sui, tactis sacro-
        sanctis envangeliis quod confederaciones et lige contente in articulis supradictis per
        ipsos dominos et eorum subditos firmiter bona fide tenebuntur. Ab istis autem
        confederacionibus et ligis excipiuntur pro parte dictorum dominorum nostrorum
        regis et principis omnes illi qui racione generis seu subjectionis, dum tamen subditi
65   prefati Henrici Lencastrie non existant aut pretextu ligarum precedencium erant
        sibi antea federati. Quequidem capitula nos Jacobus de Borbonio, comes Marchie,
        necnon Griffinus Yonge et Johannes de Hanmer, procuratores et nuncii supradicti,
        dominorum nostrorum regis Francorum et principis Walliarum predictorum nomi-
        nibus, rata et grata habentes ipsa omniaque et singula in eis et quolibet ipsorum
70   contenta et declarata alter alteri quisque videlicet pro suo dominorum nostrorum
        predictorum et nomine ipsius et pro ipso promittimus bona fide juramusque in ani-
        mas eorundem dominorum ad sancta Dei envangelia per nos et utrumque nostrum
        tacta, bene et fideliter tenere, attendere et complere ac eciam firmiter et inviola-
        biter observare.
75   "In quorum omnium et singulum fidem et testimonium presentes litteras seu
        presens publicum instrumentum fieri et dupplicari et per notarios publicos infra-
        scriptos publicari mandavimus et sigillorum nostrorum una cum signis et subscrip-
        cionibus dictorum notariorum publicorum fecimus appensione muniri."
            Tenor vero litterarum procuratoriarum dicti domini nostri Francorum regis
80   sequitur et est talis:
            "Karolus Dei gratia Francorum rex, universis presentes litteras inspecturis
        salutem. Notum facimus quod nos de fidelitate diligenti et industria dilectorum et
        fidelium consanguinei et consiliariorum nostrorum Jacobi de Borbonio comitis
        Marchie et Johannis episcopi Carnotensis plenissime confidentes ipsos facimus,
85   constituimus, nominamus et eligimus procuratores nostros generales et certos nun-
        cios speciales et eorum quemlibet in solidum ita quod non sit melior condicio occu-
        pantis, sed quod unus eorum inceperit alter prosequi valeat et finire, ad tractandum
        nomine nostro et pro nobis cum dilectis nostris magistro Griffino Yonge et Johanne
        de Hanmer, consanguineis magnifici et potentis Owyni principis Walliarum et ejus
90   ambaxiatoribus et nunciis, habentibus ad infrascripta a dicto principe potestatem
        per litteras ipsius principis sigillo suo sigillatas, ligas, confederaciones, et amicicias
        perpetuas vel ad tempus inter nos ex una parte et dictum principem Walliarum ex
        altera, prout eisdem procuratoribus utriusque partis videbitur faciendum de et

officers, and under their subjection and fidelity. Again, that if strife, violence, battle, riot, pillage, or other injury whatever, and may that not happen be committed or caused to arise, upon sea or land, between the subjects of the said lords, and should a pretext appear over this, let it be treated amicably according to their merits and extent of places where the offences were committed by the lords of both parties, or their justiciars or officers to whom that pertains, and that offences of every kind committed by them shall be legitimately reformed, and the aforesaid strife pacified. Again, that whosoever of the aforesaid lords on his part shall have required of the other, he will be held by his letters to ratify, confirm, and even to make valid with biding promises that aforesaid covenants thus begun and completed by their ambassadors. Again, that whatever one of the aforesaid ambassadors will promise and vow instead of his lord, having touched the sacrosanct gospels, those covenants and binding league in the aforesaid articles shall be held firmly in good faith by those lords and their subjects. However, all those who by reason of their race or subjection, while subjects of the aforesaid Henry of Lancaster, shall not appear, or by pretext of former treaties previously federated, shall be excepted from these covenants and leagues. We, James de Bourbon, count of March, and Gruffudd Yonge, and John de Hanmer, ambassadors and special nuncios aforesaid, of the lords, the king of the French, and the prince of Wales aforesaid by name, having each, all and singular in them accepted and received, and in each of them is satisfied, and the one has declared to the other; and we each promise, in good faith, on his own behalf and of our aforesaid lords, and in his name and for himself, and we swear for our masters, the holy gospels of God having been touched by us and each of us, each article well and faithfully to hold, keep, comply, and even firmly and inviolably observe.

"In faith and testimony of each and all of which, we have commanded that these present letters or present public instrument to be made and duplicated, and to be published by the public notaries undermentioned, and we have caused them to be confirmed by appending our seals together with the marks and signatures of the said public notaries."

The true tenor of the letters of commission of our lord, the king of the Franks, follows, and is of this nature:

"Charles, by the grace of God king of the French, to all these present letters may come, greeting. We make known that we, on account of the faithful diligence and industry of our beloved and faithful kinsman, and our councilors, James de Bourbon, count of March, and John, bishop of Chartres, having our fullest confidence, we make, constitute, name, and elect them our general ambassadors and assured special nuncios, and each of them, in the whole matter, thus that there may not be a better condition of negotiations, but that which one of them may commence, the other shall have power to follow and complete, for the purpose of negotiating in our name and for us with our beloved friends, Master Gruffudd Yonge and John Hanmer, kinsmen of the magnificent and powerful Owain, prince of the Cymry, and his ambassadors and nuncios, having for the undermentioned purpose, power, from the said prince, by letter sealed by the seal of the prince himself, to make leagues, covenants, and perpetual or temporary friendships between us on the one part, and the said prince of the Cymry on the other part, as it may seem to the same ambassadors of both parties, concerning and over the same leagues, cove-

95   super ipsis ligis confederacionibus et amiciciis et de modis ipsorum conveniendum
        ipsasque cum illis modis convencionibus et permissionibus de quibus ipsi procura-
        tores utriusque partis invicem convenerint firmandum, concludendum, ac quod-
        cumque licitum et debitum juramentum in animam nostram necnon quamcumque
        securitatem ad hoc necessarium querendum, inveniendum, prestandum atque dan-
        dum; similesque a parte dicti principis querendum, recipiendum et acceptandum;
100   dantes et concedentes dictis procuratoribus nostris et eorum cuilibet in solidum ple-
        nam generalam et liberam potestatem et mandatum speciale premissa et generali-
        ter omnia et singula faciendi, gerendi, exercendi et expediendi que circa ea et eo-
        rum dependencias necessaria fuerint et quomodolibet oportuna et que nos facer-
        emus et facere possemus si presentes ad hec personaliter interessemus eciamsi man-
105   datum exigerent magis speciale, promittentes bona fide ratum, gratum et firmum
        habere quidquid per predictos procuratores nostros et eorum quemlibet in solidum
        in premissis et circa premissa actum factumque fuerit ac eciam firmatum et conclu-
        sum sub ypotheca et obligacione omnium bonorum nostrorum presencium et futu-
        rorum.
110   "In cujus rei testimonium nostrum presentibus litteris fecimus apponi sigillum.
        Datum Parisius die xiiija junii, anno Domini millesimo quadringentesimo quarto
        et regni nostri xxiiijo."
            Item sequitur tenor litterarum procuratoriarum dicti domini principis Walli-
        arum in hec verba:
115   "Owynus Dei gratia princeps Wallie, universis has litteras nostras inspecturis
        salutem. Noveritis quod propter affectionem et sinceram dilectionem quas erga nos
        et subditos nostros illustrissimus princeps dominus Karolus eadem gratia Franco-
        rum rex hactenus gessit et sui gratia in dies gerit sibi et suis prout merito ad hoc
        tenemur adherere desideramus. Quapropter magistrum Griffinum Yonge, decre-
120   torum doctorem, cancellarium nostrum et Johannem de Hanmer, consanguineos
        nostros predilectos, nostros veros et legitimos procuratores, actores, factores, nego-
        ciorum gestores ac nuncios speciales facimus, ordinamus et constituimus per pre-
        sentes, dantes et concedentes eisdem procuratoribus nostris et eorum utrique per
        se et in solidum potestatem generalem et mandatum speciale ita quod non sit
125   melior condicio occupantis sed quod unus eorum inceperit alter eorum prosequi
        valeat, mediare et finire pro nobis ac nomine nostro de et super liga perpetua vel
        temporali cum prefato illustrissimo principe tractandi ipsamque ligam ex parte
        nostra iniendi, faciendi et firmandi ac quodcumque licitum juramentum in ea parte
        necessarium in animam nostram prestandi, litterasque obligatorias hujusmodi
130   ligam concernentes faciendi et quamcumque aliam securitatem in ea parte forte
        necessariam pro nobis inveniendi et prestandi, necnon consimilem securitatem in
        materia premissa necessariam a prefato illustrissimo principe domino Karolo Dei
        gratia Francorum rege ex parte sua nobis faciendam petendi et recipiendi cetera-
        que omnia et singula faciendi, exercendi et expediendi que in premissis et circa ea
135   necessaria fuerint seu quomodolibet oportuna eciamsi mandatum exigant speciale
        et que nos facere possemus si personaliter hujusmodi tractatui interessemus; pro
        dictis vero procuratoribus nostris et eorum utroque rem ratam habere, judicio sisti
        et judicatum solvi sub ypotheca et obligacione omnium bonorum nostrorum pro-
        mittimus et cauciones exponimus per presentes.

nants, and treaties, and concerning the manner of arranging of them, meetings and concerts concerning which the same ambassadors of both parties will meet mutually for the purpose of confirming, concluding, and of binding whatsoever lawful or due in our stead, seeking, finding, securing, and giving whatsoever security necessary for this purpose; and in like manner seeking, receiving, and accepting from the part of the said prince; giving and conceding to our said ambassadors, and to each of them complete, full, general, and free power and command by special permission, both for making, negotiating, exercising, and preparing generally each and every thing which shall be necessary, both for those purposes and their dependencies, and in whatever manner suitable, and that we shall cause and are able to cause, if we shall be interested personally, for this present purpose even if they require a very special command, promising in good faith to have ratified, accepted, and confirmed whatever shall be made and completed in full by our aforesaid ambassadors, and whoever of them in or around these premises , and even confirm and conclude under conditions and obligation of all our goods present and future.

"In testimony whereof we have caused our seal to be attached to these present letters. Dated at Paris the 14th day of June, 1404, and the twenty-fourth year of our reign."

Again, the tenor of the letters of proxy of the said lord prince of Wales follow in these words:

"Owain, by the grace of God, prince of Wales, to all who will examine these our letters, greeting. Know ye that on account of the affection and sincere regard which the illustrious prince, the lord Charles by the same grace, king of the French, has up to the present time borne towards us and our subjects, and of his grace bears daily, we desire to cleave to him and to his subjects, as by merit we are held to this purpose. Wherefore, we make, ordain, and constitute by these presents Master Gruffudd Yonge, doctor of Canon Law, chancellor, and John de Hanmer, our well-beloved kinsmen, our true and legal ambassadors, proctors, factors, negotiators, and special nuncios, giving and conceding to our same ambassadors, and to both of them by himself, and in full general power and special command, in such manner that there shall not be a better condition of negotiation, but that which the one of them shall commence the other of them has power to follow, consider, and complete for us, and in our name concerning and over a perpetual or temporal league with the aforesaid most illustrious prince, and of conducting, commencing, making, and confirming the same league on our part, and of undertaking whatsoever suitable oath necessary in that part in our stead, and of the making of letters obligatory of this kind concerning the league, and of giving or granting for us whatsoever other security may incidentally appear necessary on their part, or of seeking and receiving the giving of similar security necessary in the material premises from the aforesaid most illustrious prince, the lord Charles by the grace of God king of the French on his part to us, and of making, granting, and expediting other, all and singular, which were necessary in the premises, and concerning them or whatsoever manner suitable, even if a special injunction appear necessary, and which we are able to make if we had been personally concerned in any way in the negotiation. For the said our true ambassadors and each of them, we promise and place our consent by these presents that ye shall decide, and your decision shall be fulfilled, and the agreement established shall be kept under the pledge and obligation of all our goods.

140   "In cujus rei testimonium has litteras nostras fieri fecimus patentes. Data apud
        Dolegelle xo. die mensis maii, anno Domino millesimo quadringentisemo quarto,
        et principatus nostri quarto."

        Actum et datum Parisius in domo habitacionis magnifici viri domini Ernaudi
145   de Corbeya militis, cancellarii Francie, anno Domini millesimo quadringentesimo
        quarto, indictione duodecima, die xiiija mensis julii, presentibus dicto domino can-
        cellario Francie, necnon reverendis in Christo patribus et dominis dominis Philippo
        Noviomensi, Petro Meldensi, et Johanne Atrebatensi episcopis ac eciam magnifico
        et potenti Ludovico de Borbonio, comite Vindocinensi, nobilibusque viris dominis
150   Roberto de Braquemont et Roberto d'Amilli, militibus dicti serenessimi principis
        regis Francorum cambellanis testibus ad promissa vocatis.
        Ego Johannes de Sanctis, Belvacensis diocesis, apostolica et imperiali auctori-
        tatibus publicus notarius prefatisque domini nostri Francorum regis notarius et sec-
        retarius qui premissis omnibus et singulis dum, ut premittitur, agerentur et fierent
155   per dominos procuratores superius nominatos una cum suprascriptis testibus presens
        fui eaque fieri vidi et audivi ad requestam et de consensu ipsorum dominorum
        procuratorum ut huic presenti publico instrumento super hiis confecto et super
        eadem forma verborum dupplicato quod scribi et grossari per alium feci, pluribus
        aliis negociis occupatus, collacione per me facta cum notario publico infrascripto de
160   originalibus litteris procuratoriarum supra insertis cum eodem presenti publico
        instrumento ipsum publicando me subscripsi et signum meum apposui consuetum.
        Et ego Benedictus Comme, clericus Assavensis diocesis publicus auctoritate
        apostolica notarius, premissis omnibus et singulis dum sic ut premictitur per dictos
        dominos procuratores agerentur et fierent una cum magnificis dominis testibus ac
165   venerabili viro notario supradicto presens interfui, eaque sic fieri vidi et audivi, et
        ideo hoc presens publicum instrumentum per alium me aliunde occupato, fideliter
        scriptum ad requisicionem et de consensu eorumdem dominorum procuratorum,
        dupplicatum publicavi, signoque et nomine meis solitis et consuetis signavi rogatus
        et requisitus in fidem et testimonium omnium premissorum."
170   Nos vero factum procuratorum nostrorum in hac parte ratum et gratum hab-
        entes ligam et confederacionem premissas quantum in nobis est ratificamus et con-
        firmamus per presentes.
        In cujus rei testimonium has litteras nostras fieri fecimus patentes. Data in
        castro nostro de Llanpadarn xijo. die januarii, anno Domini millesimo quadrin-
175   gentisimo quinto et principatus nostri sexto.

47. *TRIPARTITE INDENTURE*   **Latin**
                                                                           28 February 1405

        Hoc anno Comes Northumbriæ fecit legiam et confederationem et amicitiam
        cum Owino Glendor et Edmundo de Mortuomari, filio quondam Edmundi Comitis
        Marchiæ, in certis articulis continentibus formam quæ sequitur et tenorem:
        Primo quod iidem domini — Owinus, Comes, et Edmundus — erunt amodo ad
5   invicem conjuncti, confœderati, uniti, et ligati vinculo veri fœderis et veræ amicitiæ,
        certæque et bonæ unionis. Iterum quod quilibet ipsorum dominorum honorem et

"In testimony whereof we make these our letters patent. Given at Dolgellau the tenth day of May, 1404, and in the fourth year of our rule."

Completed and given at Paris in the house of his magnificence Lord Arnaud de Corbie, knight, chancellor of France, on the fourteenth day of July, 1404 in the twelfth cycle, being present the said lord chancellor of France and the reverend fathers and lords in Christ, Lord Philip Noyon, Peter Meux, and John bishop of Arras, and even the eminent and powerful Louis de Bourbon, count of Vendôme, and the noble lord Robert de Braquemont and Lord Robert d'Amilly, knights of the chamber to the said most serene prince, the king of France, as witnesses to the premises named.

I, John de Sanctis, of the diocese of Beauvais, notary public by apostolic and imperial authority, notary and secretary to the aforesaid and our lord king of France, was present while each and every of the premises as it was brought forward, discussed, and agreed upon by the above-named lords ambassadors, together with the above-mentioned witnesses. I saw and heard them made at the request and with the consent of the same lords ambassadors, as in this present public instrument above, drawn up and under the same form of words duplicated; which I have written and caused to be engrossed by another, being myself occupied with many other negotiations, an examination being made by me, together with the notary public undermentioned of the original letters of commission above inserted, the same being published with this present public instrument, I therefore have subscribed myself and placed my accustomed sign.

And I, Benedict Comme, clerk of the diocese of St. Asaph, notary public by apostolic authority, was present while each and every of the premises as thus set forth, were discussed and completed by the said lords ambassadors, together with the eminent lords witnessing and the venerable notary aforesaid, and I saw and heard them thus made; and I have caused this present public instrument to be faithfully written by another, as I was occupied in another manner, and with the consent of the same lords ambassadors duplicated. I have signed with my sign and name, as is customary, being asked and required in faith and testimony of all the premises."

We truly ratify and confirm as far as in us lies the premises containing the league and covenant made, established, and accepted on our part by your ambassadors.

In testimony whereof we cause these to be made our letters patent. Given in our castle of Llanbadarn on the twelfth day of January, A.D. 1405, and the sixth of our rule.

47. *Tripartite Indenture*   **Notes: pp. 341–42**

In this year the Earl of Northumberland made a league and confederation and friendship with Owain Glyndŵr and Edmund Mortimer, son of Edmund earl of March, in certain articles of the following form and tenor:

In the first place that these lords — Owain, the Earl, and Edmund — shall henceforth be joined to one another, confederate, united, and bound by the bond of a true federation and true friendship, and certain and good union. And furthermore that

commodum alio volet et prosequetur, ac etiam procurabit, dampnaque et gravamina quæ ad unius ipsorum notitiam devenerit, per quoscumque alicui ipsorum
inferenda, impedient bona fide. Quilibet quoque ipsorum apud alium aget et faciet
10   ea omnia et singula quæ per bonos, veros, et fidos amicos, bonis, veris, et fidis
amicis agi et fieri debent et pertinent, fraude et dolo cessantibus quibuscumque.
Item, si et quotiens aliquis ipsorum dominorum sciverit vel cognoverit aliquid gravaminis sive dampni procurari sive ymaginari per quoscumque contra alium, ipse
aliis, quam citius commode fieri poterit, ea significabit, et ipsos de et super hoc ad-
15   juvabit, ut adversus malicias hujusmodi, prout ei visum fuerit, sibi valeat providere.
Solliciti quoque erunt quilibet ipsorum dominorum impedire dampna et gravamina
prædicta bona fide. Item, quilibet ipsorum dominorum in tempore necessitatis,
prout decet, juxta posse, alium adjuvabit. Item, si disponente Deo apparent præfatis
Dominis ex processu temporis, quod ipsi sunt eædem personæ de quibus Propheta
20   loquitur, inter quos regimen Britanniæ Majoris dividi debeat et partiri, tunc ipsi
laborabunt et quilibet ipsorum laborabit, juxta posse, quod id ad effectum effica-
citer perducatur.

Quilibet quoque ipsorum contentus erit portione regni prædicti sibi ut infra
scribitur limitata, absque ulteriori exactione seu superioritate quacunque. Ymmo
25   quilibet ipsorum in portione hujusmodi sibi limitata æquali libertate gaudebit. Item,
inter eosdem Dominos unanimiter conventum et concordatum existit, quod præfatus Owinus et hæredes sui habeant totam Cambriam sive Walliam, sub finibus,
limitibus, et bundis infrascriptis, a Leogrea, quæ vulgariter Angliam nuncupatur,
divisam; viz. a mari Sabrino sicut flumen Sabrinum ducit de mari, descendendo
30   usque ad Borialem Portam civitatis Wigorniæ; et a porta illa directe usque ad ar-
bores fraxineas in lingua Cambriensi sive Wallensi Onnene Margion vulgariter
nuncupatas, quæ in alta via de Brigenorth ad Kynvar ducente crescunt; deinde
directe per altam viam, quæ vetus sive antiqua via vulgariter nuncupatur, usque ad
caput sive ortum fluminis de Trent; deinde directe usque ad caput sive ad ortum
35   fluminis Meuse vulgariter nuncupati; deinde, sicut illud flumen ad mare ducit, descendendo infra fines, limites, et bundas suprascriptas. Et præfatus Comes North-
umbriæ habeat sibi et hæredibus suis comitatus infrascriptas; viz. Northumbr.,
Westmorland., Lancast., Ebor., Lincolniam, Notyngam, Derb., Stafford., Leycestr.,
Northampton, Warwic., et Norffolch. Et dominus Edmundus habeat totum residu-
40   um tocius Angliæ integre sibi et successoribus suis.

Item, quod pugna, riota, seu discordia inter duos dominorum ipsorum — quod
absit — oriatur, tunc tertius ipsorum dominorum, convocato ad se bono et fideli
consilio, discordiam, riotam, seu pugnam hujusmodi debite reformabit; cujus laudo
sive sententiæ discordante hujusmodi obedire tenebuntur. Fideles quoque erunt ad
45   defendendum regnum contra omnes homines, salvo juramento ex parte præfati
domini Owini illustrissimo principi, Domino Karolo, Dei gratia Francorum regi, in
ligea et confederatione inter ipsos initis et factis præstito.

Et ut prædicta, omnia et singula, bene et fideliter observentur, ipsi domini —
Owinus, Comes, et Edmundus, ad sacrum corpus dominicum quod perseverant jam
50   contemplans et ad sancta Dei Evangelia per eosdem corporaliter tacta — jurarunt
præmissa, omnia et singula, sicut posse eorum, inviolabiliter observare, et sigilla sua
alternatim præsentibus in testimonium apponi fecerunt.

each of these lords shall will and pursue, and also procure, the honor and advantage of one another, and they shall in good faith prevent any losses and distresses that shall come to the knowledge of any of them, by anyone whatsoever, intended to be inflicted on any of them. Each of them also shall act and do with one another each and all of those things that ought to be observed and done by good, true, and loyal friends to good, true, and loyal friends, laying aside all fraud and deceit. Also, if and whenever any of these lords shall know or learn of any loss or damage brought about or intended by anyone against another of them, he shall signify it to the others as quickly as possible, and he will help them in this matter, in order that against malice of this kind each might take such measures as he is able to provide. Each of these lords shall also take care to prevent damage and injuries to each other in good faith. Also, each of these lords shall in time of need help each other, as is fitting, as they are able. Also, if by God's dispensation it should appear to these lords in process of time that they are the same persons of whom the Prophet speaks, between whom the government of Great Britain ought to be divided and partitioned, then they, each alone and together, shall labor to their utmost so that it may be brought about effectually.

Each of these shall also be content with the portion of the kingdom aforesaid, assigned as described below, without further charge or superiority among them of any kind. In fact, each of them in the portion assigned to him shall enjoy equal liberty. As such, between these lords it is unanimously covenanted and agreed that the aforementioned Owain and his heirs shall have the whole of Cambria or Wales, within the borders, limits, and boundaries underwritten, divided from Loegria, which is commonly called England; namely, from the Severn coast where the River Severn leads from the sea, going down to the North Gate of the city of Worcester; and from that gate directly to the ash trees commonly called Onnenau Meigion in the Cambrian or Welsh language, which grow on the high road from Bridgnorth to Kinver; thence directly by the high road, which commonly is called the old or ancient way, as far as the head or source of the River Trent; thence directly to the head or source of the river commonly called the Mersey; and thence, as that river leads to the sea, going down within the borders, limits, and bounds written above. And the aforesaid Earl of Northumberland shall have to himself and to his heirs the counties written below; namely, Northumberland, Westmorland, Lancashire, Yorkshire, Lincolnshire, Nottinghamshire, Derbyshire, Staffordshire, Leicestershire, Northamptonshire, Warwickshire, and Norfolk. And the lord Edmund shall have the whole of the remainder of England entirely to himself and his successors.

Also, should any battle, riot, or discord arise between two of these lords — God forbid it — then the third of these lords, calling to himself good and faithful counsel, shall duly rectify such discord, riot, and battle; his commendation or condemnation of such a dispute they shall be bound to obey. Faithful they shall also be to defend the kingdom against all men; excepting only the oath on the part of the aforesaid lord Owain given to the most illustrious prince, Lord Charles, by the Grace of God king of the French, in the league and covenant between them begun and executed.

And in order that the aforesaid things, each and all, be well and faithfully observed, these lords — Owain, the Earl, and Edmund, now continually contemplating the sacred body of the Lord and touching the Holy Gospels of God — have sworn to observe inviolably the premises all and each to their utmost and have caused their seals to be mutually affixed hereto.

48. PRINCE HENRY, *BATTLE OF GROSMONT*   **Anglo-Norman**
                                                                            11 March 1405

Moun tresredoute et tressoverein seigneur et piere,

Le plus humblement que en moun cuer je scey penser me recomande a vostre roiale majestee humblement requerant vostre graciouse benisoun. Moun tresredoute et tressoverein seigneur et piere je supplie vraiement que Dieu monstre graciousement pour vous soun miracle en toutes parties.

Loez soit il en toutes ses oevres. Car Mescredy le xi. jour de cest present moys de Mars voz rebelx des parties de Glomorgan, Morgannok, Uske, Netherwent, et Overwent feurent assemblez a la nombre de oyt mil gentz par leure aconte, demesne et senalerent le dit Mescredy par matyn et arderent part de vostre ville de Grosmont dedeinz vostre seigneurie de Monmouth. Et jenvoia tantost hors moun treschier cousin, le Sire de Talbot, et moun petit meigne de moun hostel et a eux assemblerent voz foialx et vaillans chivalers William Neuport et Johan Greindre. Lesqueux ne feurent qun trespetit pouoir en tous, mes il est bien voirs que la victoire nest pas en la multitude de poeple, et ce feut bien monstre illoeques: mes en la puissance de Dieu et illoeques par laide de la benoite Trinitee voz gens avoient le champs et vainquerent tous les ditz rebelx et occirent de eux par loial aconte en le champs a leure revenue de la chace aucuns dient viiic et aucuns dient mil sur peine de lour vie. Nientmeins soit il lun ou lautre en tiel aconte je ne vuille pas contendre, et pour vous enformer pleinement de tout cest fait je vous envoie vne homme de credence, en ce cas moun loial serviteur le portour de cestes, qui feut a le fait et fist tresagreablement soun devoir sicome il fait a tout temps. Et tiels amendes Dieu vous a ordenne pour larsure de quatre maisons de vostre subdites ville. Et prisoners ne fuerent pris, forsque un qui feu un grant chiefteyn entre eulx, luy quel je vous voudroie avoir envoie mes il ne poet chivacher uncore a soun aise.

Et touchant la gouvernance quele je me propose affaire apres cestes, plese a vostre hautesse adjouster ferme credence a le portour de cestes en ce quil monstrera a mesme vostre hautesse de ma part. Et pri a Dieu quil vous sauve tousdys en joie et honneur et moy doynt pour vous solacer en haste ovec autres bonnes nouvelles.

Escrit a Hereford le dit Mescredy deinz nuyt.

49. JOHN STANLEY, *HARLECH PARLIAMENT*   **Anglo-Norman**
                                                                            30 July 1405

Tresexcellent, trespuissant, et tresredoute Seigneur liege,

Je me recomant a vostre roial Mageste en tanque je say ou ose, vous esmerciant si humblement et en tanque je suffice, de voz honourables lettres, a moy ja tarde depar vostre dite Mageste envoiez. Par les nouvelles des queux toutz voz lieges ces parties et moy sumes graundement comfortez, et voz rebelx ces Marches esbahiez, c'est assavoir, si bien de vostre honourable et hastive venue vers ces ditz Marches, come de vostre gracious esploit en lez parties de Northe, comme en voz ditz lettres appiert pluis au plein.

48. PRINCE HENRY, *BATTLE OF GROSMONT*   Notes: pp. 342–44

My most dread and most sovereign lord and father,

I recommend myself to your royal majesty in the most humble way I know in my heart, humbly seeking your gracious blessing. My most dread and most sovereign lord and father, I plead honestly that God graciously shows you his wonders in all directions.

Praised be he in all his works. For on Wednesday the 11th day of this present month of March your rebels of the parts of Glamorgan, Morgannwg, Usk, Netherwent, and Overwent assembled to the number of eight thousand men by their own account, and went on that said Wednesday morning and burned part of your town of Grosmont within your lordship of Monmouth. And I immediately sent out my most dear cousin, the Lord Talbot, and a small company of my household and with them assembled your faithful and valiant knights, William Newport and John Greyndour. They were only a very small force in all, but it is very true that victory is not in the numbers of men, and this was well shown there: in the power of God and by the aid of the blessed Trinity your men won the field and vanquished all the said rebels and killed by reliable account on the battlefield at their return from pursuit, some say 800 and some 1000, on pain of their life. Nevertheless I would not wish to contend whether it be one or the other in such an account, and in order to inform you fully of all that was done I send you a trusty messenger, in this case my loyal servant the bearer of these letters, who was at the battle and did his duty very creditably as he does at all times. And such amends God has ordained for you for the burning of four houses of your above-named town. And no prisoners were taken, apart from one who was a great lord among them, whom I would have wished to send but he cannot yet ride comfortably.

And touching the governance which I propose to make after this, may it please your highness to give firm credence to the bearer of these in what he will show to your same highness on my behalf. And pray God that he will keep you always in joy and honor and grant me to comfort you soon with more good news.

Written at Hereford on the said Wednesday at night.

49. JOHN STANLEY, *HARLECH PARLIAMENT*   Notes: pp. 344–45

Most excellent, most mighty, and most dread liege lord,

I commend myself to your royal majesty as far as I know how or dare, thanking you as humbly and as far as I can, for your honorable letters, recently sent by your said majesty to me. All your lieges in these parts and I are greatly comforted by the news contained in them, and your rebels in these Marches are frightened, that is to say both on account of your honorable and speedy coming to these said Marches, and for your gracious success in Northern parts, as appears more fully in your said letters.

Quelles lettres moy viendront le darrein semaigne, sicome je gisoie malade en
10   lez accesses en moun maisoun a Lathum. Et en mesme le jour, sicome fortune le
voilloit, qu'un David Whitmore et Yevan ap Meredithe, deux de les pluis suffisantz
persones de le Countee de Flynt, y furent venuz de parler a moy de lour governance, estat, et lez nouvelles de Gales, c'est a dire, coment le dit Countee est enqore
en boun pees, attendant et expectant toutz foitz le gracious socour, comfort, et
15   venue as ditz Marches de vous, tresredoute Seigneur; et voillant d'estre toutdis voz
humbles et foialx lieges et subgetz, sitost come ils purront estre socorez et salvement
gardez del malice de voz autres rebelx Galoies illeoques eux enviroun par mesme
vostre graciouse et hastive venue as Marches sus ditz. Et auxi ils m'ont dit coment
Owene de Glendoredee ad somone une parlement de present, a teigner a Harde-
20   laghe, lou serront quatres des pluis suffisantz persones de checune Comote parmy
tout Gales, soubz sa obbeisance esteantz.

Et auxi, tresredoute Seigneur, lez ditz David et Yevan m'ount dit, q'en taunt q'ils
puissent savoir a celle temps, que le dit Owen, meis q'il poet estre seure a soun dit
Parlement d'avoir trop fort poveir et graunde eide hors de Fraunce, il soy purpose
25   d'envoier a vous, trespuissant Seigneur, apres celle soun Parlement avantdit, pour une
treite; et mesmes lez David et Yevan sont alez au dit Parlement pour ent savoir tout
le purpos et esploit d'icelle, et de moy reencontrer al Countee a tenir le Marsdy
proschein en Cestre, pour moy ent certifier tout la verite et purpos de dit Parlement.

Sour qoy, tresredoute Seigneur, pleise a vostre Mageste avandite de moy ren-
30   voier voz graciouses pleisers par voz honorables lettres ove le portour de cestes; si
j'envoiera a vostre Hautesse le purpos du dit treite si ascun tiel moy viendra, ove les
autres novelles du dit Parlement si plesir vous soit, et que vous pleist que je ferra,
si bien touchant le dit Countee de Flynt, et toutz autres Marches icy environ, some
toutz voz autres pleisirs icy accomplier ces parties tanque, ove les counfortables
35   novelles que vous sont sourvenuz celles parties, si pleisir soit a vostre Hautesse
susdite, tanque vostre venue a ces ditz Marches.

Que Luy tout-puissant envoie en hast, a vostre haut honour demesne! Et vous
ottroie graciouse vie a treslong durer, en toutz honours, joies, et prosperites, ove
la sovereine victorie de toutz voz ennemys, et gracious accomplicement de voz
40   honourables desirs.

Escrite al Abbeie de Valleroial, le xxx. jour de Juyllet.

50. HENRY IV, *RESISTING THE FRENCH INVASION*   **Latin**
                                                                  7 August 1405

Rex vicecomiti Herefordiae, salutem.

Quia ad nostrum jam noviter pervenit intellectum quòd dominus de Hugevyle
et plures alii inimici nostri Franciae, in portu de Milford, ad rebelles nostros Wallenses pro posse suo fortificandum, et cum certa classe navium applicuerunt, et cum
5   eisdem rebellibus nostris regnum nostrum Angliae et Marchias Walliae, ad mala
quae poterunt nobis et fidelibus ligeis nostris regni et marchiarum praedictorum
inferendum, hostiliter ingredi intendunt, nos, malitiae ipsorum inimicorum nostrorum (Gratiam favente divinam) resistere, ac pro salvatione et defensione regni
et marchiarum praedictorum ac fidelium ligeorum nostrorum eorumdem ordinare

Those letters reached me last week as I was lying ill of the ague at my house at Lathom. And on the same day as luck would have it, one David Whitmore and Ieuan ap Maredudd, two of the most influential people in the county of Flint, came there to talk to me about their governance, their condition, and the news from Wales, that is to say, how that the said county is still well at peace, always expecting and awaiting the gracious aid, comfort, and arrival in the said Marches of you, most dread lord; and willing to be at all times your humble and loyal lieges and subjects, as soon as they can be helped and safely protected from the wickedness of your other Welsh rebels in those parts around them by your gracious and speedy arrival in the above named Marches. And they have also told me how Owain Glyndŵr has now summoned a parliament to be held at Harlech, where there will be four of the most influential persons from each of the commotes throughout all Wales which are under his sway.

Also, most dread lord, the said David and Ieuan have informed me that as far as they have been able to gather up to now, the said Owain proposes to send to you, most mighty lord, for a treaty, after this his above named parliament, provided he can be assured at his said parliament of having a very great force and considerable support from France. The same David and Ieuan have gone to the said parliament to find out all its aims and results, and will meet me again at the county court to be held next Tuesday in Chester, to inform me of the truth of it and the purpose of the said parliament.

Most dread lord, may it please your aforesaid majesty to send me your gracious pleasure concerning this by your honorable letters, with the bearer of these; so I shall send to your highness the aim of the said treaty, if anything of the kind shall reach me, with other news of the said parliament, if it please you. And what is your pleasure that I should also do concerning the said county of Flint and all the other Marches around it, to accomplish all your other wishes for these parts up to now, together with the comforting news that has come to you from these parts, if it please your above named highness, until your coming to these said Marches.

May He who is Almighty send you quickly, to your own high honor. And may He grant you a gracious and very long life to remain in all honors, joy, and prosperity, with sovereign victory over all your enemies, and gracious fulfilment of your honorable wishes.

Written at the abbey of Vale Royal on the 30th day of July.

50. HENRY IV, *RESISTING THE FRENCH INVASION* Notes: pp. 345–46

The king to the sheriff of Hereford, greetings.

Because we have just recently received the information that the lord of Hugueville and others of our French enemy sailed with a fleet of ships into the port of Milford to strengthen those in Wales rebelling against us, and since these rebels intend to enter into our kingdom of England and the Welsh Marches in a hostile matter, to do what evil they can upon us and our faithful lieges of the kingdom and said marches, we command you to resist (by the grace of God) the evil of those our enemies, ordering this for the salvation and defense of our kingdom and those marches

10   volentes, tibi praecipimus, firmiter injungentes, quòd statim, visis praesentibus, in
      singulis civitatibus, burgis, et villis mercatoriis, et aliis locis, infra ballivam tuam, tàm
      infra libertates, quàm extra, ubi meliùs expedire videris, ex parte nostra, publicè pro-
      clamari facias, quòd omnes et singuli milites, armigeri, valetti, et alii homines defens-
      abiles, de dicta balliva tua, super fide et ligeantia suis, ac sub forisfactura omnium
15   quae nobis forisfacere poterunt, se parent, arraient, et armis muniant (videlicet) qui-
      libet eorum juxta statûs sui exigentiam, ipsique, sic parati, arraiati, et muniti, versus
      civitatem nostram Herefordiae cum omni festinatione se trahant, properent, et festi-
      nent, nobiscum, ad malitiam et proterviam dictorum inimicorum nostrorum (Deo
      dante) reprimendum et viriliter resistendum, profecturi. Et hoc, sicut nos, et honorem
20   nostrum, ac salvationem et defensionem regni et marchiarum praedictorum, et lige-
      orum nostrorum eorumdem, diligis, nullatenus omittas.
          Teste rege apud Castrum de Pountfreyt, vij. die Augusti. Per ipsum regem et
      concilium.
          Consimilia brevia diriguntur vicecomitibus subscriptis etc.

51. OWAIN GLYNDŴR, *PENNAL LETTER I* Latin
31 March 1406

    Serenissimo et illustrissimo principi domino Karolo, Dei gracia, Francorum
regi,
    Serenissime princeps, humili recommendacione premissa scire dignemini quod
nacio mea per plures annos elapsos per rabiem barbarorum Saxonum suppeditata
5   fuit; vnde ex quo ipsi regimen habebant licet de facto super nos oportuit cum eis
ambulare. Sed nunc, serenissime princeps, ex innata vobis bonitate, me et subditos
meos ad recognoscendum verum Christi vicarium luculenter et gratiose multipliciter informastis. De qua quidem informacione vestre excellencie regracior toto
corde; et quia prout ex huiusmodi informacione intellexi, dominus Benedictus,
10   summus pontifex, omnibus viis possibilibus offert se ad vnionem in ecclesia Dei faciendam, confidens eciam in iure eiusdem et vobiscum, quantum michi est possibile
concordare intendens, ipsum pro vero Christi vicario pro me et subditis meis per
litteras meas patentes hac vice maiestati vestre per latorem presencium presentan-
das recognosco. Et quia, excellentissime princeps, rabie barbarica, vt prefertur, hic
15   regnante, ecclesia Menevensis metropolitica violenter ecclesie Cantuarensi obedire
coacta fuit et in subiectione huiusmodi adhuc de facto remanet et alia quamplura
in convenientia per huiusmodi barbaros ecclesie Wallie illata extiterunt que pro
maiori parte in litteris meis patentibus de quibus prefertur plenius sunt inserta,
super quorum expedicione penes dominum summum pontificem habenda mages-
20   tatem vestram actencius deprecor et exoro, vt sicut nos a tenebris in lucem erigere
dignati estis, similiter violenciam et oppressionem ecclesie et subditorum meorum
extirpare et aufferre, prout bene potestis, velitis. Et vestram excellentissimam magestatem in prosperitate votiua diu conseruet Filius Virginis gloriose.
    Scriptum apud Pennal, vltimo die marcii.

and our faithful lieges, firmly enjoining you that, immediately after you have seen this, you publically proclaim in each of the cities, towns, markets, and other places within your bailiwick, both within and without your liberties, wherever it seems most expedient, that each and every knight, esquire, yeoman, and militiaman from your bailiwick, on their faith and allegiance, and on pain of forfeiting everything that they might forfeit to us, prepare, array and arm themselves with whatever is required of their status, that they, thus ready, arrayed and armed, might bring themselves, hurrying and hastening with all due speed to our city of Hereford, and with us to set out to reprimand and strongly resist (God willing) the evil and arrogance of our enemies. And this for failing to appear: may you be bound, as we are upon our honor, to the salvation and defense of the kingdom and the aforementioned marches, and these our lieges.

Witnessed by the king at Pontefract Castle, 7 August. For the king and council. Similar letters were directed to the sheriffs listed below, etc.

51. Owain Glyndŵr, *Pennal Letter I*   Notes: p. 347

To the most serene and most illustrious prince, Lord Charles, by the grace of God, king of France,

Most serene prince, you have deemed it worthy on the humble recommendation sent, to learn how my nation, for many years now elapsed, has been oppressed by the fury of the barbarous Saxons; whence because they had the government over us, and indeed, on account of that fact itself, it seemed reasonable with them to trample upon us. But now, most serene prince you have in many ways, from your innate goodness, informed me and my subjects very clearly and graciously concerning the recognition of the true Vicar of Christ. I, in truth, rejoice with a full heart on account of that information of your excellency, and because, inasmuch from this information, I understood that the lord Benedict, the supreme pontifex, intends to work for the promotion of a union in the church of God with all his possible strength. Confident indeed in his right, and intending to agree with you as far as is possible for me, I recognize him as the true Vicar of Christ, on my own behalf, and on behalf of my subjects by these letters patent, foreseeing them by the bearer of their communications in your majesty's presence. And because, most excellent prince, the metropolitan church of St. Davids was, as it appears, violently compelled by the barbarous fury of those reigning in this country, to obey the church of Canterbury, and de facto still remains in this subjection. Many other disabilities are known to have been suffered by the church of Wales through these barbarians, which for the greater part are set forth fully in the letters patent accompanying. I pray and sincerely beseech your majesty to have these letters sent to my lord, the supreme pontifex, that as you deemed worthy to raise us out of darkness into light, similarly you will wish to extirpate and remove violence and oppression from the church and from my subjects, as you are well able to. And may the Son of the Glorious Virgin long preserve your majesty in the promised prosperity.

Dated at Pennal the last day of March.

52. OWAIN GLYNDŴR, *PENNAL LETTER II*   **Latin**
                                                                31 March 1406

Illustrissimo principi domino Karolo Dei gracia Francorum regi, Owynus eadem gracia princeps Wallie, reverencias tanto principi debitas cum honore. Noverit excellencia vestra nos articulos infrascriptos ex parte vestra per fratrem Hugonem Eddouyer, ordinis predicatorum et Mauricium Kery, familiares et nun-
5   cios nostros nobis viijo die marcii anno a Nativitate Domini millesimo quadringen-tesimo sexto presentatos recipisse formam continentes infrascriptam et tenorem:

Et primo premissa cordiali salutacione ex parte domini nostri regis et presen-tatis ejus litteris exponent dicto domino principi qualiter dominus noster rex mul-tum desiderat scire bonum statum suum et felices successus in negociis suis, rogat-
10 que eum ut quociens se facultas offeret de hoc velit sibi scribere quoniam recipiet magnam complacentiam; et demum informabit eum de bono statu dicti domini regis, regine et liberorum suorum ac aliorum dominorum principum regalis prosa-pie et quomodo dominus rex et alii domini regalis prosapie habent et habere pro-ponunt sinceram dilectionem et cordialem amicitiam ad dictum principem, zelantes
15 ejus honorem, statum prosperum et bonum, et de hoc dictus dominus princeps potest securissime confidere. Item exponent eidem domino principi qualiter dominus noster rex, qui sincere et caritative diligit eum, multum desiderat quod sicut sunt colligati et confederati in temporalibus quod ita essent in spiritualibus et in factis ecclesie ut unanimes in domo Domini valerent ambulare. Ideoque rogat
20 dominus rex eundem dominum principem affectuose ut velit attendere ad justiciam domini pape Benedicti tercii decimi, universalis ecclesie summi pontificis, ac ipsam agnoscere et ab omnibus subditis suis agnosci facere, et tenet dominus rex quod erit ad salutem anime sue et subditorum suorum, et securitatem ac firmitatem status sui et eorum confederationes in utilitate fidei et caritate Christi fundate erunt firmiores
25 et vallidiores. Item licet omnes fideles christiani teneantur se informare de veritate scismatis, tamen inter omnes magis tenentur principes, et quia eorum opinio potest plures trahere in errorem et maxime subditos qui se habent conformare cum opin-ione sui superiores et quia eorum eciam interest ex debito procurare totis conatibus ut tale scisma totaliter extirpitur paxque et unio in Dei ecclesia habeatur et quod
30 ille qui verus est Christi vicarrius a cunctis Christi fidelibus agnoscatur et recipiatur et ille qui est intrusus et conatur ansu nephario sanctam sedem apostolicam usur-pari expellatur et ab omnibus fidelibus abiciatur ut antichristus et ad hoc posse-thenus laborare astringuntur secundum decreta sanctorum patrum, ad quod non sine magnis sumptibus et expensis laboravit dictus dominus rex et laborat indefesse.

· · ·

52. Owain Glyndŵr, *Pennal Letter II*   Notes: pp. 347–50

To the most illustrious prince, the lord Charles, by the grace of God, king of the French, Owain by the same grace, sends the reverence due to such a prince with honor. Be it known to your excellency that we have received from you the articles following, brought to us by Hugh Eddowyer, of the Order of Predicants, and Morris Keri, our friends and envoys, on the eighth day of March, A.D. 1406, the form and tenor of which follow:

In the first place they express the cordial greeting on the part of our lord the king, and of his present letter to our said lord the prince. In this manner, our lord the king greatly desires to know of his good state and the happy issue of their negotiations. He requests Owain, that he will write as often as an opportunity offers, as he will receive great pleasure, and he will inform him, at length, concerning the good state of the said lord, the king, of the queen, their children, and of the other lords, the princes of the royal family, how my lord the king, and the other princes of the royal family have and intend to have sincere love, cordial friendship, zeal for his honor, the prosperity and well-being of the state of the said prince, and in this they said lord, the prince, can place the most secure faith.

They also explain to the same lord, the prince, how our lord, the king, who esteems him with sincerity and love, greatly desires that, as they are bound and united in temporal matters, so also will they be united in spiritual things, and they may be able to walk to the house of the Lord together. My lord, the king, also requests the same lord, the prince, that he wishes him to consider, with a favorable disposition, the rights of my lord, the pope, Benedict XIII, the supreme pontiff of the universal church, that he may himself learn and cause all his subjects to be informed. Because my lord the king, holds that it shall be to the health of his soul and of the souls of his subjects, to the security and strength of his state, and that their covenants shall be laid in a stronger and more powerful foundation in the advantage of faith and in the love of Christ. Again, even as all faithful Christians are held to keep themselves well informed concerning the truth of schisms. Princes, however, are so held even more than others, because their opinion can keep many in error, especially their subjects, who must conform with the opinion of their superiors. It is, also, even to their advantage, on account of their duty, to keep themselves informed in all things, that such a schism may be entirely removed and that the Church may have unity in God. Because he, who is the true Vicar of Christ, should be known and acknowledged by all the faithful in Christ, while he, who is an intruder, and known to have by nefarious means usurped the holy apostolic see, shall be expelled and cast aside, by all the faithful, as anti-Christ. To this purpose they should bind themselves to strive, to their utmost, according to the decrees of the holy fathers. To which purpose the said lord, the king, has striven, not without great burdens and expense, and will strive unweariedly.

. . .

35   Et subsequentur ex deliberacione consilii nostri convocari fecimus proceres de
        prosapia nostra et prelatos principatus nostri ac alios in hac parte evocandos et tan-
        dem post diligentem examinacionem et disputacionem articulorum premissorum
        et materie eorumdem per prelatos et clerum sufficienter factas, concordatum et
        conclusum existit quod nos, confidentes in jure domini Benedicti, sacrosancte
40   Romane ac universalis ecclesie summi pontifices, presertim eo quod pro pace et
        unione ecclesie prosequtus est et in dies, ut intelleximus, prosequitur, consideran-
        tesque duram servitiem, adversarii ejusdem Benedicti tunicam Christi inconsutilem
        dillacerantis ac ob sinceram dilectionem quam erga vestram excellenciam gerimus
        specialem, predictum dominum Benedictum ut verum Christi vicarium in terris a
45   nobis et subditis nostris recognoscendum fore duximus et recognoscimus per pre-
        sentes. Et quia, illustrissime princeps, infrascripti articuli statum nostram et ecclesie
        Wallie refformacionem et utilitatem notorie concernunt, vestram regiam magesta-
        tem humilime rogamus quatinus expedicionem eorumdem graciose penes prefatum
        dominum Benedictum summum pontificem promovere dignemini. Et primo si sen-
50   sure ecclesiastice contra nos et subditos nostros seu terram nostram per prefatum
        dominum Benedictum aut Clementem predecessorem suum late existant, quod ipse
        Benedictus easdem relaxet. Item quod quecumque et qualiacumque juramenta per
        nos seu quoscumque alios principatus nostri illis qui se nominaverunt Vrbanum et
        Bonifacium nuper deffunctos seu eisdem adherentibus qualitercumque prestita re-
55   laxat. Item quod confirmet et ratificet ordines collatos, titulos prelatorum, dispensa-
        cionesque et officia tabellionum ac alia quecumque in quibus periculum animarum
        aut prejudicium nobis et subditis nostris in ea parte evinire seu generari possent a
        tempore Gregorii xi. Item quod ecclesia Menevensis que a tempore sancti David
        archiepiscopi et confessoris fuit metropolitana et post obitum ejusdem successerunt
60   eidem archiepiscopi ibidem xxiiij, prout in cronicis et antiquis libris ecclesie Mene-
        vensis nomina eorumdem continentur et hic pro majori evidencia eadem exprimi
        fecimus, videlicet, Eliud, Keneu, Morwal, Menevie, Haerunen, Elwayd, Gvrnuen,
        Llevdiwyt, Gvrwyst, Gvgavn, Cledavc, Ainan, Elave, Maelyswyd, Sadernuen, Catul-
        lus, Alathvy, Nouis, Sadernuen, Diochwael, Asser, Arthuel, David secundus, et
65   Sampson, pristina statui restituatur; quequidem ecclesia metropolitana infrascriptas
        habuit et habere debet ecclesias suffraganeas, videlicet, Exoniensem, Battoniensem,
        Herefordensem, Wygorniensem, Legicestrensem, cujus sedes jam translata est ad
        ecclesias Coventrensem et Lichfeldensem, Assavensem, Bangorensem, et Landaven-
        sem; nam ingruente rabie barbarorum Saxonum qui terram Wallie eisdem usur-
70   parunt, ecclesiam Menevensem predictam suppeditarunt et eam ancillam ecclesie
        Cantuariensis de facto ordinarunt. Item quod idem dominus Benedictus provideat
        de metropolitano Menevensi ecclesie et aliis ecclesiis cathedralibus principatus nos-
        tri, prelaturis, dignitatibus et beneficiis ecclesiasticis, curatis scientibus linguam nos-
        tram dumtaxat. Item quod dominus Benedictus in corporaciones, uniones, annex-
75   iones, et appropriaciones ecclesiarum parrochialium principatus nostri, monasteriis
        et collegiis anglicorum quorumcumque auctoritate hactenus factas revocet et an-
        nullet et quod veri patroni earumdem ecclesiarum locorum ordinariis ydoneas per-
        sonas presentare valeant ad easdem seu alias conferre. Item quod dominus Bene-
        dictus concedat nobis et heredibus nostris principibus Wallie quod capella nostra
80   de cetero sit libera et gaudeat privilegiis, exempcionibus et immunitatibus quibus

Following the advice of our council, we have called together the nobles of our race, the prelates of our Principality and others called for this purpose, and, at length, after diligent examination and discussion of the foregoing articles and their contents being thoroughly made by the prelates and the clergy, it is agreed and determined that we, trusting in the rights of the lord Benedict, the holy Roman and supreme pontiff of the universal Church, especially because he sought the peace and unity of the church, and as we understood daily seeks it, considering the hard service of the adversary of the same Benedict, tearing the seamless coat of Christ, and on account of the sincere love which we specially bear towards your excellency, we have determined that the said lord Benedict shall be recognized as the true Victor of Christ in our lands, by us and our subjects, and we recognize him by these present [letters]. Whereas, most illustrious prince, the underwritten articles especially concern our state and the reformation and usefulness of the Church of Wales, we humbly pray your royal majesty that you will graciously consider it worthy to advance their object, even in the court of the said lord Benedict:

First, that all ecclesiastic censures against us, our subjects, or our land, by the aforesaid lord Benedict or Clement his predecessor, at present existing, the same shall by the said Benedict be removed. Again, that he shall confirm and ratify the orders, collations, titles of prelates, dispensations, notorial documents, and all things whatsoever, from the time of Gregory XI, from which, any danger to the souls, or prejudice to us, or our subjects may occur, or may be engendered. Again, that the Church of St. Davids shall be restored to its original dignity, which from the time of St. David, archbishop and confessor, was a metropolitan church, and after his death twenty-four archbishops succeeded him in the same place, as their names are continued in the chronicles and ancient books of the church of Menevia, and we cause these to be stated as the chief evidence, namely, Eliud, Ceneu, Morfael, Mynyw, Haerwnen, Elwaed, Gwrnwen, Llewdwyd, Gwrwyst, Gwgawn, Clydâwg, Aman, Elias, Maeslyswyd, Sadwrnwen, Cadell, Alaethwy, Novis, Sadwrnwen, Drochwel, Asser, Arthwael, David II, and Samson; and that as a metropolitan church it had an ought to have the undermentioned suffragan churches, namely, Exeter, Bath, Hereford, Worcester, Leicester, which see is now translated to the churches of Coventry and Lichfield, St. Asaph, Bangor and Llandaff. For being crushed by the fury of the barbarous Saxons, who usurped to themselves the land of Wales, they trampled upon the aforesaid church of St. Davids, and made her a handmaid to the church of Canterbury. Again, the same lord Benedict shall provide for the metropolitan church of St. Davids and the other cathedral churches of our principality, prelates, dignitaries, and beneficed clergy and curates, who know our language. Again, that the lord Benedict shall revolve and annul all incorporations, unions, annexations, appropriations of parochial churches of our principality made so far, by any authority whatsoever with English monasteries and colleges. That the true patrons of these churches shall have the power to present to the ordinaries of those places suitable persons to the same or appoint others. Again, that the said lord Benedict shall concede to use and to our heirs, the princes of Wales, that our chapels, &c., shall be free, and shall rejoice in the privileges, exemptions, and immunities

gaudebat temporibus progenitorum nostrorum principum Wallie. Item quod habe-
amus duas universitates sive studia generalia, videlicet unum in Northwallie et aliud
in Swthwallie, in civitatibus villis seu locis per ambaxiatores et nuncios nostros in
hac parte specifiendis et declarandis. Item quod dominus Benedictus contra Henri-
85   cum Lencastrie intrusorem regni Anglie et usurpatorem corone ejusdem regni et
sibi adherentes, eo quod ecclesias tam cathedrales quam conventuales et parochiales
voluntarie combusit et comburi procuravit, archiepiscopos, episcopos, prelatos,
presbyteros, religiosos tam possessionatos quam mendicantes inhumaniter sus-
pendi, decapitari et quartirizari fecit et fieri mandavit et quod scismaticus existit,
90   cruciatam concedere dignetur in forma consueta. Item quod idem dominus Benedictus concedat nobis et heridibus nostris, subditis et adherentibus nobis cujuscum-
que nacionis fuerint dumtamen fidem teneant ortodoxam, qui guerram contra prefatum intrusorem sustinemus plenam remissionem omnium peccatorum et quod
remissio hujusmodi duret guerra inter nos, heredes, et subditos nostros et prefatum
95   Henricum, heredes et subditos suos durante.

In cujus rei testimonium, has litteras nostras fieri fecimus patentes. Data apud
Pennal ultimo die macii anno a Nativitate Domini millesimo quadringentesimo
sexto et principatus nostri sexto.

53. MADOG AP GRONW GETHIN, *I AFON DYFRDWY*   **Welsh**
                                                                    1402 x 1415?

*Cowydd i Afon Ddyfyrdwy i ddiolch iddi am lifhau, a boddi llawer o'r llu Seisnig a oedd yn
pebylhaw ar i glann, a'i llesteir drosti i Faelawr (yn erbyn Ywain Glyñdwr) i ddistrywio y
wlad yn amser Mongymbry: a hyny fy yr haf heb law ond drwy wynt y dehau rhwn a yrr Lynn
Tegid i'r afon i beri iddi lifhau (ac a barhaodd y llif yn yr afon yn hir, hyd oni caffodd Ywain
5   rybydd o'r brad oedd yn ei erbyn ef).*

        Dyfrdwy fawr, ganawr gynnyrch,
        dwfr gwrdd a lvdd, Deifr a gyrch;
        dewr a chadarn i'th varnwyd:
        dwfr rhyfeldwrdd, agwrdd wyd.
5   Ban fu fwya, caetha cad,
        bygwth Saesson, a'i bygad,
        o ladd a llosgi ar lenn
        Maelawr, oleuwawr lawen,
        doethost, dan agwrdd duthiaw,
10   ar vrys, rhag bod arnam fraw,
        yn argae brwydr rhwng dwydref,
        yn gaer gron, yn gowair gref,
        yn llidiog ruthr, uthr wythi,
        yn llawn o fordwy a lli.
15   Mefyl i'r Sais a'n treisiai,
        hir i druth a hwyr i drai;
        pan ddelai, erfai aerfaeth,

in which they rejoiced in the times of our forefathers the princes of Wales. Again, that we shall have two universities or placed of general study, namely, one in North Wales and the other in South Wales, in cities, towns, or places to be hereafter decided and determined by our ambassadors and nuncios for that purpose. Again, that the lord Benedict shall brand as heretics and cause to be tortured in the usual manner, Henry of Lancaster, the intruder of the kingdom of England, and the usurper of the crown of the same kingdom, and his adherents, in that of their own free will they have burnt or have caused to be burnt so many cathedrals, convents, and parish churches; that they have savagely hung, beheaded, and quartered archbishops, bishops, prelates, priests, religious men, as madmen or beggars, or caused the same to be done. Again, that the same lord Benedict shall grant to us, our heirs, subjects, and adherents, of whatsoever nation they may be, who wage war against the aforesaid intruder and usurper, as long as they hold the orthodox faith, full remission of all our sins, and that the remission shall continue as long as the wars between us, our heirs, and our subjects, and the aforesaid Henry, his heirs, and subjects shall endure.

In testimony whereof we make these our letters patent. Given at Pennal on the thirty-first day of March, A.D. 1406, and in the sixth year of our rule.

53. MADOG AP GRONW GETHIN, *PRAISE OF THE RIVER DEE*　　　Notes: pp. 350–54

A cywydd to the River Dee to thank it for flooding and drowning many of the English host which was encamped on its bank and blocking it from crossing to Maelor (against Owain Glyndŵr) to lay waste to the country in the time of Montgomery; and that was in the summer without rain, but because of the south wind, which drives Llyn Tegid to the river to cause it to flood (and the flood continued in the river for a long time, until Owain received warning of the treachery that was against him).

Great Dyfrdwy, product of the white wave,
fierce water that hinders, that attacks the English,
you were judged brave and strong.
Water with the roar of war, you are mighty.
5　　When the threat of the Englishmen, most grievous strife,
and their host, was greatest,
of killing and burning on the borders
of Maelor, at the cheerful light of dawn
you came, in a mighty rush,
10　　swiftly, lest terror come upon us,
like a battle-embankment between two towns,
like a round fortress, well-formed, strong,
in an angry rush, terrifying streams,
full of flood and deluge.
15　　Shame to the Englishman who would oppress us,
long his deceit and slow to ebb.
When the men, splendid, battle-trained,

             y gwyr i'r cyrch, gwewyr caeth,
             mud glud glodrudd, treiddydd tref,
20   o nidr, nid ai yr un adref:
             rhai a faeddüd, glüd glodlif,
             a'r llaill a foddyd ar llif.
             Mongymbry ffo, cyn tro trai:
             maith yw'r sarn, methu'r siwrnai;
25   dibrin, ban i'th ddadebrwyd,
             o'r llynn fu'r tafarnwr llwyd.
             Da fû'r âl rhag Plant Alis
             o'th law dwys braw, nid oes bris;
             darllaw teg, dwfr dinegyn,
30   gwell rhag y drin no'r gwin gwyn.
             Gwythen o'r uchel Geli,
             gwrthiau yw d'anwydau di:
             garw distrych, llwythwrych llathrwawr,
             Aerfen bengrech felen fawr.
35   Ban glywaist vod, cydfod cam,
             bu gaeth orn, bygwth arnam,
             brochaist, dan daflu brychau
             broch rhom a'r aer, taer fu'r tau;
             llwybr disathr, treiglathr tragloyw,
40   llithr hyppynt deheuwynt hoyw.
             Cadw a wnayt, rhag hoccedau,
             swyddwyr cowir y tir tau,
             o Gaer hyd y Llynn, ar gyrch,
             Tegid, lle y delid elyrch.
45   Boddud, be rhaid, bob byddin,
             baedd rhwym drud, bydd rhom a'r drin;
             bydd i'n cadw rhag i bradwdrais,
             bydd raglaw er syddaw Sais.
             Mawr ddolau gais, drais drosgraig,
50   mammaeth llywodraeth, lle'r aig;
             mud, rhed i ddeuled ddyli:
             bydd bob pyrnhawn yn llawn lli.
                 Madog ap Gronw Gethin a'i kant (oddeutu 1404).

54. LLYWELYN AB Y MOEL, *BRWYDR WAUN GASEG*   **Welsh c.1410 x c.1416**

             Da'dd oeddem y dydd heddiw,
             deulu rhwydd, ar dâl y rhiw,
             arddyfrwys, pobl aur ddifreg,
             yn cychwyn o fryd tyn teg
5   ar odde cael, arwydd cain,
             mwya' chwedl am Owain.
             Gwneuthud, cyn pwlfryd apêl,

came to the attack, with sharp spears,
unremitting famed movement, penetrator of a town,
20   through hindrance, not one went home.
Some you beat, unremitting famed flood,
and the others you drowned in the flood.
Montgomery fleeing, before the turn of the ebb —
extensive is the destruction — the journey failing.
25   Unstinting, when you were aroused,
with drink was the holy tavern-keeper.
Choice was the ale against the Children of Alice
from your hand of weighty proof; there is no charge!
A fair brew, abundant water,
30   better against battle than white wine.
Stream from Heaven on high,
your passions are miracles;
harsh foam, bristling load of bright hue,
great yellow curly-headed Aerfen.
35   When you heard there was — false compact,
grievous blasphemy — a threat against us,
you raged, flinging the stains
of spume between us and the battle — you were fervent,
an untrodden path, a bright shining course,
40   the flowing thrust of the lively south wind.
You would protect against deceits
the true officials of your land,
on a journey from Chester to Llyn
Tegid, where swans are caught.
45   You would drown, if necessary, every army.
Fierce bound boar, be between us and the battle;
be our protection against their shattering violence;
be a deputy for sinking an Englishman.
Seek great meadows, violence over rocks,
50   foster-mother of government, place of shoals,
move, race to twice the width of a flood;
be full of flood every afternoon.
        Madog ap Gronw Gethin sang it, about 1404

54. LLYWELYN AB Y MOEL, *BATTLE OF WAUN GASEG*   Notes: pp. 354–57

We were fine today,
a ready war band, on the brow of the hill,
strong, faultless fine folk,
setting out with fair, resolute determination,
5   with the intent of getting — splendid portent —
the greatest news about Owain.
We held, before any dull-witted complaint,

              fwting cyn cyrchu'r fatel,
              dodi'n hamcan ar rannu
10   proffid o lleddid y llu;
              rhoi o bawb o ryw bybyr
              eu cred, cyn gweled y gwŷr,
              na chilyn', rhyglyddyn' glod,
              o'r maes fyth er ymosod.

15   A ni felly gwedy gwawd
              yn dadlau am enw didlawd,
              nacha', gwelem o'n hemyl
              ellwng i'n plith (chwith fu'r chwŷl)
              ar hyd gorlechwedd rhedyn
20   o feirch mwy no chanmeirch ynn,
              a chyda hwynt, pwynt apêl,
              awchus leferydd uchel.
              Simwned eurged arwgainc
              (sym brochwart ffromart o Ffrainc,
25   gên âb, yn canu tabwrdd)
              o glariwn uwch no gwn gwrdd.

              Nawd salw, anodus helynt,
              ninnau, wedi'r geiriau gynt,
              ni bu'n bryd ar hyd y rhos
30   yn yr aer unawr aros,
              na phraw ar arf, llymdarf llam,
              na phais oni ffoasam.
              Y llu a dducsem ar llid
              yno'n aml yn ein ymlid,
35   traws yr oeddynt i'n trosi,
              trosasant tros nawnant ni,
              tresor gwŷr esgor Gaer Wysg,
              trosiad geifr, trwsiad gofrwysg.
              Twrn girad, traw i'n gorwyf,
40   tost oedd ynn weled, tyst wyf,
              ar Waun Gaseg, wen gysellt,
              wewyr ein gwŷr yn y gwellt.

              Minnau, rhagorau girad,
              mawntais a gefais o'r gad,
45   cyrchu'n fuan anianol
              ceunant a mawrgant i'm ôl,
              a phawb i'm dangos yn ffo
              dan fy adnabod yno.
              Pŵl fydd ar lethr mynydd maith
50   peiswen ŵr, anhapuswaith;
              wrth hyn, dyfyn diofwy,

a discussion before engaging in battle,
declaring our purpose of sharing
10   the profit if the host was slain.
All those of eager sort gave
their oath, before seeing the men,
that they would not ever — they would deserve fame —
retreat from the field, because of an attack.

15   And as we were thus, after a song of praise,
debating about abundant fame,
behold, we could see close by us,
set loose amongst us — strange was the turn of events —
along the bracken-covered slope,
20   horses, more than a hundred of them,
and with them — grounds for complaint —
a high, piercing cry.
A splendidly advantageous harsh tune was raised
(an odious French badger-keeper leers,
25   ape's jawbone playing a tabor)
from a clarion louder than a mighty gun.

Disheartened spirit, sally with no losses,
we, for our part, after our earlier words,
had no intent, along the moorland,
30   to stay in the battle for a moment,
or to have a trial of arms — swift scattering attack —
or to use a cuirass until we fled!
The host that we had angered
was there in great numbers chasing us.
35   They were energetic in chasing us;
they chased us across nine streams,
the pick of men from Caer Wysg's fort,
a goat chase, heady in their attire.
A sorry turn of events, a blow to our pride,
40   it was painful for us to see — I am a witness —
at Waun Gaseg, unbloodied bundle,
the spears of our men in the grass.

As for me — sad bravado —
I gained an advantage from the battle,
45   making at breakneck speed
for a ravine with a great host behind me,
and all of them pointing me out fleeing,
recognizing me there.
Dull-witted, on the slope of a big mountain,
50   is a man with unstained cuirass — unfortunate event!
Because of this — summons without encounter —

delwynt, pan ei mynnwynt, mwy,
oerfel i mi o'm gwelant
a'r wen bais ar y Waun Bant!

55. LLYWELYN AB Y MOEL, *I GOED Y GRAIG LWYD*   **Welsh**
                                                                    c.1410 x c.1416

*Moliant i'r Coed y buasai'r Bardd yn ymguddio ynddo ac eraill hefyd yn Amser Owain
Glyndwr.*

Rho Duw, Goed, rhydeg ydwyd,
y Graig, Llech Ysgar, grug Llwyd!
Rhod o ddail, rhawd Wyddelig,
rhad Duw fry ar hyd dy frig!
5   Rhestrog fagadog ydwyd,
rhysfa, gwarwyfa gwŷr wyd.
Rhedynglos, diddos dyddyn,
rhyfedd oedd, yr haf, i ddyn
(eurai latai ddiletyb)
10   allel bod hebod i'm tyb.

      Dy gaerau di a gerais
dan llaw i ransymiaw Sais,
dy weuad ar dy wiail,
dy frynau, mydylau dail,
15   dy ogofau digyfyng,
dy ddiell gangell rhag yng,
dy bur osgedd, dy brysgoed
i drais a rodiais erioed.
Gwell o'r hanner no chlera
20   i ddyn a chwenychai dda
dwyn Sais a'i ddiharneisio
dan dy frig, dien dy fro.

      Fy mharch diymgel, fy mhwys,
fy mhôr wyd, fy mharadwys,
25   fy mabsant a'm gwarant gwir
a'm neuadd-dŷ a'm nodd-dir.
Fel gwaith, hyder maith, ym wyd,
am ael rhiw y'm olrhewyd;
dinam faeth, da iawn ym fu
30   dy gael i'm diogelu:
yn befrglos, diddos dudded,
yn berth glaear glynnerth gled,
yn dyno glas i danadd,
yn dir mwyn ir a main nadd,

let them return, when they wish;
I'll be damned if they see me
and my unbloodied cuirass in the hollow on the Waun!

55. LLYWELYN AB Y MOEL, *PRAISE OF THE REBELS' LAIR*   Notes: pp. 358–61

Praise of the wood the poet had been hiding in, and others also, in the time of Owain Glyndŵr.

Between me and God, you are too fair,
Coed y Graig Lwyd — Llech Ysgar — grey hillock!
Circle of leaves, a wild plenty,
the grace of God on high be upon your branches!
5   You are arrayed in close ranks;
a fortification, a playground for men are you.
A bracken bower, a cozy cottage,
it would be extraordinary, in the summer, for a man
— he would enrich with gold an undoubting love messenger —
10   to manage without you, in my opinion.

     Your fortresses I have cherished
to ransom an Englishman by stealth,
your interwoven branches,
your hills, your piles of leaves,
15   your spacious caves,
your faultless chancel to protect from trouble,
your fair form, your undergrowth
that I have always trod with force.
Better by half than minstreling
20   for a man who desired wealth,
to take an Englishman and despoil him
under your branches — you of fair surroundings.

     My pride and joy, my spouse,
you are my lord, my paradise,
25   my patron saint and my true guarantee
and my great hall and my refuge.
Like a fortress — great confidence — are you to me,
I was pursued about the brow of a hill.
Faultless nurture, it was very good for me
30   to have you to keep me safe:
a radiant bower, a cozy shelter,
a pleasant, tightly-woven, snug thicket,
a green meadow beneath,
a gentle, verdant land and hewn stones,

35   yn drwsiad y Tad dien,
        yn dywyll bebyll uwchben,
        yn ddiogel i'm gwely,
        yn annhebyg dy frig fry
        i dŷ taeog do tyweirch,
40   diwael wedy cael y ceirch!

        Digrifach, deg arofun,
        oedd i fab arab a bun
        ar hynt ar ben yr hwntian
        orwedd ymysg irwydd mân
45   a gwrando, y gawr iawndeg,
        coeth lwys dôn cathl eos deg,
        a tharfu llid a therfysg,
        a thorri dail (uthr eu dysg!),
        ac edrych, befrddrych y byd,
50   ar y sêr eres wryd.

        Eres, bychan anianawl,
        ydoedd i mi oed dydd mawl!
        A gwiw olwg y gwelwn
        gaerau'r rhiw o'r goror hwn,
55   lle nid rhaid, llonaid rhedyn,
        llechu'r dydd, lle dichwerw dyn,
        lle dirffyrdd, lle diarffordd,
        lle'r nos ni thramwy llu'r Nordd.
        Llydan sercl uwch y berclwyd,
60   Llundain gwerin Owain wyd,
        llwyn hirwydd yn llawn herwyr,
        lled no maes, lleuad na mŷr.
        Llwyr fendith i blith dy blaid,
        llawn dâl, llu Owain delaid.
65   Llwyr ystad, lloer ystodiau,
        llwyddid Duw'r llueiddiaid tau!

56. *ROLLS OF PARLIAMENT, 1407*   **Anglo-Norman**
                                                       14 November 1407

        17. Item, lundy le xiiijme. jour de Novembre, les communes viendrent devaunt
le roy et les seignurs en parlement, et illeosqes le dit parlour monstra et rehercea
plusours grandes meschiefs q'ore tarde avoient avenuz a roialme, et en especiale
pur defaute de la saufegarde du meer, sibien par tuer des gentz, come par prise des
5   gentz, et des merchandises qe s'amonte as grandes sommes. Et auxint touchant la
rebellion de Gales, coment ils ne sont ascunement tenuz ne obligez pur celles
guerres sustenir, mais q'ils soyent dischargient de cell jour enavaunt. Et coment,
pur defaute de les bonnes ordinances et estatuitz faitz devaunt ces heures, de ce qe

35   a garment from the comely Father,
        a dark canopy overhead,
        a safe place for my bed,
        your fine branches on high unlike
        the sod roof of a churl's house,
40   splendid after having oat bread!

            More pleasant — fair intent —
        was it for a cheerful lad and a maiden,
        straightway after wandering about,
        to rest among the green saplings
45   and listen — beautiful cry —
        to the excellent fine tune of a handsome nightingale's song,
        and banish anger and commotion,
        and break leaves — tremendous their learning! —
        and look — brilliant form of the world —
50   at the marvelous span of stars.

            Strange, remarkably short,
        for me was a tryst on a day of praise!
        And a fitting sight did I see
        the hillside's forts from this quarter,
55   where there is no need — abundance of bracken —
        to lie hidden all day, a sweet place for a man,
        a place of difficult paths, an inaccessible place,
        a place the host of the North does not traverse by night.
        Broad circle of the firmament above the perch,
60   you are the London of Owain's men,
        grove of tall trees full of outlaws,
        broader than meadow, moon, or seas.
        A complete blessing be on your party,
        full payment, Owain's fair host.
65   A complete estate, for months,
        may God prosper your soldiers!

56. *ROLLS OF PARLIAMENT, 1407*   **Notes: p. 361**

17. Request of the commons. Also, on Monday 14 November, the commons came before the king and the lords in parliament, where their speaker set out and rehearsed a number of great wrongs which had occurred in the kingdom, most notably through failure to keep safe the seas, as well as killing of people, and seizures of people and of merchandise amounting to great sums. Also, concerning the rebellion in Wales, he said that they were not in any way obliged or bound to support these wars, but should in future be discharged from doing so. Also, he said that because various good ordinances and statutes previously made (namely that every

chescun seignur et autres aiantz possessions sur les marches serroient continuele-
ment receantz et demurrantz sur icelles, pur resistre la malice de tieulx rebealx, ne
sount pas duement executz, mesmes les Galoises sont devenuz pluis rebealx qe ne
furent par devaunt, a grant damage et disease de tout le roialme d'Engleterre.
Paront pria le dit parlour, el noun des ditz communes, a mesme nostre seignur le
roy, qe luy plese charger les ditz seignurs et autres d'ordeigner pur la garde d'icelles
marches a lour peril demesne: et qe les ditz communes ent soient outrement dis-
chargiez. Purveux toutesfoitz, qe nulle damage ne disheritesoun aviegne ascunement
par ceste ordinance a les heirs esteantz deinz age, et en la garde nostre seignur le
roy, et de les autres seignurs. A quoy feust responduz de par nostre seignur le roy,
coment il avoit bien entenduz lour request, et surce il vorroit estre avisez ovesqe les
seignurs, et ent faire ce qe serroit pur le meillour, par l'aide de Dieu.

. . .

Rebelles de Gales.
    41. Item, de ceo qe les rebelx de Gales, et autres larouns, veignont en le counte
suisdit, et prendront des lieges demurantz deins le dit counte, sibien par jour come
par noet, et eux amesnent hors du dit counte as diverses parties de Gales adjoig-
nantz mesme le counte, et la eux deteignent en prison tanqe ils ount fait fyn et
raunceon ove les ditz rebelles et larouns a lour volunte, ou autrement tueront les
ditz lieges ensi prisez; et ensi ils fount larcine et robberie comunement, sibien des
biens et chateux, come de prise des ditz lieges, et les amesnent hors du dit counte.
Et nonobstant qe mainteignant apres tielx felonies sount faitz deinz le dit counte,
et gentz de mesme le countee pursuent les larouns ove hu et cri hors du dit counte
as parties marchees, nulle Galoys demurrant deinz aucune seignurie marchee ne
voet socurer n'aider les ditz lieges pur prendre mesmes les larouns, mez pluistost
manacent les ditz lieges de eux tuer, s'il fount ascune suyte pluis. Et si lettres soient
envoiez par le viscount du dit counte as officers et ministers des lieux ou les ditz
rebelles et larons sount recettez et herbergez, et teignent en prisone les ditz lieges,
nulle livere de mesmes les prisoners est fait, mez les officers doignent a tieux
larouns foie en manere de sauf condit: et ensi succurent les larons, nonobstant qe
les officers et ministres savoient bien qe les larons ount en garde et en prisone les
ditz lieges, et auxi biens et chateux prisez par larcine et robberie. Dont ils prient
remedie en cest present parlement.

Responsio. Le roy voet, qe les seignurs marchees en lour presence compellent et
facent lour officers d'estre aidantz as parties grevez, d'avoir restitucione solonc la
contenue de cest peticione.

. . .

    51. Item, priount les communes pur les poveres burgeis et comunes de la ville
de Salop': qe come la dit ville et les enhabitantz en ycelle ount estee graundement
empoverez et anientesez par diverses causes, pointz, et articles q'ensuent. En
primes, qe la demy parte du dit ville fuist ore tarde par fue de fortune ars, ove toutz

lord or other person who had possessions in the marches ought continually to remain and reside there in order to resist the malice of those rebels), had not been properly enforced, the aforesaid Welsh had grown even more rebellious than before, to the great damage and injury of the whole realm of England. And the said speaker prayed our lord the king, therefore, in the name of the aforesaid commons, that it might please him to charge the aforesaid lords and others to make provision for the keeping of these marches at their own peril, and that the said commons be entirely discharged from this obligation; provided always that as a result of any such ordinance, no damage or disinheritance should in any way befall heirs who were under age and in the wardship of the king or of other lords. To which reply was given on behalf of our lord the king that he fully understood their request, and that he wished to consult with the lords on this subject before deciding, with the help of God, what to do for the best.

· · ·

[Rebels of Wales in the county of Hereford].

41. Rebels of Wales. Also, whereas rebels from Wales and other thieves come into the aforesaid county and seize the lieges residing in the said county, both by day and by night, and remove them from the said county to various parts of Wales adjoining the same county, and detain them in prison there until such time as they make fine or ransom with the said rebels and thieves at their will, failing which they kill those lieges whom they have seized; and since, moreover, they habitually commit larceny and robbery not only of goods and chattels but also as a result of their seizure of the said lieges, and take them out of the county; and yet (notwithstanding the fact that, straight after such felonies are committed in the county, the people of the same county pursue the thieves with hue and cry beyond the said county into parts of the march), none of the Welshmen residing in any of the lordships of the march tries to help or assist the said lieges to apprehend these thieves, but instead they threaten to kill the said lieges if they persist any further in their pursuit; and if letters are sent by the sheriff of the said county to the officers and ministers of the areas where the aforesaid rebels and thieves are received and harboured, and where they hold the said lieges in prison, nevertheless these prisoners are not released, but instead the officers entrust these thieves with safe-conducts, thus assisting the thieves, despite the fact that the officers and ministers are well aware that the thieves have the said lieges in their keeping and in prison, and that they also have goods and chattels seized by larceny and robbery. Whereof they pray for a remedy in this present parliament.

Answer. The king wills that the marcher lords compel and force their officers, in their presence, to assist the aggrieved parties, so that they shall have redress according to the contents of this petition.

· · ·

51. On behalf of the town of Shrewsbury. Also, the request of the commons on behalf of the poor burgesses and commons of the town of Shrewsbury: whereas the town and its inhabitants have been greatly impoverished and ruined in the following ways and by the following means. Firstly, half of the said town was recently,

les biens des burgeys en ycelle partie esteantz, a graund anientisment de tout la ville. Item, al parlement tenuz a Salop' en temps le Roy Richard second l'an de son
50   regne .xxi., tout la armure et la defens des ditz burgeys furont prises, et as diverses persones donez, issint perduz, a damage des ditz burgeys de ccc marcz et outre. Item, l'ou le dit ville fuist principalment encresce par merchaundise, servoise, et autere vitaill, les berbys du dit pays sount prises et destruitz par les rebelles de Gales, et les vitaillers de dit ville sount destruitz et anientisez, a cause qe ne poient
55   avoir deliverance de lour vitailles, a graund damage et destructione du dit ville. Item, qe Owen de Glendour, traitour et rebell, ad ars .viij. villages deins la fraunchise de la dit ville et les suburbes d'icelle, tanqe a les portz, a graund anientisment de tout la dit ville.

57. Gruffudd ap Dafydd, *Defying Lord Grey of Ruthin*   Middle English
                                                                          11 June 1411

Worschipfull lord I recomande me to you and to your lordschip, and I would pray you hertli that ye wold her how the fals John Wele serued me, as al men knowyn wel. I was under the protexion of Mered ap Owein, he sende to me be trety of my cosynes, Maester Edward and Edward ap Dauid, and askyt gyf I wold cum in
5   and he wold gete me the kings charter, and I schuld be maester forster and keyshat in Chirkeis lond, and other thinges he behiht me the qwich he fulfullyt not. Afterward he askyt me qwether I wold go ouer see with hym, and he wold gete me my charter of the kynge, and bringe me to hym sounde and saff, and I schuld haue wages as muche as any gentilman schuld haue that went with hym; and ouer this he
10   seide befor the byschop of Seint Assaph, and befor my forsaede cosynes, that rather then I schuld fael he wold spene of his own godde xx. marke. Her apon I trust, and gete me ij. men, and boht armery at all pees, and horses, and other araement, and come to Oswestre a nyht befor or thei went; and on the morw ther after I send Piers Cambr the reseuor of Chrikeis lond, thryes to him, for to tel him that I was redy. He
15   saed that I schuld speke no word with him; and at the last he saed that he hade no wages for me; and that he hade al his reteneu; but bade me go to Sir Ric. Kakin to loke qwether he hade nede of me. With the qwych I had neuer ado nor no covenande made, for I wold a gon for no wages with hym ouer see, but for to haue my charter of the kyng and sum leuying that I myht dwel in pees and in rest. And this,
20   as a wytnes of Sir Ric. Lakyn and of Strange, I was redy and wylly for to a gon with hym hedde he be truw. He come and saed priuely to Sir Ric. and to Straunge, "Her is Gruffuth ap David ap Gruffuth in this town, and has no sauecondyt but in Chirkeis lond, and ye mown take hym and ye wolle." And a gode frende come and told me this, and I hert this and trust me thens in al the haste that I myht, and so I was be-
25   gyllyd and deseyued of that fals wele as al men knoyn welle. And so I hade no leuyng worth, qnowth no werche, but take my leuyng as gode wolle ordeyn for. And as I herd ther ben taken ij. horses of your men that wen pyte in your parke, thoo horsys I wod qwer thei ben; but for no hatered that I hade to you or your lordschip thei wern taken, but my men toke ham, and boht ham of hem. And hit was told me

by ill fortune, burnt, along with all the goods of the burgesses which were in that part of it, to the great ruin of the whole town. Also, at the parliament held at Shrewsbury in the time of King Richard the Second, in the twenty-first year of his reign [1398], all the armour and other means of defence of the said burgesses were taken and given to various persons, and thus lost, resulting in damage to the said burgesses amounting to 300 marks and more. Also, whereas the town prospered principally through merchandise, beer and other victuals, the sheep of the surrounding country have been seized and destroyed by the rebels of Wales, and the victuallers of the town are ruined and destroyed on account of the fact that they cannot secure delivery of their victuals, to the great damage and ruin of the said town. Also, the traitor and rebel Owain Glendŵr has burned eight villages within the franchise of the said town, as well as its own suburbs right up to the gates, to the great destruction of the whole town.

57. GRUFFUDD AP DAFYDD, *DEFYING LORD GREY OF RUTHIN*   Notes: pp. 361–62

Honored lord, I recommend myself to you to your lordship, and I heartily pray you to hear how the false John Wele injured me, as all men know well. I was under the protection of Maredudd ab Owain when Wele contacted me under truce through my cousins, Master Edward and Edward ap Dafydd, and asked if I would come in and he would get me the king's pardon, and I should become master forester and warden in Chirkland, and other things he promised me that he did not fulfill. Afterward he told me that if I would go overseas with him, he would get me my pardon from the king, and bring me to him safe and sound, and I should also be paid as much as any gentleman should be paid who went with him. All this he said before the bishop of Saint Asaph, and before my aforesaid cousins, that rather than see me fail he would spend his own goods 20 marks. I trusted all this, and I procured two men and bought the required armor and horses and other array, and I came to Oswestry the night before they departed overseas. In the morning I thrice sent word by Piers Cambre, the receiver of Chirkland, to tell Wele that I was ready to go. He said that I should speak no word with him; and at the last he said that he had no wages for me and that he already hade all his retinue. But he suggested I go to Sir Richard Lakin to inquire whether he had need of me. I had never spoken nor made a covenant with him, but I was not going to go overseas with him for wages, but only in order to have my pardon from the king and some means of living that I might dwell in peace and in rest. Sir Richard Lakin and Le Strange will witness: I was ready and willing to go with him if he had been true. But he came and said privately to Sir Richard and to Le Strange, "Here is Gruffudd ap Dafydd ap Gruffudd in this town, and he has no safe-conduct except in Chirkland, so you may seize him if you can." A good friend came and told me this, and I heard this and fled away from there as quickly as I could, and so I was beguiled and deceived of that false promise as all men know well. So I had neither pardon nor work, and I had to take my leave as God ordained. And as I heard there had been taken two horses from your men that were supposed to be in your park, those horses I would return there: for no hatred that I had of you or your lordship did I take them; my men took them, and I bought them from them. And it was told to me that you are

30   that ye ben in purpos for to make your men bran and sle in qwade soeuer cuntre
      that I be, and am sesened in. Withowten doute as mony men that ye sleu and as
      mony howsin that ye bran for my sake, as mony wol I bran and sle for your sake.
      And doute not I wolle haue both bredde and ale of the best that is in your lordschip.
      I can no more, but Gode kepe your worschipfull astate in prosperite.
35   Iwrettin in grete haste at the parke of Brinkiffe the xj. day of June.

58. LORD GREY OF RUTHIN, *WELSH OUTLAWRY*   Middle English
                                                                  23 June 1411

          Right heigh and myghty prynce, my goode and gracious lorde, I recomaund to
      you as lowly as I kan or may with all my pouer hert, desiryng to hier goode and
      gracious tydynges of your worshipfull astate and welfare, which I prey to Allmyghty
      God as goode mot thei be as ye in your gracious hert kan best deuyse vnto the
5   plesaunce of God and of you. And, gracious lorde, pleseþ hit vnto your heigh astate
      to witte that I have resceyued our liege lordes pryve seal with your oun worshipfull
      lettres to me sent, comaundyng me unto see, and to apees the misgouvernance and
      the riote wich ye heiren that is begunnen heer in the marches of Norþ Wales. Pleseþ
      unto your gracious lordshipe to witte that I have do my power, and woll doo fro day
10   to day by our liege lordes comaundement and by youres. But, my gracious lorde,
      plese hit you to witte þat ye wiþ avise of our liege lordes counsaile most giffe me a
      moore pleyner commyssioun þen I have yit, to taken hem in the kynges grounde,
      other in the erles ground of the March, other in the erles of Arundele, or in any
      lordes grounde of North Wales; and by the feith that I owe unto my ligeaunce I
15   shall trewely do my power to do our liege lorde the kynges comaundement and
      youres: but worshipfull and gracious lorde ye most comaunden the kynges officeres
      in every cuntree to do the same. Also, my gracious lorde, ther been many officeres,
      sume of our liege lord the kynges lond, sume of the erles of the Marche es lond,
      sume off the erle es londe of Arundele, sume of Powise lond, sume of my lond, sume
20   of other lordes londes heer aboute, that ben kynne unto this meignee that be rissen.
      And tyll ye putte thoo officeres in bettere gouvernance, this cuntre of North Gales
      shall nevere haue peese. And if ye hadde tho officeres under your gouvernance, thei
      koude ordeyn remedy, wherthrogh thei sholde be taken. And, gracious lorde, plese
      hit you to witte that the day that the kynges messagere cam with the kynges lettres
25   and with youres to me, the strengest thiefe of Wales sent me a lettre, which lettre
      I send to you, that ye mowe knowen his goode wyll and gouvernance, with a copie
      of another lettre that I have send to hym agayn of an answare. And also, gracious
      lorde, I besech you lowely that ye wolde vouchsaufe to giffe feith and credence to
      a pouere squyer of myn, Richard Donn, of that he shall enfourme you of by mowthe
30   touchyng tydynges of this cuntree; and that ye wolde take to you our liege lordes
      counsaile and ordeyn other remedie for hem then we been of powere for to do,
      other elles trewely hitt woll be an unruely cuntree within short tyme. My gracious
      lorde I kan no more write at this tyme, but God that is our elder sovereigne gife you
      long lyve and well enduryng.
35   Written at Ruthyn the xxiij. day of June.

intending to make your men burn and murder in whatsoever country that I dwell and am seiseined in. Know without doubt that as many men as you slay and as many houses as you burn for my sake, just as mony will I burn and slay for your sake. And doubt not that I will have both bread and ale of the best that is in your lordship. I can say no more now, but God keep your honored estate in prosperity.

Written in great haste at the park of Bryncyffo on the 11th day of June.

58. Lord Grey of Ruthin, *Welsh Outlawry*   Notes: pp. 363–64

Rightfully high and mighty prince, my good and gracious lord, I commend myself to you as humbly as I can with all my poor heart, desiring to hear good and gracious news of your honored estate and welfare, which I pray to Almighty God are as good as you in your gracious heart can best devise to the pleasure of God and of yourself. And, gracious lord, may it please your high estate to know that I have received our liege lord's private seal along with your own honorable letters, commanding me to see and to correct the misgovernance and the riot that you hear has begun here in the marches of North Wales. May it be pleasing unto your gracious lordship to know that I have done what is in my power, and will do so daily by our liege lord's commandment and by yours. But, my gracious lord, please know that you, with advice of our liege lord's counsel, must give me a more complete commission than I have at this time, to take the rebels in the land of the king, or in the ground of the earl of March, or in the earl of Arundel's, or in any lord's ground of North Wales; and by the faith that I owe unto my allegiance I shall truly do all in my power to do our liege lord the king's commandment and yours. But, honorable and gracious lord, you must command the king's officers in every part of the country to do the same. Also, my gracious lord, there are many officers, some of the land of our liege lord the king, some of the land of the earl of March, some of the land of the earl of Arundel, some of the land of Powys, some of my land, some of the lands of other lords around here, that are kin unto this crowd that has risen up. And until you put those officers in better governance, this country of North Wales shall never have peace. And if you had those officers under your governance, they could ordain a solution, through which the rebels would be taken. And, gracious lord, may it please you to know that the day that the king's messenger came with the king's letters and with yours to me, the strongest thief of Wales sent me a letter that I now send to you, so that you may know his good will and governance, along with a copy of another letter that I have sent to him in reply. And also, gracious lord, I beseech you humbly that you would vouchsafe to give faith and credence to a poor squire of mine, Richard Donn, of what he shall inform you of by mouth regarding the news of this country; and that you would take to you our liege lord's counsel and ordain other remedies for them than we are empowered to do, or else truly it will be an unruly country within a short time. My gracious lord I can write no more at this time, but may God who is our elder sovereign give you long life and good health.

Written at Ruthin on the 23rd day of June.

59. *ROLLS OF PARLIAMENT, 1411* **Anglo-Norman**
November 1411

42. Item, priount les communes de les countees de Gloucestre, Wyrcestre, Hereford, Bristuit, Somerset, et d'autres plusours countees, villes, et burghs, auxibien
deins la marche de Gales come de les countees suisditz, et lour compleynont de les
graundes mieschiefs et damages q'ils ount euez et sustenuz devant ces heures, et un-
5 qore ount de jour en autre, par les rebelx et larouns de diverses seignuries de Gales,
qi tout temps gisont en agaite en hautes chymyns, et preignent plusours des ditz
suppliantz, et d'autres lieges nostre seignur le roy, auxi bien deins les countees suisditz, come en les ditz seignuries de Gales, eux amesnantz en diverses seignuries de
Gales, en boys et disertes, et la les lient as arbres, et eux gardent par deux moys ou
10 trois come en prisone et peyns jesqes q'ils soient raunsonez a le pluis outre de lour
biens et pluis, a graund damage et destruccion des ditz suppliantz et de lour amys.
Les queux rebelx apres le dit treson, qe appartient a la corone, sount resceux, vitaillez, et soeffrez en les avantditz seignuries, et ount diverses trewes et sauf con-
duyt, et fount lour fyns et gree ovesqe les ministres des ditz seignuries a lour vol-
15 unte; et ensy sount supportez, vitaillez, et soeffrez par les ministres des ditz seignuries et autres lour amys, qe nulle remedie, correccion, ne deliverance des prisoners suisditz, saunz graund raunceon devant mayn paie, en nulle manere poet estre
fait, mays a demurrer en graund peyne jesqe a mort, a graund destruccion et anientisment des plusours lieges nostre seignur le roy.

60. HENRY IV, *GENERAL AMNESTY TO REBELS* **Latin**
22 December 1411

Rex vicecomiti Kantiae, salutem.

Cum, ob reverentiam Dei, et ad specialem requisitionem, dominorum spiritu-
alium et temporalium, ac Communitatis regni nostri Angliae, in ultimo parliamento
nostro existentium, necnon pacem et quietem populi nostri, pardonaverimus uni-
5 versis et singulis ligeis regni nostri Angliae, Owino de Glendordy de Wallia, et
Thoma de Trumpyngton, ac aliis adversariis nostris, in partibus transmarinis et cismarinis, vel alibi, sibi falso adhaerentibus, exceptis, sectam pacis nostrae, quae ad
nos versus ipsos pertinet, pro omnimodis proditionibus, insurrectionibus, rebel-
lionibus, feloniis, mesprisionibus, offensis, impetitionibus, transgressionibus, et con-
10 temptibus, per ipsos, ante decimum nonum diem Decembris, ultimo praeteritum,
factis sive perpetratis (murdris et raptibus mulierum exceptis) dumtamen iidem
ligei nostri, probatores, latrones, vel depraedatores, aut in prisona pro latrocinio
vel roberia, absque debita manucaptione seu traditione in ballium, seu de felonia
de recordo convicti seu attincti non existant, nolumus tamen quod officiarii, minis-
15 tri nostri, seu alii quicumque, qui nobis debitores, aut aliqualiter computabiles existunt, in debitis et compotis suis praedictis beneficium, colore praesentis Pardonationis, habeant ullo modo, tibi praecipimus quod prodonationem praedictam in singulis locis, infra ballivam tuam, ubi magis expediens fuerit et necesse, publice proclamari et eisdem ligeis nostris notificari facias quod ipsi literas inde, citra Festum
20 Nativitatis Sancti Johannis Baptistae, proximo futurum, separatim prosequantur,
si ipsi beneficium hujusmodi pardonationis voluerint optinere.

59. *Rolls of Parliament, 1411*   **Notes: p. 364**

42. Commons of the counties of Gloucester etc. Also, the request of the commons of the counties of Gloucester, Worcester, Hereford, Bristol, Somerset and various other counties, towns, and boroughs, both in the March of Wales and in the aforesaid counties: they complain of the great wrongs and damage which they have had and borne before this time, and still have daily, at the hands of rebels and robbers from various lordships in Wales who continually lie in wait on highways and seize many of the said supplicants and other lieges of our lord the king, both within the aforesaid counties and in the said lordships in Wales, and take them into various lordships in Wales, to woods and uninhabited places, and tie them to trees there, and keep them for two or three months in prison and torture them until they are ransomed with all of their goods and more, to the great damage and destruction of the said supplicants and their kinsmen. Which rebels, following such treason (which pertains to the crown), are harboured, fed, and supported in the aforesaid lordships, and enjoy various truces and safe-conducts, and make their fines and agreements with the officers of the said lordships at their pleasure; and so they are harboured, fed, and supported by the officers of the said lordships and their other kinsmen, and there is no redress, correction, or freedom for the aforesaid prisoners under any circumstances unless a large ransom is paid beforehand, but they remain in mortal danger, to the great harm and ruin of many of our lord the king's lieges.

60. Henry IV, *General Amnesty to Rebels*   **Notes: pp. 364–65**

The king to the sheriff of Kent, greetings.

When, out of reverence for God, and by special request of the lords, both spiritual and temporal, and of the Commons of our Kingdom of England, in the last Parliament, and for the peace and quiet of our people, we pardon each and every liege of our Kingdom of England, with the exception of Owain Glyndŵr of Wales, Thomas of Trumpington and our other adversaries, both in England and France, or elsewhere, except those who joined it falsely, our surety of peace, that pertains to us against them, for all kinds of treasons, insurrections, rebellions, felonies, kidnappings, offenses, assaults, transgressions and contempts, made by them, before the nineteenth day of December, recently past, done or perpetrated (except for murders and the rape of women) provided that our lieges themselves did not support brigands, robbers or plunderers or were in prison for banditry, or robbery, without owing writs for or surrendering bail and are not convicted of or held for a felony of record. However, we do not wish that officials, our ministers or any others who are debtors or otherwise accountable to us, by debt or in possession of an aforementioned benefice, have any part of the present pardon. We command that this pardon be proclaimed publicly in every place in your bailiwick where it is more expedient or necessary, and that you notify each of our lieges that the letters be filed separately by them from before the upcoming Feast of the Nativity of St. John the Baptist, if they wish to obtain the benefit of such Pardon.

Teste rege apud Westmonasterium, vicesimo secundo die Decembris per ipsum regem, de gratia sua in parliamento.

Consimilia brevia diriguntur singulis vicecomitibus per Angliam, ac cancellario
25   regis in Comitatu Palatino Lancastriae.

61. HENRY IV, *LICENCE TO TREAT WITH OWAIN*   Latin
14 June 1412

Rex Omnibus, ad quos etc., salutem.

Monstravit nobis, dilectus armiger noster, Luellin ap Howel, Pater, dilecti armigeri nostri, David Gamme, ac tenens infra dominium nostum de Brech', qualiter praefatus David, per Owinum de Glendourdy, rebellem et proditorem nostrum, vio-
5   lenter captus, et per eundem Owinum forti et dur prisonâ positus extitit, de qua, absque eo quod ipse finem ad voluntatem praefati Owini facere velit, deliberari minime potest, nos (ad hoc considerationem habentes) de Gratia nostra speciali, concessimus et licentiam dedimus, dilecto et fideli militi nostro, Johanni Tiptofte, senescallo de Brech', et Willielmo Botiller, receptori ibidem, quod ipsi, ac illi, quos,
10   cum assensu praedicti Lewellini, et aliorum amicorum praefati David, assignare voluerint, tractare possint cum praefato Owino, ac aliis, quos ipse pro se assignare voluerit, ad faciendum finem et concordiam inter ipsos, de redemptione et deliberatione praedicti David, meliori modo quo ipsi inde poterunt concordari, et ulterius, de habundanti gratia nostra, concessimus et licentiam dedimus praefatis, Johanni
15   et Willielmo, ac caeteris amicis praefati David, quod, si ipsi seu eorum aliquis capiant vel capiat aliquos seu aliquem Wallensium, de adhaerentibus, favorantibus, succurentibus, seu auxiliantibus praefato Owino, quod ipsi hujusmodi Wallenses, sic captos, eidem Owino, pro deliberatione praedicti David, deliberare possint.

In cujus etc.
20   Teste rege apud Westmonasterium, decimo quarto die Junii, per breve de privato sigillo.

62. ADAM OF USK, *CHRONICLE, PART 3*   Latin
February 1414

Captiuitas Edmundi Mortemer. In festo sancti Albani, iuxta Knyghton in Wallia, inter Anglicos sub domino Edmundo Mortemere et Wallicos sub Oueno Glyndour quam graui innito conflictu, et miseranda cede ad octo milia inde contingente, dicto O cessit uictoria. Et heu me, dictus dominus meus Edmundus, cuius me pater
5   et dominus de Vsk ad scolas exhibuit, belli fortuna abducitur captiuus; qui eciam per emulos in Angl' omnibus bonis priuatus ac redimi impeditus, captiuitatis dolores mitius ut euaderet, dicti Oweni filiam, de qua filium nomine Leonellum et tres filias, licet iam cum matre extra una filia mortuos, procreauerat, ad magnum populi rumorem noscitur duxisse uxorem. Ac demum in castro de Hardeleghe, per exerci-
10   tum Angl' obcesso, de (quo) adhuc mira canuntur in festo, dies suos quam doloroso

Witnessed by the king at Westminster, on the 22 December on behalf of the king by the grace of his parliament.

Similar letters are directed to each sheriff in England, and to the chancellor of the king in the County Palatine of Lancaster.

61. HENRY IV, *LICENCE TO TREAT WITH OWAIN*   Notes: p. 365

The king of all to whom, etc., greetings.

Our beloved esquire, Llywelyn ap Hywel, father of our beloved esquire, Dafydd Gam, and holding Brecknockshire in our dominion, has shown to us how the aforesaid Dafydd was violently taken by Owain Glyndŵr, rebel and traitor to us, and was placed by Owain in a strong and indestructible prison, from which he is able to communicate only a little, despite the fact that he would like to put an end to the aims of Owain. Considering this, we have conceded our special grace and give license to our beloved and faithful knight, John Tiptoft, steward of Brecknockshire and William Botiller, receiver of the same, that they, and others, who, with the consent of Llywelyn, and other friends of Dafydd, are so designated to negotiate with Owain, and others who are assigned this on his behalf, to put an end to this situation and make peace between them, for the redemption and deliberation of the said Dafydd, in whatever better way that they might be able to make peace. And otherwise, in our abundant grace, we concede and give license to the said John and William, and to other friends of Dafydd, that, if they capture any of the adherents, favorites, followers or abettors of Owain, anywhere in Wales, that those captives might be used to exchange for Dafydd.

In whose, etc.

Witnessed by the king at Westminister, 14 June, by letter with private seal.

62. ADAM OF USK, *CHRONICLE, PART 3*   Notes: p. 366

The capture of Edmund Mortimer. On the feast of St. Alban [22 June 1402], a fierce battle was fought near Knighton in Wales between the English under Sir Edmund Mortimer and the Welsh under Owain Glyndŵr, in which as many as eight thousand persons died miserable deaths before Owain emerged victorious. And it grieves me to relate that this Edmund, my lord, by whose father, the lord of Usk, I was supported at the schools, was by the fortunes of war taken captive; whereupon, having been deprived of all his goods and prevented from ransoming himself by his enemies in England, and in order to mitigate the rigours of his captivity, he married Owain's daughter, which occasioned a great deal of murmuring amongst the people; he fathered three daughters by her, as well as a son called Lionel, although all of them, including their mother are now dead, apart from one daughter. He eventually ended his unhappy life in Harlech castle, besieged by an English army;

finiuit. Isto anno eciam dominus Grey de Ruthyn ad duorum milium de suis necem
per eundem Owenum captus, mancipatur et carceribus, sed sexdecim milium librarum auri redempcione ab eisdem liberatus exstitit. De tanto infortunio Angl' dominio per dictum Owenum causato mea, dum cogito, uiscera contremiscunt; name
15   totam Walliam cum eius marchia, triginta milium de cauernis exeuncium consorcio
stipatus, omnia parcium castra, inter que de Vsk, Carlyon et Nuportus, subuertit ac
opida succendit. Ouid mora? Velut alter Assur, furoris Dei uirga, inauditam tyran-
nidem ferro et flamma miserime uibrauit.

. . .

Hoc anno rex, cum centum milibus et ultra in tres partes diuisis, Walliam mili-
20   tariter contra Owenum inuadit; sed ipso cum suis miseris in cauernis et nemoribus
delitescentibus, rex, deuastata patria, et cum infinita animalium preda, gloriose
rediit ad propria.

. . .

Post dictam cedem inter regem et dictum dominum Henricum Persy contingen-
tem, Owenus cum homunculis cauernas et nemora (relinquens), quasi oportunita-
25   tem captans, in multitudine glomerata usque ad Sabrinum mare totam circuit Walliam, et quosque sibi resistentes, aut ultra idem mare, ubi per pagenses tanquam
Wallici expliati erant, (propulit), aut ferro et flamma, eciam ecclesiis non parcendo,
unde et ad ruinam finaliter deuenit, ad sui dedicionem subegit. Et cum maxima
preda ad suas aquilonares Wallie partes, unde panditur omne malum Wallie, cum
30   interna adulteriorum suorum publicorum malediccione, pro suo tutamine, et ad
montes rediit Snowdonie. Homines Bristoll', cum armata classe sub capitaneis
Iacobo Clyfford et Willelmo Rye, armigeris, Glanmorgancie partes, ecclesiam Lan-
dauens' spoliando, inuadunt; sed per miraculum sancti Theliai a pagensibus diuicti,
cum eorum ruina non modica, confuse sunt repulsi.
35   Suspensio fratrum. Prior de Latunde et dominus Rogerus Claryndon, miles fra-
terque regis Ricardi spurius, ac undecim de ordine fratrum minorum, in theologia
dotores, quia dicto Oweno confederati, per proprios socios regi detecti, apud Ty-
born' London' post tractum crudeliter furcis sunt suspensi; multique domini et
somine, eciam comitisse, eadem causa carceribus sunt mancipate.
40   Inuasio Brutonum. Rex ducis Brytanie relictam, regisque Nauarie sororem, per
eam releuari sperans, duxit in uxorem. Sed statim, spe frustrata, Britones, nupcias
detestantes, una cum Gallicis, comite marescallo Aquitanie et domino de Huguyle
Normannie eorum ducibus, in magno exercitu in succursum et expedicionem
Oweni intrarunt Walliam, et totam marchiam ferro et flamma deustando nocu-
45   menta non modica intulerunt Anglicis.

. . .

and these remarkable events are still to this day sung about at feasts. Lord Grey of Ruthin was also captured and imprisoned by Owain this year, two thousand of his men being slaughtered in the process, but he regained his liberty by paying a ransom of sixteen thousand pounds in gold. My heart trembles when I think of this dire blow against English rule inflicted by Owain; backed by a force of thirty thousand men who would issue forth from their caves, he seized castles everywhere throughout Wales and the march — including Usk, Caerleon, and Newport — and burned the towns. What more can I say? Like another Assyrian, the rod of God's anger, he vented his fury with fire and sword in unprecedented tyrannies.

. . .

This year [Sept. 1402] the king led a force of a hundred thousand men and more, in three divisions, to attack Owain in Wales, but Owain and his wretches remained in hiding in the caves and forests, so the king devastated the land and returned home in great pomp, taking with him an enormous booty in animals.

. . .

[1403] Following the battle mentioned above between the king and Sir Henry Percy, Owain, seizing his chance, emerged with his manikins from the caves and the woods and marched with a great host right across Wales as far as the Severn sea; those who resisted him he either drove across the sea-where, being Welsh, they were persecuted by the local people — or forced with fire and sword into surrender; nor did he spare even the churches, which ultimately was to lead to his downfall. Then, taking enormous quantities of booty with him, he returned to the safety of the mountains of Snowdonia in the north of Wales, the source of all the evils in Wales, while the people silently cursed his flagrant barbarities. The men of Bristol, captained by the esquires James Clifford and William Rye, took an armed fleet and raided Glamorgan, plundering the church of Llandaff, but through a miracle of St. Teilo they were defeated by the local people and driven off in confusion, with considerable loss.

Friars are hanged. The prior of Launde and Sir Roger Clarendon, a knight, the natural brother of King Richard, along with eleven friars of the Franciscan order who were doctors of theology, were betrayed to the king by their fellows as being in alliance with the aforesaid Owain, and were drawn to Tyburn in London and cruelly hanged at the gallows there; and many lords and ladies, even countesses, were sent to prison for the same reason.

The invasion of the Bretons. The king took as his wife the widow of the duke of Brittany, who was also the sister of the king of Navarre, hoping through her to gain some assistance. His hopes were promptly dashed, however, because the Bretons, disapproving of the marriage, allied themselves with the French under the command of the count marshal of Aquitaine and the lord of Hugueville in Normandy, and took a large force to Wales to help and support Owain [1405], devastating the entire march with fire and sword and inflicting substantial losses on the English.

. . .

In Anglia interim parliamenta celebrantur multa, in quibus et contra prouisiones apostolicas strictiora sunt statua, et plus solito clerus et populus grauiori taxantur collecta. Et nemirum, quia ita graunantur et guerra contra Franciam, Scociam, Hiberniam, Walliam et Flandriam se defensando, ac sexaginta milibu auri libris a Wallia eis solui consuetis guerra causante destituti. Owenus apud Machenllith et montanis sua eciam miseria cum duellorum et aliarum regaliarum usurpacione, licet ad sui confusionem, celebrat-ymmo symulat seu confyngit parliamenta.

. . .

Capiture filius Oweni. Cedes apud Vscam. In festo sancti Gregorii, Giffinus, prinogenitus Oweni, in multitudine magna castro de Vsk, aliqualiter ad defensionem reparato, in quo tunc erat dominus Grey do Codnore, dominus Iohannes Greyndour, et multi alii regis soudati, in mala sua insultauit hora; quia dicti domini, uiriliter exeuntes, ipsum captiuarunt et suos ipsos usque ad montana superioris Wencie per Vsce flumen, ubi plures, et presertim abbas de Lanterna, tam fluminis quam gladii ore ceciderunt, et per monachorum siluam, ubi dictus Griffinus erat captus, indefesse contriuerunt. Ac uiuos captos, in numero trecentum, ante dictum castrum prope Ponfaldum decapitarunt; et quosdam nobiliores ad regem cum dicto Grifino captiuos duxerunt. Qui Grifinus, per sex annos in captiuate existens, finaliter in London' turri morbo extinguitur pestilenciali; et de cetero in illis partibus uiluit sors Oweni.

. . .

Vxor Oweni, cum eius duabus filiabus et tribus neptibus, domini Edmundi Mortemeri filiabus, et omnibus laruibus, captiuatur, et London' ad regem transmittitur; Owenus cum unico filio suo, Meredyth nomine, in terre cauernis et montium fruticibus delitet miserime. Ad bonam cautelam, regis expensis, per eius soldatos (ad) rebelliones nouas refrenandas, de Snowdon et aliorum montium ac siluarum Northewall' saltus et passus custodiunt.

63. *ROLLS OF PARLIAMENT, 1414*   **Anglo-Norman**
                                                       November 1414

41. Item priont les communes, qe come puis le rebellioun de Gales, ore tarde par vous, nostre soveraigne seignour et vostre puissante governaunce refourme, plusours des ditz rebelles, ove autres a eaux adherantz, ove force et armes, en manere de guerre, ascun foitz par jour, et ascun foitz par noet, ount venuz en les countees de Salop', Hereford, Gloucestr', et en autres a mesme la paiis adjesantz, et en diverses boys et autres lieux en ycelles parties mussiez et loggez, ount treterousement et felenousement pris plusours de voz foialx lieges, ascunz chivechant entour lour merchan-

Meanwhile, in England several parliaments were held, in which even stricter decrees against papal provisions were passed, and even harsher taxes than usual were imposed on the clergy and the people; and no wonder, for they were hard pressed to hold their own in the wars against France, Scotland, Ireland, Wales and Flanders, and were also, as a result of the war, deprived of sixty thousand pounds of revenue which they used to receive from Wales. Owain, in his wretchedness, held — or rather aped, or mimicked — parliaments at Machynlleth, and in the mountains, where he would usurp rights of combat and other royal privileges, although it did him no good.

· · ·

The son of Owain is captured. Deaths at Usk. Gruffudd, the eldest son of Owain, attacked Usk castle with a great host on the feast of St. Gregory [1405] — an evil hour for him; however, the defences there had been considerably strengthened, and Lord Grey of Codnor, Sir John Greyndour, and many more of the king's soldiers were there, and they made a sortie in force from the castle and captured him and his men, driving them relentless through the river Usk, where many of them — most notably the abbot of Llantarnam — were killed either at the point of a sword or by drowning in the river, through Monkswood, where Gruffudd himself was captured, and on to the mountains of Upper Went. Of those whom they took alive, three hundred were beheaded in front of the castle, near Ponfald, although some of the nobler ones, including Gruffudd, were sent as prisoners to the king. This Gruffudd remained in captivity for six years, eventually dying of the plague in the Tower of London; and from this time onwards, Owain's fortunes began to wane in the region.

· · ·

Owain's wife, together with her two daughters and three granddaughters — the daughters of Sir Edmund Mortimer — and all their goods, was captured and sent to the king in London; and Owain in his misery hid himself away with his only son, called Maredudd, in remote caves and wooded mountainsides. In order to prevent any fresh outbreaks of rebellion, the king for better security paid his soldiers to guard the valleys and passes of Snowdon and the other mountains and forests of North Wales.

63. *ROLLS OF PARLIAMENT, 1414*   Notes: p. 367

41. XI. Concerning the rebels in Wales. Also, the commons pray that whereas, since the rebellion in Wales recently put down by you, our sovereign lord, and by your forceful government, many of the said rebels, with others who are their adherents, have come into the counties of Shropshire, Herefordshire, Gloucestershire and others adjacent to the same land, with force of arms and in a warlike manner, sometimes by day and sometimes by night, and, hiding and encamped in various woods and other places in those parts, they have treacherously and feloniously taken many of your faithful lieges, sometimes when they were riding with their merchandise and going

dises, et lour autres busoignes faisantz, et ascunz en lour maisons, ou ils furent demurantz faisantz lour overaigne et lour housbondrie en le peas de Dieu, et le vostre,
10 et mesmes voz tielx lieges ensi prisez ont amenez hors de lour dit paiis as diverses
parties de Gales, et les eient gardez et detenuz ovesqe eaux en les mountaignes
d'icelles parties de Gales par un demy an, ascun foitz pluis, et ascun foitz meyns,
tanqe ils ount raunsonez ascun de voz ditz lieges a cli. et ascun pluis, solonqe lour
afferant, en semblable manere come est use en terre de guerre, et unqore font;
15 issint par celle cause, voz ditz foialx lieges n'osent pas demurer a lour houstelle demesne, ne pres bordures de Gales, par my les countees suisditz, a cause suisdite, a
lour tresgraunde anientisment et finalle destruccioun pur toutz jours, si due remedie ne soit purveu en ceste partie, a cause qe tielx malfaisours maintenaunt sur
lour malfait soy retrahent en Gales, ou le brief du roy ne court.

64. HENRY V, *LICENCE TO TREAT WITH OWAIN* | Latin
5 July 1415

Rex Omnibus, ad quos etc., salutem.

Sciatis quod nos, de fidelitate, circumspectione, et industria, dilecti et fidelis
nostri, Gilberti Talbot Chivaler plenius confidentes, commisimus et deputavimus ipsum Gilbertum ad comunicandum et tractandum cum Owino Glendourdy de Wallia
5 de et super certis materiis, praefato Gilberto per nos injunctis, Et tam ad praedictum
Owinum, quam alios rebelles nostros Wallenses, ad obedientiam et Gratias nostras,
si se ad eas petendum optulerint, nomine nostro admittendum et recipiendum, et alia
omnia et singula faciendum et exercendum, quae in praemissis et circa ea necessaria
fuerint seu quomodolibet oportuna, promittentes nos ratum, gratum, et firmum habi-
10 turos quicquid praefatus Gilbertus fecerit in praemissis, vel aliquo praemissorum.
In cujus etc.
Teste Rege apud castrum regis de Porchestre quinto die Julii.

65. HENRY V, *LICENCE TO TREAT WITH OWAIN'S SON* | Latin
24 February 1416

Rex Omnibus, ad quos etc., salutem.

Sciatis quod nos, de fidelitate, et circumspectione, et industria, dilecti et fidelis
nostri, Gilberti Talbot Chivaler, plenius confidentes, assignavimus et deputavimus
ipsum Gilbertum ad communicandum et tractandum cum Meredith ap Owyn, filio
5 Owyni de Glendourdy, de et super certis materiis, praefato Gilberto per nos injunctis et declaratis, et tam ad praedictum Owinum, quam alios rebelles nostros Wallenses, ad obedientiam et Gratias nostras, si se ad eas petendum optulerint, nomine
nostro admittendum et recipiendum, caeteraque omnia alia et singula faciendum
et excercendum, quae in praemissis et circa ea necessaria fuerint seu quomodolibet
10 oportuna, promittentes, nos ratum, gratum, et firmum habituros quicquid praefatus
Gilbertus fecerit in praemissis, vel aliquo praemissorum.
In cujus etc.
Teste Rege apud Westmonasterium xxiv. die Februarii.

about their other business, and sometimes when they were in their houses where they were living, doing their work and their husbandry, in the peace of God and yours; and they have taken or carried your same such lieges in this way out of their said countries into the various regions of Wales, and have kept and held them with them in the mountains of those regions of Wales for half a year, or at times more and at times less, until they have ransomed your said lieges, sometimes for £100 and sometimes more, depending on what seemed appropriate, just as if they were in a land at war, and they still do this; so that for this reason your said faithful lieges do not dare to live in their own households or near to the borders of Wales in the aforesaid counties, for the aforesaid reason, to their very great ruin and final destruction forever, if a due remedy is not provided for this matter; because such malefactors immediately after their crimes retreat into Wales, where the king's writ does not run.

64. HENRY V, *LICENCE TO TREAT WITH OWAIN*   Notes: p. 367

The king of all, to whom etc., greetings.

Know that we, by faithfulness, circumspection, and work, having complete confidence in Gilbert Talbot, Knight, commission and deputize Gilbert to communicate and negotiate with Owain Glyndŵr of Wales concerning certain matters. We order Gilbert to the said Owain, as well as other rebels of our Wales, to ask them to offer themselves to our obedience and grace, and, in our name, to admit and receive all things, each and every deed and action which may be necessary in the matter. We promise our reason, grace and confirmation to whatever Gilbert does in this matter or all other matters.

In whose, etc.

Witnessed by the king at the royal castle of Porchester on 5 July.

65. HENRY V, *LICENCE TO TREAT WITH OWAIN'S SON*   Notes: p. 367

The king of all, to whom, etc., greetings.

Know that we, by faithfulness, circumspection, and work, having complete confidence in Gilbert Talbot, Knight, assign and deputize Gilbert to communicate and negotiate with Maredudd ab Owain, son of Owain Glyndŵr, concerning certain matters. We order Gilbert to the said Owain, as well as other rebels of our Wales, to ask them to offer themselves to our obedience and grace, and, in our name, to admit and receive all remaining things, each and every deed and action which may be necessary in the matter. We promise our reason, grace and confirmation to whatever Gilbert does in this matter or all other matters.

In whose, etc.

Witnessed by the king at Westminister on 24 February.

66. MICHEL PINTOIN, *CHRONICLE OF CHARLES VI*   **Latin**
                                                             1420

Capitulum ix. Ad arma comparanda Parisius princeps Wallie misit.

    Inter plures generosos qui regem Anglie ad regni fastigium ascendisse injus-
tissime abhorrebant, solus princeps Wallie Glindour nomine. Non modo eidem
viribus contradicendo, sed et contra eum levando calcaneum, nunc marte claro
5   nunc obscuro Angliam hucusque infestaverat pro posse. Videns tamen opus tam ar-
duum inchoatum sine exterorum auxilio et mercenario conductu se continuare non
posse, nec suam tueri auctoritatem, ad Francos decrevit recurrere, arma et auxilium
poscere, quos super omnes mortales in armis strenuos reputabat. Et quamvis vere-
cundum reputaret, quia alias inauditum, scuto Francie protegi Walenses petere, ad
10 id tamen audaciam prestitit quod famosus quondam armiger Yvo de Wallia, cui jure
consanguinitatis successerat, in servicio regis Francie Karoli nuper deffuncti occu-
buerat. Ideo fratrem proprium in Franciam mense mayo destinavit.

    Ut semper regi et de regio sanguine procreatis moris fuit de longinquis partibus
accedentes ad eos propensius honorare, sic et istum excipientes honeste, quamdiu
15 in regno mansit, curaverunt dapsiliter, et, audiencia concessa, duo sequencia que
petebat liberaliter annuerunt. Primo namque concesserunt ut, arma bellica Parisius
ad sufficienciam comparantes, eligerent qui hec imposita navibus de Sequana per
mare usque ad Walliam secure conducerent. Addentes ulterius quod opportuno
tempore in subsidium principis armatos viros mitterent, qui sub vexillo comitis
20 Marchie militarent. Nec existimo silendum celandum quod, cum rex sanus effectus
legatum donis uberio ribus cumulasset, et inquirens de statu, vita, et moribus Wallensium familiariter, ipsi interroganti que fratri inter caduca omnia plus placerent,
respondisset arma bellica, eidem sic statuit complacere. Nuncio namque vale
dicens, cassidem regiam deauratam, loricam et ensem loco enceniorum principi
25 presentandam nomine suo misit, que quidem, prout a Francis qui tunc interfuerunt
didici, cum tanta genuum flectione humili totque devotis osculis hoc gratum donum
recepit, ac si regem personaliter recepisset. Insuper et de pugnatoribus mittendis
graciarum ingentes referens actiones, ipsi comiti Marchie et suis commilitonibus
venturis scripta misit, que perlegi, portus famosiores Wallie, plana quoque itinera
30 et plagas uberiores patrie continencia, per quos ingredi possent liberius et ubi possent habundancius refoveri.

    Infinitorum hominum sibi favorem acquisivit princeps dictus litteris divulgatis,
et expedicionem illam bellicam multipliciter attollentes, innumerabiles nobiles
affuerunt, qui ad illam modis omnibus anhelabant, indignum ducentes in regno
35 marcessere ocio, cum ibi reperire sperarent materiam triumphorum. Gratum eciam
habentes ducem exercitus, ipsum multis laudibus attollebant, cum adhuc existens
in juvenili etate non solum in Hungaria sed et alibi quamplura marina et terrestria
peregerat periculosa itinera, et ideo affectabant sub tam famoso comite et de regio
sanguine procreato militare. Grato igitur assensu insignes duces Francie, Biturie,
40 de Borbonio et Aurelianis, rege tenebris ignorancie detento, auctoritate ipsius,
classem sexaginta duarum navium ordinantes, octingentos pugiles ad transfretan-

66. Michel Pintoin, *Chronicle of Charles VI*   **Notes: pp. 368–69**

Chapter 9. The prince of Wales requests military relief from Paris.

Of all the nobles who abhorred the unjust usurpation of the king of England, none showed more animosity than Glyndŵr, the prince of Wales. He not only refused to recognize it, but he openly raised the banner of revolt, and he attacked England several times with varying success and failure. However, seeing that he could not continue this perilous work, or maintain his own authority, without calling for foreign aid and mercenary troops, he resolved to ask for men and arms from the French, who of all peoples were said to be the most strong of arms. It was the first time that the Welsh demanded the protection of France, so he felt at first some qualms. But he was encouraged in this approach by the example of the famous esquire Owain Lawgoch, who died in the service of the late King Charles and whom he had succeeded by right of inheritance. He thus determined in the month of May to send his own brother to France.

The king and the princes of the blood, who always received with honor envoys from distant countries, made for this ambassador a most gracious host and treated him lavishly as he remained in the kingdom; and, having given him an audience, they freely agreed to two requests made of them. First they consented that he would have in Paris what weapons he needed, that he would then embark by ship on the Seine and thus be conducted safely by sea to Wales. They also promised to send in a timely manner more aid to the prince, a body of troops under the leadership of the count de La Marche. I record this embassy because of the fact that the king, who was in good health and who had completed this present business, was chatting with the embassy about the state, the life, and the manners of the Welsh, and the king asked him what his brother loved best in the world. The envoy answered that it was weapons of war; the king, to please the Prince of Wales, gave the ambassador at the time of his departure a royal gilded helmet, a shield, and a sword, and he charged him to offer his hand to his brother. I knew by the French who were found there that when the presents were handed over he received them humbly, kneeling and covering them with kisses, as if he had received the king himself. As a token of gratitude for the help that the king had intended, the envoy sent to the count de La Marche and the armed men who were to accompany him a message that I have read, in which he told them the best ports in Wales, the safest and most useful routes, and the districts that were the most fertile and best stocked.

This message concealed a great favor to him. It boasted everywhere about the expedition, and noble lords came forward in droves, asking to go with all the more eagerness because they were bored of the idleness in which they languished, and they hoped to find in this war the opportunity to be made illustrious through victories. They also were pleased to see that the army was commanded by a knight whose valor was known, and who when he was young had more than once taken part in dangerous expeditions on land and sea, both in Hungary and in other countries, and they burned all of them with the desire to fight under a leader from the already famous and royal blood. The illustrious duke of Berry, of Bourbon and of Orleans hastened to raise up, in the name of the king, who was held in the darkness of ignorance, a fleet of sixty-two sails, and with these embarked eight hundred men-

dum statuerunt cum multis balistariis. Eciam inter istos multi, non multum divites, sed tamen strenuitate conspicui milites et armigeri habebantur, qui sua libere expo
45 suerunt ut honestius illuc tenderent armis et necessariis instructi. Et hii, ut jussi fuerant, ad portum famosum de Brest in Britania applicuerunt circa medium augusti.

                                        . . .

Capitulum xviii. De hiis que marescalus de Ryeux in Wallia gessit.

Ut quod principi Wallie domini duces Francie, in regni regimine principales, de subsidio mittendo adimplerent, et ut quodam notabili facto comitis Marchie,
50 quem antea miserant, ignominia tegeretur, inelitos milites dominum marescallum de Rieux, dominum de Hugevilla, magistrum ballistariorum Francie, et dominum Strabonem de Laheuse capitaneos elegerunt pugnatorum mittendorum. Ex Britania igitur et Normania, mandatis obtemperantes, cum sexeentis balistariis, mille ducentis servientibus levis armature, octingentos electos pugiles collegerunt, qui
55 cum elasse duarum magnarum et rostratarum navium ac triginta mediocrium in Walliam transmearent. Et hii omnes, circa finem jullii navigium ascendentes, cum per mensem mare placidum ex aspero factum expectassent, tandem portum de Willeforde, situm in comitatu de Pennebroc, attingentes, mox decem mille Wallenses missos a principe repererunt, quorum ope libere principatum intrarent,
60 et si impedimentum occurreret, eos potenter juvarent.

Ex tunc Gallici cum ipsis Walensibus campestrem patriam ceperunt destruere, et flamma voraci consumere, recte tendentes ad villam de Heleford, que castro munitissimo subjacebat, unde protinus exierunt cum multis sagittariis fere trecenti homines ad unguem omnes loricati et ad resistendum prompti; cum quibus inito
65 prelio, mox victi sunt, et ex eis sexdecim captis et quadraginta interfectis, ceteros fugere compulerunt. Inde ad villam tendentes, insultus multos fecerunt; sed ex castrensibus septuaginta interfectis, eum propter fortitudinem loci illam capere nequirent et obsidionalia instrumenta per mare ducere ad loca alia ordinassent, mox obsidionem relinquerunt. In hiis tamen assultibus quamvis perpauci ex Francis
70 ceciderint, ibi tamen quidam miles famosus, nomine Patroullart de Trya, occubuit, cujus interitum graviter omnes Gallici tulerunt.

Eadem eciam die ad castrum nomine Picot ad custodiam pabulatorum deputati perrexerunt, quod primo assultu ad dedicionem venire coegerunt. Loco igitur, onusti preda, cedentes, et per adjacentem patriam, nulla incolumi relicta re, cui
75 ferro aut igni noceri posset, ad villam maritimam et muratam nomine Canneby pervenientes, ipsam de communi consilio omnium et assensu obsidione cingere et capere viribus decreverunt, per circuitum balistarios et obsidionalia instrumenta commode colloeantes. Cum autem ad id diligentissime instarent, nundum primo assultu inchoato, a longe classem triginta navium appropinquare viderunt, armatis
80 viris et victualibus munitam, que ad succurrendum incolis mittebatur. Quod cum per exploratores veraciter didicissent, subito tantus pavor et formido super eos irruit, ac si omnes interitum sentirent imminere, et quia majorem partem navigii habebant super arenam, quam et nequibant ad mare impellere, cum non navigio se salvare, mox evacuatis vasis, illa igne combusserunt, ne ad manus hostium deve-
85 nirent. Moxque adhuc nemine persequente, sic contabuerunt eorum corda pre

at-arms with many crossbowmen. Among them there were many knights and squires renowned for their value, who had willingly made the sacrifice to equip themselves honorably and provide their weapons and all the necessary things. As they were ordered, they went forth from the famous port of Brest in Brittany around the middle of August.

. . .

Chapter 18. Expedition of the marshal de Rieux in Wales.

The dukes of France, who had the direction of affairs, desiring to fulfill the promise made to aid the Prince of Wales, and to repair through some notable feat of arms the shame of the failure of the count de La Marche, who had formerly been in charge of this mission, resolved to send to this country auxiliary troops under the leadership of illustrious knights, the marshal de Rieux, the lord de Hugueville, grand-master of the crossbows of France, and the lord Borgue de la Heuse. These three captains, in accordance with orders they had received, gathered in Brittany and Normandy eight hundred handpicked men, six hundred crossbows and twelve hundred light troops, and they prepared to cross over to Wales with a fleet composed of two large warships and thirty small vessels. They all embarked in late July. After waiting for a month for a favorable wind, they finally arrived at the port of Milford Haven, in the county of Pembroke. They found that the prince of Wales had sent ten thousand Welsh to facilitate their entry into the land and to lend their support if they met with any obstacle.

Then the French and Welsh began to set the country ablaze, and they advanced right up to the town of Haverfordwest, which is dominated by a castle, from which nearly three hundred men armed from head to toe, followed by a host of archers, made a sortie, determined to fight. They came to blows. The French had the advantage, and they killed forty men, made sixteen prisoners, and compelled the rest to flee. Then they approached the town and made several assaults. But the fortifications were too strong; they could not gain the upper-hand, even though they had also carried by sea all their siege artillery. So they raised the siege, after having killed seventy defenders and losing very few people themselves. Among the French dead was a famous knight named Patrouillart de Trie, who was deeply mourned by all his companions.

On the same day, a detachment guarding the foragers drove forward as far as the castle of Picot, and forced it to surrender after the first assault. The French went away laden with booty from ravaging the surrounding country, and they put everything to fire and sword and then came to a fortified port, called Tenby. Having resolved by mutual agreement to besiege and take this town, they surrounded it with their crossbows and placed their siege engines. They were actively making their preparations, and were about to deliver the first assault, when they saw from afar a fleet of thirty ships, well supplied and full of men of war, which was coming to the rescue of the townspeople. The reports of their scouts having left them no doubt about the intentions of the enemy, they were all seized with fear and dread and believed they would be lost without their provisions. Most of their ships were beached, and they could not make them float and consequently escape by sea, so they withdrew from the ships their provisions and set fire to them. Soon fear grew even

timoris augustia, et fugere sic inordinate et cum tanta celeritate decreverunt, ut obsidionalia instrumenta et maximam missilium partem cum sarcinis hostibus distrahenda relinquerent, quamvis tunc secum haberent duo mille equestres Walenses.

90   Post hanc ignominiosam fugam, cum more suo villagia comburendo ad castrum Sancti Clari fortissimum pervenissent, illud obsidione cingere statuerunt. Sed tandem ad dedicionem venire promiserunt, si bona villa propinqua vocata Callemardin ad eorum obedienciam veniret. Ex hac villa populosa, quam et muri fortissimi ambiebant, rex Anglie multa percipiebat commoda, et ex ea sagittarii cum cohorti-
95   bus armatis sepius erumpentes Walensibus multa dampna inferebant. Quapropter princeps jurejurando firmavit se inde non discessurum, donec viribus caperetur. Ibi in una parte Francigenis et altera Walensibus locatis, cum dies quatuor in obsidione exegissent, Gallici cum fossoriis et celtibus ferreis muros ilico suffoderunt, ut sic plane possent et manutentim pugnare. Ibique multis ex hostibus sauciatis et occisis,
100   secundo reiterato assultu, cum jam Franci murorum altitudinem occupare conarentur, oppidani pro tractu pacifico componendo mutuo consuluerunt. Obtulerunt siquidem ut, salvis armis et quantum quisque posset de mobilibus secum ferre, in urbe manerent salva vita, ut sic juramentum principis compleretur, et sibi atque Gallicis liber daretur ingressus. Quam oblacionem princeps et Walenses, qui nun-
105   dum pedem murorum attingerent, acceptantes, et Gallicorum laudantes strennitatem, sicut condictum fuerat, villam princeps cum suis libere est ingressus. Ex tunc villa predalis Walensibus effecta, cum se spoliis uberrimis onerassent, muros per circuitum in parte niaxima destruxerunt, in cunctis compitis ville et in suburbiis flammam voracem ponentes. Inde ambo exercitus ad Cardinguan castrum vallidum
110   tendentes, ex eventu vicinorum infausto territi oppidani dedicionem mox acceptaverunt iinperatam.

        Et tandem Gallici, cum fere per sexaginta leucas per regionem grassati fuissent hostiliter, principi requisierunt ut ab invicem divisi ob sterilitatem patrie loca eis assignarentur ad habitandum opportuna, donec classe conquisita repatriare
115   valerent. In tribus igitur locis usque ad festum omnium Sanctorum remanserunt; et tunc cum sex parvis navibus milites et armigeri disposuerunt redire, in Wallia mille ducentos levis armature servientes et quingentos balistarios relinquentes, quemdam armigerum nomine Blesum de Belay Picardum statuentes, cui omnes obedirent, donec navigium ad redeundum transmisissent.

120   Hoc in dedecus redeuncium versum fuit, cum sic relinquissent qui propter eorum gloriam dimicantes in assultibus fuerant semper primi, eos ex multis periculis sepius eruentes. Quibus tamen recommendati fuerant nobiles cum eisdem remanserunt fideliter, et necessitatibus eorum benigne succurrerunt, et eos undecunque collectis navibus circa carnisprivium reduxerunt.

among them, even though they had with them two thousand Welsh horsemen, and they became so frightened that even without being pursued they fled hastily in the greatest disorder and so abandoned their siege engines and the greater part of their artillery and their luggage.

After this shameful flight, having burned, according to their custom, the villages they met on the way, they arrived before the strong castle of St. Clears and prepared to besiege it. The garrison there promised to surrender if Carmarthen, located in the vicinity, likewise did so. This city, which was well populated and surrounded by good walls, offered great benefits to the king of England. The archers and men-at-arms, who formed the garrison there, often made frequent sorties and inconvenienced the Welsh very much. The prince of Wales swore an oath that he would not go away without making himself master of the place. The French posted themselves on one side, the Welsh on the other. After four days of siege, the French undermined the walls with picks and hoes; they made a breach and fought melee. Many of the defenders died or were wounded in the first assault. When they saw that the French were preparing to give a second assault and scale the walls, they decided to enter into talks. They offered to release the prince from his oath, to receive him and the French, and to abandon their weapons and all their goods as plunder, provided that their lives were spared and they could remain in the city. The prince and the Welsh, who had not yet reached the foot of the walls, accepted the offer, praised the French for their valor, and then went freely in the city, as had been agreed. The Welsh soon commenced looting, then, after having been gorged with booty, they razed most of the walls, and burned the streets and town. From there the two armies marched to a castle named Cardigan, whose inhabitants, frightened by the fate of their neighbors, hastened to capitulate.

The French, after marching into the country for sixty leagues, fearful of having to suffer from famine because of lacking food, begged the prince of Wales to provide different places for them to camp until they could have a fleet to return to their homeland. They were assigned three separate quarters, where they remained until the feast of All Saints [1 Nov]. Then the knights and esquires embarked on six small vessels, leaving in Wales twelve hundred light troops and five hundred crossbows under the command of a Picard squire named le Begue de Belay, to stay until they had sent their ships back for them.

We must strongly blame those who returned to France for having abandoned the men who had fought for their glory, who had always been the first in the attacks and who had saved them from many dangers. However, the nobles, under whose command the armed men had been placed, remained faithfully with them; they generously provided for their needs, gathered vessels from all parts, and then brought them back to France around Lent.

67. ADAM OF USK, *CHRONICLE, PART 4* — Latin, Summer 1421

Moritur Owenus de Glyndor post quatuor annos quibus a facie regis et regni latitasset, et sub noctis tempestate per suos fautores sepilitur. Sed per suos emulos funere detecto, sepulture restituitur, sed ubi receptatus erat nesciri poterit. Rex cum magna deuocione ad fontem sancte Wenefrede in Northwalia et pedes a Salopia
5 peregre proficiscitur.

68. THOMAS WALSINGHAM, *ST. ALBANS CHRONICLE* — Latin, Before 1423

De Gleyndor inuasorum incendio.
   Interea [1400] Wallici, nacta occasione de regis absencia, rebellare ceperunt, duce quodam Howeno de Gleyndor. Hic primo iuris apprenticius fuit apud West-monasterium, deinde armiger non ignobilis regi moderno ante susceptum regnum
5 laudabiliter militauit; sed orta discordia inter eum et dominum Reginaldum Grey de Ruffyn pro terris quas asseruit hereditario iure sibi competere, cum raciones suas et allegaciones paruipensas cerneret, primo in dominum de Grey hostilia commouit arma, uastans possessiones eius per incendia et ferro perimens plures de sua familia nimis crudeliter et inhumane. Que cum rex audisset, mox statuit eum persequi
10 tanquam pacis patrie perturbatorem. Quamobrem collecta multitudine armatorum et architenencium, Walliam est ingressus. Sed Wallici cum duce suo montes Snow-donie occupantes, intentate uindicte se subtraxerunt. Rex uero, combusta patria, et quibusdam peremptis quos sors pro tunc gladiis euaginatis obtulit, predaque capta nonmodica animalium, et iumentorum, in Angliam est regressus.

. . .

15 Efferatur Gleyndor.
   Hoc in tempore [1401] Howenus Gleyndor, collecta turba Wallensium, predatur patriam, quosdam capciuans, quosdam uero perimens inhumano more.

. . .

Cometa.
   Cometa apparuit mense Marcio [1402], primo inter Corum et Septentrionem,
20 uidelicet in Circio, flammas emittens terribiles, in altitudine magna porrecta, pos-tremo comas in boream transferens, in qua plaga ultimo uideri desiit, presignans, ut opinor, humanum sanguinem effundendum circa partes in quibus apparuit, Wallie uidelicet, et Northanhymbrie, ut dicemus.

67. ADAM OF USK, *CHRONICLE*, PART 4   Notes: p. 369

After four years in hiding from the king and kingdom, Owain Glyndŵr died, and was buried by his followers in the darkness of night. His grave was discovered by his enemies, however, so he had to be re-buried, though it is impossible to discover where he was laid.

68. THOMAS WALSINGHAM, *ST. ALBANS CHRONICLE*   Notes: pp. 369–71

The conflagration created by those attacking Glyndŵr.

In the meantime the Welsh had taken advantage of the king's absence and begun hostilities under the leadership of Owain Glyndŵr. He had originally been an apprentice-at-law at Westminster, then a distinguished esquire of the present king before he had succeeded to the throne, and had served him commendably. However, a dispute arose between him and Reginald, Lord Grey of Ruthin, over lands which he declared belonged to him by hereditary right. When he realized that his explanations and assertions were being treated with contempt, he took the initiative in beginning hostilities against Lord Grey, devastating his possessions by fire and killing many of his family in the fight with great cruelty and brutality. When the king heard what had happened, he took an immediate decision to arraign him as a disturber of the country's peace. He accordingly gathered a large force of men-at-arms and archers and invaded Wales. However, the Welsh took to the mountains of Snowdonia with their leader and withdrew from the punishment which threatened them. The king destroyed their land by fire, killed those who were unlucky enough at that time to come up against their drawn swords, and after plundering a not inconsiderable haul of cattle and pack-animals, he then returned to England.

. . .

Glyndŵr acts like a barbarian.

Also at this time Owain Glyndŵr gathered a mob of Welshmen and devastated the land, taking some men captive and killing others in a barbaric manner.

. . .

A comet.

In the month of March [1402] a comet appeared, at first between Capricorn and the Bear, that is in the north-west, emitting awesome flames, and travelling at a great height. Eventually it changed direction to the north, but finally ceased to be visible in that region of the sky, portending, in my opinion, the shedding of human blood in the vicinity of those regions in which it appeared, Wales and Northumberland, as we shall be describing.

Capitur dominus de Grey.

25   Per hoc tempus Houenus Gleyndor, congregatis suis Wallicis, uastauit terras domini Reginaldi Grey, qui in castro de Riffyn eo tempore morabatur, qui, putans eum adesse cum manu permodica, exiuit estimans se posse capere dictum Houenum, et leui negocio subiugare. Sed longe aliter euenit quam sperauerat, nam cum manus conseruissent, dominus de Grey captus est, et de parte sua plurimi interfecti.
30   Quod infortunium Wallicos extulit in superbiam, et eorum auxit insaniam, ut in sequentibus elucebit.

. . .

Capitur dominus Edmundus Mortimer.

         Per idem tempus Howenus Gleyndor cum turba Cambrensium assuetis intendens irrupcionibus, pene totam miliciam Herefordensis et armigeros comitatuum
35   prouocauit ad arma. Exiuerunt ergo, duce Edmundo de Mortuo Mari, milites et armigeri Howeno in obuiam, ualenciores uidelicet regionis, qui nichil maius metuebant quam Cambrorum fugam. Sed proh dolor! prodicione mediante, qui uicisse sperauerant, insperato uicti sunt, propriis sagittariis in suos manus uertentibus, et occidentibus cum quibus stare debuissent. Sicque perempti sunt ibidem
40   plures quam mille centum de nostratibus, et Edmundus de Mortemer captus est cum quibusdam aliis militibus et scutiferis atque ualectis, quorum nomina non tenemus. Ibique perpetratum est facinus a seculis inauditum, nam femine Wallencium post conflictum accesserunt ad corpora peremptorum et, abscindentes membra genitalia, in ore cuiuslibet posuerunt membrum pudendum, inter dentes
45   testiculis dependentibus, supra mentum, et nasos abscissos presserunt in culis eorundem. Nec passe sunt corpora mortuorum sepulture commendari sine precio grauique redempcione. Extiterunt qui asserebant dominum Edmundum Mortimer non inuitum fuisse captum, sed ex condicto premeditataque prodicione.
         Quorum asseuerauit opinionem ipsius expost Edmundi cum Howeno satis
50   infamis conuersacio, ut inferius patebit.

. . .

Rex intrat Walliam.

         Rex Anglie circa festum Assumpcionis sancte Marie, collectis exercitibus, profectus est in Walliam, committens unum exercitum filio suo, principi, alium uero Arundelie comiti, tercium secum detinens, ut in diuersis partibus Wallie, si quasi
55   inopinate subintrantes, Howenum Gleyndor et suos complices sic conclusissent, ut euadendi copiam minime reperissent, sed nichil profuit tantus armorum strepitus, quia Wallicus in noua latibula se recepit. Quin pocius, ut putatur, arte magica regem pene perdidit cum exercitu quem ducebat, nam a die quo ingressus est fines Cambrensium, usquequo loca dicta relinqueret, nunquam sibi arrisit aura serena,

Lord Grey is captured.

At this time Owain Glyndŵr gathered together an army of his Welshmen and devastated the lands of Reginald, Lord Grey, who was staying in the castle of Ruthin at that time. Thinking that Owain had arrived with only a modest force, he left the castle believing that he could capture Owain and subdue him on easy terms. But things turned out very differently from what he had hoped, for when they engaged in battle, Lord Grey was captured and very many of his men killed. This defeat of the English stirred the pride of the Welsh and heightened their madness, as will appear in later narrative.

. . .

Sir Edmund Mortimer is captured.

It was around this time that Owain Glyndŵr intensified his customary attacks [upon England] with a mob of Welshmen, and forced almost the whole of the knighthood of Hereford and esquires of the counties into armed conflict. These knights and esquires, being the strongest soldiers of the region, set out under the leadership of Edmund Mortimer to meet Owain, and feared nothing of any greater consequence than the flight of the Welsh. But alas! an act of betrayal intervened in affairs, and those who had hoped to gain a victory were unexpectedly defeated, for their own archers turned their bows against their own force and killed those with whom they should have been standing firm. So on that occasion more than one thousand one hundred of our soldiers were slain, and Edmund Mortimer was captured with certain other knights, esquires, and yeoman, whose names we do not possess. There an atrocity never before heard of was perpetrated, for after the battle Welsh women went to the bodies of the slain, cut off their genitalia, placed the penis of each man in his mouth with the testicles hanging between the teeth and above the chin, and then cut off the dead men's noses and pressed them into their anuses. They then refused to allow the bodies of the dead to be given up for burial without payment of a large ransom. There were those who alleged that Edmund Mortimer had not been a reluctant captive, but that this had been an agreed and premeditated act of treason.

Edmund Mortimer's subsequent notorious association with Owain confirmed the opinion of these people, as will be revealed below.

. . .

The king enters Wales.

At the time of the festival of the Assumption of St. Mary the king of England collected his forces and set out for Wales. He entrusted one army to his son, the prince, a second army to the earl of Arundel, and took possession of a third army himself. His aim was to infiltrate Wales by different routes unexpectedly, as it were, and thus blockade Owain Glyndŵr and his confederates, so that they would not find any way of escape. However, all this great sound of arms achieved nothing at all, for the Welshman withdrew into fresh hiding places. More to the point, indeed, he virtually defeated the king with the army which he was leading by magic, it is thought, for from the day he entered the territory of Wales up to the time he left those regions behind, no bright weather ever favoured the king, but every single

60   sed totis diebus ac noctibus pluuie mixte cum niuibus atque grandine sic afflixerunt exercitum, quod sustinere non poterant intemperanciam frigoris excessiui. In uigilia uero Naciuitatis sancte Marie, cum rex in amenissimo prato fixisset tentoria, ubi iuxta loci naturam nichil suspectum, nichil formidabile, sed summa requies sperabatur, repente in ipsius noctis prima uigilia tanta descendit aquarum abun-

65   dancia, ut pene putarent Anglici se mergendos. Superuenerunt insuper tanti uentorum turbines, ut ipsum regis tentorium rumperent, dissiparent, et prosternerent, et lanceam regis impetu uehementi deiicerent et in regali armatura defigerent; fuissetque ipsa nox regi ultima si non quieuisset armatus. Nec meminerunt Anglici, quanquam assueti rebus bellicis ab antiquo, se unquam tantum uexatos, periculis

70   tantis expositos, in ulla expedicione, ut eis uisum fuerat, sine humano ingenio extitisse. Vnde plures, si fas sit credere, opinati sunt hec mala arte Fratrum Minorum contra regem et suos fuisse commentata atque suscitata, qui parti Wallici fauere dicebantur. Sed absit hoc ab hominibus tam sanctam professis regulam, ut cum demonibus tantam contraherent familiaritatem, ut ponerent in gloria sua

75   maculam, nullo seculo detergendam! Rex autem, necessitate cogente, rediuit in Angliam post incensam patriam et predatam, de dictis infortuniis contristatus.

. . .

Edmundus de Mortuo Mari, iuuenis, quem diximus ante captum ab Howeno Gleyndor, uel tedio dire captiuitatis, uel metu mortis, uel ex aliqua nescitur causa, conuersus retrorsum, cum Howeno contra regem Anglie se sentire professus est;

80   dum nuptias satis humiles, et sue generositati impares, contrahit cum filia dicti Howeni. Et huius, ut fertur, natiuitatis exordia dira comitata sunt prodigia, cum nocte qua in lucem effusus est, in hyppodromo patris sui omnes equi patris eius reperti sunt in alto cruore stetisse, usque ad pedum et iuncturarum demersionem; quod tunc plurimi sinistrorsum interpretati sunt.

85   Eodem tempore, dominus Reginaldus de Grey, pacta solucione decem millium marcarum pro sua redempcione et exinde, solutis pre manibus sex milibus Howeno Gleyndor, de captiuitate solutus est.

. . .

Rebellio domini Henrici Percy.

Eodem tempore [1403] dominus Henricus Percy iunior, cui serena fronte

90   fortuna per ante blandita fuerat in operibus marciis in opinione uulgi rebusque temporalibus, repente — nescitur quo spiritu — et clam confederatis sibi plurimis, hostis apparuit regi Anglie manifestus; et in partibus Salopie, prout putatur, sperans in auxilio Howeni Gleyndor et Edmundi Mortimer, Cestrensium et Wallensium architenencium et hominum armatorum exercitum adunauit. Cui dominus

95   Thomas Percy, auunculus suus, comes Wygornie, quem rex filii sui primogeniti, principis Wallie, custodem constituerat et gubernatorem, relicto puero, et animum dedit et uires rebellandi, subtractis thesauris suis de Londoniis, et domo principis

day and night rain mingling with snow and hail so afflicted his army that the men could not endure the rigor of the extreme cold. On the eve of the feast of the Nativity of St. Mary, when the king had pitched his tents in a most pleasant meadow, where nothing was to be suspected, nothing feared by reason of the nature of the place, and where a time of rest could be expected, such torrential rains suddenly fell during the first watch of that very night that the English as good as thought they would be drowned. In addition such gales assailed them that these tore through the king's tent, scattered it, and left it lying flat on the ground; also in their ferocity they dislodged the king's lance, pinning it to the royal armour. That very night would have been the king's last if he had not gone to bed armed. The English, although they were accustomed to warfare from of old, did not remember that they had ever had so much trouble, or been exposed to such perils, in any other expedition that had not been, they thought, the result of human cunning. Hence many were of the opinion, if be right to have such a belief, that these occurrences had been contrived and stirred up by the magic arts of the Franciscan friars and directed against the king and his men, for the friars were said to favour the Welsh side. But God forbid that men who have professed so holy a rule should have entered into such an association with demons as to put a stain on their glory that could never again be removed! However, the king, by force of necessity, returned to England after the countryside had been ravaged by fire and plundered, saddened by the adversity that has been described.

. . .

The young man Edmund Mortimer, who we said previously had been captured by Owain Glyndŵr, changed sides, either because of weariness at his dreadful captivity, or through fear of death, or for some other reason unknown, and acknowledged that he had joined Owain in hostility towards the king of England. He also contracted a marriage with Owain's daughter, which was an inferior match and did not befit his noble position. It is said that dire portents accompanied his entry into life at birth, for on the night on which he was born into the light, it was discovered that all the horses in his father's stables had been standing in pools of blood that covered their hoofs up to their hocks. Many at that time interpreted this as a bad omen.

At that time Reginald, Lord Grey agreed a payment of ten thousand marks for his ransom, and after paying six thousand marks in advance to Owain Glyndŵr was accordingly released from captivity.

. . .

The rebellion of Sir Henry Percy.

At the same time Sir Henry Percy the younger, who had previously enjoyed the flattery of the people for his successes in warfare and in affairs of state, suddenly — it is not known what spirit motivated him — appeared as an undoubted enemy of the king of England, a large army of men having secretly joined forces with him. Relying, it is thought, on the help of Owain Glyndŵr and Edmund Mortimer, he collected an army of Cheshire and Welsh archers and men-at-arms. Thomas Percy, his uncle, the earl of Worcester, whom the king had made guardian and mentor of his eldest son, the prince of Wales, abandoned the boy, and gave his mind and resources to the rebellion, for he had withdrawn his fortune from London and had

satis occulte; et se iungens Henrico, nepoti suo, uiribus quas contrahere poterat ad eundem.

. . .

100   Rex se confert ad partes Walliarum.

Reuersus rex de partibus Aquilonis, uersus Walliam iter uertit ad comprimendas insolencias Howeni Gleyndor, qui multa dampna patriotis intulerat post recessum regis.

. . .

Filius Glenydor captus est.

105   Eo anno, die cinerum, facta est magna strages Wallensium, et quinto die mensis Marcii, altero facto conflictu apud Husk inter Wallicos et Anglicos, familiares domini principis, captus est filius Oweni Gleyndor, captis cum eo uel peremptis mille quingentis de parte rebellium. Expost circa festum sancti Dunstani captus est, in bello cancellarius Oweni Gleyndor, multis ex Wallensibus interemptis. Et eodem
110   anno captus est Iohannes Hanmere, gener eius, in bello; qui omnes ducti sunt Londonias et in Turri clausi.

. . .

Gallici uenerunt in Walliam et capiunt Kaermerdyn.

Circa dies istos Galli, facto grandi apparatu, uenerunt cum centum quadraginta nauibus ad succursum Howeni Gleyndor, et applicuerunt in portu de Milleforde,
115   amissis primo, pre defectu aque recentis, pene omnibus equis suis. Dominus de Berkle et Henricus Pay combusserunt ex eisdem nauibus quindecim in eodem portu. Gallici cum uenissent ad Howenum, animauerunt eum ad obsidionem urbis Merlini, que nunc Kaermerdyn appellatur. Cuius defensores, cum non possent resistere, reddiderunt urbem, saluis bonis omnibus, et personis, et optinuerunt
120   patentes litteras ab Howeno libere et sine indempnitate recedendi ad alia loca regis in Wallia, uel in Angliam si maluissent.

Capcio nauium Gallicorum.

Sub eodem tempore capte sunt naues quatuordecim per dominum de Berkle et dominum Thomam Swynbourne et Henricum Pay, que uelificauerunt uersus
125   Walliam in subsidium dicti Howeni. In quibus captus est senescallus Francie, et septem capitanei nominati.

. . .

Sternuntur Wallici et filius Gleyndor.

Per id tempus [1406] in die sancti Georgii conflixerunt cum Wallicis Anglici, et ceciderunt ex Wallicis mille uiri, inter quos filius alter Howeni Gleyndor occisus est.

. . .

it securely hidden in the house of the prince. He then joined his nephew Henry with the forces he had been able to muster for him.

. . .

The king marches to regions of Wales.

After the king returned from his northern territories, he marched towards Wales with the intention of curbing the insolent activities of Owain Glyndŵr, who had inflicted considerable harm upon his countrymen while the king was away.

. . .

The son of Glyn Dwr is captured.

That year [1405] on Ash Wednesday a great slaughter of the Welsh took place, and then again on the fifth of March in a second battle fought at Usk between the Welsh and the English, who were the prince of Wales's household troops, the son of Owain Glyndŵr was captured, and with him fifteen hundred on the rebel side were captured or killed. After this, at around the feast of St. Dunstan, Owain Glyndŵr's chancellor was captured in battle, and many of the Welsh killed. That same year John Hanmer, Glyndŵr's brother-in-law, was captured in battle. All these were taken to London and imprisoned in the Tower.

. . .

The French come to Wales and capture Carmarthen.

It was about this time [August 1405] that the French, having made huge preparations, came to the aid of Owain Glyndŵr with a hundred and forty ships, and landed in the harbour of Milford, though they had first lost almost all their horses because of the lack of fresh water. Lord Berkeley and Henry Pay set fire to fifteen of those ships in that very harbour. When the French reached Owain, they urged him to attack the town of Merlin, which is now called Carmarthen. Those defending it were not able to withstand the attack and surrendered the town in order to save all their possessions and their lives. They received letters patent from Owain, which allowed them freely, and without having to pay compensation, to depart to other of the king's lands in Wales, or to England if they preferred.

The capture of French ships.

At this time fourteen ships, which were sailing to Wales to aid Owain, were captured by Lord Berkeley, Sir Thomas Swinburn, and Henry Pay. In these ships a steward of France was captured along with seven men called captains.

. . .

The Welsh are slaughtered in battle, including Glyndŵr's son.

On St. George's day this year the English engaged the Welsh in battle, and a thousand Welsh soldiers were killed, amongst whom one of Owain Glyndŵr's sons was slain.

. . .

130   Naues capte.
         Eo tempore uelificauerunt uersus Walliam naues Gallicas uiginti octo, ex quibus
         capte sunt octo cum multis armatis, reliqueque in Walliam euaserunt.

                                              . . .

         [An agreement to surrender Aberystwyth]
              Hac estate [1407] obsedit princepts Wallie castrum de Aberustwith et sic artauit
         obsessos ut supplices precarentur inducias, ut patet in indenturis, sub hac re confectis.
135   "Hec indentura, facta, coram castro de Arberustwith iuxta nouam uillam de
         Lampadere situatam, illustrissimi regis Henrici quarti post conquestum anno .viii.
         mense Septembri die .xii. inter serenissimum principem Henricum dei gracia dicti
         regis Anglie et Francie primogenitum, principem Wallie, ducem Aquitannie, Lan-
         kastrie, Cornubie ac comitem Cestrie illustrissimique preexcellentissimi regis Anglie
140   et Francie locumtenentem, ex parte una, et Rees apud Gruffydd apud Llywelyn apud
         Ieuan, alias Rees apud Llywelyn Cadagan, Redderuch apud Thomas, Heire Ewyn,
         magistrum Ludwycum Mone, Ieuan apud Gruffydd, Rees David apud Gruffydd apud
         Iehun, Gruffydd apud Dauid apud Ieuan apud Madok, Meredith apud Res apud
         Roderagh, Owen apud Gruffydd apud Ieuan Blont, ex parte altera, testatur quod
145   predicti Rees et complices sui, super Corpus preciosum dominicum quod et rece-
         perunt et quilibet eorum recepit, ministratum eis per manus uenerabilis uiri magistri
         Ricardi Courteney uniuersitatis Oxoniensis cancellarii in presencia nobilium uirorum
         Edwardi ducis Eboraci, Ricardi comitis Warwyci, Iohannis domini de Furneuale,
         Thome baronis de Karrew, Iohannis domini de Audeley, Willelmi Baurchier, Francisi
150   de Court, Willelmi de Harrington, Thome Gunstalle, Rogeri Leche, Iohannis Seyn
         Iohn, Iohannis Oldecastelle, Iohannis Greindre, Iohannis Blount, Ricardi Kighley,
         Humfridi Stafforde, Willelmi Newport, militum, et aliorum fidedignorum quam-
         plurium: iuramentum prestiterunt et eorum quilibet prestitit corporale, quod si
         illustrissimi principes Henricus dei gracia rex Anglie et Francie et dominus Hibernie,
155   et Henricus eadem gracia princeps Wallie, seu alter eorum, aut eorum seu alterius
         eorundem locumtenens, deputatus seu deputandus, uel locumtenentis deputati seu
         deputandi, sint uel sit in uel coram uilla de Abrustwith, alias noua uilla de Lampader
         nuncupata, .xxiiii. die mensis Octobris proximo future tempore orti solis et ibi uel
         prope circa continuent uel continuet usque ad festum omnium sanctorum extunc
160   proximo sequens cum tali ac tanto numero pugnatorum, quod Owenus apud Gruff-
         ydd de Glendord uel eius locumtenens uel locumtenentes deputati seu deputandi non
         arcet seu arcent fuge prefatos illustres principes, Henricum aut Henricum seu eorum
         aut alterius eorum locumtenentem per uim belli seu recursus sic quod per eorum uim
         solum et acceptum et illatum arceantur demittere inter prefatum .xxiii. diem mensis
165   Octobris et prefatum festum omnium sanctorum tunc proximo sequens, quod extunc
         eodem festo omnium sanctorum, quod primo die mensis Nouembris contigerit,
         predictus Rees et prefati socii sui omnes et singuli et eorum quilibet, tenentur uirtute
         prestiti iuramenti, absque dilacione quauis seu ulteriore requisicione alia, dolo et
         fraude quibuscunque cessantibus dictum castrum de Abrustewith predictis illustribus
170   principibus Henrico et Henrico, eorum alteri seu alterius eorundem locumtenenti seu
         locumtenentibus, in possessionem pacificam mittere absque impedimento seu contra-
         diccione qualicunque.

Ships are captured.

Also at this time twenty-eight French ships set sail for Wales, but eight of these were captured along with many men-at-arms; the rest escaped to Wales.

. . .

[An agreement to surrender Aberystwyth]

That summer the prince of Wales besieged the castle of Aberystwyth and so constricted those being besieged that in submission they begged for a truce, as is apparent in the document completed in the following terms.

"This document was drawn up outside the gates of Aberystwyth castle situated not far from the new town of Llanbadarn on 12 September, in the eighth year of Henry IV after the Conquest, between the most high prince Henry, by the grace of God, eldest son of the said king of England and France, on the one part, and Rhys ap Gruffudd ap Llywelyn ab Ieuan, otherwise named Rhys ap Llywelyn Cadwgan, Rhydderch ap Tomas, Heire Ewyn, Master Lewys of Anglesey, Ieuan ap Gruffudd, Rhys Dafydd ap Gruffudd ab Ieuan, Gruffudd ap Dafydd ab Ieuan ap Madog, Maredudd ap Rhys ap Rhydderch, Owain ap Gruffudd ab Ieuan Blount, on the other part; and this document witnesses that the aforesaid Rhys and his associates took an oath over the precious Body of our Lord, which they and others individually received, administered to them by the hands of the venerable Master Richard Courteney, chancellor of the University of Oxford, in the presence of the noblemen Edward duke of York, Richard earl of Warwick, John Lord Furnivall, Thomas Baron Carew, John Lord Audley, the knights William Bourchier, Francis Court, William Harrington, Thomas Tunstall, Roger Leche, John Saint John, John Oldcastle, John Greyndour, John Blount, Richard Kighley, Humphrey Stafford, William Newport, and a large number of other trustworthy men: each and every one of them swore this corporal oath that, if the most illustrious princes, Henry, by the grace of God king of England and France and lord of Ireland, and Henry, by the grace of God prince of Wales, or either one of them, or someone representing them both or one of them, so deputed or to be deputed, or a man deputed or to be deputed in place of their representative, be outside the town of Aberystwyth, otherwise called the new town of Llanbadarn, at sunrise on the day following the twenty-fourth day of the month of October, and continue to be there or nearby until the next feast of All Saints, with such and such a number of soldiers, and Owain ap Gruffudd Glyndŵr or his representative or representatives, deputed or to be deputed, do not drive off the aforesaid illustrious princes Henry [the king] and Henry [his son] or any representative of them or of either of them, or compel them to take flight by force of battle or withdrawal, so that through their force they be constrained to abandon the soil, received and bestowed between the aforesaid twenty-fourth of October and the aforesaid feast of All Saints, which would occur on the first day of November, the aforesaid Rhys and each and every one of his associates are under obligation by virtue of the oath they have taken, without any delay or any further request, all deceit and treachery ceasing, to hand over the said castle of Aberystwyth into peaceful possession of the aforesaid illustrious princes [King] Henry and [Prince] Henry or to their representatives, without impediment or any kind of opposition.

"Preterea predicti Rees apud Gruffydd apud Llywelyn apud Ieuan et prenominati sui iurati sunt et iuramento astricti quod, a data presencium indenturarum nec illi,
175   nec ille, nec aliquis eorum, qui est aut sunt, erit aut erunt, in prefato castro continue manentes usque ad tempus reddicionis eiusdem, liberum ingressum et egressum habentes cuiuscunque status, gradus seu condicionis existant, solum exceptis illis quos a dicto castro per ordinacionem et uocacionem dicti Rees pro dicti castri securitate pleniori expelli continget, dictum castrum exibit, nec exibunt in releuamen seu
180   adiutorium dicti Oweni nec suorum nec sibi adherencium contra prefatos illustres principes Henricum et Henricum, nec aliquem eorum, seu eorum seu alterius eorumdem locumtenentis seu locumtenentium, nec contra aliquem eorum seu alterius eorumdem ligeum seu ligeos, nec specialiter contra eos qui rebellione dimissa, se ad graciam prefatorum regis et principis submiserunt.
185   "Preterea concordatum et iuratum est quod habitaciones et hospicia infra uillam predictam senecta reparata seu de nouo constructa tempore obsidionis facte coram dicto castro de Abrustewith per prefatum principem illustrissimum Henricum principem Wallie per dictum Rees nec aliquem seu aliquos destruentur nec peiorabuntur quoquo modo. Insuper si naues alique maris tempestate artate seu
190   aliquo quoquomodo ad portum siue districtum dictorum uille uel castri deueniant, per prefatum Rees, socios, seu eorum aliquem non molestari debent nec grauari nec bona contenta nec homines in eisdem.
"Insuper predicti Rees et socii sui et eorum quilibet iurati sunt quod predictum castrum in adeo bono statu uel meliore seruabunt, custodient et liberabunt, sicut die
195   confectionis presencium extat, nec persona seu persone aliqua seu alique, cuiuscunque status, gradus, nacionis seu condicionis existat seu existant, debet nec debent a data presencium usque ad dictum festum omnium sanctorum gubernare, preter predictum Rees, socios, seu eorum aliquem, qui super corpus dominicum sunt iurati, et illud conformiter receperunt, quorum ut supra nomina recitantur. Preterea
200   concordatum et iuratum est quod predictus Rees et predicti complices sui, seu eorum aliquis, tempore reddicionis eiusdem castri facient seu faciet liberacionem plenam canonum seu instrumentorum, Anglice gunnes uocatorum, arcuum, sagittarum, balistarum et aliorum instrumentorum infra dictum castrum a tempore quo per eum seu per eos extitit occuppatum, contentorum et ad dictum castrum ab antique
205   competencium.
"Et pro pleniore securitate articulorum omnium premissorum, predicti Rees et prefati socii sui, super obsidibus seu ostagiis non coacti et non compulsi, fecerunt liberacionem personarum sequencium, non coactarum, non compulsarum, uidelicet honorabilis in Christo et religiosi uiri Ricardi apud Gruffydd, abbatis de Stratflorida,
210   Iankyn apud Rees apud Dauid, Meredithe apud Oweyn Gruffydd, Thomas apud Roderiche apud Ieuan Blount, armigerorum comitatus de Cardigan. Et ex alia parte, prefatus illustrissimus princeps Henricus, princeps Wallie, etc. ob reuerenciam Dei et omnium sanctorum, necnon specialis patroni sui, Iohannis de Bridelingtone, in saluacionem humani sanguinis, cuius effusioni uigorose compatitur, necnon ad
215   humilem requisicionem et instanciam prefatorum Ricardi abbatis de Stratflorida, Rees apud Gryffydd apud Llywelyn apud Ieuan et omnium ualenciorum infra

"Furthermore, the aforesaid Rhys ap Gruffudd ap Llywelyn ab Ieuan and his aforenamed associates have taken an oath, and are bound by that oath, that from the date of the present document neither he, nor those associates, nor any of the men who are or will be in the aforesaid castle, remaining up to the time of its surrender, having free ingress and egress, no matter what their status, position, or fortune may be, will leave the said camp to gain relief or support for the said Owain, his associates, or those supporting him against the aforesaid illustrious princes [King] Henry and [Prince] Henry, except for those alone who must be expelled from the said castle through command or summons of the said Rhys for the fuller security of the said castle, or any one of those, or more than one, representing them, nor against any liegemen or either, nor especially against those who, having abandoned rebellion, have submitted to the grace of the aforesaid king and prince.

"Moreover it has been agreed and sworn that the dwellings and the hospitals within the said town, old, repaired or newly built at the time of the siege established before the castle of Aberystwyth by the aforesaid illustrious Henry, prince of Wales, should neither be destroyed by the said Rhys, or any man or men, nor impaired in any way. Furthermore, if any ships that have been afflicted by storm at sea or hindered in any other way whatsoever come to the harbour or the vicinity of the said town or castle, they must not be troubled or harmed by the aforesaid Rhys, his comrades, or any one of those men, nor the goods contained within the ships, nor the men manning them.

"Furthermore, the aforesaid Rhys, his comrades, and every man of theirs have taken an oath that they will keep guard and deliver up the aforesaid castle in as good a condition as, or better than, it is at the time this present document is completed, and no person or persons of any sort, no matter what estate, position, race, or fortune, must, from the date of this present document up to the feast of the said All Saints, govern the castle, except the aforesaid Rhys, his associates, or a representative of them, who have sworn upon the Body of our Lord and received it in a spirit of concord, and whose names are recorded above. Moreover, agreement has been reached and an oath taken that the aforesaid Rhys and his aforesaid associates, or one of their representatives, will, at the time of the surrender of the castle, deliver up in full the cannons or weapons called in English 'guns', bows, arrows, crossbows, and other weapons that have belonged to the castle from of old, contained inside the said castle since it was occupied by Rhys, or by the other men.

"In order to ensure more fully that all the aforementioned clauses are carried out, the aforesaid Rhys and his aforesaid associates, though not coerced or compelled over pledges or hostages, have handed over the following persons, without those persons being coerced or compelled: namely, the honourable brother in Christ and religious man Richard ap Gruffudd, abbot of Strata Florida, and the esquires of the county of Cardigan, Siancyn ap Rhys ap Dafydd, Maredudd ab Owain Gruffudd, and Tomas ap Rhydderch ab Ieuan Blount. On the other part, the most illustrious prince Henry, prince of Wales, etc., out of reverence for God and all the saints, as well as for his special patron, John of Bridlington, to save the spilling of human blood, the spilling of which he strongly pities, and at the humble request and plea of the aforesaid Richard, abbot of Strata Florida, Rhys ap Gruffudd ap Llywelyn ab Ieuan, and all the magnates within the said castle, is granting out of the abundance of his grace, to them

dictum castrum existencium, ex habundanti gratia sua, concedit eisdem et eorum cuilibet, qui pro tempore reddicionis eiusdem castri ligeus seu ligei deuenient prefati illustrissimi principis Henrici regis Anglie et Francie, gratiam et perdonacionem
220   speciales uite, membrorum, terrarum, bonorum et reddituum.

"Concedit insuper idem illustrissimus princeps ex gratia sua speciali eidem Rees et nominatis sociis suis infra dictum castrum existentibus, a data presencium usque ad dictum festum omnium sanctorum, quod ipse, ipsi et eorum quilibet, absque impechiamento, impedimento, arrestacione quauis libere uehere, mittere et
225   disponere poterunt omnia eorum bona mobilia a tempore date presencium infra castrum existencia, tam per mare quam per terram, et quod predicta bona per predictum illustrissimum principem, nec aliquem alium, quantum in eo est, grauari et arrestari nec ab eis alienari seu distrahi debent quouis modo; et quod eorum et eorum cuiuslibet seruientes liberum egressum et ingressum, tam per terram quam
230   per mare habeant, quantum in eo est, ut super continetur. Et si aliqua bona, ad dictum Rees uel aliquem sociorum suorum prefatorum pertinencia, per aliquos dicti illustrissimi principis subditos et subiectos infra tempus predictum uiolenter rapiantur ab eis, idem illustrissimus princeps, excessus, delicta et rapinas huiusmodi debite, prout decet, faciet castigari.

235   "Et si predictus Owynus, deputatus seu deputati sui, ui seu uirtute belli aut recursus dicti castri, arceant seu compellant ad fugam prefatos illustrissimos principes Henricum et Henricum, eorum alterum, eorum aut alterius eorundem locumtenentem seu locumtenentes, deputatum seu deputandos, a prefato .xxiiii. die mensis Octobris usque ad proximum extunc sequens festum omnium sanctorum, quod tunc
240   prefati obsides seu hostagii supradicti, prefato Rees, deputato seu deputatis suis cum eorum seruientibus, bonis mobilibus et immobilibus consequenter et indilate liberabuntur sine fraude. Preterea uult et finaliter concedit idem illustrissimus princeps Henricus etc., quod, a data Presencium, usque ad dictum proximum festum omnium sanctorum, non fiet per eum dicto castro insultus quiuis, per media, fraudes,
245   et subtilitates quascumque, neque infra tempus predictum illud obtinere contendet.

"In quorum omnium et singulorum premissorum fidem, securitatem et testimonium, prefatus illustrissimus princeps Henricus princeps Wallie et prenominati Rees et socii sui et eorum quilibet, hiis indenturis sigilla sua alternatim apposuerunt anno mense et loco supradictis."
250   Sed nil ualvere pacta nil promissa principe recedente. Nam Oweynus Gleyndor mox castrum de premissorum manibus extorsit astu, et eos, qui hec pacta pepigerant, non sine nota prodicionis, expulit et alios ad custodiam subrogauit: factus est nouissimus error peior priore.

. . .

[1412] Dauid Gamme fraude capitur amici sui et uenit, ut fertur, in manus Oweni
255   Gleyndor.

and all their dependents who at the time of the surrendering of the same castle will become liegemen of the aforesaid most illustrious prince Henry, king of England and France, special pardon and remission in respect of their life, limbs, lands, possessions, and revenue.

"The same most illustrious prince is in addition granting, out of his special grace, to those same Rhys and his named associates being within the said castle, that, from the date of this present document until the said feast of All Saints, he, his associates, and all their dependents will be able to move, send, and dispose of, freely, by both land and sea, without any hindrance, impediment, or arrest, all their movable possessions that are in the camp at the time this present document is dated, and that the aforesaid possessions must not in any respect be harmed, seized, or taken away from these men or pillaged by the aforesaid most illustrious prince, or by any other person, no matter what his rank; also that all their servants should have unimpeded egress and ingress, both by land and sea, to the extent that this accords with what is stated above. Indeed, should any possessions belonging to the said Rhys or any of this aforesaid associates be seized forcibly from them within the aforesaid time by any of the subordinates or subjects of the aforesaid most illustrious prince, he will make it his business to punish them duly for such outrages, offences, and thefts, as is fitting.

"However, if the aforesaid Owain, his deputy or his deputies, either by force or by virtue of war or by relief of the said castle, should resist, or force the most illustrious princes [King] Henry and [Prince] Henry to take flight, or either one of them, or their lieutenant or lieutenants deputed or to be deputed, after the aforesaid twenty-fourth day of October until the next day after the feast of All Saints, the aforesaid hostages and pledges, the man or men deputizing for the aforesaid Rhys with their servants, their movable and immovable possessions will, in consequence and without delay, be rightfully taken from them. Furthermore, the same most illustrious prince, [King] Henry, etc., desires and grants in conclusion, that from the date of this present document until the said next feast of All Saints, no assault of any kind will be made by him upon the said castle through mediation, trickery, or any sort of guile, and he will not during that period of time attempt to occupy that said place.

"To secure the trust of each and every one of the aforesaid, the most illustrious prince Henry, prince of Wales, and the aforenamed Rhys and each and every one of his associates have in turn fixed their seals to these documents in the aforesaid month and place."

However, nothing came of the matters agreed, nothing of the promises made, as the prince withdrew. For Owain Glyndŵr instantly wrested the castle from the hands of the aforesaid men by an adroit move, banishing those who had made this pact, stigmatizing them as traitors, and imprisoning others. So it was that the last wrong act of that man was worse than the first.

. . .

Dafydd Gam was captured through the treachery of his friend, and fell into the hands of Owain Glyndŵr.

69. PIERRE COCHON, *CHRONIQUE NORMANDE*   **French**
                                                          1430

Item, à la Saint Jehan l'an mil .cccc. et .iiij. ou environ, se commencha une très grant armée pour aller aidier au prince de Gallez contre le roy Henrry d'Engleterre, auquel y portoit guerre, de laquelle armée estoit capitaine le compte de la Marche acompaignié de grandement de grans seigneurs, nobles, grant quantité de jeunez
5   gens, arbalestiers, et archiés. Et commencherent les unz à asembler à Harefleu, à la myaost, et les autres à Bret en Bretaigne. Et là vint .xx. grosses nés d'Espaigne et des Bretons grant quantité, et là rechurent leur garnisons, et ourent .cm. lb. Et fu enchiés la Saint-Martin d'iver qu'il partissent de Bret; et furent .viij. jours sus mer, et arriverent en Engleterre, et ardirent .j. povre village où il y out fait grant
10   quantité de chevaliers en ce beau fait; et puis s'en retournerent sans plus rien faire. Ainsi furent les .cm. franz despendus. Ainsi se despendoit l'argent du propre [for povre] peupple de France.

                                      . . .

Item, en ce temps [1405], le jour de la Magdeleine ensuiant, messire Jehan de Hangest, mettre des arballestiers et le Borgne de la Heuse dit des Ventez, capitaines
15   d'une grant armée faicte et assemblée pour aller aidier au prince de Gualles contre le roy d'Engleterre; et partirent ce jour .xvj. gros vessiax et .ij. carraquez garniez de gens d'armez det de vitallez, et passerent la mer, et là furent ou pais, jusques à la Toussains ensuiant; et firent de belles besongnez et de fait d'armes et merveilles, et puis s'en revindrent.

70. *ANNALES OWENI GLYNDWR*   **Welsh**
                                                 1422 x 1450

MCCCC ydd aeth Hari i Prydain a llv mawr gidac ef. A phan ytoed ef ar wastad yno y dywedodd vn o'r arglwyddi wrthaw ydd oedd reidach iddaw vod diwydwyr iddaw y Nghymrv, a dywedyd y kyvodai Owain ap Gruff[udd] i ryvelv yn i erbyn. Ac oddyno ydd anvoned Arglwydd Talbod ac [p. 60] Arglwydd Grei o Ruthvn i vod yn
5   ddiogel o Ywain, a hwynt a'i kymerassant arnaddunt. Eissioes y gwr a ddiangawdd i'r koed, a hynn oedd Gwyl Vathav yn y kynhayaf. Yr haf nessaf wedi hynny y kyvodes Ywain ar y chwigeinved o ddireidwyr a lladron ac y ddaeth ef ac wynt ar ryvel i flaenav Keredigion, ac yno ydd ymgynvllawdd mil a haner o wyr bro Geredigion a Rros a Phenfro ac y ddaethant i'r mynydd i geissiaw dala Owain. Ac
10   ar Vynydd Hyddgant i bv yr ymgyfarvod ryddynt, ac yn gytnaid ac y troes y llv Seissnic eu kefnav y ffo y llas CC o honyw. Ac yna y ddaeth gair mawr i Owain ac i kyvodes attaw ran vawr o'r yfiengtid a'r direidwyr o bob gwlad o Gymry oni oedd gidac ef llu mawr.

      MCCCCij flynedd ydd aeth Owain a'i lv i wneuthur kyrch i ystlys Rrvthvn a
15   Dyffryn Klwyd, ac y kyvodes Reinallt Grei, [p. 61] arglwydd y tir hwnnw, i'r maes yn i erbyn. Ac yno i dalwyd Arglwy[dd] Grae yn garcharawr ac i bv mewn hir garchar gan Owain mewn diffeithwch a tharenni. Ac o'r diwedd gwnaeth aranswn er vn vil ar ddeg o vorkav.

69. Pierre Cochon, *Normandy Chronicle*   Notes: p. 371

In the year 1404 or thereabouts, there commenced a grand army in order to aid the prince of Wales against King Henry of England, which suffered war at that time, for which army the count de La Marche was chosen to lead the great lords, nobles, and many young men, crossbowmen, and archers. And they began to assemble themselves, most going to Harfleur, and the others going to Brest in Brittany. And to Brest came twenty large ships from Spain and a great number more from the Britons, and there they fitted out their stores, and they used 100,000 francs to do so. It was St. Martin's Day [11 November] before they finally left Brest, and they were eight days at sea, and they arrived in England, and they burned one poor village, where this fine thing was done by a great number of knights; and then they returned without doing anything more. Thus did they spend 100,000 francs. Thus was spent by them the gold of the poor people of France.

. . .

At that time, following the day of the Magdalene, lord Jean de Hangest, master of the crossbows, and Le Borgue de la Heuse of Ventes, were made captains of a great army and were assembled to go for the aid of the prince of Wales against the king of England; on that day there departed sixteen great vessels and two carracks loaded with men-at-arms and provisions, and they passed over the sea, and they were there in that country, up to the following All Saints' Day [1 November]; and they did fine work, both in feats of arms and marvels, and then they returned.

70. *Chronicle of Owain Glyndŵr*   Notes: pp. 371–79

1400. Henry went to Scotland, and a great host with him. And when he was at rest there, one of the lords said to him that he had better have faithful men in Wales and he said that Owain ap Gruffudd would rise up to wage war against him. And from there Lord Talbot and the Lord Grey of Ruthin were sent to make sure of Owain, and they took it upon them. However, the man escaped to the woods, and that was on the Feast of Matthew in the autumn. The next summer after that, Owain rose up with six score wicked men and thieves, and he brought them as to war into the uplands of Ceredigion. And fifteen hundred men from the lowland of Ceredigion and Rhos and Pembroke assembled there and they came to the mountain to try to capture Owain. And on Hyddgant Mountain was the encounter between them, and as soon as the English host turned their backs to flee, two hundred of them were killed. And then great praise came to Owain, and there rose up with him a great part of the youth and the wicked men from every region of Wales until there was a great host with him.

1402 years. Owain went with his host to make an attack beside Ruthin and Dyffryn Clwyd, and Reginald Grey, lord of that land, took to the field against him. And there Lord Grey was taken prisoner, and he was kept in prison by Owain for a long time in the wilderness and rocky hills. And in the end he made ransom for 11,000 marks.

MCCCCiii y kyvodes Owain a llu mawr gydac ef o Wynedd a Phowys a Dehev-
20   barth, ac i Velenydd y kyrchodd. Yna ydd ymgynvllassant marchogion swydd Hen-
ffordd yn i erbyn ac yn ystlys Pilale i bv y kyfarvod y ryddvnt. Ac yno y llas Sr Robert
o Chwitnei a Sr Ginarc Dyladr ac y dalwyd Sr Emwnt Mortimer a Sr Tomas Klannow
ac i lladdwyd y llv Seissnic kyn mwyaf. Yr Awst nessaf wedi hynny y doeth Owain i
Vorganwc ac y kyvodes holl Vorganwc y gydac [ef] ac y llosged Kaerddydd a
25   Gevenni.

MCCCCiiij y kafas Owain y kestyll nid amgen Harddlech, Aber Ystwyth. [p. 62]
Yn yr vn flwyddyn hono i bv y lladdfa ar Gymrv ar Vynydd Kamstwn, a'r llall ar y
Saesson ar Graic y Dorth rrwn Pen y Clawdd a Thref Vynwy. Yno y llas y Saesson
gan mwyaf oll ac i bv y dilyn arnynt hyd y mhorth y dref.

30   MCCCC.v y bv y lladdfa yn Ghymry ar Vynydd y Pwll Melyn wrth Frynn Bvga,
ac yna y delid Gruff[udd] ap Owain. Yna y bv dechrav yr ymchwel ar Owain a'i wyr.
Yna ir ymroddes holl Vorgannwc i'r Saesson, dieithr rrivedi bychan aeth i Wynedd
at i harglwydd.

MCCCCvj yr ymroddes Gwyr ac Ystratowi a chan mwyaf Garedigion yn Seissnic.
35   MCCCCvi[i] y doeth y twysoc Sais a llv mawr gidac ef i osod sits [p. 63] ar gastell
Aber Ystwyth ac nid aeth oddiwrtho oni kavas eddewid ar y kastell mewn oed tydd
byrr, a phedwar o'r gorevgwyr mwyaf i gallv ar oedd o vewn y'r kastell yn wystl drostaw. O vewn i hynn myned Rrys Du i Wynedd i ovyn kennad y Owein i roddi y
kastell i'r Saesson. Kadw o Owain Rs gidac ef yni gavas i nerth attaw a myned y gida
40   Rrys i Aber Ystwyth a gosod ar dorri pen Rrys oni cheffid y kastell. Ac ar hynt
rroddi y Owain y kastell.

MCCCCviii y doeth yr ail sigy ar y kastell vchod ac i henillwyd kyn myned o
iwrtho. Ac oddyno y ddaeth y llv i Harddlech. Ac yno i bv varw llawer o voneddigion
[p. 64] Kymry ac o'r diwedd gorvod rroddi y kastell i'r Saesson.

45   MCCCCix i gwnaeth gwyr Owain gyrch i ystlys swydd Ymwythic, ac yno i dalodd
y Saesson Rys Dv a Ffylpott Ysgidmor ac ydd aeth yr vn i Lundain a'r llall i Amwythic i'w llusgaw ac i'w chwartoriaw. Ac o hynny allan ni wnaeth Owain gyrch mawr
oni aeth mewn difant.

(Ano Dni 1412 i daliod Rys ap Tudur o Von ag Ednyfed i frawd ag y Nghaer
50   Lleon i dihenydhwyd hwynt.)

MCCCCxv ydd aeth Owain mewn difant y Gwyl Vathe yn y kynhayaf. O hynny
allan ni wybvwyd i ddifant. Rrann vawr a ddywaid i varw; y brvdwyr a ddywedant na
bv.

71. *PROSE BRUT (COMMON VERSION TO 1419)*   **Middle English** **after 1419**

Than began the discencion and debate yn the cuntre of Walis betwene the
Lorde Grey Rithyn and Oweyn of Glyndore, squier of Walis. And this Oweyn rerid
a nownbyr of Walschemen, and kept that cuntrey about ryht strong, and dede
myche harme, and destroyed the kingis tounez and lorschippez throuhout Walis,
5   and robbyd and slowgh the kingis pepil, both Englisch and Walsch; and thus he
endured xij. yere large. And he toke the Lorde Gray of Rithyn presoner, and kept

1403. Owain rose up, and a great host with him from Gwynedd and Powys and Deheubarth, and he made for Maelienydd. There the knights of Herefordshire assembled against him, and near Pilleth was a battle between them. And there Sir Robert Whitney and Sir Kynard de la Bere were killed, and Sir Edmund Mortimer and Sir Thomas Clanvowe were captured, and the English host was killed for the most part. The next August after that, Owain came to Glamorgan, and all Glamorgan rose up with him, and Cardiff and Abergavenny were burned.

1404. Owain took the castles, none other than Harlech [and] Aberystwyth. In that same year there was a slaughter of the Welsh on Campston Hill and another of the English on Craig-y-dorth, between Pen-y-clawdd and Monmouth town. There the English were killed for the most part, and they were pursued up to the gates of the town.

1405. There was a slaughter in Wales on Pwll Melyn Mountain near Brynbuga [Usk], and there Gruffudd ab Owain was captured. It was then the turn [of fortune] began for Owain and his men. Then all of Glamorgan submitted to the English, except for a small number who went to Gwynedd to their lord.

1406. Gower and Ystrad Tywi and most of Ceredigion submitted as English.

1407. The English prince came, and a great host with him, to lay siege to Aberystwyth castle, and he did not cease that until he received a promise for [the surrender of] the castle in a short period of time, with four of the most powerful noblemen who were within the castle as pledges for it. Within this [period] Rhys Ddu went to Gwynedd to ask permission of Owain to give the castle to the English. Owain kept Rhys with him until he had gathered his force to him, and he went with Rhys to Aberystwyth and he threatened to cut off Rhys's head if he did not get the castle. And upon that the castle was given to Owain.

1408. A second siege came to the above castle, and it was won before leaving it. And from there the host came to Harlech. And there died many of the nobles of Wales, and in the end [they were] forced to give the castle to the English.

1409. Owain's men made an attack on the borders of Shropshire, and there the English captured Rhys Ddu and Philip Scudamore, and the one was sent to London and the other to Shrewsbury to be drawn and quartered. And from then on Owain made no great attack until he went into hiding.

(Anno Domini 1412. Rhys ap Tudur of Môn was captured, and Ednyfed, his brother, and they were executed in Chester.)

1415. Owain disappeared on the Feast of St. Matthew in the autumn. From then on (the place of) his disappearance was not known. A great many say he died; the seers say he did not.

71. *Prose Brut (Common Version to 1419)*   **Notes: pp. 379–81**

Then began the dissension and debate in the country of Wales between Lord Grey of Ruthin and Owain Glyndŵr, a squire of Wales. This Owain raised a number of Welshmen, and he strongly held the country around him and did much harm, and destroyed the king's towns and lordships throughout Wales, and robbed and killed the king's people, both English and Welsh; and he remained 12 years at large. He took Lord Grey of Ruthin prisoner, and he kept him imprisoned until he

hym fast yn holde tylle he was raunsonde of prysoners of the March, and kept hym
long tyme yn holde; and at the last he made hym wedde on of his douhtris, and
kepte hym stylle there with his wiff, and sone after he deyed.

10   And thanne the king, knowyng this myschef, destruccion and treson, that this
Oweyn hade y-wrouht, then anon he ordeyned a strong power of men of armez and
of archers, and moche other stuffe that longis to warre, for to abate and destroye the
malice of the fals Walschemen. And thanne the king come ynto Walys with his power,
for to destroy this Owen and other rebellis, fals Walschmen. And anon thei fledden
15   ynto the mountaynez; and there myhte the kinge do hem non harme yn no maner
of wyse; but ofte thei toke the kingis cariage, and euery day destroyed his peple. But
Oweyn and his men, the moste parte, ascapid harmelez, ffor the king ne his meyne
myht not come to hem yn no maner of wise for the mountaynez; and so the king
come to Engelond ayen, for lesyng of moo of his peple, and thus he spedde not there.

72. *CONTINUATIO EULOGII*   **Latin**
                                                                   after 1426

Ad hoc parliamentum venit Audoenus de Glendour Wallicus qui fuerat armiger
comitis Arundell', conquerens quod dominus de Grey Ruthyn quasdam terras suas
in Wallia usurpavit, sed contra dominum de Grey nihil profecit. Episcopus de Santo
Assaf consuluit in parliamento quod non omnino contemnerent præfatum
5   Audoenum ne forte Wallici insurgerent. Et illi de parliamento dixerunt se de scurris
nudipedibus non curare.

· · ·

Anno Domini 1401, Wallici contra regem Henricum Quartum rebellant et bona
Anglicorum undique diripiunt. Rex autem transivit in Walliam Borealem et Insulam
de Anglesey, ubi Fratres Minores de conventu Lamasiæ et Wallici cum aliis Regi
10   resistebant, et ideo exercitus regis fratres occidebant et captivabant ac conventum
spoliabant. Et, Audoeno non comparente, revertitur Rex. Et dominus le Gray
manucepit tuitionem patriæ. Rex vero tradidit ministerio Ordinis fratres captivatos,
et jussit omnia restitui conventui, et voluit quod conventus ille inhabitaretur ab
Anglicis fratribus.

· · ·

15   Audoenus de Glendour dominum le Grey in bello cepit. Et eodem anno [1401]
capitulum generale Fratrum Minorum celebratur Leycestriæ in festo Assumptionis,
in quo prohibitum est sub pœna perpetui carceris ne aliquis fratrum loquatur
verbum quod possit sonare in præjudicium Regis. Et quod quilibet præsidens
haberet potestatem talem incarcerandi qui ausus esset in hoc culpari.
20   Hoc insuper anno post Natale Domini apparuit quaedam stella comata aspectu
terribilis in Occidente, eujus flamma magna sursum ascendebat.

· · ·

was ransomed for prisoners of the March, and he kept him imprisoned a long time, and in the end made him wed one of his daughters, and kept him there with his wife. Soon afterwards he died.

The king, knowing the mischief, destruction, and treason that this Owain had wrought, at once gathered a strong power of men-of-arms and archers, and many other armaments that are needed for war, in order to stop and destroy the malice of the false Welshmen. Then the king came into Wales with his power, to destroy this Owain and other rebels, false Welshmen. But they fled into the mountains; and there the king could do them no harm in any way. Still, they often seized the king's carriage, and every day they destroyed his people. Owain and his men, for the most part, escaped harmless, for neither the king nor his company could reach them in any way because of the mountains. And so the king returned to England again, due to the loss of his people, and thus he did not succeed there.

72. *Continuation of the Eulogium historiarum*   Notes: pp. 382–83

To this parliament came the Welshman Owain Glyndŵr, who had been an esquire of the earl Arundel, complaining that the Lord Grey of Ruthin, had forcibly taken some of his lands in Wales, but he had no advance against the Lord de Grey. In parliament the bishop of St. Asaph advised that they should not altogether dismiss the commander Owain, lest by chance the Welsh might rise. And concerning this the members of the parliament said that they did not care about barefooted buffoons.

. . .

In the year of our Lord, 1401, the Welsh rebelled against King Henry and snatched away the goods of the English everywhere. Moreover, the king crossed into Northern Wales and the Isle of Anglesey, where the Minorite Friars from the convent of Llanfaes and the Welsh with others were resisting the king and for that reason the army of the king began to kill and capture the friars and loot the convent. And, although Owain had not appeared, the King turned back. And Lord Grey took up the defense of the fatherland. The King however handed over to the ministry the captured brothers of the Order and commanded that everything be returned to the convent and wanted the convent to be occupied by English Brothers.

. . .

Owain Glyndŵr took the Lord Grey captive in battle. And in the same year [1401] a general chapter of the Minorite Friars was held at Leicester on the feast of the Assumption, at which it was prohibited on pain of life imprisonment that any of the Brothers speak a word which could be taken against the king. And they ruled that each had sufficient power to incarcerate anyone who had dared to offend in this matter.

Moreover in this year, after Christmas, appeared a certain comet-star, horrible to look upon, in the west, whose great flame rose on high.

. . .

Hoc insuper anno [1402], Audoenus de Glendour cepit Edmundum de Mortuo Mari, multis Anglicis de marchia Walliæ interfectis. Et Rex congregato exercitu transivit in Walliam, ubi, prohibentibus maximis tempestatibus in Septembri
25   tonitruorum, imbrium, et grandinis, equitare non potuerunt, et multi de exercitu frigore mortui sunt.

. . .

Henricus Percy, et avunculus ejus Thomas Percy, quem Rex Ricardus fecerat comitem Wigorniæ et domus suæ senescallum, collegerunt exercitum in marchia Scociæ, dicentes quod contra Scotos bellare oporteret; et venerunt ad comitatum
30   Cestriæ et Cestrenses secum assumpserunt. Miseruntque ad Audoenum ut veniret. Sed Audeonus, cognoscens quod callidi erant, non confidebat in illis. Wallicos tamen multos assumpserunt, et venerunt omnes in Lichfeld insignati signis Regis Ricardi, videlicet, cervis.

. . .

Hoc anno [1403], Rex transiit in Walliam, et quia terra est inequitabilis cito
35   revertitur.

. . .

Edmundus de Mortuo Mari in Wallia, non valens se redimere, dixit se nunquam velle subesse sub Henrico rege, sed filam Audoeni cum magna solemnitate duxit in uxorem. In nativitate autem hujus Edmundi mirabile accidit portentum. In arena stabuli sui patris sanguis manabat ita alte ut pedes equorum co-operiret. Vaginæ
40   omnes gladiorum et pugionum sanguine plenæ erant. Secures sanguine rubuerunt. Princeps jacens in cunis dormire non poterat nec a vagitu cessare nisi gladius sibi ostenderetur. Et in sinu nutricis positus non poterat quietari nisi aliquod instru-mentum bellicum sibi traderetur.

. . .

Anno Domini 1404, et anno 4 Regis, Audoenus Glendor partes Australes Walliæ
45   incendit et villam de Kaierdief et castrum obsedit. Qui vero intus erant miserunt ad regem petentes auxilium, sed ipse nec venit neque succursum misit. Audoenus villam cepit, et incendit præter unum vicum in quo Fratres Minores habitabant, quem amore fratrum cum conventu stare permisit. Cepit insuper castrum et des-truxit, multasque divitias ibi repositas abstulit. Et cum Fratres Minores peterent ab
50   eo libros suos et calices quos in castro deposuerant, respondit: "Quare posuistis bona vestra in castro? Si ea retinuissetis apud vos salva vobis fuissent."

. . .

Hoc anno [1404], filius Audoeni ab Anglicis capitur, et in Turri Londoniæ capti-vatur. Tunc hæredes comitis Marchiæ duo filli existentes in warda Regis, quos quidam dixerunt veros esse hæredes regni de proxima linea de stirpe domini Leonelli, ab-

Moreover in this year [1402], Owain Glyndŵr captured Edmund Mortimer, when many Englishmen from the marches of Wales had been killed. And the King assembled an army and crossed into Wales, where, when very great storms in September of thunder, heavy rains and hail prevented them from riding, many of the army even died of cold.

· · ·

Henry Percy, and his uncle Thomas Percy, whom King Richard had made Earl of Worcester and seneschal of his own house, gathered an army in the march of Scotland, saying that they ought to make war against the Scots; and they came to the county of Chester and they took some men of Chester with them. And they sent a message to Owain to come. But Owain, knowing that they were cunning, had no trust in them. Nevertheless they took many Welshmen along, and they all came to Lichfield, decorated with the standards of King Richard, that is, with stags.

· · ·

This year [1403], the king crossed into Wales, and he had to retreat quickly because the land was unfit for riding over.

· · ·

Edmund Mortimer, in Wales, not being able to redeem himself, said that he would never be able to submit to King Henry, but he took, with great solemnity, the daughter of Owain as his wife. Moreover at the birth of this Edmund a remarkable portent occurred. In the area of the sand in the stables of his father blood flowed so deeply that it covered the feet of the horses. All the sheaths of the swords and daggers were filled with blood. The axes were red with blood. The prince lying in his cradle could not sleep nor cease from moving about unless a sword was shown to him. And placed in the breast of his nurse he was not able to be quiet unless some instrument of war was given to him.

· · ·

In the year of our lord 1404, and the fourth year of the King, Owain Glyndŵr burned the southern parts of Wales and the town of Cardiff and besieged the castle. Indeed those who were inside sent to the king asking for help, but he himself did not come nor did he send aid. Owain captured the town (of Cardiff), and he burnt it except for one area in which the Minorite Friars were living, which he allowed to stand along with their monastery out of love of the brothers. Moreover, he took the castle and destroyed it and took away a great deal of wealth that was deposited there. And when the Minorite Friars asked him for their books and chalices which they had deposited in the castle, he responded: "why have you placed your belongings in the castle? If you had retained them with you they would have been safe with you."

· · ·

In this year [1404], the son of Owain was captured by the English, and was held captive in the Tower of London. Then the heirs of the Earl of March, his two surviving sons in the ward of the King, were abducted from the court of the King by a cer-

55   ducti fuerunt a curia Regis per quandam damicellam de camera reginæ, et ipsa ac-
     cusavit de hoc ducem Eborum. Et dux in castro de Pevenesey aliquandiu detentus est.

                                          . . .

     Et reversus transiit in Walliam Australem, et castrum de Coyfy, diu a Wallicis ob-
     sessum, liberavit. Et in redeundo cariagium suum et jocalia sua Wallenses spoliabant.

73. PROSE BRUT (PECULIAR VERSION TO 1437)   Middle English
                                                                      after 1437

     This same yere [1400] wasse holden a parlement atte Westmynstre, and thedur
     came Owenn off Glyndore, a Walsshmon, that sumtyme hadde be a squier of the
     erle of Arundell, complaynynge how that the Lorde Grey off the Ruthyn hadde take
     fro hym wrongefulli a parte of his londe, but he myght haue no remedy. And the
5   bisshoppe off Seynt Assaph off Wales counseled the lordes off the parlemente that
     thei shulde not mystrete the seide Owen, leste he made the Walshmen arise. And
     thei answered and seid they sette noht be hym.

                                          . . .

     This same yere the Walshmen beganne to arise agaynes Kynge Henry, and also
     a grete debate beganne betwexe the Lorde Grey off the Ruthyn and the seide Owen
10   off Glyndore. And the Walshmen destroied the kynges tenauntes and lordeshippez
     in Walez, and robbed and slogh the kyngez peple bothe Englissh and Walshe; and
     this endured xij. yere. And the kynge wente into Walez with a grete power, but he
     myght not take Owen that wasse chief capteyn off the Walshmen, for he fledde into
     mounteynesse and the kynge myght do ham no harme. But ofte thei toke the
15   kyngez cariage and destroied dayli his peple. And when the kynge myght not spede
     off his purpose, he retourned home agayne and the Lorde Grey vndurtoke forto
     keepe the cuntre. And sone after the seide Owen toke the seide Lorde Grey pri-
     soner. And he wasse raunsoned for prisoneres of the Marche. And atte the laste,
     Owen made the seide Lorde Grey to wedde one off his doghtres, and kepte hym
20   their with his wife, and sone after he died.

                                          . . .

     And this same yere Oweyn off Glendour toke Ser Edmunde Mortymer pri-
     souner in Wales, and because the kynge wolde not pay his raunson, he wolde neuer
     be vndir hym, but wedded on off Oweyn doghtres.
         In the birthe off this Edmunde fell mony wondur tokenes; for oute off the flore
25   off his fadurs stable welled bloode so high that yt couered the hors feet, and alle the
     shethes off swerdes and daggares in the house were full of bloode, and all the axez
     were reede off bloode. And when the seide Edmunde lay in his cradell, he myghte
     not slepe ne sese off cryinge till he sawe a sworde or sum instrumente off batayll.
     And when he sate in his norse lappe he wolde not be still till he hadde sum instru-
30   mente off warre to play with.

tain servant from the chamber of the Queen, and she herself accused the Duke of York of this. And the duke was detained for some time in the castle of Pevensey.

. . .

And turning back he crossed into South Wales, and freed the castle of Coity, long held by the Welshmen. And while he was returning the Welsh despoiled his carriage and his jewels.

73. *Prose Brut (Peculiar Version to 1437)* Notes: p. 382

This same year a parliament was held at Westminster, and Owain Glyndŵr came there, a Welshman who had once been a squire to the earl of Arundel, complaining how Lord Grey of Ruthin had wrongfully taken from him a part of his land, but he could fine no remedy for it. The bishop of St. Asaph of Wales counseled the lords of the parliament that they should not mistreat Owain, lest he make the Welshmen arise. They answered and said they set nothing by him.

. . .

This same year the Welshmen began to arise against King Henry IV, and also a great debate began between Lord Grey of Ruthin and Owain Glyndŵr. And the Welshmen destroyed the king's towns and lordships in Wales, and robbed and slew the king's people both English and Welsh; and this lasted 12 years. The king went into Wales with a great power, but he could not seize Owain, who was the leader of the Welshmen, for he fled into the mountains and the king could do them no harm. But often the Welsh took the king's carriage and destroyed his people daily. And when the king could not succeed in his purpose, he returned home again and Lord Grey undertook to keep the country. Soon afterward Owain took Lord Grey prisoner. And he was ransomed for prisoners of the March. In the end, Owain made Lord Grey wed one of his daughters, and he kept him there with his wife, and soon after he died.

. . .

And this same year Owain of Glyndŵr took Sir Edmund Mortimer prisoner in Wales, and because the king would not pay his ransom, Edmund would never be under him, but wedded one of Owain's daughters.

In the birth of this Edmund befell many wondrous signs; for out of the floor of his father's stable welled up blood so high that it covered the feet of the horses, and all the sheaths of the swords and daggers in the house were full of blood, and all the axes were red with blood. And when Edmund lay in his cradle, he would not sleep nor cease crying until he saw a sword or some instrument of battle. And when he sat in his nurse's lap he would not be still until he had some instrument of war to play with.

. . .

And he and his vncle, Ser Thomas Percye, whom Kynge Richarde hadde made erle off Worcestre, gedred a grete hoste in the north cuntre and seide they moste feght agaynes the Scottes, and wende into Chesshire and toke with ham Chesshire-men and sende to Owen off Glyndoure forto com and helpe hym. But Owen wasse
35   aferde off treson and camme not, but mony off the Welshmen camme vnto thaym, and so they camme to Lichefelde. And the seide Ser Henry Percye and all his men were arayed in the livery of the hertis, the whiche wasse Kynge Richardes livery.

74. WIGMORE CHRONICLE

Latin
c.1440

Hic [1402], proditione praehabita inter Owenum Glendortewyth — praeten-dentem se principem Walliae — et quosdam de Melenyth, in quodam bello inter dictum dominum Edmundum et dictum Owenum pro jure regni Angliae inito, super montem vocatum Brynglase infra Melenyth juxta Knyghton, captus est una
5   cum praemaxima populi multitudine interfectis. Paucis elapsis die, viz. Jovis in festo St. Albani martyris, anno regni regis Henrici quarti, quarto.

75. LONDON CHRONICLE OF HARLEY 565

Latin
c.1443

In this yere [1401] Kyng Herry rood in to Wales be the excitacion of the lord Grey Ruthyn for to distroye Owan of Glondere.

76. GLYNDWR

Welsh
mid-15th c.

Pan goronet Harri vrenin y pedwerydd oet yr Iessv m cccc excepto duo anno. Y gwannwyn nessa i llosget Aberconwy. Y vlwyddyn nessa i kyvodes Ywain ap Gruff tridiev kyn gwyl Vathev, a'r gwyl Vathev hwnnw i llosges ef Ruthyn. Duw Gwener nessa ar hynny i bv y lladdva yn y Vyrnwy. M cccc iiij pan losges Ywain Ddinbech.
5   Anno m cccc vj ar Dduw Kalan Mai i llosges y Sayson ysgopty Llanelwy.

. . .

And Hotspur and his uncle, Sir Thomas Percy, whom King Richard had made earl of Worcester, gathered a great host in the north country and said they must fight against the Scots, and they went into Cheshire and took with them Cheshire-men and sent to Owain of Glyndŵr to come and help them. But Owain was afraid of treason and came not, though many of the Welshmen came unto them, and so they came to Lichfield. And Sir Henry Percy and all his men were arrayed in the livery of the hart, which was King Richard's livery.

74. *WIGMORE CHRONICLE*   **Notes: pp. 382–83**

At this time, planned betrayal between Owain Glyndwr — pretending to be prince of Wales — and people of Maelienydd, a battle for the right to enter the kingdom of England was waged between Lord Edmund and Owain on the mountain called Bryn Glas within Maelienydd near Knighton. Mortimer was captured, and a very large number of people were slain. This was during the last days, namely, on the Thursday of the feast of St. Alban the Martyr, in the fourth year of the reign of King Henry IV.

75. *LONDON CHRONICLE OF HARLEY 565*   **Notes: p. 383**

In this year King Henry IV rode into Wales due to the provocation of Lord Grey of Ruthin, in order to destroy Owain Glyndŵr.

76. *GLYNDŴR*   **Notes: pp. 383–84**

When King Henry IV was crowned, the age of Jesus (was) 1400 minus two years. The next spring Aberconwy was burned. The next year Owain ap Gruffudd rose up three days before St. Matthew's Day. And that St. Matthew's Day he burned Ruthin. The next Friday after that there was the slaughter on the Efyrnwy. 1404 when Owain burned Denbigh. The year 1406, on the first day of May, the English burned the bishop's palace of Llanelwy.

77. JEAN JUVENAL DES URSINS, *HISTOIRE DE CHARLES VI*   **French**
                                                                   c.1440

[1404] Despuis la mort du roy Richard, qui estoit fils du vaillant prince de
Galles, les Gallois faisolent guerre aux Anglois. Et envoya le prince de Galles en
France devers le Roy, pour avoir argent, et du harnois, et aide de gens. Dont le Roy
fut content, et luy envoya un beau bassinet bien garny, un haubergeon, et une
5   espée. Et au surplus dit aux messagers, que tres-volontiers il l'aideroit et confort-
eroit, et luy envoyeroit gens. Et pour y aller ordonna le comte de la Marche de son
consenternent, lequel assembla navires et gens, et trouva soixante et deux vaisseaux
d'armes garnis de toutes choses, qui se rendirent tous à Brest en Bretagne.

. . .

Le comte de la Marche, comme dessus est dit, avoit assemblé plusieurs navires
10   vers Brest en Bretagne, pour aller en Galles. Et se mit sur mer, et y fut depuis la my-
aoust jusques à la my-novembre, attendant tousjours nouvelles de par les Gallois,
pour scavoir ou il descendroit, mais oneques n'y vint personne à luy. Et tousjours
estoit sur les rivages de la mer d'Angleterre, ou il fit aucuns exploicts de guerre,
puis s'en revint sans aucun fruict. Ils avoient mis en un vaisseau d'armes leurs
15   harnois, et autres biens: mais le vaisseau perit, et fut perdu dans la mer.

. . .

[1405] Le comte de la Marche, comme dessus a esté touché, avoit esté ordonné
d'aller en Galles, et ne fut pas sa faute. Car luy, ny ses gens ne pouvolent avoir
aucun payement, dont il eut grande desplaisance. Le mareschal de Rieux, et le seigneur de Hugueville, considerons que grand deshonneur seroit au Roy, si on n'alloit
20   aider aux Gallois, veu que le Roy l'avoit promis, ils delibererent et conclurent d'y
aller, et de faict y allerent. En allant ils eurent diverses rencontres sur mer, et aussi
quand ils furent arrivez au pays de Galles, desquelles ils sortirent à leur honneur.
Ils furent receus grandement et honorablement par les seigneurs et gens dudit
pays; et requirent lesdits seigneurs François, que le plustost qu'on peust ou les mit
25   en besongne. De faict ils mirent la siege devant une ville fermée, estant esdites marches de Galles, tenue par les gens de Henry, qui estoit située assez prés de la mer.
Ils n'y eurent pas esté longuement, qu'ils apperceurent sur mer assez prés navires,
ou il y avoit par apparence gens de guerre. Quand les Gallois les virent approcher
des rivages de la mer, il leur sembla qu'on venoit lever le siege, et bien soudaine-
30   ment se leverent, et partirent. Et quand les François les virent, aussi se partirent-ils
dudit siege, et se retirerent ou il leur fut ordonné. Esdites marches y avoit une autre
ville bien forte, tenue par les gens dudit Henry de Lancastre, laquelle nuisoit fort
au pays de Galles, elle fut assiegée par les François et Gallois. Et se defendirent fort
les Anglois, et faisoient de saillies, mesmement du costé de François, et de belles
35   armes. Et s'esmerveilloient fort ceux de dedans la place, et les Gallois aussi, de la
vaillance des François, lesquels s'y porterent fort vaillamment. Finalement les Anglois rendirent la place par certaine composition; icelle estant rendue, prirent ce
qu'ils peurent prendre, et y bouterent les Gallois se feu, et mirent en feu et en

77. Jean Juvenal des Ursins, *History of Charles VI*

Notes: p. 385

Since the death of King Richard, who had been the son of the proper prince of Wales, the Welsh made war on the English. And the prince of Wales sent into France, to the king, in order to acquire money and armor and help for the people. The king was pleased with this, and he sent him a beautiful bascinet well garnished, a hauberk, and a sword. And more than this he said to the messengers, that he would very willingly aid and comfort them, and he sent these things to the people. And in order to proceed in this he informed the count de la Marche of his consent, upon which were assembled ships and people, and he found sixty-two vessels filled with weapons of all kinds, which were all sent to Brest in Brittany.

. . .

The count of the Marche, as it is said, had assembled several ships at Brest in Brittany, in order to go to Wales. They put to sea, but from the middle of August until to the middle of November they all waited for news on the part of the Welsh, in order to know where he should attack, but no person ever came to him. And all was restricted to the shores of the sea of England, where he managed no exploits of war, until they returned without any fruits of their work. They had put their arms and armor and other goods in a vessel, but the vessel sank, and all was lost in the sea.

. . .

The count of the March, as we have already shown, had been ordered to go to Wales, and it was not his fault. For neither him nor his people would there be payment, which was a great displeasure to him. The marshal of Rieux, and the lord of Hugueville, considering that it would be a great dishonor to the king, if no one went to aid the Welsh, which thing the king had promised, deliberated and determined to go themselves, and in fact they went. In going they had several encounters at sea, and also when they were arrived in the land of Wales, where they went to their honor. They were received grandly and honorably by the lords and the people of that country, who requested the said lords of the French to engage immediately where they were in difficulty. So in fact they set siege before a walled city, that being in the aforesaid marches of Wales, held by the people of Henry, which was situated quite near the sea. They had not been there long when they perceived there were ships approaching, in which it appeared there were men of war. When the Welsh saw them approaching the shores of the sea, it seemed to them that they would raise the siege, and very suddenly they arose and departed. And when the French saw them, they also departed the said siege, and they retired to where they were ordered. In the aforesaid marches there was another strongly fortified city, held by the people of Henry of Lancaster, the most strong in the land of Wales, and it was besieged by the French and Welsh. It was strongly defended by the English, who made sallies from it, and they fought separately with the French, and with beautiful arms. And those within that place marveled greatly at the valor of the French, and the Welsh did, too, because they carried out their business very valiantly. Finally the English surrendered the place by a certain document, which was agreed to, and they took and seized it, and then invading there the Welsh burned it: they put to

40 flamme toute la ville, et raserent les murs. Et ce faict, pource qu'il estoit hyver, les
François furent logez en divers lieux, et passerent l'hyver, sans ce qu'on les em-
besongnast en aucune maniere. Et pour ce environ l'entrée de caresme se mirent
sur mer, et s'en retournerent en leur pays de France.

78. *POLYCHRONICON CONTINUATION*   **Middle English**
1432 x 1450

And so the kynge returnede from Scottelonde and commen to Leicestre herde
straunge tythynges, how that men of Wales were gedrede in a grete multitude, and
hade erecte into theire prince an esqwyer Owyn Glyndor by name, and trowbled the
pease. The cause of that insurreccion folowethe. When that the kynge wente into
5   Scottelonde, he sende letters to the seide Owyn Glyndor, in that he was a esqwyer
of grete fame, that he scholde comme to hym in eny wise. The lorde Grey of Ruthyn
was assignede to bere the letters, whiche delyverede not the letters to the seide
Owen untylle the day afore that the kynge toke his iourney unto Scotlonde. The letters taken and redde he excusede hym, seyenge that hade not a competente moni-
10 cion for such a iourney. And so the lorde Grey levynge hy in Wales made grete haste
unto the kynge, þat tyme in Scottelonde, sayenge to hym that the seide Owyn des-
pisynge his letters wolde not come in eny wyse. And so the kynge beynge stylle as
for the tyme, made provision to go to that cuntre after his departynge from Scottelonde. And so the kynge entrede into Wales cowthe not fynde hym and his men, for
15 they were hydde in caves and in mowntanes. Then the kynge seenge that he cowthe
not prevayle, and þat his hoste pereschede for hungre, gafe to the lorde Gray the
tenementes and londes of that esqwyer Owyn Glyndor, and returnede into Ynglonde. But the grawnte of þat londe caused grete trowble and hurte, as hit schall be
schewede hereafter, ffor after the departynge of þe kynge from Wales, Owyne
20 Glyndor did aryse with his companye and wente to Ruthyn, a towne in Wales long-
ynge to the seide lorde Gray, whom he spoylede firste, and that doen he destroyede
hit utterly by fyre.

. . .

The kynge purposynge to correcte the men of Wales, causynge grete trowble
come in the same yere to Evisham in the secunde tyme with a grete companye of
25 knyhtes and oþer peple, taryenge þer into the thrydde day aftre dyner, and after
that to Worcestre, and so into Wales. Whiche taryenge þer by a monethe, profite
lytelle for the cause of his commynge, but that he did sle oon man of Wales whiche
promysede to brynge the kynge to Owen Glendor, and he performede not his
promyse. The man inquirede why that he fullefyllede not the promise made to the
30 kynge, answerede sayenge he hade lever suffre dethe then to detecte the secrete
cownsayle of the seide Owyn, in that had ij. sonnes with hym. In whiche tyme the
kynge made poore þe monastery of Stretflur, insomoche that he lefte not oon
monke in hit; were oon of the monkes was heded in that he bare armoure ageyne
the kynge and pease. Neverthelesse the kynge see not the seide Owyn Glyndor
35 neiþer hade understongynge where he was or in what place; and so certeyne men
putte in diverse castells of Wales, the kynge returnede to London with his hoste.

the torch and burned all the town, and they razed the walls. And in fact, because it was winter, the French were lodged in various places, and they spent the winter without what things that were necessary in any way. And around the beginning of Lent they put to sea, and they returned to their country of France.

78. *POLYCHRONICON CONTINUATION*   Notes: pp. 385–86

And so the king, returning from Scotland to Leicester, heard strange news about how the men of Wales were gathering in a great multitude and had raised to be their prince a squire named Owain Glyndŵr, and they now troubled the peace. The cause of that insurrection follows. When the king went into Scotland, he sent letters to the said Owain Glyndŵr, because he was a squire of much fame, commanding him to come to him at once. The Lord Grey of Ruthin was assigned to bear the letters, which he did not deliver until the day before the king took his journey to Scotland. The letters received and read, he excused himself, saying that he had no supplies prepared for such a journey. And so the Lord Grey, leaving him in Wales, made great haste to the king, now in Scotland, saying to him that the said Owain, despising his letters, would not come in any way. And so the king, after being quiet for a time, made provision to go to that country after his departure from Scotland. But when the king entered into Wales he could not find him and his men, for they were hidden in caves and in mountains. Then the king, seeing that he could not prevail, and that his army was perishing from hunger, gave to the Lord Grey the tenements and lands of that squire Owain Glyndŵr, and returned into England. But the grant of that land caused great trouble and pain, as it shall be shown hereafter, for after the departure of the king from Wales, Owain Glyndŵr did arise with his company and went to Ruthin, a town in Wales belonging to the said Lord Grey, which he despoiled and then utterly destroyed by fire.

. . .

The king, intending to correct the men of Wales who were causing such trouble, came in the same year to Evesham for a second time with a great company of knights and other people, tarrying there until the third day after dinner, then journeying after that to Worcester, and so into Wales. He tarried there for a month, and little was gained for the cause of his coming, though he did slay one man of Wales who had promised to bring the king to Owain Glyndŵr and did not do so. The man, when asked why he had not fulfilled the promise made to the king, answered that he would prefer to suffer death than to betray the secret counsel of Owain because he had two sons with him. During this time the king made poor the monastery of Strata Florida: he left not one monk in it; one of the monks was beheaded because he bore arms against the king and the peace. Nevertheless the king neither saw the said Owain Glyndŵr nor had any notion where he was. And so, having put certain men in the diverse castles of Wales, the king returned to London with his army.

Owyn Glyndor understondynge the departynge of the kynge, spoylede a towne callede Poole, and did grete hurte, and brente mony places of hyt.

. . .

40   The kynge intendynge to destroye the seide Owyn Glyndor wente towarde Wales in the thrydde tyme, and come to Evysham, taryenge þer by thre dayes, and after that he wente to Worchestre in the viij.the day of October, taryenge þer by ix. dayes. Neverthelesse hit was not seen afore that tyme, a kynge of Ynglonde to have taryede thryes in þat monastery in oon yere afore that tyme. Where diverse noble men movede the kynge that he scholde commaunde lordes and oþer gentyll men that

45   hade eny lyvelode þer to kepe þat cuntre for theire awne avayle; that doen the kynge departede unto London. A blasynge sterre was seene in the weste in this yere abowte the feste of the Purificacion of oure Lady, contynuynge and apperynge in diverse tymes unto Ester nexte folowynge. And in the same yere in Lente the lorde Gray of Ruthyn, beynge in his castelle at Ruthyn in Wales, hade knowlege that Owyn Glyn-

50   dor was nye to hym with fewe men, and so he made hym redy with a certeyne nowmbre of men, and wente to fighte with hym. The seide Owyn Glyndor seenge hym, fledde untylle þat he was by a certeyne space from the castell, that the lorde scholde not escape, for he lade mony men of Wales secretely in diverse places, and so that lorde Grey was compassede abowte by his enemyes, and taken and bownde faste in

55   cheynes and broughte unto Snawdon hilles. And so the seide lorde Grey intendynge to have hade a grete pray, was made a pray to his adversaryes. Also syr Edmund Mortymere, knyghte, was taken by the seide Owyne Glendor; for the seide knyghte beynge in Ludlowe hade worde that the seide Owyn Glyndor was on a hylle nye to Ludlowe, with a fewe men in his companye. Wherefore the seide knyghte sende to

60   his tenauntez in Milenythe in Wales, that thei scholde comme to hym in armes in alle haste. Those men commen the knygte wente to that hille boldely, and gafe batell to þeim, but the seide men of Wales that come with hym returnede to Owyn Glendor, and faughte ageyne theire lorde, and so he was taken þer and mony other with hym. But þer was oon man of Wales þer soe myghty and cruell, that was callede Rees, a

65   Gythe, which did sle, wounde, or take into captivite every an þat gafe resistence to hym. In whiche conflicte iiij. [c.] men of Ynglonde were sleyne, and iiij. knyghtes: where men lay dedde in theire awne bloode under the feete of horses, and were prohibite to be beryede by a certeyne season. And a certeyne signe schewede in the byrthe of the seide syr Edmunde semede to be fullefyllede in that tyme, for when he

70   come into this worlde from the wombe of his moder, the horses in the stable stode in bloode unto the knees. Neverthelesse Owyn Glendor entretede hym lyke a gentylman, thenkynge that he scholde reioyce the crowne of Ynglonde after kynge Henricus þe iiij.the. And from that tyme Owyn Glendor encreasede in powere and in myghte, and the power of men of Ynglonde decreasede.

. . .

75   And in the same yere [1402], abowte the Feste of Seynte Martyne bischop, the seide Grey of Ruthyn was delyverede from Owyn Glendor, v. m. marke payede afore, and ij. of his sonnes lefte in the kepynge of the seide Owyn for oþer v. m. marke to be payede to hym. In whiche yere syr Edmund Mortymere, of whom we

Owain Glyndŵr, learning of the departure of the king, despoiled a town called Welshpool, and he did great harm, and he burned many parts of it.

· · ·

The king, intending to destroy the said Owain Glyndŵr, went toward Wales for a third time, and came to Evesham, tarrying there for three days. After that he went to Worcester on the eighth day of October, tarrying there for nine days. Never before that time had it happened, for a king of England to have tarried thrice in that monastery in one year. There diverse noble men moved the king that he should command the lords and other gentlemen who had any livelihood there to keep that country for their own profit; that done, the king departed to London. A comet was seen in the west in this year around the Feast of the Purification of Our Lady, continuing and appearing in diverse times until the following Easter. And in that same year at Lent the Lord Grey of Ruthin, being in his castle at Ruthin in Wales, became aware that Owain Glyndŵr was close to him with a few men, and so he readied himself with a certain number of men, and he went to fight with him. The said Owain Glyndŵr, seeing him, fled until he was some distance from the castle in order to keep the lord from escaping, for he had secretly placed many men of Wales in diverse places. Thus Lord Grey was surrounded by his enemies, and taken and bound fast in chains and brought to Snowdonia. And so the said Lord Grey, intending to have caught a great prey, was instead made a prey to his adversaries. Also Sir Edmund Mortimer, knight, was taken by the said Owain Glyndŵr; for the said knight being in Ludlow had word that the Owain Glyndŵr was on a hill near to Ludlow, with a few men in his company. Therefore the said knight sent to his tenants in Maelienydd in Wales, saying that they should come to him in arms in all haste. Those men having arrived, the knight went to that hill boldly and gave battle to them, but the said men of Wales who had come with him returned to Owain Glyndŵr, and fought against their lord, and so he was taken there along with many other men. But there was one man of Wales there who was terrible and cruel, called Rhys Gethin, who did slay, wound, or take into captivity everyone who gave resistance to him. In this conflict 400 men of England were slain, and four knights. Men lay dead in their own blood under the feet of the horses, and they were prohibited from being buried in proper time. A certain sign that was shown in the birth of the said Sir Edmund seemed to be fulfilled at that time, for when he came into this world from the womb of his mother, the horses in the stable stood in blood to the knees. Nevertheless Owain Glyndŵr treated him like a gentleman, thinking that he should wear the crown of England after king Henry IV. And from that time Owain Glyndŵr increased in power and in might, and the power of the men of England decreased.

· · ·

And in that same year, around the Feast of St. Martin the Bishop, the said Grey of Ruthin was delivered from Owain Glyndŵr for 5000 marks paid beforehand, and two of his sons left in the keeping of the said Owain as ransom for the further 5000 marks to be paid to him. In this year Sir Edmund Mortimer, of whom we have made

80   have made mencion afore, maryede the doghter of Owyn Glendor abowte þe Feste
      of Seynte Andrewe th'Apostle, with grete solennite; and so that knyghte turnede
      holly to men of Wales, as hit was seide.

79. WALTER BOWER, *SCOTICHRONICON*   **Latin**
                                                                   1441–45

*26. Quomodo rex Anglie Henricus pater cum filio subjugare nisus est Walliam que prodi-
cione propria subversa est.*

       Circa illud tempus vel paulo ante post tamen bellum de Schrewisbiri attendens
       Henricus de Loncaster rex Anglie quod Wallenses insurexerant cum Henrico Percy
5   junior contra eum (qui tamen si expectasset per xii horas adventum ducis Eboracen'
       comitis de Arundel et de Stafford cum ipsorum sequelis usque in crastinum qui de
       nocte promiserunt regem deserere et sibi Henrico adherere cum exercitu Wallensi-
       um sibi occurrencium, rex non fuisset compos congredi contra eos), ob hoc nimium
       stomochatus guerram omni annisu movit contra Walliam. Quam per se et filium
10   suum Henricum vigram furoris Domini contra Francos continuavit per xv annos
       donec in exterminium et servitutem quasi novissimam redacti sunt. Cum igitur bina
       vice rex in propria persona vel per filium suum Henricum per annos premissos
       omni anno Valliam hostiliter intrasset et plurima dampna inibi perpetrasset, novis-
       sime disposuit se omnia solo coequare. Unde collecta sua maxima potencia centum
15   et quadraginta milium armatorum rubeum vexillum sive draconem in signum ex-
       cidii et internicionis extreme sexus utriusque erexit, et tamquam leo rugiens per
       terram Wallen' deseviens ad viginti miliaria combussit et destruxit. Sic proponens
       a fine usque ad finem omnia conterere fortiter et pro libito suo perdere crudeliter.
       Tandem circa festum Sancti Michaelis tanta et tam vehemens pluviarum inundacio
20   subito de celo cecidit ut decem milia de suis cum summis et hernesiis preter cariagia
       et sarcinas alluvione pluvali et undis mergerentur. Propter quod vix valens rex ex-
       ercitum suum inter fluvios et fluenta salvare citatis amfractibus ultra quam creditor
       perteritus Angliam peciit, plus dampni sustinens quam pro tunc intulit inimicis.
       Dehinc in propria persona non audens illuc revertere commisit filio suo primo-
25   genito Henrico execucionem sui propositi. Qui callide valenciores sic saltem putatos
       viros Vallie illos scilicet de Morgannoch donis et promissis corruptos allexit, ut cum
       multitudo Wallensium contra eum si contingeret congregaretur ipsi prius fugam
       arriperent ad quorum exemplum ceteri aufugerent. Quod et factum est; nam cum
       isdem Henricus princeps Anglie et qui eciam Wallie titulo potitus cum grandi exer-
30   citu Walliam funditus destructurus petivisset, misit dominos de Coboham et Gray
       Codnore et David Gam ad exterminandum eos. At ipsi Wallenses magna multi-
       tudine contra eos insurgentes campestri pugna secum certare disposuerunt. Unde
       cum perventum fuerat ad aciem belli illi domestici proditores de Morgannoch, qui
       vangardiam regere sperebantur prout antea fuerat conductum, terga dederunt et

mention before, married the daughter of Owain Glyndŵr around the Feast of St. Andrew the Apostle, with great solemnity. Thus that knight turned wholly to the men of Wales, as it was said.

79. WALTER BOWER, *SCOTICHRONICON*   Notes: pp. 386–88

26. *How Henry king of England with his son strove to subjugate Wales which was disrupted by treason of its own.*

About that time or a little earlier (but after the battle of Shrewsbury) Henry of Lancaster king of England, considering that the Welsh had rebelled against him along with Henry Percy the younger — if nevertheless Percy had waited for twelve hours until the morning for the arrival of the duke of York, the earl of Arundel, the earl of Stafford and their followers who promised to desert the king during the night and join up with him along with the army of the Welsh who were meeting him, the king would not have been sane to fight against them — for this reason the king was much angered and put every effort into starting a war against Wales. Both by his own efforts and those of his son Henry he maintained the staff of the fury of the Lord against the Franks for fifteen years until they were reduced to destruction and absolute subjection. When therefore for the second time the king in person (or represented by his son Henry as happened nearly every year throughout these years) entered Wales as an enemy and caused a great deal of damage there, he planned to level everything completely to the ground. Thus after assembling his greatest strength of 140,000 armed men he raised his red standard or dragon-banner as a sign of destruction and utter extermination for both sexes, and like a roaring lion he raged through the land of Wales burning and harrying for twenty miles. His aim was to pound everything powerfully to pieces from one end to the other, and at his pleasure to cause cruel destruction. At length about Michaelmas such a great and heavy deluge of rain fell suddenly from the sky that 10,000 of his men were drowned in the floods and waves of rainwater along with their pack-horses and equipment, waggons and baggage. On this account the king, now scarcely able to save his army between the rivers and floodwaters, called for a retreat and sought England, more frightened than can be believed and suffering more damage than for the time being he inflicted on his enemies.

Thereafter not daring to return there in person he entrusted his eldest son Henry with the execution of his plan. Henry cunningly attracted to his side some men of Wales who were at least reputed to be powerful (that is those from Morgan-nwg) by corrupting them with gifts and promises, so that if and when a multitude of Welshmen happened to be assembled against him, they would be the first to take to flight and the rest would follow their example. And this is what happened; for when the same Henry, prince of England (who also held the title of prince of Wales) sought with a large army to destroy Wales completely, he sent Lord Cobham and Lord Grey of Codnor and Dafydd Gam to wipe them out. But the Welsh themselves rose in a great multitude against them and planned to fight them in a battle on open ground. When it came to the actual battle, those native traitors from Mor-gannwg, who were expected to form the vanguard as had previously been arranged,

35   sic ad ignominiosam fugam ceteros suos comprovinciales instruxerunt; sed verius
      quod deflendum est destruxerunt. Ubi quampluribus cesis et occisis captus est
      princepis Wallie filius illustris Griffeth hopBowan necnon belliger insignis Hopkin
      apthomas cum multis aliis, et abhinc totam Walliam de facili Angli sunt conquesti.
      Huius simile habes supra libro iiii. capitulo xvi.

40   27. *De succursu misso Wallie per Karolum regem Francie.*
              Sed quamdiu ipsa Wallia stetit indivisa modicum contra eam profecit Anglia.
      Sed illi de Morgannoch habentes latens odium contra principem suum proprium
      facilius inclinaverunt se inimicis et principi Henrico qui valde ingeniosus fuerat in
      malo sicut patuit in omnibus suis actis bellicis in Francia et Normannia quas atrocis-
45   sime castigavit donec respectus ab Altissimo tirannus sublatus est e medio. Hic finxit
      artem ex malicia qua forte divisa est Wallia sicut et per eundem ipsa Francia. Nescio
      si Vegecium studuit qui practicare docuit ubi de re militari libro suo tercio capitulo
      x. sic scribit dicens: "Inter hostes discordiarum procurare causas dolosi ducsi est.
      Nulla enim quamvis minima sit nacio potest ab adversariis perdeleri nisi prorpriis
50   simultatibus seipsam consumpserit. Nam civili odio ad inmicorum perniciem nichil
      efficacius" . . .
              Sic et ipsa ut premisimus Wallia stetit in se firme radicata donec simultates et
      prodiciones conciperentur intra se. Nam in principo sue guerre cum seniore Hen-
      rico mote possessiones suas egregie sunt defensi. Ad quorum tunc supplementum
55   Karolus rex Francie misit principi Wallie tamquam suo ab antiquo confederato in-
      clitum bellatorem baronem de Rocheford Britannum marescallum tunc Francie
      cum armatorum duobus milibus, quorum quingenti erant milites et lanciferi mille
      eciam et quingenti valetis armez et albalastrarii, una cum magna summa auri et di-
      versis apparaturis armorum preter stipendia navigii et victualia missorum. Que
60   tamen victualia una cum classe Francorum Anglici magno navigio insequentes
      prope Mylford in Sowt Wallia destruxerunt, Francis remanentibus fere per annum
      in Wallia et honorifice remissis per principem ad propria.

                                           . . .

      28. *Quomodo predicacione abbatis Wallici humiliati recuperaverunt possessiones.*
              Reliquiis igitur Wallen' nondum Anglis adhuc subiectis omni spe proprie pos-
65   sessionis et libertatis recuperande destitutis, tandem suscitavit Dominus spiritum
      cuiusdam religiosi patris canonici regularis Sancti Augustini Johannis Powal nomine
      qui fuit tunc abbas Glomorgancie prope urbem Legionum. Qui assumpto sibi pre-
      dicatoris officio palam in ecclesiis paucissimis Deo derelictis orphanis Wallen' ut
      olim Jonas Ninivitis predicare cepit et dicere: "Adhuc modicum et Wallia subver-
70   tetur nisi ad Dominum suum cicius convertatur. Propter peccata enim vestra inven-
      erunt vos mala. 'Convertatur igitur vir unusquisque a via sua mala et ab iniquitate
      que est in manibus sius.' Usquequo claudicatis in duas partes? Si Henricus Anglie
      invasor rex vester est, sequimini eum. Si autem princeps Wallie, sequimini eum. Sed

turned tail and so gave a lesson in ignominious flight to the rest of their country-men; but in reality, sad to say, they destroyed them. Very many fell and were killed there, and Gruffudd ab Owain the illustrious son of the prince of Wales was cap-tured, along with the famous fighting-man Hopcyn ap Tomas with many others. Thenceforward the English easily conquered all Wales. For something similar see above Book IV, Chapter 16.

27. *Help sent to Wales by Charles king of France.*

As long as Wales remained undivided, England made little progress against her. But the men of Morgannwg, with their secret hatred for their own prince, preferred to align with their enemies and Prince Henry, who was most inventive in evil-doing, as was clear in all his later acts of war in France and Normandy, which he chastised most cruelly until the Almighty interfered and the tyrant was plucked from the midst. This man cunningly worked at a scheme whereby it chanced that Wales was divided, just as France itself was later divided by the same man. I do not know whether he studied Vegetius who taught the practice in the third book of his *De re militari* at chapter 10 where he writes: "It is the duty of an astute leader to stir up disagreements among his enemies. Not even a very small nation can be wholly de-stroyed by its adversaries unless it is devoured by its own internal dissensions; for nothing works more powerfully towards the ruin of enemies than civil hatred" . . .

Thus as we have said Wales stood firmly rooted among her people until rivalries and treasons were conceived among them; for at the start of their war fought against the elder Henry of England they defended their possessions with distinction. As an addition to their forces Charles king of France sent to the prince of Wales (his long standing ally) a famous fighting man, the Breton baron de Rochefort who was then a marshal of France, with two thousand armed men (of whom 500 were knights and lancers, and 1500 were men-at-arms and cross-bowmen), along with a great amount of gold and various pieces of military equipment, besides pay and supplies for those sent in the fleet. These supplies, however, along with the ships of the French were destroyed by the English who followed with a large fleet near Milford in South Wales. The French remained for nearly a year in Wales and were then honorably sent home by the prince of Wales.

. . .

28. *How the humiliated Welsh regained their possessions through an abbot's preaching.*

The remaining Welshmen therefore who were still not yet subjected to the English were devoid of all hope of recovering their own property and liberty. At last the Lord stirred the spirit of a certain monastic father, a regular canon of St. Augus-tine called John Powal, who was then abbot of Llantarnam near the city of Caerleon. Taking on the office of preacher he began to preach openly in a limited number of churches to the orphan Welsh who had been abandoned by God, as Jonah once did to the men of Nineveh, saying: "A little while from now Wales will be overthrown unless she is quickly turned towards her Lord. It is because of your sins that misfor-tunes have come upon you. 'Let every man therefore abandon his wicked ways and the iniquity for which he is responsible.' For how long do you limp along between two sides? If Henry of England the invader is your king, follow him. But if the

75

80

85

90

95

100

quia princeps vester est et ipse in manibus inmicorum detentus est, non minus pug-
nemus pro patria nostra. Humiliemus Deo animas nostras et serviamus ei in timore;
et promitto vobis auxilium provenire de excelso. Si autem voluerimus peccata
nostra confiteri et de cetero vitam nostram proponere sine fictione emendare, facile
est concludi multos injustos in manu paucorum Deo famulari studencium. Quia ut
inclitus testatur Machabeus: 'Non est differencia in conspectu Dei celi liberare in
multis aut in paucis, quia non in multitudine exercitus victoria belli, sed de celo for-
titudo est.' Inimici nostri inveterati Anglici veniunt ad nos in multitudine contumaci
et superbia, cum tamen nichil juris in nos habere dinoscantur ut spolient et dis-
perdant nos et hereditatem nostram. Quod si volueritis et me audieritis pugnantes
pro patria vestra et hereditate paterna terram vestram recuperabitis et in ea absque
pavore inimicorum habitabitis. Convertimini ergo ad Dominum et ipse convertetur
ad vos et conteret inimicos vestros ante faciem vestram. Eque potens est nunc ut in
diebus antiquis quia manus eius non est abbreviata." Ad huiusmodi itaque exhor-
taciones et crebras abbatis predicaciones pauci illi qui adhuc liberate sunt potiti
aliquantulum resipiscentes et plus solito spiritum aspirantes spem suam in Altissimo
juxta verba viri Dei ponentes et curam suam in Domino jactantes bis aut ter in
septimana, sed et aliqui quorum ad hoc dictabat consciencia quasi omni die, pure
peccata sua sunt confessi. Jejuniis et oractionibus ac misericordie operibus propensius se dantes semel omni septimana de sacramento altaris communicati sunt,
et sic in nomine Domini inimicos suos qui in terra sua plantati fuerant invaserunt
et tam acriter vexaverunt ut interdum centum de Wallia de facilit vincerent vel
fugarent millenos de Anglia, mille eciam de Wallia Anglorum decem milia. Sicut
patuit per dominum Grai de Ruthin habentem secum ii. armatorum qui devictus
est per ducentos Wallie et captus ac redemptus ceteris cesis et fugatis. Unde factum
est ut, Deo sibi propicio, infra tres annos de Wallia expellerent cunctos inimicos, et
eciam dilatarent marchias suas ad ulteriorem terminum prime institucionis eiusdem
per Brutum qui Britanniam inter fratres primo dividebat. Omnia eciam castra per
Anglos restaurata forti manu et feliciori omine ceperant, et tribus dumtaxat exceptis
scilicet Abirhustwith Conwai et Hardlawch solotenus destruxerunt.

105

110

29. *Quomodo Wallici prevaricatores amiserunt terram suam.*
      Propter huiusmodi prosperos eventus sibi ad votum succedentes erigebant se
fatui Wallici supra se exaltantes corda sua in superbiam immemores beneficiorum
Dei in luxum et luxuriam paulatim defluxerunt, obliti confessionis et pristine peni-
tencie ac si Deus ignosecret vel dormiret aut impunitatis obliviceretur. Sic sic cor-
rupti sunt et abhominabiles facti sunt in studiis suis reliquentes ecclesias frequenta-
bant tabernas quibus sermo divinus sermo divinus ulterius non sapuit, sacrosancta
communio sacramentit eis omnio desipuit, deciis et ludicris se dedicantes crapulis
et ebrietatibus sese voluntantes. Cum prius cognovissent Deum non tunc sicut Deum
glorificaverunt aut gracias egerunt; sed evanuerunt in cogitacionibus suis et obscur-

prince of Wales is your natural lord, follow him. But because he is your prince and
he is unjustly detained in the hands of enemies, we should fight no less for our
fatherland. Let us humble our souls to God and serve him in fear, and I promise
you that help will appear from on high. If indeed we are willing to confess our sins
and propose without dissimulation to amend our lives in future, it is easy for many
unworthy men to be overpowered by the few who are striving to become servants
of God. As the celebrated Maccabeus bears witness: 'It makes no difference to the
God of heaven to save with many or with a few. Victory in battle does not depend
on numbers; strength comes from heaven.' Our enemies of long standing, the
English, come to us in insolent numbers and arrogance, though they are known to
have no right over us to despoil and destroy us and our heritage. But if you have the
will and listen to me, as fighters for your fatherland and ancestral heritage you will
recover your country and live in it without fear of enemies. Turn therefore to the
Lord and he will turn towards you and will crush your enemies before your eyes. He
is just as powerful now as in days gone by, for his hand is not so short that he cannot
save." In response to exhortations of this kind and to the repeated sermons of this
abbot the few who still enjoyed liberty recovered a little, and becoming more
spirited than was their wont put their trust in the Most High in accordance with the
words of the man of God. Committing their burden to the Lord they were straight-
forward in confessing two or three times a week — there were some whose con-
science dictated confession nearly every day. Devoting themselves readily to fast-
ings, prayers and works of mercy they took holy communion once every week. Then
in the name of the Lord they attacked their enemies who had been settled in their
country and harried them so fiercely that sometimes a hundred from Wales easily
defeated or put to flight a thousand from England, or a thousand from Wales ten
thousand Englishmen. This was illustrated by the case of Lord Grey of Ruthin who
was defeated, then captured and ransomed, by two hundred men of Wales when he
had two thousand armed men with him, the others being killed or forced to flee. It
turned out that with God on their side they expelled all their enemies from Wales
within three years and pushed their boundaries back to the further limit established
when the country was first set up by Brutus, who made the initial division of Britain
among brothers. They had taken also by then all the castles which the English had
rebuilt by brave force of arms and a happy omen, and destroyed them all to the
foundations except only three, namely Aberystwyth, Conway and Harlech.

29. *How the apostate Welsh lost their country.*

As a consequence of these successes which matched their wishes the foolish Welsh
got above themselves, exalting in their hearts with pride. Forgetful of God's favors
they gradually descended into excess and luxury, disregarding confession and their
former penitence, or whether God was forgiving or sleeping or paying no heed to
their unpunished state. Thus were they corrupted and became abominable in their
activities; deserting churches, they frequented taverns. For them divine discourse had
lost its savor: they found the holy communion of the sacrament wholly insipid as they
gave themselves over to dice and sports, wallowing in bouts of drinking and
drunkenness. Though previously they had known God, they did not now glorify him
as God nor offer thanks to him; instead they became light-minded in their thoughts

atum est insipiens cor eorum; "dicentes se esse sapientes, stulti facti sun." Nam quia
115   terga Deo dederunt, suscitavit contra eos denuo premissos inimicos Anglos qui subito eos humiliaverunt, ut unus de Anglia fugaret decem de Wallia, et centum millenos, quia "incrassatus est dilectus et recalcitravit et recessit a Deo salutari suo."
Propterea vidit Deus et ad iracundiam provocatus est et conclusit Wallicos in manibus inimicorum suorum; receptaverunt castra et rearsierunt, et hucusque remanet
120   Wallia eis sub servitute tributaria. Ecce quomodo isti Wallici! Propter ingratitu-
dinem suam et quia Deo digne gracias non egerunt pro multiplici victoria eis de
Anglis collata, "defecerunt in vanitate dies eorum et anni eorum cum festinacione."

Exemplum ad istud possumus adducere de Ezechia de quo Isaias xxxvii. legitur
quod cum angelus Domini occidisset de exercitu superbi Senachirib centum octa-
125   ginta quinque milia, quia extitit ingratus, Ezechias egrotavit usque ad mortem.
Unde sicut dicit Josephus: "Licet hostias cum populo Deo immolasset non tamen
digne gracias egit nec laudis canticum inde cantavit sicut patres eo tempore facere
consueverunt."

Commentator Juvenalis scribit quod quedam domina Nephastes nomine im-
130   pregnata et vicina partui ingressa est templa ut consuleret eos super fetum an
marem vel feminam foret paritura ut signulis eorum divina peteret dona. Cui
primus: "Tuus fetus erit filius, et sibi concedo pulcritudinem." Secundus concessit
fortitudinem; tercius dividiarum plenitudinem. Hiis acceptis responsis non tamen
acceptatis mulier indignata est eo quod nullus eorum concessit filio vite longitu-
135   dinem. Sed, ut moris fuit, templum egressa et denuo regressa ut deos pro beneficiis
honoraret sacrificiis, optulit eis contraria dona scilicet pro pulcritudine lutum, pro
fortitudine sputum, pro divicarum copia derisionis nutum. Quibus sic oblatis dii
nimium offensi mutaverunt fetum in utero. Name pro dono pulcritudinis protavit
caput simie, pro dono fortitudinis branchias anseris, pro dono diviciarum pellem
140   excoriatam. Sic moraliter isti Wallici pro pulcrituidne militari optulerunt lutum
luxurie, pro fortitudine victoriali sputum discordie, pro opulencia virtuali nutum
superbie. Et sic justo Dei judicio ut simie viluerunt per luxuriam, ut anseres debili-
tati sunt per discordiam. Et tandem tamquam nudi excoriati sunt per proprie libertatis et patrie amissionem et carenciam. Prolixiorem me forte debito premissis
145   insteti ut horum exemplo cautelam in similibus sumant Scoti levitatibus huiusmodi,
quod dolenter refero nimium dediti, quia ut scribit Leo papa: "Validiora sunt
exempla quam verba, et plenius opere docetur quam voce." Quia:

Tunc tua res agitur paries cum proximus ardet.

30. *De eodem et morte abbatis de Glomorganc'.*
150   De infelici regimine horum Wallensium doluit ultra modum dictus abbas
Johannes Powal. Qui nec valuit predicacione vel exhortacione eos a via sua pessima
revocare per quam incederant viciose. Sed propter hoc non cessavit predicare et

and their senseless judgement was clouded. "While boasting of their wisdom, they made fools of themselves." For because they turned their backs on God, he stirred up against them again their aforesaid English enemies, who suddenly humbled them, so that one from England put ten from Wales to flight and a hundred routed a thousand, because "the favored son became fat and petulant, and departed from God his savior." For this reason God took note, was moved to anger, and cooped up the Welsh in the clutches of their enemies who easily recaptured and repaired the castles; and right up till now Wales remains in tributary servitude to them. Note how it is with these Welshmen! On account of their ingratitude and because they did not offer thanks worthily to God for the multiple victory over the English that had been granted to them, "their days were consumed in vanity and their years in haste."

We can find a parallel to this in Hezekiah king of Judah, regarding whom Isaiah in Chapter 37 states that when the angel of the Lord had killed 185,000 of the splendid army of Sennacherib king of the Assyrians, Hezekiah fell dangerously ill as a result of his ingratitude. Hence as Josephus says: "Although he had offered animals as sacrifices to God with his people, he did not, however, offer thanks worthily nor sing then the song of praise as his forefathers of that time had usually done."

The author Juvenal writes that a certain lady called Nephastes when pregnant and near delivery entered the temples of the gods to consult them about her baby, on whether she was to bear a boy or a girl, so that she might seek divine gifts for her baby from each of them. The first said to her: "Your baby will be a boy, and I give him beauty." The second gave courage, and the third abundance of wealth. On hearing these answers the woman did not accept them, for she was indignant that none of them had given long life to her son. But, as was the custom, she left the temple and came in again to honor the Gods with sacrifices for their favors, offering contrary gifts to them, namely mud for beauty, spittle for courage, an arrogant nod for abundance of wealth. The Gods were greatly offended by these offerings and changed the baby in the womb: instead of the gift of beauty it bore the head of an ape; instead of the gift of courage the wings of a goose; instead of the gift of riches a flayed skin. So allegorically did these Welshmen offer the mud of luxury for knightly beauty, the spittle of discord for the courage that brings victory, a gesture of pride for abundance of good qualities. Thus by the just judgment of God as apes they became worthless through luxury, as geese they were crippled by discord; and at length as if stripped bare they were flayed by the loss and lack of their own liberty and fatherland. I have pursued the aforesaid matters at greater length perhaps than is suitable so that by their example the Scots may be wary of similar light-mindedness of this kind, because, I painfully note, they are too given over to it. As Pope Leo writes: "Examples to follow are more effective than words, and one learns more from action than talk." Hence the poet's words:

When your neighbor's wall is burning, then it is your business.

30. *The same topic, and the death of the abbot of Glamorgan.*
The said Abbot John Powal grieved excessively over the calamitous way of life led by these Welshmen. He could not persuade them by preaching or exhortation to withdraw from the abominable way along which they had wickedly proceeded.

clamare donec rauce facte sunt fauces sue et pro studiosioribus vigiliis defecerunt
oculi sui, vix valens inducere sordescentes reliquias Britonum ad Saxonibus resis-
155   tendum. Unde cum semel sicut solito Saxones Walliam intraverunt adhortacionibus
dicti abbatis congregati sunt Britones septuplo plures Anglico. Quos quidem Britones fiducialiter animavit pugnare pro patria, terras suas et possessiones defen-
dere, natos suos et conjuges salvare, ac pro libertate paterna usque ad mortem
agonizare. Quorum quidem ipse abbas in propria persona ante certamen confes-
160   siones audiebat et absolucionem impendebat, incessanter clamitans et instanter predicare non cessans quousque acies in procinctu attingere contingebant. Propter hoc
abbas in nullo consternatus sed in tantum zelatus est patrie libertatem et gentis
quod, quamvis licite potuit, tamen ei aufugere non libuit, quin cum ceteris suis Wallensibus Britonibus Saxones acriter cedens apud Brinbiga super aquam de Wske
165   doctilogus et armilogus regularis ut ita dicam canonicus mortem temporalem cum
septingentis Britonibus subiit et vitam inde sempiternam mercatus est ut speratur.
    Non enim sic ille frater fecit de quo huiusmodi suscepimus esse relatum, qui
dum exercitui predicaret et confessiones audiret ad congressum perventum est.
Propter quod frater finem faciens sermoni clamavit elata voce dicens: "Viri estote,
170   confortamini, et viriliter agite. Quia habetis justiciam et pro defensione partis
vestre, si quosquam contingat occumbere in hoc prelio, fidejubere audeo et in fide
qua astatis promitto ipsos hac eadem nocte antequam sanguis eorum innocuus ab
inimicis effusus infrididetur cenare cum Christo." Sed statim cum perventum fuerat
ad verba, cessabant fratris verba, propter quod frater se a periculo salvare festinans
175   fugam precinctis lumbis arripuit et in auram dilapsus est. Ad quem cum clamatum
foret a dicentibus: "O sancte frater, expectes et revertaris in prelio, ut juxta promissum tuum hac vice merearis cenare cum Christo," illum semper fugitando fertur
respondisse: "Proficiat vobis obsecro quia hodie revera jejuno et ideo non convenit
mihi hac nocte cenare cum Domino." In hoc patet hunc fratrem unum esse de illis
180   de quibus dixit Christus: "Dicunt et non faciunt. Alligant enim onera gravia et im-
portabilia et imponunt in humeros hominum, sed ipsi digito suo nolunt movere
ea." In isto fratre verificatur quod scribit Gregorius in pastorali: "Si necligas im-
plere quod doces, aliis messem seminas, et ipse a frumenti participacione jejunas."
    Adhuc etenim Wallia jacet sub gente Saxonica squalida et oppresa. Sperat se
185   tamen aliquando respirare meritis Cadvaladri post illud fatale tempus de propheciis
aquile et quod Merlinus Arthuro prophetaverat, maxime propter promissum angeli
dissuadentis pro tunc Cadvaladrum ab Armorica Britannia ad suam Britanniam se
transferre. Dicunt tamen Wallici se numquam posse jura sua ad plenum recuperare
sinc adjutorio sue ab antiquo confederate gentis Albanice. Nam quod sequitur apud
190   se reputant pro diffinito:

But he did not leave off preaching and speaking on this account until his throat was sore and his sight failed as the consequence of zealous nights of prayer. He was now scarcely strong enough to urge the vile remainder of the Britons to resist the Saxons. When therefore the Saxons entered Wales on one occasion in the usual way, the Britons were assembled at the urgings of the said abbot to the number of more than seven times the English, and by inspiring confidence he put spirit into these Britons to fight for their fatherland, to defend their lands and possessions, to save their children and wives, and to suffer even death for their ancestral freedom. The abbot in person heard the confessions of these men before battle and granted them absolution while constantly declaiming and not ceasing his earnest preaching until they came to form up in battle array at the ready. On this account the abbot was not at all afraid, but was so eager for the freedom of his fatherland and people that, although it would have been acceptable, he nonetheless did not choose to withdraw, but along with others of his fellow-Welshmen [i.e. Britons] he fiercely cut down the Saxons at Brynbuga on the river Usk. As a man skilled in learning as well as in arms, and a canon regular (as I say), he met his temporal end along with seven hundred Britons; and it is hoped that in consequence he has earned eternal life.

This was not the behavior of a friar of whom we have heard tell, who mustered with the army as a preacher and hearer of confessions. This friar, in ending his address, shouted out at the top of his voice saying: "Be men, be comforted, and act in manly fashion! Because your case is just and you are fighting for the defense of your side, I dare to stand surety and promise in the faith by which you stand that if it turns out that some fall in this battle, they will dine with Christ this very night before their innocent blood shed by the enemy grows cold." But immediately he had pronounced these words, the exhortations of this friar came to an end, because in hurrying to save himself from danger he took eagerly to flight with girded loins and melted away into thin air. When some people shouted at him saying: "Holy friar, wait and return to the battle so that in accordance with your promise you may this time earn the reward of dining with Christ," he is said to have answered while still running away: "Please understand that today I am keeping a fast so that it is not appropriate for me to dine with the Lord tonight." From this it appears that this friar was one of those of whom Christ said: "They say one thing and do another. They make up heavy and unbearable packs, and pile them on men's shoulders, but will not raise a finger to lift the load themselves." The case of this friar proves what Gregory writes in his *Pastoral Care*: "If you fail to fulfil what you teach, you are planting a harvest for others, and you are yourself abstaining from sharing in the crop."

Wales still lies wretched and oppressed under the Saxon people. Yet she hopes sometime to recover through the merits of Cadwaladr after the fated time mentioned in the prophecies of the Eagle and which Merlin prophesied to Arthur, especially in accordance with the prediction of the Angel who dissuaded Cadwaladr for the time being from moving from Armorican Brittany to his own Britain. Yet the Welsh say that they can never recover their rights in full without the help of their ally from long ago, the people of Scotland. They reckon among themselves that what follows sums it up:

Te cor clam cruciet; laus Cristi virginis instet;
      hoc quando fiet Saxia gens periet.
Wallia revera pacieris bella severa.
Scocia te serva ne fias subdita serva.
195   Wallia dampna feres; tum de relevamine speres.
Scocia fine bono pocieris celebri dono.
Quos tibi serviles reputabis, Anglice miles,
hiis dum tu viles opus est fatearis heriles.
Bruti posteritas Albanis associata
200   Anglica regna teret marte labore nece.
Flumina manabunt hostili tincta cruore.
      Perfida gens omni lite subacta ruet.
Quem Britonum fundet Albani juncta juventus;
      Sanguine Saxonico tincta rubescet humus.
205   Historie veteris Gildas luculentus orator
      Hoc retulit parvo carmine plura notans.
Vigebunt Britones Albanie gentis amici.
      Antiquum nomen insula tota feret.
Ut profert aquila veteri de turre locuta,
210   Cum Scotis Britones regna paterna regent.
Regnabunt pariter in prosperitate quieta
      Hostibus expulsis judicis usque diem.

Ad idem:

Voci verisone Merlini spem prope pone.
215   Scoti cum Britone sternent Anglos in agone.
Flumina manabunt de sanguine; quos superabunt
montes planabunt Britones, diadema levabunt.
Insula tunc uti sic debet nomine Bruti,
cum Scoti tuti vivent Angli quasi muti.

80. Enguerrand de Monstrelet, *Chronicle*   French
1444

En cest an, messire Jaques de Bourbon, conte de La Marche, acompaigné de ses deux frères, c'est assavoir Loys et Jehan, et douze cens chevaliers et escuiers, fut envoiez de par le roy de France au port de Breth en Bretaigne, pour aler en Gales en l'aide des Galois contre les Anglois. Et là, monta ou navire qui apresté lui estoit, très bien garni et pourveu de toutes besongnes neccessaires. Si cuida aler au port de Tordemue, mais le vent lui fut contraire, par quoy il n'y peut aler. Et adonc vid icellui conte partir sept nefz ui estoient pleines de diverses merchandises et aloient au port de Pleinemue. Si les suivirent hastivement, et tant que les hommes qui estoient dedens les sept nefz dessusdictes entrèrent dedens leurs petis basteaulx et

The heart may secretly torment you; the praise of Christ may press upon a virgin;
    when this happens, the Saxon people will perish.
Wales, indeed you will suffer dreadful wars.
Scotland, save yourself lest you are made a subject serf.
Wales, you will suffer injuries; then you may hope for relief.
Scotland, you will acquire a good end, a renowned gift.
Those whom you will reckon as servants, English knight,
while you consider them of no account, you must recognize them as your masters.
The successors of Brutus, allied with the men of Scotland,
    will grind down the English kingdoms with warfare, suffering and slaughter.
Rivers will flow stained with enemy blood.
    A treacherous people will tumble to ruin, subdued by every kind of strife.
The youth of Britain joined with those of Scotland will rout them;
    the earth will turn red, stained with Saxon blood.
Gildas the splendid spokesman of ancient history
    recorded this, noting many details in a short poem.
The Britons will flourish as friends of the people of Scotland.
    The whole island will bear its ancient name.
As the Eagle proclaims, speaking from the old tower,
    the Britons with the Scots will rule their ancestral kingdoms.
They will reign in like manner in quiet prosperity
    until Judgment Day, once their enemies have been expelled.

To the same effect:

Trust in the true-sounding voice of Merlin nearby.
The Scots with the Britons will scatter the English in battle.
Rivers will flow with blood; the mountains which they conquer
the Britons will lay flat; they will raise the diadem.
The island then ought to use the name of Brutus
when the Scots live in safety and the English are like dumb beasts.

80. ENGUERRAND DE MONSTRELET, *CHRONICLE*   Notes: pp. 388–89

    In this year [1404], sir James de Bourbon, count de la Marche, accompanied by his two brothers, Louis and Jean, with twelve hundred knights and esquires, were sent, by orders from the king of France, to the port of Brest in Brittany — thence to embark for Wales, to the succor of the Welsh against the English. They found there a fleet of transports ready provided with all necessaries, on board of which they embarked, intending to land at Dartmouth, but the wind proved contrary. Having noticed seven sail of merchantmen coming out of this harbor, fully laden, making sail for Plymouth, they chased them so successfully that their sailors abandoned their ships, and, taking to their boats, made their escape as well as they

10   se saulvèrent au mieulx qu'ilz porent. Et ledit conte et ses gens prindrent et em-
      menèrent lesdictes nefz et tous les biens, et puis alèrent audit port de Pleinemue et
      le exilla par feu et par espée, et de la ala à une petite isle nommée Salemine, laquelle
      pareillement fut destruicte. A laquelle isle prendre, furent fais nouveaulx chevaliers
      les deux frères du dessusdit conte, c'est assavoir, Loys, conte de Vendosme, et Jehan
15   de Bourbon qui estoit le plus jeune avec plusieurs autres de leur compaignie. En
      apres, quant ledit conte de La Marche et ses gens en eurent la seigneurie par trois
      jours, doubtans que les Anglois qui s'assembloient pour les combatre ne venissent à
      trop grant puissance sur eulx, sortirent de là pour aler en France. Mais quant ilz
      furent entrez en mer, une grande tempeste se leva qui leur dura par trois jours, de
20   laquelle furent péries douze de ses nefz et ceulx qui estoient dedens. Et ledit conte,
      à tous le surplus, s'en vint à grant péril pour ladicte tempeste, arriver au port de
      Saint-Maclou, et de là s'en ala à Paris devers le roy de France.

                                          . . .

      Chapitre xv. *Comment le mareschal de France et la maistre des arbalestriers alèrent en
      Angleterre en l'aide du prince de Gales.*
25   Environ ce temps, le mareschal de France et le Maistre des arbalestriers, par le
      commandement du Roy et à ses despens, assemblèrent douze mille combatans, si
      vindrent à Breth en Bretaigne pour secourir le prince de Gales contre les Anglois.
      Si eurent six vings nefz à voile qu'ilz y trouvèrent, et pour le vent, qui leur fut con-
      traire, demourèrent par quinze jours. Mais quant ilz eurent vent qui leur fut pro-
30   pice, si arrivèrent au port de Harfort en Angleterre, lequel ilz prindrent tantost, en
      occiant les habitans excepté ceulx qui tournèrent en fuite; et gastèrent le pays d'en-
      tour. Puis vindrent au chastel de Harford, ou quel estoit le conte d'Arondel et plu-
      siers hommes d'armes et gens de guerre. Et quant ilz eurent ars la ville et les faulx-
      bourgs dudit chastel, ilz se partirent de là, destruisant tout le pays devant eulx par
35   feu et par espée. Puis alèrent à une ville nommée Tenebi, située à dix huit lieues
      près dudit chastel, et là, trouvèrent, lesdiz François, ledit prince de Gales à tout dix
      mille combatans qui là les actendoit. Adonc alèrent tous ensemble à Calemarchin
      à douze lieues près de Tenebi, et de là en entrant ou pays de Morgnie, alèrent à la
      Table ronde, c'est assavoir l'abbaye noble, puis prindrent leur chemin pour aler à
40   Vincestre. Si ardirent les faulxbourgs et le pays environ, et trois lieues oultre encon-
      trèrent le roy d'Angleterre qui venoit contre eulx à grant puissance; là se arres-
      tèrent l'un contre l'autre et se mirent franchement en bataille, chascune d'icelles
      parties, sur une montaigne, et y avoit une grande valée entre les deux ostz. Si con-
      voitoient chascun d'eulx que sa partie adverse l'alast assaillir, ce que point ne fut
45   fait. Et furent par huit journées en cest estat que chascun jour au matin se mectoient
      en bataille l'un contre l'autre et là se tenoient toute jour jusques au soir. Durant
      lequel temps y eut plusieurs escarmouches entreulx, èsquelles furent mors environ
      deux cens hommes des deux parties et plusieurs navrez. Entre lesquelz, de la partie
      de France furent mors trois chevaliers, c'est assavoir messire Patroullart de Troies,
50   frère dudit mareschal de France, mons. de Mathelonne et mons. de La Ville. En
      oultre, avec ce, les François et Galois furent fort traveillez de famine et autres més-

could. The count de la Marche took possession of the vessels and all they contained, and then entered Plymouth harbor, which they destroyed with fire and sword. Thence he sailed to a small island, called Sallemue; and having treated it in the same manner as Plymouth, he created some new knights — among whom were his two brothers, Louis count de Vendôme, and Jean de Bourbon his youngest brother, and many of their companions. When the count de la Marche had tarried there for three days, suspecting that the English would collect a superior force to offer him battle, he set sail for France; but shortly after a tempest arose that lasted for three days, in which twelve of his ships and all on board perished. With much difficulty, the count reached the port of St. Malo with the remainder, and thence went to Paris to wait on the king of France.

. . .

Chapter 15. *The Marshal of France and the master of the crossbows, by orders from the king of France, go to England, to the assistance of the prince of Wales.*

Around this time [1405], the marshal of France and the master of the cross-bows, by orders from the king of France, and at his expense, collected 12,000 fighting men. They marched to Brest, in Brittany, to embark them, for the assistance of the Welsh against the English, on board of six score vessels with sails, which were lying there. As the wind was contrary, they there remained fifteen days; but when it became favorable, they steered for the port of Haverfordwest — which place they took, slaying all the inhabitants but such as had fled. They wasted the country round, and then advanced to the castle of Haverford, wherein was the earl of Arundel, with many other men at arms and soldiers. Having burnt the town and suburbs under the castle, they marched away, destroying the whole country with fire and sword. They came to a town called Tenby, situated eighteen miles off, where they found the prince of Wales [Owain Glyndŵr], with ten thousand combatants, waiting for them, and thence marched together to Carmarthen, twelve miles from Tenby. Thence they marched into the country of Morgannwg, went to the Round Table, which is a noble abbey, and then took the road to Worcester, where they burnt the suburbs and adjoining country. Three leagues beyond Worcester, they met the king of England, who was marching a large army against them. Each party drew up in order of battle on two eminences, having a valley between them, and each waiting for the attack of its opponent. This contest, who should commence the battle, lasted for eight days; and they were regularly every morning drawn up in battle array, and remained in this state until evening — during which time there were many skirmishes between the two parties, when upwards of two hundred of either side were slain, and more wounded. On the side of France, three knights were slain, namely, Sir Patrouillart de Trie, brother to the marshal of France, the lord de Martelonne, and the lord de la Valle. The French and Welsh were also much oppressed by fa-

aises. Car à grant peine povoient ilz recouvrer de vitaille, pour ce que les Anglois gardoient de près les passages. Finablement quant icelles deux puissances eurent esté l'une devant l'autre ainsi comme dit est, ledit roy d'Angleterre voiant que ses
55   adversaires ne l'assauldroient pas, se retrahit le soir à Vincestre. Mais il fut poursuy par aucuns François et Galois lesquelz destroussèrent dix huit charretes chargées de vivres et d'autres bagues. Si se retrahirent iceulx François et Galois ou païs de Gales. Et pendant que ce voiage se faisoit, le navire des François vaucroit sur la mer, et y avoit dedens aucun nombre de gens d'armes pour le garder. Lequel navire se
60   tira vers Gales, à ung port qui leur avoit esté ordonné, et là les trouvèrent les François, c'est assavoir l'admiral de France et la maistre des arbalestriers, lesquelz avec leurs gens se mirent en mer et singlèrent tant qu'ilz arrivèrent sans fortune à Saint-Pol de Léon. Toutesfoiz quant ils furent descendus et qu'ilz eurent visité leurs gens, ils trouvèrent qu'ilz en avoient bien perdu soixante, desquelz les trois
65   chevaliers dessusdiz estoient les principaulx. Et après se partirent de là et retournèrent en France, chascun en leurs propres lieux, réservé les deux officiers royaulx, qui alèrent à Paris devers le Roy et les autres princes de son sang, desquelz ils furent receuz à grant léesse.

81. John Capgrave, *Liber de Illustribus Henricis*   Latin
                                                                          c.1446

Et post hæc quasdam animi perturbationes habuit idem rex cum uno armigero Ricardi, comitis Arundell, qui armiger dictus est Glendore, quem rex sæpius quæ-sivit et nunquam invenit. Nam in montibus et cavernis Walliæ circumvagans, nunquam certum locum habuit, nec a quoquam capi potuit.

82. Jehan de Waurin, *Collection of Chronicles*   Latin
                                                                          1455

Ceste conclusion prinse entre ceulz de Persy, ilz manderent tous leurs amis et alyez, par tous lieux où ilz cuidoient estre amez, pour les servir à leur besoing; puis s'en allerent ou pays de Galles, sans monstrer samblant de ce qu'ilz pensoient; et là, trouverent aucuns grans seigneurs du pays, lesquelz ilz scavoient estre de la
5   partie du roy Richard, pour le tempz qu'il estoit en vie, et que tres fort avoient prins en hayne le roy Henry, disant à yeeulx seigneurs que, se ilz voulloient, leur aideroient à boutter hors de Galles tous ceulx quy estoient es chasteaulz et villes de par ledit roy Henry, et à remettre leur droit heritier de la princhaulté de Galles en possession, et les autres sei gneurs en leurs patrimones, lesquelz en avoient jadis
10   esté deboutez par le roy Edouard II de ce nom, qui les avoit desheritez, et apliquié le pays de Galles à la couronne d'Engleterre.

Ces seigneurs de Galles, oians ces Persias ainsi parler, furent moult joieux; car, à la verité dire, oncques les Gallois n'amerent naturelement les Anglois; car ilz se dient entreulx estre plus nobles de progeniture que les Anglois, pour ce qu'ilz sont
15   issus et extrais des anchiens Bretons, lesquelz jadis tindrent toute la grant Bretaigne

mine and other inconveniences; for with great difficulty could they gain any provision, as the English had strongly guarded all the passes. At length, on the eighth day that these two armies had been looking at each other, the king of England, seeing the enemy were not afraid of him, retreated in the evening to Worcester, but was pursued by some French and Welsh, who seized on eighteen carts laden with provision and other baggage; upon which the French and Welsh then marched back to Wales. While these things were passing, the French fleet was at sea, having on board some men at arms to defend it, and made for a port which had been pointed out to them, where they were found by their countrymen on their retreat from England. The marshal de Trie and the master of the cross bows, having embarked with their men on board this fleet, put to sea, and made sail for the coast of France, and arrived at St. Pol de Léon without any accident. However, when they were disembarked, and had visited their men, they found they had lost upwards of sixty men, of whom the three knights before mentioned were the principal. They thence departed, each man to his home, excepting the two commanders, who went to wait on the king and the princes of the blood at Paris, by whom they were received with much joy.

81. John Capgrave, *Liber de Illustribus Henricis*   Notes: pp. 389–90

And after these things the same king [Henry IV] had certain worries of his mind with one esquire of Richard, the earl of Arundel, called Glyndŵr whom the king rather often sought, and never found. For wandering about in the mountains and caverns of Wales, he never had a certain location nor could he be captured by anyone.

82. Jehan de Waurin, *Collection of Chronicles*   Notes: p. 390

This resolution [to depose Henry IV as a result of his demand for the captive earl of Douglas] being taken by the party of Percy, they sent for all their friends and allies in every place where they thought themselves beloved to serve them in their need, and then went into the country of Wales without giving any sign of their intentions, and there found some great lords of the country, who they knew were of the party of King Richard when he was living, and had taken a great hatred against King Henry, telling these lords that if they liked they would help them to drive out of Wales all those who were in castles and towns on the part of King Henry, and to replace their rightful heir of the principality of Wales [i.e., Owain Glyndŵr] in possession and the other lords in their patrimonies from which they had formerly been driven out by King Edward the Second of this name, who had disinherited them and annexed the country of Wales to the crown of England.

These Welsh lords hearing the Percies speak in this manner were rejoiced, for sooth to say the Welsh never naturally loved the English, for they thought themselves more noble by extraction than the English, for that they issued and descended from the ancient Britons, who formerly held all Great Britain, which now the

que maintenant occupent les Anglois; laquele, comme en ceste histore est cy devant
contenu ou premier volume, ung grant prince, nommé Englist, conequesta sur les
Bretons, si le repeupla de diverses nations: c'est à scavoir de Saxons, d'Allemans,
Flamens, Picars, Northmans et autres peuples. Si fut le pays nommé Engleterre,
20   pour Englist, lequel nom luy a duré jusques aujourd'huy.

Or donc, pour retourner à nostre propos, ceulz de Galles, moult joieuz de l'aliance faite et enconvenenchié au conte de Northumberland, et aux seigneurs de
Persy, requirent que de ceste aliance lettres feussent faites, escriptes et scellees des
seaulz des deux parties. Et, avec ce, pour plus fermement entretenir celle alyance,
25   jurerent et promisrent, sur le corpus Domini, d'icelles convenences entretenir
jusques à mort souffrir.

Les choses ainsi passees, chascun, de sa partie, manda gens, amis et alyez endroit
soy. Et les seigneurs de la princhauté de Galles assemblerent leur povoir, prindrent
jour, lieu et place pour eulz tous assambler en ung ost, adfin d'entrer en pays.

83. JOHN HARDYNG, *CHRONICLE*   **Middle English**
                                                           1436 x 1464

The ccii. chapiter. *Howe Owen of Glendoure rose in Wales againe the king, and made
warre on the lorde Gray Ruthin, and toke the lorde Graye and syr Edmonde Mortymer.*

The king came home and to London went
at Michelmasse, wher then he had message
that Owen Glendoure then felly blent
in Englande sore, and did full great damage
5   for cause the lorde Graye helde his herytage;
and to the kyng of it full sore had playned,
no remedye gate so was he then demeaned.

The lorde Gray Ruthin did hym great wrong,
destroyed his lande and he did hym the same.
10   So both Marches destroyed were full longe.
But Owen wanne himselfe eche day great name
of vasselrie, of gentyls, and of fame
that he them did, for whiche to him they drewe
and became his men & to him were full trewe.

15   So on a daye the lorde Graye and he met
with great power vpon eyther syde
where then they faught in batayle sore bet.
And toke hym then his prysoner that tyde
and there the felde he had with mikyll pryde
20   greate people toke and slewe & home he went.
The lorde Graye he raunsomed at his entent.

English occupy, and which as in this history if above contained in the first volume a great prince named Hengist conquered from the Britons, and repeopled with divers nations, that is to say, with Saxons, Germans, Flemings, Picards, Normans, and other people, and thus was the country called England from Hengist, which name has remained to it to this day.

So then to return to our history, the men of Wales, very glad of the alliance made and agreed upon with the earl of Northumberland and the Lords Percy, asked that letters of this alliance might be made, written, and sealed with the seals of both parties, and moreover the more firmly to maintain this alliance they swore and promised on the Body of Our Lord to keep these agreements unto death. These matters thus passed, each one on his side sent for friends, followers, and allies round about, and the lords of the principality of Wales assembled their power and appointed day and place for assembling in one army in order to take the field.

83. JOHN HARDYNG, *CHRONICLE*   Notes: p. 391

Chapter 202. *How Owain Glyndŵr rose in Wales against the king, made war on Lord Grey of Ruthin, and seized Lord Grey and Sir Edmund Mortimer.*

The king came home and went to London
at Michaelmas, where he heard the news
that Owain Glyndŵr was then cruelly agitating
against England, and he did great damage there
5   because Lord Grey withheld his heritage;
and when Owain complained of it to the king,
instead of a remedy he was demeaned.

Lord Grey of Ruthin did him great wrong,
destroyed his land and so he did the same.
10   So both Marches were ravaged up and down.
But Owain won for himself each day a great name
of martial might, of gentility, and of fame
for what he did for them, for which to him they drew
and became his men and to him were most true.

15   One day Lord Grey and he met
with great power upon either side.
There they fought in a terrible battle.
Owain took him prisoner at that time
and won the field with much pride.
20   Great people were taken and slain and home he went.
Lord Grey he ransomed at his intent.

Syr Edmonde then Mortimer warred sore
vpon Owen and dyd hym mekyll tene,
but at laste Owen laye hym before,
25   where in batell they faught as well was sene,
where Owen toke him prisoner as then ful kene
with mekell folke on eyther syde slayne,
and set Edmonde in prysone and great payne.

He wrote vnto the kyng for great socoure,
30   for he had made with Owen his fynaunce,
to whom þe kyng wolde graunt then no fauoure,
ne nought he wolde then make him cheuesaunce
for to comforte his foes disobeysaunce.
Wherfore he laye in feters and sore prysone,
35   for none payment of his greate raunsone.

The ccii. chapiter.

. . .

15   The kyng Henry thryce to Wales went,
in the haye tyme and haruest dyuers yere.
In euery tyme were mystes and tempestes sent
of wethers foule that he had neuer power
Glendour to noye, but euer his caryage clere
20   Owen had at certayne straites and passage,
and to our hoste dyd full greate damage.

The king had neuer but tempest foule & raine
as longe as he was ay in Wales grounde
rockes & mystes windes stormes euer certaine.
25   All men trowed þe witches it made that stounde.
the commens all then of all Englande grounde
warred his gate to Wales euery yere
for haye and corne were loste both two in fere,

whiche made greate derth & of catell morayne
30   and euen ay in hylles and in mountaynes
kepte him ful strong; þe king ay wrought in vaine:
the king might not but euer more held þe pleines
and waste his owne lordshippes & his demaines.
And full great parte Owen had and occupyed
35   by processe so in Wales and victoryed.

Th'erle Henry then of Northumberland
brought to the kyng his owne prisoner,
th'erle of Fyffe was then I vnderstand,
heire vnto the duke of Albany clere,

Sir Edmund Mortimer made hard war
upon Owain and did him much harm,
and at last Owain lay before him,
25   where in battle they fought as is well known.
Owain tooke him prisoner in that event
with many folk on either side slain,
and he set Edmund in prison and great pain.

He wrote unto the king for great succor,
30   for he had agreed with Owain on his ransom,
to whom the king would grant then no favor,
nor make for him any provision
to comfort his foe's disobedience.
Therefore he lay in chains and gravely in prison,
35   for he could not pay his great ransom.

Chapter [203].

. . .

15   King Henry thrice to Wales went,
during the hay time and the harvest in diverse years.
Every time mists and tempests were sent
of such foul weather that he never had the power
to disturb Glyndŵr, whereas his carriage
20   Owain had at certain straits and passage,
and to our army did full great damage.

The king had nothing but foul tempest and rain
as long as he was upon Welsh ground,
rocks, mists, winds, and storms ever constant.
25   All men believed the witchcraft made it so.
The commons from all English lands
warred his gate to Wales every year
for hay and corn were both lost together,

Which brought a great famine and dead cattle,
30   yet ever in the hills and mountains
Owain stayed strong. The king thus labored in vain:
he could do nothing but hold the plains
and waste his own lordships and domains.
And a large part Owain held and did occupy
35   by process so in Wales and in victory.

Earl Henry of Northumberland
brought to the king his own prisoner,
the earl of Fife, as I understand,
heir to the duke of Albany,

40   regent that was of Scotland without pere.
          But Sir Henry his soonne then would not bryng
          his prisoners in no wise to the kyng.

          But the kyng he prayed for Mortimer,
          that raunsomed might he been wiþ his frendes so.
45   He saied hym nay, for he was taken prisoner
          by his consent and treson to his foo,
          whom he would not comfort for to ouergoo
          the prince his landes ne his owne to destroye,
          for ay he had greate trust þat he should hym noye.

50   The kyng hym blamed for he toke not Owen
          when he came to hym on his assurance.
          And he aunswered then to the kyng again,
          he might not so kepe his affiaunce
          to shame hymself with suche a variaunce.
55   The kyng blamed hym for his prisoner
          th'erle Douglas for cause he was not there,

          and saied he should hym fette, but he hym sede:
          Sir Henry sawe no grace for Mortimer,
          his wifes brother, he went awaye vnkende
60   to Berwyk so, and after came no nere,
          afore thei mette at Shrowesbury in fere,
          wher then thei faught for cause of his entent,
          he purposed had Mortimer his coronoment.

          The lordes all of England had hym hight
65   and Owayn also on Seuerne hym to mete,
          except th'erle of Stafford young to fight,
          by their letters vnder their seales mete.
          But in the poinct thei brake all their behete,
          and he was slain and all the cause conselid
70   why he the field tooke and the kyng appelid.

. . .

The ccvi. chapter. *Howe the kyng his soone of Scotland and heire James was taken on the sea and brought unto the kyng and then dyed Owayn and the kyng of Scotland.*

. . .

          The tenth yere then of the kyng his date
          the kyng of Scotland, and Owayn of Glendor
10   his soonne also, the world forsoke then algate
          and dyed awaye, of theim then was no more
          the prince of Scotland then was kyng therfore
          and Wales all became the kyng his menne
          in rest and peace without rebellion then.

40   the regent of Scotland who was without peer.
     But Hotspur his son would not bring
     his prisoners in any way to the king.

     Instead he begged the king for Mortimer,
     to ransom him so that he might be with his friends.
45   He told him no, for Edmund was taken prisoner
     by his own consent and was in treason with his foe,
     whom the king would not comfort by giving
     the prince his lands nor his own to destroy,
     for ever he had great trust that he should him annoy.

50   The king blamed Hotspur for he did not seize Owain
     when he came to him on his assurance.
     And Hotspur answered then to the king again
     that he might not thus keep his allegiance
     to shame himself with such a variance.
55   The king blamed him for his prisoner
     the earl of Douglas because he was not there,

     and said he should give him over, but he said to him:
     Hotspur saw no grace for Mortimer,
     his wife's brother. He went away angry
60   to Berwick then, and afterward came no nearer
     until they met at Shrewsbury together,
     where then they fought because of his intention:
     Hotspur was going to give Mortimer his coronation.

     The lords all of England had assured him —
65   and Owain also on the Severn — to meet him,
     all except the earl of Stafford, who was too young to fight,
     by their letters under their seals affixed.
     But in the point they broke all their promises,
     and Hotspur was slain and all the cause concealed
70   why he took the field and to the king appealed.

              . . .

Chapter 206. *How the son and heir of the king of Scotland, James, was taken on the sea and brought to the king, and then died Owain and the king of Scotland.*

              . . .

     In the tenth year of the king's date,
     the king of Scotland, and Owain Glyndŵr,
10   His son also, the world forsook then together
     And died, of them then was no more.
     The prince of Scotland then was king therefore
     and the Welsh all became to the king his men
     in rest and peace without rebellion then.

84. GUTUN OWAIN, *YSTORIA BRENHINEDD SAESON*   **Welsh**
                                                                1461 x 1470

A gwedi digoroni Richart yr Ail y koroned Henrri Bedwerydd Ddugwyl Saint
Edwart. Oed Krist yna MCCCLxxxxix o vlynyddoedd.

Y vlwyddyn gyntaf o'i vrenhinaeth ef, pann oedd oed Krist MCCCC, noswyl
Vathav, yr vgeinved dydd o vis Medi, y kyvodes Owain ap Gruffydd, arglwydd Glynn
5   Dyfrdwy, a'r Kymry gyd ac ef ac y llosges Rvthvn. Ac ni bu bell gwedy hynny oni
ddaliodd Owain ap Gruffydd arglwyd Rvthvn a Syr Edmwnt Mortmer, iarll y Mars,
a'i karcharv yn y koed hyd pann ffiniasant i Owain ddec mil o vorkiav. Ac Owain a
gynhaliodd ryvel a'r Saeson.

A phann oedd oed Krist Mil CCCCiii blynedd y bu y vattel yn y Bwl Ffilt yn
10 emyl y Mwythic y rwng Harri Bedwerydd, brenin Lloegr, a Syr Harri Persi, marchog
vrddol a phenn kyngor i vrenin Richart yr Ail, yr hwnn a vv anghywir y'w vrenin.
Ac yny vattel honno y llas yr Harri Persi hwnnw a llawer gyd ac ef o bobl.

A dwy vlynedd gwedy hynny y tored penn Richart Ysgrwp, archesgob Iork, a
Thomas Mwmbraey, iarll marsial, yn ymyl Iork. A'r Richart hwnnw sydd yn
15 gwnevthur llawer o wyrthav, herwydd yr ys yn i ddywedud yny wlad honno.

A phann oedd oed Krist MCCCCxiij o vlynyddoedd y bu varw Harri Bedwerydd, brenin Lloegr, a'i gladdv yNghaer Gaint. Ac iddo y bu bedwar mab a dwy
verched, nid amgen Harri Bymed, brenin Lloegr; Tomas, duc o Klarans; John, duc
o Betfford; Wmffrey duc o Glosedyr; ac o'r merched vn oedd Blanch, gwraic
20 ymerodyr yr Almaen; a Phelipa.

A phann oedd oed Krist Mil CCCCxiii o vlynyddoedd, Sul y Meibion, y koroned
Harri Bymed yn vrenin Lloegr a Chymry.

85. *GREGORY'S CHRONICLE*   **Middle English**
                                                         c.1470

And that same yere [1400] the kynge roode in to Schotlonde. And there he beganne
the werre at Walys by Gwyn Glandowre, squyer, ayenste the Kyng of Inglonde,
Harry the iiij, &c.

86. *ALLAN O HEN GRONICL 1471*   **Welsh**
                                                         c.1471

Yr ail flwyddyn o frenhiniaeth Harri Bedwerydd i cyfodes terfysc mawr y Nghymru rhwng arglwydd Ruthun ag Owain ap Gruffudd, arglwydd Glyndyfrdwy. A'r
un amser hwnnw ir aeth y brenin a llu mawr gantho i Brydyn, ac ef a anfonasai
lythyr gyd ac arglwydd Ruthun at Owain i orchymmyn iddo ddyfod gyd ac ef i
5   Brydyn. A'r arglwydd a gedwis hwnnw ganthaw oni gychwynnodd y brenin, ac yna
ir anfones y llythr at Owain.

A phan weles Owain y gorchymmyn caled oedd yn y llythr, syn fu gantho na
allai mewn modd o'r byd ymbarattoi wrth urddas y brenin mor fyr a hynny i siwrnai
mor gostfawr a honno. A phan ddoeth yr arglwydd o Ruthun at y brenin, ef a
10 ddywed anufuddhau o Owain i'w orchymyn ef dan ddywedyd geiriau hagr dirmygus

84. Gutun Owain, *History of the Kings of the English*   Notes: pp. 391–93

And after the deposing of Richard the Second, Henry the Fourth was crowned on the Feast of St. Edward. The age of Christ then was 1399 years.

The first year of his kingship, when the age of Christ was 1400, on the eve of St. Matthew, the twentieth day of September, Owain ap Gruffudd, the lord of Glyndyfrdwy, rose up, and the Welsh with him, and burned Ruthin. And it was not long after that until Owain ap Gruffudd captured the lord of Ruthin and Sir Edmund Mortimer, earl of the March, and imprisoned them in the wood until they paid a ransom to Owain of ten thousand marks. And Owain waged war with the English.

And when the age of Christ was 1403 years, there was the battle in the Bullfield, beside Shrewsbury, between Henry the Fourth, king of England, and Sir Henry Percy, an ordained knight and chief counsel to king Richard the Second, he who was untrue to his king. And in that battle that Henry Percy was killed, and many people with him.

And two years after that the heads of Richard Scrope, archbishop of York, and Thomas Mowbray, earl marshall, were struck off beside York. And that Richard is performing many miracles, according to what is said in that land.

And when the age of Christ was 1413 years, Henry the Fourth, king of England, died and was buried in Canterbury. And he had four sons and two daughters, none other than Henry the Fifth, king of England; Thomas, duke of Clarence; John, duke of Bedford; Humphrey, duke of Gloucester; and of the daughters, one was Blanche, wife of the emperor of Germany; and Philippa.

And when the age of Christ was 1413 years, on the Sunday of the Innocents, Henry the Fifth was crowned king of England and Wales.

85. *Gregory's Chronicle*   Notes: p. 393

And that same year the king rode into Scotland. And then also began the war in Wales by Owain Glyndŵr, a squire, against the king of England, Henry IV.

86. *Out of an Old Chronicle 1471*   Notes: pp. 393–94

The second year of the reign of Henry IV a great tumult arose in Wales between the lord of Ruthin and Owain ap Gruffudd, lord of Glyndyfrdwy. And at that time the king, and a great host with him, went to Scotland, and he sent a letter with the lord of Ruthin to Owain to command him to come with him to Scotland. And the lord kept that with him until the king set out, and then he sent the letter to Owain.

And when Owain saw the stringent command that was in the letter, he was bewildered that he could in no way in the world prepare himself in accordance with the king's dignity as quickly as that for a journey as costly as that. And when the lord of Ruthin came to the king, he said Owain refused to obey his command, say-

am y brenin. A hynny a gredodd y brenin ac a'i cedwis yn ei gof yn gyfrinachol oni ddoeth adref i dref Leysedr ar fedr myned am ben Owain i Gymru. Ac er hynny ni ddoeth eithr ymchwelyd i Loegr a rhoi holl diroedd Owain i arglwydd Rhuthun, a'r rhoddiad hwnnw a beris llawer o flinder a drygioni rhwng Cymru a Lloegr, canys
15   noswyl Fathau nessaf at hynny y doeth Owain am ben tref Ruthun a'i llosgi a lladd cymmaint a[c] a gavas o wyr ynthi. Ac o hynny hyt y mhen y pumtheng mlynedd i'r un noswyl Fatheu ni bu heddwch gwastad y Nghymru, canys yna y bu varw Owain.

87. JOHN ROUS, *HISTORIA REGUM ANGLIAE*
Latin
1480–86

Circa initium regni sui apparuit stella comata, rosa, secundum astronomos, dicta, de natura solis. Rotunda erat & miræ magnitudinis. Statim surrexit magna rebellione quidam Wallicus dictus Owen de Glendour, qui totam Angliam multum inquietavit. Regio exercitui nunquam obviare ausus in certis castris erat sæpius
5   obsessus, castris ipsis captis inveniri non potuit. Dictum erat tunc commune quod lapidem habuit eum reddentem invisibilem, qui lapis, ut dicitur, quondam erat Ricardi comitis Arundeliiæ per regem Ricardum crudeliter decapitati. Comes Arundelliæ prædictus, ut asseritur, habuit corvum de majori corum genere autonomatice a Ravyn. Qui corvus erat nutritus in curia sua, & dum quadam vice luderet ad scac-
10   carium in quodam orto, dictus corvus vel spiritus in specie corvina coram comite lapidem eructavit invisibilitatis habentem virtutem. Comes lapidem non appreciavit contra consilium nobilium suorum, & cito post dictus comes manu potenti arestatus ad carceres deputatus finaliter decapitatus est.

88. RHYS PENNARDD, *RHYFEL GLYNDŴR*
Welsh
c.1480

Mil a phedwar cant, heb ddim mwy — cof ydyw —
   cyfodiad Glyndyfrdwy,
  a phymtheg, praff ei saffwy,
  bu Owain hen yn byw'n hwy.

89. *BEAUCHAMP PAGEANT*
Middle English
1485 x 1490

Here shewes howe at thies daies appered a blasyng sterre called *stella comata* which after the seiyng of clerkys signyfied greet deth and blodeshede. And sone uppon beganne the Warre of Wales by oon Owen of Glendour their chief capteyn. Whom emonges other Erle Richard so sore sewed that he hadde nerehande taken hym and
5   put hym to flight and toke his baner and moche of his people and his banerer.

ing foul, contemptuous words about the king. And the king believed that and he kept it in his mind privily until he came homewards to the town of Leicester, intending to descend upon Owain in Wales. And despite that he did not come, but returned to England and gave all Owain's lands to the lord of Ruthin, and that grant caused much affliction and evil between Wales and England, since the next St. Matthew's Eve Owain descended upon the town of Ruthin and burned it and killed as many men as he took in it. And from then until the end of fifteen years to the same St. Matthew's Eve there was no peace and quiet in Wales, since then Owain died.

87. John Rous, *Historia regum Angliae*   Notes: pp. 394–95

Around the beginning of his [Henry's] reign appeared a comet, red, according to the astronomers said to be of the nature of the sun. It was round and of an extraordinary size. At once, a certain Welshman called Owain Glyndŵr rose up in a great rebellion, who much disquieted the whole of England. He never dared to meet in battle the king's army, and he was often besieged in a stronghold. The castle having been captured, he could not be found. It was a common rumor at that time that he had a stone which rendered him invisible, which stone, as it is said, once belonged to Richard, earl of Arundel, who was cruelly beheaded by King Richard. The aforesaid earl of Arundel, so it is reported, had a crow of the greater sort of them, which are called ravens. This crow was raised in his court and when on a certain occasion he was playing chess in a certain garden, the so-called crow or spirit in the form of a crow, in the presence of the earl, noisily spat out a stone which had the virtue of invisibility. The earl did not use it, contrary to the advice of his nobles, and soon after the said earl was forcibly arrested, sent off to prison and finally decapitated.

88. Rhys Pennardd, *Glyndŵr's War*   Notes: pp. 395–96

One thousand four hundred, without any more — there is remembrance —
   of the uprising of Glyndyfrdwy,
   and fifteen years, stout his spear,
   old Owain lived afterwards.

89. *Beauchamp Pageant*   Notes: pp. 396–98

Here is shown how during these days there appeared a blazing star called a comet that, according to wise men, signified great death and bloodshed. And soon after it appeared there began the War of Wales by Owain Glyndŵr, their chief captain. Along with others, Earl Richard fought him so hard that he very nearly seized him and he put him to flight and took his banner along with many of his people and his standard bearer.

90. *ENGLYN RHYBUDD I OWAIN GLYNDŴR*

Welsh
15th–16th c.

Davydd ap Grvffydd ap Llewelyn ap Iorwerth Drwyndwn pan ddihenyddwyd
yn Amvythic ac wrth i ddihenyddv y kymerth i kigidd i galon ac a'i tafles i'r tan ac
a neidiodd y galon o'r tan ac a drawodd y kigidd ar i lygad ac a dynnodd i lygad.
A Harri Bedwerydd, Brenin Lloegyr, a ysgrifennodd at Arglwydd Grae o Rvthvn i
5   erchi iddo ef trwy ryw ystryw vradychv Owen Glyndwr. Ac yno y gyrrodd Arglwydd
Rvthvn at Owain i ddoedvd iddaw y byddai yn kiniawa gidac Owain y dydd ar dydd.
Ac yr attebodd Owain y bydde roessaw wrthaw oni ddygai gidac ef vwch benn dengwr ar hvgain. Ac a ddoeth yr arglwydd yn yr oed terfynedic ac ychydic kwmpeini
gi[d]ac ef (a gallv mawr yn arfoc tan lech yn dyfod ar i ol). A phan aeth Owen i gin-
10 iawa, ef a ossodes wersyll ar benn brynn i wersylly tra vyddai Owen ar ginio. A phan
oedd Ywain ar ganol kiniaw, nychaf y gwelynt y gwersyllwyr lonaid y ddol heb enni
o wyr arfoc ac y doedassant i Iolo Goch i rvbyddio Owain. Ac yna y doeth Iolo i
mewn, kanys didyb oedd ef, ac y kanodd ar ddamec yr englyn rhybydd yma ar ostec,
rhac tybied yr arglwydd bod twyll ynddo: er bod yr arglwydd yn dallt traethawd
15 Kymraec, nid oedd vo yn dallt yn mydyr ni:

Koffa benn a llen a llywenic — lys
a las nos Nadolic;
koffa golwyth Amwythic,
o'r tan a neidiodd naid dic.
Iolo Goch a'i kant.

91. *Y DDYFADEN AR BEN OWAIN GLYNDŴR*

Welsh
15th–16th c.

Ar ol marwolaeth Owen Glyndwr a dug un Madyn ben i'r brenin gan ddywedyd
mae'r pen hwnnw oedd ben Owen. A'r brenin a ymofynodd a'r Cymry a adwaenen
hwy ben Owain. Ac un a ddywawd os cai ef ei weled ir adwaenai fo, achos bod daf-
aden ar ei iad. A phan welwyd y pen hwnnw a gwybod nad pen Owain oedd, y
5   canodd un o lys y brenin fal hyn:

Celwydh a dhywad Madyn
Ogloph am Arglwydh y Glyn,
am na chad y dhavaden
garllaw tal y gwr llwyd hen.

Pen Tudur ap Gruffudd Vychan o Ragad, brawd Owain Glyndwr oedd hwnn. *Gefeilliaid*
oeddynt ac ni adwaeniad neb y naill rhagor y llall ond wrth y ddyfaden. Yn y Gâd
ar *Fynydd Pwll Mellyn* y Mrecheiniog i llas y Tudur . . . nid oedd Owain yn y Gâd.

90. *A POEM OF WARNING TO OWAIN GLYNDŴR*   Notes: pp. 398–99

Dafydd ap Gruffudd ap Llywelyn ab Iorwerth Drwyndwn was executed in Shrews-bury, and at his execution the executioner took his heart and threw it into the fire, but the heart leapt from the fire and struck the executioner in his eye and put out his eye. And Henry IV, King of England, wrote to Lord Grey of Ruthin to ask him, through some trick, to betray Owain Glyndŵr. And then Lord Grey sent to Owain to tell him that he would be dining with Owain on such and such a day. And Owain answered that there would be a welcome for him if he would not come with over thirty men. And the lord came at the appointed time and a small company with him (and a great armed force under cover coming after him). And when Owain went to dine, he set a lookout on top of a hill, to watch while Owain would be at dinner. And when Owain was in the middle of dinner, behold the lookouts saw the meadow over-flowing with armed men, and they told Iolo Goch to warn Owain. And then Iolo came in, for he was beyond suspicion, and he sang as a parable this warning *englyn* openly, lest the lord should suppose there was treachery in it, for though the lord could understand spoken Welsh, he did not understand our meter:

> Remember a head, and a mantle and a rejoicing court,
> which was struck off on Christmas night;
> remember the cutlet of Shrewsbury,
> from the fire it leapt, an angry leap.
> > *Iolo Goch sang it.*

91. *THE WART ON OWAIN GLYNDŴR'S HEAD*   Notes: pp. 399–401

After the death of Owain Glyndŵr one Madyn brought a head to the king, say-ing that that head was Owain's head. And the king asked the Welsh if they would recognize Owain's head. And one said if he could see it he would recognize it, be-cause there was a wart on his crown. And when that head was seen and it was known that it was not Owain's head, one of the king's court sang thus:

> Madyn the Lame told a lie
> about the Lord of the Glyn,
> because the wart was not found
> near the brow of the old grey-haired man.

This was the head of Tudur ap Gruffudd Fychan of Rhagad, the brother of Owain Glyndŵr. They were twins and no one could tell the one from the other except by the wart. Tudur was killed in the battle on Pwll Melyn Mountain in Brycheiniog . . . Owain was not in the battle.

92. *I'R KORNWYD KYNTA*   **Welsh**
                                                                         15th–16th c.

Englyn i'r kornwyd kynta a vv erioed y Nghymrv; y vlwyddyn honno y ganed Owen Glyndwr.

Marwolaeth a wnaeth Duw Naf — anwedig
    pan vv'r nodav gyntaf,
   mil a thrychant, gwarant a gaf,
   naw a deugain, y tygaf.

93. *MIDDLE ENGLISH VITA HENRICI QUINTI*   **Middle English**
                                                                         1513–14

    Manie Welshmen, and in a manner the greater parte of all Wales, were confed-
erate with these rebbells, and were present at the insurrection. And for because they
percevered in theire obstinacie the kinge deliuered the prince, his sonn, a greate
armed bande, and sent him into Wales to subdue those falsh Welsh rebellions, who,

5   at his comminge into Wales, destroyed theire lande with sworde and fyre. And after
longe and manie cruelties by them done for theire defence, the prince slewe part
of them by battaile, and part he took and punished them after there deserts. And
part he droue into stronge holds and castles, whome finallie at all times he subdued
to his fathers dominion. How so be a greate part of them, seeinge their confederats

10   thus vanquished, and themselues thus oppressed by the prince, fledd for refuge into
a greate and stronge castle in Wales called Amberrstmuch, wherevnto the prince
layed his siege, and assaulted it by mynes and all manner of engins that were
thought needfull for the distruccion of them and of there castle; he made manie
vigorous assaults and skirmishes for the oppression of them. And on his partie the

15   siege was not without the paine and disease of the prince and his companie, but in
so much the more noyous vnto them that were lodged within the castell, not in
plaine fields but in roughe and thicke woods, for with such manner woods and castells it was environed. And also it was that time winter, which was cause to them of
incredible colde and paine. Neuertheles this most virtuous prince, not wearied with

20   paine, after he had longe assieged this castell to the kings greate cost and expences,
and not without the effusion of much bloud, obtayned the castell, and subdued the
residue of Wales vnder the kings obeysance, except on person, whose name was
Owann, which was principall chieftaine of the Welsh rebellions. This Owann, for
feare and in dispaire to obtaine the kinges pardon, fledd into desart places without

25   companie; where in caues he continued, and vppon the topp of Lawton's Hope Hill
in Herefordshire, as is there obserued and affirmed, finished his miserable life.
Neuertheles his sonn afterward was taken into seruis with the prince. And this suffi-
ceth of the Welsh conspiracies and battailes, which this victorious prince right val-
liantlie vanquished, and reduced the people to the kinge his fathers obeysaunce.

92. *On the First Plague and Owain's Birth*   **Notes: pp. 401–02**

An englyn on the first plague that was ever in Wales; that year Owain Glyndŵr was born.

The eminent Lord God brought about death
    when the plague first began,
      in one thousand and three hundred, I am assured,
      and two score and nine, I swear.

93. *Middle English Vita Henrici Quinti*   **Notes: p. 402**

Many Welshmen, and in one sense the vast majority of all the Welsh, were confederate with these rebels and were present at the insurrection. And because they persevered in their obstinacy the king delivered to the prince, his son, a great armed band and sent him into Wales to subdue those false Welsh rebellions, who, at his coming into Wales, destroyed their lands with sword and fire. And after a long struggle with many cruelties done by them for their defense, the prince slew part of them by battle, and another part he captured and punished as they deserved. And another part he drove into their strongholds and castles, which finally at all times he subdued to his father's rule. As a result a large number of them, seeing their confederates thus vanquished, and themselves thus oppressed by the prince, fled for refuge into a great and strong castle in Wales called Aberystwyth, to which the prince laid siege and assaulted by mine-works and all manner of engines that were thought necessary for the destruction of them and of their castle. He made many vigorous assaults and skirmishes for the oppression of them. And the siege was not without pain and disease on the part of the prince and his company, but it was much more terrible for those who were lodged within the castle, not in plain fields but in rough and thick woods, for with such manner woods and castles it was environed. And also it was winter at that time, which was the cause of incredible cold and pain to them all. Nevertheless this most virtuous prince, not wearied with pain, after he had long besieged this castle to the king's great cost and expense, and not without the effusion of much blood, obtained the castle, and subdued the residue of Wales under the king's obedience, except one person, whose name was Owain, who was the principal leader of the Welsh rebellions. This Owain, for fear and in despair that he could not obtain the king's pardon, fled into deserted places without company; where in caves he continued to live, and upon the top of Lawton's Hope Hill in Herefordshire, as is there observed and affirmed, he finished his miserable life. Nevertheless his son afterward was taken into service with the prince. And this is enough to say of the Welsh conspiracies and battles, which this victorious prince right valiantly vanquished, and which reduced the people to his father the king's obedience.

94. JOHN LELAND, *ITINERARY IN WALES*   **Middle English**
                                                                    1536 x 39

[p. 10] New Radnor towne hathe be metly well wallyd, and in the walle appere
the ruines of iiii. gates. . . . The buildynge of the towne in some parte meatly good,
in moste part by rude, many howsys beinge thakyd. The castle is in ruine, but that
a pece of the gate was a late amendyd. The towne was defacyd in Henry the fowrthe
5   dayes by Owen Glindowr.

                                        . . .

[p. 41] Montgomerike deflorichid by Owen Glindour.
      Radenor partely destroied by Owen Glindour, and the voice is there that after
he wonne the castel he tooke a iii. score men that had the garde of the castel, and
causid them to be heddid on the brinke of the castel yarde, and that sins a certen
10   bloodeworth growith ther wher the bloode was shedde.

                                        . . .

[p. 52] Comehere an abbay of White Monkes stondith betwixt ii. great hilles in
Melennith in a botom wher rennith a litle brooke. It is a vii. miles from Knighton.
The first foundation was made by Cadwathelan ap Madok for lx. monkes. No chirch
in Wales is seene of such leght as the fundation of walles ther begon doth show; but
15   the third part of this worke was never finisched. Al the howse was spoilid and de-
facid be Owen Glindour.

                                        . . .

[p. 70]Dinas Brane Castel on a rokky hille stondith almost as neere as Vallis
Crucis to Dee ripe, and going up on De water is sumwhat lower then the abbay.
      Owen Glindour had a place yn Yale apon the north side of De caullid Ragarth
20   v. mile above Dinas Brane.
      Almost in the midle way betwixte Llanegwhist and Rithyn appere vestigia of a
castel of Owen Glindour (as it is saide) caullid Keuen De, i.e. the bakke of the Blake
Hille, wher now shepardes kepe shepe.

                                        . . .

[p. 78] Deyrnion commote lyith thus on the est side of Penthline, and hath on
25   the north side Denbighland, and Yale on the north est side, and hath on the south
side Powys lande. . . .
      Owen Glyndour dwellid yn this commot.
      Lluelin ap Irrwarth Droyndon Prince of al Wales, had Grifith. Grifith had
Lluelin. Lluelin had Catarine his heire. Catarine had Eleanor. Eleanor had Helene

94. JOHN LELAND, *ITINERARY IN WALES*   Notes: pp. 403–07

New Radnor town was once well fortified, and in the wall appear the ruins of four gates. . . . The buildings of the town in some parts appear suitably good, but in most areas are crude, many houses being thatched. The castle is in ruin, except that a part of its gate was recently repaired. The town was defaced in the days of Henry IV by Owain Glyndŵr.

. . .

Montgomery was ravaged by Owain Glyndŵr.

Radnor was partly destroyed by Owain Glyndŵr, and the rumor there is that after he won the castle he took sixty men who had been guarding the castle and had them beheaded on the side of the castle yard, and that ever since a certain blood-wort grows there where the blood was shed.

. . .

Cwm-hir, a Cistercian abbey, stands between two large hills in Maelienydd, on the valley floor where a little brook runs. It is about seven miles from Knighton. The first foundation was made by Cadwallon ap Madog for sixty monks. No church in Wales has such a length as is shown by the foundation of walls begun there shows, but a third of this work was never completed. All of the abbey was spoiled and defaced by Owain Glyndŵr.

. . .

Castell Dinas Brân stands on a rocky hill almost as close to the River Dee as is Valle Crucis Abbey, and going up the Dee, is somewhat downstream from the abbey.

Owain Glyndŵr had a home in Iâl on the north side of the Dee called Rhagad, five miles west of Dinas Brân.

Almost halfway between Llanegwystl and Ruthin can be seen the remains of a castle of Owain Glyndŵr (so it is said) called Cefn Du, that is to say, the ridge of the Black Hill, where now shepherds keep sheep.

. . .

The commote of Edeirnion lies on the east side of Penllyn, and it has on the north side Denbigh, and Iâl on the northeast side, and on the south side Powys. . . .

Owain Glyndŵr dwelled in this commote.

Llywelyn ab Iorwerth Drwyndwn, prince of all Wales, had Gruffudd. Gruffudd had Llywelyn. Llywelyn had Catherine his heir. Catherine had Elinor. Elinor had

30   and Catarine. This Helene was mother to Owen Glindoure. Catarine had Meredik. Meredik had Owen. Owen had Edmunde Erle of Richemonde, and Gasper Erle of Penbroke. Edmunde had Henry the VII. Henry was, as I hard, posthumus.

. . .

[p. 108] The tenantes of Dinas hold of the Walsche tenor. It is set by like of one of the hilles caullid Chathedrales. The people about Dinas did burne Dinas Castel
35   that Oene Glindour shuld not kepe it for his forteres.

. . .

[p. 111] The toun of the Hay yet hath a market, but the toun within the waulles is wonderfully decaied. The ruine is adscribid to Oene Glindour.

95. EDWARD HALL, *CHRONICLE*   English
                                                                1548

Owen Glendor a squire of Wales, perceivyng the realme to be unquieted, and the kyng not yet to be placed in a sure and unmovable seate, entendyng to usurpe and take upon hym the principalitie of Wales, and the name and preheminence of the same, what with faire flatteryng wordes and with large promyses, so envegled
5   entised and allured the wilde and undiscrite Welshmen, that they toke hym as their prince and made to hym an othe of allegeance and subjeccion. By whose supportacion, he beyng elated and set up in aucthorite, to the intent to bee out of all doubte of his neyghbors, made sharpe warre on Reignolde Lorde Grey of Ruthen and toke hym prysoner, promysing hym libertee and dischargyng his raunsome, yf he would
10   espouse and marie his doughter, thinkyng by that affinitye, to have greate ayde and muche power in Wales. The lorde Grey beeyng not very riche nether of substance nor of frendes, consideryng this offer to be the onely waye of his releffe and deliverance, assented to his pleasure and maried the damosell. But this false father-in-lawe, this untrew, unhonest and perjured persone, kept hym with his wife still in
15   captivitee till he dyed. And not content with this heynous offence, made warre on Lorde Edmond Mortimer erle of Marche, and in his owne lordship of Wigmore, where in a conflict he slewe many of th'erles men and toke hym prisoner, and feteryng hym in chaynes, cast hym in a depe and miserable dongeon. The kyng was requyred to purchase his delyverance by dyverse of the nobilitie, but he could not
20   heare on that syde, rather he would and wished al his linage in heven. For then his title had been out of all doubt and question, and so upon this cause as you heare, after ensued great sedicion.
    Thus Owen Glendor, glorifiyng hym self in these twoo victories, invaded the Marches of Wales on the West side of Severne, robbed vilages, brent tounes, and

---

4 envegled, inveigled. **5 undiscrite**, indiscreet (i.e., barbarous). **7 elated**, raised up. **17 th'erles men**, the earl's men.

Elen and Catherine. This Elen was mother to Owain Glyndŵr. Catherine had Maredudd. Maredudd had Owen Tudor. Owen Tudor had Edmund, earl of Richmond, and Jasper, earl of Pembroke. Edmund had Henry VII. Henry was, as I have heard, posthumous.

. . .

The tenants of Dinas are of the Welsh tenure. It is set beside one of the hills called Mynydd y Gadair. The people around Dinas burned Dinas Castle so that Owain Glyndŵr could not keep it for his fortress.

. . .

The town of Hay still has a market, but the town within the walls is terribly decayed. The ruin is ascribed to Owain Glyndŵr.

95. Edward Hall, *Chronicle*

Notes: pp. 407–08

[continued from previous page]

25   slewe the people, and laden with praies and bloudy handes returned agayn into Wales, never desistyng to do evill till the next yere, that the kyng reised a greate armye and puyssance to resist and defende his malicious attemptes and sedicious invasions, as after shall be declared.

. . .

King Henry forgat not his enterprise into Wales, but made provision for menne,
30   municions and artyllary mete and convenient for so great a businesse, whereof the Frenche kyng beyng advertised, sente privilie Lorde James of Burbone earle of Marche and his two brethren Jhon and Lewes, with xii. c. knightes and esquiers to aide Owen Glendor against the invasions of Kyng Henry, he toke shippyng with xxx. sayle at the mouthe of Seine, and the wynd was not favourable to his purpose
35   for he coulde never approche the coaste of Wales but came before the towne of Plimmouthe in Devonshire, and there leavyng his great shippes liyng at ancre, in the nyghte toke land and brent, spoiled and destroyed divers small villages, and poore cotages, and robbed, v. or vi. littell craiers and fisherbotes laden with fysshe and corne. But while he and his companie like gredy wolfes were sekyng after their
40   praye the wynde rose highe and a great tempesteous rage and furious storme sodaynely flusshed and drowned xii. of his great shippes whiche laye in the mouthe of the haven for his savegard and defence. Whereof when the erle was advertised, and perceivyng by the firyng of the beacons that the people began to assemble in

---

25 praies, commendation. **27 puyssance**, strength. **30 mete**, proper. **31 beyng advertised**, being made aware; **privilie**, secretly. **32 xii. c. knightes and esquiers**, 1200 knights and squires. **33–34 toke shippyng with xxx. sayle**, took to sea with 30 ships. **36 liyng at ancre**, lying at anchor. **37 brent**, burned; **divers**, many. **38 craiers**, small ships. **42 advertised**, made aware. **43 firyng**, firing.

45 plumpes to encounter with hym, and also seyng his purpose sore diminished as well by the slaughter of suche as ranged abrode in hope of spoyle and praye, as by the furious rage of the unmercifull see and hydeous tempest, with muche paine and great labour toke his shippes agayne, and was not without jeopardie of hys lyfe dryven on the coast of Britayne and landed at Sainct Malos. The French kyng per-
50 ceivyng that this chance had il successe appointed one of his marshals called Memo-rancie, and the master of his crosbowes with xii. m. men, to sayle into Wales, which toke shippyng at Brest and had the wynde to them so prosperous that they landed at Milford Haven, and leavyng the castell of Penbroke unassaulted, because it was well fortified, manned, and vitayled, besieged the towne of Harforde West whiche
55 was so well defended by the erle of Arundell and his power that they much more lost then gayned. And from thence they departed towarde Owen Glendor whome they nominated prince of Wales, and founde hym at the towne of Dinbigh abidyng their commyng with ten thousand men. They wer of hym lovyngly receyved, and gentelly interteyned, and when all thynges were prepared, they passed by Gla-
60 morgan shire toward Worcester and there brent the suburbes, but hearyng of the kynges approchyng sodaynly returned into Wales. The kyng with a great puys-saunce followed and founde them embattayled on a highe mountayne, and a gret valey betwene bothe the armyes, so that eche armye playnely perceyved other, and every hoste loked to be assauted of his adversary, and of the ground to take the most advauntage: thus they continued eight dayes from mornyng to nyght ready to
65 abyde but not to geve battayle. There wer many fearce skirmyshes and many propre feates of armes daily done, whiche the French croniclers more then the Englishe writers can reporte. For there were slayne the Lorde Patrioles of Tries, brother to the marshall of France, the Lord Mattelone and the Lord Vale and the bastarde of Burbon, with v. hundred gentelmen.
70   The Frenche men and Welshe men were sore trobled and afflicted with famine, that their hertes were appalled and their corages sore abated, for the kyng had so stopped the passages that nether vytayll nor succour could by any way be con-veighed to them. Wherfore of very necessitie they were compelled eyther to fyghte or flee: And so by the advisement and councell of the marshall of Fraunce, whiche
75 put not to muche confidence in the waveryng Welshemen, the hole hoste departed theight day at midnight in the most secretest maner that they could devyse. The Frenche men with littell rewardes and no gayne returned into Britayne makyng small boast of their paynfull journey.
     The kyng seyng them departed, folowed them into Wales, and chasing them
80 from hilles to dales, from dales to woddes, from woddes to marishes, and yet could never have them at any advauntage. A world it was to see his quotidiane removyng, his paynfull and busy wanderyng, his troblesome and uncertaine abidyng, his con-tinuall mocion, his daily peregrinacion in the desert, felles and craggy mountains

---

44 plumpes, crowds. **49 il successe**, little success. **50 xii. m. men**, 12,000 men. **53 vitayled**, supplied with food; **Harforde West**, Haverfordwest. **56 nominated**, called. **58 gentelly interteyned**, properly (genteelly) entertained. **60–61 puyssaunce**, strength. **71 hertes**, hearts; **corages sore abated**, courage sorely waned. **72 vytayll nor succour**, food nor aid. **76 th'eight**, the eighth. **80 woddes**, woods; **marishes**, marshes. **81 quotidiane removing**, daily moving about. **83 peregrinacion**, wandering; **felles**, fells.

85 of that bareine unfertile and depopulate countrey. And thus beyng tossed from countrey to countrey, from hyll to valey, from marishe to wod, from noughte to worsse, without gayne or profite, withoute vitayle or succour he was of necessitie compelled to retire his armye and retourne agayne to Worcester, in whiche retournyng the Welshemen knowyng the passages of the countrey, toke certaine car-riages of his laden with vitayle to his great displeasure, and their great comforte.

90 When he came to Worcester perceivyng winter to approche whiche season of the yere is not convenient and proper for men of warre to lie in the feldes, and specially in suche a barraine and hill countrey as Wales is, dispersed his armie for that time and returned to London.

Wherwith they [the earl of Northumberland and his son Henry Hotspur] beyng
95 sore discontent, by the councell of Lord Thomas Percy erle of Worcester, whose study was ever to procure malice, and to set all thinges in broile and uncertaintie, fainyng a cause to prove and tempte the kyng, came to hym to Wyndsor, requityng hym by raunsome or otherwise to cause to bee delivered out of prison Edmond Mortimer erle of Marche their cosyn germayn whome (as they reported), Owen
100 Glendor kepte in filthy pryson shakeled with yrons, onely for that cause that he toke his parte, and was to hym faithfull and trewe. The kyng began not a litell to muse on this request, and not without a cause, for in dede it touched him as nere as his sherte, as you well may perceive by the Genealogy rehersed in the beginnyng of this story. For this Edmond was sonne to Erle Roger whiche was sonne to Lady Philip
105 doughter to Lionel duke of Clarence, the third sonne to Kyng Edward the Third, whiche Edmonde at Kyng Richardes goyng into Ireland, was proclaimed heire ap-parant to the croune and realme, whose aunt called Elinor this Lord Henry Percy had maried. And therfore the kyng litell forced although that that lignage were clerely subverted and utterly extincte.
110 When the kyng had long digested and studied on this matter, he made aun-swere and sayd that the erle of Marche was not taken prisoner for his cause nor in his service, but willyngly suffered hym selfe to be taken, because he woulde take no parte agaynste Owen Glendor and his complices, and therfore he would nether raunsome nor releve hym, [which] fraude the kyng caused openly to be published
115 and divulged, with whiche aunswere yf the parties were angry doubt you not. But with the publyshyng of the cautell, that the erle of Marche was willyngly taken, they ten tymes more fumed and raged in so muche that Sir Henry Hotspur sayd openly: "Behold the heire of the realme is robbed of his righte, and yet the robber, with his owne, wyll not redeme hym." So in this fury the Percies departed, nothyng more
120 myndyng then to depose Kyng Henry from the high tipe of his regalitie, and to deliver and set in his trone their cosyn frende and confederate Edmonde erle of Marche, whome they not onely delivered oute of the captivitie of Owen Glendor, but also entered into a leage and amitie with the sayd Owen against Kyng Henry and all his frendes and fautours, to the great displeasure and long unquietyng of
130 Kyng Henry and his partakers. Here I passe over to declare howe a certayne writer

96 in broile, in disturbance. **97 fainyng**, pretending; **requityng**, urging. **99 cosyn ger-mayn**, first cousin. **106–07 heire apparant**, heir apparent. **116 cautell**, ruse. **120 mynd-yng**, determined to do; **tipe**, tip. **121 trone**, throne. **128 a leage and amitie**, an agreement and friendship. **129 fautours**, supporters.

writeth that this earle of Marche, the lorde Percy and Owen Glendor wer unwysely made beleve by a Welch prophecier, that King Henry was the Moldwarpe, cursed of Goddes owne mouth, and that they thre were the Dragon, the Lion and the Wolfe, whiche shoulde devide this realme betwene them, by the deviacion and not

135   devinacion of that mawmet Merlyn. I wyll not reherse howe they by their deputies in the howse of the archdeacon of Bangor, seduced with that falce fained prophesie devided the realme amongest them, nor yet write howe by a Tripartite Endenture sealed with their seales, all Englande from Severne and Trent South and Eastward, was assigned to the erle of Marche: Nor how all Wales and the landes beyond Se-

140   verne Westward, were appoyncted to Owen Glendor, and all the remnaunt from Trente Northwarde to the lord Percie. But I will declare to you that whiche was not prophesied, that is the confusion destruccion and perdicion of these persones, not onely gevyng credite to suche a vain fable, but also settyng it forwarde and hopyng to attayne to the effecte of the same whiche was especiall of the lorde Percey and

145   Owen Glendor. For the erle of Marche was ever kepte in the courte under suche a keper that he could nether doo or attempte any thyng agaynste the kyng without his knowledge, and dyed without issue, levyng his righte title and interest to Anne his sister and heyre, maried to Rycharde erle of Cambrige father to the duke of Yorke, whose offspryng in continuaunce of tyme, obteygned the game and gat the

150   garland. O ye waveryng Welshmen, call you these prophesies? Nay call theim un-profitable practises. Name you them divinacions? Nay name them diabolicall de-vises, say you they be prognosticacions? Nay they be pestiferous publyshinges. For by declaryng and credite geving to their subtyl and obscure meanynges, princes have been deceyved, many a noble manne hath suffred, and many an honest man

155   hath been begyled and destroyed.

. . .

[Among the Percies' published articles of grievance against the king:]
Also we do alledge, saie and intende to prove, that where Edmond Mortimer earle of Marche and Ulster, was taken prysoner by Owen Glendor in a pitched and foughten fyeld, and cast into pryson and laden with yron fetters, for thy matter and cause, whom falsely thou hast proclaymed willyngly to yelde hymselfe prisoner to the

160   saied Owen Glendor, and neither wouldest deliver hym thy self, nor yet suffre us his kinsmen to raunsome and deliver hym: Yet notwithstandyng, we have not onely con-cluded and agreed with the same Owen for his raunsome at our propre charges and expences, but also for a peace betwene thee and the said Owen. Why hast thou then not onely publyshed and declared us as traytours, but also craftely and deceitfully

165   imagened, purposed and conspired the utter destruction and confusion of our per-sones. For the whiche cause we defy thee, thy fautoures and complices as commen traytoures and destroyers of the realme, and the invadours, oppressoures and con-founders of the verie true and right heyres to the croune of Englande, whiche thing we entende with our handes to prove this daie, almyghty God helpyng us.

. . .

170   After this greate battaill [of Shrewsbury], he [i.e., Henry IV] like a triumphant conqueror returned with greate pompe too London, where he was by the senate and magestrates solemply receyved, not a little rejoysyng of his good fortune and fortunate victorie. But before his departure from Shrewesbury, he not forgettyng his enterprise againste Owen Glendor, sent into Wales with a great armie Prynce Henry
175 his eldest sonne against the said Owen and his sedicious fautours, whiche beyng dismaied and in maner desperate of all comfort by the reason of the kynges late victory, fled in desert places and solitary caves, where he received a finall reward mete and prepared by Goddes providence for suche a rebell and sedicious seducer. For beyng destitute of all comforte, dreadyng to shewe his face to any creature, lackyng
180 meate to sustaine nature, for pure honger and lacke of foode myserably ended his wretched lyfe. This ende was provided for suche as gave credence to false prophesies. This ende had they that by diabolicall devinacions were promised great possessions and seigniories. This ende happeneth to suche as beleving suche fantasticall folies, aspire and gape for honoure and high promocions. When the prince
185 with lytle labour and lesse losse, had tamed and brideled the furious rage of the wyld and savage Welshemen, and lefte governours to rule and governe the countrey, he returned to his father with great honour and no small prayse.

175 sedicious fautours, rebellious supporters. **177 mete**, fitting. **183 seigniories**, lordships. **184 gape**, reach.

96. ELIS GRUFFUDD, *CHRONICLE*   **Welsh**
                                                                                1548 x 1552

Heuaid ynn y vlwyddyn yma i torres yr argae o'r hen gaas a'r gynuigen a viasai
ir ynn hir o amser yn y blaen hrwng ysgwier o Gymru, yr hwn a elwid Owain Glyn
Dyuyrdwy ac arglwydd Hrwthun, y neb, megis ac i mae llyure Kymru yn dangos, a
ddaliodd Owain yn garcharor garllaw llys Maes Mynnan ynn y lle ir ydoedd yr
5   arglwydd yn kynnal i lys. O'r man ir arweddodd ef yr arglwydd i vynnydd Berwyn.
Ar hyd y goror ir arweddodd ef yr arglwydd ynn garcharor oni gordies yr arglwydd
a'i gennedyl ar roddi triffwn maeirch in aur bathol i Owain yn arianswm dros yr
arglwydd erbynn serttein o ddydd ac amser. Y rhain, megis ac i mae'r llyuyr ynn
dangos, a ddanuoned ar dri march i Gymru att Owain. Yr hwn gwedi iddo ef edrych
10   ar y da a ganuu yn vuan nad oedd y ddegued rann ohonnaunt twy yn aur da. O'r
achos ynn gydrym ac i Ywain ddyalld y modd ir ydoedd gennedyl arglwydd Hruthun ymkanv i dwyllo ef drwy gyurwysdra o'r achos y vo. A gymerth allan ohonnaunt twy kymaint ac a vedrodd ef i deffol ynn aur da a'r llaill a ddeliurodd ef i'r
genniad y'w dwyn y'w meisder dracheuyn drwy roddi gorchymyn ar y genniad
15   annerch i meistyr oddiwrtho ef a dywedud wrtho ef ynn y modd hwn, "Bid ysbys a
diogel i bawb ohonnoch i ar y sydd o byrthynnas ac o gyrennydd ac arglwydd Hruthun ac yn enwedig i'r kyuriw wyr ac a vu o'r kyngor ac o'r bwriad i'm shiomi i, nad
ydwyf i a'm kenedlaeth mor ddissynwyr ac na vedrwn i adnabod aur oddiwrth met-
tel arall a deffol yr aur da o vysg yr hrai drwg, ir vy mod i a'm kennedlath yn dlawd
20   o aur. Ac ynn gymaint ac ichwi vyn gwattwar i ynn y modd hwn, myui a dyngaf i
Dduw na ollyngaf i arglwydd H[r]uthun byth ynn vyw allan o'i garchar nes y'w
gennedyl ef dalu i mi ddau kymaint o aur batthol ynn arianswm drostaw ef."
    Yr holl brosses yma a ddangossed i'r brenin, y neb a gymerth mwy o lid wrth
Ywain, y neb a gedwis yr arglwydd ynn garcharor ir maint bygwth y brenin a'i
25   gyngor. O vewn yr amser i gordderchodd yr arglwydd verch i Owain. Yr hon a oruu
ar yr iarll i ffriodi hi ynn y karchar. Ynn yr hwn o vewn ychydig o amser ynn ol a vu
uarrw ynn i garchar yn ol maruolaeth y mab. I dannuones y brenin lu mawr o bobyl
i ddistrowio Ywainn, yr hwn a oedd ynn ymgadw y mynnydd Berwyn ynghylch goror
main Gwynnedd.
30   O'r man, megis ac i mae llyure Kymrv yn dangos, i diulanodd ef o vysc i bobyl
oherwydd serttein o eirriau a ddyuod abaad Glyn Egwysdyr wrtho ef ar voregwaith.
Yr hwn a oedd wedi kyuodi ohir vore ac ynn kerdded ar hydd llethyr bron ac ynn
dywedud i blygain. Yr hwn a gyuaruu ac Ywain, yr hwn a ddyuod, "A, Syr Abaad,
chychwi a godasogh yn hry fore." "Nag e," hebyr yr abad, "chychwi a gyuodes yn
35   hry uore o gan mhlynnedd." "Ie," heb yr Ywain. Ac ynn ol opiniwn hrai o'r Kymru
y vo a golles ac a ddiulannodd ymaith o vysg i bobyl hrag kaffel kywilidd kanis wrth
ymadrodd yr abaad y vo a ydnabu yn hysbys nad y vo ydoedd yr Ywain ir ydoedd
ef ynn ymkanv i vod ir hwn ir ydoedd y brudiau yn addo dwyn koron Lloygyr. O'r
achos i kolles ac i diualannodd ef yn ddisdaw o blith i bobyl drwy ordeino i serttein
40   o wyr o'i gyurinach gymerud korf gwr a viasai varw y nosol hono a dywedud mae i
gorf ef ydoed hwnnw hrag ovyn i neb i geishio ef o'r ddydd hwnw allan. Yr hyn a
wnaeth i wassnaethwyr ef drwy gladdv y korf hwn o'r ttu dehau i Eglwys Lanhrayadyr y Mochnant. Neithyr hrai eraill o'r bobyl y ssydd ynn tybiaid ynn sickyr mae
o eishiau arian i dalu i'r gwyr o ryuel i diulanodd ef o'i mysg wynt ynn y modd yma.

96. Elis Gruffudd, *Chronicle*   **Notes: pp. 408–11**

Also in this year the dam of the ancient hatred and malice broke that had been for a long time in the fore between a squire of Wales, who was called Owain Glyndyfrdwy, and the lord of Ruthin, the one whom, as books of Wales show, Owain took prisoner near the court of Maes Mynan, in the place the lord held his court. From there he conveyed the lord to the Berwyn mountains. Along the border he conveyed the lord as a prisoner until the lord and his kin agreed to give three pack horses of gold coin to Owain as ransom for the lord by a certain day and time. These, as the book shows, were sent on three horses to Wales to Owain. He, after looking at the goods, perceived straightway that not a tenth part of them was good gold. Because of that in an instant Owain understood how the lord of Ruthin's kin intended to deceive him through cunning, if it might be. And he took out from them as much as he could of his choice of good gold, and the rest he delivered to the messenger to take it back to his master, commanding the messenger to greet his master for him and to say to him thus, "Let it be known and certain to each of you who is related and kin to the lord of Ruthin, and especially to the sort of men who were of the counsel and the intent to cheat me, that neither I nor my kin is so foolish that we are not able to distinguish gold from another metal and choose the good gold from amongst the bad, though I and my kin are poor in gold. And as much as you mock me in this way, I, in turn, swear to God I shall never release the lord of Ruthin alive out of his prison until his kin pay me twice as much in gold coin as ransom for him."

This whole matter was revealed to the king, who became more angry with Owain, who had kept the lord as a prisoner despite the great threat of the king and his council. During this time the lord had an affair with a daughter of Owain. She prevailed upon the earl to marry her in the prison. There a short time afterwards he died in his prison, after the death of the child. The king sent a great host of people to destroy Owain, who was keeping himself safe in the Berwyn mountains around the boundary of Maen Gwynedd.

From this spot, as books of Wales show, he vanished from amongst his people because of certain words which the abbot of Glynegwestl spoke to him one morning. He had risen in the early morning and was walking along the slope of a hill and saying his matins. He met with Owain, who said, "Ah, Sir Abbot, you rose up too early." "No," said the abbot, "it is you who have risen up too early by a hundred years." "Yes," said Owain. And in the opinion of some of the Welsh, it may be he disappeared and vanished away from amongst his people lest he incur shame, since from the speech of the abbot it may be he recognized clearly that he may not have been the Owain he was intending to be, the one the prophecies were promising to take the crown of England. Because of that he disappeared and vanished silently from the midst of his people by ordaining certain men of his fellowship to take the body of a man who had died that night and say that that was his body, lest anyone seek him from that day on. His servants did that by burying this body on the south side of the church of Llanrhaeadr-ym-Mochnant. But some others of the people suppose that surely it is from lack of money to pay the men of war that he vanished from amongst them in this way. And others say that he died without doubt, truly.

45   Ac eraill a ddywaid mae marw a wnaeth ef ynn ddiddowt onid ynn wir. Ni wna ma-
      ter pa un o'r tri modd hwn i kolles ef o vysc i bobyl. Y rhain yn gydrym a'i ddiulanv
      ef o'i mysg wynt a ymadewis a'r maes o'r lle. Ir aeth pawb ar i uan o eissiau kap-
      pitten i gyuaruod a'i gelynnion ar y maes. Y rhain ynn gydrym ac vddunt twy glywed
      ddaruod i Ywain a dori'r maes ynn yr vn modd. Ir ymchwelodd pawb o'r Ssaeson
50   ar i kynneuinoedd i Loygyr. Ac ynn y modd hwn i diweddodd Ywain Glyn Dyuyr-
      dwy, yr hwn a viasai dan gnwck Brenin Ritshart a Brenin Hari gymaint a xij. o
      vlynnyddoedd.

97. POLYDORE VERGIL, *HISTORIA ANGLICA*   **Latin**
                                                               1555

      Interea ut spes nulla requietis esset, Wallia quae semper ad novos motus intenta
      erat, mutuis quorundam nobilium dissidiis exagitata, ad defectionem propemodum
      spectare uidebatur. Quod ubi rex cognouit, eo celeriter cum exercitu proficiscitur,
      qui uix aberat bidui, cum Walli perterriti sese raptim in syluas atque paludes ab-
5   diderunt, copiis regiis posse se resistere, non dubitanter desperantes: non omnibus
      tamen fuga saluti fuit, quippe aliquot in ea capti merita poena afficiuntur.

                                        . . .

      Rex interim, certior factus a comitibus in se bellum parari, quam citissime potest,
      militem suum cogit, praesentemque tumultum Wallico anteuertendum ratus,
      Salopiam reuertit, ueritus se a tergo ab inimicis intercluderetur: uix eo peruenerat,
10   cum intellexit comites instructo agmine aduentare, qui tanta ferocia accedebant ad
      dimicandum, ut in propinquo castris positis, ausi sint incursare in hostes. Rex ubi
      propiorem spe dimicationem uidet, ut ne militum uirtuti mora damno sit, aciem
      instruit: instruuntur contra et hostes animis et uiribus pares, datoque utrinque
      signo, initur magnis sublatis clamoribus praelium: primo congressu, regia prima
15   acies quae peditum erat, a Scotis qui initium pugnae fecerunt, paululum loco cedere
      cogitur, sed confestim centurionum opera et iussu, pro se quisque rursus in eum
      locum unde erat egressus, reuertens non parum fortiter resistit. Interim Walli qui
      post regis discessum, ex syluis ac paludibus egressi de nouo bello audierant, subinde
      uenientes ad comites, fessis integri ac recentes subibant.

                                        . . .

20   Princeps Henricus secundum hanc victoriam, in Wallum exercitum duxit, quem
      patris belli fortuna secunda perterritum, nullo fere labore domuit, Ouino viro
      natura seditioso tumultuosoque, qui factionum caput fuerat, exilium ultro adire
      coacto, ubi vitae exitum suis factis dignum habuit: nam rerum omnius egens miser-
      rime mortem obiit. Haec domi, at foris longe maior belli motus impendebat. Equi-

It does not matter in which one of these three ways he disappeared from amongst his people. These, as soon as he vanished from amongst them, abandoned the field immediately. Everyone went on the spot, lacking a captain, to meet with his enemies in the field. These, as soon as they heard of the end of Owain, quit the field in the same way. All of the English returned to their usual abodes in England. And in this manner Owain Glyndŵr came to an end, he who had been under the lash of King Richard and King Henry for as much as twelve years.

97. POLYDORE VERGIL, *HISTORIA ANGLICA*   Notes: p. 412

Meanwhile, so there would be no hope for quiet, Wales, ever prone to new risings, was troubled by the mutual bickering of certain nobles and seemed almost to look towards rebellion. When the king found this out, he hastened there with an army, and was scarce two days away when the terrified Welsh swiftly stole away to their forests and marshes, no doubt despairing that they could resist the royal forces. But this flight was not the salvation of them all, since some were captured there and suffered their deserved comeuppance.

. . .

Meanwhile when the king was informed by his earls that he should prepare himself for war, he brought together his soldiers as quickly as he could. Considering the present tumult to be more important than the Welsh one, he turned back to Shrewsbury, fearing that he might be cut off from behind by his enemies: barely had he come there, when he perceived that his earls had arrived with battle lines drawn up, who had approached with such ferocious eagerness for battle, that, since the camps had been pitched close to each other, they dared to strike against the enemy. When the king saw that battle was closer than he had hoped, he drew up his battle line, so that delay would not do harm to the courage of his soldiers: they were drawn up, both enemies in spirit and in strength equal, and when the signal was given on both sides, battle was joined with a great clamour: in the first part of the engagement, the king's first battle line, which was on foot, was driven to yield a little ground, by the Scots who made a start of the battle. But quickly, by the work and the orders of the centurions, each for himself made back the ground from which he had withdrawn, and turning back each resisted with not a little bravery. Meanwhile the Welsh, who after the withdrawal of the king had emerged from their forests and marshes and had heard about the new war, came unhurt and fresh to the aid of those who were weary.

. . .

After this victory Prince Henry led the army into Wales, and, since it was terrified by his father's good fortune in war, he subdued it with next to no effort. Owain, the leader of the faction, a man seditious and riotous by nature, was forced to go into voluntary exile, where his life had an ending worthy of his deeds. Reduced to extreme poverty, he died a wretched death. These were the things done

25   dem ubi Carolus rex Francus de defectione Wallorum cognovit (nam, uti supra
       docuimus, induciae inter reges in paucos dies convenerat) statim Iacobum Borbon-
       iensem comitem Marchiae cum mille ducentibus equitibus ac magno peditum nu-
       mero in Walliam traiicere seque quamprimum cum Wallis contra Henricum coniun-
       gere iubet. Comes, ut erat iussus, ex Sequanae ostio solvens cum classe cui praeerat
30   navium triginta, vento non adverso, in Cornubiam venit. Inde parum progressus
       Plimuthum portum occupat, relictisque aliquot maioribus navibus in anchoris con-
       tra portum et noctu in terram egressus vicos spoliat, incendit, complanat. Sed dum
       milites in agris praedantur, orta subito tempestate, duodecim naves ex illis quae ad
       custodiam portus in anchoris stabant pereunt. Quo accepto detrimento, comes
35   exercitus infirmitate laborans colligit repente milites ac in Britanniam se refert,
       amissis bene multis ex suis qui ab agricolis dum populabantur interfecti fuere. Qua
       re nuntiata, rex Henricus Thomam filium cum classe multarum navium in altum
       mittit qui, si fuerit occasio, manu, sin minus, populatione iniuriam ulciscatur. Ille
       postquam aliquot portus secundum Normaniae oram spoliavit ac nonnullas one-
40   rarias naves qui in mari casu offenderat cepit, praeda onustus pari propedum cel-
       eritate atque ierat domum reversus est. Quo etiam tempore Valleranus comes divi
       Pauli pagum ad tria millia passuum a Caleto distantem, quem Marchum vocant,
       subito accessu diripuit. Sed cum cognovisset Ricardum Aschtonum praefectum
       Caleti cum expedita militum manu adventare, relicta praeda celeriter fugit. Cae-
45   terum Franci posthac seditionibus domesticis maxime laborantes externo bello ab-
       stinere coacti sunt. Idem quoque facere compulsus est Henricus, suorum crebris
       coniurationibus vexatus. Quibus de causis reges in aliquot menses inter se inducias
       pepigerunt.

98. WILLIAM BALDWIN, *MIRROR FOR MAGISTRATES*   English
                                                                        1559

       Whan [Sir Thomas Chaloner] had ended this so wofull a tragedy [the previous
       poem cast in the voice of King Richard II's ghost], and to all Princes a ryght worthy
       instruction, we paused: having passed through a miserable time full of piteous tra-
       gedyes. And seing the reyne of Henry the Fourth ensued, a man more ware and pros-
5   perous in hys doynges [than King Richard] although not untroubled with warres both
       of outforth and inward enemies, we began to serch what piers were fallen therin,
       wherof the number was not small. . . . And finding Owen Glendour next, one of
       fortunes owne whelpes, and the Percyes his confederates, I thought them unmete to
       be over passed, and therefore sayde thus to the silent company: what my maysters is
10   every man at once in a browne study, hath no man affeccion to any of these storyes?
       You minde so much sum other belyke, that these do not move you: And to say the
       troth there is no speciall cause why they should. Howbeit Owen Glendour because he
       was one of fortunes darlings, rather than he should be forgotten, I wil tel his tale for
       him under the privilege of Martine Hundred: whych Owen cumming out of the wilde
15   mountaynes like the Image of death in all poyntes (his dart onely excepted) so sore
       hath famine and hunger consumed hym, may lament his folly after thys maner.

6 **piers**, peers. 8 **unmete**, improper. 11 **belyke**, perhaps.

These were the things done at home, but a much greater movement towards war threatened abroad. For when King Charles of France learned of the Welsh mutiny (for, as I showed above, the truce between the kings was only for a few days), he at once commanded Jacques de Bourbon, earl of Marche, with 1,200 horsemen and a great number of men to cross over to Wales and join with the Welsh as soon as possible, to fight against Henry. Doing as he was told, the earl came to Cornwall. And, progressing a little further, he occupied the port of Plymouth; he left a few ships of war at anchor opposite the port and, making a night-landing, plundered, burned, and leveled a number of villages. But while his soldiers were ravaging the countryside a sudden storm brewed up and twelve of the ships guarding the port were lost. Having suffered this loss, the earl, a victim of camp-fever, gathered his soldiers and promptly went back to Brittany, having lost a large number of his men who had been slain by farmers while harrying the fields. Hearing the news of this, King Henry sent out his son Thomas with a fleet of ships, to avenge this insult with a battle, or, if he could not, by making depredations. After he had pillaged several ports along the Norman coast, as well as some merchantmen he happened to catch at sea, he returned home nearly as fast as he had come, laden down with spoils. At the same time, the count of Walleran made a sudden descent on the village of St. Paul, three miles from Calais, which they call Marche, and sacked it. But when he learned that Richard Ashton, the governor of Calais, was approaching with a fast-moving company of men, he abandoned his prizes and fled at once. After this the French greatly suffered from domestic sedition and were obliged to refrain from external wars. Henry, vexed by his subjects' frequent risings, was compelled to do the same. For this reason the kings pledged a truce for several months.

98. William Baldwin, *Mirror for Magistrates*   Notes: pp. 412–14
[continued from previous page]

Howe Owen Glendour seduced by false prophesies tooke upon him to be prince of Wales, and was by Henry then prince therof, chased to the mountaynes, where he miserably dyed for lacke of foode.

20	I Pray the[e] Baldwin sith thou doest entend	
	to shewe the fall of such as clymbe to hye,	
	remember me, whose miserable ende	
	may teache a man his vicious life to flye:	
	oh Fortune, Fortune, out on her I crye,	
25	my body and fame she hath made leane and slender	
	for I poore wretch am sterved Owen Glendour.	*starved*
	A Welshman borne, and of a gentle blud,	
	but ill brought up, wherby full wel I find,	
	that neither birth nor linage make us good	
30	though it be true that Cat wil after kinde:	
	fleshe gendreth fleshe, so doeth not soule or minde,	

they gender not, but fowly do degender,   *degenerate*
when men to vice from vertue them do surrender.

Ech thing by nature tendeth to the same
35   wherof it came, and is disposed like:
downe sinkes the mold, up mountes the fiery flame,   *soil*
with horne the hart, with hoofe the horse doth strike:
the Wulfe doth spoyle, the suttle Fox doth pyke,   *steal*
and generally no fish, flesh, fowle, or plant
40   doth any property that their dame had, want.

But as for men, sith severally they have
a mind whose maners are by learning made,
good bringing up alonly doth them save
in vertuous dedes, which with their parentes fade.
45   So that true gentry standeth in the trade
of vertuous life, not in the fleshly line:
for blud is Brute, but Gentry is divine.

Experience doth cause me thus to say,
and that the rather for my countreymen,
50   which vaunt and boast their selues above the day
if they may strayne their stocke for worthy men:
which let it be true, are they the better than?
Nay farre the wurse if so they be not good,
for why they steyne the bewty of theyr blood.   *stain*

55   How would we mocke the burden bearing mule
if he would brag he wer an horses sunne,
to presse his pride (might nothing els him rule,)
his boast to prove, no more but byd him runne:
the horse for swiftenes hath his glory wunne,
60   to which the mule could never the more aspier
though he shold prove that Pegas was his sier.   *Pegasus*

Ech man may crake of that which is his own,   *boast*
our parentes vertues theirs are and not oures:
who therfore wil of noble kind be knowen
65   ought shine in vertue like his auncestors,
gentry consisteth not in landes and towers:
he is a churle though all the world be his,
he Arthurs heyre if that he live amys.   *even if he is Arthur's heir who lives amiss*

For vertuous lyfe doth make a gentleman
70   of her possessour, all be he poore as Job,
yea though no name of elders shewe he can:
for proofe take Merlyn fathered by an hob.   *hobgoblin*

But who so settes his mind to spoyle and rob,
although he cum by due discent fro Brute,   *descent from Brutus*
75   he is a chorle, ungentle, vile, and brute.

Well thus dyd I for want of better wyt,
because my parentes noughtly brought me up:
for gentle men (they sayd) was nought so fyt
as to attaste by bolde attemptes the cup
80   of conquestes wyne, wherof I thought to sup:
and therfore bent my selfe to rob and ryve,   *pillage*
and whome I could of landes and goodes depryve.

For Henry the Fourth did then usurpe the crowne,
despoyled the kyng, with Mortimer the heyre:
85   for whych his subjectes sought to put him downe.
And I, whyle Fortune offred me so fayre,
dyd what I myght his honour to appeyre: *impair*
and toke on me to be the prynce of Wales,
entiste therto by many of Merlines tales.

90   For whych, such Idle as wayte upon the spoyle,
from every parte of Wales unto me drew:
for loytring youth untaught in any toyle
are redy aye all mischiefe to ensue.   *ready always*
Through help of these so great my glory grew,
95   that I defyed my kyng through lofty hart,
and made sharp warre on all that tooke his part.

See lucke, I tooke Lord Reynolde Grey of Rythen,
and him enforst my doughter to espouse,
and so unraunsomed held him still: and sithen
100   in Wygmore land through battayle rygorous
I caught the ryght heyre of the crowned house
the erle of March Syr Edmund Mortymer,
and in a dungeon kept hym prysoner.

Then al the marches longyng unto Wales
105   by Syverne west I did invade and burne: *Severn*
destroyed the townes in mountaynes and in vales,
and riche in spoyles did homward safe retourne:
was none so bold durst once agaynst me spurne.
Thus prosperously doth Fortune forward call
110   those whom she mindes to geve the sorest fall.

Whan fame had brought these tidings to the king
(although the Skots than vexed him ryght sore)
a myghty army agaynst me he dyd bryng:

wherof the French kyng beyng warned afore,
115 who mortall hate agaynst Kyng Henry bore,
to greve our foe he quyckely to me sent
twelve thousand Frenchmen armed to war, and bent.

A part of them led by the erle of Marche   *comte de La Marche*
Lord James of Burbon, a valiaunt tryed knyght
120 withheld by winds to Wales ward forth to marche,
tooke lande at Plymmouth pryvily on a nyght:
and when he had done al he durst or myght,
after that a mayny of his men were slayne
he stole to shyp, and sayled home agayne.

125 Twelve thousand moe in Mylford dyd aryve,
and came to me, then lying at Denbygh
with armed Welshmen thousandes double five:
with whom we went to Wurcester well nigh,
and there encampte us on a mount on high,
130 to abide the kyng, who shortly after came
and pitched his feild, on a hyll hard by the same.

Ther eyght dayes long, our hostes lay face to face,
and neyther durst the others power assayle:
but they so stopt the passages the space
135 that vitayles coulde not cum to our avayle,
wherthrough constrayned our hartes began to fayle
so that the Frenchmen shrancke away by night,
and I with mine to the mountaynes toke our flight:

The king pursued us, greatly to his cost,
140 from hyls to wuds, fro wuds to valeyes playne:
and by the way his men and stuf he lost.
And whan he see he gayned nought save payne,
he blewe retreat, and got him home agayne:
then with my power I boldly came abrode
145 taken in my cuntrey for a very God.

Immediatly after fell a Ioly Iarre
betwene the king, and Percies worthy bluds,
which grew at last unto a deadly warre:
for like as drops engendre mighty fluds,
150 and litle seedes sprut furth great leaves and buds,
even so small strifes, if they be suffred run
bre[e]de wrath and war, and death or they be don.

The kyng would haue the raunsum of such Scots
as these the Percyes had tane in the feeld: *taken*

155   but see how strongly Luker knits her knottes,
         the king will have, the Percies wil not yeeld,
         desire of goodes soone craves, but graunteth seeld: *seldom granted*
         oh cursed goods desire of you hath wrought
         all wyckednes, that hath or can be thought.

160   The Percies deemed it meter for the king   *more fitting*
         to have redeemed theyr cosin Mortymer,
         who in his quarel all his power did bryng
         to fight with me, that tooke him prisoner
         than of their pray to rob his Souldier:
165   and therfore willed him to see sum mean wer found,
         to quit furth him whom I kept vily bound.

         Because the king misliked their request,
         they came them selves and did accord with me,
         complayning how the kyngdome was opprest,
170   by Henries rule, wherfore we dyd agre
         to put him downe, and part the realme in three:
         the North part theirs, Wales wholy to be mine
         the rest to rest to th'erle of Marches line.

         And for to set us hereon more agog
175   a prophet came (a vengeaunce take them all)
         affirming Henry to be Gogmagog
         whom Merlyn doth a Mouldwarp ever call,   *mole*
         accurst of god, that must be brought in thrall
         by a wulf, a Dragon, an a Lyon strong,
180   which should devide his kingdome them among.

         This crafty dreamer made us thre such beastes
         to thinke we were these foresayd beastes in deede:
         and for that cause our badges and our creastes
         we searched out, whych scarcely wel agreed:
185   howbeit the haroldes redy at such a neede,
         drew downe such issues from olde auncestors,
         as proved these ensignes to be surely oures.

         Ye crafty Welshemen, wherfore do you mocke
         the noble men thus with your fayned rymes?
190   Ye noble men why flye you not the flocke
         of such as have seduced so many times?
         False Prophecies are plages for divers crymes
         whych god doth let the divilish sorte devise
         to trouble such as are not godly wyse.

195   And that appered by us thre beastes in dede,
through false perswasion highly borne in hand
that in our feat we could not chuse but spede
to kyll the kyng, and to enjoye his land:
for which exployt we bound our selves in band
200   to stand contented ech man with his part,
so fully folly assured our folysh hart.

But such they say as fysh before the net
shal seldome surfyt the pray they take,   *surfeit with*
of thinges to cum the haps be so unset
205   that none but fooles may warrant of them make: *assurance*
the full assured, succes doth oft forsake.
For Fortune findeth none so fyt to flout,
as suresby sots whych cast no kinde of doute.   *dependable fools*

How sayest thou Henry Hotspur, do I lye?
210   For thou right manly gavest the king a feeld,
and there was slayn because thou wouldest not fly:
Sir Thomas Percie thine uncle (forst to yeeld)
did cast his head (a wunder seen but seeld)
from Shrewsbury town to the top of London Bridge.
215   Lo thus fond hope did theyr both lives abridge.

Whan Henry king this victory had wunne,
destroyed the Percies, put their power to flyght,
he did appoynt Prince Henry his eldest sunne
with all his power to meete me if he might:
220   but I discumfit through my partners fight
had not the hart to mete him face to face,
but fled away, and he pursued the chase.

Now Baldwin marke, for I cald prince of Wales,
and made beleve I should be he in dede,
225   was made to flye among the hilles and dales,
where al my men forsooke me at my nede.
Who trusteth loyterers seeld hath lucky spede:
and whan the captaynes corage doth him fayle
his souldiers hartes a litle thing may quayle.

230   And so Prince Henry chased me, that loe
I found no place wherin I might abide:
for as the dogges pursue the selly doe,
the brach behind the houndes on every side,   *dog that hunts by scent*
so traste they me among the mountaynes wide: *traced*
235   wherby I found I was the hartles hare
and not the beast Colprophete did declare.   *false prophet*

And at the last: like as the little roche,   *roach (a fish)*
    must eyther be eat, or leape upon the shore
    whan as the hungry pickrel doth approach,   *pike*
240   and there find death which it eskapte before:
    So double death assualted me so sore
    that eyther I must unto my enmy yeeld,
    or starve for hunger in the baryane feeld.

Here shame and payne a whyle were at a strife,
245   payne prayed me yeeld, shame bad me rather fast: *bade*
    the one bad spare, the other spend my life,
    but shame (shame have it) overcam at last.
    Than hunger gnew, that doth the stone wall brast   *gnawed*
    and made me eat both gravell, durt and mud,
250   and last of all, my dung, my fleshe, my blud.

This was mine ende to horrible to heare,
    yet good ynough for a life that was so yll.
    Wherby (O Baldwin) warne all men to beare
    theyr youth such love, to bring them up in skill.
255   Byd Princes flye Colprophetes lying byll:
    and not presume to clime aboue their states,
    for they be faultes that foyle men, not their fates[.]

99. ROBERT GLOVER, *STEMMA ALICIAE*

**Latin
1570–77**

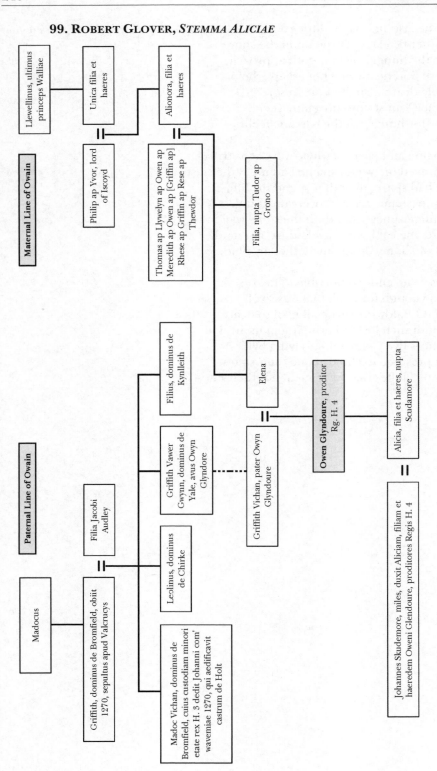

Maternal Line of Owain

Llewellinus, ultimus princeps Walliae

Unica filia et haeres

Alionora, filia et haeres

Philip ap Yvor, lord of Iscoyd

Thomas ap Llywelyn ap Owen ap Meredith ap Owen ap [Griffin ap] Rhese ap Griffin ap Rese ap Thewdor

Filia, nupta Tudor ap Grono

Paternal Line of Owain

Filius, dominus de Kynlleith

Elena

Owen Glyndoure, proditor Rg. H. 4

Alicia, filia et haeres, nupta Scudamore

Griffith Vawer Gwynn, dominus de Yale, avus Owyn Glyndore

Griffith Vichan, pater Owyn Glyndoure

Filia Jacobi Audley

Leolinus, dominus de Chirke

Madocus

Griffith, dominus de Bromfield, obiit 1270, sepultus apud Valcrucy's

Madoc Vichan, dominus de Bromfield, cuius custodiam minori etate rex H. 3 dedit Johanni com' wavemiae 1270, qui aedificavit castrum de Holt

Johannes Skudemore, miles, duxit Aliciam, filiam et haeredem Oweni Glendoure, proditores Regis H. 4

99. ROBERT GLOVER, *GLYNDŴR'S PEDIGREE*

Notes: pp. 414–18

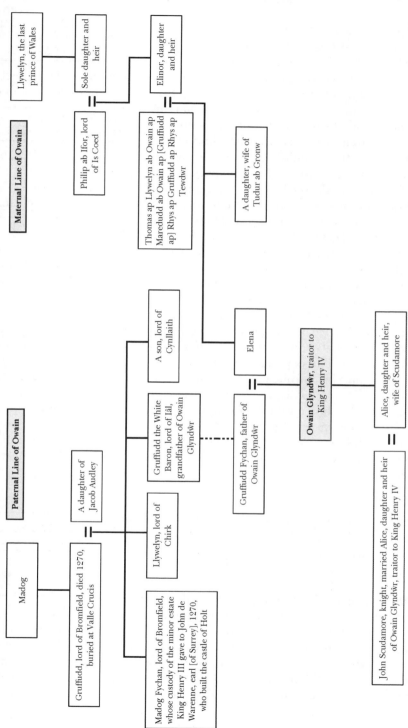

100. RAPHAEL HOLINSHED, *CHRONICLES*

English
1587

In the kings absence, whilest he was foorth of the realme in Scotland against his enimies [in August 1400], the Welshmen tooke occasion to

The Welshmen rebell by the setting on of Owen Glendour.

rebell under the conduct of their capteine Owen Glendouer, dooing what mischeefe
5   they could devise, unto their English neighbours. This Owen Glendouer was sonne
to an esquier of Wales, named Griffith Uichan: he dwelled in the parish of Conwaie, within the countie of Merioneth in Northwales, in a place called Glindourwie,

John Stow. Owen Glendour what he was.

which is as much to saie in English, as The vallie by the side of the water of Dee, by
10   occasion whereof he was surnamed Glindour Dew.

He was first set to studie the lawes of the realme, and became an utter barrester, or an apprentise of the law (as they terme him) and served King Richard at Flint Castell, when he was taken by Henrie duke of Lancaster, though other have written that he served this King Henrie the Fourth,

Tho. Wals.

15   before he came to atteine the crowne, in roome of an esquier, and after, by reason of variance that rose betwixt him and the lord Reginald Greie of Ruthin, about the lands which he claimed to be his by right of inheritance: when he saw that he might

The occasion that mooved him to rebel.

not prevaile, finding no such favor in his sute as he looked for, he first made warre
20   against the said Lord Greie, wasting his lands and possessions with fire and sword, cruellie killing his servants and tenants. The king advertised of such rebellious exploits, enterprised by the said Owen, and his unrulie complices, de-

The king entreth into wales, meaning to chastise y rebels.*

termined to chastise them, as disturbers of his peace, and so with an armie entered
25   into Wales; but the Welshmen with their capteine withdrew into the mounteines of Snowdon, so to escape the revenge, which the king meant towards them. The king therefore did much hurt in the countries with fire and sword, sleing diverse that with weapon in hand came foorth to resist him, and so with a great bootie of beasts and cattell he returned.

. . .

30   About the same time [as Richard II's wife Queen Isabel was returned to France, in June 1401], Owen Glendouer and his Welshmen did much hurt to the kings subjects.

Anno. Reg. 3.

Owen Glendour.

. . .

In the moneth of March [1402] appeared a blasing starre, first betweene the east part of the firmament and the north,

A blasing starre.

35   flashing foorth fire and flames round about it, and lastlie, shooting foorth fierie beams towards the north, foreshewing (as was thought) the great effusion of bloud that followed, about the parts of Wales and Northumberland. For about the same time, Owen Glendouer (with his Welshmen) fought with the lord Greie of Ruthen, comming foorth to defend his possessions, which the same Owen wasted and des-

22 advertised, made aware. **27 sleing**, slaying. **33 blasing starre**, comet.

40   troied: and as the fortune of that daies worke
fell out, the lord Greie was taken prisoner, and
manie of his men were slaine. This hap lifted

> The lord Greie of Ruthen taken
> in fight by Owen Glendour.

the Welshmen into high pride, and increased mervelouslie their wicked and presumptuous attempts.

. . .

45   Owen Glendouer, according to his accustomed manner, robbing and spoiling
within the English borders, caused all the forces of the shire of Hereford to
assemble togither against them, under the conduct of Edmund Mortimer earle of
March. But comming to trie the matter by battell, whether by treason or otherwise,
so it fortuned, that the English power was dis-

50   comfited, the earle taken prisoner, and above
a thousand of his people slaine in the place.

> The earle of March taken prisoner
> in batell by Owen Glendour.

The shamefull villanie used by the Welshwomen towards the dead carcasses, was
such, as honest eares would be ashamed to heare, and continent toongs to speake
thereof. The dead bodies might not be buried, without great summes of monie

55   given for libertie to conveie them awaie.
    The king was not hastie to purchase the deliverance of the earle March, bicause
his title to the crowne was well inough knowen, and therefore suffered him to re-
maine in miserable prison, wishing both the said earle,
and all other of his linage out of this life, with God and

> The suspicion of K.
> Henrie grounded upon
> a guiltie conscience.

60   his saincts in heaven, so they had beene out of the waie,
for then all had beene well inough as he thought. . . .
About mid of August, the king to chastise the presumptuous attempts of the
Welshmen, went with a great power of men into Wales, to pursue the capteine of the
Welsh rebell Owen Glendouer, but in effect he lost his labor; for Owen conveied

65   himselfe out of the waie, into his knowen lurking places, and (as was thought)
through art magike, he caused such foule weather of
winds, tempest, raine, snow, and haile to be raised, for the

> Intemperat weather.

annoiance of the kings armie, that the like had not beene heard of; in such sort,
that the king was constreined to returne home, having caused his people yet to

70   spoile and burne first a great part of the countrie.

. . .

    [The English defeat a Scottish invading force and besiege Cocklawes castle.]
The first two moneths passed, and no likelihood of rescue appeared; but yer the
third moneth was expired, the Englishmen being sent
for to go with the king into Wales, raised their siege and

> The earle of March
> marieth the daughtre
> of Owen Glendour.

75   departed, leaving the noble men prisoners with the
earle of Northumberland, and with his sonne the lord
Persie, to keepe them to the kings use. . . . Edmund Mortimer earle of March, prisoner with Owen Glendouer, whether for irkesomnesse of cruell captivitie, or feare
of death, or for what other cause, it is uncerteine, agreed to take part with Owen,

80   against the king of England, and tooke to wife the daughter of the said Owen.

42 hap, event. **53 honest eares**, virtuous ears. **69 constreined**, forced. **72 yer**, ere.

Strange wonders happened (as men reported) at the nativitie of this man, for the same night he was borne, all his fathers horsses in the stable were found to stand in bloud up to the bellies.

. . .

[Henry IV demands the prisoners captured by the Percies in their recent encounter with the Scots]: wherewith the Persies being sore offended, for that they claimed them as their owne proper prisoners, and their peculiar preies, by the counsell of the lord Thomas Persie earle of Worcester, whose studie was ever (as some write) to procure malice, and set things in a broile, came to the king unto Windsore (upon a purpose to proove him) and there required of him, that either by ransome or otherwise, he would cause to be delivered out of prison Edmund Mortimer earle of March, their cousine germane, whome (as they reported) Owen Glendouer kept in filthie prison, shakled with irons, onelie for that he tooke his part, and was to him faithfull and true.

The request of the Persies.

The king began not a little to muse at this request, and not without cause: for in deed it touched him somewhat neere, sith this Edmund was sonne to Roger earle of March, sonne to the ladie Philip, daughter of Lionell duke of Clarence, the third sonne of King Edward the Third; which Edmund at King Richards going into Ireland, was proclamed heire apparant to the crowne and realme, whose aunt called Elianor, the lord Henrie Persie had married; and therefore King Henrie could not well heare, that anie man should be earnest about the advancement of that linage. The king when he had studied on the matter, made answer, that the earle of March was not taken prisoner for his cause, nor in his service, but willinglie suffered himselfe to be taken, bicause he would not withstand the attempts of Owen Glendouer, and his complices, and therefore he would neither ransome him, nor releeve him.

The Persies with this answer and fraudulent excuse were not a little fumed, insomuch that Henrie Hotspur said openlie: "Behold, the heire of the relme is robbed of his right, and yet the robber with his owne will not redeeme him." So in this furie the Persies departed, minding nothing more than to depose King Henrie from the high type of his roialtie, and to place in his seat their cousine Edmund earle of March, whom they did not onlie deliver out of captivitie, but also (to the high displeasure of King Henrie) entered in league with the foresaid Owen Glendouer. Heerewith, they by their deputies in the house of the archdeacon of Bangor, divided the realme amongst them, causing a tripartite indenture to be made and sealed with their seales, by the covenants whereof, all England from Severne and Trent, south and eastward, was assigned to the earle of March: all Wales, and the lands beyond Severne westward, were appointed to Owen Glendouer: and all the remnant from Trent northward, to the lord Persie.

The saieng of the L. Persie.

The conspiracies of the Persies with Owen Glendouer.

An indenture tripartite.

A division of that which they had not.

This was doone (as some have said) through a foolish credit given to a vaine prophesie, as though King Henrie was the moldwarpe, curssed of Gods owne mouth, and they three were the dragon,

A vaine prophesie.

86 preies, prizes. **109 type**, tip.

the lion, and the woolfe, which should divide this realme betweene them. Such is
125 the deviation (saith Hall) and not divination of those blind and fantasticall dreames
of the Welsh propheciers. King Henrie not knowing of this new confederacie, and
nothing lesse minding than that which after happened, gathered a great armie to
go againe into Wales, whereof the earle of Northumberland
and his sonne were advertised by the earle of Worcester, and
130 with all diligence raised all the power they could make, and

> The Persies raise their powers.

sent to the Scots which before were taken prisoners at Homeldon, for aid of men,
promising to the earle of Dowglas the towne of Berwike, and a part of Northumberland, and to other Scotish lords, great lordships
and seigniories, if they obteined the upper hand. The

> They crave aid of Scots.

135 Scots in hope of gaine, and desirous to be revenged of their old greefes, came to the
earle with a great companie well appointed.

The Persies to make their part seeme good, devised certeine articles, by the
advise of Richard Scroope, archbishop of Yorke, bro-
ther to the lord Scroope, whome King Henrie had
140 caused to be beheaded at Bristow. These articles being
shewed to diverse noblemen, and other states of the

> The archbish. of Yorke of counsell with the Persies in conspiracie.

realme, mooved them to favour their purpose, in so much that manie of them did
not onelie promise to the Persies aid and succour by words, but also by their
writings and seales confirmed the same. Howbeit when the matter
145 came to triall; the most part of the confederates abandoned them,

> Thom. Wals.

and at the daie of the conflict left them alone. Thus after that the conspirators had
discovered themselves, the lord Henrie Persie desirous to proceed in the enterprise,
upon trust to be assisted by Owen Glendouer, the earle of March, and other, assembled an armie of men of armes and archers foorth of Cheshire and Wales. Inconti-
150 nentlie his uncle Thomas Persie earle of Worcester,
that had the governement of the prince of Wales, who
as then laie at London in secret manner, conveied
himselfe out of the princes house, and comming to

> The earle of Worcester governour to the prince slippeth from him. Hall.

Stafford (where he met his nephue) they increased their power by all waies and
155 meanes they could devise. The earle of Northumberland himselfe was not with
them, but being sicke, had promised upon his amendement to repaire unto them
(as some write) with all convenient speed.

. . .

The king returning foorth of Yorkeshire [after the Battle of Shrewsbury], determined to go into Northwales, to chastise the presumptuous dooings of the unrulie
160 Welshmen, who (after his comming from Shrewesburie, and the marches there) had
doone much harme to the English subjects. But now
where the king wanted monie to furnish that enterprise,
and to wage his souldiers, there were some that coun-

> The Welshmen molest the English subjects.

selled him to be bold with the bishops, and supplie his want with their surplusage.
165 But as it fortuned, the archbishop of Canturburie was there present, who in the
name of all the rest boldlie made answer, that none of his province should be

---

129 advertised, made aware. **145 triall**, a fight. **147 discovered**, exposed.

spoiled by anie of those naughtie disposed persons;
but that first with hard stripes they should under-

It was spoken like a prelat.

stand the price of their rash enterprise. But the king neverthelesse so used the mat-
170   ter with the bishops for their good wils, that the archbishop at length to pleasure
him, calling the cleargie togither, got a grant of a

A tenth levied of the cleargie.

tenth, towards the kings necessarie charges.

. . .

In the meane time, to wit the fifteenth of March [1405] at a place in Wales
called Huske, in a conflict fought betwixt the Welshmen and certeine of the princes
175   companie, the sonne of Owen Glendouer was taken, and fifteene hundred Welshmen taken and slaine. Also in Maie about the feast daie of S. Dunstane, was the
chancellor of the said Owen taken prisoner, and a great number of other taken and
slaine. The prisoners were brought up to London, where the chancellor was committed to safe keeping in the Tower.
180   This was a shrewd discomfiture to the Welsh by the English, on whome sinister
lot lowred, at such time as more than a thousand of them were slaine in a hot skirmish; and such shamefull villanie executed upon the car-
casses of the dead men by the Welshwomen; as the like (I

Abr. Fl. out of Thom.
Wals. *Hypod.* pag. 159.

doo beleeve) hath never or sildome beene practised. For
185   though it was a cruell deed of Tomyris queene of the

*Iust. lib. 1. Herod. lib.
1.Val. Max. lib. 8. cap. 7.*

Massagets in Scythia, against whome when Cyrus the
great king of Persia came, and had slaine hir sonne, she
by hir policie trained him into such streicts, that she slue him and all his host; and
causing a great vessell to be filled with the bloud of Cyrus and other Persians, did cast
190   his head thereinto, saieng; Bloud thou hast thirsted and now drinke thereof thy fill:
againe, though it was a cruell deed of Fulvia the wife of Marcus Antonius (at whose
commandement Popilius cut off the head and hands of that golden mouthed orator
Tullie, which afterwards were nailed up over the place of common plees at Rome) to
hold in hir hands the toong of that father of eloquence cut out of his head after the
195   same was parted from his shoulders, and to pricke it all over with pins and needels:
yet neither the crueltie of Tomyris nor yet of Fulvia is comparable to this of the
Welshwomen; which is worthie to be recorded to the shame of a sex pretending the
title of weake vessels, and yet raging with such force of fiercenesse and barbarisme.

. . .

After that the king had disposed things in such convenient order as stood with
200   his pleasure at Berwike, he came backe, and had the
castell of Alnewike delivered unto him, with all other

The castell of Alnewike
yeelded to the king.

the castels that belonged to the erle of Northumberland
in the north parts, as Prodhow, Langlie, Cockermouth, Aluham, and Newsteed.
Thus having quieted the north parts, he tooke his journie directlie into Wales,
205   where he found fortune nothing favourable unto
him, for all his attempts had evill success, inso-

The king passeth into Wales.

174 Huske, Usk [or Pwll Melyn].

somuch that lossing fiftie of his cariages through abundance of raine and waters, he returned; and comming

He looseth his cariages.
He returneth.

210 to Worcester, he sent for the archbishop of Cantur-
burie, and other bishops, declaring to them the misfortune that had chanced to
him, in consideration whereof he requested them to helpe him with some portion
of monie, towards the maintenance of his warres, for the taming of the presumptuous and unquiet Welshmen.

215 In the meane time, the French king had appointed
one of the marshals of France called Montmerancie, and
the master of his crosbowes, with twelve thousand men to

Hall. The marshall
Montmerancie sent to
aid Owen Glendouer.

saile into Wales to aid Owen Glendouer. They tooke
shipping at Brest, and having the wind prosperous, landed at Milford haven, with
an hundred and fourtie ships, as Thomas Walsingham saith; though Enguerant de
220 Monstrellet maketh mention but of an hundred and twentie. The most part of their
horsses were lost by the waie for lacke of fresh water. The lord Berkleie, and Henrie
Paie, espieng their advantage, burnt fifteene of those French ships, as they laie at
road there in the haven of Milford: and shortlie after the same lord Berkleie, and
Sir Thomas Swinborne, with the said Henrie Paie, tooke other fourteene ships, as
225 they came that waie with provision of vittels and munition foorth of France to the
aid of the other.

In the meane while the marshall Montmerancie, with his
armie, besieged the towne of Carmarden, and wan it by composition, granting to the men of warre that kept it against

Carmarden woone
by the French.

230 him, licence to depart whither they would, and to take with them all their mooveve-
able goods: the castell of Penbroke they assaulted not, esteeming it to be so well
manned, that they shuld but lose their labour in attemp-
ting it. Notwithstanding they besieged the towne of Hereford west, which neverthelesse was so well defended by the

Hereford west man-
fullie defended.

235 earle of Arundell and his power, that they lost more than they wan, and so they
departed towards the towne of Denbigh, where they found Owen Glendouer
abiding for their comming, with ten thousand of
his Welshmen. Here were the Frenchmen joifullie
received of the Welsh rebels, and so when all

Enguerant de Monstrellet
saith they burnt the townes
but could not win the castell.

240 things were prepared, they passed by Glamorgan-
shire towards Worcester, and there burnt the
suburbes: but hearing of the kings approch,

The suburbs of Worcester burnt.

they suddenlie returned towards Wales.

The king with a great puissance followed, and found them imbattelled on a
245 high mounteine, where there was a great vallie betwixt both the armies, so that
either armie might plainelie perceive the other, and either host looked to be
assailed of his adversarie, and therefore sought to take the advantage of ground.
Thus they continued for the space of eight daies from morning till night, readie to
abide, but not to give battell. There were manie skirmishes, and diverse proper
250 feats of armes wrought in that meane while, in the which the French lost manie of

---

217–18 tooke shipping, took sail. **222 espieng**, seeing. **225 vittels**, food. **228–29 composition**, mutual agreement. **233–34 Hereford west**, Haverfordwest. **244 puissance**, strength.

their nobles and gentlemen, as the lord Patroullars de
Tries, brother to the marshall of France, the lord Mate-
lonne or Martelonne, the lord de la Valle, and the bastard of Bourbon, with other,
to the number (as some have written) of five hundred. But Enguerant de Monstrel-
255   let affirmeth, that upon their returne into France, there wanted not aboue three-
score persons of all their companies.

French lords slaine.

    After they had laine thus one against an other the space of eight daies (as before
is said) vittels began to faile, so that they were inforced to dislodge. The French and
Welshmen withdrew into Wales, and though the Englishmen followed, yet impeached
260   with the desart grounds and barren countrie, thorough which they must passe, as
ovr felles and craggie mounteins, from hill to dale, from marish to wood, from
naught to woorsse (as Hall saith) without vittels or succour, the king was of force
constrained to retire with his armie, and returne againe to Worcester, in which
returne the enimies tooke certeine cariages of his laden with vittels. The French-
265   men after the armies were thus withdrawne, re-
turned into Britaine, making small brags of their
painefull journie.

The Frenchmen returne home.

. . .

    The same time [March 1406] the earle of Northumberland, and the lord
Bardolfe, warned by the lord David Fleming, that there was a conspiracie practised
to deliver them into the king of Englands hands, fled into Wales to Owen Glen-
270   douer. This cost the lord Fleming his life: for
after it was knowne that he had disclosed to
the earle of Northumberland what was meant
against him, and that the earle thereupon was
shifted awaie, certeine of the Scots slue the
275   said lord Fleming.

The lord Fleming lost his life for
giving knowledge to the earle of
Northumberland of that which
was meant against him.

. . .

    The lord Henrie prince of Wales this yeare [1407] in the sum-
mer season besieged the castell of Abiruscwith, and constreined
them within to compound with him under certeine conditions for truce; but the
prince was no sooner from thence departed, but that Owen Glendouer by subtill
280   craft entered the castell, put out the keepers, and charging
them with treason for concluding an agreement without his
consent, placed other in that fortresse to defend it to his use.

Abiruscwith.

Owen Glendour.

. . .

    The Welsh rebell Owen Glendouer made an end of his wretched life in this tenth
yeare of King Henrie his reigne [1408–09], being driven now
285   in his latter time (as we find recorded) to such miserie, that in
manner despairing of all comfort, he fled into desert places
and solitarie caves, where being destitute of all releefe and suc-
cour, dreading to shew his face to anie creature, and finallie lacking meat to susteine
nature, for meere hunger and lacke of food, miserablie pined awaie and died.

Owen Glendouer
endeth his life in
great miserie.

259 impeached, hindered. **261 ovr**, over.

101. WILLIAM SHAKESPEARE, *1 HENRY IV*, ACT III, SCENE I   **English**
                                                                      1596–97

Enter HOTSPUR, WORCESTER, LORD MORTIMER, OWEN GLENDOWER

	MOR. These promises are fair, the parties sure,
	And our induction full of prosperous hope.
	HOT. Lord Mortimer, and cousin Glendower
5	Will you sit down? And Uncle Worcester—
	A plague upon it! I have forgot the map!
	GLEN. No, here it is.
	Sit cousin Percy, sit good cousin Hotspur,
	For by that name, as oft as Lancaster doth speak of you,
10	His cheek looks pale, and with a rising sigh
	He wisheth you in heaven.
	HOT. And you in hell,
	As oft as he hears Owen Glendower spoke of.
	GLEN. I cannot blame him. At my nativity
15	The front of heaven was full of fiery shapes
	Of burning cressets, and at my birth
	The frame and huge foundation of the earth
	Shaked like a coward.
	HOT. Why, so it would have done
20	At the same season, if your mother's cat
	Had but kittened, though yourself had never been born.
	GLEN. I say, the earth did shake when I was born.
	HOT. And I say, the earth was not of my mind,
	If you suppose, as fearing you, it shook.
25	*GLEN.* The heavens were all on fire, the earth did tremble.
	HOT. O, then the earth shook to see the heavens on fire,
	And not in fear of your nativity.
	Diseased nature oftentimes breaks forth
	In strange eruptions. Oft the teeming earth
30	Is with a kind of colic pinch'd and vex'd,
	By the imprisoning of unruly wind
	Within her womb, which, for enlargement striving,
	Shakes the old beldame earth, and topples down
	Steeples and moss-grown towers. At your birth
35	Our grandam earth, having this distemp'rature
	In passion shook.
	GLEN. Cousin, of many men
	I do not bear these crossings. Give me leave
	To tell you once again, that at my birth
40	The front of heaven was full of fiery shapes,

---

2 promises, commitments. **3 induction**, first steps. **15 front**, face. **16 cressets**, torches (see Notes). **29 teeming**, pregnant. **33 beldame**, grandmother, aged matron. **35 distemp'rature**, sickness, disordered condition. **38 crossings**, contradictions.

The goats ran from the mountains, and the herds
Were strangely clamorous to the frighted fields.
These signs have mark'd me extraordinary,
And all the courses of my life do show
45 I am in not in the roll of common men.
Where is he living, clipp'd in with the sea,
That chides the banks of England, Scotland, Wales,
Which calls me pupil, or hath read to me?
And bring him out, that is but woman's son,
50 Can trace me in the tedious ways of art,
And hold me pace, in deep experiments.
HOT.   I think, there's no man speaks better Welsh.
I'll to dinner.
MOR.   Peace, cousin Percy, you will make him mad.
55 GLEN.   I can call spirits from the vasty deep.
HOT.   Why, so can I, or so can any man.
But will they come, when you do call for them?
GLEN.   Why I can teach you cousin, to command the devil.
HOT.   And I can teach thee, coz, to shame the devil,
60 By telling truth. Tell truth and shame the devil!
If thou have power to raise him, bring him hither,
And I'll be sworn, I have power to shame him hence.
Oh while you live, tell truth and shame the devil.
MOR.   Come, come, no more of this unprofitable chat.
65 GLEN.   Three times hath Henry Bolingbroke made head
Against my power; thrice from the banks of Wye,
And sandy-bottomed Severn have I sent him
Bootless home, and weather-beaten back.
HOT.   Home without boots, and in foul weather too?
70 How scapes he agues, in the devil's name?
GLEN.   Come, here is the map, shall we divide our right,
According to our threefold order ta'ne?
MOR.   The Archdeacon hath divided it
Into three limits, very equally.
75 England from Trent, and Severn hitherto,
By South and East, is to my part assigned;
All westward, Wales beyond the Severn shore,
And all the fertile land within that bound,
To Owen Glendower; and, dear coz, to you,
80 The remnant northward, lying off from Trent.
And our indentures tripartite are drawn,
Which being sealed interchangeably —

---

48 read to me, instructed me. **50 trace**, follow; **art**, magic art. **51 hold me pace**, keep up with me, keep pace with me. **68 bootless**, without success. **70 How scapes he agues . . . ?** How did he avoid sickness? **71 right**, rightful claims, property. **81 And**, i.e., when; **indentures tripartite**, contract of our three parties. **82 sealed interchangeably**, agreed to by all parties.

A business that this night may execute —
To morrow, cousin Percy, you and I,
85   And my good Lord of Worcester, will set forth
To meet your father, and the Scottish power,
As is appointed us, at Shrewsbury.
My father Glendower is not ready yet,
Nor shall we need his help these fourteen days.
90   Within that space, you may have drawn together
Your tenants, friends, and neighboring gentlemen.
GLEN.   A shorter time shall send me to you, Lords,
And in my conduct shall your ladies come,
From whom you now must steal, and take no leave,
95   For there will be a world of water shed,
Upon the parting of your wives and you.
HOT.   Me thinks, my moiety north from Burton here,
In quantity equals not one of yours.
See, how this river comes me cranking in,
100   And cuts me from the best of all my land,
A huge half moon, a monstrous cantle out.
I'll have the current in this place dammed up,
And here the smug and silver Trent shall run
In a new channel, faire and evenly.
105   It shall not wind, with such a deep indent,
To rob me of so rich a bottom here.
GLEN.   Not wind? It shall. It must. You see it doth.
MOR.   Yet, but mark, how he bears his course, and runs me up,
With like advantage on the other side,
110   Gelding the opposed continent, as much
As on the other side he takes from you.
GLEN.   Yea, but a little charge will trench him here,
And on this north side, win this cape of land,
And then he runs straight and even.
115   HOT.   I'll have it so. A little charge will do it.
GLEN.   I'll not have it altered.
HOT.   Will not you?
GLEN.   No, nor you shall not.
HOT.   Who shall say me nay?
120   GLEN.   Why, that will I.
HOT.   Let me not understand you then. Speak it in Welsh.
GLEN.   I can speak English, lord, as well as you,
For I was trained up in the English Court,
Where, being but young, I framed to the harp,
125   Many an English ditty, lovely well,

93 conduct, escort. **97 moiety**, part. **99 cranking**, zig-zagging. **101 cantle**, projecting angle. **103 smug**, smooth; also, "neat" because the new bed evens out the river. **106 bottom**, low-lying (hence richly alluvial) land. **112 charge**, expenditure.

And gave the tongue a helpful ornament —
A virtue that was never seen in you.

HOT.   Marry, and I am glad of it, with all my heart,
I had rather be a kitten and cry mew,

130   Than one of these same meter ballet-mongers.
I had rather hear a brazen cansticke turned,
Or a dry wheel grate on the axle-tree,
And that would set my teeth nothing on edge,
Nothing so much as mincing poetry —

135   'Tis like the forc'd gait of a shuffling nag.

GLEN.   Come, you shall have Trent turned.

HOT.   I do not care, I'll give thrice so much land,
To any well deserving friend.
But in the way of bargain — mark ye me —

140   I'll cavil on the ninth part of a hair.
Are the indentures drawn? Shall we be gone?

GLEN.   The moon shines faire, you may away by night.
I'll haste the writer, and withal,
Break with your wives, of your departure hence.

145   I am afraid my daughter will run mad,
So much she doteth on her Mortimer.   *Exit.*

MOR.   Fie, cousin Percy, how you cross my father.

HOT.   I cannot choose, sometime he angers me
With telling me of the moldwarp and the ant,

150   Of the dreamer Merlin and his prophecies,
And of a dragon and a finless fish,
A clip-wing'd griffin and a moulten raven,
A couching lyon, and a ramping cat,
And such a deal of skimble skamble stuff,

155   As puts me from my faith. I tell you what —
He held me last night at least nine hours,
In reckoning up the several devils' names
That were his lackeys. I cried "Hum," and "Well, go to,"
But marked him not a word. O, he is as tedious

160   As a tired horse, a railing wife,
Worse than a smoky house. I had rather live
With cheese and garlic in a windmill, far,
Than feed on cates, and have him talk to me
In any summer-house in Christendom.

165   *MOR.*   In faith he is a worthy Gentleman,

126 helpful ornament, useful embellishment (see Notes). **130 ballat-mongers**, makers of ballads. **131 cansticke turned**, candlestick turned (on a lathe). **133 nothing**, not a bit. **144 Break with**, i.e., tell; **of**, i.e. the news of. **149 moldwarpe**, mole (see Notes). **152 griffin**, a mythical beast, half lion, half eagle; *clip-wing'd*, i.e., tamed(?); **moulten**, having molted. **153 couching**, couchant, lying down; **ramping**, rampant, standing erect. **154 skimble skamble**, nonsensical. **155 puts me from my faith**, i.e., undermines my belief. **158 lackeys**, servants. **163 cates**, delicacies. **164 summer-house**, i.e., pleasant dwelling.

Exceedingly well read, and profited
In strange concealments, valiant as a lion,
And wondrous affable, and as bountiful
As mines of India. Shall I tell you, cousin?
170 He holds your temper in a high respect,
And curbs himself, even of his natural scope,
When you come 'cross his humor, faith he does.
I warrant you, that man is not alive
Might so have tempted him, as you have done,
175 Without the taste of danger and reproof.
But do not use it oft, let me entreat you.
WOR.   In faith, my lord, you are too willful blame,
And since your coming hither have done enough
To put him quite beside his patience.
180 You must needs learn, lord, to amend this fault,
Though sometimes it show greatness, courage, blood,
And that's the dearest grace it renders you,
Yet oftentimes it doth present harsh rage,
Defect of manners, want of government,
185 Pride, haughtiness, opinion and disdain,
The least of which, haunting a nobleman,
Loseth men's hearts, and leaves behind a stain
Upon the beauty of all parts besides,
Beguiling them of commendation.
190 HOT.   Well I am schooled. Good manners be your speed,
Here come our wives, and let us take our leave.

Enter GLENDOWER with the LADIES

MOR.   This is the deadly spite that angers me,
My wife can speak no English, I no Welsh.
195 GLEN.   My daughter weeps — she'll not part with you.
She'll be a soldier too — she'll to the wars.
MOR.   Good father, tell her, that she and my Aunt Percy
Shall follow in your conduct speedily.

GLENDOWER speaks to her in Welsh, and she answers
200   *him in the same*

GLEN.   She is desperate here, a peevish self-willed harlotry —
One that no persuasion can do good upon.

167 strange concealments, extraordinary secret arts. **170 temper**, character. **171 curbs himself**, restrains himself; **natural scope**, rightful freedom of action (in this case, to respond angrily). **175 taste**, i.e., experience. **181 blood**, aristocratic birth. **185 opinion**, conceit. **189 beguiling**, depriving. **190 Good manners be your speed**, May you thrive by good manners (and not deeds). **193 spite**, vexing situation. **201 desperate**, despairing; **harlotry**, i.e., rebellious woman (because she wants to follow him to the wars).

The LADY speaks in Welsh.

MOR. I understand thy looks, that pretty Welsh,
205   Which thou pourest down from these swelling heavens,
       I am too perfect in, and but for shame
       In such a parley should I answer thee.

The LADY again in Welsh.

MOR. I understand thy kisses, and thou mine,
210   And that's a feeling disputation.
       But I will never be a truant love,
       Till I have learn'd thy language, for thy tongue
       Makes Welsh as sweet as ditties highly penn'd,
       Sung by a faire Queene in a summers bower,
215   With ravishing division to her lute.
GLEN.   Nay, if you melt, then will she run mad.

The LADY speaks again in Welsh.

MOR. O, I am ignorance itself in this!
GLEN.   She bids you on the wanton rushes lay you down,
220   And rest your gentle head upon her lap,
       And she will sing the song that pleaseth you
       And on your eyelids crown the god of sleep,
       Charming your blood with pleasing heaviness,
       Making such difference twixt wake and sleep,
225   As is the difference betwixt day and night,
       The hour before the heavenly-harness'd team
       Begins his golden progress in the East.
MOR. With all my heart, I'll sit and hear her sing.
       By that time will our book, I think, be drawn.
230 GLEN.   Do so,
       And those musicians that shall play to you,
       Hang in the air a thousand leagues from hence.
       And straight they shall be here. Sit and attend.
HOT.   Come, Kate, thou art perfect in lying down. Come, quick, quick, that I may
235   lay my head in thy lap.
LADY PERCY. Go, ye giddy goose.

The music plays.

---

204 Welsh, i.e., the language of her tears. **206 I am too perfect in**, I know only too well.
215 ravishing division, charming variation (see Notes). **216 melt**, i.e., in tears. **219
wanton**, i.e., soft, pleasant (with a mild sexual association). **223 heaviness**, drowsiness. **226
heavenly-harness'd team**, i.e., of Apollo, the sun god. **229 drawn**, written out. **234
perfect**, well versed.

HOT.   Now, I perceive the devil understands Welsh,
     And 'tis no marvel he is so humorous,
240   By'r Lady, he is a good musician.
LA.   Then should you be nothing but musical, or you are altogether governed
     by humors. Lie still, ye thief, and hear the lady sing in Welsh.
HOT.   I had rather hear, lady, my brach howl in Irish.
LA.   Would'st thou have thy head broken?
245 *HOT.*   No.
LA.   Then be still.
HOT.   Neither, 'tis a woman's fault.
LA.   Now God help thee.
HOT.   To the Welsh lady's bed.
250 *LA.*   What's that?
HOT.   Peace, she sings.

          Here the LADY sings a Welsh song.

HOT.   Come, Kate, I'll have your song too.
LA.   Not mine, in good sooth.
255 *HOT.*   Not yours in good sooth? Heart, you swear like a comfit-maker's wife. "Not
     yours in good sooth," and "as true as I live," and "as God shall mend me," and
     "as sure as day,"
     And givest such sarcenet surety for thy oaths,
     As if thou never walk'st further than Finsbury.
260   Swear me, Kate, like a lady as thou art,
     A good mouth-filling oath, and leave "in sooth,"
     And such protest of pepper gingerbread
     To velvet guards, and Sunday citizens.
     Come, sing.
265 *LA.*   I will not sing.
HOT.   'Tis the next way to turn tailor, or be redbreast teacher. And the indentures
     be drawn, I'll away within these two hours, and so come in when ye will.   *Exit.*
GLEN.   Come, come, Lord Mortimer, you are as slow,
     As hot Lord Percy, is on fire to go.
270   By this our book is drawn. We'll but seal,
     And then to horse immediately.
MOR.   With all my heart.   *Exeunt.*

---

239 humorous, capricious, fantastical. **242 humors,** moods, caprices. **243 brach,** bitch (dog). **247 Neither,** i.e., On the contrary. **254 in good sooth,** i.e., in truth. **255 comfit-maker's,** confectioner's. **258 sarcenet surety,** i.e., softly feminine guarantees (see Notes). **262 pepper gingerbread,** i.e., "sweet" bourgeois oaths. **263 velvet guards,** overskirts (see Notes). **266 and,** if. **270 book,** compact.

NOTES TO THE TEXTS

1. *PROPHECY OF SIX KINGS*

Adapted and trans. by Michael Livingston, from *Brut*, ed. Brie, 1.72–76.

Manuscripts: Oxford, Bodleian Library MS Douce 323 (base text), Bodleian Library MS Rawlinson B.171, and Dublin, Trinity College MS 490.

It is arguable whether this source should be included in this volume at all, much less where it should fall within the list of contents: *The Prophecy of the Six Kings to Follow King John* (as it is often more fully titled) comes in many forms, is variously dated, and is not actually "about" Owain Glyndŵr.

Based on the prophecies of Merlin in the seventh book of Geoffrey of Monmouth's *Historia regum Britanniae*, this prophecy exists in, according to Smallwood's classifications, at least eight distinctive versions, beginning with an "Original Prose Version" in Anglo-Norman executed around 1312. From this text derived the "Revised Prose Version" written "about the time of Edward II's death (1327)" and incorporated into the Anglo-Norman *Brut* ("Prophecy," p. 572). Doig has subsequently suggested that the detail in this revised version that the Boar (i.e., King Edward III) would go on Crusade (lines 80–81) may well point to a later date of composition, most likely in 1336 ("Prophecy of the Six Kings," p. 258n10). Regardless, it was in the last decades of the fourteenth century that this revised version was translated into English as part of the text now commonly called the *Prose Brut* (see note to line 72, below; for more on the *Prose Brut*, see headnote to Item 71). It is this third "English Prose Translation" that is presented here (Smallwood, "Prophecy," p. 572). Subsequent versions followed over the next century or more in prose and verse, in Middle English, Welsh, and Latin.

Smallwood's fourth version, the "English Couplet Version," was at one time thought to have been composed as a work of propaganda used against Henry IV by the allied forces of Percy and Glyndŵr. Indeed, it was once common to imagine that this poem was the very "skimble skamble stuff" about the Welshman referred to in Shakespeare's *I Henry IV* (III.ii, see Item 101.154 in this volume). This was the opinion, for instance, of Scattergood, who pictured Owain actively rewriting "the traditional source prophecy in his own terms" (*Politics and Poetry*, p. 118). However, Smallwood's dating and discussion of the contents of the poem has made such an argument untenable and even "perverse" ("Prophecy," p. 586). No known version of the *Prophecy of Six Kings* was written by or for Owain.

Nevertheless, we cannot deny the possibility that Glyndŵr — or those surrounding him — could have used the atmosphere of such pre-existing prophecies to further his cause within the turbulent political events of the early fifteenth century. *Prophecy of Six Kings* was a clearly popular text, most especially in the version preserved here from within the *Prose*

Brut, and other sources hint at Glyndŵr's public willingness to accept prophetic authorities. In Item 36 in this volume, for instance, Owain is reported to have consulted the diviner (a "Master of Brut") Hopcyn ap Thomas in 1403. Indeed, more than one scholar has suggested that one of the manuscripts containing the long Welsh version of the present text — Small-wood's seventh version — is based on the prophecies of this very same individual (see Lloyd, *Owen Glendower*, pp. 68–69, and Lloyd-Morgan, "Prophecy," p. 26n40). We know, too, that this prophetic strain in turn accepted him (see the essay by Fulton in this volume). In addition, at least two of our early sources independently point to the idea that Glyndŵr traded on the idea presented in texts like the *Prophecy of Six Kings* that England would be broken into three parts: "one to the Wolf, one to the Dragon, and one to the Lion" (lines 126–27); compare this to Owain's letters to the kings of Scotland and Ireland (Item 22.62–117) and the partitions described in the so-called *Tripartite Indenture* (Item 47.18–22).

As Strohm observes, however, we probably ought not conclude from this potential openness to prophecy that Owain was a great part "the fulminating seer" made so famous by Shakespeare; Glyndŵr instead appears to maintain "a slightly provisional stance in relation to prophecy, but a determination not to forgo the practical and argumentative advantages that prophecy might confer" (*England's Empty Throne*, p. 17).

Put simply, the political use of prophecy might just have been useful politics.

1	The manuscript contexts from which the text of this version is drawn present this prophecy of Merlin as wisdom imparted to King Arthur ("Sire, quod Merlyn, "In þe yere . . .). It is here removed from that narrative context for the purpose of presentation and to reflect the independent form in which such prophecies would have circulated at the end of the fourteenth century.
3	*a Lambe oute of Wynchestre*. I.e., King Henry III.
6	*he shal make one of þe faireste places of þe worlde*. Henry III directed the rebuilding of Westminster Abbey, though he would not live to see its completion.
7–8	*a Wolf of a straunge lande*. I.e., Simon de Montfort, 6th earl of Leicester, a nobleman of Anglo-Norman descent who led the barons in opposition to Henry III.
9	*a rede Fox*. I.e., Gilbert de Clare, 6th earl of Hertford, 7th earl of Gloucester, a nobleman who switched his allegiance to Henry III prior to the Battle of Evesham in 1265. He was often called the "red earl."
10	*þe Wolfe shal dye in water*. Simon de Montfort died in the midst of a torrential thunderstorm at the Battle of Evesham, 4 August 1265.
11	*in*. So Brie. MS omits.
12–13	*His sede þan shal bene in strange lande, and þe lande shal bene wiþout a governoure a litil tyme*. Henry III's eldest son and heir, Edward, was on his way home from an ineffectual crusade in the Holy Land when he was informed of his father's death in 1272. He did not return to England, however, for another two years.
14	*a Dragoun*. I.e., King Edward I.
16	*o foote shal be sette in Wik*. Prophecy is often intentionally variable in its interpretation, and *Prophecy of Six Kings* introduces additional difficulties given the various

forms in which it circulated. In the present text, Edward I's foot in *Wik* is a reference to Berwick-upon-Tweed, which figured prominently in his Scottish wars.

17   *he shal unbrace iij habitacions.* Over the course of his long reign, Edward I engaged in wars for control of England, Wales, and Scotland.

22–23   *a peple out of þe Northwest duryng his regne þat shal bene lade þrouh an wickede Hare.* The rule of Scotland was much in dispute after the death of King Alexander III, and Edward I of England was asked to arbitrate over the matter of succession in 1292. His choice was John Balliol, who went on to ally Scotland with France — making him the *wicked Hare* of the *Prophecy* — before being deposed by Edward and banished across the sea to France.

28   *an Hare þat shal meve ageynes him werr in þe ende of his lif.* I.e., Robert the Bruce, who had himself crowned king of the Scots in 1306.

30   *Þis Dragoun shal bene holden in his tyme þe best body of al þe worlde.* Like his nickname "Longshanks," this passage is very likely a reference to the fact that Edward I was a tall man for his time.

30–31   *he shal dye bisides þe marche of a straunge lande.* Edward I died at Burgh by Sands in 1307, traveling north to engage Robert the Bruce in Scotland.

31–32   *faderlesse.* So Brie. MS: *fadelesse.*

35   *a Gote oute of a kar.* I.e., King Edward II, who was born at Caernarfon Castle and the first English prince to hold the title Prince of Wales.

39   *þe Floure of Lif and of Deþ.* I.e., Isabella of France.

40   *an Egle in Cornewaile þat shal have feþeres of golde.* I.e., Piers Gaveston, a nobleman who was created earl of Cornwall a month after Edward II's coronation. The close relationship between the two men — and Gaveston's extravagant spending at the sake of the king's wealth — was a source of great tension in the realm at the time and has subsequently been the source of many questions about the king's sexuality. Gaveston's coat of arms was a gold-feathered eagle.

42   *he shal flee shamefully by a Bere at Gaversiche.* The Bere is Thomas, earl of Leicester and Lancaster, who came to lead much of the baronial opposition to Edward II. He had a direct hand in the death of Gaveston in 1312, who was executed on his lands at Blacklow Hill (*Gaversiche*).

46   *þe white bataile.* Probably a reference to the Battle of Bannockburn ("white stream"), fought off the Forth on 24 June 1314, in which Edward II's forces suffered a disastrous defeat at the hands of Robert the Bruce.

51–52   *he shal avenge him oppon his enemys, þrouh conseil of ij Oweles.* I.e., Hugh Despenser and his father, Hugh le Despenser, earl of Winchester. The two Despensers became favorites of Edward II and had great influence in his efforts to wrest control of the kingdom back from Thomas of Lancaster and the barons. Their greed and corruption soon made them the focus of baronial discontent, leading first to their exile and then, after Edward II had purged many of their enemies from the nobility, to their recall from France and the so-called Despenser War.

53   *straunge*. So Brie. MS: *staunge*.

58   *Bur-up-Trent*. Thomas of Lancaster entered into open rebellion against Edward
          II and the Despensers in 1321. The king, moving north with his army, was for
          a time delayed when Lancaster attempted to prevent the loyalists from crossing
          the Trent by fortifying the important bridge at Burton-upon-Trent in the so-
          called Battle of Burton Bridge.

58–59   *for drede þe Bere shal flee, and a Swan wiþ him, for his company, to Bur towarde þe*
          north. Unable to stop the king at Burton Bridge (see note to line 58, above),
          Thomas of Lancaster fled north. The *Swan* is likely a reference to Humphrey
          de Bohun, 4th earl of Hereford, who accompanied him. The rebels were caught
          at Boroughbridge.

60–63   *þe Swan shal bene slayne wiþ sorwe, and þe Bere taken and biheuedede . . . meny shal him*
          seche, for vertu þat fro hym shal come. The Battle of Boroughbridge, 16 March 1322,
          was a tremendous victory for Edward II. Humphrey (here the *Swan*) died on the
          bridge, trying to break through the royalist forces (many accounts describe how
          he was killed when a pikeman underneath the bridge thrust a spear through the
          boards and into his anus). Thomas of Lancaster (the *Bear*) was captured and sub-
          sequently beheaded in front of his home at Pontefract Castle (*alþer nexte his neste*).
          The *Prophecy* seems to make garbled reference to the setting of Lancaster's head
          on a pike, before noting how there soon arose a cult around the "Martyr" and
          "Saint" Thomas of Lancaster. This cult was popular for more than a century.

61   *stand*. So Brie. MS omits.

66–67   *þe forsaide Floure of Lif . . . shal passe over into Fraunce, forto make pees bituene þe*
          Gote and þe Flour Delice. Isabella returned to France in 1325 to make peace be-
          tween Edward II and her brother, King Charles of France (*þe Flour Delice*).
          Isabella, however, who reviled the Despensers, took the occasion to join forces
          with Roger Mortimer and return to England at the head of an army.

69–70   *þai shul seche the Owelyn, and put ham unto despitous deþ*. After they were captured
          by Mortimer and Isabella, the Despensers were both quickly sentenced to
          death. After judgment the elder Despenser was immediately hanged, then be-
          headed and fed to dogs. The younger Despenser's death was far more grue-
          some: he was dragged to his place of execution, where he was stripped and had
          condemnations carved into his skin. He was then hung from a 15m gallows but
          cut down while still alive. According to Froissart, Despenser's genitals were then
          cut off and burned in front of him before he was disemboweled. He died when
          his heart was removed, after which his body was quartered and beheaded.

70–71   *after shal þis Goot bene brouht to disese*. Edward II, captured by Mortimer and Isa-
          bella, was forced to abdicate in favor of his son. He was then imprisoned at
          Berkeley Castle where he was murdered — likely by suffocation, though accor-
          ding to later accounts by the thrusting of a red-hot poker into his anus.

72   *shal come out of Wyndesore a Boor*. I.e., King Edward III, who was born at Windsor
          (many other versions of this prophecy term him not the Boar but the Lion). It
          seems clear that this version of the *Prophecy of Six Kings* was written during his

long reign (1327–77): the poet recognizes the king's very real chivalric and military accomplishments — it was Edward III who began the Hundred Years' War and saw some of its greatest triumphs — but at the same time he seems to fantasize about many others: actions in Jerusalem and the seeming mastery of all Europe. The *Prophecy*'s claim that this king would be buried alongside the legendary three kings of Cologne is fanciful in the extreme (and in any case wrong, as Edward III was buried at Westminster). The 1370–80 dating of the *Prose Brut* (Smallwood, "Prophecy," p. 572) thus leads us to favor a ca. 1370 dating for the execution of this work, though the Anglo-Norman text being translated might well date, as Doig argues, from 1336 ("Prophecy of the Six Kings," p. 258n10).

92   *a Lambe*. I.e., King Richard II. Other versions of the text term this figure the Boar, though here that label is reserved for Edward III (see note to line 72).

101   *a Moldewerpe*. I.e., King Henry IV.

107–12   *a Dragoun in þe North . . . a Wolf þat shal come oute of the West . . . a Lyon oute of Irlande*. Identifying the Dragon, Wolf, and Lion who would successfully defeat the Mole and put an end to the kingdom of England as it was then known was surely a matter of some interest during the reign of Henry III. If Owain and his supporters accordingly made use of this popular prophecy (on which question see the headnote above), the Wolf would presumably be Owain (despite his dragon banner), the Lion the anti-English lords in Ireland, and the Dragon the anti-English lords of Scotland, perhaps combined with English allies such as the Percies and Mortimers.

2. IOLO GOCH, *CONVERSATION BETWEEN THE SOUL AND BODY*

Ed. Dafydd Johnston. Trans. and notes, John K. Bollard.

Manuscripts: There are 18 manuscript copies, of which four (Johnston's MSS A–D) contain a version of 124 lines and the remainder a shorter version of 82 lines. The passage included here is found near the end of the longer version.

The Welsh text is taken from Iolo Goch, *Gwaith*, ed. Johnston, p. 67. The text and a translation of the entire poem may also be found in Iolo Goch, *Poems*, ed. and trans. Johnston, pp. 56–62. The following notes on the text often reflect editorial choices and comments in Johnston's textual notes, and similarly the general observations and interpretations owe a great debt to his careful analysis.

While poems structured as a conversation between the body and the soul were common in medieval Europe, Iolo Goch's use of this topos is unique. Typically, such poems present a debate in which the soul exhorts the body or castigates it for its attachment to this world rather than preparing to enter the next. Examples can be found in Welsh in the *Black Book of Carmarthen* (see Haycock, *Blodeugerdd*, pp. 203–33), and in Old and Middle English (see Krapp, *Vercelli Book*, pp. 54–59; Krapp and Dobbie, *Exeter Book*, pp. 174–58; Moffat, *Soul's Address*; Moffat, *Body and Soul*). In Iolo's poem, however, the Soul describes its travels throughout Wales searching for the Body, which lies drunk somewhere: *Mae ydd wyd, y corff meddw iawn?* "Where are you, quite drunken body?" (Iolo Goch, *Poems*, 14.6). Thus the poem gives a lighthearted description of the wanderings of the poet from the house of one patron to another, praising the land and the generosity of his patrons. The Body, in turn, maintains the conversation with such questions as "Did you go to the land of Buellt (Builth)?" "Did you see the men of Cydweli (Kidwelly)?" and "What did the abbot of wine-drinking Whitland ask you?" (ibid., 14.43, 57, 67–68). The soul then suggests that they go to Ceredigion, to Strata Florida Abbey, and to other welcoming places and patrons.

In the final section of the poem, from which the present extract is taken, the Body recommends that the Soul visit Sycharth, Owain Glyndŵr's home, and gives pride of place finally to a visit to Ithel ap Robert in Coedymynydd. Johnston notes that the entire poem is "an elaborate compliment to Ithel, since once he has reached his house Iolo need journey no more" (Iolo Goch, *Poems*, p. 168). Ithel ap Robert (fl. 1357–1382) was a canon of Bangor Cathedral from 1357, and, in addition, a canon of St. Asaph's cathedral and archdeacon of that diocese from 1375 until 1382. As well as being a patron of Iolo, he was also a friend, for in his poetic request for the gift of a horse from Ithel, Iolo records that as youths they had been pupils of the same master (Iolo Goch, *Poems*, 12.45–48). Iolo also composed a poem of thanks and an elegy for Ithel (Iolo Goch, *Poems*, Poems 13, 15).

This extract is included here as the earliest known, albeit implicit, poetic reference to Owain as lord of Sycharth. Because a new archdeacon of St. Asaph was appointed in 1382 and we hear no more of Ithel ap Robert after that date, we may assume that the poem was written between 1375 and 1382, or soon afterward. Owain would have been somewhere between the ages of twenty-three and thirty-three, depending on what we accept as the year of his birth (see Items 7.1 and 92). Sycharth itself, as the family seat, may have had greater fame than its chief resident at the time, for it would be two or three years yet before Owain's service in the north brought his military accomplishments to the attention of the poets. But it is not unlikely that Owain's reputation as lord of Sycharth and especially as a patron of poets, was already sufficiently well established that he need not be mentioned by name, under the assumption that the pronoun alone in line 106 is sufficient.

104	*pa waeth*. This phrase is composed of the interrogative pronoun *pa* [what?] + *gwaeth* [worse], the irregular comparative of *drwg* [bad], but the sense is clearly not "What [is] worse than Sycharth?" Following Johnston, I translate this as "Why not?" The idiom *pa waeth* is generally used in the sense of "What does it matter?" or "What difference does it make?" (see *GPC*, s.v. *gwaeth*), but the context here is clearly less equivocal than those renderings would suggest.
	i [to]. The preposition *i* does not occur in the MSS, but the emendation improves both the sense and the length of the line.
	Sycharth. On the name *Sycharth*, see the note to Item 8.92.
106	*od gwn* [indeed]. This had become a set phrase in Middle Welsh; the literal meaning is "if I know it," but it fossilized into an idiom largely independent of its verbal force, with the sense of "surely, assuredly, indeed."
	gydag ef [with him]. This, of course, is a reference to Owain Glyndŵr.
107	*Duw fydd*. All four MSS read *Duw a fydd*, though the inclusion of the preverbal particle makes the line a syllable too long.

110　　'*r Berfeddwlad* [the Perfeddwlad]. '*r* is a postvocalic form of the definite article
　　　　y. *Y Berfeddwlad* [lit., the Middle Country], is an earlier name for the region be-
　　　　tween Gwynedd and Powys, comprising the cantrefs of Rhos, Rhufoniog, Dyffr-
　　　　yn Clwyd, and Tegeingl. After the area came under the power of Gwynedd, it
　　　　was called *Gwynedd Is Conwy* (G. below Conwy); see the note on Item 6.47.

113　　*dwg . . . Ithel*. This line is a syllable short in all the manuscripts.

114　　Coedymynydd was Ithel ap Robert's home a few miles north of Ruthin.

3. GRUFFUDD LLWYD, *OWAIN'S EXPLOITS IN SCOTLAND*

Ed. Rhiannon Ifans. Trans. and notes, John K. Bollard.

Manuscripts: There are forty-seven manuscripts of this poem, the majority of which were
written in the sixteenth and seventeenth centuries. The earliest is perhaps the nearly illegible, cropped, and partly erased fragment of some twenty lines in a fifteenth- or sixteenth-
century hand in the margin of British Library MS Cotton Caligula A.iii, fol. 151v (Ifans' MS
H), a thirteenth-century Welsh law text. Three of the best manuscripts used for Ifans's
edition are **A**: Bangor University MS 703, p. 13 (1790); **B**: Bangor University MS 704, p. 96
(1780s); and **C**: British Library, London, Additional MS 14866, fol. 45v (1587). For details
and a list of all the manuscripts, see Gruffudd Llwyd, *Gwaith*, ed. Ifans, pp. 136, 345.

　　The Welsh text is taken from Gruffudd Llwyd, *Gwaith*, ed. Ifans, pp. 134–36. Many of the
following notes reflect Ifans' editorial choices and comments in her textual notes. Similarly my
own observations and interpretations owe a great debt to her careful analysis, though the
translation does not necessarily follow Ifans' punctuation or understanding of the original.
　　That this poem was written before 1400 may be inferred from the facts that (a) there is
no mention of rebellion or war with the English, only the Scots (see lines 16, 84), and (b)
while he is given the title *Mur Glyn . . . Dyfrdwy* (lines 5–6), there is no indication of the position or title he assumed in September 1400 as *Princeps Wallie*. The subject of the poem is restricted to his absence in Scotland and his heroic deeds there. The poet, according to pane-
gyric tradition, may have been exaggerating his exploits, for, as Davies points out, Owain's
service with Sir Gregory Sais in the garrison at Berwick during 1384 "was prosaic, verging
on the dull," and Richard II's expedition to Scotland in the summer of 1385 "was short-
lived; it burnt and plundered its way to Edinburgh and then retired" (Davies, *Revolt*, pp.
146, 147). The poem makes no mention of Owain's service in Flanders in the personal retinue of the Earl of Arundel in late March 1387, which may suggest that Gruffudd Llwyd composed this poem before that time. Thomas Roberts suggests that this poem was composed
in late 1385 or early in the following year (Lewis et al., *Cywyddau*, p. xiv).
　　As is usual, there is no known contemporary title for the poem. Many of the manuscripts
give a variant of a short title rubric similar to that of MS A, from which the title *I Owain
Glyndŵr* is taken, and MS B, *Cywydd moliant Owain Glyn Dyfrdwy, o waith Gruffydd Llwyd* [A
cywydd of praise for Owain Glyndŵr, from the work of Gruffudd Llwyd]. The note printed
at the head of the poem is taken from MS C, written by Dafydd Johns in 1587; variants are
also found in MSS G, V, X, c, s. The endnote is found only in MSS C and G (1800).

1   *Eryr* [Eagle]. As a figurative term for a chief, prince, or great warrior, *eryr* [eagle] appears frequently in Welsh, as early as *The Gododdin* (c.600), where Buddfan is described as *eryr tith tirion* [the eagle of graceful movement]; Gwyddien simply as an eagle, *eryr Gwyddien*; Rhys as *Eryr brwydrin, trin tra chwardd* [A fierce eagle, laughing in battle]; and Eiddef as *Diechyr eryr gwŷr gofaran* [An invincible eagle of wrathful men] (Aneirin, *Gododdin*, lines 274, 440, 508, 828). In her ninth-century lament for her sister Ffreuer and her brothers, Heledd mourns, . . . *mor yw gwann heno. / gwedy agheu eluan. / ac eryr kyndrwyn kyndylan* [how sad it is tonight / after the death of Elfan / and the eagle of Cyndrwyn, Cynddylan] (Rowland, *Early Welsh Saga Poetry*, pp. 437, 488; Rowland translates *eryr* here as "hero"). On the death of his patron Gronwy Fychan, the Anglesey poet Gruffudd ap Maredudd (fl. 1352–1382) laments, *Marw eryr Penmynydd* [Dead is the eagle of Penmynydd] (Evans, *Poetry in the Red Book*, col. 1322.36). Within this long tradition, *eryr* can be understood as a particularly powerful and evocative first word for the present poem.

3   *eurfab* [golden son]. See note to line 20 below.

3–4   While *ei* [his] in line 4 might conceivably refer to Gruffudd Fychan, it is more likely, as suggested by the syntactic parallelism of *agwrdd ei arfod* [mighty his stroke] and *glân ei glod* [fair his fame], that both phrases refer to Owain in line 2.

5   *mur* [protector]. Like *eryr* in line 1, *mur* [wall] is a long-standing metaphor for a leader or steadfast warrior. It occurs in this sense no fewer than seven times in *The Gododdin* (Aneirin, *Gododdin*, lines 8, 310, 406, 411, 575, 598, 608). The perhaps twelfth- or thirteenth-century poem *Marwnat Ercwl* [Elegy for Hercules] in the *Book of Taliesin* names *Ercwlf mur ffossawt* [Hercules, the rampart of battle] (Haycock, *Legendary Poems*, Poem 19.19). Iolo Goch uses the same metaphor in his poem to Owain composed during the revolt: *Pen nen pur, mur, mawr waladr* [a pure chief lord, a rampart, a great spear] (Item 27.45).

     menestr [cupbearer]. *Menestr* (MS J: *mynistr*) [cupbearer, servant] is a borrowing through Old French *menestre* or perhaps directly from Latin *minister*, and thereby cognate with English *minister*. Some twenty manuscripts read *meistr/maistir* [master, ruler], but *menestr* is numerically, metrically, and semantically the stronger reading. In addressing Owain as *menestr*, Gruffudd may possibly be evoking the poem *Hirlas Owain* ["Owain's Long Blue (Drinking Horn)"], by Owain Cyfeiliog (c.1130–1197), ruler of the commote of Cyfeiliog in western Powys, or perhaps by or in collaboration with the preeminent court poet of the period, Cynddelw (fl. 1155–1200). *Hirlas Owain* is a dramatic monologue in which Owain enjoins his own cupbearer to pass the drinking horn to each member of his war band as he praises them for their heroic deeds after a successful expedition and laments those who died.

5–6   *Glyn . . . Dyfrdwy* [Glyndyfrdwy]. A particularly effective form of tmesis or parenthesis (see p. 516) is the interpolation of a descriptive phrase between a personal name and a patronymic, as in lines 2–4 above, or as here between the elements of a compound name. Gruffudd Llwyd similarly divides *Glyn Dyfrdwy* in Item 5.64; that identical line also occurs in Iolo Goch's praise of Owain in

Item 4.16. Compare also, Iolo's *Owain, glain dwyrain, Glyndŵr* [Owain, ascendant jewel, Glyndŵr] (Item 27.19).

9   *fy nghrair* [my treasure]. This phrase is redolent with connotation. The core sense of *crair* is a "relic, holy thing, . . . talisman," extending to "object of admiration or love, darling," and in some instances it carries the sense of "safeguard, strength" (*GPC*, s.v. *crair*). Gruffudd uses this word again as a term of endearment for Owain in line 56. In her modern paraphrase of the text, Ifans renders it as *anwylyd*, i.e., "dear one, loved one" (*Gwaith*, ed. Ifans, pp. 134.9, 135.56).

11   *medd fynfyr* [Lord of the mead]. Literally, "miniver of mead." *Mynfyr* [miniver] is a white fur that was worn by medieval nobles, especially on robes of state. Here it is a synecdoche for the lord who wore it, appropriate here as Gruffudd recalls the mead and wine he has received from Owain's hand. Compare also Item 5.72 and note.

16   *Prydyn* [Scotland]. Ifans suggests that we should not put too much weight on this as a reference to Owain's service with Richard II in Scotland in 1385, but that it might rather be understood as a poetic reference to some far-off place, perhaps Berwick, where Owain served in 1384. Given the shifting fortunes and competing Scottish and English claims to Berwick, we might wonder to which country Owain and/or Gruffudd Llwyd thought the town belonged (*Gwaith*, ed. Ifans, p. 252). Berwick might not have been "in Scotland" in any definitive sense, but it looked like it was, especially when viewed from distant Wales, and Owain certainly went there in opposition to the Scots. For uncertainty and ambiguity between the forms *Prydyn* and *Prydain*, see Item 6.55n.

17   *hiraeth* [longing]. *Hiraeth* is a term that has long been redolent in Welsh culture as a sense of an otherwise inexpressible, untranslatable, and particularly Welsh grief, sadness, or yearning for home or loved ones. Gruffudd's expression of *hiraeth* here heightens the sense of a close personal relationship between him and Owain.

20   *aur* [gold]. For the figurative use of *aur* in the sense of "excellent," see line 3 above and Items 6.39, 83; 8.24; 27.9; 54.3.

24   *y tad hael* [a generous father]. Literally, "the generous father"; while English prefers an indefinite construction here, the referent is definite, i.e. Gruffudd Fychan (see line 4 above).

25   *cefais* [I received]. Twenty-four of the manuscripts read *klywais* [I heard].

     o ben [from the mouth]. Literally, "from the head."

27   *yn yr aer* [in battle]. Literally, "in the battle," but here an example of the definite article used as in indefinite; see Item 4.47n.

29   *Daroganawdd* [prophesied]. This verb takes on considerable significance, especially given the persistence of the theme of prophecy in connection with Glyndŵr (see Fulton's essay in this volume) and the poet's reference to himself as *dewin* [sage, magician] in line 33. This is the earliest clear poetic reference connecting Owain and prophecy; see also Item 27.12.

drymlawdd [profound praise]. From *trwm* [heavy] + *llawdd* [praise]. Alternatively, as a noun *trwm* can also mean "battle;" thus we might understand *drymlawdd dro* to mean "a time for battle-praise." Ifans suggests the further possibility that understanding *trymlawdd* as a compound of *trwm* + *blawdd* [tumult, commotion, terror, fright] would suit the context, but if such were the case, we would expect *trymflawdd* rather than *trymlawdd* (*Gwaith*, ed. Ifans, p. 253n29).

31   *faenawr* [lordship]. Lenited form of *maenawr, maenor*. *Maenor* carries wider implications than English *manor* and Old French *manoir*. It is not related to these forms etymologically, though under the influence of their similarities it developed a similar range of meanings (see Jenkins, *Hywel Dda*, p. 363, s.v. *maenol*).

33   *Dewin* [A sage]. *Dewin* is a borrowing from Latin *divinus* (through a form such as *deuinus*), and it is often used in collocation with *Duw* [God], but elsewhere it also carries connotations of "sage, wise man, wizard, magician, prophet." The legendary "Taliesin" (as distinct from the sixth-century historical Taliesin), describes himself as *Bran bore dewin* [the early-rising sage of Brân], and in another wisdom poem (not necessarily by the same poet), the narrator states *Mydwy Taliessin / areith lif dewin* [I am Taliesin / with a sage's flow of eloquence] (Haycock, *Legendary Poems*, Poems 14.38, 25.58–59). Gruffudd taps into this tradition, which is rich in prophecy and magic, by naming himself similarly, if with some hesitation (see note 29 above).

35   *ramant* [tale]. Welsh *rhamant* is cognate with French *romans* and English *romance*, in the sense of a tale of history, knighthood, valor, love, war, etc. The story of how Uthr/Uther avenged the treacherous death by poison of his brother Aurelius Ambrosius (Welsh: *Emreis Wledig*) is told by Geoffrey of Monmouth in his *Historia regum Britanniae* (Book 8, chapters 14–16), which had been translated into Welsh no fewer than three times by the end of the thirteenth century (Geoffrey of Monmouth, *Historia*, pp. 143–45; *History*, pp. 199–202; *Brut*, ed. Lewis, pp. 130–33; *Brut*, ed. Parry, pp. 147–49; on the date, see *Brut*, ed. Roberts, p. xxix).

39–44   In these lines the poet compares Owain's exploits in Scotland to those of his namesake Owain ab Urien in the *Tale of the Countess of the Spring*, also known simply as *Owain*, as also in the French *Yvain* of Chrétien de Troyes and the Middle English *Ywain and Gawain*. At a spring, Owain encounters a knight attired in black on a black horse and with a black pennon on his spear and they break their two spears (see p. 503; Thomson, *Owein*, lines 269–82; Bollard, *Tales of Arthur*, p. 74). The broken spear and the chase both resonate with the accounts of Owain Glyndŵr's exploits in this poem and in the other poems addressed to him (see Item 4.52, 59–60, and Item 27.49).

39   *Hwyliaist, siwrneiaist* [You sailed, you journeyed]. The motif of the battle as a journey as Owain cuts a path through the enemy reappears in lines 47–48, 67–70, 75–76; see also the note to line 48.

42   *y marchog duog* [the Black Knight]. In the tale of *Owain*, the Black Knight whom Owain encounters at the spring is twice referred to as *y marchawc duawc*. For the significance of *duog*, see p. 503n21.

o'r dŵr [from the water]. The water is that of the *ffynnon* [spring, fountain] of line 44, the setting of the encounter in the tale.

43–44   *gŵr fu ef . . . a phen draig* [He was a man . . . and chief warrior]. The referents for these lines are ambiguous; it is not clear whether Owain or the Black Knight of the Spring is meant. Alternatively we might understand the *A* as *â* [with], rather than *a* [and], and read these lines as "He (Owain) was a man for fighting with the chief warrior of the fountain (the Black Knight)." The reading of line 52 might suggest that we should take line 44 as a reference to the Black Knight.

44   *a phen draig* [and chief warrior]. Literally, "and head dragon/leader." *Draig* has a long history as a term of praise for a battle leader; it is cognate with *dragon*, which has a similar range of senses, as in the compound *pendragon*.

45–46   *gwŷr a fuant* [They were men]. Given the positive connotations of *llwyddiant llu* [(with) the success of a host/army], the reference here seems to point to Uthr and Owain ab Urien as models of comparison with Glyndŵr. On the other hand, if perhaps less likely, the description might apply to Owain ab Urien and the Black Knight as renowned and, up to the final blow Owain strikes in their encounter, both successful fighters. The tale is explicit that they both broke their spears and then fought with swords: *A'e erbynnyeit a oruc Owein, ac ymwan ac ef yn drut, a thorri y deu baladyr a orugant, a dispeilaw deu gledyf a wnaethant ac ymgyfogi* [And Owain encountered him and jousted with him fiercely, and they broke the two spears, and they drew two swords and smote each other] (Thomson, *Owein*, lines 271–72; Bollard, *Tales of Arthur*, p. 74).

48   *drafn, â llafn* [lord, with a sword]. *Trafn* is a poetic word for "leader, lord," and *llafn* might be more literally rendered "blade;" it is translated "sword" here to approximate the internal rhyme of the original.

llwybr [path]. With the image of forging a track or path through a battle, compare Iolo Goch's passage on the devastation that Owain, like Arthur, left in his wake (Item 4.61–64), and see pp. 505–06.

49–52   *mab Urien hir* [tall son of Urien]. This passage continues the comparison of Owain with Owain ab Urien. There are no other examples of *hir* [tall] applied to either Owain or Urien in the earlier poems and tales in which they appear.

53   Note the parallelism with line 23 above.

56   On the use and meaning of *crair*, see the note to line 9 above. Ifans points out that this line draws a twofold picture of Owain as gentle and beloved, on the one hand, and dreadful in battle, on the other (*Gwaith*, ed. Ifans, p. 255n56).

57   *Ffwg*. Fulk III Fitzwarin of Whittington in Shropshire is a historical figure and the outlaw hero of the Old French prose romance, *Fouke le Fitz Waryn*, written in the first half of the fourteenth century (see *Fouke le Fitz Waryn*, trans. Kelly). The Fitzwarin family held lands in Shropshire for 400 years after the Norman Conquest, and every heir to the estate for at least nine generations bore the name Fulk (Welsh *Ffwg*). Indeed, R. R. Davies points out that a Fulk Fitzwarin served alongside Glyndŵr in the personal retinue of the earl of Arundel in 1387

— a very short time after the likely date of composition of the present poem (Davies, *Revolt*, p. 148). Fulk III aided Llywelyn ab Iorwerth against Henry III in 1217 but reconciled with the crown in 1218. He is named frequently by Welsh poets of the fourteenth and fifteenth centuries, including Dafydd ap Gwilym (see *Welsh Biography Online*, s.n. *Fitz Warin*; Dafydd ap Gwilym, *Gwaith*, Poem 6.37n; Lloyd-Jones, *Geirfa*, p. 504, s.n. *Ffawc*).

60 *gwayw ufeldan* [fiery spear]. Literally, a "spear of sparking fire." *Ufeldan* is a compound of *ufel* [fire, sparks] + *tân* [fire]; compare the nearly synonymous *Gwayw ufelfellt* [flashing spear] (Item 5.46).

68 *gyriad ychen llog* [a driving of hired oxen]. Though the general intent is clear, there are multiple ambiguities depending on our interpretation of *gyriad*. The root (also that of the verb in line 67) is the noun *gyr* [drive, thrust; rush onset] + *-iad*, which may be either an abstract noun suffix or an objective suffix; thus, *gyriad* here may be either "a driving, a sending, expulsion" or "driver, drover." In the former case, *gyriad* could describe the *llu* [the host, the army] as oxen being driven away by Owain, or it might refer to Owain as having the strength or the effect of a team of oxen plowing through the enemy; in the latter case, it would designate Owain as the driver/drover of oxen. Ifans points out that *ychen llog* [hired oxen] may refer to the hired soldiers of the enemy (Ifans, *Gwaith*, p. 256n65).

71–78 This sentence, with its multiple *sangiadau* (parentheses) and complex, disordered syntax, replicates the very rush of Owain's attack that it describes. It can be more or less disentangled thus: "You come from a proud line, and your poet says that, should [the call to] battle come (fair summons), your attack with a two-edged sword will be remembered as remarkable until Judgment Day by the inhabitants of Britain, as you cut a path in your white garments, your rush to the field with your lance, your bloody thrusting-spear, and your fame and your ability, afflicting a hundred."

72 *hanwyd o feilch* [you come from a proud line]. *Beilch* is the plural of the adjective *balch* [proud]; hence, more literally, "you are descended from proud (ones)."

74 *Brydain* [Britain]. As Ifans suggests, *Prydain* here refers to the inhabitants of Wales, England, and Scotland, though sometimes the term excludes Scotland (*Gwaith*, ed. Ifans, p. 256n74).

75 *(g)wisg wen* [white garments]. Compare line 11 above, in which *mynfer* [miniver] is used as a synecdoche for Owain.

79 *ddaioni* [bravery]. *Daioni*, literally "goodness," is used similarly in the sense "bravery, valor" three times in the fourteenth-century Welsh translation of the romance of Otuel, as in the passage introducing the impetuous Estut o Lengrys (Estuyt of Legiers) as *marchawc prouedic y dayoni* [a knight of proven bravery], where "goodness" *per se* can hardly be meant (Williams, *Ystorya*, pp. 46, 103, 106).

80 *hort teg* [a fair declaration]. *Hort*, a borrowing from ME *hurt*, generally has negative connotations and is glossed unambiguously so in *GPC*: "reproach, censure, slander, defamation, aspersion, abuse, taunt, detraction, disparagement, calum-

ny" (*GPC*, s.v. *hort*). However, its use here in reference to Owain and especially as modified by the adjective *teg* [fair], suggests that we should read it in a positive light. Ifans renders the phrase in Modern Welsh as *datganiad clodforus*, i.e., "a praiseworthy declaration" (*Gwaith*, ed. Ifans, p. 144, line 80).

81   *ddursiamp* [coat of mail]. The compound *dursiamp*, from *dur* [steel] + *siamp* [field, surface] is known only here, though there are other compounds with the fairly uncommon term *siamp*, which is probably a borrowing from ME *chaumpe* [a field for a battle or tournament, or the field of a shield or banner] (*MED*, s.v. *chaumpe*). The phrase *diarswyd ddursiamp* is a synecdoche for Owain himself.

86   *ŵyth archoll brwydr* [wrath of the wound of battle]. This is another phrase applied to Owain, as the one who causes wounds in battle. The word *ŵyth* is the lenited form of *gŵyth* [anger, wrath], with lenition caused by the vocative. Alternatively, the *wyth* of the manuscripts may be read as *wyth*, literally "eight," but often used to mean "many," giving the sense "(one who causes) many battle wounds."

88   *marchog o'r Glyn* [knight of the Glyn]. With this construction, compare *Arglwydd terwyn o'r Glyn glwys* [a fiery lord from the fair Glyn] (Item 4.5), *pôr y Glyn* [lord of the Glyn] (Item 27.37) and *Beli y Glyn* [(a) Beli of the Glyn] (Item 6.54). A poem to Rhys Gethin, Owain's deputy, states, *Milwr yw â gwayw melyn / Megis Owain glain y Glyn* [He is a soldier with a yellow spear / like Owain, jewel of the Glyn]; though no longer attributed to Iolo Goch, this is one of the few surviving poems that may have been composed during the rebellion (Lewis et al., *Cywyddau*, Poem 37.27–28). Later poets, too, often refer to Owain as *Owain y Glyn*; e.g. Hywel Cilan in the late fifteenth century: *Nai . . . Owain y Glyn* [nephew of O. y G.] (Jones, *Gwaith Hywel Cilan*, Poem 23.22). Tudur Aled (fl. 1480–1526) calls him *Owain Glyn* (Tudur Aled, *Gwaith*, Poems 13.77, 46.28, 77.77), as well as *Owain Glyn Dwfr* (ibid., Poem 20.91–92). The *glyn* [valley, glen] in question is, of course, Glyndyfrdwy, the valley of the Dee, which residents of the area often call simply *y Glyn* (Williams, *Adolygu*, p. 70).

89   *Teityl Owain . . .* [Owain's title . . .]. On this colophon, see the note Headnote and colophon above.

4. Iolo Goch, *Owain's Exploits in Scotland*

Ed. Dafydd Johnston. Trans. and notes, John K. Bollard.

Manuscripts: There are nine manuscripts, which represent two versions; each version is defective in parts, and thus the present text is a critical text combining the best readings of the two. After line 64 some manuscripts of one version conclude with lines 85–92 of Item 6; two copies of the other version end with a corrupt text of the opening couplet of an anonymous prophetic poem attributed to Iolo Goch in the manuscripts [see note 64 below].

The Welsh text is taken from Iolo Goch, *Gwaith Iolo Goch*, ed. Johnston, pp. 43–44. Some of the following notes reflect Johnston's editorial choices and comments in his textual notes, and similarly the general observations and interpretations below owe a great debt to his careful analysis. The translation does not necessarily follow Johnston's punctuation or understanding of the original.

The detailed treatment in lines 43–64 of Owain's service in Berwick and Scotland with Sir Gregory Sais during 1384 provides an earliest date for the poem's composition, and the absence of reference to any later episodes in his life suggests that it was written shortly afterwards (Iolo Goch, *Gwaith*, p. 228). If Gruffudd Llwyd borrowed line 16 — *Iôr Glyn, daeardor, Dyfrdwy* [Lord of Glyn, narrow valley, Dyfrdwy] — from Iolo Goch, then this poem, too, must have been written prior to Dafydd Hanmer's death in 1388, but neither poem gives any indication as to who borrowed from whom (Item 5.64).

The poem is divided evenly into two parts. The first thirty-two lines outline the more courtly qualities of a nobleman whose authority stems from his lineage. Most striking, perhaps, is the device of imagining Owain as a boy — a prudent, mild, gentle, fair lad, wise enough to love a poet, who in turn, of course, will ensure his reputation. The next thirty-two lines stress Owain's martial status, prowess, and accomplishments.

1–2	The significance of the opening couplet is unclear. It is perhaps best understood as general praise of the deeds of Owain as the ideal lord.
4	*bual*. Literally, "buffalo, bison, wild ox" [< Latin *bubalus, bufalus*]; metaphorically, "lord;" other poets of the period use the same metaphor. As well as a term for the animal, *bual* is a synechdoche for a drinking horn in *The Gododdin* and later sources (Aneirin, *Gododdin*, lines 153, 166, 1071; *GPC*, s.v., *bual*). Judging by the evidence from Sutton Hoo and elsewhere (see Carver, *Sutton Hoo*, p. 30), the aurochs horn was used for this purpose at least into the 7th century, though the aurochs had been extinct in Britain since the Bronze Age (i.e., before 700 BCE). Iolo, however, refers to the color of the *bual* itself; thus it is more likely that the animal in question was the European bison or wisent (though that, too, disappeared from Britain in the twelfth century), or more generally, adopting Proinsias Mac Cana's phrase, a "foreign, exotic ox" (Mac Cana, "Ir. *buaball*, W *bual*," p. 81). Rather than search for the precise species, we should recognize that Iolo is drawing on a long-standing bardic tradition and vocabulary.
	gwineuddu [bay-black, auburn-black]. In Middle Welsh, adjectives of color following nouns in reference to people usually refer to hair color, e.g. *gwas gwinau* [an auburn-haired youth], *gwr gwynllwyd* [a grey-haired man]; thus here we might translate "dark-auburn-haired lord." If we take *bual* [bison] literally, of course, *gwineuddu* refers to the animal's color in general, but if we understand *bual* as metaphor for Owain, might this, then, be an indication of Owain Glyndŵr's hair color? Iolo also uses *gwinau* [auburn-haired] to describe Glyndŵr in Item 27.49.
6	*Pywer Lew*. Pywer (or Bywyr) the Brave, one of the legendary forebears of the line of Powys; see Item 6.32n.
9	*gwyarllwybr*. This is the only known example of this compound, from *gwyar* [blood; battle] + *llwybr* [path, track].
9–10	A very similar couplet, with the identical second line, occurs in Item 6.7–8.
10	*mab Llŷr*. In *The Mabinogi*, Llŷr is the father of Bendigeidfran, the giant king of the Island of the Mighty (i.e., Britain), and of Manawydan. Either or both may

be invoked here: though Bendigeidfran is the more likely by virtue of his crown and his might, Manawydan is an exemplar of wisdom and good counsel. Most significantly, the reference implicitly links Owain's authority to the deep traditional history and cultural ideals of Wales.

11–12   The same couplet occurs in Item 6.43–44.

16   This line refers here to Owain Glyndŵr's father. However, the same line appears also in Gruffudd Llwyd's poem to Owain, where it is clearly a reference to Owain himself (Item 4.64 above).

17   *Hiriell*. Hiriell is a legendary hero of Gwynedd of whom little is known, but who, like Arthur (and later Owain Glyndŵr himself), was prophesied to arise someday from a long sleep to save his land (see Bartrum, *Welsh Classical Dictionary*, pp. 365–66).

    ddihaereb. Here *dihaereb* [exemplar] is a noun; compare Item 6.65, where it is adjectival.

24   *clêr* [poet]. See the note to Item 8.44.

26   *fwbach*. Lenited form of *bwbach* [bugbear, bogey(man), ghost, scarecrow], i.e., a source of fear; in the present context of boyhood, "bully" seems an appropriate rendering.

31   *ni chamodd fys* [he never beckoned]. Literally, "he did not bend (or crook) a finger"; the idiom appears elsewhere during the period, e.g. in Iolo's "Description of a Girl," "If a finger is crooked suddenly / In front of her . . . / She almost falls like an ear of barley" (Iolo Goch, *Poems*, 24.47–50).

33   *gwroliaeth*. GPC cites this line as an example of the frequently occurring sense "valour, manliness, fortitude, prowess," but Johnston points out that it makes better sense understood as "manhood," also an attested sense.

34   *gorugwr*. Four manuscripts read *goreugwr* [best man, nobleman], and this reading was adopted by earlier editors, but Johnston (Iolo Goch, *Gwaith*, p. 229n34) points out Iolo's use elsewhere of the verb *gorugo* [to stab] and suggests that *gorugwr*, literally "stabbing man," should be accepted as the *lectio difficilior*.

36   *gwrmseirch* [dark armor or horse trappings]. This is an ancient poetic compound of *gwrm*, a dark color word that ranges from "black" through "grey, brown, dusky, reddish" to "blue" + *seirch* [armor, trappings, harness]. It occurs three times in the later A text of *The Gododdin*, always, as here, in conjunction with *meirch* [horses] (Aneirin, *Gododdin*, lines 357, 500, 688). Thus, it may refer to protective armor or trappings on the horses, rather than to personal armor.

38   Compare Item 6.56: *Llew siaced tew soced dur*.

39   *phenffestin*. Penffestin developed the sense of "helmet," but the earlier, more specific designation was for the coif or hood of mail worn under the helmet (see Bollard, "What is a *baryflen*?," p. 219).

41   *nen* [roof, roof-ridge, housetop; head, crown of head]. Frequently used meta-
          phorically, as translated here, in the sense "lord," but a more literal rendering
          "crown, head" would also suit the present context.

42   *adain* [plume]. Literally, "wing," most likely used here, *pars pro toto*, for the bird
          itself (see the next note).

          edn yr Aifft. While *GPC*, following the interpretation of Lloyd, posits the possi-
          bility that the red "bird of Egypt" in this unique reference was perhaps a flam-
          ingo, Breeze argues that Owain's crest was the figure of a phoenix, a recognized
          heraldic device, vaunting in Owain's case, perhaps, the wearer's excellence non-
          pareil (*GPC*, s.v. *edn*; Lloyd, *Owen Glendower*, p. 22; Breeze, "Glendower's crest,"
          pp. 99–102; see also pp. 504–05).

44   Sir Gregory Sais was a knight from Flintshire with a distinguished military
          career in France and England. In 1384 Owain served under Sir Gregory when
          the latter was dispatched to Berwick-upon-Tweed as captain of the garrison
          there. For more on Sir Gregory, see the note to Item 5.44.

45   *hirdrig herwdref*. The phrase has proved troublesome to both early scribes and
          modern editors. The four elements are *hir* [long], *trig*, the root of *trigo* [to re-
          main] and *trig* [dwelling-place], *herw* [an attack, raid, plundering], and *tref*
          [town]. The *herwdres* of four manuscripts can be easily emended to *herwdref* on
          the basis of the consistency of -*dref* in all other copies and the ease of confusing
          f and long-*s*. Three manuscripts read *herwdrig hirdref*, adopted in both editions
          of *Cywyddau Iolo Goch ac Eraill* (ed. Lewis et al., 1925, 1972), as well as by the
          editors of *GPC*, interpreting the otherwise unknown *herwdrig* nominally as
          "haunt or den of outlaws, pirates or bandits" or adjectivally as "frequented or
          inhabited by outlaws, pirates or pillagers, pirate-ridden" (*GPC*, s.v. *herwdrig*),
          giving the phrase the sense of "a pirate-ridden long-town," though, as Johnston
          points out, it is difficult to understand the function of *hir* [long] in this configur-
          ation (Iolo Goch, *Gwaith*, p. 230n45). (There is no entry for *hirdref* in *GPC*.) On
          the other hand, nominal or adjectival *hirdrig* [(a) long abiding, (a) long tarrying,
          (a) long lasting] is known from several sources as early as the late twelfth cen-
          tury (*GPC*, s.v. *hirdrig*). Johnston glosses *hirdrig herwdref* as "tref a fu'n gwr-
          thryfela'n hir" [lit., a town that was rebelling for a long time], and he translates
          it as "stubborn defiant town" (Iolo Goch, *Gwaith*, *loc. cit.*; Iolo Goch, *Poems*, p.
          36). However, by 1384 Berwick-upon-Tweed, the northernmost town in
          England, had been secure in English hands for over fifty years, and the trans-
          lation 'a town long subject to raids' is adopted here to suggest the reason for the
          garrison maintained there to protect the town and the border. Alternatively, we
          might read it as "garrison town," with the implication that it served as a base
          from which English forces could raid (*herwa*) into Scotland while protecting the
          border from Scottish raids into England. I am grateful to Dafydd Johnston for
          the suggestion that Iolo might have had in mind Edward III's siege of Berwick
          in 1333, which Iolo himself cites in his poem to Edward, composed between
          1347 and 1356 (personal communication, November 2010; for the poem, see
          Iolo Goch, *Poems*, ed. and trans. Johnson, Poem 1, esp. lines 33–34).

47   *y gŵr march* [a horseman]. Literally, "the horseman," but the definite article *y* may be used in Middle Welsh "to indicate a person or thing which is determinate for the author, but otherwise indefinite" (Evans, *Grammar*, p. 24); compare Item 8.18.

54   *cannwyll brwydr* [candle of battle]. The metaphoric use of *cannwyll* [candle] to mean "leader, hero, best" appears as early as the tenth century in the prophetic poem *Armes Prydein* in reference to the redeemer Cynan: *canhwyll yn tywyll a gerd genhyn* [a candle in the darkness will go with us] (see *Armes Prydein*, ed. Williams, line 88, pp. 8–9; Livingston, *Brunanburh*, line 88, pp. 32–33). It appears in a more courtly context closer to the age of Owain in the Arthurian tale of *Peredur* in a greeting to the young hero, "God's welcome to you, fair Peredur son of Efrawg, flower of warriors and candle of knights!" (Bollard, *Tales of Arthur*, p. 26). The metaphor may be a "Celtic" one, for Irish *caindel* is similarly used for a hero (see *Armes Prydein*, ed. Williams, p. 45n88).

       Brydyn. On confusion between *Prydyn* [Scotland] and *Prydain* [Britain], see the note to Item 6.55.

58   *i Ddeifr*. Literally, "to [the men of] Deira," the ancient Anglian kingdom that was merged with Bernicia to form Northumbria in the seventh century; see also Iolo's later poem to Owain, Item 27.22. While the later medieval poets generally use *Deifr* and *Brynaich* [Bernicia] *pars pro toto* as terms for the English in general, Iolo seems to be drawing more on the northerly implications of the name, for he uses it here to mean the Scots, as he similarly uses *Brynaich* in Item 6.79 and in his poem to Edward III (Iolo Goch, *Poems*, 1.30). In Madog ap Gronw Gethin's poem to the River Dee (Item 53.2), we find *Deifr* in the more usual sense of "English."

61–64   These lines compare Owain to four of the great heroes of Welsh myth and legend; they echo the version of the triad of the Three Red Ravagers found in the mid-fourteenth-century *White Book of Rhydderch*; see pp. 505–06.

64   *Faesbwrch*. Maesbury is a small community in Shropshire, south of Oswestry and about eight miles by road east of Owain's home at Sycharth.

       Four manuscript copies continue with lines 85–92 of Item 6; two others end with a corrupt version of the opening couplet of a prophetic poem wrongly attributed to Iolo Goch in the manuscripts. Rather than being simply the result of faulty or confused copying, these additional lines indicate and illustrate the effects of a long period of oral transmission of Iolo's poetry.

5. GRUFFUDD LLWYD, *I KNOW NO GREATER LORD*

Ed. Rhiannon Ifans. Trans. and notes, John K. Bollard.

Manuscripts: There are two manuscripts of this poem: **A**. British Library Add 14967, fol. 60v, a manuscript in an unknown hand from the sixteenth century after 1527 (Gruffudd Llwyd, *Gwaith*, ed. Ifans, p. 346). A heavy line has been drawn through each line of the poem, and some words are difficult to make out. It is attributed to Iolo Goch. **B**. National Library of Wales Peniarth 55, fol. 9, a manuscript of c.1500, also in an unknown hand (p. 354). It is attributed to Gruffudd Llwyd. Significant manuscript variants are given in the notes below, in the orthography of the manuscripts.

The Welsh text is taken from Gruffudd Llwyd, *Gwaith*, ed. Ifans, pp. 146–47. Many of the following notes reflect Ifans' editorial choices and comments in her textual notes. Similarly my own observations and interpretations owe a great debt to her careful analysis, though the translation does not always follow Ifans' punctuation or understanding of the original.

The key to dating this poem is found in the reference to Dafydd Hanmer, Owain Glyndŵr's father-in-law, in lines 41–43. Hanmer was knighted in 1386 and died in 1387. Since he is identified here as a knight in a context in which it is clear that he is alive, the poem must have been written between those dates. If line 64, *Iôr Glyn, daeardor, Dyfrdwy* [Lord of Glyn — narrow valley — Dyfrdwy], was borrowed from Iolo Goch's poem to Owain, then that poem, too, must have been written prior to Hanmer's death, but neither poem gives any indication as to who borrowed from whom (Item 4.16).

2   *daw* [shines]. Literally, "comes."

3   A: *llawnn iawn ac ni llawen neb* [very full and no one is happy].

6   *mileiniaid* [villains]. Plural of *milain / bilain* [villein], a borrowing from OF or ME *vilein*, with the "false radical" forms in *m-* and *b-* generated because /v/ is not a native Welsh initial phoneme. The Welsh villein is well defined by Lloyd, drawing on the evidence of the early Welsh law texts: he "was distinguished in many ways as belonging to an inferior social grade. He was subject to a lord, or one of the free landowners. . . . He might not leave the tillage of the soil for any liberal occupation. . . . He might not, indeed, quit the community in which he was bred and born . . . and if he took flight and deserted his lawful station, he paid forfeit with all his possessions, which were immediately seized by his lord" (Lloyd, *History*, p. 294). Like English *villain*, *milain / bilain* often took on the even stronger derogatory connotations of "knave, churl, scoundrel," or worse. See also Item 6.76 note.

10   *cenedl* [kindred]. In modern Welsh *cenedl* means "nation" or "(grammatical) gender," but in medieval Wales it denotes a group of people who are related in any way, not unlike modern English *clan* or *tribe* (see Jenkins, *Hywel Dda*, p. 325).

    fal brain brwysg [like drunken crows]. The reversal inherent in this simile is heightened with the recognition that *brân* [crow, raven], pl. *brain*, and *branhes* [a flight of crows] were often used as laudatory terms for warriors; e.g., in the description of the army of Alexander the Great in the *Book of Taliesin*: *O gadeu a For pan adrodet / digonynt brein, gwnëint pen brithret* [It was recounted, with regard to the battles with Porus, / that the warriors (*brein*, lit. "crows, ravens") took action, that they wrought great disaster] (Haycock, *Legendary Poems*, p. 413). In the parodic tale of *The Dream of Rhonabwy*, the author dismantles this metaphor and presents the war band of Owain ab Urien as literal ravens that fly aloft with their opponents and drop them: "And then the squire said to Owain, 'Lord, is it with your permission that the emperor's young lads and his squires are contending with and harassing your ravens?'. . . And there was a great commotion in the air with the fluttering of the exultant ravens and their croaking" (Bollard, *Companion Tales*, pp. 108–09).

11–12   *gallwn . . . eu galw yn gallor goludd* [I could . . . call them a kettle of tripe]. The image of these lines is of tripe rising, sinking, and roiling about in a boiling kettle, a striking metaphor for the social turmoil and shifting status boundaries of the late fourteenth century. The phrase *gallor goludd* [kettle of tripe] is similarly used to describe an army in turmoil in the NLW Peniarth MS 3 text of the "Prophecy of Myrddin and Gwenddydd, his Sister," possibly composed before 1100 but certainly by the early fourteenth century (Williams, "Y Cyfoesi," p. 119).

13–16   These lines are the most direct expression of the "world turned upside down" topos, continued in the following two couplets with much more specific, even graphic metaphoric reversals.

13   *foesau* [mores]. Lenited pl. of *moes* [customs, manners, behavior].

16   *ac ufyddaf* [and most humble]. B: *ac vyddaf.*

17–18   *dincwd, hwd . . . bencwd, tancwd.* This couplet provides the earliest citations for each of the words *tincwd, hwd, pencwd,* and *tancwd* (to give their unmutated forms). The imagery centers on *cwd* [pouch, bag, sack (cognate with Latin *cutis,* perhaps borrowed from English *cod*)] compounded with *tin* [bottom (of bag or person), breech, rump], *pen* [head, top], and *tan-* [sub-, under-]. *Tincwd* is generally taken to mean, as it certainly does later, "(contents of) the bottom of a bag or sack; small amount, remainder, *also fig.*; bottom, buttocks" (GPC, s.v. *tincwd*). The absence of mutation of the second element, *cwd* (rather than leniting to *-*gwd*) in both *tincwd* and *pencwd* suggests that *tin* and *pen* denote parts of a bag, or by extension the contents of that part, rather than different kinds of bag, though by the same logic we might expect *tangwd rather than the well-attested *tancwd* [scrotum] (Dafydd Johnston, personal communication; Morgan, *Treigliadau,* pp. 99–100). The later usage *tin y cwd* [bottom of the sack; the end of one's resources] suggests similarly that the compound is not tightly bound into a differentiating sense. Thus, the *tincwd – pencwd* opposition contrasts "(someone/something at) the bottom of the bag" with "(someone/something at) the top of the bag," and for "bag" in the present metaphoric context we might read "social order." It is likely that Gruffudd Llwyd is reflecting a preexisting proverbial contrast. The *tincwd – pencwd* pairing occurs in Thomas ap Wiliam's autograph collection of proverbs in NLW MS Mostyn 204 (1620), p. 16: *A vo bencwd, y sydd dincwd / A vo dincwd, y sydd bencwd* [Who would be a *pencwd* is a *tincwd* / Who would be a *tincwd* is a *pencwd*]), and in Dr. John Davies' collection of some two thousand proverbs in NLW MS Brogyntyn 11 (1632–44), p. 29: *A fu bencwd aeth yn dincwd* [Who (or what) was a *pencwd* became a *tincwd*], which he glosses, somewhat literally, in Latin, "*Rythm. Quod fuit os sacculi. factum est postremum sacculi. postremo, fundo, quod fuit consuitur &c fit fundus*" (GPC, s.v. *tincwd*). A triad of somewhat later but indeterminate date (possibly late seventeenth or eighteenth century) employs the same metaphoric notion: *Tri thincwd a dybiant eu hunain yn bencwd; cyvoethog o ledrad a chribddail, gwybodus ar ddichell-*

ion dihirdawd, a mab a gredwys y cyvan a ddywed ei vam am dano [Three "of low status" who suppose themselves "high status": one wealthy by theft and extortion, one expert in deceits and wickedness, and a boy who believed everything his mother said about him] (Jones et al., *Myvyrian Archaiology*, p. 896, no. 68).

Gruffudd Llwyd then draws on the extended sense of *tincwd*, "rear end, bottom," reinforced by (the metrically tempting) *tancwd* [scrotum], to give stronger, more explicit, even anatomical overtones to his use of the proverb than its usual "bottom/top of the barrel" implications. Gruffudd's appositive use of *hwd* [hood, from ME *hōd*] (albeit a magical or deceiving one) suggests that he is drawing on the literal sense of "a head covering" for *pencwd*, to which the *sangiad* or parenthesis refers. Thus, to contrast with the concrete image of *pencwd* as a hood for the head, *tincwd* is here translated as a similarly hoodlike or baglike item of nether clothing: a codpiece. However, because the codpiece was a fifteenth-century sartorial development, *tincwd* here might also mean simply "scrotum," which, as a derogatory metaphor, would have the advantage of attaching even greater opprobrium to the usurpers Gruffudd has in mind. In two later bawdy satirical poems, the poets Dafydd ab Edmwnd (fl. 1450–1490) and Llywelyn ap Gutun (fl. c.1480) also couple *tincwd* and *tancwd* (see Johnston, *Canu Maswedd*, pp. 126, 114).

19–20   The kite was common in medieval Britain and well known as a scavenger, as evidenced by its Welsh names, *bery*, and *barcud* [kite; *fig.*, plunderer], both from the Brythonic root **berg-*, *barg-*, attested also in Cornish *barges*, *bargos*, Middle Breton *barquet*, and Modern Breton *barged* [kite], and related to Irish *bergg* [spoiler, robber]. The element *-cud* is a borrowing from OE *kyta*, ME *kite* (*GPC*, s.v. *bery*, *barcud*). As a scavenger the kite is an apt metaphor for the oppressors who are the object of the poet's scorn; i.e., the scavenging kites are trying to behave like the more noble hawk or falcon, Welsh *gwalch*, pl. *gweilch*, long a bird of favorable comparison, as it is in Gruffudd ab yr Ynad Coch's famous elegy for Llywelyn ap Gruffudd (d. 1282): *Gwae fi am arglwydd, gwalch diwaradwydd* [Alas for a lord, hawk beyond reproach] (Parry, *Oxford Book*, p. 46; Clancy, *Medieval Welsh Poems*, p. 171), to give just one of many possible examples.

Alternatively, in MS A line 20 reads *bryhyrion kulion kwyl*, from which we might tease a quite different, if less likely, reading. *Bryhyrion* (usually *brehyrion*) is the plural of *brëyr* [nobleman], which Dafydd Jenkins defines as a "freeman who has come into his patrimony in land because all his ancestors in the direct male line are dead" (Jenkins, *Hywel Dda*, p. 320). Thus, if we take *kulion* as a figurative instance of the plural of the adjective *cul* [slender, narrow; *fig.*, narrowminded] and *cwyl* as a variant or misformation of *cŵl* [fault, blame, offence; sin, wrong], we have "faulty or blameworthy, narrow(minded) noblemen acting like hawks (i.e., predators?) at every chance."

22   *Pa fyd a fydd?* [What sort of world is to come?]. Literally, "What world will there be?" A: *pa ryw vyd vydd* [What sort of world will be?].

24   *hyd nad* [so that]. The construction *hyt na(d)* can express either a negative causation ("because . . . not") or a negative result ("[so] that . . . not,") (see Evans, *Grammar*, p. 238); either interpretation is possible here.

28   *cyfoedion* [contemporaries]. Plural of the adjective *cyfoed* [of the same age], hence, "(persons) of the same age (as)." A: *kywoedran* [(person) of the same age].

Caw. Caw o Brydain or *o Brydyn* [of Prydyn (= Scotland)] was a legendary figure of the fifth century, reputed to be the progenitor of numerous saints. In the *Vita Cadoci* (The Life of St. Cadog), Caw is a giant and an oppressive ruler. The two *Lives of St. Gildas* agree that the saint's father, Caunus (v.r. Cawus?) ruled in Scotland (see Bromwich, *Trioedd*, 1978, pp. 301–03; Bromwich and Evans, *Culhwch*, pp. 128–29). The genealogist Lewys Dwnn (c.1550–c.1616) compiled a list of Caw's twenty-two sons and three daughters from whom all the saints and many of the kings of Britain were descended (Dwnn, *Heraldic Visitations*, 2.104). Caw also appears as the father of nineteen sons and as a hero himself in *How Culhwch Got Olwen* (Bollard, *Companion Tales*, pp. 29, 41, 53, 70). Gruffudd invokes him here as the first of a series of representatives of the powerful heroes of the past.

30   *onaddun'* [from them]. A: *o honvn*. The forms *onaddunt* and *ohonunt* are variants of the third person plural of the preposition *o* [from]; the former has survived primarily in poetry.

31–32 *Brân . . . brawd Beli*. This is a reference to the story of Brân son of Dyfnwal Moelmud and his brother Beli as told in *Brut y Brenhinedd*, the Welsh translation of Geoffrey of Monmouth's *Historia regum Britanniae*. The names correspond to Geoffrey's Belinus and Brennius, sons of Dunwallus Molmutius, whose tale Geoffrey has blended with that of the Gaulish leader Brennus, who sacked Rome in 390 BCE (Bartrum, *Welsh Classical Dictionary*, p. 50). According to the *Brut*, Brân and Beli were reconciled after a period of discord and war, and together they went on to conquer France *ar holl wledydd hyt yn ruvein* [and every country as far as Rome]. After conquering the city of Rome, Beli returned to Britain and Brân remained as emperor (*Brut*, ed. Parry, pp. 45–52). (Brân and Beli ap Dyfnwal Moelmud should not be confused with the more widely known Brân Fendigaid / Bendigeidfran [Brân the Blessed], whose fate is told in *The Mabinogi*, and Beli Mawr [B. the Great], the ancestral progenitor claimed by all the early Welsh dynasties.)

33   *Custennin*. In *Brut y Brenhinedd*, Custennin Fendigaid [the Blessed] is the Welsh name corresponding to Geoffrey's *Constantinus*, the brother of Aldroen and grandfather of Arthur. Geoffrey seems to have conflated two or three historical figures with that name: Constantine (Welsh: *Custennin Gornau*), the sixth-century ruler of Dumnonia (Devon), who was attacked by Gildas in his *Epistle*; Constantine, the first Christian emperor (whose mother Helena was conflated in Welsh tradition with Elen Luyddog [of the Hosts], the heroine of *The Dream of Maxen Wledig*; and Constantine III the Usurper, whose troops in Britain proclaimed him emperor in 407 (Bartrum, *Welsh Classical Dictionary*, p. 157).

34   *Arthur*. Arthur is called *ameraudur llywyawdyr llauur* [emperor, ruler of battle toil] independently of (and probably earlier than) Geoffrey of Monmouth's *Historia* in a poem on Geraint ab Erbin (Rowland, *Early Welsh Saga Poetry*, pp. 240–43, 459, 505; Bollard, "Arthur," p. 15). Rowland points out that the phrase *amer-*

audur llywyawdyr was a poetic commonplace used by several court poets of the thirteenth and fourteenth centuries and "most probably a formula for a powerful leader without specific political or dynastic connotations" (*Early Welsh Saga Poetry*, pp. 639, 242); however, such a reference dovetails neatly with Geoffrey's extension of Arthur's career to the continent in his war against the emperor Lucius (*Brut*, ed. Parry, pp. 172–90). This account became a foundation stone of Welsh traditional history, especially through *Brut y Brenhinedd*. The inclusion of these three emperors in lines 29–34 and perhaps the reference to five score kings in lines 35–38 make it clear that Gruffudd Llwyd was acquainted with that work. Arthur is also referred to as *amherawdyr* in the (probably post-Galfridian) tales of *Peredur*, *Owain*, and *Geraint* (see Bollard, *Tales of Arthur*).

36–38   *brenhinoedd . . . bum hugain . . . coronog* [five score crowned kings]. This may be a reference to the approximately 100 kings of Britain listed throughout Geoffrey's *Historia regum Britanniae* and *Brut y Brenhinedd*. As Roberts notes, "The concept of a succession of single kings, sovereigns of Britain, is at the root of Geoffrey's view of the path of British history" ("Geoffrey," p. 102). It is worth noting here, too, that *Brut y Brenhinedd* reads *Llundein* [London] where Geoffrey uses the earlier name *Trinovantum* through the death of Vortimer and London afterward.

36   *bro iawn hynod* [quite remarkable region]. A: *in bro hynod* [our(?) remarkable region].

40   *tros Gymry* [in all of Wales]. Literally, "across Wales."

41–43   *Dafydd . . . o Hanmer*. Dafydd (or David) Hanmer was descended from a family of English origin in Flintshire, though from the reign of Edward I his forefathers had taken Welsh wives, as he did himself, and Owain Glyndŵr married his daughter, Margaret. The family remained supporters of Glyndŵr after 1400. Dafydd Hanmer was made a justice of the king's bench in 1383 and was knighted in 1386. His death in 1387 puts the dating of this poem within a fairly narrow time span.

44   *Grigor . . . Sais*. Sir Gregory Sais (aka Degory Sais, Desgarry Seys, etc.), a native of Flintshire, was the most prominent Welsh soldier in the English service during the second half of the fourteenth century. He first appears as a captain of Beaumont-le-Vicomte in Maine in 1360 and served in France, England, Wales, and Scotland. He was in Pembroke in 1377, and Owain Glyndŵr served under him at the northern border garrison in Berwick in 1384. In 1386 Sir Gregory was in Calais and in 1387 he was appointed to a command in Queenborough on the Isle of Sheppey in Kent. He died in 1390 (see Chapman, "David le Hope and Sir Gregory Sais"). The epithet or surname *Sais* means "Englishman" and was adopted by or given to some Welshmen who spoke English, adhered to English ways, lived for a time in England, or were in service to the English court or bureaucracy. Gruffudd Llwyd's description of Sir Gregory as *ail Sain Siôr* [a second St. George] certainly suggests his long career in and dedication to his service to the English court.

46   *gwayw ufelfellt* [lightning-sparked spear]. Literally, a "spear of sparking lightning." With this image of sparks from a shattered spear, compare Item 3.59–66, espe-

cially line 60, *gwayw ufeldan* [a fiery spear], and Iolo Goch's earlier poem to Syr Hywel y Bwyall, *A'r gŵr llwyd cadr paladrddellt / Yw Syr Hywel, mangnel mellt* [And the stout grey man with shattered spear / is Sir Hywel, lightning-throwing catapult] (Iolo Goch, *Poems*, pp. 6–7; trans. Johnston).

47   *phensel* [pennon]. The spirant mutation of *pensel*, a borrowing from OF *pen(on)cel* [small banner, pennon, standard], possibly through ME. Sir Hywel's standard is twice described in Iolo Goch's poem to him: *Ac ystondardd hardd hirddu / Yn nhâl tŵr, da filwr fu, / A thri blodeuyn gwyn gwiw / O'r unllun, dail arianlliw* [and a beautiful long black standard / on a tower top, he was a good soldier, / and three fine white flowers / of the same shape, silver-coloured leaves]; *Ystondardd – ys hardd o sud; / Pensel Syr Hywel yw hwn; / Myn Beuno, mae'n ei benwn / Tri fflŵr-dy-lis, oris erw, / Yn y sabl, nid ansyberw* [a standard – beautiful decoration; / this is Sir Hywel's pennoncel; by Beuno, in his pennon / Are three *fleurs-de-lis*, iris field, / in the sable, not uncourtly] (Iolo Goch, *Poems*, pp. 6–9, lines 23–26, 48–52; trans. Johnston). The conjunction of the images of lightning sparks and the pennon strongly suggests that Gruffudd Llwyd was familiar with Iolo's poem.

Syr Hywel. Sir Hywel y Fwyall [of the Axe] (d. c.1381) gained fame in the wars of Edward III in France. One tradition holds that he was knighted and made constable of Cricieth castle as reward for his deeds at the battle of Poitiers in 1356, where his battle-axe also earned him his nickname (see Iolo Goch, *Poems*, p. 158). An alternative, more likely, tradition suggests that he commanded a Welsh contingent at the battle of Crécy in 1346; he was receiving a knight's fee in the king's service at least a year before the battle of Poitiers (National Library of Wales Web site, Welsh Biography Online, s. n. *Hywel ap Gruffydd*).

48   *Otiel*. This is a variant of *Otuel*, the more usual Welsh form (also found in Norse and English) of the French *Otinel*, the name of the noble Saracen who converts to Christianity while in combat with Roland and who marries Charlemagne's daughter Belisent in the *chanson de geste* of the same name, which was translated into Welsh before 1336. When he first appears in the Welsh version he is described as *gwr a wedei yn anrydedus o bedeir ford, o arderchogrwyd pryt, a chedernit yn arueu, a chenedyl, a doethineb* [a man who deserved honor in four ways: for excellence of form, for strength in arms, and kindred, and wisdom] (Williams, *Ystorya*, p. 44). Cherrell Guilfoyle argues that Otuel was also a model for Shakespeare's Othello (Guilfoyle, "Othello").

aur ei otoyw [gold his spur]. This phrase could be in reference to Sir Hywel; in support of this reading compare Iolo Goch's exhortation to Sir Roger Mortimer, *A rho eto eur otoyw* [and put on again a gold spur] (Iolo Goch, *Poems*, 20.100), as well as Dafydd ap Gwilym's declaration that the gift of a kiss he received was *gwell no ruddaur otoyw* [better than a red-gold spur] (see Gruffydd, "Englynion y Cusan," p. 4). On the other hand, in the *Ystorya de Carolo Magno*, at the description of the arming of Otuel we are told, *A Roos o Rinuel a wisgwys am y draet dwy yspardun oedynt gywyrthyd a ryw gastell* [Rossete de Ruissel put on his feet two spurs that were as valuable as any castle] (Williams, *Ystorya*, p. 56). A golden spur, of course, is a hallmark of excellent knighthood in all these instances.

51   *Profyns* [Provence]. Sir Hywel, along with Sir Grigor Sais, served in Edward III's
            wars in France, though probably not as far to the southeast as Provence. Ifans
            suggests that *Profyns* might be a synecdoche (to fulfil the rhyme) or perhaps a
            reference to a force from Provence fighting with the king of France against
            Edward (*Gwaith*, ed. Ifans, p. 265).

52   *pryns*. I.e., Edward, Prince of Wales ("the Black Prince," 1330–1376), son of
            Edward III.

55–58   These lines are not in B.

55   *Ednywain*. This is possibly a reference to Ednywain Bendew ap Cynon, cited in
            Lewys Dwnn as the head of one of the fifteen tribes of Gwynedd, who held
            courts at Ysgeifiog and Whitford in Flintshire, or alternatively if even less likely
            to Ednywain ap Bradwen, lord of Dolgellau, and head of another of the fifteen
            tribes (Dwnn, *Heraldic Visitations*, 2.22, 83, 302–05; Lloyd-Jones, *Geirfa*, sv.
            Ednywein). Ifans points out that Hywel is an indirect descendant of Ednywain
            Bendew (*Gwaith*, ed. Ifans, p. 265).

59–60   These lines are not in A.

62   Following this line B includes lines 81–84 of Iolo Goch's poem in praise of
            Owain (Item 4); see also the note to lines 65–72 below. Such cross-pollination
            as we see in these poems is not evidence of one poet borrowing from another
            (though line 64 below may be such a case); rather, it is most often the effect of
            a long period of oral (and manuscript) transmission, as is also clear from the
            frequent variation in the order and sometimes the absence of lines of the same
            poem in different manuscripts.

64   *iôr Glyn, daeardor, Dyfrdwy* [the Lord of Glyn — narrow valley — Dyfrdwy]. This
            same line appears in Iolo Goch's poem in praise of Owain, but in reference to
            Owain's father (Item 4.16); there is no telling evidence in regard to this line
            that gives priority of date to one poem or the other. A reads *penllad glyn davyr-
            dad dyfrdwy* [the *summum bonum* of Glyn . . . (?) . . . Dyfrdwy]; the reading and
            sense of *davyrdad* are uncertain (Lewis et al., *Cywyddau*, p. 358n127.2).

65–72   These lines do not appear in A, which includes in their place lines 81–88 of Iolo
            Goch's poem on Owain's genealogy (see Item 6 below).

66   *cadfuarth* [fortress]. Literally, 'battle-yard,' from *cad* 'battle' + *buarth* (< *bu* 'head
            of cattle' + *garth* 'enclosure'). On Sycharth, Glyndŵr's fortified residence, see
            especially the elaborate description by Iolo Goch, Item 8, and the note to *buarth
            y beirdd* in line 92.

            ced fawr [of great bounty]. This phrase, *ced* 'gift, bounty' + *mawr* 'great, large,'
            most likely refers to *cadfuarth* [battle yard, fortress], but possibly to *Sycharth* or
            arglwyddfab [lord's son]; certainly Owain is meant by implication.

67   *hen* [old]. B: *hyn* [older].

70   *wrls* [borders]. A borrowing from OF *orl*, *url*; pl. *ho(u)rles*, or possibly from ME (see *MED*, s.v. *ourlen*). Decorative, especially gilded or fur edging was the legal prerogative of nobility in the Middle Ages, as is reflected in early Welsh law: *Try peth ny dele brenhyn e rannu ac arall: eursullt ac aryant, a kyrn bual, a guysc e bo urles eur urthy* [Three things a king ought not to share with another: gold treasure and silver, and buffalo horns, and clothing that has (gold) borders on it]; only one manuscript, from the thirteenth century, includes the word *eur* [gold] in the last phrase (Wiliam, *Llyfr Iorwerth*, p. 23; my translation; see also Jenkins, *Hywel Dda*, p. 41).

      ysgarlad [scarlet]. A borrowing from ME *scarlet* or OF *escarlate* (from Latin *scarlatum*); originally a rich cloth, usually but not invariably red, that was a symbol of high status; as in English it became a word for the red color itself.

      On the social significance of clothing and sumptuary laws in the fourteenth century, Barbara Tuchman points out that "exact gradations of fabric, color, fur trimming, ornaments, and jewels were laid down for every rank and income level" (Tuchman, *Distant Mirror*, p. 19; and see also pp. 20–21).

72   *gra* [fur]. A borrowing from ME *grai*, *grei* [gray; a gray fur]; *MED* identifies the fur as "prob. the fur of the back of the Russian gray squirrel in winter" (s.v. *grei*). Compare *mynfyr* [miniver] in Gruffudd's other poem to Owain (Item 3.11 and note).

      barwn [baron]. On the significance of the word *barwn* in Welsh context, see Item 6.1 note.

76   *cordwalfrith* [speckled cordovan]. From *cordwal* [cordovan (leather), cordwain] + *brith* [speckled]. In MW the form with -*l* is more common than that with -*n*, though *cordwan* also occurs. Though not noted in the *OED* or *MED*, the English forms *cord(e)wale*, -*wal(l)*, are recorded from the sixteenth century, originally an adjectival derivative of *Cordoba*; e.g., "Item . . . twa cordwale skynnis to cover ane sadill of the Frenche fassoun to the Kingis grace, price of the pece x s[hillings]" (Paul, *Accounts*, p. 205, also pp. 327, 425). This may have been the origin of the Welsh form. Leather from Córdoba, Spain, is a soft, fine-grained leather of goatskin or horsehide that was highly prized by European nobility in the Middle Ages.

79   *ar osteg* [at the call to silence]. One of the traditional court officers was the *gostegwr* (from *gosteg* [(call to) silence] + *gwr* [man]): "It is right for him to give service and to call for silence and to strike the post above the priest of the household. . . . His protection is from the first silence he proclaims [*o'r ostec kentaf*] until the last" (Jenkins, *Hywel Dda*, p. 21).

81   A reads, somewhat provocatively: *Add*[. . .] *gan loegr ni oddef*. The first word is hard to read, and the earlier editors, Henry Lewis et al., suggest *Addos?* or *Addic?* [angry?]. Thus, A may mean something like "He will not tolerate anger(?) by/from England."

6. IOLO GOCH, *OWAIN GLYNDŴR'S LINEAGE*

Ed. Dafydd Johnston. Trans. and notes, John K. Bollard.

Manuscripts: There are 33 manuscripts with considerable variation amongst them, with no one manuscript suitable as a base. Some couplets are missing in most manuscripts, e.g., lines 61–64 and 69–72. Lines 93–96 occur in only two manuscripts, but variation in line order and vocabulary throughout provides strong evidence of oral transmission, suggesting that it is quite possible for genuine lines to survive in only two copies.

The Welsh text is taken from Iolo Goch, *Gwaith*, ed. Johnston, pp. 36–38. Many of the following notes reflect editorial choices and comments in Johnston's textual notes, and similarly the general observations and interpretations below owe a great debt to his careful analysis.

Line 79, with its reference to Owain's service with Sir Gregory Sais in northern England and Scotland, dates the poem after 1385. References such as that to Sycharth (line 92), the bounds of Owain's inheritance and lands (e.g., lines 9–16, 60–64, 77, 93–94), and the lack of any reference to the stunning events of 1400 and afterwards, clarify definitively that the poem was composed before September 1400, at the very latest. Johnston argues that "Iolo is not urging Owain to rebel against English rule, but rather to demand his legal rights under that rule" (Iolo Goch, *Poems*, p. 163; see also the discussion on p. 510).

Genealogy was an important fact of life, especially among landowners, in medieval Wales, and as the living repositories of tradition and history, the poets give much attention to descent and relationships in their eulogies and elegies to their patrons. Owain's lineage was, naturally, a crucial aspect of his claims to rule over lands in Wales, whether limited to the various territories inherited from his parents or extending throughout the country. Iolo Goch's tribute to Owain's lineage is a prime example of the blending of genealogy, poetic praise, and perhaps political aspirations. In it is outlined Owain's descent from the dynasties that formerly ruled the three major divisions of medieval Wales. Genealogical records give Owain's descent from Bleddyn ap Cynfyn, the founder of the Powys dynasty, as follows, where *ap, ab* = "son of"; *ferch* = "daughter of"; and boldface indicates names cited in Iolo's poem (for the sources of these genealogies, see Iolo Goch, *Gwaith*, ed. Johnson, pp. 220–21):

> **Owain** ap **Gruffudd** ap **Gruffudd** ap **Madog Fychan** ap (Madog Crupl ap) Gruffudd ap Gruffudd ap Madog ap **Gruffudd Maelor** ap **Madog** ap **Maredudd** ap **Bleddyn** ap **Cynfyn**.

Lloyd puts forward the argument that Madog Grupl ("the Cripple;" or unlenited as *Crupl*, as listed above) is the same person as Owain Glyndŵr's great grandfather (*Owen Glendower*, p. 12n4). Bleddyn himself is traced elsewhere to **Teon** ap **Gwinau Dau Freuddwyd** ap **Pywyr Lew** and **Beli Mawr**, taking the line back to its legendary and mythological origins. Owain's descent from the rulers of Deheubarth is traced through his mother:

> Elen ferch Thomas ap Llywelyn ab Owain ap Maredudd ab Owain ap Gruffudd ab **Yr Arglwydd Rhys** ap Gruffudd ap Rhys ap **Tewdwr Mawr**.

Owain's connections to the ruler of Gwynedd are more distant, though crucial to his later claim to the title *Princeps Wallie*. Through the father of his great-grandmother, Gwenllian, the wife of Madog Fychan, he is related to an important family of Tegeingl, the northeastern-most cantref (analogous to the English "hundred") of Gwynedd:

Gwenllian ferch Ithel Fychan ab Ithel Gam ap Hen Ithel Gam ap Maredudd ap **Uchdryd** ab Edwin ap Goronwy.

And importantly, through her mother Adles, Gwenllian could trace her descent from Gruffudd ap Cynan, the great ruler of Gwynedd in the late eleventh and early twelfth centuries:

Adles ferch **Richard** ap Cadwaladr ap Gruffudd ap **Cynan**.

(For the sources of the above genealogies, see Iolo Goch, *Gwaith*, pp. 220–21, and Bartrum [1974], s.n. Bleddyn ap Cynfyn 5, 1.32.)

1 *farwn*. Lenited form of *barwn* [baron], a borrowing from ME *barun, baron, baroun*. On the appropriateness and the implications of this title in Wales, especially as applied to Owain Glyndŵr, Davies points out that "Owain belonged to a small, and diminishing, group of Welshmen most of whom were descended from the pre-Conquest native dynasties who held by the distinctive Welsh tenure of *pennaethium*, translated by English officials as 'Welsh barony'. . . . [These rulers] still proudly called themselves barons (W *barwniaid*)" (*Revolt*, pp. 133–34). See also lines 41–43 below and Items 5.11, 14; 8.19.

2 *dyhuddiant* [solace]. *GPC* glosses *dyhuddiant* as "solace, consolation; appeasement, pacification; reconciliation; propitiation; recompense, reward." The poet offers his praise especially, perhaps, to bolster Owain's outstanding claims to lands from his mother's family in southwest Wales (see lines 59–64), as well as to his broader claims as a descendant from the royal lines of Powys (lines 9–14), Deheubarth (lines 25–26), and even of Gwynedd (lines 43–46) (see the discussion on pp. 509–11). Johnston translates "reassuring praise" (Iolo Goch, *Poems*, 8.2).

6 *paun y Sirwern* [the peacock of Sirwern]. I.e., Owain. Sirwern was a cantref in southern Ceredigion, divided into the commotes of Is Coed and Gwynionydd and in which Owain inherited lands through his mother; see line 77.

7 *Faelawr*. Maelor was a commote in northeast Powys bordering England, bounded on the south and east by the Dyfrdwy. It was given the name *Maelor Gymraeg* (Welsh Maelor) to distinguish it from *Maelor Saesneg* (English Maelor). When the Anglo-Normans established their lordship there, they changed the name to Bromfield (Richards, *Enwau*, p. 29).

9 *ped fai fyd*. Literally, "if it were (a/the) world", but as Johnston points out, *byd* [world] often carries a positive connotation in the works of the poets of the period (Iolo Goch, *Poems*, p. 164); compare Dafydd ap Gwilym's "Elegy for Madog Benfras": *Gwladaidd oedd gwledydd, eddyw, / O bai fyd, na bai ef fyw* "[All] lands would be boorish — he has gone — / if it were a (fair) world, were he not alive" (see Dafydd ap Gwilym, *Poems*, 48.45–46, and dafyddapgwilym.net; my translation).

9–10   A very similar couplet, with the identical second line, occurs in Item 5.7–8.

11   *Y ddwy Faelawr* [the two Maelors]. See the note to line 7.

            mâl. Literally, "tax, rent," i.e., the wealth produced by rents from the region.

12   *Mathrafal*. Mathrafal was the principal seat of the medieval princes of Powys
            and, with Aberffraw in Gwynedd and Dinefwr in Deheubarth, one of the three
            royal residences of Wales (Lloyd, *History*, p. 249). In this and the following four
            lines Iolo suggests strongly that Owain has some claim to the rule of all Powys.

16   *Owain Gruffudd*. Might the absence of *ap* between these names suggest that
            Gruffudd is being used as a surname, after the English fashion? See the note to
            lines 63–64, below.

            Nudd. Nudd Hael [N. the Generous] is often named as a model by the poets of
            the period. In the Triads, he appears first among the "Three Generous Men of
            the Island of Britain" (Bromwich, *Trioedd*, Triad 2). In all likelihood, Nudd was
            a historical figure living in the north of Britain in the sixth century. The histor-
            ical poet Taliesin names "the sons (or descendants; lit., whelps) of Nudd Hael"
            (Williams, *Taliesin*, 8.45), and an early-sixth-century inscribed stone at Yarrow-
            kirk, Selkirkshire, has been translated in part to read, ". . . in this place lie the
            most famous princes Nudus and Dumnogenus; in this tomb lie the two sons of
            Liberalis." The connection between the names Nudus and Liberalis and the fact
            that the Welsh genealogies show that all Three Generous Men in the triad were
            first cousins suggest a family or clan noted for generosity (Bromwich, *Trioedd*,
            pp. 476–77). See also Item 27.25, 47.

18   *gryfgorff . . . gall*. Compare Dafydd ap Gwilym's pseudo-elegy for Rhydderch ab
            Ieuan Llwyd: *A'i gryfgorff gwyn digrifgall* "[and] his strong white body, merry and
            astute" (Dafydd ap Gwilym, *Poems*, ed. and trans. Bromwich, 46.36).

19–20   If we understand *iôr medeingl* and *yn ymseingian Eingl* as referring to Owain, the
            term *Eingl* [Angles] is best understood as a general reference to the northerners
            Owain opposed on the Scottish border in 1384–85; compare the similar use of
            Deifr in Item 5.58. On the other hand, if these phrases are descriptive of Madog
            Fychan, Owain's great-grandfather, they may, perhaps be taken more more
            generally as referring to the English.

19   *orwyr*. Lenited form of *gorwyr* [great-grandson]; see the note to lines 21–22.

21–22   *goresgynnydd* [descendant]. *Goresgynnydd* more specifically means "great-great-
            grandchild; grandchild of a grandchild; descendant in the fifth degree" (*GPC*,
            s. v. *goresgynnydd*). If the word is understood in this more specific sense, Iolo has
            skipped either one or more generations (depending on which Gruffudd Maelor
            he means), perhaps inadvertently, though he may not have intended to enu-
            merate every generation.

            Ruffudd . . . Maelor. Gruffudd Maelor (d. 1191) reunited much of northern
            Powys, which had been subdivided after the death of his father, Madog ap
            Maredudd.

23   *Madog.* Madog ap Maredudd (d. 1160), the last king of a united Powys. The line is ambiguous and might be read as "of the long-lived ancient line of Madog."

25   *hwyliwr.* Literally, "sailor," but often used more generally as "leader, guide, governor." Johnston quite elegantly translates it as "helmsman" (Iolo Goch, *Poems*, 8.25).

26   *Arglwydd Rhys.* Rhys ap Gruffudd ap Rhys ap Tewdwr became the sole ruler of Deheubarth in 1155, and after his act of homage to Henry II of England in 1158, he dropped the styling *brenin* [king]; in the chronicles he is henceforth known as *Yr Arglwydd Rhys* "the Lord Rhys." In 1164–65 he regained Ceredigion and the parts of Ystrad Tywi of which Henry had deprived him, and until his death in 1197 he was the most powerful magnate in Wales.

27   Bleddyn ap Cynfyn (d. 1075) and his brothers ruled Powys as vassals of Edward the Confessor. Within a few years after Bleddyn was killed by noblemen from Deheubarth in 1075, his sons had gained control of all of Powys. Bleddyn is consequently remembered as the founder of the line of Powys.

28   *Aedd.* This is probably a reference to Aedd Mawr [A. the Great], who is named in the medieval tract *Enweu Ynys Brydein* (*The Names of the Island of Britain*), which begins: "The first name that was upon this island before it was seized or settled: Myrddin's Cloister. And after it was seized and settled: The Honey Island. And after it was conquered by Prydain son of Aedd the Great the name 'The Island of Britain' was given to it" (Bollard, "Myrddin," p. 53; see also Bromwich, *Trioedd*, pp. 228, 263–64).

29   Maredudd ap Bleddyn, *Dux Powisorum*, died in 1132 (Lloyd, *History*, pp. 464–65).

30   *Carneddau Teon* [The Cairns (or Mounds) of Teon]. The Welsh name given to the Stiperstones in Shropshire, a five-mile ridge topped with several impressive natural outcrops some ten miles southeast of Welshpool. In the genealogies Teon is the son of Gwinau Dau Freuddwyd and the progenitor of several tribes, especially in Powys (Bartrum, *Welsh Classical Dictionary*, p. 609).

31   *Gwinau Dau Freuddwyd* [Gwinau Two Dreams]. The son of Pywer Lew and one of the legendary forebears of the line of Powys. Early Welsh genealogical tracts place him in the second half of the seventh century. The story behind the epithet *Dau Freuddwyd* is not known. He is named as an ancestor of the mid-ninth-century saint Llywelyn o'r Trallwng (of Welshpool) (Bartrum, *Welsh Classical Dictionary*, p. 327). Dafydd ap Gwilym cites Gwinau Dau Freuddwyd as an ancestor of Hywel ap Goronwy, Dean of Bangor (Dafydd ap Gwilym, *Gwaith*, 15.5–6).

32   *Bywer Lew.* Pywer (or Bywyr) the Brave was one of the legendary forebears of the line of Powys. Early Welsh genealogical tracts place him in the first third of the seventh century (Bartrum, *Welsh Classical Dictionary*, p. 72).

    fy llew llwyd [my tawny lion]. The poet refers to Owain as a lion three more times in this poem (lines 55, 56, 77), and four times in his later poem during the rebellion (Item 27.25, 30, 31, 46). Gruffudd Llwyd uses the same comparison once (Item 2.52).

33   *Ednyfed*. This may be a reference to Ednyfed Fychan (d. 1246), the steward of
      Llywelyn the Great. His relationship to Owain Glyndŵr can be traced through
      Owain's paternal great-great-grandmother, Adles, the wife of Tudur ab Edny-
      fed Fychan (Bartrum [1974], s.n. Marchudd 5, 4.672).

34   *Uchdryd lwyd*. Uchdryd ab Edwin ap Goronwy was a forebear of Owain's great-
      grandmother Gwenllian, through whom Owain is connected to the rulers of
      Gwynedd. The term *llwyd* literally means "grey" (and other pale colors),
      through which it developed the senses "grey-haired, old, ancient, senior." Be-
      cause of the eight generations between Owain and Uchdryd, it has been inter-
      preted in the translation in the literal sense "grey," rather than the genera-
      tional sense "senior." There is also a sense "holy," as Johnston translates it in
      this line; the evidence cited for this sense in *GPC*, however, is markedly reli-
      gious in content (*GPC*, s.v. *llwyd* [d]; see also Item 53.26).

35   *Dewdwr Mawr* [Tewdwr the Great]. Probably Tewdwr ap Cadell, the father of
      Rhys ap Tewdwr (eleventh-century king of Deheubarth), is meant. Elsewhere
      he first appears with the cognomen *Mawr* in the genealogies of Gutun Owain
      in the late fifteenth century (Bartrum, *Welsh Classical Dictionary*, p. 612).

37   *Faig Mygrfras*. Maig Myngfras [Thick-/Long-haired (< *mwng* "mane" + *bras*
      "thick")] appears in genealogical tracts as the brother of Brochwel Ysgithrog ap
      Cyngen, legendary king of Powys in the fifth century, and his name is preserved
      in that of the region of Meigen in Powys. He is cited by the poets as a model of
      comparison as early as the mid thirteenth century, and he is named in Triad
      79 as the father of Afan, one of the Three Lively Maidens of the Island of Bri-
      tain (Bartrum, *Welsh Classical Dictionary*, p. 445; Bromwich, *Trioedd* (1978), pp.
      199, 455–56). The epithet *myngfras* is a fairly uncommon term that appears in
      Y Gododdin and other sources as descriptive of horses, as in *Aduwyneu Taliessin*
      [Taliesin's Pleasant Things], a poem possibly by Llywarch ap Llywelyn (Prydydd
      y Moch; fl. c.1174/5–c.1220): *Atwyn march mygvras mangre* [Fair is the thick-
      maned stallion in the stud] (Haycock, *Legendary Poems*, 3.11). There is, however,
      sufficient agreement among the manuscripts to suggest that the form *mygrfras*
      [fine and stout] (< *mygr* [fine, beautiful] + *bras* [thick, stout]), is intentional and
      probably original with Iolo Goch.

39   *eurddor*. Literally, *eur*- [gold(en)] + *dôr* [door]; both elements are frequently used
      metaphorically, and the compound itself occurs in poems by Einion ap Madog
      (c.1237), Casnodyn (fl. 1320–40), and Gruffudd ap Maredudd (fl. 1352–82).

40   Richard ap Cadwaladr, a forebear of Owain's great-grandmother Gwenllian,
      through her mother.

42   *bybyrach*. The lenited comparative of *pybyr*, for which *GPC* gives a striking range
      of positive renderings almost any of which would suit the context here: "lively,
      eager, zealous, staunch, enthusiastic, ardent; vigorous, strong, mighty, valiant,
      brave; fine, splendid, bright, shining, clear." Johnston translates "mightier"
      (Iolo Goch, *Poems*, 8.42). In origin, the adjective may be a reduplication of the
      root of the verb *peri* [to make, cause, prepare]; less likely is a derivation from
      the noun *pybyr* [pepper], a borrowing from Latin *piper*.

43–44 The same couplet, with trivial variation, occurs in Item 5.11–12.

45 *gorwyr*. See the notes to lines 20 and 21–22.

dioer. From *Duw a wyr* [God knows] translated etymologically here, though it may also carry the attenuated, generalized sense of "certainly, indeed."

47 *y ddwy Wynedd* [the two Gwynedds]. Gwynedd was broadly divided into *Gwynedd Uwch Conwy* [Gwynedd above the Conwy] to the west of that river and *Gwynedd Is Conwy* [Gwynedd below the Conwy] to the east. Iolo also mentions *y ddwy Wynedd* in line 16 of the "Conversation between the Soul and the Body" from which a passage is included herein as Item 2.

50 *Arth o Ddeheubarth*. This may echo a passage from the prophetic poem in the *Black Book of Carmarthen* known as the *Oianau*, the "Oian, Little Pig" stanzas attributed to Myrddin [= Merlin]: *Arth o deheubarth a dirchafwy. / Rylletaud y wir ew tra thir mynvy* [A bear from Deheubarth will arise; his justice will spread beyond the land of Mynwy] (Jarman, *Llyfr Du*, p. 33; Bollard, "Myrddin," p. 28).

54 *Beli*. Owain is identified here with the legendary Beli Mawr [B. the Great], king of Britain before the coming of the Romans. He figures significantly in the genealogies as the ancestor of Cunedda and Coel Hen (= "Old King Cole") (Bartrum, *Welsh Classical Dictionary*, pp. 38–39). Beli is named several times as a forebear in the second and third branches of *The Mabinogi*, in *How Culhwch Got Olwen*, and as the father of Lludd and Llefelys in *The Story of Lludd and Llefelys* (Bollard, *Mabinogi*, p. 125; Bollard, *Companion Tales*, pp. 30, 89). In *The Dream of Maxen Wledig* it is said that Maxen "conquered the island by force from Beli son of Manogan and his sons, and he drove them over the sea . . ." (Bollard, *Companion Tales*, p. 81). For the construction *y Glyn* [of the Glyn] in reference to Owain, see the note at Item 3.88.

55 *Prydain*. This is the only instance of *Prydain* in the works of Iolo Goch. There is often confusion in Middle Welsh texts and later manuscripts between *Prydain* [Britain] and *Prydyn* [Pictland, Scotland]. Johnston translates as "Scotland" and interprets it as a reference to Owain's service there. However, while this line is found in only five manuscripts, they consistently read *Prydain*, and the six references to Scotland in four of his poems regularly read *Prydyn*. Thus, though either interpretation is possible here, a more general and broader note of praise is conveyed through the rendering "Britain."

Peredur. Peredur is the hero of the Welsh Arthurian tale known by his name, *The History of Peredur*, analogous to Perceval in Chrétien de Troyes' *Conte du Graal* (Bollard, *Tales of Arthur*, pp. 21–62; Bollard, "Theme"). The comparison with Peredur here, in conjunction with Iolo's evocation of Owain's spear (*soced dur* [socket of steel] in the next line, is apt given Peredur's epithet *Paladr Hir* [Long Spear] (Bollard, *Tales of Arthur*, p. 52).

56 Compare Item 4.38: *Soced dur a siaced tew*.

siaced [jacket, tunic]. A borrowing from ME *jaket* [jacket], itself from a diminutive of Old French *jaque*. It is a lexical curiosity that *siaced* in this poem appears perhaps sixty years earlier than English *jaket* (cited from 1451), which in turn is known earlier than French *jaquette*, not cited until the late fifteenth-century (see *GPC*, s.v. *siaced*; *MED*, s.v. *jaket*).

soced. A borrowing from ME or Anglo-French *soket* [a spearhead, originally shaped like a plowshare] (*MED*, s.v., *soket*).

58   *Lloegr*. Originally the Welsh name for the area known to the Anglo-Saxons as Mercia, *Lloegr* became generalized to refer to England as a whole, though its derivation from the name for that part of England bordering Owain's territory is worth noting in the present context.

59   *edling*. A borrowing from Old English *æðeling* [man of royal blood, chief, prince]. In early Welsh law, the *edling* is equated with the *gwrthrych(iad)*, the heir apparent (see lines 63–64 and the note below): "The heir-apparent, to wit the edling, who is entitled to reign after the King, is entitled to be the most honoured in the court, except the King and Queen. It is right for him to be a son or a nephew of the King" (Jenkins, *Hywel Dda*, p. 6). In *How Culhwch Got Olwen*, Arthur accords to Culhwch "the privilege of a prince [*edling*], the heir of a kingdom, upon you as long as you may be here" (Bollard, *Companion Tales*, p. 27).

60   *Tref y Traeth*. Literally, "settlement/farm/estate on the beach;" Trefdraeth/Newport in Dyfed.

62   *Tref y Garn*. Trefgarn-Owen in Brawdy Parish, Dyfed, where Owain's aunt, Margaret, held land. Lloyd comments, "Iolo's line implies, I think, a claim, and not ownership"; the name comes not from Owain Glyndŵr, but from Owain ap Llywelyn ab Owain, who inherited it in 1309 (*Owen Glendower*, p. 19n3).

63–64   *gwrthrych(iad)*. The native Welsh legal term for the presumptive heir to a throne, literally, "one who looks forward, or who expects or anticipates" (cognate with Old Irish *frescissid). The ending *-iad* is a derivative noun ending. The use of the legal terms *edling* and *gwrthrych(iad)* highlights Owain's claim to lands in Pembrokeshire, though that claim, coming through his mother's family as it did, would not pertain according to Welsh legal tradition, which did not recognize the right of women to hold land; however, Owain's grandfather and father had gained the privilege of English legal status (Davies, *Revolt*, p. 136), which would have meant that Owain could inherit his mother's lands according to English law. It is perhaps also pertinent that these terms are used in Welsh legal texts and elsewhere to identify specifically the heirs of kings and rulers, and they may thus serve here to bolster Owain's proposed status as a ruler over all Wales (see line 97), even if that was meant by Iolo only as a poetic fiction at the time of composition.

64   *Acharn*. Henry Lewis posits that the name *Talacharn* (Eng., *Laugharne*) is a compound of *tâl* [end] and an earlier name, *Acharn* [Iolo Goch, *Cywyddau*, ed. Lewis et al., p. 346]. Richards, however, suggests somewhat inconclusively that *Talacharn* "appears to be a compound of the word *tâl* and the noun *lacharn*, whatever that is" (Richards, *Enwau*, p. 49; my translation). Iolo Goch's use of *Acharn* here would seem to support the former.

65	*dihaereb*. Here *dihaereb* [exemplar] functions adjectivally; compare Item 4.17.
67	*gŵr . . . a grybwyllir*. Iolo uses this same line in his "Praise of Sir Roger Mortimer" (Iolo Goch, *Poems*, 20.20); see also the note to line 96 below.
69	*marchog*. Marchog (< *march* "horse" + the agentive suffix *-og*) carries a range of meanings from the literal "horseman, rider" to "mounted warrior" to "knight" that often raises difficulty in translation. Certainly it was often understood as "knight" in the fourteenth century, as it is in the Welsh Arthurian tales such as *The History of Peredur*: "'Say, friend,' asked Owain, 'have you seen a knight [*marchog*] going past here either today or yesterday?' 'I do not know,' he replied, 'what a knight is.' 'The sort of thing I am,' said Owain" (Bollard, *Tales of Arthur*, p. 23). While Owain Glyndŵr was not an ordained knight as that office is generally understood (especially in relation to the English crown), he is, of course, consistently described as an accomplished warrior, and his status as a nobleman clearly qualifies him, in Welsh eyes at least, for knighthood; compare Gruffudd Llwyd's promotion of Owain following his complaint that there were but three ordained knights in Wales in Item 5, especially lines 39–48.
71–72	This couplet is obscure. The *sangiad* (parenthesis) of line 71, *asgwrn nerth esgud* [bone of quick strength], refers to Owain; elsewhere Iolo describes Sir Hywel y Bwyall as *Asgwrn hen yn angen in* [old bone in our time of need] (Iolo Goch, *Poems*, 2.60). The phrase *o'i droed* [from his foot] might be understood as part of the main clause: "His war cry rose up from his foot," i.e., from deep within him.
73–76	Iolo Goch adopts this contrastive device in two other poems (Iolo Goch, *Poems*, 11.63–70, 16.89–92). An important stylistic antecedent is found in the elegy by Cynddelw Brydydd Mawr for Owain Gwynedd (d. 28 Nov. 1170):

> *Gwlyt wrth wlyt wrth wlad gyuanhet.*   Mild to the mild in a pleasant land.
> *Garw wrth arw wrth awr gyminet.*   Harsh to the harsh at the hour of battle.

This passage continues in the same mode with the same grammatical construction for five more lines (Morris-Jones, *Llawysgrif Hendregadredd*, fol. 36b.33–39). Along with other features, this demonstrates the degree to which a poet of Iolo's skill was steeped in a deep poetic tradition; see also, for example, the notes on lines 18, 39, 50, 79, 87, 92.

76	*aflonydd* [ungentle, severe, harsh]. The negative of *llonydd* [still, calm, tranquil, peaceful, courteous, gentle], etc., as in lines 74–75.
	fileiniaid [villains]. The Welsh term underwent a semantic development similar to the English: "an unfree person" > "a person of low status" > "an uncouth person, a churl" > "a rascal, a villain." Given the implications of the present contrastive context, the English cognate is retained in the translation. See also Item 6.6 note.
77	*Is Coed*. A commote in southern Ceredigion, where Owain's maternal line held land; see the note to line 6 above.
79	*llithio'r brain* [feeding the ravens]. Twice elsewhere Iolo makes striking use of the ancient "beasts of battle" motif. In his poem to Edward III, the army itself

becomes the ravens: *Llithio dy fyddin, lin lem, / Frain byw, ar frenin Böem* [You fed your army, cruel battle-line, / human crows, on the king of Bohemia] (Iolo Goch, *Poems*, 1.41–42). The coupling of the image of the ravens with that of the heavy spear (line 80) is also found in Iolo's elegy for Tudur Fychan of Penmynydd: *Yswain wayw lithfrain lwythfraich* [a squire's crowfeeding armburdening spear] (Iolo Goch, *Poems*, 4.78).

Brynaich. Originally meaning "the land or people of Bernicia (the Anglo-Saxon kingdom in northeastern England and Scotland), *Brynaich* came to refer to the English generally. Here, however, Iolo intends the Scots inhabiting the same area; compare his use of *Deifr* in Item 5.58, and see the note there, also Item 27.29. As a reference to Owain's service in Berwick with Sir Gregory Sais this dates the poem later than 1384.

81–88   A version of lines 81–88 is appears in one of Gruffudd Llwyd's poems to Owain (Item 4) following line 64 in MS A and of lines 81–84 following line 66 in MS B; for details, see the note to Item 4.65–72. This is evidence, not of priority of date for either poem, but rather of later oral transmission.

83   *eurddrem* [beautiful visage]. Literally, "golden aspect/sight." For *eur-* as a metaphor for brightness, beauty, or excellence, see the note to line 39 above and Item 8.24.

          hwyl [temper, mood; nature, disposition]. Johnston translates this as 'course', drawing on the related sense of 'rush, attack' in line 40.

84   *Maig*. See the note to line 37.

85–92   These lines form two interlacing sentences, further complicated by the *sangiad* or insertion of *coel a honnir* [belief is declared] of line 89. Disentangling them gives us, "Teeth are good in front of the tongue in the depths of an unskilled mouth. A day will come when he shall get (the belief is declared) the heart of Is Aeron and its cheer, and health," etc. These same lines are added to the end of four manuscript copies of Item 5, *q.v.*

87   *da . . . tafod*. This is a traditional proverb found in manuscript collections from the mid thirteenth century and later. Its earliest surviving citation is as the last line of the poem of the poet-prince Hywel ap Owain Gwynedd (d. 1170) praising (or boasting of) women he has known: *Cefais saith, ac ef gwaith gorddygnawd; / Cefais wyth yn nhâl pwyth; peth o'r wawd yr gaint; / Ys da daint rhag tafawd* [I had seven and an arduous business it was; / I had eight, repaying some of the praise I sang; / teeth are good to keep the tongue quiet!] (Parry, *Oxford Book*, p. 27; trans. Williams, *Welsh Poems*, p. 38).

90   *Is Aeron*. Southern Ceredigion below [W *is*] the river Aeron, which includes the eastern portion of the commote of Is Coed and the western portion of the commote of Gwynionydd, where Owain held claim to lands through his mother and her sister.

          sir. Pronounced like English *sheer*, this is a borrowing from ME *chere* [cheer, kindness, friendliness, hospitality], or possibly ME *shire* [shire, region, district, area].

92   *Sycharth*. Owain's home in Cynllaith, described at length in Item 8 below.

     buarth y beirdd. *Buarth Beirdd* is the title of one of the vaunting poems of the legendary, all-knowing poet Taliesin in the *Book of Taliesin*, and the phrase also occurs in line 6 of that poem. The basic meaning of *buarth* is "an enclosure or pen for cattle or other animals; a farmyard." *GPC* (s.v., *buarth*) also identifies the sense of a "place of resort or assembly, rendezvous," which Haycock sees as the likely meaning in *Buarth Beirdd*, where Taliesin claims to best 15,000 less capable poets (Haycock, *Legendary Poems*, pp. 79, 82 title note). Similarly, Iolo Goch elsewhere uses *buarth* as a gathering place for poets: *Buarth clyd i borth clêr / Heb wrthod neb a borther* [a snug enclosure to nurture poets / without refusing anyone who would be nurtured] (Iolo Goch, *Poems*, Poem 5.45–46). See also Gruffudd Llwyd's reference to Sycharth as *cadfuarth* (Item 5.66).

93–96   These four lines are found in only two manuscripts, but as they are completely characteristic of Iolo's style, Johnston sees no reason to reject them (Iolo Goch, *Gwaith*, p. 227 note, and see the headnote above).

93   *Corwen, Dyfrdwy, Conwy, Cain*. This line maps out Owain's territory in Powys, bounded by the valley of the Dyfrdwy (Dee) to the north, the Cain to the south, and the Conwy to the west. Located where the Dyfrdwy turns from flowing generally northeast to east, Corwen had been a significant ecclesiastical center with as many as sixteen clerics in the early thirteenth century, and lands in the area owed rents held by Owain's estate (see Davies, *Revolt*, p. 131).

95   This line continues the comparison to Cai, who, in contrast to his later reputation for surliness as Sir Kay in French and English romance, was one of the earliest and greatest of Arthur's warriors in early Welsh poetic and narrative tradition. Iolo's comparison may not be simply generic; the Arthurian poem known as *Pa gur* or "What man is the porter?" says of Cai, "Vain was an army / compared to Cei in battle. / He was a sword in battle; / he pledged with his hand" (Bollard, "Arthur," p. 18); compare also the attention to Cai's hands in the flamboyant tale of *How Culhwch Got Olwen*: "there will be no warmth in his hands . . . . when the rain was hardest, whatever was in his hand would be dry a hand's breadth above his hand and another below his hand, so great was his heat" (Bollard, *Companion Tales*, pp. 31, 34).

96   A nearly identical line occurs in Iolo's "Praise of Sir Roger Mortimer": *ŵyr burffrwyth iôr Aberffraw* [descendant of the pure-fruited lord of Aberffraw] (Iolo Goch, *Poems*, 20.14); see also the note to line 67 above. Given the effects of oral transmission and the fact that the line occurs in only two manuscripts, Johnston queries whether *eur* [gold(en)] should not be amended to *ŵyr* [descendant] or *aer* [heir], (the latter a borrowing from Middle English). Note that such an emendation would change *purffrwyth* from a noun referencing Owain as a descendant of the *iôr Aberffraw* to an adjective modifying *iôr Aberffraw* itself. The "lord of Aberffraw" would be Gruffudd ap Cynan, the renowned king of Gwynedd (d. 1137) (Iolo Goch, *Gwaith*, p. 227).

Aberffraw. The chief court of the rulers of Gwynedd in southwestern Anglesey, which claimed preeminence over the other courts in Wales; see the note to line 12 above.

99   *caith*. Literally, "slaves," but here, like *bilainiaid* in line 76, it is a more generalized term of opprobrium.

7. SCROPE-GROSVENOR TRIAL REPORT

Adapted and trans. by Michael Livingston, from *De controversia*, ed. Nicolas, 1.254–55.

The Scrope-Grosvenor trial is one of the most famous heraldic law cases in history. During Richard II's 1385 invasion of Scotland, Richard Scrope of Bolton and Robert Grosvenor of Cheshire discovered that they were bearing the same coat of arms blazoned *azure a bend or* (see note to line 3, below). Scrope brought an action against Grosvenor, who made the claim that the arms went back to a member of his family who had come to English shores with William the Conqueror. When the case went to trial, hundreds of witnesses were called, including John of Gaunt, Geoffrey Chaucer, and both Owain Glyndŵr and his brother, Tudur. The case was decided in 1389 in Scrope's favor.

The trial is remarkable in part for the record of its proceedings, which give us insight into biographical and at times historical details that would otherwise elude us. It is here, for instance, that we get the most direct information about Owain's age (see line 1). As Lloyd observes, the transcript reveals much about how Owain was set in "a crowd of well-born young squires, learned in heraldic distinctions and the customs of chivalry. This is his world, and he is perfectly at home in it" (*Owen Glendower*, p. 24).

1   Of present interest in Owain's testimony is the report of his age, which is given as "twenty-seven years and more." The trial took place between 1386 and 1389, but Owain was among the early witnesses called: his testimony took place in Chester on 3 September 1386 (Lloyd, *Owen Glendower*, p. 23). Thus the latest year of his birth would be 1359. His brother, Tudur, is described in the same records as being over the age of twenty-four, while his brothers-in-law John Hanmer and Robert Puleston were twenty-two and twenty-eight.

3   *azure a bend or*. Such is the heraldic language. In layman's terms, the arms in question were a blue (*azure*) background with a single golden stripe (*a bend or*) running from top left to bottom right.

9   This invasion of Scotland occurred in August 1385.

8. IOLO GOCH, OWAIN GLYNDŴR'S COURT

Ed. Dafydd Johnston. Trans. and notes, John K. Bollard.

Manuscripts: There are 24 manuscripts; the best are British Library MSS B 23 and B 24, which are the basis for this text. There are some couplets missing in B 23, but none in B 24.

The Welsh text is taken from Iolo Goch, *Gwaith*, ed. Johnston, pp. 46–50. Many of the following notes on the text reflect editorial choices and comments in Johnston's textual notes, and similarly the general observations and interpretations below owe a great debt to his careful analysis.

Internal evidence provides some help in establishing an approximate date for the poem. Owain's wife is referenced in lines 81–84, and it is believed that he married Margaret Hanmer around 1383 (Lloyd, *Owen Glendower*, p. 25; Iolo Goch, *Gwaith*, p. 231). Margaret Hanmer's father was probably knighted in 1386–87, which establishes a *terminus post quem* for the poem. Lines 85–86 suggest that Margaret may have had four, possibly more, children by the time of composition, which also suggests 1387 at the earliest. There is not the slightest hint in the poem of the troubles of 1400 and afterward, much less the destruction of Sycharth in 1403. Thus, the most likely period fitting the poem would be from the late 1380s to the late 1390s.

The motte-and-bailey castle at Sycharth may have been built as early as the twelfth century, but there is little evidence prior to this poem. Excavations of the motte have revealed the remains of two earth-and-timber buildings. A larger hall and other structures may have been built within the bailey (RCAHMW, s.n. *Sycharth*; for details, see Hague and Warhurst, "Excavations").

1–4	The implication of the first four lines is that Iolo Goch has promised, and presumably twice kept his promise, to visit Owain's home at Sycharth, most likely as he makes his poetic circuit to various noble houses and patrons.
1	*hyd* [as far as]. This is the reading of B 23 and B 24. Most of the other manuscripts read *Addewais yt hyn* 'I have promised you this,' but nowhere else in the poem does the poet address Owain (or anyone else) directly. The reading *yt* 'to you' probably arose during oral transmission, for a final *-d* before *h-* becomes voiceless *-t* (Iolo Goch, *Gwaith*, p. 231). Similarly, *h-* after *-s* might not be heard.
3–4	Literally, "Let each one pay, paying as far as may be / his promise that he may promise."
5	*ffyddlawn*. *Ffyddlawn* may be the adjective 'faithful', but it might also be nominal 'a faithful person/servant', giving the reading "the (good) fortune of a faithful one" (i.e., Iolo himself).
6	*mawr iawn*. "Very great," modifying *pererindawd* 'pilgrimage'.
7	*eidduned*. Perhaps 'oath, promise,' as translated here, but 'desire' is the sense of earlier instances of the word; it is derived from the same root as *addaw* 'to promise', *addewid* 'a promise', which occurs five times in lines 1–4.
7, 9	*oddáin*. This is a rare word, and all the manuscripts read *ddain*. The original form is *eddëin* 'foreign, strange, unfamiliar, wondrous'. With the stress remaining on the final syllable as *ë-i* became the diphthong *ai*, the initial vowel became obscured and, in some cases, lost. However, B 23 and B 24 are both a syllable short in these lines, and on this basis, reinforced by Iolo's use of the form *oddáin* elsewhere, also with the sense 'swift', the emended reading has been adopted here (see Iolo Goch, *Poems*, 23.45). It is not easy to account for the semantic shift from 'foreign, strange' to 'swift', but the latter is clear in other examples (see *GPC*, s.v. *dain*).

12   Johnston comments, "It is an honor for Iolo that Owain and he greet each other as friends" (Iolo Goch, *Gwaith*, p. 232n12; my translation).

14   *cleiriach* [decrepit old man]. This borrowing from Irish *cléireach* [cleric] seems to be one of Iolo's favorite words, occurring (once in the form *cleirch*) no fewer than eight times in his poetry. Six of these are in humorous reference to himself; the remaining examples are found in two of his biting satires and clearly show the term's pejorative connotations. Somewhat earlier Dafydd ap Gwilym has a similar sardonic, self-referential use of *cleirch* in "The Magpie's Advice": "It is but vain for you . . . / despicable grey old man, half imbecile / . . . to rave about a sparkling girl" (Dafydd ap Gwilym, *Poems*, ed. and trans. Bromwich, 25.44–48).

18   *o'r deucant.* Literally, 'of the two hundred,' but the definite article *y/'r* may be used as an emphatic indefinite; see the note at Item 4.47.

19   *barwn* [baron]. On the significance of this word, see Item 6.1 note.

            syberwyd [nobility]. Literally, "pride" (here in a good sense). For the range of its implications, compare this description of Arthur's court from one of the Welsh versions of Geoffrey of Monmouth's *History of the Kings of Britain*: *A chymeint oed syberwyt llys Arthur o uoes a gvybot a haelder a daeoni a dewred a milwraeth ac nat oed dim gan neb o'r a'e clywhei ony allei ymgyffelybu vrthi* ["And so great was the nobility/pride of Arthur's court in manners and courtesy and generosity and goodness and bravery and prowess that there was nothing that anyone had heard of that could compare with it"] (*Brut Dingestow*, ed. Lewis, pp. 153–54; my translation).

21   *gwawr* [queen]. The ultimate source of *gwawr* is the Indo-European root that also gives us Latin *aurora*. The literal sense of "dawn, sunrise, break of day" is often used figuratively, and *gwawr-* is also used for both "lord, chieftain, hero, etc." and "queen, princess, lady, noblewoman, etc." If we accept this reading, such personification of the court is very striking.

24   *eurgylch.* Literally, "a golden circle"; for *eur-* "gold(en)" as a metaphor for brightness, beauty, or excellence, compare line 14 above and Item 6.39, 83.

27–28   *cyplau . . . cwplws . . . cwpledig . . . cwpl. Cwpl* (pl. *cyplau*), like ME *couple* from which it is borrowed, is an architectural term for one of a pair of joined rafters or for the pair together. *Cwplws* is a Welsh spelling of the ME plural *couples*; *cwpledig* is *cwpl* + the adjectival ending *-edig*. These lines provide a fine example of both Iolo Goch's readiness to borrow English terms and his delight in clever wordplay. Though some poets were opposed to the use of English vocabulary, incorporating English terminology into the complexities of *cynghanedd* (see pp. 516–17) must have had a satisfying, often humorous, effect on both the poets of the period and their listeners.

29–30   In these lines, Iolo compares Sycharth to two of the finest and most impressive examples of fourteenth-century architecture in the British Isles.

29   *clochdy Padrig* [Patrick's bell-house]. The belltower of St. Patrick's Cathedral, Dublin, was built between 1363 and 1370. According to Bernard, "This great work of Archbishop Minot's is unrivalled in Ireland, and unsurpassed as a

belfry in the United Kingdom. It stands 147 feet in height from the nave floor to the battlements, and is 39 feet square at the base, with walls 10 feet thick of Irish limestone. No unskilled labourers like those of whom tradition speaks could have executed such work, and Minot must have employed as foremen the best masons of his time" (*Cathedral*, pp. 31–33).

Ffrengig ffrwyth [French fruit]. Johnston notes that "*Ffrengig* is often used by the poets as a term of praise" (Iolo Goch, *Poems*, p. 165), but we may have here a more particular allusion to the renown of French architecture and architectural developments of the thirteenth and fourteenth centuries.

clostr Wesmustr [Westminster Cloister]. After the great fire at the abbey in 1298, much of the cloisters of Westminster Abbey were rebuilt, with work completed by 1364.

34   *daeardy* [earthen house, dungeon]. A compound of *daear* [earth] + *tŷ* [house]. Johnston suggests that the idea here is that there are no chinks or open spaces in the walls (Iolo Goch, *Gwaith*, p. 234).

37   *tai nawplad* [nine-plate houses]. *Plad* [plate] is an architectural term borrowed from ME: "A horizontal beam at the top of the lateral walls of a house upon which the bottom end of the rafters rests, a wall plate" (*MED*, s.v. *plate* 7). Interestingly, the earliest citation in the *MED* is from 1428. The number nine is probably used here as an ideal number, as also in lines 49–50, though there may be a connection to the nine "houses," actually rooms, chambers, or areas with specific functions, not necessarily separate buildings, enumerated in early Welsh law: "There are nine houses which it is right for the King's villeins to make: hall, chamber, food-house, stable, porch, barn, kiln, latrine, dormitory or sleephouse" (Jenkins, *Hywel Dda*, p. 441).

deunawplas [eighteen mansions]. *Plas* is a borrowing from ME *place*, "A house, manor house; mansion, palace" (*MED*, s.v. *place* 6a), as in *Sir Gawain and the Green Knight*, "Iwysse þou art welcom, wyȝe, to my place" (ed. Tolkien and Gordon, line 2240). The number eighteen (twice nine) provides further hyperbolic comparison between Sycharth and other great houses.

42   *llofft*. From ME *loft* [an upstairs room, upper room, bedroom]; compare *Sir Gawain and the Green Knight*, "ȝe schal lenge in your lofte & lyȝe in your ese" (ed. Tolkien and Gordon, line 1096).

44   *clêr* [poets]. See also Item 5.24. The collective noun *clêr* (perhaps a borrowing from Middle Irish *cléir* [poets, minstrels, priests]) refers both to poets in general and more particularly to poets of lower status than either a *pencerdd* [chief of song], i.e., a learned court poet recognized as a bardic teacher, or a *bardd teulu* [household bard], the official poet of a Welsh lord's retinue. These *clêr* were poets or minstrels who traveled from one noble household to another, somewhat analogous to the *clerici vagantes* or *joculatores* on the continent. *Clêr* was, therefore, sometimes used by poets of the higher orders as a term of opprobrium to identify those who composed low verse and satire, but following the collapse of the traditional Welsh social structure after the Edwardian conquest, it

became, during the fourteenth century, an acceptable term for the poets who sang to and praised patrons among the surviving, if lesser, aristocracy in different parts of the country (see Lloyd, *Gogynfeirdd*, pp. 37–38, and Bromwich, "Dafydd ap Gwilym," p. 121). Except in one of his biting satires, Iolo Goch regularly uses the word as an unmarked or positive term for poets, most often in contexts similar to this, in which a poet is made welcome at a patron's home.

47   *teils*. A borrowing of the plural of ME *tile*, "A roofing tile; a stone slate used as a roofing tile" (*MED*, s.v. *tile*, n.2 [2]).

       talwg. A *hapax legomenon*; Johnston suggests it is a compound of *tâl* [forehead, brow, gable end] + *gwg* [frown] (Iolo Goch, *Gwaith*, p. 236).

48   *magai*. The third-person imperfect of *magu* [to nurture, grow, increase]; the basic idea is that smoke rising from a chimney is a sign of warmth and welcome.

50   *gwardrob*. A borrowing from ME *wardrobe*, "A room for the storage of clothing, armor, and similar articles; a closet" (*MED*, s.v. *warde-robe*).

51–52   *siopau . . . siop*. *Siop* (sg.), *siopau* (pl.), is a borrowing from ME *shop(pe)*. This is descriptive of the contents of the wardrobes; there were, of course, no actual shops at Sycharth.

52   *Siêp Lundain*. *Chep(e)* (from OE *ceapan* [to buy]) or *Chep-side*, modern Cheapside, is a street in London where markets were held in the Middle Ages (*MED*, s.v. *chep*, n.4); compare the General Prologue to Chaucer's *Canterbury Tales*: "A fairer burgeys was ther noon in Chepe" (I[A]754).

53   *croes eglwys* [cruciform]. Literally, the "cross of a church," here a metaphor for the shape of the house, carried through the next line.

59   *Pysgodlyn* [fishpond]. "There are traces of two fishponds to be seen at Sycharth still today" (Williams, *Owain y Beirdd*, p. 6; my translation).

63   *dir bwrdd*. *Tir bwrdd* was most likely understood as a compound of *tir* [land] + *bwrdd* [board, table], but in all likelihood it is a calque on ME *bord-land* [land held in bordage], i.e., certain lands held by a villein (more specifically a *bordar*) at the will of his lord (see *OED*, s.v. *bord-land*, *bordar*). The term also occurs in medieval Welsh law texts (Jenkins, *Hywel Dda*, p. 125).

72   *cyfar*. Co-tillage, joint ploughing, or a contract for the same; a legal term for the system of sharing oxen for ploughing tracts held or worked by different bondmen (see Jenkins, *Hywel Dda*, pp. 198–202). The implication of the couplet is that Owain's workers do everything necessary for the running of his estate.

73   *blaendrwyth*. Literally, the first decoction or infusion (of a liquor); hence, the best draft.

74   *bragodau*. Plural of *bragod*, *bragawd* [bragget], a drink made from the fermentation of a mix of ale, honey, and spices.

81–84   Owain's wife was Margaret Hanmer (Marred ferch Dafydd), the daughter of Dafydd Hanmer, a judge in king's bench. Owain and Margaret had six sons (including Gruffudd and Maredudd), of whom only Maredudd seems to have survived him, and several daughters (including Alice and Catrin).

82 *Gwyn fy myd* [I am blessed]. Literally, "blessèd [is] my world," an idiom in Middle Welsh and later for expressing great happiness; the pronoun is variable. Compare *Gwyn eu byt wy Gymry* "Blessèd will the Welsh be" in the tenth-century prophecy *Armes Prydein*, line 97 (Livingston, *Brunanburh*, pp. 32–33), and the Beatitudes in Bishop William Morgan's translation of the Bible (1588): *Gwyn eu byd y tlodion yn yr yspryd, canys eiddynt yw teyrnas nefoedd* "Blessèd are the poor in spirit, for theirs is the kingdom of heaven" (National Library of Wales website).

83–84 If these lines can be taken to imply that Margaret's father had been ordained (*urddo*) as a knight (*marchog*), we must date the poem after 1387, when that event took place.

86 *nythaid* [brood]. Literally, "nestful."

88 *chliced*. *Cliced* [latch] is a borrowing from ME *cliket* or OF *cliquet*, a latch, especially a kind of latch that can be locked with a key (*MED*, s.v. *cliket*).

89 The function of the porter, of course, was to challenge the right of anyone to enter.

92 *Sycharth*. Another name for Cynllaith Owain, the hilly region that was one of the chief holdings of Owain Glyndŵr, his father, and his grandfather (see Lloyd, *Owen Glendower*, pp. 10–12), *Sycharth* [from *sych* "dry, parched" + *garth* "hill, ridge"] became also the name of the principal manor house for the region. Alternatively, understanding *garth* in its sense of "enclosure, garden," the name of the manor house may have been applied, *pars pro toto*, to the region over which it held authority.

94 *Pywer Lew*. On this legendary forebear of the line of Powys, see the note to Item 6.32.

96 *hoff* [renowned]. *Hoff* is a common adjective with broad but strong pleasant and positive connotations. Among the English equivalents given in *GPC* are "beloved, dear, favourite, pet; lovely, choice, desirable, pleasant, delightful, fine, agreeable, admirable, praiseworthy, remarkable, renowned, famous" (*GPC*, s.v. *hoff*). Any of these, except perhaps the rather diminutive "pet," would serve equally well here.

9. OWAIN GLYNDŴR, *GRANT OF LANDS*

Ed. and trans. Michael Livingston.

Manuscript: National Library of Wales, MS Bachymbyd 216.

  This document was first noted by J. Conway Davies, who identified it among the papers in the Bagot Collection at the National Library of Wales. Then listed as MS Bagot 216, the grant was dated by Davies to 16 June 1392 ("Some Owen Glyndŵr Documents," p. 48). As it turns out, this dating was in error by a day: the grant is dated to a Sunday in 1392, which would have been 17 June. The grant is one of the few records we have of Owain's time as lord of Glyndyfrdwy in peace with the English crown, and it provides an interesting look at the man at home among his people.

2–4   About the individuals named in this grant, the new tenant Gruffudd ap Ieuan Llwyd and the former tenant Dafydd Goch ap Madog, nothing else is known, though a "David ap Madock" appears in Item 11.87 along with five sons of Ieuan Llwyd (11.107, 114, 129, 133).

4   *Mystwyr*. Mwstwr is a township near Corwen in Merionethshire, part of Owain's holdings as lord of Glyndyfrdwy (Richards, *Welsh Administrative and Territorial Units*, p. 161). The town's odd name appears to derive from Latin *monasterium* [monastery], probably because the lands were formerly in the possession of Valle Crucis Abbey (Pierce, "Welsh *mystwyr*," pp. 135–37).

8, 14   *Ieuan*. MS: *Ieua*.

8   *libere, quiete, bene, et in pace*. Medieval grants are distinctly formulaic, often preserving phrases as standard language long after the phrases ceased having pertinence. This particular phrase, as Kaye points out, is by this time "a conventional jingle" that served as "words of comfort" but lacked substance (*Medieval English Conveyances*, p. 87). For the reader's convenience they are nonetheless translated here according to their general intent.

16–19   Among those named are Owain's steward and his *rynghill*, the military officer in charge of protecting the manor. Nothing more is known of these individuals.

19–21   As is often the case with legal documents of the period, the grant is dated relative to the ecclesiastical calendar and the regnal year. As noted above, this date is, in modern terms, 17 June 1392.

10. HENRY IV, *CONFISCATION OF OWAIN'S LANDS*

Adapted and trans. by Kelly DeVries, from Rymer, *Foedera*, 8.163–64.

This edict from Henry IV, our earliest verifiable documentary evidence for the revolt in Wales, reveals how early the crown recognized Owain Glyndŵr's role in the initial actions of the rebellion: here, in one stroke, the king summarily confiscates all of Owain's estates and grants them to his half-brother, the earl of Somerset (on whom, see note to lines 2–3, below).

1   *ad quos etc*. This formula is used in the greetings of most royal letters and documents to include all to whom the document pertains. Modern English translators generally leave it in the Latin or translate it, as above, "to whom etc."

2–3   *carissimo fratri nostro Johanni, comiti Somersetiae*. John Beaufort (1373–1410) was, technically speaking, only Henry's half-brother: he was the eldest of the Beauforts, the initially illegitimate offspring of John of Gaunt (Henry's father) and his mistress, Katherine Swynford. At Gaunt's request, the Beauforts were declared legitimate by Richard II in 1390, and Gaunt married Katherine in 1396, after which a Papal Bull likewise legitimated them. Parliamentary action confirmed the same (though it barred them from succession), and John Beaufort was made the first earl of Somerset on 10 February 1397. John was very supportive of Richard II, even after the king exiled his half-brother Henry, but there appears to have been few ill feelings among the Lancastrians: after the usurpation, Henry allowed him to maintain his earldom, and he became a constable of England in 1404. Henry's decision to grant him the whole of Owain's Welsh holdings was a mark of obvious favor — even if he could not, for obvious reasons, take possession of them for quite some time.

4   *ratione*. MS: *ratine*.

27   *In cujus etc.* is an abbreviation for *in cujus re testimonium huic testamento meum siglium apparui* [in witness of which thing I have affixed my seal to this]. This formula appears on almost all royal documents.

11. *DE OWEINO GLENDWOREDY*

    Ed. and trans. Graham C. G. Thomas ("Oswestry 1400"). Adaptation and notes, John K. Bollard.

Manuscript: National Library of Wales, Sir John Williams Deeds and Documents No. 126, back flyleaf.

    Graham C. G. Thomas's edition and translation are reprinted here, with minor adaptations, and the following discussion and notes owe a great deal to his research and analysis.

    The text appears in a seventeenth-century hand on the back flyleaf of "a volume containing 59 folios with a limp vellum cover; the word 'Evidences' appears on the spine. Printed on each page are the outlines of indentures and seals, all of which are empty. . . . In addition to the Oswestry document, the same scribe has copied on the front fly-leaf letters patent, dated 5 May 1604, granting the barony of Le Despenser to Mary Fane, a descendant of Hugh le Despenser" (Thomas, "Oswestry 1400," p. 117n2). It is an incomplete copy of a document, written sometime after 11 November 1400, but apparently derived from the court rolls for 6 (or possibly or 27) October 1400 from the General and First Court of the town of Oswestry. Following an inquest on 6 October to discover who from the lordship of Oswestry and Kynardley had taken part in Owain's campaign the preceding month, those named were summoned to appear in person and to receive judgement on the 27 October, and that judgment is recorded here.

    Lines 11–41 of the introductory paragraph present a summary of the events of 16–24 September that is nearly identical to that in the record of the trial on 25 October 1400 of John Kynaston, the son of John Kynaston, senior, the steward of Maelor Saesneg, Moldsdale, and later Ellesmere, and the maternal uncle of Owain's wife (Coram Rege Roll, no. 560 [Easter 1401] in Sayles, *Select Cases*, pp. 114–17, designated in the following notes as S; Davies, *Revolt*, p.139). This brief account of the outbreak includes the names of fifteen men believed to have been present at the meeting of 16 September when Owain was declared *Princeps Wallie*, Prince of Wales, though in the present document the name of Philip Hanmer has been omitted through homoioteleuton, skipping from the first *Hanemer* to the second. That these fifteen were regarded as leaders of or as noteworthy among others gathered that day is implied by the phrase *et multi alij Wallicorum* [and many other Welshmen]. The document then diverges from S to name those who gave relief to the rebels in the "mountains and woods of Wales" for a period at least through the feast of St. Martin, 11 November. Thus, while the actual date the original of this document is uncertain, it is undoubtedly after 11 November 1400. In this regard, it is worth noting that S, recording the trial on 25 October, appears in the Coram Rege Roll for Easter 1401. The present record, then, may date from that period.

The subsequent lists in this document are also significant in that they record the names of 34 additional men believed to be involved in the initial campaign and who were summoned therefore by name; the names of 147 others who appeared, declared that they were "compelled through fear of death and arson," and were pardoned; and 35, most of whom appear in one of the preceding lists, who did not appear and were thus declared traitors.

2–3   *Anno regni [Regis] Henrici iiij^{ti} secundo.* Henry IV was crowned on 30 September 1399; thus while the rebellion began in the first year of his reign (see lines 22–24), this trial three weeks later took place in the second year of his reign.

4   *Essonie.* An essoin is an excuse for not appearing in an early English court at an appointed time, especially for such reasons as illness, being overseas, or being in the king's service.

10   *Johanne Gouch.* Here *Gouch* may represent Welsh *Goch* [Red-haired], as it certainly does in several Welsh names below, though in this case it might also be a surname as in English usage. That he may have been anglicized himself is also suggested by his appearance in this list of men with English names giving testimony against the Welsh. Note that the only two figures listed as *Johannes* in the following lists of rebels, *Johannes Estewike* (line 15), and *Johannes Symond/ Symons* (lines 53–54, 130), have English surnames, compared to the numerous instances of the Welsh form, *Ieuan.*

11   *Owen de Glyndowerdey.* S: *Oweyn Glyndour.* The names listed here are assumed to be the prominent members of the meeting at Glyndyfrdwy of 16 September 1400 at which Owain was declared *Princeps Wallie*; see the headnote above. From here through *fuerunt* (line 41) the text is very close to that of S.

11–12   *Griffinus filius eius.* S: ditto. Both manuscripts here identify Owain's son Gruffudd with the common Latin variant form. His name was omitted in lines 42–43.

12   *Griffith Hanemer, [Phillippus Hanemer].* Gruffudd and Philip Hanmer were the brothers of Owain's wife. Philip, who appears in the nearly identical list in S, was probably omitted inadvertently; see the headnote above.

12–13   *Robertus Pulesdon.* Robert Puleston was the husband of Owain's sister, Lowri (Davies, *Revolt*, pp. 139, 147).

14   *Madoc ap Ieuan ap Madoc.* Madog ap Ieuan ap Madog was descended from a distinguished Welsh family in the lordship of Bromfield and Yale. His wife was the sister of Owain's brother-in-law, and he was present at Glyndyfrdwy on 16 September 1400 (Davies, *Revolt*, p. 142).

15   *Ieuan ap Howell Pichull.* MS: *Ieuan ap Howell Howel Pichull.* Ieuan ap Hywel Pickhill was a prominent landowner in the lordship of Bromfield and Yale (Davies, *Revolt*, p. 142).

    Ierwerth. On the numerous variants of the name Iorwerth, see Morgan and Morgan, *Welsh Surnames*, pp. 139–40.

    Johannes Estewike. S: *John Eftewyk.* According to Thomas, he appears in the King's Bench verdict as John Astewick ("Oswestry 1400," p. 118). He has not been identified, but there is an Eastwick in Shropshire a couple of miles north of Ellesmere and just east of Dudleston; early spellings include Astwick' 1279–80, Astwik 1280, Estwic c.1561, and others, for which Eftewyk is also a plausible variant (Paul Cavill, Institute for Name Studies, University of Nottingham, personal communication).

15–16   *Craghe Ffynnant eorum propheta* [Crach Ffinnant, their prophet]. Though none of his poetry is known to have survived, Crach Ffinnant was a poet, trained undoubtedly in the tradition of prophetic verse, who was also with Owain in Berwick in 1384. He was probably somewhat older than Owain, having served as an archer under Sir John de Charlton in Edward III's naval expedition of 1372 (*Soldier in Later Medieval England*, s.n. Crach Yffynnant; on his role as "prophet," see Williams, "Gwrthryfel Glyndŵr," pp. 180–87). This reference to him as "their prophet" has been accorded considerable weight in assessing Glyndŵr's relationship to prophecy. Crach is a nickname from Welsh *crach* [scab; scabby; contemptible; little, dwarfish] (*GPC*, s.v. *crach*). The name is a reference to his size, rather than his character; compare the bardic names of three other fourteenth-century poets of Powys, Sypyn Cyfeiliog [literally, "(little) parcel of C."], Cnepyn Gwerthrynion [literally, "(little) lump of G."], and Y Poesned [literally, "the little pot," from AF or ME *posnet*]. The name Ffinnant (from *ffin* [border] + *nant* [stream]) is especially common in the region of the former Montgomeryshire, but it also occurs in six other counties (Williams, "Gwrthryfel Glyndŵr," p. 180n6). In a poem addressed to Sir Dafydd Hanmer, Owain's father-in-law, Gruffudd Llwyd asks that Judge Hanmer hear the case of one Morgan ap Dafydd, and he names eleven contemporary poets who would be a suitable panel of jurors, including *Nid amheuwn, gwn gannair, / Lw'r Crach a'i law ar y crair* [I would not doubt (I have heard a hundred declarations) / the oath of Y Crach with his hand on the relics] (Ifans, *Gwaith*, Poem 10.51–52n).

17   *domini regis predicti.* S: *domini Henrici, regis Anglie.*

18   *ac.* S: *necnon.*

20–21   *necnon . . . tocius lingue Anglicane.* The complaint that an enemy wished to annihilate one's people and language is a common trope; compare this statement and the similar one in Item 16.6 with the entries in *Brut y Tywysogion* for the year 1114, which states of the English that *aruaethu a wnaethant o gytundep mynnv dileu yr holl Bryttannyeit o gwbyl hyt na choffeit Brytannyawl enw ynn tragywydawl* [they planned by agreement to exterminate all the Britons (i.e., the Welsh) completely, so that the Britannic name should never more be remembered], and for 1165, where it is said that Henry II *dyuot hyt yg Kroes Oswald, gann darparu alldudyaw a diuetha yr holl Vryttannyeit* [came as far as Oswestry, purposing to carry into bondage and to destroy all the Britons] (Jones, *Brut* [1952], pp. 78–79, 144–45).

21   *erexerunt.* S: *errigerunt.*

22   *Glyndouerdey.* S: *Glyndour.*

23   *anno regni [Regis] Henrici.* S: *anno regni regis.*

24   *constentandam.* S: *sustendendum.*

25   *[de].* Also missing in S.

28   *omnibus.* S: *simul.*

29   *prodiciose combusserunt.* S: *comburerunt.*

31   *proximis.* S: *proximo.*

34   *combusserunt.* S: *comburerunt.*

35   *ad villam de la Pole* [to the town of the Pool]. The town of Welshpool may have been an English settlement; as Lloyd states, "It would otherwise have hardly had an English name." It was originally called Pool, but in the nineteenth century the name was expanded to Welsh Pool to distinguish it from Poole in Dorset (*History*, p. 248). The name may have been simply descriptive or a translation from the earlier Welsh *Trallwng Llywelyn* [Ll.'s boggy place] or *Y Trallwng* [The Boggy Place]. As William Camden noted in his *Britannia* 1586 [ed. 1695], *Trallwng* or "*Trallwn . . .* in some parts of Wales [is] a common appellative for such soft places on the Roads or elsewhere as travellers may be apt to sink into" (*GPC*, s.v. *trallwng, trallwn*).

36   *ac.* S: *et.*

37   *modo hostilando.* S: *modo guerrino hostilando.*

38   *proximum.* S: *proximo*

        quo die. S: *quando.*

38–39   *Hugonem Burnell.* At the beginning of S, Hugh Burnell also appears in the list of five judges assigned to hear the complaints against Glyndŵr and the case against John Kynaston.

39   *eius Regis.* S: *domini regis*

        Salope. Salop is an abbreviation of *Salopesberia*, which developed through Anglo-Norman phonetic dissimilation from OE *Scrobbesbyrig* [Shrewsbury].

41   *et dissipati fuerunt.* S: *ac desceperati fuerunt.* From this point S deals with different matters altogether.

43   *[Griffith filius].* A scribal omission through homoioteleuton.

46   *festum Sancti Martini.* The feast of St. Martin is 11 November.

49   *Madoc ap Enion.* He appears in line 126 as Maddoc ap Eynus.

50   *Ieuan Werth*. He appears in lines 126–27 as Ieuan Wethe.

54   *William Twiford*. There is a Twyford in Shropshire about five miles southeast of
            Oswestry.

            de duabus partibus de Ossestry. The lordship of Oswestry was divided into two
            parts, the larger, southern being *Deuparth*, literally "two parts (of three)," which
            became *Duparts* in official records, and to the north, *y Traean* (lines 88–89)
            literally "one-third" (see Richards, *Enwau*, 34).

56   *Madoc ap Ieuan Gruffith*. He appears in line 133 as Madoc ap Ieuan ap Grono.

57   *Gruffith ap Ieuan ap Rees de Malveley*. He appears in line 134 as Gruffith ap
            Ieuan ap Richard de Malverdeley. Melverley is a village in Shropshire near the
            confluence of the Efyrnwy and the Severn rivers, about ten miles south and east
            of Oswestry.

59   *Kynardisley*. Kynnersley is a village in the borough of Telford and Wrekin, about
            7 miles north of Telford and 14 miles east of Shrewsbury.

87   *Deio o'r Wawn. Y Waun*, is the Welsh name for Chirk, a parish adjoining
            Oswestry. Compare *Swydd y Waun*, Chirkland.

88–89   *de tribus partibus hundredi de Ossestry*. On the Traean (Traian, Tryan) of Oswestry,
            see the note on line 54 above. *Traean* is the Welsh word for "one-third."

100   *Ienna*. Emend to *Ieuan*?

109   *?Ybole*. The meaning is unclear; possibly a portly man's nickname, *Y Boly* [The
            Belly]?

126   *Maddoc ap Eynus*. He appears in line 49 as Madoc ap Enion.

126–27   *Ieuan Wethe*. He appears in line 50 as Ieuan Werth.

133   *Madoc ap Ieuan ap Grono*. He appears above (line 56) as Madoc ap Ieuan ap
            Gruffith.

134   *Gruffith ap Ieuan ap Richard de Malverdeley*. He appears above (line 57) as
            Gruffith ap Ieuan ap Rees de Malveley.

12. HENRY IV, *PROTECTION FOR SUBMITTING REBELS*

Adapted and trans. by Kelly DeVries, from Rymer, *Foedera*, 8.167.

On 8 November the king had confiscated Owain's lands, concurrent with a sequence of
efforts to ascertain and punish the guilty ringleaders of the Welsh rebellion (see Items 10 and
11). By the end of the month, if this edict is any indication, Henry apparently felt confident
that his justice was complete. Here, in a sweeping act that greatly belies any impulse to paint
him in outright tyrannical terms, Henry IV offers blanket forgiveness to the country and
people of Wales — provided they submit themselves to the crown. Henry would essentially
repeat these terms on 10 March 1401, this time including specific mention of those few to
whom it was denied: Owain Glyndŵr, Rhys ap Tudur, and Gwilym ap Tudur (Item 14).

1   *universis et singulis*. This adjectival phrase is formulaic for legal documents, but
            its meaning is clearer than many other legalistic terms and phrases. It is here
            translated with a more common modern English idiom, although the emphasis
            has been changed from "whole" to "singular" rather than "each and every."

24   *In cujus etc*. This is an abbreviation for the *testimonium*, a formulaic statement
            concluding a legal document that signifies that it has been properly executed
            and is authenticated by the listed authority. In its most common medieval form
            the *testimonium* begins "in cuius rei testimonium" [in witness of which thing],
            often followed by — as it would have been in the present instance — a reference
            to the affixation of an authenticating seal.

13. *ROLLS OF PARLIAMENT, 1401*

From *PROME*, ed. and trans. Chris Given-Wilson. Notes by Michael Livingston.

The parliament that met at Westminster between 20 January and 10 March 1401 was
recognized even in its time as a noteworthy event. As Chris Given-Wilson has observed, it
was one of those somewhat rare proceedings afforded "considerable interest" among contemporary chroniclers (*PROME*). The wide interest was perhaps predictable, as the parliament came at a dramatic moment for King Henry IV: any grand hopes for his reign had fallen to new lows for the crown in the eighteen months since Henry had returned to England
to usurp it. The king by mid-January 1401 was haunted by conspiracies (most dangerously
the Epiphany Rising a year earlier), incessant rumors (mostly of Richard II's survival), and
a royal treasury that was depleted by a poor economy (at least partly the fault of the un-
settled government), the new regime's expenditures (at times extravagant, as during the
entertaining of the Byzantine Emperor Manuel II in December 1400), and the costs of battle
(in Scotland, Northumberland, and Wales). At the same time, his conservative archbishop
of Canterbury, Arundel, was leading a charge against perceived heresy in the country, particularly in the form of Lollardy. As Given-Wilson observes, there were thus three "main
points of interest of the parliament, namely: (i) the debate over taxation and conciliar
appointments; (ii) the passing of *de heretico comburendo*; and (iii) the legislation relating to
the Welsh" (*PROME*). The eleven petitions regarding this latter subject, mostly connected
to actions taken on 21 February (line 1), are reproduced here.
    While the fires of Owain's initial revolt had been quickly put down in September, the
lingering English unease about matters in Wales is made clear in the severely anti-Welsh
sentiment of the parliament. The fact that Owain himself remained at large was no doubt
a concern, but it is interesting to note that he goes unnamed in both the petitions of the
commons and the king's replies. Of more concern, apparently, was the perception that
Owain had, as Given-Wilson puts it, "caught the mood of his people" (*PROME*). Owain may
well have been considered less the cause of the revolt than a symptom of it.
    If that is so, then it is all the more ironic that the passage of a sequence of anti-Welsh
legislation appears to have had an effect quite different from that intended: instead of
ending the troubles, Davies rightly observes that these statutes and ordinances "convinced
the Welsh that they were right to regard themselves as second-class citizens and they drove
the remnant of unreconciled desperadoes of the September [1400] uprising into further
desperation" (*Revolt*, p. 103).

At the same time, while the parliamentary selections reproduced and translated here have rightly drawn attention for their anti-Welsh sentiment — including the declaration that the Welsh could no longer own land, bear arms, or have citizenship in England or in English towns just over the border (lines 119–25) — it is worth observing that, as Davies has suggested, "the moving spirit behind these statutes and ordinances may not have been the government itself, so much as English public opinion as expressed by the commons in parliament. This suggestion seems amply confirmed by the royal response to many of the petitions presented in parliament. Some were accepted, but only after they had been hedged about with important qualifications by the king" (*Revolt*, p. 287).

3–5	The commons, in framing its petition, is careful to praise the king's successful actions against the Welsh the prior September, before observing that the job was not yet finished.
6–14	The number of Welsh students at Oxford and Cambridge who were fleeing to Wales, along with the number of skilled Welsh laborers across the realm doing the same, is difficult to ascertain. It was, at any rate, significant enough to confirm in English eyes a fear — probably longstanding — that a great Welsh army might take arms and rise up across the border. This fear would only have been furthered by rumors about Welsh barbarism, culminating in Henry IV's anxiety a few months later that Owain and the Welsh were coming across the border determined to wipe out the English language itself (see Items 11.20–21 and 16.6). For Owain's part, the return of the Welsh students and laborers to Wales would have underscored how powerful the nationalistic forces were that were beginning to rally to him.
62–64	The phrasing of this petition seems to imply that specific names of the "foundours" of the Welsh rebellion were circulating, though they go unnamed here. Judging from Henry's subsequent pardon, those names were likely Owain Glyndŵr, Rhys ap Tudur, and Gwilym ap Tudur (Item 14.16–17).
76–77	Much of what the commons requested was granted by the king, but it is interesting to observe where he modified their requests or, as here, delayed them. At the end of November Henry had essentially granted pardon to any Welsh rebels who submitted themselves to his authority (Item 12); this decision was either not well-known or (more likely) not well-received on the part of the English — especially, one imagines, those lords and landowners along the border who had been most severely effected by the Welsh raids in September. In either case, the commons asked that the Welsh make reparations prior to being restored to the king's grace. Henry's reply that he would grant clemency when and how he saw fit speaks volumes about his sense of his own authority and his unwillingness to use the rebellion as a pretense for punishing the people of Wales. At the same time, the king is politically shrewd, observing that he still desires to listen to "bon advis" [good advice]; it is thus interesting to note that the day parliament ended, the king re-offered pardon to the Welsh who would submit, only this time specifically omitting Owain Glyndŵr, Rhys ap Tudur, and Gwilym ap Tudur (Item 14.16–17); these three men were probably those considered by the commons to be "foundours des ditz hautes tresons et insurreccions" [originators of the said high treasons and insurrections] (line 63).

113–16   Here again, the king tempers the request of the commons, which asked that no
           Englishman be convicted on charges brought by a Welshman in Wales — a
           request that harshly emphasizes the anti-Welsh nature of the parliament. Henry
           decrees that this be temporary (lasting only for three years), not permanent.

14. HENRY IV, *PARDON FOR WELSH REBELS*

Adapted and trans. by Kelly DeVries, from Rymer, *Foedera*, 8.181–82.

This pardon, according to the copy now surviving, was composed in general on 10 March
1401, after which *consimiles literas* [similar letters] of the same content were produced specifically for the king's subjects in the county of Flint (also sent on 10 March), in "the dominion of Thomas, the earl of Arundel, of Chirk, and Chirkland in Wales" (6 May), in "the
dominion of the dear and faithful cousin of the king, Thomas, earl of Arundel, of Bromfield,
Yale, and the hundred of Oswestry in Wales" (10 May), in "the dominion that belonged to
John late lord Lestrange of Knockin deceased, of the hundred of Ellesmere in Wales" (16
May), and in "the dominion of Fulk Fitz Waryn, knight, of his hundred of Whittington in
Wales" (25 June). Like Henry IV's earlier offer of forgiveness to the Welsh rebels (Item 12),
this pardon is striking for its sweeping universality, though here the king notably singles out
three exceptions: those perceived as the ringleaders of the revolt. This change might well be
an acquiescence to the mood of parliament on 21 February (see note to Item 13.76–77).

15–16   *de praemissis vel aliquo praemissorum*. This is a legal phrase meant to include the
           whole as well as each one singly.

15. ADAM OF USK, *CHRONICLE, PART 1*

From Adam of Usk, *Chronicle*, ed. and trans. Given-Wilson, pp. 100–01, 126–27. Notes
by Michael Livingston.

Manuscript: London, British Library, Add. MS 10,104, fols. 166v, 170r.

Adam of Usk (d. 1430) is one or our most essential chroniclers for the revolt of Owain
Glyndŵr. He is also among the most fascinating, for his chronicle is a personal document,
in many ways a kind of diary for his actions and reactions between the years 1377 and 1421.
The editorial work of Given-Wilson has revealed that Adam's chronicle was written in multiple, datable stages: the first part runs from June 1377 to March 1401; the second from
April 1401 to February 1402; the third from February 1402 to February 1414; and the
fourth from April 1414 to June 1421 (Adam, *Chronicle*, p. xlvi). Selections from all four
stages are reproduced in this volume, appearing as separate sources (Items 15, 22, 62, and
67). All four stages were written in England or Wales, though for the events of the third
stage Adam was himself in distant Rome, hearing of the events that he would later incorporate into the chronicle at several removes from their original source (a fact that is also of
some use in judging the "international" knowledge about the Welsh revolt).
    Born in Usk, Adam was a Welshman by blood and tongue and an Englishman by career
advancement as a clerk and ecclesiast; as a result, the revolt of Owain confronted him with

a "virtually insuperable . . . conflict of loyalties": by his own account Adam "bitterly resented the English attempt in 1401 to suppress the Welsh tongue," yet at the same time "he was capable of talking about 'our side, the English'" (Adam, *Chronicle*, p. xxiii). It may be that these divided allegiances led him to support Owain initially; certainly this accusation was made against him and may have played a role in his decision to try to find advancement in Rome — though independent documents show that suspicions about his loyalty followed him there (Adam, *Chronicle*, pp. xxv–xxvi). His allegiances were so equivocal, in fact, that when he explains how he volunteered in the summer of 1408 to join Owain and the rebels as an English spy, there remain lingering uncertainties about which side he served in his web of espionage (Adam, *Chronicle*, pp. xxix–xxxiii).

1 *in festo decollacionis sancti Iohannis baptiste.* I.e., 29 August 1400.

1–2 As Given-Wilson notes, "the revolt erupted on 16 Sept. 1400, with Glendower proclaimed prince of Wales at Glyn Dyfrdwy; Henry heard of it at Northampton, not Leicester, on 19 Sept." (Adam, *Chronicle*, p. 100).

4–11 On the sequence of events, Given-Wilson notes that "Hugh Lord Burnell hanged ten rebels at Ruthin on 28 Sept.; Henry arrived at Shrewsbury on 26 Sept., toured North Wales, and arrived back at Shrewsbury on 15 Oct. (Davies, *Revolt*, p. 102). Glendower lay low until May 1401" (Adam, *Chronicle*, pp. 100–01).

12 The Parliament to which Usk refers is that of 1401, whose relevant contents are given in Item 13, above.

16. HENRY IV, *COMMISSION: THREAT OF OWAIN*

Adapted and trans. by Michael Livingston, from *PPC*, ed. Nicolas, 2.54–56.

Manuscript: London, British Library, MS Cotton Cleopatra F.iii, fol. 115.

By this commission King Henry IV summoned the full military might of fourteen counties to meet him at Worcester with all possible speed in order to resist the rumored assault of Owain Glyndŵr. The counties so summoned are Berkshire, Oxfordshire, Wiltshire, Somerset, Gloucestershire, Herefordshire, Worcestershire, Shropshire, Warwickshire, Leicestershire, Lancashire, Derbyshire, Nottinghamshire, and Staffordshire. Lloyd surmises that the sudden and shocking news that has provoked the king to this action must have been brought by Sir Hugh Waterton and John Leventhorpe, who would recently have arrived from Brecon (*Owen Glendower*, p. 40n1).

6 The commission includes rumor that Owain intends to destroy the English tongue, thereby suggesting that the rebels were perceived — at least to some degree — as a significant threat to do just that. It was this rumor — associated with the rebellion from its earliest days (see Item 11.20–21) — that Owain would subsequently deny in his parleys with Henry Percy and give as a reason for his failure to negotiate in person on English soil (see Item 24.13–15). It is an interesting (if unanswerable) question whether or not the king believed these rumors to be true or simply understood that they were likely to galvanize his subjects by

preying on their prejudicial fears. Regardless of the rationale, placing the rumors in the commission underscores the panic felt in England at the time.

17. JOHN CHARLTON, *BATTLE WITH OWAIN*

Adapted and trans. by Michael Livingston, from *Anglo-Norman Letters*, ed. Legge, p. 292.

Manuscript: All Souls MS 182, fol. 273v.

As Legge observes in printing it, this "letter, though clear, is ungrammatical, and gives the impression of having been written or dictated by [John Charlton, lord of] Powys himself in some haste" (p. 293). On 4 June Hotspur had reported from Denbigh to the king and his Council that he had defeated a Welsh force at Cader Idris five days earlier, and that he had heard that John Charlton had recently engaged in a combat with Owain himself (*PPC* 1.152–53). This letter appears to confirm this report.

The information here, combined with Hotspur's report "that Powys was on his way to join Worcester and himself" at Denbigh, suggests to Legge "that Powys would be moving north-east from his own country" in western Powys. Hodges therefore speculates that the mountainous region of *M.* in which Charlton engages Owain (line 5), therefore, is likely to be Mawddwy, on the southern edge of Snowdonia. If this is so, then Hodges is probably correct in his assumption that the *M.* in which Charlton subsequently lodged himself (line 16) might be Machynlleth, and the *K.* towards which Owain appears to have fled (line 13) is likely to be Carmarthen (English *Kermerdyn*) (Hodges, *Owain*, pp. 49–50). Owain's subsequent actions, at any rate, did indeed occur in that direction, if not as far south: the next major action in Owain's rebellion would be the mysterious Battle of Hyddgen, fought in the mountains of Plynlimon (for which see Item 70.8–13).

There is interesting correlation between Charlton's description of this engagement — the mountain terrain, the splitting of English troops, the capturing of Owain's banner and bannerman — and the text and accompanying drawing in the *Beauchamp Pageant* (Item 89).

3   *yce lundy darrein* [this past Monday]. If indeed this encounter is the same as that reported by Hotspur (see above), then the encounter must have occurred on 1 June 1401.

18. HOTSPUR, *BATTLE AT CADER IDRIS*

Adapted and trans. by Michael Livingston, from *PPC*, ed. Nicolas, 1.152–53.

Manuscript: London, British Library, MS Cotton Cleopatra F.iii, fol. 27r.

Henry Percy, more commonly known as "Hotspur," was the eldest son of Henry Percy, the powerful earl of Northumberland whose support was vital to Henry IV's usurpation of the crown. The new king had placed the Percies in the position of controlling effectively the entirety of England's border with Scotland, and Hotspur (so called because he reportedly would drive his horses so hard his spurs became "hot" with blood) proved himself a highly capable military commander in the field there, most famously at the Battle of Homildon Hill in September 1402. Percy lordships also extended into the March and North Wales, including the castle of Conwy, which was captured by the Welsh at Easter 1401; Hotspur took command of the successful siege to retake the castle, and he stayed in Wales for several more months as the overseer of the English response to the revolt. It is during this time that he writes the present letter regarding English successes against the Welsh.

These efforts drained the Percy coffers, and in the letter Hotspur is at pains to emphasize how his service has been not just for the recovery of his own lands but for the recovery of English rule in general; thus, he reasons, the king should pay for his many expenses, money that has not yet materialized. Such monetary frustrations were a cause of festering resentment on the part of the Percies, and they played a clear role in their decision to revolt against the crown themselves in 1403.

1   *et treshonurez.* MS: *et ~~mez~~ treshonurez.*

10   *moun treshonure uncle.* Thomas Percy, earl of Worcester.

21–23   The news of Owain's defeat at the hands of John Charlton, lord of Powys, is undoubtedly regarding the same battle that Charlton himself describes in a hasty letter written to the prince (Item 17).

19. HENRY IV, *PROCLAMATION AGAINST OWAIN*

Adapted and trans. by Kelly DeVries, from Rymer, *Foedera*, 8.225.

This proclamation of the king is perhaps the closest thing we have to an official declaration of war upon Owain and the rebellious Welsh. The preserved text is that of the letter sent to the sheriff of Devonshire, but notes in the manuscript relate that on the same day "consimilia brevia" [similar letters] were sent to the sheriffs of Gloucestershire, Oxfordshire and Berkshire, Worcestershire, Bedfordshire and Buckinghamshire, Cambridgeshire and Huntingdonshire, Northamptonshire, and Shropshire. Also on the same date letters were sent "mutatis mutandis" [with some changes] to the sheriffs of Nottinghamshire and Derbyshire, Staffordshire, and Warwickshire and Leicestershire; so, too, were letters "omissa illa clausula et quod venire facias, usque ibi, comitatus tui" [omitting the clause that you should come there all the way from your county] sent to the sheriffs of Somersetshire and Dorcestershire, Wiltshire, Herefordshire, Lincolnshire, Rutland, and Yorkshire, along with a similar letter that was directed to the chancery in the County Palatine of Lancaster.

6–7   In the Roman law used in medieval England, as in modern law, consent to rebellion was the same as participation in rebellion.

7   *de die in diem.* This phrase continues to be used in English legal documents to indicate "constant" or "daily" activity.

15   *in personis ad laborandum potentes.* This phrase is frequently used in documents summoning the military for their obligated service to the crown.

16   *qui annua feoda vel vadia de nobis percipiunt* [who take an annual fief or wages from us]. Both terms needed to be specified as the older system of military obli-

gation based on land grants was in the process of being supplemented by one of occupation for wages.

17   *se trahant, properent, et festinent.* Yet another phrase found frequently in English military summons throughout the Middle Ages. It could be simply translated as a single word summoning the soldiers to travel to the designated location.

20. *OWAIN AT A FUNERAL*

Adapted and trans. by Michael Livingston, from *Anglo-Norman Letters*, ed. Legge, p. 281.

Manuscript: All Souls MS 182, fols. 270v–271r.

This brief letter — written either to the English prince of Wales or to the king himself — must have been composed in haste and under some duress: the anonymous writer states his intention to ride out against a much larger Welsh contingent under the control of Owain Glyndŵr and another Welsh commander (likely Rhys Gethin; see note to line 3). Owain and the rebels have, he says, come to his jurisdiction to attend the funeral of two fellow Welsh rebels, but they are spending the night nearby and will, he is certain, raze his lands in the morning. The writer undertakes his fight against them out of a sense of duty, but he also seems resigned to the fact that his combat will end in defeat. Indeed, the fact that the writer goes on to suggest where the rebels might strike next may well indicate that he has little hope for surviving, much less achieving victory.

The identity of the two slain men that Owain has come to honor is, like the writer of the letter, unknown. During his October invasion of Wales the king informed his son that he executed two rebels at Hereford (*Anglo-Norman Letters*, ed. Legge, pp. 302–03). The unnamed monk of Evesham also relates that the king ravaged the abbey of Strata Florida, decapitating at least one of the monks there for standing with the rebels (Item 28.42–44). Perhaps most famously, Adam of Usk reports that it was at this time that Llywelyn ap Gruffydd Fychan of Caeo in Carmarthenshire was gruesomely executed along with his eldest son before the king at Llandovery (see Item 22.31–36). It is tempting to associate the funeral with the burial of Llywelyn and his son in particular — and it would fit with the possibility that the letter is written from nearby Builth or Brecon — but we cannot be sure.

3   *O. de G. et R. de B.* That the first abbreviation is meant for Owain Glyndŵr (as it is throughout this manuscript; see also Items 17 and 21) is clear, but the identity of the second rebel leader is less certain. The suggestion here is that it is Rhys Gethin of Builth, one of the most recognizable of Owain's Welsh supporters.

5–6   Henry IV led punitive expeditions into Wales in October of 1400 (responding to attacks on English communities in the north of Wales and the Marches) and again in October of 1401 (responding to a more widespread resurgence in the revolt). It is likely that it is this second expedition referred to here, for which reason the writer must speak of it being the "most recent" one. This would certainly be the case if, as suggested above (and see note to lines 7–8), the writer is located close to South Wales: the king's *chevauchée* ran from Worcester to Carmarthen.

7–8   *la seignurie de C . . . de ceste part de le B.* The anonymous writer is in a lordship that starts with the letter *B*, which is near another lordship that begins with the letter *C*, and these abbreviated locations probably ought to be associated with one of Henry's expeditions into Wales (like that of October 1401, see note to lines 5–6). It is also possible that the writer's location might be in some way an entry point to South Wales: he suggests that the rebels might proceed there after leaving his lands. One possible solution would be that the writer is located in Brecon, and he refers as well to nearby Crickhowell. In November 1401, the royal castle at Brecon was assigned 20 men-at-arms and 40 archers (*PPC* 1.174). Another possibility would be Builth Wells, which would explain the writer's lack of surprise at the presence of Rhys Gethin of Builth. As it happens, either location would be close to Llandovery, site of the well-known execution of Llywelyn ap Gruffydd Fychan and his son, who may (or may not) be the individuals being buried.

21. HENRY PERCY, *OWAIN'S PARLEY*

Adapted and trans. by Michael Livingston, from *Anglo-Norman Letters*, ed. Legge, pp. 308–09.

Manuscript: All Souls MS 182, fol. 279r.

This letter, written by the earl of Northumberland to the English prince of Wales, was dated by Legge to November 1401, noting that it "cannot be later than 1401, for the reference to Mortimer shews that he was still at liberty and was still loyal" (p. 309). A November writing makes sense in light of the fact that the earl goes on in the letter to inform the prince that he would not spend Christmas with the king on account of the Sessions. The letter concludes with some of the earl's recommendation for a Welsh strategy built on a simultaneous triple advance into the mountains of Wales from east, west, and north. These plans, as Hodges points out, were "to be put into practice by Prince Henry in 1405 with decisive results" (*Owain*, p. 58).

7–9   Owain's reported concern about *grandes seignurs* [great lords] being executed by the commons without trial and against the wishes of the king might not have been without reason. Only the year before the earl of Salisbury was thus killed at Cirencester.

17–18   The prince's garrisons at *C.* and *H.* likely refer to Harlech and either Conwy or (more likely) Caernarfon.

19   Hotspur will invade and utilize as his base *M.* This is likely to mean Môn (Anglesey), which was granted to the Percies in the first year of Henry IV's reign.

22. ADAM OF USK, *CHRONICLE, PART 2*

From Adam of Usk, *Chronicle*, ed. and trans. Given-Wilson, pp. 128–29, 134–35, 144–53.
Notes by Michael Livingston.

Manuscript: London, British Library, Add. MS 10,104, fols. 170r–170v, 171v–172v.

For general information on Adam of Usk and his chronicle, see the headnote to part
1 (pp. 306–07). This second part contains several accounts of importance for Owain and his
revolt, including his (perhaps first) usage of the standard of Uther Pendragon (lines 44–47).
Also of note is Adam's inclusion of what appear to be copies of two letters from Owain to
potential allies in Scotland and Ireland. Adam insists that the messengers were beheaded,
but we know that other Welsh messengers at least got through to Scotland and found an
audience there who might have been receptive to prophecies of English doom (see Item
79.191–219). Adam's possession of these letters were once thought to be "indicative of his
collusion" with Owain at this stage of the revolt (see, e.g., Williams, "Adam of Usk"), but
Given-Wilson points out that "it is perfectly possible that he acquired copies of them
through his contacts at the English court" (Adam, *Chronicle*, p. xxiv).

6–7   Given-Wilson notes that "the siege probably ended in late June, not May"
             (Adam, *Chronicle*, p. 128).

15–16   This sentence is a much later insertion into the chronicle. Lord Grey's capture
             occurred in April 1402, and he was ransomed at the end of the year. The
             amount Owain received varies in the sources, though the records of parliament
             show an agreement for 10,000 marks (Item 25.4), which would equate to some
             10,000 pounds less than the report here.

34   *festo sancti Dionysii* [feast of St. Denis]. I.e., 9 October.

36   *testum sancti Michaelis* [feast of Michaelmas]. I.e., 29 September.

39–43   Given-Wilson observes: "There is no surviving record of a decree suppressing
             the Welsh language, though the blatantly racist legislation of 1401–2 would
             have made it easy to believe in one" (Adam, *Chronicle*, p. 147); see Davies, *Con-
             quest*, pp. 458–59. For the legislation, see Item 13.

44–47   This scene of a relatively small engagement in which Owain raises his standard
             might seem of little consequence at first glance, but it is, in fact, a heavily sym-
             bolic moment — one whose importance the chronicler would have well recog-
             nized. The standard that Owain here displays, for what is apparently the first
             time, is that of "a golden dragon on a white field." It is, in other words, the
             standard of the legendary Uther Pendragon. There may well be significance in
             the time chosen, as well: it is 2 November 1401, the day after All Saints Day, the
             first full day of the New Year according to the Celtic calendar.

68–69   As Given-Wilson notes, Owain "tactfully makes Albanactus the eldest son of
             Brutus, whereas Geoffrey of Monmouth had him as the youngest" (Adam,
             Chronicle, pp. 148–49).

NOTES TO ITEM 23: HENRY IV, *BATTLE OF BRYN GLAS*

23. HENRY IV, *BATTLE OF BRYN GLAS*

Adapted and trans. by Rhidian Griffiths, from *PPC*, ed. Nicolas, 1.185–86.

Manuscript: London, British Library, MS Cotton Cleopatra F.iii, fol. 121r.

The Welsh victory at the Battle of Bryn Glas, near the village of Pilleth, on 22 June 1402, and their capture of Edmund Mortimer, was a severe blow to royal authority in Wales. The tone of these instructions suggest that Henry IV believed that a major punitive expedition of the array of the midland counties of England would quell the rebellion. In this hope he was to be seriously frustrated. Moreover, the request to the Council to issue writs to the sheriffs of the northern counties of England, to combat unrest on the Marches towards Scotland, and of the southern counties, to resist possible invasion by sea, underlines the precarious nature of his kingship, which faced constant crises during its early years. Owain's insurrection was only one of these.

4   *Esmon Mortymer et pluseurs autres*. Sir Thomas Clanvowe, the sheriff of Hereford-shire, was one of those captured along with Mortimer (see Item 70, s.a. 1403, and notes 21–22).

24. HENRY PERCY, *OWAIN DENIES GENOCIDE*

Adapted and trans. by Michael Livingston, from *PPC*, ed. Nicolas, 2.59–60.

Manuscript: London, British Library, MS Cotton Cleopatra F.iii, fol. 114r.

Though Nicolas places this amid his undated material from the reign of King Henry IV, he hazards a guess that it must date to early 1401, a dating that appears to have been followed by most subsequent scholars as unquestioned fact (see, e.g., *Hodges*, Owain, p. 57, and Davies, *Revolt*, p. 151) or emended to November of that year, associating it with the attempts of the Percies to parley with Owain (see Item 21). As Lloyd observes, however, this report must instead belong to a date after summer of 1402, since, "previous to his capture, Edmund Mortimer had no special access to Glyn Dwr and Northumberland would not have required leave from the king to send him a message" (*Owen Glendower*, p. 58n1). Even further, one might suppose that this exchange is most likely to have occurred before Mortimer publicly changed his allegiance to the Welsh cause; we might thus date it to the months between July and November 1402.

Among the more interesting tidbits gleaned from this report of a report is the fact that Owain understood that certain parties among the English were convinced that he and his forces intended nothing less than the eradication of the English language, which was an early rumor in the conflict (see Item 11.20–21). For the king's own acceptance of these rumors (or at least his utilization of them), see Item 16.

25. *ROLLS OF PARLIAMENT, 1402*

From *PROME*, ed. and trans. by Chris Given-Wilson. Notes by Michael Livingston.

The anti-Welsh statues and ordinances passed during the parliament of January-March 1401 (Item 13) and in the weeks following it did little to stem the growing Welsh revolt. To the contrary, this legislation appears to have only made the situation worse. As Davies observes, historical precedent had already left the Welsh with a sense that "[t]heir status was that of political outsiders vis-á-vis the English kingdom and that of second-class citizens within their own country, at least theoretically. All that Henry IV's legislation did was to codify and fortify these discriminations and exclusions" (*Revolt*, p. 284). The Welsh revolt grew, and so, too, did the disasters for the English as Owain Glyndŵr captured first Lord Grey of Ruthin and then, at the Battle of Bryn Glas, Edmund Mortimer. Predictably, perhaps, the October-November 1402 parliament thus served to introduce yet more anti-Welsh measures that formalized the 1401 ordinances into statutes.

The first passage reproduced here is the plea of the commons for ransom for Lord Grey of Ruthin; that this was the first item on the parliamentary agenda after the commendation of the king speaks to the seriousness with which parliament was taking the revolt. Concerns over the fate of Edmund Mortimer went unspoken.

The second item included here concludes the long list of anti-Welsh legislation; this declaration is noted for naming Owain Glyndŵr, a name conspicuously missing from the earlier parliament (Item 13). Mortimer married Owain's daughter on 30 November 1402.

5   *le jour de Seint Martyn proscheyn* [Martinmas following]. That is, 11 November.

26. EDMUND MORTIMER, *DEFECTION TO OWAIN*

Adapted and trans. by Rhidian Griffiths from *Original Letters*, ed. Ellis, 2.1.24–26.

Manuscript: London, British Library, MS Cotton Cleopatra F.iii, fol. 122v.

Edmund Mortimer was the brother of Roger Mortimer, Earl of March (d. 1398), and the uncle of Edmund Mortimer (d. 1425), the heir to the Earldom of March, who was a minor at the time of the rebellion. At the battle of Bryn Glas or Pilleth on 22 June 1402, the elder Edmund, at the head of an army of Herefordshire men, was heavily defeated by Owain and taken prisoner, a significant prize for the Welsh. Later in 1402 Edmund cast his lot with his captor by marrying Owain's daughter, and he was to remain an adherent of the Welsh cause until his death during the siege of Harlech in 1409. This letter announces to his tenants his change of allegiance. But in spite of the apparent intimacy of *treschiers et bien amez* [dearest and well-beloved] (lines 1, 14) and *vous empriant chierement de cuer* [entreating you dearly from my heart] (line 7), this letter is neither a simple statement of his personal re-alignment nor a politely hopeful request; it is, rather, notice from a lord to his stewards to protect his properties, his tenants, and his interests in Wales and, in spite of his avowed intention to "remain outside the said dispute," to supply him with assistance in *mon dit querele* [my said grievance] (line 8). That his plea did not succeed on all counts is clear from the subsequent career of Sir John Greyndour (see note to line 18 below).

2–3   *si le roy Richard soit en vie*. Richard II is thought to have died a prisoner in 1400, but that may not have been widely known. Rumors to the effect that he was still alive persisted well into the fifteenth century, and it is interesting that even Mortimer could suggest the possibility that Richard was still alive.

3   *et sinoun qe* [and if that is not so]. More literally, "and if not that."

     mon honoure Neuewe. The younger Edmund Mortimer, heir to the Earldom of March, had a claim to the throne by virtue of his descent from Lionel of Clarence, the second surviving son of Edward III. Lionel's daughter Philippa was the mother of his father, Roger Mortimer.

4–5   *son droit en Gales*. It is not clear what exactly is meant by Owain's right, whether the restoration of lands taken from him by Reginald de Grey, earl of Ruthin, or a right to political power as a native Prince of Wales.

9–10   *Mellenyth . . . Kereynon*. The lordships named here were Mortimer lands in the central March.

18   *Johan Greyndor*. Sir John Greyndour was a prominent knight of Herefordshire who began his career as a servant of John of Gaunt. In September 1402 he was given custody of the castle and lordship of Radnor in order to resist the rebels (*Calendar of Patent Rolls 1401–05*, p. 120). In spite of Mortimer's plea, he remained loyal to the king, fought at Shrewsbury, served under the prince of Wales during the summer of 1403, played a prominent part in the defeat of the Welsh at Grosmont in March 1405, and was active in the siege of Aberystwyth castle in 1407 and the defence of a number of the border castles. Davies concludes, "It was men such as Sir John Greyndour who had saved the English king's bacon in Wales during the Glyn Dŵr revolt" (*Revolt*, p. 245). He died in September 1416 (*Calendar of Close Rolls 1413–19*, p. 338).

19   *Preshemde*. Presteigne (Welsh, Llanandras [= the church of St. Andrew]) was likely an Anglo-Saxon settlement, as indicated by the early forms Preshemde, Presthende, and Presthemede, "a household of priests" (Soulsby, *Towns*, p. 219).

27. IOLO GOCH, *WHEN HIS AUTHORITY WAS GREATEST*

Ed. Gruffydd Aled Williams. Trans. and notes, John K. Bollard.

Manuscripts: There are thirty-five manuscripts, ranging from the first quarter of the sixteenth century to the beginning of the nineteenth century, containing thirty-six copies of this poem, but not every manuscript includes a complete transcript of the poem, and two manuscripts contain only very brief fragments.

While this poem was rejected from the Iolo Goch canon in the 1920s and from Dafydd Johnston's editions of Iolo's complete works in 1988 and 1993, Gruffydd Aled Williams has more recently presented a set of compelling arguments for reinstating it in "Adolygu'r Canon," in which is included the edited text reproduced herein. Williams's arguments are summarized briefly in the essay below (see p. 315), and the translation and following discussion and notes are heavily indebted to his notes, ideas, and analysis, as well as to his thoughtful suggestions and corrections.

Thirty-four of the manuscripts attribute the poem to Iolo Goch; the thirty-fifth contains only the first two lines with no attribution. In and of themselves, these attributions are inconclusive as to authorship, as many later poems were attributed to him. Seven manuscripts date from the sixteenth century. The NLW Llanstephan MS 7 (1500–25?) text, written in a remarkably small hand, difficult to read, is possibly the earliest, and it contains some good readings not found in later versions; unfortunately the manuscript has been damaged by rot and the beginnings and endings of the lines have been lost. Another early manuscript, valuable for its textual evidence, is NLW Peniarth MS 189, written by the Elizabethan poet Simwnt Fychan. Williams points out the striking fact that nearly a third of the manuscripts containing this poem include collections of poems, authentic and inauthentic, to Owain Glyndŵr. The largest of these collections, with nine poems in NLW MS 8330B, is followed by a copy, in the original Latin, of the agreement (see Item 46) made between Glyndŵr and Charles VI of France (Williams, *Adolygu*, p. 62).

Title	Twenty-nine manuscripts include a heading connecting the poem with Glyndŵr, ten of which describe the poem as made for Owain *pan oedd fwyaf i rwysg* [when his authority was greatest]. This title, however, does not appear before c.1600; see the note to line 24 below.
1	*Llyma* [Behold!]. *Llyma* is not a verb form *per se*, but an interjection derived from *syll* [look!] (imperative of *syllu* [gaze]) + *yma* [here], thus meaning "lo!, lo here!, behold!;" see Evans, *Grammar*, p. 246.
	rhag sythfryd Sais [caused by English arrogance]. More literally, "from an Englishman's arrogance." *Sythfryd* is a compound of *syth* [stiff, stubborn; contemptuous, swaggering, proud] + *bryd* [mind, thought], hence "arrogance, haughtiness, pride." *Sais* (pl. *Saeson*) [Englishman, Saxon] is taken here as a rhetorical use of an indefinite singular to mean the plural in general.
3	*llain* [blade]. Here *llain* [blade, sword] is a metonymy for a leader, establishing the Owain/weapon metaphor carried throughout the poem.
5	*pybyr* [mighty]. For the wide range of positive and apt senses for this adjective, see the note to Item 6.42, Iolo's poem on Owain's genealogy; see also lines 9, 35.
7	*waedlain* [bloody blade]. This is the lenited form of *gwaedlain*, from *gwaed* [blood] + *llain* [blade], an extension of the metonymy in line 3.
8	*ymwan naw tarian llu* [contend with many shields of a host]. Literally, "joust with nine shields of a host." *Naw* [many; lit., nine] here, as elsewhere, means "a large number." In her commentary on the line *ar naw bystylat* [trampling nine (at a time)] in the *Book of Taliesin*, Haycock notes, "The idea of defeating nine(s) and its multiples is frequent, and she references eight additional examples from early Welsh poetry (Haycock, *Legendary Poems*, pp. 302–03). Thus, *naw tarian* [nine shields] may be understood metonymously as "many defenders or opponents."

11   *braw geinbryd gân* [terror of a finely formed song]. Williams interprets this phrase as "a well-formed song that causes terror," with the suggestion that it refers to the effect of poetic prophecies about Owain (*Adolygu*, p. 68n11 [my translation]).

12   *darogan* [prophecy]. On the linking of Owain and prophecy in the poetry contemporary with him see Fulton's essay in this volume and Item 3.29 note.

14   *Yn dial cam y Deau* [avenging the wrong of the South]. Williams (*Adolygu*, pp. 47–48, 60) suggests the possibility that this is a reference to Glyndŵr's campaigns in the South in 1401, 1402, and 1403, but inclines towards the two latter years.

17   *gyrcher* [may be engaged]. Lenited form of *cyrcher*, present subjunctive impersonal of *cyrchu* [to attack].

18   *o'r tri Owain* [by the three Owains]. Owain Glyndŵr is named explicitly, but the identities of the other two to whom he is compared are less certain; perhaps the most likely are the legendary Owain ab Urien and the historical Owain Lawgoch; see the notes to lines 21, 23–25. The former appears earlier in prophetic context in the *Oianau*, the "Little Pig Stanzas" attributed to Myrddin in the *Black Book of Carmarthen* (Jarman, *Llyfr Du*, 17.148–49; Bollard, "Myrddin," p. 28). An otherwise unspecified Owain is named in "The Prophecy of Myrddin and Gwenddydd, His Sister": "Decreed is the coming of Owain, / who will conquer as far as London / and give the Welsh the object of their desire" (Bollard, "Myrddin," p. 40; Evans, *Poetry in the Red Book*, col. 581.5–6). It may be purely coincidental that this passage contains the verb *goresgyn* [conquer], which underlies Iolo Goch's *[g]oresgynnwr* [conqueror]; see the note to lines 23–25 below. As Margaret Griffiths summarizes, "Owain became one of the most popular long looked-for deliverers of later vaticinations, and the prophecy of his return was applied to more than one Owain in succession" (Griffiths, *Early Vaticination*, p. 100).

19   *glain dwyrain* [ascendant jewel]. The word *dwyrain* is literally "east" or "eastern," whence the figurative sense of "rising, ascending, triumphant." Alternatively, might it mean "a jewel of the east," a more literal reference to Glyndŵr's origins in eastern Wales?

20   *Baun* [peacock]. Lenited form of *paun*. Iolo also refers to Owain as a peacock in line 39 below and earlier in Items 4.8, and 6.6, 8.

21   *Owain*. Williams (*Adolygu*, p. 68) proposes that the use of *Deifr* in the next line suggests that this might be a reference to Owain ab Urien, the northern sixth-century prince Taliesin praises and who in later lore became one of the heroes of Arthur's court (see Williams, *Taliesin*, Poems VI, X; Thomson, *Owein*; Bollard, *Arthur*, pp. 65–91, 150–53).

     arglwyddlain [lordly jewel]. This compound could be either *arglwydd* [lord] + *glain* [jewel] (see lines 17, 19), or *arglwydd* + *llain* [blade, sword] (see lines 3, 7); if the latter, translate "lordly blade."

22   *Derfysgwr* [troublemaker]. The lenited form of *terfysgwr*, literally, "one who causes a commotion or strife," from *terfysg* [tumult, commotion] + *gŵr* [man].

          Deifr [Deirans]. On Iolo's use of *Deifr*, see Item 4.58 note. In the present context, as there, it may retain its northern connotation; see also the note on line 29 below.

23–25   *Owain . . . oresgynnwr* [Owain . . . conqueror]. Williams (*Adolygu*, p. 68) suggests that *(g)oresgynnwr* [conqueror] is an apt word to describe Owain Lawgoch (d. 1378), a descendant of the royal house of Gwynedd, who led a "free company" to fight with the French against the English in the Hundred Years' War. He planned two invasions to drive the English out of Wales; the first, in 1369, was foiled by bad weather, and he was assassinated in Poitou in 1378 before the second expedition was mounted. In later tradition, it was prophesied that he, like Glyndŵr, would return.

24   *rwysg* [authority]. Lenited form of *rhwysg*. The occurrence of this word here and in the compound *rhwysgwr* [ruler] (*rhwysg* + *gŵr* [man]) in line 38 probably inspired the rubric at the head of the poem in some later manuscripts; see the note on the title above. *Rhwysg* has a wide range of meanings and connotations; the relevant sense is glossed in *GPC* as "power, authority, rule, dominion, influence, majesty, dignity, glory, splendour, pomp, ostentation, pride," of which any but the last three would fit the present context.

25   *llew* [lion]. Iolo compares Owain to a lion three more times in this poem (lines 30, 31, 46) and four times in his earlier poem on Owain's genealogy (Item 6.32, 55, 56, 77).

          Nudd. Iolo also compares Owain to Nudd Hael (the Generous) in the same poem (see Item 6.16 and note).

26   *Llyrf* [spears]. *Llyrf* is the plural of *llorf*, which generally means "post, piller; supporter, defender" (see *GPC*, s.v. *llorf*). However, in his elegy to Sir Rhys ap Gruffydd of Llansadwrn (d. 1356), Iolo uses *llorf* in the sense "spear, lance" (Iolo Goch, *Poems*, 7.18).

          ffyrf [mighty]. Not unlike English "stout," *ffyrf* can connote strength or thickness or both. The sense of the line is that Owain was endowed with his father's martial attributes.

27   *wrth wŷr â llediaith* [towards men with a foreign accent]: One might reasonably translate this more specifically as "towards men with an English accent."

29   *Brynaich* [Bernicians]. Perhaps *Brynaich* here is a term for the English in general, or a reference to Owain's earlier successes on the Scottish border; see Item 6.79 note and the note to line 22 above.

31   *aergroch* [battle's uproar]. Twenty-seven of the thirty-three complete texts read *eurgroch* (i.e., *eur* [gold] + *croch* [loud]), which is meaningless in this context. However, orthographic variation between *aer* and *eur* is not unusual, and Williams (*Adolygu*, p. 69n31) is confident that the two texts reading *aergroch* both by learned scribes, have retained the correct reading, which he interprets as "hand causing uproar in battle" or "hand causing loud crying in battle" (my trans.).

32   *goch* [bloody]. Lenited form of *coch*, literally, "red;" this adjective could modify either (*g*)*wŷr* [men] or *Lloegr* [England].

33   *Llurig Dduw* [God's breastplate]. The general sense of this phrase is "God's protection." *Llurig*, literally, "breastplate," is a borrowing from Latin *lorica* [a leather cuirass, a defence] which developed in Christian tradition a secondary sense of "a prayer or charm of protection." A well-known example is the Lorica of St. Patrick or St. Patrick's Breastplate. Iolo Goch also uses the phrase *llurig Dduw* in a poem to Ieuan Trefor, bishop of St. Asaph, to reassure him and to act as a protective charm on the bishop's journey to Scotland as ambassador for Richard II in 1397: *Gwisg lurig Dduw . . . / pan gyfotych* [put on God's breastplate . . . / when you arise] (Iolo Goch, *Poems*, 17.41). The phrase occurs earlier in a poem by Einion ap Gwgawn to Llywelyn ab Iorwerth (d. 1240): *llurig Dduw amdanad* [God's breastplate upon you] (Morris-Jones and Parry-Williams, *Hendregadredd*, p. 53), and in a seventeeth-century manuscript in an anonymous poem that begins *Croes Crist a wisga / Lluruc duw amdana* [I will put Christ's cross, / God's breastplate, upon me], and whose title, *Llurig Alexander*, was probably drawn from an earlier poem with that title in the *Book of Taliesin*, and which contains the line *Croes Crist glaear, lluryc llachar rac pob aelet* [The gentle cross of Christ, resplendent breastplate against every pain] (Haycock, *Blodeugerdd*, pp. 23–29).

34   *iôr Rhufain* [lord of Rome]. This reference identifies Owain with Cadwaladr Fendigaid, whose death in Rome in 689 is recounted in Geoffrey of Monmouth's *Historia regum Britanniae* (*Historia* 12.18; *History*, p. 283). There were pre-Galfridian traditions that Cadwaladr would return to lead the Welsh against the English, as can be seen in the tenth-century poem *Armes Prydein*: *Bydinoed Katwaladyr kadyr y deuant* [The armies of Cadwaladr, bravely will they come] (see Williams, *Armes Prydein*, and Livingston, *Brunanburh*, line 81, also lines 91, 163, 184). Williams (*Adolygu*, p. 70) notes that the fifteenth-century poet Dafydd Llwyd ap Llywelyn ap Gruffudd refers to the *mab darogan* [the son of prophecy] as *Owain o Rufain* [of Rome].

35   *pybyr* [mighty]. See the note to line 5 above.

36   *tair talaith* [three diadems]. I.e., the crowns of the three major historical kingdoms of Wales, as enumerated, for example, in the *Llyfr Blegywryd* version of the laws: *teir ran Kymry, Gwyned, Powys, Deheubarth* [the three parts of Wales: Gwynedd, Powys, and Deheubarth] (Williams and Powell, *Cyfreithiau*, p. 2).

37   *y Glyn* [the Glyn]. The *glyn* [valley, glen] is, of course, Glyndyfrdwy (see Item 3.88 note).

38   *rwysgwr* [ruler]. See the note to line 24.

41   *mewn ymladdgors* [in the battle-bog]. This seems to be a reference to the prophetic tradition that Cors Fochno ("the bog or marsh of Mochno" in northern Ceredigion, now known in English by the less euphonious name Borth Bog) was to be the site of the battle in which the Welsh would finally be victorious over the English. References to Cors Fochno are frequent in prophetic poetry both before and after the time of Owain Glyndŵr; the earliest is found in the *Black Book of Carmar-*

then in the "Oian, little pig!" stanzas, composed no later than the mid-thirteenth century but attributed to Myrddin (Merlin), in a list of battles to come that includes *cad Cors Mochno* [the battle of Cors Fochno] (Jarman, *Llyfr Du*, p. 34; Bollard, "Myrddin," p. 29; Griffiths, *Vaticination*, index, s.v. Cors Fochno).

42   *hil Hors* [of Horsa's line]. Hengist and Horsa were the first Saxons invited to Britain by Gwrtheyrn (Vortigern) to Britain, where they settled on the Isle of Thanet, as recounted in the *Historia Brittonum* (see Williams, *Armes Prydein*; Livingston, *Brunanburh*, pp. 28–29; and Morris, *Nennius*, pp. 26, 66–67).

44   *pais dewddur* [a thick iron surcoat]. Iolo uses the same phrase, with the compound of *tew* [thick] + *dur* [steel] reversed to *durdew*, in Item 6.58.

48   *gwinau* [auburn-haired]. On the color of Glyndŵr's hair, see the note to Item 4.4.

49   *paladr briwdwn* [a shattered spear]. On the significance of the image of a shattered spear, see Items 3.46, 55, 59–66; 4.52.

52   *pumoes* [five ages]. I.e., a very long life.

28. *HISTORIA VITAE*

Adapted and trans. by Alicia Marchant, from *Historia vitae*, ed. Stow, pp. 167–68, 170–75.

Manuscripts: Fourteen surviving manuscripts, including London, British Library, MS Cotton Claudius B.ix (c.1404) and MS Cotton Tiberius C.ix (c.1413).

The *Historia vitae et regni Ricardi Secundi* is thought to have been produced in two parts at the Abbey of Evesham, in Worcestershire, sometime before 1413. The first section, which covers the history of England from 1352 to 1392, appears to have been authored by Nicholas Herford, the prior of Evesham (Gransden, *Historical Writing*, pp. 157–58). The second section covers the years 1390 to 1402 and was written by an unknown author during the reign of Henry IV (1399–c.1413). Despite the narrative ending in 1402, the chronicler provides unique insight into the revolt; the account of its initiation is of particular note. The fourteen surviving manuscripts of the *Historia vitae* point to a degree of popularity (*Historia vitae*, ed. Stow, pp. 22–29). Also notable is its apparent use by later writers, including the anonymous composer of the English *Polychronicon Continuation* (Item 78). On the dating of the chronicle, see Livingston's essay in this volume, pp. 472–74.

31–32   *uigilia Corporis Christi* [the evening of Corpus Christi]. I.e., 2 June.

42   *Stretflur*. This is an interesting combination of the Welsh and Latin; the Latinate is *Strata Florida*, and the Welsh is *Ystrad Fflur*. The Welsh-born chronicler Adam ofUsk also uses the form *Stratflur* (Item 22.22).

45   *Exercitus*. Stow: *Excercitus*.

58   Easter Sunday fell on 26 March in 1402. According to Stow, Lord Grey must have been captured sometime after 7 February 1402 (*Historia vitae*, p. 213).

76   *festo Sancti Albani* [the feast of Saint Alban]. I.e., 22 June.

83–85   In this colorful account of the defection of Mortimer's Welsh tenants to Owain Glyndŵr, the Welsh of Maelienydd are described not only as traitors to their immediate overlord, but more broadly are constructed as an isolated pocket that is detached ethnically, religiously and culturally. As the descendants of Judas this community is destined for damnation; Judas was held to have committed the mortal and unforgivable sin not only of betraying Christ, but of despairing of God's mercy (hence his suicide).

103   *festum Decollacionis beati Iohannis Baptiste* [the feast of the Beheading of the Blessed John the Baptist]. I.e., 29 August.

108   *festum Sancti Martini episcopi* [the feast of Saint Martin the Bishop]. I.e., 11 November.

112–13   *festum Sancti Andree Apostoli* [the feast of Saint Andrew the Apostle]. I.e., 30 November.

29. *TERROR IN SHROPSHIRE*

Adapted and trans. by Michael Livingston, from *PPC*, ed. Nicolas, 2.77–78.

Manuscripts: London, British Library, MS Cotton Cleopatra F.iii, fol. 41r.

Though we know the day and month on which this damaged but fascinating letter was written to King Henry IV, we do not know the year. Nicolas, in printing the text, placed it among those materials of Henry IV's reign for which he had no clear date, but in the brief few lines of his headnote to the letter he speculated that the document should be dated to 1403. The likelihood that the letter obliquely refers to the Battle of Bryn Glas (see line 9) indeed suggests a date of 21 April 1403 at the earliest, and the reference to a recent and comforting visit from Prince Henry would match well (see lines 12–17). While this date for the letter is accepted here, it is not accepted without some reservation (see note to line 13).

No matter the date, the letter is a superb attestation to not only the physical damage but also the psychological damage wrought by the Welsh rebels in Shropshire: nearly every line drips with the panic of those writing the letter to the king.

9   *archers estraungers* [non-local archers]. The fact that the citizens of Shropshire specifically ask for non-local archers could indicate a very present awareness on their part of the disaster at the Battle of Bryn Glas, in which local archers turned against the English and joined the Welsh, resulting in a catastrophic slaughter. For more on this fascinating battle, see Livingston's essay herein.

10–11   *mettre voz . . . mayns a voz lieges* [your hands . . . to your lieges]. The letter's writers here trade upon the language of feudalism: the rite of allegiance required the placement of the liege's hands (or symbol) literally within the hands of the liege-lord.

12–17   Prince Henry was in Shrewsbury in March of 1403, which might well have led
          Nicolas to assume an April 1403 date for this letter. The prince did, however,
          make subsequent visits to Shropshire, any one of which could be the visit in
          question. No matter the date, his presence, and that of his non-local and trusted
          military retinue, was clearly of some psychological and practical effect for the
          English in the city.

13   The reference to a French presence alongside the Welsh rebels is intriguing to
          say the least. One explanation for these lines is that the citizens are referring
          to reports of French units engaging with the sieges of northern Wales, or to
          heretofore unknown (and nowhere else recorded) early French parties on the
          ground in England. Another possibility would be that the document has been
          misdated, and that it belongs to the period of 1405 or 1406, when the presence
          of French on English soil in aid of the Welsh was either an imminent threat or
          a frightening memory. Alternatively, the people of Shropshire could be report-
          ing on rumors that had no basis in fact but were no less powerfully provocative.

21   The devastation of a third of the county may not be an exaggeration. See
          Hodges, *Owain*, pp. 111–12.

30. PRINCE HENRY, *RAZING OF OWAIN'S HOMES*

Adapted and trans. by Rhidian Griffiths from *PPC*, ed. Nicolas, 2.61–62; *Original Letters*,
ed. Ellis, 2.1.11–13. Variants from the latter are designated OL in the notes below.

Manuscript: London, British Library, MS Cotton Cleopatra F.iii, fol. 117v.

This letter was written, presumably to his father Henry IV, during the Prince's sojourn
at Shrewsbury while fulfilling his commission as his father's lieutenant in Wales for a year
from 1 April 1403 (Rymer, *Foedera*, 8.291; *Calendar of Patent Rolls 1401–05*, p. 216). The
intention was to establish a frontier line of strong garrisons from north to south as bases for
attacks on the rebels, but it was only partially fulfilled owing to a lack of money to pay the
wages of armies and garrisons, and effectively came to an end in July 1403 following the
rebellion of the Percies and the Battle of Shrewsbury. Henry had as the nucleus of his army
the men of his own household and the retinues of some of his associates, including the earl
of Worcester, Gilbert Talbot, and Sir John Stanley. This letter describes a raid into Owain's
own country of Cynllaith and attacks on his two main residences; scorched earth tactics were
employed, but Owain himself proved elusive.

3   *consideracioun*. OL: *consideracion*.

          les bosoignes. OL: *la bosoignes*.

5   *pardecea*. OL: *par decea*.

7   *povair dautres*. OL: *pouair d'autres*.

9   *par quoy*. OL: *per quoy*.

          noz gens. OL: *nos gens*.

11   *Sagherne*. OL: *Saghern*. I.e., Sycharth, Owain's residence in the valley of the river Cynllaith, near Llangedwyn in Powys, described (c.1387–95) in some detail by Iolo Goch in Item 8. The site of Owain's manor is still visible, though none of the buildings remain. Numerous aerial photographs, plans, and views of excavations are available at RCAHMW, s.v. Sycharth (see also Roberts, "Tŷ pren").

Sycharth Today. Clearly visible in the center of the picture is the flat-topped mound, surrounded by earthworks. At far right are the remains of what was once a fishpond.

11   *vousist*. OL: *voussit*.

12–13   *nul homme*. OL: *nul home*.

13   *pluseurs*. OL: *plusieurs*.

14   *Glyndourdy*. A ditched mound on the south bank overlooking the Dee about a mile west of the present village of Glyndyfrdwy is traditionally Owain Glyndŵr's ancestral castle site. It is associated with a roughly triangular moat some 300 feet to its east, the site of what is thought to have been one of Owain's houses destroyed in 1403 (RCAHMW, s.vv. Owain Glyndwr's Mount, Owen Glyndwr's House [sic]).

17   *illeoques*. OL: *illoeques*.

17   *un grand gentil*. This influential follower of Owain has not been identified. Owain did command a significant following among the squirearchy (see Davies, "Owain Glyn Dŵr and the Welsh Squirearchy").

18   *ransom*. OL: *ranson*.

19   *davoir*. OL: *d'avoir*.

         dite some. OL: *dit somme*.

20–21   *compaignouns que feurent*. OL: *compaignons que furent*.

21   *le dit journe*. OL: *la dit journee*.

22   *commote d'Edirnyoun*. OL: *Commote Dedirnyon*. Commote is a borrowing from the Welsh *cwmwd*, a medieval Welsh territorial unit, two (or more) of which form a cantref, analogous to the English hundred. At the eastern extreme of Edeirnion, Glyndyfrdwy was a "quasi-autonomous islet of Welsh rule" (Davies, *Revolt*, p. 134).

     Merionyethe. OL: *Merionnyth*. Prior to the Edwardian conquest, Edeirnion was a commote in the cantref of Penllyn. In 1284 under the Statute of Rhuddlan, Penllyn was combined with Meirionydd to form the administrative county of Merionethshire.

24   *pur*. OL: *por*.

     ovec. OL: *ove*.

25   *par*. OL: *per*.

26   *[de] touz*. OL: *de touz*.

     pardecea. OL: *par decea*.

     pardevers vous notre. OL: *pardevers notre*.

27   *Johan de Watertoun*. OL: *John de Waterton*. John de Waterton was a member of a staunch Lancastrian family who had been servants of Henry IV's father, John of Gaunt. John Waterton was a member of the prince's council, keeper of his secret treasury and his receiver in the Duchy of Cornwall.

     foy. OL: *foye*.

29   *sainte*. OL: *sante*.

31. OWAIN GLYNDŴR, *LETTER TO HENRY DWN*

Adapted and trans. Matthews, in Rees and Jones, *Thomas Matthews's Welsh Records in Paris*, pp. 105–06, 113–14. Notes by John K. Bollard.

Manuscript: The original source, now lost, was reportedly in the possession of Robert Pugh of Cefn-y-Garlleg in Llansantffraid, Denbigshire, around 1700, and was itself "apparently a copy of something 'lately seen by Mr. Owen Lloyd in London'" (Lloyd, *Owen Glendower*, p. 40n4; Owen and Blakeney, *History of Shrewsbury*, 1.181–82n).

Henry Dwn (or Don) of Kidwelly was a powerful leader in South Wales, a descendant of Llywelyn ap Gwrgan, progenitor of the Welsh lords of Kidwelly in the eleventh-century. He served under John of Gaunt in Normandy and Picardy in 1369, and in 1388–89 he was appointed Gaunt's steward of the lordship of Kidwelly. Dwn was a strong, even harsh, leader, evicting tenants and seizing lands, undeterred by legal proceedings against him. For his cause to succeed in the south, Owain would need Henry Dwn as an ally, and the present letter was sent to secure Dwn's aid. That this letter — and other negotiations unknown to us today — served its purpose is evident from the fact that Henry Dwn and his son gathered a force to attack Kidwelly in June 1403 (giving us a *terminus ad quem* for this letter), Dinefwr castle on 2 July, and Kidwelly once more on 13 August, and yet again, joined by French and Breton forces, in late September or October, also capturing the ship of a Llanstephan merchant in Carmarthen. As one of Owain's most zealous supporters, Dwn's lands were officially forfeited to the crown in 1407, and he himself spent time in prisons in Kidwelly and Gloucester. He was pardoned in 1413 for a fine of £200, the largest fine against a rebel — and one he never paid. After regaining his lands, he rather audaciously levied fines on tenants who had failed to support him in rebellion (Davies, *Revolt*, pp. 200–01, 305, 307, 311; Lloyd, *Owen Glendower*, pp. 40–41).

2   *auxilio Dei et vestro* [by God's help and yours]. Owain begins by addressing Dwn as a fellow Welshman to enlist him his aid, though he later expresses his hopes as a command: *mandamus, et requirimus, et supplicamus* [we command, require, and enjoin] (lines 9–10).

13–14   *et non admiramini* [do not be surprised]. With the verb *admiror* [to wonder at, be astonished at, to regard with admiration] it is clear that Owain is not telling Henry Dwn about the rebellion — he would certainly have heard the news much earlier — but is rather apologizing and admonishing him not to be offended that he had not earlier enlisted Henry's aid. This justification for not having apprised Dwn of his plans because of the need for surprise also suggests a hasty period of planning and preparation in September 1400.

17   *Dominum de Glyn Dwfrdwy*. It is indicative of Owain's relationship with, and understanding of, Henry Dwn that he styles himself, "lord of Glyndyfrdwy" in this letter, rather than *Princeps Wallie*, which he had adopted in 1400 and which he used in his international correspondence (see Items 46.1, 52.1, 4).

32. JOHN SCUDAMORE, *PLEA FOR AID*

Ed. and trans. by Michael Livingston.

Manuscript: London, British Library, MS Cotton Cleopatra F.iii, fol. 120r. First printed in *Original Letters*, ed. Ellis, 2.1.19–20; variants from the latter are designated OL in the notes below.

    This letter to John Fairford, the receiver of Brecknock, from John Scudamore, who had been given custody of Carreg Cennen on 2 May 1402, introduces a sequence of striking letters written over the course of days in the south of Wales. These original letters grant us multiple English viewpoints with which to gauge the advance of Owain's assault on Carmarthenshire in particular. This present letter shows that Owain's advance southward was taking place with high speed, leaving Scudamore in real fear for his safety and that of his family: Scudamore reports that Owain refused safe-conduct from the castle for his wife and mother-in-law. (In a strange twist, Scudamore would later marry once more — after the presumed death of the wife referred to here — this time to Owain's daughter; indeed, there are lingering rumors that Owain's last years were thus spent in hiding under Scudamore's protection.) We also learn that Scudamore believed that Owain's next destination was Pembrokeshire, which would indeed prove the case (see Items 35 and 36).

2   *kyng*. So MS. OL: *king*.

4   *and require yow*. MS: *and require ~~and requ~~ yow*.

9   *aboute the towne*. MS: *aboute the ~~tone~~ towne*.

13   The fact that Scudamore asks Fairford to contact Sir Hugh Waterton in order
           to press upon the king the seriousness of the situation perhaps reveals how well
           it was known by Henry IV's subjects that the king was slow to action.

           al thilke. So MS. OL: *all thilke*.

15   *traytours*. So MS. OL: *traytors*.

19   *Wreten*. So MS. OL: *Written*.

33. Jankyn Havard, *Plea for Aid*

   Ed. and trans. by Michael Livingston.

Manuscript: London, British Library, MS Cotton Cleopatra F.iii, fol. 111r. First printed in
Original Letters, ed. Ellis, 2.1.13; variants from the latter are designated OL in the notes
below.

   Jankyn Havard (or Hanard) was constable of Dinefwr Castle, just outside the town of
Llandeilo in Carmarthenshire, Wales, a fortress that Owain quite possibly viewed as both a
strategic and a symbolic target (see note to Item 35.15). As Ellis observes in first printing it,
this letter from Havard was addressed to John Fairford, then receiver of Brecknock, who
sent it on to the King's Council.

1   *Oure*. So MS. OL: *Dure*.

3   *Kermerdin*. So MS. OL: *Kermerdyn*.

6   *wydd*. So MS. OL: *wydde*.

7   *woll*. So MS. OL: *well*.

           ows. So MS. OL: *owss*.

9   *coming*. So MS. OL: *comig*.

12   *Gruff*. So OL. MS: *Grufff*.

13   *lettre*. So MS. OL: *letter*.

15   *yn hast and*. MS: *yn hast ~~ad~~ and*.

           fest of Seint Thomas the Martyr. There were two yearly feasts in honor of Thomas
           Becket at this time: the Feast of St. Thomas the Martyr, 29 December, and the
           Feast of the Translation of St. Thomas the Martyr, 7 July. Context makes clear
           the summer date, and so Havard is thus writing on a Saturday, a fact somewhat
           relevant to the details of his subsequent letter (Item 35).

Martyr. So MS. OL: *Martir*.

34. RICHARD KINGSTON, *PLEA FOR AID*

Ed. and trans. by Michael Livingston.

Manuscript: London, British Library, MS Cotton Cleopatra F.iii, fol. 121v. First printed in *Original Letters*, ed. Ellis, 2.1.17–19; variants from the latter are designated OL in the notes below.

Richard Kingston, on the Sunday he wrote this letter, was archdeacon and clerk of the royal castle at Hereford, as well as the dean of Windsor. He was, through and through, a king's man, which is more than evident in his signing this letter *votre petite creature*. This fascinating letter was written, it seems, in two phases. The initial letter, written in great haste (line 14) was intended to pass the news he had just received from John Scudamore in a letter written on 5 July: Carmarthen was surrounded by Welsh rebels and in grave danger of falling (Item 32). Before Kingston could send his impassioned plea to the king, however, he apparently received a further letter, this one written on 6 July by Jankyn Havard to John Fairford (who dutifully passed it on): not only had Carmarthen fallen to Owain and his men, but so, too, had Newcastle Emlyn (Item 33). This additional news apparently so shocked the archdeacon that his postscript abandoned linguistic proprieties and addressed the king directly in Middle English.

4	*contenantz lettre*. MS: *contenantz leftre*.
5	*hastifment*. MS: *hastifment ~~atte~~*.
7	*pur salvacioun*. So MS. OL: *pour salvacion*.
	est. Inserted above the line.
8	*ou suffrez estre perduz*. Inserted above the line.
9	*per*. So MS. OL: *pour*.
11	*d'une lettre . . . de John Skydmore*. I.e., Item 32.
14	*grant haste*. Inserted above the line.
16	*alle*. So MS. OL: *all*.

35. JANKYN HAVARD, *PLEA FOR AID*

Ed. and trans. by Michael Livingston.

Manuscript: London, British Library, MS Cotton Cleopatra F.iii, fol. 123v. First printed in *Original Letters*, ed. Ellis, 2.1.15–16; variants from the latter are designated OL in the notes below.

This letter, if indeed written on a Wednesday (see line 18), must have been written on 11 July 1403. On the actions narrated, see the notes to Item 36.

2, 4   *Clere*. So MS. OL: *Cler*.

5   *Lacharn*. So MS. OL: *Locharn*.

            miles. So MS. OL: *myles*.

10–13   Havard either surmises or has received official word that reinforcements are not yet coming due to logistical concerns over supplies. He is thus at pains to emphasize how many food stocks are available in the countryside alone.

10   *hast₂*. So MS. OL: *haste*.

15   *for that was the chef plas in old tyme*. In addition to controlling a significant and important expanse of the Tywi valley, the castle of Dinefwr was traditionally regarded as the chief seat of Hywel Dda (r. 942–950), who was widely considered one of the greatest of Welsh kings. For Owain it thus served a symbolic purpose in addition to a strategic one, a fact not lost upon his enemies.

16   *seyyn*. MS: *seyþyn*, with the thorn marked for deletion.

            viij. mill. and xij. xx. spers. I.e., eight-thousand and twelve-score (8,240) men with spears.

18   *Dynevour*. So MS. OL: *Dynevor*.

36. BURGESSES OF CAERLEON, *OWAIN AND THE PROPHET*

Ed. and trans. by Michael Livingston.

Manuscript: London, British Library, MS Cotton Cleopatra F.iii, fol. 116r. First printed in *Original Letters*, ed. Ellis, 2.1.22–23; variants from the latter are designated OL in the notes below.

This letter, from *le maire et les burgeis de Kairlyon* [the mayor and burgesses of Caerleon], presents several difficulties of interpretation, not least because it is missing several words in two locations. The letter appears to be written in some haste, speaking of matters that must have made more contextual sense in the moment than they do at a remove of six hundred years. The letter, written from Caerleon to Monmouth, brings news of two events that had just occurred to the west: Owain's defeat at the hands of Lord Carew and his meeting with Hopcyn ap Tomas, a man apparently well-known for his vatic powers. That these matters were of some urgent news for both the people of Caerleon and of Monmouth helps us to recognize the contextual action: Owain and his men had blitzed down the Afon Tywi and Afon Teifi in twin raids that had left him in control of much of Carmarthenshire. The fear in South Wales was that he would now sweep eastward, unchecked through the coast before retreating up the River Wye toward his mountain hideouts, no doubt destroying Caerleon and Monmouth along the way. The two events in the letter are thus related: Carew's actions had at last stopped Owain's forces and prevented him from pursuing a course to the east, while Hopcyn's clever use of prophecy had played on Owain's fears and prevented him from riding west into Gower and on to the rest of the southern coast.

As it happens, the confidence of the burgesses was apparently ill-founded. On 23 July William Beauchamp reported from Abergavenny that he was under distress and that the rebels had captured one of his soldiers between his castle and Hereford (*Royal Letters*, ed. Hingeston, pp. 152–54). On 3 September, Archdeacon Kingston reported hundreds of rebels were raiding Herefordshire (Item 37), and Adam of Usk suggests they raided as far as the Severn sea (Item 62.23–28).

2	*Glyndour*. So MS. OL: *Glyndor*.
4–12	This passage is confusing at best. We know something of Owain's actions from Jankyn Havard's letter of 11 July, which reports that Thomas Lord Carew rose up out of Pembrokeshire with a force of men to fight the Welsh rebels; Owain, who had been planning to sweep east toward Kidwelly was thus forced to move west to face this new threat to his rear. Owain and Carew held talks outside of St. Clears, after which the two forces apparently withdrew: Owain lodged at Laugharne before returning to Carmarthen (Item 35). It may be, then, that the *hull* [hill] referred to here does not mean, as previous scholars have understood it, "the hill country north of Carmarthen" (so, e.g., Lloyd, *Owen Glendower*, p. 68, and Hodges, *Owain*, p. 102). Instead, it may be, as the singular form of the noun implies, a specific hill, one west of St. Clears where Owain and Carew met (perhaps Brandy Hill?). Regardless of the specific location, it seems that Owain attempted to split his forces the next day: the idea that Owain was attempting a tactical retreat, as reported here, cannot be ruled out, but — since this information comes from the English — it seems likely to be wishful thinking on the part of his enemies; certainly Jankyn Havard paints a picture of Owain well at ease as he takes stock of how best to divide the spoils at Carmarthen.
4	*wordes*. So MS. OL: *words*.
5	*baroun*. So MS. OL: *baron*.
	Glyndour. So MS. OL: *Glyndor*.
7	*y-purpos*. MS: *y purpos do*.
10	*serche*. MS: *r* is a superscript correction.
11	*barones*. So MS. OL: *barons*.
12	MS deteriorated; two or three words are lost.
13	*hit*. So MS. OL: *it*.
	undirstonde. So MS. OL: *understonde*.
14	MS deteriorated; two or three words are lost.
	Thomas. MS: *a* is a superscript correction.
14–21	Owain's exchange with Hopcyn ap Tomas of Gower has been a source of much interest: it is one of our clearest pieces of evidence that Owain himself traded

in the swirl of prophecy and poetry that made him an object of fascination for the Welsh and an object of derision for the English. Of Hopcyn himself we know little, but the report here that he is a "master of Brut" (line 16) indicates that he was considered well-versed in the so-called prophecies of Merlin most commonly associated with Geoffrey of Monmouth — prophecies that had become by the time of Owain a kind of common stock of vatic pronouncement subject to wildly diverse interpretation and reimagination (as in the *Prophecy of Six Kings*, Item 1). Ellis observes that subsequent history "shews that Hopkin . . . was not infallible as a seer," understanding that Hopcyn was prophesying in predicting that Owain would be captured, an event that did not subsequently come true (*Original Letters* 2.1.22). In their review of Ellis, Griffiths and Griffiths argue that the story "exhibits master Hopkin to have been, if not an infallible seer, at least the author of a very ingenious and malicious device for retaliating upon the superstitious fears" of his enemy, Owain (Review of *Original Letters*, p. 225). Such an interpretation might help to make sense of this otherwise difficult passage, yet the reference to Hopcyn in the *Scotichronicon* makes clear not only that he was a fighting man in addition to a seer, but also that he was a partisan for Owain (Item 79.37–38; see Williams, "*Gwrthryfel Glyndŵr*," pp. 181–82). It appears, then, that the account of the burgesses of Caerleon is garbled and distorted: Hopcyn's message may have been formed of prophetic language, but first and foremost it was likely a warning from one of Owain's military allies.

15   *uppon*. So MS. OL: *upon*.

18   *witterliche*. So MS. OL: *wittliche*.

23   *tydynges*. So MS. OL: *tydyngs*.

37. RICHARD KINGSTON, *PLEA FOR AID*

Ed. and trans. by Rhidian Griffiths from *Royal and Historical Letters*, ed. Hingeston, 1.155–59.

Manuscript: London, British Library, MS Cotton Cleopatra F.iii, fol. 79r.

Richard Kingston was granted the deanery of the king's free chapel and castle of Windsor in July 1402. He was also archdeacon of Hereford, which accounts for his presence there (*Calendar of Patent Rolls 1401–05*, pp. 91, 107, 135). He was commissioned in September 1403 (along with the Herefordshire knight, Sir John Cheyney) to raise a loan of 2000 marks for the king, to be sent to him at Carmarthen (*Calendar of Patent Rolls 1401–05*, p. 293), and again in June 1404 to receive money from the subsidy granted by parliament in the counties of Gloucester, Hereford, and Worcester and use it to pay the wages of men at arms and archers fighting the rebels in Wales (*Calendar of Patent Rolls 1401–05*, p. 398).

This excitable letter, written "in great haste," indicates the often precarious position of the March and border country during the revolt in Wales. It also suggests that Owain was at this time able to command significant forces, if Kingston's estimate of a raiding party of 400 Welshmen is correct. Cross-border devastation is a frequently recurring theme in the sources for the history of the rebellion, as much of the warfare engaged in by both sides took the form of punitive attacks on townships, castles and lands. Kingston was over-optimistic in assuming that the arrival of the king himself would bring an end to the uprising.

5   *Talgard*. Hingeston interprets this as a personal name, which makes 'Talgard' appear as a companion of "Owyne Glyn"; but it could be that there is a word missing between *Glyn* and *Talgard* and that *Talgard* refers to the township of Talgarth in the lordship of Brecon. If that is the case, it is likely that Talgarth was the assembly point for this army of rebels, not that they all came from there.

9   *Miles Walter*. This is possibly the same king's esquire who (described as Miles Water) was on 1 December 1403 granted lands worth £47 6s. 8d. in the lordship of Brecon, in recompense for the losses he had sustained to his own lands and goods, provided he defend the town of Brecon and the surrounding country at his own expense (*Calendar of Patent Rolls 1401–05*, p. 320).

9–10   *vous dira . . . a present*. Added above the line.

23   *Mestre Beauford*. This is presumably John Beaufort, earl of Somerset, who was appointed the king's lieutenant of South Wales with full power to receive rebels into grace on 28 September 1403 (*Calendar of Patent Rolls 1401–05*, p. 298).

24   *et dc. archiers*. Altered from *et sufficiauntz archiers*.

38. WILLIAM VENABLES, *OWAIN THREATENS HARLECH*

Ed. and trans. Michael Livingston.

Manuscript: London, British Library, MS Cotton Cleopatra F.iii, fol. 39v.

This note is one of a series of primary documents associated with the sieges of Harlech and Caernarfon Castles (see also Items 39 and 41). Written to the king by William Venables and Roger Brescy, respectively the constable and under-chamberlain of Chester, this particular item efficiently makes clear how desperate the situation was at Harlech Castle in early 1404: the king's constable had been seized by the enemy, and at most twenty-one men remained inside the walls to defend it — sixteen of them, Venables observes, being Welshmen whose loyalties, at least from afar, might well be subject to question. The note summarizes another letter, this one from Reynald Baildon, that was also being passed along to the king (see note to lines 4–5 below).

4–5   *le conestable de Hardelagh en Northgales et deux valletz ovesque lui* [the constable of Harlech in North Wales and two servants with him]. This note was composed on the dorso of a longer, more detailed letter about the situation written to Venables and Brescy by Reynald Baildon, one of the two wardens of the town of Conway (fol. 39r; printed in Ellis, *Original Letters*, 2.1.35–37). Baildon reports that the town of Caernarfon is wracked by disease, and the Welsh in the area are planning to remove the people and cattle from Anglesey into the mountains, a sign of impending attacks: the mountains provided safety for the Welsh people, and removing the livestock to them gave the Welsh vital foodstocks while denying them from the English. Baildon also passes along more confirmation that Frenchmen are aiding the Welsh (see Item 39 below). Though Baildon could not know it, the French and Welsh had already on 14 January joined together on Anglesey to attack the loyal defenders of Beaumaris Castle: they ambushed a deputy collecting taxes, killing dozens of men and capturing the deputy himself, Maredudd ap Cynwrig (the letter imparting this information is dated 21 January and appears on fol. 40r of the present manuscript; it has not been printed). At any rate, Baildon goes on to provide an account of the seizure of the constable of Harlech and the deplorable condition of its defense — the material summarized in this present letter. From Baildon's more detailed letter we learn that this unfortunate constable was William Hunt and that the two "yeoman" captured with him were Jak Mercer and Harry Baker. More than this, we learn that the lieutenant of Owain who captured them was Robin Holland (Lloyd posits that he is the same Robin Holland of Eglwys Fach found in some documents of the time; *Owen Glendower*, pp. 78–79), and that this was the second constable of Harlech he had so captured: the first being Hunt's predecessor, John Hennore.

39. WILLIAM VENABLES, *OWAIN ATTACKS CAERNARFON*

Ed. and trans. Michael Livingston.

Manuscript: London, British Library, MS Cotton Cleopatra F.iii, fol. 39v.

This letter to the king is written by William Venables and Roger Brescy, respectively the constable and under-chamberlain of Chester, explaining the perilousness of the English situation at Caernarfon in particular. It is one of a series of primary documents associated with the sieges of Harlech and Caernarfon Castles (see also Items 38 and 41).

Given its dominating size, its strategic location in northern Wales, and its symbolic significance, Caernarfon Castle had been an important goal for the Welsh rebels from early in the rebellion. As a matter of fact, it was at the Battle of Tuthill, an attack on Caernarfon on 2 November 1401, that Owain apparently first flew the golden dragon banner of Uther Pendragon. That assault, Adam of Usk reports, was turned back with the loss of 300 rebels (Item 22.44–47), but Owain clearly had not given up on seizing the castle. In November of 1403 the Welsh returned in force, this time aided by ships from France under the leadership of a French knight named Jean d'Espagne (on whom see also the headnote to Item 41). Caernarfon successful defense was this time led by William of Tranmere, whose accounts survive (see Lloyd, *Owen Glendower*, p. 77n1). What Venables and Brescy report here is that Owain and the French had returned for a third attempt on the town and castle, one that appears likely to succeed since there are no more than 28 able men left for the defense.

6   *ouesque les Fraunceys* [with the French]. On this French force, see above.

8   *esgynes, sowes, et laddres de tresgrand longure* [engines, sows, and ladders of great length]. The attacking rebel force is apparently well-equipped, and it is interesting to note that the writer expresses no significant surprise in this fact. The *sowes* referred to are roofed structures of some kind: perhaps covered battering rams or constructions to shield sappers and miners who work to undermine a

fortification's wall. The observation that the ladders are of great length led Hodges to wonder if this implied that the ladders used in the November siege were of insufficient length (*Owain*, p. 109).

16–18   The letter referred to is printed in Ellis, *Original Letters*, 2.1.35–37. See note to Item 38, lines 4–5, above.

40. *ROLLS OF PARLIAMENT, 1404*

From *PROME*, ed. and trans. Chris Given-Wilson. Notes by Michael Livingston.

The parliament that began on 14 January 1404 came at a difficult time for Henry IV. He had defeated the rebellion of Hotspur and the Percies at Shrewsbury on 21 July 1403, but the fate of Hotspur's father and likely co-conspirator, the earl of Northumberland, had not yet been decided, and the loyalties of several castles in the north were still committed to the Percy cause. To the west, the Welsh rebellion had grown stronger despite the king having undertaken four recent punitive expeditions in the country. French forces were not only aiding the Welsh now, but they were also independently striking at English shores in raids of their own: most recently an attack by the count of St. Pol. The summary of these threats is the initial excerpt provided here.

Henry IV was not only beset on all sides, he was apparently out of money. And the commons, led by Arnold Savage, fought hard against the king's attempts to extract more funds. As the second excerpt here shows, they demanded an audit of royal accounts, especially those pertaining to the crown's engagement with the Welsh rebellion. As Given-Wilson notes, "remarkably little was said" on the matter of Wales, especially in comparison to the previous two parliaments (Items 13 and 25), and at least some of what was said — including the general pardon announced on the last day of parliament, the third excerpt provided here — was far less antagonistic than the previous parliamentary proceedings: "perhaps it was because the government reasoned that where the stick had failed, the carrot deserved at least to be tried" (*PROME*). Interestingly, while the king named three exceptions to the pardon, not one of them is associated with the Welsh rebellion. It seems that Owain, if he had wished, could have sued for and attained royal pardon.

41. HENRY SCARISBREC, *HARLECH NEAR SURRENDER*

Ed. and trans. Michael Livingston.

Manuscript: London, British Library, MS Cotton Cleopatra F.iii, fol. 40v.

Written by "Henry of Scharisbrec," the lieutenant of Sir John of Bolde at Conwy, this letter is addressed to William Venables and Roger Brescy, respectively the constable and under-chamberlain of Chester. They, in turn, passed the missive on to the king at midnight on 29 February (fol. 40r). It is one of a series of primary documents associated with the sieges of Harlech and Caernarfon Castles (see also Items 38 and 39).

Short though this letter is, it interestingly reveals the kind of "backdoor" dealings that are often forgotten in war. From what Scarisbrec reports, Harlech was not long for English hands at the end of February 1404, though we are relatively certain it was still held by the king on 23 April, when John Stevens of Bristol and Lord Thomas Carew were ordered "to array five ships and vessels at Bristol with men-at-arms and archers" for the purpose of relieving the castles of Cardigan, Aberystwyth, Harlech, and Caernarfon, which were all besieged; in particular, the two men were ordered to drive off Jean d'Espagne, "a knight of France, who with certain ships and vessels has besieged the castles of Caernarfon and Harlech" (*PPC*, ed. Nicolas, 1.221; see Item 39, above). How long afterward Harlech fell into Owain's hands, we do not know, though both it and Aberystwyth were under Welsh control by the end of 1404 (Item 70.26).

42. *Chronicle of Dieulacres Abbey*

Adapted from *Chronicle*, ed. Clarke and Galbraith; trans. Alicia Marchant.

Manuscript: London, Gray's Inn MS no. 9, fols. 129–47.

The Chronicle of Dieulacres Abbey was composed sometime before 1413 at Dieulacres Abbey in Staffordshire, England (Clarke and Galbraith, p. 131). Tensions within the political arena caused by the deposition of Richard II in 1399 are played out within the one chronicle text, which was written in two parts by two different authors. The first author wrote the section from 1381 to 1400, and appears to have favored the deposed Richard II. The second author, who wrote the narrative for the years 1400 to 1403, including the narratives of Owain Glyndŵr's revolt, was a supporter of the new king Henry IV. The Dieulacres chronicler displays greater knowledge of Wales and its history and geography than many contemporary chronicles, and is at times sympathetic towards the Welsh revolt. For instance, the Dieulacres chronicler makes an explicit connection between the terrible weather experienced by the English in Wales and their questionable right to rule that country.

2   The use of phrase *Wallencium de genere Britonum* [the Welsh of the race of the Britons] is a significant departure from the more common use of the term "Welsh" used by the English chroniclers to describe the participants of the revolt. From the twelfth century the Welsh more commonly referred to themselves as *Brytaniaid* [Britons] and *Cymry* [compatriots], terms that express a sense of self, as well as notions of community and a shared ancestry. The term *Welsh* was itself derived from the Anglo-Saxon word for "foreigner" (*Wealh*), and although it came to be largely adopted by the people of Wales, the origins of this term embodied a sense of otherness (see Smyth, "Emergence," p. 28; Davies, *Conquest*, p. 19).

3   This account of Owain Glyndŵr drawing upon "the law of his ancestors" to cement his legitimacy as Prince, is a significant recognition of the duality of the legal system in Wales by the unknown Dieulacres chronicler. Legal processes in Wales between 1284 and 1536 were complex; following the conquest of Wales by Edward I and the resulting Statute of Wales of 1284, English and Welsh laws existed side by side, although English law was followed in matters of criminal law. This legal duality was abolished in the Act of Union in 1536, when English law was formally introduced into Wales. However, in Owain Glyndŵr's day,

there were two separate court systems that dealt with either Welsh law or English law. Within this system, being "Welsh" was legally defined (see Davies, "Twilight"; Williams, *Renewal*, p. 35; Prestwich, *Edward I*, pp. 206 ff.; Davies, "Race Relations," pp. 39–44).

13–15 On the 1st April, 1401, two brothers, Rhys and Gwilym ap Tudur captured Conwy Castle in North Wales, and manage to hold the castle until about May or June, despite the best efforts of the English soldiers. They were first cousins to Owain Glyndŵr, and their brother Maredudd was the great-grandfather of the first Tudor king, Henry VII.

19 I.e. 24 June.

31 Clarke and Galbraith suggest *acreari*, thanking one Mr. Charles Johnson. It is unclear from their edition whether this is a manuscript reading for which Johnson has offered an explanation, or a conjecture, but in either case it is not a good one. I would suggest *arceri* makes good sense, unlike the non-word *acreari*, the proposed meaning of which ('destroyed') does not fit the context in any case, even if it is a possible meaning of this otherwise unattested word.

43. OWAIN GLYNDŴR, *AUTHORIZING AMBASSADORS TO FRANCE*

Ed. Michael Livingston; trans. Helen Fulton. Notes by John K. Bollard.

Manuscript: Paris, Archives Nationales, MS J392.27.

This letters patent appoints Gruffudd Yonge and John Hanmer as Owain Glyndŵr's ambassadors to negotiate fully, together and separately, in his name as Prince of Wales with the ambassadors similarly appointed by Charles VI of France to establish "a permanent or temporary allegiance with the aforementioned most illustrious prince" (lines 12–13). There had been some prior aid from France, who shared a common enemy in the English, though it had not been formalized by treaty. French ships under the command of Jean d'Espagne took part in an attack on Caernarfon in November 1403, in January 1404 a company of some 200 of these French forces waylaid a troop of fifty or sixty from Beaumaris, and, as they continued to cruise Welsh waters, they planned a second attack on Caernarfon (see Item 39; Lloyd, *Owen Glendower*, pp. 77–81). However, this letter opened formal negotiations between the rulers of two states, as indicated by the title Owain has adopted. Owain's chosen ambassadors are named on the dorso of the manuscript: *Procuratio magistri Griffini Yonge, decretorum doctoris, et Johannis Hangmer ambaxiatorum domini Owini principis Walliarum* [Procuration of Master Griffith Yonge, doctor of decrees, and John Hanmer, ambassadors of Lord Owain, prince of Wales]. The manuscript is sealed with Owain's privy seal, bearing, beneath a princely coronet, an escutcheon with the four lions rampant of Llywelyn Fawr and Llywelyn ap Gruffudd of Gwynedd, supported by a dragon on the left and a lion(?) on the right (see p. 5).

1 *Owynus, Dei gratia princeps Wallie*. This is the earliest surviving example of Owain's own use of the title Prince of Wales. In 1301 Edward I appropriated the title *princeps Wallie* for his son, and it remained the title of the first-born son of English kings; it was conferred on Henry IV's son Henry in October 1399. (On

the prior Welsh use of the title, see p. 425.) Thus, Owain was formally challenging the English usage as well as their hegemony, and to emphasize the implications of his claim he was the first Welsh leader to incorporate directly into his official title the highly resonant phrase *Dei gratia* [by the grace of God], thus claiming the same right to authority as the kings of England and France, as well as other potentates (see Lloyd, *Owen Glendower*, p. 83).

5   Gruffudd Yonge (c.1370–c.1435) was probably the illegitimate son of Morgan Yonge ab Iorwerth ap Morgan, who served alongside Glyndŵr in Scotland in 1385 and was sheriff, under-sheriff, and viceroy of Flintshire. Gruffudd was educated at Oxford as *decretorum doctor* [doctor of decrees (i.e., canon law)], and became a prominent churchman. During the early years of the rebellion he was a canon and prebend of Bangor, while simultaneously holding several other ecclesiastical positions. In 1401 he remained in good standing with the English court, but by 1404 he had changed allegiance and become a member of Owain's inner circle, where it is likely that he played a major hand in crafting both the ecclesiastical and the political policies recorded in the "Pennal Letters" (Items 51, 52), and probably in drafting the *Tripartite Indenture* as well (Item 47). He served as Owain's chancellor from 1404, avoiding capture throughout the war, and he was provided to the see of Bangor by Benedict XIII in 1407. The papal schism was resolved in 1417, and in 1418 Pope Martin V selected Yonge, unable to return to Wales, as bishop of Ross, in Scotland, after which in 1423 he became bishop of Hippo in North Africa. He still called himself bishop of Ross in 1430 and was alive in 1432 (see Lloyd, *Owen Glendower*, pp. 121–22; Davies, *Revolt*, p. 214; *Y Bywgraffiadur Cymraeg*, s.n. Gruffydd Young). Gruffudd Yonge's seal, a shield with a lion rampant within a border dancetté, is attached with three other seals to the original copy of the treaty with France (see Item 46), Paris, Archives Nationale, MS J623.96bis.

6   John Hanmer was the son of Dafydd Hanmer and hence Owain Glyndŵr's brother-in-law. He too testified at the Scrope-Grosvenor trial (see Item 7), whose records show that he was five years Owain's junior. It appears that he took no part in the events of 1400, though like Gruffudd Yonge he had become a close confidant of Owain's by 1404 (Lloyd, *Owen Glendower*, pp. 24, 34).

12   *super liga*. There is a substantial gap between these two words as the text moves around damage in the parchment.

20   *excercendi*. So MS. Matthews: *exercendi*.

22   *interessmus*. So MS. Matthews: *interressmus*.

23   *vtraque*. So MS. Matthews: *utroque*.

44. PRINCE HENRY, *DEFENDING THE MARCH*

Ed. and trans. Rhidian Griffiths from *PPC*, ed. Nicolas, 1.229–31. Substantive variants from the very similar letter to the Council on the same date are drawn from PPC, ed. Nicolas, 1.231–32, and are designated C in the notes below.

Manuscript: **C**: London, British Library, MS Cotton Cleopatra F.iii, fol. 57r.

This is one of a number of communications sent by Prince Henry to his father which underline his precarious position as defender of the March at a time when the Welsh rebels were powerful and confident. On the same date the prince sent a duplicate letter, *mutatis mutandis*, to the Council, major variants from which are included in these notes. During the summer of 1404 the Prince maintained his household at Hereford and Leominster, at his own cost, in an attempt to contain the Welsh, who were attacking the English border counties. Owing to the frequency of Welsh attacks, it was also becoming difficult to collect taxes in the western parishes of Shropshire and Herefordshire (see Watt, "On Account"). The major differences between the version sent to the king and that sent to the council (C) are the additional detail and the increased rhetorical pressure the prince applies at the end of the latter.

1–19	*Moun . . . Wircestre*. C: *Depar le Prince. Treschiers et de nostre entier cuer tresbien amez. Nous vous salvons tressouvent en vous signiffiant que a le hault commandement du Roy nostre tresredoubte seigneur et pere nadegaires par ses gracieuses lettres / nous suymes remue ovec nostre hostiel a la ville de Wircestre* [From the Prince. Most dear and greatly loved of our whole heart. We greet you fervently and notify you that at the high command of the King, our most dread lord and father, by his gracious letters of late, we removed with our household to the town of Worcester].
6	*Pontfreyt*. Pontefract, near Wakefield in West Yorkshire, was one of the principal castles of the Duchy of Lancaster, and a favorite residence of John of Gaunt, the father of Henry IV. Richard II is believed to have died a prisoner at Pontefract.
10	*Conte de Northumbr'*. Henry Percy (1341–1408), earl of Northumberland, was an ally of King Henry IV but rebelled against him in 1403. He was pardoned, but rebelled again in 1405, was attainted the following year, and was killed in battle at Bramham Moor in 1408. His son, Henry "Hotspur" Percy (1364–1403), and his brother Thomas Percy (1343–1403), earl of Worcester, were prominent in the early campaigns against Owain, Hotspur as justiciar of North Wales and Worcester as the king's lieutenant in South Wales. Both rebelled against the king in 1403. Hotspur died at the battle of Shrewsbury on 21 July 1403, and Worcester was executed two days later.
11	*William Clifford*. A northern knight and retainer of Richard II and a close ally of the earl of Northumberland, Clifford was later implicated in Archbishop Scrope's rising in 1405.
11–12	*vostre adversaire d'Escoce*. Robert III, king of Scotland.
20	*Conte de Warrewyk*. Richard Beauchamp, earl of Warwick, a close associate and retainer of Prince Henry, was lord of Elfael in the March of Wales. He served regularly in the campaigns against Owain and his followers, and latterly under Henry V in France, where he died in 1439.
24–25	*je feu certiffiez que lez Galoys*. C: *nous estions certiffiez depar les gentils et comenes du countee de Hereford que les rebelx Galoys* [we were informed by the gentlemen and commons of the county of Hereford that the Welsh rebels].

32–33   *Richard d'Everwyk*. Richard of York, brother of Edward, duke of York, who as earl of Cambridge was executed in 1415 for his part in a conspiracy against Henry V.

33   *Conte Mareshcal*. Thomas Mowbray, earl of Norfolk, was Earl Marshal of England and had landed interests in the March as lord of Gower and lord of Strigoil (Chepstow).

34   *Joedy prouchain*. 26 June 1404 was a Thursday; the following Thursday would therefore be 3 July.

43–48   *Et fere vuillez . . . Juyn*. C: *Et que vuillez ainsi ordenner pour nous en haste, que nous purrons fere honoure et service au Roy, nostre seigneur et pere suisdit, prouffit au royaume et sauver nostre estat, entendans que nous navons riens dont nous sustener icy sinon que nous avons mys en gage noz petitz vesseaulx et joiaulx et ent faite chevance de monoie. Et ovec ce nous ne purrons que brief temps continuer, et apres, ce si vous nordeignez pur nous, il nous covient departir ove hount et meschief et la paiis serra outrement perduz, que Dieux ne vuille. Ore puis que nous vous avons declare les perils et meschiefs, pur Dieux faites vostre ordenance par temps en sauvacioun de lonnour du Roy, nostre suisdit seigneur et pere, et de nous et de tout le royaume. Et nostre seigneur vous garde et doint grace de bien fere. Donne soubz nostre signet a Wircestre le xxvi jour de Juyn* [And we trust that you will so ordain for us quickly, so that we will be able to do honor and service to the King, our lord and father aforementioned, for the benefit of the kingdom and the saving of our estate, it being understood that we have nothing with which to support ourselves here except that we have pledged our smaller vessels and jewels and have raised a money loan. With this we will only be able to continue for a short time, and afterwards, if you do not make ordinance for us, we will have to depart in shame and disgrace and the country will be totally lost, which God forbid. Now that we have explained to you the dangers and threats, for God's sake make your ordinance with speed to save the honor of the King, our aforesaid lord and father, and of ourselves and all the kingdom. And may our Lord keep you and give you grace to act wisely. Given under our signet at Worcester on the 26th day of June].

45. LOUIS OF BOURBON, *LETTER TO HENRY III OF CASTILE*

Ed. and trans. Matthews, in Rees and Jones, *Thomas Matthews's Welsh Records in Paris*, pp. 106–08, 114–15. Notes by John K. Bollard.

Manuscript: Paris, Archives Nationale, MS K 1482.B1.11.

   This letter, composed during the negotiations of Owain's ambassadors with the court of Charles VI of France, is a request to Henry III of Castile to send forty ships to aid a planned French expeditionary force to Wales in support of Owain Glyndŵr. The letter is dated 7 July 1404, seven days earlier than the treaty between Wales and France was formally drawn up, witnessed, and sent to Owain for confirmation (Item 46.146). The signature line *Loys, duc de Bourbonnais, conte de Fourez et seigneur de Beaujeu* [Louis, Duke of Bourbon, Count of Fourez, and Seigneur de Beaujeu], is accompanied by his signature, *Loys — De Bor*. On the dorso is the address: *A très hault et très excellent prince et mon chier sires et cousins le roy de Castielle et de Léon* [To the most high and most excellent prince, and my dear lords and cousins, the king of Castile and León].

Louis II de Bourbon (1337–1410) became the third duke of Bourbon on the death of his father in 1357; he was uncle to Charles VI and one of the king's regents before his majority. Henry III of Castile (1379–1406) succeeded to the crown of Castile in 1390. Charles VI of France had ordered the muster of 1,000 lances and 500 archers to sail to the aid of Wales, hence the request for ships in this letter. According to the *Chronique Normande* of Pierre Cochon (Item 69.6), twenty ships from Spain were among the expedition that sailed from Brest in November 1404. The expedition itself, led by Louis's cousin, Jacques II (or James) de Bourbon (1370–1438), count of La Marche, was delayed either for lack of money or lack of a specific destination, and rather than sail to Wales it was decided to "explore the coast of England." After pursuing seven merchant vessels, they attacked and burned the town of Plymouth, and on their return they lost twelve ships and sixty men to foul weather. On this expedition, see also the *Chronique* of Jean Juvenal des Ursins (Item 77), and Matthews, *Welsh Records*, pp. xxix–xxx).

46. *CONFEDERATION BETWEEN WALES AND FRANCE*

Ed. and trans. Matthews, in Rees and Jones, *Thomas Matthews's Welsh Records in Paris*, pp. 32–39, 75–82. Notes by John K. Bollard.

Manuscript: Paris, Archives Nationale, MS J623.96.

This document, signed and sealed by Owain Glyndŵr on 12 January 1405, confirms an earlier agreement of confederation between Wales and France that was executed on 14 July 1404. The majority of this present document reproduces, formalizes, and finalizes that earlier text, quoted in its entirety here (lines 6–169) and which in turn contains a copy (lines 81–112) of Charles's appointment of his ambassadors Jacques de Bourbon, count of La Marche, and Jean, bishop of Chartres, and a copy (lines 115–43) of Owain's letters patent confirming his ambassadors (Item 43). Owain's great seal (see pp. 423–24) is attached to this copy of the treaty. Because the earlier text of the agreement survives in Paris, Archives Nationale, MS J623.96bis, we can compare the two versions; the very few deviations between the texts are noted below.

The framework of this document consists of Owain's greetings and acknowledgment of receipt (lines 1–5) and his ratification and dating of the treaty (lines 170–75). The form and language of the treaty itself is that of an agreement between heads of state, thus showing that Owain formally assumed such a position in Wales and that France recognized him as such. Its significance, too, is indicated in the status of the witnesses; it was executed in Paris at the house of the French chancellor, witnessed by three bishops, a duke, and two lords knights of the chamber, and notarized by the king's secretary and a Welsh clerk, Benedict Comme of St. Asaph. The nine articles of the treaty establish a Franco-Welsh union against "Henry of Lancaster," with pledges of mutual support and defense, in particular stipulating that neither party shall separately enter into a peace or truce with Henry without giving the other a month to decide whether or not he wishes to be included.

6–169   *Nos Jacobus de Borbonio . . . et testimonium omnium premissorum*. Aside from orthographical differences — and a few significant differences noted below — this
is the verbatim text of the agreement between the Welsh and French ambassadors on 14 July 1404.

6   *Jacobus de Borbonio*. This opening paragraph makes it clear that Jacques II (or
James) de Bourbon, count of La Marche, was the chief negotiator of this treaty
for King Charles. He had earlier been appointed to lead an expedition to
Wales; see the headnote to Item 45 above.

8–9   On Gruffudd Yonge and John Hanmer, see Item 43, notes 5, 6.

10   *domini nostri Owyni principis Walliarum*. Here and throughout this document
King Charles recognizes Owain's title of *Princeps Wallie*, whereas Henry IV of
England, whom France did not acknowledge as king, is named only "Henry of
Lancaster" (e.g., lines 21, 29).

13   *specialiter*. Not in the 14 July 1404 agreement.

72   *dominorum ad sancta*. The 14 July 1404 agreement reads *dominorum nostrorum ad
sancta*.

81–112   This passage reproduces a letter of 14 June 1404 from Charles VI authorizing
the Count of March and the Bishop of Chartres as his ambassadors to negotiate
with Owain's representatives.

84   *Johannis episcopi Carnotensis*. Jean VI (or John), bishop of Chartres, was translated to the archbishopric of Sens in 1406 until his death in 1415. Though
named here as one of the king's ambassadors in this matter, his name does not
appear elsewhere in the text of the agreement or in the list of witnesses, suggesting that he played little or no part in the negotiations.

115–42   This passage is a copy of Owain's letter of 10 May 1404 to Charles VI, naming
his ambassadors (see Item 43 and notes).

144–45   *Ernaudi de Corbeya militis, cancellarii Francie*. Arnaud de Corbie (1325–1414) was
counselor to both Charles V and Charles VI. He was knighted by the former in
1373, named chancellor by the latter in 1388; he was removed from office at a
remarkable old age in 1413.

147–48   *Philippo Noviomensi*. Philippe de Moulins was bishop of Noyon from 1388–1409.

148   *Johanne Atrebatensi*. Jean Canard was bishop of Arras from 1391/92–1407.

150   *Roberto de Braquemont*. Robert de Bracquemont (c.1360–1419) served with Henry
III of Castile (see Item 45) in his war with Portugal (1396–1402). He became
governor of the city of Honfleur 1415–1417, and was elevated to the rank of
Admiral of France in 1417.

173–74   *in castro nostro de Llanpadarn*. Owain signed this treaty at Aberystwyth Castle, which
had been captured sometime after April 1404 and remained in Welsh hands until
1408 (see Item 70.26, 42–43). The castle and borough, originally called Llanbadarn from their proximity to the ancient church and settlement of that name,

were founded in 1277 by Edward I to replace the original Anglo-Norman castle of Aberystwyth across the Ystwyth valley at Tan-y-Castell (1110–c.1200).

47. *Tripartite Indenture*

Adapted and trans. by Michael Livingston, from Ellis, *Original Letters*, 2.1.27–28.

Manuscripts: London, British Library, Sloane MS 1776 [oldest MS, base-text for Ellis], and Royal MS 13 [base-text for *Chronicon Incerti Scriptoris*, ed. Giles, pp. 39–42]. The two Cotton manuscripts of this chronicle (Julius E.iv and Titus F.iii) are fragmentary and do not include this passage.

For discussion of the authenticity, date, authorship, and intentions of this famous document, see the short essay by Livingston in this volume.

1   *Hoc anno*. See Livingston's essay herein for the dating of this event.

19–20   *de quibus Propheta loquitur* [of whom the Prophet speaks]. This section of the *Indenture* points to the prophetic tradition that the governance of England would come to be divided into three parts. The most popular version of this vision is that contained in the *Prophecy of Six Kings*, which identifies the three leaders who would bring about this change as the Dragon, Wolf, and Lion. See Item 1.121–28.

27–29   *totam Cambriam sive Walliam . . . a Leogrea, quæ vulgariter Angliam nuncupatur, divisam* [the whole of Cambria or Wales . . . divided from Loegria, which is commonly called England]. The use of the ancient names for the realms of England and Wales (Loegria and Cambria) establishes the historical precedent on which the future border will be based according to the *Indenture*. In Owain's day the line between the realms had long been the River Wye in the south, but in the older traditions — still present in his day within the stories of King Arthur — the geographical boundary between Loegria and Cambria was the Severn (see, e.g., Geoffrey of Monmouth's *History of the Kings*, trans. Thorpe, p. 75). The *Indenture* seeks to re-establish this older boundary in the south, combining it with a line across the north that follows not the River Dee but a persistent and powerful memory of the great Welsh kings who commanded territories well into "England" (see note to line 31, below).

30   *ad Borialem Portam civitatis Wigorniæ* [to the North Gate of the city of Worcester]. The description of the border of the Welsh governance zone is fascinating for its specificity. There were three main gates in the medieval walls of Worcester, the North Gate, St. Martin's Gate, and Sidbury Gate. That the *Indenture* fixes the border at the northern gate is an indication that it is the road north — what would today be the A449 — that is the main demarcation line for this part of the border.

31   *Onnene Margion*. Perhaps more than any other detail, it is the hyperspecificity of Onnenau Meigion [ash trees of Meigion] that helps not only to give this document an air of authenticity, but also to indicate that Owain (or Welsh rep-

resentatives on his behalf) had an integral and probably leading role in the crafting of the agreement (see Livingston's essay herein). The site, as the *Indenture* describes it, is a stand of ash trees on the road between Bridgnorth and Kinver; Lloyd assumed this to be near "the hamlet of Six Ashes, standing on the crest of a hill 500 feet high" where, "according to local tradition, there were formerly here some very old ash trees, now fallen or cut down" (*Owen Glendower*, p. 95n1). Alternatively (or additionally), the site might have been associated with Four Ashes, only a mile further on the road to Kinver. Regardless, it would hardly be a significant monument in English eyes. To the Welsh, however, it appears that this mysterious location was more well-known in the fifteenth century, especially within the context of prophetic traditions and ancient histories of a more glorious, farther-reaching Wales. Lloyd notes "a prophetic dialogue" in Peniarth MS 94 (c.1600) in which "the ash trees of Meigion" will be the gathering point "where the Great Eagle musters his host of Welsh warriors" for battle. The earlier Peniarth MS 26, "written for the most part about 1456," contains a similar passage: "Ac yna y marchoga yr eryr gwr [v.r. mawr?] hyt onnenev meigion" [And then the great eagle rode as far as Onnenau Meigion] (Evans, *Report on Welsh I*, p. 351; trans. Bollard). The name *Meigion* is apparently derived from or related to that of the legendary Maig Myngfras of Powys, whose name is cited several times by Iolo Goch in his poems to Owain Glyndŵr (see Item 6.37 and note); Davies notes that in the form *Meigen* it would also have "had a further historical resonance since it was the name of one of the great battles in which the heroic British king, Cadwallon, had triumphed over the Saxons." In sum, as Davies has noted, the accumulation of these mythological, historical, and cultural threads "would have been part of the common coin of [Welsh] literary discourse and a wonderfully reassuring indication that past, present, and future were at last to be brought into alignment" (*Revolt*, p. 169).

45   *defendendum regnum* [defend the kingdom]. As noted in the essay below (p. 494), the use of the singular noun here underscores that the *Indenture* does not divide the kingdom into three new kingdoms; rather, it splits the kingdom into three autonomous governmental zones within one confederated state.

45–47   On Owain's agreement with King Charles VI of France, see Item 46.

48. PRINCE HENRY, *BATTLE OF GROSMONT*

Adapted and trans. Rhidian Griffiths from *PPC*, ed. Nicolas, 1.248–50.

Manuscript: London, British Library MS Cotton Cleopatra F.iii, fol. 59.

This rather breathless letter containing the prince's account of the English victory at Grosmont is interesting for the light it casts on the nature of campaigning during the rebellion. It was largely a war of raids and individual offensives, and pitched battles were relatively few and far between. It is also instructive to have estimates of the numbers of soldiers taking part in the battle. Davies shrewdly points out that Henry here magnifies the size of Welsh forces in order "to exaggerate the scale of his own victory," but stresses that even if the figures here quoted are divided by ten, "we are still left with the impression that during 1402–06 Owain Glyn Dŵr was indeed able to muster substantial armies" (*Revolt*, p. 231).

It is a measure of the real threat which Owain and his followers had posed to the authority of the English crown that after receiving this letter on 13 March the King thought it necessary to broadcast the news of the victory at Grosmont to the city of London:

> Most dear and faithful, we greet you heartily. And because we well know that you are well pleased and happy at all times to hear good news of things concerning the safeguarding of our honour and estate and especially the common good and honour of all our kingdom, we are sending you for your comfort a copy of a letter sent to us by our most dear son the Prince concerning his governance in the Marches of Wales and the news from him. By means of this copy you will be able to know that same news for which we give thanks to our Lord Almighty God. We ask you to make this news known to our most dear and faithful mayor and good men of our city of London, so that they may take comfort with us and praise our Creator for it. (trans. Griffiths, from *PPC*, ed. Nicolas, 1.248)

By such evidence it is clear that Grosmont was "a victory of which the moral effect might be expected to be considerable" (Lloyd, *Owen Glendower*, p. 96).

7   *Glomorgan, Morgannok*. Glamorgan and Morgannwg are names for the same general region in southeast Wales, and it is difficult to know what distinction the prince is making here. The Welsh kingdom of Morgannwg (earlier Glywysing) was conquered by the Normans in the 1080s and King William Rufus installed Robert fitz Hamo as lord of Glamorgan. The lordship of Glamorgan, with its center at Cardiff, had come into royal custody after the beheading of its lord, Thomas Despenser, for his part in the Epiphany Uprising of January 1400. The upland regions in particular preserved much of their Welsh culture and perspective through the fourteenth century, as is notably evident from Gruffudd Llwyd's poem of praise "To the Sun and to Morgannwg," which he concludes by saying that even if a poet were banned from the whole world and exiled, *Ef a gâi, heb ofwy gwg, / Ei gynnal ym Morgannwg* [He would receive, without a frown, / support in Morgannwg] (Ifans, *Gwaith*, p. 114).

7–8   *Uske, Netherwent, et Overwent*. The early Welsh kingdom of Gwent was divided by the forest of Wentwood into the cantrefi of Gwent Iscoed [= Gwent below the wood] and Gwent Uwch Coed [= Gwent above the Wood]. After the Norman conquest, Gwent was eventually split into separate lordships, including Abergavenny, Caerleon, Monmouth, and Usk. This passage indicates that Owain drew followers from a wide area across southeastern Wales.

10   *Grosmont*. Grosmont castle, originally built on the west bank of the Monnow in the twelfth century, was "an important key to the control of upper Gwent," and a borough of perhaps as many as 160 plots developed there in the thirteenth century (Soulsby, *Towns*, pp. 137–38). The subsequent decline of the town (the current population is approximately 300) is largely attributed to the effects of the destruction wrought by Glyndŵr's rebels during the attack and battle described in this letter.

vostre seigneurie de Monmouth. The lordship of Monmouth was held by the king as duke of Lancaster.

11   *le Sire de Talbot*. Gilbert, Lord Talbot, had landed interest in the March as lord of Goodrich and Archenfield. He fought extensively on the Welsh borders and organized a relief expedition to Beaumaris at the end of 1403. With his brother John he recaptured Harlech castle from the Welsh early in 1409. In July 1415 he appointed to treat with Owain and receive his submission, though this was never fulfilled (*Calendar of Patent Rolls 1413–16*, p. 342).

12   *William Neuport*. Sir William Newport was a Staffordshire knight and long-standing servant of the house of Lancaster who had served with Prince Henry's household on the defense of the Welsh border in the summer of 1404. He was rewarded with a life grant from the prince of the manor of Aber in Caernarfonshire (*Calendar of Patent Rolls 1416–22*, p. 119).

   Johan Greindre. Sir John Greyndour was a prominent knight of Herefordshire who remained loyal to the king in 1402, in spite of Edmund Mortimer's entreaty to assist him in his alliance with Glyndŵr (See Item 26n18).

49. JOHN STANLEY, *HARLECH PARLIAMENT*

Adapted and trans. Rhidian Griffiths from *Royal and Historical Letters*, ed. Hingeston, 2.76–79.

Manuscript: London, British Library MS Cotton Cleopatra F.iii, fol. 58r.

Sir John Stanley of Newton in Macclesfield, Cheshire, was a loyal servant of the House of Lancaster, who served as steward of the household of Henry, prince of Wales, and as steward of the king's household. He served extensively in the campaigns against Owain, and under Henry V became king's lieutenant in Ireland. His descendants became earls of Derby. This rambling letter is valuable particularly for its evidence of Owain's parliament at Harlech, but also for the suggestion that Henry IV was expected to go to Wales in person to defeat the rebels, a hope that was not to be realized.

10   *Lathum*. Stanley acquired his manor of Lathom in west Lancashire by his marriage to Isabella, the heiress of Sir Thomas Lathom.

11   *David Whitmore et Yevan ap Meredithe*. David Whitmore and Ieuan ap Maredudd, prominent Flintshire landowners, were "English moles in the Welsh camp," ostensibly supporting Owain while relaying information about his activities to the English authorities (Davies, *Revolt*, p. 164). Whitmore was the sole freeholder in Whitford Llan in 1407, and Ieuan ap Maredudd had been steward of Hope and Hopedale in May 1397 (Lloyd, *Owen Glendower*, p. 101n2, 3).

19–20   *Hardelaghe*. Harlech castle had fallen to the Welsh in 1404. This was the second of Owain's known parliaments, the first having been held at Machynlleth, according to Adam of Usk, probably in 1404. The evidence of this letter would suggest that the Harlech parliament was held around 1 August 1405.

24   *graunde eide hors de Fraunce*. Owain's ambassadors had been favorably received at the court of Charles VI of France in 1404, but a promised French expedition apparently never reached Wales. In the following year, however, a French force did reach Milford Haven early in August and made its mark in south-west Wales, penetrating as far as Carmarthen (Davies, *Revolt*, pp. 193–95).

27–28 *le Marsdy proschein*. 30 July 1405, the date on which the letter was written, was a Thursday; the following Tuesday, the date of the county court, would therefore be 4 August.

42   *Abbeie de Valleroial*. Vale Royal abbey was a Cistercian house in Whitegate, between Northwich and Winsford, Cheshire.

50. HENRY IV, *RESISTING THE FRENCH INVASION*

Adapted and trans. Kelly DeVries, from Rymer, *Foedera*, 8.406–07.

There is remarkably little surviving primary documentation on the French invasion of England in support of the Welsh rebellion in 1405; for much of the story we must rely on the chronicle accounts, such as those of Pintoin (Item 66), Walsingham (Item 68), Jean Juvenal (Item 77), and Monstrelet (Item 80). What seems clear is that the French force was led by three main figures: Jean de Rieux, marshal of France; Jean VI de Hengest, lord of Hugueville and master of crossbows; and Robert de la Heuse, lord of Ventes and known as *Le Borgue* [one-eyed] (see note to line 2, below). Their gathered French forces — well over 2500 troops — waited some weeks in Brest for favorable winds, but by the end of July they had set sail, and they arrived in Wales at Milford Haven in the first days of August. They met Owain's forces not long afterward (Pintoin tells us he was waiting at Milford Haven, while Monstrelet reports that he was at Tenby), and the combined force began to assault those positions held by the English. They besieged Haverfordwest but failed to take it, but Picton Castle soon fell, followed by other towns, including Carmarthen. The Franco-Welsh army marched on, ultimately passing through much of south Wales (the alliance noting many Arthurian monuments along with way), before they turned northeast, toward Worcester. It was outside this city, hard upon the fertile heart of England, that Owain and his allies at last encountered the forces of Henry IV — who had been called to arms and gathered in Hereford by command of this present letter.

Interestingly, a hoard of eighty-six silver coins (pictured below) was discovered near Hereford at the village of Canon Pyon in 1997. These coins, which date from the late-thirteenth to the late-fourteenth centuries, appear to have been buried in the early years of the fifteenth century, and they may well be associated with the revolt of Owain Glyndŵr. If this is so, it might well be fitting to imagine the coins being hidden by someone either heading off to answer the king's call or, alternatively, someone preparing to flee from the advancing Franco-Welsh army. In any case, they never returned.

2   *dominus de Hugevyle*. This was Jean VI de Hengest, lord of Hugueville, then governor of Brittany. He had served as ambassador from Charles VI to England at least twice before this attack, in 1400 and 1404 (on the first of these see Pistono, "Diplomatic Mission"). Although only second in command of the French forces,

he acted as general due to the ill health and old age of the commander, Jean de Rieux, marshal of France (Webb "Translation of a French Metrical History," p. 227.

13–14　　*alli homines defensabilis*. The Latin phrase denotes the others besides knights, men-at-arms and yeomen who were responsible for defense in the province of Hereford. I have translated it with the generic term "militiamen."

17–18　　*cum omni festinatione se trahant, properent, et festinent* [hurrying and hastening with all speed]. The king's emphasis on speed is obvious, underscoring the very real threat of the French invasion.

19–21　　*Et hoc . . . nullatenus omittas* [And this for failing to appear]. This Latin phrase is often used in legal documents in concert with a *sub poena* punishment (i.e. failure to appear would result in the stated punishment). In the present case the penalty is the material between the two halves of the phrase: a recollection of the obligations upon both lord and lieges, who are bound by their oaths to uphold the system of mutual protection between and among them. The king's threat is thus an implied loss of position and the king's favor, which could be devastatingly painful to the social, economic, and political standing of a family.

Canon Pyon Hoard, perhaps associated with Glyndŵr's revolt. Courtesy of the Hereford Museum and Art Gallery.

51. Owain Glyndŵr, *Pennal Letter I*

> Ed. Michael Livingston; trans. Matthews, in Rees and Jones, *Thomas Matthews's Welsh Records in Paris*, pp. 40–41, 83–84. Notes by John K. Bollard.

Manuscript: Paris, Archives Nationales, MS J516 B.40.

On the last day of March 1406 in the village of Pennal, about four miles west of Machynlleth, Owain Glyndŵr signed two letters to Charles VI, King of France. These have come to be known as the "Pennal Letters," and they are our best documentary evidence of Owain's vision for an independent Wales. The present source, the shorter of the two, is Owain's personal letter to the king in which he assures Charles that he will recognize Benedict XIII, the pope in Avignon, as "the true Vicar of Christ." Owain does this to align himself "as far as is possible" with the king, certainly in order to assure continued assistance from France; however, he also takes this opportunity to put forward part of his own agenda. He opens energetically with a reminder of how Wales (*nacio mea* [my nation]), has long suffered *per rabiem barbarorum Saxonum* [from the fury of the barbarous Saxons] (Item 51.4), and later, in accordance with the ecclesiastical subject at hand, he directs his argument to the oppression of the Welsh church and a renewed hope for independent metropolitan (i.e., archiepiscopal) status for the bishop of St. Davids, treated in greater detail in Pennal Letter II (Item 52.58–71; see also Lloyd, *History*, pp. 480–83; Gerald of Wales, *Journey*, Book II, ch. 1).

4   *suppeditata*. So MS. Matthews: *suppedita*.

9–10   *dominus Benedictus, summus pontifex*. On Benedict XIII, see the notes to Item 52 below.

12   *pro me et*. MS: *me* inserted above the line.

52. Owain Glyndŵr, *Pennal Letter II*

> Ed. and trans. Matthews, in Rees and Jones, *Thomas Matthews's Welsh Records in Paris*, pp. 42–54, 85–99. Notes by John K. Bollard.

Manuscript: Paris, Archives Nationales, MS J516.29.

The second and longer Pennal letter, executed on the same day as Pennal Letter I (Item 51), deals largely with the matter of accepting the authority of the pope in Avignon. Owain responds to the appeals of Charles VI to consider the history of the claims of Benedict XIII and to cast his lot in favor of Benedict (Item 52.1–34). Omitted here is the lengthy middle portion of the letter, in which Owain's envoys reproduce that history by giving a detailed account of the Papal Schism. The king then promises to make every effort to ensure that the Welsh appointments made earlier by the "pope of Rome" will not be threatened if Owain acknowledges Benedict, and that any new appointments will be to Owain's satisfaction.

The included text resumes with Owain's declaration of intent, with certain provisos, and this important passage gives us a sense of both his diplomatic skill and his hopes for the future of Wales (Item 52.35–98). He begins with his acknowledgment, both for himself and his subjects, of Benedict XIII as the true pope (Item 52.35–46). To this promise he appends a series of nine articles which he asks Charles VI to promote to Benedict on his behalf. Several of these articles pertain to the church in relation to the war: Owain asks that any censures declared against him or his subjects by Benedict or his predecessor Clement be removed, that Henry and his adherents be branded as heretics, and that for as long as the war lasts Benedict grant remission of all the sins of those who fight against Henry. Other articles are concerned with the independence and continuity of the Welsh church: that Benedict recognize any appointments, titles, dispensations, etc., from the time of Gregory XI (1370–78) prior to the schism, that the revenues of Welsh parish churches should go to their original Welsh patrons, not to English monasteries and colleges; and that future bishops, clergy, and other church dignitaries be Welsh speakers. Of particular note is Owain's extended request for metropolitan status for the see of St. Davids, especially with the stipulation that suffragan bishoprics under the authority of St. Davids should include not only the Welsh dioceses of St. Asaph, Bangor, and Llandaff, but also several English sees (see note to lines 65–66 below). The quest for the restoration of archiepiscopal status to the see of St. Davids had a considerable history, and Owain's resurrection of the matter after nearly 200 years is remarkably ambitious. Clearly an independent Wales whose church was in thrall to an English archbishop would be unpalatable to Owain politically as well as ecclesiastically. Similarly, the establishment of universities in Wales would provide educated clerics and officials to serve both in church positions and in governmental roles, not unlike Gruffudd Yonge himself. Even so, as Davies points out, "to establish one, let alone two universities, in a thinly populated and economically poor country like Wales was certainly extraordinarily ambitious" (*Revolt*, p. 172).

St. David and the twenty-four bishops after him were traditionally called *archi episcopus*, but that was more an honorary title than an indication of metropolitan authority (Lloyd, *History*, p. 204n43). However, coupled with the early independence of the Welsh bishoprics, this title provided a core element of the argument for archiepiscopal status for St. Davids in Wales. There is also some , though limited, evidence that St. Davids held jurisdiction over other Welsh bishoprics (see Davies, *Archbishopric of St Davids*). The last Welsh bishop of St. Davids completely free of the influence of Canterbury was Sulien (d. 1091), whose son Rhygyfarch, in the early 1090s, wrote a *Life of St. David* in which he states that David was "appointed archbishop (*archiepiscopus constituitur*) by the consent of all the bishops, kings, princes, nobles, and all ranks of people of the whole British nation (Sharpe and Davies, "Rhygyfarch's *Life*," pp. 146–47). This *Life* may, indeed, have been written to promote the recognition of St. Davids as an independent metropolitan see. In 1115, by command of King Henry I, Bishop Bernard was consecrated by Archbishop Ralph of Canterbury, thus formally putting the Welsh church under Canterbury jurisdiction. Though a Norman, Bernard himself subsequently took up the cause of metropolitan status in letters and visits to Popes Honorius II, Innocent II, Lucius II, and Eugenius III, who seem to have been favorably disposed to his claim. Unfortunately, Bernard died in 1148, before Eugenius made a final ruling and the case was dropped. Towards the end of the century and the beginning of the next, the cause is once again pursued vigorously by Giraldus Cambrensis. Giraldus had long set his sights on the bishopric of St. Davids; he was nominated for the position in 1176 and was elected unanimously in 1198 but never installed. He researched and published much of the historical information about the metropolitan claim in his various books (Richter, *Giraldus Cambrensis*, pp. 38–48 and passim; Lloyd, *History*, pp. 447–61). In his *Itinerarium*, Giraldus includes a list of the twenty-five "archbishops" who occupied the see, though there are some variations between the lists in the three versions of his text (see Gerald, *Journey through Wales*, pp.

161–62 and note 263). The list in the Pennal letter also varies from those lists, suggesting they may derive from different sources or perhaps from oral tradition (Item 52.62–65).

4   *Hugonem Eddouyer*. In addition to delivering from France the articles referred to herein, Hugh Eddowyer (or Hywel Edwere) served as Owain's envoy on several other missions (Davies, *Revolt*, pp. 187, 212).

    ordinis predicatorum. The Order of Predicants, i.e., the Dominican Order of Friars Preachers.

    Mauricium Kery. Morris Kery is not otherwise known.

19–34   The language of these lines is closely replicated in the *Tripartite Indenture* (Item 47.4–17). For the implications of this parallelism, see Livingston's essay herein.

58   *ecclesia Menevensis*. The church of Mynyw, i.e., the cathedral of St. Davids; see note 62 below.

62–65   This list of twenty-four archbishops after David is largely, but not entirely, in agreement with those in the three versions of Giraldus Cambrensis' *Itinerarium Kambriae*; each is missing names found in the other, though all end with Samson (of Dol), following the tradition that Samson took with him the pallium (the white stole worn by an archbishop) when he went to Brittany. However, Samson was a contemporary of David and lived almost four centuries earlier than this list suggests, thus pointing toward the role of tradition and legend in compiling such a list.

62   *Eliud*. Eliud was a contemporary of David, better known by his cognomen St. Teilo. He founded a monastery on the site of the church at Llandeilo Fawr, and his cult spread throughout South Wales and Brittany.

    Morwal, Menevie. No equivalent to *Menevie* occurs in Giraldus'e lists. Latin *Menevia*, Welsh *Mynyw*, is the native name for the area around St. Davids, and it is likely that here *Menevie* is an epithet to the previous name, i.e., "Morwal/ Morfael of Mynyw," misinterpreted perhaps to make up the required number of twenty-four names.

64   *Asser*. Asser (d. 909/10) was the bishop and scholar who was enlisted by King Alfred of Wessex in 884 to divide his time between St. Davids and Alfred's court and who in 893 wrote the famed *Vita Ælfredi regis Angul Saxonum*. There is no direct evidence that he was bishop of St. Davids, though he himself implies that he was (Davies, "Archbishopric," p. 299).

    David secundus. This name does not occur in Giraldus's list or elsewhere as an early "archbishop." Might it be a faulty memory and misplacement of David fitz Gerald, the uncle of Giraldus Cambrensis, who succeeded Bernard in 1148? If so, it is somewhat ironic that at his consecration he took an oath, which he subsequently kept, not to pursue the metropolitan question (Richter, *Giraldus Cambrensis*, p. 8).

66–68   *Exoniensem . . . Lichfeldensem*. Davies notes that "The ecclesiastical mythology current at St. David's in the medieval period claimed that these five English bishoprics had indeed been within the ambit of the archbishopric of St. David's from the time of St. David himself to that of his twenty-fifth successor, Samson of Dol" (*Revolt*, p. 172). Lloyd comments, "If we doubt whether so wide a claim was seriously put forward, the pretensions of the Tripartite Indenture should be recalled; Glyn Dŵr was still confident of a success which would extend beyond the borders of Wales and make him the arbiter of the western Midlands" (*History*, p. 120).

68   *Assavensem, Bangorensem, et Landavensem.* Though St. Davids was recognized as the preeminent see in Wales, the dioceses of St. Asaph, Bangor, and Llandaff had been similarly independent of metropolitan oversight prior to the late eleventh century.

78–81   Owain's stipulation that Benedict grant for his and his successor's personal chapel the same free status enjoyed by the royal chapels in England further demonstrates the extent to which Owain was adopting the practices and trappings of sovereignty. Naming himself and his heirs as princes of Wales and coupling this right with that of "our forefathers the princes of Wales" places him firmly in the succession of the independent princes of Wales, further revealing his hope to reestablish Wales as a free nation.

53. MADOG AP GRONW GETHIN, *PRAISE OF THE RIVER DEE*

Ed. Dafydd Huw Evans ("Incident"); trans. John K. Bollard.

Manuscripts: There are fourteen manuscripts, designated A–N by Evans, ranging in date from 1587 to the early 18th century. The present edition is based on the earliest copy, A: British Library Add. MS 114,866, "The Book of David Johns, vicar of Llanfair Dyffryn Clwyd," written in June 1587 (Evans, "Incident," p. 33).

The text is that edited and discussed by Evans, and the present translation and the following notes owe a great deal to his research, his careful analysis of the poem and its setting, and his thorough notes and discussion. The translation does not necessarily follow Evans' punctuation or interpretation of the original.

The incident described in this poem cannot be verified in the historical record, and hence the date of the composition is uncertain. If we accept the connection made in the headnotes in several manuscripts between the flooding of the Dee and Owain's rebellion, then perhaps the earlier years might be more likely, but nothing explicitly excludes the later years as the rebellion devolved into a period of skirmishes and outlawry, or perhaps even the middle decades of the troubled fifteenth century. But whether the poem is based on an actual incident during the war or was applied to it retroactively, it is the type of event (or tale) that gave rise to Glyndŵr's reputation as a conjuror who could "call spirits from the vasty deep" and who "Thrice from the banks of Wye / And sandy-bottomed Severn" sent King Henry "Bootless home and weather-beaten back" (Shakespeare, *1 Henry IV* 3.1.53, 65–67; see Item 101). On the subject of this poem, see also Oram's essay in this volume.

Notes on the headnote:

1   *Cowydd*. On the form of a *cywydd*, see p. 515.

Seisnig [English]. This is the adjectival form, derived from Latin *Saxonicus*, generally meaning 'English', or more literally and especially in the earlier periods, 'Saxon', as distinct from *Saesneg* [the English language], and *Sais* [Englishman, a Saxon], pl. *Saeson* [the English or Saxons].

2 *i Faelawr* [to Maelor]. The area of Maelor in northeast Wales was divided by the Dee into *Maelor Gymraeg* [Welsh-speaking Maelor] to the west of the river and *Maelor Saesneg* [English-speaking Maelor] to the east. In 1397 the latter was incorporated into the newly formed Principality of Chester. Here the scribe or original writer of the headnote, like the poet in line 8, clearly means Maelor Gymraeg.

yn erbyn Ywain Glyñdwr [against Owain Glyndŵr]. Added from C, NLW Peniarth 112 (c.1610).

3 *yn amser Mongymbry* [in the time of Montgomery]. See the note to line 23 below.

rhwn [which]. From *yr hwn*, the definite article *yr* + *hwn* [this], commonly used in relative clauses in apposition to the real antecedent, here *gwynt* [wind], and sometimes regarded as a proper relative pronoun (Evans, *Grammar*, pp. 68–69).

3–4 *Llynn Tegid*. Llyn Tegid (Bala Lake) is a lake in Gwynedd through which the Dyfrdwy flows. The lake is about four miles long and a mile wide, stretching from the southwest to the northeast. This orientation makes it prone to flooding in the north when the wind blows from the southwest. In his *Tours of Wales*, Thomas Pennant comments, "In stormy weather, its billows run very high, and incroach greatly on the north east end, where, within memory of man, numbers of acres have been lost. It rises sometimes nine feet, and rains and winds jointly contribute to make it overflow the fair vale of Edeirnion" (Pennant, *Tours*, p. 213). In 1188 Gerald of Wales commented similarly, "The river has its source in Lake Bala. . . . You will find it true that the Dee is never swollen by rain but that it often rises when the winds blow" (Gerald, *Journey*, p. 198).

4–5 *ac a barhaodd y llif . . . yn ei erbyn ef* [and the flood continued . . . against him]. Added from C, NLW Peniarth 112 (c.1610).

Notes on the poem:

1 *ganawr*. Lenited form of *canawr*, a hapax legomenon that Evans tentatively identifies with *kannaw* [white wave]; see Lloyd-Jones, *Geirfa*, s.v. *kannaw*.

2 *dwfr . . . lvdd*. A: *dyfr . . . lwydd*.

Deifr [the English]. See the note to Item 4.58.

4 *dwfr rhyfeldwrdd*. A: *dwr ryfelddwrf*.

7 *ar lenn* [on the borders]. *Llen* more literally denotes a sheet, veil, curtain, mantle, etc., but it is also used figuratively as a divider, not unlike "Iron Curtain," hence Evans' suggestion of "borders."

16 *hir i druth a hwyr i drai*. A: the original reading has been altered to *hir ar draeth a hwyr ar drai* [long on (the) beach and slow to ebb]; C has been similarly revised, and this is also the reading of most other MSS.

17   *aerfaeth* [battle-trained]. A: *aerfaith* altered to *aerfaeth*.

18   *gwewyr caeth* [sharp spears]. A: *ai gwewyr caith*, with *ai* cancelled and *caith* altered
            to *caeth*.

20   *o* [of, from]. A omits *o*, which is in JKLN; the other MSS have different readings.

21   *faeddüd* [you beat]. Lenited imperfect 2nd singular of *maeddu* [to beat, conquer,
            foul], emended from A: *faeddyd*.

23   *Mongymbry*. Montgomery, also named in the headnote to the poem, appears to
            be either an otherwise unidentifiable leader of the English force or possibly an
            equally obscure reference to (the men of) the lordship of Montgomery. Evans
            suggests that it may be, in effect, a synecdoche for the English, stemming from
            the long-term Welsh hatred of Roger Montgomery, earl of Shrewsbury (d.
            1093) and his descendants. As Lloyd puts it, "The name of Montgomery be-
            came, indeed, one of mournful import throughout the whole of Mid Wales"
            (*History*, p. 389; Evans, "Incident," pp. 19–24). In general support of this last
            interpretation, we might remind ourselves of the similar *pars pro toto* use of *Deifr*
            in line 2, also used, along with *Brynaich*, by Iolo Goch and other poets, long
            after they had become defunct as geographical or political referents (see Items
            4.58; 5.79; 23.22, 29, and the accompanying notes). The writer of the headnote
            seems to have understood *Mongymbry* in this line as the name of a person who
            fled at the time of the incident.

26   *o'r llynn*. Literally, "from the lake," but there is a play on the homonyms *llyn*
            [lake] and *llyn* [drink, beverage, intoxicating liquor]; compare English "drink."

            tafarnwr llwyd. Extending the drink metaphor, the "holy tavern-keeper" is God.
            On *llwyd* in the sense of "holy, blessed," see the note to Item 5.34 above.

27   *Plant Alis* [Children of Alice]. A metonymy for "the English." Marged Haycock
            and Michael Livingston each independently suggested that the Alis in question
            is perhaps Alys, Countess of the Vexin (personal communications). Alys (1160–
            c.1220), a daughter of Louis VII of France and his second wife, Constance of
            Castile, was betrothed at the age of eight to Richard (later Richard I), the son of
            Henry II of England, and it was rumored that during her engagement she be-
            came mother of a child fathered by Henry himself (Saul, *Three Richards*, 136–
            39). Though still engaged to Alys, Richard married Berengaria of Navarre in
            1191. Alys' half-brother, Philip II of France, offered her in marriage to Prince
            (later King) John, but the marriage was prevented by Richard's mother, Eleanor
            of Aquitaine. In 1195, Alys married William IV Talvas, count of Ponthieu, and
            through that marriage she became the grandmother of Eleanor of Castile, who
            married the future Edward I in 1254. Alys thereby may be considered a pro-
            genitor of the English royal family, and hence the English as a whole become
            plant Alis to the Welsh. Other than the present instance, Dafydd Llwyd of Matha-
            farn (c.1420– c.1500) provides the earliest recorded instance of *plant Alis* as a
            derogatory term for the English: *Nid un dwyll na dyn na dis / Onid diawl a phlant
            Alis* [(There is) no treachery of either man or dice, / Except for the devil and the
            children of Alis] (*GPC*, s.v. *plant*). Other poets similarly use either or both *plant*

Alis and *plant Rhonwen*. An anonymous and vituperous sixteenth-century poem protesting the felling of Coed Glyn Cynon (Glyn Cynon Forest) as fuel for iron works implores that for destroying the homes of the wild birds, *Boed yr anras yn eu plith / Holl blant Alis ffeilsion* [Let there be a curse amongst them, / All the false children of Alis] (Parry, *Oxford Book*, p. 207; my translation). In the eighteenth century, Alis came to be known as *Alis y biswail* [Alice of the dunghill], and she was conflated by Iolo Morganwg with Rhonwen (or Ronnwen, Renwein, etc.), the daughter of the Saxon Hengist, whose warning to her father that her husband Vortigern planned to drive the Saxons out of Britain resulted in the permanent settlement of Saxons in Britain (Geoffrey of Monmouth, *History*, p. 163); thus Iolo's "Alice Ronwen," though adopted by others, is a spurious name.

31　　*Gwythen* [stream]. The core sense of *gwythen* is "vein, blood vessel, artery"; not until the late fifteenth century do we begin to find the sense of "a small natural channel through which water flows" (*GPC*, s.v. *gwythïen*), which may be meant here, though the implications of the original sense may also be felt.

　　o'r [from the]. A: *yr*, altered to *or*; BEFGHIJKLMN: *or*.

34　　*Aerfen*. A: *Aerdden*, altered to *Aerfen*; BCDEIJKLM: *aerfen*; F: *aerdden*; GH: *aerden*; N: *Aerddon*. On the alternation between *f* [v] and *dd* [ð], J. Morris Jones notes that these two sounds "were liable to be confused; and so we find one substituted for another as in . . . Late Mn. W. *Caer Dydd* for *Caer Dyf* 'Cardiff'" (Morris Jones, *Welsh Grammar*, p. 177). *Aerfen* is another name for the Dyfrdwy/Dee. Melville Richards explains, "When they [the Romans] arrived, the thing that struck them most was the broad estuary of the river, and upon asking the inhabitants, they learned that it was a river dedicated to the British goddess of war. The form closest to the word for goddess [*duwies*] was *Deva*, and that was adopted by the Romans as the name of their camp. *Deva* gave the form *Dwfw*, *Dwy* in Welsh, and that is why we still talk about the *Dyfrdwy*, the holy river. The name of this particular goddess was Aerfen, a name that contains the well-known word *aer*, which means 'battle, slaughter'. On the tongues of the English more recently, Deva turned into Dee" (Richards, *Enwau Tir*, p. 68 [my translation]; see also Rhys, *Celtic Folklore*, p. 441, and Evans, "Incident," p. 10). The second element of *Aerfen* is in all likelihood the same as that in *tynghedfen* [fate], from *tynged* [destiny, fate] and perhaps the same as that in the name *Ceridfen*, *Ceridwen*, who brewed the cauldron of inspiration from which Taliesin gained his prophetic powers (see Haycock, "Cadair Ceridwen," esp. p. 172n33).

37　　*brochaist* [you raged]. The verb *brochi* is doubly apt here; it derives from the noun *broch*, which means both "foam, froth, spume" and "anger, wrath, rage" (*GPC*, s.vv. *broch*, *brochaf*).

38　　*broch* [spume]. AC originally: *brych*; BDEIJKLM: *broch*.

41　　*a* (particle). Not in AI.

42–43　　In manuscript B (late sixteenth century) the following note appears between these lines: *pyryddon / aerven / dwfrdwy val dyma i tri henw ar avon ddwfrdwy* [Peryddon, Aerven, Dyfrdwy; these are the three names of the river Dyfrdwy].

44   *elyrch* [swans]. ACIN: *eleyrch*; BDEFGHJKLM: *elyrch*. The flat wetlands around
            Llyn Tegid remain the habit of numerous waterfowl, including the relatively
            uncommon Bewick Swan.

48   *raglaw* [deputy]. Welsh *rhaglaw* [deputy, viceroy] (from *rhag* [before, in front of]
            + *llaw* [hand]) was Latinized as *raglotus* and became the title of an administrative
            office in late medieval Wales (*GPC*, s.v. *rhaglaw*; Jenkins, *Law*, p. 270). In *How
            Culhwch Got Olwen*, Glewlwyd Mighty-Grasp announces, "I am Arthur's porter
            each first day of January, and my deputies [*raclouyeit*] during the year except for
            that" (Bollard, *Companion Tales*, p. 25; Bromwich and Evans, *Culhwch*, line 85).

52   Evans notes, "The implication of this reference surely is that the disaster
            described in the *cywydd* occurred in the afternoon" ("Incident," p. 11n37).

Colophon   This is a common form of attribution in Welsh manuscripts.

            oddeutu 1404 [about 1404]. Not in A; from three late manuscripts: J (1739–60),
            K (2nd half of 18th century), and L (1769–1804).

54. LLYWELYN AB Y MOEL, *BATTLE OF WAUN GASEG*

Ed. Iestyn Daniel, *Gwaith*, pp. 94–95; trans. John K. Bollard.

Manuscripts: There are eight manuscripts, designated in Iestyn Daniel's edition as A-H, and
ranging from 1599 to the early nineteenth century. The texts are very similar to each other,
suggesting that they derive ultimately from a single source; C is a copy of B, and E of D; F
is similar to ABC in places, though it has some independent readings. H, NLW Llanstephan
118, p. 186 (1600–1620), is perhaps the earliest, but lines 32–54 are quite worn; however,
its readings are not likely to be significantly different from the edited text.

    Many of the following notes reflect editorial choices and comments in Daniel's textual
notes, and similarly the general observations and interpretations below owe a great debt to
his careful analysis. For more information on the poet and this poem, see pp. 519–21.
    This poem is remarkable not only for the excellence of its verse, but especially as a rare
first-person account of a battle, albeit one told through a light-hearted, ironic persona worthy of Dafydd ap Gwilym or Geoffrey Chaucer. The only other medieval Welsh poem that
comes close to such a direct witness is perhaps that by Madog ap Gronw Gethin in praise of
the river Dee (Item 53). Llywelyn ab y Moel, or Llywelyn ap Moel y Pantri, was born probably around 1395–1400 and died in 1440. As a young man he joined the ranks of Glyndŵr's
rebellion in its later stages, and he lived as an outlaw in the forests, preying on the English,
for some time, as portrayed in his poem to Coed y Graig Lwyd (Item 55). In his elegy to Llywelyn, Guto'r Glyn calls him *bronfraith Owain* [Owain's songthrush], almost certainly a reference to Owain Glyndŵr, as in line 6 of the present poem and line 60 of Item 55. The reference in line 6 of this poem reveals that Llywelyn knew or believed that Owain was alive at
the time of the incident the poem describes. This suggests that the skirmish took place before 1416 at the very latest, perhaps closer to c.1410. Though the poem, of course, could
be somewhat later, it would be odd for Llywelyn to produce such a humorous and self-mock-
ing poem shortly after Owain's death (had he heard of it).

3   *aur* [fine]. Literally, "gold(en)," see Item 3n20.

5–6   There are two ways of reading this couplet, depending on the interpretation of
           chwedl [story, tale; tidings, news]. The lines may mean that the band was expec-
           ting news (*chwedl*) of Owain's arrival or, alternatively, that they hoped through
           their success to increase Owain's reputation (i.e., his story).

           Line 6 is a syllable short, unless *chwedl*, technically a monosyllable, is counted
           as two syllables as a result of the tendency of postconsonantal final -*l* to become
           syllabic or to generate an epenthetic vowel in the consonant cluster *dl*.

7   *Gwneuthud*. This is a variant form of the verbnoun *gwneuthur*, *gwneud* [make,
           do]. The construction is a nominal sentence with no inflected verb, hence the
           translation "We held."

           apêl [complaint]. A borrowing from ME *ap(p)el* [accusation, appeal]. Presum-
           ably, the discussion was meant to forestall any complaints about the spoils they
           hoped to win.

8   *fwting* [discussion]. Lenited form of *mwting*, from ME *muting*, a Northern variant
           of *moting* [discussion; conference, council], the gerundive of *moten* [speak, talk,
           complain]; see *MED*, s.v. *moting(e*.

           fatel [battle]. Lenited form of *batel*, from ME *batayle*.

9   *dodi* [declaring]. Literally, "place, give, set."

11   *o ryw bybyr* [of a brave sort]. See Item 5n42.

15   *gwawd* [a song of praise]. The Welsh Laws state, *Os bard teulu a gan bardoni y gyt
           a theulu y brenhin vrth dwyn anreith, y llwdyn goreu o'r anreith a geiff; ac or byd dar-
           par ymlad arnunt, canet y canu a elwir "Vnbeinyaeth Prydein" racdunt* [If the bard of
           the bodyguard declaim poetry with the king's bodyguard at the taking of spoil,
           he receives the best animal of the spoil; and if they are preparing for battle, let
           him sing the poem called "The Chieftainship of Britain" before them] (Williams
           and Powell, *Cyfreithiau*, p. 22; Richards, *Laws*, pp. 38–39). Might this be the
           song Llywelyn has in mind — and might he be the one who sang it? It has been
           suggested that the song in question might be *Armes Prydein*, the earliest Welsh
           prophecy, composed probably shortly before the Battle of Brunanburh (Jen-
           kins, *Law*, pp. 227–28; for the poem, see Livingston, *Brunanburh*, pp. 28–37).

22   *awchus leferydd uchel* [a high, piercing cry]. I.e., the war-cry, trumpets, drums,
           etc., of the English.

24   *ffromart* [odious]. *GPC* glosses this as "stubborn, wilful, perverse; huge, repug-
           nant." It is a borrowing from ME *frommard*, a variant of *froward* [unruly, intract-
           able, disobedient; stubborn, willful, perverse], from OE *fromweard* [about to
           depart or pass away] (*MED*, s.v. *froward*).

           o Ffrainc [French]. Literally, "from France." It is not clear whether a French or
           Norman drummer was accompanying the clarion player or *ffromart o Frainc* is
           meant as an anti-English slur.

25   *tabwrdd* [tabor]. A small drum.

26   *glariwn* [clarion]. Lenited form of *clariwn*. The clarion is a medieval trumpet
            with clear shrill tones.

            gwn [gun]. This is perhaps the earliest instance of this borrowing from ME
            gonne, gun(ne); see *GPC*, s.v. *gwn*[1]. The nearest contender, also used as a point
            of hyperbolic comparison, is in *Y Dilyw* [The Deluge], a humorous poem on
            lovers fleeing a thunderstorm, sometimes attributed to Dafydd ap Gwilym (fl.
            1340–1370), but more likely to be by Maredudd ap Rhys (fl. 1440–1483): "I
            went mad, with my hair askew, / from the roar of a gun in the air" (see Fulton,
            Apocrypha, pp. 122–23, 235).

29   *bu'n* [was . . . our]. A contraction of *bu ein* [was our].

37   *Caer Wysg*. The fortress and town of Usk (*Brynbuga*).

36   *tros nawnant* [across nine streams]. This should be understood as hyperbole,
            rather than taken literally.

38   *trwsiad gofrwysg* [heady in their attire]. *Trwsiad* refers to the attire of the English
            soldiers, but *gofrwysg* to their behavior. A compressed phrase.

39   *Twrn* [turn of events]. Here Llywelyn borrows the ME *turn*; cf. *chwŷl* in line 18
            above; and see also John Lydgate, *Troy Book* (c.1420): "O Ioie vnstable of veyn
            ambicioun, With vnwar [= sudden, unsuspected] torn reuersed vp-so-doun!"
            (*MED*, s.v. *turn(e*, 9).

            traw [blow]. So F; DGH: *yw* [is]. The reading *traw* occurs only in F, a late eigh-
            teenth- or early nineteenth-century manuscript, but this better fits the require-
            ments of the *cynghanedd* than the *yw* of DGH, giving us a line in which all the
            consonants but the last one before the caesura are matched in the same order
            in the second half of the line: t rn g ' r (d) | tr n g ' r (f); see pp. 516–17.

40   *tost* [painful]. *Tost* has a broad range of denotation and connotation, glossed in
            GPC as "severe, harsh, hard, vehement, furious, bitter, cruel; painful, sore,
            hurt, sick, ill; troubled, sad; pitiful."

41   *Waun Gaseg*. There were three places with the name *Waun Gaseg* [mare's
            meadow], one in Llanbadog, just across the river from the town of Usk, another
            at Aber-carn, between Caerphilly and Pontypool, and a third in Cwmcyncoed
            in Radnorshire, about a mile north of Cwm-hir Abbey. Enid Roberts identifies
            the Waun Gaseg in Llanbadog as the site of this incident, but she argues that
            the poem was a description of the battle of Pwll Melyn in 1405, which is un-
            likely for several reasons, including the age of Llywelyn ab y Moel. Cledwyn
            Fychan, on the other hand, notes that the geographical descriptions in lines 2,
            19, 29, 46, and 49 correspond very well to the geography of the Waun Gaseg
            above Cwmcyncoed. The presence of soldiers from Usk (line 37) can be ex-
            plained by the possibility that they were billeted at Cwm-hir Abbey in order to
            keep the peace in Maelienydd, even after the rebellion wound down (Daniel,
            Gwaith, p. 139; Roberts, "Uchelwyr y Beirdd," p. 72; Fychan, "Llywelyn ab y
            Moel," pp. 292–93).

wen gysellt [unbloodied bundle]. *Cysellt* is a term used for a bundle of straw, as in Dafydd ap Gwilym's address to the haycock in which he is hiding in the rain in hopes of seeing his girl: "I tried to get a bundle [*cysellt*] from you, / flimsy dovecote of straw" (Dafydd ap Gwilym.net, Poem 66.15–16). The image, then, is of a sheaf-like bundle of unused and unbloodied spears left behind in the grass by the Welsh. *Wen*, the lenited form of *gwen*, fem. of *gwyn* [white, shining, bright], is used here in the sense of "unstained by blood," hence the translation here and in lines 50 (*peiswen*, from *pais* + *gwen*) and 54 (*a'r wen bais*).

44   *mawntais* [advantage]. A variant of *mantais*, a borrowing from ME *vauntage, vantage* [a position from which some benefit can be acquired or derived; benefit] (*MED*, s.v. *vauntage*).

45   *cyrchu* [making . . . for]. Llywelyn's use of this word is suitably sardonic, for it is frequently used in the sense "to attack, attacking."

47   *phawb* [all of them]. Spirant mutation of *pawb*, literally, "all, everyone," i.e., the English.

48   Whether or not the English know who is hiding in the ravine, Llywelyn feels like they do.

50   *peiswen ŵr* [a man with unstained cuirass]. See the note to *wen gysellt*, line 41.

        anhapuswaith [unfortunate event]. This hapax legomenon is a compound of *anhapus* [miserable, wretched, unhappy, unlucky] + *gwaith* [work, act, deed]. *GPC* (s.v. *anhapuswaith*) glosses it as "misfortune, mishap."

51–54   Daniel points out that in these lines Llywelyn is boasting of his escape from the enemy, rather than expressing his fear (Daniel, *Gwaith*, p. 142).

51   *dyfyn diofwy* [summons without encounter]. Literally, "unvisited summons." This anticipates the final couplet, i.e., he will not be there if they are commanded to "visit" him.

53   *oerfel i mi* [I'll be damned!]. The idiom *oerfel i*, literally "coldness to" is used to mean "a curse upon," as in several instances by Dafydd ap Gwilym, e.g. *Oerfel i'r carl gwasgarlun, / Amên, a wylltiodd fy mun* [A curse on the slovenly churl, / Amen!, who frightened my girl] (Dafydd ap Gwilym.net, Poem 62, also Poems 106, 142).

54   *a'r wen bais* [and my unbloodied cuirass]. Literally, "and the white cuirass." See the note to *wen gysellt*, line 41.

        y Waun bant. Cledwyn Fychan notes that this is probably a place name, and he suggests that it may have been a farm formerly named Waun-bant (more recently, "The Grove"), about two miles south of Abbey Cwm-hir (Fychan, "Llywelyn ab y Moel," p. 293).

55. LLYWELYN AB Y MOEL, *PRAISE OF THE REBELS' LAIR*

Ed. Iestyn Daniel, *Gwaith*, pp. 96–97; trans. John K. Bollard.

Manuscripts: There are fourteen manuscripts, designated by Iestyn Daniel as A-M (including H[1] and H[2]); they range in date from 1527 to c.1800 and fall into two classes, α: ACDEG H[1]IJKL, and β: BFH[2]. H[2] is a marginal addition to H[1] of only the twenty lines not in the latter; M contains only the first two lines and is therefore not classifiable.

Many of the following notes reflect editorial choices and comments in Daniel's textual notes, and similarly the general observations and interpretations below owe a great debt to his careful analysis. For more information on the poet and this poem, see pp. 519–21.

Version β, presented here, contains twenty lines not found in α, and the order of lines after line 10 is quite different in the two. Unless the poet himself is responsible for both versions, it would seem that β, though it does not always have the best readings, is the original and α is a later abridgement. Version β was first edited by Daniel; it was not known to the editors of *Cywyddau Iolo Goch ac Eraill*, both editions of which contain the 46 lines of version α (Lewis et al., *Cywyddau*, pp. 198–99). There are no lines in α not represented in β, and Daniel suggests that as poetry β is more satisfying and has a deeper appeal than α, not to mention that it includes additional autobiographical references, as in lines 17–18, 51–52 (Daniel, *Gwaith*, p. 143).

The poem is an encomium to Coed y Graig Lwyd [literally, "wood of the grey rock"], to which Llywelyn also refers in poems to his purse (ibid., Poem 11.25–26) and to his tongue (ibid., Poem 12.53–54). The wood in question is that at Craig Llanymynech, on the Welsh-English border, now the Shropshire Wildlife Trust's Llanymynech Rocks Nature Preserve, about five miles south of Oswestry. Here, in the later years of the rebellion, Llywelyn and others sheltered under the protection of the wood as they harried English travelers and residents. The narrator of this poem is more confident than in the previous poem (Item 54), and he combines elements familiar from battle poetry, nature poetry, and even love poetry in this paean to his favorite hiding place.

The headnote is taken from manuscripts B (second half of the 18th cent.) and F (1644/6–1660).

Headnote   *Moliant* [Praise]. B: Mol.; F: Cyw. mol. (i.e., *Cywydd moliant* [A poem of praise]).

1   *Rho Duw* [Between me and God]. This is a common asservation in Middle Welsh, occurring no fewer than nine times in the poetry of Dafydd ap Gwilym, and thirty-one times, in the fuller form *y rof i a Duw*, in *The Mabinogi*. *Rho/rhof* is the first person singular form of the preposition *rhwng* [between].

1–2   *Coed . . . y Graig . . . Lwyd.* Llywelyn accomplishes a metrical tour de force in his opening couplet, twice using the device of tmesis or descriptive parenthesis within a single place name, added to which the final element, *Llwyd* [grey] does double duty as a modifier of *crug* [hill, hillock, knoll] to create a phrase that is a description of the place itself. In the translation this is indicated (somewhat awkwardly) by inserting an extra "grey," which seems preferable to translating the name literally but misleadingly into a form that is not an existing English place name. That *Llwyd* is an integral element of the name is clear from its inclusion in the two instances in other poems mentioned in the headnote. To heighten the effect even further, the poet embeds within the name another place name, Llech Ysgar.

2   *Llech Ysgar*. This the name of one of the courts of Madog ap Maredudd (d. 1160), the last prince of a united Powys, which was apparently at the same or a nearby location. *Llech* is a term for stone, especially slate or other stone with a flat face; the sense of *ysgar* is perhaps "split, division, separation; separated, divided," descriptive of the cliffs of Craig Llanymynech, though John Lloyd-Jones suggests *esgar/ysgar* "enemy, foreigner, stranger" (*Geirfa*, s.v. *escar*[1]; Daniel, *Gwaith*, p. 145n2).

3   *Wyddelig*. Lenited form of *Gwyddelig*, literally, "Irish" (adj.), used here in the sense of "wild."

4   *brig* [branches]. *Brig* is more specifically a term for the smaller upper or outer branches at the tops of trees or other plants.

9   "It is understood that the poet is the subject of the verb. He is thinking of Coed y Graig Lwyd as his faithful lover and saying that he would confidently send it a *llatai* [a love messenger] if he were separated from it in the summer" (Daniel, *Gwaith*, pp. 145–46n9; my translation).

latai. Lenited form of *llatai* [love messenger, go-between]. In the fourteenth century Dafydd ap Gwilym, in particular, popularized the convention of sending an imaginary messenger to one's love. While often a bird, the *llatai* could be another animal, such as a horse or a roebuck, or something inanimate, such as the wind or a wave.

11   *gaerau*. Lenited form of *caerau* [fortresses]. Llywelyn is probably referring to the natural defenses of the place, rather than to any man-made structures.

14   *mydylau* [piles]. Literally, "haycocks."

16   *gangell*. Lenited form of *cangell* [chancel]. Here Llywelyn compares the safety of the wood to the sanctuary of a church.

21   *ddiharneisio* [despoil]. Lenited for *of diharneisio*, literally, "unharness," though it can also carry a force as strong as "mutilate" (see Llywelyn ap Gutun, *Gwaith*, ed. Daniel, Poem 4n11).

23   *Fy mharch diymgel*. Literally, "my unhidden (object of) respect"; the English idiom "pride and joy" seems to convey something close to Llywelyn's sentiment here.

fy mhwys. The noun *pwys*, literally "(a) weight" and figuratively "importance, significance, authority," can also mean "a person in authority" and by extension "a spouse" (Daniel, *Gwaith*, p. 146n23); see especially Mac Cana, "Poet as Spouse."

31   Compare line 7 above.

34   *main nadd* [hewn stones]. "Craig Llanymynech is limestone, and its face is like many rows of square or angular large stones on top of each other. Perhaps therefore the face of the crag is meant — or else, since the stones are men-

tioned along with *tir mwyn* [gentle land] in the same line, the pieces of the Craig that have fallen off over the ages and can be seen resting on the ground here and there" (Daniel, *Gwaith*, p. 147n34; my translation).

40   *diwael* [splendid]. "*Diwael* is a kind of exclamation, for Llywelyn is saying what a great place the wood is, especially after having had oats to eat" (Iestyn Daniel, personal communication).

48   *a thorri dail* [and breaking leaves]. The reference may be to lovers making a bed of leaves or a shelter of leaves, or less likely, perhaps, making a garland of leaves.

      uthr eu dysg! [tremendous their learning!]. BF: *vthr iw dysc*; ACDH¹I-L: *dail athro dysc* [leaves of a master of learning]. The *dysg* [learning] is presumably that which comes from "breaking leaves."

51–52 The poet seems to be recalling a woodland meeting with his love, cut short perhaps by the calls upon him as a soldier (Daniel, *Gwaith*, p. 158n51). In four of his poems, Llywelyn names his sweetheart Euron (p. 209).

58   *llu'r Nordd* [the host of the North]. Prior to the modern era, the term *y Nordd* generally referred to the north of England (see *GPC*, s.v. *nordd*, north). As E. D. Jones explains, "Of all the English the worst [to the Welsh] were the men of the North, the inhabitants above the river Trent, and in this the English of the southeast would agree with the [Welsh] poets" (quoted by Daniel, *Gwaith*, p. 149n58; my translation).

59   The interpretation of this line is difficult. In the present translation, *perclwyd* [perch] (possibly from ME *perk* [perch] + *clwyd* [roost, perch]) is understood as referring to a position at the top of the Craig, with a broad view of the *sercl*, i.e., the sky, the firmament, the arc of the heavens, and of the surrounding lands. The only other citation for *berclwyd* in *GPC* is from Dafydd ap Gwilym's address to the lark: *Mawr yw'r sercl yt o berclwyd* [Large is the sky for you from a perch] (five manuscripts read . . . *sercl dy berclwyd* [Large is the sky of (= which is?) your perch]) (Dafydd ap Gwilym, *Gwaith*, Poem 114.57; Dafydd ap Gwilym.net, Poem 44.57; both sources list variants).

60   *Llundain*. I.e., the wood is a place to which many people would flock.

63   *i blith dy blaid* [amidst your party]. ACDH¹IKL: *ymhlith ymlaid* (= *[ffy mhlaid*) [amongst my party]; however, note that line 66 identifies the men not as the poet's, but as *llueiddiaid tau* [your soldiers], i.e., soldiers of Coed y Graig Lwyd.

64   *llawn dâl* [full payment]. I.e., the poet is not short of money as an outlaw in Coed y Graig Lwyd as he is in the poem to his purse, composed c.1421 (Daniel, *Gwaith*, p. 150, and Poem 11, *I'r pwrs*, pp. 100–01).

65   *Llwyr ystad* [A complete estate]. I.e., "the poet had everything he could wish for in Coed y Graig Lwyd" (Daniel, *Gwaith*, p. 150n65; my translation).

      lloer ystodiau. Literally, "courses/periods of the moon." *Ystod* [course, route, path, length (of time), duration, etc.] also has adverbial force, especially in the combination *yn ystod* [during]. Thus, *lloer ystodiadau* [(during or through) the phases of the moon] implies a long period of time.

66   *llwyddid*. Third person sg. imperative of *llwyddo* [to bring or give success to, make prosperous, bless] (*GPC*, s.v. *llwyddaf*).

56. *ROLLS OF PARLIAMENT, 1407*

From *PROME*, ed. and trans. Chris Given-Wilson. Notes by Michael Livingston.

The parliament of 1404 (Item 40) had been reticent to provide the king with the funds he demanded of them, noting that the realm had proved hardly secure under his leadership; among their foremost concerns were the deteriorating conditions in Wales. The parliament of 1407, held between 20 October and 2 December, saw much of the same dynamic. It was held in Gloucester rather than Westminster, a decision that Given-Wilson suspects was tied to Owain's rebellion. The prince of Wales had been besieging rebel-held Aberystwyth since August, and in September the Welsh commander, Rhys Ddu, had made an agreement (Item 68.133–254) to surrender the town by 1 November if he was not relieved by Owain: when parliament opened "no doubt Henry IV hoped soon to have news of its recovery"; Owain's successful — and little understood — relief of Aberystwyth, however, dashed these hopes and is no doubt "reflected in the occasionally recriminative tone in which Welsh affairs were discussed during the parliament" (*PROME*). The elected speaker of parliament was Thomas Chaucer, the son of Geoffrey Chaucer. It was the first of five times he would hold the office, which is a testament to how well he handled his duties from the outset: on some matters he drew a strong line against the king, including his observation that conditions in Wales were at least partly the responsibility of English lords of Wales and the March who were derelict in their duties; on other matters he was clearly willing to work with the king, resulting in a stronger relationship between the commons and the crown.

57. GRUFFUDD AP DAFYDD, *DEFYING LORD GREY OF RUTHIN*

Ed. and trans. Michael Livingston, from Ellis, *Original Letters*, 2.1.5–7.

Manuscript: London, British Library, MS Cotton Cleopatra F.iii, fol. 72r.

This letter and the following one (Item 58) were once thought to have been written at the outbreak of Owain's rebellion (so Ellis, *Original Letters*, 2.1.1). More recent scholars have backed a date in 1411. As Davies observes, this "extraordinary exchange of letters between Reginald Grey and Gruffudd ap Dafydd ap Gruffudd, a Welsh bandit and doubtless erstwhile rebel, lifts the veil on the sort of bargains and cajoleries which lay behind the ending of the revolt" (*Revolt*, p. 297). Here, Gruffudd excuses his most recent wrong-doings as the fault of dishonest Englishmen; he then makes direct threats against Grey if he does not receive what he wants: a royal pardon, a job, and overseas military service.

Of Gruffudd himself, little is known beyond what is contained or can be extrapolated from his exchange with Grey. The English lord calls him "the strengest theife of Wales" (Item 58.25), and scholars have long accepted Grey's statement about Gruffudd's outlawry without question (as in Davies, cited above). Ellis, in editing this exchange, took Grey's position so thoroughly to heart that he characterized one of these letters as "of a barbarous character, and [it] breathes more of savage warfare than of chivalry" (*Original Letters*, 2.1.5); alas for Ellis, he had misread the authorship of the letter: it was written by Grey, not Gruffudd (for the clever conclusion to this epistle, see note to Item 58.25 below). Stenroos and Mäkinen, in a fascinating study of the linguistic and formal contents of the letters, have concluded that Gruffudd is hardly the "barbarous" thief that critics have long assumed him to be: "the stereotypical characterisation of Gruffuth in modern historiography is a remarkable example of the communication of politically charged texts to readers across several centuries. It derives from readings that take Grey's letters largely at face value, without considering critically the political agenda behind them. The image of Gruffuth as a bandit has, in its turn, coloured the interpretation of the historical happenings referred to in the texts" ("Defiant Gentleman," p. 83). To the contrary, Stenroos and Mäkinen argue, all signs point to Gruffudd being "regarded as a member of the gentry," a man with "considerable literacy skills, familiarity with English letter-writing conventions and a fluent command of English" ("Defiant Gentleman," p. 100).

In addition to the general impression of the continuing troubles in Wales, the present letter is interesting for Gruffudd's claim that he has been under the protection of *Mered ap Owein* (line 3), by which most have assumed is meant Owain Glyndwr's son, Maredudd. If this is so, then it implies that by this date Owain had largely retired from the field of the Welsh uprising he had begun over a decade earlier.

3   *Mered ap Owein*. Presumably, this is Owain Glyndwr's son, Maredudd.

4   *Maester Edward and Edward ap Dauid*. Of Gruffudd's cousins little is known, except that the title "Master," as Stenroos and Mäkinen point out, "suggests either university learning or, more generally, high social status; the English name probably indicates intermarriage between Welsh and English families" ("Defiant Gentleman," p. 100).

5   *keyshat*. The term, as Stenroos and Mäkinen note, "seems to represent a Welsh official's title, corresponding approximately to Middle English *serjeant*" ("Defiant Gentleman," p. 85n3).

34   *Gode kepe your worschipfull astate in prosperite*. This is a polite and common concluding phrase, but in light of what Gruffudd has just said it can take a humorously insulting edge: if Gruffudd is preying on Grey's estates than he has good reason for wishing for those estates to prosper.

35   *the parke of Brinkiffe*. Davies notes that this is likely to mean Bryncyffo in Dyffryn Clwyd (*Revolt*, p. 266). If this is so, then this may be a kind of veiled insult: Gruffudd is hiding out within Grey's own jurisdiction.

58. Lord Grey of Ruthin, *Welsh Outlawry*

Ed. and trans. Michael Livingston.

Manuscript: London, British Library, MS Cotton Cleopatra F.iii, fol. 70r. First printed in *Original Letters*, ed. Ellis, 2.1.3–4; variants from the latter are designated OL in the notes below.

In addition to those reasons already noted (for the initial facts of this document, see headnote to Item 57), this letter is here included in part for the fact that it does *not* mention Owain Glyndŵr: we would expect that in his accounting of local events in the rebellion, Lord Grey — who in the standard accounts is the reason for Owain's rebellion and had in fact been held prisoner by him in 1402 — would mention Glyndŵr by name. Indeed, the one rebel he does refer to, and whom he terms "the strengest theife of Wales," is not Owain but Gruffudd ap Dafydd ap Gruffudd (line 25). Along with Gruffudd's statement that he was under the protection of Owain's son Maredudd rather than that of Owain himself, this provides further evidence that Owain Glyndŵr — if he was still alive — now served the Welsh rebellion for the most part in a symbolic role.

4   *your gracious*. MS: your inserted above the line.

7   *comaundyng*. So MS. OL: *commaundyng*.

    misgouvernance. So MS. OL: *misgouernance*.

13   *erles of Arundele*. Lord Grey's concerns regarding the lands of the earl of Arundel are most likely centered upon the fortress of Castell Dinas Brân, which even today is a prominent feature above the town of Llangollen in Denbighshire. The hilltop location, which commands views of both the Dee Valley and the route north past Valle Crucis Abbey to Ruthin over what is now called Horseshoe Pass, has been recognized since at least the Iron Age. The medieval ruins date to a castle built by Gruffydd II ap Madog during the rule of Llywelyn ap Gruffydd (c.1223–1282), the last prince of an independent Wales. Though Dinas Brân was partially destroyed in the war with Edward I and ultimately allowed to fall into ruin by the time of the Glyndŵr Rising, it would have remained a key strategic location for any rebel actions in the area.

15   *comaundement*. So MS. OL: *commaundement*.

16, 17 *officeres*. So MS. OL: *officers*.

18   *the marche es lond*. So MS. OL: *the Marches lond*.

20   *rissen*. So MS. OL: *risen*.

21   *officeres in bettere gouvernance*. So MS. OL: *officers in better governance*.

    Gales. So MS. OL: *Wales*.

24   *messagere*. So MS. OL: *messager*.

25   *the strengest thiefe of Wales.* So MS. OL: *the strengest theife of Wales.* Here not Owain but Gruffudd ap Dafydd ap Gruffudd. For Gruffudd's letter, see Item 57. Grey's reply, long thought to be another letter from Gruffudd (see headnote to Item 57) essentially responds to the several points Gruffudd makes before stating that Gruffudd has essentially confessed himself to be a horse-thief, no matter his rationale. And so, Grey concludes (in verse written as prose): "we hoepe we shall do the a pryve thyng: a roope, a ladder, and a ryng, heigh on gallowes for to henge and thus shall be your endyng. And he that made the be ther to helpyng, and we on our behalfe shall be welle willyng" [we hope to do you a secret thing: a rope, a ladder, and ring, high on the gallows to hang, and that shall be your ending. And may he who made you be there to help you, and we, for our part, will be more than willing] (fol. 70v).

26   *you.* MS: inserted above the line.

29   *pouere.* So MS. OL: *pour.*

59. *ROLLS OF PARLIAMENT, 1411*

From *PROME*, ed. and trans. Chris Given-Wilson. Notes by Michael Livingston.

By the time parliament opened on 3 November 1411, the rebellion in Wales had been much in retreat. Owain Glyndŵr appears to have given up some (if not all) personal control over the Welsh rebels (see the headnote to Item 58, above), who had by now lost much of their conquests and large-scale capacities. The Welsh rebels were, by all indication, reduced to banditry and brigandry — compare the actions of Llywelyn ab y Moel (Items 54, 55). Their appearance here in the parliament rolls very much underscores this view.

60. HENRY IV, *GENERAL AMNESTY TO REBELS*

Adapted and trans. by Kelly DeVries, from Rymer, *Foedera,* 8.711.

This amnesty claims to have been composed at the urging of the Commons at parliament, but there is little in the rolls of the previous parliament (which began a month earlier in November) to match the particulars of this amnesty. In fact, the closest request on record is from several years earlier, at the 1404 parliament (Item 40.44–69), which similarly excepted Thomas of Trumpington (see note to line 6 below) but interestingly made no exception for the rebels of Wales.

6   Thomas Ward of Trumpington appears often in the English record between 1402 and 1419 as a "pseudo-Richard": in Scotland, perhaps under the protection of the duke of Albany, he was impersonating the dead Richard II.

6–7   *in partibus Transmarinis et Cismarinis.* This is a legal phrase, meant to include English nobles and troops in England as well as in France; the terms could also be divided to refer only to those in England or in France. (Interestingly, *in partibus transmarinis* never refers to nobles and garrisons in Ireland.)

7   *sectam pactis nostrae* [our surety of peace]. A formulaic legal phrase appearing in many medieval English pardons.

11   *factis sive perpetratis*. This phrase appears frequently in legal documents to include both those who performed and those who initiated the deeds.

20   *Festum Nativitatis Sancti Johannis Baptistae* [Feast of the Nativity of St. John the Baptist]. I.e., 24 June.

61. HENRY IV, *LICENCE TO TREAT WITH OWAIN*

Adapted and trans. by Kelly DeVries, from Rymer, *Foedera*, 8.753.

It can be all too easy to paint the rebellion of Owain Glyndŵr in simple terms as the Welsh against the English (terms which have indeed been used in this book as a kind of short-hand to refer to the two antagonist sides in the conflict). The reality was not nearly so tidy, however: intermarriage left many families with loyalties on both sides, and even "pure-blood" families were not a certainty to join one side or another.

One of the more interesting figures caught in "profound paradoxes of loyalty and contradictions of conviction" as a result of the struggle is Dafydd Gam, whose name is often anglicized to Davy Gamm or David Gamme: as Davies describes him, he was "the most redoubtable and famous of Owain's opponents," despite the fact that he was, like Owain, unquestionably Welsh and even a claimant "of princely descent" in Wales (*Revolt*, p. 225). Dafydd's family had long served the English lords of Brecon, and they cast their lot with the English early in the revolt. Dafydd Gam himself proved a remarkable military man whose loyalty to the crown was unflinching; he ultimately "acquired a legendary status as one of the most implacable and daredevil Welsh opponents of Owain" (*Revolt*, p. 227).

Perhaps it is fitting, then, that the last relatively firm record we have of Owain Glyndŵr still being active is his spring 1412 seizure of Dafydd Gam, reported here through the king's license to treat with Owain for his release. Subsequent to this document, Dafydd was quickly ransomed at an estimated cost of 200–700 marks, the money coming from the royal estates. A valued leader in the field, his loyalty to the English kings, including his bravery and death at the Battle of Agincourt in service of Henry V, became so well-known that Shakespeare named him on the brief list of English dead delivered to the crown at the end of that battle (*Henry V* 4.8.102).

8   This is likely John, first baron of Tiptoft, who held a number of important positions in his long life (d. 1443), including Speaker of the House of Commons, Treasurer of the Household, Chief Butler of England, Treasurer of the Exchequer and Seneschal of Lands and Aquitaine.

9   William Botiller was a servant of Henry V who had been with him for many years before he was made king. Because of his loyalty and service Henry elevated him above his station to perform a number of duties, including the one listed here. See Griffiths, "William Botiller."

62. ADAM OF USK, *CHRONICLE*, PART 3

Adapted from Adam of Usk, *Chronicle*, ed. and trans. Chris Given-Wilson, pp. 158–63, 172–77, 212–13, 242–43. Notes by Michael Livingston.

Manuscripts: London, British Library, Add. MS 10,104, fols. 173r–173v, 174v–175r; Belvoir quire, fols. 1v, 4r.

For general information on Adam of Usk and his chronicle, see the headnote to part 1 (pp. 306–07). This third part contains many accounts of importance for Owain and his revolt, from the Battle of Bryn Glas in 1402 to the imprisonment of Owain's family in 1409 and Owain's present (1414) inability to do more than hide in the mountains.

5–9   Edmund Mortimer died at Harlech Castle in 1409 (whether from illness or wounds is unknown). The rest of Owain's family was captured when the castle was subsequently taken by the English. Imprisoned in the Tower of London, they died in 1413 (see the chronology in this volume, p. 4).

17–18   Adam's comparison of Owain with an Assyrian acknowledges the rebel leader's impact but does so in damning fashion. See Isaiah 10:5.

35–39   Given-Wilson notes: "Roger Clarendon, . . . Walter de Baldock, prior of Launde (Leics.), and their accomplices were hanged in May 1402 for proclaiming that Richard II was still alive. . . . The mention of 'countesses' probably refers to the conspiracy of the countess of Oxford in 1403–4" (Adam, *Chronicle*, p. 174).

41–45   Adam here refers to the August 1405 French invasion of England. For more on this attack, see Items 50 and 66 in particular.

50–52   There is some question about where and when Owain held his Welsh parliaments; we are relatively certain he held a parliament at Machynlleth in summer 1404 (as stated here), and that a subsequent one was held in 1405 at Harlech (see Item 49). It is possible that a third parliament was held in 1406 at Pennal, which produced the so-called Pennal Letters (Items 51, 52).

53–62   Adam here conflates two different battles. The first, with the prince and the date given here, is Grosmont, which occurred on 11–12 March 1405 (see Item 48). The second, with the death of the abbot and capture of Owain's son, is Pwll Melyn, which Walsingham also conflates with Grosmont but records for 5 March (Item 68.104–08). The fact that both were significant English victories — after many defeats — no doubt caused confusion between them. Walsingham's 5 March date, and his record of a similar battle on St. George's Day, 6 May 1406 (Item 68.127–29), may well indicate that Pwll Melyn occurred on 5 May 1405.

58   *abbas de Lanterna* [abbot of Llantarnam]. This is John ap Hywel. For more on this charismatic figure, see Item 79.63–103, 150–166.

62–63   Given-Wilson notes that "Griffith spent most of his captivity at Nottingham castle, being moved to the Tower in Mar. 1411, shortly before his death" (Adam, *Chronicle*, pp. 212–13).

63. *ROLLS OF PARLIAMENT, 1414*

From *PROME*, ed. and trans. Chris Given-Wilson. Notes by Michael Livingston.

The second parliament of Henry V's reign was held between 30 April and 29 May 1414. For the present purposes, the official roll of the proceeding is interesting for claiming in a petition, quite baldly, that the Welsh rebellion was finished (line 1). That being said, the petition proceeds to describe the still relatively lawless condition of the border counties and Wales itself, where former rebels had become bandits and brigands — a complaint much like that which was made in the parliament of 1411 (Item 59).

64. HENRY V, *LICENCE TO TREAT WITH OWAIN*

Ed. and trans. Kelly DeVries, from Rymer, *Foedera*, 9.283.

This license of 5 July 1415 is the last surviving document that appears to be written under the belief that Owain was still alive. The next time that the crown attempted to enter into talks with the rebel leadership, it would do so with Owain's son, Maredudd ap Owain (Item 65).

3   Sir Gilbert, the fifth baron of Talbot, was the elder brother of Sir John Talbot, one of the most famous English leaders of the Hundred Years' War. His career in France began in 1419, after which he fought in almost every major siege and battle; it would include capture by Joan of Arc at the Battle of Patay in 1429 and death at the battle of Castillon in 1453, the last major engagement of the war. Gilbert also met death in the Hundred Years' War, at the siege of Rouen in 1418.

65. HENRY V, *LICENCE TO TREAT WITH OWAIN'S SON*

Ed. and trans. Kelly DeVries, from Rymer, *Foedera*, 9.330–31.

There are several small differences between this license to negotiate with Owain's son, Maredudd ap Owain, and the earlier licence to negotiate with Owain himself (Item 64). Why Henry waited more than seven months between issuing the two licenses is not known, though many have speculated that this second licence, by turning from Owain to his son, marks an awareness on the part of the English court that Owain had died in the interim, generally assumed to be September of 1415.

66. Michel Pintoin, *Chronicle of Charles VI*

Adapted and trans. by Michael Livingston from Pintoin, *Chronique*, ed. Bellaguet, 3.164–68, 322–28.

The chroniclers of the Abbey of St. Denis in France are among our most important sources for the study of the late Middle Ages. Most famous among their works are perhaps the *Grandes Chroniques de France*, which served as an "official" chronicle for the realm beginning in the reign of Louis IX and lasting until 1461. Among the many continuations or additions to this work produced at the abbey is the *Chronicle of Charles VI*, a work that covers the reign of this French king from 1380 to 1422. For centuries the author of this work was lost, so that it promulgated under the anonymous authorship of the *Religieux de St Denis* [the Monk of St. Denis], but in 1976 Grévy-Pons and Ornato revealed that the author of the work to 1420 was named Michel Pintoin (d. 1421), and that Pintoin had likely composed it as a single unit at around that point ("Qui est l'auteur?").

This French chronicle provides a number of interesting perspectives on Owain Glyndŵr and his revolt, including an account of the French invasion of England in July of 1405 that is more detailed and likely more accurate than that found in Walsingham or Monstrelet (Items 68 and 80). Before that, however, it also provides us with a glimpse at the earlier failed invasion by Bourbon in August 1404, in addition to a fascinating account of Owain's ambassadors in Paris.

10	*Yvo de Wallia* [Owain Lawgoch]. Owain ap Thomas ap Rhodri (d. 1378) was one of the most famous soldiers of his day. Known as Owain Lawgoch in his Welsh homeland, he fought for the French (who knew him as Yvain de Galles) against the English (who called him Owain of the Red Hand) in the Hundred Years' War.
12	*fratrem proprium* [his own brother]. It is unlikely that Owain sent his own brother by blood (Tudur), who was one of his military commanders in the field. To the contrary, the phrase is surely meant to refer to John Hanmer, Owain's cousin and brother-in-law, who was one of the two ambassadors authorized by Owain to treat with the king of France (Item 43).
19–20	*comitis Marchie* [the count La Marche]. I.e., James II of Bourbon-La Marche (1370–1438). On his experience, see the following note.
35–39	The adventures of the count de La Marche were, in fact, little to boast about: his experience on crusade in Hungary, for instance, was to have fought at the disastrous Battle of Nicopolis in 1396.
40	*rege tenebris ignorancie detento* [who was held in the darkness of ignorance]. Bellaguet (3.167) assumed that this refers to the on-and-off madness of King Charles VI of France ("était alors privé de sa raison" [he was at this time deprived of his reason]), but the Latin is far less direct. More likely, the chronicler is only trying to point out that his king was not aware of the plans that were carried out in his name — whether due to madness or treachery — and is thus not guilty for the ultimate failure of them.

49–52   The three leaders of this French invasion were Jean de Trie (the marshal of Rieux), Jean of Hengest (the lord of Hugueville and master of the crossbows of France), and Robert of La Heuse (the lord of Ventes), who was also called *Le Borgue* [One-eyed]. Cochon names the second two men, but he omits the marshal (Item 69.13–14); Monstrelet says that the leaders are the marshal de Trie and the master of crossbows (Item 80.3–4).

101–11   The surprisingly civilized nature of Owain's agreement with the citizens is noted by Walsingham. See Item 68.117–21.

112–13   The push of the French force to Worcester, and the long stand-off with Henry IV that followed, is here glossed over by the chronicler.

118   *armigerum nomine Blesum de Belay Picardum* [a Picard squire named le Begue de Belay]. About this figure, who is here lauded for his dedication to the troops, nothing more is known. It is uncertain, in fact, if le Begue is his name or an epithet, meaning "the Stammerer."

124   *circa carnisprivium* [around Lent]. The fifty days preceding Easter, a period formally called in Latin *Quinquagesima* [the Fiftieth], was a time of fasting and preparation for that most holy of days. For this reason, an alternative Latin name for the period is *carnisprivium* [the depriving of flesh], which could indicate either an abstinence from eating meat (as it often was) or a spurning of the body's physical needs. Because the medieval calendar revolved so resolutely around such liturgical concepts, Lent (as it is more commonly called today) became synonymous with the season of spring more generally. It is thus impossible to determine, from the data provided here, any specific date for the final departure of the French forces beyond "Spring 1406."

67. ADAM OF USK, *CHRONICLE, PART 4*

From Adam of Usk, *Chronicle*, ed. and trans. Chris Given-Wilson, pp. 262–63.

Manuscript: Belvoir quire, fol. 5v.

For general information on Adam of Usk and his chronicle, see the headnote to part 1 (pp. 306–07). This fourth part contains his account of the death, burial, and secret re-burial of Owain. Most historians have set the events in this passage in 1415, though Adam himself is somewhat unclear on their chronological location: it is set between events in 1415 and those in early 1416.

68. THOMAS WALSINGHAM, *ST. ALBANS CHRONICLE*

Adapted from *St Albans Chronicle*, ed. and trans. Taylor, Childs, and Watkiss, pp. 304–05, 314–17, 320–27, 336–39, 358–59, 380–81, 434–35, 462–65, 470–71, 474–75, 518–29, 602–03. Notes by Michael Livingston.

Manuscript: Oxford, Bodleian Library, MS Bodley 462, fols. 258r, 259r–261r, 262r–262v, 265v, 268v, 276v, 281r, 282r, 289v–291r, 302r.

The *St. Albans Chronicle* is without doubt one of the most important contemporary records of the end of the fourteenth century and the beginning of the fifteenth, yet the full text of this fascinating book has been printed only recently, in the 2011 edition and translation by Taylor, Childs, and Watkiss. As these modern editors reveal, what scholars have long considered a "school" of writers who produced several different chronicles of the period at St. Albans was, in fact, a team of scribes, led by Thomas Walsingham, who produced a single great chronicle: previous printings of what were thought to be a multiplicity of chronicles — and known in scholarship under various names, including *Walsingham's Chronicle*, *Chronica maiora*, *Historia Anglicana*, and *Chronicon Angliae* — are now understood to be abbreviated copies of this one originating text.

This full chronicle gives a wide look at the revolt of Owain, and it includes several rare or unique pieces of information, including a copy of the agreement through which the Welsh surrendered Aberystwyth to the English.

5–6	Walsingham passes over the "withheld letter" story about the origin of the dispute between Owain and Lord Grey in order to focus on a struggle over the inheritance of lands. Interestingly, Owain apparently emphasized this very same issue — though the particulars are not now clear — in his dialogue with Henry Percy (Item 24.11–12).
52	*festum Assumpcionis sancte Marie*. I.e., 15 August 1402.
54	*Arundelie comiti*. Thomas FitzAlan.
62	*uigilia uero Naciuitatis sancte Marie*. I.e., 7 September.
85–87	Lord Grey's ransom occurred on 11 November; see *Rot. Parl.* 3.487, *PROME* 8.162 (13).
100–03	3 September muster of troops at Worcester, followed by mid-September march to Carmarthen and back to Hereford; in October Henry IV returned toward London.
105	*die cinerum* [Ash Wednesday]. I.e., 4 March 1405.
	facta est magna strages Wallensium [a great slaughter of the Welsh took place]. The event referred to is the Battle of Grosmont.
105–06	*quinto die mensis Marcii, altero facto conflictu apud Husk* [the fifth of March in a second battle fought at Usk]. This appears to refer to Pwll Melyn, though other sources indicate that this engagement occurred in May (see Item 62.53–62n).
108	*festum sancti Dunstani* [feast of St. Dunstan]. I.e., 19 May.
109–10	The capture of John Hanmer occurred in June 1405.
128	*die sancti Georgii*. I.e., 23 April 1406. On this battle, see Item 62.53–62n.
135–36	*castro de Arberustwith iuxta nouam uillam de Lampadere situatam* [the gates of Aberystwyth castle situated not far from the new town of Llanbadarn]. Taylor et al. trans-

late *Lampadere* as "Lampeter" rather than "Llanbadarn." The town of Aberystwyth, at the mouth of the river Rheidol, was founded by Edward I, who both built the castle and chartered the borough in 1277. The town and castle originally took the name Llanbadarn from that of the ancient settlement of Llanbadarn Fawr, about a mile inland. Latin documents from the 13th century regularly use the spelling *Lampader* or *Lampaderuaur* for Llanbadarn (Fawr) (Edwards, *Littere Wallie*, pp. 131, 188, 196, 201). On the other hand, Lampeter (Welsh: Llanbedr Pont Steffan), which is some 25 miles away, appears in Latin documents of the same period as *Lampeter, Lampet[er]*, and *Lampater* (Edwards, *Littere Wallie*, pp. 80, 164). (Note that in each case the *-t-* is preserved, showing the English pronunciation of Lampeter.) The castle and town subsequently took the name Aberystwyth from the earlier fortification about a mile and a half to the south across the Ystwyth valley at the site now known as Tan-y-castell; this original Aberystwyth castle was destroyed in 1143 (Lloyd, *History*, 426, 490).

141–42   *Rees apud Gruffydd apud Llywelyn apud Ieuan, alias Rees apud Llywelyn Cadagan.* I.e., Rhys Ddu.

157   *noua uilla de Lampader.* See note to lines 135–36, above.

251–54   Walsingham refers to Matthew 27:64. Taylor et al. note that "While this type of arrangement to end a siege was not unusual, it was more unusual that Glyn Dwr successfully relieved the castle within the specified time. His anger with Rhys Ddu is confirmed in the Welsh Annals of Owain Glyn Dwr. Aberystwyth did not fall to the English until the Autumn of 1408 or the spring of 1409."

255–56   The capture of Dafydd Gam by Owain is accounted twice in the chronicle: once here (fol. 302v) and again later, in the same year, at fol. 305r.

69. PIERRE COCHON, *NORMANDY CHRONICLE*

Adapted and trans. Michael Livingston, from Cochon, *Chronique*, ed. Beaurepaire, pp. 209–11.

Manuscript: Paris, Bibliotheque Nationale, MS fds. Francais 9859. 3.

Pierre Cochon (1390?–1456?) was a priest and *notaire apostolique* of Rouen; it was in this position that he wrote a continuation of the *Chronique normande* to 1430. He should not be confused with the more famous Pierre Cauchon of Beauvais, associated with Joan of Arc.

13   *jour de la Magdeleine* [day of the Magdalene]. I.e., 22 July 1405.

18   *Toussains* [All Saints' Day]. I.e., 1 November.

70. *CHRONICLE OF OWAIN GLYNDŴR*

Ed. and trans. John K. Bollard.

Manuscripts: **α**: Aberystwyth, National Library of Wales, MS Peniarth 135, pp. 59–64; **A**: Aberystwyth, National Library of Wales, MS Panton 23, pp. 223–228; **B**: Aberystwyth, National Library of Wales, MS Panton 22, fols. 1–4.

The text is edited from a fresh transcription of MS α, written between 1556 and 1564 in the hand of the poet, genealogist, and herald Gruffudd Hiraethog (d. 1564). The language of the text suggests that he was copying an original from the early fifteenth century, making this one of the earliest Welsh accounts of the rebellion (Lloyd, *Owen Glendower*, p. 149). Substantive variants are shown from MS A (1770s) and MS B (dated to 1776), both in the hand of Evan Evans (Ieuan Fardd), a noted scholar and copyist of Welsh manuscripts. The orthography of the manuscripts has been retained, though modern capitalization and punctuation have been supplied. Except in the case of proper names, simple orthographic variants are not indicated.

Title   B: *Annales Oweni Glyndwr ex liber vet: script: per Lewys Morgannwg* [The Annals of Owain Glyndŵr, from an old book written by Lewys Morgannwg]. Lewys Morgannwg was a notable poet of Glamorgan who flourished 1520–1565. There is no title in α or A, where these annals are embedded in a longer chronicle.

1   *MCCCC.* B: *[A PHAN OEDD OET] MCCCC.*

            Hari. B: *Harri.*

            Prydain. A: *Prydyn.* Clearly Scotland is the intended meaning here. On variation between *Prydain* [Britain] and *Prydyn* [Pictland, Scotland], see the note to Item 6.55. Henry IV made a punitive expedition to Scotland in the summer of 1400, to which Glyndŵr had been summoned, though Lord Grey's failure to deliver the summons in a timely fashion may have contributed not only to Glyndŵr's failure to comply, but also to his reasons for mounting his rebellion. For more on this supposed cause, see Items 78 and 86.

1–2   *a phan ytoed ef ar wastad yno* [and when he was at rest there]. The primary sense is *gwastad* is "flat, level, smooth, even", with a secondary sense of "quiet, peaceful, tranquil, placid." Here it seems to imply "when things were settled there." Lloyd translates, "While he was unoccupied there" (*Owen Glendower*, p. 150).

2   *y dywedodd vn o'r arglwyddi* [one of the lords said]. A: *un o'r arglwyddi a ddywedodh;* B: *dywaid* [said].

            ydd oedd reidach iddaw [he had better]. More literally, "it was more necessary for him;" *reidach* is the comparative of *rhaid* [necessity], taken adjectively.

            diwydwyr [faithful men]. Though Lloyd prints *dieydwyr*, the distinction between Gruffudd Hiraethog's *e* and *w* is at times unclear in certain contexts, and the manuscript reading, though ambiguous, seems closer to *diwydwyr* than *dieydwyr*. MSS A, B read *diwydwyr*. Both forms derive from *diwyd* [faithful] + *gwŷr* [men].

3   *dywedyd y kyvodai Owain* [he said that Owain would rise up]. In indirect speech the imperfect in Welsh often carries a future sense, as in the present translation, following Lloyd's: "he said that Owen . . . would wage war" (*Owen Glendower*, p. 150). This reading implies a predictive element to the lord's statement which is

not borne out elsewhere in the historical record, but which is understandable in the present context, and indeed there may have been some audible grumblings from Wales before September 16 that have not survived in the historical record. On the other hand, the imperfect in indirect speech may also indicate the present indicative in direct speech, suggesting that we might alternatively translate "he said that Owain . . . was rising up to wage war." The chronology of this chronicle is not precise, but we know from other sources that Henry learned of the rebellion on September 19 at Northampton on his way back from Scotland, only three days after Owain was proclaimed prince of Wales.

4   *ydd anvoned* [were sent]. A: *i danvonwyd* [were sent].

Arglwydd Grei [Lord Grey]. α: These words are repeated at the end of p. 59 and the beginning of p. 60.

5   *Ywain*. B: *Owein*.

hwynt a'i. α: *hwynt a*; A: *hwynt ai*, B: *hwy ai*.

6   *i'r koed* [to the wood]. B: *i coet* [to a wood].

Gwyl Vathav [the Feast of St. Matthew]. September 21.

Yr haf nessaf [the next summer]. A: *1401. / Yr haf nessaf.*

7   *ar y chwigeinved* [with six score]. A, B: *ar y chweugeinved*. *Chweugeinved* is the ordinal form of *chweugain* (*chwe* [6] + *ugain* [20, a score]). More literally, "upon his six score of;" this is the usual idiom for expressing "as one of (a number)."

ddireidwyr a lladron [wicked men and thieves]. *Direidwyr* is a compound of *dir(i)aid* [evil, wicked, villainous, dire, terrible, mischievous] + *gwŷr* [men]. Might this choice of words suggest an English source for the original Welsh text, or perhaps a degree of English sympathies (or political expedience) on the part of the Welsh author? Of course, not all the Welsh were favorably disposed towards the rebellion and its effects. Whereas in modern Welsh *direidu* connotes "making mischief" in a somewhat lighter tone, compare Gwydion's rebuke of Aranrhod in the Fourth Branch of *The Mabinogi*: *"Dygaf y Duw uyg kyffes,"* heb ef, *"direit wreic wyt . . . "* ["I confess to God," he said, "you are a wicked woman"] (Williams, *Pedeir Keinc y Mabinogi*, p. 79). All the major translations agree in rendering *direit wreic*, the feminine sg. equivalent of *direidwyr*, as "wicked woman" (see Bollard, *Mabinogi*, p. 95; Davies, *Mabinogion*, p. 55; Ellis and Lloyd, *Mabinogion*, p. 117; Ford, *Mabinogi*, p. 99; Gantz, *Mabinogion*, p. 107; Guest, *Mabinogion*, p. 422; Jones, *Mabinogion*, p. 58). A less critical translation of *direidwyr* in the present context might be "mischief makers" or "troublemakers;" Lloyd translates as "reckless men" in line 6 and as "fighting men" in line 10 (Lloyd, *Owen Glendower*, pp. 150, 151). On the other hand, we might similarly reinterpret the phrase from *The Mabinogi* as "You are a troublesome woman."

ac y ddaeth ef ac wynt [and he brought them]. B: *ag ydd aeth ef ag wynt* [and he went with them]. The form *daeth* is a later development from the more usual MW *doeth/deuth* (Morris Jones, *Welsh Grammar*, p. 364). This development can thus lead to ambiguity in the interpretation of *yddaeth* in manuscript, for it can be read either as *y ddaeth* [he came] or *ydd aeth* [he went]. The choice between "came" and "went" is often subjective and does not greatly affect our understanding of the larger context. *Dyfod â* [to come with] is a common expression for "to bring," though it can also be understood literally.

7–8   *ar ryvel* [as to war]. Not in A.

8   *Keredigion*. A: *Garedigion*, B: *Caredigion*. Ceredigion is the coastal region of mid Wales, formerly an independent kingdom, bounded by the river Dyfi in the north and the river Teifi to the east and south.

    mil a haner [fifteen hundred]. B: *1500*. *Mil a haner* is literally "a thousand and a half."

    bro [lowland]. *Bro* [region, vale, lowland] contrasts here with *blaenav* [uplands] in the preceding line.

9   *Rros* [Rhos]. A cantref (from *cant* [100] + *tref* [town], a regional unit analogous to the English hundred) in the southwestern tip of Wales, just north of the cantref of Penfro.

    Phenfro. The spirant mutation of *Penfro*, the southernmost cantref of the southwestern peninsula, containing the castle and town of Pembroke, which gave its name to the entire region under English rule as Pembrokeshire. The Primitive Welsh form of the name, **Pennbroʒ*, lost its final consonant very early, but the Anglo-Saxons, hearing something of its remains, adopted the form *Penbroc*, ultimately *Pembroke*, probably through folk etymology, interpreting the final syllable with Old English *broc* [brook] (Jackson, *Language*, pp. 458–59).

    i geysiaw dala Owain [to try to capture Owain]. So α, B. A omits.

10   *ar Vynydd Hyddgant* [on Hyddgant Mountain]. The river Hyddgen and the mountain alongside which it runs, now known as Carn Hyddgen, lie just north of the slopes of Pumlumon (Plynlimon) and across the river Hengwm, into which the Hyddgen runs (see p. 442 for an image of the area today).

    ryddynt [between them]. A: *rydhant*, B: *rhynthunt*. All are forms of the third person plural of the preposition *rhwng* [between].

    yn gytnaid ac [as soon as]. *Cydnaid* is an adjective compounded of *cyd-* [co-, together] + *naid* [a leap], hence "leaping forward together, simultaneous, immediate." The construction *yn gytnaid ac* also occurs in the tale of *The Dream of Rhonabwy*, *Ac yn gytneit ac yd aeth hun yn y lygeit* [And as soon as sleep came into his eyes] (Richards, *Breudwyt Ronabwy*, p. 3), and in *Chwedlau Odo*, a late fourteenth-century Welsh translation of the fables of Odo of Cheriton, *Ac yn gytneit ac y gyhyrdawd a'r we* [And as soon as she touched the web] (Williams, *Chwedlau Odo*, p. 19). The reading in B *yn gynted ac* seems to be a conflation of this construction and the more usual *cyn X â/ac* [as X as] (in which X represents the equative form of an adjective); *cynted* is the equative of *cynnar* [early, quick] and *buan* [swift].

11   *CC o honyw* [200 of them]. A: *200 o honynt*; B: *o honynt CC*.

    gair [praise]. Literally, "word," hence "report, reputation, praise."

i Owain [to Owain]. A: *am Owain* [for Owain].

12   *o'r yfiengtid a'r direidwyr* [of the youth and the wicked men]. B: *o jeuenctid a direidwyr* [of youth and wicked men]; see note 16–17 below.

o bob gwlad o Gymry [from every region of Wales]. More specifically *gwlad* means "country, land," and thus, especially to a fifteenth-century Welsh ear, it might invoke a clearer sense of the distinct, once independent, kingdoms and territories of Wales than does the translation given here.

14   *flynedd* [years]. A omits. Lenited form of *blynedd*, a form of *blwyddyn* [year] used after cardinal numbers.

15   *Dyffryn Klwyd*. Dyffryn Clwyd was the cantref with Ruthin at its center and through whose valley [*dyffryn*] runs the river Clwyd.

Grei. B: *Gray*.

17   *a tharenni* [and rocky hills]. B: *a thrueni [Leg a tharenni]*. The reading of B, *a thrueni* [and misery/wretchedness], looks like an attempt to make sense out of an illegible or unfamiliar term, *tarenni*, in an earlier exemplum. The correction in brackets is included in the line of running text in Evan Evans' hand.

aranswn [ransom]. A: *aranswm*. This is a borrowing from ME *ra(u)nsoun, -sum, -som(e)*, or possibly directly from OF. The earliest form ending in *-m* cited in *GPC*, s.v. *ranswm, ranswn, rhanswm*, is 1547, after which no citations for *-n* are noted. The unstressed initial *a-* was likely generated in reaction to the late medieval adoption of this word with a non-native initial /r-/, which only occurs in borrowings, as distinct from the unvoiced Welsh /hr-/; compare the forms *yreiol, yreial*, borrowed in the sixteenth century from English *royal* [*GPC*, s.v. *yreiol*]. For the later form *arianswm*, see *Cronicl Elis Gruffudd*, note to Item 96.7.

gwnaeth. A: *i gwnaeth*.

19   *MCCCCiii*. The chronology for this entry is off by a year. Owain moved into Maelienydd in June 1402, and the Battle of Bryn Glas, near Pilleth, took place on 22 June. In August that same year, he moved into Glamorgan.

20   *Velenydd*. A: *Vaelienydh*, B: *Felenydd*. Lenited forms of *Maelienydd*. Maelienydd was a large cantref on the eastern border of mid Wales, stretching from the precinct of Cwm Hir Abbey in the west to Knighton on the English border in the east. At the time of Glyndŵr's incursion it was part of the extensive territories held by the Mortimer family, as it had been since the twelfth century. After the Act of Union in 1536, it formed the northern portion of the county of Radnorshire.

21   *Pilale* [Pilleth]. A: *Pilalei*; B: *Pilalai*. Pilleth is first mentioned in the *Domesday Book* in the form *Pelelei* (fol. 183v). On the Battle of Bryn Glas at Pilleth, see Livingston's essay in this volume.

y kyfarvod [a battle]. Literally, "the battle/meeting," though here and in both instances of *y lladdfa* [the/a slaughter] in lines 27 and 30, the definite article *y* may function as an intensifying indefinite; see the note on Item 4.47, and Item 8.18.

yno [there]. B: *yna* [then].

21–22   *Sʳ Robert o Chwitnei*. A, B: *Chwitnai*. Sir Robert (de) Whitney, Lord of Pencombe, Little Cowarne, and Whitney, in Herefordshire, was born in Whitney in 1348. The castle at Whitney was burned in 1402 during the Welsh incursions into Herefordsire.

22   *Sʳ Ginarc Dyladr*. A: *Sʳ Ginart Dyladr*; B: *Ginarc Dyladyr*; the final *-c* in the *Ginarc* of α and B may simply be a misreading of an original *-t*, given the paleographic similarity of these letters. Sir Kinard (or Kynard) de la Bere, also of Herefordshire, is listed as a man-at-arms probably for King Henry's expedition to Scotland in 1400 ("Kynard," *Soldier in Medieval England Database*). He was made a knight sometime before 20 November 1462, and served as sheriff of Herefordshire (Shaw, *Knights*, 2.10).

        Emwnt. A: *Edmwnd*, B: *Edmwnt*.

        Sʳ Tomas Klannow. A: *Sʳ Thomas Clannow*, B: *Syr Thomas Clanow*. Sir Thomas Clanvowe, sheriff of Herefordshire, was made a knight some time before 30 September 1399 (Shaw, *Knights*, 2.11). His wife, Perine, was the sister of Sir Robert Whitney (see Powell, "Clanvowes," p. 22). Though Lloyd, in accord with scholarly opinion at the time, identifies Sir Thomas Clanvowe as the author of *The Cuckoo and the Nightingale*, it is more likely that the author of this Middle English poem was John Clanvowe, who died in 1391 (Lloyd, *Owen Glendower*, p. 52n2; see Scattergood, "Authorship").

23   *kyn mwyaf* [for the most part]. A: *cann mwyaf*, B: *gan mwyaf*.

24   *y gydac* [*ef*] [with him]. α: *y gydac*, A: *i gyd ag ef*, B: *gyt ac ef*.

        Kaerddydd. A: *Caer Dydh*, B: *Caer Dydd*.

26   *Harddlech, Aber Ystwyth*. α: *Harddlech Aber Ystwyth*, A *Harddlech, Aberystwyth*, B: *Harddlech ag Aberystwyth*.

27   *Yn yr* [In the]. Thus α, A. B: *Ag yna yn yr* [And then in the].

27, 30 *y lladdfa* [a slaughter]. A, B: *lladdfa*. Here in α literally "the slaughter"; though it may be correctly read as a definite noun, the indefinite force of *y* is supported by the readings in A and B. See the note to 21 above.

27   *ar Vynydd Kamstwn* [on Campston Hill]. The *Mynydd Camstwn* [Campston Hill] battle site is located about two and a half miles south of Grosmont in Monmouthshire.

28   *ar Graig y Dorth*. B: *at Graig y Dorth*. *Craig-y-dorth* is located south of the present A-40 halfway between Monmouth and Pen-y-Clawdd.

        rrwn [between]. A, B: *rhwng*; see the note on *ryddynt*, line 8.

        Pen y Clawdd. Pen-y-Clawdd, formerly a small parish, about five miles southwest of Monmouth.

29   *y dilyn*. A, B: *dilyn*.

30 *wrth Frynn Bvga*. B: *wrth Fryn Puga*. This is one of the earliest records of *Bryn-buga*, the Welsh name for the town of Usk. It translates as "Buga's Hill"; the identity of Buga, however, is not known.

31 *yna* [there]. A: *yno* [there].

Gruff[udd] ap Owain. A: *Gruffudh*, B: *Gruffudd*. Owain Glyndŵr's eldest son.

Yna y bv . . . ar Owain. A: passage omitted through homeoteleuton.

34 *ac* [and]. B omits. Without *ac* the phrase *gwyr Ystrad Tywi* can be understood as "the men of Ystrad Tywi. In the absence of modern capitalization and diacritics *gwŷr* [men] and *Gŵyr* [Gower] may be easily confused.

Ystratowi. A, B: *Ystrad Tywi*. Ystrad Tywi [the Tywi Vale] is the region comprised of the three eastern cantrefi of Deheubarth (Richards, *Enwau*, pp. 50–54), most particularly Cantref Mawr and Cantref Bychan, which are separated by the river Tywi.

yn Seissnic [as English]. The translation given, while a bit awkward, hopes to convey a distinction made in the Welsh as compared to the similar phrase in line 32 above. *Seisnic*, modern spelling *Seisnig* [English] is an adjective, as distinct from the nouns *Sais* [Englishman], pl. *Saesson*, *Sayson*, modern *Saeson* [the English, Saxons], and *Saesneg* [the English language].

35–41 *MCCCCvi[i]*. α: *MCCCvi*; A, B: *MCCCVII*. This account of Prince Henry's failed siege of Aberystwyth Castle is sufficiently lacking in detail to be ambiguous of interpretation on its own. Owain's threat to behead Rhys Ddu was presumably addressed not to the English besieging the castle (who would be only too glad to see Rhys Ddu executed, as indeed he was two years later), but to — and extending to — those Welshmen within the castle who may have been considering Prince Henry's offer of pardon and indemnity in hopes of ending the rebellion. If it did not simply cow them into obedience, such a threat would show Owain's determination to his men and thereby hearten them, and it may have also impressed the twenty-year-old Prince Henry and his captains. There was a degree of dissension among the English commanders, whom Lloyd suggests were looking for an honorable way to extricate themselves from a hopeless expedition (Lloyd, *Owen Glendower*, pp. 131–33), and thus Owain's threat, along with the additional forces accompanying him, may indeed have been a factor in convincing them to abandon the siege.

35 *sits* [siege]. B: *gwarchae* [siege]. The reading in α, A is a direct borrowing from English *segge*, *siege*. See also the note to line 42 below.

36 *oni kafas eddewid* [until he received a promise]. A: *yni gafas adhewid*, B: *yni chafas addewid*.

tydd [time]. A: *dydh*; B: *dydd*. *Dydd* [lit., day] becomes *tydd* through provection or unvoicing, in which /-d/ + /d-/ becomes /t/, though the phonetic change is not always shown orthographically as here.

37   *gorevgwyr mwyaf i gallv* [the most powerful noblemen]. Literally, "noblemen, (the) greatest their ability."

          y'r kastell. A: *y castell.*

38   *i hynn.* B *hyn.*

          Rrys Du. B: *Rhys Ddu.* Rhys ap Gruffudd ap Llywelyn ab Ieuan Fychan ab Ieuan, known as Rhys Ddu (R. the Black, probably in reference to his hair color, though possibly to his armor or attire), and as "Rys ap Gryvyth de Cardigan" by Adam of Usk (see Item 67), had been the royal sheriff of Cardigan before becoming one of Owain's most loyal captains (Lloyd, *Owen Glendower*, p. 131n2; Davies, *Revolt*, p. 199).

39   *Kadw o Owain.* The subject of a verbal noun used transitively, here *cadw* [(to) keep], often follows the verbal noun governed by the preposition *o* [of]. When the verb is intransitive there is usually no preposition, as in *myned Rrys Du i Wynedd* [Rhys Ddu went to Gwynedd], in the previous line (see Evans, *Grammar*, p. 161). In such cases the verbal nouns carry verbal force and are understood to have the same tense as the surrounding context.

          i nerth [his force]. B: *nerth.*[(a) force].

          attaw [to him]. A omits.

42   *sigy* [siege]. So α; A: *sige*, B: *gwarchaedigaeth* [siege]. See also the note to line 35 above.

44   *Kymry* [Wales]. This word is repeated as a catchword at the end of p. 63.

45   *Ymwythic.* B: *Amwythig. Amwythig* is the Welsh name for Shrewsbury; *Swydd Amwythig* is the county name (*swydd* = "county"). Variation in the spelling of an unstressed initial vowel /ə ~ ɑ/ before a stressed syllable is not uncommon in early Welsh.

46   *Ffylpott Ysgidmor.* B: *Philpot Yscidmor.* Philip Scudamore (or Skidmore) was a member of the prominent Herefordshire family that included John Scudamore, who held the castle of Carreg Cennen against Glyndŵr in 1402–03, who secretly married Glyndŵr's daughter Alys in 1410, and who may have harbored him in his final years; see p. 579. Lloyd notes that *Philpot* was a common form of *Philip* during the fifteenth century in West Herefordshire (*Owen Glendower*, p. 142n2). On the form of the surname *Ysgidmor*, a prosthetic *y-* develops regularly before *s* + consonant; compare *yspryt*, ultimately from Latin *spiritus*.

          ydd aeth [was sent]. A: *ir aeth. Aeth* is literally "went."

          yr vn [the one]. B: *un* [one].

47   *i'w llusgaw* [to draw]. α: *i llusgaw*; A, B: *i'w llusgaw* [to draw them].

49–50   This passage is found only in MS A, p. 228. *Rys ap Tudur . . . Ednyfed.* Gwilym, Rhys, and Ednyfed, sons of Tudur ap Goronwy of Penmynydd, were members of an ancient and important family in Anglesey and cousins, through their mother, of Owain. They rose in rebellion within the same month (September

1400) as Glyndŵr (Lloyd, *Owen Glendower*, p. 33), and led the attack that captured Conwy Castle on Good Friday, 1 April 1401, an act which Davies sees as independent of Owain's campaign, but which infused the rebellion with new energy. The brothers were pardoned by the English government in July 1401, but later reverted to Owain's cause. It is not known whether they were executed because they refused to be reconciled to the crown or they were not given the chance to do so (Davies, *Revolt*, pp. 103–04, 199, 311).

51   *ydd aeth Owain mewn difant* [Owain disappeared]. Literally, "Owain went into disappearance." We might understand *difant* as a euphemism much like "passing" in English, but certainly in the 1420s, and perhaps even through the 1440s, it might not have been unreasonable to hope or even believe that Owain was still alive. Nevertheless, such statements as this both reflect and contribute to the developing tradition that Owain is or would become the hoped for redeemer who will return.

    Gwyl Vathe. A: *Gwyl Vathau*, B: *Gwyl Fathau*. For another early statement that Owain died or disappeared on the same day the rebellion began, see Item 86.

    yn y kynhayaf [in the autumn]. The *yn* [in] is inserted superscript in the same hand.

52   *y brudwyr* [the seers]. The sense of *brudwyr*, sg. *brud(i)wr* (from *brud* [chronicle, history, brut] + *gŵr* [man]) can range from "chronicler, historian" to "predictor, soothsayer, sorcerer, magician." In the fifteenth and sixteenth centuries the term was often used of the poets who composed *cywyddau brud*, prophetic poems, which became increasingly popular as the fifteenth century progressed.

    a ddywedant [(they) say]. B: *a ddywaid*.

    MS B includes a colophon in a flourished script: *Finis Oweni Glyndwr ex Lib. Lew. Morgannwg*.

71. *PROSE BRUT* (COMMON VERSION TO 1419)

Adapted and trans. Michael Livingston, from *Prose Brut*, ed. Brie, pp. 362–63.

Manuscripts: Cambridge University Library MS Kk I 12; MS Rawlinson B.173 (for fuller version below, after 1431).

    The *Prose Brut* is one of the most popular and important works of the Middle Ages, all deriving from an original version written in Anglo-Norman after 1272 that propagated and metamorphosed into hundreds of copies in multiple languages in a bewildering array of versions: "It occurs in over 240 manuscripts, written in the three major literary languages of medieval England; it was the first chronicle of England to be printed, going through thirteen early printed editions, and in both the Middle Ages and the early Renaissance it served as the standard account of English history" (Matheson, *Prose Brut*, p. 1). In Middle English alone the *Prose Brut* exists in more manuscript copies than any text outside of the Bible. It is especially unfortunate (and regretfully expected given the task), therefore, that it should be in such need of a modern edition: many manuscripts, and a far greater understanding of their relationships, have been discovered since the only modern printing of the *Prose Brut*, edited by Brie and published in two volumes in 1906 and 1908. The most thorough accounting of the Middle English manuscripts is that of Matheson, who was able to divide the extant copies into over forty versions, of which Brie's text (reproduced here) is designated as a particular branch of the Common Version to 1419 ("CV–1419 [r&g]:A"; see Matheson, *Prose Brut*, p. 69). Another, later rendition of the *Prose Brut*, designated by Matheson as the Peculiar Version to 1437 ("PV–1437:A"; see *Prose Brut*, p. 75), is produced here as Item 73. The multiplicity of copies makes precisely dating the origin of any single version of the *Prose Brut* a daunting if not impossible task; as such, these versions are dated by their earliest possible date.

5–9   *And he toke the lorde Gray of Rithyn presoner, and kept hym fast yn holde tylle he was raunsonde of prysoners of the March, and kept hym long tyme yn holde. And at the last he made hym wedde on of his doughtris, and kepte hym stylle there with his wiff, and sone after he deyed.* The tradition that Lord Grey married one of Owain's daughters while imprisoned, only to die shortly afterwards while still in Owain's custody, has no historical basis. The married Lord Grey was captured by Owain in early 1402 and held in prison until his ransom later in the year (at considerable cost in gold); released from captivity, Grey returned to his estates, eventually married a second time (in 1415), and died as an old man in 1440. The legendary alternative tradition captured here — and included in many later sources — appears to begin with a scribal error in the copying of manuscripts of the present text, whose popularity insured a subsequent wide dissemination of the mistake. Manuscript copies of the *Prose Brut* survive, however, that reveal the original form of the narrative and make clear how the error was introduced. Brie, who chose (understandably) in his modern edition of the text to present the more widely preserved (and in this case erroneous) version of the text, includes in Appendix C of his edition text from MS Rawlinson B.173, which he calls a "fuller version of the time from 1399–1401" (p. 392). Matheson identifies part of this manuscript copy (including the material at hand) as a different branch of the Common Version to 1419 ("CV–1419 [men]:A, Subgroup b"; see Matheson, *Prose Brut*, p. 69). Included in this copy is the following passage:

> And he toke þe lorde Grey Ryffyn prisoner, and kept him ffast in holde tyll he was raunsomed. **And in the iij yere of King Henry, Owen brent a towne of the Erles of March in Walys, þat hight Knighton. And on the morowe after Seint Albones Day, was the batayle bitwene Sir Edmond Mortymere and Owen. And þis bataile was on the blacke hyll beside Pymaren. And þer Owen toke Sir Edmond Mortymer, þe Erles brother** of the Marche, prisoner, and kepte him long tyme in holde. And at the laste he made him wedde one of his doughtris, and kept him there styll with his wiffe; and sone after he died. (*Prose Brut*, ed. Brie, p. 393)

Comparison of this text with that of the popular manuscript record presented by Brie (and followed in this present volume) reveals that scribal eyeskip has likely caused the omission of Owain's battle with and capture of Edmund Mortimer at Bryn Glas (placed here in bold face), thus misappropriating the marriage and death of Mortimer to Lord Grey. In addition, it appears that the false idea that Lord Grey was ransomed in a prisoner exchange (rather than coinage) may well be due to the copyist picking up the last details pertinent to Mortimer.

72. *CONTINUATION OF THE EULOGIUM HISTORIARUM*

Adapted and trans. Alicia Marchant, from *Eulogium*, ed. Haydon, 3.388–89, 394, 396, 398, 401–02, 408.

Manuscript: London, British Library, MS Cotton Galba E.vii.

The oldest surviving manuscript copy of this work is associated with the *Eulogium historiarum*, though whether the so-called *Continuatio Eulogii* (or, as here, the *Continuation*) originated in this context is unknown: "it may have been composed with such a role in mind, or it may have seemed a suitable continuation when completed" (Clifford, "An Edition," p. 20). It has been suggested that parts of the *Continuation*, including those pertinent to Owain Glyndŵr's actions in Wales from 1401–1405, are the work of John Trefor, bishop of St. Asaph (see Jones, "Authorship of the Continuation"), which would make this a most intriguing source for the revolt. The most current theory of the making of the *Continuation*, however, is that the section from 1401–1405 was composed and incorporated into the source chronicle (which is perhaps not the extant text) around the year 1405 but did not reach its final form until after 1426 (Stow, "Continuation of the *Eulogium Historiarum*"). Recent studies have indicated that the author was most likely attached to the Franciscan order (Friars Minorite), based at either Canterbury or at London Greyfriars (see, e.g., Gransden, *Historical Writing*, p. 158; Taylor, *English Historical Literature*, p. 106, and Catto, "Alleged Great Council," p. 766).

The *Continuation* offers a rich account of Owain Glyndŵr's revolt, and on the whole is quite sympathetic in its portrayal. The author shows detailed knowledge of the events of the revolt, particularly the circumstances which prompted its initiation, and is the only chronicle in which Owain Glyndŵr is recorded via the medium of direct speech. The *Continuation* appears to have been used by the compiler of later versions of the *Prose Brut* (see Item 73).

3–5   The bishop of St. Asaph was John Trefor (Siôn Trefor), d.1410/1412. Trefor allied himself to Owain Glyndŵr after 1404, primarily because he was dissatisfied with the support he received from Henry IV after the Welsh rebels burnt his cathedral and several of his manor houses. Trefor subsequently acted as a diplomat and administrator for Owain. Adam of Usk notes that Trefor traveled on two occasions to France to secure support for the Welsh cause (Adam, *Chronicle*, ed. Given-Wilson, p. 218). Trefor was also prominent in negotiations with the Avignon papacy, and was perhaps involved in the drafting of the *Tripartite Indenture* (Item 47) at the house of the archdeacon of Bangor (on which issue, see Livingston's brief essay in this volume). He also made at least one visit to Scotland as an ambassador for Owain, and may have been the originator of the reports of the rebellion recorded by Walter Bower in his *Scotichronicon* (see headnote to Item 79).

20–21   Comets were frequently connected to rebellions and had long been considered signs of impending war, famine and plague. Here, the appearance of the comet in the "west" points to the location of troubles both in Wales and also the site of the Battle of Shrewsbury, which was fought in 1403 in Shropshire in the west of England near the Welsh border, and which ended with the death of Henry "Hotspur" Percy.

27–30   The Percy family found particular support against Henry IV from Cheshire because of the popularity of Richard II in that region. From the late 1390s, Cheshire archers were employed by Richard II as his bodyguards (see Morgan, *War and Society in Medieval Cheshire*).

38–39   *In arena stabuli*. Haydon: *In area stabuli*. The phrase *in area stabuli* sounds rather vague, especially as the horses are apparently standing in the stable when the portent takes place. *In arena stabuli* [on the sand of the stable] is much more vivid, and not at all a difficult correction.

36–38   Owain Glyndŵr's daughter's name was Catrin. She, along with her three daughters, was captured at the siege of Harlech Castle in 1409, where Edmund Mortimer was killed. She died in the Tower of London before the year 1413 (Davies, *Revolt*, p. 326).

52–53   Owain Glyndŵr's eldest son Gruffudd was held in the Tower of London from 1405 until his death c.1412.

73. *Prose Brut* (Peculiar Version to 1437)

Adapted and trans. Michael Livingston, from *English Chronicle*, ed. Marx, pp. 28–29, 32–33.

Manuscripts: Aberystwyth, National Library of Wales MS 21068 and Oxford, Bodleian Library MS Lyell 34.

For information on the multiple versions of the *Prose Brut*, see the headnote to Item 71.

17–20   For an explanation of how Lord Grey became confused with Edmund Mortimer in regards to becoming a husband to Owain's daughter, see the note to 71.5–9. Note that in this version of the *Prose Brut* scribes have added the marriage of Mortimer back into the text (lines 21–23), with the result that both Englishman have married into Owain's family!

74. *Wigmore Chronicle*

Adapted and trans. by Michael Livingston, from Dugdale, *Monasticon Anglicorum*, 6.1.354.

Manuscript: Chicago, University of Chicago MS 224.

The so-called *Wigmore Chronicle* has never been edited in full, though the portion printed here was published in Dugdale's multi-volume collection *Monasticon Anglicorum*. Though brief, it is an important source for recording the location of the Battle of Bryn Glas, at which Edmund Mortimer was captured. Not only does it appear that the chronicle was produced at Wigmore Abbey, not far from the site of the engagement, but it was also composed as a kind of family history of the Mortimers. Its clear record that the battle occurred upon the mountain of Bryn Glas (line 4), rather than in the valley nearby or upon the nearby Black Hill, must be given some weight in our efforts to locate and understand that important event.

75. *LONDON CHRONICLE OF HARLEY 565*

Adapted and trans. Michael Livingston, from McLaren, *London Chronicles*, p. 181n160.

Manuscript: London, British Library, MS Harley 565.

As McLaren has shown, there is a remarkable proliferation of chronicles written in London in the fifteenth century, among which the most famous is likely the so-called *Gregory's Chronicle* (Item 85), once ascribed to William Gregory, an identification now somewhat in doubt (see McLaren, pp. 29–33). There is a great deal of repetition among these chronicles, which are typically sparse in their detail about the events they record.

The chronicle chosen for inclusion here comes from a less well-known tradition recorded in Harley 565, which was described by McLaren (pp. 103–04). It is chosen here not only to represent the simultaneous pervasiveness and dismissiveness of the recording of the threat of Owain and his rebellion (given the meager lines it is accorded), but also to record its statement about the influence of Lord Grey of Ruthin on the outset of hostilities.

76. *GLYNDŴR*

Ed. and trans. John K. Bollard.

Manuscripts: **A**: stray leaf from NLW Peniarth MS 52, possibly in the autograph of the poet Dafydd Nanmor (fl. 1440–90), bound as fol. 49 in NLW Peniarth MS 44, a thirteenth-century copy of *Brut y Brenhinedd* (*The Chronicle of the Kings*). The page is stained and very difficult to read. **B**: Bound immediately after A is a paper sheet containing a transcription with the following note, *Hyn a achubwyd o'r rhagdalen gann Wiliam Maurice 1660* [This was recovered from the preceding page by Wiliam Maurice, 1660]. **C**: NLW Peniarth MS 267, p. 11, a transcription of A made by John Jones of Gellilyfdy in January or February, 1635, to which he appends the note, *Hynn uchod a gefais yn esgrifenedig ar ddolen o lyfr memrwn* [The above I found written on a leaf from a vellum book].

Title   *Glyndwr*. This is written and underlined at the top of the page, though the top half of the letters have been cut off by the binder's knife. Maurice's transcription has the underlined title *Glynndwr*; Jones' bears the heading *Am Owain Glynn dwr o Sycharth* [Concerning Owain Glyndŵr of Sycharth].

1   *m cccc excepto duo anno* [1400 minus two years]. B: *uno*, with *duo* added above it;
         C (in right margin): 1398. Henry IV was actually crowned on 13 October 1399.

2   *Y gwannwyn nessa* [The next spring]. C (in right margin): 1399.

         Aberconwy. The castle of Conwy at the mouth [*aber*] of the river Conwy was cap-
         tured by allies of Owain, Rhys and Gwilym ap Tudur ap Goronwy of Anglesey
         on Good Friday, 1401, some months after Owain's uprising in September 1400.

         Y vlwyddyn nessa [The next year]. C (in right margin): 1400.

3   *gwyl Vathev* [St. Matthew's Day]. Literally, the "feast of Matthew," which falls on
         21 September.

         i llosges ef Ruthyn [he burned Ruthin]. On the burning of Ruthin, about ten
         miles from Glyndyfrdwy, during the events of 18 September, see Davies, *Revolt*,
         pp. 102, 266.

4   *y lladdva yn y Vyrnwy* [the slaughter on the Efyrnwy]. From its headwaters in the
         Berwyn Mountains, dammed in the 1880s to form Lake Vyrnwy, the river
         Efyrnwy wanders eastwards across Powys to join the Severn near the village of
         Melverley. Its last eight miles now form the Welsh-English boundary.

         M cccc iiij pan losges Ywain Ddinbech [1404 when Owain burned Denbigh]. C (in
         right margin): 1404. Owain attacked and burned Denbigh during the events of
         18–23 September 1400 (Davies, *Revolt*, p. 102); but afterwards, Ruthin re-
         mained under English control. This might an error for Cardiff, which the
         account in the Continuation of the *Eulogium* places in 1404 (Item 72), though
         the brief mention in the *Annales Oweni Glyndwr* puts it in 1403 (Item 70).

5   *Anno m cccc vj* [The year 1406]. C (in right margin): 1406.

         ar Dduw Kalan Mai [on the first day of May]. Literally, "on the day of the
         calends of May," i.e., May-day.

         Llanelwy. The Welsh name for the cathedral and city of St. Asaph. Owain's men
         wrought considerable damage to the cathedral in 1402, but by the end of 1404,
         Bishop John Trefor was an acknowledged ally. Browne Willis's *Survey of St.
         Asaph* includes a transcript of a letter of King Henry VI, dated 13 July 1442, to
         his chancellor, the bishop of Bath, which describes "howe the Chirch Cathedrall
         of Saint Assaph, with the Steple, Bells, Quere, Porch, and Vestiary, with all
         other Contentis, Bokes, Chaliz, Vestimentis, and other Ornaments, as the
         Bokes, Stalles, Deskes, Altres, and all the aparaill longying to the same Church,
         was brent and utterly destroyed, and in likewys the Byshop's Palays and all his
         other three Mannoirs no Styk laft in the last werre tyme of Wales" (Edwards,
         Willis' Survey, pp. 116–17). Davies comments that "Ecclesiastical buildings seem
         to have been the targets for English forces rather than Welsh rebels, more often
         than not as a direct punishment for the support that the clerics had given to the
         Rebel cause. . . . At the cathedral of St. Asaph the destruction was attributed to
         the Welsh rebels; but after the defection of Bishop John Trefor in 1403–04 it
         would hardly be surprising if the English did not likewise take their revenge on
         his episcopal see" (Davies, *Revolt*, p. 279).

77. JEAN JUVENAL DES URSINS, *HISTORY OF CHARLES VI*

> Adapted and trans. Michael Livingston, from Jean Juvenal des Ursins, *Histoire de Charles VI*, ed. Michaud and Poujoulat, 2.429, 431, 437.

It is unclear exactly when Jean Juvenal des Ursins wrote his *Histoire de Charles VI*, or even if he wrote it at all. If it *is* Jean's composition, then we know at least that our author was a loyal advocate of Charles VII, under whom he served as bishop of first Beauvais (1432) and then Laon (1444), before becoming archbishop of Reims in 1449. He is widely considered to be a meticulous researcher, who combined his own first-hand knowledge of events with interviews and documentary sources — likely including the famous chronicle of St. Denis that was probably written by Pintoin (see Item 66). The relationship between Jean's text and that of Monstrelet (Item 80) is difficult to assess given our uncertainties about the composition date of this present source: it could be that it should date later than Monstrelet's chronicle and made use of it, or the opposite could be true. Regardless, it is worth noting that Jean and Monstrelet take up opposing points of view on many of the matters they report, as Jean was strongly anti-Burgundian.

4   *bassinet* [bascinet]. Pintoin (Item 66.24) more generically calls the helmet a *cassidem* [helmet].

11–12   Jean places blame for the tardiness of the expedition on the Welsh: the count de la Marche was awaiting further information from them which never came. This stands rather directly at odds with Pintoin's early report that he had seen with his own eyes a letter from the Welsh to the count providing the necessary information about conditions in Wales (Item 66.27–31). For his part, Cochon (Item 69) leaves the reason for the delay unexplained.

78. *POLYCHRONICON CONTINUATION*

> Adapted and trans. Michael Livingston, from *Polychronicon Continuation*, ed. Babbington and Lumby, 8.513–18.

Manuscript: London, British Library, MS Harley 2261, fols. 442–45.

The first folios of British Library MS Harley 2261 identify it as a translation from Latin into Middle English of the *Polychronicon*, an influential history of the world written by Ranulf Higden (d. 1364). The manuscript also informs us that it was copied out by Jacobus Ravenscroft (fol. 1r). Because the manuscript includes a short poem on the English kings since the Conquest that concludes with Henry VI, scholars have assumed that Jacobus accomplished his work during that king's reign (1432 x 1450).

The manuscript is actually one of two Middle English translations of the *Polychronicon*, and it was for this reason that the Rolls Series commissioned the text to be edited, along with Higden's original Latin text and the more famous translation of John Trevisa (d. 1402), in the middle of the nineteenth century. As its editors realized, however, the translator of MS Harley 2261 did more than merely translate Higden: he continued his text well beyond Higden's conclusion. Most interesting for our present context, it is clear that this anonymous continuation makes heavy use of the *Historia vitae*, revealing something of the wide readership for that early chronicle (Item 28).

79. WALTER BOWER, *SCOTICHRONICON*

Ed. and trans. Bower, *Scotichronicon*, ed. Watt, 8.94–111. Notes by Michael Livingston.

While much of Walter Bower's *Scotichronicon* is an elaboration of John of Fordun's earlier work, there is no known source for his discussion of the Welsh revolt, some details of which are uniquely his. In his monumental edition of Bower's work, Watt suggests that "it is at least possible" that this material "was derived from the two envoys from Owen Glendower who visited the court of Governor Albany in Scotland" (8.xix). These envoys, who were certainly in Scotland "sometime 16 Mar. 1406/07 x 27 Mar. 1408" (8.179), were probably the same as the two bishops whose visit Bower relates around 1407:

> dominus Griffinus episcopus Bangorens' et alius episcopus scilicet Assavens'
> [sir Griffin bishop of Bangor and another bishop, namely St. Asaph] (8.64–65)

Watt tentatively identifies these men as Gruffudd Yonge, bishop of Bangor, and John Trefor of St. Asaph (8.179). Whatever his source or sources, Bower's reason for relating these Welsh events is clear: "He says himself that his purpose is to warn the Scots to avoid the mistakes of the Welsh in resisting English aggression" (p. xix).

The events that Bower relates all seem to occur in 1405 and include a detailed look at the Battle of Pwll Melyn, probably fought on 5 May (see Item 62.53–62n).

3–5   It is possible that some contingent of Welsh fought alongside Hotspur at the Battle of Shrewsbury on 21 July 1403, but it is hardly true that Owain himself took any part in the conflict: the available evidence points to his campaigning in South Wales at the time (see Items 36, 37). Regardless, Bower is quite incorrect in claiming that the Welsh rebellion began after Shrewsbury. It had in fact started three years earlier, and by July 1403 Henry IV had already made three (largely unsuccessful) invasions of Wales to combat it.

9–11   As Watt notes, Bower here echoes Isaiah 10:5: "The whole phrase was originally apparently used as a description of Saracen attacks on the Franks in 731, and is here used in connection with the wars of Henry IV and Henry V against the Welsh, which did in fact last from 1400 to ca 1415" (Bower, *Scotichronicon*, p. 193).

11–12   Bower's confused understanding of Henry IV's Welsh expeditions reveals the second- or third-hand nature of his sources. According to Bower's chronology, the king's "second" invasion here ought instead to be his third (into North Wales in 1402); according to Bower's description, it is in fact an even later invasion, into South Wales in 1405.

15–16   The dragon standard was (and is) a powerful sign of Welsh nationalism; Owain had first flown it (described as a golden dragon rather than red) at the Battle of Tuthill on 2 November 1401.

16–17   In describing Owain as a raging lion, Bower may well be waxing poetic. It is also possible that he knew (directly or indirectly) that Owain's personal arms consisted of four lions rampant in red and gold.

19   *festum Sancti Michaelis* [feast of St. Michael]. I.e., 29 September.

30–31   *dominos de Coboham et Gray Codnore et David Gam* [Lord Cobham and Lord Grey of Codnor and Dafydd Gam]. That is, John Lord Cobham (1355–1408), Richard Lord Grey of Codnor (1392–1418), and Dafydd Gam; for more on the latter figure, see headnote to Item 61.

31–38   This is the Battle of Pwll Melyn, probably fought on 5 May 1405 (see Item 62.53–62n). Owain's son was indeed captured, and he would remain a prisoner of the English until his death in 1411. Also killed (but unnoted by Bower) was Owain's brother, Tudur.

37–38   *belliger insignis Hopkin apthomas* [the famous fighting-man Hopcyn ap Thomas]. This is likely the same "prophet" whom Owain had consulted in South Wales in 1403 (see Item 36). For Hopcyn's reputation as a "fighting-man" among the Welsh, see "*Gwrthyfel Glyndŵr*," pp. 181–82.

39   Watt: "The cross-reference is to a story of similar treachery during a battle, when some Picts deserted the Scots when both were fighting the Danes. Bower's interest . . . is to draw lessons for Scotland" (Bower, *Scotichronicon*, p. 194).

51–52   Omitted here is a tangential discussion on the divisions within France during the first decades of the fifteenth century.

56   Bower includes but a single leader for the French forces, John de Rieux, lord of Rochefort-en-Terre, Brittany, but other leaders were involved; see headnote to Item 50.

66–67   Bower makes several mistakes in introducing John ap Hywel, a central figure in his retelling of these events. Beginning in 1400 John ap Hywel was abbot of Llantarnam (not Glamorgan) near Caerleon, and his order was Cistercian (not Augustinian). Lloyd memorably describes this fascinating abbot as "a Welsh Savonarola" (*Owen Glendower*, p. 97).

69   Compare Jonah 3–4.

71–72   The quoted passage here is not the preaching of Jonah; rather, it is the proclamation of the king of Nineveh (Jonah 3:8).

73–74   The abbot's speech seems to indicate that Owain was prisoner to the English, which is nowhere else claimed.

79–86   Much of this passage is adapted from 1 Machabees 3:18–22.

87   Compare Isaiah 59:1.

114   Compare Romans 1:22

117   Compare Deuteronomy 32:15.

122   Compare Vulgate Psalm 77:33.

123–48   On the sources of Bower's tangent, which include the Bible, Josephus, *Gesta Romanorum*, Leo the Great, and Horace, see Bower, *Scotichronicon*, pp. 196–97.

155–56   Bower here returns to the English expedition described in lines 31–38.

164   *Brinbiga* [Brynbuga]. This is the Welsh name for Usk. The fact that Bower uses here the Welsh form, as Watt notes, "is strong evidence that his source was a Welsh informant" (Bower, *Scotichronicon*, p. 197).

165–66   John ap Hywel's death at the Battle of Pwll Melyn is also noted by Adam of Usk (see Item 62.58).

180–82   Compare Matthew 23:3–4.

182–84   As Watt notes, this quotation appears among Gregory the Great's homilies, not in his *Regula Pastoralis* (Bower, *Scotichronicon*, p. 197).

185–89   Cadwaladr (along with Cynan) is first mentioned as a deliverer of the Britons in *Armes Prydein Vawr*, but by the fifteenth century had become a standard figure of national redemption in Welsh prophetic poetry (see the poem and notes by John K. Bollard in Livingston, *Battle of Brunanburh*, esp. pp. 161–62). For the story of Cadwaladr, the angelic voice, Merlin, and the eagle, see Geoffrey of Monmouth, *History*, trans. Thorpe, pp. 282–83.

191–98   Watt observes that "no source is known for these lines. They were probably composed by Bower himself for this chapter. Mention of a virgin [line 224] seems to be a reference to Joan of Arc" (Bower, *Scotichronicon*, p. 198).

199–212   Watt: "These lines are a version of the late 13c 'prophetie de l'espoir breton' attributed to Geoffrey of Monmouth. . . . perhaps from the Welsh source used for these chapters; if he composed [lines 224–31] himself, he may also have tinkered with the text of these lines" (Bower, *Scotichronicon*, p. 198).

214–19   "This version of Merlin's prophecies has been taken as composed by Bower himself" (Bower, *Scotichronicon*, p. 198).

80. ENGUERRAND DE MONSTRELET, *CHRONICLE*

Adapted by Michael Livingston, from Monstrelet, *Chronique*, ed. d'Arcq, 1.81–84, and Monstrelet, *Chronicles*, trans. Johnes, 1.28–29.

Enguerrand de Monstrelet (c.1400–1453) was born in Picardy and rose to become a minor official of the crown in Cambrai. His chronicle, which covers the years 1400–1444, is an important source for the events of the Hundred Years' War and served as a primary source for many subsequent chroniclers in both France and England.

12   *Salemine* [Sallemue]. There is some question about the identity of the island to which Monstrelet refers; early editors suggested Saltash, and no other explanation has been put forward.

25   *Environ ce temps* [Around this time]. Within Monstrelet's text this is 1403, which is clearly a mistake. The year is 1405.

        le mareschal de France et le Maistre des arbalestriers [the marshal of France and the master of the crossbows]. I.e., John de Hangest, lord de Huqueville.

30   *port de Harfort* [port of Haverfordwest]. Though Haverfordwest stands at the tidal limit of the western Cleddau river, it is doubtful that the French fleet would move so far inland before disembarking. More likely, the forces came ashore at Milford Haven, the important port at the mouth of the Cleddau, seven miles away.

38–39   *pays de Morgnie* [country of Morgannwg]. Johnes translates "country of Linorquie," which he then queries as possibly meaning Glamorgan; more probably the French simply mangles the spelling of the Welsh county name.

39   *Table ronde* [Round Table]. Very probably the town and castle of Caerleon, which has strong Arthurian ties: it was King Arthur's capital according to Geoffrey of Monmouth's *History of the Kings of Britain*, and its Roman amphitheater may well have been the origin for the legends of the Round Table (Castleden, *King Arthur*, p. 148).

50   *mareschal de France* [marshal of France]. I.e., Regnault de Trie, lord of Fontenay, admiral of France.

81. JOHN CAPGRAVE, *LIBER DE ILLUSTRIBUS HENRICIS*

From Capgrave, *Liber de Illustribus Henricis*, ed. Hingeston, p. 110; trans. Alicia Marchant.

Manuscripts: London, British Library, MS Cotton Tiberius A.viii (1459–1500); Cambridge, Corpus Christi College, MS 408 (1446–47).

John Capgrave (d. 1464) was born in 1393, he tells us, in "Northfolke, of the town of Lynne" (Capgrave, *Life of Saint Katherine*, p. 16), and it was there that he lived for most of his life as an Augustinian friar. His family background is largely unknown. Capgrave undertook study away from Lynn from c.1416 to c.1421 in London and later at Cambridge. Capgrave's literary output was astounding; it is believed that he produced around 41 texts of commentary on scripture and theology, hagiography, and several chronicles (Lucas, "John Capgrave," p. 23, and *From Author to Audience*, pp. 310–14; see also Gransden, *Historical Writing*, 2.390). Capgrave's two major chronicles were the *Liber de Illustribus Henricis*, as well as the *Abbreuiacion of Cronicles*. The *Liber de Illustribus Henricis* was written in Latin, around 1446 or 1447, and was dedicated to Henry VI (Lucas, *From Author to Audience*, p. 310). The form that the *Liber de Illustribus Henricis* takes is somewhat unusual; the narrative is presented with the markings of a chronicle, but contains biographical reflections on various "illustrious" Henries of Europe. His account of the revolt of Owain Glyndŵr is found in his discussion of Henry IV, and although his account is quite small, it is illuminating: Capgrave's entire entry on the Welsh revolt is framed by Owain Glyndŵr's connection to Richard, Earl of Arundel, who had been executed by Richard II in 1397. Moreover, Capgrave actively leaves his narrative of the Welsh revolt open-ended, with an account of Owain Glyndŵr still *circumvagans* [wandering about] (line 3) in an imagined landscape of timeless mountains and caverns.

For a further discussion of the significance of providing (or not providing) a conclusion to the Welsh revolt in English chronicles, see my article in this volume.

2	*Ricardi, comitis Arundell.* The earl of Arundel, Richard Fitzalan, was one of the Lords Appellant and spoke openly against Richard II's tyrannical style of kingship. Arundel was executed by Richard II in 1397. Evidence suggests that Owain Glyndŵr trained as a boy in the household of Richard Fitzalan, whose Marcher landholdings bordered Owain Glyndŵr's family estate at Glyndyfrdwy in north Wales. "Oweyn Glyndouredy" and his brother "Tudour de Glyndore" are listed amongst the 25 squires in Arundel's retinue for the Scottish campaign in March 1387. He is listed as a squire in exchequer accounts (P.R.O, Exchequer, Various Accounts, 40/33). It is possible that Owain Glyndŵr was still in his service at the time of Arundel's execution. See Goodman, "Owain Glyndŵr before 1400," p. 68, and Skidmore, *Owain Glyndŵr*, p. 17.
4	It is interesting that Capgrave does not provide a conclusion to his narrative of the Welsh revolt, but rather leaves it open-ended. Capgrave suggests that Owain Glyndŵr is hiding somewhere in Wales; the implication is that the rebel may arise once more.

82. JEHAN DE WAURIN, *COLLECTION OF CHRONICLES*

Adapted by Michael Livingston, from Waurin, *Anchiennes Cronicques*, ed. Renouard, 1.179–80, and Waurin, *Collection of the Chronicles*, trans. Hardy, 40.2.56–57.

Jehan de Waurin (or Wavrin) (1398–c.1474) was a French soldier who fought at the Battle of Agincourt in 1415 and went on to compile a massive history of England, completed around 1455, entitled *Recueil des croniques et anchiennes histories de la Grant Bretaigne*. This collection of chronicles is highly (and self-admittedly) derivative of previous works: it contains two passages concerning Owain Glyndŵr, and the second one is a copy of Monstrelet (Item 80). The first passage, however, has no known source and is reproduced here. This unique account of the relationships between Owain, Mortimer, and the Percies in 1402–03 includes details of an alliance between them that sounds suspiciously like the broad terms of the *Tripartite Indenture*, including the detail of their concluding seals and oaths upon the agreement (Item 47.48–52). It is likewise of some interest that Waurin places this agreement before the Battle of Shrewsbury rather than after it, a chronological matter that has occasioned some disagreement even among scholars who accept the validity of a Glyndŵr-Mortimer-Percy alliance. It is thus tempting to view this correspondence as an independent confirmation of the authenticity of these older traditions, though we cannot discount the possibility that Waurin (or his unknown source) had simply read the preserved text of the Tripartite Indenture and created this scene accordingly.

10	*le roy Edouard II de ce nom* [King Edward the Second]. The extant text of Waurin is in clear error here, as King Edward I is no doubt meant.

83. JOHN HARDYNG, *CHRONICLE*

Ed. and trans. Michael Livingston, from the print of Grafton, 1543.

Manuscript: London, British Library, MS Harley 661, fols. 99–101.

The metrical chronicle of John Hardyng (1378–1465) is a fascinating, if oddly neglected fifteenth-century source. To begin with, the chronicle exists in two versions. The first version (c.1437) is dedicated to Henry VI and reveals a Lancastrian bias. The second version (c.1464) is heavily revised and dedicated to Edward IV. Examination of the changes made between the versions provides an intriguing glimpse into the ways in which socio-political pressures shaped the making of history for at least one historian. The chronicle is additionally interesting for the fact that although the first version is dedicated to the Lancastrian heir, Hardyng's second version includes a prose passage that reveals no small level of enmity for Henry IV. By his own account, Hardyng explains that from the age of twelve he was a member of Hotspur's house, and that he fought beside him at the Battle of Homilden Hill, the Siege of Cocklaw, and the Battle of Shrewsbury at age 25, where Hotspur died.

Chapter 206

8–12   This sequence of events is an odd conglomeration. Robert III of Scotland died on 4 April 1406 (his son James I having been captured at sea by English forces only days earlier on 22 March). This was Henry's seventh regnal year, not his tenth (which would be 1409). By most accounts Owain died in September of 1415, the third regnal year of Henry V. It may be that Hardyng has conflated the Welsh loss of Harlech Castle in February 1409 with the end of the revolt: the reported death of Owain's son (line 10) would thus be that of Edmund Mortimer, his then son-in-law.

84. *HISTORY OF THE KINGS OF THE ENGLISH*

Ed. and trans. John K. Bollard.

Manuscript: National Library of Wales MS 7006D (*Llyfr Du Basing* / *The Black Book of Basingwerk*), pp. 306b.2–307a.25.

Llyfr Du Basing / *The Black Book of Basingwerk* is a manuscript completed not long after 1461 by the nobleman, poet, and scribe Gutun Owain (Gruffudd ap Huw ab Owain, fl. 1460–1500), who transcribed pages 89–308. The manuscript contains three of the received texts recording legendary and chronicled Welsh history: *Ystoria Dared*, a translation of Dares Phrygius' Latin recounting of the fall of Troy; *Brut y Brenhinedd*, a translation of Geoffrey of Monmouth's *Historia regum Britanniae*; and *Ystoria Brenhinedd Saeson* (or as it is more generally known, *Brenhinedd y Saesson*), a chronicle of events in Wales and England up to 1198, with a continuation to 1332 based on two texts of *Brut y Tywysogion* (*The Chronicle of the Princes*), and a further continuation of brief annals from 1346, recording the battle of Crécy, to 1461, recording the deposition of Henry VI and the coronation of Edward IV. The lack of any notice of the restoration of Henry VI in October 1470 might reasonably be taken to imply that the manuscript (or possibly its exemplar) was written before that date. While the manuscript has been connected with the Cistercian abbey of Basingwerk at least since the early seventeenth century, it was most probably written at Valle Crucis Abbey in Denbighshire, where one of its sources, NLW MS Peniarth 20 (c.1330), was also written. Gutun Owain's poetry and scribal activities are more closely linked to Valle Crucis than to Basingwerk (Huws, *Welsh Manuscripts*, p. 190). All other manuscripts containing the text of *Brenhinedd y Saesson* for the period 1198–1461 are direct or indirect copies of this manuscript (Jones, *Brenhinedd*, pp. xv–xxv).

With the exception of the entry on Owain Glyndŵr's uprising in 1400 and a brief notice of Sir John Oldcastle's flight to Wales in 1413 (not included here), the entries for 1346–1461 make no mention of events in Wales. While Thomas Jones comments that "the annals for 1377 and 1413 have been duplicated" (Jones, *Brenhinedd*, p. l), it is rather the case that in these instances the chronicler has added information about the offspring of Edward III and Henry IV, leading him to repeat the date when recording the accessions of Richard II and Henry V, respectively. This strongly suggests that these entries derive from an English source.

Title	MS: *Ystoria Brenhinedd Saeson* [*The History of the Kings of the English*]. This is the title rubricated on p. 199 of the manuscript. The text is more generally known to modern readers as *Brenhinedd y Saesson*, which Jones took from the incipit of the earlier incomplete copy in London, British Library, MS Cotton Cleopatra B.v, fol. 109a. Though *Saes(s)on* is literally "Saxons" and is translated as such by Jones in his title, "English" is a more fitting term for the inhabitants of England in the later Middle Ages.
1	*digoroni* [deposing]. Verbnoun (lit., "to uncrown; uncrowning"), from *di-* [neg. prefix] + *coroni* [to crown; crowning].
7	*ffiniasant* [they paid a ransom]. The third pl. preterite of *finio*, "to fine, to pay a fine."
	The chronicler has conflated the capture of Lord Grey of Ruthin in April 1402 and that of Edmund Mortimer at the Battle of Bryn Glas (Pilleth) in June. Grey was ransomed by the king for 6,000 or 10,000 marks (Davies, *Revolt*, p. 233), while the king refused to aid in the ransom of Mortimer, who famously defected to Owain's cause and married his daughter. The chronicler has also conflated Mortimer with his nephew (also Edmund), the earl of March: this mistake was later repeated by Hall, from whom it passed to many later writers, including Shakespeare; see Item 95n15–18.
9	*Bwl Ffilt*. A rendering in Welsh orthography of English "Bull Field." The site, on the northeastern outskirts of Shrewsbury, is now known as "Battlefield."
10	*y Mwythic*. Modern *Amwythig*, the Welsh name for Shrewsbury.
	Harri. MS: *harr*.
12	*Richart Ysgrwp, archesgob Iork, a Thomas Mwmbraey*. Richard le Scrope, the Archbishop of York, and Thomas de Mowbray, Earl Marshal, were summarily executed as traitors by order of Henry IV on 5 June 1405. Clement Maidstone's fifteenth-century *Martyrium Ricardi Archiepiscopi* recounts Scrope's death and the

subsequent miracles attributed to him, with only passing reference to the Earl Marshal (Maidstone, *Martyrium*, online).

14   *A'r Richart hwnnw* [And that Richard]. MS: *A Richart hwnnw*; the grammar requires the definite article *'r* here.

15   *gwneuthur*. MS: *gwneuthu*.

17–18   *dwy verched* [two daughters]. In Middle and Modern Welsh, numerals are generally followed by a singular noun, as in the preceding *pedwar mab* [lit., four son], and we might expect *dwy verch* here, but in Middle Welsh there are also numerous examples of plural nouns in this position (Evans, *Grammar*, p. 47).

21   *Sul y Meibion*. Henry V was crowned on 9 April 1413, two Sundays before Easter. Thomas Jones translates *Sul y Meibion* as "the Sunday of the Innocents" (Jones, *Brenhinedd*, p. 275). The significance of the term *Sul y Meibion* [lit., Sunday of the Sons] remains uncertain, though it is corroborated elsewhere from the nineteenth century as a term for the second Sunday before Easter, which also came to be known as as Mothering Sunday and more recently as *Sul y Dioddefaint* [Passion Sunday] (see Fisher, *Welsh Calendar*, p. 116). Confusion between *Sul y Meibion* and *Gwyl y Fil Veibion*, the Feast of the Holy Innocents, which is commemorated on 28 December, seems unlikely.

85. GREGORY'S CHRONICLE

Adapted and trans. Michael Livingston, from Gairdner, *Historical Collections*.

Manuscript: London, British Library MS Egerton 1995.

Perhaps the most famous of the London chronicles (for another, see Item 75), this manuscript has long been associated with William Gregory, mayor of London in 1451, who may well have authored a good portion of the original text, though certainly not all of it: Gregory died in 1467, but the chronicle continues through 1469. Modern scholarship has also revealed evidence that our extant text shows some signs of later revision, leaving us with little choice but to date its contents here to a post-completion date for the whole.

86. OUT OF AN OLD CHRONICLE 1471

Ed. and trans. John K. Bollard.

Manuscript: NLW MS 1980B (Panton MS 11), (last half of 18th c.), fol. 67, in the hand of Evan Evans.

This extract derives from, or is related, directly or indirectly, to the account that first appeared in the mid-fifteenth-century anonymous continuation of Higden's *Polychronicon*, dated c.1432–50 (see Item 78). The first known appearance of the story in Welsh was in a fifteenth-century copy of *Brenhinedd y Saesson* by the poet and historian Gutun Owain (fl.

c.1460–c.1498). That manuscript has been lost, but in the seventeenth century Robert Vaughan copied extracts from it and included the incident in his English "History of Owain Glyndŵr." He also copied it into the margins of David Powel's *History of Cambria*, from which Evan Evans transferred it into Panton MS 11 (Henken, *National Redeemer*, pp. 14–15).

Title *Allan o Hen Gronicl 1471* [Out of an Old Chronicle 1471] appears as a title at the head of the extract.

7   *caled* [stringent]. Literally, "hard," hence "hard to bear, strict, stringent." The implication is that the command imposes hardship on Owain, especially given the lateness of its delivery.

       syn [bewildered]. The implications and connotations of the adjective *syn* are quite strong, as evidenced by the glosses in *GPC*: "astonished, astounded, amazed, dazed, stunned, stupified, senseless, aghast, frightened."

9   *gostfawr* [costly]. Lenited form of *costfawr*, a compound of *cost* (an earlier borrowing from ME or OF) + *mawr* [great]. The earliest citation in *GPC* is from Elis Gruffudd's autograph history, c.1552–53 (Item 96). The *Polychronicon* continuation also mentions the prohibitive expense to Owain of preparing in such haste (Item 78.8–10).

12   *myned am ben* [to descend upon]. Literally, "to go upon."

15   *noswyl Fatheu* [St. Matthew's Eve]. This account shares with the *Annales Oweni Glyndwr*, the tradition that the troubles ended on the same day that they began (see Item 70).

       y doeth Owain am ben [Owain descended upon]. Literally, "Owain came upon."

87. JOHN ROUS, *HISTORIA REGUM ANGLIAE*

From Rous, *Historia regum Angliae*, ed. Hearne, pp. 206–07, trans. Alicia Marchant.

Manuscripts: London, British Library, MS Cotton Vespasian A.xii.

John Rous (d. c.1492) was a historian and antiquarian. After studying at Oxford, he held the position of chantry priest at Guy's Cliffe (or Gibcliff) outside Warwick, a foundation set up by Richard Beauchamp, earl of Warwick (d. 1439). Rous wrote several works of local history, including that of Warwickshire, as well as the universities of Oxford and Cambridge. His major work was the *Historia regum Angliae*, written between 1480 and 1486 and dedicated to Henry VII. Rous's account of the Welsh revolt is notable for its rich imagery; the narrative weaves between two striking images that revolve around Owain Glyndŵr's escapes from numerous castles of Wales during his revolt, and of the earl of Arundel, Richard Fitzalan (d. 1397) playing chess in a garden. While the passage is a visual feast, the Welsh revolt is itself a sideline event; central to this image is a discussion of the nature of rebellions. Arundel shows his understanding of what rebellion entails by playing chess, the objective of which is to catch the opposing king. Moreover, the characteristics of Arundel and Owain Glyndŵr are juxtaposed via the protagonist's use or rejection of the magical stone; Owain Glyndŵr's decision to use the magical stone shows him to be a man who will use any means, including unorthodox ones, to gain an advantage. Arundel, on the other hand, accepts his fate and refuses to use the stone of invisibility.

5   *castris ipsis captis inveniri non potuit* [the castle having been captured, he could not be found]. After 1406, it was the policy of the English army, led by Henry of Monmouth, to focus their efforts upon securing the castles. In 1407, for instance, the English besieged Aberystwyth Castle, which had been a Welsh stronghold since 1404. It is possible that Rous had the siege of Aberystwyth Castle in mind here. The episode appears in several other English chronicles also, all of which refer to an element of trickery in the capture of the castle and Owain getting away. Thomas Walsingham discusses a treaty in which Owain Glyndŵr was to give Aberystwyth Castle back to the English; this concludes that the castle was "wrested the castle from the hands of the aforesaid men by an adroit move" (Item 68.252).

10–11   *corvina coram comite lapidem eructavit.* Rous cleverly conveys the sound of the crow by alliterations of *c* in this phrase.

88. Rhys Pennardd, *Glyndŵr's War*

Ed. and trans. Gruffydd Aled Williams; notes by John K. Bollard.

Manuscripts: There are twenty-six manuscript copies of this poem. The earliest is NLW Cwrtmawr MS 3, fol. 172v, written by William Salesbury, c.1564; the present text is derived from a comparison of all known manuscripts.

Various manuscripts give the poem the title *Rhyfel Glyndŵr* [Glyndŵr's War], which has been adopted here. A few late manuscripts attribute the poem to Iolo Goch, but many poems are falsely attributed to him, and it is not surprising that the connection here with Owain would attract his name. More interesting, in a manuscript of c.1597 written by Siôn Dafydd Rhys (Dr. John Davies of Brecon), is the attribution to Rhys Pennardd (fl. c.1480), who wrote in praise of Elisau ap Gruffudd, the son of Lowri, Glyndŵr's niece (see the discussion on p. 546). Though it occurs in only one manuscript, this attribution to a lesser-known poet is here tentatively accepted as a *lectio difficilior*.

Some copies of this poem are found in series with other chronological *englynion* (sg. *englyn*, a three- or four-line stanza with any of several metrical structures), and this particular poem is of interest as Welsh evidence for and recognition of an approximate date for Glyndŵr's death. The poem is an *englyn unodl union*, a form with lines of 10, 6, 7, and 7 syllables (see the note on line 1), in which the end-rhyme of lines 2, 3, and 4 is established in the first line, here at syllable 7, and in which there is consonantal correspondence between the rest of line 1 and the first part of line 2, here *c-f-d*. The requirements of this form are instrumental in arriving at the edited text.

1   *heb ddim mwy* [no more]. The line as it stands is a syllable too long, but *heb ddim mwy* (or a corrupt version of this) is the reading in eighteen of the manuscript copies. An alternative possibility is *nid mwy*, found in three copies (Peniarth 90

[early 17th cent.], and two in NLW 8330B), which read *Mil a phedwar cant nid mwy*. Some late 18th- and 19th-century manuscripts (BL Add. 14873 and Cardiff 4.9) read *Mil pedwar cant heb ddim mwy*, but it would be risky to base a text on such late manuscripts. We can similarly disregard the readings of Cardiff 18, p. 222 (1588), *Mil a ffedwarkant heb mwy*, and Panton 53, fol. 59v (Evan Evans, 18th cent.), *Mil a phedwarcant dim mwy*.

4   *Owain hen* [old Owain]. This poem shares with Item 91 the description of Owain as old, a practice also seen elsewhere (see Williams' essay in this volume).

Beauchamp Pageant: The earl drives the Welsh to flight. Courtesy of the British Library.

89. *BEAUCHAMP PAGEANT*

Ed. and trans. Michael Livingston.

Manuscript: London, British Library, MS Cotton Julius E.iv, fol. 3v (see facing page).

This fascinating manuscript preserves 53 outline drawings on 28 leaves, measuring 11 by 8 inches. These sketches, along with short accompanying textual narrations, illustrate the life and death of Richard Beauchamp (1382–1439), 13th earl of Warwick. While Richard Beauchamp had a life of some interest himself, he is likely known most predominantly today as the father-in-law of Warwick the Kingmaker.

Of present interest, however, is the fact that Beauchamp was engaged in military actions against Owain Glyndŵr as early as 1402 (Carpenter, "Beauchamp," p. 592). He fought on the side of Henry IV at the Battle of Shrewbury — the day after which he was made a Knight of the Garter according to the *Pageant* (fol. 4r; see Rous, *Pageant*, p. 13) — and in the summer of 1404 was the leader of the king's forces that attacked Glyndŵr at the Battle of Mynydd Cwm-du on the fields near Abergavenny. The Welsh fled this assault, down the valley of the River Usk, where they eventually counterattacked the English below the hill of Craig-y-Dorth near Mitchel Troy, forcing Beauchamp to retreat to Monmouth (see Item 70.26–29).

The illustration that the text presented here is meant to accompany (facing page) shows the earl's standard and the blazing comet, below which is depicted the apparent moment of Beauchamp's triumph against the Welsh: he is charging on horseback at the head of the English cavalry, his lance lowered against Glyndŵr's retreating banner bearer.

This illustration has been interpreted by critics, including Davies, who reproduces the illustration, as a somewhat hagiographic interpretation of Beauchamp's 1404 actions — one that would thereby wholly neglect the Welsh counter-attack, boastfully add Owain's near-defeat and the seizure of his standard-bearer, and inexplicably present the fight in the mountains (*Revolt*, pp. 243–44 and plate 7). It is far more plausible, however, that the illustration depicts earlier actions in Wales. In particular, the text and image both fit almost precisely the engagement described by John Charlton as occurring on 1 June 1401, where English riders in the mountains surprised Owain himself, dispersing the Welsh in two separate strikes — in the background of the *Pageant* image there is a second onslaught taking place — and in the process seizing Owain's banner and standard-bearer (see Item 17). That this 1401 event would be connected with the comet of 1402 (a problem equally faced by the 1404 speculation) is presumably due to how heavily connected this celestial event was to Owain's rebellion on the whole (on which, see Brindley, *Richard Beauchamp*, p. 29).

1   *stella comata*. This comet was visible from February to early April of 1402 and is marked across many chronicle accounts of the time: from England to Asia (Kronk, *Cometography*, pp. 260–64). In England, its presence is typically associated with the rise of Glyndŵr in Wales. In a note, the editor of the *Pageant* identifies this comet as Halley's Comet (Rous, *Pageant*, p. 12), but this cannot be so: Halley's has a known orbital period between 74 and 79 years since its first known appearance in 240 BCE; it was seen in 1378 and then again in 1456.

4   *Erle Richard*. Beauchamp became the 13th earl of Warwick on the death of his
           father, Thomas, in April 1401, but he not receive his full estates until February
           1403.

90. *A POEM OF WARNING TO OWAIN GLYNDŴR*

Ed. and trans. John K. Bollard.

Manuscripts: **A**: NLW MS 3039B (Mostyn MS 131), pp. 565–67; **B**: NLW MS 1980B (Panton
MS 11 [last half of the 18ᵗʰ cent.]), fol. 67.

There are fifteen copies of this poem in twelve manuscripts (four of them in NLW MS
3039B), dating from the 1560s to the nineteenth century, with considerable variation especially in the first line. The accompanying prose account is taken from NLW MS 3039B, pp.
565–67, transcribed in 1618 by the noted scribe and calligrapher John Jones of Gellilyfdy,
edited here in the original orthography, with variants given below from the eighteenth-
century version in NLW MS 1980B in the hand of Evan Evans.
       Given the tale attached to this poem, it is not surprising that ten of the manuscripts
(including A and B) attribute the poem to Iolo Goch. However, there is doubt as to whether
Iolo Goch lived into the early years of the rebellion, when the incident recounted would
have taken place. Gruffydd Aled Williams has argued recently that the poem presented
herein as Item 27 may indeed be by Iolo (see p. 513), but even if Williams is right and Iolo
was alive in 1400–02, it is far from certain that he composed this *englyn* or that this particular story is true. It looks very much like an example of the tale type demonstrating a
hero's ability to escape from difficult situations (see Henken, *National Redeemer*, pp. 100–05),
and as Johnston points out, it is likely that the poem would be attributed to Iolo because of
his known connection with Owain Glyndŵr (Iolo Goch, *Gwaith*, p. 174).

1   *Davydd ap Gruffydd*. Dafydd was the brother of Llywelyn ap Gruffudd, the last
           recognized Welsh prince of Wales. After the death of Llywelyn in December of
           1282, Dafydd held out against Edward I for some months and adopted his
           brother's title, identifying himself as *Dauid filius Gryffini princeps Wallie et domi-
           nus Snaudonie* [Dafydd son of Gruffudd, prince of Wales and lord of Snowdonia]
           in a letter of 2 May 1283 (Edwards, *Littera Wallie*, p. 77). He was captured later
           that summer, betrayed *per homines lingue sue* [by men of his own tongue], and
           on 3 October 1283 he was tried and hanged in Shrewsbury, after which his body
           was disemboweled, dismembered, and scattered to the four corners of the king-
           dom (Morris, *Welsh Wars*, p. 195; Smith, *Llywelyn*, p. 390).

           pan ddihenyddwyd [was executed]. Literally, "when (he) was executed."

2   *i kigidd* [the executioner]. The primary sense of *cigydd* is "butcher." Though the
           writer of this account may not have known it, the name of this executioner sur-
           vives in the Public Record Office — one Geoffrey of Shrewsbury, who was paid
           20 shillings for executing Dafydd (Smith, *Llywelyn*, p. 390n210).

3   *drawodd* [struck]. B: *darawodd*.

         a dynnodd i lygad [put out his eye]. B: *a'i tynnodd* [put it out].

6   *ddoedvd* [said]. B: *ddywedyd*.

         y dydd ar dydd [on such and such a day]. B: *y dydd hwnnw gan henwi rhyw dydd* [that day, naming some day]. For the idiom in MS A, compare *y da yn lledrat or lle ar lle, y dydd ar dydd, y nos ar nos, ar wythnos* [the property stolen from such and such a place, such and such a day, such and such a night, and such a week] (Owen, *Ancient Laws*, 2.676–77).

7   *wrthaw* [for him]. B: *iddaw* [to him], with *wrth* written above it.

7–8   *dengwr ar hvgain* [thirty men]. B: *30 wr* [30 men].

9   (*a gallv mawr . . . ar i ol*) [(and a great force . . . after him)]. The parentheses are lightly inscribed in A.

12   *doedassant* [they said]. B: *i dywedassant*.

14   *dallt* [understood]. B: *deall* (both instances).

16   The first line as given here appears in A and three other manuscripts (one of which copied from A). In his edition of the poem, Dafydd Johnston, drawing on a mare's nest of readings from other manuscripts, gives the first line (in modern orthography) as *Coffa ben, perchen parch urddedig — lys* [Remember a head, the revered owner of an honored court] (Iolo Goch, *Gwaith*, p. 173).

         llywenic. The meaning of *llywenic* is doubtful, though it is perhaps an adjectival derivative from *llawen* [joyful, merry].

18   *golwyth Amwythig* [the cutlet of Shrewsbury]. *GPC* glosses *golwyth* as "chop, cutlet, collop, slice, rasher (of bacon); portion of meat cooked or for cooking." The text in A has light square brackets around these words, with the clarifying note, *i kalon Dd ap Gr* [i.e., Dafydd ap Gruffudd's heart] in the right-hand margin, in John Jones' distinctive hand. Similarly, MS B has the marginal note, *sef calon Dd ap Gr* [that is, Dafydd ap Gruffudd's heart].

91. *THE WART ON OWAIN GLYNDŴR'S HEAD*

Ed. and trans. John K. Bollard.

Manuscripts: **A**: BL Add. MS 31055 (1594–96), fol. 226; **B**: NLW MS 1980B (Panton MS 11), (last half of 18th c.), fol. 69; **C**: NLW Peniarth MS 240 (mid 18th c.), fol. 3. The variants from C are taken from J. Gwenogvryn Evans's transcribed extract in the *Report on Manuscripts in the Welsh Language*, 1.3.1066.

     The text of the poem is that of A, the earliest manuscript; the variants in B and C are merely orthographic. The prose passages before and after the poem are taken from B and C, as noted below. The headnotes in B and C are clearly derived from the same or a closely related earlier source; the afternote is found only in C. The distinguishing wart that is the subject of this stanza in *cywydd* meter is also mentioned in the English account of Glyndŵr's career compiled by Robert Vaughan of Hengwrt in the 1660s. In his account of the battle at Pwll Melyn we are told,

> Among the dead bodies besides was found one much like unto Owain, whom they supposed and gave out to be Owain, and that he was there slain, but upon further enquiry it was not him but his brother Tudur who very much resembled him, and was often taken for him, being hardly distinguished asunder, only Owain had a little wart above his eyebrows, which Tudur had not. (NLW 2021B [Panton MS 53], fol. 56b., qtd. in Henken, *National Redeemer*, p. 120)

1   *Ar ol . . . ben* [After . . . head]. C: *Un Madyn Glôff a ddug Ben* [One Madyn the Lame brought a head].

2   *mae'r pen . . . Owen*. C: *mai Pen Owain Glyndwr ydoedd* [that it was O. G.'s head]

        'r Cymry [the Welsh]. C: *'r Cymru o'i Lys* [the Welsh of his court].

3   *os cai ef ei weled* [if he could see it]. Not in C.

        ir adwaenai fo, achos [he would recognize it, because]. C: *ir adwaenai o achos* [he would recognize, because].

4   *iad* [crown]. *Iad* is a term for the crown or top of the head.

        welwyd [was seen]. C: *welpwyd* [was seen].

        nad pen Owain oedd [that it was not Owain's head]. C adds: *o achaws nad oedd un Ddyfaden* [because there was not a single wart].

6   *Celwydd* [lie]. B: *celwydda*, the *-a* is unclear and may have been cancelled as a simple dittography. C: *celwydd*.

7   *Ogloff* [the Lame]. This is the lenited form of *gogloff* [halting, lame, limping], from *go-* [rather, somewhat] + *cloff* [lame]; B: *Gloff*.

10–12   Not in B.

10   *Tudur ap Gruffudd Vychan*. Tudur was Owain's younger brother by two or three years. In the 1380s they served together at Berwick, in Scotland, and in the retinue of the earl of Arundel (Davies, *Revolt*, pp. 139, 326). There is some confusion in this account; assuming that Owain died c.1415, it is unlikely that his brother Tudur's head would still be identifiable, if kept at all, for he died in the battle of Pwll Melyn in May 1405; J. E. Lloyd notes the related tradition that there had been "a moment of ecstatic joy" after that battle, when Tudur's corpse was briefly thought to be that of Owain (*Owen Glendower*, pp. 96–97).

       Ragad. Rhagad, formerly in Merioneth (now in Denbughshire), up the valley from Glyndyfrdwy, was one of the vills on Owain's estate (Davies, *Revolt*, p. 131). Rhagatt Hall, a post-medieval, two-story house, stands on the site, just west of the village of Carrog (RCAHMW website, s.n. *Rhagatt Hall*).

       Gefeilliaid [twins]. *Gefeilliaid* might be best understood here in the sense of "close look-alikes," rather than "genetic twins." Or might there have been, at some point, confusion between *gefeilliaid*, plural of *gefell* [twin], and *gyfeilliaid*, the lenited form of *cyfeilliaid*, a plural of *cyfaill* [companion]?

12   *y Mreicheiniog* [in Brycheiniog]. Brycheiniog was an independent realm in southeast Wales, divided into three cantrefi, founded according to legend by one Brychan (Lloyd, *History*, p. 270). It was conquered fairly early by the Normans and became the lordship of Brecon.

92. *ON THE FIRST PLAGUE AND OWAIN'S BIRTH*

Ed. and trans. John K. Bollard.

Manuscripts: **A**: NLW MS 3039B (Mostyn MS 131), (July 1618), p. 615; **B**: NLW Peniarth MS 172 (1582), p. 267; **C**: BL Add. MS 14967 (before 1587); **D**: NLW MS 253 (1618–22), p. 343.

The text given here is that of manuscript A. While the *englyn* itself is not about Owain Glyndŵr, it is included here because of the headnote stating the supposed year of his birth. For a differing record of Owain's age, the account of his testimony at the Scrope-Grosvenor trial places his age at *xxvij anz plus*, "27 years and more," in 1386, which would put his birth in 1359 or a bit earlier (Item 7.1).

1   *kornwyd* [plague]. The generalized sense of *kornwyd* as "plague, pestilence" is an extension of its specific sense "boil, abscess, sore," from *corn* [horn; corn callus] + an obscure ending (*GPC*, s.v. *cornwyd*). Compare *nodav* in the note below.

1–2   *y vlwyddyn honno y ganed Owen Glyndwr* [that year O. G. was born]. The degree of reliability for this statement, of course, is brought into question by the lack of certainty as to the date the note (rather than the *englyn*) was originally written.

3   *Marwolaeth* [death]. *Marwolaeth* [death, suffering; deadly plague or pestilence] is a compound from *marwol* [deadly, fatal] (from *marw* [dead]) + the abstract noun suffix -*aeth*. Compare *Pedwar vgein mlyned a chwechant ac vn oyd oed krist pan vv varwolaeth vawr yny* [sic] *ynys brydein. . . . Dwy vlyned wedy hynny y bu varwolaeth yn ywerdon* [Six hundred and eighty one was the year of Christ when there was a great mortality in the island of Britain . . . .Two years after that there was a mortality in Ireland] (Jones, *Brut* [1941], p. 1; Jones, *Brut* [1952], p. 1).

Duw Naf [Lord God]. C: *duw nef* [God of Heaven].

4   *nodav* [plague]. *Nod* [bubo, (bubonic) plague] is often used in the plural *nodau* [lit., buboes] as a term for the disease designated by its most distinctive symptom. It may derive from the general term *nod* "mark or a sign" (from Latin *nota*), or from ME *knotte* [knot, protuberance, node].

5–6   *mil a thrychant . . . naw a deugain* [1349]. The plague reached England in 1348 and Wales in 1349–50. In his continuation of *Brenhinedd y Saesson*, written in the period 1461–c.1470, the poet Gutun Owain describes the battle of Crécy in 1346 and continues, *A thair blynedd gwedy hynny y bu y varwolaeth gyntaf* [And three years after that, was the first plague] (Jones, *Brenhinedd*, pp. 272–73; and the headnote to Item 84).

5   *gwarant a gaf* [I am assured]. Literally, "I have a warrant."

6   *tygaf* [I swear]. The Early Modern Welsh orthography of the manuscripts generally reads *ng* where earlier Middle Welsh has simply *g*, allowing for the context to make the phonology clear to the reader; *tygaf* rather than *tyngaf* here might be an indication that this englyn was copied from a fifteenth-century original.

93. *MIDDLE ENGLISH VITA HENRICI QUINTI*

Adapted and trans. Michael Livingston, from *First English Life*, ed. Kingsford, pp. 9–10, 191.

Manuscripts: Oxford, Bodleian Library MS Bodley 966 and London, British Library MS Harley 35.

The Venetian Tito Livio Frulovisi traveled to England around the year 1436. There, under the employ of Humphrey, duke of Gloucester, Frulovisi composed an influential biography of the duke's recently deceased brother, King Henry V. This work, *Vita Henrici Quinti*, is that for which he is most known, though scholars now view it as largely derivative of another work, *Vita et Gesta Henrici Quinti* (once ascribed to Thomas Elmham). Frulovisi's Latin text was translated into European vernaculars on several occasions, including a Middle English version executed in 1513 by an anonymous translator that is preserved in two extant manuscripts: MS Bodley 966 and MS Harley 35. The text presented here follows that of the Bodley manuscript, which Kingsford edited under the title *The First English Life of Henry V*. In addition to being adapted to fit the editorial practices of this volume, Kingsford's text has been here emended by the inclusion of additional material from the Harley manuscript, which Kingsford had included in an appendix; it is in these materials that we have a unique report of Owain Glyndŵr's death (see note to lines 25–26, below).

14–18   *And on his partie . . . it was environed.* As Kingsford notes, this "obscure sentence is an addition of the Translator" to Frulovisi's text (p. 10).

15–16   *companie, but in so much.* So Harley 35. Bodley 966 omits *but*.

25–26   *where in caues he continued, and . . . finished his miserable life.* So Harley 35. The Bodley 966 text reads simply *where in caues he continewed and finished his misserable life*. The extra detail in Harley 35, that Owain died on the hill of Lawton's Hope in Herefordshire, is nowhere else recorded. It is interesting that this scribal insertion — for this is found in neither Frulovisi's text nor in the otherwise parallel Middle English translation found in the Bodley manuscript — is defended as being a fact well-known to and reported by the local populace, though we are not now in a position to deny or affirm that claim. Nevertheless, this detail is intriguing for its potential correspondence to other legends that report Owain living his last years in Herefordshire, perhaps in the company of one of his daughters.

94. JOHN LELAND, *ITINERARY IN WALES*

Adapted and trans. Michael Livingston, from Leland, *Itinerary*, ed. Smith, 3.10, 41, 52, 70–71, 78, 108, 111.

John Leland (c.1503–1552) was a prolific writer and an able poet, but he is most remembered today as an antiquary with a passion for books. This interest led him to search out old libraries and other sources of history throughout the realm, journeys for which he kept meticulous notebooks of observations and gathered rumors and records. These "Itineraries" have been a rich quarry for later writers, as they often preserve information (whether accurate or not) that is found nowhere else. Such is the case with several items reproduced here, which report an otherwise unknown slaughter of Englishmen by Owain and several reminders of the destructiveness of his rebellion. For such references as those here to Radnor, Montgomery, Cwm-hir, and Hay, and often elsewhere in lore and local tradition, in which Owain is scapegoated — deservedly or not — as the cause of destruction, decay, and the diminishment of numerous locations in Wales or in the Marches, see Henken, *National Redeemer*, 126–30.

1   *New Radnor*. The town of New Radnor was founded in the early thirteenth century some two miles northeast of the village of Old Radnor. The "gate" that was recently repaired in Leland's time may in fact have been the prison (see Howse, "New Radnor Castle," p. 24).

3–10   On the decline of the formerly thriving town, for which Glyndŵr seems to have been at least partly responsible, see Soulsby, *Towns*, p. 208. However, this massacre by Owain of the English garrison at Radnor Castle in 1401, which first appears here and is subsequently picked up by many writers, is of questionable authenticity: if indeed Owain and his men not only invaded Radnorshire at this time, but also publicly beheaded sixty of the king's men at Radnor, one would expect there to have been an English response. There was none. Edmund Mortimer, whose lands would have been under assault, shows no reaction to the raid, and the slaughter — which plays well to an anti-Welsh bias — is not mentioned in any chronicle of the period. Excavations of the Radnor church in 1845 uncovered, according to the *Illustrated London News*, "proofs of the sad story of the garrison . . . in a mass of human bones in one spot: in another of a corresponding collection of skulls only" (4 Oct., pp. 223–24; see Howse, "New Radnor Castle," pp. 24–25), but no scientific analysis was made to tie the remains to each other or to the time and method of death. Our only other evidence of such a raid — much less the massacre — comes from records from early 1401 showing that rent incomes had fallen in the area because "tenements were destroyed and burnt by a rebel" (see Williams, *Renewal*, p. 19). Hodges, like many other writers, nevertheless opines that "the story is too emphatic to dismiss" (*Owain*, p. 54), but on balance it would be difficult to accept Leland's rumor as truth without a great deal of qualification.

10   Bloodwort is a name formerly applied to various plants with red roots, veins, or flowers, or that were believed efficacious in stanching the flow of blood, especially Red-veined dock (*Rumex sanguineus*), Danewort (*Sambucus ebulus*), and

Great Burnet (*Sanguisorba officinalis*) (see *OED*, s.v. *bloodwort*; Keble Martin, Plates 74, 41, 26).

11   *Comehere*. Cwm-hir, near Llandrindod Wells, was founded by Cadwallon ap Madog, lord of Maelienydd, in 1176. It is likely that Llywelyn ap Gruffudd was buried there in 1282 (see note on line 28, below; Smith, *Llywelyn*, p. 383).

12   *vii. miles from Knighton*. Cwm-hir Abbey is about 20 miles west of Knighton.

19   *Yale*. Iâl, from which comes the name Yale, is a commote to the north of the Dee and northeast of Edeirnion.

19–23   Though he never uses the name, Leland is speaking here of Owain's estates in the area of Glyndyfrdwy, which is itself almost exactly five miles up the River Dee from Castell Dinas Brân. Strikingly, however, he ignores the location that is most often associated with Owain's manor — the remains of a motte (no bailey has been positively identified) on the south side of the Dee one mile further west between Glyndyfrdwy and Carrog. Instead, Leland identifies Owain's manor as being located on the north side of the river at Rhagad, which is likely on or near the site of the post-medieval Rhagatt Hall further up the river near Corwen, about nine miles from Castell Dinas Brân. Other sources indicate that this location was associated with the lordship of Owain's brother, Tudur (who would have nevertheless held his lands under Owain; see Item 91). The other location in the area most commonly associated with Owain in popular legend is the so-called *carchardy* [prison-house] that disappeared in the early twentieth century. It stood on the banks of the Dee in what is today Carrog (Henken, *Redeemer*, p. 148).

21   *Llanegwhist*. Llanegwystl, later reduced to Llanegwest, is the old Welsh name for Valle Crucis abbey, in Llandysilio, a mile and a half north of Llangollen.

22   *Keuen De*. Leland's report of a castle of Owain's called *Cefn Du* [Black Ridge] has a parallel nowhere else. A location halfway between Llangollen and Ruthin via a direct road (today's Horseshoe Pass) would place it well outside of Owain's lands and therefore a surprising place to find him keeping a castle (but if true a strong reason to have run-ins with Lord Grey of Ruthin). It is possible that Leland has misunderstood some local legends, perhaps in associating the ruin at Tomen-y-rhodwydd with Owain Glyndŵr rather than Owain Gwynedd: the site is well-known and stands roughly between the two towns, though there is no toponymical evidence that this or any nearby location has been associated with a black ridge or black hill.

More likely, however, one ought to imagine a route to Ruthin that travels around Llantysilio Mountain by continuing up the Dee as Leland's itinerary proceeds in that direction (in today's terms, taking the A5 to the A494). By this path, the halfway point would be north of Gwyddelwern, the lordship of Tudur, Owain's brother. Just north of this small village there are numerous place-names with the element *du* [black], including the wide hill still called Cefn Du, above the Nant Du [Black River] west of Clocaenog. Leland almost surely has in mind a location somewhere in this area, though exactly where is not now known.

24 *Penthline*. Penllyn is a commote to the west of Edeirnion. Here Leland uses -*thl*- to approximate the sound of Welsh *ll*.

25 *Denbighland*. By Denbighland, it is likely that Leland means the lordship of Denbigh, created in 1284 by Edward I; the county of Denbighshire was created by the Laws in Wales Acts (Acts of Union) of 1535 and 1542, which abolished the Marcher lordships.

28 *Lluelin ap Irrwarth Droyndon*. Llywelyn ab Iorwerth Drwyndwn (c.1172–1240), commonly known as Llywelyn Fawr or Llywelyn the Great, established and maintained effective control over all of independent Wales (Gwynedd, Powys, and Deheubarth) from 1216 until his death. For a more detailed discussion of the spurious claim of Owain Glyndŵr's descent from Llywelyn ap Gruffudd, see pp. 427–30).

 Grifith. Gruffudd ap Llywelyn ab Iorwerth (c.1198–1244) was Llywelyn's first son, but he was born illegitimate. While illegitimate sons had a right to inheritance according to Welsh law and tradition, Llywelyn favored his legitimate son Dafydd for succession, especially to maintain the unity of Wales. Even before Llywelyn died, Dafydd stripped Gruffudd of all his territories and imprisoned him. When Dafydd submitted to Henry III, Gruffudd was transferred to the Tower of London, where he died in an attempt to escape. Dafydd died without heir, however, and Gruffudd's son Llywelyn subsequently gained the rulership of Wales.

29 *Lluelin*. Llywelyn ap Gruffudd (c.1223–1282) was the last independent Welsh Prince of Wales recognized by the English crown. After some fragmentation of power following the death of Dafydd, Llywelyn reconsolidated the unity of independent Wales, declaring himself Prince of Wales in 1258. He retained his title, but lost much of his lands in his war with Edward I in 1277. When he was killed in a skirmish at Irfon Bridge, near Builth, during renewed hostilities in 1282, Welsh independence came to an end, paving the way for the events of 1400.

 Catarine. In declaring Catherine to be the heir of Llywelyn ap Gruffudd, Leland is drawing on a tradition that differs from the more likely genealogy of Owain, for Llywelyn and his wife Eleanor had only one child, Gwenllian (1282–1337), who was a few months old when her father was killed. In 1283 Gwenllian was forcibly committed to a convent in far away Lincolnshire on order of the king, where she died without issue (see Item 99 and the note to *Unica filia et haeres*, pp. 417–18; Smith, *Llywelyn*, pp. 344–45, 391, 405). *Glyndŵr's Pedigree* similarly shows Owain as a direct descendant of Llywelyn's "sole daughter and heir" (for discussion, see pp. 427–30).

 Eleanor. Owain's grandmother Elinor was the wife of Thomas ap Llywelyn ab Owain (d. 1343); both she and her husband were descended from the dynasty of Deheubarth established by Rhys ap Tewdwr (d. 1093). On the uncertainties of her ancestry, see pp. 427–30.

 Helene. Elen was one of two daughters of Thomas ap Llywelyn. She married Gruffudd Fychan, who was a direct male descendant of the dynasty of Powys.

Combined with a more distant connection to the line of Gwynedd, this heritage led their son Owain Glyndŵr to claim to the title Prince of Wales (for this claim, see pp. 425–30 and Item 6).

30   *Catarine*. Leland is in error here in naming the other daughter of Thomas ap Llywelyn as Catarine. Owain Glyndŵr's aunt was, in fact, Marged, who married Tudur ap Goronwy (d. 1367); on the introduction of the name Catherine, see pp. 429–30.

     Meredik. Maredudd ap Tudur (d. 1406) and his brothers Rhys (d. 1409) and Gwilym (d. 1413) were among the most loyal supporters of Owain Glyndŵr's rebellion.

31   *Owen*. Owen Tudor (c.1400–1461) had two children with Catherine of Valois (widow of King Henry V); whether or not they were secretly married at the time (thus legitimizing the children) has been a subject of some interest for those interested in royal genealogies. He took on the English surname of Tudor in order to be disassociated from his family's rebellious past. He fought at the Battle of Agincourt, was subsequently granted full rights as an Englishman, and is considered the progenitor of the Tudor dynasty in England.

     Edmunde. Edmund Tudor, earl of Richmond (1430–1456), was also known as Edmund of Hadham. Because of the lingering uncertainty of his parents' relationship at his birth, he was declared legitimate in 1453. He died of the plague while imprisoned by the Yorkists during the Wars of the Roses.

     Gasper. Jasper Tudor, earl of Pembroke (c.1431–1495). As the uncle of Henry VII and a descendant of Ednyfed Fychan, Llywelyn the Great's powerful seneschal, he was instrumental in helping the king press his claims in Wales in 1485.

32   Henry VII (1457–1509) was the only child of Edmund Tudor and Margaret Beaufort, who was thirteen at the time of his birth and through whose ancestry he lay claim to the throne of England that he seized from Richard III at Bosworth Field in 1485. Leland is correct in observing that Edmund died almost three months before his son's birth.

33   *Dinas*. Castell Dinas or Dinas Castle (not to be confused with Castell Dinas Brân in Denbighshire) is just east of Pengenffordd, in Brecknockshire. The idea that the local populace destroyed it to keep it out of Owain's hands is not otherwise recorded (and seems doubtful). It is worth noting that this is within the area mentioned in Item 20.

34   *Chathedrals*. This is Leland's translation of *Mynydd y Gadair* (literally, "mountain of the chair"), which he identified earlier: "Atterel Hylles, the wich be cawlled in Walsch Meneth e Cadair, id est montes alti instar cathedrarum" (ed. Smith, p. 104). *Cadair* [chair] is a common term for a mountain top or ridge more or less in the shape of a seat; compare Cadair Idris and Cadair Fronwen in Meirionnydd and Arthur's Seat in Edinburgh.

36   *the Hay*. There is evidence from the early twelfth century of a Norman motte at Hay-on-Wye, also known as "the Hay," in Brecknockshire (Soulsby, *Towns*, p. 142–44).

95. EDWARD HALL, *CHRONICLE*

Ed. Scott Lucas, from Hall, *The Vnion*, fols. 16v–19v, 22r–23r.

The lawyer, London official, and parliamentarian Edward Hall composed his account of English affairs c.1399–1509 in the early 1540s, completing it only shortly before he was stricken by a debilitating illness in late 1546. It was published posthumously, along with his uncompleted account of Henry VIII's reign, in 1548. A second edition appeared in 1550.

Hall's chief source for his fifteenth-century material was Polydore Vergil's *Historia Anglica* (first printed in Basle in 1534, here reproduced in its final 1555 edition as Item 97); however, he drew as well from a number of English, French, Scottish, and Burgundian chronicles and primary documents in composing his work. Much of his information about Owain Glyndŵr's rising appears to have come from a manuscript source, anti-Lancastrian in its bias, that is now lost.

Hall was a fervent admirer of his own monarch Henry VIII, a strong proponent of Henry's break with Rome, and a proud English chauvinist. His hostility toward any who opposed English claims to sovereignty over them colors his accounts of the Welsh, French, and Scots in his narrative. The anger Hall evinces at the conspirators' belief in the so-called *Prophecy of the Six Kings* (Item 1), furthermore, is almost certainly heightened by the fact that this prophecy had been recently employed against Henry VIII by Catholics opposed to the king's repudiation of papal authority. No less than three men were executed between 1535 and 1539 for asserting that King Henry was the moldwarp foretold in that text.

8–15   The claim that Lord Grey married one of Owain's daughters and died in captivity is common to all the printed English chronicles consulted by Hall. See *The Cronycles of Englonde* [a version of the *Brut* prepared by William Caxton] (London, 1528), fol. 141r; Robert Fabyan, *The Chronicle of Fabyan* (London, 1542), p. 344; and *Polycronycon* (London, 1527), fol. 326r. This tradition appears to originate in a copyist's error in the *Prose Brut* (see Item 71, note to lines 7–9).

15–18   Hall conflates the captured Sir Edmund Mortimer (b. 1376) with his nephew, Edmund Mortimer, earl of March (b. 1391), who held the strongest rival claim to Henry IV's throne. Hall's confusion passed into Holinshed's *Chronicles* and thus into Shakespeare. While it is possible that the blending of the two Mortimers originated in a now lost Yorkist source designed to attack the Lancastrian right to the throne, it was quite possibly just the result of confusion due to their names (as in an earlier Welsh source, Item 84.7). Hall's claim that Mortimer was captured near Wigmore likely refers to the historical events at Battle of Bryn Glas.

30–69   Hall's primary source for the two French attempts to aid Glyndŵr is Enguerrand de Monstrelet's *Chronique*. He departs from Monstrelet in his account of Bourbon's attack on the English coastline, however, to follow instead Polydore Vergil's assertions that Bourbon destroyed only a few English villages, that he lost many men during his expedition, and that Bourbon had twelve ships sunk in Plymouth harbor. Monstrelet himself correctly records that the French sacked and burned the town of Plymouth and lost their twelve ships only in crossing the channel after an entirely successful harrying of the English coast. Hall's count of thirty French "sayle" (line 34) and his claim that the English marshaled forces to threaten Bourbon while he was in Plymouth are found in neither Monstrelet or Vergil.

49–50   Jean de Rieux and Jean de Hangest, respectively. In a slip of the pen, Hall replaces de Rieux's name with that of the celebrated French marshal of his own time, Anne de Montmorency (made marshal of France in 1522).

65–69   Monstrelet counts a total of 200 or more men slain on each side in the skirmishes between the French, Welsh, and English, and he offers no specific count of gentlemen lost, as Hall does. The death of the "bastarde of Burbon" (lines 68–69), Rieux's lack of confidence in his Welsh allies, and the French forces' retreat (rather than their pursuit of a retreating Henry IV as recorded by Monstrelet) are Hall's interpolations, perhaps drawn from another French or Burgundian chronicle. Compare Monstrelet's original account, Item 80.

67   *Lorde Patrioles of Tries*. Monstrelet's mistake for the admiral of France, Regnault de Trie.

130   The *certayne writer* whom Hall credits for his account of the *Tripartite Indenture* (Item 47) and the influence of the *Prophecy of the Six Kings* on its signers has not been identified. Hall's descriptions of the indenture, its creation before the Battle of Shrewsbury, Henry Percy's participation in it, and the prophecy that allegedly occasioned the pact were adopted by Holinshed for his own chronicle, and by means of both Hall and Holinshed they were transmitted to Shakespeare for his *1 Henry IV*.

156–69   Hall's source for the Percies' articles is a prose note included in manuscripts of the second version of John Hardyng's *Chronicle* (see Hardyng, *Chronicle*, ed. Ellis, pp. 351–54). Hall rewrites the article as recorded by Hardyng so that it identifies Sir Edmund Mortimer, brother to the former earl of March and Ulster ("Edmundus Mortymere, frater Rogeri Mortymere nuper comitis Marchie et Ultonie") as Roger's son Edmund Mortymer, earl of March.

96. *CHRONICL ELIS GRUFFUDD*

Ed. and trans. John K. Bollard.

Manuscript: National Library of Wales MS 3054D (Mostyn 158), in the autograph of Elis Gruffudd, fols. 285a.10–286a.3.

Elis Gruffudd (or Gruffydd) was born between 1490 and 1500 in Flintshire. In the "envoy" to his chronicle, he styles himself as *Ellis gruffyth sawdiwr o Gallis*, "Elis Gruffudd, soldier of Calais." He served with Sir Robert Wingfield in Calais at "The Field of the Cloth of Gold" in 1521, and with the Duke of Suffolk's army in France during 1523. In 1529 he accompanied Wingfield to Calais and spent the rest of his life in Calais and various parts of France. The date of his death is not known, but his chronicle ends with the executions of Sir Ralph Vane, Sir Miles Partridge, Sir Michael Stanhope, and Sir Robert Arundel on 25 [*recte* 26] February 1551/2 (*Welsh Biography Online*, s.n. *Elis Gruffydd*; Thomas Jones, "Elis Gruffydd").

After completing a work on the virtues and medicinal uses of plants in 1548, he wrote his extensive chronicle of world history, gathered for the most part from English and French sources, but also from unspecified *llyfre o Gymru* [books from Wales], though not from *Brut y Tywysogion, The Chronicle of the Princes*. The latter years of the history draw heavily on his personal experience. He completed this work in 1552 or shortly thereafter. The first part, contained in NLW MS 5276D, is an account of world history from the Creation to the Christian Age; the second part, in NLW MS 3054D (Mostyn MS 158), covers the years 1066 to 1552.

Gruffudd is not so much interested in outlining the course of Owain's rebellion, its battles and other events, as in recounting incidents indicating something about the character and reputation of Owain. The narratives he includes we would consider today to be of a legendary nature, as, for example, the earliest surviving version of Owain's encounter with the abbot of Glynegwestl.

In the present text, word division, capitalization, punctuation, and paragraphing are editorial. Gruffudd's orthography has been retained with the exception of a few emendations which are recorded in the notes. He regularly writes *hr* for modern *rh*, as in *hrwng* [between] and *Hruthun* [Ruthin], but *Jr hain* for *y rhain* [these]. He often uses capital *J* for *i*, *y*, and for the 3rd person singular possessive pronoun *y* (ModW *ei*), printed herein as *i*.

1   *Heuaid ynn y vlwyddyn yma* [Also in this year]. Gruffudd's chronology is imprecise here. The passage on Owain Glyndŵr follows his notice of the execution of Sir Roger Clarendon "in the second year of the rule of King Henry the Fourth," i.e., 1400. Clarendon, however, was executed in 1402; Lord Grey of Ruthin was captured by Owain in April 1402 and ransomed in October. A marginal note in Gruffudd's hand to the right of the present passage reads *Owain gly[n]dwr 1400*.

2   *ysgwier* [squire]. The *i* is inserted superscript in the MS. The Welsh borrowing carries much the same range of senses as English *squire*, and in this sixteenth-century context is perhaps best understood to mean a gentleman, especially the chief landowner of a region.

4   *Maes Mynnan*. The present-day Maes Mynan Hall nursing home and farm is just SW of Caerwys on the A541, about 12 km north of Rhuthun. The court rolls of Dyffryn Clwyd for 1407 record the lease of the manor, park, and demesne of Maesmynan and include a clause giving a rebate on the lease-rent if the manor could not be occupied "on account of war and rebellion" (Davies, *Revolt*, p. 267).

5   *mynnydd Berwyn*. The Berwyn range (*Y Berwyn*) runs from southwest to northeast south of the river Dee, separating the cantrefs of Penllyn and Mochnant. After Penllyn fell to the men of Gwynedd under Llywelyn ab Iorwerth in the thirteenth century, Y Berwyn formed the boundary between Powys and Gwynedd.

7   *arianswm* [ransom]. This form, first cited in *GPC* from 1552 as well as from elsewhere in Gruffudd's *Chronicle*, is a development from the earlier borrowing (*a*)*ranswn, -swm*, by folk etymology assuming the elements to be *arian* [silver,

money] + *swm* [sum]; see the note on *aranswn* in *Annales Oweni Glyndwr*, Item 70.14.

8   *Y rhain*. MS: *yr hain*, as also in line 38. This division is typical of Gruffudd's orthography; compare notes to line 8.

10   *nad oedd* [that not . . . were]. MS: *na doedd*.

         ohonnaunt twy [from them]. This is Gruffudd's usual orthography, which recognizes the aspirate effect of *-t* + *h*-; the standard modern form is *ohonynt hwy*.

12   *ymkanv*. Variant spelling of *amcanu* [to intend]; also in line 38.

16   *o gyrennydd ac*. The *ac* is added superscript.

17   *enwedig* [especially]. MS: *wnwedig*.

18   *adnabod* [to know, recognize]. MS: *ednabod* .

         aur. MS: *aur h*.

19   *deffol*. A variant spelling of *dethol* [to choose, select].

25–27   The inclusion of this curiously worded reference to a marriage between Owain's daughter and Lord Grey suggests a source in one of the English accounts that confused the capture and subsequent marriage of Mortimer with the capture of Grey. For the likely origins of this a-historical marriage account, see the note on lines 5–9 of the *Prose Brut* (Item 71); for other versions, see Items 95, 98, and 100 (see also Lloyd, *Owen Glendower*, p. 49n2).

24   *ir*. A variant of *er* [despite].

25   *gordderchodd*. The noun *gordderch*, attested from the twelfth century, has a range of possible interpretations ranging from "lover, paramour, mistress" to "concubine, adulteress, whore," and the derivative verb *gordderchu* covers a similar span from "woo" to "have sexual intercourse with" and "fornicate." Adding further ambiguity, the subject of the sentence could be either *yr arglwydd* [the lord] or *verch* [daughter]. The latter, however, is much the less likely. The next sentence might best be understood to imply that she was pregnant, which would account for the subsequent reference to *maruolaeth y mab* [the death of the child].

26   *iarll* [earl]. Though first appearing in a mid-thirteenth-century law text, *iarll* may be a direct borrowing from Old Norse *earl*, *iarl* [earl] or an indirect borrowing through Old English *eorl* [earl]. The semantic range of *iarll* in Welsh, however, did not narrow to a specific title as did *earl* in English, and thus in Middle Welsh it is often, as here, used in the general sense of "nobleman."

         hi [her]. Added superscript in MS.

26–27   *Ynn yr hwn . . . y mab*. The absence of an explicit subject pronoun leaves it ambiguous as to who dies in this sentence, which might alternatively be translated as "There a short time afterwards she died in his prison, after the death of the child." Note that "she" is the subject of the immediately preceding sentence. Furthermore, the feminine reading might provide a better context for the phrase "after the death of the child"; the child is not mentioned in the English versions, which simply say, "sone after he deyed" (e.g., *Prose Brut*, Items 71.9 and 73.20). On the other hand, it is likely that Gruffudd took the idea of Lord Grey's marriage to a daughter of Owain from one of the English chronicles; thus, the masculine reading is the more likely (see note 25–27 above). Alicia Marchant (in a personal communication) raises the question of whether the phrase *ar ol maruolaeth y mab* [after the death of the child] might stem from a misreading of *sone* as "son" rather than "soon" as in the account in the various versions of the *Prose Brut*; on the other hand, Gruffudd's *o vewn ychydig o amser ynn ol* [a short time afterwards] corresponds to the *sone* in these chronicles. All of this raises the question of whether Gruffudd was trying to reconcile the information he had found with his more Welsh-oriented perspective, as he seems to do by coupling this marriage reference with the tale of the counterfeit ransom payment, which is not found in earlier texts.

27   *mab* [child]. MS: *meb*.

29   *main Gwynnedd*. "Maen Gwynedd is a prehistoric standing-stone alongside the ancient pathway which crosses the Berwyn mountain southwards from the Dee Valley. It is thought to mark the boundary between Gwynedd and Powys. The part of the Berwyn where the stone stands is very remote and wild — a good place for Owain to hide, but rather wind-swept in winter (but possibly wooded in the Middle Ages, of course)! This is exactly the type of place where you would expect Welsh partisans to go into hiding (I know of few more remote place in Wales). Elis Gruffudd could well have heard of a genuine tradition in this respect" (Gruffydd Aled Williams, personal communication). The stone in question is located near Bwlch Maen Gwynedd, between Craig Berwyn and the peaks of Cadair Bronwen (W *Cadair Fronwen*) and Tomle. A roughly rectangular slab a little over 8 feet long, 1.5 feet wide, and 8 inches thick, it was a prominent monument when standing, though it has fallen in recent years. The national grid reference is SJ 081 337.

33   *Syr* [Sir]. Abbreviated *S*[r] in the MS.

35   *hrai*. MS: *hraii*.

42–43   *Eglwys Lanhrayadyr y Mochnant*. Llanrhaeadr-ym-Mochnant is a village about 12 miles to the west of Oswestry. The present church [W *eglwys*], dedicated to St. Dogfan, dates from the thirteenth century.

48   *a'i* [with his]. MS: *ai ai*.

51   *gnwck* [knock, blow, lash]. Lenited form of *cnwc*, a borrowing from Middle English *knok(ke)* "a blow" [*MED* s.v. *knok(ke)*]. The *-ck* shows the influence of English spelling.

97. POLYDORE VERGIL, *HISTORIA ANGLICA*

Adapted and trans. Alicia Marchant, from Vergil, *Historia Anglica* (1555), pp. 432–34.

Manuscripts: Vatican BAV, Cod. Urb. Lat 497 and 498 (from c.1512); three printed revisions dated 1534 (in Basel), 1546, and 1555.

Polydore Vergil was born around the year 1470, near the town of Urbino in Italy. After being sent to England by the Vatican, he became involved in the English court. Vergil was encouraged by Henry VII to complete his history of England, and he produced the first version of his *Historia Anglica* sometime between 1512 and 1513 (Gransden, *Historical Writing*, 2.425). Vergil wrote and re-edited his *Historia Anglica* over a thirty-year period, resulting in the publication of a third edition in 1555. Vergil's chronicle has been of particular interest in modern scholarship (see, e.g., Hay, *Polydore Vergil*). He is considered among the most influential humanist scholars of his day, but he was also controversial, particularly with regards to his scepticism of the authenticity of Geoffrey of Monmouth's version of early British history (see Lupack, "Arthurian Legend," p. 341, and Grandsen, *Historical Writing*, 2.436–37). Vergil's discussion of Owain Glyndŵr's revolt is striking in its portrayal of the Welsh as a community that was fractured and divided. Vergil's depiction can, in part, be explained by his involvement in Tudor propaganda, particularly his role in justifying The Act of Union, introduced between 1536 and 1543 in the reign of Henry VIII, which established the formal assimilation of England and Wales. The representation of Wales pre-1485 as in a state of chaos and disorder allowed Tudor chroniclers to justify the Union of Wales, and indeed celebrate the accession of the Tudor monarchs, who were, of course, Welsh themselves (see, e.g., Fox, *Politics and Literature*, pp. 110–13).

1–6   Here, Vergil suggests that the Welsh revolt was caused by internal problems, namely, the "mutual bickering of its nobles." This is a significant shift away from the notion of the rebellion as initiated because of conflicts between Owain Glyndŵr and Lord Grey or Henry IV, which implicitly frames the conflict as "Welsh" against "English." In Vergil the cause of the rebellion was internal to Wales.

98. WILLIAM BALDWIN, *MIRROR FOR MAGISTRATES*

Ed. Scott Lucas.

Print: William Baldwin et al., *A Myrroure for Magistrates* (London,1559), fols. 18v–23v.

In 1554, the printer John Wayland determined to publish a new edition of John Lydgate's fifteenth-century classic *The Fall of Princes*, a work comprising poems narrating the tragic ends of famous men and women from the beginning of time to the fourteenth century. Wayland commissioned the celebrated mid-Tudor author William Baldwin and seven other poets to create a specifically British continuation of Lydgate's *Fall*, one he could append to his new edition. Titling their work *A Memorial of suche Princes, as since the tyme of king Richard the seconde, haue been vnfortunate in the Realme of England*, Baldwin and his fellow authors followed Lydgate's practice of presenting ghosts of famous historical "princes" whose stories exemplified either the cruel vicissitudes of fortune or the tragic consequences of evil living. The *Memorial* authors departed from Lydgate's model, however, by presenting their poems in the voices of the ghosts themselves, by offering prose discussions of the tragedies as a means of linking the poems to each other, and by handling only fallen British figures.

Several of the authors who contributed poems to the *Memorial* were fierce opponents of the political policies of their current monarch, Queen Mary I, and their use of their supposedly historical tragedies to protest obliquely against political actions of their own time led to the suppression of the *Memorial* before it could be released to the public. Its poems were only published in 1559, the year after Mary's death, under the new title *A Mirror for Magistrates*. The work became an immediate best seller. In response to its popularity, Baldwin offered a new volume of *Mirror* tragedies in 1563, and over the following sixty years poets unconnected with the original group of authors contributed numerous new pieces to this ever-expanding collection.

Baldwin's source for his Glyndŵr poem is Edward Hall's *Union of the two noble and illustre famelies of Lancastre & Yorke* (Item 95). As a man of Welsh ancestry, Baldwin tempers Hall's blanket condemnation of the Welsh as a "wyld and savage" race (Item 95.186). Instead, Baldwin praises the men and women of Wales for "the bewty of theyr blood" (line 54) and their noble descent from Britain's first civilized people, the Britons. When he does condemn Welshmen, he condemns most strongly only particular individuals who choose to do wrong, namely false prophets and the riotous Glyndŵr and his followers, whose malicious activities he blames on their poor upbringing rather than on any defect in the Welsh national character.

12–16   In the suppressed 1554 edition, Baldwin begins this sentence with "Howbeit Owen Glendour because he is a man of that countrey whence (as the welchmen beare me in hand) my Petigre is discended, althoughe he be but a slender prince, yet rather then he should be forgotten, I wyll tell his tale for him vnder the priuilege of Martin Hundred." *Martin Hundred* is likely a colloquial name for Castlemartin Hundred, a jurisdictional unit of Pembrokeshire located in the Anglophone section of Wales known as Little England beyond Wales. Baldwin's family apparently had its roots in this area.

41–47   Baldwin's claim that Glyndŵr was poorly reared is his own creation, one that allows him to promote the humanist credos that "good bringing up" makes the man and true nobility is found only in character and not in blood. In his collection of classical adages *The Treatise of Morall Philosophie* (1548), Baldwin included the maxims "It is a shame for a man to desyre honor because of his noble progenitours, & not to deserue it through his owne vertue"; and "he that to his noble lynage addeth vertue and good condicions is to be praysed."

68   I.e., even Arthur's heir is a churl if he lives amiss. To convey better this sense, Baldwin changes "He Arthurs" to "Yea Arthurs" in the second edition of the *Mirror* (1563). The Welsh understood themselves to be the direct descendants of King Arthur's race, the Britons.

72   According to Geoffrey of Monmouth, Merlin was fathered by an incubus.

74–75   According to Geoffrey of Monmouth, the Welsh are the progeny of the original Britons, whose line originated with the Trojan Brutus. Baldwin playfully rhymes the name of this progenitor (*Brute*) with what Owain became (*a brute*), no doubt also thinking of how this story is told in British histories (each called a *Brut*).

160–64   I.e., the Percies deemed it fitter for Henry IV to redeem Mortimer than to "rob" a man who fought in his service ("his Souldier," Lord Henry Percy) of his prisoners.

174–80   For this prophecy, often called the *Prophecy of the Six Kings*, see Item 1.

176   The prophet's characterization of Henry IV as Gogmagog is Baldwin's own invention. According to Geoffrey of Monmouth, Gogmagog was the only one of the original Albion race of giants not slain by Brutus and his men in their conquest of Britain. He was later killed during a wrestling match with the Trojan Corineus. In August 1554, just at the time Baldwin and his fellow authors were composing their poems, London officials placed a statue of Gogmagog at the entrance to London Bridge as part of the pageantry welcoming Queen Mary I and her new husband Philip of Spain on their first royal entry into the city. Baldwin characterizes Gogmagog as "accurst of god" (line 178) not based on Geoffrey but almost certainly on the words of Revelation 20:8, which identify Gog and Magog as agents of Satan.

248–50   These horrific details are apparently Baldwin's own creations.

99. ROBERT GLOVER, *GLYNDŴR'S PEDIGREE*

Adapted and trans. John K. Bollard, from Rees and Jones, *Thomas Matthews's Welsh Records in Paris*, p. 122.

Manuscript: London, British Library, Harleian MS 807, fol. 95.

British Library Harleian MS 807 is a folio book of pedigrees written for the most part by Robert Glover, Somerset Herald, during the years 1570–1577. For a discussion of this pedigree and its relation to other records of Owain's ancestry, see pp. 425–30. Matthews comments somewhat vaguely, "The pedigree is almost contemporaneous, and seems to have been drawn up for the Scudamore family" (*Records*, p. 129). This suggests the possibility that the pedigree may have been drawn up c.1430–33 to illuminate Alice's (or her husband's) rights of inheritance in regard to her father's confiscated lands (see note on *Johannes Skudemore* below and Item 10). Of the six sons and five daughters of Owain and his wife Margaret (not to mention three other children of Owain), the *Stemma Aliciae* names only Alice (for the others, see Bartrum [1974], s.n. Bleddyn ap Cynfyn 5, 1.32). Owain's sole surviving son, Maredudd, was offered a pardon in April 1417 which he accepted in April 1421 (Lloyd, *Owen Glendower*, p. 144n2; Davies, *Revolt*, p. 310), thus, no claim to Owain's patrimony could have been made effectively by Scudamore before then, nor indeed before Maredudd's death at some now unknown date. If the *Stemma* was designed to further Alice's and her husband's claims to her father's estates, it would seem rather counter-productive to identify Owain twice as *proditor Rg. H. 4* [traitor to King Henry IV]. The wording of a notice of 1433 in the *Calendar of Patent Rolls* naming Alice as "daughter and heir of Owen ap Glendourdy the traitor" is sufficiently close to that of the *Stemma* to suggest that the latter derives from or is closely related to some such

English official record (see note to *Johannes Skudemore* below). The Scudamore connection might also account for the absence of Owain's other children in the *Stemma*.

Whatever the reason for producing it, the pedigree's central feature is that it lays out the lines through which Owain Glyndŵr was believed to be descended from the three major major Welsh dynasties: Powys, Deheubarth, and Gwynedd. But while Matthews further notes that the pedigree "is not strictly in accord with others in the paternal line," he says nothing about the highly questionable maternal line which appears here and in other sources, and which is in accord with the propagandistic version of the Tudor pedigree claiming direct descent from Llywelyn ab Iorwerth (*Records*, p. 129).

The following notes attempt to identify the listed names, separated for ease of discussion into the paternal and maternal lines. The repetition of names in the family, especially Gruffudd and Madog, seems to have led to some confusion or elision of generations.

Paternal line:

Madocus. Owain's paternal lineage begins here with Madog ap Gruffudd Maelor ap Madog ap Maredudd. Madog ap Maredudd died in 1160, the last ruler of a united Powys, and through him comes Owain's claim to the rule of Powys. Madog ap Gruffudd Maelor died in 1236 and was buried at Valle Crucis abbey, which he had founded in 1201, the last Cistercian foundation in Wales.

Griffith, Dominus de Bromfield. Gruffudd ap Madog (d. 1269/70) was also known as Gruffudd Maelor (see Lloyd, *History*, Index, s.v. *Gruffydd ap Madog ap Gruffydd [Maelor II]*). Bromfield is the English name of Maelor Gymraeg (see Item 5n7).

Filia Jacobi Audley. After her husband's death, the dowager Emma Audley inherited Maelor Saesneg, which never again came under Welsh rule (Lloyd, *History*, p. 746).

Madoc Vichan. Vichan (Welsh *Fychan*, from *bychan* [small]) as a name element has no reference to size; it is generally used, much like modern English *junior* to specify the son of a father with the same name. But this Madog's father was named Gruffudd, not Madog; thus, *Fychan* in this case may represent confusion with his father's brother Madog (d. 1269), who was known as Madog Fychan (Lloyd, *History*, p. 747n162).

Johanni Com' wavemiae. John de Warren, the 5th Earl of Surrey, was married to Henry III's half sister. He served Edward I during his Welsh wars and was subsequently awarded the lordships of Bromfield and Iâl.

Leolinus. Llywelyn ap Gruffudd ap Madog (d. 1282) inherited the region south of the Dee, becoming the Lord of Chirk. His holdings included Glyndyfrdwy and half of Cynllaith (Lloyd, *History*, p. 747–48 and n166; *Owen Glendower*, p. 9).

Griffith Vawer Gwynn. The second element in *Griffith Vawer Gwynn* as printed in Matthews should be emended to *Varwn* (i.e., *Farwn*, from *barwn* [baron]). He was also known as Gruffudd Fychan and was one of the very few of princely lineage to survive the Edwardian conquest of 1282. On 12 February 1283 King Edward I granted Glyndyfrdwy to him, to hold as tenant at will, though on 22 July 1284, letters patent revised that holding to *per baronium* [as a baron], as his ancestors had held it before him. Thus, while he still held his lands *ad voluntatem Regis* [at the will of the King], it was through the traditional Welsh tenure of *pennaethium* or "Welsh barony" (see Item 5n1; Lloyd, *Owen Glendower*, pp. 10–11, 13–14; Davies, *Revolt*, pp. 133–34). The epithet *Gwyn(n)* [white] is a not uncommon descriptive term, meaning "white-haired." "Gruffudd Fychan, the third son of Gruffudd ab Madog, Lord of Dinas Brân and Prince of Powys Fadog, was surnamed "Y Barwn Gwyn", or the White Baron, and had the lordships of Glyndfrdwy and Iâl for his share of his father's territories (Lloyd, *History of . . . Powys Fadog*, p. 194; see also Bartrum [1974], s.n. Bleddyn ap Cynfyn 4, 1.131).

avus Owyn Glyndore. Though *avus* might be understood (somewhat redundantly) in the broad sense of "descendant," by naming the White Baron as Owain's "grandfather," the compiler of the *Stemma* seems to have confused him with Gruffudd ap Madog, known as Gruffudd o'r Rhuddallt (see p. 427). There are thus two or three generations missing, depending on whether Madog Grupl and Madog Fychan are one person or two (probably one; see p. 426; Item 5 headnote; Lloyd, *Owen Glendower*, p. 12n4). Assuming only one Madog in this gap, Gruffudd Farwn Gwyn was Owain's great-great-grandfather. Iolo Goch may have similarly skipped three earlier generations in his poem, conflating the present Gruffudd with Gruffudd Maelor (see Item 5n21–22).

Filius, Dominus de Kynlleith. Owain (d. 1282), the fourth son of Gruffudd, inherited half of Cynllaith, including Bangor Iscoed (Bangor-on-Dee), south of Oswestry (Lloyd, *Owen Glendower*, p. 9; *History*, p. 748).

Griffith Vichan. Owain's father, Gruffudd Fychan, died before 1370–71, when his wife is described as "lately (*jadis*) the wife of Gruffudd of Glyndyfrdwy" (Smith, "Glyn Dŵr").

Alicia, filia et haeres. Alice (or Welsh, Alys) appears in some genealogical sources as Elizabeth, though she is named Alice in several official English records (see *Rotuli Parliamentorum*, 4.440; *Calendar of the Patent Rolls*, 2.286; Bartrum [1974], s.n. Bleddyn ap Cynfyn 5, 1.32; and the note on *Johannes Skudemore* below). The use of the phrase *filia et haeres* here and with Llywelyn's only daughter and Thomas ap Llywelyn's wife, suggests that inheritance rights might indeed be a concern of this pedigree (see notes on *Johannes Skudemore*, *Unica filia*, and *Alionora* below).

Johannes Skudemore. Sir John Scudamore (later Skidmore) was King Henry's steward of Kidwelly castle and was custodian of Carreg Cennen castle in 1403 when it was attacked by Glyndŵr (see Item 32). His marriage to Glyndŵr's daughter Alice can hardly have been prior to this time, and may have been considerably later. The tradition persists that Owain spent his last years in hiding with one of his daughters, and a branch of that tradition suggests the Scudamore family seat at Kentchurch, Herefordshire, as the location (Davies, *Revolt*, pp. 318, 322; *NLW Biographies Online*, s.v. *Scudamore family*). In 1430 Scudamore attempted to have the decree of outlawry against Glyndŵr reversed, in order to recover his wife's rights to inheritance of her father's lands; this plan backfired in 1433, however, when Scudamore was removed from office for having married in contravention of the 1401 statute (4 Hen. IV, c.34) forbidding an Englishman to marry a Welshwoman (Lloyd, *Owen Glendower*, p. 144n6; Davies, *Revolt*, p. 322). Scudamore's loss of status is recorded in the *Calendar of Patent Rolls* for 8

August 1433: "Granted, during pleasure, by advice of the council, to Edmund Beauford, count of Mortayn, of the offices of constable of the castle of Kermerdyn [*Carmarthen*], and of the stewardship of 'walstot' of the commotes of Whigidada [W *Gwidigada*] and Elvet [W *Elfed*] in South Wales, to be discharged by him or his deputies, with the accustomed wages, fees and profits; John Skydemore, knight, as the said Edmund has shewn, being no longer eligible to hold the premises under the ordinance made in the Parliament of 4 Henry IV, he having married Alice daughter and heir of Owen ap Glendourdy the traitor" (*Calendar of the Patent Rolls, Henry VI*, 2.286). For the office of 'walstot,' from W *gwalstod*, lit. "interpreter," *GPC* notes that the Latinized form *Walstottus* appears in the fourteenth century as the title of "a special official in the Welshry of Carmarthen" (*GPC*, s.v. *gwalstod*).

Maternal line:

The confusion in this branch of the *Stemma* is discussed in greater detail on pp. 427–30. A significant contributing factor seems to have been a faulty memory of Philip ab Ifor's marriage to the daughter of Llywelyn ap Iorwerth (not Llywelyn ap Gruffudd). Another may have been the fact that one of Owain's paternal great-grandmothers shared the name Gwenllian with Llywelyn ap Gruffudd's only daughter; it is she who provides Owain's connection to the Gwynedd dynasty; she was descended from Gruffudd ap Cynan, king of Gwynedd from 1079 to 1137, through her mother Adles, daughter of Richard ap Cadwaladr ap Gruffudd ap Cynan (see also the headnote to Item 5).

Llewellinus. Llywelyn ap Gruffudd (d. 1282) was the last independent Welsh Prince of Wales. He is first seen using the title *Princeps Wallie* in a treaty with a group of noblemen of Scotland in 1258 (Edwards, *Littere*, p. 184). Owain's claim to Llywelyn's title and the rule of all Wales derives not from Llywelyn directly, but from Owain's paternal great-grandmother's relationship to the Gwynedd dynasty through Gruffudd ap Cynan.

Philip ap Yvor. Philip ab Ifor was clerk to Dafydd ap Llywelyn ab Iorwerth in 1241 and was married to Llywelyn ab Iorwerth's daughter, Angharad (Edwards, *Littere*, pp. 18, 153; Bartrum [1974], s.n. Gruffydd ap Cynan 4, 3.446).

Lord of Yscoyd. Is Coed is a commote in southern Ceredigion, a portion of which Owain laid claim to through the joint inheritance of his mother and her sister (see Item 5n90). Might the fact that Philip's title is given in English indicate a later addition to an earlier pedigree?

Unica filia et haeres. Gwenllian, the only child of Llywelyn ap Gruffudd, was born in June 1282, just six months before her father's death. After the capture and execution of her uncle, Dafydd ap Gruffudd, in 1283, Gwenllian was commited by the king to the Gilbertine convent at Sempringham in Lincolnshire, far from Wales, as is summarized in *Brut y Tywysogion*, "And a marriage was solemnized between Llywelyn and Eleanor. . . . And by her the prince had a daughter, who was called Gwenllian. And Eleanor died giving birth to her. . . . And that Gwenllian, after the prince's death, was taken into captivity to England; and before her coming of age she was made a nun against her will" (Jones, *Brut* [1952], p. 117). On her entry into this pedigree, see pp. 427–30.

Thomas ap Llywelyn. Owain was descended through his maternal grandfather from Rhys ap Gruffudd, now known as *yr Arglwydd Rhys* [the Lord Rhys] (d. 1197), and through him from Rhys ap Tewdwr (d. 1093), who established the dynasty of Deheubarth.

Owen ap Rhese. Emended to *Owen ap [Griffin ap] Rhese.* Gruffudd (d. 1201), the son of the Lord Rhys has been omitted.

Alionora, filia et haeres. Thomas ap Llywelyn's first wife was indeed Elinor, but she was not a granddaughter of Llywelyn ap Gruffudd. Bartrum notes that her ancestry is in doubt and lists her as possibly Thomas's niece as well, the daughter of his sister Lleucu and her husband, Maredudd ab Owain ap Maredudd. Bartrum does not list any children for Philip and Angharad, and he notes, "There is much disagreement in the genealogies about the ancestry of Thomas's wife Elinor, sometimes made into two. Some versions are definitely fictitious, the others (shown here) open to doubt" (Bartrum [1974], s.n. Rhys ap Tewdwr 7, 4.782).

Elena. Owain's mother; see the notes on *Griffith Vichan* and *Thomas ap Llywelyn* above (see also Bartrum [1974], s.n. Rhys ap Tewdwr 7, 4.782).

100. RAPHAEL HOLINSHED, *CHRONICLES*

Ed. Scott Lucas.

Print: Raphael Holinshed et al., *The first and second [and third] volumes of Chronicles . . . first collected and published by Raphaell Holinshed, William Harrison, and others: now newlie augmented . . . to the yeare 1586* (London, 1587), vol. 6, pp. 518–24, 527–28, 530–31, 533. This 1587 edition of Holinshed's *Chronicles* divides its text into six sections, which it calls volumes; confusingly, its title page uses the same word "volumes" to denote the three larger divisions, each with its own title page, in which the six volumes of text itself are contained. The Glyndŵr material is found in volume 6 of the text, which is contained in volume 3 of the larger division of the material.

Raphael Holinshed (c.1525–1580) was an employee of the learned London printer Reyner Wolfe. Together, Wolfe and Holinshed undertook to compose a comprehensive historical and geographical account of the entire world. Wolfe's death in 1573 ended hopes for this work; however, a new group of printers and booksellers soon encouraged Holinshed to continue the project as a history and description solely of the British Isles. In composing the historical sections of his text, Holinshed wove together the work of numerous earlier chroniclers, exercising himself more as an editor and synthesizer of other men's writings than as a creator of new material. Holinshed's *Chronicles of England, Scotland, and Ireland* came from the press in 1577, and such was its popularity that after Holinshed's death in the early 1580s a new consortium of authors formed to create a second edition of Holinshed's massive production. Led by Abraham Fleming, these augmenters added new matter to the 1577 text gleaned either from authorities unused by Holinshed or, as is the case with Fleming's description of the desecration of the corpses at the Battle of Bryn Glas, from material found in Holinshed's own sources that Holinshed himself had simply omitted. The second edition of Holinshed's *Chronicles* appeared in 1587; soon after, Shakespeare employed it as the chief source for his history plays, including *1 Henry IV* (Item 101).

5–10   *This Owen Glendouer . . . was surnamed Glindour Dew.* Holinshed credits the sixteenth-century antiquarian and chronicler John Stow for his information about Glyndŵr's parentage and the etymology of his name. Three years after the first edition of Holinshed's work, Stow himself would refer to Glyndŵr uniformly as "Glendouerdew" in his own *Chronicles of England* (London, 1580).

11–29   Holinshed derives this information and much of that in the paragraphs that follow from Thomas Walsingham, *Chronica maiora*, a contemporary account of English affairs from 1376 to 1420 recorded in the famous *St. Albans chronicle* (Item 68).

45–55   Holinshed's primary source for this information is Walsingham, *Chronica maiora* (Item 68). Holinshed, however, adds to Walsingham's simple mention of "Edmundus de Mortemer" the words *earle of Marche*, in order to assert that it was Edmund Mortimer, earl of March, whom Glyndŵr captured rather than the man he actually seized: the earl's uncle, Sir Edmund Mortimer. Holinshed makes this change in order to align Walsingham's text with his chief source for his fifteenth-century material, Edward Hall's *Union of the two noble and illustre famelies of Lancastre & Yorke* (Item 95). It was Hall who first put into print the confusion between the two Mortimers that Holinshed and Shakespeare both famously introduced into their own works.

56–70   This paragraph and those following weave together information derived from both Hall (Item 95) and the *St. Albans Chronicle* (Item 68).

81–83   Holinshed's direct translation of Walsingham's "huius" as *this man* here leaves potentially unclear just who experienced the prodigy of the bloody stables at his birth. The reference is in fact to Mortimer (see Items 28 and 68); however, Holinshed's phrasing might be misread to suggest that it was Glyndŵr who received this sign. It was possibly such a misunderstanding of Holinshed's ambiguous language that led Shakespeare to have his own Owen Glendower insist that his birth was marked by prodigies and wonders (see *1 Henry IV*, 3.1; Item 101).

87–88   *(as some write).* I.e. Edward Hall, whom Holinshed follows for his information about the Percies and their quarrels with Henry IV.

121   *(as some have said).* Namely Edward Hall and the unnamed "certayne writer" Hall follows for his claims about the *Tripartite Indenture* (Item 47) and the false prophecy that allegedly occasioned it (see Items 82 and 95).

137–57   Holinshed's sources for this paragraph are Thomas Walsingham and Edward Hall. However, the marginal ascriptions are reversed: Hall supplies the opening and closing material of this paragraph, while Walsingham provides the information about the origin of Henry Percy's army and Worcester's departure from the Prince of Wales's household.

158–72   Holinshed's source for this and the next paragraph is Walsingham, *Chronica maiora* (Item 68).

180–98   This paragraph is the work of Holinshed continuer Abraham Fleming, who draws on Thomas Walsingham, *Ypodigma Neustriae* (London, 1574), a printed abridgment of the *Chronica maiora*. Fleming oddly places Walsingham's count of more than 1,000 dead at the Battle of Bryn Glas (fought in the year 1402) and his description of the Welsh women's desecration of the English corpses there only after Holinshed's account of the later Battle of Pwll Melyn and the capture of Glyndŵr's chancellor (both events of 1405).

184–95   Fleming's classical sources are M. Junianus Justinus, *Historiarum Philippicarum . . . libri XLIV*, and Herodotus, *Histories*, for the story of Tomyris; and Valerius Maximus, *Factorum et dictorum memoribilium libri IX*, for the account of Fulvia and Cicero.

199–213   Holinshed's source for this paragraph is Walsingham, *Chronica maiora*.

214–17   Holinshed follows Walsingham in placing this French expedition in the year 1405. Both Enguerrand de Monstrelet and Edward Hall place it in the year 1403 (see Items 80 and 95). Holinshed follows Hall exclusively, however, for much of his account of this expedition, and he thus repeats Hall's error in identifying the leader of the French forces as the sixteenth-century marshal Anne de Montmorency rather than the fifteenth-century marshal Jean de Rieux.

251–52   In naming Patrouillart de Trie the brother of the marshal of France, Holinshed repeats an error shared by both Monstrelet and Hall: Patrouillart de Trie's brother Regnault de Trie was the admiral, but not marshal, of France.

254   *to the number (as some have written) of five hundred*. The author who claims 500 French gentlemen were lost is Edward Hall.

264–67   Compare Monstrelet's account, Item 80.

268–76   Holinshed's source for this and the next paragraph is Walsingham, *Chronica maiora*.

283–89   For the details of Glyndŵr's demise, Holinshed follows Edward Hall. Hall presents Glyndŵr's death as occurring shortly after the Battle of Shrewsbury (1403), however, and not, as Holinshed does, in the year 1409.

101. WILLIAM SHAKESPEARE, *HENRY IV, PART 1*

    Ed. by William A. Oram

Text: The copy-text, designated as **Q1** below, is the digital reproduction of the 1598 Quarto (STC 22280) made by Early English Books On Line. Three probable misprints (on lines 101, 130 and 133) have been corrected in accordance with the 1623 Folio, designated **F** below. Spelling and punctuation have been modernized.

The first part of *Henry IV* was very likely performed in 1587, and a few pages remain of a quarto (Q0) published in 1598; the first quarto of which we have a complete copy (Q1) was published later that year, with the compendious title *The history of Henrie the Fourth; vvith the battell at Shrewsburie, betweene the King and Lord Henry Percy, surnamed Henry Hotspur of the north. VVith the humorous conceits of Sir Iohn Falstalffe [sic]. Newly corrected by W. Shake-speare.* Contemporary references suggest that it was a popular work, and there were subsequent quartos in 1599, 1604, 1608, 1613 and 1622. The play appears in the first folio of Shakespeare's works in 1623. In addition to these printed text, around 1522 Sir Edward Dering commissioned a manuscript compilation of the two parts of *Henry IV*. Dering was concerned above all with the political content of the plays and cut much of the rest; in III.i he omitted the section in which Glendower's daughter sings to her husband.

1	*Hotspur*. Henry Percy, nicknamed "Hotspur" for his speed and readiness in battle, was born in 1364, though Shakespeare portrays him as about the same age as Prince Henry (Prince Hal), who was 16 at the time of the Battle of Shrewsbury in 1403. He was brother-in-law to Sir Edmund Mortimer.
	Worcester. Thomas Percy, 1st Earl of Worcester, was Hotspur's uncle. He was beheaded for his part in the rebellion two days after the battle of Shrewsbury, in which his nephew was killed (Davies, *Revolt*, p. 185).
	Lord Mortimer. Sir Edmund Mortimer (d. 1409) was the uncle of Edmund Mortimer, 5th Earl of March (d. 1425), and became in 1402 the husband of Owain Glyndŵr's daughter, Catrin. In naming Sir Edmund as earl of March, Shakespeare confuses uncle and nephew.
16	*cressets*. A cresset is an iron cup or basket holding oil or pitch and hung or mounted on a pole as a torch or lantern.
26–36	The passage treats wind trapped in and eventually escaping from the earth (commonly thought to cause earthquakes) as both a sickness ("colic") and a birth, paralleling Glendower's.
59	*shame the devil*. Proverbial. The devil is the father of lies and hence to tell truth is to shame him.
101	*cantle*. From F; Q1: *scantle*.
126	*helpful ornament* [useful embellishment]. I.e., he added music to the words, and new poetry to the language.
130	*meter*. From F; Q1: *miter*.
133	*on*. From F; Q1: *an*.
149	*moldwarpe* [mole]. Holinshed comments on the "vaine prophesie" "as thugh King Henrie was the moldwarpe, cursed of Gods owne mouth, and they three were the dragon, the lion and the wolfe, which should divide this realme betweene them. Such is the deviation (saith Hall) and not divination of those blind and fantasticall dreames of the Welsh prophesiers" (Item 100.121–26).

153   *couching . . . rampant*. Couching [couchant, lying down] and ramping [rampant, standing erect] are heraldic terms. Hotspur's account of the prophecies parodies heraldic insignia.

195   *My daughter*. Edmund Mortimer married Owain Glyndŵr's daughter Catrin in the autumn of 1402, after he had been captured in the summer at the Battle of Bryn Glas and subsequently joined Owain in rebellion.

215   *ravishing division*. In the 16th and 17th centuries a variation on a tune was known as a division, because usually each repetition of a tune was played by breaking up a melody into quicker phrases with more notes to a measure, i.e., "dividing" quarter notes (crotchets) into eighth notes (quavers) and sixteenth notes (semiquavers), etc.

234   *Kate*. Elizabeth Mortimer (b. 1371), the sister of Sir Edmund Mortimer, was the child-bride of Henry Percy, and was thus somewhat older than she is portrayed in the play. Shakespeare, however, has Hotspur call her "Kate"; Hall names her "Elinor," which Holinshed renders as "Elianor" (Maguire, "'Household Kates,'" p. 131).

247   *'tis a woman's fault*. I.e., it is women who are too silent (Hotspur's characteristic irony).

255–62   This passage mocks the supposed bourgeois restraint of Kate's language.

258   *sarcenet*. Sarcenet was a soft silk dress-material.

259   Finsbury was a field outside London where its inhabitants might walk; hence Kate is like a middle-class Londoner instead of an aristocratic northern Lady.

263   *velvet guards*. Rather grand overskirts, to protect a woman's dress from the mud, hence the wives of bourgeois "Sunday citizens."

266   *'Tis the next . . . teacher*. Neither acting like a tailor (supposed to sing at his work) nor teaching a bird to sing is fit occupation for a noble wife.

ESSAYS ON OWAIN GLYNDŴR

Great Seal of Owain Glyndŵr (obverse). Comparison with the reverse side reveals that the full legend read *Owenus Dei gratia princeps Wallie* [Owain, by the grace of God prince of Wales]. Owain is depicted enthroned holding a scepter, his feet upon two lions, his arms upon two wolves (or perhaps dragons). Behind him two angels raise up a cloth with the arms of the Gwynedd dynasty: four lions rampant. Courtesy of the National Museum of Wales.

Great Seal of Owain Glyndŵr (reverse). Comparison with the obverse side reveals that the full legend read *Owenus Dei gratia princeps Wallie* [Owain, by the grace of God prince of Wales]. Owain is depicted astride a charging mount, and both he and his horse wear a dragon crest. On his shield are four lions rampant, the arms of the Gwynedd dynasty that became his own. Courtesy of the National Museum of Wales.

John K. Bollard
Owain Glyndŵr, *Princeps Wallie*

On 16 September 1400, at a fateful meeting with important supporters and kinsmen, Owain ap Gruffudd, lord of Glyndyfrdwy, was declared *Princeps Wallie* [Prince of Wales], a title that appears in subsequent documents and on the Great Seal that Owain began to use not long afterward (see previous pages).[1] In order to give validity to his claim to that title, Owain would need to demonstrate his descent from the ruling lines of Powys, Deheubarth, and — perhaps most importantly — Gwynedd.[2] Llywelyn ap Gruffudd of Gwynedd (known to posterity in Welsh as *Llywelyn ein Llyw Olaf* [Llywelyn, our last ruler] and in English as Llywelyn the Last), had been the first to use the title *Princeps Wallie* as early as 1258, later styling himself *Princeps Wallie et Dominus Snaudonie* [prince of Wales and lord of Snowdonia], as also adopted by his brother Dafydd after Llywelyn's death in December 1282.[3] After Dafydd's capture and execution six months later, the title was no longer used in Wales.

Whether Owain had a legitimate claim to this title according to Welsh law and custom is a matter of some complexity: as we will see, his descent from two of the three major Welsh dynasties is traced through female members of his ancestry. While there are conflicting statements in the Welsh law texts regarding the ability of women to inherit land, the ancient practice, as R. R. Davies states succinctly, was that "a woman of Welsh status could *not* inherit land nor could a title to land be inherited through the female line."[4] As English law was imposed to varying degrees after 1282, it became increasingly important to establish whether a woman had English or Welsh status, for English law *did* recognize a woman's right to inherit land.[5]

---

[1] For names of those believed to be principals at this meeting, see Item 11.11–16. For Owain's use of the title, see, e.g., Items 43.1, 46.1, 52.1. On Owain's name, see Williams' essay in this volume.

[2] The significance of Gwynedd to Owain's assumption of the title to all Wales is evidenced not least by his adoption of the Gwynedd coat of arms, which appears on his Great and Privy Seals and on the armorial decorative harness mounting found at Harlech Castle, shown on the cover of this book.

[3] Edwards, *Littere Wallie*, pp. 74, 184; Smith, *Llywelyn*, pp. 2, 161–62. The prefaces to the Welsh and Latin law texts all identify Hywel Dda (d. 950) as *rex totius Wallie* or *tywysog Cymry oll* [king/prince of all Wales], though the earliest manuscripts are from the thirteenth century, and this may not represent Hywel's own style.

[4] Davies, "Status of Women," p. 100, his italics. See *Llyfr Iorwerth*: "According to the men of Gwynedd a woman is not entitled to have patrimony, since she is not entitled to two status in one hand, that is, her husband's patrimony and her own"; *Llyfr Blegywryd*: "If an owner of land has no other heir than a daughter, the daughter will be heir of all the land" (both translations from Jenkins, *Law*, p. 107; Wiliam, *Llyfr Iorwerth*, p. 56, and Williams and Powell, *Cyfreithiau*, p. 75).

[5] In the Statute of Rhuddlan (1284), Edward I made provision for Welsh women to receive dower land from their husband's estates which they could continue to hold after a husband's death; however, this provision was not applied equally throughout the principality or in the Marcher lordships

425

When the system began to change in the fifteenth century, we find the phrase "Welsh custom to the contrary as used from ancient time notwithstanding" appended to deeds of enfeoffment allowing daughters to succeed in the absence of male heirs.[6] But Owain Glyndŵr was not making a claim of inheritance to land; rather he was assuming the title *Princeps Wallie* as the closest surviving descendant of all three princely lines. In this instance his legal status, and even that of his mother and aunt, may not be strictly relevant as a matter of heritable rights according to Welsh law; subsequent events show that it was sufficient that other Welsh leaders and much of the populace recognized Owain, presumably through his descent as well as his military prowess, as their best representative for regaining independence. Regardless of our present uncertainties over how Owain made his claim during his own lifetime, there is no indication that his comrades-in-arms accepted it as anything but legitimate.

Three sources in this book present versions of Owain's genealogy, though they do not fully agree on the details: *Achau Owain Glyndŵr* (or *Owain Glyndŵr's Lineage*, Item 6), Iolo Goch's detailed poem on the subject, composed for and undoubtedly sung to Owain himself in the 1380s; *Stemma Aliciae* (or *Glyndŵr's Pedigree*, Item 99), set out in a book of pedigrees collected by Robert Glover, Somerset Herald, dated 1570–1577, but undoubtedly from an earlier unknown source; and a brief genealogical statement in John Leland's *Itinerary of Wales*, dated 1536–1539 (Item 94). These are representative in general terms of the various pedigrees and other sources for Owain's lineage. The most thorough and reliable modern compendium and collocation of Welsh genealogical sources (including some of the items discussed here) is that of Peter C. Bartrum, recorded in the *Welsh Genealogies, A.D. 300–1400* in 1974. That the early genealogical sources are not in complete agreement with each other, as discussed below, is as much a reflection of the reasons for which such pedigrees are drawn up as it is the result of faulty memory or record keeping.

Owain's descent from the line of Powys is relatively consistent in the surviving pedigrees, in which his paternal ancestry is traced back directly through nine, or possibly eight, generations to Madog ap Maredudd, *Rex Powissentium*, the last ruler of a united Powys, who died in 1160.[7] The uncertainty as to the number of generations results from the possibility that Owain's great-grandfather, Madog Fychan (whose heraldic slab appears at the end of this essay), may be the same person as *Madog Grupl* [Madog the cripple], who appears in some sources as the father of Madog Fychan.[8] On the other hand, if Madog Fychan were the same person as Madog Grupl, it is difficult to account for the use of Fychan, an appellative (from Welsh *bychan* [small]), used in early Welsh as a form somewhat analogous to English "Junior."[9] In the *Stemma Aliciae* (Item 99) if we understand *avus* to mean specifically "grandfather" rather than "forebear," then the *Stemma* skips one or two generations in the paternal line by making Gruffudd Farwn Gwyn the father of Gruffudd Fychan, rather than of Madog Grupl (= Madog Fychan?). There is a similar ambiguity regarding the interpretation of *goresgynnydd* [great-great-grandchild; descendant] in Iolo Goch's poem (Item 6n21–22).

(Davies, "Status of Women," pp. 101–03).

[6] Davies, "Status of Women," pp.100–01.

[7] Lloyd, *History*, pp. 492–93 and note 24.

[8] Lloyd, *Owen Glendower*, p. 12n4.

[9] As the English use of surnames spread to Wales during the fifteenth century, *Fychan* developed into the family name Vaughan.

Owain's descent from the line of Deheubarth is not quite as strong as that from the line of Powys, because it is through his mother's side of the family. Owain's mother Elen was the daughter of Thomas ap Llywelyn, and he is directly descended in the male line through six generations from the Lord Rhys, *Princeps Sudwallie* [ruler of Deheubarth], the grandson of Rhys ap Tewdwr, who established that southern dynasty.[10] Thomas's wife Elinor is in all likelihood also descended from the Lord Rhys, as discussed below.

Owain's descent from the Gwynedd dynasty is yet more distant. Though on his father's side, it passes through two of his female forebears. The wife of Madog Fychan, and hence Owain's great-grandmother, was Gwenllian, and her mother was Adles, the daughter of Richard ap Calwaladr ap Gruffudd ap Cynan. It was Gruffudd ap Cynan (1055–1137) who definitively established the powerful line of rulers of Gwynedd which came to an end with the deaths of Llywelyn ap Gruffudd in 1282 and his brother Dafydd in 1283. Iolo Goch emphatically declares Owain to be the "great-grandson, God knows . . . / of Gwenllian descended from fair Cynan," and he further highlights this Gwynedd connection explicitly in the next three lines: "Our two Gwynedds say, / 'He is good — may God keep him for us — / to everyone in his patience and his understanding' " (Item 6.45–49). Owain, therefore, appears to be descended directly from Gruffudd ap Cynan through Gwenllian and her mother Adles, who was a second cousin of Llywelyn the Great, Gruffudd ap Cynan's great-grandson.

Below are listed the lines through which Owain is descended from these three major Welsh dynasties, based on the pedigrees coordinated by Bartrum (Bartrum [1974], s.n. Bleddyn ap Cynfyn 5, 1.32 et al.). Female names are printed in *italics*; = represents a marriage; + links siblings; names marked with an asterisk are mentioned by Iolo Goch in his poem.

Owain Glyndŵr's Probable Genealogy		
GWYNEDD Owain's paternal great-grandmother's line	**POWYS** Paternal Line	**DEHEUBARTH** Maternal Line
	Cynfyn*	
	Bleddyn*	Tewdwr*
	Maredudd*	Rhys
	Madog*	Gruffudd
Cynan*	Gruffudd Maelor*	The Lord Rhys*
Gruffudd	Madog	Gruffudd
Owain + Cadwaladr	Gruffudd Maelor (II)	Owain
Iorwerth Richard*	Gruffudd Farwn Gwyn	Maredudd
Llywelyn *Adles*	Madog Grupl	Owain
Gruffudd *Gwenllian**	= Madog Fychan*	Llywelyn
Llywelyn, d. 1282	Gruffudd* o'r Rhuddallt	Thomas
Dafydd, d. 1283	Gruffudd Fychan*	= *Elen*
	Owain	

At some point a tradition arose tracing Owain's Gwynedd descent on his mother's side directly from Llywelyn ap Gruffudd. While there is no evidence of this tradition prior to Owain's death, c.1416, it is reflected in the *Stemma Aliciae*, in Leland's list of Owain's maternal relatives, and in numerous genealogies of the English Tudor monarchs. The Tudor

---

[10] Smith, "Treftadaeth," esp. p. 34.

connection stems from Owain's mother's sister Marged, perhaps the daughter of Thomas's second wife Isabel rather than his first wife Elinor; Marged became the wife of Tudur ap Goronwy, and the English Tudor dynasty is descended from this union. Whether or not it was produced for the Scudamore family, as Matthews suggests, it is possible that the *Stemma Aliciae*, known only from Glover's late sixteenth-century copy, is a representative of the same (perhaps Tudor) genealogical tradition preserved by Leland.[11] The endnote that appears in a 1587 manuscript copy of a poem by Gruffudd Llwyd to Owain also reflects this tradition: "Owain's title to the Principality was that he was descended from a daughter of Llywelyn ap Gruffudd, who was slain by treachery at Builth" (Item 3.89).

The genealogical memory or record seems to have become confused especially in regard to Owain's maternal grandmother Elinor. Bartrum includes a note stating, "There is much disagreement in the genealogies about the ancestry of Thomas's wife Elinor, sometimes made into two. Some versions are definitely fictitious, the others (shown here) open to doubt."[12] Those in the *Stemma* and in Leland's *Itinerary* are almost certainly among the "definitely fictitious." According to Bartrum, the best evidence — though still "open to doubt" — shows Elinor as the daughter of Maredudd ab Owain ap Maredudd (i.e., the brother or half-brother of Llywelyn ab Owain in column 4 above), and his wife Lleucu (the daughter of the same Llywelyn). Elinor was thus removed six generations from the Lord Rhys on her father's side and seven generations on her mother's.

If there were a demonstrable line of descent from Llywelyn ap Gruffudd to Owain Glyndŵr, it would have been so important to Owain that we cannot doubt that Iolo Goch would have alluded to it in his poem. The absence of any reference to Llywelyn in the poem strongly suggests that such a relationship is highly unlikely. The following is an attempt to unravel some of the confusion; the columns below represent Owain's maternal line as it appears in the *Stemma* and in Leland.

The Spurious Gwynedd Line	
Stemma Aliciae (Item 98)	Leland's *Itinerary* (Item 93)

Llywelyn, d. 1282
a daughter = Philip ab Ifor, Lord of Is Coed
Elinor = Thomas ap Llywelyn
Elen + a daughter, wife of Tudur ap Goronwy
Owain
	Llywelyn ap Iorwerth
	Gruffudd
	Llywelyn
	Catherine
	Elinor
	Elen + *Catherine*
	Owain Maredudd
	               Owen Tudor
	               Edmund, earl of Richmond
	               Henry VII

[11] "The pedigree is almost contemporaneous, and seems to have been drawn up for the Scudamore family" (Rees and Jones, *Thomas Matthews's Welsh Records in Paris*, p. 129). With the explicit naming of Owain's *avus* [grandfather] and *pater* [father], as well as the inclusion of Alicia and her husband, John Scudamore, it is clear that the primary interest of the *Stemma* is in Owain's family; on the other hand, while it may be earlier than or independent of the Tudor genealogies, the appearance of Tudur ap Goronwy suggests possible Tudor influence.

[12] Bartrum [1974], s.n. Rhys ap Tewdwr 7, 4.782; Bartrum's parenthesis.

Llywelyn ap Gruffudd married Eleanor de Montfort by proxy in 1275 and in person in 1278. Llywelyn had no illegitimate children, at least none who are documented in known records, and thus he was without an heir until Eleanor gave birth to a daughter in June 1282.[13] Eleanor died in childbirth or very soon thereafter, and Llywelyn himself was killed in December that year. His daughter Gwenllian was given into the custody of her uncle Dafydd, but after Dafydd was captured and executed, Gwenllian and various girls and women in Dafydd's family were forcibly sent to convents in England. In 1327 Edward III granted Gwenllian an annual pension of £20, and she was kept at Sempringham Abbey in Lincolnshire until she died, c.1337.[14]

The *Stemma Aliciae* lists Owain's mother Elen as the daughter of Thomas ap Llywelyn and his wife Alionora (i.e., Elinor). Alionora, in turn, is listed not as the daughter of Maredudd ab Owain ap Maredudd, but as the daughter of Philip ab Ifor and *unica filia et haeres* [the only daughter and heir] of Llywelyn, *ultimus princeps Walliae*, making her (i.e., Gwenllian) Owain's great-grandmother. Llywelyn, *princeps Wallie*, thus becomes Owain's great-great-grandfather.

Various points now come into play. First, it is quite possible that Elinor's grandfather Llywelyn ab Owain became confused with Llywelyn ap Gruffudd. Second, we see in Iolo Goch and other sources that Owain indeed had a great-grandmother named Gwenllian, but on his father's side. Might it be that someone, remembering that Owain had claimed descent from the Gwynedd dynasty, but not knowing the details, confused (accidentally or deliberately) the two Gwenllians? Third, Philip ab Ifor is listed as the husband of Llywelyn ap Gruffudd's "only daughter." Philip ab Ifor was lord of Is Coed and in 1241 served as clerk to Dafydd ap Llywelyn ab Iorwerth.[15] Philip was indeed married to a daughter of Llywelyn, but not Gwenllian, and not Llywelyn ap Gruffudd. His wife was Angharad, the daughter of Llywelyn ab Iorwerth (d. 1240), known as Llywelyn the Great, and his wife Joan, the daughter of King John.

Though each of the pedigrees in Leland and in the *Stemma Aliciae* has details not in the other, they must share some source or influence. The major difference between their common portions is that Leland names both Elen's sister and her grandmother as Catherine, while the *Stemma* leaves them unnamed. Leland's list appears in a passage dealing with Owain Glyndŵr, but it is clearly drawn from a source recording the Welsh pedigree of the Tudors. According to tradition, upon his succession Henry VII had a commission formed to establish his Welsh ancestry, with a panel that included the Welsh poet, genealogist, and polymath Gutun Owain (fl. 1450–1498).[16] The pedigrees for Henry VII recorded by David

---

[13] Bartrum lists an illegitimate son Madog and his descendants, but notes, "This Madog is probably an error for Madog ap Llywelyn ap Maredudd" (Bartrum [1974], s.n. Gruffudd ap Cynan 5, 3.447). In October-November 1282, Archbishop Peckham tried unsuccessfully to negotiate peace with an offer from the king of a lordship in England worth 1,000 that Llywelyn's son would inherit, should Llywelyn remarry and have a son; also his daughter would be provided for in a suitable manner. Thus there was no other known candidate to succeed Llywelyn (Smith, *Llywelyn*, p. 366; Davies, *Age*, p. 351).

[14] Patent Rolls, 1 Edw III 1.21.

[15] Edwards, *Littere Wallie*, pp. 18, 153; Bartrum [1974], s.n. Cydifor ap Gwaithfoed 1, 1.177.

[16] Sydney Anglo outlines the propagandistic purposes behind Henry's claim to an ancient British (and thence Trojan) heritage, though he accepts Henry's descent from Llywelyn ap Gruffudd ("Early Tudor Propaganda," p. 19). For doubts that Henry ever appointed such a commission, see Chrimes, *Henry VII*, p. 4.

Holland of Ruthin, for example, include numerous marginal notes reading "by gyttyn owen bok."[17] Among these are three lines listing "katryn verch lly ap gruff last prynce of wales" as the mother of Elinor, as does the pedigree in Leland, though Owain's aunt remains Margaret in Holland's account (fol. 8r).

It is not known how the name Catrin or Catherine might have been drawn into these pedigrees. However, the fact that Owain Glyndŵr had a daughter Catrin, who married Edmund Mortimer in 1402, suggests there may have been an earlier Catrin in the family, and indeed Bartrum records a Catrin as sister to Elinor's grandfather, Owain ap Maredudd (Bartrum [1974], s.n. Rhys ap Tewdwr 6, 4.781). The *filia* given twice in lieu of names in the *Stemma Aliciae* may represent an earlier stage in the corruption of the pedigree, before the introduction of the name Catrin, or perhaps it simply reflects ignorance of or doubt about these names.

While we cannot establish all the details of Owain's lineage with absolute certainty, such confusions as those outlined here remain the most likely explanation for differences and discrepancies among the various pedigrees of Owain Glyndŵr and of Henry VII, his cousin three times removed. The personal and political uses to which genealogical information — historically accurate or otherwise — is put are multifarious. We can surmise that Owain used Iolo Goch's poem, with its glorious rhetorical and imaginative embellishments, and other more prosaic pedigrees to further his political ambitions. Though Iolo Goch may not have seen the rebellion coming as he composed his genealogical poem, it undoubtedly helped focus attention on the lord of Glyndyfrdwy as *un pen ar Gymru* — "the one head of Wales" (Item 6.97). That generations after Owain had their own reasons for preserving (and even, on occasion, altering) his pedigree is perhaps an inevitable consequence of his prominence as the last Welshman to be called *Princeps Wallie*, *Tywysog Cymru*, Prince of Wales.

Heraldic slab of Madog Fychan. Found in 1956 before the front altar at the Abbey of Valle Crucis, this stone marked the grave of Owain's great-grandfather. The inscription reads *Hic iacet Madoc fil' Grifini dci Vychan* [Here lies Madog ap Gruffudd, called Fychan]. On the shield is the lion rampant, the arms of Powys, one of the three kingdoms of Wales.

---

[17] London, British Library MS Royal 18 A.lxxv, fols. 2–10; transcribed by Jason O'Rourke on the Imagining History Portal website, s.v. Henry VII.

GRUFFYDD ALED WILLIAMS
OWAIN GLYNDŴR: THE NAME

The cognomen *Glyndŵr*/*Glendower* derives from the name of the small lordship of Glyn-dyfrdwy (lit., "the glen of the Dee")[1] in the Merioneth commote of Edeirnion, which formed part of the ancestral lands of Owain ap Gruffudd Fychan, who came to be known as Owain Glyndŵr. The full name of the lordship occurs in late thirteenth- and fourteenth-century Latin and Anglo-Norman records in various forms (*Glyndeuerdey, Glyndoverde, Glindoverdy, Glendeverdoye*, etc.).[2] The full form is also used in documents when attached to the names of Owain's ancestors, his great-grandfather Madog ap Gruffudd and his grandfather Gruffudd ap Madog: the latter features as *Griffin de Glyndouerde* in 1328, *Griffinus ap Madok de Glyndouerde* in 1334, and *Griffith de Glyndorde* in 1343.[3] In 1370–71 Owain's mother is cited as the widow of *Gruffudd de Glindorde*.[4] In muster rolls relating to Owain's military service in Scotland in 1384 his name occurs as *Owen Glyndourdo* and *Owen Glyndouido*,[5] and similar sources relating to his participation in the earl of Arundel's naval expedition in 1387 and his aborted participation in the earl's expedition of 1388 refer to him as *Owen Glyndouerdy*.[6] Legal documents from 1386 and 1387 concerning the properties of Owain's Hanmer in-laws cite him as *Oweinus*/*Owenus Glyndoueredoy*,[7] and in a grant of land by Owain himself in 1392 he is styled *Oweyn ap Gruffuth, dominus de Glyndyvyrdoy* (Item 9 above).

I have found no evidence that *Glyndŵr*, as opposed to *Glyndyfrdwy*, was used as a stand-alone territorial name until modern times;[8] examples of such modern usage include the application of the name to a local council authority established in 1974 by way of honoring

---

[1] The river name *Dyfrdwy* (English *Dee*) means 'sacred water' (< *dwfr* [water] + *dwyw* [god, goddess].

[2] See e.g. Edwards, *Calendar of Ancient Correspondence Concerning Wales*, pp. 85, 107, 108; *The Welsh Assize Roll*, ed. Davies, p. 247; *Calendar of Chancery Rolls, 1277–1326*, p. 266; *Calendar of Fine Rolls, 1272–1307*, pp. 286, 304; *Calendar of Close Rolls, 1288–1296*, p. 235; *Rotuli Parliamentorum* 1.306.

[3] *Calendar of Patent Rolls, 1327–1330*, p. 314; *Rotuli Scotiae*, 1.284, 294–95; "Roll of Fealty," ed. Banks, p. clvi.

[4] Jack, "New Light," p. 164.

[5] www.icmacentre.ac.uk/soldier/database (Universities of Reading and Southampton), citing TNA E101/39/39 m 1 and TNA E101/39/40 m 1. Tudur, Owain's brother, is listed in 1384 as *Tedyr Glynderdo* (TNA E101/39/39 m 1; TNA E101/39/40 m 1).

[6] www.icmacentre.ac.uk/soldier/database, citing TNA/E101/40/33 m 1, TNA/E101/40/34 m 2i, and TNA/E101/41/5 m 1.

[7] National Library of Wales, Bettisfield documents 425, 426.

[8] There are no authentic examples of *Glyndŵr* as a territorial name in the Melville Richards Archive, the Welsh place-name database at Bangor University. An apparent example from *The Welsh Assize Roll*, ed. Davies, is cited in error: the correct citation from that source (p. 247) is *Glyndeuerdey*.

Owain Glyndŵr in his own locality.[9] Historically, it appears that the name *Glyndŵr* (in various orthographical representations) was first used in reference to Owain Glyndŵr himself and to his brother Tudur, and that it was subsequently exclusively deployed until modern times in references to Owain, not independently as a territorial designation. The earliest extant example, in the form *Glyndore*, occurs in an Anglo-Norman record of testimony given by Owain to the Court of Chivalry in 1386 in connection with the Scrope-Grosvenor controversy, where Owain is cited as *Oweyn, sire de Glendore* (Item 7.1). The record of Tudur's testimony to the same hearing refers to him as *Tuder de Glyndore*;[10] he is similarly cited as *Tudor de Glyndore* in a muster roll relating to the naval expedition of 1387.[11] Whilst the loss of the medial *-f-* of *Glyndyfrdwy* indicated by *Glendore/Glyndore* is unexceptional, being probably a reflection of contemporary local Welsh pronunciation,[12] the loss of the final syllable *-dwy* is unexpected and appears somewhat contrived.[13] A crucial consideration in explaining these forms is the context within which they occur. Did they result from a perception by clerks, familiar with Anglo-French, Latin, or English but not with Welsh, or by Owain and Tudur's English military and civil acquaintances, that *Glyndyfrdwy* — with its alien medial consonant cluster *-frd-* and final syllable — was a somewhat intractable form? Was the simpler *de Glendore/Glyndore* style explicitly sanctioned by the Welsh brothers themselves conscious of the "foreignness" of *Glyndyfrdwy* and possibly motivated at that stage of their careers by a desire to ease their way into English military and chivalric society?[14]

English state records (such as Patent Rolls, Close Rolls, and Parliament Rolls) from the time of the Glyndŵr revolt usually append the name *Glyndyfrdwy* in referring to Owain (the many variants include *Owyn de Glyndordo*, *Owen de Glyndordy*, *Owyn Glyndourdy*, and *Owin Glendourdy*).[15] These sources occasionally, however, use forms corresponding to *Owain Glyndŵr*, such as *Owen de Glyndour*, *Owin Gleyndour*, *Owin Glendore*, and *Owin Glyndour*:[16] in the published *Calendars of Patent Rolls* of the reign of Henry IV over a fifth of all cited references to Owain use such forms. But in contemporary or near contemporary chronicles (Items 15,

---

[9] The Cyngor Dosbarth Glyndŵr / Glyndŵr District Council was absorbed into Denbighshire County Council in 1996. Other modern examples of the local territorial use of the name inspired by the fame of Owain Glyndŵr were its adoption as a telephone exchange name for the Glyndyfrdwy area in the 1950s and the establishment of a male voice choir, the Côr Meibion Bro Glyndŵr, in 1973.

[10] *De controversia*, ed. Nicolas, 1.260.

[11] www.icmacentre.ac.uk/soldier/database, citing TNA E101/40/33 m 1d and TNA E101/40/34 m 2i.

[12] *f* was more of a bilabial in Middle Welsh, and *dwfr* regularly became *dŵr* [water]. This change is suggested by some of the fourteenth-century documentary forms of *Glyndyfrdwy* cited above, although the orthographical ambiguity of *u* and *v* renders strict classification difficult.

[13] It should be noted that as a stand-alone river name *Dyfrdwy* has never been shortened. But by the fourteenth-century it is highly unlikely that the meaning of the final *-dwy* (< *dwyw*) would be apparent and it could have been viewed as a superfluous affix. This would have facilitated the back-formation *Glendore/Glyndore* if a more amenable form of *Glyndyfrdwy* were desired (e.g. for status purposes), but the historical persistence of *Dyfrdwy* shows that the dropping of *-dwy* was exceptional.

[14] For comments on Owain's outlook c.1386–87 as reflected in the poetry of Gruffudd Llwyd, see my "More than "skimble-skamble stuff," pp. 22–24.

[15] The examples cited are from *Calendar of Patent Rolls, 1399–1401*, pp. 370, 386; *1401–1405*, pp. 261, 420.

[16] Examples cited from *Calendar of Patent Rolls, 1401–1405*, pp. 155, 322, 347, 409.

22, 28, 42, 62, 67, 68, 72 above) the full form *Glyndyfrdwy* is typically not attached to Owain's name: he is styled *Oweyn Klyndor, Owyn Glendor, Owinus de Glyndour, Howenus Gleyndor, Audoenus de Glendour* or other variants employing the shorter two-syllabled cognomen.[17] The chronicle and record evidence taken together indicates that Owain was probably usually known in England in various anglicized representations corresponding to *Owain Glyndŵr* during the time of his revolt, the *(de) Glyndyfrdwy* style probably being largely reserved for formal record purposes.

Was the leader of the 1400 revolt commonly known as *Owain Glyndŵr* in Welsh during his own lifetime? The only relevant contemporary Welsh language sources are the bardic eulogies addressed to Owain. In the poetry addressed to him before the revolt by Iolo Goch and Gruffudd Llwyd it is noteworthy that he is not designated *Owain Glyndŵr*. Although both these poets were able, with some ingenuity — such as employing the devices of tmesis and enjambment — to accommodate the name *Glyndyfrdwy* within the tight constraints imposed by the heptasyllabic *cywydd* line and the demands of *cynghanedd*,[18] when they sought a more amenable shorter form it was not *Glyndŵr* they used but *[y] Glyn* [the Glyn], describing Owain as *[y] marchog o'r Glyn* [the knight from the Glyn], *arglwydd . . . o'r Glyn* [the lord from the Glyn] and *Beli y Glyn* [the Beli of the Glyn].[19] Generalization based on limited evidence is patently hazardous, but it could be speculated that the *Glyndŵr/Glendore/Glyndore* cognomen — possibly an innovation of the mid-1380s and derived from an Anglo-Norman cultural milieu — may have been relatively unfamiliar to these poets.[20] Or, if known to them, did it hold little attraction because it was perceived to be a somewhat alien Frenchified style, less preferable in reference to Owain than the palpably Welsh *Owain y Glyn*? It must be noted, however, that in a poem composed during the revolt (c.1402–1403), Iolo Goch, employing tmesis, does refer to Owain as *Owain . . . Glyndŵr*, although he also refers to him as *pôr y Glyn* [the lord of the Glyn].[21] It may be that the *Glyndŵr* style — demonstrably widely current in contemporary England — also gained currency in Wales and in Welsh during the revolt.[22] Whether the style *Owain Glyndŵr* or *Owain y Glyn* predominated in Welsh at the time cannot be determined.[23]

Fifteenth-century Welsh chronicles do not refer to Owain as Glyndŵr, preferring the patronymic style *Owain ap Gruffudd* or the more extended *Owain ap Gruffudd, arglwydd Glyndyfrdwy*.[24] As for poetry, what may well be the earliest extant example of the use of *Glyndŵr*

---

[17] Examples cited from Items 22.12, 28.2, 42.2, 68.16, 72.1 above.

[18] Items 3.5–6, 4.16, 5.64, 6.8 above.

[19] Items 3.88, 4.5, 6.54 above. On Beli, see Bartrum, *Welsh Classical Dictionary*, pp. 38–39.

[20] Of the five poems in question, two (Items 3 and 4 above) are datable to 1385, thereby predating the Scope-Grosvenor record of 1386. A third (Item 5) almost certainly dates to 1386–87.

[21] Item 27.19, 37 above.

[22] For examples of *Glyndour* forms emanating from sources opposed to Owain in Wales see Items 33, 36, and 38 above. For a possible instance of the use of *Owain Glyn* in a source from the Welsh marches, see Item 37.5, although it is not impossible that the *Glyn* here may represent a scribal contraction.

[23] It is not unexpected that in diplomatic documents emanating from his chancery Owain was formally styled *Owynus princeps Wallie*, compare Items 43, 46, and 52 above. Compare also *Yweun ap Gruffuth, Dominus de Glyn Dwfrdwy* (Item 31 above, and compare Item 9).

[24] See Items 70, 84, and 86 above.

after Owain's time occurs in an elegy for Gwenllian, an illegitimate daughter of Owain, in which Lewys Glyn Cothi refers to her as *Luned wen o Lyndŵr* [the fair Luned issuing from Glyndŵr].[25] It may be significant, however, that in the ten poems addressed to Gwenllian and her husband by three poets — Lewys, Llawdden and Ieuan Gyfannedd — this is the only instance of the use of *Glyndŵr*; other citations in these poems refer to Gwenllian as *o Owain y Glyn* [issuing from Owain y Glyn], *merch o'r Glyn* [a daughter from the Glyn], *ar-glwyddes o'r Glyn* [the lady from the Glyn], *merch glaer, hil Marchog y Glyn* [the bright daughter of the line of the Knight of the Glyn], *Gwenfrewy Glyn Dyfrdwy dir* [the Saint Winifred of the land of Glyndyfrdwy], and *o Lyn Dyfrdwy dad* [issuing from a father from Glyn Dyfrdwy][26] Indeed, until the closing decades of the fifteenth century it appears that Owain was more often designated in poetry as being of *y Glyn* than as *Glyndŵr* in genealogical citations.[27] In the sixteenth century, however, particularly during its second half, Welsh poets came to refer more frequently to him as *Glyndŵr* in such instances.[28] Their ability to freely deploy this form despite the constraints of meter and *cynghanedd* demonstrates that metrical considerations would not have deterred their predecessors from using it.

English Tudor writers, such as Leland, Hall, Baldwin, and Holinshed (Items 94, 95, 98, and 100), following the usage of fifteenth-century vernacular chroniclers (Items 71, 73, 75, 78, 83, and 85), used various English orthographical representations of *Glyndŵr* (*Glindour, Glendor, Glendour, Glendouer*). It was Holinshed's most commonly used form — *Glendouer* — which prompted Shakespeare's *Glendower* spelling in *1 Henry IV* (Item 101), the predominant anglicized form in subsequent centuries.

Owain's Mount in Glyndyfrdwy, the ancestral seat of his patrimony. His manor close by was razed by Prince Henry.

---

[25] Lewys Glyn Cothi, *Gwaith*, ed. Johnston, 188.60, p. 413. Luned features as a kindly handmaiden in the romance of *Owein*.

[26] Lewys Glyn Cothi, *Gwaith*, ed. Johnston, 187.21, p. 410; Ieuan Gyfannedd in Payne, *Crwydro Sir Faesyfed*, p. 114; Llawdden, *Gwaith*, ed. Daniel, 11.35, p. 59; 12.42, p. 63; 13.22, p. 65; 14.40, p. 68. As Gwenllian's mother hailed from Genau'r Glyn in Ceredigion it is not impossible that the second and third of these references convey a double meaning (*Glyn*dyfrdwy/Genau'r *Glyn*), but there is no doubt that Glyndyfrdwy is primarily intended (compare the last two citations).

[27] In the fifteenth-century poems before c.1480 that I have examined *y Glyn* references occur roughly twice as often as *Glyndŵr* references. Whilst this sample may well be indicative, it should be noted that much of the poetry of the period remains unedited.

[28] I have gathered examples of the use of *Glyndŵr* in genealogical citations by some twenty sixteenth- and early seventeenth-century poets. For examples in published editions see Gruffudd Hiraethog, *Gwaith*, ed. Bowen, 16.52, p. 63; 21.26, p. 77; Siôn Tudur, *Gwaith*, ed. Roberts 31.37, p. 131; 65.22, p. 266; 106.14, p. 417. It should be noted, however, that y *Glyn* citations remain common during this period.

KELLY DEVRIES
OWAIN GLYNDŴR'S WAY OF WAR

The Defining of a Leader

War requires and produces leaders who can command the power of their forces in any arena of military conflict. If an engagement ends in victory, it is this leader who typically gets the credit, no matter how many decisions he (or, on rare occasions like Joan of Arc, *she*) really made. If the engagement ends in defeat, it is this same leader — no matter the real culpability — who typically gets the blame. (Although if the general is also the central political or religious authority, and not killed or decisively defeated, blame is often accorded elsewhere, especially if the health or well being of the "blamer" is at stake!) When it comes to conflict, then, the difference between winning and losing is very often perceived as a difference in leadership.

Military legacies for leaders are thus defined by fairly simple rules: the good ones win, the bad ones lose. To this simple dichotomy we can add further complexity in terms of what one wins: the great leaders win battles and sieges, the greater leaders go on to win campaigns, and the greatest leaders go on to win wars.[1] In ancient times Alexander the Great won battles, sieges, campaigns, and wars, and he has unquestionably gone down as one of the greatest of leaders. So, too, Scipio Africanus and Julius Caesar. In the Middle Ages, Charlemagne, William the Conqueror, and Mehmed the Conqueror likewise won all four levels of conflict (which no doubt explains their cognomens), as did Saladin (although without the cognomen). Edward III and Joan of Arc, like Hannibal long before them, thus qualify as greater but not the greatest of leaders: they won battles, sieges and campaigns, but they did not win wars. And Richard the Lionheart, intriguingly like Pyrrhus, is a "merely" great leader: for he won only battles and sieges.[2]

Can pre-modern leaders lose an individual engagement and still make this rarified list of great, greater, or greatest? Yes they can, at least when it comes to battles, sieges, and even campaigns. Charlemagne's loss at Roncevalles, celebrated as it is in *The Song of Roland*, does not tarnish his reputation as one of the greatest leaders in history. Similarly, the losses of Edward III at the siege of Tournai or Joan of Arc at the sieges of Paris and La Charité do nothing to tarnish their greater leader status. Some pre-modern leaders even started out

---

[1] Rarely in ancient or medieval warfare is a coalition of leaders given credit or blame for battle and siege victories or defeats, although it is not entirely unknown: such is the case of the First Crusaders at Nicaea, Dorylaeum, Antioch, Jerusalem, and several other smaller engagements. It is more common for a coalition of leaders to be given credit for successful campaigns and wars, but still far less frequent than assigning credit or blame to a single general.

[2] Pyrrhus is famed for giving his name to those battles that cost one so much in victory that the wars are lost: "If we are victorious in one more battle with the Romans, we shall be utterly ruined," he is alleged to have said (Plutarch, *Pyrrhus*, 21.9).

as losers in military conflict only to rebound with major victories that earned them legacies as great or greater leaders. For example, John the Fearless, duke of Burgundy from 1404 to 1419, started his military career by leading the Crusaders to disastrous defeat at the Battle of Nicopolis in 1396, only to bounce back with significant and very victorious campaigns against the Liégeois in 1407–08 and the Armagnacs in the French Civil War (also called the Armagnac-Burgundian War) from 1407 until his murder in 1419. His legacy for future generations rested not on what had resulted at Nicopolis, but on the number of battles, sieges, and campaigns he had won in Liège and France, defining him as a greater leader, although his inability to end the French Civil War victoriously before his death (despite his victory in the Liège Rebellion) probably denies him the status of greatest leader.[3] Thus it is that results in pre-modern conflicts have come to define military leaders, both to contemporary reporters and modern commentators.

Set against these leadership criteria, the Welsh rebel leader Owain Glyndŵr comes off quite well, fitting easily into the great leader category as a winner of battles and sieges, and very probably into the greater leader category, too, as a winner of campaigns. He might even have some claim to the greatest leader category — he certainly has been so determined in some Welsh nationalist literature — although even his staunchest supporters would have to admit that this could only be accorded if one defines his "victory" as not entirely losing a war that his opponent had deemed largely irrelevant. Regardless, as a military leader his legacy is undoubtedly secure.

Becoming a leader at all, of course, can be the result of many different forces: birth and opportunity being foremost among them. Even so, great leadership, the kind displayed by Owain during his fifteenth-century rebellion against the English, has proven to be essentially innate. It cannot be effectively learned or taught. Certain aspects — basic strategy, tactics, logistics, chivalry, and the "laws of war" — can certainly be learned by reading, and as a result books on the subject, like those written by ancient authors, Frontinus and Vegetius, and later by Geoffroi de Charny, Honoré Bouvet, Christine de Pisan, the Chevalier de la Tour Landry, and Jean de Bueil, among several others, proliferated during the late Middle Ages.[4] But that type of training can only go so far. Placed in a military leadership position, anyone incapable of more than "book learning" will quickly be found out and, even if not removed — a difficulty if that leader was a member of the royal family or entourage — will be sidelined, with better leadership sought elsewhere by captains and common soldiers. (Increasingly, in the later Middle Ages those replacements often were non-noble figures like John Hawkwood, Robert Knolles, Hugh Calveley, Ponton de Xantrailles, La Hire, Joan of Arc, Jan Žižka, and Jean Bureau.) In the end, only military leaders with innate abilities survived and won. Birth may have given Owain Glyndŵr some claim to leadership (as seen in several essays in this volume), but it was his own innate leadership abilities that made that leadership real and lasting.

The Training of a Leader

Long before he could become a leader in war, however, Owain first had to be trained in the wearing of armor and the wielding of weapons and shield that were used in waging it. In the Middle Ages, these martial skills — unlike innate leadership — could be taught, and a sig-

---

[3] The other leaders mentioned above do not need biographical citations, as they are numerous. For John the Fearless, unjustly less well known, see DeVries, "John the Fearless' Way of War."

[4] Contamine, *War in the Middle Ages*, pp. 210–18.

nificant portion of a noble male's adolescence would be spent learning them through an education that would be continued, and hopefully enhanced, while serving as squire for a more experienced soldier on campaigns and conflicts.[5] Sometimes a noble was simply unable to learn these military skills; sometimes he was unable to find conflicts in which to apprentice sufficiently. The former could be a lack of talent or interest, the latter a lack of war — although this was hardly an issue from the middle of the eleventh to the end of the fifteenth centuries, a time when wars were plentiful. A young noble could find combat near to home — inter-European wars too numerous to list here — or in exotic locales much further abroad — Spain, North Africa, the Holy Land, the Eastern Mediterranean, the Balkans and/or Northeastern Europe. Some would travel very far indeed just to practice their military skills.[6] After the beginning of the twelfth century there were even opportunities for the young noble who had both a destiny by devotion or family for religious service and an inclination or talent for military skills to unite these paths by joining one of the Military Orders: the Templars (until 1307), the Hospitallers, the Teutonic Knights, or sundry Iberian Orders.[7]

Unfortunately, details of Owain Glyndŵr's childhood and adolescence, when such training would have been done, have not survived. Owain's grandfather, Gruffudd ap Madog, was a renowned soldier, with service dating to the 1330s, but his death c.1370 would have kept him from having much influence; and Owain's father, Gruffudd Fychan, as far as is known, was not a soldier, so it is likely that he also did not oversee his son's training. Perhaps the task of training the young Welsh nobleman fell to one of his cousins, Rhys or Gwilym ap Tudur, who had impressive military careers of their own before leading Welsh rebels early in support of Owain's rebellion. They are recorded, for instance, as serving in the retinue of Edward, the Black Prince, in Gascony in 1369, taking 120 archers from Caernarfon to the southern English coast in anticipation of a French attack in 1386, and taking archers to Ireland in 1394. Their military services were worthy enough, in fact, that in 1398 both received an annuity of £10 from the English crown.[8] While entirely speculative, in between their early years of service it is certainly possible that they could have supervised Owain's adolescent training in arms: their "brothers in arms" relationship would further explain the military support they gave their much younger cousin in defending his claim as Prince of Wales in 1400.

Based on more firm evidence is Owain Glyndŵr's next military tutor, Sir Gregory Sais, the captain whose retinue Owain and his brother, Tudur, joined at Berwick in 1384. By this time Gregory — also Welsh; on the epithet *Sais* [Englishman] see Item 5.44n — had a distinguished and lengthy military career. He had fought in many military campaigns, both as a member of the Free Companies in France during the early 1360s and as a member of the English army in France, Spain, Wales, and Scotland from the late 1360s through the 1380s. Although specifics of Owain's service to him have been lost, other than the muster rolls which record him becoming a captain at an early age, Gregory's assignment to secure Pembrokeshire in 1377 against a French invasion suggests a high degree of confidence in his leadership abilities.[9]

---

[5] See Rogers, *Soldiers' Lives Through History*, pp. 3–10 for a good overview of this type of training.

[6] The best general work on medieval military skills remains Contamine, *War in the Middle Ages*, although Nicholson's *Medieval Warfare* is also quite good.

[7] Again, works on the military orders are numerous. Forey's *Military Orders* is a good synthesis.

[8] Davies, *Revolt*, p. 52.

[9] See Carr, "A Welsh Knight in the Hundred Years' War." A record of his military service drawn from the muster rolls can be found on the *Soldier in Later Medieval England Database*.

Owain and Tudur were listed as esquires among the 99 men-at-arms and 280 archers who served in the Berwick garrison under Gregory. During their tenure they participated in garrison duty, border raids, and an invasion of Scotland, during which they raided the Scottish countryside all the way to Edinburgh but failed to bring any sizeable army to battle. This service was, in the words of R. R. Davies, "an important part of [Owain's] military apprenticeship."[10]

By Spring 1387 Owain had graduated from Gregory's tutelage to that of Richard Fitzalan, earl of Arundel.[11] At the time, Arundel was Admiral of the West and North, and he led a sizeable military force of 2500 men divided into 27 retinues. Owain served as an esquire in Arundel's personal retinue of 4 bannerets, 32 knights, 127 esquires and 217 archers. Arundel also commanded 60 ships. To this were added 70 German and Dutch vessels that joined Arundel's fleet at the beginning of a naval battle off Sluys on 24 March against a large Franco-Flemish fleet that still outnumbered the English even after the defection of Germans and Dutch.[12] This Franco-Flemish fleet had been charged with keeping the English from landing, but instead it was completely routed, with around 50 ships captured and another 12 sunk, in what was described by a contemporary chronicler as the worst Flemish naval disaster in history.[13]

For the next three weeks Arundel's army conducted a *chevauchée* in the northwestern Flemish countryside, a means of engagement that had become the "way" of English warfare during this phase of the Hundred Years' War. The purpose of the *chevauchée* was not to besiege any large town or fortification, nor even to engage an army in battle (in this case a French army), but rather to raze small unprotected villages, to steal animals and crops (or destroy them), and to terrorize the inhabitants — thus depriving the enemy from resources and favor in the region.[14] It was a style of fighting that Owain had already seen in action in Scotland, and one that he would learn well, as he would utilize it often against the English in his later rebellion.

J. J. N. Palmer is justifiably critical of the results of Arundel's campaign in Flanders, for even though it was economically profitable for the short term — mostly because of the captured ships — it was a long-term strategic and economic loss, as it drove Flanders, a strong ally for most of the war up to that point, further from the English. Any experience in war can likely be turned to the benefit of a young military leader, but it is difficult to see how Arundel's Flemish campaign taught the young Owain much new aside from negative example: mistakes made by Arundel do not appear to have been duplicated by the Welsh leader. It is also true that Owain did meet several men who would be instrumental in his later rebellion, some

---

[10] Davies, *Revolt*, p. 146.

[11] While Davies (*Revolt*, p. 146) asserts that Owain served with Arundel first during the Scottish invasion of 1385, there is no evidence to confirm this. He is not listed on the muster rolls.

[12] The Flemish rebellion against the French had ended in 1385, and they had joined the latter in fighting the English, made a more suitable enemy due to the bishop of Norwich, Henry Despenser, and his laughably misguided "Crusade" of 1383 — he attacked fellow supporters of Roman Pope Urban VI rather than supporters of Avignonese Pope Clement VII. See DeVries, "Reasons for the Bishop of Norwich's Attack on Flanders in 1383."

[13] Palmer, *England, France and Christendom*, pp. 92–93. The contemporary chronicler was the anonymous author of the *Croniques de Tournai*.

[14] On *chevauchées* during the period see Contamine, *War in the Middle Ages*, pp. 122–25, and on this particular *chevauchée* see Palmer, *England, France and Christendom*, pp. 92–96.

fighting for and some against him. Even so, Owain's time with Arundel was certainly not "the experience which was transferring his contacts and horizons," an exaggeration by Davies.[15]

The death of his father-in-law, Sir Dafydd Hanmer, forced Owain to break his contract with Arundel and return to Wales, thus missing out on the earl's French expedition in 1388. (That this was even more, and more quickly, disastrous than his 1387 campaign might suggest that Owain's absence was an opportune one.)[16] Several of Arundel's esquires had been knighted after his naval victory, but Owain, rather conspicuously, was not among them. In his poem on Owain's exploits in Scotland, dated to 1385–86, Gruffudd Llwyd nevertheless calls him *marchog*, which is usually translated as "knight" (Item 3.88), although he is listed as an esquire on Arundel's muster rolls of 1387 and 1388 (his name on the last being crossed out as he had returned to Wales), and he is never called a knight in English documents. If, when, or by whom he was knighted is thus unknown; it may be, in fact, that he never was "officially" dubbed a knight at all despite his services — and despite that being the title carried by him in some sources. It also may not matter, since in 1392 we know that he was already referring himself as *lord* of Glyndyfrdwy in a granting of lands to Gruffuydd ap Ieuan Llwyd, a title that assumes more authority, legally if not militarily, than *knight* (Item 9.1).

What Owain Glyndŵr did militarily between 1387 and 1400 is uncertain. His lack of activity in any "army" of the period may not mean inaction so much as inopportunity. His first captain, Gregory Sais, died in 1390. His second, the earl of Arundel, never recovered from his 1388 disgrace in France and would never again lead an army; he was beheaded in 1397 for treason against Richard II. Owain attached himself to no one else.[17] The period was certainly tumultuous, with Henry, duke of Lancaster's, rebellion against Richard II attracting nobles throughout England and Wales to either side.[18] But Owain does not seem to have been among them.

Owain was not at Westminster when Henry IV was crowned king on 13 October 1399. Probably he did not think much of this new king, although that is an assumption made largely due to our hindsight awareness of his own declaration less than a year later, on 16 September 1400, that he was Prince of Wales. That act of rebellion was a move that Owain must have known would incite an armed response from a king who had so recently shown himself to be a victorious military leader. It was, as far as we know, Owain's next major military endeavor after his service with Arundel. What made Owain so confident to think that his military leadership would succeed over Henry's?

---

[15] Davies, *Revolt*, pp. 147–48. Davies often exaggerates the earl of Arundel's influence. "The years 1387–8 could have made Glyn Dŵr," he writes, doubting only its positive influence because Arundel did not knight him and because the death of his father-in-law caused him to break off his service with the earl.

[16] Palmer, *England, France and Christendom*, pp. 122–41.

[17] Hodges (*Owain*, pp. 22–23, 191) suggests that Owain served with Henry IV during his military usurpation of Richard II's crown, misreading Walsingham's *armiger non ignobilis regi moderno ante susceptum regnum laudabiliter militauit* [a distinguished esquire of the present king before he had succeeded to the throne, and had served him commendably] (Item 68.4–5) to mean actual service with the future king. As he does not appear in any of Henry's muster rolls or other records, this is unlikely.

[18] The usurpation of Henry IV is yet another event that is covered by many historical studies. Bennett's *Richard II and the Revolution of 1399* is a solid synthesis, but for the military history see Biggs, *Three Armies in Britain*.

The Forging of a Leader

Assessing military confidence can be tricky for the historian. Ensuing victory means that confidence was warranted, that the leader was *bold*, while defeat means that the confidence was not warranted, that the leader was *rash*.[19] There is no doubt that Owain's confidence in this decision was risky: he was assessing not only his own military leadership capabilities, but also the military capabilities of others who had already pledged their arms to him. In following him, they, too, showed their confidence that he could lead them successfully against a much more numerous and better funded army. Recruitment of followers, an important part of military leadership, thus seems not to have been much of a problem for Owain. Many appear to have already flocked to his cause even before his declaration, although the sources are unclear how the message of rebellion was spread or why so many decided to follow this specific rebel leader at this time.

It should hardly surprise us that the Welsh rebellion's initial military action, the week after he declared himself Prince, was a series of *chevauchée*-style attacks against Ruthin, Denbigh, Rhuddlan, Flint, Hawarden, Holt, Oswestry, Felton, and Welshpool (Item 11). The goals of the Welsh were clear: to gather supplies, destroy, and confuse. Contemporary sources claim that the first two goals were quite successful: the country was laid in waste, and all the supplies were gathered to the rebels' stores. The effectiveness of the final goal, confusion, is evidenced by a number of proclamations condemning only a few named rebels in the wake of this *chevauchée*; a pardon was offered in March of the following year to anyone, other than Owain Glyndŵr and the two brothers Rhys and Gwilym ap Tudur, should they submit to the king of England (Item 14). Rhys and Gwilym had been excluded no doubt because they had attacked and captured Anglesey: only Beaumaris Castle, which had also been attacked but had not fallen, remained in English hands on that island.

These rebel soldiers also, for the most part, avoided battle with any English force. When one was encountered, after their sacking of Welshpool, the rebels were defeated by militias drawn from the counties of Salop, Stafford and Warwick, led by Hugh Burnell. Although, to be fair, the only report of this engagement, attested to at a General and First Court on 6 October in Oswestry, suggests simply that the rebels "fled, seeking the mountains and woods, and very many of the said rebels returned to their own manors, behaving just as if they had not previously been in the forests" (Item 11.38–42) — hardly the "sound" defeat one recent author, William E. Baumgaertner, has described.[20]

Neither the rebels fleeing when encountering a force, nor the absence of Owain from among them, can be seen as a failure of Glyndŵr's military leadership. On the contrary, it appears that this *chevauchée* into Northern Wales was a calculated attack, meant to get the attention of the king, who was then traveling to Shrewsbury. Once Henry had discovered what had happened, he decided to divert his force from there to Wales in order to search out and punish the rebels. For three weeks the king campaigned, but little was accomplished. He did leave troops as garrisons in several of his castles there — although adding only 20 men-at-

---

[19] The perfect example of this might be Charles, duke of Burgundy, whose cognomen is sometimes *the Bold* (le Hardi), but, due to his military ineptitude, is also sometimes *the Rash* (le Téméraire). See Vaughan, *Charles the Bold*.

[20] Baumgaertner, *Squires, Knights, Barons, Kings*, n.p. (ebook). Baumgaertner claims that the River Vyrnwy, where the battle was fought, ran with blood, although this is not cited and appears nowhere in the sources.

arms and 80 archers barely increased the numbers of English already garrisoned throughout the region — and he executed 8 suspected rebels — the body of one, Gronw ap Tudur, being quartered and sent to four border towns — but in actuality nothing else was accomplished upon the ground. Of the results, Davies writes that the "authorities showed they were firmly back in control . . . [they] put fear into the hearts of the rebels and resolve into those of nervous English burgesses," but this is a gross exaggeration of English effectiveness.[21] To the contrary, as in the case of most of these early English reprisals, the English only succeeded in doing the opposite of their intent, putting fear into the hearts of the English burgesses and strengthening the resolve of the rebels. Some of Owain's early adherents did back down, including one of his sons, but rebel numbers appear to have increased markedly afterwards. During the early rebellion this was the pattern: one or two prominent rebels would surrender themselves to the English in exchange for their lives and property, only to be replaced by four or five new rebels of equal or greater status. Owain's way of recruiting soldiers, strictly calculated by him or not, had enlarged the rebellion, even before the end of its first few months.

It took little time for Owain's forces to show how ineffective the king's answer to their initial *chevauchée* had been. On 1 April 1401 a small group of rebels, only 40 men, led once again by Rhys and Gwilym ap Tudur, captured the very important castle and walled town of Conwy, one of the strongest fortifications in North Wales. Strikingly, they captured it not by conventional siege — it is likely, in fact, that the rebels did not yet have the means of laying a conventional siege — but by clever stratagem. According to the chronicler Adam of Usk, Rhys and Gwilym meant only to raid the countryside, but, seeing the castle meekly guarded, the rebels enlisted a carpenter who did work in the castle to enter it on the pretext of "simply coming to do his usual work." They then killed two of the watch he had deceived and captured the courtyard and some of the buildings. The rest of the garrison retreated into the bowels of the castle — likely the king's apartments, although Adam does not specify — where they remained for more than a month before surrendering the rest of the castle in exchange for their lives, except for nine "whom the prince [Owain] particularly loathed," who were drawn, disemboweled, hanged, beheaded and quartered (Item 22.1–11).

The capture of Conwy was more symbolic than anything else, as on 24 June it would be handed over to the care of Sir Henry Percy (Hotspur), the son of the earl of Northumberland — a later ally of Owain's and rebel leader against Henry IV, but then acting as an agent of the king — whom Owain and the brothers Rhys and Gwilym knew from their days at Berwick. But as a symbol of the strength of the rebellion and the impotency of the king, as well as the stupidity of his soldiers garrisoning Wales, it was incredibly effective. Hotspur's letter to the king written before he received Conwy, on 4 June, described seeing "much pillaging and mischief in the country," against which he recommends both military and naval action, as Wales was "without doubt in great peril of being destroyed by the rebels" (Item 18.4–7).

Owain and his rebel soldiers were spotted and chased in several places, but they were never caught. Nor were their numbers ever whittled down much. Hotspur's troops defeated a Welsh rebel force on 31 May at Cader Idris, which he claimed was personally led by Owain Glyndŵr; Hotspur noted that his forces wounded "many of his men," but apparently they killed or captured no one. A day later John Charlton wrote to the king that he had "defeated" the rebels, again supposedly led by Owain, at what has been called "the battle" of Mawddwy, there capturing only one "henchman," along with some of Owain's armor, horses, lances, and

---

[21] Davies, *Revolt*, pp. 102–03. For an account of the king's actions, see Item 28.

a drapery "painted with maidens with red hands" (Item 17). Whether Owain was actually at either or both of these battles (fought one day apart), or whether this was just mirage-like conjecture by these two English leaders, neither of whom admitted to seeing the rebel Prince, is uncertain.

The English were doing themselves little favor with these actions. Their higgledy-piggledy chasing after men who quickly disappeared into the mountains and forests of Wales only emboldened and added to the number of rebels and increased the stature of their leader. When Owain did appear at the head of an army, as at the Battle of Hyddgen, fought on an undetermined date in the Summer of 1401, he seemed to have had no problem defeating his foes; nor was he frightened of appearing even in an area seemingly controlled by the English, as evidenced by his and his army's attendance at the funeral of two slain compatriots during that same summer.[22] In 1401 he was invincible, while the English king was impotent. Perhaps it was, as the anonymous reporter of the funeral visit claimed, a case of having not "enough Englishmen with me to manage a *chevauchée* against them" (Item 20.10–11), but even after the king personally invaded Southern Wales, hanging rebels, devastating the lands (including those of the Strata Florida abbey, some of whose monks supported Owain), reinforcing the garrisons of castles (which the *Historia vitae* calls "evidently insufficient"), and forcing the people to migrate to England, the rebellion only increased in magnitude.[23]

Mynydd Hyddgen, framed by the valleys of the rivers Hyddgen (rising to the left) and Hengwm (passing and up to the right). Owain won a great victory amid these slopes and valleys in 1401.

Military matters continued to go well for Owain throughout the end of 1401 and into 1402. The rebels led, and the English were forced to follow. Even when the Welsh ostensibly lost, as in their failure at the siege of Harlech Castle, the English were forced to expend a

---

[22] See Item 70.8–13 (and Davies, *Revolt*, p. 266) for Hyddgen, and Item 20 for the funeral.

[23] See Adam of Usk (Item 22); *Historia vitae* (Item 28); and Davies, *Revolt*, p. 105.

large amount of men and money to prevent catastrophe.[24] And when they won, as at the skirmish fought on Tuthill, outside of Caernarfon, on 1 November 1401, the whole of Wales seemed to rejoice at the news. Knowing this, Owain started to fight under a new banner, reported by Adam of Usk to be a "golden dragon on a white field." He knew the value of theater: showing confidence yields confidence in others.[25]

The Success of a Leader

Owain Glyndŵr's greatest victory came at the Battle of Bryn Glas, fought on 22 June 1402. There is no doubt that Owain was at this battle and that he led his army personally. It was a battle decided not by luck, happenstance, numbers, technology or nature, but by superior leadership. As will be seen in the subsequent essay by Michael Livingston in this volume, Owain Glyndŵr's tactical expertise greatly exceeded that of his opposing general, Edmund Mortimer, leading to that general's capture and the massacre of a large number of his soldiers. Mortimer was the second major prisoner captured by Owain that year, joining Reginald Grey, baron of Ruthin, taken during a rebel *chevauchée* through his barony.[26]

These two Englishmen would prove to be a valuable duo of captives, although in ways that none likely envisioned at the time of their capture. Grey would be released, but only after Henry IV paid a huge ransom on behalf of the captured baron (10,000 marks or pounds, authorized at Parliament on 16 October). Grey would be nearly bankrupted in trying to pay the king back, while the funds covered rebel logistics costs for a very long time.[27]

The cost of Mortimer's freedom was, as it turned out, even more beneficial to the rebels and costly to the English than money. In November he married Owain's daughter, and in December he publicly defected to the Welsh side. "Treason" and "notorious" is what the English called it; being convinced of the justice of Owain's cause is how Mortimer described it: "the grievance is good and reasonable."[28] Showing wisdom, and perhaps mercy, in the capture of these two English lords once again proved the maturity of Owain's military leadership. Their immediate execution might have brought short-term pleasure among the Welsh and anger among the English; that they were instead kept alive consequently added an important ally while filling the coffers of the rebellion, thus bringing much longer-lasting results.

Owain's successes at this time may also have encouraged the exportation of rebellion elsewhere. Such is the greatest worry of those targeted by rebels. Should they not put down the rebellion quickly and ruthlessly, there is a good chance of its exportation to other parts of their principalities. Should the rebellion continue, as this one had for more than two years by the time of Mortimer's defection, and should it record military victories, as Owain had in numerous engagements, the chances of exportation increase exponentially.

---

[24] Davies, *Revolt*, p. 105.

[25] See Item 22.44–47 and Davies, *Revolt*, p. 105. Although historians have come to look at this as a Welsh victory, the place where Owain unfurled his banner, Adam has it as a loss, with the rebels losing 300 men before being driven off. That Owain was unable to advance on the town or castle following the battle might suggest that to the English this was indeed their victory. On the rejoicing of Wales, see Item 27.

[26] For accounts of their captures, see Items 22, 28, 42, and 68, as well as Davies, *Revolt*, p. 107.

[27] See Items 25, 28, 42, 68, and Davies, *Revolt*, p. 233.

[28] Item 26. See also the *Historia vitae*, Item 28, and Walsingham's chronicle, Item 68.

Before the end of 1401 Owain had sent letters to the king of Scotland and the lords of Ireland asking them to rise up against the English (Item 22.62–117). Forcing Henry IV to fight rebellions in those arenas would obviously lessen any pressure on Wales. Even more significant were Owain's negotiations with his former foe, Hotspur, which the young Henry Percy reports in a letter to his father had begun in November 1401. He had rebuffed them, Hotspur writes, and recommends that more be done to put down the rebellion (Item 21), but as history will soon record, clearly these negotiations were not forgotten by the young general. Although for the next year and a half he became concerned with Scottish military matters, on 10 July 1403 he declared himself a rebel against Henry IV. Less than two weeks later, on 21 July, the English king, leading the largest army he had ever assembled, would remove him as a rebellious threat at the famous Battle of Shrewsbury.[29]

Obviously Henry IV saw Hotspur as a great challenge to his kingdom, evidently far greater than he ever had Owain Glyndŵr. The king had certainly sent several armies against the Welsh rebels, but they were never very large, and they were never very well led. Hotspur was certainly experienced, but by the end of 1401 he had been removed to Scotland from fighting in Wales. Among his replacements, neither Grey nor Mortimer had much military experience. In fact, other than being guardian of his nephew the earl of March (also named Edmund), Mortimer had very little personal leadership experience at all. This had clearly been shown at Bryn Glas. (Indeed, that he had defected to Owain's rebellion gave him more importance than he had ever been accorded in England, which might have been one of his motives in making the switch.) Even Henry's own forays into Wales seemed half-hearted, even lazy, raising the anonymous author of the *Historia vitae* to make the following criticism of the king's *chevauchée* in the Summer of 1402 — although it could just as easily have been made of any of Henry's responses during the first three years of Owain's rebellion:

> the king came down with a strong force once again into Wales against . . . the Welsh who were still rebelling against him. He remained in the same place for twenty days, not only achieving nothing, but bearing many misfortunes and injuries through the storms of airy malignities. So the same man returned from there ignominiously.[30]

Even the naming of his son, the future Henry V, as royal lieutenant for Wales on 8 March 1403 was ineffective, as the Prince was quickly pulled back to England by Hotspur's rebellion.

In the meantime, Owain continued his rebellion. In April 1403 his rebels waged a *chevauchée* throughout Shropshire, prompting the very despondent and frightened Shrewsbury residents to plead for the king's aid:

> your loyal lieges of your county of Shropshire are in great doubt and despair every day because of the malice and [mischief that] your Welsh rebels and their adherents

---

[29] There is desperate need for a new history of the battle of Shrewsbury, especially in light of the recent, although fairly inconclusive, excavations conducted by Pollard and Oliver there (reported in *Two Men in a Trench*). Accounts by Morgan (*Battle of Shrewsbury*), Maxfield (*Battlefield of Shrewsbury*), Priestley (*Battle of Shrewsbury*), and Boardman (*Hotspur*, pp. 157–206) are incomplete and error-filled.

[30] Item 28.104–07. The *Dieulacres Chronicle* (Item 42) tries to suggest the opposite, that the *chevauchées* of Henry IV and Prince Henry had been very effective in quelling the rebellion, although even that author must admit that earlier responses had not been so: "because they had not worked sufficiently at these things in the first place" (Item 42.25–26). See also the accounts in Item 68.

are intending to commit or later will commit . . . a third part of your said county at present [has been] destroyed and devastated. (Item 29.3–6, 21–22)

Many similar pleas would soon follow.[31] Henry's response was weak and ineffectual: in May he had his son attack and raze several of Owain Glyndŵr's houses (Item 30), perhaps dealing a personal blow to the rebel leader, but doing little to his resolve or to his rebellion at large, as evidenced in Owain's confident letter to Henry Dwn shortly afterwards: "their [the English] time draws to a close . . . success turns toward us" (Item 31.5–7).

It was not until 12 July 1403, near St. Clears in South Wales, that Owain suffered his first significant military setback in the rebellion. Not much is revealed about the battle in the contemporary sources, and what is given lacks the detailed reporting that, for example, enables a relatively secure reconstruction of the Battle of Bryn Glas. What is said by contemporaries is that a part of Owain's army — numbering 700 according to the burgesses of Caerleon — became divided from the main body, possibly to scout out escape routes from the area and were attacked by an army led by Thomas, Lord Carew, who, again according to the burgesses, "killed every one."[32]

This was hardly the defeat needed to destroy the rebellion, however, considering that around the same time Owain's forces were busy conquering English castles: Dryslwyn, Newcastle Emlyn, Carmarthen, and Llandovery all fell before the end of Summer 1403, and Aberystwyth and Harlech, much bigger prizes, fell sometime before the end of 1404. The town of Kidwelly was also sacked and burned on 20 August 1404.[33] The rebels fought sieges very well by this time, with sufficient men, ladders and artillery to bring their surrender — they no longer had to rely on tricks, as Rhys and Gwilym ap Tudur had to take Conwy in 1401. The garrisons of these sites, on the other hand, were small and demoralized. William Venables' pleas to the king concerning Harlech and Caernarfon Castles, written on 15–16 January 1404, claim that Harlech was manned only by 5 English and 16 Welsh soldiers and Caernarfon only by 28, their nationalities not identified.[34] Unlike the battle at St. Clears, however, the capture of castles and the sacking of Kidwelly were important victories, showing Owain's continued strength and Henry's continued weakness.

It comes as little surprise, then, that the French would take an interest in what was happening in Wales. The Hundred Years' War was in stasis, the truce signed between the English and France at Leulinghem in 1389, unlike all previous treaties, actually bringing peace for a number of years.[35] But, by 1403 the French were willing to break it. Henry IV's usurpation of Richard II's crown, Owain's continued success in Wales, and Hotspur's less successful rebellion all indicated an English weakness that France was determined to exploit. The same thought apparently occurred to Owain. Exploratory French voyages and raids along the Welsh coast in late 1403 and early 1404 prompted the rebel leader to write a letter to King Charles VI on 10 May 1404, suggesting an alliance between them. Accompanying the letter

---

[31] See, for example, Items 32–35, 37.

[32] See Jankyn Havard, Item 35, and the Burgesses of Caerleon, Item 36. Davies dates this engagement to 11 July, apparently misreading Havard's account (*Revolt*, p. 112). For the correct sequence, see Item 36, note to lines 4–12.

[33] Davies, *Revolt*, p. 116.

[34] See Items 38 and 39.

[35] Palmer, *England, France and Christendom*, pp. 147–79.

Harlech Castle. Owain's seizure of this strategically important location was a triumph of his rebellion. So important was the fortification to his cause, that he summoned parliament here in 1405.

were two of his most diplomatically-experienced comrades, John Hanmer and Gruffudd Yonge (Item 43). The result was a treaty, agreed to on 14 July.[36] Seven days previously, Louis de Bourbon, cousin to Charles and his chief councillor, had agreed to send 1000 men-at-arms and 500 crossbowmen on 40 ships from Brittany to Wales under the leadership of yet another cousin, Jacques II Bourbon, count of La Marche (Item 45). All was in place for a joint Franco-Welsh expedition against England.

This treaty was a major coup for Owain. Not only did it supply him with needed weapons and reinforcements — although the latter would likely be used elsewhere than next to his troops in Wales — it also gave him recognition as Prince of Wales from a major European kingdom. The French were an enemy of the English, it was true, and they may not have agreed to an alliance had there not been a common enemy; nevertheless it was recognition that he was the legitimate ruler of a sovereign Wales.

Nor did Owain's enthusiasm decline when, after he had dutifully sacked and burned Plymouth, the count of La Marche retreated to France, his fleet decimated by a storm, especially as the French became very embarrassed by this result — Michel Pintoin describes it as the "shame of the failure of the count" — and became determined to follow it with the outfitting of a new expedition.[37] Another 800 men-at-arms, 600 crossbowmen and 1200 light

---

[36] The best account is in Michel Pintoin's *Chronicle of Charles V*, Item 66. See also Davies, *Revolt*, pp. 192–93.

[37] See Pintoin, Item 66. This treaty is Item 46.

troops would to be mustered, according to Pintoin, and sent to Wales on a fleet of 2 large warships and 30 smaller vessels (Item 66).

The second treaty came just before the *Tripartite Indenture* was agreed to on 28 February between Owain, his son-in-law, Edmund Mortimer, and Henry Percy, the earl of Northumberland, who was still smarting from the loss of his son, Hotspur, a year and half previously. Northumberland, not condemned by his son's rebellion after he declared his ignorance and disapproval to Henry IV, clearly regretted that declaration and sought to change it. What better way to do so than to align himself with the most successful rebel in the kingdom?

The *Tripartite Indenture* is above all a military agreement. Not only did it divide the Kingdom of England into three relatively equal parts to be ruled each by one of them, it pledged that the three were "joined to one another, confederate, united, and bound by the bond of a true federation and true friendship, and certain and good union" (Item 47.4–6), that they were to keep the others informed about possible military incursions, and that they would come to each other's aid when required. Should two of them personally differ to the point of military action — battle is mentioned specifically here — the third should step in to settle the discord.

Owain was riding high, the most successful rebel leader since the Norman Conquest. For four and a half years he had been active, the self-declared Prince of Wales. He had men, resources, non-combatant support, castles, arms, armor, and even a few gunpowder weapons.[38] He had won battles and sieges; his *chevauchées* terrorized the English marches. He had alliances with the biggest enemy of England and one of the most powerful and wealthy English lords. He was recognized far and wide as Prince of Wales. It would not be long before the English king also recognized his royalty. Sovereignty for Wales was just around the corner.

The Failure of a Leader

Then the wheel of fortune, which had been stuck in the up position for Owain Glyndŵr since September 1400, not only turned down to a much lower position, but completely fell apart. The promised French troops did not arrive until Summer 1405, which would not have been a problem had it happened any time between 1400 and 1404. But this year, by the time they did arrive, the rebellion had already begun to collapse. On 11 March a large army of Welsh soldiers, as many as 8000 according to the sources, led by Rhys Gethin, a trusted rebel leader who had fought beside Owain at the battle of Bryn Glas, attacked Monmouthshire, sacking and burning the town of Grosmont. In response, Prince Henry immediately sent an army to the region. It was a "very small force," admitted Prince Henry in a letter written to his father shortly after the battle (Item 48), but among them were some experienced knights, and it was led by Gilbert Lord Talbot, who had distinguished himself while leading troops at Shrewsbury. Talbot's soldiers moved quickly and encountered the rebels before they could once more disappear into the mountains and forests; they then annihilated them. Between 800 and 1000 rebels were killed, and Rhys Gethin was captured.

The rebellion recovered somewhat a few days later, when Owain defeated a small English force at Craig-y-dorth — although the evidence for the battle is slim. It was, however, but a respite before the rebels faced a second, more major defeat at Pwll Melyn on 5 May. In this battle the rebels once again took a heavy toll: 1500 killed, including Owain's

---

[38] A number of stone cannonballs, of varying sizes, buried in a side-room at Harlech Castle are identified as those left behind by Owain Glyndŵr's rebels. See, for example, Taylor, *Harlech Castle.*

brother, Tudur, or captured, including one of Owain's sons, Gruffudd. A few weeks later his brother-in-law, John Hanmer, was also captured at another engagement lost by the rebels.[39]

Owain had been riding high, but his power, as with most rebel leaders, rested on the thinnest of foundations. The problem, at least in part, was one of population. No matter how enthusiastic the rebels, or how great their support among non-combatants, there were still far too few of them to face the large English population. Their only chance was, and had always been, to keep moving, to launch *chevauchées* against English-populated towns in Wales and the marches bordering Wales, and, above all, to avoid risky battles. Victories, such as those at Hyddgen and Bryn Glas, had perhaps made Owain and the rebels overly confident in their own abilities. They simply could not keep facing English armies, especially when taking losses as they had at Grosmont and Pwll Melyn.

They had also to hope that other forces, the French, or rebels, like Hotspur, would divert attention from Wales, which the English had, at least so far, seen as less valuable. But even that did not save the rebellion after 1405. The French landed in Southwest Wales, joined forces with some of the rebels, and made a *chevauchée* through Pembrokeshire. Haverford was burnt, but their siege of Tenby was raised only a short time afterwards when a few English ships appeared off the coast and threatened them. They showed no greater courage against the castle of St. Clears, which they attacked but did not capture. They did sack the important town of Carmarthen, although being merciful to the townspeople, whom they allowed to flee. Many chronicles report that this combined Franco-Welsh force may have marched on into England, to the very edge of Worcester, but even if true (there are remarkable few English accounts of what should have been a frightening invasion) this ended with a whimper rather than a roar: the English army met them, and after facing each other for some days the invading force retreated without giving battle. Some of the invaders returned to France, while others sat out the winter at Carmarthen. French reinforcements sent early in 1406 were captured or turned back.[40] In March 1406 Owain wrote yet again to the French king, in the Pennal Letters, even pledging his allegiance to the Avignonese Popes over the Roman ones (Items 51 and 52). These pleas went unanswered. And, eventually those few French soldiers remaining in Wales returned to France. By the beginning of 1407 the alliance was finished.

As for further English rebellions, these also did not help rebuild or turn the wheel of Owain's fortune. The rebellion of Richard le Scrope, archbishop of York, was defeated with very little fanfare or military action in 1405; the leaders — Scrope, Thomas of Mowbray, earl of Norfolk, and Sir William Plumpton — were beheaded. And the rebellion of Henry Percy, earl of Northumberland and one of the "tripartite" who signed the *Indenture* with Owain and Mortimer, was ended at the battle of Bramham Moor, with Northumberland killed at the latter stages of the battle.[41] Neither Owain nor Mortimer had gone to help him.

To be fair, it is doubtful that either of them could have gone to Henry Percy's aid had they wanted to. They were in hiding. Their rebellion had gone sour so quickly that neither

---

[39] See Item 68 and Davies, *Revolt*, p. 119. On the date of Pwll Melyn, see Item 62.53–62n.

[40] Pintoin's account (Item 66) of this invasion is the most complete, but see also those by Jean Juvenal des Ursins (Item 77) and Thomas of Walsingham (Item 68). Davies (*Revolt*, pp. 193–95) is the best modern account.

[41] As with Hotspur's rebellion, these two rebellions are badly in need of more detailed investigations, although Christopher Given-Wilson's anticipated biography of Henry IV for the Yale English Monarch Series may fill some of these scholarly gaps.

had been captured, but their support had also dwindled to only a few. These allies mostly kept them hidden, with few *chevauchées* even attempted. Those that were waged, such as into Shropshire in 1409, often ended disastrously for the rebels (Item 70.45–48). No larger military action could have been attempted; there were simply too few rebels to lay a siege, fight a battle, or even hold on to a castle. By the beginning of 1409 almost all of the castles once occupied by rebel garrisons were back in the hands of the English, although some were too damaged to care about anymore. Aberystwyth and Harlech were recaptured in late 1408 and early 1409.[42]

By this time the English had apparently ceased caring. It cannot be a rebellion if there is nothing to rebel against. Henry IV finally realized that and started issuing pardons to everyone other than the Owain (Item 60). Many took advantage of these. Even Owain's capture of Dafydd Gam, a prominent Welsh loyalist to the English crown, in Spring 1412, warranted little attention and even less action (Item 68.254–55). Henry died on 20 March 1413, and was replaced by Prince Henry. Owain remained at large, but Henry V had other business: an invasion of France was more on his mind. He even offered the old rebel leader a pardon on 5 July 1415, although it was not accepted (Items 64 and 65).

Owain Glyndŵr died at the end of September 1415, perhaps on the 20th or 21st.[43] Henry V probably never heard about it. He was then in France, and a month later, on 25 October, he fought the battle of Agincourt, certainly the greatest English victory in the Hundred Years' War, if not in the entire Middle Ages. In an interesting twist, Dafydd Gam was with him; perhaps the only man on the battlefield who had ever met the great Welsh rebel leader, he was among the very few *English* casualties.[44]

During his lifetime, Owain Glyndŵr was lauded for his military leadership. His ambassadors to the French court had described him as a great soldier and a great leader of soldiers. Welsh poet Iolo Goch called him "the candle of battle" (Item 4.54), who

> did nothing but ride horses . . . in dark armor, carrying a lance, a brave proper lord, an iron socket and a thick jacket, a spear rest and a mail coif and a fair helmet . . . and on its top . . . a red plume of the bird of Egypt. He was the best soldier of the time. (Item 4.35–43)

Even Owain's enemies marveled at his martial prowess and military leadership: he was a *armiger formosus* [a handsome esquire], wrote the author of the *Historia vitae* (Item 28.5). Of course, historians looking back, now more than 600 years, are too cynical to accept what was written contemporaneously, even when both sides in this conflict seem to agree. Maybe they are only reacting to a Welsh nationalism that has built century after century on a mythological foundation that began to be laid not long after Owain's death. For Welsh nationalists he thus remains the very example of a military leader, compared easily to those great names mentioned at the beginning of this article: Alexander the Great, Caesar, Hannibal, Scipio Africanus, Pyrrhus, Charlemagne, William the Conqueror, Saladin, Richard the Lionheart, Edward III, John the Fearless, Mehmed the Conqueror. He was clearly none of these. Maybe the most apt comparison is to that French general of a generation later than Owain,

---

[42] Davies, *Revolt*, p. 125. On the surrender of Aberystwyth, see Item 68.133–253.

[43] Sources vary, but this is the traditional — if unlikely — date.

[44] Jones, *Agincourt 1415*, p. 118, and Barker, *Agincourt*, pp. 319–20.

a leader like him who would arise suddenly to capture castles, win battles, inspire troops to great victories against huge odds, and then, when it seemed that nothing could defeat them, fall almost as quickly as (in this case) she had arisen: Joan of Arc.[45]

There was also one other similarity between these great heroes of the Welsh and French: even if only for a little while, they made life very miserable for the English.

Aberystwyth Castle. Despite extensive English efforts to drive them out, Owain's rebels held this important fortification from 1404 to late 1408.

---

[45] DeVries, *Joan of Arc: A Military Leader*.

MICHAEL LIVINGSTON
THE BATTLE OF BRYN GLAS, 1402

Christe, Dei Splendor, tibi supplico, destrue Gleendor.
Iste versus fuit scriptus in fine chori Monachorum Sancti Albani.

[Christ, Splendor of God, I beg you, destroy Glyndŵr.
This verse was written at the end of the choir of the monks of St. Albans.]

These two simple lines — likely recording a piece of choir graffiti no longer in existence — give us a surprising insight into the psychological impact that Owain Glyndŵr's Welsh rebellion had in the heart of England: they are scribbled into the bottom margin of the entry for 1403 in a copy of Thomas Walsingham's *Chronica Maiora* housed at the Benedictine Abbey of St. Albans just north of London in Hertfordshire, some two hundred miles from the action of the Welsh rebellion.[1] Yet we see here that, far away from any physical threat, the monks were praying that divinity would succeed where royalty had failed. They were praying for God to destroy Owain Glyndŵr.

It is a kind of historical commonplace to disregard Owain Glyndŵr's revolt today, to view the Welsh rebellion as an essentially inconsequential blip in the mainline history of England. To King Henry IV and the men and women of England at the time, however, the rebellion in Wales was nothing less than a threat to the very existence of the realm. This is, in retrospect, a simply remarkable fact in and of itself: on paper, after all, Wales was hopelessly outmatched against the power of the English crown. And in truth the rebellion began — despite the high solemnity and symbolism of declaring Owain the rightful prince of Wales on 16 September 1400 — with what appeared to be a rather localized issue, a squabble over lands and rights between the English Lord Grey of Ruthin and the Welsh Lord Owain of Glyndyfrdwy.[2] The initial damage was confined to a small district of North Wales, and it seemed to be quickly defused by the king's rapid reaction, along with the lesser-known but perhaps more essential actions of some of his subjects, like Hugh Burnell of Shropshire, who defeated Owain on the banks of either the Severn or the Vyrnwy near

---

[1] Cambridge, Corpus Christi College MS 7, fol. 3r, quoted by Marchant, "*In Loco Amoenissimo*," who provides an interesting discussion of the local ramifications of the marginalia.

[2] There are long-standing questions regarding the specific cause of Owain's rebellion, whether it was a political land dispute with Ruthin (as in Item 68.5–6) or a personal character dispute with him (as in Item 28.6–14). The truth, no doubt, lies in the fact that then, as now, the personal often was the political. Their close border across Llantysilio Mountain would have inevitably given rise to economic frictions between Ruthin and Glyndyfrdwy, tensions that would no doubt have been exacerbated by the cultural divide between the neighboring English and Welsh lords. On the proclamation of Owain as prince of Wales, see Item 11.

Welshpool on 24 September 1400.[3] Henry IV invaded the area in October, and while he never encountered Owain himself, the king apparently thought that his show of power was enough to settle things down. By November Welshmen were being brought to trial for their part in the nascent rebellion (Item 11). Henry IV had confiscated Owain's lands (Item 10), and he was handing out general pardons to those Welsh who would willingly submit to the crown (Item 12). The king was moving on to other matters of state: stamping out the last supporters of the deposed King Richard II, quelling religious dissent that the new English administration considered tantamount to anti-State proclivities, reconsidering relationships with the Continent, and dealing with the incessant rumblings of Scotland in the north. To Henry IV and his advisors Owain's revolt must have seemed a small plot indeed against such grand theater, especially given the historical tendency on the part of the English to disregard the Welsh anyway: it is not difficult to imagine how easily many of the English might have shrugged off the early months of Owain's actions as a laughable bit of barbaric nonsense and nuisance "over there." After all, it was just this kind of attitude that may have helped give rise to Owain's struggle in the first place, as his complaints to the crown about Ruthin went unheeded by Lord Grey's fellow Englishmen, who reportedly considered the Welsh "barefooted buffoons" (Item 72.6).

But to the king's apparent surprise — and perhaps hinting at the possibility that the local squabble was more a pretext for rebellion than an actual cause for it — these local struggles quickly metastasized into something far more fearsome and frightening. On 1 April 1401 Owain's cousins Rhys and Gwilym ap Tudur seized Conwy Castle, prompting Henry IV to appoint Henry "Hotspur" Percy to take command of the English forces in Wales (Item 22.1–11). Less than two months later, the continuing news from Wales was that the situation was deteriorating. On 26 May of 1401 we find Henry IV writing an anxiety-ridden letter to fourteen counties of the realm, summoning men and arms to Worcester in response to reports "that Owain Glyndŵr and other of our rebels from our country of Wales are raising themselves and forming a new assembly on the marches of Carmarthen with the intention to enter into our realm with a strong force in order to destroy our English tongue and all our loyal lieges and subjects" (Item 16.3–7). In less than a year the conflict between Ruthin and Glyndyfrdwy had somehow become — at least in rumor, since Owain reportedly denied these accusations (Items 21 and 24) — a war whose aim was nothing less than the destruction of England.

To the crown's great relief, subsequent dispatches from Wales brought good news for the English: Hotspur had defeated a Welsh force near Cader Idris on 31 May (Item 18). Even more importantly, John Charlton reported that he and his men had beaten Owain himself on 1 June, seizing the rebel's banner and a number of prisoners in a battle likely near Mawddwy (Item 17). The Welsh threat, once again, seemed to dissipate. The king's force in Worcester disbanded two weeks later, and on 24 June Hotspur at last took back Conwy Castle from Rhys and Gwilym ap Tudur. The revolt struggled on, and Henry IV would indeed make another punitive raid into Wales that September, but there appears little sense that Owain's rebellion was a cause for national concern in England. The Battle of Hyddgen in the summer of 1401, for instance, large though it looms in the national memory of Wales, goes entirely unnoted in the English chronicles of the day: our only

---

[3] We have little information about many of the battles in Owain's rebellion, but the sources for this engagement are particularly slight: see Lloyd, *Owen Glendower*, p. 32n3.

contemporary source attesting to the battle is the important anonymous Welsh text *Annales Oweni Glyndwr* (Item 70).[4] For a time, one might say, only one side was really showing up for the war. Yet by 1403 the monks at distant St. Albans were scared, apparently frightened enough to appeal to God for vengeance. What, one wonders, had happened?

The change, at least in part, was undoubtedly due to the Battle of Bryn Glas, perhaps the most striking Welsh victory in history — without question the most important success they had achieved against the English since the Battle of Llandeilo Fawr in 1282. In this engagement, on 22 June 1402, St. Alban's Day, Owain Glyndŵr's Welsh army defeated the English forces of Sir Edmund Mortimer, one of the most powerful lords of England. More than that, Owain obliterated them. Six hundred years later, a headline in London's *Daily Telegraph* would look back on the battle and declare it "Wales's Finest Hour."[5]

Even in the contemporary aftermath of the engagement people understood that what had happened at Bryn Glas might well be a turning point in English history, and from our historical perspective we can see that it no doubt was: news of this single crushing blow ran like wildfire through Wales, England, and indeed the rest of the world. For the Welsh, it was a triumph that reignited a flagging cause: without it one doubts that Owain's rebellion could have lasted much longer; with it, the rebellion would last another ten years and would see Owain negotiating treaties with foreign leaders and overseeing an oft-forgotten French invasion of England. For the English, however, it was a strike that spurred new fears about the safety and security of the realm. The crushing defeat led the English poet John Gower, for instance, then in apparent retirement in London, to rouse himself to write a Latin poem, "Presul, ouile regis," that questioned the effectiveness of the crown.[6] Beyond the raw emotions of the outcome, the Battle of Bryn Glas set in motion a series of events that brought Henry IV to the brink of disaster: the king refused to ransom Mortimer from Glyndŵr's hands, ultimately leading him to join Owain's cause and eventually sign the so-called *Tripartite Indenture* — or something very much like it — with Glyndŵr and Henry Percy, the earl of Northumberland, a document that aimed at nothing less than a dissolution of the English crown (Item 47). And even before that, Mortimer's capture and the king's refusal to ransom him had no small part in pushing the Percies into open rebellion against the crown, resulting in the Battle of Shrewsbury, the tragic, calamitous fight in which thousands of Englishmen died and King Henry IV very nearly lost his life and his kingdom.

The connection between these two battles — Bryn Glas and the far more famous Shrewsbury, separated by a mere thirteen months — would eventually become so ingrained in the English consciousness that 192 years later Shakespeare opened his dramatization of the period with the Earl of Westmorland bringing the news of Bryn Glas to King Henry IV:

> My liege, this haste was hot in question,
> And many limits of the charge set down
> But yesternight, when all athwart there came
> A post from Wales loaden with heavy news,

---

[4] It is possible that there is oblique reference to this early battle in Adam of Usk's *Chronicle* (see Item 22.12–15), but this is far from certain.

[5] Rogers, "Wales's Finest Hour," p. 12. The phrase has subsequently stuck; see Rees, "Battle."

[6] Gower, "Presul ouile regis," in *Minor Works*, ed. and trans. Yeager, pp. 50–51. That this poem was written in response to Owain's victory at Bryn Glas has not previously been observed.

> Whose worst was that the noble Mortimer,
> Leading the men of Herefordshire to fight
> Against the irregular and wild Glendower,
> Was by the rude hands of that Welshman taken,
> A thousand of his people butchered —
> Upon whose dead corpse there was such misuse,
> such beastly shameless transformation,
> By those Welshwomen done as may not be
> Without much shame retold or spoken of. (*1 Henry IV*, I.i.34–46)

The "misuse" of the dead of which Westmorland will not speak is the supposed desecration of the English corpses in the aftermath of the battle: later English chronicles, starting with Walsingham's *St Albans Chronicle*, report that Welsh women moved over the field, cutting the genitals off the dead and stuffing them into the dead men's mouths, then cutting their noses off and stuffing them into the dead men's anuses (see Item 68.42–46) — a gruesome image, astonishing even against the background of the bloody butchery that is medieval warfare.

Alicia Marchant has argued strongly that Walsingham's presentation of these acts is unlikely to be true, that it is a means by which the chronicler worked to "emphasise the alterity of Wales and its inhabitants," painting them in the most uncivilized, barbaric, and backward light.[7] Perhaps this is so. Still, the fight was a brutal one, all the more so for its lopsided outcome, and there are indeed multiple reports of the mistreatment of the English dead after Bryn Glas, if not necessarily of the same inhumanity that Walsingham imagines. The accusation is present, in fact, in what appears to be our earliest description of the battle in any detail, the account preserved in the *Historia vitae*, which appears to date to the first months of 1403.[8] In this chronicle the anonymous compiler records that while Owain himself was a gentleman to the defeated men, one of his fellow Welsh leaders, Rhys Gethin, was not:

> This one either killed or mutilated or captured all those resisting him. Thus in that conflict around four hundred Englishmen were slain, among whom were four knights. . . . Therefore the bodies were lying amongst the feet of the horses, red with their own blood, being forbidden to be buried for a long time afterwards. (Item 28.88–93)

Bishop David Thomas, speaking six hundred years later at a service of reconciliation on the site of the battle, observed that it cannot have been "Wales's finest hour" in 1402 "to leave hundreds dead on the hillside."[9] At the same time, the rumors of the aftermath underscore the impact of the battle itself, which makes it all the more important that we work to understand what happened on this field, on this bloody ground, on St. Alban's Day, 1402.

The Combatants: Owain and the Welsh

Even before Bryn Glas, Owain Glyndŵr appears to have been having a good summer in 1402. Following up on his success at the Battle of Hyddgen, in which he had managed to fight his way out of what was apparently an English ambush on the high slopes of Plyn-

---

[7] Marchant, "*In Loco Amoenissimo*."

[8] See "A Note on Dating the *Historia vitae*," at the end of this essay.

[9] Boobbyer, "Second Battle of Pilleth," p. 21.

limon, Owain chose to launch an ambush of his own. In mid-April, Glyndŵr descended on Ruthin in northern Wales. In a brilliant bit of maneuvering and plotting, he managed to capture Lord Grey, his arch-enemy and perhaps the Englishman who had done the most to draw him into rebellion against the crown (see Item 28.6–14). With this valuable hostage in tow, Owain apparently retreated at once to the mountains of Snowdonia, securing his prisoner as far from English eyes as possible.[10]

True to his eventual magical reputation, Owain Glyndŵr had disappeared into the mists, but it would not be for long. Only a few weeks later he descended into Mortimer's lands in Maelienydd (formerly a cantref of the Welsh region of *Rhwng Gwy a Hafren* [Between Wye and Severn], later northeast Radnorshire). It is tempting to imagine that Maelienydd was the Welsh leader's destination, especially given the remarkable success he would have at Bryn Glas. This is, for instance, the opinion of the writer of the *Annales Oweni Glyndwr*, who reports that "Owain rose up, and a great host with him from Gwynedd and Powys and Deheubarth, and he made for Maelienydd" (Item 70.19–20). At the same time, this appears to be a case of biased hindsight driven by his shocking victory over Mortimer. Rather more likely is Geoffrey Hodges' theory that Owain's move into Maelienydd was the initial action toward a sweeping raid on horseback — in medieval terminology, a *chevauchée* — through Glamorgan and then Gwent in southern Wales: only the "good fortune" of Owain's encounter with Mortimer on 22 June led him to end these larger plans and delay the southern *chevauchée* until August, since the subsequent priority of the Welsh "would surely have been to take their prisoners and plunder back to north Wales first."[11] Regardless of Owain's initial aims for his raiding this strategically important area of Wales right at the doorstep of Herefordshire, then, it is safe to say that he probably had no intentions of engaging in a pitched battle in Maelienydd. He could hardly have been planning, in other words, the kind of engagement that was subsequently fought there at Bryn Glas.

Owain's army, such as it was, was probably a confederation of what might today be termed bands of guerrilla fighters. Owain, then in his forties, had a long track record of military service and command, and the spirits of his men were probably high after his success at Hyddgen. Among its other leaders was the aforementioned Rhys Gethin (later called Rhys "the Fierce").[12] The Welsh under their direction at the Battle of Bryn Glas could hardly have numbered more than a few hundred men, many of them using ponies — cheaper, more durable, and in need of less food than warhorses — in order to move more quickly across the hilltops of Wales. Less wealthy than their English foes and more reliant on the maneuverability required by their guerilla tactics, there would have been few if any among their numbers who could boast the kind of tank-like armor that no doubt shone upon the English nobles that they would face in battle. Owain and at least some of his men probably wore mail shirts, with a breastplate at best: it was far less comforting than full plate upon the field, but it was far more comfortable off it. There would have been a contingent of foot-soldiers to go with the mounted men — though nothing quite the same in numbers or armament as the

---

[10] And valuable Lord Grey was: in the November parliament Henry IV would agree on a ransom of some 10,000 marks for his safe return (Item 25.4).

[11] Hodges, *Owain*, p. 67.

[12] Famous as he was, it is uncertain whether this war-leader was Rhys Gethin ap Gruffudd of Nantconwy, a descendant of prince Dafydd ap Gruffudd, or Rhys Gethin ap Rhisiart of Builth, whose family were deprived of their lands for supporting Glyndŵr; see Fychan, *Pwy Oedd Rhys Gethin?*

English, as we will see — but it is probable that a good number of Owain's men were Welsh archers whose skills with the longbow were already the stuff of legend. The collected power of the Welshmen lay not in their quantity, therefore, but in the lightning speed of their raids, the devastating accuracy of their longbows, and their intimate knowledge of the lands through which they moved — a knowledge that had much to do with what the English perceived as their "magical" ability to melt into the countryside. The Welsh forces had proven to be fast, unpredictable, and efficiently deadly.

The Combatants: Mortimer and the English

At the time of the battle Edmund Mortimer was twenty-five years old. Since the death of his elder brother Roger in Ireland in 1398, he had been placed in charge of the vast estates of the Mortimer family, holding them in guardianship for Roger's underage son, the 5th earl of March (b. 1391). This young nephew was also named Edmund Mortimer, which has been a source of confusion for many historians and writers, including Shakespeare, who conflates the uncle and nephew in *1 Henry IV*. The Mortimer lands were substantial enough to make the elder Edmund one of the most powerful Marcher lords in the realm in 1402. At the same time, however, the very bloodlines that brought the family wealth and power were a threat to no less than the king himself: young Edmund Mortimer had been heir presumptive to Richard II, and there were many in the realm who might not have been opposed to Henry of Lancaster's deposition of that king who nevertheless *did* oppose Henry's usurpation of his throne; the crown should have fallen not to Henry IV, they might have thought, but to young Edmund Mortimer. No surprise, then, that after Henry IV's coronation, the young boy, not yet eight years old, found himself and his brother in the king's custody, his eponymous uncle left in the odd position of overseeing the Mortimer lands in his name. It would not have been lost on Henry IV that the Mortimer family might thus have had some common cause with Owain Glyndŵr in desiring his overthrow. Though there is no evidence to support them, rumors spread soon after Bryn Glas that Edmund Mortimer had purposely led his men to slaughter there, conspiring all along to join Owain in his rebellion; those rumors, in turn, no doubt factored in the king's decision not to ransom Mortimer and all that followed from it.

All that, though, was yet to come when Mortimer set out from his castle at Ludlow in order to engage Owain Glyndŵr. How many men he had with him is uncertain. Walsingham informs us that the Welsh incursion "forced almost the whole of the knighthood of Hereford and esquires of the counties into armed conflict" (Item 68.34–35), but what did this mean in practice? Our earliest reference to the battle, a letter of Henry IV's written on 25 June, only a few days after the slaughter, speaks only of the news that "our rebels there have lately taken our very dear and well beloved cousin Edmund Mortimer and several other knights and esquires in his company" (Item 23.3–5): the fate of the hundreds of common folk who died around these high-born figures goes unobserved by the king. Our only textual evidence for the numbers involved in the battle must come, therefore, from the chronicles. This is unfortunate, because the chronicles, despite their often coldly aloof appearances, are rarely (if ever) unbiased accountings.[13] The texts are flawed to one degree or another, which makes it all the more important that we look to those few other pieces of evidence that remain. In particular, we must look to the ground. While vegetative patterns can change and roads can be built, major terrain features do not alter over the small timescale of human history,

---

[13] For more on ways to read the chronicles, see Marchant's essay in this volume.

setting aside the rather pronounced exception of events like Krakatoa. Bryn Glas remains where it was over six hundred years ago. Drains have helped bring more tillable land to bear for the farmers, and tractors now roll amiably where the ground was once too marshy for oxen to pull a plow, but on the whole the topography has little changed. This gives us some key insights into what happened here, allowing us to flesh out the textual evidence and put us on solid footing indeed. For the numbers, though, even the ground will not help us, and we are left with only speculation.

The *Historia vitae*, writing within a year of Bryn Glas, tells us that four hundred English-men died (Item 28.90; compare 78.66). The contemporary *Dieulacres Chronicle*, however, paints a far more grim picture of fifteen hundred slain upon the field (Item 42.40). News of the defeat was so staggering, so shocking, that it even reached Adam of Usk, who was then in distant Rome. More than a decade after the battle, he reported that "as many as eight thousand persons died miserable deaths before Owain emerged victorious" (Item 62.3–4). More realistic, one suspects, is Thomas Walsingham's eleven hundred dead on the English side (Item 68.40). The truth is no doubt far short of Adam of Usk's extreme figure, and the even fifteen hundred total in the *Dieulacres Chronicle* has the appearance of being a rounded-up count (Item 42.40). The truth is likely somewhere between the early reports of four hundred slain and Walsingham's eleven hundred. The chronicles all agree that the loss for the English was in the end almost total — a statement of approximate astonishment that rarely equates with actual reality — so we might speculate that Mortimer set out with, at best, less than two thousand men. More likely he had not much more than a thousand, as our sources are in agreement that Mortimer mobilized quickly in response to news of Owain's proximity. There simply was no time to gather a larger force. Even so, the English-men apparently far outnumbered the Welsh.

Not only did Mortimer's men outnumber their Welsh adversaries at the Battle of Bryn Glas, but they were also likely to be better armed and far better armored. Mortimer, the knights, and the wealthier men upon the field would surely have worn plate armor over their mail — a breastplate or brigandine on the torso, with various smaller plates strapped to their extremities — and they would have ridden upon horseback as the kind of heavy cavalry whose use reached back through the distant days of William the Conqueror. They would have favored swords for melee combat, but their initial weapon of engagement would have been the lance. The great helm was by this time being replaced by more advanced helmets like the visored bascinet, but this rural fight, which all accounts agree was fought on short-notice, would surely have brought out a mix of the most state-of-the-art military technologies with arms and armor that were a generation or more out-of-date. Most of the infantry men, often called men-at-arms, would have worn mail sleeves and collar under-neath a brigandine or breastplate. They would likely have had a simple, open-faced bascinet for a helm, and they would have been armed with a mix of staff-weapons (polearms): spears and halberds backed by daggers, intermixed with the occasional poleaxe and sword. Where the mounted men might have had the archetypical curved-triangle shield — by this time likely notched in the corner in order to better control and support a lance — the foot-soldiers would have had a motley of shields in nearly every shape and size.[14] Though it dates from the late fifteenth century, the sketches in the *Beauchamp Pageant* reveal something of

---

[14] For descriptions and examples of these and other terms of military materials, see DeVries and Smith, *Medieval Military Technology*, particularly pp. 85–93.

the noticeable contrast between the forces. One of the more interesting images depicts Richard Beauchamp among John Charlton's Englishmen riding against Owain and his Welshmen on 1 June 1401.[15] The English cavalry wear full plate and ornate helms, and their steeds are adorned with armor plates upon their heads. The Welshmen wear simple mail, simple helms, and wield simple weapons. It is a contrast of power, of wealth, and of fighting styles. In 1401 that contrast spelled victory for the English as they drove the Welsh into full retreat. In 1402 at Bryn Glas that contrast would spell something far different.

The Site of the Battle

Somewhat rare among medieval battles, the battlefield at Bryn Glas can be localized to at most a square mile. The early account in the *Historia vitae* attests that the fight happened "on one of the mountains . . . not far from the said town of Ludlow" (Item 28.77–79; compare 78.58–59); this affiliation with the castle at Ludlow, which occurs elsewhere, is almost assuredly due to this being the Mortimer family seat of power, where Edmund himself was born and from which he departed in June 1402 in order to attack the Welsh. Adam of Usk, writing a dozen years later, is more specific as to the local ground, informing us that the battle happened "near Knighton in Wales" (Item 62.1). Forty years after the event, the anonymous composer of the *Wigmore Chronicle*, who lived within perhaps fifteen miles of the site, is even more precise: the battle happened, he writes, "upon the mountain called Bryn Glas within Maelienydd near Knighton" (Item 74.4). Written around the same time, the Welsh text *Annales Oweni Glyndwr* concurs, locating the battle "near Pilleth," the town that sits in the Lugg river valley, right at the foot of Bryn Glas (Item 70.21). By the middle of the fifteenth century, then, a location near Bryn Glas (Welsh for "blue-green hill," presumably referring to its lack of trees in the period, as now) appears to be accepted essentially without doubt. Of those sources written within a century of the battle, only the *Prose Brut*, composed some eighty years after the event, provides an alternative location we will discuss below: the great slaughter occurred on Black Hill, it says, a slightly taller summit beside Bryn Glas (note to Item 71.5–9). Later legends would place the battle upon the valley floor below Bryn Glas — and this is indeed the site on many maps, including those of the Ordnance Survey — but our early sources repeatedly emphasize a location on Bryn Glas, not below it. To this we can add as corroborating evidence a number of local stories about mass burials associated with the hill. In 1847, Evan Williams of nearby Knighton observed that at Pilleth church "the funerals do not average more than two a year, this parish being one of the smallest in the Principality. In digging out graves here, great quantities of human bones are always discovered," a fact he associated with "the severe conflict" that had occurred there in 1402.[16] Not long afterward, a mass burial was found higher up on the hillside above the church; six sequoia trees were planted in pairs on the spot by Sir Richard Green-Price, Bart., of which four still stand today, prominently marking the location.[17] If the tale of the sequoias is true

---

[15] This image has previously been regarded by critics as depicting Beauchamp's fight with Owain near Abergavenny in 1404; see the notes to Item 89.

[16] Williams, "On the Church," p. 330.

[17] Some of the bones from the hillside were apparently reburied in the churchyard in a location marked by a stone slab, but there is no contemporary written record of these excavations or indeed of any of these discoveries. Today the location of the church burial is marked by a simple flat stone, reading "May all who fell in the Battle of Pilleth, 1402, rest in peace." The trees above, which are

— and we have no reason at all to doubt it — then there is no question that a significant portion of the fighting took place high upon the side of Bryn Glas itself: there would be no reason to drag the dead up such a slope, passing the consecrated ground of the church along the way, in order to bury them. They were buried, it would seem, more or less where they lay. Such a scenario would fit, too, the evidence of our sources, which emphasize the hill itself as the location of the battle. In recording the event in the *Historia vitae*, for instance, the chronicler makes clear that Mortimer "fearlessly ascended the said mountain" in order to attack the Welsh (Item 28.82–83).

The notion that the fight took place on the fields below seems likely to be the result of the existence of at least four mounds that appear to be tumuli — known today as Cuckoo Pen Mounds I–IV — that are scattered along the north bank of the River Lugg. (These mounds, along with other features and important locations are marked on the map below; the fourth mound is located within the earthworks of Castell Foel-Allt.) Though these earth mounds have never undergone formal archaeological investigation, the Royal Commission on the Ancient and Historical Monuments of Wales (RCAHMW) has concurred with long-standing local tradition in associating them with "the burial places of the slain."[18] As we will see, however, the hillside and valley floor battle locations may not be mutually exclusive: a fluid battle, the kind of fight that Bryn Glas might have been, would have ranged across a wide ground before or after the primary engagement, resulting in several mass burials.

The Theories of the Battle

As we have already seen, the precipitating event for the Battle of Bryn Glas was Owain's incursion into Maelienydd, where the Welsh raided English settlements. As Thomas Wal-singham writes in his *St Albans Chronicle*, "Owain Glyndŵr intensified his customary attacks" there (Item 68.33–34), and Edmund Mortimer, as soon as he heard of the raid in nearby Ludlow Castle, immediately sent out a call for men to rush toward his side. The *Historia vitae* hints at the possibility that it was known that Owain was making a pilgrimage to the church at Pilleth, "where a certain image of the blessed virgin Mary was greatly honored" (Item 28.78), but this seems suspicious in the extreme: it requires the entire operation to be an elaborate ambush with a high degree of foresight and false intelligence. While only a couple of months earlier Owain had proven capable of similar plotting in his homelands of north Wales by drawing Lord Grey of Ruthin out of his castle and into an ambush — aided, it seems, by "some members of his household" in a remarkable case of espionage (Item 28.59) — it would be remarkable indeed to imagine the Welsh leader simultaneously constructing an even more complex operation in the heart of the English March. It is far more likely that the *Historia*'s tale of Owain's pilgrimage — which is nowhere else in the sources — is either a confusion of facts or a construction meant to explain the seemingly inexplicable obliteration of so many Englishmen.

native to the Sierra Nevada Mountains of California, are often called "Wellingtonias" in the literature of the battle. The original name of the species, given by John Lindley in 1853, was, in fact, *Welling-tonia gigantea*, but this was quickly shown to be invalid (the name *Wellingtonia* was already in use for another plant). It was not until the twentieth century that a new binomial name was made standard: *Sequoiadendron giganteum*. The continuing use of the name *Wellingtonia* is not only scientifically in-correct, it is considered by many international botanists to be a sign of lingering cultural imperialism (Ornduff, "A Botanist's View," pp. 11–12).

[18] RCAHWM, *Radnorshire Inventory*, 1913, p. 135n558. For questions of authenticity, see note 38.

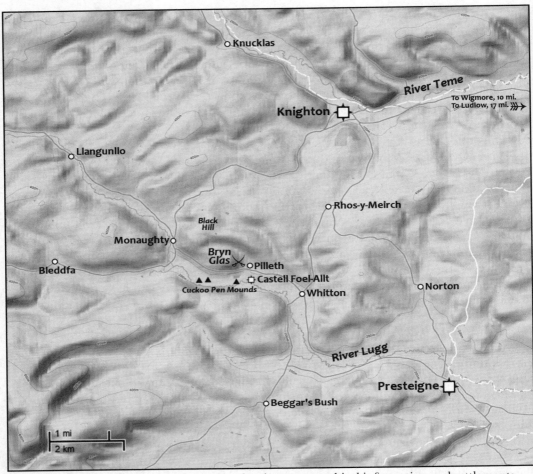

Map of Bryn Glas and surrounding areas, showing topographical information and settlements.

At any rate, the standard reconstruction of the battle has Mortimer quickly gathering a large army from Herefordshire and the surrounding area, then marching from Ludlow to the valley of the River Lugg. Perhaps gathering more men at Presteigne, his forces then continued up the valley, roughly following the path of the modern road, B4356, to meet Owain's men on the hillside above Pilleth. There are several possible routes to be taken from Ludlow to the Lugg valley, but no matter the path the English would have had to cover at least twenty miles before they reached Pilleth, uphill essentially all the way. Owain, seeing the advancing English at a distance, smartly positioned himself upon the treeless mount of Bryn Glas, raising his banners in view of Mortimer below him. As the English closed in, the Welsh archers began to fire down upon their enemy, and because of their higher position they were able to strike before the English could even bring them within range. Even when they did get close enough to return fire, Mortimer's own archers — who were gathered from the surrounding Welsh lands of Maelienydd — were ineffective in their fusillade, either due to the difficulty of ranging a bow uphill or because of a prior agreement to betray the English. Mortimer, forming up ranks, then ordered his army in a standard frontal charge directly up the steep grade, through the continuing assault of Owain's archers above. At this point, according to the standard account of the battle, Mortimer's Welsh archers abruptly switched sides, turning and firing point-blank into the English ranks. The English army was pinned down and slaughtered, and Mortimer was captured. The dead were left to rot for some time before they were interred on the hillside, and Owain retreated to Snowdonia to hide Mortimer, his prisoner, alongside the earlier captured Lord Grey of Ruthin.

This is, to be sure, a rather compelling and even cinematic reconstruction of what happened on 22 June 1402. There are several difficulties that stand in the way of viewing this traditional account as the full story of the Battle of Bryn Glas, however, starting with Mortimer's route to the battle. The *Prose Brut* provides us a key piece of evidence in our effort to track the actions of Mortimer and Owain, informing us that before the battle "Owain burned a town of the earl of March in Wales, that was called Knighton" (note to Item 71.5–9). Associations of the battle with Knighton (though not necessarily with that town's burning) are also found in Adam of Usk's *Chronicle* and the anonymous *Wigmore Chronicle* (Items 62.1 and 74.4).[19] If Owain had indeed attacked Knighton on the River Teme, then it is little wonder that Mortimer reacted with such urgency at Ludlow, sending "a message there quickly to the men and those who were attached to him in Maelienydd in Wales, asking that they not neglect to come to his aid in this dire necessity" (Item 28.79–81): Ludlow Castle is only 17 miles down the River Teme, and one of his secondary castles, Wigmore, lay between them. Mortimer knew that if Knighton fell then Owain was a very real threat to the heartland of his family estates. Counter to the traditional reconstruction of the battle, however, the only sensible response to such a present danger would have been for Mortimer to move his army directly up the threatened valley of the Teme from Ludlow rather than marching over the hills south to Presteigne and then up the still-unthreatened valley of the Lugg.

Hodges, observing just this problem, resolved that Mortimer must logically have driven his forces up the Teme, but that he then abandoned this valley and crossed the hillsides down into the valley of the Lugg — perhaps following the line of Offa's Dyke to do so — when he became aware that Owain had retreated from Knighton and moved south. Hodges surmised that Mortimer camped near the present town of Whitton on 21 June, watching the Welsh gather on the hillside ahead of them, and he then led the ill-fated assault in the early morning.[20] While such a reconstruction admirably resolves one problem with the traditional account, it only intensifies another: the foolishness of Mortimer's charge up the hill. The traditional account *might* allow one to conclude that the decision was made in haste as the English marched up the valley; however, if Mortimer had indeed crossed the hills himself and then encamped in the valley of the Lugg — giving up, we might add, any of his own tactical advantage upon the heights — he would have had ample opportunity to consider the likely outcome of a headlong charge up a steep grade against a well-placed enemy.

There are, sadly, many medieval examples of forces charging uphill against highly defensed positions and paying a terrible price. In some cases it is difficult to discern a reason

---

[19] Previous scholars (see, e.g., Hodges, *Owain*, p. 75, and Noble, "Further Excavations," p. 61) have also attributed as evidence for a Knighton assault a mysterious source quoted by local historian William Hatfield in 1947 regarding a pre-battle Welsh raid on the town (*Knighton*, pp. 10–11). I have now identified Hatfield's source, however, as G. A. Henty's 1899 juvenile novel *Both Sides of the Border*, a historical fiction retelling of the early fifteenth century. See Livingston, "Hatfield's Mystery Source."

[20] Hodges, *Owain*, p. 76.

to explain the decision of the field commanders (as at Neville's Cross on 17 October 1346), but in most cases historians have been able to identify reasonable (if incorrect) explanations for such assaults. In the case of Bryn Glas, attempts to explain what was a disastrous uphill charge appear to be as old as the battle itself. After all, Henry IV's conspiratorial suggestions that Mortimer had secretly been in league with the Welsh, while perhaps politically expedient, also served to explain the seemingly unexplainable: Mortimer knew the ground, he knew the enemy, and yet he charged.[21]

One cannot discount the impact of foolishness on the course of human affairs, and this appears to have been one of the main ways that historians have endeavored to explain Mortimer's action: he was either not a military man or he was driven to act by the same kind of "aggressive pride" that caused the French charges to fail against the brave and well-commanded English troops at Morlaix on 30 September 1342.[22] This is the implication, for instance, of Jon Latimer, who writes that the young Mortimer "rashly ordered a direct uphill charge."[23] Inexperienced in war, perhaps Mortimer simply did not know any better than to run his tired army directly up an open hillside under a heavy rain of arrows. It was foolish, but Mortimer was a foolish leader. Perhaps this is so, though it is quite clearly a circular argument: Mortimer is considered a failure on the field because he failed so badly on the field. The argument informs us only about the outcome of the engagement, in other words; it tells us nothing about the rationale for the decisions that led up to it.

An appeal to Mortimer's presumed ignorance (or arrogance) also works under the assumption that he was the only man involved in making the tactical decisions on the ground, and that his decisions, even when alarmingly misguided, were carried out without question. Yet there were, by all accounts, a number of knights on the field, many of whom were "men of proven military experience, whose families had long traditions of service," and who were surely anxious to share their knowledge base with the commander who had their lives in his hands.[24] Ian Skidmore — though supporting the traditional account of Mortimer marching up the valley of the Lugg and ordering "an immediate charge up the slopes of Bryn Glas" — nevertheless notes how preposterous it is that such an order — one that ignored the "basic axiom" of medieval tactics "that attacks were not launched on an enemy occupying higher ground" — was actually carried out: "In the massacre which followed, in which the Welsh archers went over to the rebels, over 1,100 of the Herefordshire levies were slain, amongst them famous soldiers of the day who must have been astounded at Mortimer's order."[25] Scholars might well debate the number of the dead (as we have seen), but there is

---

[21] The subsequent relationship between Owain and Mortimer also had much to do with rumors that Mortimer had planned all along to side with the Welsh: his foolish assault was part of an elaborate plan not only to switch allegiances but also to destroy a significant portion of the English forces en route. This is unlikely to be true. Quite to the contrary, Owain's sudden retreat once he had Mortimer, followed by the many months of delay between Mortimer's capture and his change of allegiance, speak to a lack of planning for such a result. More likely, the Lancastrian regime encouraged such conspiratorial rumors both to mitigate the military failure and to cast aspersions against Mortimer's character and prevent others from joining his banner.

[22] On this earlier battle, see DeVries, *Infantry Warfare*, pp. 142–44.

[23] Latimer, "Last Prince," p. 45.

[24] Hodges, *Owain*, p. 70.

[25] Skidmore, *Owain Glyndŵr*, p. 83.

no debating the names and accomplishments of some of the English commanders who died in the slaughter: Robert Whitney of Whitney Castle, Sir Kynard de la Bere of Kinnersley, who had thrice been sheriff of his county (1387, 1396, and 1401) and been knight of the shire in 1399, and Sir Walter Devereux of Frome, also a sheriff and knight of the shire (1401).[26] In addition to the dead, there were those who were captured, which included Thomas Clanvowe, himself a sheriff (1399).[27] Walsingham calls them "the strongest soldiers of the region" (Item 68.36), and it was these heavy losses, we might recall, that were on the mind of the king three days afterwards.

We might also note that Owain himself does not seem to have taken Mortimer for a fool: some months later, in November, the imprisoned Englishman would switch sides to the Welsh cause, marry Owain's daughter Catrin, and give military support to his new father-in-law. Owain subsequently placed Mortimer in charge of the important Welsh-held castle of Harlech until his death there from disease in 1409; such trust would be strange indeed if Mortimer were entirely blameworthy for the charge at Bryn Glas.

On balance, then, we must assume that something must have driven Mortimer to consider such an assault to be reasonable. One possible rationale is that Mortimer was simply desperate: he saw Owain, determined that it was "now or never," and so made the assault. In a famous and perhaps instructive historical example to which we will return, Philip IV and his tired French forces were most likely prompted to make the ill-fated charges uphill at Crécy on 26 August 1346 as a result of concerns about Flemish forces that might arrive to reinforce the English; it could be that Mortimer was similarly worried about reinforcement arriving to aid the Welsh.

This is quite possible, though in the standard account of the battle it really does nothing to allay the issue at hand; if Owain wanted to leave, he could simply have easily moved west and retreated back to the battered Knighton or even further up the Lugg valley toward Bleddfa, closer and closer to his own territory. The fact that Owain instead stayed and fought indicates that either he was supremely confident in his position (and Mortimer was once again a fool) or he himself had no choice, which is hardly the case if the English had made the difficult trek across the hillsides and then encamped in the valley before them as Hodges imagines. More likely, Mortimer's assault was excusable to Owain because Mortimer and his men had good reason to *think* they had all the advantage when they very much did not. Owain had outsmarted the English forces, trapping them into an ambush not at all dissimilar to the one that he had sprung a few months earlier on Lord Grey at Ruthin.

Not all scholars have been willing to accept an account of the battle revolving around this kind of action. Davies, for instance, seems to be hesitant to accept that Owain might have conducted an "ambush" of Mortimer, as if such a designation would demean the accomplishment of the Welsh.[28] Nevertheless, it has become increasingly common to view

---

[26] Lloyd, *Owen Glendower*, p. 51.

[27] Lloyd, *Owen Glendower*, p. 52. Many historians, including Lloyd, also identify Thomas Clanvowe as a poet, author of "The Cuckoo and the Nightingale," but this is a nineteenth-century misidentification. It was Thomas' father, John Clanvowe, who was a close friend of Geoffrey Chaucer and the author of several works of Chaucerian poetry. See Symons, *Chaucerian Dream Visions*, p. 29n38.

[28] *Revolt*, p. 107. This hesitancy is no doubt driven in large measure by nationalistic pride, which is ironic: to assume that Owain could only be a success if he met the English army in a traditional English engagement is to assume that the English tactics are perforce normative, the standard by

Mortimer's actions as indicative of some kind of clever stratagem on the part of the Welsh. According to a recent reconstruction dramatized by the BBC for its *Battlefield Britain* series (and accompanying book), for instance, Owain divided his forces on Bryn Glas as soon as he became aware of Mortimer's approach up the valley. First, Owain placed his line of archers near the summit of the hill, keeping them hidden from the English but still giving them range over the approaching slope, which is roughly 300 meters from summit to base — which they claim (wrongly in my estimation) to be the lethal range of the period long-bow.[29] Second, he moved a substantial part of the Welsh forces down into a small ravine on the north side of Bryn Glas that separates it from the higher Black Hill. Third, Owain himself took a small party down the slopes, making his personal presence clear to the advancing English. Mortimer, seeing his prize with such a small number of Welsh rebels, chased them up Bryn Glas. Once on the slopes, however, he came under fire from Owain's archers. Next, Mortimer's own contingent of archers, which the BBC depicted upon the English left flank, turned on him.[30] Then, as the English labored up the increasingly steep hillside under the aerial onslaught from above and to the left, the hidden part of the Welsh force sprang up from the ravine and charged into the English right flank. The resulting devastation would have been, as the chronicles report it, essentially total, and Mortimer would have been overcome by superior generalship, not undone by foolish stupidity.

Such a reconstruction suitably attempts to explain both Mortimer's decision and the totality of the Welsh victory. It also perhaps coincides with the tactics deployed by Owain at Ruthin, where he drew Lord Grey out into the countryside under a feigned retreat, only to have the greater part of his forces waiting for him in the mountains, where they cut off the Englishman's retreat and captured him.[31] At the same time, a visit to the battle site reveals at least one significant issue: the flanking theory depends upon Owain hiding hundreds of his men in the ravine in order to have them surprise the English in a dramatic flanking action, yet this ravine is visibly open to the valley floor as the road passes up from Whitton. Brough, one of the foremost academic proponents of this theory, surmises that there may have been more vegetation in the ravine in Owain's day, but even if such a hypothesis is true it seems a stretch to imagine it would be dense enough to hide any kind of useful force.[32] After all, even the slightest hint of their presence would presumably end the ambush before it began.

---

which actions should be judged. It is, therefore, an odd position to take, especially as the matter relates to a man leading a rebellion against England.

[29] Snow, *Battlefield Britain*, pp. 71–75. The effective range of the longbow remains a point of much contention both inside and outside of academia, due in large part by debates about the draw weight of medieval bows. Modern forensic studies from the Battle of Towton (1461) and the wreck of the *Mary Rose* (1545), however, have helped to answer many of our questions about bow manufacture and usage. As a result, 200 yards now appears to be useful approximation of the maximum range for the typical medieval longbowman (not far from the "eleven score yards" in a statute from Henry VIII's reign); see Waller, "Archery," pp. 131–32.

[30] The sudden turn of Mortimer's bowmen against him, like Mortimer's charge itself (see note 20), has been the subject of some conspiratorial theorizing. Brough, for instance, imagines how they might have been "alerted or recruited initially by Glyn Dŵr's agents who had infiltrated the area the year before" (*Glyn Dŵr's War*, p. 87), which is a grandiose vision to say the least.

[31] This earlier ambush likely took place in the area of the small hamlet of Bryn Saith Marchog.

[32] Brough, *Glyn Dŵr's War*, pp. 88–89.

Bryn Glas from the East, showing the superiority of the Welsh position upon the hilltop, and the open ravine along its flank. The church is the white building at center.

Short of revising geography or simply declaring Mortimer and his men imbeciles, therefore, how can we account for the actions at Bryn Glas? What happened here? And what of the Cuckoo Pen Mounds, possibly associated with the battle?

The Battle of Bryn Glas Reconstructed

In the end there are only two plausible English routes to the battlesite, paths that make sense of most of the evidence at hand.

The first, which is discussed by Hodges before being abandoned in favor of his theory that Mortimer crossed the hills between the valleys of the Teme and Lugg near Whitton — not seeing the far greater flaws with that argument — is that Mortimer's route up from Presteigne followed not the northern bank of the River Lugg, where the modern road is today, but the *southern* bank. This was indeed, according to local traditions, the route of the "old" road, which ran along the lower slopes of the hills on that side of the valley, far above the marshy floor. Mortimer would have made his crossing at a ford — or perhaps even a bridge — that has vanished but whose existence might be inferred from the ruins of Castell Foel-Allt, an old earthwork and timber fortification that may have been built to protect a crossing here during the Early Middle Ages but was, by Owain's time, in disuse.[33] A distinct mark in favor of this theoretical route for the English forces is that approaching Bryn Glas from this direction more adequately hides the ravine from view. Thus Owain would be more able to place troops there and mask the size of his command, a fact that could have excused Mortimer's charge. A mark against this route, however, as Hodges rightly observed, is that the English would have been crossing a river within sight of the Welsh forces — a dangerous operation under any conditions, but particularly difficult with the enemy so close at hand.[34] There is, too, the problem that has already been raised with the traditional account: it is highly likely that Owain and his Welsh forces assaulted Knighton prior to the battle, and that it was this attack that brought Mortimer and his army of Englishmen marching forth from Ludlow Castle.

---

[33] Wiles, J. "Castell Foel-Allt," in Coflein, 2002 <http://www.coflein.gov.uk/en/site/92400/>. For many details of the local topography I am grateful to a July 2011 visit with Peter Hood of Pilleth.

[34] Hodges, *Owain*, p. 73.

Bryn Glas from Castell Foel-Allt (and the site of Cuckoo Pen Mound IV), south-east near the River Lugg. In the foreground, running from lower left to upper right is a farmtrack that may correspond to a road and river crossing protected by this fortification. **A**: West, up the Lugg valley; it is in this area that Cuckoo Pen Mounds I–III are located; Black Hill is out of sight behind the summit of Bryn Glas. **B**: Pilleth Oaks, site of the battle according to Ordnance Survey maps. **C**: The slope of Bryn Glas, with the lone stand of trees marking the site of the mass burial associated with the battle; further to the right, running down to D is the ravine that may have served to hide some of Owain's men. **D**: Partially hidden in the trees is the church supposedly burned at the time of the battle (and in the churchyard of which is another mass burial); below and to the right is Pilleth Court and the base of the slope.

The second plausible route for the English forces — one not yet considered by scholars, yet perhaps the one which best accounts for the facts both within the sources and on the ground itself — is that Mortimer approached the battle not from the east, but from the west.

In this scenario, Mortimer and the English would have marched with all haste up the south bank of the River Teme— essentially though not exactly following the path of the A4113 today — with the primary aim of securing the town. Owain, on their arrival or just prior to it, fled south, toward the valley of the River Lugg. If there is any truth to the *Historia vitae*'s report that Owain helped set his trap in claiming that he was making a pilgrimage to the church at Pilleth, "where a certain image of the blessed virgin Mary was greatly honored" (Item 28.78), then this might well have happened at the time of this retreat. At any rate, though, he would have moved along the old road to the south over the low hills and down upon Monaughty, roughly five miles from Knighton. (The modern A488 takes a lower path than the medieval track, which still winds along the hillsides to its east.) He may have continued two miles onward, possibly burning the tower at Bleddfa at this time.[35]

The author of the *Prose Brut* states that the Battle of Bryn Glas occurred the morning after the burning of Knighton, and this makes good sense (note to Item 71.5–9). Only after being sure of the safety of that beleaguered town did Mortimer turn from a defensive strategy to an offensive one and set off to the south after his prey. Intriguingly, coming to Bryn Glas from Knighton via Monaughty would have brought the English forces around the sides of Black Hill, the taller summit beside and behind Bryn Glas that was, according to the *Prose Brut*, the location of the battle (note to Item 71.5–9). As noted above, the traditional account of the

---

[35] See Noble, "Further Excavations," pp. 60–61. It is more probable, thogh, that this destruction (if even associated) occurred after the battle, as Owain retreated toward Snowdonia with his prize.

English forces coming up the Lugg would have done nothing to prevent Owain from escaping if he so chose. But if Owain had fled south from Knighton, Mortimer might well have thought that he had the chance to cut off Owain's escape by pursuing him. Should Owain by chance move down the Lugg, then Mortimer would be at his back, pinning the Welsh between his own army and any additional forces gathering a short six miles down the river at Presteigne — which is never mentioned once in the sources (yet another mark against theories of the English routing through an eastern direction), but surely would have been put on high alert. And Owain did indeed move down the Lugg: when the English followed them to Monaughty, the Welsh hurried east down the valley: it is less than a mile and a half from Monaughty to Pilleth church at the foot of Bryn Glas. Mortimer and his veteran knights would surely have been elated. They had trapped the rebel. They had him on the run.

Whichever of these alternative routes Mortimer took — and the evidence (particularly that in the *Prose Brut*) seems to favor the western approach through Monaughty — the English would have arrived at essentially the same point: the southeast corner of the base of Bryn Glas. They could have had no idea that the Battle of Bryn Glas, which now began, would end so horrifically. They had no idea the ambush that Owain had set ahead of them. Whether coming from the west or the south, they could not see it.

What happened next has an interesting precursor and an intriguing successor in two of the most famous battles of the Hundred Years' War: Crécy and Agincourt. At the early conflict at Crécy in 1346, Edward III had taken the high ground from the French. The approaching slope, though slight compared to the greater advantage the Welsh would have at Bryn Glas, managed to slow the advancing French at the very same time that it served to increase the range advantage of the English longbowmen, who shot wave after wave of arrows into the enemy in what became a legendarily lopsided battle. At Bryn Glas, Owain, who might well have had men at his side whose fathers had served the English in France, similarly seized the high ground and put his enemy at a disadvantage that would, he no doubt hoped, work to cancel out the enemy's advantage in numbers and arms.

In fact, the Welsh in 1402 outdid the English position at Crécy. The terrain that Owain had chosen not only gave his men the higher position, but it also naturally hemmed in the field of battle: to the Welsh left was a long ravine that would stall or prevent any English attempt to flank on that side; to the Welsh right was an even steeper slope than the one faced by the English center — it might even have been the case that then, as now, the trees grew heavy on that south-facing slope, which would take an unlikely chance of flanking and render it impossible. The English thus had a front before them that was only two hundred meters wide, a breadth that greatly restricted their ability to use their numbers to any positive effect. Indeed, the funneling of Mortimer's men, combined with the exhausting slope, would no doubt have caused the advancing force to pile up as the men in front stumbled from the steep climb or from the steady onslaught of arrows that the Welsh longbowmen began to rain down upon them. The scene, in fact, has striking familiarity with the position taken by Henry V and the beleaguered English forces at Agincourt in 1415, a mere thirteen years later. There, too, an outnumbered force used the natural terrain — in Henry's case, the forests to his left and right — to hem the greater numbers of the enemy into a killing field where ranks of longbowmen had an integral role in sending them into oblivion. The future Henry V made his mark as a field commander combating against Owain in Wales, and he no doubt had ample opportunity (and a powerful motive) to learn what had happened at Bryn Glas. As it happens, the majority of his longbowmen at Agincourt were also Welshmen — no small number of whom might well have served at Bryn Glas and could not have mistaken the irony. It would not be surprising, in fact, if the arrangement of English forces at Agincourt gives us an insight into the arrangement of Welsh forces at Bryn Glas: foot-soldiers forming a strong middle rank, with wings of longbowmen stretched out and forward to either side. As the enemy struggled up the steep grade, advancing toward the middle and Owain's bright banner, the wings of Welsh longbowmen would be striking them from both left and right.

The ravine to the Welsh left at Bryn Glas may have been used simply as a geographical obstacle to an English flanking maneuver. If it was not, if there is any truth to the theory of Owain hiding forces within it — which is impossible with the traditional route of the English, is just possible with a route on the southern bank of the Lugg that crosses at Castell Foel-Allt, and is wholly plausible with the western route through Monaughty — then these "reserve" forces were more likely to be a cavalry than the second wave of footmen imagined by the BBC: it would be a poor strategy indeed that required your flanking force to clamber onto the field by climbing the very same steep embankment that served to dismay the enemy's flanking action in that same direction. A mounted force would be more flexible, and its aim would hardly have been to rise up into the English flank upon the hillside. To the contrary, it would have been aimed at the English flank at the *base* of Bryn Glas. The English would not have sent all their men in a single mad rush up the slope — as the BBC insensibly portrays. Most medieval battles happened in organized waves, often with the commanders among the reserve units directing the engagement. As Edward the Black Prince had done at Poitiers in 1356, Owain might have used a hidden cavalry to ride out and flank the enemy command as soon as the advantage on the field was revealed. For the Black Prince, this maneuver had won him the king of France as a prisoner. For Owain, it would win him the prize of Edmund Mortimer.

Visiting Bryn Glas today reveals a pleasant stretch of countryside, green and quiet, but by noon on St. Alban's Day, 1402, it would have been awash in the sound of trumpets and hooves, steel and screams. The Welsh forces had moved up the hillside ahead of the English, their archers setting positions and firing down upon the English. The banners signaling Owain's personal presence were no doubt provocative enough to goad them into the attack, but it may be that Mortimer was further provoked when Owain burned the church at Pilleth, which stands on the lower slopes of Bryn Glas.[36] The church does indeed seem to have been razed at this time; the current church has undergone extensive recent restoration.[37]

Mortimer had Owain nearly in his grasp, and according to the chronicles he clearly thought he had the advantage: he "went to that hill boldly," and he "feared nothing of any greater consequence than the flight of the Welsh" (Items 78.61, 68.36–37). The *Historia vitae* relates how Mortimer "fearlessly ascended the said mountain" (Item 28.83). He may have been confident that the numbers were heavily on his side, but the Welsh position was not as weak as it seemed. As the English made their assault, the Welsh arrows ripped holes through their ranks. Owain himself might have retreated back and back, egging the enemy forward, until with a roar his men rushed down the slope into the English as "the two forces came together with a great charge" (Item 28.83). It would have been then, as Mortimer's men began to break and run, that their archers, Welsh tenants of Mortimer's lands whose feudal obligations had made them a party to the fight, turned on the English: "Alas!" Wal-

---

[36] Brough, *Glyn Dŵr's War*, p. 90.

[37] For a synopsis of the restoration efforts, see Boobbyer, "The Second Battle of Pilleth."

singham laments, "an act of betrayal intervened in affairs, and those who had hoped to gain victory were unexpectedly defeated, for their own archers turned their bows against their own force and killed those with whom they should have been standing firm" (Item 68.39–42). It is possible that then, in a final *coup de grace*, Owain's cavalry could have ridden forth, smashing into Mortimer's command and causing his army to be "deceptively surrounded," as the author of the contemporary *Dieulacres Chronicle* writes (Item 42.39–40).

Though the Cuckoo Pen Mounds have not yet been excavated, if the RCAHMW and local traditions are correct in associating them with the battle then it is possible we can trace the bloody next steps by the four tumuli that dot the valley floor: they mark at least four occasions when men fell in rough groupings. It is dramatic to imagine these deaths happening during the initial stage of the battle — especially if the English came from the west, and perhaps caught bands of Welsh that were harrying the English, trying to draw Mortimer into the trap at Bryn Glas — but it is far more likely that the tumuli (if associated with this event) represent post-battle deaths as the English who fled the slaughter on the hillside were struck down. In terror and confusion, the English would have fled in three directions: back up the valley toward Monaughty (Cuckoo Pen Mounds I and II), straight away from the sudden cavalry charge into their flank (Cuckoo Pen Mound III), and finally toward the river crossing at the ruins of Castell Foel-Allt.[38] Caught in such an elegant and effective Welsh ambush, though, it hardly would have mattered where the English went. Death followed them all.

Mortimer had done his best — had done, one might say, what almost any other commander at the time would have done — but the results were an English tragedy. It was a massacre perhaps not on the numerical scale of Agincourt or Crécy, but as a measurement of total loss it was every part the equal if not the better of those more famous engagements.

The Aftermath

The stunning news of Mortimer's resounding defeat at the Battle of Bryn Glas moved swiftly through England. No longer could Glyndŵr's rising be treated as a matter confined to the distant wilds of Wales. Owain had destroyed an English county levy on the very doorstep of the realm, a mere twenty miles from Leominster. R. R. Davies calls the battle "one of the most momentous in the revolt," pointing out how, after Bryn Glas, "the Welsh rebels could no longer be dismissed," and that "the alleged mutilation of the bodies confirmed contemporary fears of the savagery of the Welsh and fed the anti-Welsh hysteria of the men of the border countries:

> The seriousness of the setback was measured in the response it elicited: steps were immediately taken to safeguard border castles such as Clifford and Radnor; Brecon was placed in a state of defence; and even in far-away Swansea a garrison was installed for twenty-eight days in July–August.[39]

---

[38] There is good reason to question the connection of the mounds with the battle, however. Recent excavations of the three "burial mounds" on the field of the 1461 Battle of Towton (so identified by both local tradition and the 1995 English Heritage Register of Historic Battlefields) have revealed "no traces of human remains . . . no evidence of underlying grave pits." Rather than battlefield memorials, the Towton mounds appear instead to be "prehistoric round barrows" (Sutherland, "Archaeological Investigation," p. 163). The same could very well be true of the Cuckoo Pen Mounds, which like much of the battlefield awaits modern forensic survey.

[39] Davies, *Revolt*, p. 107.

Only three days after the battle, Henry IV was writing to his council from Berkhamstead in Herefordshire, notifying them that he would lead the effort "to resist and combat the wickedness of our aforesaid rebels" (Item 23.14–15). And so he did: on the very same day the king sent urgent orders to his sheriffs, summoning those men in the crown's employ — knights, squires, and yeomen from various parts of the country — to move at once to Lichfield in preparation for an assault on Owain Glyndŵr and the rebellious Welsh.[40] Meanwhile, the Welsh cause had new hope, new inspiration for the future. Men flocked to Owain's banner, and Adam of Usk reports that the Welsh rebels were making a frightening raid into south Wales, directly threatening the prosperous towns of Usk, Caerleon, and Newport (Item 62.15–17).

There was, too, the political and social fallout from Owain's capture of Mortimer, the king's refusal to ransom him, and then the earl's subsequent joining with the Welsh cause. E. F. Jacob observes that the "capture and defection of Mortimer meant that Maelienydd and the Mortimer lordships of the middle and upper Wye as well as that of Blaenllyfni on the upper Usk were lost to the English cause and a great hole had been made in the loyal marcher centre."[41] Moreover, Owain now had a political pawn of staggering influence. After his defection, Mortimer wrote a letter to his Marcher tenants urging them to support Owain (Item 26), and he was clearly a central figure in opening up dialogue with the Percies.

St. Alban's Day 1402 was a dramatic event, and how deeply the shock of it penetrated the English psyche can be seen in how quickly the English chroniclers began to associate Owain's physical victory — like William the Conqueror's victory over Harold Godwinson at Hastings three-and-a-half centuries earlier — with metaphysical signs: celestial phenomena and mystical prophecies about the doom of Edmund Mortimer himself. For example, the anonymous author of the *Historia vitae* reveals a fascinating mix of skepticism and belief in these superstitions, along with a genuine fear of Owain, when he writes about the aftermath:

> Therefore the bodies were lying amongst the feet of the horses, red with their own blood, being forbidden to be buried for a long time afterwards. Here it is supposed, according to the opinion of certain people, that that prodigy, which had occurred at the birth of the said Edmund, was fulfilled in this conflict. For when he had been given forth into this light from his mother's insides, his own horses were found standing in the stables in blood almost up to their knees. But may it be so that it was fulfilled in this way, lest something worse happen to us in some other matter, through that very man and on account of that very man. (Item 28.92–97)

Later accounts only increased the ominous portents at Mortimer's birth, no doubt casting his personal doom as a way of defending the resounding English failure at Bryn Glas. An English chronicle of the mid-fifteenth century, for instance, reports:

> In the birth of this Edmund befell many wondrous signs; for out of the floor of his father's stable welled up blood so high that it covered the feet of the horses, and all the sheaths of the swords and daggers in the house were full of blood, and all the axes were red with blood. And when Edmund lay in his cradle, he would not sleep nor cease crying until he saw a sword or some instrument of battle. And when he sat

---

[40] For the text of Henry's orders, see Rymer, *Foedera*, 8.264–65.

[41] Jacob, *Fifteenth Century*, p. 42.

in his nurse's lap he would not be still until he had some instrument of war to play with. (Item 73.24–30)

Other sources not only repeated this association between the supposed signs at Mortimer's birth and the bloody results of the conflict at Bryn Glas, but they also went further by connecting the trauma of the battle with the appearance of a comet that had been visible across much of Europe in March of 1402.[42] Walsingham writes in his *St Albans Chronicle*:

> In the month of March a comet appeared, at first between Capricorn and the Bear, that is in the north-west, emitting awesome flames, and travelling at a great height. Eventually it changed direction to the north, but finally ceased to be visible in that region of the sky, portending, in my opinion, the shedding of human blood in the vicinity of those regions in which it appeared, Wales and Northumberland. (Item 68.19–23)

Walsingham includes the blood spilled in the north, but other writers honed in more fully on the conflict in Wales. Thus we find in the *Beauchamp Pageant* that

> at thies daies appered a blasyng sterre called *stella comata* which after the seiyng of clerkys signyfied greet deth and blodeshede. And sone upon beganne the Warre of Wales by oon Owen of Glendour their chief capteyn. (Item 89.1–3)

The bloodshed at Bryn Glas had become, it seems, a matter of supernatural reckoning, a connection that was no doubt strengthened by the rumors of Owain's apparently magical ability to disappear into the Welsh hillsides when cornered, or to control even the weather itself. Henry IV's subsequent late-summer campaign, for example, ended in disappointment and near disaster when the weather in Wales turned "phenomenally bad, and rain, hail, and snow conspired to make the three weeks which the English spent in the country a time of hardship, loss, and misadventure."[43] As a kind of microcosm of the campaign, on 7 September the king himself "encamped for the night in a most pleasant meadow; he had not long retired to rest when a sudden storm arose which, amid torrents of rain, blew down the tent in which he was sleeping and put him in peril of his life — he was only saved because he had taken the precaution to sleep in his armour."[44] Little wonder, then, that for the English Owain would quickly grow to become the supernatural figure that he is in William Shakespeare's *I King Henry IV*.

The Battle of Bryn Glas was a significant turning point in the rebellion of Owain Glyndŵr, a catalyzing moment in the struggle for an independent Wales. What happened there among the now-quiet hills and fields was surely reason enough for the distant monks of St. Albans to pray for divine retribution upon the magical Welsh warrior who could melt in and out of the mists, leaving little behind but the dead.

---

[42] This comet was visible from February to early April of 1402 and is marked across many of the chronicle accounts of the time: from England to Asia (Kronk, *Cometography*, pp. 260–64).

[43] Lloyd, *Owen Glendower*, p. 54.

[44] Lloyd, *Owen Glendower*, pp. 54–55.

To the Welsh, Bryn Glas was victory and pride, great banners gold and red. To the English, it was nightmares and fears, darkness and dread.

Owain Glyndŵr had come like a bolt from the sky, and what he left behind in his wake depended — as history so often does — on whose book you read.

A NOTE ON DATING THE *HISTORIA VITAE*

George B. Stow, Jr., in his introduction to the standard edition of the work, observes that "of all he chronicles covering the reign of King Richard II, the *Historia Vitae et Regni Ricardi Secundi* survives in the largest number of manuscripts, making it more popular than even Walsingham's histories."[45] The *Historia vitae* (also called, confusingly, the *Vita Ricardi*, and extracted as Item 28 in this volume) is, without question, an important source for our understanding of not only Richard II's reign, but also the first years of Henry IV's: the chronicle reports events from 1377 to 1402, providing at times what Stow reveals to be "significant original information" and "a totally independent history" (p. 4) that proves "especially valuable" on many subjects and events (p. 10). As Stow reveals, the text as we have it is not a unified work. What was previously considered a single-authored chronicle is almost assuredly composed by two hands: one from 1377 to 1390 (and probably to be identified with Nicholas Herford, prior of Evesham) and the other from 1390 to 1402 (an unnamed monk of Evesham) (p. 3). Attempting to date the work of the second author of this chronicle — and thus date the *Historia vitae* as an extant text — Stow writes:

> Internal evidence again indicates a structural independence for the *Vita Ricardi* from 1390 to 1402. Although there are occasional back-references in the later part of the text, none refers to a point before 1390. Other references show that this half of the text was written during the reign of Henry IV. Under the year 1399, for instance, the *Vita Ricardi* contains two references to Henry IV "qui nunc est" [who now is (king)]. More particularly, mention of the punishment of Gloucester's murderers in Claudius B.ix permits us to date this manuscript no earlier than 1404, but Tiberius C.ix can be shown to have been written as late as 1413 since it refers to Richard II's burial at Westminster. (p. 3)

Dating the *Historia vitae* through these two manuscripts — the earliest surviving examples of the two families of the chronicle's manuscript tradition as identified by Stow (pp. 23–24) — has, since the publication of his edition in 1977, resulted in a standard dating of the *Historia vitae* between 1404 and 1413. Stow's dating of the Tiberius manuscript is without question, since Richard II's body was indeed moved from the church at Kings Langley to Westminster Abbey in 1413. For all the strengths of his valuable editorial work, however, Stow has likely erred in his *terminus post quem* dating of 1404 based on the fate of Gloucester's murderers in the Claudius manuscript. In a later footnote he says more precisely that Claudius B.ix was "probably written c.1404" (p. 40n180), yet even this, as we will see, is too late. The second part of the *Historia vitae* should instead be dated to the first months of 1403, making it very important in gauging the English reaction to (and understanding of) the early events of Owain Glyndŵr's rebellion.

---

[45] *Historia Vitae et Regni Ricardi Secundi*, ed. Stow, p. 1. All subsequent parenthetical citations are to this book.

The *Historia vitae* ends with events at the end of 1402 or the first month of 1403: the robberies of shrines of the Holy Blood at Hailes and of St. Edward at Westminster, the former dated specifically by the chronicler to "hoc etiam anno, 17 Kalendas Ianuarii," i.e., 16 December 1402 (p. 175).[46] Interestingly, its account of earlier events shows no awareness of the later evolutions of them. Adam of Usk, for instance, when he presents the capture of Edmund Mortimer at the Battle of Bryn Glas on 22 June 1402, takes the opportunity to explain how he would go on to marry Owain Glyndŵr's daughter, father four children by her, and then die at Harlech Castle during the English siege (Item 62.1–11). Thomas Walsingham does much the same in his recounting of the capture, hinting at "Mortimer's subsequent notorious association with Owain" (Item 68.49–50). Even more common are attempts on the part of the chroniclers to foreshadow the fall of the Percies and the future bloodshed at Shrewsbury when reporting the Percy victory over the Scots at Homildon Hill. There is nothing of this sort in the *Historia vitae*. To the contrary, this chronicle ends on the "high note" of upward trajectory for the Welsh rebellion, which is much to be expected in the months after Bryn Glas but in the main becomes less sensible the further one is removed from that battle. On the basis of content alone, then, the *Historia vitae* must date to after 16 December 1402, and we might have reason to think that a time closer to that date is preferable to one much later: if nothing else, it would be surprising for any chronicler writing after the Battle of Shrewsbury on 21 July 1403 to have failed to account for that event in any way whatsoever.

Stow argues, nevertheless, that the chronicle must be after 1404 because the chronicler thanks God that the murderers of Thomas, duke of Gloucester, did not escape without vengeance: "Carnifices uero omnes non sine uindicta euadere a Deo permissi sunt. Per omnia benedictus, qui perdidit impios" (p. 161). The murder of Gloucester in 1397 was quickly suspected to have been the work of Thomas de Mowbray, duke of Norfolk. It was this very accusation that lay behind the challenge that Henry Bolingbroke — Gloucester's nephew — made to Mowbray in 1398, the challenge that led to the banishment of both men and thus set the stage for Henry's return and the deposition of Richard as king. Mowbray died in exile on 22 September 1399, but a month later Parliament heard how his former valet, John Hall, confessed not only to his own involvement, but also that of several other men, including Mowbray, William Serle, and Nicholas Colfox (who is misidentified in the Rolls as Johan Colfox). Hall was executed immediately after his confession (in rather grotesque fashion), as were, apparently, many of the other conspirators.[47] Though he was not executed, Nicholas Colfox was, within three weeks, stripped of his titles and properties by the king.[48] William Serle escaped justice by fleeing to Scotland. Though he does not provide his specific rationale, Stow's assumption that the *Historia vitae* must be written after 1404 is presumably due to the fact that Serle was at last captured and executed for his role in the murder in June 1404.[49] This is logical enough on its surface, yet some weeks before Serle's capture, on 31 March

---

[46] The chronicle edited by J. A. Giles gives the date of the spoliation of Hailes as 27 January 1403, and states that the robberies at St. Edwards occurred shortly afterward; see *Incerti Scriptoris Chronicon Angliae*, p. 30.

[47] *Parliament Rolls*, ed. and trans. Given-Wilson, 3.452–53. These events are summarized (and the evidence that Johan is Nicholas is given) by J. Leslie Hotson in his argument that Chaucer's Nun's Priest's Tale is an allegory of the murder; see "Colfox vs. Chauntecleer,"pp. 769–71.

[48] *Cal. Pat. Rolls*, 1 Henry IV, 2.57.

[49] *Close Rolls*, 5 Henry IV, 2.1.

1404, the conspirator Colfox had been pardoned by the king for his part in the murder: "Pardon, out of reverence of Good Friday last, to Nicholas Colfox, 'chivaler', for the death of Thomas, late Duke of Gloucester, the king's uncle."[50] Indeed, Colfox was subsequently pardoned again, even more generally, in 1405.[51] The chronicler's high opinion of God's justice for the killers would seem hardly justifiable after these occurrences, in which case March 1404 ought probably to be viewed as a date *before* which the *Historia vitae* was written, not after. That Serle had been forced to flee the country to Scotland was perhaps a sufficient sign of God's justice for the chronicler (especially in light of the executions of Hall and the others), who no more needed proof of vengeance in Serle's capture and execution in 1404 than he must have needed that of the title-stripped Colfox, which never came.

Contra Stow, therefore, our outside dates of composition for the *Historia vitae* appear to be mid-December 1402 (the last events in the chronicle) and the end of March 1404 (the pardon of Colfox for Gloucester's murder). Less conservatively, we might further narrow the range of composition to the first months of 1403. Such a dating would allow time for the dissemination of news regarding the robberies at Hailes and Westminster, and it would readily explain why the chronicler takes no opportunity to foreshadow the Battle of Shrewsbury.

If indeed the *Historia vitae* was completed between January and July 1403, when the Percies arose in revolt, then this chronicle becomes all the more important as a contemporary record of the final events of Richard II's reign and the early events of Henry IV's. Such a dating might also enable us to determine more closely the interactions between this chronicle and those of other writers, like Adam of Usk (whose stages of composition have been superbly revealed by Chris Given-Wilson's recent edition) and Thomas Walsingham (who is seeing new light through the editorial work of John Taylor, Wendy R. Childs, and Leslie Watkiss).[52] In addition, it is possible that a more precise date for the conclusion of the *Historia vitae* may help researchers to identify its author.

For our present purposes, this revised date for the *Historia vitae* makes it contemporaneous to the first years of Owain Glyndŵr's revolt — and the earliest narrative account of the Battle of Bryn Glas.

---

[50] *Cal. Pat. Rolls*, 5 Henry IV, 2.381. Colfox's petition is in *Ancient Petitions*, File 254, no. 12671.

[51] *Cal. Pat. Rolls*, 7 Henry IV, 1.80.

[52] The *Historia vitae* is also utilized, it seems, by the writer of the chronicle edited by Giles (see note 45 above) and by the writer of the English *Polychronicon Continuation* that is preserved in London, British Library, MS Harley 2261 (Item 78 in this volume).

HELEN FULTON
OWAIN GLYNDŴR AND THE PROPHETIC TRADITION

In a court case of October 1400 brought against John Kynaston and others who had proclaimed Owain Glyndŵr 'prince of Wales' earlier that year, Kynaston and the others were accused of *machinantes, conspirantes et proponentes mortem et exheredacionem domini Henrici, regis Anglie* [plotting, conspiring and supporting the death and disinheritance of the lord Henry, king of England]. In the deposition, one of Owain's followers is called "Eragh Fynant, eorum propheta" [Crach Ffinnant, their prophet].[1] Whether the force of this reference is indeed "prophet" or something more innocuous such as "spokesman," it forms part of a popular account of Owain Glyndŵr as a man swayed by prophecy, a man who, as Shakespeare put it, listened to "'the dreamer Merlin and his prophecies" (Item 101.150).

I have already argued elsewhere that rumors of Owain's belief in prophecy have been greatly exaggerated, then and now, mainly for political or ideological effect.[2] The reputation of the Welsh as disseminators of false prophecies, regarded as treasonable if not actually heretical, was well-established by the fifteenth century. It was further entrenched as part of the anti-Welsh rhetoric of Tudor chroniclers such as Edward Hall and Ralph Holinshed and is regularly refurbished as historical fact by modern historians. While not denying the importance of prophecy as part of a medieval worldview (and by no means exclusive to the Welsh), I would argue that there is effectively only one prophecy that mattered to the Welsh, and that was the identity of the *mab darogan*, the "son of prophecy," the leader who would return to rout the Saxons, unite the island of Britain, and restore the Welsh to their rightful place at the center of political power.[3] Earlier Welsh prophecies such as the tenth-century *Armes Prydein*, "The Prophecy of Britain," and a number of those incorporated by Geoffrey of Monmouth

---

[1] Sayles, ed., *Select Cases*, 2.114, and compare Item 11.15–16. Sayles translates *propheta* as "spokesman," though Lloyd has no hesitation in interpreting it as "prophet" (*Owen Glendower*, p. 31). The form *Eragh* seems to be a misreading of *Crach* [W 'scab']; Item 11.15 reads *Craghe*.

[2] "Owain Glyn Dŵr and the Uses of Prophecy." Gruffydd Aled Williams has since argued that I have overstated the case that the evidence connecting Owain Glyndŵr with prophecy is very slim ("Gwrthryfel Glyndŵr," pp. 183–86). The fact remains, however, that only five contemporary documents connect Owain with prophecy, and three of these were produced by his enemies, who had every reason to discredit him. Prophecy was without doubt a key political discourse throughout the Middle Ages, and while I do not deny that Owain made use of prophecy (as he clearly did), it seems to me that the extent of his use of it, and belief in it, has been exaggerated. My reading of Owain's letters is that, far from being in the grip of superstition, he used the prophecy references very strategically and with great political astuteness.

[3] For the relevance of this prophecy to Owain Glyndŵr, see Henken, *National Redeemer*. It should be pointed out, too, that though the notion is undoubtedly earlier, the first known instance of the term *mab darogan* is found in a poem composed later in the fifteenth century, well after the end of the revolt; see below.

into his *Vita Merlini* and *Historia regum Britanniae* pin their hopes on a variety of legendary heroes — usually Cynan, Cadwaladr, or Owain — who will drive the Saxons out of Wales, and even out of Britain entirely, and lead the Welsh to a triumphant return to sovereignty.[4]

As the Norman and then English royal hegemony established itself in the centuries after the conquest, this kind of prophecy appeared increasingly to challenge the legitimacy of the English kings who claimed sovereignty in both England and Wales. The *Prophecy of the Six Kings*, one of the most enduring prophecies of the medieval and early modern centuries, emerged in an Anglo-Norman version around the time of Isabella's deposition of her husband, Edward II, in favor of her son Edward III, and reappeared in a Middle English version during the precarious decades leading up to the deposition of Richard II in 1399.[5] Circulating originally to support the cause of the future Edward III, who deposed his father in 1327, the prophecy describes the succession of English kings after Henry III using the kind of animal imagery familiar from Galfridian tradition and drawing on Geoffrey's Merlinian prophecy of *sex posteri* [six successors] of the Boar of Cornwall and the heroic leader *Sextus* [lit., the sixth], who will defeat Ireland and be crowned with a lion's head.[6] Though Owain Glyndŵr's knowledge and use of this prophecy was overstated by Tudor writers, its circulation at the time of his rebellion illustrates the close link between prophecy and political commentary on the legitimate succession of kings.

With the deposition of Richard II in 1399, an event of cataclysmic and long-lasting significance which led directly to the rebellion of Owain Glyndŵr and his English supporters, the legitimacy of the monarchy of Henry IV came under extreme scrutiny and was explicitly challenged by the rebellion. Small wonder, then, that a number of parliaments under Henry IV issued acts against "false prophecies" by the king's enemies, including Lollards and the Welsh, whose revival of ancient grudges about English rule and insinuations that Richard was still alive were likely to be particularly unwelcome. In 1402, in the heady days of Owain's rebellion when Wales was on fire, parliament decreed that "no wasters, rhymers, minstrels or vagabonds should be tolerated in Wales," since their "divinations, lies and incitements" were the direct cause of the uprisings across the country.[7]

When we look at the evidence for Owain's use of prophecy, it becomes clear that he used it only on formal occasions as a kind of political shorthand to seek support for his claim to

---

[4] Williams, *Armes Prydein*. This prophecy names Cynan and Cadwaladr as the returning heroes, and their names are also found in a number of the Myrddin poems in the *Black Book of Carmarthen* (c.1250), one of the earliest surviving manuscripts containing poetry in Welsh; see Bollard, "Myrddin in Early Welsh Tradition," pp. 24 and 28. The figure of Owain, associated with an historical sixth-century British prince of northern Britain, appears as a returning leader in the poetry of the Welsh princes and gentry from the twelfth to fifteenth centuries; see Bromwich, *Trioedd*, pp. 479–83 and 560–61. There are some twelfth-century Latin references to a Welsh belief that Arthur will return, but Arthur is not otherwise represented as the *mab darogan* in Welsh literature; see Bullock-Davies, "*Expectare Arturum*," pp. 432–40; Loomis, "Legend of Arthur's Survival," pp. 64–71. Faletra has argued that, although Geoffrey of Monmouth refers to the Welsh claim of original sovereignty over the whole island of Britain, it is not a claim which he endorses ("Narrating the Matter of Britain," pp. 60–85).

[5] See Item 1. For a history of the prophecy and its transmission, see Smallwood, "Prophecy."

[6] I have discussed the prophecy and its Welsh versions in *Welsh Prophecy and English Politics*. For Geoffrey's references in the *Prophetiae Merlini*, see Geoffrey of Monmouth, *History*, ed. Reeve, pp. 145, line 43, and 149, lines 99–100.

[7] *PROME*, ed. and trans. Given-Wilson. See also Strohm, *England's Empty Throne*, p. 15.

power, drawing on what seems to be a common discourse of the prophecy (originating in Geoffrey's *Historia*, drawing on earlier Welsh tradition) of a united Britain from which the English have been expelled. From a considerable corpus of contemporary and near-contemporary documents relating to Owain's rebellion, ranging from government records to chronicles and letters, there are only five which refer directly to Owain's use — or alleged use — of prophecy, not an overwhelming body of evidence to suggest that prophecy was rife among the Welsh. I have already mentioned one of these references, to Crach Ffinnant, and I will go on to discuss the other four examples before looking at the general context of disaster portents and then the aftermath of Owain's association with prophecy.

Key References to Prophecy in Contemporary Documents

Owain makes three explicit references to prophecy in three formal documents: his letters of 29 November 1401 addressed to Robert III, king of Scotland, and the lords of Ireland, and the *Tripartite Indenture* of 28 February 1406.[8] In his letter to the king of Scotland, in which he reminds the king of their common descent from Brutus, he asks for military support against the "Saxons," drawing on the traditional discourse of British history derived from Geoffrey of Monmouth:[9]

> Des quex oppressions et bondages le prophecie dit que je serray delivere par eid et socour de vostre dit roial mageste. (Item 22.75–76)

> [The prophecy states that, with the help and support of your royal majesty, I shall be delivered from this subjection and bondage.]

Owain strikes a similar note in his letter to the lords of Ireland — not surprisingly as the letters bear the same date and are clearly part of a strategic attempt to gather a significant army of allies to fight against Henry IV:

> Sed, quia uulgariter dicitur per propheciam quod, antequam nos altiorem manum in hac parte haberemus, quod uos (et) uestri carissimi consanguinei in Hibernea ad hoc manus porrigetis adiutrices. (Item 22.96–99)

> [It is commonly said in the prophecy, however, that, before we can gain the upper hand in this contest, you and your noble kinsmen in Ireland shall come to our aid in this matter.]

Both references assume a shared understanding of a particular strain of prophecy by which Wales, Scotland, and Ireland will unite to throw off the shackles of English rule. The letters may be referring to one specific prophecy, but it seems just as likely that they are referring to the general tenor of the Merlinic prophecies derived directly from Geoffrey of

---

[8] Adam of Usk included copies of the two letters in his chronicle (Item 22.62–117); for the *Tripartite Indenture*, see Item 47. It should be remembered that neither of the two letters to Scotland and Ireland appear to have been delivered into the right hands, but were intercepted en route, perhaps in Ireland (Lloyd, *Owen Glendower*, p. 47).

[9] See, for example, *Historia regum Britanniae*, Book 2, ch. 1.

Monmouth's *Historia regum Britanniae*. The *Historia* circulated in both Wales and Scotland, had been assimilated into their native histories, and was the basis of Owain's claim that the two countries should work together to achieve a common goal of shaking off English overlordship. He begins his letter to Robert III by invoking their shared kinship from the line of Brutus, implicitly referring to Geoffrey's account of the founding of Britain:

> Et, tresredoute seigneur et tressovereygn cosin, pleser seyt a vous et a vostre dit treshautisme majeste dasavoyr que Brutus, vostre tresnoble auncestre et le meyn, estoyt le primer roy corone qui primerment enhabita deinz cest realme dengleterre, qui jadis fuist nomme Brataygne graunt; le quel Brutus engendera trois fitz, cest assavoir Albanactus, Loctrinus et Kamber; de quel dit Albanactus vous estez descenduz par droit lyne, de quel dit Kamber les issuez ount reygnes roialment tanque a Kadualadir, qui estoit le darrein roy coronne de ma dit nacioun, dount je, vostre simple cosin, suy descenduz par droit lyne. Apres que decese mes auncestres et tout ma dit nacion avons este et ore sumes en oppression et bondage desouz mes et vostres morteles enimys Sacsouns. (Item 22.64–73)

> [Most esteemed lord and royal cousin, may it please you and your royal excellence to know that Brutus, your most noble ancestor and mine, was originally the first crowned king to live in this kingdom of England, which used to be known as Great Britain. Brutus fathered three sons, namely Albanactus and Locrinus and Kamber; you are descended from the direct line of this Albanactus, while the descendants of this Kamber ruled as kings until the time of Cadwaladr, who was the last crowned king of my people, and from whose direct line I, your humble cousin, am descended. Since his death, however, my forbears and all my people have been, as we still are, subjected and held in bondage by my and your mortal enemies the Saxons.]

This, then, is the context in which Owain goes on, almost at once, to write about "the prophecy" which says that he will be released from the oppression of the Saxons with the help of the Scots. It is noticeable, too, that when writing to his friend and ally, Henry Dwn, in 1403, Owain refers in the same terms to the long history of Saxon oppression which is now coming to an end:

> Vobis narramus quod speramus auxilio Dei et vestro posse liberare progeniem Wallicanam de captivitate inimocorum nostrorum Anglicorum, qui oppresserunt nos et antecessores nostros a multo tempore jam elapso. (Item 31.2–4)

> [We inform you that we hope to be able, by God's help and yours, to deliver the Welsh race from the captivity of our English enemies, who, for a long time now elapsed, have oppressed us and our ancestors.]

We know, from the evidence of the Welsh poem *Armes Prydein* and other early verse that prophecies of Welsh liberation from English oppression were circulating in Wales well before Geoffrey published his *Historia*, and it seems likely that Geoffrey was drawing on this Welsh tradition of prophecy to shape his account of British history and Merlin's prophecies. There was no need, then, for Owain Glyndŵr to look to an English prophecy such as the *Six Kings* to justify his rebellion; he had only to refer to the ancient Welsh tradition of deliverance from Saxon oppression under a chosen leader, a tradition popularized by Geoffrey and disseminated throughout Britain, certainly to Scotland, if not Ireland.[10]

The third document in which Owain refers explicitly to prophecy is the *Tripartite Indenture* (Item 47), the alliance made between Owain, Edmund Mortimer, and Henry Percy, the earl of Northumberland, on 28 February 1405. The reunited kingdom of Britain was to be divided into three parts: Northumberland would receive the north of England and much of the north Midlands; Mortimer would receive southern England (and his nephew, the young Earl of March, would be made king); Owain himself would possess all of Wales and the Marches as far north as the river Mersey.[11] The written contract drawn up between them refers not to a prophecy but to 'the prophet':

> Item si disponente Deo apparent praefatis Dominis ex processu temporis, quod ipsi sunt eædem personæ de quibus Propheta loquitur, inter quos regimen Britanniæ Majoris dividi debeat et partiri, tunc ipsi laborabunt et quilibet ipsorum laborabit, juxta posse, quod id ad effectum efficaciter perducatur. (Item 47.18–22)

> [Also, if by God's dispensation it should appear to these lords in process of time that they are the same persons of whom the Prophet speaks, between whom the government of Great Britain ought to be divided and partitioned, then they, each alone and together, shall labor to their utmost so that it may be brought about effectually.]

In this document, the "Propheta" almost certainly refers to Merlin, as W. T. Matthews suggests,[12] with the added reference to God as the legitimating force behind the plan. In the prophecies of Merlin included by Geoffrey in his *Historia*, there are references to a tripartite division of Britain which follow on from Geoffrey's earlier claim that the rule of Britain was divided between the three sons of Brutus. Thus Merlin refers to three springs of water dividing the country into three, though the fate of those who try to benefit from the division is not one to be desired:

> Tres fontes in urbe Wintonia erumpent, rivuli quorum insulam in tres partes, seu portiones, secabunt. Qui bibet de uno, diuturniori vita fruetur nec supervenienti languore gravabitur. Qui bibet de altero, indeficienti fame peribit et in facie ipsius pallor et horror sedebit. Qui bibet de tertio, morte subita periclitabitur nec corpus ipsius subire poterit sepulchrum.[13]

> [In the city of Winchester there will erupt three fountains whose waters will divide the island into three portions. Whoever drinks from one will enjoy a long life and will not be oppressed by unexpected illness; whoever drinks from the second will die of

---

[10] There is no evidence of a translation of Geoffrey's *Historia* into Irish.

[11] Williams makes the point that the *Indenture* was in fact a two-way agreement between Owain and Northumberland to give themselves the largest share of land (*Owain Glyndŵr*, pp. 39–40).

[12] Rees and Jones, *Thomas Matthews's Welsh Records in Paris*, p. 126.

[13] *Historia regum Britanniae*, ed. Hammer, 7.6, lines 147–52.

insatiable hunger, and pallor and fright will mark his face. Whoever drinks from the third will fall victim to sudden death, and no one will be able to bury his body.][14]

There is an even closer reference to such a division in Geoffrey's earlier work, *Vita Merlini*, where Merlin speaks of the English oppression and the restoration of Britain by Welsh heroes:

Insuper incumbit gens Saxona marte feroci, que nos et nostras iterum crudeliter urbes subvertit legemque Dei violabit et edes. . . . Tres tamen ex nostris magna virtute resistent, et multos periment et eos in fine domabunt. Set non perficient quia sic sententia summi judicis existit, Britones ut nobile regnum temporibus multis amittant debilitate, donec ab Armorica veniet temone Conanus et Cadualadrus Cambrorum dux venerandus, qui pariter Scotos Cambros et Cornubienses Armoricosque viros sociabunt federe firmo amissumque suis reddent diadema colonis, hostibus expulsis renovato tempore Bruti, tractabuntque suas sacratis legibus urbes.

[For the Saxon, warlike and ferocious, descends on us, savagely overthrows our cities and ourselves once more, and will violate God's law and his house. . . . Three of our men will resist with great bravery, however; they will kill many of the invaders and in the end overcome them. But they will not complete their task. It is the will of the most high Judge that the British shall be without their kingdom for many years and remain weak, until Conan in his chariot arrives from Brittany, and that revered leader of the Welsh, Cadwalader. They will create an alliance, a firm league of the Scots, the Welsh, the Cornish and the men of Brittany. Then they will restore to the natives the crown that had been lost. The enemy will be driven out and the time of Brutus will be back once more. The natives will administer their own cities by the time-hallowed laws.][15]

This prophecy, reminiscent of the Welsh *Armes Prydein*, fits the language of Owain in his letters fairly closely, including the reference to Cadwaladr, the alliance with the Welsh and Scottish, and the restoration of the "crown that had been lost."

While G. W. S. Barrow has suggested that Owain was rather out of touch in using the gambit of the common descent of the Welsh and Scots from Brutus, arguing that the Scots had rejected the legend of Brutus as their own foundation myth and preferred to trace their descent from Pharaoh's daughter Scota, it is clear that Owain was drawing on a well-established tradition of Welsh and Scots co-operation against the English.[16] A late thirteenth-century poem titled *Prophetia Sibillae et Merlini vatis de Albania et Anglia, et eorum eventibus* ["The Prophecy of the Sibyl and the seer Merlin regarding Scotland and England and their

---

[14] Galyon and Thundy, trans., "History of the Kings of Britain," p. 64.

[15] *Life of Merlin*, pp. 102–05.

[16] "Wales and Scotland in the Middle Ages," p. 306. Davies takes a similar line, saying that the Welsh "would have been wise not to have mentioned the Brutus legend at all" (*Revolt*, p. 158). Lloyd points to the chronicle of Walter Bower, written in the mid-fifteenth century, as evidence that "the valiant struggle of the Welsh was watched with close attention and whole-hearted sympathy in the North" (*Owen Glendower*, p. 47), but Walter's comments on the Welsh during the uprising are far from complimentary. For the legend of Gaythelos and Scota as the founding ancestors of the Gaels and Scots, see Bower, *Scotichronicon*, 1.27–45, especially p. 45.

relations"] found in the manuscript attributed to Walter of Coventry, a compilation derived from Geoffrey of Monmouth, Henry of Huntingdon, and other chronicles, refers directly to such co-operation in a prophecy known elsewhere as *Regnum scotorum* ["The Kingdom of the Scots"].[17] Following an opening summary of Scotland's foundation history and its subjugation by the English, the anonymous poet says:

> Bruti posteritas cum Scotis associata
>   Anglica regna premet marte, labore, nece.
> Flumina manabunt, hostili tincta cruore,
>   Perfida gens omni lite subacta ruet.
> Quem Britonum fundet Albanis juncta juventus
>   Sanguine Saxonico cuncta rubebit humus.
> Regnabunt Britones Albanae gentis amici,
>   Antiquum nomen insula tota feret.
> Ut profert Aquila, veteri de turre locuta,
>   Cum Scotis Britones regna paterna regent.[18]

[The descendants of Brutus, allied with the Scots, will overwhelm the English realm with warfare, toil, and slaughter. Rivers will flow, stained with enemy blood. The treacherous people, subdued by every confrontation, will be ruined. The youth of Britain, joined with the Scots, will rout them, the entire land will turn red with Saxon blood. The Britons will rule as allies of the Scottish people, the whole island will bear its ancient name. As the Eagle declares, speaking from the old tower, the Britons with the Scots will rule the ancestral kingdom.][19]

A version of the same prophecy, giving a more subtle emphasis to the role of the Scots, is recorded by Walter Bower in his *Scotichronicon*, where he adds an additional section of unknown origin, to bring in a Merlinian angle:

> Voci verisone Merlini spem prope pone.
> Scoti cum Britone sternent Anglos in agone.
> Flumina manabunt de sanguine; quos superabunt

---

[17] On the uses of the prophecy for anti-Scottish propaganda, see Coote, *Prophecy and Public Affairs*, pp. 71–73. See also Tatlock, "Geoffrey of Monmouth and the Date of Regnum Scotorum."

[18] Coventry, *Memoriale Fratris Walteri de Coventria*, p. 26. At the end of this poem, the author attributes it to Gildas to indicate its antiquity and veracity. For other versions in Latin, see Skene, *Chronicles*, p. 117; Langtoft, *Chronicle*, 2.448. The prophecy was also translated into Welsh and is found in a number of manuscripts including a fragment in National Library of Wales, Peniarth MS 16, fol. 20 (mid-fifteenth century).

[19] The reference to *Aquila* [the Eagle], may be a reference to the *Historia*, where Geoffrey says that Cadwaladr, the last British king, consults Alanus, king of Brittany, who "gathered various books of prophecies, uttered by the eagle which prophesied at Shaftesbury, by the Sibyl and by Merlin" (*History*, ed. Reeve and Wright, p. 280). The reference also suggests a later Merlinian prophecy, the "Prophecy of the Eagle," a thirteenth-century Latin compilation referring to the kings of England from the Norman conquest to the reign of John. See Coote, *Prophecy and Public Affairs*, pp. 61–64; Sutton and Visser-Fuchs, "Richard III's Books."

montes planabunt Britones, diadema levabunt.
Insula tunc uti sic debet nomine Bruti,
cum Scoti tuti vivent Angli quasi muti. (Item 79.214–19)[20]

[Trust in the true-sounding voice of Merlin nearby.
The Scots with the Britons will scatter the English in battle.
Rivers will flow with blood; the mountains which they conquer
the Britons will lay flat; they will raise the diadem.
The island then ought to use the name of Brutus
when the Scots live in safety and the English are like dumb beasts.]

Given the evidence for a robust tradition of prophecy concerning the alliance of the British and the Scots — and it may well be the *Regnum scotorum* that Owain was thinking of when he referred to "the prophecy" in his letter to Robert III — it is hard to share T. M. Smallwood's conviction that the *Tripartite Indenture* alludes to the *Prophecy of the Six Kings*.[21] The reference to the "prophet" in the *Tripartite Indenture* seems rather to invoke the spirit of Merlin as the one who foretold the restoration of Britain from English oppression with the aid of the Scots, in much the same way that Owain situates his own rebellion in his skilfully-worded letter to Robert III.

A fourth document which implicates Owain in the workings of prophecy is the letter from the mayor and burgesses of Caerleon to their counterparts in the city of Monmouth, written in July 1403 to report a confrontation between Owain and the baron of Carew, near Kidwelly in Pembrokeshire (Item 36). As Englishmen loyal to the crown, the burgesses were pleased to report that 700 of Owain's men had been ambushed and cut down by the baron's army. Towards the end of the letter, they report that Owain, while in Carmarthen,

sende after Hopkyn ap Thomas of Gower to come and speke with him uppon trewes [truce]. And when Hopkyn come to Owein, he priede hym, in as meche as he huld hym maister of Brut, that he schuld do hym to understonde how and what maner hit schold befalle of hym. (Item 36.14–17)

Hopcyn ap Tomas ap Einion of Ynys Forgan, near Swansea in south Wales, in the lordship of Gower, was a prominent member of the Welsh *uchelwyr*, or landed gentry, and a well-known patron of Welsh literature. A number of Welsh poets of the late fourteenth and early fifteenth centuries composed praise poems to him, in recognition of his patronage, and he was almost certainly the man who commissioned and designed the Red Book of Hergest, one of the most important anthologies of medieval Welsh prose and poetry.[22] The reference

---

[20] The poem is inserted in the section which covers the rebellion of Owain (without naming him), an account which is highly critical of the Welsh. Matthews also cites this poem as evidence that Merlin is the "prophet" referred to in Owain's letter, but he does not give the source (Rees and Jones, *Thomas Matthews's Welsh Records in Paris*, p. 126). See also Kelly, "Arthurian Material in the *Scotichronicon* of Walter Bower."

[21] Smallwood, "Prophecy," pp. 590–92.

[22] The main scribe of the Red Book was Hywel Fychan ap Hywel Goch, known to have copied other work for Hopcyn ap Tomas. See Daniel Huws, *Medieval Welsh Manuscripts*, p. 80; Roberts, "Hopcyn ap Tomas ap Einion"; Fulton, "Literature of the Welsh Gentry."

to Hopcyn as "master of Brut" has been almost universally taken to mean that Hopcyn was an expert in prophecy, and indeed Owain's reported request that Hopcyn should tell him what will befall him indicates that Owain wants Hopcyn to foretell his fate (which he apparently does, saying, according to the burgesses, that Owain would be captured between Carmarthen and Gower under a black banner).

While Hopcyn took an antiquarian interest in both history and prophecy — and the two genres were almost indistinguishable for many medieval writers, hence the conflation of the two Welsh terms *brut*, 'history', and *brud*, 'prophecy' — he was evidently associated with prophecy in the popular mind.[23] Gruffydd Aled Williams cites references to Hopcyn by contemporary poets Llywelyn Goch ap Meurig Hen and Dafydd y Coed (who both flourished in the second half of the fourteenth century), describing Hopcyn as someone who could interpret prophecy, though this would have been an obvious consequence of his scholarly interests and does not mean that Hopcyn regarded himself, or was regarded by others, as a "prophet" of the same type as Merlin.[24] Given that the Red Book of Hergest contains copies of the Welsh version of Geoffrey's *Historia*, *Brut y Brenhinedd*, and the other major native chronicle, *Brut y Tywysogion*, as well as ancient prophecies associated with Merlin, it is easy to see why Hopcyn might have been called 'master of Brut', and if Owain wanted to draw on ancient prophecy to authorize his appeals to Scotland and Ireland, then Hopcyn may well have been the obvious expert to call. Unfortunately, we only have the somewhat partial account of the burgesses that Hopcyn actually foretold Owain's fate (inaccurately) and was summoned for that purpose. What is interesting about the letter from the burgesses is not whether Hopcyn actually claimed to be a prophet or not (and the evidence is inconclusive), but that they were eager to believe that prophecy was both a privileged form of knowledge and a marker of Owain's exceptional (if transgressive) nature.

The Context of Belief

A trust in prophecy as a meaningful adjunct to history was part of a medieval worldview which embraced the supernatural as part of a particular kind of piety. The turbulence of Owain Glyndŵr's rebellion, which coincided with a number of natural phenomena such as the comet of 1402, triggered a wave of alarm about Owain's association with magic and the supernatural. The comet, reported by Adam of Usk among others, appeared in March 1402, its fiery tail terrorizing all who saw it:

> Tam de nocte quam eciam de die, solem precedentem cometam terribilem, solis scilicet cleri et lune scilicet milicie mundi terrorem, ipsius ducis cito post defuncti mortis prefiguracionem, conspexi.

---

[23] Already by the late fourteenth century, the form *brut* was being used to denote primarily a historical chronicle, while *brud* was customarily used for 'prophecy'. See Jerry Hunter, *Soffestri'r Saeson*, pp. 78–79. *GPC* gives both meanings for the entry *brud/brut* and says that "fel rheol" [as a rule], the form *brut* refers to a historical chronicle and the form *brud* refers to prophecy. On the Welsh tradition of *cywyddau brud* [prophetic poetry], see Evans, "Prophetic Poetry," pp. 278–97. On the slippage between history and prophecy in medieval historiography, see Southern, "History as Prophecy."

[24] Williams, "Gwrthryfel Glyndŵr," p. 186.

[I could see both at night and during the daytime a fearsome comet, which moved ahead of the sun, spreading terror throughout the world, among both the clergy, who are the sun, and the knighthood, who are the moon, and foreshadowing the death of the above-mentioned duke [of Milan] — who did in fact die soon after this.][25]

The Welsh saw it as being in the shape of a dragon, the symbol of Welsh nationalism, while the English saw it as pointing towards either Wales or Scotland as a portent for the battles to come that year.[26] The St. Albans chronicle links the appearance of the comet to the capture of Sir Reginald Grey in April 1402, as a portent of Owain Glyndŵr's malign activities and of bloodshed in Northumberland as well (Item 68.18–23).

Thomas Walsingham, the chronicler most associated with the abbey of St. Albans, records a series of turbulent events after 1400, including plots against the king's life, the appearance of the devil at Danbury in Essex, and violent thunderstorms. He suspects that Owain prevails against the English in 1402 because he had direct access to the arts of magic:

. . . sed nichil profuit tantus armorum strepitus, quia Wallicus in noua latibula se recepit. Quin pocius, ut putatur, arte magica regem pene perdidit cum exercitu quem ducebat, nam a die quo ingressus est fines Cambrensium, usquequo loca dicta relinqueret, nunquam sibi arrisit aura serena, sed totis diebus ac noctibus pluuie mixte cum niuibus atque grandine sic afflixerunt exercitum, quod sustinere non poterant intemperanciam frigoris excessiui. (Item 68.56–61)

[However, all this great sound of arms achieved nothing at all, for the Welshman [Owain] withdrew into fresh hiding places. More to the point, indeed, he virtually defeated the king with the army which he was leading by magic, it is thought, for from the day he entered the territory of Wales up to the time he left those regions behind, no bright weather ever favoured the king, but every single day and night rain mingling with snow and hail so afflicted his army that the men could not endure the rigor of the extreme cold.][27]

Prophecy clustered around a number of the key players in the rebellion and was an indicator of political and social importance. Describing the death of the younger Henry Percy in the Battle of Shrewsbury in 1403, the author of the St. Albans chronicle recounts that Hotspur knew of a prophecy that he would die at Berwick. Thinking this meant the city of Berwick on the Scottish border, Hotspur was aghast to discover that Berwick was also the name of a village near Shrewsbury where he was about to lead his troops into battle against the king.[28] Hotspur did indeed die at the battle of Shrewsbury in July 1403, in which the English were victorious.[29] Adam of Usk refers to another prophecy being fulfilled on the

---

[25] Adam of Usk, *Chronicle*, p. 155.

[26] Bradley, *Owen Glyndwr*, pp. 163–64.

[27] John Hardyng also mentions the bad weather: "All men trowed þe witches it made that stounde" (Item 83.25).

[28] *St Albans Chronicle*, pp. 364–67. Berwick, Shropshire, is just north of Shrewsbury, very near the battle site.

[29] Davies, *Revolt*, p. 112.

deaths of Hotspur and his uncle, Thomas Percy, earl of Worcester, at Shrewsbury, the prophecy that *bestia abiecta duo lune cornua sibi auferet*, [the outcast beast shall bear away with him
the two horns of the moon], referring to the Percy livery bearing the crescent moon.[30]

This then is the context in which Owain made use of prophecy, a powerful discourse,
in order to authorize his actions. Prophecy was used, not just to explain and give weight to
unexpected events, but as a political tool to justify specific actions. If Owain did indeed
summon Hopcyn ap Tomas to foretell his future, he may not have known where Hopcyn's
real talents lay; nonetheless he showed a keen awareness of the role prophecy played in the
public imagination in conferring legitimacy on those who were prepared to acknowledge
its truth value.

The Aftermath

Somewhere between the mid-fifteenth century, when contemporary or near-contemporary accounts of Owain's rebellion ceased, and the time when Edward Hall wrote his
chronicle in the 1540s, the great plan outlined in the *Tripartite Indenture* to divide Britain
into three under Owain Glyndŵr, Edmund Mortimer, and the earl of Northumberland became conflated with the *Prophecy of Six Kings* (Item 1). Hall's chronicle seems to have been
the first to state, with apparent authority, that the three rebel leaders, in agreeing on the
terms of the *Indenture*, were "seduced" into identifying themselves as the dragon, lion, and
wolf mentioned in that prophecy, which was, inevitably, attributed to Merlin:

> Here I passe over to declare howe a certayne writer writeth that this earle of
> Marche, the lorde Percy and Owen Glendor wer unwysely made beleve by a Welch
> prophecier, that King Henry was the Moldwarpe, cursed of Goddes owne mouth,
> and that they thre were the Dragon, the Lion and the Wolfe, whiche shoulde devide
> this realme betwene them, by the deviacion and not devinacion of that mawmet
> Merlyn. (Item 95.130–35)[31]

It was Hall's account which influenced Ralph Holinshed in his chronicle of 1577, and
which led from there to Shakespeare's invention of the Welsh dreamer, Owen Glendower,
in *Henry IV Part I*. Since neither Owain himself nor any of his chroniclers associate the
Tripartite Indenture with the *Prophecy of Six Kings*, why would these Tudor historians decide
that Owain had been influenced by this prophecy?[32] There is no definitive answer, but it
probably has to do with the increasing popularity of the *Six Kings* prophecy during the fifteenth and sixteenth centuries, an English resistance to the Welsh myth of the returning
king, and the ideological function of prophecy as a political discourse. The *Prophecy of Six
Kings*, emerging first as an Anglo-Norman prose text around 1312, became attached to the

---

[30] Adam of Usk, *Chronicle*, pp. 170–71.

[31] Hall's *Chronicle* was first published in 1548, a year after Hall's death, and included many passa-
ges copied verbatim from earlier sources, including Polydore Vergil, John Hardyng and Robert
Fabyan, none of which mention prophecy. Hall's printer, Richard Grafton, lists his sources on p. viii.
See also Dillon, *Performance and Spectacle in Hall's Chronicle*, pp. 4–5.

[32] Hall and Holinshed claimed that Owain Glyndŵr was directly influenced by the *Prophecy of Six
Kings*, but there is little evidence for this; see the discussions by Doig, "Prophecy," and Fulton, "Owain
Glyn Dŵr and the Uses of Prophecy."

Anglo-Norman *Brut* and was then translated with it into English some time after 1350.[33] In its English form, the prophecy names six kings as different types of animals, and by 1400 these were interpreted as the six kings from Henry III to Henry IV, namely the Lamb (Henry III), the Dragon (Edward I), the Goat (Edward II), the Boar (Edward III), the Ass (Richard II) and the Mole (Henry IV). The imagery throughout is clearly Galfridian in origin, with many of the same animals occurring in Geoffrey's *Historia*, and the attribution to Merlin also echoes Geoffrey's most famous prophet.

The prophecy emerged into popular circulation at the time of the deposition of Richard II in 1399; while some versions of it celebrate the heroic Mole who sees off the weak and ineffectual Ass, other versions assert that the Ass is destined to return to the throne after the wicked Mole, or Moldwarp, is overthrown: "acursede of Godes mouþ. . . . and vengeance shal fal uppon him for synne" (Item 1.101–03). The version contained in the Middle English *Brut* was appropriated after 1399 as an anti-Lancastrian text which describes the evil Moldwarp being destroyed and the land then being divided into three:

> And after þat shal þe Moldewerp dye aventurly and sodeynely: allas þe sorwe, for he shal bene drenchede in a flode of þe see. His seede shal bicome pure faderles in straunge lande forevermore, and þan shal the lande bene departede in iii parties. Þat is to seyn, to the Wolf, to þe Dragoune, and to þe Lioun. And so shal it bene forevermore. And þan shal þis land bene callede "þe lande of conquest," and so shal þe riht heires of Engeland ende. (Item 1.123–28)

According to the prophecy, the dragon comes from the north, the wolf from the west, and the lion from Ireland, locations which are hard to assign to Owain and his two allies. If any of them might be the dragon, it should be Owain, and yet the dragon comes from the north, not the west. It seems that Edward Hall, familiar with the prophecy, attached it to the memory of the *Tripartite Indenture* and claimed that the three rebels were deliberately trying to fulfill the prophecy. Hall's gambit was, in fact, a piece of Tudor anti-Welsh propaganda which made a striking anecdote but which misrepresented Owain as a man driven by a particular prophecy. In political terms, Hall succeeds in discrediting Owain as a failed rebel, and at the same time he discredits the prophecy which Owain was apparently enacting — the same prophecy which denounced Henry IV, ancestor of Hall's king, Edward IV. Dismissing both Owain's master plan and the prophecy as the ravings of a madman, Hall authoritatively asserts the legitimacy of Henry IV's kingship and that of his heirs and pours scorn on what he clearly interpreted as an anti-Lancastrian prophecy.

Among Welsh writers, Owain seems to have been remembered with caution and possible disapproval on the one hand, and as the noble ancestor of leading Welsh families on the other. As in the English sources, there is virtually no reference to prophecy in relation to Owain, except his function as the *mab darogan*. The Welsh chronicle *Annales Oweni Glyndwr* (Item 70), compiled soon after the accession of Henry VI in 1422 (but surviving only in a manuscript of the sixteenth century), gives an abbreviated account of the whole rebellion without offering any evaluation as to Owain's heroism or otherwise, though this comment

---

[33] The history and transmission of the prophecy have been described by Smallwood, "Prophecy." See also Marvin, "Arthur Authorised," and the very useful discussion by Coote in *Prophecy and Public Affairs*. On the dating of the English version in the *Brut*, see Matheson, *Prose 'Brut'*.

for the year 1400, *yna y ddaeth gair mawr i Owain ac i kyvodes attaw ran vawr or yfiengtid a'r direidwyr o bob gwlad o Gymry oni oedd gidac ef llu mawr* [Owen now won great fame, and a great number of youths and fighting men from every part of Wales rose and joined him, until he had a great host at his back], could be construed as revealing a certain admiration.[34] Though the chronicle makes no mention of prophecy, it does say, for the year 1415, that Owain went into hiding on St. Matthew's Day (September 21): *O hynny allan ni wybvwyd i ddifant. Rrann vawr a ddywaid i varw; y brvdwyr a ddywedant na bv* [From then on (the place of) his disappearance was not known. A great many say that he died; the seers say he did not] (Item 70.51–53). The use of the word 'brudwyr', which Lloyd also translates as "seers," could also imply men who knew about prophecy or who claimed a particular knowledge about future events.

Elis Gruffudd, writing in the sixteenth century, gives a different account of Owain's disappearance after 1415. According to Elis's chronicle (Item 96), an abbot at Valle Crucis, one of the Welsh Cistercian monasteries located near Owain's home at Glyndyfrdwy, persuaded Owain that he was not, after all, the same Owain as the one long prophesied to return to save Wales from English oppression. As a result of this conversation, Owain staged his own disappearance to avoid the shame of seeming to be an impostor.[35] This is a nice story, which belongs to a range of anecdotes about the likely fate of Owain whose exact time and place of death are unverified, and it feeds on the continuing myth of a Welsh return to power, but again there is no explicit contemporary evidence that Owain saw himself as, or even knew of, the historical Owain of ancient Welsh prophecy.

Finally, it is worth drawing attention to the number of poetic prophecies in Welsh during the fifteenth century which commemorate Owain Glyndŵr and his rebellion as fulfillments of the ancient prophecy of a British return to power. Taking up the old theme of the armed liberation of Wales from the oppression of England, these Welsh prophecies seem to represent the rebellion — despite its ultimate failure — as an exemplar for future action, much of it located in the context of the Wars of the Roses. The anonymous prophecies in National Library of Wales, Peniarth MS 50, dating from the middle of the fifteenth century, refer repeatedly to 'Owain' (*Mi a welaf rythreu Owein o'r dwyrein y'r gorllewyn* [I see Owain's attacks from the east to the west]) or to 'the Boar' (*Yna y bydd Lloegr yn ddiras, a Seis heb gyweithas / A baedd Glyn Dyfwrdwy yn rannu'r teyrnas* [Then shall England be wicked, and Englishman without grace, And the boar of Glyn Dyfrdwy dividing the kingdom]).[36]

Among the Welsh gentry-poets of the fifteenth and early sixteenth century, Owain was glorified as the ancestor of leading families, with occasional oblique references to his legend. In a praise poem to Humphrey Kynaston, the rebellious son of a north Wales Marcher family, Siôn Ceri (fl. c.1500) described Humphrey thus:

---

[34] The translation given here is that of Lloyd (*Owen Glendower*, p. 151). On the tone in this passage, much depends on our understanding of the word *direidwyr*, which Lloyd renders here as "fighting men," though he translates it earlier in this passage as "reckless men." For a contrasting view that makes the matter somewhat more cloudy, see the translation at Item 70.11–13 and the note to Item 70.7.

[35] See Item 96.30–43; also Phillips, "When did Owain Glyndŵr Die?"

[36] Jenkins, "Aspects of the Welsh Prophetic Verse Tradition," pp. 399 and 264. As Owain's home region, Glyndyfrdwy is often used to signify him. On the Peniarth MS 50 poetry, see further Williams, pp. 525–27, below.

Y ddraig wen a dd'roganwyd,
Dâr Owain wych y drin wyd.

[The white dragon which was prophesied, warrior of excellent Owain of the rebellion are you.][37]

A fifteenth-century *cywydd brud* or prophetic poem by Ieuan ap Rhydderch, probably
addressed to Jasper Tudor, less likely to his father Owain Tudor, in 1465–70, hails him as
the *mab darogan* who has inherited the role of his namesake, Owain Glyndŵr, in driving the
English out of power:

Tri o enwau, gleiniau glân,
A drig ar y mab drogan.
Mae arnad, ganiad, od gwn,
Tri o henwau tra honnwn:
Cadwaladr, liw taradr tân,
Owen, cain awen, Cynan . . .
Dos a chymell yr Ellmyn,
Na weinia gledd Owain Glyn;
Pâr ynn bacs o dir Macsen,
A chwncwest Hors Hinsiest hen.[38]

[Three names, like pure jewels, are attached to the son of prophecy. You have,
surely, in song three names, as I declare them: Cadwaladr, color of piercing fire,
Owain, object of great inspiration, and Cynan . . . Go and drive out the English [lit.,
"foreigners"], do not put the sword of Owain Glyndŵr in its sheath; make peace for
us in the land of Maxen, and make a conquest of ancient Hors and Hengist.][39]

All the traditional imagery is here in this poem — the comet; the *mab darogan* as bear, wolf,
stag, and dragon; Cornwall, Scotland, and Ireland as the allies of Wales; and finally the call
to expel the English. Half a century after Owain's death, the memory of his triumphs as the
son of prophecy reinvigorates Welsh hopes during another struggle — the fight to put a
Tudor on the throne of England.

---

[37] *Gwaith Siôn Ceri*, ed. Lake, p. 79. The reference to 'white dragon' may indicate that Humphrey's family was English rather than Welsh.

[38] Ieuan ap Rhydderch, *Gwaith*, pp. 65–67. The poem's editor, Iestyn Daniel, makes the suggestion that the subject of this praise poem might be Owain Tudor or Owain ap Gruffudd ap Nicolas
(pp. 155–56), but see p. 529n64.

[39] According to the tale of *The Dream of Maxen Wledig*, Macsen or Maxen Wledig was a Roman
emperor who became ruler of Wales when he dreamed of and then married a beautiful Welsh woman;
the character is based on Magnus Maximus, the Roman official in Britain who was declared emperor
by his troops in 407.

Michael Livingston
An "Amazing" Claim: *The Tripartite Indenture*

Though it is perhaps the most famous document associated with Owain Glyndŵr, there has been uncertainty among scholars whether the so-called *Tripartite Indenture* (Item 47 in this volume) should be accepted at face value as an authentic artifact of Owain's rebellion, when and by whom it would have been composed (if genuine), and what this astonishing agreement was really intended to accomplish. This brief essay will address these issues.

The Authenticity of the Indenture

For the most part, doubts about the *Indenture*'s authenticity rest on both the generally sub-par reputation of the chronicle in which it is found — J. E. Lloyd amusingly refers to its author as a "not over-accurate chronicler" — and the generally astonishing scope of its content, since "in its terms" the *Indenture* "is more than a little amazing."[1]

To the first objection, R. R. Davies has more recently observed that while the anonymous work often termed *Giles's Chronicle* (after its early editor) "has not been highly regarded by historians for its reliability . . . it is particularly well informed about events in the north of England and its summaries and citation of official documents for the reign of Henry IV are generally accurate and are one of its distinguishing features." To the second objection, Davies concludes that "the apportionment of England and Wales" described within the *Indenture* "is certainly surprising, but it was not beyond the ken of political dreamers."[2] Lloyd likewise favored the document's ultimate authenticity "at any rate as a programme of Welsh ambitions; it breathes the spirit of divination and prophecy in which the Welsh leader was so peculiarly at home at all periods of his career."[3] Certainly, as the notes to the text in this volume show, the *Indenture* is keenly specific in its references to geography, particularly when it comes to the boundaries of Wales: some of the locations mentioned are mysterious now and probably would have been equally so to anyone outside the direct circle of Welsh influence in the fifteenth century. To imagine it an English forgery would be to imagine a complex scheme indeed. Thus, while a minority of scholars remains skeptical, it would seem that scholarship is increasingly regarding the *Indenture* as a genuine record — and potentially even a word-for-word accounting — of at least part of the unprecedented agreement made between Owain Glyndŵr, Edmund Mortimer, and Henry Percy to defeat the house of Lancaster and, if successful, organize the kingdom of England into three confederated states (on the relationship of which, see below).

---

[1] Lloyd, *Owen Glendower*, p. 93.

[2] Davies, *Revolt*, pp. 166, 168.

[3] Lloyd, *Owen Glendower*, p. 93.

The Date of the Indenture

Even among those who accept it as an authentic report, the date and circumstance of the *Indenture* has been a matter of debate. Shakespeare, in his dramatic reconstruction of the meeting at which the agreement was struck in *I Henry IV*, III.i (see Item 101), envisions the *Indenture* as taking place between the battles of Homildon Hill (14 September 1402) and Shrewsbury (21 July 1403). Interestingly, our only fifteenth-century account that might corroborate the authenticity of this remarkable agreement between Owain, Mortimer, and Percy might give weight to such a scenario. Under the years 1402–03, Jehan de Waurin's *Chronique* includes a passage (Item 82) that is not found in the chronicle of Monstrelet, the source he otherwise relies upon for his accounting of Wales (Item 80). In this passage Waurin relates that the Percies, angry at Henry IV's demands after the Battle of Homildon Hill, resolved to betray the king. Henry Percy himself went to "some great lords" in Wales (Item 82.4) and made a pact with them to join forces against the English king:

> the men of Wales, very glad of the alliance made and agreed upon with the earl of Northumberland and the Lords Percy, asked that letters of this alliance might be made, written, and sealed with the seals of both parties, and moreover the more firmly to maintain this alliance they swore and promised on the Body of Our Lord to keep these agreements unto death. (Item 82.21–26)

Other sources from the period — Hardying's *Chronicle*, for instance (Item 83.203.64–65) — mention that there were agreements between Owain and the Percy faction to fight against Henry IV, but none share the specificity of Waurin as it relates to the *Indenture*: the men involved, the highlighting of the seals, and the circumstances of the swearing. Mortimer is not mentioned by name in Waurin's account, but then neither is Owain, who is surely meant. Besides which fact, by the time the earl of Northumberland would have come to Wales in this scenario, he arguably would have found Mortimer no longer counted as a lord of England but as a son-in-law and lord of Wales. That said, it is possible that the event related by Waurin never occurred. And even if it did occur, it is wholly plausible that it refers to a separate agreement from that recorded in the *Indenture*.

The text of the *Indenture* itself has been preserved without any of the initial or concluding clauses that would typically provide much detail about its composition, including the firm date for such a text. Within the chronicle context in which it survives, the document occurs with only an "in this year" tag, which would appear to place the agreement among those events that the anonymous writer records as taking place in the fifth regnal year of Henry IV (i.e., 1403–04). Of the text manuscripts that preserve this part of the chronicle, one (the Royal MS) adds the detail that the agreement took place on 28 February, while the other (the Sloane MS) says 18 February, either of which results in a calendar date of 1404. There is good reason, however, to suspect that this is a false conclusion. The preceding report in the chronicle is the election of Pope Innocent IV, which occurred in October 1404 (Henry IV's sixth regnal year), and the next item after the *Indenture* is an account of the revolt of the earl of Northumberland and Lord Bardolf, which occurred in the summer of 1405 (Henry IV's seventh regnal year); this framing would logically point to an intermediary date of 18 or 28 February 1405 for the agreement. Also adding to the difficulty of a 1404 date, Lloyd rightly comments that it would be "impossible" to imagine the earl of Northumberland taking part in such an agreement at that time since he was then "in the king's power and suing for pardon."[4] A 1404 date is thus accepted by few scholars, if any. J. H. Wylie and Chris Barber, among others, place the agreement in 1406 because the three conspirators could not have met in person in either February of 1404 or 1405, but we have many precedents that such a personal meeting would not be necessary — including, as it happens, the so-called *Pennal Letters* in which Owain brokered agreements with the distant king of France regarding a similarly fantastic vision of the future (Items 51 and 52, to which we will return below).[5] A 1403 date, as Shakespeare and some of the later chroniclers would have it, makes for an intriguing and dramatic scene, and it is undoubtedly true that the kind of kingdom-altering future that the *Indenture* envisions would have seemed well within the conspirators' grasps before the Battle of Shrewsbury in 1403. At the same time, we know that hopes for defeating the Lancastrians did not perish at Shrewsbury; even in the aftermath of that defeat and Hotspur's death, the struggles of the three men named in the *Indenture* continued. In addition, the *Indenture* itself makes clear reference to Owain's agreements with the king of France, agreements that were not formalized until 12 January 1405, and which do not seem to have even begun until 10 May 1404 (see Items 43 and 46).

The vast majority of scholars, therefore, have favored a date of 28 February 1405.[6] Such a date fits well with the chronicle context in which it is found, and it coincides well with Owain's treaty with France. The *Indenture* would thus serve as a striking component in the 1404–05 foreign policy efforts of the Welsh leader, efforts that culminated in the August landing of a French army to help Owain press his claims (see Items 50, 66, 68, 69, 77, 80, 82). Intriguingly, a February 1405 date for the *Indenture* could also establish some connection between the conspiracy it contains and the foiled plot by Lady Despenser and Duke Edward of York to smuggle Mortimer's nephews, the young earl of March (a potential rival claimant for the throne of Henry IV) and his brother Roger out of the Tower of London, which occurred earlier in the same month: the failure of that effort might well be what caused it to be the elder Mortimer who is named as the third party in the tripartite governance of the kingdom, rather than the more rightful but hopelessly imprisoned young earl.[7]

If the *Indenture* indeed dates to 1405, as here assumed, then the agreement to which Waurin refers, taking place between the lords of Wales and the Percies in 1402–03, is likely an entirely separate event, marking an earlier agreement from which no specific documentation survives. Indeed, it is quite probable that this is the very same event to which Hardyng refers when he writes of Hotspur meeting with Owain and Mortimer on the Severn and sealing an agreement with them that led to the Battle of Shrewsbury (Item 83.203.64–65).

The Author of the Indenture

Viewed against the background of Owain's rebellion in 1405, the *Indenture* is revealed for what it was: a breathtaking step in his political efforts to stabilize an independent Wales. As such, he could have trusted the task of composing the document to relatively few people,

---

[4] Lloyd, *Owen Glendower*, p. 93n1.

[5] See Wylie, *History of England*, and Barber, *In Search*, p. 170.

[6] See, e.g., Davies, *Revolt*, p. 166.

[7] On this aborted plot, see Pugh, *Henry V*, pp. 78–79. It is tempting to imagine some communications between these efforts — in which case the forces arrayed against Henry V in the spring of 1405 might have been far more organized than many have heretofore assumed — but there is no evidence to support such a conspiracy.

and foremost among them would have been Gruffudd Yonge, who "had a brilliant career and a panoply of degrees to his name" along with a "rich haul of ecclesiastical livings, canonries, and prebends" before he defected to Owain's cause in 1403–04.[8] Gruffudd was Oxford-trained, and he quickly became vital to Owain's programs both foreign and domestic: Davies writes that this learned man was "quite likely the mastermind behind his more ambitious policies."[9] In authorizing Gruffudd as one of his two ambassadors to France in 1404, Owain himself describes him as "Magistrum Griffinum Yonge, decretorum doctorem, cancellarium nostrum" [Master Gruffudd Yonge, doctor of decrees, our chancellor] (Item 43.5–6; compare Item 46.8). Around 1407 he would serve an ambassadorial role in Owain's administration: he was, no doubt, the "Dominus Griffinus episcopus Bangoren" [Lord Gruffudd bishop of Bangor] who served as one of Owain's two envoys to Scotland at that time.[10] Gruffudd Yonge was clearly a man deeply trusted by Owain to engage with the foreign powers that he hoped would empower his rebellion to turn toward true independence for Wales. As such, he would have been the ideal and expected man to engage with Henry Percy and Edmund Mortimer in the negotiations that led to the *Tripartite Indenture*.

There is additional reason for supposing Gruffudd Yonge to be the hand behind the *Indenture*. As we have already seen, Gruffudd was one of the two ambassadors negotiating on Owain's behalf with King Charles VI of France (the other being Owain's brother-in-law, John Hanmer). It was in this role that, as Lloyd surmised, he "may reasonably be regarded as the author of the Pennal policy" — that is, the second *Pennal Letter* (Item 52) that alludes to the details of the alliance between Wales and France and the coinciding "transference" of Welsh religious allegiance from the papacy of Rome to that of Avignon.[11] As Davies has observed, that text has much in common with the *Indenture*: "the most puzzling features of both documents are woven from the same weft and bear the stamp of the same author."[12]

Davies is probably right to suppose shared authorship between these texts, and we can probably extend this common hand at work in a third document: the *Confederation between Wales and France*, which is attributed to Gruffudd Yonge in his role as chancellor (Item 46.8). Side-by-side comparison reveals that the *Confederation* and the *Indenture* share far more than the same weft. What follows is a lengthy passage of the two documents: bold face indicates identical text; *italics* indicate variant word form, alternate word choice, and, in one instance, a change of word order; *square brackets* […] indicate words or passages not in the other text.

Confederation Between Wales and France (Item 46.16–38)	Tripartite Indenture (Item 47.1–18)
. . . **confederacionibus et amiciciis** [parties involved] **in certis** capitulis seu **articulis continentibus formam que sequitur et tenorem:**	. . . **confederationem et amicitiam** [parties involved] **in certis articulis continentibus formam que sequitur et tenorem:**

---

[8] Davies, *Revolt*, pp. 212–13.

[9] Davies, *Revolt*, p. 143.

[10] See Bower, *Scotichronicon*, ed. Watts, 8.64–65. Gruffudd had become bishop of Bangor by decree of the Avignon Pope Benedict XIII in February 1407 (Lloyd, *Owen Glendower*, p. 122).

[11] Lloyd, *Owen Glendower*, pp. 121–22; see also Davies, *Revolt*, p. 214.

[12] Davies, *Revolt*, p. 172.

Primo quod *ipsi* **domini** [parties involved] **erunt amodo ad invicem conjuncti, confederati, uniti et ligati vinculo veri federis et vere amicicie certeque et bone unionis** [parties involved]. *Item* **quod** *alter* **ipsorum dominorum honorem et commodum** *alterius* **volet, prosequetur ac eciam procurabit, dampnaque et gravamina que ad unius noticiam devenerint per** [parties involved] **quoscumque** *alteri* **inferenda impedient bona fide**, *alter* **quoque ipsorum apud** *alteram* **aget et faciet ea omnia et singula que per bonum verum et fidum amicum bono, vero et fido amico agi et fieri debent et pertinent fraude et dolo cessantibus quibuscumque. Item si et quociens** *alter eorum* **sciverit vel cognoverit** [parties involved] **aliquid gravaminis sive dampni procurare** *vel machinari* **contra alium, ipse** *sibi* **quam cicius commode fieri poterit ea significabit et ipsum de et super hoc** *advisabit* **ut adversus malicias** *suas* **prout ei visum fuerit sibi valeat providere; soliciti quoque erunt quilibet ipsorum dominorum impedire gravamina et dampna predicta bona fide. Item** *quod* **quilibet dominorum** . . .	**Primo quod** *iidem* **domini** [parties involved] **erunt amodo ad invicem conjuncti, confoederati, uniti, et ligati vinculo veri foederis et veræ amicitiæ, certæque et bonæ unionis.** *Iterum* **quod** *quilibet* **ipsorum dominorum honorem et commodum** *alio* **volet et prosequetur, ac etiam procurabit, dampnaque et gravamina quæ ad unius** [parties involved] **notitiam devenerit, per quoscumque** *alicui* **ipsorum inferenda, impedient bona fide.** *Quilibet* **quoque ipsorum apud** *alium* **aget et faciet ea omnia et singula quæ per bonos, veros, et fidos amicos, bonis, veris, et fidis amicis agi et fieri debent et pertinent, fraude et dolo cessantibus quibuscumque. Item, si et quotiens** *aliquis ipsorum* [parties involved] **sciverit vel cognoverit aliquid gravaminis sive dampni procurari** *sive ymaginari* [per quoscumque] **contra alium, ipse** *aliis*, **quam citius commode fieri poterit, ea significabit, et ipsos de et super hoc** *adjuvabit*, **ut adversus malicias** *hujusmodi*, **prout ei visum fuerit, sibi valeat providere. Sollicti quoque erunt quilibet ipsorum dominorum impedire dampna et gravamina præderta bona fide. Item,** *quilibet* **ipsorum dominorum** . . .

Without question, the person who wrote the *Tripartite Indenture* had seen first-hand the text of the *Confederation*. Very likely this was because he was the very man who had helped to compose the earlier text in the court of Charles VI, and who subsequently drafted the second Pennal Letter, as well: Gruffudd Yonge.[13]

Lloyd opined that the Welsh representatives to the meeting at which the *Indenture* was agreed upon would have been bishops Lewis Byford of Bangor and John Trefor of St. Asaph, but it appears that he was too far driven by the chronicler Edward Hall's report about the circumstances of the composition of the *Indenture*: Hall claims that the meeting took place between the "deputies" of the three parties involved, "in the howse of the archdeacon of Bangor" (Item 95.135–36). Lloyd speculated that "Byford may well at this time have been in residence" in that house, and thus must have been a key figure.[14] Perhaps he was there, but far more evidence points to Gruffudd Yonge as the drafting hand, a man whose position as archdeacon of Merioneth and later bishop of Bangor might well have led to Hall's confusion with an archdeacon of Bangor.

---

[13] John Bollard (private communication) points out that a few of the passages isolated here are closely matched, though not verbatim, by the 7 January 1398 treaty between Charles VI and Jacques I of Cyprus (printed in de Mas Latrie, *Histoire*, 2.439–40). This may well indicate that at least some of the phrasing utilized by Gruffudd Yonge is borrowed from the secretary of the French court.

[14] Lloyd, *Owen Glendower*, p. 94.

The Intent of the Indenture

It is a common misconception both in the popular imagination and in scholarship to view the *Indenture* as an agreement that "divided England and Wales into three kingdoms," one each to Owain, Mortimer, and Percy.[15] This is not, however, the vision described in the document. To the contrary, the *Indenture* calls for three autonomously independent dominions within one confederated kingdom (Item 47.41–47), not unlike the relationship that England would have with some of its former colonies on the way to the creation of today's Commonwealth. That this divided realm is still envisioned as a singular kingdom after the fulfillment of the agreement is made visible at the end of the *Indenture*, when the singular *regnum* [the kingdom] is used in the Latin, rather than the plural (Item 47.45).

It has also been common among many historians — perhaps due to some habitual disregard of the Welsh — to assume that the "principal architect" of the *Indenture* was Henry Percy.[16] Yet one can hardly imagine that the earl of Northumberland would (or even could) craft a document so specific in its Welsh demarcation, which stands very much in contrast to the "shire" descriptions utilized for Percy's own border. To the contrary, it is far more likely that Owain took the lead in these negotiations (as he also does in Shakespeare's account of them in *I Henry IV*; see Item 101). It is Owain's claim that is first drawn in the document, his claim that is most specific in its delineation (see Item 47.27–36 and note to line 31), and his claim that has raised the most eyebrows, since it would expand "Wales" to include the whole of Cheshire, Shropshire, and Herefordshire, in addition to significant parts of Gloucestershire, Worcestershire, and Staffordshire (see the map opposite). That Owain would be driving the negotiations should not surprise us. At the time that the document was being composed, after all, it was Owain who stood most in strength among the collaborators. He held significant portions of Wales in his control, and he had more than once defeated the English armies in open battle. Even more vitally, he had now concluded a formal alliance with the king of France, giving him a powerful international ally to support his cause. In contrast, Mortimer had been defeated by Owain before marrying his daughter and was now almost wholly dependent on the Welsh; he had no power to muster on his own behalf. For his part, Percy had only recently managed to convince Henry IV to spare his life after the defeat of his forces and his son Hotspur at Shrewsbury; as he would show later in the summer of 1405 during the northern rebellion of Richard le Scrope, the once-powerful earl now had effectively little of substance to offer on the field. In 1405 Owain Glyndŵr held all the cards.

It should also be noted that Owain's claim to such a large swath of England's western counties may not be as "amazing" as Lloyd once surmised. One of the central locations marking the proposed Welsh border are the ash trees of Meigion (see Item 47, note to line 31). By the fifteenth century this site had numerous connections to Welsh prophecy and history as a border to a grander vision for Wales returning to past glories associated with figures of history and legend such as Maig Myngfras of Powys, along with Cadwallon ap Cadfan of Gwynedd and his son, Cadwaladr ap Cadwallon, the latter of whom was the last of the high kings of native Britain according to the imaginative but highly influential account of Geoffrey of Monmouth (*Historia regum Britanniae*, Book 12). In the eyes of the Welsh at least, Owain's "amazing" claim (to return to Lloyd's description) was perhaps less an overreach into English territories than it was a rebalancing of English overreach into

---

[15] See, e.g., Skidmore, *Owain*, p. 137.

[16] Skidmore, *Owain*, p. 137.

Welsh ones. Indeed, when weighed against the kind of restorative vision for Wales espoused in popular works such as the earlier *Armes Prydein Vawr* — which called for nothing less than "to expel [the Saxons] from Britain" — Owain's expanded homeland seems a somewhat conservative construction.[17]

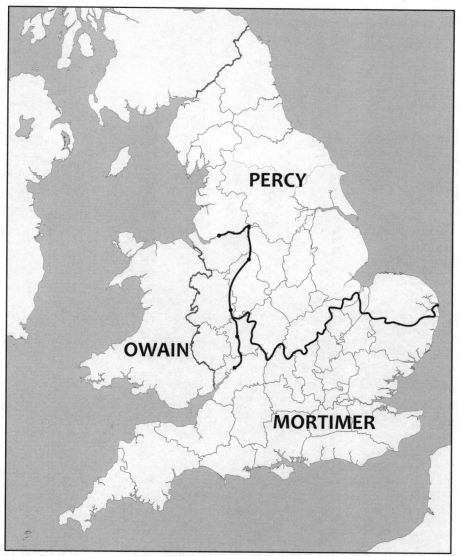

Map of the Division of England according to the *Tripartite Indenture*, superimposed on the modern counties of England.

---

[17] Trans. John K. Bollard, in Livingston, *Battle of Brunanburh*, p. 35. The same theme, if not *Armes Prydein Vawr* itself, is invoked by Iolo Goch in his poem to Owain during the rebellion (Item 27.41–42 and notes).

Valle Crucis Abbey, only a few miles from Glyndyfrdwy. Among those buried here were some of the Owain's ancestors, along with contemporary poets Guto'r Glyn and (according to some) Iolo Goch.

JOHN K. BOLLARD
OWAIN GLYNDŴR AND THE POETS

Caru clêr, felly ceir clod! [To love poets – thus is fame achieved!]
— Iolo Goch[1]

Until your artists have conceived you in your unique and supreme form you can never conceive yourselves, *and have not, in fact, existed.* . . . the poet becomes truly the creator by offering that form which allows *man* of the period *to be.*
— William Carlos Williams[2]

The loss of Welsh independence in 1282 brought about profound changes in the social and political structures in Wales. Centuries of struggle to maintain secular and ecclesiastical autonomy and native laws, customs, and liberties gave way, perforce, to the need to accommodate to foreign rule, which bred a growing resentment at territorial and economic domination. Many Welsh did adjust successfully to these new circumstances, but R. R. Davies aptly sums up the general effect: "The conquest of Wales left a deep legacy of despair and bitterness among Welshmen."[3] One of the significant cultural effects of conquest was that the long tradition of Welsh court poetry was broken, for the very courts themselves ceased to be.

The heroic age of the poets Taliesin and Aneirin in the late sixth and early seventh centuries provided models of praise and lament for many generations of poets in the courts of rulers and military leaders.[4] The *Beirdd y Tywysogion*, the "Poets of the Princes," in the eleventh through the thirteenth centuries further developed the poetry of eulogy and elegy in a style imbued with *gravitas*, sonority, and a remarkably rich vocabulary to extol their leaders and to express their religious faith.[5] Upon the fall of Llywelyn ap Gruffudd, however, Welsh royal patronage was no longer available to these poets. After the powerful and plaintive laments for Llywelyn by Bleddyn Fardd and Gruffudd ab yr Ynad Coch, the tradition of the Poets of the Princes rapidly waned.[6]

---

[1] See Item 4.24 in this volume.

[2] *English Institute Essays*, p. 60 (italics original).

[3] Davies, *Age of Conquest*, p. 379.

[4] See Ifor Williams, *Poems of Taliesin*; seven of the twelve poems are translated in Clancy, *Medieval Welsh Poems*, pp. 39–44. For the poetry of Aneirin, see A. O. H. Jarman's edition and translation of *Y Gododdin*; the full text has also been translated by Clancy, pp. 45–76.

[5] For an introduction to early Welsh poetry, see *Guide to Welsh Literature*, ed. Jarman and Hughes, vol. 1, chs. 1–7; Jarman, *Cynfeirdd*; J. E. Caerwyn Williams, *Poets of the Welsh Princes*.

[6] To a list of thirty-one Poets of the Princes compiled by J. Lloyd-Jones, Thomas Parry adds six fourteenth-century poets who maintained the earlier traditions in the face of profound social and poetic change (Parry, *History*, p. 66).

As their successors in the fourteenth and fifteenth centuries, the *Beirdd yr Uchelwyr*, the "Poets of the Nobility," sought patronage from and offered their poetry to the class of nobles known as *uchelwyr*, descended from the remaining lesser branches of the ancient royal and noble families.[7] Many members of this rising class served as government officials, often as intermediaries, and at times as buffers between the English rulers and the Welsh people. These *uchelwyr* served the crown while both regulating and protecting their subjects. However, they also preserved much of Welsh culture and tradition, especially through their patronage of poets. The poets themselves travelled from one noble house to another offering poems of praise, request, and thanks that served to enhance the reputations of their hosts.[8]

The Welsh poetry of praise had developed in an unbroken tradition for possibly seven hundred years, and much of what had been true in the work of the Poets of the Princes remained true for the Poets of the Nobility, though differing in degree and emphasis. Many of the thematic conventions of praise poetry remained relatively stable, and poetry continued to be an important medium through which the idealized relationship between the rulers and the ruled was expressed and disseminated. The poets learned, preserved, and embedded in their poetry references to the legendary, historical, and genealogical information that gave legitimacy and status to the Welsh nobility. Thus, through their poetry, the poets helped keep alive the memory of a glorious Welsh past, while simultaneously expressing the qualities expected of those in authority and, with frequent optimism, voicing hope for the future.

In addition to the profound social and political changes wrought by the Edwardian conquest, there were significant developments in the art of poetry itself that are worth noting because they help us to understand the role and the effect of the poems addressed to Owain Glyndŵr. Most important among these was the development of a new form, the *cywydd*.[9] The arrival of the *cywydd* is significant in part because it is in many ways a simpler form, not as dependent as earlier praise poetry on abstruse vocabulary and profundity of theme. Dafydd ap Gwilym (fl. 1340–70), the greatest poet of the period, introduced with this new form a range of new themes, especially matters of nature and love (often treated with great humor). As a result, poetry became more accessible to a wider range of people, and the poets and professional reciters could reach a broader audience, especially within the newly evolving social and class structures in a subjugated Wales. This would make it easier for the popular conception of Owain to be influenced directly by the poems in his praise, especially in regions distant from Glyndyfrdwy and Sycharth, and this image of a leader of promise would in turn have its effect when the revolt began and Owain was in need of support.

The portraits that medieval Welsh poets provide of their subjects tend to be conventional and highly idealized, following models and poetic traditions developed over generations. The conventions of praise that a poet might choose from are categorized in the fourteenth-century *Gramadegau'r Penceirddiaid* [*Grammars of the Chief Poets*], a handbook not only of grammatical principles and poetic meters, but also a guide to the proper subject matter of poetry. In a section on how subjects should be praised, we find the following instruction:

---

[7] *uchelwyr*, lit. "high men"; sg. *uchelwr*.

[8] On the *Beirdd yr Uchelwyr* and the changes in poetic practice in the 14th century, see *Guide to Welsh Literature*, ed. Jarman and Hughes, vol. 2, especially chs. 1, 4, 6.

[9] The *cywydd* and its major features are described briefly in the Note on Prosody below.

Arglwyd a uolir o uedyant, a gallu, a milwryaeth, a gwrhydri, a chedernyt, a balchder, ac adfwynder, a doethineb, a chymhendawt, a haelyoni, a gwarder, a hegarwch wrth y wyr a'e gyueillon, a thegwch pryt, a thelediwrwyd corff, a mawrurydwch medwl, a mawrhydri gweith-redoed, a phetheu eraill adfwyn enrydedus.

[A lord is to be praised for authority, and ability, and skill at arms, and valor, and strength, and dignity, and gentleness, and wisdom, and discretion, and generosity, and mildness, and amiability towards his men and his companions, and fairness of face, and beauty of body, and grandness of thought, and majesty of deeds, and other pleasant, honorable things.]

An *uchelwr* or *breyr* [nobleman (the terms are synonymous)] is to be praised similarly, though perhaps a bit less effusively:

Brehyr a volir o dewrder, a glewder, a chedernit, a chryfder, a chywirdeb wrth y arglwyd, a doethineb, a chymhendawt, a haelyoni, a digrifwch, a thelediwrwyd corff, a boned, a phetheu ereill kanmoledic.[10]

[A nobleman is to be praised for bravery, and courage, and strength, and loyalty to his lord, and wisdom, and discretion, and generosity, and agreeableness, and beauty of body, and lineage, and other praiseworthy things.]

As can be seen in the poems to Owain Glyndŵr, the poets use these categories creatively to provide portraits that are by no means as wooden or static as such lists might seem to suggest. At the same time, it is not surprising, given the times, to find that subjects are most often praised for their martial skills and military successes, counterbalanced by praise for their gentleness and kindness towards their friends and for their generosity — especially, of course, to poets!

That Owain Glyndŵr was an up-and-coming figure amongst the *uchelwyr* by his late teens or early twenties, even before establishing his military credentials in Scotland, is hinted at in the earliest known reference to him in Iolo Goch's "Dialogue between the Soul and the Body," composed in the period 1375–82. Four additional poems by Iolo Goch (c.1325–c.1403) and two by Gruffudd Llwyd (fl. c.1380–1410), all composed between 1385 and 1403, have Owain as their central subject.[11] Although they do not focus on Owain, three poems composed during the rebellion are included in this casebook for the light they shed on the war itself. Madog ap Gronw Gethin's praise of the river Dee for its help in the war effort was most likely composed during the early years of the rebellion, and two poems by Llywelyn ab y Moel reference events during the later years, though the date of their composition is not known.[12]

Iolo Goch's "Dialogue between the Soul and the Body" is a light-hearted poem of 124 lines that recounts the Soul's itinerary through Wales in search of the reprobate Body, thus providing the poet an opportunity to offer brief moments of praise to patrons throughout

---

[10] Williams and Jones, *Gramadegau'r Penceirddiaid*, p. 16. The terms *uchelwr* and *breyr* are synonymous and designate a freeman who has inherited ancestral land through the direct male line (Jenkins, *Law*, pp. 320, 389).

[11] Iolo Goch: Items 2, 4, 6, 8, 27; Gruffudd Llwyd: Items 3, 5.

[12] Madog ap Gronw Gethin: Item 53; Llywelyn ab y Moel, Items 54, 55. For a discussion of the poems by Llywelyn ab y Moel, see pp. 519–21.

the country. The poem describes his visits to various nobles in their houses, towns, and abbeys, giving us a representative précis of the travels of a poet in mid-to-late fourteenth century Wales. The penultimate stop in his wanderings is the *tŷ teg* [fair house] (Item 2.111) at Sycharth, though the poet refers to Owain only pronominally in the line *Trig, od gwn, tro gydag ef* [Stay, indeed, a while with him] (Item 2.106). Iolo does, however, note the abundance of the place and the generosity that a visitor will receive there; he then ends his circuit at the home of his longtime friend Ithel ap Robert, archdeacon of St. Asaph. Thus, in our very first glimpse of Owain Glyndŵr we see him as a wealthy and welcoming nobleman and a patron of poets.

This brief mention of Owain's home at Sycharth is filled out in exquisite detail in Iolo Goch's renowned poem on *Owain Glyndŵr's Court* (Item 8), c.1387–95, which provides a portrait of Owain Glyndŵr's home and family life.[13] Here Owain's court is *Llys barwn, lle syber-wyd, / lle daw beirdd aml, lle da byd* [A baron's court, a place of nobility, / a place where many poets come, a place of the good life] (Item 8.19–20), and *pebyll y beirdd* [a shelter for poets] (Item 8.77). The architectural wonders of the court are enumerated at length as Iolo takes us from the bright moat through the gate "where a hundred packloads could go," to its coupled rafters, joists, and beams, its sleeping lofts, its tiled and gabled roofs, its chimneys, its halls with wardrobes as full as a London shop, and its splendid glass windows. And in a widening vision Iolo guides us through the estate, from the bakeries in the court to a vineyard, a mill, a dovecote, a well-stocked fishpond, peacocks and herons abounding, and beyond that pastures, hayfields, corn fields, a rabbit park, a deer park, and plows and horses, mentioning finally the serfs or bondmen who keep it running, before bringing us back to *tecaf llys bren . . . / o'r deyrnas, nawdd Duw arnai* [the fairest wooden court . . . / of the kingdom, God's protection be upon it!] (Item 8.79–80). Iolo then praises Owain's wife, *gwraig orau o'r gwragedd* [the best woman among women] (Item 8.81), and his children *a ddeuant bob dau* [who come by twos] (Item 8.85). The poem reaches its thematic climax in lines 90–92:

> ni bydd eisiau, budd oseb,
> na gwall na newyn na gwarth,
> na syched fyth yn Sycharth.
>
> [There will be no need — beneficial gift —
> nor want, nor hunger, nor shame,
> nor thirst ever in Sycharth.][14]

In the poem's final lines Iolo even gives us a brief hint of Owain's physical appearance: *Gorau Cymro . . . / piau'r wlad, . . . / gŵr meingryf, . . . / a phiau'r llys, hoff yw'r lle* [The best Welshman . . . / owns the land, . . . / a strong, slender man, . . . / and owns the court. The place is renowned] (Item 8.93–96).

---

[13] This poem may be representative of a custom of writing poems in praise of a new building (Williams, "More than 'skimble-skamble stuff,'" p. 14). This suggests that Owain may have rebuilt or made some renovations or additions to Sycharth during the 1380s.

[14] In line 92 Iolo puns on *syched* [dryness, thirst] and the name *Sycharth*, etymologically "a dry promontory or hill."

This poem, like many praise poems, takes full advantage of the rhetorical effects of hyperbole and exaggeration; for example, Sycharth is compared favorably to the new bell tower of St. Patrick's cathedral in Dublin, built in the 1360s, and the restored cloisters of Westminster Abbey, completed in 1364 (Item 8.29–30).[15] Though Iolo is clearly overstating its glories, much of the architectural and personal detail in this poem rings true. Life at Sycharth may not have been as sumptuous as Iolo makes it sound, but the overall picture is of a well-appointed estate, offering welcome hospitality to visitors. This should serve to remind us that though Wales was a relatively poor country suffering oppression from without, Welsh nobles participated in many of the refinements of culture enjoyed by the nobility of England and other European countries at the time. Owain Glyndŵr was no simple rustic country squire; though his estate and holdings may seem small compared to those of the most powerful English barons, he was, nevertheless, a member of that class, as we see also in other poems addressed to him. Indeed, in a couplet that appears in two of his poems to Owain, Iolo Goch turns this comparison on its head, making Owain the standard of baron-hood: *Anoberi un barwn / ond y rhyw yr henyw hwn* [Any baron is a man of no account / but one of the lineage that this one is descended from] (Items 4.11–12, 6.43–44). And in the final line of one of his poems to Owain, Gruffudd Llwyd concurs: *ymysg ieirll ydd ymwaisg ef* [He will include himself among earls] (Item 5.82).

Two poems, one each by Gruffudd Llwyd and Iolo Goch, praise Owain's military exploits in Scotland, where he served on two occasions. Owain served with Sir Gregory Sais in the garrison at Berwick on the Scottish border in March 1384, and he also took part in Richard II's Scottish campaign in August 1385, serving under the earl of Arundel.[16] Gruffydd Aled Williams presents a strong argument that the opening lines of Iolo Goch's poem on Owain's exploits in Scotland (Item 4) reflect the bustle and tumult of armies gathering for Richard II's campaign in Scotland in the summer of 1385: *Mawr o symud a hud hydr / a welwn ni ar welydr* [Great movement and mighty magic / do we see among lords] (Item 4.1–2).[17] However, as is clear from the mention of Sir Gregory Sais and Berwick immediately

---

[15] Owain himself would have seen the newly refurbished Westminster cloisters during his time in London.

[16] Davies, *Revolt*, p. 139; Williams, "More than 'skimble-skamble stuff,'" p. 10; Iolo Goch, *Gwaith*, p. 228.

[17] "The opening couplet seems to me to refer to a momentous event and the mention of *gwelydr* ('lords') is significant. Departure for routine garrison duty in Berwick (as in 1384) would not amount to a momentous event, and Sir Gregory Sais (a mere knight) would hardly be reckoned a *gwaladr*. However, the 1385 Scottish expedition was a very different matter. It was the last summons of the English medieval levy and the first such summons to be issued for 58 years. All the king's tenants- in-chief (56 lay and 36 ecclesiastical) were summoned, i.e. all the leading magnates of England (for which *gwelydr* would be an extremely appropriate term). The army assembled was the second largest English army of the fourteenth century, and the chronicle accounts of the expedition make it clear that its mustering was regarded as a wondrous event, e.g. Knighton, who refers to "flos militiae Angliae, comitum, baronum, militum, armigerorum, valettorum" (Knighton, *Chronicon*, p. 204; there are similar remarks by Walsingham and the Monk of Westminster). Iolo's use of the present tense (*a welwn ni* [do we see]) in the opening couplet is significant. He is referring to the event which was the immediate occasion of the *cywydd*, and what an event it was!" Williams also notes the contrasting use of the past and imperfect tenses in describing Owain's exploits the previous year in lines 33–64 (personal communication); see also Williams, "More than 'skimble-skamble stuff,'" p. 10.

before the introduction of Owain's encounter, Iolo Goch's composed in 1385, refers back to the same events of 1384 praised by Gruffudd Llwyd in Item 3. Davies notes that "Owain's own initial military assignment was prosaic, verging on the dull," although "a posting to Berwick at this stage was certainly no military holiday." As corroboration, in a reference to these very poems, he points out, "His household bards back in Wales found themselves torn between exaggerated fears for their patron's safety in such outlandish parts and even more exaggerated praise of his military feats there."[18] Williams similarly recognizes that "in view, too, of John of Gaunt's *chevauchée* into Scotland from Berwick in the spring of 1384 and the fighting that occurred in the East March that summer it is conceivable that Glyndŵr may have seen some military action."[19]

Gruffudd Llwyd's poem on Owain's exploits in Scotland, beginning *Eryr digrif afrifed* [Eagle delightful beyond measure] (Item 3), is a second-person poem addressed directly to Owain. Lines 1–14 make reference to a feast, ostensibly on the previous evening, *lle cawn win o'th law* [where I had wine from your hand] (Item 3.10). While the gift of wine and mead is a stock trope of praise poetry, the apologetic tone in which Gruffudd admits his own volubility and some undefined discourtesy on that occasion has a specificity that rings true:

> . . . mwy oedd f'anfoes
> a gwaeth dros fy maeth fy moes,
> nêr mawlair nawrym milwr,
> nag ar fy nhad, arnad, ŵr. (Item 3.11–14)

> [. . . greater was my discourtesy
> and my behavior towards you worse,
> lord of great praise with nine times the strength of a warrior,
> in return for my support, man, than towards my father.]

This is followed by an expression of the poet's longing (*hiraeth*, Item 3.17) as soon as Owain departs for Scotland. The grief and weeping the poet claims to have experienced may also have a foundation in the reality of their relationship, but it is typical of the hyperbole with which poets often expressed an intimacy with their patrons. The passage begins:

> Yr awr yr aethost ar ŵyth
> dir Prydyn, darpar adwyth,
> agos i hiraeth, gaeth gad,
> a'm dwyn i farw amdanad. (Item 3.15–18)

---

[18] Davies, *Revolt*, p. 146. In regard to the tendency to exaggeration, Williams reminds us that "the presence of hyperbole should not lead us to think that poems were shameless constructs of unalloyed mendacity. Whilst a certain amount of hyperbole was expected and, no doubt, humorously appreciated by the gathered audience at a patron's court, what might be identified as blatant untruths would have fatally undermined a poet's offering. In reading this poetry, whilst being aware of hyperbole, we should beware too of adopting a posture of outright disbelief and cynicism" (Williams, "More than 'skimble-skamble stuff,'" p. 7).

[19] Williams, "More than 'skimble-skamble stuff,'" p. 11. Though Berwick was an English town, as Iolo Goch notes (Item 4.63), it was an oft-contested border town and would be viewed from distant Wales as the point of contact with the Scottish enemy, as in Iolo's early poem to Edward III, whom he praises for *Curo â blif . . . / Cerrig Caer Ferwig furwelw* [battering with a catapult . . . / the stones of pale-walled Berwick] (Iolo Goch, *Poems*, pp. 2–3).

[The hour you went in anger
to the land of Scotland, intending destruction,
nearly did longing, fierce struggle,
bring me to death because of you.]

Fortunately for the poet, when his sorrow is heaviest a messenger arrives from Scotland to say that Owain is safe and that he has won great fame ([*m*]*awrglod*, Item 3.28) in battle.

The remaining sixty lines comprise the detailed description of the poem's key encounter, either imagined or drawn from accounts coming back from Scotland, elaborated in terms of fulsome praise. Owain is compared first (Item 3.35–38) to Uther Pendragon, who, according to Geoffrey of Monmouth, avenged in battle the death of his brother Aurelius Ambrosius.[20] In an extended comparison (Item 3.39–52), Owain is then likened to his namesake from Arthurian legend, Owain ab Urien, in that hero's encounter with the Black Knight of the Spring, a central episode in *Owain* or *The Tale of the Countess of the Spring*. For Gruffudd Llwyd's purposes, the pertinent elements of that incident are the breaking of spears and the subsequent chase: "And Owain encountered him and jousted with him fiercely, and they broke the two spears, and they drew two swords and smote each other. . . . And then the Black Knight knew he had received a mortal blow, and he turned his horse's head and fled, and Owain pursued him."[21] While the trope of the breaking spear is a very common narrative convention, as is the detail of sparks given off at the strike, Gruffudd Llwyd amplifies the moment in an elaborate description, as if in slow-motion, of the splintering of the *gwayw ufeldan* [fiery spear] (Item 3.60) with sparks flying like *pyst mellt* [lightning bolts] (Item 3.66). During the telling of this moment, Owain is compared to yet another legendary figure, the thirteenth-century Shropshire outlaw Fulk III Fitzwarin, who became the hero of the eponymous early fourteenth-century Old French prose romance, *Fouke le Fitz Waryn*.[22] As a result of this encounter, the Scots fled before Owain like *gyriad ychen llog* [a driving of hired oxen] (Item 3.68). This feat will be remembered *hyd Ddydd Brawd, medd dy wawdydd* [until Judgment Day, says your poet] (Item 3.71). And with a touch of national pride, Gruffudd has the herald *a chrio i Gymro'r gamp* [crying that the contest goes to a Welshman] (Item 3.82), thus ensuring Owain's reputation *a'r gwiw rwysg, a'r goresgyn, / a'r glod i'r marchog o'r Glyn* [and the fitting authority, and the conquest, / and the fame of the knight of the Glyn] (Item 3.87–88).[23]

---

[20] Geoffrey of Monmouth, 8.16; Thorpe, pp. 201–02; Lewis, *Brut Dingestow*, pp. 132–33.

[21] Bollard, Tales of Arthur, p. 74. *A'e erbynnyeit a oruc Owein, ac ymwan ac ef yn drut, a thorri y deu baladyr a orugant, a dispeilaw deu gledyf a wnaethant ac ymgyfogi. . . . Ac yna adnabot a oruc y marchawc duawc ry gaffel dyrnawt agheuawl ohonaw, ac ymchoelut penn y varch a oruc a ffo* (Thomson, *Owein*, lines 270–72, 275–77). That Gruffudd Llwyd was drawing on his knowledge of a Welsh version of this tale is indicated by his use of the rare form *duog* [black] in naming *y marchawc duog o'r dŵr* [the Black Knight from the water], a form known elsewhere only from the *White Book of Rhydderch* and the *Red Book of Hergest* copies of the tale (in the earlier spelling *duawc*), where other versions have the simplex *du*; see Thomson, *Owein*, lines 276n and 281.

[22] See Item 3.57n. This reference may not be entirely by chance, for a direct descendant with the same name was in company with Owain at Berwick (see Davies, *Revolt*, p. 148).

[23] Williams suggests that this poem, with its references to Glyndyfrdwy in lines 5–6, 31, and 88, was first recited to Owain at his court in Glyndyfrdwy, the only poem that can be so specifically located ("Owain y Beirdd," p. 5; "More than 'skimble-skamble stuff,'" pp. 12–13).

Iolo Goch's poem on Owain's exploits in Scotland (Item 4) describes the same incident. After the opening couplet discussed above, Iolo invokes Mary's protection for Owain, whom he equates with the legendary Powys forebear Pywer Lew. In doing so, he leaves it ambiguous as to whether the phrase *iôr Powys* [lord of Powys] (Item 4.6) refers to Pywer Lew or to Owain. He then poses and answers a rhetorical question to establish the perceptivity that underlies Owain's moral authority as a leader: *Pwy adwaenai bai'n y byd, / pwy ond Owain, paun diwyd?* [Who would recognize a fault in the world — who but Owain, faithful peacock?] (Item 4.7–8). Iolo also compares Owain with Llŷr's son (*mab Llŷr*, Item 4.10), Bendigeidfran, the mythological giant king of the Island of the Mighty (i.e., Britain) in the second branch of *The Mabinogi*, thus linking Owain to the deepest traditional history and cultural values of Wales.[24] After brief references to Owain's lineage, Iolo exemplifies his gentler qualities with a portrait of Owain as a young boy who was fair and kind and considerate to others. In this context it is noteworthy that Iolo describes Owain as *mab yn adnabod / caru clêr* [a boy who knew / to love poets], for as this couplet concludes: *Felly ceir clod!* [Thus is fame achieved!] (Item 4.23–24). This states directly the mutually dependent relationship between a nobleman or noblewoman and a poet, for while the poets needed patrons to support them with their generosity, so too the secular leaders of society, in particular, needed the poets to put into words their importance, their character, and their qualities as leaders not merely to satisfy their egos but also to provide the medium through which their reputations were spread. Owain, it seems, understood this at an early age. It is not unlikely that Iolo Goch, born c.1325, knew Owain during the latter's childhood, which may account for the air of specificity, even affectionate intimacy, in this passage.

The second half of this poem, however, opens with a strikingly abrupt shift in the characterization of Owain: *Pan aeth mewn gwroliaeth gwrdd, / gorugwr fu garw agwrdd* [When he reached stout manhood, the slashing man was a rough, mighty one] (Item 4.33–34). The remainder of the poem portrays Owain as a soldier — *Gorau sawdwr gwrs ydoedd* [He was the best soldier of the time] (Item 4.43) — and as in Gruffudd Llwyd's poem it centers on an encounter during Owain's time in Berwick. Lines 35–42 give us a description of him, armed and on horseback, with particular attention to his fair helmet (*helm wen*, Item 4.40).[25]

Iolo gives us an image for the crest on Owain's helmet with sufficient specificity to be based on fact: *ac yn ei phen, nen iawnraifft, / adain rudd o edn yr Aifft* [and on its top — finely-plumed lord — / a red plume of the bird of Egypt] (Item 4.41–42). Andrew Breeze presents a convincing argument that the device on Owain's crest was a phoenix, rather than flamingo feathers, as originally suggested by J. E. Lloyd.[26] What then might have been its significance? Breeze suggests, somewhat tentatively, "Some may feel that the implication of that crest is perhaps not the resurrection of the flesh (as in most Christian texts), but the unique excellence of the bearer, with no peer or parallel for valour." However, he goes on to say that "it is possible that Glendower's use of the phoenix had an implication more spiritual than laudatory," especially in the light of the bird as a device for Joan of Arc later in the fif-

---

[24] Alternatively, *mab Llŷr* might refer to Manawydan son of Llŷr, the main figure in the third branch of *The Mabinogi*, traditionally known for his wise counsel; it is also possible that Iolo intentionally leaves it up to us to decide which son of Llŷr is meant.

[25] Gruffudd Llwyd also mentions his helmet in the opening couplet of the poem discussed above: *Owain helm gain* [fine-helmed Owain] (Item 3.2).

[26] Breeze, "Owen Glendower's Crest"; Lloyd, *Owen Glendower*, p. 22.

teenth century (accompanied by the motto "Invito funere vivat"), and for Mary Queen of Scots in the sixteenth (with the motto that had also been her mother's, "En ma fin est mon commencement").[27] One might note, of course, that any crest is meant to reflect the excellence of the bearer, though the phoenix, as an *unica avis*, is perhaps particularly appropriate in this regard. But dare we go a step farther to suggest that a phoenix crest might simultaneously imply uniqueness, invincibility, and the wearer's hopes or aspirations for himself as a representative of Wales?[28] However it is interpreted, we should note that Owain chose a different device in his later career. The reverse of his Great Seal shows him mounted with a dragon crest, undeniably emblematic of Wales, above the crown on his helmet.[29]

Iolo Goch then briefly describes in conventional terms two of Owain's encounters at Berwick. In the first of these he throws his opponent "to the ground, with his shield in bits" (Item 4.50). In the second, which may be a rout following upon the first, "he broke his spear with his ferocity" (Item 4.52), followed by a chase. These encounters are remembered as a reproach to the Scots, who fled, not like oxen, as in Gruffudd Llwyd's poem, but *yn gweiddi megis gwyddeifr* [bleating like wild goats] (Item 4.57). Just as Gruffudd Llwyd comments on the path that Owain cut through the battle (Item 3.47–48), so too does Iolo, not without exaggeration: *Mawr fu y llwybr drwy'r crwybr crau, blwyddyn yn porthi bleiddiau* [Great was the path through the bloody hoar-frost, / a year feeding wolves] (Item 4.59–60).

The last four lines of the poem expand this image with a hyperbolic expression of Owain's heroic stature, a description that is consistent with, and may have contributed to, Owain's later reputation for devastation:

Ni thyfodd gwellt na thafol
hefyd na'r ŷd ar ei ôl,
o Ferwig Seisnig ei sail
hyd Faesbwrch, hydr fu ysbail. (Item 4.61–64)

[Neither grass nor dock grew,
nor corn, in his track
from Berwick, English its foundation,
to Maesbury, mighty was the spoil.]

These lines bring Owain back as far as Maesbury, on the Welsh-English border just eight miles from his home at Sycharth, but they also provide another significant link to Welsh legendary history. Iolo Goch implicitly compares Owain with the heroes whose names are combined in the triad of the *Tri Ruduoavc Ynys Prydein* [Three Red Ravagers (or Bloody Reapers) of the Island of Britain]. The earliest version of this triad, from the thirteenth century, names the three as Arthur, Rhun son of Beli, and Morgant the Wealthy, but the later

---

[27] Breeze, "Owen Glendower's Crest," p. 101. Breeze also notes that "the interpretation 'phoenix' suits Iolo's images of heat and fire at this point of his poem" (p. 100).

[28] John Vinycomb notes a comparable case: "Queen Elizabeth placed a phoenix upon her medals and tokens with her favourite motto: 'Semper eadem' ('Always the same'), and sometimes with the motto 'Sola phoenix omnis mundi' ('The sole phoenix of the world'); and on the other side, 'Et Angliae gloria' ('And the glory of England'), with her portrait full-faced" (*Fictitious & Symbolic Creatures*, p. 175).

[29] See p. 424.

fourteenth-century expanded version found in the *White Book of Rhydderch* and the *Red Book of Hergest* elucidates for us Iolo's reference in the poem:

> Tri Ruduoavc Ynys Prydein: Run ap Beli, a Llew Llaw Gyffes, a Morgan Mwynuawr, ac vn a oed ruduogach no'r tri. Arthur oed y henw; blvydyn ny doy na gvellt na llysseu y ford y kerdei yr vn o'r tri. a seith mlyned ny doy y ford y kerdei Arthur.

> [Three Red Ravagers of the Island of Britain: Rhun son of Beli, and Lleu Skilful Hand, and Morgan(t) the Wealthy. But there was one who was a Red Ravager greater than all three: Arthur was his name. For a year neither grass nor plants used to spring up where one of the three would walk; but where Arthur went, not for seven years.][30]

Little is known of Rhun ap Beli, partly because the name Rhun is common in early Welsh and identification without a patronymic is uncertain. His father may be Beli Mawr [Beli the Great], who was claimed as a forebear by all of the major Welsh dynasties, though there are other possibilities. Lleu Llaw Gyffes has mythological origins — his name is cognate with that of the god known in Irish as Lugh, in Gaulish as Lugus, also represented in the names of the cities of Lyon, Laon, and Leiden. The tale of Lleu's birth, youth, marriage, and betrayal, as it was known in medieval Wales, is told in the fourth branch of *The Mabinogi*, which ends "And as the tale says, he was lord over Gwynedd after that."[31] Morgant the Wealthy was, in all likelihood, a figure from the "Old North," i.e., one of the leaders of the Brythonic kingdoms of northern Britain, perhaps the Morcant of the ninth-century *Historia Brittonum* who joined Urien Rheged and other kings in the war against Bernicia in the sixth century. Arthur, of course, needs no introduction, and we need only recognize that coupling Owain's name with him and the other Red Ravagers, even indirectly, is a considerable accolade.[32]

While the descriptions of the encounters in these poems are conventionalized, the central underlying event can not be entirely discounted as apocryphal, especially when these two poems are considered side by side. It seems likely that both poets are responding to the same or similar accounts. Both tell of an encounter in which Owain's lance was broken, in both poems this is followed by a chase couched in terms of animals (cattle or wild goats) fleeing, both mention the path that he cut through the battle, though only Iolo mentions Sir Gregory Sais and Berwick. Only the opening couplet of Iolo Goch's poem (Item 4) so much as hints at any subsequent campaign or later event. Especially given the relatively short time span within which these poems were probably produced, we might even wonder whether they were composed in poetic competition, either implicit or acknowledged, or one in response to the other, to celebrate Owain Glyndŵr's burgeoning reputation as a soldier. It is an added benefit that both poems also preserve for us a glimpse of each poet's personal feelings for Owain: Gruffudd Llwyd after his evening of drinking and jesting with his patron and Iolo Goch in his charming evocation of Owain's character as a boy.

The two poems discussed above present us with a view of Owain at an important and promising stage in his career, praised by his poets, in his role as "an upper-class Welshman fully and comfortably assimilated to the conditions of English rule, an eager participant in

---

[30] Bromwich, *Trioedd*, Triad 20W, p. 35.

[31] Bollard, *Mabinogi*, p. 108.

[32] For more on these four heroes in Welsh tradition, see Bromwich, *Trioedd*, pp. 500–01; 420–22; 465–67; 274–77.

English armies in their imperial mode, . . . at ease, like his English squirely counterparts, in the enjoyment of the good life."[33] But though he participated as a nobleman of some (albeit "colonial") status in the hierarchy of English rule, Owain was nevertheless "far from being a fully fledged Englishman."[34] Another poem by Gruffudd Llwyd gives a different view of Wales, and, to a degree, of Glyndŵr as well. The opening of the poem beginning *Byd dudrist, bywyd hydraul, / ydyw hwn* [A gloomy world, a transitory life, / is this"] (Item 5) is an unrelenting expression of tensions in Wales, couched in terms similar to the "world turned upside down" topos also found in John Gower's Latin poem *Vox Clamantis*, written during the period 1377–82 and outlining the conditions in England that led to the Peasants' Revolt of 1381.[35] Gruffudd Llwyd's poem describes a harsh world (*byd gogaled*, 5.8) in which no one is happy (*nid llawen neb*, Item 5.3). The scope of the poet's discontent, and its cause, is expressed in a pair of remarkably striking images:

> Cymry, rhag maint eu camrwysg,
> cenedl druain fal brain brwysg.
> Gallwn, nid erfynnwn fudd,
> Eu galw yn gallor goludd. (Item 5.9–12)

> [The Welsh, because their oppression is so great,
> are a kindred of wretches like drunken crows.
> I could — I would not beg for gain —
> call them a kettle of tripe.]

As Professor Williams points out, the *mundus inversus* topos is "often used historically to express upper class discomfiture"; however, these lines, which would have been insulting to the Welsh had the poet not explicitly laid the blame on the oppression, cast the motif rather in the role of a more general, national complaint.[36] The image of the crows is best understood in light of the Welsh poetic tradition of using *brân* (crow, raven, pl. *brain*) as a laudatory term for warriors.[37] This makes even more stark the contrast with actual ravens, which are cacophonous and seemingly disorganized and directionless even without being drunk. The unusual image of tripe roiling in a kettle, too, is emblematic of the social turmoil and uncertain, shifting social boundaries of the late fourteenth century. The "world turned upside down" motif is then employed explicitly in a series of reversals expressed both directly ("Whoever was lowest in his mores / is highest . . . / and the highest before midday / will be

---

[33] Williams, "More than 'skimble-skamble stuff,'" p. 20.

[34] Williams, "More than 'skimble-skamble stuff,'" p. 20. Williams draws on Davies's identification of post-conquest Wales as a colony in "Colonial Wales," and on the modern postcolonial theory of Homi Bhabha ("Of Mimicry and Man," pp. 85–92) to explore the complexity of Owain's position vis-à-vis the English court.

[35] "The bitter thing is now becoming sweet, the sweet is now becoming bitter. . . . Servants are now masters and masters are servants" (Gower, *Major Latin Works*, pp. 208, 259; quoted in Williams, "More than 'skimble-skamble stuff," pp. 21–22). Chaucer, too, complains that "turned up-so-doun / Is al this world for mede [payment, bribery] and wilfulnesse" ("Lak of Stedfastnesse," lines 5–6, in *Riverside Chaucer*, p. 654).

[36] Williams, "More than 'skimble-skamble stuff,'" p. 21.

[37] For examples, see the note on this line.

lowest and most humble" [Item 5.13–16]), and metaphorically ("The slender feathered kites are behaving like hawks at every turn" [5.19–20]). The poet then states his complaint forthrightly and asks a troubling question:

> hyn a wna, hen a newydd,
> y drygfyd. Pa fyd a fydd? (Item 5.21–22)

> [It is this that causes, old and new,
> the troubled world. What sort of world is to come?]

Gruffudd Llwyd's final reversal encompasses the Welsh people as a whole, contrasting them with the former greatness of the Britons, familiar to his audience through historical tradition, and he recalls that greatness in the persons of three British leaders whose rule extended even beyond the island of Britain: Brân, the son of Dunwallus Molmutius (in Welsh, Dyfnwal Moelmud), who became emperor of Rome in Geoffrey of Monmouth's *Historia regum Britanniae*; Custennin, a conflation of a sixth-century ruler of Devon, Constantine, the first Christian emperor, and Constantine III the Usurper, whose troops in Britain proclaimed him emperor; and Arthur, whose title *ameraudur* [emperor] predates Geoffrey of Monmouth's *Historia*.[38]

Returning to his own time, Gruffudd registers a more specific complaint – that there are only three Welsh knights and one of them, Sir Hywel of the Axe, is now dead. He asks directly, "Who now, since he has gone, / will hold the office" (Item 5.61–62), and he confidently answers his own question:

> Owain, mael ni wn i mwy,
> iôr Glyn, daeardor, Dyfrdwy. (Item 5.63–64)

> [Owain, I know no greater lord,
> the Lord of Glyn — narrow valley — Dyfrdwy.]

He then praises Owain's lineage, his prowess, and his elegant dress, pointedly naming him a powerful baron (*barwn grym*, Item 5.72), and closing with a couplet that hints at Owain's ability to redress the harsh conditions so graphically outlined at the poem's beginning:

> anneddf a cham ni oddef,
> ymysg ieirll ydd ymwaisg ef. (Item 5.81–82)

> [He will not tolerate lawlessness and wrong.
> He will include himself amongst earls.]

Throughout this poem there is no hint of rebellion, no suggestion that Owain openly oppose the powers that be. The poet does, however, call for Owain to be recognized by those powers as one of the foremost Welshmen of his day, and this at a time when Owain was at his prime, probably in his late twenties or early thirties. The point would surely not be lost on a sympathetic Welsh audience that Gruffudd Llwyd is speaking on behalf of Wales against wrongs they are suffering under English rule and that Owain Glyndŵr is the best

---

[38] Item 5.25–28; see also the notes to these lines.

man to lead them. Rebellion was at least twelve years in the future and is not the subject of this poem, but we see here laid bare in stark imagery the discontent born of oppression that drew many to Owain's cause when rebellion came.

For it to gain broad support among the Welsh and, perchance, to be successful, the legitimacy of that revolt must be based, however, not only on the wrongs, real and perceived, done to the Welsh; it must also be evident in the person and descent of Owain as their leader. Both Iolo Goch and Gruffudd Llwyd refer briefly to Owain's lineage in the two poems discussed above (Items 4.11–18, 5.65–69), but during the same period, sometime after 1385, Iolo wrote an important poem outlining Owain's genealogy more fully (Item 6).[39] There is no precedent for this poem, which names no fewer than twelve of Owain's historically documented ancestors, reaching back eleven or twelve generations to the mid eleventh century. Four legendary forebears ranging from the fifth to the seventh century are also named. Of the known ancestors seven are in the Powys line, two from the Deheubarth line, and three from Gwynedd, each line culminating in a key figure who established dynastic stability in his rule: Bleddyn ap Cynfyn in Powys, Rhys ap Tewdwr in Dehebarth, and Gruffudd ap Cynan in Gwynedd.[40] The purpose of the poem, beyond the general glorification of Owain, is a matter of some debate, and interpretation hinges on our understanding of the poet himself.

Iolo Goch's career extended for more than fifty years over the last half of the fourteenth century and, it appears, into the early years of the fifteenth. Like Owain Glyndŵr as noted above, Iolo moved in the circle of Welsh gentry in a multicultural, albeit English-dominated, Wales. In an important article, Dafydd Johnston presents strong evidence that Iolo was consistently concerned "with the maintenance of law and order by rightful authority."[41] Nor was he adverse to composing poems in praise of prominent Englishmen. Indeed, one of his early poems — and significantly the earliest known use of the *cywydd* for serious praise poetry — was addressed to the English king, Edward III, sometime between 1347 and 1356.[42] The poem praises Edward for his military prowess and successes and encourages him to go on crusade as foretold in the *Prophecy of the Six Kings*.[43] Considerably later, between 1394 and 1398, Iolo composed a *cywydd* to Roger Mortimer, fourth Earl of March and heir apparent of Richard II (as well as Iolo's feudal lord), prophesying for him success in the Irish wars. Sir Roger had noble Welsh blood in his veins (his great-grandfather married Gwladus Ddu, daughter of Llywelyn the Great), and this made it easy for Iolo to delight in the fact that he stood in line

---

[39] The thirty-three manuscript copies of this poem attest to its later popularity, and the considerable variation in readings and line order reveal that it had enjoyed a long period of oral transmission (see Williams, "More than 'skimble-skamble stuff,'" pp. 26–27; Johnston in Iolo Goch, *Gwaith*, p. 221).

[40] For names and further details, see pp. 425–30 and the notes to Item 6.

[41] "Iolo Goch and the English," p. 89.

[42] Iolo Goch, *Poems*, pp. 2–5. Johnston suggests that while it may be that Iolo expected Edward to understand his Welsh poem on the basis that it is couched in the second person and that lines 16–17 extol Edward's knowledge of "every angelic language," it is more likely that both points should be laid at the door of convention and hyperbole ("Iolo Goch and the English," pp. 81, 84). As it is plausible, too, that this poem was instigated by Sir Rhys ap Gruffudd, a strong supporter of (and recruiter for) the king, it may have served in Wales as a vehicle to garner support for Edward's prophesied crusade (Iolo Goch, *Poems*, p. 157). Iolo composed an elegy for Sir Rhys on his death in 1356.

[43] See Item 1.78–91; Johnston concludes that Iolo's source "seems to have been the Anglo-Norman French version, written soon after 1312" (Iolo Goch, *Poems*, p. 157).

to become king, even stating that "it would be fitting for you to get the crown / of Aberffraw, my tall liege-lord," though that hope came to nought when Earl Roger died in Ireland in 1398.[44] Johnston also stresses that underlying Iolo Goch's famous poem to the plowman is a "deeply conservative social philosophy" calling for the maintenance of the social order, traditionally represented as consisting of three classes or estates (warriors, clergy, laborers), especially following the Peasants' Revolt of 1381 in England.[45] Rather than rising up in opposition, the plowman is expected to pay his tithes and gain his reward at Judgment Day.

The question at hand, then, is to what degree Iolo Goch's conservatism informs his poem on Owain Glyndŵr's genealogy? While acknowledging that "the poem does convey very clearly a leading Welshman's dissatisfaction with the condition of his country," Johnston sees as the "immediate practical occasion of the poem" the legitimization of Owain's claims of inheritance through his mother and aunt to lands in Pembrokeshire, as stated in lines 59–62:[46]

> edling o hen genhedlaeth
> yw ef o ben Tref y Traeth;
> ei gyfoeth, ef a'i gofyn,
> Tref y Garn, a'i farn a fyn.

> [heir of an ancient clan
> is he, from the head of Tref y Traeth.
> His realm — he claims it —
> is Tref-y-Garn, and he desires his judgment.]

The reference to his desire for judgment might imply that there was a legal claim pending, and the same claim might be alluded to in line 68: *ni wneir dwyn un erw o'i dir* [Not one acre of his land will be taken]. Johnston recognizes that "[i]n view of Owain's connections with all three royal lines Iolo is fully justified in calling him 'un pen ar Gymru' (sole leader of Wales)." "But," he continues, "Iolo does not go on to make clear any practical consequences of this exalted status, presumably because he abhorred the idea of rebellion against the rightful authority of the Crown."[47]

However, rebellion is not necessarily the only expectation we might draw from Iolo's characterization of Owain. In this genealogical poem, the greatest attention is paid to Owain's descent from the once-powerful rulers of Powys, though at the time his inherited lands comprised only a small portion of the former kingdom. But Powys was no longer a formally recognized entity; rather all of Wales was under English control, be it in the royal principality or Marcher lordships. Given Owain's very real, if weaker, claims of descent from the lines of Deheubarth and Gwynedd, the absence of any other Welshman of comparable ancestry, and the oppression the Welsh were experiencing under English rule, it is not unlikely that Iolo Goch and Gruffudd Llwyd could envision Owain as a sympathetic intercessor for and defender of Wales *de facto*, should his status as the preeminent Welsh leader be suitably recognized and rewarded by the crown.

---

[44] Iolo Goch, *Poems*, p. 84. The "crown of Aberffraw" is shorthand for the rule of all Wales; see below.

[45] Iolo Goch, *Poems*, p. 180, also pp. 14–15; see also Johnston's "Iolo Goch and the English," pp. 94–96.

[46] "Iolo Goch and the English," pp. 92, 91.

[47] "Iolo Goch and the English," p. 93.

In his later poem to Roger Mortimer, Iolo identifies him as *ŵyr burffrwyth iôr Aberffraw* [descendant of the pure-fruited lord of Aberffraw], borrowing this line, with one change, from the earlier poem to Owain (Item 6.96).[48] Though the specific lord of Aberffraw intended in these poems may differ (Gruffudd ap Cynan in Owain's case, Llywelyn the Great in Mortimer's), it is striking that in regard to Wales, Iolo sees both Owain and Mortimer in the same position, poised to be the preeminent Welsh leader — certainly so for Mortimer should he become king, quite possibly so for Owain were he given suitable preferment by the king — while leaving the English crown in place over all of Britain. Central to both these poems are Iolo's hopes for Wales, but with the benefit of hindsight we might also see in them, with their shared lines, a hint of the pre-war social connections that may make more understandable the change of allegiance and marriage to Owain's daughter Catrin by Edmund Mortimer, Roger's brother, after his capture by Owain at Bryn Glas in 1402. At the very least, Owain and Sir Roger shared the same poet; this perhaps suggests some shared sympathies between their families.

Iolo also recycled another line, *gŵr bellach a grybwyllir* [as a man is he praised henceforth] (Item 6.67) in his poem to Mortimer (*Poems*, 20.20), in both poems contrasting it with their boyhood and in conjunction with a reference to the acquisition and ownership of land.[49] We do not know precisely when the poem on Owain's genealogy was written, nor do we know when Owain's dispute began with Lord Grey. Iolo's insistence in the very next line of his poem to Owain that *ni wneir dwyn un erw o'i dir* [Not one acre of his land will be taken] (Item 6.68), however, suggests that, even if this particular reference is interpreted as limited to his land claims in the south (see Item 6.61–64), the preservation of his estates was a matter of no small importance to Owain, and provides us with some further understanding of his response when the spark touched the kindling in September 1400.

Gruffydd Aled Williams brings another perspective to our understanding, pointing out that this poem "which epitomised Owain's claim to be Prince of Wales . . . was eminently fitted to elicit support for Owain and could well have been used to this end both before and during the revolt."[50] Williams notes that lines 93–96, including the highly resonant reference to Owain as *aur burffrwyth iôr Aberffraw* [golden pure fruit of the lord of Aberffraw] (Item 6.96), appear in only two of the thirty-three manuscript copies of the poem.[51] Williams and Dafydd Johnston agree that these lines are fully consistent with Iolo Goch's style and that they may indeed be original to the poem, but Williams suggests that they might also be "a propagandistic interpolation added — as an afterthought by Iolo Goch himself or by someone else — in order to specifically highlight Owain's claim to be the *de facto* heir of the princes of Aberffraw, a potent aspect of his eventual call to arms directed at his fellow countrymen."[52]

---

[48] Iolo Goch, *Poems*, 20.14. Johnston raises the possibility that *ŵyr* [descendant] might also have been the original reading in the poem to Owain, rather than *aur* [golden]; see Item 6.96n.

[49] This demonstrates, at the least, that Iolo must have had his poem to Owain in mind as he praised Mortimer, and perhaps that he had found in Mortimer an even more promising candidate to take on the role of *iôr Aberffraw*, at least until Mortimer's death in 1398.

[50] "More than 'skimble-skamble stuff,'" p. 27.

[51] These two manuscripts, NLW Peniarth 96 (late 16th century) written by Lewys Dwnn and NLW Llanstephan 53 (c.1647) by James Dwnn, who may have been Lewys Dwnn's son, are closely related and share many variant readings; thus they may derive from a common source.

[52] Williams, "More than 'skimble-skamble stuff'"; Johnston in Iolo Goch, *Gwaith*, p. 227.

While it is likely that neither Iolo Goch nor Gruffudd Llwyd had rebellion in mind as they composed their poems, it can hardly be doubted that, as events moved toward and into armed revolt, these poems proved useful in legitimizing Owain's claims to the title *Princeps Wallie*, Prince of Wales, and illuminating his military credentials. And though these poets may not have been inciting action directly, there is little question that their poems, and perhaps others now lost, helped lay the seeds of the revolt that came into full flower in September 1400. Nor would it be surprising that the increase of social and inter-cultural tensions during the late fourteenth century might also lead to a change of perspective in the minds of the poets themselves. They certainly would not advocate an overthrow of the entire social order, but the weight of Welsh history, the pressure of events (many now unknown to us), and the existence of such an undoubtedly charismatic leader as Owain, whom they clearly loved and respected, might very well have led them to support the idea of an armed resistance perhaps even before it became a fact.

The poems discussed above played a significant role in presenting Owain Glyndŵr to Wales in the later fourteenth century. But prior to their public dissemination, they presented Owain to himself. By holding up a mirror to the man, the poets showed him the qualities he should embody, and such public praise must have some effect on its object, thereby helping to create the man he was to become. It is in no small measure through the poets that Owain achieved such stature as a Welsh leader — one who ultimately risked all not simply for personal gain, but to regain the status and recognition that Wales had lost in 1282.

The comfortable life of a Welsh baron at home in Sycharth and Glyndyfdrdwy was not to last, and we have now come to 1400 and the turbulent years to follow, years in which poets certainly played a part, though little poetry of the period has survived. As purveyors of praise, news, rumor, and potentially sedition, bards of all classes became especially suspect to the English during the rebellion. Certainly, the fear of poets as a vehicle of encouragement, recruitment, or propaganda is demonstrated by a statute enacted, amongst other anti-Welsh laws, by Parliament in 1402:

> Item, qe nulls westours, et rymours, mynstrales, ou vacabundes, ne soient sustenuz en Gales, pur faire kymorthas ou quyllages sur le commune poeple, les queux par lour divinaciones, messonges, et excitacions, sont concause de la insurrectioun et rebellioun q'orest en Gales.

> [Also, that no wasters, rhymers, minstrels or vagabonds should be tolerated in Wales to make *kymorthas* or exactions on the common people, for, by their divinations, lies and incitements, they are a cause of the present insurrection and rebellion in Wales.][53]

There is no reason to believe that at this time Parliament could (or cared to) make distinctions between higher and lower grades of Welsh poets and their social functions, and this statute continued to echo in England for the next two centuries. Richard Suggett and Eryn White note in their discussion of the persecution of Welsh minstrels as vagabonds under the Tudors that "the idea of the minstrel as a seditious vagabond had a long historical

---

[53] *PROME*, ed. and trans. Chris Given-Wilson. English *kymortha(s)* derives from W *cymortheu*, pl. of *cymorth* [help, support], which developed the sense of "a gathering together of people for a benevolent purpose," and thence "tribute, subsidy" (*GPC*, s.v. cymorth; see also Suggett and White, "Vagabonds and Minstrels," pp. 156–57).

pedigree in the administration of Wales reaching back to the legislation enacted in the aftermath of Owain Glyndŵr's revolt."[54]

Of the few poems from the years of the rebellion that have survived, one must have been quite popular, judging by the number of surviving manuscript copies.[55] This the only poem of the period whose subject throughout is Owain *pan oedd fwyaf i rwysg* [when his authority was greatest], as the headnotes to ten manuscripts state (Item 27). Though thirty-four of the thirty-five manuscripts attribute this poem to Iolo Goch, in 1922 Ifor Williams published an article rejecting it from the Iolo Goch canon, ascribing it to Lewys Glyn Cothi (fl. 1447–1486) and arguing that the subject of the poem was Owain ap Gruffudd ap Nicolas, a relatively minor figure in southwest Wales in the mid fifteenth century. Through a careful analysis of the poem's poetics, however, Gruffydd Aled Williams has demonstrated that its style is more consistent with earlier poetry than with that of the 1450s, and more specifically that it shares numerous similarities with Iolo Goch's work, including some strikingly close parallels, not to mention one entire line (Item 27.50) also found in Iolo's "Thanks for a Horse."[56] Thus the evidence that this poem is correctly ascribed to Iolo Goch is as strong as, or stronger than, that for many other poems and poets, and we can reasonably accept that Iolo's long life extended into the early years of the fifteenth century.[57]

We do not know whether Iolo came to regret the loss of the hopes he earlier held for law, order, and justice through accommodation to English rule, but once hostilities have broken out he is forthright in revealing his wishes, focusing squarely on Owain Glyndŵr's martial skills. Like Gruffudd Llwyd's poem on "the world turned upside down" (Item 5), this poem composed in the early years of the war begins with a dark and unequivocal expression of dissatisfaction with the state of affairs (and the affairs of state) in Wales: *Llyma fyd rhag sythfryd Sais!* [Behold a world caused by English arrogance!] (Item 27.1). The second line of the opening couplet then ties this complaint to the poet's long-standing wish for a lord *ohonom ni ein hunain* [from amongst us ourselves], Item 27.4), and the answer to that wish is named straightaway:

> . . . pawb adwaen pwy —
> arf glân dewrdarf Glyndyfrdwy,
> Owain, loyw waedlain lidlorf. (Item 27.5–7)

> [. . . everyone knows who:
> the fair, brave and fear-inspiring weapon of Glyndyfrdwy,
> Owain, bright bloody blade, ferocious defender.]

The poem continues, unrelenting in its fervor and its delight in Owain's ferocity, declaring "A well-made song about him will be meaningful" (*Deall a wnair gywair gân / ohono ef ei*

---

[54] Suggett, "Vagabonds and Minstrels," p. 162.

[55] Madog ap Gronw Gethin's poem (Item 53) praising the river Dee for its active participation in the war does not name Owain and hence is not discussed in this essay. It does, however, give a sense of the intensity of feeling that must at times have been pervasive amongst those hoping for Owain's success. The poems by Llywelyn ab y Moel composed in the later years of the rebellion (Items 54 and 55) are discussed in Gruffydd Aled Williams's essay below.

[56] Iolo Goch, *Poems*, 13.104: *Poed gwir, bywyd hir i hwn!* [May it be true, long life to him!].

[57] The proof, of course, is not absolute, and as Dafydd Johnston has reminded me in conversation, the possibility remains that another poet imitated and drew on Iolo Goch's style and earlier poetry.

hunan, Item 27.15–16). Depth of meaning (*dyfynder ystyr*) is one of the three chief attributes that strengthen a poem,[58] and we can be confident that Iolo Goch saw this poem as meaningful in extolling Owain with such martial intensity as to encourage and raise the spirits of his followers. Owain Glyndŵr is again named explicitly in line 19, and the Owains in lines 21 and 23 may be comparisons with Owain ab Urien, the Arthurian hero, and Owain Lawgoch, whose plan to invade from France in 1369 to drive the English out of Wales was foiled by foul weather; alternatively, especially given a certain syntactic ambiguity, these lines may be a tripled description of Glyndŵr himself.[59] Iolo asks for the protection of *Llurig Dduw . . . am Owain* [God's breastplate . . . for Owain] (Item 27.33–34), and then he reminds his listeners, with audacious hyperbole, of the deep legendary history of former Welsh hegemony over Britain and of the coming of the Saxons, in a couplet describing Owain that is reminiscent of the call to drive out the English in the tenth-century prophecy *Armes Prydein*:[60]

> Pôr a ladd mewn ymladdgors
> pedwar can mil o hil Hors. (Item 27.41–42)

> [Lord who kills in the battle-bog
> four hundred thousand of Horsa's line.]

As in his poem on Sycharth, Iolo gives us near the end one more detail of Owain's personal appearance: *pôr dôr dâr, gwanar gwinau* [an oak door of a lord, an auburn-haired chief] (Item 27.48), and he then returns to the familiar, almost defining, image of Owain's broken lance, before closing with a prayer for a long life for him:

> Pleidiwr brwydr, paladr briwdwn,
> poed gwir, bywyd hir i hwn!
> Pedr i'w borth pa dir y bo,
> pe mau swydd pumoes iddo! (Item 27.49–52)

> [A supporter of battle with a shattered spear,
> may it be true — long life to him!
> St. Peter as his support wherever he may be.
> If mine were the office — five ages to him!]

The poems discussed above are by poets who knew Owain Glyndŵr personally, but the conventions of fourteenth-century Welsh poetry are such that we learn little about his personal appearance and demeanor, other than the interesting though rather meager details that he was strong, thin, and auburn-haired. More of the physical man we may never know, but this poetry does help us to see how Owain became the preeminent Welshman of his day and the multi-variate hero for centuries after his death. While Owain Glyndŵr's greatness can be ascribed in good measure to his genealogy and circumstances, we might also look to his character, and it is here that the poetry becomes particularly relevant.

---

[58] *Tri pheth a gadarnhaa kerd: dyfynder ystyr, ac amylder Kymraec, ac odidawc dechymic* [Three things that strengthen a poem: depth of meaning, and copious Welsh, and wonderful imagination] (Williams and Jones, *Gramadegau'r Penceirddiaid*, p. 17).

[59] See the notes to lines 18, 21, 23–25, and 26.

[60] See Livingston, *Brunanburh*, pp. 28–37; *Armes Prydein Vawr*, ed. Williams.

The use of conventional praise *topoi* has been noted several times above, and on the surface such praise may seem generic and *de rigueur*, especially as similar *topoi* and comparisons are used in multiple poems to different patrons. But the poets had a great deal of freedom in the choice of both characteristics to stress and images in which to couch them, and there is indeed remarkable imagination (*odidawc dechymic*) evident in these poems of praise, among the earliest in the new *cywydd* form. Part of the deep meaning (*dyfynder ystyr*) of a poem, too, lies in the effect it has or might have on the object of that praise.[61] The poets do not simply reflect his own image back to their subject; they also hold up a vision before him, one that reiterates, often in very specific and striking terms, the ideals which he is thereby encouraged to incorporate into his own character. Insofar as those ideals were adopted by or reinforced in Owain Glyndŵr, to that extent — as William Carlos Williams defines the poet's role in the quotation at the head of this essay — Iolo Goch and Gruffudd Llwyd played a significant part in creating the man, the leader, and the legend that he became.

A NOTE ON WELSH VERSE

Medieval Welsh poetry was meant to be declaimed, and the surviving manuscript copies of many poems contain evidence of a period of oral transmission before a poem was written down. The audiences listening to this poetry would know many, if not all, the principles of Welsh verse, and they would appreciate the poet's skill in constructing the complexity of the sound patterns as much as (at times even more than) they would the overt meaning of a poem. As an early proverb decrees, *Deuparth kerdd i gwrando* [Two thirds of a poem is listening to it].[62]

To the modern reader, medieval Welsh poetry is quite difficult, both in the original and in translation. There are several features that are all but impossible to translate into English, and others that make the flow of thought seem disjunctive and hard to follow. There is insufficient space here to explain Welsh prosody in full, but the following brief comments should help the non-Welsh reader to appreciate some of the formal complexities that make Welsh poetry simultaneously so tightly controlled and so imaginative, and hence to better understand these poems to Owain Glyndŵr.[63] We might state at the outset that medieval Welsh verse is not narrative as we generally think of that term, though there may be a narrative element to a poem, as in Llywelyn ab y Moel's account of the battle of Waun Gaseg (Item 54). It should also be noted that the translations in this book are not meant to be poetic in any way; rather an attempt has been made to render them into acceptable English while staying as close to meaning of the original as possible.

Cywydd

A *cywydd* (etymologically, "harmony") is a poem comprised of a series of any number of couplets of seven-syllable lines, either one of which must end on a stressed syllable and the other on an unstressed syllable, as well as the requirement that every line be in *cynghanedd* (see below).

---

[61] See note 58 above.

[62] Salesbury, *Oll Synnwyr*, B.iv.verso.

[63] For greater detail, see Eurys Rowlands, "Cynghanedd, Metre, Prosody," and also his *Poems of the Cywyddwyr*, pp. xx–xlix.

Englyn

An *englyn* (pl., *englynion*) is an epigrammatic stanza of three or four lines, composed according to strict rules. A common form of *englyn*, as found in Items 88, 90, and 92, is the *englyn unodl union* [lit., "straight, single-rhyme *englyn*], which has four lines of 10, 6, 7, 7 syllables, in which the end-rhyme of lines 2-3-4 is established in syllable 7, 8, or 9 of the first line, and the consonants in the remaining syllables of line 1 are matched in the beginning of line 2.

Cymeriad

Even the untrained eye will be able to recognize a certain fondness for what is known as *cymeriad*, the linking together of lines by beginning each with the same letter or word, as in Item 53.1–4, or more strikingly, in Item 6.25–40, all but one of which begin with the letter H, ten of them with the word *hil* [lineage].

Sangiad

Sangiad (pl. *sangiadau*) is a form of parenthesis — the interruption of a line, sentence, or thought with another phrase or thought. *Sangiad* often serves to facilitate the *cynghanedd* of a line and the sense is frequently subordinate to the sound. Multiple *sangiadau* might form their own sentence, alternating phrases with the one they are interrupting. This requires the reader or listener to hold two ideas in mind simultaneously as each thought progresses independently. A fine example is found in Item 6.87–90, in which two sentences are intertwined and the second is itself interrupted by another. Unraveling them, these become (1) "Teeth are good in front of the tongue in the depths of an unskilled mouth"; (2) A day will come when he shall get the heart of Is Aeron and its cheer"; and (3) "The belief is declared." But, of course, by doing so all the poetry is lost. In the translations in this casebook, the *sangiadau* are often set off by dashes. Often a poet will use tmesis between the two parts of a name, as in a line used by both Iolo Goch and Gruffudd Llwyd: *iôr Glyn,* **daeardor**, *Dyfrdwy* [lord of Glyn — narrow valley — Dyfrdwy] (Items 4.16, 5.64).

Dyfalu and metaphor

Dyfalu [imagine; compare] is the describing of an object with a string of multiple comparisons. The poets became particularly adept at this device, as in the passage in which Iolo Goch describes Owain as "a bear from Deheubarth . . . / a young wolf . . . angry cub / . . . a beautiful bison, / lion of Britain, hand of Peredur, / thick-jacketed lion with a socket of steel, / pestle of battle, a brave lordly father, / pillar of the region of Lloegr, a thick iron surcoat" (Item 6.50–58). Single metaphors are also frequent: Iolo Goch is fond of calling Owain a peacock (Items 4.8; 6.6, 8, 10; 27.20, 40), but he is also a "bay-black bison" (4.4), "the candle of battle" (4.54), "my tawny lion" (6.32), a "whetted blade" (6.33), and to Gruffudd Llwyd he is an "eagle delightful beyond measure" (3.1), a "cupbearer of abundant drink" (3.5), and a "bold powerful stag" (5.76).

Cynghanedd

Cynghanedd ("harmony, concordance, agreement") is an elaborate system, refined in the fourteenth and fifteenth centuries, whereby a poetic line must exhibit one of several patterns of consonantal correspondence, internal rhyme, or both. The four basic types of *cynghanedd* are described here in brief, ignoring many subtleties, variations, complications, and refinements:

1. Consonants before the final stress in the first half of a line must be **matched** in order in the second half:

   Archwn i Fair, | arch iawn fu   [Let us ask Mary — it was a proper request] (4.3)

2. Like the above, except one or more consonants in the beginning of the second half can be *unmatched*:

   caru clêr, *felly* ceir clod!   [to love poets — thus is fame achieved!] (4.24)

3. The first third of a three-part line <u>rhymes</u> with the second, and the second and third have **matching** consonants:

   cenedl dru<u>ain</u> | fal **br**<u>ain</u> | **br**wysg   [a kindred of wretches like drunken crows] (5.10)

4. The final or only syllable of the first stressed word in a line <u>rhymes</u> with the next-to-last syllable of the last word:

   Eryr di<u>grif</u> af<u>rif</u>ed   [Eagle delightful beyond measure] (3.1)

Late medieval and Tudor Wales, constrained by the lack of a favorable political context and developed poetic narrative genres, did not produce the equivalent of Barbour's *The Brus* or Blind Harry's *The Wallace* or even of the Border Ballads in celebration of Owain Glyndŵr. Yet Glyndŵr is a persistent presence in fifteenth- and sixteenth-century Welsh poetry, intruding intermittently into various poetic genres and different levels of poetic activity. Whilst political and cultural developments and the simple passage of time inevitably meant that this presence eventually diminished — not to recover until relatively modern times — it merits attention in any serious evaluation of Glyndŵr's posthumous renown amongst his countrymen.

THE LATER STAGES OF THE REVOLT AND ITS AFTERMATH

Although they cannot be ascribed to specific dates, there are poems extant which can be confidently judged to belong broadly to what J. E. Lloyd once called "the end of the rebellion, when its fires were dying down, but were not yet extinguished."[1] Their author was Llywelyn ab y Moel, a poet from Arwystli in north-western Powys who was probably born during the last decade of the fourteenth century.[2] As a youth during the last phase of the revolt he was probably a Glyndŵr partisan, later becoming an outlaw like many of Owain's unreconciled former adherents.[3] His poem to the Battle of Waun Gaseg (Item 54) — a skirmish with English troops from Usk probably fought in the remote hill-country of Maelienydd (later north Radnorshire) a short distance north of Abbey Cwm-hir[4] — is a noteworthy account by an active participant in a military action associated with the revolt.[5] The poem — self-deprecatingly humorous rather than heroic — depicts Llywelyn and his companions awaiting news of Owain — implying that he was yet alive — and before the engagement boldly affirming their intent not to retreat before the enemy. But faced with a large approaching enemy force Llywelyn recalls how he and his companions were routed and — deciding that discretion was the better part of valor — how he fled ignominiously across hill country. It has been rightly remarked that a coward would be unlikely to sing of his coward-

---

[1] Lloyd, "Trouble in Wales," p. 155.

[2] Williams proposes 1395–1400, but 1400 is almost certainly too late (*Cywyddau Iolo Goch ac Eraill*, ed. Lewis et al, p. lviii).

[3] For the poet's biography see Daniel, *Gwaith Dafydd Bach*, pp. 75–82; *Cywyddau Iolo Goch ac Eraill*, ed. Lewis et al, pp. liv–lxii.

[4] The location was established by Fychan, "Llywelyn ab y Moel," p. 292.

[5] For a discussion of the likely date of the poem see Llywelyn ab y Moel, *Gwaith*, ed. Daniel, p. 139. He proposes 1410–16, favoring a date nearer 1410. If Llywelyn's proposed birthdate of c.1395 is accepted a date nearer to the middle of the decade is more likely.

ice,[6] and the poem — possibly only loosely rooted in military actuality — was probably intended as humorous entertainment for an audience of fellow combatants. It may too, of course, reflect Llywelyn's realization, derived from experience, that participation in warfare was not always unremittingly heroic.

Other poems also reflect Llywelyn's adherence to Owain. In a poem in praise of the birch-wood, he imaginatively conceived of its branches as *Gwewyr goreuwyr Owain* [the spears of the fine men of Owain].[7] This may well relate to his time as an outlaw, as two other poems undeniably do, being in all likelihood composed after the revolt.[8] The first eulogizes Coed y Graig Lwyd [the Wood of the Grey Crag] or Crickheath Hill at Llanymynech in the borderland to the south of Oswestry, idealized as an outlaw haunt.[9] Not unexpectedly, the poem reflects the racial antagonism of the times: the wood is depicted as a stronghold where an Englishman could be held to ransom, the poet asserting that capturing and despoiling an Englishman was more profitable than plying his itinerant bardic craft;[10] neither would the remote wood allow a night attack by a force of the hated English *llu'r Nordd* [host of the North] (Item 55.58). Exuberant evocations of the wood and its thick cover, often echoing the imagery of love and nature poetry and employing the technique of *dyfalu* — description by extravagant comparison — climax with its designation as *Llundain gwerin Owain* [the London of Owain's men] (Item 55.60) and by an invocation of a blessing on *llu Owain delaid* [Owain's fair host] (Item 55.64). In another poem, cast in the form of a dialogue between the poet and his empty purse, the complaining purse urges the poet to resort to his former haunt of Coed y Graig Lwyd claiming that there were rich pickings to be had by raiding the nearby Shropshire settlement of Ruyton XI Towns in Arundel territory.[11] In reply the poet resists, citing the danger of capture in the English borderland, asserting his intention to move southwards and afterwards to progress to Maelienydd, where patrons were plentiful. It has been suggested by Cledwyn Fychan that these would have included the locally prominent descendants of Phylip Dorddu of the line of Elystan Glodrydd, a family renowned for its literary patronage,[12] and that another of Llywelyn's patrons not far from Maelienydd may have been Phylip ap Rhys of St. Harmon in the adjoining commote of Gwrtheyrnion, Glyndŵr's son-in-law.[13] A later eulogy by Lewys Glyn Cothi to a descendant of Phylip Dorddu is strongly suggestive of sentiments

---

[6] *Cywyddau Iolo Goch ac Eraill*, ed. Lewis et al, p. lx.

[7] Llywelyn ab y Moel, *Gwaith*, ed. Daniel, 8.18, p. 91.

[8] Daniel, in Llywelyn ab y Moel, *Gwaith*, p. 145, tentatively dates the poem to 1410–16, but also admits the possibility that the poem may postdate Owain's likely death in 1415 (compare Fychan, "Llywelyn ab y Moel," p. 289).

[9] See Item 55. The location of Coed y Graig Lwyd was established by Roberts, "Uchelwyr y Beirdd," p. 72.

[10] Compare the reference in Item 63.5–6 to the incursions of Welsh rebels and their adherents "hiding and encamped in various woods and other places" into English border counties, including Shropshire, and their seizure and holding to ransom of the king's subjects in those counties.

[11] Llywelyn ab y Moel, *Gwaith*, ed. Daniel, 11, pp. 100–01.

[12] "Llywelyn ab y Moel," pp. 290–92. Poems by Llywelyn to Maelienydd patrons have not survived, but, significantly, a later poet, Gwilym ab Ieuan Hen (fl. 1435–70), addressing a great-grandson of Phylip Dorddu, lists Llywelyn ab y Moel among poets who had previously addressed members of the family.

[13] Fychan, "Llywelyn ab y Moel," pp. 302–05. Fychan notes that Phylip ap Rhys also may have been of the line of Elystan Glodrydd and Phylip Dorddu.

current in Maelienydd and the area's likely attraction for a man of Llywelyn's sympathies: Maelienydd, claimed Lewys, was not enamored of the English, and, just as Cornwall hoped for Arthur's second coming, fondly hoped for the resurrection of *Owain hen* [old Owain], as Glyndŵr was sometimes designated in poetry.[14] Interestingly, too, Fychan cites folk traditions, traceable to the late seventeenth century, which identify caves in the neighborhood of Llanddewi Abergwesyn in the cantref of Buellt, south-west of Maelienydd, as the haunts of a certain Lewsyn ap Moelyn or Moilsin, seemingly hypocoristic forms of the poet's name; this figure is described in Edward Lhuyd's *Parochialia* as "a Raparee" and in a nineteenth-century Welsh source as an *ysbeiliwr*, both terms meaning "bandit." Whilst such evidence may be historically problematic, the testimony of Llywelyn's poetry is of a different order. It demonstrates at first hand Owain's ability to engender a loyalty focused on his person, one which inspired men such as the poet to engage in military action and to endure the uncertainties of outlawry sustained by memories of their leader.

Llywelyn's military fame endured beyond the revolt and its aftermath: Rhys Goch Eryri, his antagonist in a bardic debate of the 1420s, felt compelled to greet him as *Llew brwydr fal llaw Beredur, / Llywelyn derwyn â dur* [The lion of battle with the hand of Peredur, / Llywelyn ardent with steel].[15] When he died, probably in 1440, Guto'r Glyn in an elegy recalled his proverbial bravery (*dewredd dihareb*), significantly characterizing his death as the silencing of *bronfraith Owain* [Owain's thrush] and hailing him too as *awdur Meredudd* [Meredudd's author],[16] a likely allusion to Llywelyn's adherence to the son of Glyndŵr who kept the flickering flame of revolt alive after his father's demise until his final acceptance of a royal pardon in 1421.

VATICINAL VOICES

The ancient tradition of prophetic poetry, which spanned both elevated and popular levels of poetic activity and which had sustained Welsh morale and expectations throughout the centuries, was undoubtedly exploited by Glyndŵr and persisted long after the end of the revolt.[17] In discussing this poetry the caveat must be entered that conclusions must often be provisional and tentative: vaticinal poetry — which as a body remains inadequately explored in Welsh scholarship — tends to pose challenging difficulties of interpretation, being frequently deliberately obscure and vague in content and only very rarely precisely datable.

---

[14] Quoted in Fychan, "Llywelyn ab y Moel," p. 291. See also Lewys Glyn Cothi, *Gwaith*, ed. Johnston, 181.11–12, 17–18, p. 397. On "Owain hen" see note 47 below.

[15] Rhys Goch Eryri, *Gwaith*, ed. Evans, 7.1–2, p. 79. Compare *llew Prydain, llaw Peredur* [lion of Britain, the hand of Peredur] (Item 6.55). Peredur was the Welsh counterpart of Chrétien de Troyes' Perceval.

[16] gutorglyn.net, 82.5, 35, 37; also Guto'r Glyn, *Gwaith*, ed. Williams, 5.5, 35, 37. The occurrence of Maredudd's name in the couplet that follows the one where Owain is named makes it likely that Glyndŵr's son is meant rather than Llywelyn's grandfather, Maredudd Benwyn, or the poet's Maelienydd patron, Maredudd Fychan of Llanbister. On the identification of Maredudd, see Fychan, "Llywelyn ab y Moel," pp. 291–92, 304; Llywelyn ab y Moel, *Gwaith*, ed. Daniel, pp. 80–81.

[17] The best overview of this tradition remains Griffiths' *Early Vaticination*. See also R. Evans, "Prophetic Poetry," pp. 278–97. Lynch's excellent *Proffwydoliaeth a'r Syniad o Genedl* examines vaticination in the context of modern historiography relating to nationalism. For a recent evaluation and affirmation of Glyndŵr's use of prophecy see my "Gwrthryfel Glyndŵr."

What is most probably an early post-revolt vaticinal poem was composed by a poet from north-west Wales, Rhys Goch Eryri, whose bardic career probably extended from the mid-1380s to c.1440.[18] No poetry by Rhys from the heyday of the revolt has survived, but folklore recorded in the nineteenth century which depicts him harboring Glyndŵr at his home in Beddgelert in Snowdonia and facilitating his escape from pursuers, though tinged with romance, may preserve a memory of the poet's support for Owain.[19] The poet's most recent editor, Dylan Foster Evans, has convincingly repudiated Sir Ifor Williams's suggestion that the somewhat enigmatic poem in question was an elegy for Sir Gruffudd Fychan — a Powys nobleman executed in 1447 — and has assigned the poem to the aftermath of the revolt, placing it within the context of the disappointed hopes of Glyndŵr's supporters.[20] Of the nineteen manuscript texts of the poem which are provided with titles, it is described as an elegy for Owain Glyndŵr in twelve and a further four copies have titles which describe it as a joint lament for the Welsh princes and for Owain.[21] Owain is not specifically named in the poem, which is certainly not a conventional elegy, but Evans considers the manuscript titles to be significant, implying that the poem was recognized as marking the *de facto* end of Owain's revolt. It might be noted too that the persistent scribal identification of the poem with Owain — the manuscripts range chronologically over three hundred years from the sixteenth century onwards — testifies to his enduring renown as the *mab darogan* [son of prophecy].[22] Cast in the form of a dialogue between the poet and Myrddin and Taliesin, revered as the founding fathers of the Welsh prophetic tradition, the poem displays much of the obscurity characteristic of vaticinal verse, but is occasionally more focused:

"Bid di-hawl gwaith nefawl naf,
A bid lle y byd lleiaf
Am roi tydwedd ar gleddyf
Noeth cyn ddisgleiried â nyf.
Ni wn paham ond amwyll
(Nid oes gan ddyn cywir dwyll)
Yr aeth i dref dan nef nen
Y sarff, lle nid oes orffen."[23]

["Let the work of the heavenly lord be unquestioned,
And let the little world be sad
Because earth has been placed

---

[18] Rhys Goch Eryri, *Gwaith*, ed. Evans, p. 12.

[19] See p. 576 below, and Henken, *National Redeemer*, pp. 100–02, and notes pp. 215–16.

[20] Text in Rhys Goch Eryri, *Gwaith*, ed. Evans, 13, pp. 116–18; for Evans's comments, see pp. 233–34, 237–38. For Williams' interpretation see *Cywyddau Iolo Goch ac Eraill*, ed. Lewis et al, pp. xlix–l.

[21] Rhys Goch Eryri, *Gwaith*, ed. Evans, p. 122. Two copies merely indicate that the poem is a *cywydd brud* (vaticinal *cywydd*) and another associates it with the two prophets. The remaining seven copies of the poem are untitled.

[22] *Mab darogan* was the term used for the national deliverer associated with vaticinal poetry. Although the concept was old (see Griffiths, *Early Vaticination*) the term itself is not recorded until the fifteenth century, see *GPC* s.v. *mab*. An alternative term, also first recorded in the fifteenth century, was *daroganwr*.

[23] Rhys Goch Eryri, *Gwaith*, ed. Evans, 13.47–54, p. 117.

On a naked sword as gleaming as snow.
I do not know why, unless it were madness,
(A rightful man is free of deceit)
The serpent went to a dwelling beneath heaven
Where there is no death."]

Evans notes that the *sarff* [serpent] in Welsh bardic tradition — unlike that of Genesis — usually had positive connotations, denoting a hero, becoming in fifteenth-century vaticination one of the terms used for the awaited national deliverer.[24] He considers that the passage refers to Glyndŵr's retreat to a hiding place after the revolt, there to await his awakening, a prominent theme in traditions concerning him.[25] In line with this interpretation, his retreat is judged to be madness (*amwyll*) as the poet perceives the immediate need for a deliverer who, it is implied, should not have gone into hiding. Whilst these lines reflect some of the depression of the years following the revolt, the poem ends on a note of exuberant hope. Having lamented the plight of the Welsh, now metaphorically cast to the floor (*ar y llawr llwm*), the poet demands of the prophets:

"A oes obaith i'n iaith ni,
Faith gof awdl, fyth gyfodi?"[26]

["Is there hope that our nation,
A poem's enduring memory, will ever arise?"]

The reply is unambiguous:

"Oes! Oes! Cwynwn anfoes caith,
Bo iawn gwbl, byw yw'n gobaith."[27]

["Yes! Yes! Let us bemoan the disrespect of serfs,
May there be full redress, our hope is alive."]

Employing imagery derived from Geoffrey of Monmouth's *Prophetiae Merlini*, the prophets then proceed to foretell the coming of the redeemer who, after fierce fighting, will restore the privileges of the Welsh and triumphally gain a ruler's scepter.

Worthy of consideration in this context too is a poem by Siôn Cent, a poet whose biography abounds with difficulties and who has sometimes been confused with other similarly named figures.[28] An association with the Scudamore family of Kentchurch Court — a daughter of Owain Glyndŵr married Sir John Scudamore of this Herefordshire line — is claimed

---

[24] Rhys Goch Eryri, *Gwaith*, ed. Evans, p. 237. Compare Evans, "Prophetic Poetry," 2.290.

[25] On this theme see Henken, *National Redeemer*, pp. 56–88, especially 70–88. Henken also notes analogues in other cultures (pp. 19–20). Arthur and Owain Lawgoch similarly feature as returning hero-deliverers, see Griffiths, *Early Vaticination*, pp. 31–36; Carr, *Owen of Wales*, pp. 92–96; Rhŷs, *Celtic Folklore*, pp. 456–97.

[26] Rhys Goch Eryri, *Gwaith*, ed. Evans, 13.79–80, p. 118.

[27] Rhys Goch Eryri, *Gwaith*, ed. Evans, 13.81–82, p. 118.

[28] For a full discussion see *Cywyddau Iolo Goch ac Eraill*, ed. Lewis et al, pp. lxx–lxxvii.

for the poet in a sixteenth-century manuscript note,[29] but this cannot be authenticated and may reflect confusion with a felon named John Kent active in Herefordshire in the 1480s.[30] Little can safely be said about the poet other than that the bulk of his output consisted of earnestly moralistic and religious verse and that he flourished during the first half of the fifteenth century. In typical admonitory mode an "Ubi sunt?" sequence in one of his poems features an unspecified Owain together with Richard II amongst famous men whose passing exemplified the transience of earthly power: *Mae Owain? Iôr archfain oedd. / Mae Risiard frenin?* [Where is Owain? He was a graceful lord. / Where is King Richard?].[31] In contradiction to Sir Ifor Williams, who favored an identification with Owain Lawgoch (d. 1378), more recent scholarship has advanced arguments in favor of Owain Glyndŵr.[32] But probably more significant than this fleeting reference is a vaticinal poem by Cent, the only one by him to survive.[33] The poet laments the reduced state of the Welsh, deprived of homes and land (*heb na thai na thir*) and akin to outlaws (*gwylliaid*),[34] drawing a parallel between the souls in Limbo awaiting redemption by Christ and the plight of his countrymen who await their national savior, an unnamed *daroganwr* (the equivalent of *mab darogan*).[35] Their present sorry state is contrasted with a glorious past; their Trojan descent is particularly emphasized with reference to the siege of Troy, drawing on the pseudo-history of Dares Phrygius, and the origin myth of Brutus narrated by Geoffrey of Monmouth. But as in Rhys Goch's poem, hope transcends despair: the line *Gobeithaw a ddaw ydd wyf* [I hope for that which is to come] recurs as a morale lifting refrain at intervals in the poem, and the poet foresees military triumph over the English.[36] Saunders Lewis has ascribed the poem to the disconsolate years following the Glyndŵr revolt, emphasizing its expressions of heartbreak and agony and describing it as *[y] farwnad fwyaf a ddaeth o fethiant Glyndŵr* [the greatest elegy issuing from the failure of Glyndŵr].[37] Whilst this overstates the poem's pessimism, Lewis' perception of the poem's political context may be correct and cannot definitely be gainsaid. However, a reference in the poem proclaiming *Gwae ddwyblaid Loegr* [woe on the two parties of England][38] — whilst conceivably merely mirroring a reference earlier in the poem to the tribulations of the two parties involved in the siege of Troy[39] — counsels caution in this regard, possibly indicating an early awareness of the division which eventually led to the Wars of the Roses. But the

[29] *Cywyddau Iolo Goch ac Eraill*, ed. Lewis et al, p. lxxix–lxxx. The manuscript is Cardiff 50 [= Phillips 12463], the note being an addition in a hand dated 1560–1620.

[30] *Cywyddau Iolo Goch ac Eraill*, ed. Lewis et al, pp. lxxvi, lxxx.

[31] *Cywyddau Iolo Goch ac Eraill*, ed. Lewis et al, p. 271, lines 5–6.

[32] For Williams' identification, see *Cywyddau Iolo Goch ac Eraill*, ed. Lewis et al, p. lxvi. Glyndŵr is favored by Lewis; see *Meistri a'u Crefft*, p. 149, and Bowen, "Siôn Cent," pp. 10–11.

[33] *Cywyddau Iolo Goch ac Eraill*, ed. Lewis et al, 88, pp. 265–67.

[34] *Cywyddau Iolo Goch ac Eraill*, ed. Lewis et al, p. 265, line 6; p. 267, line 13,

[35] *Cywyddau Iolo Goch ac Eraill*, ed. Lewis et al, p. 267, lines 23–30. Johnston, *Llên yr Uchelwyr*, p. 227, considers these lines to refer exclusively to religious rather than political salvation, but references elsewhere in the poem and its general tone invalidate this interpretation.

[36] *Cywyddau Iolo Goch ac Eraill*, ed. Lewis et al, p. 267, lines 20–21.

[37] Lewis, *Meistri a'u Crefft*, p. 150.

[38] *Cywyddau Iolo Goch ac Eraill*, ed. Lewis et al, p. 267, line 21.

[39] *Cywyddau Iolo Goch ac Eraill*, ed. Lewis et al, p. 266, line 6.

emergence of such an awareness is difficult to date precisely,[40] and such an interpretation of the phrase in question — invalidating Lewis' reading — might necessitate an extension of Siôn Cent's floruit beyond that which has been generally accepted in Welsh scholarship.[41]

The vaticinal poems so far considered were composed in the *cywydd* meter employing the metrical embellishment of full *cynghanedd*, a marker of high status poetry. Yet vaticination — much of it anonymous or ascribed to Myrddin and Taliesin — employing looser metrical forms long preceded the fourteenth-century evolution of the *cywydd* and enjoyed an enduring popular currency for generations beyond the Glyndŵr revolt.[42] An important source in this respect is National Library of Wales MS Peniarth 50 ("Y Cwta Cyfarwydd"), a Glamorgan manuscript where the dates 1445, 1451 and 1456 occur, but part of which may have been written as early as 1424.[43] Whilst some of its contents indicate a learned ecclesiastical provenance — it has been proposed that its scribe was a monk of Neath Abbey[44] — it preserves a mass of miscellaneous vaticinal poetry of a probably relatively popular origin deriving from various periods.[45] The poems abound with references to an unspecified Owain as *mab darogan*: some of the poetry probably pre-dates the revolt, and this figure must often be the generic deliverer

---

[40] For a nuanced discussion, see Griffiths, "Duke Richard." He tentatively concludes (p. 202) that "Some pre-conditions of civil war were present in England by the end of 1450, and the duke of York was beginning to emerge as the acknowledged leader of protest."

[41] Williams suggests a floruit of 1400–30, but opines that the poem in question could have been composed at any time between 1420 and 1440 (*Cywyddau Iolo Goch ac Eraill*, ed. Lewis et al, pp. lxix–lxx). Lewis, *Meistri a'u Crefft*, p. 148, dates Cent's poetry to 1412–45. An extension of his floruit to the early1450s by which time Richard, Duke of York may be said to have developed an embryonic opposition to the Lancastrian faction controlling the Crown (compare previous note), would not be impossible, though difficult to reconcile with the conjectural birthdate of c.1367 which Williams proposes for Cent (*Cywyddau Iolo Goch ac Eraill*, ed. Lewis et al, p. lxvi). The suggestion by Bowen, "Siôn Cent," p. 11, that the English *dwyblaid* may refer to the English divisions of 1403, when the Percies rebelled against Henry IV, would, of course, have radical implications for the dating of the poem, but this suggestion is unlikely.

[42] The popular provenance of much vaticination is a theme rightly stressed by Lynch, *Proffwydoliaeth*, pp. 36–38.

[43] The manuscript is described by Evans, *Report on Manuscripts*, 1.389–99. A note inserted by Evans at the beginning of the manuscript in 1886 states that "This MS appears to have been written at various times between 1424 & 1456. Folio 34b bears the date of a prophecy to happen in 1425 thus seemingly arguing that it was written before that year." I have been kindly allowed to consult a draft copy of the description of the manuscript in the forthcoming *Repertory of Welsh Manuscripts* by Daniel Huws deposited at the Centre for Advanced Welsh and Celtic Studies, Aberystwyth. Huws is more cautious than Evans, dating the manuscript to c.1445.

[44] The scribe records his name as "Davyd" on p. 114. Evans (*Report on Manuscripts*, 1.389) was the first to suggest an association with Neath Abbey, and this association has generally been accepted, see Morgan, "Prophecy and Welsh Nationhood," p. 20 and n26. His motivation in compiling Peniarth 50 is indicated in a poignant passage on pp. 87–89, which deplores English cruelty in depriving the Welsh of their princes and the reduction of his people to indigence and nakedness (quoted in full by Lynch, *Proffwydoliaeth*, pp. 34–35, and in part by Morgan, "Prophecy and Welsh Nationhood," pp. 24–25).

[45] Williams, *Traddodiad Llenyddol Morgannwg*, p. 11, suggested that some of the vaticinations in Peniarth 50 may derive from a collection owned by Hopcyn ap Tomas, the literary patron and "maister of Brut" consulted by Glyndŵr in 1403 (see Item 36.16) and also his military supporter. Though possible in view of the Glamorgan provenance of Peniarth 50 and Hopcyn's expertise in vaticination, this, as Morgan notes ("Prophecy and Welsh Nationhood," p. 26n40) cannot at present be proven.

so named — an inherited amalgam of past heroes such as Owain ab Urien, Owain Gwynedd, and Owain Lawgoch — but it is also likely that Glyndŵr is sometimes subsumed in this multiple personage and that occasionally he may even be its main referent. Citations of an unnamed hero of advanced age may conceivably refer to Glyndŵr,[46] whose designation as *Owain hen* is elsewhere attested.[47] There are some poems, however, where an association with Glyndŵr can be more definitely asserted.[48] One such anonymous poem ends as follows:

A chyuodi Arth o Sycharth o Eryri llechua,
Y G6yl Veir ddiwetha, a dial ar Seis y dreis a'y dra.
Yna y bydd Lloegr yn ddiras, a Seis heb gyweithas,
A baedd Glyn Dyf6rdwy yn rannu'r teyrnas.[49]

[And the rising of a Bear of Sycharth from a lair in Snowdonia,
On Mary's Day, and revenge on the Englishman for his violence and excess.
Then shall England be wicked, and Englishman without grace,
And the boar of Glyn Dyfrdwy dividing the kingdom.]

Whilst poetry in a broadly similar vein would undoubtedly have been employed to rouse passions during the revolt, the reference to Owain's rising from a lair in Snowdonia — which is preceded by a reference to the resurrection of Hiriell, a traditional returning hero of vaticination — indicates a post-revolt date,[50] when the myth of Owain's retreat into hiding to await a later awakening had developed.[51] Another poem in the manuscript prophesies the coming of warriors from Edeirnion — where Owain's Glyndyfrdwy patrimony was situated — led by him in person:

Ac yn yr oes oesoedd, gwerinoedd gwirion
A geyf y gorvot, yn dyuot o [E]deyrnion . . .

---

[46] Noted by Jenkins, "Aspects of the Welsh Prophetic Verse Tradition," p. 229. Examples occur on pp. 410, 416, 417, 450. Jenkins edits and translates the vaticinal poetry from Peniarth MS 50, and it is from her edition that I quote the texts and translations. Occasionally where Peniarth 50 is now illegible because of gall stains, Jenkins silently supplies text from a transcript of the manuscript by John Jones of Gellilyfdy in NLW MS Peniarth 311, written c.1635–40 when Peniarth 50 was more legible.

[47] E.g. Items 88 and 91 above, along with Lewys Glyn Cothi, *Gwaith*, ed. Johnston, 186.6, p. 408, 188.4, p. 412; Tudur Penllyn and Ieuan ap Tudur Penllyn, *Gwaith*, ed. Roberts, 42.18, p. 76.

[48] Identified by Jenkins, "Aspects of the Welsh Prophetic Verse Tradition," p. 229.

[49] Peniarth 50, p. 18; text and translation from Jenkins, "Aspects of the Welsh Prophetic Verse Tradition," p. 264. A variant version of this poem — demonstrating the fluidity of such vaticinal texts — occurs in two seventeenth-century manuscripts, NLW 3077B and NLW 9169B. In the latter manuscript the poem is ascribed to Taliesin.

[50] Compare Johnston, *Llên yr Uchelwyr*, p. 353. On Hiriell, a hero of north Wales, see Bartrum, *Welsh Classical Dictionary*, pp. 365–66. He is featured in a vaticinal poem in the Black Book of Carmarthen, *A civod hirell oe hir orwet. / y amvin ae elin terwin guinet* [Hiriell will arise from his long sleep / to defend the border of Gwynedd against his enemy], Jarman, *Llyfr Du Caerfyrddin*, 17.91–92, p. 31. Iolo Goch cites him in a poem to Glyndŵr, Item 4.17 above.

[51] On the myth, see Henken, *National Redeemer*, pp. 64–88.

Ac Ywein val bleidd ymlaen marchogyon,
A chat yn y amgylch gweilch g6isc rydyon.[52]

[And for ever, true peoples
Will have the victory, coming from Edeirnion . . .
And Owain as a wolf in the van of the warriors,
And a host around him [of] red-robed noblemen.]

Other poems refer to an Owain attacking from the east, and the fact of the north-east Wales origin of the leader of the revolt together with a mention in one of these poems of an attack on Ruthin — the target of the first military action of the revolt in 1400 — makes it likely that Glyndŵr is indicated:[53]

Mi a welaf veibion kywir yn kael tir tref Rythyn.
Mi a welaf rythreu Owein o'r dwyrein y'r gorllewyn.[54]

[I see true young men securing the land of the town of Ruthin,
I see Owain's attacks from the east to the west.]

Not only does the vaticination preserved in Peniarth 50 indicate that a mood of unreconciled disaffection persisted in some circles in Wales in the early decades after the revolt, but some of the material also reflects unambiguously the potency of the memory of Owain and his elevation in popular imagination into the pantheon of vaticinal heroes.

The Wars of the Roses stimulated a huge outpouring of new vaticination, mostly in the *cywydd* meter.[55] This was generally more focused than most of the prophecy preserved in Peniarth 50 and usually designed to elicit support for individual protagonists in the contemporary dynastic struggle, notably Jasper Tudor, earl of Pembroke, leader of the Lancastrian party, and his nephew Henry Tudor, the young earl of Richmond. The Tudors could claim kinship with Glyndŵr,[56] a factor which, in addition to a generalized appreciation of their Welsh antecedents, may have accounted for some of their support in Wales, including the overwhelming support of the bards. Though not primarily a vaticination, a poem overshadowed by the vaticinal tradition and which anticipated later political and poetical developments was an elegy for Owain Tudur [= Owen Tudor], father of Jasper and grandfather of Henry, composed after his execution by the Yorkists following the battle of Mortimer's Cross in 1461. Its author, Ieuan Gethin ab Ieuan ap Lleision, a gentleman-poet from Gla-

---

[52] Peniarth 50, p. 228; Jenkins, "Aspects of the Welsh Prophetic Verse Tradition," pp. 392–93. The emendation "[E]deyrnion" is unnecessary in view of the manuscript reading *or deyrnnion*.

[53] Peniarth 50, pp. 67d, 229, 291; Jenkins, "Aspects of the Welsh Prophetic Verse Tradition," pp. 304, 399, 440.

[54] Peniarth 50, p. 229; "Aspects of the Welsh Prophetic Verse Tradition," p. 399.

[55] For an overview, see my "Bardic Road to Bosworth"; also Evans, "Prophetic Poetry," 2.278–97. Over 200 vaticinations by some 50 poets relating to the Wars of the Roses are extant in manuscripts ("Bardic Road to Bosworth," p. 14).

[56] Marged, the sister of Glyndŵr's mother, Elen, married Tudur ap Goronwy of Penmynydd, ancestor of the Tudors, see Bartrum (1974). s.n. Rhys ap Tewdwr 7, 4.782.

morgan who as a young man had fought for Glyndŵr,[57] laments the repeated disappointments of vaticinal hopes, of which the latest was the demise of Owain Tudur, the third
successive Owain to excite frustrated expectations:

> Gwae ni'n darogan Owain
> Annoeth rwysg a wnaeth y rhain;
> Gwae Wynedd ddaroganwyr
> Gan Saeson, galon y gwŷr:
> Owain dywysawg Lawgoch,
> Owain y Glyn onwayw gloch;
> Owain Tudur, fur ar Fôn,
> A hwn aeth â'r henw weithion.
> Felly'r âi'r rheiny i'r rhwyd;
> O'n tri Owain y'n treiwyd.[58]

> [Woe unto us our prophesying of Owain,
> These made a rash presumption;
> Woe to the prophets of Gwynedd
> Because of the English, the foes of these men:
> Prince Owain Lawgoch,
> Owain of the Glyn with his ashen spear and bell;
> Owain Tudur, Anglesey's rampart,
> It was he who bore the name latterly.
> Thus were those overcome [lit. went into the net];
> From losing our three Owains we have been destroyed.][59]

But vaticinal hopes were not to be lightly abandoned: frustration is replaced by defiance as
the poet proceeds to extol the potential of the surviving Tudors:

> Mae gobaith i'n hiaith yn ôl,
> A byw aeth yn obeithiol;
> A clybod darfod â dur,
> Newid hoedl Owain Tudur,
> Gwylio Siasbar a Harri,
> Ei ŵyr a'i fab, yr wyf i.[60]

> [Hope remains for our nation,
> And life has become hopeful;

---

[57] See Huws, "Dyddiadau Ieuan Gethin," p. 47. Ieuan and his wife received a royal pardon in
1410 for various offences committed during the revolt.

[58] Scourfield, "Gwaith Ieuan Gethin," 11.43–52, p. 41.

[59] The reference to the bell of Owain of the Glyn [= Owain Glyndŵr] is an early instance of the
conception of him as a sleeping cave-dwelling redeemer-hero to be awakened at the opportune time
by the ringing of a bell. The bell appears in later folklore featuring Owain in this connection, see
Henken, *National Redeemer*, pp. 81, 87; it also occurs in folklore featuring Arthur and Owain Lawgoch
as sleeping redeemer-heroes, see Rhŷs, *Celtic Folklore*, pp. 459–60, 463, 474, 477.

[60] Scourfield, "Gwaith Ieuan Gethin," 11.53–58, p. 41. Another elegy for Owain Tudur by Robin
Ddu similarly emphasizes Jasper's future potential role with accompanying vaticinal imagery, see
Ceinion Llenyddiaeth Gymreig, ed Jones, 2.219–20.

Having heard of an end through steel,
Owain Tudur's passing from life,
I contemplate Jasper and Henry,
His son and grandson.]

A vaticinal *cywydd* by Ieuan ap Rhydderch was once thought to relate to the Glyndŵr revolt, being described by J. E. Lloyd as "the one poem which may without hesitation be connected with the wars of Glyn Dŵr,"[61] a conclusion he partly based on the poet's reference to a "Stella cometa," which he thought to be the 1402 comet interpreted by contemporaries as heralding the success of Glyndŵr.[62] Thomas Roberts, however, cogently argued that the poem related to the Wars of the Roses,[63] and later advances in our knowledge of *cywydd* stylistics confirm his conclusion regarding the poem's later date. Roberts identified the comet as that of 1465 and the poem's addressee — a composite *mab darogan* designated as "Owain" and also as Cadwaladr and Cynan — as Jasper Tudor rather than Glyndŵr.[64] The poem is, however, relevant to the topic of this essay, for it ends with an exhortation that the *mab darogan* should continue the struggle of Owain Glyndŵr by avenging himself on the English, designated by the poet as "Ellmyn" [foreigners]:

Dos a chymell yr Ellmyn,
Na weinia gledd Owain Glyn;
Pâr ynn bacs o dir Macsen,
A chwncwest Hors Hinsiest hen.[65]

[Go and drive away the foreigners,
Do not sheathe the sword of Owain Glyn;
Bring about peace for us from the land of Macsen,
And the conquest of ancient Horsa and Hengist.][66]

---

[61] Lloyd, *Owen Glendower*, p. 156. For a text of the poem, see Ieuan ap Rhydderch, *Gwaith*, ed. Daniel, pp. 55–57.

[62] On the comet of 1402, see Items 42, 68, 72, 78, 87, 89, and 100 above.

[63] Roberts, "Pedwar Cywydd Brud," pp. 231–41; see also *Cywyddau Iolo Goch ac Eraill*, ed. Lewis et al, pp. xxvii–xxviii.

[64] Roberts, "Pedwar Cywydd Brud," pp. 234–35. In *Cywyddau Iolo Goch ac Eraill*, ed. Lewis et al, p. xxvii, Roberts revises his earlier suggestion that the poem was addressed to Henry Tudor (1st ed., pp. xci–xcii). Daniel, whilst not rejecting Roberts' identification of the poem's addressee as Jasper Tudor, raises the possibility that he may have been Owain Tudur or Owain ap Gruffudd ap Nicolas (Ieuan ap Rhydderch, *Gwaith*, ed. Daniel, pp. 155–56). But this is most unlikely, as the poem's addressee is referred to as having been in hiding in Scotland, where Jasper is known to have been in 1462–63. It might also be objected that Owain ap Gruffudd ap Nicolas, a figure of merely local eminence in south-west Wales, was of insufficient political stature to have inspired the extravagant expectations apparent in the poem.

[65] Ieuan ap Rhydderch, *Gwaith*, ed. Daniel, 4.77–80, pp. 66–67.

[66] "The land of Macsen" equates with Rome, by way of reference to Magnus Maximus, Western Roman Emperor 383–88, known in Welsh legend as Macsen Wledig. The *mab darogan* was sometimes portrayed in poetry as coming from Rome, influenced by Geoffrey of Monmouth's account that Cadwaladr retreated to Rome and that British hegemony would not be restored until his body had been removed from Rome to Britain (*Geoffrey of Monmouth*, ed. Reeve, trans. Wright, 205.563–73, p. 279). Horsa and Hengist are reputed to have led the Germanic invasion of Britain in the time of Vortigern, their story being popularized through Geoffrey's *Historia* (98.249–50, pp. 123–24).

Ieuan ap Rhydderch was probably a child during the Glyndŵr revolt,[67] and this poem of his old age interestingly indicates his lingering admiration for Owain as the avenger of his people. The rhetoric of vaticination notwithstanding, it also suggests that some in Wales unrealistically perceived the Tudor participation in the struggle for the English Crown as a renewal of Glyndŵr's war and an opportunity to redress national wrongs through the agency of new protagonists of Welsh descent. In this context it may be noted that kinsmen of Owain (who were also distant kinsmen of the Tudors) — such as the Pulestons of Emral and Gruffudd Fychan of Corsygedol — were among the most active Lancastrian supporters in north Wales.[68]

Among the vaticinal poems of the Wars of the Roses there are numerous mentions of an unspecified Owain; this was a name frequently used for the *mab darogan* at this time, reflecting perhaps the living memory of Owain's revolt at the beginning of the century. But it would be hazardous to identify all such references as applying to Glyndŵr: as in the case of some of the Peniarth 50 vaticinations, the Owain of the *cywyddau brud* is often likely to be a composite figure, incorporating the various historically famous Welsh personages of that name, sometimes, no doubt, including Owain Glyndŵr. It may be significant that the Owain of these poems is sometimes portrayed as a figure emerging from death or hiding, an attribute which could imply both Owain Lawgoch and Owain Glyndŵr. This is the Owain to whom Lewys Glyn Cothi alludes in a vaticinal passage in a poem addressed to Dafydd Goch ap Meredudd, a patron from near Presteigne, where he asserts *fo gyfyd i'r byd o'r bedd / cnawd Owain cyn y diwedd* [Owain will eventually arise in the flesh from the grave to the world].[69] The two leading vaticinal poets of this period — Dafydd Llwyd of Mathafarn and Robin Ddu of Anglesey — both portray an Owain in this vein: in one poem Dafydd Llwyd's emergent Owain is transposed into a thinly veiled all-conquering Henry Tudor.[70] A poem by Robin Ddu, with its reference to a *mab darogan* who is a *gŵr gwyn hen* [a white[-haired] old man] — whilst influenced by the *niueus . . . senex* of Geoffrey of Monmouth's *Prophetiae Merlini*[71] — almost certainly alludes to Glyndŵr, echoing allusions to him elsewhere in poetry. Interestingly the poet associates him with Maelienydd, an area where Lewys Glyn Cothi indicates that traditions about Owain's awaited second coming were in circulation:[72]

---

[67] His father Rhydderch ab Ieuan Llwyd died in 1398–99 (Ieuan ap Rhydderch, *Gwaith*, p. 16).

[68] For references to the Pulestons and Gruffudd Fychan (Vaughan) in this context, see Evans, *Wales and the Wars of the Roses*, pp. 242–43. Their kinship with Glyndŵr derived from the marriage of Lowri, Owain's sister, with Robert Puleston (Bartrum [1974], s.n. Bleddyn ap Cynfyn 5, 1.32; s.n. Puleston, 4.741). Their kinship with the Tudors derived from the marriages of the two daughters of Thomas ap Llywelyn with Tudur ap Goronwy of Penmynydd and with Gruffudd Fychan, father of Owain Glyndŵr, see Bartrum (1974), s.n. Rhys ap Tewdwr 7, 6.782.

[69] Lewys Glyn Cothi, *Gwaith*, ed. Johnston, 173.37–38, p. 382. Another poem to the same patron (174.454–50, p. 384), with its explicit reference to one of Iolo Goch's poems to Glyndŵr, makes it likely that the reference is to Owain Glyndŵr, compare Johnston's notes, p. 607. Interestingly, the poem in question was addressed to a Yorkist patron.

[70] See Dafydd Llwyd o Fathafarn, *Gwaith*, ed. Richards, 8.28, p. 38; compare 12.33–34, p. 45, where the poet refers to an Owain who is prophesied to arise *o gudd* [from hiding].

[71] *Geoffrey of Monmouth*, ed. Reeve, trans. Wright, 115.108, p. 149.

[72] Lewys Glyn Cothi, *Gwaith*, ed. Johnston, 181.17–18. Compare also the reference to Owain's resurrection in Lewys' poem to Dafydd Goch ap Meredudd cited above (Dafydd lived in the commote of Llythyfnwg which adjoined Maelienydd). It may be very tentatively suggested that the association

Mae gŵr hen ym Maelienydd
A'r gwallt megis blodau'r gwŷdd. . . .
Mi a glywais, magl awen,
Ganu hir i ŵr gwyn hen,
Ac os hwn a gais ei hawl
Ydyw'r gwyn daroganawl,
Bwyall a chledd heb ohir
A estyn terfyn ein tir. . . .
Owain yno a 'nynnir,
Abl ei hawl, a Beli Hir.
Llawer drwg yn amlwg nod
A oddefir i ddyfod.
Un gŵr a wna iawn i gyd
Ac ef o farw a gyfyd.[73]

[There is an old man in Maelienydd
With hair like the blossom of trees. . . .
Ensnared by the muse, I have heard
Persistent poetry about a white-haired old man,
And if this one who will seek his right
Is the prophesied white one,
Axe and sword without delay
Will extend the boundary of our land. . . .
Owain then will be aroused,
His claim being powerful, together with Beli Hir.
Many a harm as a manifest sign
Will be suffered in time to come.
One man will bring about full redress
And he will arise from the dead.][74]

Other references in the poem to the redeemer's coming across the sea (*O'r môr y daw'r ymwared*) display the propagandistic conflation of the risen Owain with either Jasper or Henry Tudor, who both spent time in continental exile. A *cywydd brud* by the Ardudwy poet Ieuan Brydydd Hir partly parallels Robin Ddu's poem in foretelling that *y gŵr hen* [the old man] will claim the boundary of his land (*A ofyn derfyn ei dir*), and concludes by prophesying the emergence of "the old white[-haired] one" from hiding (*Yr hen gwyn ar hyn o gudd*).[75] Bardic propagandists such as these inherited a well established myth of Owain as a national deliverer who would eventually arise to lead his people, skillfully exploiting it for Tudor ends. In such a way did the enduring memory of Owain help to project a descendant of his Anglesey kinsmen to ultimate triumph at Bosworth Field.

---

of Owain's resurrection with Maelienydd by both Lewys and Robin Ddu may have implications relevant to the story of Owain's last days. Was there a tradition that he died or was buried in Maelienydd, which was in close proximity to the home of his daughter Gwenllian in Gwrtheyrnion?

[73] I have edited this extract from the nineteen manuscript copies of the poem (Robin Ddu's vaticinal poems remain unedited). The text of this poem published in *Ceinion Llenyddiaeth Gymreig*, ed. Jones, 2.215, is unsatisfactory.

[74] On Beli Hir as a hero of prophecy, see Griffiths, *Early Vaticination*, p. 166.

[75] Ieuan Brydydd Hir, *Gwaith*, ed. Bryant-Quinn, 4.49–50, 61–62, p. 35. Also Evans, "Cywydd Brud."

INCIDENTAL REFERENCES

Isolated, but not insignificant, incidental references relating to Owain occur in fifteenth-century poetry. A number of them evoke Owain's court at Sycharth, famously portrayed in its heyday by Iolo Goch.[76] The memory of the past glories of Sycharth — undoubtedly bolstered by Iolo's *cywydd* — furnished poets with a ready source of comparisons when they portrayed the newly-built halls of their patrons, celebration of such new edifices — numerous in an age of much rebuilding — being sanctioned by contemporary bardic protocol.[77] Guto'r Glyn in celebrating the new hall of Edward ap Hywel at Berriew in mid-Wales emphasized its magnificence by claiming that it surpassed even Sycharth in eminence:

Os uchel oedd dai Sycharth
A'i fryn gynt yn nwyfron garth,
Os mawr tai Powys a Môn,
Ys mwy nef is Manafon.[78]

[If the buildings of Sycharth were on high,
And its mound formerly on two breasts of a hill;
If the houses of Powys and Anglesey are large,
Greater is the heavenly dwelling below Manafon.]

Guto, in evoking Hywel ab Ieuan's new hall at Moelyrch, Llansilin — possibly replacing one destroyed during the revolt — compared its whitewashed brightness to that of *seren Owain* [the star of Owain], the allegedly portentous comet which appeared in 1402;[79] the deliberately ambiguous comparison also undoubtedly implied a resemblance to the former glories of Sycharth less than two miles away, and would have pleased a patron whose father, uncle, and grand-uncle had been amongst Owain's gathered supporters at Glyndyfrdwy in September 1400.[80] Ieuan ap Hywel Swrdwal, in 1436 or soon afterwards, similarly invoked *seren Owain* — extravagantly coupled in significance with the Star of Bethlehem — in depicting the refulgence of newly-built Bryndraenog in Maelienydd, the most impressive of surviving medieval Welsh hall-houses.[81] Tudur Penllyn employed the same comparison in describing

---

[76] See Item 8 in this volume.

[77] The bardic statute of Gruffudd ap Cynan (1523) noted that the former bardic right to visit a patron on the occasion of the building of a new house had been rescinded and replaced by allowing them to visit on the occasion of local patronal saints' feasts, see *Records of Early Drama*, ed. Klausner, pp. 164, 355.

[78] gutorglyn.net, 38.51–52 (which has the reading *tai* [houses, buildings] in the first line as opposed to the *tŷ* [house] of Guto'r Glyn, *Gwaith*, ed. Williams, 21.51–52, p. 58). Poets often used the plural *tai* in referring to their patrons' courts. The neighboring parish of Manafon is four miles west of Berriew.

[79] gutorglyn.net, 90.38; Guto'r Glyn, *Gwaith*, ed. Williams, 41.36, p. 110. On the comet of 1402, see Items 42, 68, 72, 78, 87, 89, and 100 above. On the likely destruction of Moelyrch by the English in 1403, see Huws, "Ailadeiladu Bywyd," pp. 106–07. Poems which employ *seren Owain* as a comparison in relation to houses are discussed by Huws on pp. 119–20.

[80] Huws, "Y Bardd a'i Noddwr," pp. 6–7; Huws, "Ailadeiladu Bywyd," p. 100.

[81] *Hywel Swrdwal a'i Deulu*, *Gwaith*, ed. Evans, 25.1–6, p. 98. The poem is discussed in the context of an architectural account of Bryndraenog by Suggett, *Houses and History*, pp. 51–54. Dendrochronological evidence dates the house to 1436 (pp. 51, 298).

the carpentry of Meredudd ap Llywelyn's new hall of Gogerddan in north Ceredigion (*Saer a wnaeth seren Owain*).[82] But for Dafydd Llwyd of Mathafarn — alleged by Llywelyn ap Gutun to have been present at the battle of Bryn Glas as a young follower of Owain (*Yn y Bryn Glas . . . yn ôl Owain*)[83] — the comet of 1402 served as more than a referent for fanciful architectural comparisons, retaining its aura as a political portent in a *cywydd* replete with prophetic imagery: *Siwrneied seren Owain* [let the star of Owain journey onwards].[84] An older Guto'r Glyn in praising Oswestry — a town whose hinterland included the former lands of Glyndŵr and which, ironically, had been "burnt, destroyed and spoiled by Welsh Rebells and enemies" during the revolt — echoed Llywelyn ab y Moel's outlaw poem by depicting it as *Llundain gwlad Owain a'i dir* [the London of Owain's country and land].[85] Guto's poem earned him burgess status at Oswestry, suggesting that his reference to Owain cannot have been unacceptable to his audience and that elements among the Welsh burgesses of the racially mixed town had retained an admiration for Owain.[86] Positive attitudes to Owain are also indicated by Lewys Glyn Cothi's rhetorical mode in praising two patrons named Owain: he elevated them by identical means, imparting glory by association, listing them in a succession of famous Owains; the name of *Owain y Glyn* (Glyndŵr) featured in each laudatory sequence.[87] Neither did Lewys forget Margaret Hanmer, evoking her as an exemplar of female hospitality by comparing the feasts of an Anglesey widow to those of *arglwyddes Sycharth* [the lady of Sycharth].[88] References such as these — and more could be cited — indicate that memories of Owain were very much alive and still sharply evocative among the bards and their Welsh gentry patrons during the century whose opening decades witnessed the revolt.

---

[82] Tudur Penllyn and Ieuan ap Tudur Penllyn, *Gwaith*, ed. Roberts, 21.52, p. 36.

[83] Llywelyn ap Gutun, *Gwaith*, ed. Daniel, 12.13–16, p. 53; Gwerful Mechain ac Eraill, *Gwaith*, ed. Howells, 8.13-16, p. 96. The context of the poem is humorous, and the reference may be designed to (over)emphasize Dafydd Llwyd's age and his unsuitability as a suitor for the young Gwerful Mechain. But Roberts argues in favor of its accuracy (*Dafydd Llwyd o Fathafarn*, p. 7). Dafydd Llwyd lived until 1485 and beyond.

[84] Dafydd Llwyd o Fathafarn, *Gwaith*, ed. Richards, 16.67, p. 53.

[85] gutorglyn.net, 102.21; Guto'r Glyn, *Gwaith*, ed. Williams, 69.21, p. 183. For the destruction of Oswestry by Owain's forces see Lloyd, *History of . . . Powys Fadog*, 6.309.

[86] On Guto's gaining of burgess status for "A songe that he made *yn lawde & prese* [= praise] aswell of the towne of oswestre as also touchyng the burges & inhabit*uns* there," see gutorglyn.net, poem 102, preliminary note. Significantly perhaps, close kinsmen of Geoffrey Kyffin, burgess and constable of Oswestry and Guto's patron, were among the core supporters of Glyndŵr who gathered at Glyndyfrdwy in September 1400, compare note 80 above, and the genealogical table in Huws, "Y Bardd a'i Noddwr," pp. 6–7.

[87] Lewys Glyn Cothi, *Gwaith*, ed. Johnston, 17.31–56, pp. 52–53 (in praise of Owain ap Gruffudd ap Nicolas), and 199.47–56, p. 435 (in praise of Owain Fychan ap Gruffudd). In both cases the rhetoric may have been inspired by the common occurrence of Owain as a name for the promised deliverer in contemporary vaticinal verse.

[88] Lewys Glyn Cothi, *Gwaith*, ed. Johnston, 228.17–18, p. 493. The poem is dated to c.1480 (p. 629).

KINSHIP WITH GLYNDŴR

Such references, however, are few indeed compared to the scores of instances — of which only a selection are here discussed — in fifteenth- and sixteenth-century eulogies where patrons' kinship with Owain is cited. It is evident that a family link with such a pre-eminent figure — however remote and tenuous — was a source of pride for his kinsmen and a ready ingredient of bardic praise for them over many generations; this was the factor above all others which maintained Owain's presence in poetry for two centuries and more after his revolt.

Of the poetry addressed to patrons of the line of Glyndŵr, a body of ten poems — the work of three poets, Lewys Glyn Cothi, Llawdden, and Ieuan Gyfannedd — associated with Gwenllian, the illegitimate daughter of Owain and her husband, Phylip ap Rhys of Cenarth in St. Harmon in Gwrtheyrnion, is notable for its insistent assertion of Glyndŵr kinship.[89] Gwenllian, born of a mother from the commote of Genau'r Glyn,[90] had probably found a husband among her father's former supporters: one of the poems which Llawdden addressed to Phylip was composed when he was an outlaw in Arwystli to the north of Gwrtheyrnion, calling, says the poet, for victory (*A galw am fuddugoliaeth*); significantly it contains what may well be a comparison of his outlawry with that of his celebrated father-in-law.[91] Another poem by the same poet suggestively states that Phylip, by then enjoying the settled life of a generous patron, had formerly experienced *hafog a thir rhyfel* [havoc and a land of war].[92] In praising Gwenllian — portrayed as a paragon of generosity and hospitality — all three poets laud her as the daughter of Glyndŵr: to Ieuan Gyfannedd she is *merch o'r Glyn* [a daughter from the Glyn] and *merch Owain* [the daughter of Owain];[93] to Llawdden she is *arglwyddes o'r Glyn* [the lady from the Glyn], *merch glaer, hil Marchog y Glyn* [the bright daughter, of the line of the Knight of the Glyn], *hyloywawr o hil Owain* [the shining lady of Owain's line], and *Gwenfrewy Glyn Dyfrdwy dir* [the Saint Winifred of the land of Glyndyfrdwy];[94] Lewys Glyn Cothi twice hails

---

[89] Lewys Glyn Cothi, *Gwaith*, ed. Johnston, poems 186–89, pp. 408–15; Llawdden, *Gwaith*, ed. Daniel, poems 10–14, pp. 56–70. Ieuan Gyfannedd's poem is edited in Payne, *Crwydro Sir Faesyfed*, pp. 114–16.

[90] Gwenllian's mother was the unnamed daughter of Ieuan ap Maredudd of the line of Ednywain ap Bradwen, see Bartrum, *Welsh Genealogies AD 300–1400, Additions and Corrections, Sixth List*, s.n. Bleddyn ap Cynfyn 5, p. 3. This supersedes idem, Corrigenda to Vol. 1, s.n. Bleddyn ap Cynfyn 5, Bleddyn ap Cynfyn 42, p. 2, where Gwenllian's mother is listed as the daughter of Tudur ap Maredudd of Mechain. Gwenllian's association with Ieuan ap Maredudd is corroborated by a poem by Lewys Glyn Cothi which cites an Aron from Meirionnydd and a Llawdden as her ancestors, see Lewys Glyn Cothi, *Gwaith*, ed. Johnston, 187.23, 25, p. 410. These were among her matrilineal ancestors, see Bartrum (1974) s.n. Ednywain ap Bradwen 4, 2.258.

[91] Llawdden, *Gwaith*, ed. Daniel, 10.47–56, p. 57. For a discussion of these lines, see ibid., pp. 168–69; the identity of Owain Glyndŵr tends to be confirmed by the mention of the advanced age (*Hen iawn*) of the former outlaw with whom Phylip ap Rhys is compared. Daniel rejects Fychan's suggestion, "Llywelyn ab y Moel," pp. 303–04, who interprets 10.51–52 to mean that Phylip assumed the rebel leadership after Maredudd, Glyndŵr's son, accepted a royal pardon in 1421.

[92] Llawdden, *Gwaith*, ed. Daniel, 13. 29–36, p. 65.

[93] Payne, *Crwydro Sir Faesyfed*, pp. 114–15.

[94] Llawdden, *Gwaith*, ed. Daniel, 11.35, p. 59; 12.42, p. 63; 12.47, p. 63; 13.22, p. 65. The comparison with Saint Winifred implies chastity and beauty.

her as the daughter of *Owain hen* [old Owain],[95] similarly alluding to an elderly Owain in his description of Phylip as *Mab yng nghyfraith . . . i'r Hen Gwyn* [the son in law of the Old White(-haired) one].[96] Phylip and Gwenllian's five sons are characterized by Llawdden as worthy of comparison with their grandfather, *Coed gwiw cyhyd ag Owain* [Fine trees as tall as Owain].[97] Not unexpectedly, the poets do not neglect to cite Gwenllian's princely lineage: Llawdden traces her descent through Owain to Gruffudd Maelor and Cynfyn of the princely line of Powys,[98] as does Lewys Glyn Cothi who additionally cites her connection with the dynasty of Deheubarth, hailing her as *merch o Rodri Mawr* [a daughter issuing from Rhodri Mawr].[99] Lewys' elegy on the death of two of Gwenllian and Phylip's sons, one of them tellingly named Owain — the poet's holograph copy of the poem is headed by an armorial shield bearing in two quarters Glyndŵr's lion rampant — cited the distress of Sycharth at their passing:[100] Owain's court was then no more, but remained a name with resonant connotations. On the death of Gwenllian a poignant elegy by Lewys highlighted her Glyndŵr connections. The poet cites the evocative names of Rhuddallt — Owain's ancestral patrimony in Glyndyfrdwy[101] — and Sycharth, and mourns Gwenllian as *[l]leuad Owain* [the moon of Owain], not neglecting to refer to her father's princely eminence: *a'i thad oedd d'wysog cadarn, / a holl Gymru fu'n ei farn* [her father was a mighty prince, / and all of Wales was under his jurisdiction].[102] Ending his poem by comparing Gwenllian to Luned, the kindly handmaiden of the romance of *Owein* (Chrétien's *Yvain*), he expresses the wish that Jesus would welcome to heaven *Luned wen o Lyndŵr* [the fair Luned issuing from Glyndŵr].[103]

Gwenllian was not the only child of Glyndŵr to feature in Llawdden's poetry. A poem requesting the gift of a shield and buckler from Phylip ap Rhys was written on behalf of one Siancyn y Glyn, the request, in line with a convention common in poems of solicitation, being couched in the *persona* of the gift-seeker, who describes himself as Phylip's brother-in-law (*Brawd o gyfraith*).[104] Genealogies record a son of Glyndŵr called John and an illegitimate son called Ieuan;[105] either name could have evolved into the hypocoristic form Siancyn [Jen-

---

[95] Lewys Glyn Cothi, *Gwaith*, ed. Johnston, 186.5–6, p. 408; 188.3–4, p. 412.

[96] Lewys Glyn Cothi, *Gwaith*, ed. Johnston, 187.17–18, p. 410. Lewys' *Hen Gwyn* echoes a Welsh translation of the *niueus . . . senex* of Geoffrey of Monmouth's *Prophetiae Merlini* (*Geoffrey of Monmouth*, ed. Reeve, trans. Wright, 115.108, p. 149), compare *Brut Dingestow*, ed. Lewis, p. 107.14.

[97] Llawdden, *Gwaith*, ed. Daniel, 13.52, p. 66.

[98] Llawdden, *Gwaith*, ed. Daniel, 11.31–36, p. 59.

[99] Lewys Glyn Cothi, *Gwaith*, ed. Johnston, 187.27–28, p. 410.

[100] Lewys Glyn Cothi, *Gwaith*, ed. Johnston, 189.21, p. 414. The arms are reproduced in an edition of the poet's work in Peniarth MS 109, see Lewys Glyn Cothi, *Gwaith*, ed. Jones, p. 41. A poem by Lewys asking for a gift of a bed from four women, of whom Gwenllian was one, is also headed by a shield bearing Glyndŵr's coat of arms (p. 102). The device of a lion rampant Sable may be differenced to signify Gwenllian's illegitimacy, see Siddons, *Development of Welsh Heraldry*, 1.93, 293–94.

[101] Lloyd, *Owen Glendower*, p. 13n1.

[102] Lewys Glyn Cothi, *Gwaith*, ed. Johnston, 188. 2, 23, 25–26, 37, pp. 412–13.

[103] Lewys Glyn Cothi, *Gwaith*, ed. Johnston, 188.59–60, p. 412.

[104] Llawdden, *Gwaith*, ed. Daniel, 14.21, pp. 67–70.

[105] Bartrum (1974) s.n. Bleddyn ap Cynfyn 5, 1.32. For Ieuan's descendants see idem (1983), s.n. Bleddyn ap Cynfyn 5(A), 1.68.

kin].[106] By way of reference to Gwenllian in this poem Llawdden again stresses the Glyndŵr connection, describing her as *o Lyn Dyfrdwy dad* [issuing from a father from Glyndyfrdwy] and of *Hil yr hydd hael o'r Rhuddallt* [the race of the generous one of Rhuddallt].[107]

The marriages of two daughters of Owain to members of Herefordshire gentry families — Alice married Sir John Scudamore of Kentchurch and Jonet married Sir John Croft of Croft Castle[108] — were not forgotten by poets who sang the praise of their descendants. Hywel Dafi, in an elegy for Thomas Scudamore of Kentchurch, a great-grandson of Glyndŵr's daughter,[109] composed before 1489, compared the mourning at his death with that after Owain (*cwyn am Owain*), and lauded his military prowess by comparison with his great-great-grandfather: his arrows were as *byllt o dân gwyllt Owain gynt* [bolts from the wild-fire of Owain of old].[110] A far more formidable martial figure, Sir Rhys ap Thomas, earned military comparison with Owain in a poem by Tudur Aled,[111] and, despite his only claim to a Glyndŵr connection being through his wife — a great-great-grandaughter of Alice Scudamore — was hailed by Lewys Morgannwg as *Câr Owain* [Owain's kinsman] when he died in 1525.[112] The poet was on firmer ground in 1541 when celebrating the newly-built court of Gruffudd Dwnn at Ystradmerthyr in Carmarthenshire as *Tŷ newydd gwaed Hen Owain* [the new house of the blood of Old Owain]. Gruffudd could rightly claim his share of *gwaed mawr Ysgudmoriaid* [the mighty blood of the Scudamores], however diluted, for his great-grandfather had married a grand-daughter of the Scudamore-Glyndŵr union.[113] It was the Croft-Glyndŵr connection that Lewys celebrated in a poem to Walter Herbert of St. Julians, *câr Owain Glyn* [the kinsman of Owain Glyn], whose mother was a grand-daughter of Sir John and Jonet Croft,[114] but the poet also recorded Herbert's descent from Dafydd Gam, the enemy of Glyndŵr.[115] A broadly contemporary poet Siôn Ceri praised the Croft wife of a patron from Clun for her Glyndŵr affiliations: she was a *Merch Edwart . . . Crofft* [daughter of Edward Croft] and a descendant of *Glyndŵr, milwr moliant* [Glyndŵr, praiseworthy war-

---

[106] Compare Llawdden, *Gwaith*, ed. Daniel, p. 181.

[107] Llawdden, *Gwaith*, ed. Daniel, 14.40, 42, p. 68. (The faulty punctuation of 14.42 has been amended.)

[108] Bartrum (1974), s.n. Bleddyn ap Cynfyn 5, 1.32. There is confusion over the name of the daughter who married Sir John Scudamore. Bartrum, ibid., lists her as Elizabeth, but a petition of 1433 in *Rotuli Parliamentorum* 4.440, which refers to her as the wife of John Scudamore, records her name throughout as Alice, and compare *Calendar of Patent Rolls, 1429–1436*, p. 286, where she is also recorded as Alice.

[109] Bartrum (1983), s.n. Scudamore, 10.1595.

[110] I wish to thank A. C. Lake for this reference and for supplying me with an edited text of the poem from his forthcoming edition of the work of Hywel Dafi. For a diplomatic transcript of the poem from manuscript, see *Peniarth MS. 67*, ed. Roberts, pp. 19–20. Compare Item 3.66.

[111] Tudur Aled, *Gwaith*, ed. Jones, 1.13.77, p. 75.

[112] Lewys Morgannwg, *Gwaith*, ed. Lake, 2.63.14, p. 377. For the descent of Efa, wife of Sir Rhys ap Thomas, see Bartrum (1974), s.n. Selyf 6, 4.845; Bartrum (1983), s.n. Elystan Glodrydd 52(B, C), 5.731; s.n. Scudamore, 10.1595.

[113] Lewys Morgannwg, *Gwaith*, ed. Lake, 57.16, 47. For the marriage see Bartrum (1983), s.n. Llywelyn ap Gwrgan 2(A), 7.1193; s.n. Scudamore, 10.1595.

[114] Bartrum (1983), s.n. Croft, 2.343; s.n. Godwin 8(A₁), 5.780.

[115] Lewys Morgannwg, *Gwaith*, 1.23.14, 22, p. 104.

rior]; unusually, the poet also records her descent from *Cyff Hanmer* [the stock of Hanmer] by way of allusion to Margaret Hanmer, the wife of Glyndŵr.[116] Bardic consciousness of the Croft-Glyndŵr connection persisted into Elizabethan times, Wiliam Llŷn citing the descent of Siôn Prys of Newtown in Montgomeryshire from the Croft bloodline *Ac o lin deg o Lynn Dwr* [and from the fair line of Glyndŵr].[117]

It was in poetry written over many generations to the descendants of Owain's siblings, however, that the Glyndŵr connection was most extensively celebrated. Lowri, daughter of Owain's brother, Tudur, was a crucial figure in this respect. She married firstly Robin ap Gruffudd Goch of the *cantref* of Rhos,[118] their daughter Marged, wife of Gruffudd ap Rhys of Dinmael, being duly hailed by Hywel Cilan as *nith Owain* [the niece of Owain], a term also applied to Marged and Gruffudd's daughter Catrin in an elegy by Tudur Aled.[119] But Lowri's second marriage to Gruffudd ab Einion of Corsygedol in Ardudwy, Merioneth, generated immeasurably more bardic interest.[120] The poetry addressed to the sons of this marriage, Gruffudd Fychan, who inherited Corsygedol, and his younger brother Elisau ap Gruffudd,[121] made much of their Glyndŵr connections. Tudur Penllyn in a joint eulogy for the brothers praised them as *[t]yrau Glyndŵr* [the towers of Glyndŵr] and *[c]eirw'r Glyn* [the stags of the Glyn],[122] whilst another Merioneth poet Hywel Cilan hailed them as *neiaint Owain* [Owain's nephews].[123] Gruffudd Fychan, like other north Wales gentry who could claim kinship with both Glyndŵr and Jasper Tudor,[124] was an active supporter of the Lancastrian cause during the Wars of the Roses, and the convergence of pride in Glyndŵr and Tudor kinship and Lancastrian partisanship is exemplified in the poetry addressed to him. He was cited as both a *[c]âr i Siasbar* [kinsman of Jasper] and *nai Owain* [the nephew of Owain] by Deio ab Ieuan Du,[125] and a poem by Tudur Penllyn in praise of Gruffudd when

---

[116] Siôn Ceri, *Gwaith*, ed. Lake, 38.39–42, p. 110. Margaret, wife of Ieuan Gwyn, was the great-great grand-daughter of Jonet Croft, see Bartrum (1983), s.n. Croft, 2.343.

[117] Wiliam Llŷn, *Barddoniaeth*, ed. Morrice, 29.47–48, p. 76. Siôn Prys was sixth in descent from Sir John and Jonet Croft (Bartrum [1983], s.n. Croft, 2.343; s.n. Elystan Glodrydd 45(A$_1$), 5.718; s.n. Hywel Fain(A$_2$), 6.1018; Dwnn, *Heraldic Visitations of Wales*, ed. Meyrick, 1.315).

[118] Bartrum (1974), s.n. Bleddyn ap Cynfyn 5, 1.32; s.n. Marchudd 22, 4.689.

[119] Hywel Cilan, *Gwaith*, ed. Jones, 14.38, p. 25; Tudur Aled, *Gwaith*, ed. Jones, 77.77, p. 312 (Catrin was wife of Ieuan ap Dafydd ab Ithel Fychan of Tegeingl). Tudur Aled also noted the Glyndŵr genealogical associations of Gruffudd and Marged's son in an elegy for Gruffudd in Tudur Aled, *Gwaith*, ed. Jones, 88.31–36, p. 351. The use of *nith* [niece] and *nai* [nephew] in genealogical references to indicate more distant kinship than the precise relationships which the terms convey today was common in medieval Welsh praise poetry.

[120] Bartrum (1974), s.n. Bleddyn ap Cynfyn 5, 1.32; s.n. Osbwrn 1, 4.727.

[121] Bartrum (1983), s.n. Osbwrn 1(A$_1$), 9.1415.

[122] Tudur Penllyn and Ieuan ap Tudur Penllyn, *Gwaith*, ed. Roberts, 3.5, 20, p. 6. They are also praised as "the descendants [lit. "grandsons"] of Gruffudd of Rhuddallt," 3. 23, by way of reference to their descent from Glyndŵr's grandfather.

[123] Hywel Cilan, *Gwaith*, ed. Jones, 26.16, p. 45.

[124] Gruffudd and Jasper could claim kinship through the marriages of the two daughters of Thomas ap Llywelyn to their great-grandfathers, see Bartrum (1974), s.n. Rhys ap Tewdwr 7, 4.782.

[125] Deio ab Ieuan Du, *Gwaith*, ed. Davies, 1.13,72, pp. 2–3.

he was among the Lancastrian defenders of Harlech castle during the 1460s both described him as *Tŵr Rhuddallt* [the tower of Rhuddallt] by way of reference to the Glyndŵr ancestral patrimony in Glyndyfrdwy and hinted at his role in aiding Jasper's flight by sea from Barmouth to France.[126] In the same vein, in a poem in praise of Gruffudd's new sea-girt tower-house at Barmouth — where it was implied that Jasper resorted — Tudur described it as *Tŵr nai Owain* [the tower of Owain's nephew].[127]

Even greater emphasis on the Glyndŵr connection appears in the poetry addressed to Gruffudd Fychan's brother Elisau, a cultivated literary patron who owned the White Book of Rhydderch,[128] the prime repository of medieval Welsh prose tales. Marriage to an heiress from the commote of Iâl having brought him to reside in a district adjoining Glyndŵr country, Elisau was hailed by Tudur Penllyn as *Eryr Glyn Dyfrdwy oror* [the eagle of the boundary of Glyn Dyfrdwy].[129] Gutun Owain, a poet from the Welsh borderland, not only praised his wide culture but also extravagantly lauded his lineage: he was *O dwf ieirll Glyn Dyfrdwy fawr* [sprung from the earls of great Glyndyfrdwy] and was *Gorwyr avr gledd i geirw'r Glyn* [the great-grandson with golden sword of the stags of the Glyn], his mother's association with Rhuddallt also being cited.[130] According to Rhys Pennardd his feasts invited comparison with those of the lords of Glyn and of Cynfyn, ancestor of the princes of Powys, and the poet extended his hyperbole to prophesy, somewhat hopefully, Elisau's recovery of the ancestral princely seat of Mathrafal.[131] When Elisau died in 1489 Lewys Môn, having mourned the loss suffered by the lands of Glyndŵr and of Iâl, was moved to assert that *ceirw Rhuddallt* [the stags of Rhuddallt] outdid in renown other stags of stunted growth.[132] But it was Gutun Owain who most powerfully expressed a sense of loss by placing Elisau's death within a wider context of Welsh history, which told of the decline of the formerly glorious *llin Troea* [line of Troy] and the loss of native princes, of whom the last in line was Owain. The death of his kinsman, Elisau, was a further blow:

> Issel ŷm, gwaith wasel oedd,
> A'n hynaif yn vrenhinoedd:
> Kan koron cyn Saesson sydd
> O'n kronigl a'nn kyrenydd,
> Kann t'wyssoc rrowioc o 'rrain,
> A'r diwedd vv hyd Ywain.

---

[126] Tudur Penllyn and Ieuan ap Tudur Penllyn, *Gwaith*, ed. Roberts, 2.8, 15–26, pp. 4–5.

[127] Tudur Penllyn and Ieuan ap Tudur Penllyn, *Gwaith*, ed. Roberts, 16.46, p. 28.

[128] Bartrum (1983), s.n. Osbwrn 1(A$_2$), 9.1416. Gruffudd Fychan and Elisau's grandfather, Einion ap Gruffudd of Corsygedol, married Tangwystl, daughter of Rhydderch ab Ieuan Llwyd (Bartrum [1974], s.n. Osbwrn 1, 4.727), the original owner of the manuscript. It was this family link which acounted for Elisau's eventual ownership of the manuscript, which may originally have passsed to his grand-uncle, the poet Ieuan ap Rhydderch, see Huws, *Medieval Welsh Manuscripts*, pp. 256–57.

[129] Tudur Penllyn and Ieuan ap Tudur Penllyn, *Gwaith*, ed. Roberts, 3.39, p. 7. Elisau married Marged ferch Siancyn ab Ieuan of Plas-yn-Iâl, Bryneglwys, but was also associated with Maerdy in Gwyddelwern and Rhagad in Corwen. It may be significant that Rhagad was an old Glyndŵr family possession (Davies, *Revolt*, p. 131).

[130] Gutun Owain, *L'Œuvre Poétique*, ed. Bachellery, 42.4, 13, 17, p. 229.

[131] Peniarth MS 239, pp. 390–91.

[132] Lewys Môn, *Gwaith*, ed. Rowlands, 69. 9–10, 17–18, p. 245.

Y kyff hwn, oedd y'n koffav,
A lâs pann aeth Elissav. . . .
Tores y llin vrenhinol,
Trist yw'n iaith trosto, — 'n i ôl.[133]

[We are laid low, it was the work of a wassail-cup,[134]
Our ancestors having been kings.
There are a hundred crowned heads before the English,
According to our chronicle, who were our kinsmen.
These were a hundred princes of noble descent,
And they ended with Owain.
This stock, which served to remind us,
Was terminated with Elisau's passing. . . .
The royal line has broken,
Our nation is sad on his account after his passing.]

Owain also featured in poetry addressed to the next generation of this line. Tudur Aled recalled the descent of Wiliam Fychan of Cilgerran, son of Gruffudd Fychan,[135] from *gweilch Glyn Dŵr* [the hawks of Glyndŵr], noting his affinity both with south Wales and with the northern territory of Glyndŵr (*gwlad Arglwydd Glyn*).[136] But the Glyndŵr connection resonated louder in the poems Tudur addressed to the sons of Elisau.[137] Gruffudd Llwyd ab Elisau, whose residence was at Rhagad in the Dee valley on land once in the ownership of Owain's family and close to his former court at Glyndyfrdwy, was portrayed as one who would hone *[c]ledd glas Arglwydd y Glyn* [the bright sword of the Lord of the Glyn] in the land of Berwyn.[138] In a remarkable passage heavy with allusion to Galfridian history, Tudur extolled him as one capable of avenging ancient wrongs and of ringing the bell associated with the myth of Owain the sleeping hero:

Ymliw âg wyrion Rhonwen,
Ymladd hwnt am y wlêdd hen;
Cân gyrn ar y cŵn o Gent,
Coffa wasel, cyffesent. . . .
Cyd chwyrner, cedwch arnoch,
Cyw Owain Glyn, cân y gloch.[139]

Rebuke the descendants of Ronwein,
Fight yonder on account of the ancient feast;

---

[133] Gutun Owain, *L'Œuvre Poétique*, ed. Bachellery, 43.2–12, 19–20. p. 233.

[134] According to Geoffrey of Monmouth, Hengist's daughter Ronwein proffered a wassail-cup to Vortigern, who, enamored of her, voluntarily ceded British territory to the Saxons (*Geoffrey of Monmouth*, ed. Reeve, trans. Wright, 100.339–67, pp. 129–31).

[135] Bartrum (1983), s.n. Osbwrn 1(A$_1$), 9.1415.

[136] Tudur Aled, *Gwaith*, ed. Jones, 108.10, 17–18, p. 421.

[137] Bartrum (1983), s.n. Osbwrn 1(A$_2$), 9.1416.

[138] Tudur Aled, *Gwaith*, ed. Jones, 47.40, p. 195. On Rhagad as a Glyndŵr family possession see Davies, *Revolt*, p. 131. It was located some one and a half miles west of the site of Glyndŵr's court. The Berwyn hills run parallel to the Dee valley to the south.

[139] Tudur Aled, *Gwaith*, ed. Jones, 47.65–68, 71–72, p. 196.

Sound trumpets on the dogs from Kent,
Remember the wassail-cup, they confessed it; . . .
Though they may snarl, take heed,
Descendant of Owain Glyn, ring the bell.

Whilst such a passage indicates the survival of racial animosities and grievances and of an acute Welsh historical consciousness, its rhetoric should be interpreted cautiously. Its political context is unknown, and could be the later stages of the Wars of the Roses or some period of military alert during the reign of Henry VII:[140] significantly, perhaps, another poem by Tudur addressed to Gruffudd Llwyd describes him as *plaid i'r Goron* [a support of the Crown].[141] Yet, paradoxically, that poem too makes much of Gruffudd's kinship with Owain. The right of *nai Owain* [Owain's nephew] to bear the arms of his famous ancestor is asserted, as is Gruffudd's fittingness to succeed to Owain's court at Sycharth, a compliment which could only have been meant metaphorically:

Darogan iwch, drwy gan iaith,
Dringo henllys draw 'Nghynllaith;
Yno bu Owain a'i barth,
A'r llys uchaf, Iarll Sycharth.[142]

[There is a prophecy about you, in a hundred languages,
That you will ascend to an old court over in Cynllaith;
It was there that Owain had his hearth,
And the highest of courts, the earl of Sycharth.]

A poem by the same poet to Gruffudd's younger brother, Dafydd Llwyd, resident in his mother's patrimony in Iâl, similarly evokes his ancestry, citing Glyndŵr himself, Lowri, and her father, Tudur:

Aeth Glyn Dŵr i'th galyn di,
Ar ôl eryr ŵyr Lowri;
Baedd Tudur, byddut waedwyllt,
Brawd Ywain, gwayw briwdan gwyllt.[143]

[Glyn Dŵr was in your retinue [of ancestors],
There behind the eagle who is the grandson of Lowri;
The boar of Tudur, you would be wild blooded,
The brother of Owain, with a wild spear flashing fire.]

---

[140] The reference to Kent may be significant and convey a double meaning. Geoffrey of Monmouth relates how the Saxons acquired Kent from the Britons by stratagem, compare note 134 above. But a contemporary allusion to the pretender Perkin Warbeck's landing at Deal in Kent in 1495 is not impossible.

[141] Tudur Aled, *Gwaith*, ed. Jones, 110.57, p. 431.

[142] Tudur Aled, *Gwaith*, ed. Jones, 100.21–24, p. 430.

[143] Tudur Aled, *Gwaith*, ed. Jones, 46.45–48, p. 191.

The poet goes on to describe how Dafydd's court overlooked the northern part of Glyndŵr's territory (*Ar ogledd gwlad Arglwydd Glyn*).[144] The poetic evidence suggests that the memory of Owain was particularly cherished among the members of this branch of his kinsmen resident in the very heart of Glyndŵr country. It was through a marriage to a grand-daughter of Elisau ap Gruffudd that the Salusburies of Rug, Corwen — who came to possess Owain's former lands shortly before the middle of the sixteenth century — could claim kinship with Glyndŵr, mentioned by a number of poets during the reign of Elizabeth.[145]

The marriages of two sisters of Glyndŵr often resulted in references to Owain in the poetry addressed to their descendants. His sister Lowri married Robert Puleston of Emral in north-east Wales, a descendant of an English settler family and one of Owain's core adherents who assembled in Glyndyfrdwy in September 1400 and who supported him during the revolt.[146] Poetry addressed to the descendants of this marriage perpetuated the memory of Glyndŵr over many generations. Guto'r Glyn addressed a *cywydd* to Elen, a daughter of Robert Puleston and Lowri who was married to Gruffudd ap Llywelyn of Llannerch in Llŷn requesting the gift of an Irish mantle, addressing her with genealogical precision as *nith Owain* [the niece of Owain].[147] Other poems by Guto, Hywel Cilan, Gutun Owain, Ieuan ap Tudur Penllyn, Rhys Goch Glyndyfrdwy, and Lewys Môn featured grandsons of Lowri and Robert. The poets mostly confined themselves to merely noting these men's kinship with Owain, Hywel Cilan's elegy for Siôn ap Madog Puleston typically lamenting *Mae'n aeaf am nai Owain* [it is winter for Owain's nephew],[148] but Rhys Goch Glyndyfrdwy in a *cywydd* addressed to Roger Puleston during his absence in Glamorgan not only hailed him as *nai Owain* [Owain's nephew], but also referred to Owain's renown in Glamorgan, *A dwedyd a da ydyw / a wnan fod owain yn fyw* [And they say, and it is good, that Owain is alive].[149] The active support given by members of the main Puleston line to the Tudor cause during the Wars of the Roses provided an opportunity for military comparisons with Owain: Ieuan ap Tudur Penllyn hailed Edward Puleston of Ruabon, brother of Siôn ap Madog Puleston, as *Blaidd Owain Hen* [the wolf of Old Owain], praising his military action on behalf of "the young earl" from Anglesey (presumably Henry Tudor, earl of Richmond),[150] whilst Hywel Cilan in a similar vein hailed him as *Nai, gwrol yn ei guras, / Owain y Glyn, onwayw glas* [the nephew, brave

---

[144] Tudur Aled, *Gwaith*, ed. Jones, 46.82. Dafydd resided at Plas-yn-Iâl in Bryneglwys.

[145] For the genealogical link with the Salusburies see Bartrum (1983), s.n. Bleddyn ap Cynfyn 21(A), 1.106; s.n. Osbwrn 1(A$_1$), 9.1415; s.n. Osbwrn 1(A$_2$), 9.1416; s.n. Salesbury 9, 9.1577. On the acquisition of lands described as "formerly of Owen Glyndwre" by Robert Salusbury (d. 1550), see Siôn Tudur, *Gwaith*, ed. Roberts, 2.58.

[146] See Lloyd, *Owen Glendower*, pp. 31, 34. His lands were declared forfeit in late 1400. A note in Dwnn, *Heraldic Visitations of Wales*, ed. Meyrick, 2.151, claims that he was slain during the revolt. For the Puleston pedigree see Bartrum (1974), s.n. Puleston, 4.741.

[147] gutorglyn.net, 53.14; Guto'r Glyn, *Gwaith*, ed. Williams, 78.14, p. 205.

[148] Hywel Cilan, *Gwaith*, ed. Jones, 22.9, p. 38; compare Guto'r Glyn's elegy for him: gutorglyn.net, 72.49; Guto'r Glyn, *Gwaith*, ed. Williams, 23.49, p. 63. For Siôn ap Madog Puleston's descent see Bartrum (1974), s.n. Puleston, 4.741.

[149] Peniarth MS 100, pp. 417–18. For Roger Puleston's descent see Bartrum (1974), s.n. Puleston, 4.741; Bartrum (1983), s.n. Puleston(C$_1$), 9.1458.

[150] Tudur Penllyn and Ieuan ap Tudur Penllyn, *Gwaith*, ed. Roberts, 42.18, 21–24, p. 76. For Edward Puleston's descent see Bartrum (1974), s.n. Puleston, 4.741; Bartrum (1983), s.n. Puleston(B), 9.1457.

in his cuirass, / Of Owain y Glyn, with his bright ashen spear].[151] The Pulestons' support for the Tudors paved the way for the successful public career of John Puleston (Siôn Pilstwn Hen), great-grandson of Robert Puleston and Lowri,[152] esquire of the body to Henry VII and chamberlain of North Wales. Tudur Aled dutifully noted that Owain's sister was his great-grandmother (*Chwaer Owain fu'ch hennain chwi*) and noted the alleged resemblance of his arms to those of Owain,[153] whilst Hywel Rheinallt compared him to his famous kinsman (*dy hap fal Glyndyfrdwy hen*) somewhat misleadingly citing his lack of English blood (*diwaed-Sais*) and contrasting him with formerly oppressive English officials.[154] To Lewys Môn he was *Nai Owain braff o nen brud* [the nephew of mighty Owain who was chief of prophecy], the poet lamenting at his death that earth had been heaped on the blood of Owain (*mae daear am waed Owain*).[155] In the next generation the kinship with Owain of John Puleston's son, Sir John Puleston, constable of Caernarfon castle and chamberlain of North Wales, did not go unrecorded by poets.[156] Not only descendants of Robert Puleston and Lowri in the male line but also those on the distaff side were regularly hailed as kindred of Owain. Gutun Owain, a poet assiduous in recording the Glyndŵr connections of patrons of the Puleston line, did not ignore those of the three sons of John Trevor of Bryncunallt, Chirk, the great-grandsons of Robert Puleston and Lowri through their daughter Angharad,[157] describing them as *Tri o gloe tyrav y Glynn* [the three locks of the towers of the Glyn] and *Trindod llewod llv Owain* [a trinity of lions of Owain's host].[158] Ieuan ap Tudur Penllyn praised three of the sons of Siôn ap Maredudd of Ystumcegid, Eifionydd, similarly descended from Robert Puleston and Lowri through their daughter Elen, as three supporters of Henry Tudor who issued from *arglwyddi'r Glyn* [the lords of the Glyn].[159] Owain Tudur Fychan of Penmynydd, Anglesey, esquire of the body to his kinsman Henry VII, could also claim kinship with Glyndŵr as the

---

[151] Hywel Cilan, *Gwaith*, ed. Jones, 23.21–22, p. 39.

[152] Bartrum (1983), s.n. Puleston(A₁), 9.1454.

[153] Tudur Aled, *Gwaith*, ed. Jones, 41.31, p. 174, 42.25–28, p. 178. For heraldic comment on the the latter reference see Siddons, *Development of Welsh Heraldry*, 1.138.

[154] For Hywel Rheinallt's poem see Lewys Môn, *Gwaith*, ed. Rowlands, Atodiad 2, pp. 367–68. The lines cited are 20, 29–32. Ironically, a Puleston ancestor, Sir Roger Puleston, sheriff of Anglesey, was hanged by the Welsh during the revolt of Madog ap Llywelyn in 1294 in revenge for his exactions on behalf of Edward I, see *Dictionary of Welsh Biography*, s.n. Puleston family, p. 816.

[155] Lewys Môn, *Gwaith*, ed. Rowlands, 71.47–48, p. 254, 73.8, p. 264.

[156] *Peniarth MS. 67*, ed. Roberts, 19.16, p. 31 (Hywel Dafi); Lewys Daron, *Gwaith*, ed. Lake, 12.13, p. 37; Mathau Brwmffild, *Gwaith*, ed. Lake, 6.31–32, p. 30. For John Puleston's descent, see Bartrum (1983), s.n. Puleston(A₁), 9.1454.

[157] Bartrum (1974), s.n. Puleston, 4.741; s.n. Tudur Trefor 14, 4.883; Bartrum (1983), s.n. Tudur Trefor 14(C₁), 10.1690.

[158] Gutun Owain, *L'Œuvre Poétique*, ed. Bachellery, 37. 48, 49, p. 211, For other references by this poet to the Glyndŵr kinship of Puleston relations, compare 15.17–18, p. 101 (Gruffudd ap Hywel ap Morgan); 17.2, p. 109 (Matthew Puleston); 38.15, p. 213 (Robert Trevor of Hope); 50.16, p. 265 (Siôn ab Elis Eutun); 53.7–8, p. 277 (Roger son of John Puleston).

[159] Tudur Penllyn and Ieuan ap Tudur Penllyn, *Gwaith*, ed. Roberts, 43.47–52, p. 78. Compare also 43.11 p. 77. The sons addressed are Morus, Owain, and Ieuan (Siôn ap Maredudd had two other sons, Robert and Gruffudd). For their descent see Bartrum (1974), s.n. Gollwyn 7, 2.434; Bartrum (1983), s.n. Gruffudd ap Cynan 15(A₂), 5.846.

son of Annes, another daughter of Robert Puleston and Lowri, and was greeted by Lewys Môn as *Owain câr Owain* [Owain the kinsman of Owain].[160] Later Pulestons and Puleston relations by marriage were greeted by poets as kinsmen of Owain throughout the sixteenth century, leading poets such as Gruffudd Hiraethog (d. 1564) and Siôn Tudur (d. 1602) being among those who acknowledged such family links.[161]

Owain's sister Isabel married Adda ab Iorwerth Ddu of Pengwern, Llangollen, a member of a prominent family in Nanheudwy which bordered on Glyndyfrdwy.[162] In a poem to Ieuan Fychan ab Ieuan ab Adda of Pengwern, a grandson of Isabel and Adda, composed after 1448, Guto'r Glyn hailed him as *nai Owain* [the nephew of Owain] and his son, Hywel, as one of *hil Owain* [Owain's race].[163] Guto also found a patron in Siôn Edward (d. 1498) of Plasnewydd, Chirk, son of Ieuan Fychan's brother, Iorwerth, describing him in a poem to celebrate his return from the battle of Bosworth as *Gwaed Owain Glyn i gadw'n gwlad* [one of the blood of Owain Glyn to defend our land].[164] Gutun Owain in a passage replete with allusions praised not only Siôn Edward's patronage for poetry — he was a veritable Ifor Hael, the patron of Dafydd ap Gwilym — but also his kinship with both Glyndŵr and the Tudors:[165]

> Gŵr mawr o oreugwyr Môn,
> Gwayw Rruddallt, vric aur rroddion,
> Ail Ivor Hael o'i ovynn
> Wyd i glêr, o waed y Glynn.[166]

> [A great man descended from the best men of Anglesey,
> The spear of Rhuddallt, the summit of golden gifts,
> A second Ifor Hael, if solicited,
> Are you for poets, of the blood of the Glyn.]

---

[160] Lewys Môn, *Gwaith*, ed. Rowlands, 22.3, p. 81. For Owain Tudur Fychan's descent see Bartrum (1974), s.n. Marchudd 6, 4.673; Bartrum (1983), s.n. Marchudd 6(A_1), 8.1263. Like other members of the Penmynydd line, he could also claim distant kinship with Glyndŵr through the marriage of Margaret, sister of Glyndŵr's mother Elen, and his great-great-grandfather, Tudur ap Goronwy (Bartrum [1974], s.n. Rhys ap Tewdwr 7, 4.782).

[161] Gruffudd Hiraethog, *Gwaith*, ed. Bowen, 48.59, p. 157; 53.29–32, p. 171; 57.17–18, p. 183; 74.28, p. 235. Siôn Tudur, *Gwaith*, ed. Roberts, 52.33.4, 84, pp. 214–15; 53.12, p. 217; 54.37, p. 222.

[162] For the marriage see Bartrum (1974), s.n. Bleddyn ap Cynfyn 5, 1.32; s.n. Tudur Trefor 13, 4.882. In Griffith, *Pedigrees*, p. 182, the wife of this marriage is named "Lowry, (Elizabeth in some books)," but this is incorrect.

[163] gutorglyn.net, 106.62, 67; Guto'r Glyn, *Gwaith*, ed. Williams, 27.62, 67, p. 75. For Ieuan Fychan's descent see Bartrum (1974), s.n. Tudur Trefor 13, 4.882.

[164] gutorglyn.net, 107.46. In Guto'r Glyn, *Gwaith*, ed. Williams, 105, pp. 270–72, the couplet which includes this line was not incorporated into the text but listed as a variant reading. For the genealogy of this branch of the family see Bartrum (1983), s.n. Tudur Trefor 13(E), 10.1686; Lloyd, *History of . . . Powys Fadog*, 4.63–66.

[165] Siôn Edward's grandmother, Angharad, wife of Ieuan ab Adda, was the grand-daughter of Tudur ap Goronwy of Penmynydd, Anglesey, ancestor of the Tudors. Siôn Edward could claim distant kinship with Glyndŵr through the Penmynydd line also, as Tudur ap Goronwy's wife, Marged, was the sister of Glyndŵr's mother, Elen. See Bartrum (1974), s.n. Rhys ap Tewdwr 7, 4.782.

[166] Gutun Owain, *L'Œuvre Poétique*, ed. Bachellery, 55.25–28, p. 287. For another reference to Siôn Edward's kinship with Glyndŵr see Deio ab Ieuan Du, *Gwaith*, ed. Davies, 14.17–18, p. 34.

Hywel Cilan in a poem addressed jointly to Siôn and his brother Ednyfed, deployed the evocative names of Glyn and Sycharth in association with imagery bearing genealogical connotations:

> Deunai, pell a adwaenir,
> Owain ŷnt hwy, enw ein tir, . . .
> Coed y Glyn ganddyn' i gyd,
> Coed Sycharth cyd oes iechyd.[167]

> [They are the two nephews, it is acknowledged afar,
> Of Owain, the renowned one of our land, . . .
> All the trees of Glyn are theirs,
> And the trees of Sycharth, may they both enjoy a healthy life.]

In the next generation Tudur Aled and Lewys Môn addressing the sons of Siôn Edwart, Wiliam ap Siôn Edwart (d. 1532) and Dafydd Llwyd ap Siôn Edwart, also cited the Glyndŵr connection,[168] Lewys similarly hailing their sister Catrin, widow of Tudur Llwyd of Bodidris in Iâl, for her consanguinity with Owain (*gydwaed Owain*).[169] Poets during the reign of Elizabeth were just as aware of the Glyndŵr associations of the line of Pengwern and Plasnewydd. A poem by Siôn Brwynog in praise of Lewys ab Owain of Fron-deg, Anglesey, composed in 1558–59, noted the Glyndŵr kinship of his wife, Alice, the great-grandaughter of Ieuan Fychan ab Ieuan ab Adda.[170] As in the case of the Puleston descendants, Gruffudd Hiraethog did not omit to mention the Glyndŵr connections of members of this line, citing them in the case of a grand-nephew of Ieuan Fychan ab Ieuan ab Adda and a grandson and granddaughter of Siôn Edwart.[171] Similarly, Gruffudd's pupil, Wiliam Llŷn, in an elegy for William Mostyn (d. 1576), head of the powerful Mostyn family and sixth in descent from Adda ab Iorwerth Ddu and Isabel, was moved to cite Mostyn's distant link with Rhuddallt, the ancestral possession of Glyndŵr and his line in Glyndyfrdwy.[172]

Mentions of kinship with Glyndŵr persisted in poetry into the late Elizabethan period and beyond. Four poets who addressed poems to Robert Salusbury (d. 1599) of Rug, Corwen, cited either his family connection with Glyndŵr or his ownership of Owain's former lands.[173]

---

[167] Hywel Cilan, *Gwaith*, ed. Jones, 21.9–10, 25–26, pp. 36–37. Compare line 49 where Ednyfed is described as having *[c]orff Owain* [the body of Owain].

[168] Tudur Aled, *Gwaith*, ed. Jones, 63.7, p. 253; Lewys Môn, *Gwaith*, ed. Rowlands, 112.23, p. 573. The two brothers (Bartrum [1983], s.n. Tudur Trefor 13(E), 10.1686) could also claim kinship with Glyndŵr through their mother, a great-grand-daughter of Robert Puleston and Lowri, sister of Glyndŵr (Bartrum [1974], s.n. Puleston, 4.741; Bartrum [1983], s.n. Tudur Trefor 25(A₁), 10.1701.

[169] Lewys Môn, *Gwaith*, ed. Rowlands, 68.60, p. 242. For a similar reference to her by Tudur Aled see *Gwaith*, ed. Jones, 52.76, p. 214;

[170] Wiliam, *Y Canu Mawl i Deulu'r Fron-Deg*, 2.67, p. 6 (on the date of the poem, see p. 32).

[171] Gruffudd Hiraethog, *Gwaith*, ed. Bowen, 16.52, p. 63 (grand-daughter of Siôn Edwart); 21.23–26, p. 77 (grand-nephew of Ieuan Fychan); 41.22, p. 135 (grandson of Siôn Edwart).

[172] Wiliam Llŷn, *Barddoniaeth*, ed. Morrice, 86.67–68, p. 236. For William Mostyn's descent, see Dwnn, *Heraldic Visitations of Wales*, ed. Meyrick, 2.307.

[173] Hughes, "Noddwyr y Beirdd," 270.61–62, p. 593 (Robert Ifans); 271.11–12, p. 594 (Rhys Cain); 272.91–92, p. 596 (Simwnt Fychan); 274.51–52, p. 601 (Edwart ap Raff).

In the new century his longer living brother William Salusbury (d. 1650) — known by his sobriquet *Yr Hen Hosanau Gleision* (Old Blue Stockings), and the doughty royalist governor of Denbigh Castle during the Civil War — was similarly hailed by Rhisiart Phylip for his kinship with Glyndŵr.[174] The kinship of the squires of Corsygedol with Owain was also long celebrated, both Lewys Dwnn and Siôn Phylip noting that Gruffudd Fychan II (d. 1616) was of the line of Glyndŵr and Rhuddallt,[175] whilst Edward Urien greeted his son William Fychan as *karw or Rhyddallt* [the stag from Rhuddallt].[176] In the eighteenth century the gentleman poet William Wynn in an elegy for Richard Vaughan, member of Parliament for Merioneth at his death in 1734, did not omit to mention his descent from *Owen Derwen Glynndŵr* [Owain, the oak of Glyndŵr].[177] But after the middle of the seventeenth century — as the tradition of praise poetry to gentry patrons waned — such references were rare: by that time Owain's presence in poetry had faded into insignificance.

MISCELLANEOUS VERSE

A small number of short items, mostly quatrains in the *englyn* meter, which appear in manuscripts from the second half of the sixteenth century onwards testify to Owain's continued impact on Welsh memory. These include three items of versified chronology, one of them being an anonymous *englyn* recording the supposed date of the death of Llywelyn ap Gruffudd but also alluding to Owain:

> Deü cant a mil myn dûcain
> oed Düw, a devddeg ar hügain,
> pen las Llywelyn, poen lain,
> ym Myellt kyn term Owain.[178]

> [Two hundred and a thousand by[?] forty
> was the age of God, and thirty-two,
> when Llywelyn, by means of a painful spear,
> was killed in Buellt before Owain's term.]

Though chronologically suspect — Llywelyn was slain in 1282, not 1272 — the *englyn*'s implication that Owain was Llywelyn's successor shows a significant historical awareness of Owain's princely claim and standing. Another *englyn* — which occurs in almost thirty manuscript copies (the earliest of them written by William Salesbury c.1564) — which is sometimes entitled *Rhyfel Glyndŵr* [Glyndŵr's War], records the date of the beginning of Owain's rising in 1400 and of his purported death fifteen years later (see Item 88). The *englyn*'s

---

[174] Hughes, "Noddwyr y Beirdd," 280.333–34, p. 615.

[175] Hughes, "Noddwyr y Beirdd," 30.51–52, p. 64 (Lewys Dwnn); 35.79–80, p. 76 (Siôn Phylip); 37.23–24, p. 80 (Siôn Phylip).

[176] Hughes, "Noddwyr y Beirdd," 43.26, p. 98.

[177] Hughes, "Noddwyr y Beirdd," 77.32, p. 181. For an even later example, compare Rhys Jones' elegy for Catrin wife of William Vaughan of Corsygedol in 1768 (104.40, p. 234). Catrin was the heiress of Nannau, her claim to Glyndŵr kinship deriving from marriages between the line of Nannau and those of Rug and Corsygedol (see Griffith, *Pedigrees*, p. 200).

[178] Edited from Peniarth MS 72, p. 418. The *myn* in line 1 is problematic.

author is not usually indicated and the few late manuscripts which ascribe it to Iolo Goch may be ignored. Its unique attribution to the fifteenth-century poet Rhys Pennardd in a manuscript of c.1597 by the humanist Siôn Dafydd Rhys (Dr. John Davies of Brecon) is, however, interesting.[179] This poet wrote in praise of Elisau ap Gruffudd of Plas-yn-Iâl (d. 1489),[180] son of Lowri, Glyndŵr's niece — praised for his knowledge of chronicles by Gutun Owain[181] — and if the attribution of the *englyn* to Rhys is correct it may reflect a tradition about the date of Glyndŵr's death current among his kinsmen.[182] A variant date of 1430 for his death versified in another *englyn* illustrates the imprecision of popular memory. It occurs uniquely among a sequence of chronological verses in a manuscript written c.1621 by the scribe and poet Thomas Evans of Hendreforfudd, Carrog, being very possibly his own work.[183] Thomas Evans lived in the very heart of Glyndŵr country — Hendreforfudd was once a Glyndŵr possession[184] — and his verse is best viewed as a token of continuing antiquarian interest in Owain in his own locality rather than as an authentic historical record:

Marwolaeth Owain Glyndwr

Mil a ffedwarcant wedi maeth — agos
      vgain bv i farfolaeth,
   a deg ar ol, deigr aeth
   a mawr wylo y marwolaeth.[185]

[*The Death of Owain Glyndŵr*

One thousand and four hundred [years], after nurture,
      and close to twenty [years] was his death,
   and ten [years] again, a tear was shed
   and great weeping occasioned by the death.]

A satirical *englyn* addressed to Dafydd Gam of Brecon, Owain's prominent enemy, also occurs in manuscripts, sometimes attributed to a poet called Gruffudd ab Owain Gethin of whom nothing is known. In Peniarth MS 94, written by Thomas Wiliems of Trefriw (1550?–1622?), it is accompanied by a short prose explanation which places it within the context of an alleged attempt to betray Owain at his Machynlleth parliament of 1404:

---

[179] Cardiff MS 18, p. 67. It is to be noted that Rhys Pennardd was a little-known poet. False attribution might be suspected if the work in question was associated with a well-known poet.

[180] Peniarth MS 239, p. 390.

[181] For Elisau's knowledge of chronicles see Gutun Owain, *L'Œuvre Poétique*, ed. Bachellery, 42.36, p. 231.

[182] The date of 1415 for Owain's death concurs with the evidence of the fifteenth-century sources Peniarth MS 26 and Jesus College MS 141 and also with that of Gruffudd Hiraethog's chronicle in Peniarth MS 135 (originally compiled in the fifteenth century), see Phillips, "When Did Owain Glyndŵr Die?" It is to be noted too that Peniarth MS 26 is possibly linked with the Chirk families of Edwards of Plasnewydd or Trevor of Bryncunallt, both descended from sisters of Glyndŵr.

[183] Evans appends his name to some of the chronological verses he includes in NLW MS 253A, pp. 334–44, although the *englyn* in question is not among them.

[184] Davies, *Revolt*, p. 131.

[185] Edited from NLW MS 253A, p. 342.

Davydh Gam, dryglam dreigldhyn — ymwan vrwydr,
       vradwr Richard frenin,
   lhwyr y troes diawl, hawl hwylvlin,
   o vath ystad, ei vys i'th din.

Pan a geisiei Ddafydd Gam d[d]ala Owein Glyndwr yMachynllaeth, ac y daliei Ywein efo, a'i
rhoi dan arianswm cyn cael myned adref i D[d]eheubarth, y canei y gefnder yd[d]aw, yr hwn
oed[d] stiward Ywein ac yn vach drostaw am drychant o vorcieu . . .[186]

[Dafydd Gam, [?]misfortunate wanderer in battle,
       a traitor to King Richard,
   utterly did the devil, [?]angrily pressing his claim,
   such was your state, turn his finger in your arse.

When Dafydd Gam tried to capture Owain Glyndŵr in Machynlleth, and Owain caught him and
held him to ransom before he could return home to south Wales, his cousin who was Owain's
steward and surety on his behalf for three hundred marks addressed him in verse . . .]

A quatrain in free verse to which Owain Glyndŵr's name is attached — as its presumed
locutor — is found in three early seventeenth-century manuscripts, twice in conjunction with
the *englyn* relating to Dafydd Gam:

O gweli di wr koch kam
yn ymofyn y gyrnig wenn,
dywaid y bod hŷ yn ochyr glynn
a nod y glo ar y ffenn.[187]

[If you see a red-haired, one-eyed man
seeking the white-chimneyed dwelling,
say that it is on the side of the valley
and the mark of charcoal on its head.]

In the 1695 edition of Camden's *Britannia* an addition to the Brecknockshire section supplied by Edward Lhuyd, based on notes by Robert Vaughan of Hengwrt, now lost, incor-
porates the above verse into a coherent narrative;[188] it tells of Dafydd Gam's bid to murder
Owain at Machynlleth and, as a result of his perfidy after returning to south Wales, how
Owain advanced southwards and burned Dafydd's house, informing one of his tenants of
the action in verse. In the eighteenth century two manuscript accounts by Evan Evans

---

[186] Edited from Peniarth MS 94, p. i (the end of the last line of the prose is illegible because of a
stain). The text of the *englyn* is unstable. In another version copied by Thomas Wiliems in Peniarth 94,
p. iv, *fileingin golesg* (= ?"loathsome dirty rag") occurs in line 1 instead of *dreigldhyn ymwan vrwydr*, a possible *lectio difficilior*. In line 4 the reading is *vasw ei waith diawl* (= "lewd was his devilish work"), a possible
attempt to remedy the faulty *cynghanedd* of *o vath ystad*. These readings are also found in other manuscripts.

[187] Edited from NLW MS 3039B (Mostyn MS 131), p. 697 (written by John Jones, Gellilyfdy,
1605–18). This text is better than those of Peniarth MS 94, p. iv (Thomas Wiliems), and Llanstephan
MS 119, p. 139 (Wiliam Phylip) where the verse is accompanied by the Dafydd Gam *englyn*.

[188] Gibson, *Camden's Britannia*, p. 591. Lhuyd acknowledges his source as "some notes of the
learned and judicious Antiquary Robert Vaughan of Hengwrt Esq."

("Ieuan Brydydd Hir") provided a more developed narrative of Owain and Dafydd Gam's enmity, probably drawing more fully on Robert Vaughan's notes and incorporating the *englyn* lampooning Dafydd as well as the verse relating to the burning of his house.[189]

Some intriguing anonymous lines in *cywydd* meter, first found in two manuscripts written during the 1590s or soon afterwards — one by Thomas Wiliems of Trefriw and the other by Edward Puleston, a distant kinsman of Glyndŵr — and included with a more extensive prose commentary — probably deriving again from Robert Vaughan's lost notes — in two eighteenth-century manuscripts, also relate to Owain (see Item 91).[190] They allude to the alleged action of a character called Madyn (= the Fox) after the battle of Pwll Melyn in 1405 when Tudur, Owain's brother, was slain. There would seem to have been a confusion of identity, some supposing that the slain man was Owain, not his brother who resembled him. A partly illegible note that follows the lines in Thomas Wiliems' manuscript states that Madyn went to the king to indicate the burial place of the supposedly slain Owain. The later manuscripts, however, relate that Madyn brought a head to the king claiming it to be Owain's, but that a Welshman at court refuted the identification because of the absence of a wart on the brow of the proffered head. The verse text in Puleston's manuscript displays minor variants, but, despite the differing prose accounts, the lines accusing Madyn of mendacity are identical in the other three manuscripts.[191] Whether what we have is pure fiction or a creative elaboration of authentic historical memory cannot be determined.

An *englyn* associated with Glyndŵr and doubtfully attributed to Iolo Goch occurs in manuscripts either on its own or, more often, with an explanatory prose narrative (see Item 90). The earliest example of this narrative occurs in an early seventeenth-century (1605–18) manuscript written by John Jones of Gellilyfdy.[192] It relates that Henry IV wrote to Earl Grey of Ruthin urging him to betray Glyndŵr by some stratagem. Having arranged to dine with Owain ostensibly promising not to bring more than thirty men in his entourage, the duplicitous Grey arranged for a large covert force to follow him. Owain's lookouts encamped on

---

[189] NLW MS 1980B (Panton MS 11), fols. 40v–42v; NLW MS 2021B (Panton MS 53), fols. 54v–55r. Henken bases her discussion in *National Redeemer*, pp. 98–99 on the NLW 1980B account. It is to be noted that Evans' account of his sources is confusing. In NLW MS 2021B, fol. 1r, he refers to "The History of Ywein Glyndwr supposed to be compiled by Mr Robert Vaughan," but states that "This copy is transcribed from a Manuscript which belonged to Bishop Humphreys." But on fol. 49r, at the beginning of his account of Glyndŵr, he refers to "W^m. Morris of Llansilin, out of whose book I transcribed this account." It may be that Bishop Humphrey Humphreys (1648–1712) had a copy of Vaughan's notes which were then transcribed by the antiquary William Maurice (d. 1680) and eventually seen by Evans. If the Dafydd Gam *englyn* occurred in Vaughan's notes, Edward Lhuyd might have omitted it from his 1695 *Britannia* account because of its scatological nature.

[190] British Library Additional MS 31055, fol. 226r (Thomas Wiliems); NLW MS 20898E, fol. 62r (Edward Puleston); Peniarth MS 240, pp. 2–3 (William Wynn); NLW MS 1980B, fol. 69r (Evan Evans). I am grateful to Bleddyn Huws for drawing my attention to Puleston's text, which is written in the margin of a heraldic manuscript, opposite the armorial shield of Gruffudd Fychan, Glyndŵr's father, and accompanied by the chronological *englyn* (Item 88 in this volume).

[191] For the prose commentary, see Item 91 in this volume. For a parallel prose account (without the poetry) supplied by Evan Evans in NLW MS 2021B, fol. 56v, see the accompanying notes. Printed prose accounts without the poetry occur in Carte, *General History of England*, p. 665; *History of the Island of Anglesey*, pp. 70–71 (Memoirs of Owen Glendowr), and Pennant, *Tours in Wales*, pp. 345–46.

[192] For the full version of the accompanying prose, see Item 90 in this volume.

a hill saw this force and sent Iolo Goch to warn Owain. He did this by reciting before Owain and an uncomprehending Grey an *englyn* pertaining to Dafydd ap Gruffudd's execution at Shrewsbury in 1283 when his executioner allegedly threw his heart into a fire only to be blinded when the heart leapt out at him. The rather oblique relation between the *englyn*'s subject matter and the narrative in which it is embedded suggests that a verse originally associated with Dafydd ap Gruffudd may have been transferred to Owain, a figure less remote in time and of greater historical resonance.[193] The story of Owain's confounding of Grey's duplicity may have its origin in folklore,[194] but the narrative prose's precise naming of historical personages and the placing of Owain within a context of Welsh princely history indicates a sophistication that might be associated with humanist antiquarian endeavor, and John Jones' own authorship cannot be discounted.

EPILOGUE

It has been shown that references to Owain Glyndŵr in fifteenth-and sixteenth- century Welsh poetry are numerous and diverse, and dispersed among various poetic genres. In the fifteenth century, whilst memories of Owain and his revolt were still alive, these references were often politically charged, reflecting the disappointments and bitterness of the post-revolt period and the frustrations which pervaded contemporary Welsh consciousness. Such references occurred in both vaticinal poems and poems addressed to patrons who were close kinsmen of Owain. During the Wars of the Roses the passions which had been generated by the revolt were reflected in modified form in vaticinal poetry, where Owain — conceived as rising from the dead or emerging from hiding — sometimes featured as the *mab darogan*. Welsh sentiment was channeled to further the Tudor bid for the English crown, one often strongly supported by members of families who could claim kinship with Owain (as could the Tudors themselves). In accord with the perceptions of the vaticinal tradition, Henry Tudor's victory at Bosworth Field in 1485 and his winning of the English crown was seen as a Welsh triumph and the fulfilment of ancient hopes. After Bosworth — with Welsh aspirations apparently satisfied — references to Owain in poetry, though plentiful, became virtually devoid of political connotation, being almost wholly confined to genealogical citations in poetry addressed to members of gentry families who could claim kinship with him. Though disparaged in print by sixteenth-century writers,[195] a de-politicized Owain often featured as a famous kinsman — usually as one amongst a cast of ancestors cited to flatter patrons' family pride — in poems whose recipients

---

[193] John Jones was not the first to associate the *englyn* with Glyndŵr. Thomas Evans of Hendreforfudd appends a note to his slightly earlier (1603) text of the *englyn* in Cardiff MS 12, p. 140 stating that it was *yn gyngor a siampl i owain glyndwr pan oedd fo yn troi i ryfela* [an advice and example to Owain Glyndŵr when he was preparing to go to war].

[194] The story is cited in the context of folklore relating to Owain by Henken, *National Redeemer*, pp. 102–03.

[195] See Items 95 (Hall), 98 (Baldwin), and 100 (Holinshed). To these may be added Powell, *The historie of Cambria, now called Wales*, pp. 385–36, who maintained that those "cunning in Merlins prophesies" brought Owain into "a fooles paradise."

were frequently pillars of the Tudor administration in Wales.[196] It is clear, as evidenced by miscellaneous items of poetry pertaining to Owain, some of a folkloric nature and placed in a narrative context, that he impacted strongly on Welsh popular memory and was long revered as a figure of renown, although such items carry little political significance. During the seventeenth and eighteenth centuries, after the decline of professional bardism and the weakening of the associated eulogistic tradition, Owain largely disappeared from Welsh poetry, though antiquarian interest in the poetry formerly associated with him persisted. It was only in the wake of the revival of Welsh national feeling in the nineteenth century and the development of a more consciously political Welsh nationalism in the twentieth century that Owain re-emerged as a significant presence in poetry, often featuring as a potent symbol of aspirational Welsh nationhood.[197]

[196] Among obvious examples were the poems addressed to members of the Puleston family prominent as holders of public office, e.g. Lewis Daron's poem to Sir John Puleston (d. 1551) where his kinship with Glyndŵr is cited but where the praise is focused on his public roles as constable of Caernarvon castle, sheriff of Caernarvonshire and sergeant in the service of Henry VIII (Lewys Daron, *Gwaith*, ed. Lake, 12, pp. 37–39).

[197] I have traced this development in my *Owain y Beirdd*, especially pp. 15–25. See also James, *Glyndŵr a Gobaith y Genedl*.

ALICIA MARCHANT
A NARRATIVE APPROACH TO CHRONICLES

At a first glance chronicles of the fifteenth and sixteenth centuries might give the impression of being simple and artless narratives. The tendency for chroniclers to present their work as unbiased and unfiltered history, means that it can be easy for readers to accept them as such. As this essay aims to show this is far from the case. Chronicles are sophisticated narratives in which chroniclers implement a range of narrative devices to help render believable their version of history. Each chronicler composes through his own biases — even at the seemingly simple level of selecting the events to be described, not to mention how to describe them. The texts that result from these labors, therefore, can be productively (and at times provocatively) viewed as narrative constructions that utilize "history" even as they seek to reform the past for their own particular purposes. Comparative readings of fifteenth- and sixteenth-century English chronicle accounts discussing the Welsh revolt of Owain Glyndŵr powerfully reveal the narratological forces at work within them — a body of evidence that is rich and detailed, but also quite diverse in its content and intention.

The unknown author of the *Historia vitae*, thought to have been completed at the abbey of Evesham in Worcestershire by the year 1403,[1] introduces "the hateful insurrection of the Welsh" by explaining how

> When the king made arrangements to hasten into Scotland he sent a letter sealed with his signet ring to the aforesaid Owain, amongst other people, because in those days he [Owain] was held to be a handsome squire, so that in no manner could he refuse to come with him. Lord Grey of Ruthin had been appointed as the carrier of this letter, who postponed delivering the accepted letter to him up until the time of the setting out of the king. Therefore at Terce on the day before setting out the aforesaid letter of the king was freed by him. He [Owain] was deeply astonished by these happenings, and replied that he had been alerted too late, suddenly and unexpectedly for such a voyage, briefly excusing himself because he was not willing, just as he had not been able, to go into Scotland at that time. In fact Lord Grey, having left that man [Owain] in Wales, told the king, who had advanced thus far into Scotland, in an incriminating fashion, that the aforesaid Owain scorned the king's letters and considered the king of no value, vehemently condemning his commands. (Item 28.4–15)

In contrast, the London-based chronicler Robert Fabyan, writing some hundred years later, begins his account of the revolt of Owain Glyndŵr in the following manner:

---

[1] See Livingston's discussion of the dating, pp. 472–74.

And in this yere began a great discencion in Walys atwene the lorde Gray Ryffyn, & a Welsheman named Howen of Glendore, which Howen gatheryd to hym great strength of Welshemen, and dyd moche harme to that countrey, not sparyng the kynges lordshyppes nor his people, and lastlye toke the sayde lorde Grey prisoner, and helde hym prisoner tyll, contrarye his wyll, he hadde maryed the sayde Howens daugher, after whiche matrimony fynysshed, he helde the said lorde stylle in Walyes, tyll he dyed, to the kynges great displeasure.

Wherfore the kynge with a stronge army spedde hym into Walys, for to subdue the sayde Howan and his adherents; but whan the kynge with his power was entred y[e] countre, he with his fawtours fledde into the mountaynes and helde hym there, so that the kynge might nat wynne to hym without distruccyon of his hoost; wherfore finally, by y[e] aduyce of his lords, he retournyd into Englande for that season.[2]

Other than agreeing on the main protagonists involved (Owain Glyndŵr, King Henry IV, and Reginald Grey of Ruthin), there are few points on which these two chroniclers concur; certainly, the role of each of these individuals in the start of the troubles is presented differently. The author of the *Historia vitae* points the blame squarely at Reginald Lord Grey, who is portrayed as a trickster and troublemaker, who purposefully sows the seeds of discord via several calculating plots. Henry IV and Owain Glyndŵr both emerge as innocent victims, and the events that follow are a "hateful" (*execrabili* [Item 28.1]) product of Grey's plot. In the *Historia vitae*, Owain Glyndŵr is a well regarded individual; indeed he is referred to as a "handsome squire" (*armiger formosus* [Item 28.5]). Owain Glyndŵr's status is recognized, albeit from an English perspective, and Henry IV's subsequent consideration of what to do with the Welshman is portrayed as carefully deliberated: if the king's choices led to death and destruction, then his guilt, if any, lies in his susceptibility to Grey's misinformation. The image of the king "considering these things in silence for a time afterwards" creates a moment of quiet before the narrative of the violence in Wales, and a humanizing image of a king faced with a tough decision. By contrast, Fabyan portrays Owain as entirely at fault for the start of the revolt, and indeed for the manner in which it continued thereafter. Fabyan's narrative focuses not on nuance and a sense of character, but on the violence and the recounting of a series of policies and events that were forcibly enacted: Lord Grey is captured and held for a long period of time; he is made to marry Owain's daughter under duress, which was to no avail as the wily Owain Glyndŵr had no intention of letting him go from the start. The marriage, conducted in captivity, reflects on the rather desperate assertiveness of Owain Glyndŵr in forming a prospectively useful marriage alliance. This sequence of events, which gets progressively worse, reveals Fabyan's view of the character of both Owain Glyndŵr and the revolt he leads, which is constructed around the actions of an individual acting to self-serving ends.

As such readings of the material demonstrate, the English chronicles offer a variety of information on the revolt of Owain Glyndŵr, with many providing unique perspectives not present in any other chronicle narrative. In some instance the events narrated are incorrect; Fabyan's account of the marriage of Reginald Lord Grey to one of Owain Glyndŵr's daughters, a point to which I will return in a moment, is one instance of this. For scholars wishing to construct empirical accounts of Owain Glyndŵr and the events of 1400 to c. 1415, there-

---

[2] Fabyan, *New Chronicles*, pp. 569–70.

fore, such chronicle accounts often prompt more questions than answers; details of exactly what was done, when, where, and by whom may not be attainable by a straight reading across a number of different chronicles. This is, of course, true of comparisons between many written sources, and it does not mean that the chronicles are of no historical value. Rather, it means that the material needs to be approached in a way that acknowledges this richness and recognises the historical specificity in which each source was produced. In other words, the chronicles need to be contextualized within their fifteenth- and sixteenth-century political and literary environments. It is essential, then, to understand the nature of chronicle writing in order to help decipher the history set within the narrative constraints of the chronicle form. Viewed as complex literary (not simple historical) artifacts, these chronicles richly reward their readers.

Authorship and Political Contexts

Fabyan's account of the marriage of Owain Glyndŵr's daughter to Reginald Grey of Ruthin, cited above, is an interesting initial example of some of the various narrative strategies adopted by the chroniclers to describe the events of the revolt, and how political concerns might affect the writing of the revolt over time. Although the chronicler Edward Hall, among others, agrees with Fabyan that the groom was Grey (Item 95.6–15), there are many other chroniclers, many of whom were writing contemporaneously to the Welsh revolt, who record that it was Edmund Mortimer (d.1409); these include the unknown writer of the *Historia vitae*, as well as Thomas Walsingham, the *Eulogium Continuation*, the *Dieulacres Chronicle*, Adam of Usk, and Holinshed.[3] The more reliable chroniclers unanimously show that it was Mortimer who married a daughter of Owain, and died during the rebellion. Grey was captured by Owain Glyndŵr, ransomed for 10,000 marks, and released in the autumn to live for several more decades (and to continue his engagement with Welsh outlawry; see Item 58).

The chronicle accounts of the marriage are an intriguing puzzle that can be approached from several scholarly directions. Via studies of the chronicle manuscripts one can trace the transmission of these inaccuracies. Indeed, we are now in a position to be able to observe the point at which the confusion between the two men arose in the manuscripts of the *Prose Brut* before being disseminated by copyists (see note to Item 71, lines 5–9). At the same time, the co-existence of the two traditions within the sources continued — including in the 1437 version of the *Prose Brut*, for example, which strikingly resolves the confusion by relating that both Mortimer and Grey married Owain Glyndŵr's unnamed daughters (Item 73.18–23).

However, when approached through a narratological lens, the Grey/Mortimer issue prompts questions as to the role of various narrative strategies in the communication of history within the chronicle form. In Edward Hall's *Chronicle*, written in the 1530s and 40s, there are several interesting narratological features with regards to the marriage of Owain Glyndŵr's daughter; he states:

> The lorde Grey beeyng not very riche nether of substance nor of frendes, consideryng this offer to be the onely waye of his releffe and deliverance, assented to his pleasure and maried the damosell. But this false father-in-lawe, this untrew, unhonest and perjured persone, kept hym with his wife still in captivitee till he dyed. (Item 95.11–15)

---

[3] See Items 28, 68, 72, 42, 62, 100, respectively.

Reginald Lord Grey and Owain Glyndŵr together are characterized in a manner that is unflattering to both of these individuals. Lord Grey is depicted as lacking in both judgement and close relationships, and his marriage to Owain Glyndŵr's daughter does not appear to do anything to change his situation. Hall's presentation of Grey as the groom is an intriguing narrative choice; Hall had clearly read and used a large number of earlier chronicle compositions written contemporaneously to the Welsh revolt. Thomas Walsingham, for instance, is acknowledged in-text many times in Hall's chronicle, showing that Hall had consulted previous chroniclers who offered the correct version of events, with Mortimer as the groom.[4]

However, Hall takes his discussion one step further, using techniques of narrative that effectively shut down any possibility of Edmund Mortimer's involvement in the marriage to Owain Glyndŵr's daughter. Immediately following his discussion of Grey's marriage he continues:

> And not content with this heynous offence, [Owain] made warre on Lorde Edmond Mortimer erle of Marche, and in his owne lordship of Wigmore, where in a conflict he slewe many of th'erles men and toke hym prisoner, and feteryng hym in chaynes, cast hym in a depe and miserable dongeon. The kyng was requyred to purchase his delyverance by diverse of the nobilitie, but he could not heare on that syde, rather he would and wished al his linage in heven. For then his title had been out of all doubt and question, and so upon this cause as you heare, after ensued great sedicion. (Item 95.15–22)

Hall's positioning of this episode directly after Grey's marriage to Owain Glyndŵr's daughter emphasises that Edmund Mortimer was in no way involved; indeed he is firmly placed away from the scene of the marriage.

Moreover, there are further discrepancies in Hall's narrative: the titles attached to Mortimer are incorrect; he was not the Earl of March. Hall records on multiple occasions in his revolt narratives, "Edmond Mortimer erle of Marche and Ulster" (see, e.g., Item 95.156–57). These titles are the product of the conflation of Edmund Mortimer and his nephew of the same name, who was indeed the earl of March. While the elder Edmund Mortimer (d. 1409) joined Owain Glyndŵr after his capture in 1402, the younger Edmund Mortimer, the earl of March (d. 1425), along with his brother Roger, was kept as a royal ward in Windsor Castle for much of his youth. Though this merger can in part be explained by the confusion caused by their shared name, for Hall there could be significant benefits to maintaining the confusion even if he was aware of their separate identities: it could be a useful strategy for negotiating the issue of the role of the Mortimer family in the revolt narratives. On his death in 1425 the title and estates of Edmund, the earl of March, passed to the son of his sister Anne Mortimer, Richard, duke of York, who became the father of Edward IV and grandfather of Elizabeth of York, the wife of Henry VII. At the start of his narrative of Henry IV's reign, in fact, Hall provides the genealogical line from Edward III, via the Mor-

---

[4] For further discussion of Walsingham as a source for later chroniclers such as Hall, Holinshed and Stow, see *Chronica Maiora*, ed. Clark, p. 1, and Marchant, "Cosmos and History." There are notable similarities, for instance, in the language of Hall's and Walsingham's descriptions of the Battle of Shrewsbury in 1403, especially in their descriptions of Henry IV's praises to God after the battle, and Douglas' injuring of a testicle. Compare Hall's *Chronicle*, pp. 30–31, with Walsingham's *Annales Henrici Quarti* edited by Riley in *Johannis de Trokelowe et al.*, 2.362–68. See also a useful discussion by Henry Ansgar Kelly, *Divine Providence*, p. 114.

timer family, to Henry VII.[5] Hall makes it clear that John of Gaunt, Henry IV's father, was the younger brother of Lionel, duke of Clarence, from whom the Mortimer family were descended.[6] Further, Hall states that the Mortimer family, and Edmund earl of March (d. 1425) in particular, had a better claim to the English crown. Hall records that Henry IV knew this, "and wished al his linage in heuen," thus cleverly blackening even further the name of the usurper of Edward III's lineage, and furthering the impression that the fifteenth century as a whole was a time of constant treachery and warfare between usurping kings and overmighty magnates, only corrected by the Tudors.

The merging of the two Mortimers has numerous implications for Hall's narratives of the Welsh revolt. Hall confirms that Owain Glyndŵr captured Mortimer. However, after Henry IV refused to pay his ransom, Mortimer was "delivered oute of the captivitie of Owen Glendor" by the Percy family, who sought to depose Henry IV and crown Edmund Mortimer (Item 95.122). Hall adamantly rejects the notion that Mortimer was involved in the *Tripartite Indenture* (Item 47) and hence formed any alliance with Owain Glyndŵr or the Percy families:

> the erle of Marche was ever kepte in the courte under suche a keper that he could nether doo or attempte any thyng agaynste the kyng without his knowledge, and dyed without issue, levyng his righte title and interest to Anne his sister and heyre, maried to Rycharde erle of Cambrige father to the duke of Yorke, whose offspryng in continuaunce of tyme, obteygned the game and gat the garland. (Item 95.145–50)

It is, of course, possible that Hall was as confused as everyone else on the matter; however, within a narratological framework, the creation of a new, composite character, can also be read as an ingenious narrative strategy implemented by Hall to deal with the complication of changes within the political sphere. The result is the creation of a new character, formed out of the selected desirable elements of the two Edmund Mortimers, giving us a sympathetically portrayed character for a narrative about a man who is noble, wronged, and long-suffering.

An analysis of the nuances or shifts in particular details narrated in the chronicles can thus reveal wider patterns at play; the transition between Edmund Mortimer and Reginald Lord Grey, or indeed chroniclers' silences on the marriage, provides an example of how changes in politics can have an impact on particular aspects of the revolt narratives over time. In this instance, changes in political alignments have direct implications for why and how particular individuals are depicted as being involved in the events of the chronicle. However, politics, or indeed the views of royalty, provide only one necessary consideration for the reader of this material; chroniclers had to negotiate many different and sometimes conflicting opinions within their narratives in order to please a whole range of individuals, including patrons and family, as well as members of their various communities. As a result, an analysis of the known biographical information on the authors, their possible participation in politics through attachment to the royal court or through their families, and their affiliations with particular monastic or learned communities not only aids in an understanding of the text's relationship to the political sphere, but also points to why particular viewpoints exist in the various narratives.

Unfortunately, collecting information about a chronicler's background is frequently easier said than done. While many of the chronicles in this collection have identified authors, others

---

[5] Hall, *Chronicle*, p. 2.

[6] Hall, *Chronicle*, pp. 2–3.

do not. A significant number of chronicles of the early fifteenth-century were composed by monks, such as the *Dieulacres Chronicle* (Item 42) and the *Historia Vitae* (Item 28). In these instances the place of composition might be known, but not the individual author within the community. The *Dieulacres Chronicle* was compiled at the Cistercian abbey of Dieulacres in Staffordshire, sometime around the year 1413, by two unknown authors.[7] Similarly, the *Historia Vitae* is thought to have been produced in two sections by at least two chroniclers at the abbey of Evesham, in Worcestershire, by 1403. On the other hand, both the author and the place or institution at which the *Eulogium Continuation* was composed are strongly disputed.

Amongst the identified authors are chroniclers such as Thomas Walsingham (c.1422 [Item 68]), John Rous (d. c.1492 [Item 87]), and Edward Hall (d. 1547 [Item 95]), to name only three. While we do not have insight into how these individuals felt and thought (insight that might be gained, to some extent, through such media as letters and diaries), we do know something of the major life experiences of these individuals through an examination of historical records, and sometimes what they say of themselves in their own writings. For instance, records of the life-events that took place between Thomas Walsingham's birth at Walsingham in Norfolk, England, in the 1350s or 60s and his death in 1422, reveal decidedly little of the man himself other than his place within the community of monks at the Abbey of St. Albans in Hertfordshire. In the *Liber Benefactorum*, which Walsingham himself compiled in 1380, Walsingham is listed as being twentieth in rank out of a community of around sixty monks.[8] Other records suggest that Walsingham was ordained as a priest in September 1364, and attended university at Oxford, finishing c.1376. After university, Walsingham devoted himself to the scriptorium at St. Albans, producing several chronicles and commentaries on classical authors, including Seneca. Walsingham seems to have stayed at St. Albans for his entire life, except between 1394 and 1400, when he served as prior at Wymondham,[9] a priory of St. Albans located nine miles from the city of Norwich.[10]

Such information, while scant, does provide a framework through which to tease out possible influences on Walsingham's depiction of the revolt of Owain Glyndŵr. Elsewhere, I have argued that Walsingham's depictions of Wales and the Welsh in his narratives of the revolt derive their meaning from St. Albans and its position relative to London and to Wales, and its social, patronage, political, and economic networks.[11] Walsingham wrote his chronicle within the walls of the Benedictine abbey of St. Albans in Hertfordshire, and certainly many of his views can be considered the product of his monastic community. St. Albans had strong ties with English royalty and received royal patronage.[12] While this con

---

[7] *Chronicle of Dieulacres Abbey*, ed. Clarke and Galbraith, p. 131.

[8] London, British Library, MS Cotton Nero D.vii, fol. 82v; compare Clark, "Thomas Walsingham," p. 838. David Knowles and R. Neville Hadcock report that in 1396 there were 51 monks at St. Albans (*Medieval Religious Houses*, p. 74).

[9] Walsingham, *Gesta Abbatum Monasterii Sancti Albani*, 3.436. See also Kingsford for details of the intrigue surrounding Walsingham's semi-banishment to Wymondham because of his tenuous relationship with the then Abbot Thomas de la Mare (*English Historical Literature*, p. 12).

[10] Knowles, *Religious Orders*, p. 41.

[11] Marchant, "*In Loco Amoenissimo*."

[12] Account rolls, letters, registers, and records of burials for the monks reveal strong links to royalty. Members of the community, particularly those who held the position of abbot, were drawn from the most influential and rich baronial families in England; see Clark, "Thomas Walsingham Reconsidered."

nection had the advantage of providing Walsingham with detailed information concerning events that were currently unfolding, including the revolt in Wales, it did assume a certain level of expectation, as patronage and prestige from wealthy benefactors were at stake for the whole abbey community — so much so, that the scholar Antonia Gransden refers to Walsingham rather unflatteringly as "his community's mouthpiece."[13] Certainly, Walsingham's revolt narratives contain recognizable Lancastrian elements; the Welsh revolt is portrayed as disruptive, violent, and unnecessary. Henry IV's supporters are depicted favorably. Reginald Lord Grey, for instance, emerges here as an innocent party in the initiation of the revolt.[14]

Like Thomas Walsingham, many of the fifteenth-century English chroniclers were writing from within monastic houses, although many of these authors remain unnamed. The *Eulogium Continuation* (Item 72), for example, has no identified author and indeed even its place of composition is debated; however, it is most likely the work of a monk of the Franciscan order (otherwise known as the Minorite Friars), based either at Canterbury, or at Greyfriars in London; there is a recognisable Franciscan voice in the chronicle. In the early years of Henry IV's reign, the Franciscans were embroiled in controversy; the order was well favored by Richard II, and their loyalty to him continued after his deposition. Many monks were arrested and some executed for their part in apparent heresy, the use of black magic, and rebellion, with several monks proclaiming Richard to be alive and plotting to overthrow the new king.[15] In the year 1402 alone the *Eulogium Continuation* records no fewer than twelve executions of Franciscan monks.[16]

It is quite probably because of the order's ambivalence towards the current king, and because several Welsh Franciscan monasteries were favorable to Owain Glyndŵr, that the Welsh revolt is presented in fairly sympathetic terms in the *Eulogium Continuation*. The narrative starts with an account of Parliament refusing to listen to a warning not to ignore the legal complaint issued by Owain Glyndŵr, to which Parliament responds (now somewhat famously) that they do not care about "barefooted buffoons" (Item 72.5–6). The revolt is thereby framed with a notion that it was directly caused by legitimate grievances on Owain Glyndŵr's part, rather than by the Welshman's aggressive ambitions, which is the central feature of Thomas Walsingham's depiction. Furthermore, the author of the *Eulogium Continuation* puts forward the complainant's nationality as an important factor determining how Owain Glyndŵr's petition was regarded by Parliament. Interestingly, the first account of

---

For registers, see London, British Library MS Harley 602 and Cambridge University Library MS Ee.4.20. For registers of burials, see London, British Library MS Harley 3775, fols. 129r–37r.

[13] "Chronicles of Medieval England and Scotland," p. 210.

[14] On Grey's culpability, see Davies, *Revolt*, p. 102.

[15] For further discussion, see McNiven, *Heresy and Politics*; and McNiven, "Rebellion, Sedition and the Legend of Richard II's Survival."

[16] According to the *Eulogium Continuation* eight friars were hanged in a location not specified (ed. Haydon, 3.389); a monk at Aylesbury for treason (p. 390); a Friar Minor of Leicester and some others hanged at Tyburn (3.393); and two friars executed at Lichfield (3.393). Furthermore, Thomas Walsingham describes how a diabolic apparition appeared in Danbury in Essex in the form of a Minorite Friar (Walsingham, *Historia Anglicana*, 2.249). Several chroniclers, including Walsingham, link the Minorites to the Welsh rebellion, stating that the Friars favored the Welsh cause (Walsingham, *Historia Anglicana*, 2.251).

violence in the *Eulogium Continuation* has Henry IV as the aggressor, and the victims are the Franciscan monks of the monastery of Llanfaes.[17]

The Generic Conventions of Chronicles

Questions of authorship are not limited to the identification of the chroniclers and their communities, but include questions about the authors' participation in the wider tradition of historical writing. This includes consideration of the generic conventions of chronicles, and also an examination of how chroniclers engaged with one another's narratives. What, then, is a chronicle? Chronicles are a form of historical writing with several defining characteristics, including a narrative that is tightly structured in a chronological arrangement, and a narrating voice that is (or presents itself as) impersonal and unemotional in style.[18] The importance of time and chronology in structuring chronicle narrative was recognized and documented throughout the Middle Ages.[19] For example, Gervase of Canterbury (d. c.1210) explains,

> A chronicle . . . reckons the years, months and Kalends from the Incarnation of our Lord, briefly tells of the deeds of kings and princes which happened at those times, besides recording any portents, miracles or other events.[20]

Adherence to a chronological organization was a fundamental generic marker, as is acknowledged by the term "chronicle" itself, taken from the Greek χρόνος (*khronos*), meaning "time." There are a number of strategies used to reckon time in chronicles; in some instances each new year is signaled by the regnal date, but more often reference is made to the *anno Domini* [year of the Lord] date: events of the year are then narrated sequentially in order of their occurrence and are arranged into discrete paragraph entries. In most cases, new events are introduced via a temporal expression, such as "meanwhile," "at the same time," or "this year." The life of Christ was central to salvation history, and the application of an *anno Domini* chronological sequence, coupled with temporal markers, provided a clear link between events of the Bible and individuals of the contemporary era. The arrangement of the narrative in chronological fashion meanwhile reflected a historical reality, at least in theory, with events documented one after the other, connected only by their proximity in time.

Time and chronology thus have significant implications for the narrative structure of chronicles. The *Historia Anglicana* of Thomas Walsingham, for instance, presents a structure that is temporally overt. That is, it has a structure in which the marking of time is a dominant narrative feature. The following summary, showing the chronological arrangement of unrelated events, covers the period from the initiation of the Welsh revolt in September 1400 to the capture of Edmund Mortimer at the Battle of Bryn Glas in June 1402. The events are summarized, with those not included in this book in square brackets. The overt chronological references are indicated in boldface.

---

[17] Item 72.7–14. The monks of Llanfaes in Anglesey were one of the first groups to pledge their support to the Welsh revolt and were subsequently one of the first targets of the English expedition into Wales in 1401; see Williams, *Welsh Church*, p. 219.

[18] For a full examination of chronicle form, see my forthcoming monograph on Owain Glyndŵr (York Medieval Press, c.2014). See also Dumville, "What is a Chronicle?" and Given-Wilson, *Chronicles*.

[19] See the discussion by Given-Wilson, *Chronicles*, pp. 113–27.

[20] *Historical Works*, 1.87.

In the meantime, Owain Glyndŵr rebels after a dispute with Lord Grey; the king invades Wales, lays waste to the land and returns to England (see Item 68.2–14).
[**This year** the bishop of Bath died. **At the same time** the emperor of Constantinople visited London. The bishop of Carlisle was removed to another bishopric.]
[**In 1401** a parliament was held in London; a statute against the Lollards was passed; a pseudo-priest was executed; the king of Letto was killed in battle. **On April 8** Thomas Beauchamp, earl of Warwick, died. **In the same year** the bishop of Bethlehem and Rochester died. Queen Isabella is returned to France.]
Also at this time Owain Glyndŵr gathered a mob of Welshmen and devastated the land, taking some men captive and killing others (see Item 68.15–17)
[Henry IV is nearly killed by a metal instrument placed in his bed.]
In March 1402 a comet appeared and is described as a portent of bloodshed.
At this time Owain Glyndŵr attacked the lands of Lord Grey. Lord Grey was captured and very many of his men killed. Welsh pride and madness is stirred, "as will appear in later narrative" (see Item 68.18–31).
[**Around Pentecost** a plot to kill Henry IV is discovered; a priest is executed for his role. **Not long after**, the prior of Launde is executed; a Franciscan monk is executed for treason; Roger Clarendon, his squire, and his valet are executed for treason. A devil appeared in a church at Dunbury in Essex **on the feast of Corpus Christi at the hour of Vespers. At the same hour** there was a terrible storm and the church was destroyed.]
It was around this time that Owain Glyndŵr intensified his attacks into Herefordshire. Edmund Mortimer was defeated and captured at the Battle of Bryn Glas (see Item 68.33–42).

This summary well illustrates the narrative impact of the overt temporal anchoring. It is clear from this example that chronicles that explicitly calculate time place limitations on the narratives they contain. Regardless of whether the entry is comprised of a pithy single line or of multiple sentences that contain rich imagery, the chronicle narrative is thereby arranged in piecemeal fragments. In the present case this makes for short, staccato entries on the revolt of Owain Glyndŵr, and Walsingham's narrative is typical of the overtly temporal chronicles under consideration in this book. For instance, the *Eulogium Continuation* (Item 72) provides a total of twelve passages on the revolt of Owain Glyndŵr, distributed over twenty pages in the Rolls Series edition. In contrast, an examination of the narrative for the same time frame in Edward Hall's *Chronicle* reveals a very different structural arrangement. The beginning of Hall's temporally covert narrative records in one paragraph under the first year of Henry IV's reign the information covered in nineteen separate entries over three years in Thomas Walsingham's chronicle (see Item 95.1–22). As a result, chronology, representations of time, and establishing a sense of duration do not appear as important to Hall's structural arrangement as they are for Walsingham. In Hall's chronicle, it is the historical subject rather than the acknowledgement of time that is the primary structural concern of his narrative. In narratological terms, this makes for larger, arguably more developed discussion of the revolt. Walsingham keeps a tighter chronology, but as a result he loses narrative flow. Hall's is one of several temporally covert chronicles in the present volume; others include John Rous's *Historia regum Angliae* (Item 87), John Capgrave's *Liber de Illustribus* (Item 81), and Polydore Vergil's *Historia Anglica* (Item 97). Such chronicles, while still maintaining a chronological arrangement, are not completely restricted by it. They favor other narrative concerns.

The temporal elements of chronicles have substantial implications for how meaning and significance are conveyed. For instance, many of the chronicles in this volume report that a comet appeared around the year 1402. Comets were not merely neutral objects in medieval thought, but were loaded with divinatory significance. They were frequently associated with rebellions and had long been considered signs of impending war, death, famine, and plague.[21] Many chroniclers do not state the exact event that this comet was thought to forewarn. The *Prose Brut*, for instance, states of the comet:

> The iij[de] yere off Kynge Henry, anon after Cristemasse wasse seen and appered a sterre in the weste whoos flames & bemes ascended vpwarde, that wasse called the blasynge sterre, and be clerkes yt wasse called stella commata.[22]

Here there is only an indirect syntactic connection between the appearance of the comet and events that it may have signified. The significance of the comet is gained through a reading of the material that surrounds it; preceding the comet's appearance is an account of an elderly Franciscan friar accused of speaking badly against the king, and following the announcement of the comet is an entry that discusses the grievances people felt against Henry IV. The description of the comet is, in fact, bracketed by expressions of discontent against King Henry, and it is not a great interpretive stretch to assume that this comet is related to future rebellions, most likely to occur in the west of the British Isles. Here, the significance of the comet is conveyed by paratactic means, according to the sequential arrangement of the material. However, this points to a need to consider the surrounding material, by examining the chronicle as a whole, rather than as isolated fragments.

One striking feature of many of the chronicles in this volume is the lack of a conclusion to the revolt. With the exception of the *Dieulacres* and the *Historia Vitae*, as their narratives cease in 1403, all of the chronicles under examination had the means to provide a conclusion to the revolt, since they were either actively composing at the time the revolt ceased or they were not yet begun. The *Eulogium Continuation*, for instance, leaves its narrative of the revolt in 1405 with an entry that first describes how Henry IV freed Coity Castle in south Wales and then records that the king had his baggage and jewels stolen from him by the Welsh (see Item 72.57–58). The loss of the king's personal possessions to his enemies is an intriguing place to cease the *Continuation's* revolt narratives; not only would this have been a potential source of embarrassment for Henry IV, but it also leaves the narrative with the Welsh holding the upper hand. Thomas Walsingham's *Historia Anglicana* and Capgrave's *Abbreuiacion* also conclude their revolt narratives with Owain Glyndŵr in control of Wales; both abruptly end their narrative with an account of the siege of Aberystwyth Castle in 1407.[23] The 1437 version of the *Prose Brut* and Robert Fabyan end their revolt narratives with the execution of Rhys

---

[21] Comets, meteors, and the like were considered to be natural phenomena that were in the wrong place, as is described in chapter 30, "Of the fyre and of the sterres that seme to falle," of Caxton's *Mirrour of the World*, p. 122.

[22] *English Chronicle*, ed. Marx, p. 29.

[23] "In this summer the Lord Henry, Prince of Wales, took by siege the castle of Aberystwyth; but not long after, Owain Glyndŵr deceitfully entered it, and placed new guardians" (Walsingham, *Historia Anglicana*, 2.277; Capgrave, *Abbreuiacion of Cronicles*, p. 232).

Ddu, Owain's captain, in 1410.[24] Exactly why these chronicles leave their narrative of the Welsh revolt at these points is not clear. Fabyan wrote his *New Chronicles* around the year 1504, almost ninety years after the rebellion had ceased and Owain Glyndŵr was long dead, yet he leaves the story of Owain Glyndŵr's revolt open. There are several possible explanations: it could be that he somehow lacked any of the many available sources that referred to its conclusion or it could be a narratological choice.

In his *Liber de Illustribus Henricis*, to take a different example, John Capgrave appears to actively construct an open-endedness to his narrative of the Welsh revolt. Completed around the year 1446 and presented to Henry VI, Capgrave, in his only entry on the revolt in the *Liber*, records:

> And after these things the same king [Henry IV] had certain worries of his mind with one squire of Richard, the earl of Arundel, called Glyndŵr, whom the king rather often sought and never found. For wandering about in the mountains and caverns of Wales, he never had a certain location nor could he be captured by anyone. (Item 81)

It is the lack of conclusion to the revolt that dominates the entire entry. The resultant image is one of Owain Glyndŵr still "wandering about" (*circumvagans*) in an imagined landscape of a Wales dominated by timeless mountains and caverns. Here, Capgrave's denial of narrative closure invites readers to imagine Owain Glyndŵr's continued presence in the wild, beyond the end of his narrative. Adam of Usk too provides a narrative ending to the revolt that seeds a degree of uncertainty. Adam records under the year 1415 that,

> After four years in hiding from the king and kingdom, Owain Glyndŵr died, and was buried by his followers in the darkness of night. His grave was discovered by his enemies, however, so he had to be re-buried, though it is impossible to discover where it was laid. (Item 67)

After a period of lying low, the rebel leader is dead. However, this certainty is undercut by Adam's subsequent report of the movement of his burial site to an unspecified location; this lack of solid and tangible evidence that Owain Glyndŵr was actually dead therefore generates a degree of open-endedness.[25] It is also, as Elissa Henken has documented, a key factor that contributes to the casting of Owain Glyndŵr into the role of the redeemer hero within the Welsh tradition.[26] As Henken comments, "the unknown grave leaves open possibilities for the hero. If the grave cannot be found, perhaps the hero does not need one."[27]

When an ending to the revolt is provided, it tends to focus on the death of Owain Glyndŵr. Polydore Vergil, Edward Hall, and Ralph Holinshed are amongst those chroniclers who describe the manner of Owain Glyndŵr's death, particularly the physical details, in-

---

[24] *English Chronicle*, ed. Marx, p. 39; Robert Fabyan, *The Newe Cronycles*, p. 576, both of which name him "Rhys ap Ddu." Rhys Ddu's full Welsh name was Rhys ap Gruffudd ap Llywelyn ab Ieuan; on him, see especially *Annales Oweni Glyndwr*, Item 70.38–46 and notes.

[25] Indeed, Owain Glyndŵr's final burial place is still the source of endless fascination and debate. See Davies, *Revolt*, p. 327; Phillips, "When Did Owain Glyn Dŵr Die?"

[26] Henken, *National Redeemer*, pp. 64–70.

[27] Henken, *National Redeemer*, p. 69.

cluding Owain's bodily suffering and starvation. Holinshed, closely echoing Hall (Item 95.179–81), records that Owain Glyndŵr, "lacking meat to susteine nature, for meere hunger and lacke of food, miserablie pined awaie and died" (Item 100.288–89). Polydore Vergil similarly resolves his narrative by stating that Owain Glyndŵr's "life had an ending worthy of his deeds. Reduced to extreme poverty, he died a wretched death" (Item 97.22–23). These three chroniclers cast Owain Glyndŵr's uncomfortable end as divine retribution for his guilty and rebellious actions.

The mode of narration used by the chroniclers to describe the events that occurred is an important generic marker. When recording his account of the initiation of the Welsh revolt, Polydore Vergil, writing around 1513, uses language meant to construct his position as narrator as covert and unobtrusive:

> Meanwhile, so there would be no hope for quiet, Wales, ever prone to new risings, was troubled by the mutual bickering of certain nobles and seemed almost to look towards rebellion. When the king found this out, he hastened there with an army, and was scarce two days away when the terrified Welsh swiftly stole away to their forests and marshes, no doubt despairing that they could resist the royal forces. But this flight was not the salvation of them all, since some were captured there and suffered their deserved comeuppance. (Item 97.1–6)

Vergil's employment of a third-person mode of narration, a combination of past tenses, and fairly simple sentence structures is a typical mode of chronicle narration and establishes an authoritative narrative voice, one without immediately obvious personal characteristics as the narrators construct distance between themselves and the material that they record. The narrating voice consistently presents itself as heterodiegetic (outside of the textual world), empirical and impersonal. In fact, it is none of these things. Close inspection reveals its perspective and cultural prejudices in such terms as "ever prone to new risings," "terrified," "stole away," "despairing," and especially "suffered their deserved comeuppance." The essential point is that the pretence of neutrality aims to naturalize these value judgements.

Within the generic conventions of chronicles, a narrative was nevertheless envisioned as objective (rather than subjective), observed (rather than engaged in), and formulaic (rather than free). Chronicles and chronicle writing were widely considered in the medieval era to be a record of humanity's progress towards divine salvation in light of the fall of humankind in the Garden of Eden.[28] For this reason, the chronicler's main purpose was to observe the world and to record events that were deemed important to this progress. Events of national and universal importance, as well as natural and supernatural phenomena such as the sightings of comets and devils, were considered key to understanding the world and humanity's place within it. While maintaining covert narration, chroniclers employed various methods to make the historical narrative vivid and persuasive; putative eyewitness accounts and quotations of direct speech are two such devices used by chroniclers.[29] These strategies, frequently used in conjunction with each other, were an important element in the recounting of events, providing the appearance of authority and an impression of accuracy.

---

[28] For further discussion see Reeves, "Originality and Influence of Joachim of Fiore," pp. 269–87.

[29] See for instance the *Eulogium Continuation* (Item 72.44–51), in which Owain Glyndŵr addresses a Franciscan Friar in the town of Cardiff.

The different modes of narration used by the chroniclers have profound implications on the representation of the revolt of Owain Glyndŵr and in particular on ways the reader is guided through the materials that are presented. While there were certain generic conventions to which a chronicler needed to adhere, there was scope for individuality. Although covert narration is the dominant mode for chronicles, there are frequent episodes in which the narrator is overt, and other modes of narration are used. The first- and second-person pronouns (we, our, and you, both singular and plural) occur throughout the chronicle narratives, and indeed there are several examples in the present volume. The first person singular "I" is not commonplace; however, the chronicle of Adam of Usk is unusual in this regard: he frequently refers to himself within his chronicle and records events which he witnessed personally or in which he took part.[30] This is a significant departure from the more usual understanding of the role of the chronicler, which was to record events of national and world significance and to do so in an unobtrusive and impersonal way. Adam narrates the capture of Mortimer in the following manner:

> On the feast of St. Alban, a fierce battle was fought near Knighton in Wales between the English under Sir Edmund Mortimer and the Welsh under Owain Glyndŵr, in which as many as eight thousand persons died miserable deaths before Owain emerged victorious. And it grieves me to relate that this Edmund, my lord, by whose father, the lord of Usk, I was supported at the schools, was by the fortunes of war taken captive. (Item 62.1–5)

In this account, Adam emphasizes his personal and emotional connection to the narrative subject through the use of the first person. Here, and in Adam's composition more broadly, we see the presence of a narrating ego. He does employ the more usual covert modes of narration, although these are interspersed with moments of overt narration in which the account is focalized through Adam himself. However, despite the numerous points of originality presented in his chronicle, which is particularly rich in its record of the Welsh revolt, Adam of Usk was to have no influence on the next generation of chroniclers. His chronicle, of which there is only one known manuscript, was not known to be in circulation in the fifteenth and sixteenth centuries.[31]

Reading through the collection of extracts in this volume, similarities among various chronicles are apparent, often as the result of direct or indirect influence. For instance, much of *An English Chronicle*'s narrative of the Welsh revolt, written sometime around 1460, relies heavily upon the earlier *Eulogium Continuation*, written sometime before 1428. Integrated throughout most of our chronicle narratives are echoes of the voices of other chroniclers: in medieval historiography, chroniclers frequently consulted, replicated, and re-

---

[30] For a fuller discussion of the unique style of Adam of Usk, see my "'Adam, you are in a labyrinth'."

[31] An analysis of the full manuscript of Adam of Usk's chronicle has only recently been possible; at some unknown point between the seventeenth and nineteenth centuries the Chronicle was split into two distinct sections; the second section was only rediscovered in 1885 at Belvoir Castle. Indeed, evidence suggests that Adam may have decided that he did not want his chronicle to be read or used by other chroniclers. He states under his discussion of the year 1400 that, "I should hate for this account of my present follies to be seen during my lifetime" (Adam of Usk, *Chronicle*, ed. Given-Wilson, p. 119; see also pp. xxxviii–xlii).

worked existing chronicle compositions; changes could involve a slight or substantial reorientation or the interpolation or excision of material large and small.[32]

Comparisons between the accounts of three different chronicles all describing the arrival of the French at Milford Haven to supply much-needed aid to Owain Glyndŵr reveal just such a pattern of narrative transmission. Thomas Walsingham, writing sometime before the year 1420, states:

> It was about this time [August 1405] that the French, having made huge preparations, came to the aid of Owain Glyndŵr with a hundred and forty ships, and landed in the harbour of Milford, though they had first lost almost all their horses because of the lack of fresh water. (Item 68.113–15)

John Capgrave's narrative, composed in the early 1460s records:

> In þis tyme a hundred schippis and xl sailed oute of Frauns into Wales, for to help Howen Glendor. They cam into Mylforth Haue; but al her hors were ded or thei cam there for defaute of fresch water.[33]

Lastly, Raphael Holinshed's *Chronicles*, first published in 1577, says:

> In the meane time, the French king had appointed one of the marshals of France called Montmerancie, and the master of his crosbowes, with twelve thousand men to saile into Wales to aid Owen Glendouer. They tooke shipping at Brest, and having the wind prosperous, landed at Milford haven, with an hundred and fourtie ships, as Thomas Walsingham saith, though Enguerant de Monstrellet maketh mention but of an hundred and twentie. (Item 100.214–20)

There are clear parallels between these three extracts. Capgrave's dependence on the earlier narrative of Thomas Walsingham is evident; it appears that Capgrave simply translates the earlier material from the Latin to include it in his account. Moreover, Capgrave retains Thomas Walsingham's entire narrative framework, using ten of the fourteen possible narrative entries on the Welsh revolt contained within Thomas Waslingham's *Historia Anglicana* in exactly the same order. Regardless, Walsingham is not named once by Capgrave, but rather exists silently in the narrative. In contrast Holinshed refers both to Thomas Walsingham and to the French chronicler Enguerrand de Monstrelet (d. 1453). Holinshed refers to many named and unnamed chronicles throughout his chronicle. While in the earlier chroniclers the narrator appears as the master of a relatively diffuse and anonymous tradition, the narrating voice of the sixteenth-century chroniclers tends to be more overtly connected to a written culture that explicitly names its sources.

To end the discussion let us return to the marriage of Owain Glyndŵr's daughter to either Edmund Mortimer or Reginald Grey discussed at the beginning of this essay. As I have argued, Hall's acceptance of the confusion of the two men — whether strategically conscious

---

[32] For a further discussion, see Constable, "Forgery and Plagiarism"; Hathaway, "*Compilatio*"; Minnis, "Late-Medieval Discussions of *Compilatio*."

[33] Capgrave, *Abbreuiacion of Cronicles*, p. 230.

or not — results in the politically convenient creation of a new Reginald Lord Grey, but also of a new hybrid character, who can function as a substitute for Edmund Mortimer, himself now a member of the royal line. Still other chroniclers writing under the York and Tudor monarchs favored a solution of complete silence on the matter of the marriage, a significant disengagement from earlier narratives.[34] Against this background, Holinshed's depiction of Edmund Mortimer is an outlying case. Holinshed's Mortimer is an uneasy mix of both Walsingham's and Hall's earlier versions. For instance, of the marriage narratives, Holinshed records:

> Edmund Mortimer earle of Marche, prisoner with Owen Glendouer, whether for irkesomnesse of cruell captivitie, or feare of death, or for what other cause, it is uncertaine, agreed to take part with Owen, against the King of England, and tooke to wife the daughter of the said Owen. (Item 100.77–80)

Here, and indeed throughout the revolt narratives, Holinshed's depiction of Edmund Mortimer is much more akin to that of the fifteenth-century chronicles, although the title of Earl of March is a notable addition.[35] Holinshed's apparent reluctance to deviate too far from Walsingham, whom he claims as his source, while adding several important new interpretations from Hall's account thus makes his narrative one of ingeniously balanced tensions that ultimately exerted a subtle, but important influence on popular depictions of these individuals. This example from Holinshed illustrates the need to consider and contextualize each chronicle individually. Though all of these chronicles draw on material from elsewhere, this material is nonetheless made to signify in new ways in its new contexts.

Conclusions

The material concerning the revolt of Owain Glyndŵr contained within these chronicles is rich and illuminating, although, as has been shown, the information they convey needs to be approached critically. It is important to note that there are multiple voices both literary and extraliterary in any chronicle text: the chroniclers themselves, their communities, and other chroniclers to name only a few. Such voices influence what is recorded and indeed how information concerning the Welsh revolt is narrated. These texts need to be individually contextualized in a way that recognizes the generic conventions within which they operate, and there are various narrative devices that must be understood in order to fully appreciate the narrative complexity of the chronicles. Though they belong to history, the chronicles cannot be read without attention to the dynamics of narrative. Through such a lens the English chronicles amply repay a close and sympathetic reading, both as sources for the revolt of Owain Glyndŵr, and as intriguing narrative texts individually and collectively illuminating the complicated processes involved in constructing and reconstructing what we call history.

---

[34] Examples of chronicles that do not report a marriage include Capgrave's *Abbreuiacion of Cronicles*, Capgrave's *Liber de Illustribus Henricis* (Item 81), Polydore Vergil (Item 97), John Rous (Item 87), and the two versions of Hardyng's chronicle (Item 83).

[35] It was via Holinshed that the merged character of Edmund Mortimer, rebel and Earl of March, made its way into more popular forms of literature. In Shakespeare's *Henry IV Part One* he is referred to as the "Earl of March" and as the heir apparent to King Richard (I.iii.154–57; see also Item 101).

Castell Dinas Brân, east of Owain's estates around Glyndyfrdwy, looking northward toward Horse-shoe Pass in the direction of Ruthin.

WILLIAM ORAM
WHAT DID SHAKESPEARE MAKE OF OWAIN GLYNDŴR?

Shakespeare wrote the first part of *Henry IV* in 1595, almost two centuries after the events that the play chronicles, and his version of Owain Glyndŵr differs fundamentally from both the figure suggested by the Welsh sources and that in Holinshed's reworking of Hall's *Chronicles*, which provided his primary source. Taking a few hints from Holinshed, he makes the scene — and Glendower — largely out of whole cloth. As R. R. Davies recognized, "Shakespeare's Glendower is thoroughly grounded in Holinshed's account; but his portrait is shot through with insight, sympathy and a human warmth altogether lacking in the one-dimensional narratives of the historians. . . . It took the genius of an Englishman to create the first credible, even attractive characterization of the Welsh leader."[1]

In fact critics have argued over whether Glendower appears here as a charismatic leader or boastful comic figure,[2] and since Davies' study, critics have tended increasingly to focus discussions of Shakespeare's Glendower on English attitudes toward the Welsh and the Welsh language.[3] Thus an often-cited article by Terence Hawkes connects Glendower to the Welsh language (spoken and sung by his daughter in the second half of the scene), which questions the claims of Anglo-Saxon Britons to possess the single language and culture of the island.[4] Further, a number of critics have seen the treatment of Glendower as shadowing current events in Ireland. Christopher Highley, among others, argued that Shakespeare's account of Glendower was a way of talking about (and denigrating) the ongoing Irish rebellion of Hugh O'Neill, earl of Tyrone.[5]

The portrait of Glendower in Shakespeare's theater was bound to touch attitudes about the sixteenth-century Welsh and Elizabeth's troublesome Irish wars. But the connection doesn't really suggest why Shakespeare should have written *this* scene in *this* play. Why, to put it differently, should he have chosen to develop a few hints in Holinshed into a scene largely unnecessary to the political action of the play — and in a work largely concerned with the transformation of Prince Hal? To understand what Shakespeare makes of Glendower in this scene, it's important to consider his function in the economy of the play.

---

[1] Davies, *Revolt*, p. 329.

[2] For the disciplined leader, see Rees, "Shakespeare's Welshmen"; for the account of him as a comic figure see Zitner, "Staging the Occult in *1 Henry IV*." Highley believes that the scene "feminizes" Glendower in order to reassure its English audience about the Irish rebellion (*Spenser, Shakespeare and the Crisis in Ireland*, pp. 95–97).

[3] See especially Lloyd, *Speak it in Welsh*, pp. 1–45, and Schwyzer, "Thirteen Ways."

[4] Hawkes, "Bryn Glas."

[5] See Highley, *Spenser, Shakespeare and the Crisis in Ireland*, p. 97.

Glendower plays an important part in the symbolic geography of *1 Henry IV*, a geography that sets an English center of civility against the threat of civil war.[6] Henry's court lies in Westminster: it is the center of English rule and the opening speech of the opening scene suggests an almost desperate need to impose a rule that will enable the English — and the Welsh — to "march all one way." Henry IV has of course precipitated this breakdown of order by usurping the throne, and Shakespeare is explicit in pointing to the resultant chaos when he has both the Bishop of Carlisle and Richard II prophesy the coming civil wars.[7] The choice of Henry — and eventually, Prince Hal — as ruler is a choice of evils. But the centralizing drive of King Henry and his son is set against the tendency to split the kingdom into pieces, a tendency that Shakespeare dramatizes when Hotspur, Mortimer, and Glendower quarrel over the division of the spoils.

The primary opponents of the king are the Percies, who operate quite literally on the periphery of the realm. Hotspur and his backers embody an older English nobility that remained under the Tudors an old-fashioned, autonomous power, given (as Mervyn James has pointed out[8]) to notions of "honor" that conflicted with complete allegiance to English law. In using his fifteenth-century materials, Shakespeare sets up a characteristic Tudor tension between a centralizing government and recalcitrant older nobility — a tension largely resolved by Shakespeare's time in favor of the central government.

But where does Glendower sit in this division? He attempts to put himself *outside* the periphery of Henry's rule: he wants an independent kingdom and represents a different way of life with radically different attitudes toward what is fit and right. He is first referred to as the irregular and wild Glendower — *irregular* because he does not abide by the rules of civilized behavior. The first thing we hear about the Welsh is that, after the English defeat at Bryn Glas, their women have inflicted on the dead English "such misuse / Such beastly shameless transformation / . . . as may not be / Without much shame retold or spoken of" (*1 Henry IV* I.i.43–46). Earlier writers, starting with Walsingham's *St. Albans Chronicle* (Item 68.42–46 in this volume), are more explicit: the Welsh women have castrated and debased the English bodies. In the play Wales is thus treated as a civilization outside the norms of English society, one in which Welsh *women* perform outrageous acts against English *men*. The play's anthropology suggests an opposition between English civility and Welsh barbarism.

Yet, as Davies stresses, Shakespeare's Glendower is no barbarian. He mentions that he has been brought up in an English court and written English poetry, and the rest of the scene suggests that he is a capable and disciplined leader. The scene opposes Glendower to Hotspur, who challenges the Welsh leader repeatedly, seemingly unwilling to allow another alpha male in the room. Yet from the beginning Hotspur's claims to dominance get undercut. In the opening lines, Hotspur finds that he has forgotten the map of Britain and Glendower produces it. Twice in the negotiations that follow Hotspur picks a quarrel — about

---

[6] Marchant argues for the opposition of center and periphery in "Cosmos and History." Wales, she argues, is constructed as a barbarous place, where wild Welshwomen castrate the bodies of Englishmen and Glendower practices magical arts. As will be clear, I agree with her about many of these claims, although I think she tends to take too literally the theological rhetoric of the play. The language insisting that rebellion is unnatural comes from the mouths of particular characters, and serves their purposes.

[7] *Richard II* IV.i.116–49; V.i.55–68.

[8] James, "English Politics and the Concept of Honor."

Glendower's claim to be a magician, and on the division of the kingdom. And in both cases Glendower is willing to put aside his differences with Hotspur to let the conspirators move forward; it is Hotspur who jeopardizes the common goal by insisting on his own priorities.

The primary disagreement, which has drawn considerable attention, is Glendower's claim to be a magician, which Hotspur mocks with gleeful humor:

> GLEN.   I can call spirits from the vasty deep.
> HOT.   Why, so can I, or so can any man.
>   But will they come, when you do call for them? (Item 101.55–57)

Before taking Hotspur's side, one should remember that Glendower's claim would not have seemed entirely absurd. Mortimer speaks admiringly of Glendower's "strange concealments" (Item 101.167), which most commentators gloss as his magical arts,[9] and early in Elizabeth's reign John Jewel preached before the Queen on the evils of witchcraft.[10] Holinshed himself is equivocal about Glendower's claims. He writes that when Henry IV attempted to come to battle with Glendower in 1402, "he lost his labor; for Owen conveied himselfe out of the waie, into his knowen lurking places, and (as was thought) through art magike, he caused such foule weather of winds, tempest, raine, snow, and haile to be raised, for the annoiance of the kings armie, that the like had not beene heard of" (Item 100.64–68). "As was thought" leaves Holinshed neutral about the truth of Glendower's arts, but the enumeration of the various kinds of bad weather and the comment that "the like had not been heard of" gives rhetorical emphasis to the idea of Glendower's potency.[11] By contrast, Holinshed contemptuously dismisses the Welsh prophecies (Item 100.121–26). Shakespeare takes the implicit uncertainty in Holinshed's account, and dramatizes the opposing views in Glendower and Hotspur.

But why then should Shakespeare concern himself with Glendower's claims to be a magician? *1 Henry IV* meditates on what one must do to become — and to stay — a king. The opening of the play shows that Henry's rule is unstable, and generations of scholars, following E. M. Tillyard, have pointed to Hal's strategy, announced in his soliloquy early in the play, to gain public approval — a kind of charismatic legitimacy — by staging his errancy and miraculous redemption:

> So when this loose behavior I throw off
>   . . .
> My reformation, glittering o'er my fault,

---

[9] It is possible that the phrase "strange concealments" could refer to Glendower's well-known ability to retreat and hide his forces from the English sent to attack him, but I think that the context favors the idea of magic. Glendower would be unlikely to boast to Hotspur of his ability to hide.

[10] Part of the sermon appears in Notestein, *History of Witchcraft in England*, pp. 16–17. The treatment of witches in sixteenth-century England was considerably less hysterical than it was in the following century, but there was an important statute against witches in 1566, and throughout the reign witches were arraigned and prosecuted. The point is that belief in magical powers was common in the period, at least as common as Hotspur's rationalism. See also MacFarlane, *Witchcraft in Tudor and Stuart England*, and Thomas, *Religion and the Decline of Magic*.

[11] The connection is made by Baker, but he argues that Shakespeare is trying to undercut Glendower ("Glyn Dwr, Glendouer, Glendourdy and Glendower," p. 49). It seems to me, by contrast, that the scene makes Glendower into a formidable leader.

> Shall show more goodly and attract more eyes
> Than that which hath no foil to set it off. (I.ii.208, 212–14)

Hal concerns himself with how his future subjects will see him. The myth of his divinely-inspired reformation will enable his success as a king.

In this way, Glendower and Hal seem more like one another than Glendower and Percy. Glendower too needs to appeal to his subjects. While we have no soliloquy from him, it is obvious that the leader of a rebel army needs all the backing he can get to inspire his followers. It helps the leader of Shakespeare's barbarous Welshmen to have them believe that he is "not in the roll of common men" — that he is a magician, and the subject of prophecies about "the moldwarp and the ant." In Glendower, Shakespeare creates another able leader like Hal, concerned like him with the public impression he makes. Whether Glendower believes in his magic is a question that the play doesn't ask.

Later in the scene, when Glendower tells his guests that he will summon musicians who "Hang in the air a thousand leagues from hence" (Item 101.232), his words seem to me a kindly joke. The audience is surely not encouraged to imagine magical spirits playing the instruments they hear. Unearthly music appears in *The Tempest*, but *1 Henry IV* is no romance. As Sheldon Zitner suggests, the audience would probably have seen the musicians who were playing, although unlike him I don't see the effect as comic.[12] Instead, the whole of this final section would have stressed, for its original London audience, the simple *foreignness* of the Welsh setting. Glendower's magical references, along with the singing of his daughter, tend to remove it from the ordinary world — to suggest the world of romance.[13] Unlike other early modern English playwrights, Shakespeare does not write out the words of Mortimer's bride: he simply stresses that she speaks and sings in Welsh.[14]

Shakespeare accentuates the extravagant romance dialogue of Mortimer, Glendower and his daughter by setting it against the comic sparring of Hotspur and his lady. *They* are emphatically English and Hotspur, elsewhere devoted to poeticized ideas of honor, here adopts the prose of a good, plain Englishman, stressing once again the distance between Glendower's world and the rest of England.[15] Yet this distance should not obscure the degree to which Glendower, far more than Hotspur, concerns himself with the here and now, and remains as shrewd a leader as Henry IV or Prince Hal. He prepares his forces for battle, whether his music is magical or not.

---

[12] See Zitner, "Staging the Occult," for a contrary view.

[13] In "Romancing the Chronicles," Greenberg argues that Hotspur stands for a single-minded "epic" mode in the scene, concerned above all with masculine power, opposed to Glendower's Welsh "romance" mode. While two different generic registers oppose one another in this final part of the scene, it seems to me too much a simplification to oppose Glendower as "romance" to Hotspur's "epic." Glendower is as formidable a warrior as Hotspur, but in Shakespeare a warrior from a distinctively different culture.

[14] Schwyzer argues that the absence of actual Welsh words suggests Shakespeare's lack of interest in Wales and Welsh culture ("Thirteen Ways," pp. 40–41). It may also stress that for Shakespeare the important point was that Glendower's wife spoke a radically different tongue — what words she used was unimportant.

[15] Highley's view, however, that the scene presents a kind of Bower of Bliss in which the unwary Mortimer is made effeminate (pp. 103–07) will stand only by ignoring the context of the rest of the play. Mortimer's warlike abilities are not, in fact, being put to sleep: despite his love for his wife he will be off within the hour to fight for his piece of the kingdom.

Elissa R. Henken
Owain Glyndŵr in Folklore and the Popular Imagination

Like many another great military leader, Owain Glyndŵr has left his mark not just in the documentary and historical records but also in the memories and imaginations of the people who inherited his world, in the folklore of people in Wales.[1] The narratives of Glyndŵr's war appear first in chronicles written by contemporaries and then in histories compiled over the following centuries. Given that the chroniclers were writing about actual events as well as borrowing from each other, it is generally impossible to determine whether a given event receives particular attention simply as an historical fact or whether it has greater traditional significance. Shifting emphases and changing details (as well as poetic references) suggest the interplay between written and oral, with the written form sometimes taking from and sometimes leading to oral traditions. Note, for example the shift in describing the origins of the war: the earliest record, *Annales Oweni Glyndwr*, reports that King Henry IV, while in Scotland, was told that Glyndŵr might rise against him and, therefore, sent Lords Talbot and Grey to make sure of him.[2] A few years later, Adam of Usk, again with no explanation for the uprising, reports that King Henry returned from Scotland, learned that Glyndŵr and his men, already having broken out in rebellion, were seizing castles, and burning and pillaging towns, and the king went in to Wales to subdue him (Item 15.1–11). The next chronicle, however, an extension of the second translation of Higden's *Polychronicon* compiled between 1432 and 1450, shows Glyndŵr as Grey's innocent victim. King Henry wrote Glyndŵr letters asking him to join him on his Scottish campaign and sent them with Grey, who did not deliver them until the day before the expedition. When Glyndŵr said he did not have enough time or money to prepare at such short notice, Grey reported back to the king that Glyndŵr had refused the summons. Angered, the king tried to capture Glyndŵr, but failing, gave his lands to Grey, and thus the ensuing enmity (Item 78.1–22). This story was reported again in a paper copy of *Brehinedd y Saesson*, which was eventually copied by Robert Vaughan in the seventeenth century, first in a compilation of texts and then in his own "History of Owen Glyndŵr."[3] It became part of subsequent histories, but at which points was this a literary or an oral tradition, a literary repetition or a traditional narrative?

The lists of battles are basically the same in the chronicles — Ruthin, Mynydd Hyddgant, Mynydd Cwm-du, Craig-y-dorth — but occasionally there is extra information that suggests greater traditional significance. Connected with Mynydd Pwll Melyn where Glyndŵr's son Gruffudd was captured and his brother Tudur was killed, we have the story that one of the slain was thought to be Owain, but it turned out to be his brother "who very much

---

[1] Many of the materials in this essay are more fully discussed in my book *National Redeemer*.

[2] See Item 70.1–5. The *Chronicle* was compiled around 1422 and preserved in the sixteenth-century manuscript, Aberystwyth, NLW Peniarth MS 135.

[3] Aberystwyth, NLW 13074D; NLW Panton MS 53.

resembled him, and was often taken for him, being hardly distinguished asunder, only Owen had a little wart above his eyebrows, which Tudur had not."[4]

Uncertainty about what exactly accounted for Glyndŵr's absence from the 1403 battle between the Percies and King Henry at Shrewsbury has given rise to several different traditions: Glyndŵr sent four thousand of his men but was himself twelve miles away in Oswestry and did not join the battle; he watched the battle in safety sitting in a tree (the Shelton Oak or Glyndŵr's Oak) across the river; he couldn't get to the battle because the river flooded and that is why he watched from a tree; Percy and Mortimer began the battle earlier than planned, giving Glyndŵr no chance to reach Shrewsbury in time.[5]

One characteristic often ascribed to military leaders but applied particularly to Glyndŵr declares his destructiveness. Iolo Goch introduces the theme in describing Glyndŵr's part in the Scottish wars:

> ni thyfodd gwellt na thafol
> hefyd na'r ŷd ar ei ôl
> o Ferwig Seisnig ei sail
> i Faesbwrch, hydr fu ysbail[6]

> [Neither grass nor dock grew,
> nor corn, in his track
> from Berwick, English its foundation,
> to Maesbury, mighty was the spoil.]

With the same idea of destruction so intense that it inverts the natural order, antiquarian Richard Fenton recorded in the nineteenth century that Glyndŵr's wars "brought great desolation on Nant Conwy, so that the green grass grew in the Market place of Lhanrwst, and the Deer out of Snowdon fed in the Church yard."[7]

Mixing historical, sometimes accurate, information with traditionally based assumptions, reports of Glyndŵr's destructiveness include towns (Ruthin at the start of the war, Cardiff except for one street of Glyndŵr's supporters, Abergavenny), estates (Gogarth manor, Tretower Court, Crickhowell, Hay), and cathedrals (Bangor, Llandaff).[8] Destructiveness as part of Glyndŵr's traditional persona and not just historical reporting shows in the place names Pentre-boeth and Tre-boeth (Hot Village and Hot Town) which, despite most likely referring to charcoal burning, were reportedly derived from having been destroyed by Glyn-

---

[4] Item 91 herein. Gruffydd Aled Williams discusses this story above (p. 548).

[5] Aberystwyth, NLW Panton MS 53, pp. 55–55b, 59; also in Wynne, *History of Wales*, p. 318; Ellis, *Memoirs of Owen Glendowr*, pp. 68–69, 73; Pennant, *Tours*, p. 326. Turner, *Narrative of a Journey*, pp. 203–04; *Archaeologia Cambrensis* 5.11 (1894), p. 56; *Baner ac Amserau Cymru* (24 Ebrill 1967), p. 5; *Y Gwyddoniadur Cymreig* 5 (1866), pp. 93–94; Lloyd, *Owen Glendower*, p. 71.

[6] Item 4.61–64. See also reference in Bollard above (pp. 505–06).

[7] Fenton, *Tours*, p. 352.

[8] For example, Aberystwyth, NLW Peniarth MS 135, p. 61; Aberystwyth, NLW Panton MS 53, p. 54; Ellis, *Memoirs*, p. 67; Pennant, *Tours*, p. 302; Evans, The Story of Glamorgan, p. 303–04; Thomas Evans, *Cambrian Itinerary*, p. 112; Hague, "Bishop's Palace," p. 10; Llywelyn-Williams, *Crwydro Brycheiniog*, pp. 46, 59, 63.

dŵr.[9] Similarly, the ruins of Cefn-y-fan, one of two estates owned by Ieuan ap Maredudd and which Glyndŵr burned "to cold ashes,"[10] were said in local tradition in the 1950s to have "smoked for a year and a day; and the field in which the remains of the site are now to be seen is called Cae Murpoeth, the Field of the Hot Wall."[11] Archaeological evidence, however, shows that not only was the place never set afire, it may not even have been built until after Glyndŵr's time.[12] All of the emphasis on Glyndŵr's destructiveness suggests that he is the Owain referred to in a proverb recorded in a 1620 fair copy of an earlier list of proverbs compiled by lexicographer Thomas Wiliems: *Ni weled y cyvriw, er pan vu ryvel Owain*[13] [The like has not been seen since Owain's war]. Without contextual evidence, nothing can be certain, but this sounds much like Southerners in the United States saying they had not seen such destruction since Sherman, or Londoners since the Blitz.

Some chroniclers associate a comet with Glyndŵr's wars. Variously reporting its appearance in 1400, 1401, and 1402, they interpret it as foretelling his uprising, a great shedding of blood, or the battle of Shrewsbury, but in general portending great events. Judging by poetic references, many Welsh people apparently took it as a sign of Glyndŵr's success.[14]

Memory of Glyndŵr is imprinted on the landscape; local lore keeps him ever present. Among the many sites are the stone bearing the impress of Glyndŵr's knees where he knelt; two different stones bearing the imprint of his horse's hooves; Tomen Glyndŵr (his Mound) where he would stand to watch for enemies and gather his men, and other mounds where he is said to have lain or addressed the people; Cwm Gwarchae (Valley of the siege) where he fought; Brynsaithmarchog (Hill of the seven knights) where seven of his men spied on Lord Grey; Bryn Owain (his Hill) and Erw Lech (Acre of the flat slab) where his men hid; Ffynnon Garreg Udfan (Fountain of the rock of wailing) where the women wept; Bwrdd y Tri Arglwydd (Table of the three lords) where he met with Lord Grey and others; Bwrdd y Brenin (the King's table) where Prince Henry refreshed himself after burning Sycharth; Cerrig Cyfamod Owain Glyndŵr (Stone of his treaty) where he made a pact with Mortimer; Y Stablau (the Stables) where he stabled his horses on Pumlumon; Ffos Owen Glyndwr (his ditch); and Cadair Glyndŵr (his seat).[15] In addition to traditions about his primary residence

---

[9] *Archaeologia Cambrensis* 5.11 (1894), p. 64; *Archaeologia Cambrensis* 6.10 (1910), p. 423.

[10] Wynne, *History of the Gwydir Family*, p. 33, quoted in Hogg, "14th Century House-Site," p. 1.

[11] Gresham, "Platform Houses in North-West Wales," pp. 36–37.

[12] Hogg, "14th Century House-Site," p. 6.

[13] Aberystwyth, NLW MS 3064B (Mostyn 204), p. 119. This proverb was brought to my attention by Mary Burdett-Jones.

[14] See Items 42, 68, 72, 78, 87, 89, and the above essay by Williams.

[15] Henken, Field notes, II, 9, 15; Cledwyn Fychan, notes on conversation with John and Jim James, December 1965; Henken, Field tapes, 1982, transcription, p. 81; Borrow, *Wild Wales*, pp. 124–25; Fenton, *Tours in Wales*, p. 343, Appendix — notes from printed sources; Hobley, *Hanes Methodistiaeth Arfon*, p. 25; Henken, Field tapes, 1982, transcription, p. 164; Henken, Field tapes, 1982, transcription, p. 138; Amgueddfa Werin Cymru, MS 2593/81, p. 90; Cledwyn Fychan, notes on conversations with Mr. Oliver (1966), Meirwen Hughes (1980), and Mrs. A. Evans (c.1967); *Y Brython* 4 (1961), 253; Aberystwyth, NLW 39B, p. 68. Folk onomastics often provide more than one explanation, as demonstrated by Brynsaithmarchog which is also said to be where Glyndŵr captured Lord Grey and seven of his men (Foulkes, "Dyffryn Clwyd," pp. 89–90), and much earlier as the place where seven men were left behind to look after the Island of Britain while the rest went off to war (Bollard, *Mabinogi*, p. 51).

at Sycharth, local lore records a variety of other residences, such as Plas Crug, a fortified mansion between Abersytwyth and Llanbadarn; Dolwen, a farmhouse in Llanarmon Dyffryn Ceiriog; a farmhouse at Carrog Uchaf in which the stairs are said to be stained with the blood of one of his soldiers and which until recently still held a table used by him; and the ruins of a house which belonged to him outside Corwen.[16] In the Corwen area, people frequently told me about Glyndŵr's deer park at Llidiart y Parc (The Park Gate) and even more frequently about his prison house.[17]

Several legends show Glyndŵr leaving his mark with his sword. In one he threw his sword against a rock, now called *Maen Cleddyf Glyn Dwr* [stone of Glyndŵr's sword], and in another he scratched the church bell tower in Corwen.[18] One of the best established local stories tells of the time that Glyndŵr, sitting on Penypigyn, the hill behind the church in Corwen, threw his sword (or dagger), which landed on a rock where it left its impress. That stone, showing the outline of a sword, has been built into the church wall, where it is still to be seen. People tell this legend in both fragmented or extended form, with Glyndŵr throwing the sword in anger at an individual or at a whole community, but in Corwen, even those who seemed to know little else about Glyndŵr and who had never even bothered to look at the stone, would tell it to me.[19]

In the Dolgellau area, the prevalent local legend, known as "Ceubren yr Ellyll" (the hollow tree of the ghost), tells about the time that Glyndŵr's cousin Hywel Sele tried to kill him. In an attempt to make peace, the two went hunting at Nannau, Hywel's estate. Pretending to aim at a deer, Hywel turned his arrow against Glyndŵr, who, fortunately, wore armor under his clothes. Enraged, Glyndŵr burned Nannau and immured Hywel in a hollow oak tree, a deed not discovered until years later.[20]

Our first records of these last two legends appeared relatively late, in the eighteenth- and seventeenth centuries, respectively, but both are still very much alive today. The stories about Dafydd Gam, however, seem no longer to survive in oral tradition. Starting in the seventeenth century and repeated up through Thomas Pennant in the late eighteenth century, the story was that Dafydd Gam, having tried to assassinate Glyndŵr, was released from prison on promises of loyalty, but again attacked Glyndŵr, who responded by burning his home and merrily reciting a verse mocking him.[21]

Much of Glyndŵr's folklore connects with his style of guerilla warfare — stories of clever tricks, traveling in disguise, narrow escapes, and sheltering in caves. Glyndŵr is a bit of a trickster, credited with internationally recognizable ruses such as turning his horse's shoes

---

[16] Evans, *Cambrian Itinerary*, p. 170; Lewis, *Born on a Perilous Rock*, p. 6; Amgueddfa Werin Cymru MS 2593/84, pp. 2–3, 7; Henken, Field tapes, 1982, transcription, pp. 112–13, 137; Henken, Field notes, II, 9; Cernyw, *Hynafiaethau Edeyrnion*, p. 9.

[17] Henken, Field tapes, 1982, transcription, pp. 116, 137, 139; Henken, Field notes, II; earlier reports appear in Pennant, *Tours*, pp. 351–52; Cernyw, *Hynafiaethau Edeyrnion*, p. 6.

[18] *Baner ac Amserau Cymru* (11 Hydref 1927), p. 6, col. 4; *Y Geninen*, 10 (1892), 6.

[19] Aberystwyth, NLW MS 39B, p. 68; Evans, *Cambrian Itinerary*, p. 266; Lewis, *Topographical Dictionary of Wales*, s.v. Corwen; Henken, Field tapes, 1982, transcription, pp. 88, 119, 145, 289.

[20] Aberystwyth, NLW Panton MS 53, pp. 53–53b; *Archaeologia Cambrensis* 9 (1863), p. 132, prepared by Robert Vaughan of Hengwrt, 1649; Pennant, *Tours*, pp. 310–11; Fenton, *Tours in Wales*, p. 127; Henken, Field notes, II, 43–45; *Y Llenor Cymreig* 1 (1882), p. 110; *Y Geninen* 26 (1908), p. 287.

[21] Aberystwyth, NLW Panton MS 11, pp. 41b–42; discussed by Williams above (pp. 546–48).

around so as to confuse his track.[22] Another common ruse has Glyndŵr dressing wooden poles with caps and jackets to look like soldiers from a distance. While the stick soldiers are consistently said to have been set up in Dôl Pennau (Meadow of the heads) near Corwen, both the exact location of the fields and the purpose of the ruse vary. According to the stories, Glyndŵr used the stick soldiers to trick his enemy Lord Grey into thinking he was home when he was not so that Grey would not attack in his absence, to trick Grey into spending his arrows on the wooden soldiers before he himself attacked Grey, or to trick the enemy into bogging down in soft ground.[23]

Glyndŵr also reportedly made use of disguise, either disguising others to look like him or disguising himself in order to pass among his enemies. According to a sixteenth-century record, he escaped the enemy cordon at Y Berwyn by disguising one of the dead as himself.[24] One person told me that Glyndŵr sent a small band with one member dressed as himself to draw Grey out of his castle and then, with a much larger group waiting in the woods, attacked.[25] Another explained,

> Glyndŵr was everywhere, and he used even to have people imitate him. This is what confused the English for so long. He used to have people masquerading as him in different parts of the country, so the English never knew where he was, you see.[26]

Moreover, Glyndŵr himself used to go about in disguise, a frequent claim for his later years after he disappeared from public life when he reportedly would wander unrecognized in the guise of a shepherd, but it was also one of his strategies at the height of his fame. Unfortunately, the most developed narrative of this kind comes to us first from Iolo Morganwg, whose mix of genuine research and clever invention leaves uncertain whether an oral narrative first seen in Iolo's works was already in oral circulation earlier or entered it only later as a result of Iolo's creativity. In this case, the story is that Glyndŵr, disguised as a Frenchman, stayed at the home of his enemy Lord Berkrolles, who kept boasting that he was about to capture Glyndŵr and encouraging his guest to stay to witness the event. After several days, Glyndŵr departed and, in his own name, thanked his host for his hospitality. Berkrolles was so dumbfounded that he never spoke again.[27] The story was published in nineteenth-century nationalist journals, histories, the Welsh encyclopedia *Y Gwyddoniadur Cymreig*, and perhaps most importantly, in the form of a ballad by Ceiriog whereby it was disseminated through the schools.[28] The ballad seems to be the primary source for people in

---

[22] Thomas, "Glyndyfrdwy."

[23] Henken, Field notes, II, 16; Henken, Field tapes, 1982, transcription, pp. 114–15; Cernyw, *Hynafiaethau Edeyrnion*, pp. 6–7; Hope Hewett, *Walking through Merioneth*, pp. 80–81; Bowen, ed., *Atlas Meirionnydd*, p. 193.

[24] Aberystwyth, NLW Mostyn MS 158, p. 285b (1548).

[25] Henken, Field notes, II, 20.

[26] Henken, Field tapes, 1982, transcription, p. 288.

[27] Iolo Morganwg, *Iolo Manuscripts*, pp. 98–99/493–94.

[28] *Y Llenor Cymreig* 1 (1882), pp. 111–12; *Y Geninen* 22 (1904), p. 108; Lloyd, *History of . . . Powys Fadog*, 3.206–07; Evans, *Story of Glamorgan*, p. 304; *Y Gwyddoniadur Cymreig* 5 (1866), p. 92; "Owain Glyn Dwr a Syr Lawrence," in Jones, ed., *Ceiriog*, p. 56. The story is told again in another ballad, "Syr

north Wales whom I interviewed, but in south Wales, in an area near where the story's events occurred, some people did claim to have learned the story orally and locally.

Folk narratives and histories repeatedly show Glyndŵr as a master of escape, particularly when surrounded by his enemies. These escapes may take place in battle as in the example mentioned above, where he disguised a corpse as himself in order to escape capture, or, as in one sixteenth-century report repeated over the subsequent centuries, when he and only 120 men set to flight the 1,500 Flemings who surrounded them at Mynydd Hyddgant.[29] A number of his escapes also have him (almost) taken unawares while dining. One rather bare form of such a narrative, appearing in a mid-seventeenth century text, reports that before the war opened, King Henry IV

> sent the Lord Talbot and Grey to reduce Owain with part of his forces, and they came so unexpectedly about Owain's house, that he had much ado to make his escape into the woods.[30]

Another story (Item 90), concerning that same period, has Grey, at King Henry's urging, invite himself to dine with Glyndŵr, with a large force secretly following. Glyndŵr's guards, seeing the gathering enemy, send the poet Iolo Goch to give warning, which he does openly in Welsh verse — a form Grey does not understand.

A much more elaborate story tells of a time when Glyndŵr had gone to seek shelter at the home of his supporter, the poet Rhys Goch Eryri. One of Rhys's servants gives timely warning of the encroaching enemy, and Rhys and Glyndŵr escape in their servants' clothes, Rhys going one way and Glyndŵr another — fleeing along the shore, swimming a tidal river at high tide, climbing a steep ravine at y Simnai (the Chimney), running across the top of y Diffwys (Steep Slope), and clambering down to a cave where he hides for six months while provisioned by the Prior of Beddgelert.[31]

Glyndŵr's use of caves forms one of his strongest recurring traditions, whether he simply shelters in them as he moves about the countryside, hides in them during a difficult middle period of his war, or retreats to them at the end when the war is essentially lost. The early fifteenth-century *Historia vitae* notes the difficulty King Henry had in fighting or even finding Glyndŵr and his men for "Owain Glyndŵr himself hid from the sight of the king in the caves and mountains of Wales" (Item 28.18–19). The king, unable to sustain his own troops, was forced to withdraw to Shrewsbury. Adam of Usk, also in the fifteenth century, describes a point in 1409 when "Owain in his misery hid himself away with his only son,

---

Lawrens Berclos," by Jones, *Caniadau*, pp. 25–26.

[29] Aberystwyth, NLW Peniarth MS 135, p. 60 (c.1560); later in Aberystwyth, NLW Panton MS 53, p. 52 (18th century); Ellis, *Memoirs of Owain Glendowr*, p. 65 (1775); Pennant, *Tours*, p. 306 (1778); *Y Llenor Cymreig* 1 (1882), p. 110, in which the numbers of men with Glyndŵr and casualties are slightly greater.

[30] Aberystwyth, NLW Panton MS 53, p. 51b; repeated in Ellis, *Memoirs of Owain Glendowr*, p. 64 (1775); Pennant, *Tours*, p. 301 (1778). The earlier text Aberystwyth, NLW Peniarth MS 135, pp. 59–60 says simply that when Grey and Talbot came for him, Glyndŵr escaped into the woods without specifying the surprise of their attack.

[31] *Y Brython* 4 (1861), pp. 212–13, with further versions in *Cymru* 10 (1896), p. 32; *Bye-Gones* 10, New Series (1907–08), p. 67; *Cymru* 50 (1916), p. 173; Firbank, *Country of Memorable Honour*, p. 70. Glyndŵr is credited in modern mountaineering books as the first to climb Simnai y Foel.

called Maredudd, in remote caves and wooded mountainsides" (Item 62.66–67). A nine-teenth-century antiquarian reported of that same period:

> Gwelwyd ef [Owain Glyndŵr], pan oedd aflwyddiant yn gwgu arno, yn grwydryn ar hyd y wlad, weithiau yn gwisgo fel bugail, bryd arall yn ffoi oddiwrth y naill gyfaill at y llall i gael lloches a thamaid o fwyd: — ei fywyd mewn cymaint o berygl weithiau, fel nad oedd yn ddyogel iddo aros mewn tŷ na chastell, ac felly ceisiai loches mewn ogofeydd; a'i wely yn fynych fyddai y graig galed a llaith.[32]

> [He (Owain Glyndŵr) was seen, when misfortune was pressing on him, wandering about the land, sometimes dressing as a shepherd, another time fleeing from one friend to another to get shelter and a bit of food — his life so much in danger at times, that it was not safe for him to stay in house or castle, and thus he sought shelter in caves; and his bed often was the hard and damp rock.]

The association of Glyndŵr with caves appears not just in the written histories and anti-quarians' reports; it lives strongly in oral tradition. The details may not always be clear, but the connection remains. Twentieth century lore reports a place above Dyffryn Hyddgen where Glyndŵr was supposed to have spent the night before the battle.[33] Ogof Owain Glyn-dŵr near Beddgelert was reported by a nineteenth-century traveler as a place where Glyndŵr, "upon one of his expeditions to harass the English forces, was fain to shelter himself from his enemies,"[34] and was described by one local person to me as a place where *"o'n medru cuddio fanno am hanner blwyddyn tra roedd y bradwyr yn chwilio amdano fo"* [he was able to hide there for half a year while the traitors were looking for him].[35] One man told me of caves above Corwen through which Glyndŵr fled straight through to Chester,[36] and a woman told me about a cave in Llanarmon where Glyndŵr hid, though she wasn't sure from whom.[37]

An associated motif, telling who provided for the hero while he hid in a cave, declares the people's general support for him, and that support is a source of family pride for his provisioners. Thus, just as the Prior of Beddgelert provided for him in one cave, Ednyfed ab Aron cared for him in another near Tywyn, a deed noted by Pennant and in the gene-alogy of the Peniarth family,[38] and Gruffudd Fychan hid him in yet another, as noted in the nineteenth-century obituary of one of his descendants.[39]

---

[32] *Y Llenor Cymreig* 1 (1882), p. 111.

[33] Cledwyn Fychan, notes on conversation with George Pugh, Rhiwgam, Aberhosan (February 1966); Henken, Field tapes, 1982, transcription, pp. 81–82.

[34] Turner, *Narrative of a Journey*, p. 104.

[35] Henken, Field tapes, 1982, transcription, p. 173.

[36] Henken, Field tapes, 1982, transcription, p. 289. Corwen is about 30 miles from Chester.

[37] Henken, Field notes, II, 13. That same cave was described in fieldwork by the Welsh Folk Mu-seum with Glyndŵr's hiding there being one of three associated traditions — the other two being that it is linked by an underground passage to another cave and that Ned Puw was last seen entering the cave piping the air "Ffarwel Ned Puw" (AWC, MS 2593/81, pp. 105–06).

[38] Pennant, *Tours*, p. 334; Lloyd, *History of . . . Powys Fadog*, 5.102, and repeated in a wide range of local histories and nationalist journals.

[39] *Baner ac Amserau Cymru* (3 Ionawr 1894), p. 4, col. 4.

Caves provide one of the clearest links to Glyndŵr's role as a redeemer-hero, the hero who will come and restore the nation to its former glory. This type of hero, which generally arises when a people has a sense of itself both as constituting a distinct group and as being oppressed by outsiders, developed in other European nations as well, but usually at a much later time than in Wales, where oppression by Romans, Saxons, and then Normans made the need felt early. Six major redeemer-heroes (Hiriell, Cynan, Cadwaladr, Arthur, Owain, Owain Lawgoch) and a number of minor ones appear in Welsh tradition before Glyndŵr, and one (Henry Tudor) after. Medieval prophecies are filled with their names. Glyndŵr's own role as *y mab darogan* [the son of prophecy] was suggested in his own time and established through vaticinatory poetry,[40] in histories compiled soon after his time, and in the traditions which developed around him. Glyndŵr himself referred to the prophecies when, asking for aid, he wrote to the king of Scotland:

> Des quex oppressions et bondages le prophecie dit que je serray delivere par eid et socour de vostre dit roial mageste. (Item 22.75–76)

> [The prophecy states that, with the help and support of your royal majesty, I shall be delivered from this subjection and bondage.]

and to the lords of Ireland:

> Sed, quia uulgariter dicitur per propheciam quod, antequam nos altiorem manum in hac parte haberemus, quod uos (et) uestri carissimi consanguinei in Hibernea ad hoc manus porrigetis adiutrices. (Item 22.96–99)

> [It is commonly said in the prophecy, however, that, before we can gain the upper hand in this contest, you and your noble kinsmen in Ireland shall come to our aid in this matter.]

Various histories through the centuries refer to Glyndŵr's attempt to fulfill prophecy, though some emphasize Glyndŵr being foolishly misled by the prophecies while others emphasize the use he made of them. David Powel in the sixteenth century writes of those "cunning in Merlin's prophesies" who put in Glyndŵr's head "that now the time was come wherein the Brytaines through his meanes might recouer againe the honour and liberties of their ancestors" and thereby "brought him into such a fooles paradise, that he neuer waieng what title he might pretend nor what right he had, proceeded and made warre upon the Earle of March."[41] A century later William Wynne continued this idea when he wrote that the "Prophecies of Merdhyn . . . made the swelling mind of Glyndŵr overflow its Banks, and gave him some hopes of restoring the Island back to the Britains."[42] Pennant, however, writes that Glyndŵr in order "to animate his countrymen, called upon the antient prophecy."[43] Shakespeare, too, refers to "the dreamer Merlin and his prophecies" when Hotspur mocks Glyndŵr for talking of them.[44]

---

[40] See the essays in this volume on poetry and prophecy by Bollard, Williams, and Fulton.

[41] Powel, *Historie of Cambria*, p. 386.

[42] Wynne, p. 317.

[43] Pennant, *Tours*, p. 322.

[44] Item 101.150. Shakespeare may have followed Holinshed in this (Item 100.121–26).

When the war ended and with it Glyndŵr's attempt to restore independence and glory to Wales, hopes were transferred to a future when *y mab darogan* might return. Glyndŵr had disappeared, but traditional expectations left it uncertain that he had died. An account compiled soon after 1422, only seven years after Glyndŵr's disappearance, records:

> MCCCCxv ydd aeth Owain mewn difant y Gwyl Vathe yn y kynhayaf. O hynny allan ni wybvwyd i ddifant. Rrann vawr a ddywaid i varw; y brvdwyr a ddywedant na bv. (Item 70.51–53)

> [1415. Owain disappeared on the Feast of St. Matthew in the autumn. From then on (the place of) his disappearance was not known. A great many say he died; the seers say he did not.]

Two strains of tradition arose, one describing his last years and death, the other insisting he was only waiting to return. The former involves several related motifs: his wandering in disguise and/or staying with one of his daughters; his death on St. Matthew's Eve, the same day he had started the war with an attack on Ruthin fifteen years earlier; and his grave site lying unknown.[45] Adam of Usk explains the unknown grave:

> After four years in hiding from the king and kingdom, Owain Glyndŵr died, and was buried by his followers in the darkness of night. His grave was discovered by his enemies, however, so he had to be re-buried, though it is impossible to discover where he was laid. (Item 67)

An unknown grave gives rise to various claimants. The most prevalent local tradition, placing his death and burial in Monnington, received quite a bit of attention in 1999/2000 when Scudamore descendants of one of his daughters were said to reveal the long-held family secret, leading to discussions about whether his bones should be re-buried in Wales.[46] Other claims support Corwen or Llanfair Caereinion as the burial place.[47]

Despite occasional intense local interest in identifying Glyndŵr's grave, the richer, more powerful strain in tradition declares that the grave is unknown because Glyndŵr never died. Rather, he will return to resume the fight and restore Wales to its former glories. However he may have used the prophecies during his lifetime, it is this role — the redeemer-hero, *y mab darogan* — which bestows on him and recognizes his symbolic power. Apparently arising immediately upon his disappearance (witness the seers' claim that he did not die), this role provides a framework for hope across the centuries. As Gruffydd Aled Williams discusses in his essay in this volume, awaiting Glyndŵr forms one of the themes in the post-war poetry.

The strongest presentation of Glyndŵr's role as a redeemer-hero appears in legendry, especially in legends of caves in which he sleeps awaiting the right moment to return. Legendry locates the cave in which he sleeps in many places, sometimes named (Craig Gwr-

---

[45] See, for example, Aberystwyth, NLW Panton MS 53, p. 58b; Aberystwyth, NLW Panton MS 11, p. 68b; William Wynne, p. 319; Pennant, *Tours*, pp. 357–58.

[46] Thomas, *Memoirs of Owain Glendower*, p. 169; *Cymru* 1 (1891), p. 224; *Western Mail* (5 January 1995 and 2 December 2000, among other dates).

[47] *Y Llenor* 9 (1897), p. 79; Aberystwyth, NLW MS 39B, p. 68.

theyrn, Mynydd yr Aran, Ogof y Ddinas[48]), but more often left unspecified. The point is that he remains waiting there. As one man told me,

> Ma' 'na chwedl 'i fod o'n cuddio ar lethr y Wyddfa rhwla mewn ogof, a 'dyn, pan fydd angen ar Gymru, bydd Glyndŵr yn codi unwaith eto ac yn ailgychwyn y gwrthryfel.[49]

> [There's a legend that he's hiding on the side of Snowdon somewhere in a cave, and after, when Wales will have need, Glyndŵr will rise once again and restart the rebellion.]

One of the more developed legends tells of a drover taking his cattle to London and on the way cutting a hazel (a typically magical plant) for a walking stick. He was crossing London Bridge when a stranger approached him, asking where he got his walking stick and could he show him. The two journeyed back together to Wales. When they reached the spot where the drover had cut his stick, the stranger pulled away a clump of bushes and a rock and led the drover into a deep cave, filled with gold and silver and jewels and a great number of sleeping men, including one especially splendid one. The stranger explained that these were Glyndŵr and his men, that the Welshman could take as much treasure as he could carry without dropping any, and that he must be careful not to wake the warriors or touch a silver bell hanging from the ceiling. The drover goes back to the cave several times, but eventually becomes greedy, takes too much, bumps into the bell, wakes the warriors, has to run from the cave, and then can never again find the entrance.[50]

Sometimes the drover takes his cattle to Bala; sometimes the stranger uproots a tree or moves a boulder; sometimes the injunction is not to mix different substances when taking the treasure; sometimes the drover is told that if the warriors awake, they will ask, "Is it day?" and he must answer, "No, it is not day. Sleep on;" sometimes the cave is found not by a drover and his guide but by a shepherd following a lost sheep; sometimes the warriors beat up the intruder and never again does he enjoy a day's health; and sometimes the sleeper is not Owain Glyndŵr but Arthur or Owain Lawgoch.

A crucial element in these cave legends is that the time must be right, whether or not the sleepers cry out, "Is it day?" Welsh legendry emphasizes that the time must be right: when Wales's need is at its greatest and when the people are ready to follow the redeemer-hero. This is best exemplified in a legend unique to Glyndŵr. The basic story relates that Glyndŵr is out walking in the hills (on Y Berwyn) early one morning, meets an abbot (from Glyn-y-groes/Valle Crucis), and says, "Good morning, father; you're up early" and the abbot replies, "No, it is you who is up early, one hundred years too early." Elis Gruffudd, in the first record we have of this legend, reports that when Glyndŵr realized he was not the Owain of the prophecies, he was ashamed and disappeared (Item 96.30–41). Since then, however,

---

[48] Rhŷs, *Celtic Folklore*, 2.487; Henken, Field tapes, 1982, transcription, p. 85; Gwyn Thomas, *Welsh Eye*, p. 110. Two other Welsh redeemer-heroes, Arthur and Owain Lawgoch, are also said to be sleeping in various caves around Wales; sometimes a single cave is even assigned to more than one hero depending on the narrator.

[49] Henken, Field tapes, 1982, transcription, p. 162.

[50] For a transcription of an actual version of this tale, see Henken, *National Redeemer*, pp. 80–82, taken from Henken, Field tapes, 1982, transcription, p. 291.

the story is usually told with the implication that Glyndŵr will return and that in this encounter he is simply taking a break from his long sleep. Each narrator presents the legend with slightly different emphases and concerns — one talks about him as a man before his time; one speaks of unrealized dreams; another says the people weren't ready to fight and that perhaps if Glyndŵr had come a couple of centuries later, Wales would already be a free nation[51] — but the point remains the same: The time is not right.

It is Glyndŵr's role as a redeemer which makes him such a potent symbol for modern Welsh nationalism. A symbol of hope for a better future, he can be adapted to whatever the current social needs. For the purposes of Welsh nationalists, however, he first had to be rehabilitated. He had never totally disappeared from Welsh consciousness, but for a few centuries he had become less important, and the histories compiled in those times depended heavily on previous works for both details and interpretations, often echoing English views. At the end of the eighteenth century, with the beginning of romantic nationalism in Wales, interest in Glyndŵr revived. Thomas Pennant re-evaluated the previous histories; Iolo Morganwg added his bits. However, for the first part of the nineteenth century, though recognized as important, Glyndŵr was still judged to have behaved improperly and, no matter how exemplary he was in other ways, was condemned for having gone against the king. An 1820 biography begins with this verse:

> And he was once the glory of his age,
> Disinterested, just, with every virtue
> Of civil life adorned — in arms excelling:
> His only blot was this, that, much provoked,
> He raised his vengeful arm against his sovereign.[52]

However, as nationalist sentiment grew, attitudes evolved: Welsh scholars gradually stopped acting as apologists and began shifting their interpretation of Glyndŵr's uprising. At the beginning of the nineteenth century, they emphasized his conflict with Lord Grey over land; at the end of the century, they emphasized the revolt against injustice and the Welsh struggle for freedom. Re-examining all aspects of Welsh culture, they disseminated their findings in histories, encyclopedias, and especially a wide selection of nationalist journals. Publishing literature, history (frequently in verse form), and as much folklore as they could collect, they worked to heighten nationalist sensibilities. And attitudes changed. In 1895, the *awdl* which won the chair at the Llangollen Eisteddfod with an interpretive history of Glyndŵr's wars, ended with the verse:

> Bu Cymru'n dysgu o dan — ei faner,
>   Drwy fynych gyflafan
> Fyw yn rhydd, fynnu ei rhan, — yn unol
>   Wlad anibynnol. Adnabu'i hunan.[53]

---

[51] Henken, Field tapes, 1982, transcription, pp. 131, 181.

[52] *Cambro-Briton*, 3.17.

[53] Eifion Wyn, "Owain Glyndwr."

[Wales learned under his banner, through frequent battles, to live in freedom, to demand its share, a united, independent land. She knew herself.]

In the twentieth century, Glyndŵr became a useful means of expressing nationalist hopes. In 1915 (the 500th anniversary of the end of Glyndŵr's war), a booklet designed for children and published in honor of St. David's Day, devoted several pages to Glyndŵr, linking the patron saint and warrior as national heroes. The article ends:

Byddin Owen Glyndwr ydym ninnau heddyw, yn ennill ei frwydr. Y mae'n cenedl yn eglwys i Grist, a'i chrefydd yn gref a phur. Y mae addysg yng nghyrraedd y tlotaf. Y mae'r llafurwr yn raddol ennill ffrwyth cyfiawn ei lafur; y mae llafur yn anrhydeddus. Y mae'n gwlad anwyl yn rhydd, ac yn deyrngarol i'r ymerodraeth rymus a gogoneddus y mae'n rhan hynaf ohoni. Ac am hyn y breuddwydiodd ac yr ymladdodd Owen Glyndwr.[54]

[We ourselves are Owen Glyndŵr's army today, winning his battle. Our nation is a church for Christ, and its religion is strong and pure. Education is within reach of the poorest. The laborer is gradually gaining the just fruit of his labor; labor is honorable. Our beloved land is free, loyal to the powerful and glorious empire of which it is the oldest part. And for this Owen Glyndŵr dreamed and fought.]

They may not have been totally ready to break from king and empire, but they were clearly ready to fight for the good of Wales. In 1931, historian J. E. Lloyd concluded his well-considered history of Glyndŵr with the statement, "He may with propriety be called the father of modern Welsh nationalism."[55] Glyndŵr's name is invoked by politicians, protest singers, and other activists, both directly and indirectly. Gwynfor Evans, a former member of Parliament and president of Plaid Cymru (the Welsh Nationalist Party) included in his 1964 book, *Rhagom i Ryddid*, a photograph of a statue of Glyndŵr and captioned it with a line taken from a Glyndŵr's Day lecture by Gwyn A. Williams: "*Goleuir y meddwl Cymreig o hyd gan luchedyn y weledigaeth o bobl a fu'n rhydd*" [The Welsh mind is still haunted by its lightning-flash vision of a people that was free].[56] Glyndŵr served as a model for twentieth-century activists. Gwynfor Evans wrote of the "young nationalist leaders of this decade [1970s] who have shown a heroic commitment not seen in Wales since the days of Owain Glyndwr";[57] the Free Wales Army explained their actions in a 1964 letter to the police with the statement, "Glyndwr had from an early period of his insurrection the aim of independence for his country; dream though it might be, we also have this in mind."[58] Meibion Glyndŵr (Sons of Glyndŵr) summoned the goals and imagery (slipping in and out of the community, burning enemies' homes) of Glyndŵr's war with their campaign begun in 1979 to drive out the English by burning English holiday homes in Wales. Part of invoking Glyndŵr is the idea that he will

---

[54] *Dydd Gwyl Dewi Sant*, p. [7].

[55] *Owen Glendower*, p. 146.

[56] Evans, *Rhagom i Ryddid*, facing p. 33.

[57] Evans, *Wales Can Win*, p. 79.

[58] Ellis, *Wales — A Nation Again!*, p. 138.

return, but only if the people are ready, if the people make it possible by their efforts—the same theme as in the cave legends and the legend in which the abbot tells Glyndŵr that he is too early. Welsh political activist Emyr Llewelyn stressed this in a 1969 speech in which he invoked Glyndŵr with the words of a *cywydd*, "*Myn Duw, mi a wn y daw*" [By God, I know he will come] and spoke of the need for courage and effort in order to make the dream come true.[59] At the same 1969 rally, protest singer Dafydd Iwan introduced a song inspired by the same *cywydd* and using "*Myn Duw, mi a wn y daw*" as its refrain.[60] Glyndŵr serves as a vital link between Wales's historical past and its future. Gŵyl Owain Glyndŵr (his Day) on 16 September provides occasion for nationalist speeches and flag-waving, and from 1986 to 2009 the Welsh history annual *Cof Cenedl* (Memory of a Nation) was dated Gŵyl Owain Glyndŵr. Examples abound both on the political stage and in private comments of people invoking Glyndŵr's return — whether metaphorically or not — to aid in their struggle for a better future.

Not all references to Glyndŵr are as high minded. His name appears on numerous inns and pubs, bottled water, and locomotive No. 7 of the Vale of Rheidol Light Railway. Nonetheless, these, too, indicate Glyndŵr's importance in the popular imagination and a pride in him. Communities link themselves to him, whether the competitive choir Côr Meibion Glyndŵr in Corwen or Prifysgol Glyndŵr (his University) in Wrexham. A national walking trail, Llwybr Glyndŵr, is named in his honor. Statues are raised to him: a 1916 statue stands in Cardiff's City Hall; a 1980s statue in Corwen was deemed to make him look too much like a farmer, and was replaced in 2007 by one of him as a war leader with raised sword on a charging horse; in 2013 plans are afoot for a new statue in Cardiff. His reputed parliament building in Machynlleth has been turned into an interpretive center featuring his history and ideas. And in 2000, he was voted in Wales the person of the millennium.

Ever adaptable, Glyndŵr continues to serve the needs of his countrymen. In the twentieth century, he served for many as a call to action, sometimes with a dangerous edge. A guerilla fighter who dealt in death and destruction, represented as he was by activists quite intent on major societal shifts, he was dangerous. As I have reported elsewhere, I met people at the height of my fieldwork in the 1980s who were afraid to talk to me about him, and one woman responded to my question about what he signified with, "*Trwbl, dim ond iwso fo fel esgus i wneud trwbl*" [Trouble, just using him as an excuse to make trouble].[61] More often, though, he was seen as leader who dared to try for a better world. That was at the core of his role as a redeemer-hero, someone who would restore the nation to its golden age. Glyndŵr had given people a glimpse of that golden age in the fifteenth century with his tripartite plan for a Welsh parliament, universities, and independent church laid out in the Pennal letters (Items 51, 52). In the twentieth century, that plan, repeatedly cited by people with whom I spoke, gave greater potency to Glyndŵr than to his fellow redeemer-heroes sleeping in their caves. Arthur, who had in any case been co-opted by the English, had a golden age too distant from current realities, and Owain Lawgoch was stopped in his attempt before he even got started. Glyndŵr, however, almost succeeded; he is the necessary model to take up the fight. In the twenty-first century, when Wales has partial devolution and its own Assembly, he is called on not as the rebel or warrior but rather as a statesman. With a slight shift

---

[59] Llewelyn, "Mi a Wn y Daw," pp. 13–16. The *cywydd* appears in Aberystwyth, NLW MS 6209, pp. 336–37.

[60] The song can be found in Dafydd Iwan, *Cant o Ganeuon*, pp. 91–93.

[61] Henken, Field notes, II, 49.

of focus, his tripartite plan becomes a modern statesmen's vision of "a strong, independent and sophisticated Wales,"[62] and of "a Welsh future in a European context."[63]

In a role shaped by prophecy and legend as well as by his own skills as a leader and warrior, Glyndŵr attempted to establish an independent Welsh state. Both his struggle and his disappearance before that goal could be accomplished gave rise to new legendry and to revived hopes. Though his image shifts with people's changing needs, he has retained a strong presence in the folk and popular imagination. Whether people need him as a warrior ready for action or as a statesman ready with ideas, whether they need the man of history or the son of prophecy, people in Wales can call on him as they create their own desired future.

Kentchurch Court in Herefordshire, the ancestral home of the Scudamores. According to family tradition, Owain spent some of his last years here, living with his daughter, Alice, and her husband, John Scudamore. The older tower in the foreground dates from Owain's time and holds what is now presented as Owain's room. Housed here is the sixteenth-century St. Jerome portrait that some have argued depicts the folkloric figure Jack of Kent, the Welsh poet Siôn Cent, or (perhaps most fantastically) even Owain himself.

---

[62] *Western Mail* (1 July 2000), p. 11.

[63] The First Secretary of the Assembly as reported in *Western Mail* (17 April, 2000), p. 12.

BIBLIOGRAPHY FOR THE VOLUME

Adam of Usk. *Chronicle*. Ed. Chris Given-Wilson. Oxford: Oxford University Press, 1997.

Aneirin. *Y Gododdin: Britain's Oldest Heroic Poem*. Ed. and trans. A. O. H. Jarman. Llandysul: Gomer, 1988.

Anglo, Sydney. "The *British History* in Early Tudor Propaganda." *Bulletin of the John Rylands Library* 44 (1961), 17–48.

Anglo-Norman Letters and Petitions from All Souls MS 182. Ed. M. Dominica Legge. Anglo-Norman Texts Series 3. Oxford: Basil Blackwell, 1941.

Annales monastici. Ed. Henry Richards Luard. 5 vols. Rolls Series 36. London: Longman, Green, Longman, Roberts, and Green, 1864–69.

Armes Prydein Vawr. Ed. Ifor Williams. In *Armes Prydein o Lyfr Taliesin*. Cardiff: University of Wales Press, 1964.

———. Trans. Rachel Bromwich. In *Armes Prydein: The Prophecy of Britain from the Book of Taliesin*. Dublin: Dublin Institute for Advanced Studies, 1972. [Based on *Armes Prydein*, ed. Williams.]

Baker, David J. "Glyn Dwr, Glendouer, Glendourdy and Glendower." In *Shakespeare and Wales: From the Marches to the Assembly*. Ed. by Willy Maley and Philip Schwyzer. Farnham: Ashgate Publishing Group, 2010. Pp. 43–57.

Barber, Chris. *In Search of Owain Glyndŵr*. Second ed. Abergavenny: Blorenge Books, 2004.

Barker, Juliet. *Agincourt: The King, The Campaign, The Battle*. London: Little, Brown, 2005.

Barrow, G. W. S. "Wales and Scotland in the Middle Ages." *Welsh History Review* 10 (1980), 302–19.

Bartrum Collection: AHRC Project on P. C. Bartrum's *Welsh Genealogies* (2010). <http://cadair.aber.ac.uk/dspace/handle/2160/4691>.

Bartrum, Peter C. *Welsh Genealogies AD 300–1400*. 8 vols. Cardiff: University of Wales Press, 1974.

———. *Welsh Genealogies AD 1400–1500*. 18 vols. Aberystwyth: National Library of Wales, 1983.

———. *Welsh Genealogies AD 300–1400, Additions and Corrections, Sixth List*. Aberystwyth: National Library of Wales, 1999.

———. *A Welsh Classical Dictionary*. Aberystwyth: National Library of Wales, 1993.

Baumgaertner, William E. *Squires, Knights, Barons, Kings: War and Politics in Fifteenth Century England*. Bloomington: Trafford Publishing, 2010.

Bennett, Michael. *Richard II and the Revolution of 1399*. Stroud: Sutton Publishing, 1999.

Bernard, J. H. *The Cathedral Church of Saint Patrick: A History & Description of the Building, with a Short Account of the Deans*. London: George Bell & Sons, 1903.

Bhabha, Homi. "Of Mimicry and Man: The Ambivalence of Colonial Discourse." In *The Location of Culture*. Abingdon: Routledge, 1994. Pp. 85–92.

Biggs, Douglas L. *Three Armies in Britain: The Irish Campaign of Richard II and the Usurpation of Henry IV, 1397–99*. Leiden: Brill, 2006.

Boardman, A. W. *Hotspur: Henry Percy, Medieval Rebel*. Stroud: Sutton Publishing, 2003.

Bollard, John K. "Myrddin in Early Welsh Tradition." In *The Romance of Merlin*. Ed. Peter Goodrich. New York: Garland, 1990. Pp. 13–54.

———. "Arthur in the Early Welsh Tradition." In *The Romance of Arthur*. Ed. James J. Wilhelm. New York: Garland, 1994. Pp. 11–23.

———. "Theme and Meaning in *Peredur*." *Arthuriana* 10.3 (2000), 73–92.

———. *The Mabinogi*. Llandysul: Gomer Press, 2006.

———. *Companion Tales to The Mabinogi*. Llandysul: Gomer Press, 2007.

———. "What is a *baryflen*? A Speculation." *Studia Celtica* 43 (2010), 213–20.

———. *Tales of Arthur*. Llandysul: Gomer Press, 2010.

Boobbyer, Juliet. "The Second Battle of Pilleth." *For a Change* (Apr/May 2005), 20–21.

Borrow, George. *Wild Wales*. Glasgow: Fontana/Collins, [1862], 1977.

Bowen, D. J. "Siôn Cent a'r Ysgwieriaid." *Llên Cymru* 21 (1998), 8–37.

Bowen, Geraint, ed. *Atlas Meirionnydd*. Y Bala: Gwasg y Sir [?1974].

Bower, Walter. *Scotichronicon*. Gen. ed. D. E. R. Watt. 9 vols. Vol. 1, ed. John and Winifred MacQueen, 1993; Vol. 8, ed. D. E. R. Watt, 1987. Edinburgh: Aberdeen University Press, 1987–1998.

Bradley, A. G. *Owen Glyndwr and the Last Struggle for Welsh Independence*. London: G. P. Putnam's Sons, 1901.

Breeze, Andrew. "Owen Glendower's Crest and the Scottish Campaign of 1384–1385." *Medium Aevum* 73 (2004), 99–102.

Brenhinedd y Saesson or The Kings of the Saxons. Ed. and trans. Thomas Jones. Cardiff: University of Wales Press, 1971.

Breudwyt Ronabwy. Ed. Melville Richards. Cardiff: University of Wales, 1948.

Brindley, David. *Richard Beauchamp: Medieval England's Greatest Knight*. Stroud: Tempus, 2001.

Bromwich, Rachel. "Dafydd ap Gwilym." In *A Guide to Welsh Literature*. 2.112–43.

———. *Trioedd Ynys Prydein: The Welsh Triads*. Cardiff: University of Wales; second ed., 1978; third ed., 2006.

Bromwich, Rachel, and D. Simon Evans. *Culhwch and Olwen: An Edition and Study of the Oldest Arthurian Tale*. Cardiff: University of Wales Press, 1992.

Brough, G. J. *Glyn Dŵr's War: The Campaigns of the Last Prince of Wales*. Glyndŵr Publishing, 2002.

The Brut or The Chronicles of England. Ed. Friedrich W. D. Brie. 2 vols. EETS o.s. 131, 136. London: K. Paul, Trench, Trübner & Co., 1906–08.

Brut Dingestow. Ed. Henry Lewis. Cardiff: University of Wales Press, 1942, rpt. 1975.

Brut y Brenhinedd: Cotton Cleopatra Version. Ed. John Jay Parry. Cambridge: Medieval Academy of America, 1937.

Brut y Brenhinedd: Llanstephan MS 1 Version. Ed. Brynley F. Roberts. Dublin: Dublin Institute for Advanced Studies, 1971.

Brut y Tywysogion: Peniarth MS. 20. Ed. Thomas Jones. Cardiff: University of Wales Press, 1941.

Brut y Tywysogion or The Chronicle of the Princes. Trans. Thomas Jones. Cardiff: University of Wales Press, 1952.

Bullock-Davies, Constance. "*Expectare Arturum*: Arthur and the Messianic Hope." *Bulletin of the Board of Celtic Studies* 29 (1982), 432–40.

Calendar of Chancery Rolls Preserved in the Public Record Office, A.D. 1277–1326. London: HMSO, 1926.

Calendar of the Close Rolls Preserved in the Public Record Office, Edward I, Vol. III, A.D. 1288–96. London: HMSO, 1904.

Calendar of the Fine Rolls Preserved in the Public Record Office, Edward I, Vol. I, A.D. 1272–1307. London: HMSO, 1911.

Calendar of the Patent Rolls Preserved in the Public Record Office, Edward III, A.D. 1327–1330. London: HMSO, 1891.

Calendar of the Patent Rolls Preserved in the Public Record Office, Henry IV. 4 vols., A.D. 1399–1401, 1401–05, 1405–08, 1408–13. London: HMSO, 1903–09.

Calendar of Patent Rolls Preserved in the Public Record Office, Henry VI, Vol. II, A.D. 1429–1436. London: HMSO, 1907.

The Cambro-Briton, Vol. 1. London: J. Limbird, 1820.

Capgrave, John. *Liber de Illustribus Henricis*. Ed. Francis Charles Hingeston. Rolls Series 7. London: Eyre and Spottiswoode, 1858.

———. *The Life of Saint Katherine of Alexandria*. Ed. F. J. Furnivall. Early English Text Society. London: 1893.

Carpenter, Christine. "Beauchamp, Richard." *Dictionary of National Biography*. 4.592–95.

Carr, A. D. "A Welsh Knight in the Hundred Years War: Sir Gregory Sais." *Transactions of the Honourable Society of Cymmrodorion* (1977), 40–53.

———. *Owen of Wales: The End of the House of Gwynedd*. Cardiff: University of Wales Press, 1991.

Carte, Thomas. *A General History of England, Vol. II*. London, 1750.

Carver, Martin. *Sutton Hoo: Burial Ground of Kings?* London: British Museum, 1998.

Castelden, Rodney. *King Arthur: The Truth Behind the Legend*. London: Routledge, 2000.

Caxton, William. *Caxton's Mirrour of the World*. Ed. Oliver H. Prior. Early English Text Society e.s. 110. London: K. Paul, Trench, and Trübner, 1913.

Catto, J. I. "An Alleged Great Council of 1374." *English Historical Review* 82 (1967), 764–71.

Ceinion Llenyddiaeth Gymreig. Ed. Owen Jones. 4 vols. London: Blackie, 1875–76.

Cernyw, Hywel. *Hynafiaethau Edeyrnion*. Corwen: R. Hughes, 1878.

Chapman, Adam. "David le Hope and Sir Gregory Sais." In *Soldier in Medieval England Database*. <http://www.icmacentre.ac.uk/soldier/database/September2008.php>.

Chaucer, Geoffrey. *The Riverside Chaucer*. Third ed. Ed. Larry D. Benson. Boston: Houghton Mifflin, 1987.

Chrimes, S. B. *Henry VII*. London: Eyre Methuen, 1972; New Haven: Yale University Press, 1999.

Chronica Maiora. See also *St. Albans Chronicle*.

The Chronica Maiora of Thomas Walsingham (1376–1422). Ed. James G. Clark; trans. David Preest. New York: Boydell Press, 2005.

The Chronicle of Dieulacres Abbey, 1381–1403. Ed. M. V. Clarke and V. H. Galbraith. In "The Deposition of Richard II." *Bulletin of the John Rylands Library* 14 (1930), 125–85.

Chronicon Incerti Scriptoris Angliae de Regnis Henrici IV, Henrici V et Henrici VI. Ed. John Allen Giles. London: Typis Editoris Apud Brampton, 1848.

Clancy, Joseph P. *Medieval Welsh Poems*. Dublin: Four Courts Press, 2003.

Clark, James G. "Thomas Walsingham Reconsidered: Books and Learning at Late-medieval St. Albans." *Speculum* 77.3 (2002), 832–60.

Clifford, S. N. "An Edition of the *Continuation of the Eulogium Historiarum 1361–1413*." Unpublished M.Phil thesis. University of Leeds, 1975.

Cochon, Pierre. *Chronique normande*. Ed. Charles de Robillard de Beaurepaire. Rouen: Brument, 1870.

Constable, Giles. "Forgery and Plagiarism in the Middle Ages." *Archiv für Diplomatik* 29 (1983), 1–41.

Contamine, Philippe. *War in the Middle Ages*. Trans. Michael Jones. Oxford: Basil Blackwell, 1984.

Coote, Lesley. *Prophecy and Public Affairs in Later Medieval England*. Woodbridge: Boydell and Brewer, 2000.

Cywyddau Iolo Goch ac Eraill. Ed. Henry Lewis, Thomas Roberts and Ifor Williams. Cardiff: University of Wales Press; new ed., 1937.

Dafydd ap Gwilym. *Gwaith Dafydd ap Gwilym*. Ed. Thomas Parry. Cardiff: University of Wales Press, 1963.

———. *Poems*. Ed. and trans. Rachel Bromwich. Llandysul: Gomer, 1982.

Dafydd ap Gwilym.net. <http://www.dafyddapgwilym.net/>.

Dafydd Llwyd o Fathafarn. *Gwaith Dafydd Llwyd o Fathafarn*. Ed. W. Leslie Richards. Cardiff: University of Wales Press, 1964.

Daniel, R. Iestyn, ed. *Gwaith Dafydd Bach ap Madog Wladaidd 'Sypyn Cyfeiliog' a Llywelyn ab y Moel*. Aberystwyth: Centre for Advanced Welsh and Celtic Studies, 1998.

Davies, J. Conway. "Some Owen Glyndwr Documents." *National Library of Wales Journal* 3 (1943), 48–50.

Davies, John R. "The Archbishopric of St Davids." In *St David of Wales: Cult, Church and Nation*. Ed. J. Wyn Evans and Jonathan M. Wooding. Woodbridge: Boydell Press, 2007. Pp. 296–304.

Davies, R. R. "The Twilight of Welsh law, 1284–1326." *History* 51 (1966), 143–64.

———. "Owain Glyn Dŵr and the Welsh Squirearchy." *Transactions of the Honourable Society of Cymmrodorion* (1968), 2.150–69.

———. "Colonial Wales." *Past and Present* 65 (1974), 3–23.

———. "Race Relations in Post-Conquest Wales: Confrontation and Compromise." *Transactions of the Honourable Society of Cymmrodorion* (1974–75), 32–56.

———. "The Status of Women and the Practice of Marriage in Late-medieval Wales." In *The Welsh Law of Women: Studies Presented to Professor Daniel A. Binchy on His Eightieth Birthday*. Ed. Dafydd Jenkins and Morfydd E. Owen. Cardiff: University of Wales Press, 1980. Pp. 93–114.

———. *The Age of Conquest: Wales 1063–1415*. Oxford: Oxford University Press, 1987.

———. *The Revolt of Owain Glyn Dŵr*. Oxford: Oxford University Press, 1995.

Davies, Sioned, trans. *The Mabinogion*. Oxford: Oxford University Press, 2007.

De controversia in curia militari inter Ricardum Le Scrope et Robertum Grosvenor milites. Ed. N. Harris Nicolas. 2 vols. London: Samuel Bentley, 1832.

Deio ab Ieuan Du. *Gwaith Deio ab Ieuan Du a Gwilym ab Ieuan Hen*. Ed. A. Eleri Davies. Cardiff: University of Wales Press, 1992.

DeVries, Kelly. *Joan of Arc: A Military Leader*. Stroud: Sutton Publishing, 1999.

———. "John the Fearless' Way of War." In *Reputation and Representation in Fifteenth Century Europe*. Ed. Douglas L. Biggs, Sharon D. Michalove, and A. Compton Reeves. Leiden: Brill, 2004. Pp. 39–55.

———. "The Reasons for the Bishop of Norwich's Attack on Flanders in 1383." *Fourteenth Century England* 3 (2004), 155–65.

———, and Robert Douglas Smith. *Medieval Military Technology*. Second ed. Toronto: University of Toronto Press, 2012.

The Dictionary of Welsh Biography down to 1940. London: The Honourable Society of Cymmrodorion, 1959.

Dillon, Janette. *Performance and Spectacle in Hall's Chronicle*. London: Society for Theatre Research, 2002.

Doig, James A. "'The Prophecy of the Six Kings to Follow John' and Owain Glyndŵr." *Studia Celtica* 29 (1995), 257–67.

Dumville, David. "What is a Chronicle?" In *The Medieval Chronicle II: Proceedings of the 2nd International Conference on the Medieval Chronicle Diebergen/ Utrecht 16-21 July 1999*. Ed. Erik Kooper. Amsterdam: Rodopi, 2002. Pp. 1–27.

Dunn, Elizabeth. "Owain Glyndŵr and Radnorshire." *Radnorshire Society Transactions* 37 (1967), 27–35.

Dwnn, Lewys. *Heraldic Visitations of Wales and Part of the Marches, Between 1586 and 1613*. 2 vols. Ed. Samuel Rush Meyrick. Llandovery: William Rees, 1846.

Dydd Gwyl Dewi Sant. Caerdydd: Western Mail, 1915.

Edwards, Edward. *Willis' Survey of St. Asaph, Considerably Enlarged*. Wrexham: John Painter, 1801.

Edwards, J. Goronwy. *Calendar of Ancient Correspondence Concerning Wales*. Cardiff: University of Wales Press Board, 1935.

———, ed. *Littere Wallie, Preserved in Liber A in the Public Record Office*. Cardiff: University Press Board, 1940.

Eifion Wyn. "Owain Glyndwr." *Cymru* 13 (1897), 188.

Ellis, Henry. *Original Letters Illustrative of English History*. 11 vols. London: Richard Bentley, 1824 (series 1), 1827 (series 2), 1846 (series 3).

Ellis, P. Berresford. *Wales — A Nation Again!* London: Tandem Books, 1968.

Ellis, T. P., and John Lloyd, trans. *The Mabinogion, Vol. I*. Oxford: Clarendon Press, 1929.

Ellis, Thomas. *Memoirs of Owen Glendowr*. In *A History of the Island of Anglesey*. London: J. Dodsley, 1775.

An English Chronicle 1377–1461: A New Edition. Ed. William Marx. Woodbridge: Boydell Press, 2003.

Eulogium Historiarum sive Temporis. Ed. Frank Scott Haydon. 3 vols. Rolls Series 9. London: Longman, Brown, Green, Longmans, and Roberts, 1858–63.

Evans, C. J. *The Story of Glamorgan*. Cardiff: Educational Publishing Company, 1908.

Evans, D. Simon. *A Grammar of Middle Welsh*. Dublin: Dublin Institute for Advanced Studies, 1964.

Evans, Dafydd Huw. "An Incident on the Dee during the Glyn Dŵr Rebellion?" *Transactions of the Denbighshire Historical Society* 37 (1988), 5–40.

Evans, Gwynfor. *Rhagom i Ryddid*. Bangor: Plaid Cymru, 1964.

Evans, Gwynfor. *Wales Can Win*. Llandybie: Christopher Davies, 1973.

Evans, Howell T. *Wales and the Wars of the Roses*. Cambridge: University Press, 1915.

Evans, J. Gwenogvryn, ed. *Report on Manuscripts in the Welsh Language*. London: HMSO, 1898–1910.

———, ed. *The Poetry in the Red Book of Hergest*. Llanbedrog: [privately printed], 1911.

Evans, R. Wallis. "Prophetic Poetry." In *A Guide to Welsh Literature.* 2.278–97.

Evans, R. Wallis. "Cywydd Brud gan Ieuan Brydydd Hir o Feirionnydd." *Journal of the Merioneth Historical and Record Society* 12 (1994–97), 189–90.

Evans, Thomas. *Cambrian Itinerary, or Welsh Tourist.* London: C. Whittingham, 1801.

Faletra, Michael. "Narrating the Matter of Britain: Geoffrey of Monmouth and the Norman Colonization of Wales." *Chaucer Review* 35 (2000), 60–85.

Fenton, Richard. *Tours in Wales (1804-1813).* London: The Bedford Press, 1917.

Firbank, Thomas. *A Country of Memorable Honour.* Bath: Cedric Chivers Ltd, [1953], 1971.

First English Life of Henry V. Ed. Charles Lethbridge Kingsford. Oxford: Clarendon Press, 1911.

Fisher, John. "The Welsh Calendar." *Transactions of the Honourable Society of Cymmrodorion* (1896), 99–145.

Ford, Patrick K., trans. *The Mabinogi and Other Medieval Welsh Tales.* Berkeley: University of California Press, 1977.

Forey, Alan. *The Military Orders: From the Twelfth to the Early Fourteenth Centuries.* Toronto: University of Toronto Press, 1992.

Fouke le Fitz Waryn. Trans. Thomas Kelly. In *Robin Hood and Other Outlaw Tales.* Ed. Stephen Knight and Thomas Ohlgren. Kalamazoo: Medieval Institute Publications, 1997. Pp. 687–723.

Foulkes, Isaac. "Dyffryn Clwyd: Ei Ramantau a'i Lafar Gwlad." *Transactions of the Honourable Society of Cymmrodorion* (1893): 88–103.

Fox, Alistair. *Politics and Literature in the Reigns of Henry VII and Henry VIII.* Oxford: Basil Blackwell, 1989.

Fulton, Helen. *Selections from the Dafydd ap Gwilym Apocrypha.* Llandysul: Gomer Press, 1996.

———. "Owain Glyn Dŵr and the Uses of Prophecy." *Studia Celtica* 39 (2005), 105–21.

———. "Literature of the Welsh Gentry: Uses of the Vernacular in Medieval Wales." In *Vernacularity in England and Wales, c.1300–1550.* Utrecht Studies in Medieval Literacy 17. Ed. Elizabeth Salter and Helen Wicker. Turnhout: Brepols, 2012. Pp. 199–223.

Fychan, Cledwyn. "Llywelyn ab y Moel a'r Canolbarth." *Llên Cymru* 15 (1987–88), 289–307.

———. *Pwy Oedd Rhys Gethin? Yr ymchwil am gadfridog Owain Glyndŵr.* Aberystwyth: Cymdeithas Lyfrau Ceredigion Gyf., 2007.

Gairdner, James. *The Historical Collections of a Citizen of London in the Fifteenth Century.* Westminster: Camden Society, 1876.

Galyon, Aubrey, and Zacharias P. Thundy, trans. "History of the Kings of Britain." In *The Romance of Merlin: An Anthology.* Ed. by Peter Goodrich. New York: Garland, 1990. Pp. 57–70.

Gantz, Jeffrey, trans. *The Mabinogion.* Harmondsworth: Penguin Books, 1976.

Geiriadur Prifysgol Cymru, A Dictionary of the Welsh Language. Cardiff: University of Wales Press, 1950–2002.

Geoffrey of Monmouth. *Historia regum Britanniae: A Variant Version.* Ed. Jacob Hammer. Cambridge: Medieval Academy of America, 1951.

———. *The History of the Kings of Britain.* Trans. Lewis Thorpe. Harmondsworth: Penguin, 1966.

———. *Geoffrey of Monmouth: The History of the Kings of Britain. An Edition and Translation of De gestis Britonum [Historia regum Britanniae].* Ed. Michael D. Reeve, trans. Neil Wright. Woodbridge: The Boydell Press, 2007.

———. *Life of Merlin. Vita Merlini.* Ed. and trans. Basil Clarke. Cardiff: University of Wales Press, 1973.

Gerald of Wales. *The Journey Through Wales and the Description of Wales.* Trans. Lewis Thorpe. Harmondsworth: Penguin, 1978.

Gervase of Canterbury. *The Historical Works of Gervase of Canterbury.* Ed. William Stubbs. Rolls Series 73. London: Longman, 1879–80.

Gibson, Edmund. *Camden's Britannia, Newly Translated into English.* London: Edmund Gibson, 1695.

Giles's Chronicle. See *Chronicon Incerti Scriptoris.*

Given-Wilson, Chris. *Chronicles: The Writing of History in Medieval England.* London: Hambledon, 2004.

Goetinck, Glenys Witchard. *Historia Peredur vab Efrawc.* Cardiff: University of Wales Press, 1976.

Goodman, Anthony. "Owain Glyndŵr before 1400." *Welsh History Review* 5 (1970–71), 67–70.

Gower, John. *The Major Latin Works of John Gower*. Trans. by Eric W. Stockton. Seattle: University of Washington Press, 1962.

———. *The Minor Works of John Gower*. Ed. and trans. R. F. Yeager. Kalamazoo: Medieval Institute Publications, 2005.

Gransden, Antonia. *Historical Writing in England, Vol. II, c.1007 to the Early Sixteenth Century*. London: Routledge and Kegan Paul, 1982.

———. "Chronicles of Medieval England and Scotland." In *Legends, Traditions and History in Medieval England*. London: Hambledon, 1992. Pp. 199–238.

Greenberg, Bradley. "Romancing the Chronicles: *1 Henry IV* and the Rewriting of Medieval History." *Quidditas* 26–27 (2005–06), 35–50.

Gregory, Donald. *Radnorshire: A Historical Guide*. Llanrwst: Gwasg Carreg Gwalch, 1994.

Gresham, Colin A. "Platform Houses in North-West Wales." *Archaeologia Cambrensis* 103 (1954), 18–53.

Grévy-Pons, Nicole, and Ezio Ornato. "Que est l'auteur de la chronique latine de Charles VI dite du Religieux de St Denis?" *Bibliothèque de l'école des Chartes* 134 (1976), 85–102.

Griffith, John Edwards. *Pedigrees of Anglesey and Carnarvonshire Families*. [Bangor]: privately published, 1914.

Griffiths, Margaret Enid. *Early Vaticination in Welsh with English Parallels*. Ed. T. Gwynn Jones. Cardiff: University of Wales Press, 1937.

Griffiths, Ralph, and George Edward Griffiths. Review of *Original Letters*, ed. Ellis. *The Monthly Review* 22 (June 1827), 220–37.

Griffiths, Ralph A. *The Principality of Wales in the Later Middle Ages, Vol. 1: South Wales, 1277–1536*. Cardiff: University of Wales Press, 1972.

———. "Duke Richard of York's Intentions in 1450 and the Origin of the Wars of the Roses." *Journal of Medieval History* 1 (1975), 187–209.

———. "Wales and the Marches." In *Fifteenth-century England 1399–1509: Studies in Politics and Society*. Ed. S. B. Chrimes, C. D. Ross, and R. A. Griffiths. Manchester: Manchester University Press, 1972. Pp. 145–72.

———. "William Botiller: A Fifteenth Century Civil Servant." In *King and Country: England and Wales in the Fifteenth Century*. Ed. Ralph A. Griffiths. London: Continuum, 2003. Pp. 179–86.

Gruffudd Hiraethog. *Gwaith Gruffudd Hiraethog*. Ed. D. J. Bowen. Cardiff: University of Wales Press, 1990.

Gruffudd Llwyd. *Gwaith Gruffudd Llwyd a'r Llygliwiaid Eraill*. Ed. Rhiannon Ifans. Aberystwyth: Centre for Advanced Welsh and Celtic Studies, 2000.

Gruffydd, R. Geraint. "Englynion y Cusan by Dafydd ap Gwilym." *Cambridge Medieval Celtic Studies* 23 (Summer 1992), 1–6.

Guest, Charlotte, trans. *The Mabinogion*. London: Bernard Quaritch, 1877.

A Guide to Welsh Literature. Ed. A. O. H. Jarman and Gwilym Rees Hughes. 2 vols. Swansea: Christopher Davies, 1976–79.

Guilfoyle, Cherrell. "Othello, Otuel, and the English Charlemagne Romances." *The Review of English Studies* n.s. 38, no. 149 (Feb., 1987), 50–55.

Guto'r Glyn. *Gwaith Guto'r Glyn*. Ed. John Llywelyn Williams and Ifor Williams. Cardiff: University of Wales Press, 1939.

gutorglyn.net. Aberystwyth: Centre for Advanced Welsh and Celtic Studies, 2012.

Gutun Owain. *L'Œuvre Poétique de Gutun Owain*. 2 vols. Ed. E. Bachellery. Paris: Librairie Ancienne Honoré Champion, 1950–51.

Gwerful Mechain. *Gwaith Gwerful Mechain ac Eraill*. Ed. Nerys Ann Howells. Aberystwyth: Centre for Advanced Welsh and Celtic Studies, 2001.

Hague, Douglas B. "The Bishop's Palace, Gogarth, Llandudno, Caernarvonshire." *Transactions of the Caernarvonshire Historical Society* 17 (1956), 9–22.

———, and Cynthia Warhurst. "Excavations at Sycharth Castle, Denbighshire, 1962–63." *Archaeologia Cambrensis* 115 (1966), 108–27.

Hall, Edward. *The Vnion of the two noble and illustre famelies of Lancastre & Yorke*. London, 1550.

Hardyng, John. *The Chronicle of Iohn Hardyng*. Ed. Henry Ellis. London: F. C. and J. Rivington et al., 1812.

Hatfield, William. *Knighton and District*. Hereford: Jakemans, 1947.

Hathaway, Neil. "*Compilatio*: from Plagiarism to Compiling." *Viator* 20 (1989), 19–44.

Hawkes, Terence. "Bryn Glas." *European Journal of English Studies* 1 (1993), 269–90.

Hay, Denys. *Polydore Vergil, Renaissance Historian and Man of Letters*. Oxford: Oxford University Press, 1952.

Haycock, Marged, ed. *Blodeugerdd Barddas o Ganu Crefyddol Cynnar*. Swansea: Cyhoeddiadau Barddas, 1994.

———. "Cadair Ceridwen." In *Cyfoeth y Testun*. Ed. Iestyn Daniel, Marged Haycock, et al. Cardiff: University of Wales Press, 2003. Pp. 148–75.

———, ed. *Legendary Poems from the Book of Taliesin*. Aberystwyth: CMCS, 2007.

Henken, Elissa R. *National Redeemer: Owain Glyndŵr in Welsh Tradition*. Ithaca: Cornell University Press, 1996.

Hewett, Hope. *Walking through Merioneth*. Newton: Welsh Outlook Press, n.d.

Higden, Ranulf. *Polychronicon Ranulphi Higden Monachi Cestrensis*. Ed. Churchill Babington and Joseph Rawson Lumby. 9 vols. Rolls Series 41. London: Longman, Green, Longman, Longman, Roberts, and Green, 1865–86.

Highley, Christopher. *Spenser, Shakespeare and the Crisis in Ireland*. Cambridge: Cambridge University Press, 1997.

Historia Vitae et Regni Ricardi Secundi. Ed. George B. Stow, Jr. Philadelphia: University of Pennsylvania Press, 1977.

The History of the Island of Anglesey. London: J. Dodsley, 1775.

Hobley, W. *Hanes Methodistiaeth Arfon*. Caernarfon: Cyfarfod Misol Arfon, 1924.

Hodges, Geoffrey. *Owain Glyn Dŵr and the War of Independence in the Welsh Borders*. Little Logaston: Logaston Press, 1995.

Hogg, A. H. A. "A 14th Century House-Site at Cefn-y-Fan Near Dolbenmaen, Caernarvonshire." *Transactions of the Honourable Society of Cymmrodorion* 15 (1954), 1–7.

Hotson, J. Leslie. "Colfox vs. Chauntecleer." *PMLA* 39.4 (1924), 762–81.

Howse, W. H. "New Radnor Castle." *Radnorshire Society Transactions* 28 (1958), 24–26.

Hughes, Arwyn Lloyd. "Noddwyr y Beirdd yn Sir Feirionnydd. Casgliad o'r Cerddi i Deuluoedd Corsygedol. Dolau-gwyn, Llwyn, Nannau, Y Rug, Rhiwedog, Rhiw-goch, Rhiwlas ac Ynysymaengwyn." MA diss., University of Wales, 1969.

Hunter, Jerry. *Soffestri'r Saeson: Hanesyddiaeth a Hunaniaeth yn Oes y Tuduriaid*. Caerdydd: Gwasg Prifysgol Cymru, 2000.

Huws, Bleddyn Owen. "Dyddiadau Ieuan Gethin." *Llên Cymru* 20 (1997), 46–55.

———. "Y Bardd a'i Noddwr yn yr Oesoedd Canol Diweddar: Guto'r Glyn a Hywel ab Ieuan Fychan o Foeliwrch." *Cof Cenedl* 16 (2001), 1–32.

———. "Ailadeiladu Bywyd ar ôl Gwrthryfel Glyndŵr." *Dwned* 13 (2007), 97–137.

Huws, Daniel. *Medieval Welsh Manuscripts*. Cardiff and Aberystwyth: University of Wales Press and the National Library of Wales, 2000.

Hywel Cilan. *Gwaith Hywel Cilan*. Ed. Islwyn Jones. Cardiff: University of Wales Press, 1963.

Ieuan ap Hywel Swrdwal. *Gwaith Hywel Swrdwal a'i Deulu*. Ed. Dylan Foster Evans. Aberystwyth: Centre for Advanced Welsh and Celtic Studies, 2000.

Ieuan ap Rhydderch. *Gwaith Ieuan ap Rhydderch*. Ed. R. Iestyn Daniel. Aberystwyth: Centre for Advanced Welsh and Celtic Studies, 2003.

Ieuan Brydydd Hir. *Gwaith Ieuan Brydydd Hir*. Ed. M. Paul Bryant-Quinn. Aberystwyth: Centre for Advanced Welsh and Celtic Studies, 2000.

Imagining History Portal website. <http://www.qub.ac.uk/imagining-history/resources/wiki/>.

Iolo Goch. *Gwaith Iolo Goch*. Ed. Dafydd R. Johnston. Cardiff: University of Wales, 1988.

———. *Iolo Goch: Poems*. Ed. and trans. Dafydd Johnston. Llandysul: Gomer Press, 1993.

Iolo Morganwg. *Iolo Manuscripts*. Ed. and trans. Taliesin Williams. Llandovery: Welsh Manuscripts Society, 1848.

Issues of the Exchequer, Being a Collection of Payments Made Out of His Majesty's Revenue, from King Henry III to King Henry IV Inclusive. Ed. Frederick Devon. London: John Murray, 1837.

Iwan, Dafydd. *Cant o Ganeuon*. Talybont: Y Lolfa, 1982.

Jack, R. Ian. "New Light on the Early Days of Owain Glyndŵr." *Bulletin of the Board of Celtic Studies* 21 (1964–66), 163–66.

Jackson, Kenneth. *Language and History in Early Britain*. Edinburgh: Edinburgh University Press, 1953.

Jacob, E. F. *The Fifteenth Century, 1399–1485*. Oxford: Clarendon Press, 1961.

James, E. Wyn. *Glyndŵr a Gobaith y Genedl: Agweddau ar y Portread o Owain Glyndŵr yn Llenyddiaeth y Cyfnod Modern*. Aberystwyth: Cymdeithas Lyfrau Ceredigion Gyf., 2007.

James, Mervyn. "English Politics and the Concept of Honor." In *Society, Politics and Culture: Essays in Early Modern England*. Cambridge: Cambridge University Press, 1986. Pp. 308–414.

Jarman, A. O. H. *The Cynfeirdd: Early Welsh Poets and Poetry* (Writers of Wales). Cardiff: University of Wales Press, 1981.

———. *Llyfr Du Caerfyrddin gyda Rhagymadrodd, Nodiadau Testunol a Geirfa*. Cardiff: University of Wales Press, 1982.

Jenkins, Dafydd. *The Law of Hywel Dda*. Llandysul: Gomer Press, 1986.

Jenkins, Manon. "Aspects of the Prophetic Verse Tradition in the Middle Ages." PhD diss., University of Cambridge, 1990.

Johnston, Dafydd. "Iolo Goch and the English: Welsh Poetry and Politics in the Fourteenth Century." *Cambridge Medieval Celtic Studies* 12 (1986), 73–98.

———. *Canu Maswedd yr Oesoedd Canol: Medieval Welsh Erotic Poetry*. Cardiff: Tafol, 1991.

———. *Llên yr Uchelwyr: Hanes Beirniadol Llenyddiaeth Gymraeg 1300–1525*. Cardiff: University of Wales Press, 2005.

Jones, Evan J. "The Authorship of the Continuation of the Eulogium Historiarum: A Suggestion." *Speculum* 12.2 (1937), 196–202.

Jones, John Morris. *Caniadau*. Oxford: Fox, Jones, & Co., 1907.

Jones, Michael K. *Agincourt 1415: Battlefield Guide*. Barnsley: Pen and Sword, 2005.

Jones, Owen (Myvyr), Edward Williams (Iolo Morganwg), William Owen Pughe (Idrison), eds. *The Myvyrian Archaiology of Wales: Collated Out of Ancient Manuscripts*. Denbigh: Thomas Gee, 1801–07; second ed., 1870.

Jones, T. Gwynn, ed., *Ceiriog*. Wrecsam: Hughes a'i Fab, n.d.

Jones, Thomas. "Elis Gruffydd, y Milwr o Galais." In *Mân Us*. Cardiff: Llyfrau'r Castell, 1949. Pp. 60–67.

———. "The Black Book of Carmarthen 'Stanzas of the Graves.'" *Proceedings of the British Academy* 53 (1968), 97–137.

Jones, Thomas, and Gwyn Jones, trans. *The Mabinogion*. New York: Alfred A. Knopf, 2000 (1949).

Juvénal des Ursins, Jean. *Histoire de Charles VI Roy de France*. Ed. Joseph François Michaud and Jean Joseph François Poujoulat. In *Nouvelle Collection des Mémoires pour Servir à l'histoire de France*. 32 vols. Paris: Commentaire Analytique du Code Civil, 1836–44. 2.323–571.

Kaye, J. M. *Medieval English Conveyances*. Cambridge: Cambridge University Press, 2009.

Keble Martin, W. *The Concise British Flora in Colour*. London: Ebury Press and Michael Joseph, 1965.

Kelly, Henry Ansgar. *Divine Providence in the England of Shakespeare's Histories*. Cambridge, MA: Harvard University Press, 1970.

Kelly, Susan. "The Arthurian Material in the *Scotichronicon* of Walter Bower." *Anglia* 97 (1979), 431–39.

Kingsford, Charles. *English Historical Literature in the Fifteenth-Century*. New York: Burt Franklin, 1913.

Knighton, Henry. *Chronicon Henrici Knighton vel Cnitthon, Monachi Leycestrensis*. Vol. 2. Ed. Joseph Rawson Lumby. Rolls Series 92. London: HMSO, 1895.

Knowles, David. *The Religious Orders in England, Vol. II: The End of the Middle Ages*. Cambridge: Cambridge University Press, 1955.

———, and R. Neville Hadcock. *Medieval Religious Houses: England and Wales*. London: Longman, 1971.

Krapp, George Philip, ed. *The Vercelli Book*. The Anglo-Saxon Poetic Records 2. New York: Columbia University Press, 1932.

Krapp, George Philip, and Elliot Van Kirk Dobbie, eds. *The Exeter Book*. The Anglo-Saxon Poetic Records 3. New York: Columbia University Press, 1936.

Kronk, Gary W. *Cometography: A Catalog of Comets*. Vol. 1: Ancient–1799. Cambridge: Cambridge University Press, 1999.

Langtoft, Pierre de. *The Chronicle of Pierre de Langtoft*. Ed. T. Wright. New York: Kraus Reprint, 1964.

Latimer, Jon. "The Last Welsh Prince of Wales." *Military History* (Dec. 2002), 42–48.

Leland, John. *The Itinerary in Wales of John Leland in or about the Years 1536–1539*. Ed. Lucy Toulmin Smith. London: George Bell and Sons, 1906.

Lewis, Henry, Thomas Roberts, and Ifor Williams, eds. *Cywyddau Iolo Goch ac Eraill*. Bangor: Evan Thomas, 1925; second ed., Cardiff: University of Wales Press, 1972.

Lewis, Samuel. *A Topographical Dictionary of Wales*. London: S. Lewis and Co., 1833.

Lewis, Saunders. *Meistri a'u Crefft: Ysgrifau Llenyddol gan Saunders Lewis*. Ed. Gwynn ap Gwilym. Cardiff: University of Wales Press, 1981.

Lewis, W. J. *Born on a Perilous Rock: Aberystwyth Past and Present*. Aberystwyth: Cambrian News, 1980.

Lewys Daron. *Gwaith Lewys Daron*. Ed. A. Cynfael Lake. Cardiff: University of Wales Press, 1994.

Lewys Glyn Cothi. *Gwaith Lewys Glyn Cothi*. Ed. Dafydd Johnston. Cardiff: University of Wales Press, 1995.

———. *Gwaith Lewis Glyn Cothi, Y Gyfrol Gyntaf, Testun Llawysgrif Peniarth 109*. Ed. E. D. Jones. Cardiff: University of Wales Press; Aberystwyth: National Library of Wales, 1953.

Lewys Môn. *Gwaith Lewys Môn*. Ed. Eurys I. Rowlands. Cardiff: University of Wales Press, 1975.

Lewys Morgannwg. *Gwaith Lewys Morgannwg*. 2 vols. Ed. A. Cynfael Lake. Aberystwyth: Centre for Advanced Welsh and Celtic Studies, 2004.

Livingston, Michael, ed. *The Battle of Brunanburh: A Casebook*. Exeter: Exeter University Press, 2011.

———. "Hatsfield's Mystery Source for the Battle of Bryn Glas." *Transactions of the Radnorshire Society* 82 (2012), forthcoming.

Llawdden. *Gwaith Llawdden*. Ed. R. Iestyn Daniel. Aberystwyth: Centre for Advanced Welsh and Celtic Studies, 2006.

Llewelyn, Emyr. "Mi a Wn y Daw." *Areithiau Cymdeithas yr Iaith*. Talybont: Y Lolfa, 1970.

Lloyd, D. Myrddin. "The Later Gogynfeirdd." In *A Guide to Welsh Literature*. 2.36–57.

Lloyd, J. E. *A History of Wales*. London: Longmans, 1911, rpt. 1967.

———. "Trouble in Wales about 1410." *Bulletin of the Board of Celtic Studies* 5 (1929–31), 155–56.

———. *Owen Glendower / Owain Glyn Dŵr*. Oxford: Oxford University Press, 1931.

Lloyd, J. Y. W. *The History of the Princes, the Lords Marcher, and the Ancient Nobility of Powys Fadog, and the Ancient Lords of Arwystli, Cedewen, and Meirionydd*. 6 vols. London: T. Richards, 1881–87.

Lloyd, Megan S. *Speak it in Welsh: Wales and the Welsh Language in Shakespeare*. New York: Rowman and Littlefield, 2007.

Lloyd-Jones, John. *Geirfa Barddoniaeth Gynnar Gymraeg*. Cardiff: University of Wales Press, 1931–63.

Lloyd-Morgan, Ceridwen. "Prophecy and Welsh Nationhood in the Fifteenth Century." *Transactions of the Honourable Society of Cymmrodorion* (1985), 9–26.

Llywelyn ab y Moel. *Gwaith*. See Daniel, ed., *Gwaith Dafydd Bach ap Madog Wladaidd 'Sypyn Cyfeiliog' a Llywelyn ab y Moel*.

Llywelyn ap Gutun. *Gwaith Llywelyn ap Gutun*. Ed. R. Iestyn Daniel. Aberystwyth: Centre for Advanced Welsh and Celtic Studies, 2006.

Llywelyn-Williams, Alun. *Crwydro Brycheiniog*. Llandybie: Llyfrau'r Dryw, 1964.

Loomis, R. S. "The Legend of Arthur's Survival." In *Arthurian Literature in the Middle Ages*. Ed. by R. S. Loomis. Oxford: Clarendon Press, 1959. Pp. 64–71.

Loth, J., ed. *Les Mabinogion, Vol. 2*. Paris: Ernest Thorin, 1889.

Lucas, Peter. "John Capgrave, Friar of Lynn." *Historian* 44 (1994), 23–24.

———. *From Author to Audience: John Capgrave and Medieval Publication*. Dublin: University College Dublin Press, 1997.

Lupack, Alan. "The Arthurian Legend in the Sixteenth to Eighteenth Centuries." In *The Companion to Arthurian Literature*. Ed. Helen Fulton. Oxford: Wiley-Blackwell, 2009. Pp. 340–54.

Lynch, Peredur I. *Proffwydoliaeth a'r Syniad o Genedl*. Bangor: Ysgol y Gymraeg, Prifysgol Bangor, 2007.

Mac Cana, Proinsias. "The Poet as Spouse of His Patron." *Ériu* 39 (1988), 79–85.

———. "Ir. *buaball*, W *bual* 'drinking horn.'" *Ériu* 44 (1993), 81–93.

MacFarlane, Alan. *Witchcraft in Tudor and Stuart England: A Regional and Comparative Study*. New York: Harper and Rowe, 1970.

Maguire, Laurie E. "'Household Kates': Chez Petruchio, Percy and Plantagenet." In *Gloriana's Face: Women, Public and Private, in the English Renaissance*. Ed. S. P. Cerasano and Marion Wynne-Davies. Detroit: Wayne State University Press, 1992. Pp. 129–67.

Maidstone, Clement. *Martyrium Ricardi Archiepiscopi*. Ed. and trans. by Stephen Wright, 1997. <http://english.cua.edu/faculty/wright/latmaidston.cfm> [Latin]; <http://english.cua.edu/faculty/wright/maidston.cfm> [English].

Marchant, Alicia."Cosmos and History: Shakespeare's Representation of Nature and Rebellion in *Henry IV Part One*." In *Renaissance Poetry and Drama in Context: Essays for Christopher Wortham*. Ed. Andrew Lynch and Anne M. Scott. Newcastle Upon Tyne: Cambridge Scholars, 2008. Pp. 41–61.

———. "*In Loco Amoenissimo*: Fifteenth-Century St Albans and the Role of Place in Thomas Walsingham's Description of Wales." *Place: An Interdisciplinary E-journal* (April 2008), 1–18. <http://www.elsewhereonline.com.au/place>. Accessed 5 May 2009.

———. "'Adam, you are in a labyrinth'": Textual Interpolation as the Nexus of Body and Spirit in the *Chronicle* of Adam Usk." In *Conjunctions: Body and Mind from Plato to Descartes*. Ed. Danijela Kambaskovic-Sawers. Forthcoming.

Marvin, Julia. "Arthur Authorised: The Prophecies of the Prose *Brut* Chronicle." *Arthurian Literature* 22 (2005), 84–89.

Mathau Brwmffild. *Gwaith Mathau Brwmffild*. Ed. A. Cynfael Lake. Aberystwyth: Centre for Advanced Welsh and Celtic Studies, 2002.

Matheson, Lister M. *The Prose Brute: The Development of a Middle English Chronicle*. Tempe: Medieval and Renaissance Texts and Studies, 1998.

Matthews, Thomas. *Welsh Records in Paris*. Reprinted in Rees and Jones.

Maxfield, Stephen. *The Battlefield of Shrewsbury*. Shrewsbury: Stephen Maxfield, 2003.

McLaren, Mary-Rose. *The London Chronicles of the Fifteenth Century: A Revolution in English Writing, with an Annotated Edition of Bradford, West Yorkshire Archives MS 32D86/42*. Woodbridge: D. S. Brewer, 2002.

McNiven, Peter. *Heresy and Politics in the Reign of Henry IV: the Burning of John Badby*. Woodbridge: Boydell Press, 1987.

———. "Rebellion, Sedition and the Legend of Richard II's Survival in the Reigns of Henry IV and Henry V." *Bulletin of the John Rylands University Library of Manchester* 76.1 (1994), 93–117.

Minnis, Alastair J. "Late-medieval Discussions of *Compilatio* and the Role of the *Compilator*." *Beiträge zur Geschichte der deutschen Sprache und Literatur* 101 (1979), 385–421.

Moffat, Douglas, ed. *The Soul's Address to the Body: The Worcester Fragments*. East Lansing: Colleagues Press, 1987.

———, ed. *The Old English Body and Soul*. Cambridge: Cambridge University Press, 1990.

Monstrelet, Enguerrand de. *The Chronicles of Enguerrand de Monstrelet*. Trans. Thomas Johnes. 2 vols. London: William Smith, 1840.

———. *La Chronique d'Enguerran de Monstrelet*. Ed. Louis Douet d'Arcq. 6 vols. Paris: Renouard, 1857–62.

Morgan, Ceridwen Lloyd. "Prophecy and Welsh Nationhood in the Fifteenth Century." *Transactions of the Honourable Society of Cymmrodorion* (1985), 9–26.

Morgan, Noel. "Owain Glyndŵr." In *The Friends of Pilleth*. Hereford: Richard Downes, 2002.

Morgan, Philip. *War and Society in Medieval Cheshire 1277–1403*. Manchester: Chetham Society, 1987.

———. *The Battle of Shrewsbury, 1403*. Stroud: History Press, 2003.

Morgan, T. J. *Y Treigliadau a'u Cystrawen*. Cardiff: University of Wales Press, 1952.

Morgan, T. O. "Historical and Traditional Notices of Owain Glyndwr," *Archaeologica Cambrensis* 2.2 (1851), 24–42, 113–22.

Morris, John. *Nennius: British History and the Welsh Annals*. London: Phillimore, 1980.

Morris, John E. *The Welsh Wars of Edward I*. Oxford: Clarendon Press, 1901, rpt. 1968.

Morris Jones, J. *A Welsh Grammar: Historical and Comparative*. Oxford: Clarendon Press, 1913.

Morris-Jones, John, and T. H. Parry-Williams, eds. *Llawysgrif Hendregadredd*. Cardiff: University of Wales Press, 1933, rpt. 1971.

National Library of Wales Web site: http://www.llgc.org.uk/index.php?id=122 (accessed 3 May 2012).

Nicholson, Helen. *Medieval Warfare: Theory and Practice of War in Europe, 300–1500*. Houndmills: Palgrave Macmillan, 2004.

Noble, F. "Further Excavations at Bleddfa Church and Associated Problems of the History of the Lordship of Bleddfa." *Radnorshire Society Transactions* 33 (1963), 57–63.

Notestein, Wallace. *A History of Witchcraft in England from 1558 to 1718*. New York: Crowell, 1968.

Ornduff, Robert. "A Botanist's View of the Big Tree." In *Proceedings of the Symposium on Giant Sequoias: Their Place in the Ecosystem and Society*. Ed. Philip S. Aune. General Technical Report PSW-GTR-151. Albany: Pacific Southwest Research Station, Forest Service, U. S. Department of Agriculture, 1994. Pp. 11–14.

Owen, Aneurin. *The Ancient Laws and Institutes of Wales*. 2 vols. London: G. E. Eyre and A. Spottiswoode, 1841.

Palmer, J. J. N. *England, France and Christendom, 1377–99*. Chapel Hill: University of North Carolina Press, 1972.

The Parliament Rolls of Medieval England. Ed. and trans. Chris Given-Wilson. Woodbridge: Boydell Press, 2005.

The Parliament Rolls of Medieval England (PROME). Ed. Chris Given-Wilson. Leicester: Scholarly Digital Editions, 2005.

Parry, Thomas. *A History of Welsh Literature*. Trans. Idris Bell. Oxford: Clarendon Press, 1962.

Parry, Thomas, ed. *The Oxford Book of Welsh Verse*. Oxford: Clarendon Press, 1962.

Paul, James Balfour. *Accounts of the Lord High Treasurer of Scotland, Vol. VII (1538–1541)*. Edinburgh: H. M. General Register House, 1907.

Payne, Ffransis G. *Crwydro Sir Faesyfed: Yr Ail Ran*. Llandybie: Llyfrau'r Dryw, 1968.

Peniarth MS. 67. Ed. E. Stanton Roberts. Cardiff: Guild of Graduates of the University of Wales, 1918.

Pennant, Thomas. *Tours in Wales*. 3 vols. London: Henry Hughes, 1778–1883.

Pennant, Thomas. *Tours in Wales*. Ed. John Rhŷs. Caernarvon: H. Humphreys, 1883. Vol. II, App. VII, "of Owen Glyndwr."

Phillips, J. R. S. "When did Owain Glyndŵr Die?" *Bulletin of the Board of Celtic Studies* 24 (1970–72), 59–77.

Pierce, Gwynedd O. "The Welsh *mystwyr*." *Nomina* 23 (2000), 121–40.

Pintoin, Michel. *Chronique du Religieux de Saint-Denys*. Ed. M. L. Bellaguet. 6 vols. Paris: Crapelet, 1839.

Pistono, Stephen P. "The Diplomatic Mission of Jean de Hangest, Lord of Hugueville (October, 1400)." *Canadian Journal of History* 13 (1978), 193–207.

Pollard, Tony, and Neil Oliver. *Two Men in a Trench: Battlefield Archaeology — The Key to Unlocking the Past*. London: Michael Joseph, 2002.

Polychronicon Continuation. See Higden, Ranulf.

Powel, David. *The Historie of Cambria, Now Called Wales*. London: Rafe Newberie and Henrie Denham, 1584.

Powell, A. D. "The Clanvowes." *Radnorshire Society Transactions* 58 (1988), 21–24.

Prestwich, M. *Edward I*. London: Methuen, 1988.

Priestley, E. J. *The Battle of Shrewsbury, 1403*. Shrewsbury: Shrewsbury and Atcham Borough Council, 1979.

Pugh, T. B. *Henry V and the Southampton Plot of 1415*. London: Sutton, 1988.

Records of Early Drama: Wales. Ed. David N. Klausner. Toronto: University of Toronto Press; London: British Library, 2005.

Rees, Joan. "Shakespeare's Welshmen." In *Literature and Nationalism*. Ed. by Vincent Newey and Ann Thompson. Savage: Barnes and Noble, 1991. Pp. 22–40.

Rees, Dylan, and J. Gwynfor Jones. *Thomas Matthews's Welsh Records in Paris: A Study in Selected Welsh Medieval Records*. Cardiff: University of Wales Press, 2010.

Rees, Owen. "The Battle of Bryn Glas, 1402: Glyn Dwr's Finest Hour." *Medieval Warfare* 2.4 (2012), 43–47.

Reeves, Marjorie. "The Originality and Influence of Joachim of Fiore." *Traditio: Studies in Ancient and Medieval History, Thought and Religion* 36 (1980), 269–316.

Rhys Goch Eryri. *Gwaith Rhys Goch Eryri*. Ed. Dylan Foster Evans. Aberystwyth: Centre for Advanced Welsh and Celtic Studies, 2007.

Rhŷs, John. *Celtic Folklore: Welsh and Manx*. Oxford: Oxford University Press, 1901, reissued London: Wildwood House, 1980.

Richards, Melville. *Welsh Administrative and Territorial Units*. Cardiff: University of Wales Press, 1969.

———. *Enwau Tir a Gwlad*. Caernarfon: Gwasg Gwynedd, 1998.

Richter, Michael. *Giraldus Cambrensis: The Growth of the Welsh Nation*. Aberystwyth: National Library of Wales, 1976.

Riley, Henry Thomas, ed. *Johannis de Trokelowe et Henrici de Blaneforde, Monachorum S. Albani, Necnon Quorundam Anonymorum, Chronica et Annales, Regnantibus Henricio Tertio, Edwardo Primo, Edwardo Secundo, Ricardi Secundo, et Henrico Quarto*. Rolls Series 28. London: Longmans, Green, Reader, and Dyer, 1866.

Roberts, Brynley F. "Geoffrey of Monmouth, *Historia regum Britanniae* and *Brut y Brenhinedd*." In *The Arthur of the Welsh*. Ed. Rachel Bromwich, A. O. H. Jarman, and Brynley F. Roberts. Cardiff: University of Wales Press, 1991. Pp. 97–116.

———. "Hopcyn ap Tomas ab Einion," *Oxford Dictionary of National Biography* [www.oxforddnb.com, accessed 7 February 2013].

Roberts, Enid Pierce. "'Tŷ pren glân mewn top bryn glas.'" *Transactions of the Denbighshire Historical Society* 22 (1973), 12–47.

Roberts, Enid. "Uchelwyr y Beirdd." *Transactions of the Denbighshire Historical Society* 24 (1975), 38–73.

———. *Dafydd Llwyd o Fathafarn*. Caernarfon: Eisteddfod Genedlaethol Cymru, 1981.

Roberts, Glyn. "Wyrion Eden." *Transactions of the Anglesey Antiquarian Society and Field Club* (1951), 34–72.

———. "The Anglesey Submissions of 1406." *Bulletin of the Board of Celtic Studies* 15 (1952), 39–61.

Roberts, Thomas. "Pedwar Cywydd Brud." *Bulletin of the Board of Celtic Studies* 7 (1933–35), 231–46.

Rogers, Byron. "Wales's Finest Hour, 600 Years On." *The Daily Telegraph* (15 June 2002), 12.

Rogers, Clifford J. *Soldiers' Lives Through History: The Middle Ages*. Westport: Greenwood Press, 2007.

"Roll of Fealty and Presentments on the Accession of Edward the Black Prince to the Principality of Wales." Ed. R. W. Banks. *Archaeologia Cambrensis* (Fourth Series) 8 (1877); "Original Documents" supplement, pp. cxlviii–clxxv.

Rotuli Parliamentorum, ut et Petitiones et Placita in Parliamento. 6 vols. [London: 1767–77].

Rotuli Scotiae in Turri Londinensi et in Domo Capitulari Westmonasteriensi Asservati. Vol. 1. Ed. David Macpherson. London: The Record Commission, 1814.

Rous, John. *Historia regum Angliae*. Ed. Thomas Hearne. Oxford, 1716.

———. *Pageant of the Birth, Life and Death of Richard of Beauchamp, Earl of Warwick K.G., 1389– 1439*. Ed. Viscount Dillon and William Henry St. John Hope. London: Longmans Green and Co., 1914.

Rowland, Jenny. *Early Welsh Saga Poetry: A Study and Edition of the Englynion*. Cambridge: D.S. Brewer, 1990.

Rowlands, Eurys I. "Cynghanedd, Metre, Prosody." In *A Guide to Welsh Literature*. 2.202–17.

———. *Poems of the Cywyddwyr: A Selection of Cywyddau c.1375–1525*. Dublin: Dublin Institute for Advanced Studies, 1976.

Royal Commission on the Ancient and Historical Monuments of Wales. <http://www.coflein.gov.uk/>.

Rymer, Thomas, ed. *Foedera*. 16 vols. The Hague, 1704–35.

Salesbury, William. *Oll Synnwyr pen Kembero ygyd*. Ed. J. Gwenogvryn Evans. Bangor: Jarvis & Foster; London: J. M. Dent, 1902.

Saul, Nigel. *The Three Richards: Richard I, Richard II, and Richard III*. London: Hambledon Continuum, 2006.

Sayles, G. O. *Select Cases in the Court of King's Bench, Volume 7*. London: Bernard Quaritch, 1971.

Scattergood, V. J. "The Authorship of *The Boke of Cupide*." *Anglia* 82 (1964), 37–49.

———. *Politics and Poetry in the Fifteenth Century*. London: Blandford Press, 1971.

Schwyzer, Philip. "Thirteen Ways of Looking Like a Welshman: Shakespeare and his Contemporaries." In *Shakespeare and Wales: From the Marches to the Assembly*. Ed. Willy Maley and Philip Schwyzer. Farnham: Ashgate Publishing Group, 2010. Pp. 21–41.

Scourfield, Nest. "Gwaith Ieuan Gethin ab Ieuan ap Lleision, Llywelyn ap Hywel ab Ieuan ab Gronw, Ieuan Du'r Bilwg, Ieuan Rudd a Llywelyn Goch y Dant." MPhil diss., University of Wales, 1992.

Sharpe, Richard, and John Reuben Davies. "Rhygyfarch's *Life* of St David." In *St David of Wales: Cult, Church and Nation*. Ed. J. Wyn Evans and Jonathan M. Wooding. Woodbridge: Boydell Press, 2007. Pp. 107–55.

Shaw, William A. *The Knights of England*. 2 vols. London: Sherratt and Hughes, 1906.

Siddons, Michael Powell. *The Development of Welsh Heraldry*. 4 vols. Aberystwyth: National Library of Wales, 1991–2006.

Siôn Ceri. *Gwaith Siôn Ceri*. Ed. A. Cynfael Lake. Aberystwyth: Centre for Advanced Welsh and Celtic Studies, 1996.

Siôn Tudur. *Gwaith Siôn Tudur*. 2 vols. Ed. Enid Roberts. Cardiff: University of Wales Press, 1980.

Sir Gawain and the Green Knight. Ed. J. R. R. Tolkien and E. V. Gordon. Second ed. Oxford: Clarendon Press, 1968.

Skene, William F. *Chronicles of the Picts, Chronicles of the Scots, and Other Early Memorials of Scottish History*. Edinburgh: H. M. General Register House, 1867.

Skidmore, Ian. *Owain Glyndŵr: Prince of Wales*. Swansea: Christopher Davies, 1978.

Smallwood, T. M. "The Prophecy of the Six Kings." *Speculum* 60 (1985), 571–92.

Smith, J. B. "The Last Phase of the Glyn Dŵr Rebellion." *Bulletin of the Board of Celtic Studies* 22 (1968–69), 250–60.

Smith, J. Beverley. *Llywelyn ap Gruffudd, Tywysog Cymru*. Cardiff: University of Wales Press, 1986.

———. "Treftadaeth Deheubarth." In *Yr Arglwydd Rhys*. Ed. by Nerys Ann Jones and Huw Price. Cardiff: University of Wales Press, 1996. Pp. 18–52.

Smith, Llinos. "Glyn Dŵr, Owain (c.1359–c.1416)." In *Oxford Dictionary of National Biography*. Oxford: Oxford University Press, 2004.

Smyth, Alfred P. "The Emergence of English Identity, 700–1000." In *Medieval Europeans: Studies in Ethnic Identity and National Perspectives in Medieval Europe*. Ed. Alfred P. Smyth. London: MacMillan, 1998.

Snow, Peter, and Dan Snow. *Battlefield Britain: From Boudicca to the Battle of Britain*. London: BBC Books, 2004.

Soldier in Later Medieval England Database. Ed. Anne Curry and Adrian R. Bell. Reading: ICMA Centre, 2006–07. <http://www.icmacentre.ac.uk/soldier/database/search_musterdb.php>

Soulsby, Ian. *The Towns of Medieval Wales*. Chichester: Phillimore, 1983.

Southern, R. W. "History as Prophecy." *Transactions of the Royal Historical Society* 5th ser. 22 (1972), 159–80.

The St Albans Chronicle: The Chronica Maiora of Thomas Walsingham. Ed. and trans. John Taylor, Wendy R. Childs, and Leslie Watkiss. Oxford: Clarendon Press, 2003–11.

Stenroos, Merja, and Martti Mäkinen. "A Defiant Gentleman or 'the Strengest Thiefe of Wales': Reinterpreting the Politics in a Medieval Correspondence." In *Communicating Early English Manuscripts*. Ed. Päivi Pahta and Andreas H. Jucker. Cambridge: Cambridge University Press, 2011. Pp. 83–101.

Stow, G. B. "The Continuation of the Eulogium Historiarum: Some Revisionist Perspectives." *English Historical Review* 119 (2004), 667–81.

Strohm, Paul. *England's Empty Throne: Usurpation and the Language of Legitimization, 1399–1422.* New Haven: Yale University Press, 1998.

Suggett, Richard. *Houses & History in the March of Wales: Radnorshire 1400–1800.* Aberystwyth: Royal Commission on the Ancient and Historical Monuments of Wales, 2005.

Suggett, Richard, and Eryn White. "Vagabonds and Minstrels in Sixteenth-century Wales." In *The Spoken Word: Oral Culture in Britain 1500–1850.* Ed. Adam Fox and Daniel Woolf. Manchester: Manchester University Press, 2002. Pp. 138–72.

Sutherland, Tim. "The Archaeological Investigation of the Towton Battlefield." In *Blood Red Roses: The Archaeology of a Mass Grave from the Battle of Towton AD 1461.* Ed. Veronica Fiorato, Anthea Boylston, and Christopher Knüsel. Oxford: Oxbow Books, 2000. Pp. 155–68.

Sutton, Anne F., and Livia Visser-Fuchs. "Richard III's Books: VIII: Geoffrey of Monmouth's *Historia regum Britanniae* with the *Prophecy of the Eagle* 2: Prophecy and Commentary." *The Ricardian* 8.107 (1989), 290–304, 8.108 (1990), 351–62.

Symons, Dana M. *Chaucerian Dream Visions and Complaints.* Kalamazoo: Medieval Institute Publications, 2004.

Tatlock, J. S. P. "Geoffrey of Monmouth and the Date of Regnum Scotorum." *Speculum* 9 (1934), 135–39.

Taylor, Arnold. *Harlech Castle.* Ed. Richard Avent. Second ed. Cardiff: CADW, 1988.

Taylor, John. *The Universal Chronicle of Ranulf Higden.* Oxford: Clarendon Press, 1966.

———. *English Historical Literature in the Fourteenth Century.* Oxford: Clarendon Press, 1987.

Thomas, Graham C. G. "Oswestry 1400: Glyndŵr's Supporters on Trial." *Studia Celtica* 40 (2006), 117–26.

Thomas, Gwyn. *A Welsh Eye.* London: Hutchinson & Co, 1964.

Thomas, Keith. *Witchcraft and the Decline of Magic.* New York: Oxford University Press, 1997.

Thomas, Owen. "Glyndyfrdwy." Y *Geninen* 10 (1892), 7.

Thomson, R. L. *Owein or Chwedyl Iarlles y Ffynnawn.* Dublin: Dublin Institute for Advanced Studies, 1968.

Thomas, Thomas. *Memoirs of Owain Glendower.* Haverfordwest, 1822.

Tuchman, Barbara. *A Distant Mirror.* New York: Alfred A. Knopf, 1978.

Tudur Aled. *Gwaith Tudur Aled.* 2 vols. Ed. T. Gwynn Jones. Cardiff: University of Wales Press, 1926.

Tudur Penllyn and Ieuan ap Tudur Penllyn. *Gwaith Tudur Penllyn ac Ieuan ap Tudur Penllyn.* Ed. Thomas Roberts. Cardiff: University of Wales Press, 1958.

Turner, Thomas. *Narrative of a Journey.* London: C. Whittingham, 1840.

Vaughan, Richard. *Charles the Bold: The Last Valois Duke of Burgundy.* London: Longmans, 1973.

Vinycomb, John. *Fictitious and Symbolic Creatures in Art, with Special Reference to Their use in British Heraldry.* London: Chapman and Hall, 1906.

Waller, John. "Archery." In *Blood Red Roses: The Archaeology of a Mass Grave from the Battle of Towton AD 1461.* Ed. Veronica Fiorato, Anthea Boylston, and Christopher Knüsel. Oxford: Oxbow Books, 2000. Pp. 130–36.

Walsingham, Thomas. *Chronica Majora.* See *St Albans Chronicle.*

———. *The Gesta Abbatum Monasterii Sancti Albani.* Ed. H. T. Riley. 3 vols. Rolls Series 28. London: Longmans, Green, Reader, and Dyer, 1867–69.

———. *Historia Anglicana.* Ed. H. T. Riley. 2 vols. Rolls Series 28. London: Longman, Green, Longman, Roberts, and Green, 1863–64.

Walter of Coventry. *Memoriale Fratris Walteri de Coventria, The Historical Collections of Walter of Coventry.* Vol. 1, ed. William Stubbs. Rolls Series 58. London: Longman and Co. and Trübner and Co., 1872.

Waurin, Jehan de. *Anchiennes Cronicques d'Engleterre.* Ed. L. M. E. Dupont. 3 vols. Société de l'Histoire de France 94, 102, 115. Paris: Renouard, 1858–63.

———. *A Collection of the Chronicles and Ancient Histories of Great Britain, Now Called England: From A.D. 1422 to A.D. 1431.* Trans. Edward L. C. P. Hardy. Rolls Series 40, part 3. London: HMSO, 1891.

Webb, John. "Translation of a French Metrical History of the Deposition of King Richard the Second." *Archaeologia* 20 (1824), 1–423.

The Welsh Assize Roll 1277–1284. Ed. James Conway Davies. Cardiff: University of Wales Press Board, 1940.

Welsh Biography Online. http://yba.llgc.org.uk/en/index.html.

Wiliam, Aled Rhys. *Llyfr Iorwerth*. Cardiff: University of Wales Press, 1960.

Wiliam, Dafydd Wyn. *Y Canu Mawl i Deulu'r Fron-Deg*. [Bodedern]: privately published, 2000.

Wiliam Llŷn. *Barddoniaeth Wiliam Llŷn*. Ed. J. C. Morrice. Bangor: Jarvis and Foster, 1908.

Williams, Evan. "On the Church, etc., at Pilleth." *Archaeologia Cambrensis* 2 (1847), 329–32.

Williams, G. J. *Traddodiad Llenyddol Morgannwg*. Cardiff: Gwasg Prifysgol Cymru, 1948.

Williams, G. J., and E. J. Jones, eds. *Gramadegau'r Penceirddiaid*. Cardiff: University of Wales Press, 1934.

Williams, Glanmor. *The Welsh Church from Conquest to Reformation*. Cardiff: University of Wales Press, 1961.

———. *Renewal and Reformation: Wales c.1415–1642*. Oxford: Oxford University Press, 1987.

———. *Owain Glyndŵr*. Cardiff: University of Wales Press, 1993.

Williams, Gruffydd Aled. "The Bardic Road to Bosworth: A Welsh View of Henry Tudor." *Transactions of the Honourable Society of Cymmrodorion* (1986), 7–31.

———. *Owain y Beirdd: Darlith Agoriadol*. Aberystwyth: The University of Wales, Aberystwyth, 1998.

———. "Adolygu'r Canon: Cywydd arall gan Iolo Goch i Owain Glyndŵr." *Llén Cymru* 23 (2000), 39–73.

———. "Gwrthryfel Glyndŵr: Dau Nodyn." *Llên Cymru* 33 (2010), 180–87.

———. "More than 'skimble-skamble stuff': The Medieval Welsh Poetry Associated with Owain Glyndŵr." *Proceedings of the British Academy* 181 (2012), 1–33.

Williams, Gwyn, trans. *Welsh Poems: Sixth Century to 1600*. Berkeley: University of California Press, 1974.

Williams, Ifor. "Y Cyfoesi a'r Afallennau yn Peniarth 3." *Bulletin of the Board of Celtic Studies* 4 (1928), 112–29.

———, ed. *Pedeir Keinc y Mabinogi*. Cardiff: University of Wales, 1951.

———, ed. *Chwedlau Odo*. Cardiff: University of Wales, 1957.

———, ed. *The Poems of Taliesin*. Trans. J. E. Caerwyn Williams. Dublin: Dublin Institute for Advanced Studies, 1968.

Williams, J. E. Caerwyn. "Guto'r Glyn." In *A Guide to Welsh Literature*. 2.218–42.

———. *The Poets of the Welsh Princes* (Writers of Wales Series). Cardiff: University of Wales Press, 1978.

Williams, Stephen J. *Ystorya de Carolo Magno*. Cardiff: University of Wales Press, 1968.

Williams, Stephen J., and J. Enoch Powell. *Cyfreithiau Hywel Dda yn ôl Llyfr Blegywryd*. Cardiff: University of Wales Press, 1961.

Williams, W. Llewelyn. "Adam of Usk." *Y Cymmrodor* 31 (1921), 135–60.

Williams, William Carlos. *English Institute Essays, 1947*. New York: Columbia University Press, 1948.

Wylie, James Hamilton. *History of England Under Henry the Fourth*. 4 vols. London: Longmans, Green, and co., 1884–98.

Wynne, Sir John. *History of the Gwydir Family*. Oswestry: Woodall, 1878.

Wynne, William. *The History of Wales*. London: M. Clark, 1697.

Zitner, Shelden. "Staging the Occult in *1 Henry IV*." In *Mirror Up to Shakespeare*. Ed. J. C. Gray. Toronto: University of Toronto Press, 1984. Pp. 138–48.

INDEX TO THE VOLUME

Variant forms of a name are listed in square brackets. Parentheses enclose references to persons who are identified but not by name or title; e.g., Margaret Hanmer; Catrin (*OG's dau.*). Only the principal names in Item 11, *De Oweino Glendworedy*, have been indexed.